GEORGINA CAMPBELL'S JAMESON GUIDE

The Best Places to Eat, Drink & Stay

IRELAND 2002

Georgina Campbell's Guides

Editor **Georgina Campbell**

Georgina Campbell's Guides Ltd.,
PO Box 6173
Dublin 13
Ireland

website: www.ireland-guide.com
email: info@ireland-guide.com
Guide recommendations for the Greater Dublin area can be found on the Dublin Live section of the Irish Times Web: www.ireland.com

Front Cover: Photograph - La Stampa, Dublin
Back Cover from top: Inchydoney Lodge and Spa, Co. Cork;
Pub Scene courtesy of Old Jameson Distillery, Dublin;
Lough Inagh Lodge, Co. Galway

Wine List Award: Photograph Joe St. Leger, The Irish Times

Design and Artwork by The Design Station, Dublin
Printed in Ireland by Beta Print Ltd.

First published 2001 by Georgina Campbell Guides Ltd.

ISBN: 1 903164-05-2

Foreword

by Dr. James McDaid T.D., Minister for Tourism, Sport and Recreation

It is again my great pleasure to greet readers of Georgina Campbell's Jameson Guide to Ireland in this, the edition for 2002. As ever, it is a publication which I know to be an objective, quality reference guide that will prove invaluable in the year ahead.

Quality is the keynote to the welcome which is highlighted here, and this quality guide is a cornerstone of all that is best in today's hospitality in Ireland. Georgina Campbell clearly has a vision for the future of Irish food at a time when dining and hospitality play an increasingly central role in this country's modern tourism. Her passion for perfection and commitment to excellence help to make her Jameson Guide 2002 to Ireland's finest places to eat, drink and stay a valued publication.

Today's best Irish dining and hospitality experiences are hallmarked by quality, diversity and value - from pubs to family-run restaurants, and from top hotels to the vast array of ethnic food now available. Inclusion in this Guide is an accolade in itself, as all the establishments are here through independent critical assessment, and I would particularly like to congratulate those chosen for special awards.

Modern Irish hospitality is a dynamic interaction between our legendary tradition of welcome, and our vibrant modern society. In a rapidly changing world, we endeavour to keep what is best of the old, yet must also readily adopt and adapt what is best of the new.

In Jameson, Georgina Campbell is linked with a classic Irish product which is now a recognised international brand, selling globally on its own merits. This Jameson Guide to Ireland 2002 is due recognition that today's Irish hospitality industry is now of truly international standard.

Dr. James McDaid T.D.
Minister for Tourism, Sport & Recreation

How to Use the Guide

Location/Establishment name

- Cities, towns and villages arranged in alphabetical order within counties, with the exception of Dublin, Cork, Belfast, Galway and Limerick which come first within their categories
- Establishments arranged alphabetically within location
- In Dublin city, postal codes are arranged in numerical order. Even numbers are south of the River Liffey and uneven numbers on the north, with the exception of Dublin 8 which straddles the river. Dublin 1 and 2 are most central; Dublin 1 is north of the Liffey, Dublin 2 is south of it. Within each district establishments are listed in alphabetical order.

Category(ies) of Establishment

Address/contact details

(please phone/fax/email ahead for additional directions if required)
- includes an email address if available

Rating - for outstanding cooking and accommodation

☆ - Demi-Star: restaurant approaching full star status
★ - For cooking and service well above average
★★ - Consistent excellence, one of the best restaurants in the land
★★★ - The highest restaurant grading achievable
- Outstanding Accommodation of its type
- De Luxe Hotel
- Outstanding Pub - good food and atmosphere
féile bia - Denotes establishments committed to the Féile Bia Charter

Maps are intended for reference only; Ordnance Survey maps are recommended and available from Tourist Information offices.

PRICES & OPENING HOURS

PLEASE NOTE THAT PRICES AND OPENING HOURS MAY HAVE CHANGED SINCE THE GUIDE WENT TO PRESS. TIMES & PRICES ARE GIVEN AS A GUIDELINE ONLY AND SHOULD BE CHECKED BEFORE TRAVELLING OR WHEN MAKING A RESERVATION.

Prices in the Republic of Ireland are given in Euros and those in Northern Ireland in pounds sterling.

Thanks and Acknowledgements

The publication of this guide would not have been possible without the support and encouragement of a large number of organisations, companies and individuals. Particular thanks must go to all the sponsors, of course, for having faith in this fourth edition which is an all-Irish project. Those who have given invaluable assistance are too numerous to mention individually but, on behalf the Guide, I would like to thank you all.

Georgina Campbell,
Editor.

Contents

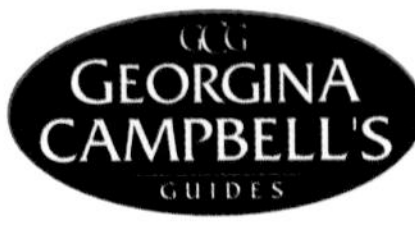
GCG
GEORGINA
CAMPBELL'S
GUIDES

A Word from the Sponsor

by Michael Murphy
Home Trade Director
Irish Distillers Wines and Spirits

A word of welcome from the distillers of Jameson Irish Whiskey.

Jameson, the world's most popular Irish Whiskey, is part of the renowned welcome and hospitality to be found in Ireland - and its roots are in Ireland at the Old Jameson Distillery in Dublin. So it is fitting that Jameson be associated with a guide which will help you find the best that Ireland has to offer in food, drink and hospitality.

A culinary revolution has taken place in Ireland during the last two decades and Irish cuisine is now taking its place among the best in the world. Good food is among the most frequently cited reasons for visitors choosing to come to Ireland and many of the most exciting eating places are to be found throughout the country, in pubs and other informal eating places as well as more formal restaurants. Add to this a high standard of accommodation, the atmosphere of Ireland's famous pubs, bars and a growing number of cafés (contemporary as well as traditional) plus a great tradition of hospitality and it becomes clear why Ireland is such a popular European destination.

Whiskey is an intrinsic part of Irish life and, whether you are enjoying the warmth of an Irish pub, relaxing in an hotel, enjoying an aperitif, or sitting back after a memorable meal, there is always an occasion to savour a glass of Jameson Irish Whiskey.

We take great pride in the quality of Jameson. From the rich countryside of Ireland comes nature's finest barley and crystal clear water. These natural ingredients are carefully distilled three times and then slowly matured for years in oak casks to produce an exceptionally smooth whiskey.

I hope you will enjoy using this Guide as you sample some of the best of Ireland's hospitality, food and - of course - Whiskey!

Michael Murphy

Home Trade Director

Introduction

by Georgina Campbell
Editorial Director

Hospitality is at the heart of the Irish psyche and, while it may seem different in today's fast-changing world - in the cities particularly - it is still very much alive and well. We see it everywhere on our travels in search of the best places to recommend in the Guide, notably in the smaller, rural and owner-run establishments but also, more surprisingly, in some of the largest hotels. What a difference it makes to be treated as an individual in a place where you might reasonably expect to feel quite anonymous; readers have related similar experiences and it is a very positive sign for the future of hospitality and tourism in Ireland if, at a time when rapid expansion has become the norm, a caring atmosphere can still prevail.

In Dublin this year, the big news has been the long-awaited opening of the two major international hotels, The Four Seasons and The Westin. While it is too soon to judge how they will eventually fit into the hierarchy, new competition has put the existing top level hotels on their mettle, which is excellent news for consumers. Their arrival has coincided with an economic downturn and a time of international uncertainty; while it will undoubtedly be a challenging year for all in the hospitality industry, there has never been a better time to visit Ireland - or for Irish people to take the opportunity to spend leisure time getting to know this extraordinarily diverse little country better.

A development that may of special interest to stressed city dwellers is the growing number of quality hotels with spas and special treatment centres; independent of season and weather, such hotels provide the ideal bolt-hole for a short break and can instantly transform a previously little-known location into a must-visit destination, as hotels with golf and leisure activities have done for the last deacde.

On the food side there are welcome signs that "tall food" may finally have gone over the top, but little indication that the dining public has yet tired of global cuisine - however, for those who long for simpler food, there are many fine restaurants recommended here where simplicity is a virtue. The success of such a philosophy depends on using first rate produce, and it is encouraging to see international groups like Euro-Toques and the Slow Food Movement working in harmony, strengthening the organic movement and, backed by the demands of increasingly well-informed consumers, opening up new oppportunities for Ireland, an island ideally placed for specialised food production, notably organic. When chefs and restaurateurs work directly with local producers it can be a rewarding partnership, socially as well as financially, and the benefits for the customer are immense. On a bigger scale, Bord Bia and other organisations are working to a similar end with Féile Bia, the national celebration of quality Irish produce and cooking, which is detailed in the guide.

Wherever your travels take you, on business or for pleasure, we hope that this Guide will lead you on many a memorable outing and that you will enjoy using it - and, of course, we always welcome your comments, good or bad, on recommended establishments.

Georgina Campbell.

The Best of the Best

STARRED RESTAURANTS

★★ / ★ / ☆

Republic of Ireland

2 Star: ★★
Dublin, Restaurant Patrick Guilbaud
Dublin,Thornton's

1 Star: ★
Dublin, L'Ecrivain
Dublin, Peacock Alley
Co Clare, Dromoland Castle, Newmarket-on-Fergus
Co Cork, Ballymaloe House, Shanagarry
Co Cork, Longueville House, Mallow
Co Kerry, Park Hotel, Kenmare
Co Kerry, Sheen Falls Lodge, Kenmare
Co Kildare, Kildare Hotel, Straffan
Co Sligo, Cromleach Lodge, Castlebaldwin

Demi-Star: ☆
Dublin, Chapter One
Co Dublin, Portmarnock Hotel, Osborne Restaurant
Dublin, Clarence Hotel, Tea Room
Dublin, The Commons Restaurant
Dublin, Mermaid Café
Dublin, Morrison, Halo Restaurant
Dublin, O'Connell's in Ballsbridge
Dublin, One Pico Restaurant
Cork city, Café Paradiso
Cork city, Jacob's on the Mall

Demi-Star *(continued)*: ☆
Cork city, Jacques
Co Cork, Casino House, Kilbrittain
Co Cork, Customs House, Baltimore
Galway city, Archway
Co Galway St Clerans, Craughwell
Co Limerick Ballingarry, Mustard Seed at Echo Lodge
Co Mayo, Ashford Castle, Cong
Co Cavan, MacNean Bistro, Blacklion
Co Kerry, Packie's, Kenmare
Co Kerry, Lime Tree, Kenmare
Co Kerry, Restaurant David Norris, Tralee
Co Limerick, Mustard Seed at Echo Lodge, Ballingarry
Co Waterford, Tannery, Dungarvan
Co Tipperary, Clifford's at The Bell, Cahir
Co Wexford, Dunbrody House, Arthurstown
Co Wexford, La Marine at Kelly's Hotel, Rosslare

Northern Ireland
2 Star: ★★
Belfast, Restaurant Michael Deane
1 Star: ★
Belfast, Cayenne
Demi-Star: ☆
Belfast, Aldens
Co Down, Shanks, Bangor

DELUXE HOTELS

Republic of Ireland

Dublin, Berkeley Court, Ballsbridge
Dublin, The Clarence, Temple Bar
Dublin, Four Seasons Hotel, Ballsbridge
Dublin, The Merrion, Merrion Street
Dublin, Morrison, Ormond Quay
Dublin, The Shelbourne, St Stephen's Green
Dublin, The Westbury, Grafton Street
Dublin, The Westin Hotel, College Green
Cork city, Hayfield Manor Hotel
Co Clare, Dromoland Castle, Newmarket-on Fergus
Co Kerry, Park Hotel, Kenmare
Co Kerry, Sheen Falls Lodge, Kenmare
Co Kildare, Kildare Hotel, Straffan,
Co Kilkenny, Mount Juliet, Thomastown
Co Limerick, Adare Manor, Adare
Co Mayo, Ashford Castle, Cong,
Co Wexford, Marlfield House, Gorey

Northern Ireland
Co Down, Culloden Hotel, Holywood

OUTSTANDING ACCOMMODATION

Republic of Ireland

Dublin, The Conrad, Earslfort Terrace
Dublin, The Towers, Lansdowne Road, Ballsbridge
Dublin, Clarion IFSC
Co Dublin, Portmarnock Hotel & Golf Links
Cork city, Maryborough Hotel
Co Cork, Aherne's, Youghal
Co Cork, Ballymaloe House, Shanagarry
Co Cork, Ballyvolane House, Castlelyons
Co Cork, Longueville House, Mallow
Co Clare, Carnelly House, Clarecastle,
Co Clare, Gregans Castle Hotel, Ballyvaughan
Co Clare, Moy House, Lahinch
Co Clare Sheedy's Hotel, Lisdoonvarna
Galway city, Killeen House, Bushypark
Galway city, SAS Radisson Hotel
Co Galway, Cashel House Hotel, Connemara
Co Galway, Dolphin Beach, Clifden
Co Galway, Fermoyle Lodge, Costello
Co Galway, The Quay House, Clifden
Co Galway, St Cleran's, Craughwell
Co Kerry, Barrow House, Tralee
Co Kerry, Caragh Lodge, Caragh Lake
Co Kerry, Emlagh Lodge, Dingle
Co Kerry, Hotel Europe, Killarney
Co Kerry, Killarney Park Hotel, Killarney
Co Kerry, Shelburne Lodge, Kenmare
Co Kildare, Barberstown Castle, Straffan
Co Kildare, Kilkea Castle, Castledermot
Co Kildare, Moyglare Manor, Maynooth
Laois, Ivyleigh House, Portlaoise
Co Limerick, Dunraven Arms Hotel, Adare
Co Limerick, Echo Lodge, Ballingarry
Co Limerick, Glin Castle, Glin
Co Mayo, Newport House, Newport
Co Monaghan, Hilton Park, Clones
Co Sligo, Coopershill House, Riverstown
Co Sligo, Cromleach Lodge, Castlebaldwin
Co Waterford, Hanora's Cottage, Nire Valley
Co Wexford, Dunbrody House, Arthurstown
Co Wicklow, Humewood Castle, Kiltegan
Co Wicklow, Rathsallagh House, Dunlavin
Co Wicklow, Tinakilly House, Rathnew

Northern Ireland

Co Antrim, Galgorm Manor, Ballymena
Co Londonderry, Ardtara House, Upperlands
Co Londonderry, Beech Hill House Hotel, Derry
Co Londonderry, Streeve Hill, Limavady
Co Tyrone, Grange Lodge, Dungannon

OUTSTANDING PUBS (for good food & atmosphere)

Republic of Ireland

Dublin, The Porterhouse
Co Cork, The Bosun, Monkstown
Co Cork, Bushe's, Baltimore
Co Cork, Mary Ann's, Castletownshend
Co Cork, Hayes Bar, Glandore
Co Galway, Moran's Oyster Cottage, Kilcolgan
Co Kerry, The Point Bar, Caherciveen
Co Kildare, The Ballymore Inn, Ballymore Eustace
Co Limerick, Arrabrook, Newcastle West
Co Offaly, The Thatch, Crinkle
Co Tipperary, The Derg Inn, Terryglass
Co Tipperary, Sean Tierney's, Clonmel
Co Waterford, Buggy's Glencairn Inn, nr Lismore
Co Wexford, Kehoe's, Kilmore Quay
Co Wicklow, Roundwood Inn, Roundwood

Northern Ireland:

Belfast, Crown Liquor Salon
Co Down, Grace Neill's, Donaghadee
Co Down, The Plough, Hillsborough

Georgina Campbell's Guides gratefully acknowledges the support of the following sponsors:

Jameson Irish Whiskey
Sponsors of:
Hotel of the Year Award
Restaurant of the Year Award
Pub of the Year Award
International Hospitality Award

Bord Bia
Sponsors of:
Féile Bia Award

Bord Iascaigh Mhara
Sponsors of:
Seafood Restaurant of the Year Award
Creative Use of Seafood Award

Bord Glas
Sponsors of:
Creative Use of Vegetables Award

Cork Dry Gin
Sponsors of:
Business Hotel of the Year Award

Jameson1780
Sponsors of:
Sommelier of the Year Award

Graham's Port
Sponsors of:
Wine List of the Year Award

Bisquit Cognac
Sponsors of:
Host of the Year Award

Rathborne Candles
Sponsors of:
Atmospheric Restaurant of the Year Award

Irish Heart Foundation
Sponsors of:
Happy Heart Eat Out Award

Electrolux & Euro-Toques
Joint sponsors of:
Natural Food Award

Kerry Foods
Sponsors of:
Denny Irish Breakfast Awards

Sharwood's
Manufacturers of quality ethnic foods.

Ireland on the Web
Dublin Live section of The Irish Times Web, www.ireland.com

Awards of Excellence

Annual awards for the best establishment and staff in a variety of categories, sponsored by leading Irish companies and organisations

JAMESON®

IRISH WHISKEY

Hotel of the Year

Three generations of experience in the hotel business show in every detail of the Treacy family's luxurious, well run hotel - which, despite its classical good looks, is just celebrating its first decade in 2002. An elegant contemporary country house style prevails, with great attention to detail throughout and, as the Treacys always make a point of anticipating demand rather than following trends, constant improvement is a major theme. A number of especially respected establishments in Ireland have become known as "hotelier's hotels" - the places visited by off-duty hoteliers and also those aspiring to higher standards and looking for examples of excellence: The Killarney Park is one such hotel and the observant traveller will recognise many of its finer features and design details in other caringly developed hotels around the country. Housekeeping is immaculate, food and service are consistently excellent - and most importantly, of course, the staff at this family-run hotel are committed to looking after guests with warmth and discretion, making it an ideal choice for both business and pleasure. It seems most appropriate that this fine example of contemporary excellence should be in Ireland's longest-established (and, many would say, most beautiful and romantic) holiday area.

2002

2001 Winner:
Tinakilly House Hotel, Rathnew

JAMESON®

IRISH WHISKEY

Killarney Park Hotel

Killarney, Co. Kerry

Jameson
congratulates

Killarney Park Hotel

winner of
Hotel of the Year

JAMESON®

IRISH WHISKEY

Restaurant of the Year

The Rankin magic is still working in Belfast's Shaftesbury Square and, behind its opaque glass façade, Cayenne may be less comfortable than Paul & Jeanne Rankins' previous restaurant, Roscoff, but it's warmer, more modest, friendlier - and the food is still superb. Fine dining this is not: eating is very definitely fun at Cayenne and the anteroom bar is filled with the hungry long before the first sitters have finished their desserts. Given the choice in Belfast these days, this says much for the quality of Paul Rankin's quick fire cooking - and it is a credit to the legendary teamwork of this kitchen that the food is equally good when he cannot be there himself. Choice is generous, with many dishes having equal appeal, and the menu is constructed to allow flexibility; flavours are strongly oriental with some Mediterranean touches and these tantalising tastes and textures from around the world are served with charm and friendliness by a mixed team of locals and 'blow-ins' in a no nonsense environment. This all has great appeal to contemporary diners who enjoy an animated environment and don't mind rubbing shoulders with neighbouring diners in the café atmosphere of this long narrow, warmly decorated dining room - and it's terrific value.

2002

2001 Winner:
Chapter One, Dublin

Chef of the Year

Rory O'Connell has been head chef at Ballymaloe House since 1995 and is doing an inspired job in the kitchen, creating generous, beautiful, daringly simple meals. A food philosophy based on using only the highest quality ingredients is central to everything done at Ballymaloe, where much of the produce comes from their own farm and gardens and the remainder - including seafood from Ballycotton and Kenmare, and meats from the trusted local butcher, Cuddigans of Cloyne - is meticulously sourced from the best local producers and suppliers. He creates fresh, strongly seasonal daily menus, using as his starting point the best fresh produce available on the day and, while the overall balance of ingredients is judicious, vegetarian dishes are predictably wonderful and specially highlighted on the menu. Ballymaloe brown bread, cruditées with garlic mayonnaise, paté de campagne with pickles, superb roast rib of Cloyne beef with three sauces (horseradish cream, béarnaise & garlic mayonnaise), Irish farmhouse cheeses (in perfect condition, served with home-made biscuits), and a dessert trolley offering irresistibly simple treats like rhubarb compôte and vanilla ice cream are typical of the truly impressive yet homely dishes that leave us lost in admiration at Ballymaloe - this is, quite simply, as good as it gets.

2002

2001 Winner:
Michael Deane, Belfast

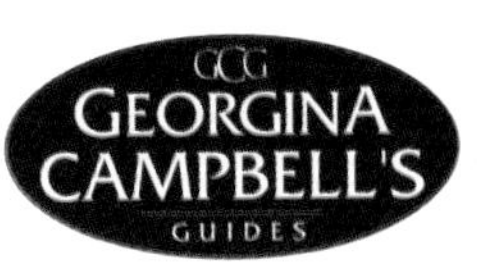

Rory O'Connell

Ballymaloe House, Co. Cork

Georgina Campbell's Guides congratulates

Rory O'Connell

winner of

Chef of the Year

Pub of the Year

Nicky and Patricia Moynihan's fine waterside pub close to the Cobh car ferry has grown a lot over the years - and, with the restaurant and accommodation growing fast and becoming an increasingly important part of the enterprise, this is now a real inn, providing food, drink and shelter. While the importance of the restaurant is steadily growing, bar food is still taken seriously, with seafood - from chowder or garlic mussels through to real scampi and chips - taking pride of place, although meat-lovers' main courses such as rack of lamb and beef stroganoff are also available. Next to the bar, the restaurant provides a more formal setting for wide-ranging menus - and also a quality Sunday lunch. Again seafood is the speciality, with starters such as crab claws or oysters worked into imaginative dishes, and main courses that include steaks and local duckling as well as seafood every which way, from grilled sole on the bone to medallions of marinated monkfish or cold seafood platters. There's always a choice for vegetarians and generous vegetables are carefully cooked. Consistent excellence is the aim at this well-run establishment and its success is down to hands-on owner-management backed up by an excellent staff.

2002

2001 Winner:
Kehoe's Pub, Kilmore Quay

The Bosun

Monkstown, Co. Cork

Jameson congratulates

The Bosun

winner of
Pub of the Year

Irish Food Board

Féile Bia Award

This accessible restaurant is run by Tom O'Connell, a brother of Darina Allen (of Ballymaloe Cookery School in County Cork). What you will get here is quality ingredient driven modern Irish cooking - simple food, with natural flavours. Head chef Brian McCarthy works closely with Rory O'Connell of Ballymaloe House and his menus, which are arranged by course and price, are extremely reasonable. Carefully sourced food is the star here and the menu not only states that beef, eggs and catering supplies are sourced using Bord Bia's Quality Assurance Schemes, but also credits a number of individual producers and suppliers: a salad is made with Fingal Ferguson's Gubbeen smoked bacon, from Schull in Co Cork, an East Cork smoked fish plate comprises a selection from Frank Hederman's smokery in Cobh and smoked salmon from Bill Casey at Shanagarry (both Co Cork), a gratin of salmon uses organic fish farmed off Clare Island, Co Mayo and beef comes from the Irish Hereford Prime Beef Society in Glencairn, Co Waterford. Irish farmhouse cheese supplied in prime condition by Sheridans cheesemongers is served with home-made biscuits and excellent classic desserts inspired by seasonal fruit, with home-made ice creams. For wonderful quality and sheer value for money this busy restaurant is a shining example of the direction Irish dining should be taking.

2002

2001 Winner:
John Howard, Le Coq Hardi

O'Connells

Ballsbridge, Dublin

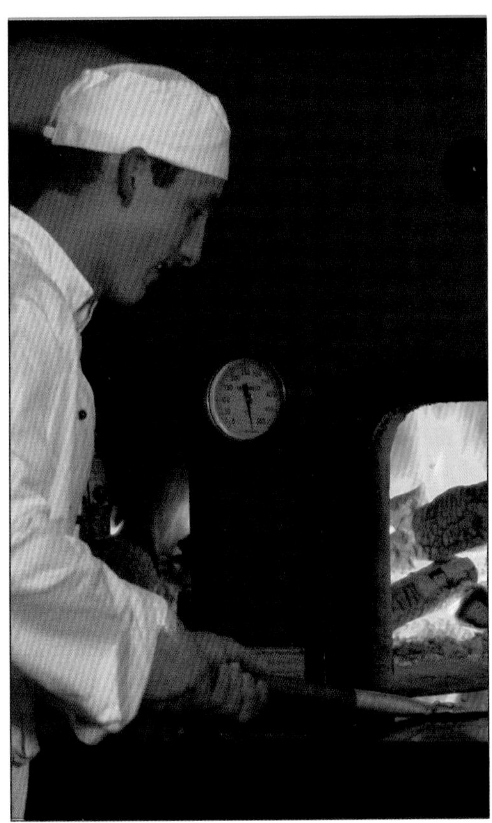

Bord Bia congratulates

O'Connells

winner of the
Feile Bia Award

Seafood Restaurant of the Year

Paul and Theresa O'Brien have been providing fine food and hospitality at their traditional, whitewashed restaurant on the cliffs just outside Lahinch for over a decade. The decor is appealingly simple and the views of Liscannor Bay - which can be magic from window tables on a fine evening - are the visual highlight. But local seafood is the star attraction and Theresa's excellent, unfussy cooking makes the most of a wide range of fish, while also offering a choice for those with other preferences, including a vegetarian menu. Main courses include lobster, when available, as well as the day's selection of other local seafood - and all at the kind of prices that many other restaurants claim to be "impossible" these days. Richly flavoured chowders, glorious crab salads with home-made mayonnaise and breads, perfectly cooked fish with excellent sauces; exact timing and perfect judgment of flavourings enhances while always allowing the fish to be "itself". Vegetables are also a strong point, served on a platter which might include beautiful Clare potatoes, wilted spinach, flavoursome flaked carrot - and some warm ratatouille as well. An interesting and keenly priced wine list, good cheeseboard, home-baked breads and aromatic cafetière coffee show an attention to detail in tune with a consistently high overall high standard.

2002

2001 Winner:
Fishy Fishy Café, Kinsale

Barrtra Seafood Restaurant

Lahinch, Co. Clare

BIM
congratulates

Barrtra Seafood Restaurant

winner of
Seafood Restaurant of the Year

Creative Use of Seafood Award

James and Tricia Kealy have a well-deserved reputation for understated excellence at their seafood restaurant on the harbour at Greencastle. Since 1989 the restaurant has been a key establishment in a major fishing port and still retains the original bar at its heart: simplicity has always been valued here. Unlike many seafood restaurants, where the emphasis on menus tends to be solely on the main ingredient (often with a rich sauce), James takes a more creative and balanced approach to this precious resource, presenting it as a component in complete dishes which are modern in tone but also often echo traditional Irish themes. House specialities demonstrating this healthy and ecologically sound philosophy include a starter of spinach wrapped seafood terrine with a tomato and chilli coulis and main courses like pan fried fillet of cod with parsley sauce on a chive and garlic champ and baked Atlantic salmon with a wholegrain mustard crust served on Irish spring cabbage and bacon. James is now developing dishes using lesser known fish, including the "new" deep sea varieties - panfried fillet of orange roughty with vegetable brunoise and vermouth sauce is now an established favourite, for example - and complementary accompaniments include local organic vegetables and farmhouse cheeses.

2002

2001 Winners:
O'Grady's on the Pier, Barna
& Cré-na-Cille, Tuam

Kealys Seafood Bar

Greencastle, Co. Donegal

BIM
congratulates

Kealys Seafood Bar

winner of the
Creative Use of
Seafood Award

JAMESON®

IRISH WHISKEY

International Hospitality Award

The Jurys Doyle Hotel Group towers over others in Ireland, not only because of the number and range of hotels encompassed, but also due to the exceptional experience of the hospitality industry personified by key staff - who, important as the industry may be, always put the emphasis firmly on hospitality. The flagship hotel, Jurys Ballsbridge, embodies the spirit of that philosophy, having the distinction of being an international hotel providing high levels of service to business and leisure guests, while also remaining a popular local hotel for Dubliners. A telling detail at the Ballsbridge hotel is how often you 'happen' to meet top personnel, including chief executive Pat McCann - who invariably has a cheery greeting for the thousand or two people he recognises. Pat joined the Jurys Hotel Group as General Manager of the Ballsbridge hotel in 1989; a real hotelier, he is highly respected within the industry: he was President of the Irish Hotels Federation fron 1996-1998 and also a member of the National Tourism Council, advising the Minister for Tourism on related matters - and very much in touch with the international aspects of the industry. Today, as Chief Executive of Jurys Doyle Hotel Group, he is responsible for thirty three properties, with 6,400 rooms and over 4,000 employees - and is a very worthy winner of our International Hospitality Award for 2002.

2002

2001 Winner:
Rory Murphy, Ashford Castle, Cong

Pat McCann

Jurys Doyle Hotel Group

Jameson
congratulates

Pat McCann

winner of the
International Hospitality Award

Cork Dry Gin

Business Hotel Award

This dashing new contemporary hotel on the river side of the Financial Services Centre is bright, airy and spacious, with an eastern feel emphasised by the food philosophy of the hotel, where Asian wok cooking provides quick healthy lunches in the bar and a smart open-plan restaurant (with admirable service) develops similar themes. Uncluttered bedrooms have 24 hour room service and much to appeal to the business traveller: keycard, security eye and security chain are reassuring features and all rooms have air conditioning, 2 phone lines, with voice mail and ISDN, also tea/coffee-making, multi-channel TV, ironing facilities, power hairdryer mini-bar and safe providing a pleasing element of self-containment. Generous semi-orthopaedic beds, good linen and bright bathrooms with power showers and bath, heated mirror, luxurious towels and top quality toiletries all add to an overall sense of thoughtful planning. There's even a 'Sleep Programme' to help stressed out executives relax before bed! Excellent leisure facilities include an 18m pool and well-equipped gym. While this is not a place for huge conferences, there are rooms with state-of-the art facilities for meetings of anything between 8 and 120 people and it is a great asset to the area.

2002

2001 Winner:
Conrad International Hotel, Dublin

JAMESON 1780

Sommelier of the Year

An especially attractive features of Eamonn O'Reilly's delightful new One Pico Restaurant is solicitous service from the charming sommelier, Julien Le Gentil. He wears his knowledge lightly, helping guests select the best wine for their choice of food in a friendly way that inspires enthusiasm - he will run through possibilities from different regions and price brackets, succinctly describing the style and explaining why it will work with, say, a combination of red meat and fish main courses. The young Breton is well-schooled - meeting Georges Dupré, chef sommelier at the Paris Ritz, when he was only 18 and in no way involved with wine studies, was crucial, and his catering studies led to specialisation at Dinard - where two teachers were also to have a great influence - then to "Le Bistrot du Sommelier" in Paris, owned by Philippe Faure Brac, holder of 'world's best sommelier' title for 1992. Luckily for us, fate next brought him to Ireland - first to Galgorm Manor, in Co Antrim, and then, for the past year, to Dublin's One Pico Restaurant. Here his wine philosophy - "wine is pleasure - always try to find new and extraordinary wines and don't be a label drinker!" - enhances the dining experience for every guest and is a great asset to this fine restaurant.

2002

2001 Winner:
Alain Bras, Sheen Falls Lodge

JAMESON
1780

Julien Le Gentil

One Pico, Dublin

Jameson 1780
congratulates

Julien Le Gentil

winner of
Sommelier of the Year

Wine List of the Year

Derry and Sallyanne Clarke's acclaimed city centre restaurant is light and airy with lots of pale wood and smoky mirrors - and seriously good food. Thoughtful little touches abound - and there are some major ones too, like the policy to add the price of your wine only after the 10% service charge has been added to your bill, instead of adding it to the total as most other restaurants do. Sommelier Martina Delaney aims to achieve an even balance to suit all palates and all pockets; keen to offer a good choice under €40, she lists about twenty imaginatively selected "Suggested Wines", providing for people who want something more challenging than the house wine but prefer somebody else to narrow down the choice a little. The list includes some great classics, also strong selections of half bottles and magnums, champagnes and ports, but the main selection is wide-ranging and Martina clearly enjoys sourcing lesser-known small producers who tend to sell on quality rather than price, saying: "I love to be able to offer a little gem for under €25". Tasting new wines is fun for this bubbly sommelier and the really exciting part is the joy of discovery: "There's always something new going on somewhere".

2002

2001 Winner:
King Sitric, Co. Dublin

L'Ecrivain

Dublin

Graham's Port congratulates

L'Ecrivain

winner of

Wine List of the Year

Host of the Year

Although small in size, this unique country restaurant on the edge of the picturesque village of Inistioge is big on personality - of the chef, Alan Walton, as conveyed through his imaginative menus and distinctive style of cooking and, especially of the host, the irrepressible Tom Reade-Duncan, who makes every guest feel as welcome as the flowers in spring and greatly adds to the enjoyment of the occasion with his offbeat humour and helpful way with local knowledge. Tom has an exceptional talent for hospitality, remembering everyone (and when they last visited, possibly even what they chose to eat) and, although he is a big man and the restaurant is quite tightly packed - with seasonal decorations, lots of flowers and wacky artefacts collected on their travels as well as the ordinary things like tables and chairs - he moves easily around from group to group, effortlessly orchestrating service while also having a chat at each table on his rounds. Everyone is relaxed, the better to enjoy Alan's fine cooking, and he makes it all seem so easy - there lies the skill. A visit to Inistioge without a meal (and a good dollop of local knowledge) at this wonderfully big-hearted restaurant would be unthinkable.

2002

2001 Winner:
Dan Mullane, The Mustard Seed

Tom Reade-Duncan

The Motte Restaurant,
Inistioge, Co. Kilkenny

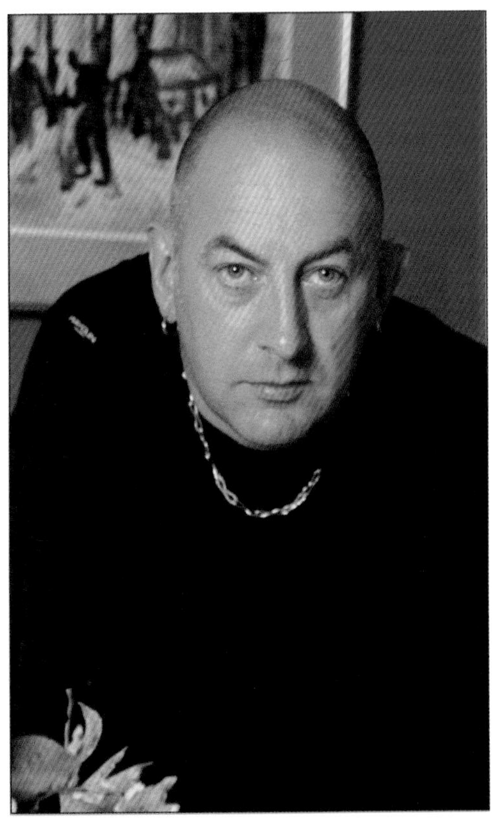

Bisquit Cognac congratulates

Tom Reade-Duncan

winner of

Host of the Year

Atmospheric Restaurant of the Year

The tall spire will lead you to the Murphy family's new restaurant in a magnificently converted church near Mullingar. The design is brilliant, with an impressive entrance foyer and thickly carpeted stairs leading off to a mezzanine floor which is luxuriously furnished with big lounge-around leather sofas, striking lamps and fresh flowers and has a bird's-eye view over the elegant candle-lit dining area below. Everything has been done to the very highest specifications, colour schemes are subtle and elegant, the whole setup is highly atmospheric and enhanced by charming service. Head chef Thérèse Gilsenan's menus are based on the best local ingredients and carefully constructed to offer a good balance of styles, to suit big country appetites and also more sophisticated urban tastes; younger guests get special choices too - a good way to introduce children to quality dining. A second staircase descends to the beautifully appointed dining area, which is very striking and extremely atmospheric, especially when seen in candlight with a room full of people enjoying themselves, with background music from the grand piano where the altar used to be - and you are invited to browse in the wine cellar if you wish, to select your own 'Wines from the Crypt'...

2002

2001 Winner:
The Cooperage, Killarney

The Belfry

Mullingar, Co. Westmeath

Rathborne Candles congratulates

The Belfry

winner of the

Atmospheric Restaurant of the Year

Happy Heart Eat Out Award

A sign on the pavement welcomes people to the friendly and informal country-style restaurant at Michael and Allison Dowling's attractive creeper-clad house in Abbeyleix. Allison's cooking is simple and wholesome, meeting the Irish Heart Foundation's definition of a Healthy Choice, i.e. dishes with lots of fruit and vegetables that are high in fibre and low in fat. Delicious morning coffee and home-bakes start off the day, then lunch brings dishes like smoked haddock chowder with freshly-baked brown bread or grilled goat's cheese and side salad followed perhaps by fish of the day, or a speciality such as stir fry beef with roast vegetables. Vegetarians do very well here, so if you're in a meat-free mood you can look forward to colourful, flavoursome dishes such as ratatouille or spinach crèpe with salad. Luscious desserts include simple, wholesome options like apple crumble. The same philosophy applies for slightly more formal dinner menus: this is deliciously healthy, well-balanced food with the emphasis on freshness and making best use of local produce. Thanks to the long opening hours and reasonable prices, it is exceptionally accessible - and it's a no smoking restaurant.

2002

2001 Winner:
Caviston's, Dublin

Preston House

Abbeyleix, Co. Laois

Irish Heart Foundation congratulates

Preston House

winner of the

Happy Heart Eat Out Award

Creative Use of Vegetables Award

Head chef Leylie Hayes has been supervising the production of the famously wholesome home-cooked food at Avoca Handweavers Restaurant since 1990 and people come from miles around to tuck into fare which is as healthy as it is delicious. Along with terrific home baking, their wonderful soups (white winter vegetable; parsnip, rosemary & fennel; mixed mushrooms), a wide range of salads (carrot & courgette; potato & mint; red cabbage with bacon & red onion) and many other imaginative ways with vegetables are the cornerstone of the Avoca style. Local produce is highly valued and traditional home cooking is the main theme - especially strong, perhaps, in simple dishes like potato & celeriac gratin and spinach omelette - but many dishes, such as piperade tartlet, have a welcome contemporary twist: strange to think that peppers were once an exotic import, while they're now an important Irish crop. Traditional hot dishes that seem especially well suited to the climate include beef and Guinness stew (with onions, carrots & garlic) and vegetarians are especially well catered for, both in special dishes – nut loaf, vegetable-based soups – and the many that just happen to be meatless. Some dishes are for sale in the delicatessen - and you can make them at home too, using the beautiful Avoca Café Cookbook.

2002

2001 Winner:
Nude Restaurant, Dublin

Avoca Café

Kilmacanogue, Co. Wicklow

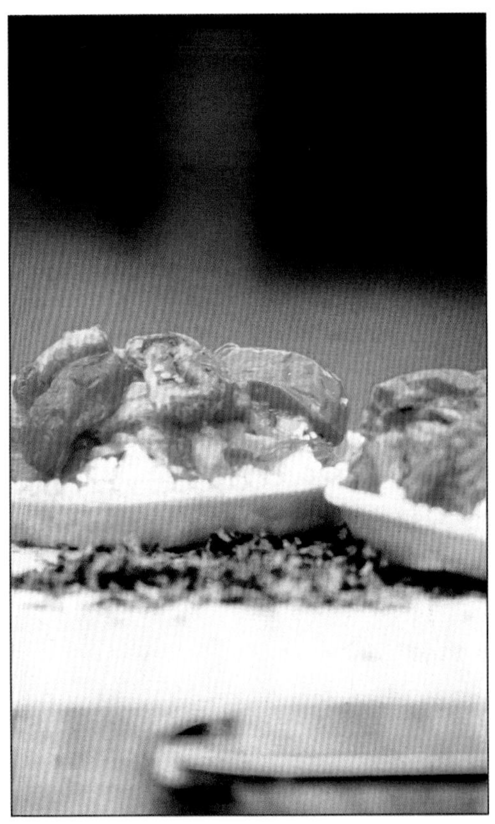

An Bord Glas congratulates

Avoca Café

winner of the

Creative Use of Vegetables Award

Natural Food Award

A must for any food lover travelling in west Cork, Hilde and Otto Kunze's restaurant is near the spot where they originally started the famous Dunworley Cottage restaurant many years ago. Deeply committed to the organic philosophy, their vegetable gardens provide a beautiful and satisfying view from the dining room, where meals of wonderful simplicity cooked by Otto are presented by Hilde. Dinner begins with a vegetarian salad platter of organic leaves and several dips, or maybe a fish plate of Anthony Cresswell's smoked wild salmon and Frank Hederman's eel and mussels, both hand processed in Co Cork. Freshly baked breads are left temptingly on the table - try to resist as there are still marvellous soups (usually based on whatever vegetable is most prolific at the time) and main courses, like wild salmon caught off the Seven Heads, panfried, or a spiced Swedish speciality such as 'Cheap', made with minced organic lamb and served with home-grown organic vegetables. As for desserts - if you are very lucky, there might be freshly picked top fruit, warm from the trees in the growing tunnels - cherries, plums, apricots, white peaches.....This wonderful food needs no embellishment - and it is extraordinarily good value too.

2002

2001 Winner:
Brid Torrades, Glebe House, Co Sligo

ELECTROLUX GROUP (IRELAND) LTD.

Otto's Creative Catering

Dunworley, Butlerstown, Co. Cork

Electrolux/Euro-Toques congratulates

Otto Kunze

winner of

Natural Food Award

Georgina Campbell congratulates

St. Clerans
Craughwell, Co. Galway
Country House of the Year

Gormans Clifftop House
Ballydavid Co. Kerry
Guesthouse of the Year

Bolton House
Kells, Co. Meath
Farmhouse of the Year

2002

2001 Winners:
Dunbrody House, Co. Wexford,
Rusheen Lodge, Co. Clare
Hillcrest House, Co. Cork

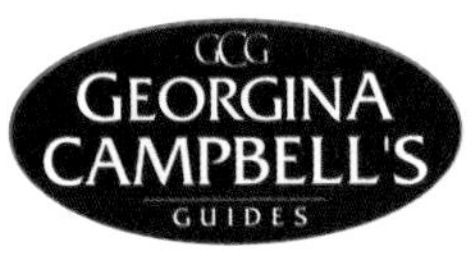

Winners 2002

St. Clerans

Gormans Clifftop House

Bolton House

Irish Breakfast Awards

Browne's Townhouse
Dublin

Dublin Winner

Ivyleigh House
Portlaoise, Co. Laois

Leinster Winner

Ballynahinch Castle Hotel
Recess, Co. Galway

Connaught Winner

Rathmullan House
Rathmullan Co. Donegal

Ulster Winner

Regional Winners 2002

Browne's Townhouse

Ivyleigh House

Ballynahinch Castle Hotel

Rathmullan House

Munster & National Winner Irish Breakfast Awards

In the beautiful Nire Valley in West Waterford, the Wall family's luxurious guesthouse and restaurant, Hanora's Cottage, is a wonderful haven renowned for good food. Mary Wall ensures that guests start the day with Hanora's legendary breakfast buffet and it takes a while to get the measure of this feast, so time must be allowed to make the most of it. Local produce and an amazing variety of exotics jostle for space on the beautifully arranged buffet. Begin in orderly fashion with fresh juices and luscious Crinnaghtaun apple juice from Lismore; next there's homemade muesli and porridge, then more fresh fruits before you reach the bread section... beginning at 6 o'clock every morning, Seamus bakes about a dozen types of bread, scones, muffins and buns, including organic and gluten free varieties, all out by 8.30am. Alongside, you'll find local farmhouse cheeses, smoked salmon and home made jams - and the hot dishes are yet to come: there's Syl Murray's home-made sausages, Clonakilty black & white puddings, Biddy Cooney's free-range eggs (various ways) and much else besides. This is truly a gargantuan feast, designed to see you many miles along the hills before stopping for a little packed lunch (based on Seamus's delicious freshly-baked breads) - and ultimately return for dinner.

2002

2001 Winner:
Rathsallagh House, Co. Wicklow

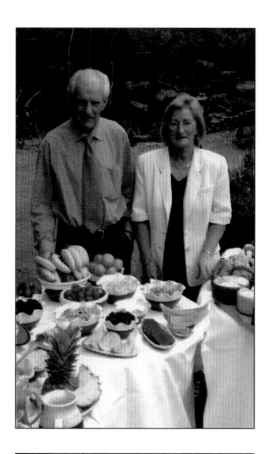

GETTING THE FLAVOUR OF IRISH WHISKEY

(With acknowledgments to John Clement Ryan and Jim Murray)

Health and long life to you
Land without rent to you
The woman (or man) of your choice to you
A child every year to you
and may you be in heaven before
the devil knows you're dead!

Portrait of John Jameson by Raeburn

Irish toasts stretch back over centuries - they're often blessings or good wishes to friends on special occasions such as weddings, but the hopes expressed only come true if your glass is filled with Irish whiskey!

Irish whiskey was invented in the 6th century, when monks from the Middle East brought with them an apparatus called the "alembic", used for distilling perfume. Irish monks soon found a better use for the alembic, which they called a "pot still", and the spirit they made in it was named "The Water of Life" (Eau de Vie) - in Irish "Uisce Beatha" (pronounced "ishka baahaa"), which was anglicised to "whiskey".

At the turn of the 19th century, Irish Whiskey was the largest selling whiskey in the world, with over 300 brands being produced here. However, during the early years of the 20th century, events beyond the industry's control caused a number of setbacks which led to its decline and the emergence of other whiskies, including Scotch. Currently Jameson Irish

Whiskey is leading the revival on the world stage and it is now the world's fastest growing whiskey. Spelling whiskey with an 'e' is far from being the main difference between Scotch and Irish - as Jim Murray points out in his book A Taste Of Irish Whiskey: "Irish is not just different from Scotch. It's a breed apart."

Ireland's temperate climate and unspoilt countryside have always ensured a plentiful supply of the natural ingredients vital to good whiskey - golden barley and pure water. Tradition plays a large part in whiskey-making in Ireland and some of its features are unique. Barley used for malt is first dried in closed kilns to ensure that the honeyed taste of the malt shines through in the whiskey. This differs from malt in Scotland where the barley is dried using smoke which gives Scotch whisky a smoky taste.

Unlike most of the world's whiskies, Jameson Irish whiskey is distilled three times, ensuring a final product that is particularly smooth and pure. During maturation in oak casks stored in dark, aromatic warehouses the whiskey mellows and takes on its rich, golden colour over the years.

Jameson's Bow Street Distillery, c. 1870

The world's oldest licensed distillery, the Old Bushmills Distillery in Co Antrim, dates back to 1608 - nearly 400 years of tradition. John Jameson's Dublin distillery was founded in 1780 and Jameson soon became the best-known Irish Whiskey in the world, a position it still holds today. A glass of Jameson makes an excellent aperitif, either on the rocks or with a little plain water, an accompaniment to smoked fish dishes, such as smoked Irish salmon - or, as a digestif, try the twelve year old Jameson 1780 and wish an old Irish Toast to your companions:

May the road rise to meet you
May the wind be always at your back
May the sun shine warm upon your face
And the rain fall soft upon your fields
And until we meet again
May God hold you in the hollow of His hand.

"Blas agus sasamh go bhfaighe tu air"

FÉILE BIA

"Blas agus sasamh go bhfaighe tu air" ("May you find it both tasty and satisfying") is the message from Féile Bia, our national celebration of Irish food and cooking.

The idea behind Féile Bia is twofold:

* to encourage chefs to make the best use of fresh local ingredients and to develop dishes with "a sense of place";
* to urge caterers to buy food produced under recognised Quality Assurance Schemes.

For Féile Bia 2001 - "A Celebration of Quality Food" - Bord Bia (the Irish Food Board) invited members of the Restaurants Association of Ireland and Irish Hotels Federation to sign up to the Féile Bia Charter, which is a serious commitment to source products from recognised Quality Assurance Schemes.

By signing the Charter, caterers are assuring consumers that they are committed to:

* Use local food and drink products
* Look for assurances, as appropriate, that products are produced under the Bord Bia or other recognised Quality Assurance Scheme
* Develop dishes and menus to profile local foods and artisan products
* Where practical identify and name the farmer/producer of ingredients used on the menu.

Consumers can identify establishments with a commitment to Quality Assured food through the display of the framed Féile Bia certificate. It's well worth looking out for, as a reassurance that the establishment you have selected sources Quality Assured key products - currently this comprises Irish beef, pigmeat and eggs, and other foods, including chicken and lamb, will shortly be joining the scheme.

Those establishments recommended by the Guide which have signed up to the Charter are listed below and are identified within the body of the Guide by the use of the Féile Bia logo.

Féile Bia Members

DUBLIN CITY

CHAPTER ONE RESTAURANT
PARNELL SQ, DUBLIN 1

JURYS CUSTOM HOUSE INN, DUBLIN 1

BROWNES BRASSERIE & TOWNHOUSE
ST STEPHEN'S GREEN, DUBLIN 2

BRUNO'S RESTAURANT
KILDARE STREET, DUBLIN 2

BUSWELLS HOTEL
MOLESWORTH STREET, DUBLIN 2

HILTON DUBLIN
CHARLEMONT PLACE, DUBLIN 2

KILKENNY RESTAURANT & CAFÉ
NASSAU STREET, DUBLIN 2

MONTYS OF KATHMANDU
EUSTACE STREET, DUBLIN 2

ONE PICO RESTAURANT
MOLESWORTH PLACE, DUBLIN 2

THE WESTBURY HOTEL
GRAFTON ST, DUBLIN 2

ANGLESEA TOWN HOUSE
BALLSBRIDGE, DUBLIN 4

THE BERKELEY COURT HOTEL, DUBLIN 4

THE BURLINGTON HOTEL, DUBLIN 4

FOUR SEASONS HOTEL
BALLSBRIDGE, DUBLIN 4

O'CONNELLS IN BALLSBRIDGE
BEWLEYS HOTEL, DUBLIN 4

JURYS BALLSBRIDGE HOTEL, DUBLIN 4

JURYS MONTROSE HOTEL, DUBLIN 4

MESPIL HOTEL, DUBLIN 4

ROLYS BISTRO,BALLSBRIDGE, DUBLIN 4

THE TOWERS HOTEL
BALLSBRIDGE, DUBLIN 4

JURYS CHRISTCHURCH INN, DUBLIN 8

NETWORK CATERING
HEUSTON STATION, DUBLIN 8

RED COW MORAN HOTEL, DUBLIN 22

JURYS GREEN ISLE HOTEL, DUBLIN 22

COUNTY DUBLIN

GREAT SOUTHERN HOTEL
DUBLIN AIRPORT, CO DUBLIN

BRASSERIE NA MARA
DUN LAOGHAIRE, CO DUBLIN

THE GRESHAM ROYAL MARINE
DUN LAOGHAIRE, CO DUBLIN

THE BLOODY STREAM RESTAURANT
HOWTH, CO DUBLIN

DEERPARK HOTEL
HOWTH, CO DUBLIN

KING SITRIC RESTAURANT
HOWTH, CO DUBLIN

BON APPETIT RESTAURANT
MALAHIDE, CO DUBLIN

CRUZZO RESTAURANT
MALAHIDE, CO DUBLIN

THE REDBANK HOUSE & RESTAURANT
SKERRIES, CO DUBLIN

STILLORGAN PARK HOTEL
STILLORGAN, CO DUBLIN

CAVAN

THE ANGLERS REST
BALLYCONNELL, CO CAVAN

MACNEAN HOUSE AND BISTRO
BLACKLION, CO CAVAN

HOTEL KILMORE, CAVAN

CLARE

FITZPATRICKS HOTEL
BUNRATTY, CO CLARE

TEMPLE GATE HOTEL
ENNIS, CO CLARE

WOODSTOCK HOTEL
ENNIS, CO CLARE

THE CONCH SHELL RESTAURANT
LISCANNOR, CO CLARE

AN CUPAN CAIFE
MOUNTSHANNON, CO CLARE

GREAT SOUTHERN HOTEL
SHANNON, CO CLARE

CORK

FENN'S QUAY RESTAURANT, CORK

JACOBS ON THE MALL, CORK, CO CORK

JURYS CORK HOTEL, CORK, CO CORK

JURYS CORK INN, CORK, CO CORK

MARYBOROUGH HOUSE HOTEL
DOUGLAS, CORK, CO CORK

Féile Bia Members

SILVER SPRINGS HOTEL
TIVOLI, CORK , CO CORK

SEA VIEW HOUSE HOTEL
BALLYLICKEY, BANTRY, CO CORK

THE MUNSTER ARMS HOTEL
BANDON, CO CORK

WESTLODGE HOTEL
BANTRY, CO CORK

BLAIRS INN, BLARNEY, CO CORK

GREGORYS RESTAURANT
CARRIGALINE, CO CORK

EMMET HOTEL, CLONAKILTY, CO CORK

DUNMORE HOUSE HOTEL
CLONAKILTY, CO CORK

ROBIN HILL HOUSE, COBH, CO CORK

INNISHANNON HOUSE HOTEL
INNISHANNON, CO CORK

ACTONS HOTEL, KINSALE, CO CORK

THE OLD BANK HOUSE
KINSALE, CO CORK

TRIDENT HOTEL
KINSALE, CO CORK

THE CASTLE HOTEL
MACROOM, CO CORK

BARNABROW COUNTRY HOUSE
MIDLETON, CO CORK

MIDLETON PARK HOTEL
MIDLETON, CO CORK

BALLYMALOE HOUSE
SHANAGARRY, CO CORK

TY AR MOR SEAFOOD RESTAURANT
SKIBBEREEN, CO CORK

DONEGAL

ST JOHNS COUNTRY HOUSE &
RESTAURANT, FAHAN, INISHOWEN
CO DONEGAL

GALWAY

TOHERS RESTAURANT & BAR
18 DUNLO STREET, BALLINASLOE
CO GALWAY

ARDAGH HOTEL, CLIFDEN, CO GALWAY

MITCHELL'S RESTAURANT
CLIFDEN, CO GALWAY

JURYS INN, GALWAY, CO GALWAY

FINN'S RESTAURANT
MILLTOWN, TUAM, CO GALWAY

MOYCULLEN HOUSE RESTAURANT,
MOYCULLEN, CO GALWAY

RENVYLE HOUSE HOTEL
RENVYLE, CO GALWAY

CRE-NA-CILLE RESTAURANT
TUAM, CO GALWAY

KERRY

THE BEAUFORT BAR & RESTAURANT
BEAUFORT, CO KERRY

DERRYNANE HOTEL
CAHERDANIEL, CO KERRY

CLEEVAUN COUNTRY HOUSE
DINGLE, CO KERRY

DOYLES SEAFOOD RESTAURANT
DINGLE, CO KERRY

LORD BAKERS RESTAURANT
DINGLE, CO KERRY

DINGLE SKELLIG HOTEL
DINGLE, CO KERRY

CASTLEROSSE HOTEL
KILLARNEY, CO KERRY

GREAT SOUTHERN HOTEL
PARKNASILLA, CO KERRY

THE ABBEY GATE HOTEL
TRALEE, CO KERRY

VAL'S BAR & BISTRO, TRALEE, CO KERRY

KILDARE

BALLYMORE INN
BALLYMORE EUSTACE, CO KILDARE

THE K-CLUB
STRAFFAN, CO KILDARE

KILKENNY

KILKENNY DESIGN CENTRE
RESTAURANT, C0 KILKENNY

THE KILKENNY RIVERCOURT HOTEL
KILKENNY, CO KILKENNY

NEWPARK HOTEL
KILKENNY, CO KILKENNY

Féile Bia Members

LIMERICK

ADARE MANOR HOTEL & GOLF RESORT, ADARE, CO LIMERICK

THE WILD GEESE RESTAURANT ADARE, CO LIMERICK

WOODLANDS HOUSE HOTEL ADARE, CO LIMERICK

THE MILL-RACE RESTAURANT CROOM, CO LIMERICK

CASTLETROY PARK HOTEL LIMERICK, CO LIMERICK

JURYS LIMERICK HOTEL LIMERICK, CO LIMERICK

JURYS INN, LIMERICK,CO LIMERICK

SOUTH COURT HOTEL LIMERICK, CO LIMERICK

LOUTH

THE OYSTERCATCHER BISTRO CARLINGFORD, CO LOUTH

QUAGLINO'S RESTAURANT DUNDALK, CO LOUTH

MAYO

HEALYS HOTEL & RESTAURANT PONTOON, FOXFORD, CO MAYO

HOTEL WESTPORT WESTPORT, CO MAYO

MEATH

BACCHUS AT THE COASTGUARD BETTYSTOWN, CO MEATH

MONAGHAN

CASTLE LESLIE GLASLOUGH, CO MONAGHAN

ANDY'S BAR & RESTAURANT MONAGHAN, CO MONAGHAN

SLIGO

AUSTIES ROSSES POINT, CO SLIGO

BISTRO BIANCONI SLIGO, CO SLIGO

COACH LANE RESTAURANT SLIGO, CO SLIGO

TIPPERARY

THE DERG INN TERRYGLASS, CO TIPPERARY

INCH HOUSE THURLES, CO TIPPERARY

WATERFORD

RICHMOND HOUSE CAPPOQUIN, CO WATERFORD

MC ALPIN'S SUIR INN CHEEKPOINT, CO WATERFORD

GATCHELLS RESTAURANT WATERFORD CRYSTAL VISITORS CENTRE, CO WATERFORD

GRANVILLE HOTEL, WATERFORD

WESTMEATH

HODSON BAY HOTEL ATHLONE, CO WESTMEATH

RESTAURANT LE CHATEAU ATHLONE, CO WESTMEATH

MANIFESTO RESTAURANT ATHLONE, CO WESTMEATH

WINEPORT LODGE GLASSON, ATHLONE, CO WESTMEATH

WOODVILLE HOUSE RESTAURANT MULLINGAR, CO WESTMEATH

WEXFORD

DUNBRODY HOUSE ARTHURSTOWN, CO WEXFORD

KELLY'S RESORT HOTEL ROSSLARE, CO WEXFORD

FERRYCARRIG HOTEL WEXFORD, CO WEXFORD

WICKLOW

DOWNSHIRE HOUSE HOTEL BLESSINGTON, CO WICKLOW

RATHSALLAGH HOUSE DUNLAVIN, CO WICKLOW

THE ROUNDWOOD INN ROUNDWOOD, CO WICKLOW

SLAINTE!

Irish food, drink & hospitality today...

As visitors to Ireland from all around the world have testified in their thousands over the last few years, Ireland has become much more than a laid-back place with pretty scenery. From the discerning traveller's point of view, the most striking change for the better has been the emergence of a new food culture that now makes Ireland a gourmet destination of the highest order - and with the high quality accommodation to match it.

Chic contemporary hotels are taking their place beside much-loved traditional establishments and the arrival of top international chains has put the leading Irish hotels on their mettle this year. But the newcomers, however prestigious their reputations may be, recognise that they have a challenge on their hands and there is fierce competition from Irish-owned hotel groups who are masters of hospitality.

Many Irish hotels now successfuly operate both fine-dining and informal brasserie-style restaurants - and there's a bevy of talented and determined owner-chefs out there too, so it's not going to be a walk-over for the big names, who have to find a balance between providing the services demanded by an international clientèle and the need to give visitors a meaningful flavour of Ireland.

For generations, Irish chefs, trained in the classical tradition, usually have gone abroad to complete their training and on their return, as surely as the invaders of earlier centuries, brought back foreign culinary influences. The process continues to this day - as a glance at any popular menu shows - but, fortunately, the demands of discerning visitors are helping to re-awaken interest in Irish food culture.

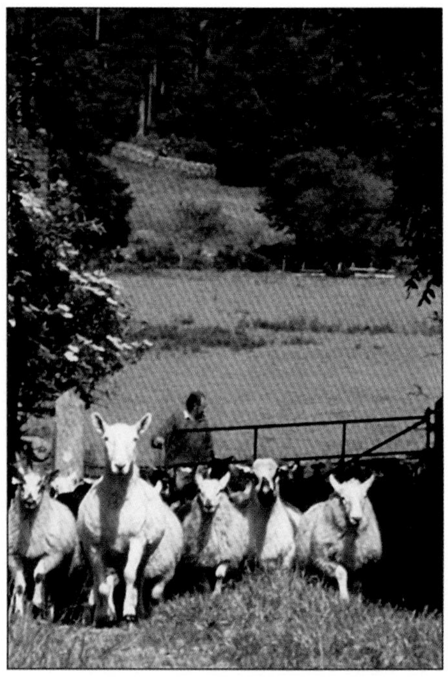

A SENSE OF PLACE

Ireland is a food exporting country and Bord Bia, the Irish Food Board, is responsible for promoting Irish food at home and abroad:their slogan "Ireland the Food Island" highlights this neatly. Although they have 700 food and drink companies to support, they are committed to the development of speciality foods, a sector that has grown in strength and variety, in particular those producers who take charge of

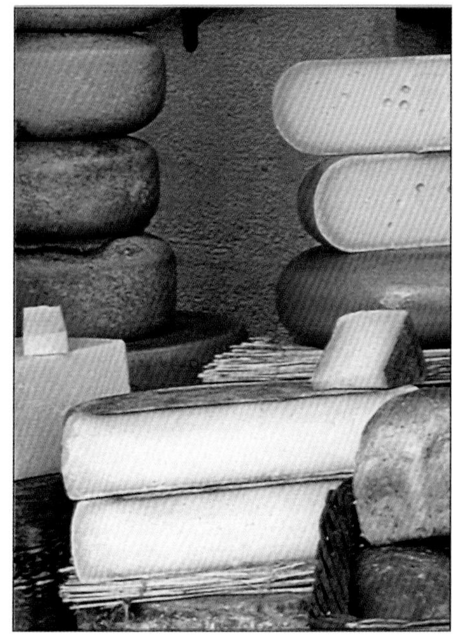

every step in the process from farm to consumer: craft sausage-makers, organic meat and poultry farmers, specialists in wild game and rare breeds, producers who work with fruits, herbs, and vegetables, and the farm cheesemakers who have gained wide respect in the international food community.

The success of niche-market foods, notably Irish farm cheeses, in recent decades has come to symbolise the hopes of food-lovers for the future of mainstream produce. It is a source of wonderment to Europeans that today's Irish farm cheeses are produced on just one farm, usually by one dedicated family. The variety and high quality is astonishing. One reason for this is the Irish climate. Our green grasslands in favoured areas are rich in wild, natural herbage and sheep, goats and cows are largely grass fed to produce flavoursome and distinctive milk. You can experience local farmhouse cheeses in restaurants, or visit local food markets in Dublin, Belfast, Cork, and many other small country markets. Food markets are a fun day out and feature innovative and traditional products from small food producers.

In the current cosmopolitan atmosphere - where global cuisine is the norm, even in many rural restaurants - the best Irish chefs are increasingly aware of the need to give the Irish table "a sense of place". The Feile Bia programme encourages chefs everywhere to think less about contemporary cooking fashions and look to their roots. Feile Bia began as a week-long festival celebrating Irish food and traditional Irish cooking has been expanded into a year-round programme. Working together, Bord Bia, the Restaurants Association of Ireland and the Irish Hotels Federation have set up the scheme, with the support of the farming community. Establishments that undertake to source and use local/quality-assured products from named suppliers, and be subject to an annual audit, may display the blue-framed Feile Bia certificate. Consumer research shows that we place a high value on quality Irish food and assume when eating out that is what we are getting. At the top end of the market, especially where the chef is a member of Euro-Toques, this is generally the case; but it is not universally true.

Feila Bia aims to provide assurance for consumers that the food they eat is quality sourced. The complications of food marketing in Ireland mean that, so far, only beef, pork, bacon, and eggs are included. It is early days yet and consumers should look out for the certificate and talk to owners or managers about their policy on sourcing other foods. Showing this interest will help the Feile Bia scheme to grow and prosper.

EURO-TOQUES

Ross Lewis, Ireland's Euro-Toques Commissioner General

Thanks to the dedication of many talented Irish chefs and small producers, progress on strengthening the regional quality of Irish food is promising. Dubbed variously "the new Irish cuisine" or "contemporary Irish cooking", a recognisably Irish cooking style is emerging, producing lighter, modern food that is still based on traditional foodstuffs and themes. Through Féile Bia, and other programmes and organisations which recognise the value of quality Irish produce and traditions, chefs are encouraged to avoid the dangers of fashionable but bland internationalism and to bring a real Irish flavour back into their restaurants. Euro-Toques, the European Community of Chefs, is an organisation with just these issues at heart - and over 200 Irish chefs are enthusiastic members. Their charter commits them to supporting the quality of natural and traditional foods, to maintaining traditional dishes and traditional ways of preparing them in order to keep regional differences alive.

Ross Lewis, chef-proprietor of Dublin's Chapter One Restaurant, is Ireland's incoming Commissioner General. He will lead a strong Irish 'chapter' which steals time to support social activities like mushroom hunts and visits to members' restaurants and to craft food producers. Euro-Toques nurtures young talent through the annual Baileys/Euro-Toques Young Chef of the Year Competition, and by selecting and coaching Ireland's representative at the world's most prestigious cooking competition, the Bocuse d'Or. But in no way is this an elitist group. All chefs are encouraged to join, providing they are prepared to follow the code of honour and use fine, non-genetically engineered, quality foods, and support local craft food producers.

SLOW FOOD

The Slow Food Movement is a focal point for small craft food producers in much the same way as Euro-Toques is for chefs. This international movement is dedicated to ensuring the future of small-scale, quality, farm-food production. Groups of small producers have formed convivia (local chapters) and hold open days throughout the country. Their goal is to spread and stimulate awareness of food culture (flavours and ancient production techniques), to safeguard the food and agricultural heritage (biodiversity, artisanal techniques and traditions), to protect the heritage of traditional eating places, and oppose the worldwide standardisation of tastes. Although only recently activated in Ireland, it is touched a chord of resonance and is, despite the name, a fast-growing movement that promises to become highly influential.

HEALTHY EATING

A youthful, health-conscious population has taken to the fashion for juices and smoothies with a vengeance and, judging by the great variety of vegetables and side salads on restaurant tables, the Bord Glas (horticultural development board) "Four or More" slogan, urging Irish people to eat more fruit and vegetables, is proving remarkably popular. Welcome mainstream trends this year include a far wider range of vegetarian dishes—often placed top of the menu; an increasing use of seasonal and named foods from local growers and producers; and the increasing availability of Irish-grown organic foods (the organic market is growing at up to 30% a year but, sadly, much is still imported). It is many an Irish food-lover's hope that we might take on the exciting challenge of turning Ireland not just into "the food island" but the "organic food island".

HAPPY HEART EAT OUT

Most visitors lose a little bit of their heart to Ireland - and it's the Irish Heart Foundation's task to keep the hearts of natives and visitors alike physically healthy. The Irish Heart Foundation's aims coincide with those of Bord Glas and other food agencies, in that they want healthy eating to be a normal, enjoyable part of life. The Happy Heart Eat Out initiative is an imaginative (and very Irish way) of doing just that and has been an annual feature for some years now. Restaurants, hotels, pubs and other eating establishments that join the programme offer healthy eating options - look out for the smiling heart-shaped face on the menu. In a country with an abundance of home-grown vegetables, fruits, herbs, seafoods, and meat, it's not difficulty to offer "healthy" menu options. Increasingly, Irish restaurants recognise the need to care for their customers' health, with dishes low in fat and sodium highlighted on the menu, and a willingness to meet special dietary requirements: if you don't see what you need on the menu "Just Ask".

Knowing that making "healthy" activities enjoyable is the secret of success, The Irish Heart Foundation invented Slí na Sláinte (the Path to Health) - a simple and successful concept that has since been adopted by 12 other countries. The signed (with a blue-pole) 1 kilometre routes allow walkers or runners to keep track of time and distance. Some run along the coast, or along lake and river banks, others go through parks and city centres. New routes are opened all the time and you'll rarely be far from one.

RICHES FROM LAND & SEA

If you wanted to create the perfect place to catch seafood - clean Atlantic waters warmed along much of the coast by the Gulf Stream - you'd probably invent Ireland: Bord Iascaigh Mhara, the Irish Sea Fisheries Board, is dedicated to developing the seafood industry and encouraging everyone to cook and enjoy seafood.

A number of developments are of interest: one innovative scheme encourages the combination of fruit and vegetables with fish, a healthy idea that makes the most of expensive seafood. Deep-water species are appearing on menus (spurred on by EU fish quotas). The development of aquaculture and the trend towards organic fish farming is growing: organic mussels, trout and salmon are already available. At Clare Island Sea Farm the demand for organic salmon outstrips supply. They are members of the Irish Seafood Producers Group which farms turbot (off Cape Clear Island) arctic char, Atlantic trout, and salmon; the shellfishes grown commercially include oysters, mussels, clams, and scallops.

With BIM's launch of The Seafood Circle (a pub-lunch programme), more pubs will be serving seafood dishes for lunch, a meal for which more and more customers prefer lighter, healthier dishes. It's a practical programme and involves workshops and on-going guidance on every aspect of buying, storing, and cooking seafood. Only pubs that meet the criteria are allowed to join the circle following annual audits by Excellence Ireland, and a striking plaque will make them easy to identify.

ETHNIC FOOD

The current fashion for global cuisine has quickened pace recently; as Ireland has become a net importer of people from all over the world, the influence of other food cultures (European, Asian, New World, and every possible fusion of cuisines from Cal-Ital to Pacific rim)

Courtesy of Sharwood's

has grown—sometimes jostling for space on the same menu. Every city street offers you a choice and few small Irish towns are without either a Chinese or an Indian restaurant (or both). Having a large cosmopolitan population with differing tastes and traditions is changing the way Irish people look at ethnic food and there is growing interest in authenticity, both in restaurants and ethnic cooking at home. Shops, supermarkets and street markets specialising in ethnic cuisines are springing up all over - a recent example is the African market in the Parnell Street area of Dublin - and mainstream supermarkets are laden down with ethnic ingredinets all all kinds. It's an exciting phase and highlights the value of restaurants that are true to a particular style or cuisine, many of which are included in the Guide - all the main cultures are well-represented with Thai and, most recently, Japanese restaurants making particular impact at the moment.

IRISH LOVE OF ATMOSPHERE

Assuming good food, atmosphere in restaurants is probably more important to the Irish dining public than anything else - and , while there's no sure recipe for making a restaurant somewhere people just love to be, genuine hospitality is the main ingredient for success. Relaxing decor and sympathetic lighting are the other magic ingredients and the Guide is privileged to have Rathborne Candles as a sponsor - Ireland's oldest established (AD 1488) surviving company, they have been lighting churches and dining rooms in the country for almost 600 years and are increasingly doing it again today as candles have become an essential "softening" feature in contemporary decor. So the next time you sit in a great candlelit dining-room overlooking a lake or a sunset-lit mountain, just think that for six centuries people have been doing something remarkably similar! Candles are also closely interwoven with traditional customs in Ireland - putting a lighted candle in the window on Christmas Eve, for example, goes back countless generations and there was also a tradition of shopkeepers and publicans giving a candle to customers at Christmas. A recent example was P.J. McCaffrey's, The Hole in the Wall pub in Dublin which is near the old candle factory at Dunsinea and continues the practice of giving out a red Rathbornes to every customer until a few years ago.

DRINK

Drink is an essential element of Irish hospitality, that some prize above food as a way of showing our pleasure in company, our delight in entertainment, and as nourishment for mind and body. The Irish have been brewing since earliest times and without a doubt, had the climate been favourable, there would have been a thriving wine industry, too. Not that the Irish did without wine. Records show that two thousand years ago French wine was being dispatched to Ireland for "feasts in the courts of the kings". Later, early Christian monks sailed to the mouth of the Loire to fetch wine for Irish monasteries and the Vikings paid tribute to Irish kings in vats of wine. The ordinary people were content with cider, ale, and later, with porter and stout.

It is generally accepted that the craft of distillation was brought to Ireland from the Mediterranean, possibly by missionary monks around fifteen hundred years ago. It was used originally to make perfumes and medicines; and later whiskey. Much as we'd like to, no one really knows the origins of whiskey. The Celtic culture was an oral one, particularly when it came to important secrets which were never written down. Historians search ancient texts for written evidence with good reason—our reputation for having invented whiskey is at stake.

We had aqua vitae of course, distilled from wine. We do know, from a wealth of written sources, that by the mid-16th Century the making of grain aqua vitae (known to the Irish as ische beatha and to English-speakers as whiskey) was widespread. Then, on Christmas Day 1661, a tax of 4p was imposed on every gallon distilled. Folklore has it that the making of the illicit spirit poitin began on St. Stephen's Day! The difference between legal and illicit whiskey was small. By the 18th Century there were 2,000 stills in operation and whiskey had become the spirit of the nation, inspiring poets and musicians and promoting friendship (and frequent disputes) between native and stranger. Irish whiskey is both spelled and made differently from other whiskeys. It is made only from kiln-dried barley (both malted and unmalted), yeast and pure Irish water. It is distilled three times in a pot still, then matured in oak barrels until judged ready for drinking. Visitors can relive this history by visiting three historic distilleries: The Old Jameson Distillery in Dublin, The Bushmills Distillery in Antrim, and the Middleton Distillery in County Cork. The tours are fascinating, covering all aspects of whiskey making - and end with a whiskey tasting.

Although whiskey is better known internationally, gin also has a long and honourable history in Ireland, and is an excellent product. It may hurt a Dubliner to admit it, but Ireland's best known gin is made, and always has been made, in Cork. Cork Dry Gin dates back to 1793 when the first stone of Cork's old Watercourse Distillery was laid. A 1798 recipe book details both the process and the recipe—grain from the rich lands of East Cork, flavoured with juniper berries (a native plant), angelica root, and citrus fruits (then a recent arrival in the port of Cork). Blending these exotic ingredients was the task of William Coldwell and his secret recipe migrated to Cork Distillers Company in 1876 inspiring the uniquely balanced taste of Cork Dry Gin.

THE GREAT IRISH BREAKFAST

If enjoyment in restaurants and pubs around the country provides memorable evening entertainment, the next morning's breakfast is no small matter for visitors to Ireland - or, indeed, for the Irish on holiday, as having the leisure to indulge in a proper breakfast seems to symbolises escape from the workaday routine.The best hosts take great pride in offering guests a breakfast to remember, whether it be a meal with little choice that is cooked to perfection or a wide range of breakfast menus - in some areas the competition between neighbouring establishments is fierce and menus can run to several pages.They offer traditional country house breakfast dishes that have fallen from favour, fresh and cured fish, European-style salami and hams, wonderful and varied breads, Irish farm cheeses, and vegetarian options. Not that the traditional Irish breakfast is neglected; how could it be when it remains (particularly with visitors) the most popular way to start to the day?

"The full Irish" as it is affectionately known, is not for the faint-hearted—bacon rashers, eggs, sausages, black and white puddings, tomatoes, and fried bread. Once cooked on a great black cast-iron frying pan over a turf fire, it is more usually grilled nowadays (or oven-baked) except for the fried egg. The truly health-conscious will be glad to know you'll be offered a choice of poached, scrambled, or baked eggs (which, just to confuse, are often cooked in thick Irish cream). The Ulster Fry, on the other hand, remains defiantly unreconstructed—at least in name! Its additional ingredients include fried potato cakes, boxty, farls of soda (griddle) bread, mushrooms, and on occasion baked beans! Small wonder that the "all-day breakfast" is widely on offer!

You can forgive visitors for being confused sometimes; not only can they eat breakfast all day but there is a growing trend of serving Sunday lunch all day, too! What's next? The all-night dinner?

IRELAND

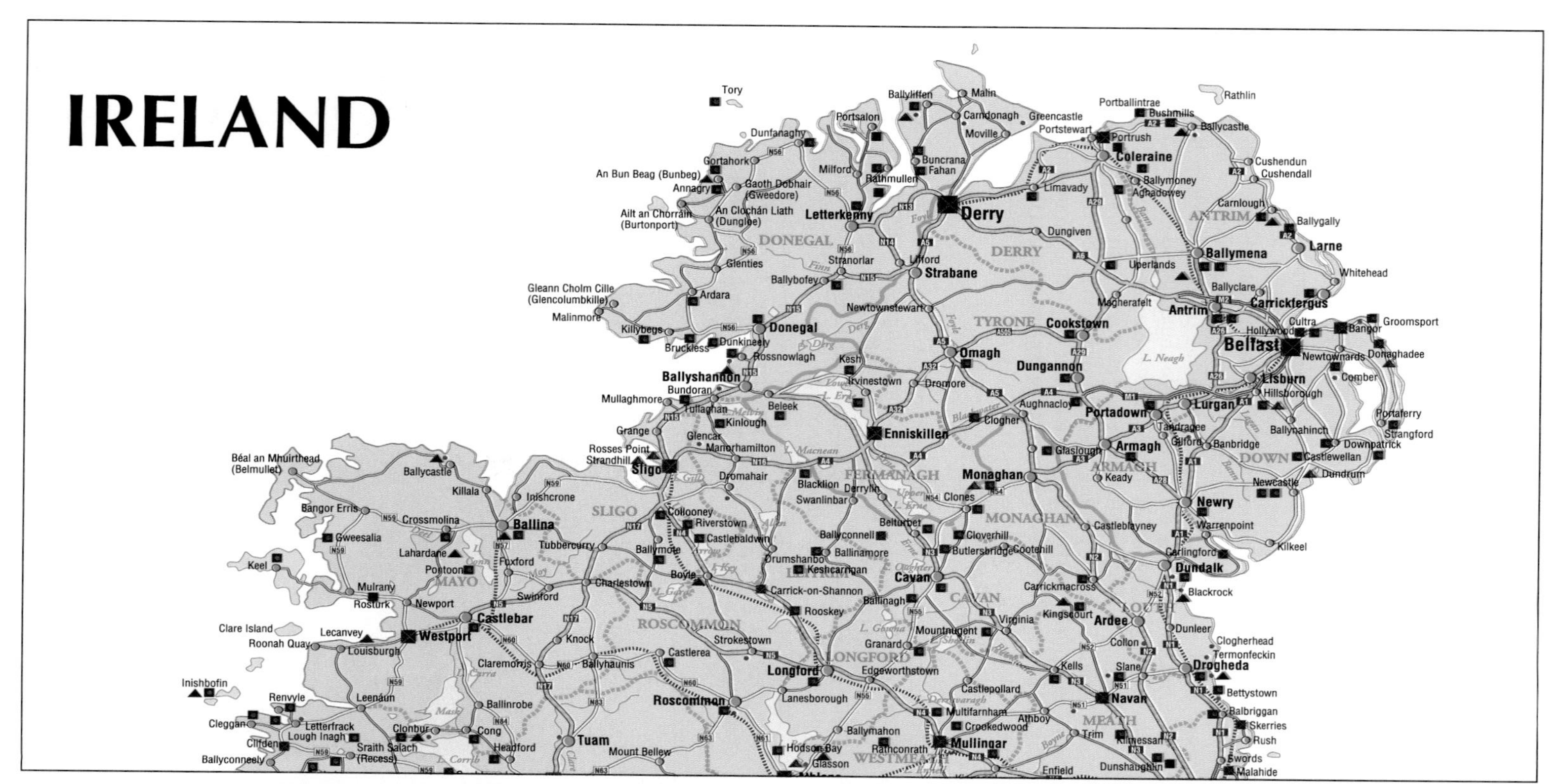
Tory
Dunfanaghy
Gortahork
An Bun Beag (Bunbeg)
Annagry
Gaoth Dobhair (Gweedore)
Ailt an Chorráin (Burtonport)
An Clochán Liath (Dungloe)
Glenties
Gleann Cholm Cille (Glencolumbkille)
Malinmore
Ardara
Killybegs
Bruckless
Dunkineely
Donegal
Rossnowlagh
Ballyshannon
Bundoran
Mullaghmore
Tullaghan
Kinlough
Beleek
Grange
Glencar
Manorhamilton
Rosses Point
Strandhill
Sligo
Dromahair
Portsalon
Milford
Rathmullen
Letterkenny
DONEGAL
Stranorlar
Ballybofey
Ballyliffen
Malin
Carndonagh
Moville
Greencastle
Buncrana
Fahan
Derry
Lifford
Strabane
Newtownstewart
Kesh
Irvinestown
Dromore
Omagh
Enniskillen
Portstewart
Portballintrae
Bushmills
Ballycastle
Rathlin
Portrush
Coleraine
Limavady
Ballymoney
Aghadowey
Dungiven
DERRY
TYRONE
Cookstown
Dungannon
Magherafelt
Uperlands
Cushendun
Cushendall
Carnlough
ANTRIM
Ballygally
Ballymena
Larne
Whitehead
Ballyclare
Carrickfergus
Antrim
L. Neagh
Hollywood
Cultra
Bangor
Groomsport
Belfast
Newtownards
Donaghadee
Comber
Lisburn
Hillsborough
Portaferry
Strangford
Ballynahinch
Downpatrick
Castlewellan
Dundrum
DOWN
Newcastle
Kilkeel
Lurgan
Portadown
Tandragee
Gilford
Banbridge
Armagh
ARMAGH
Keady
Glaslough
Aughnacloy
Clogher
Newry
Warrenpoint
Carlingford
Dundalk
Blackrock
Monaghan
Clones
MONAGHAN
Castleblayney
FERMANAGH
Blacklion
Derrylin
Swanlinbar
Belturbet
Ballyconnell
Cloverhill
Butlersbridge
Cootehill
Ballinamore
Keshcarrigan
Drumshanbo
LEITRIM
Cavan
CAVAN
Carrick-on-Shannon
Ballinagh
Rooskey
Carrickmacross
Kingscourt
Virginia
Ardee
LOUTH
Dunleer
Clogherhead
Termonfeckin
Drogheda
Collon
Slane
Kells
Navan
MEATH
Bettystown
Balbriggan
Skerries
Rush
Swords
Malahide
Mountnugent
Granard
L. Gowna
LONGFORD
Longford
Edgeworthstown
Castlepollard
Multifarnham
Crookedwood
Athboy
Trim
Kilmessan
Dunshaughlin
Enfield
Mullingar
WESTMEATH
Rathconrath
Ballymahon
Lanesborough
Hodson Bay
Glasson
Strokestown
ROSCOMMON
Roscommon
Castlerea
Ballyhaunis
Claremorris
Knock
Charlestown
Boyle
Ballymote
Riverstown
Collooney
Castlebaldwin
SLIGO
Tubbercurry
Inishcrone
Ballina
Killala
Ballycastle
Béal an Mhuirthead (Belmullet)
Bangor Erris
Crossmolina
Gweesalia
Lahardane
Foxford
Swinford
Pontoon
MAYO
Keel
Mulrany
Rosturk
Newport
Castlebar
Westport
Clare Island
Lecanvey
Roonah Quay
Louisburgh
Inishbofin
Renvyle
Leenáun
Cleggan
Letterfrack
Lough Inagh
Clifden
Ballyconneely
Sraith Salach (Recess)
Clonbur
Cong
Ballinrobe
Headford
Tuam
Mount Bellew

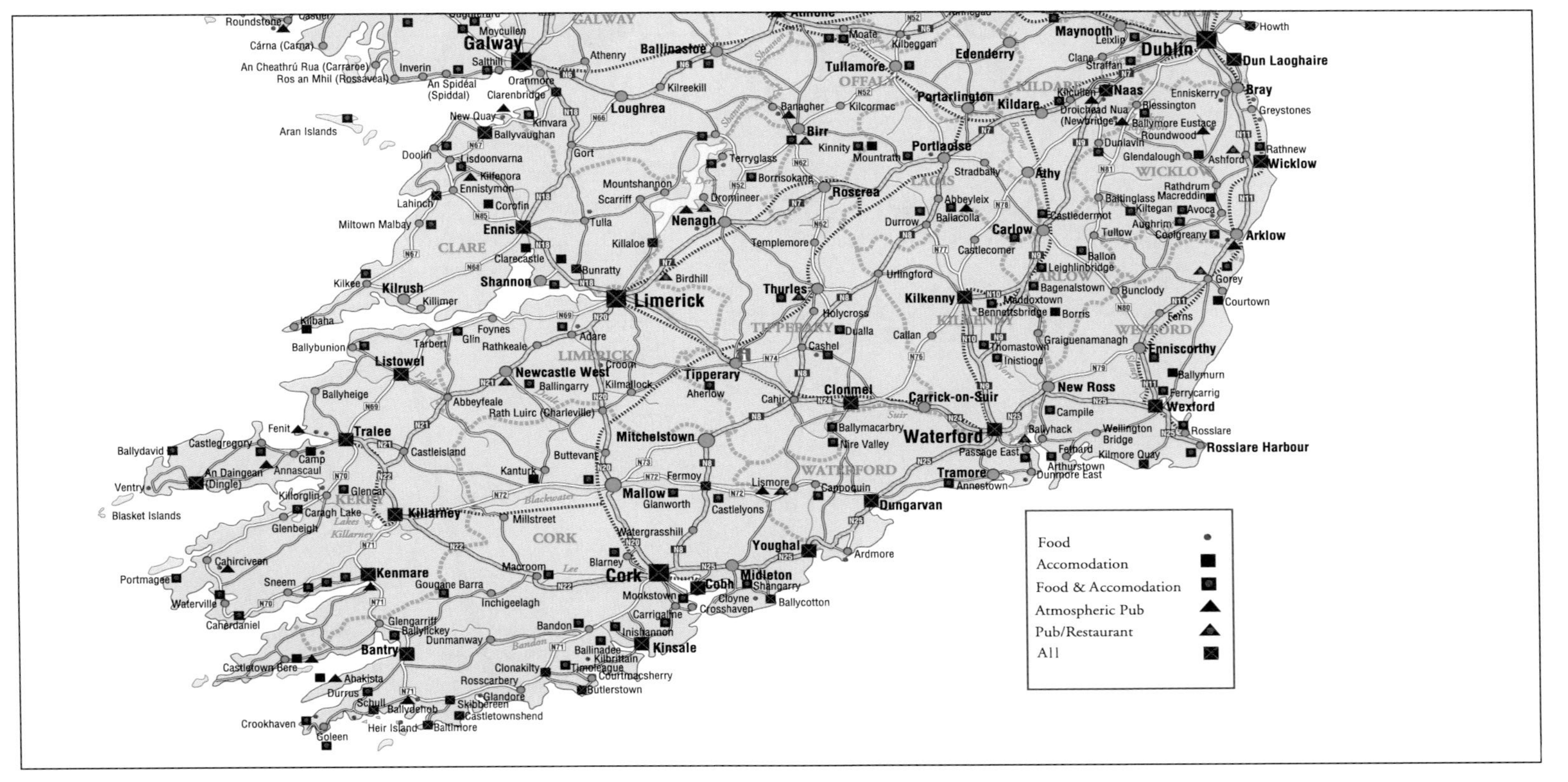
Food
Accomodation
Food & Accomodation
Atmospheric Pub
Pub/Restaurant
All
Galway
Dublin
Dun Laoghaire
Howth
Maynooth
Leixlip
Bray
Greystones
Wicklow
Rathnew
Arklow
Gorey
Courtown
Enniscorthy
Wexford
Rosslare
Rosslare Harbour
New Ross
Waterford
Tramore
Dungarvan
Kilkenny
Carlow
Athy
Kildare
Naas
Portlaoise
Portarlington
Tullamore
Edenderry
Birr
Roscrea
Nenagh
Thurles
Limerick
Shannon
Ennis
Kilrush
Tipperary
Clonmel
Carrick-on-Suir
Cahir
Cashel
Mitchelstown
Mallow
Fermoy
Youghal
Midleton
Cobh
Cork
Kinsale
Bandon
Clonakilty
Skibbereen
Baltimore
Bantry
Kenmare
Killarney
Tralee
Listowel
Newcastle West
An Daingean (Dingle)
Aran Islands
Blasket Islands
Loughrea
Ballinasloe
Athenry
Oranmore
Clarenbridge
Kinvara
Ballyvaughan
Lisdoonvarna
Doolin
Ennistymon
Lahinch
Miltown Malbay
Kilkee
Ballybunion
Abbeyfeale
Adare
Kilmallock
Castleisland
Killorglin
Glenbeigh
Cahirciveen
Portmagee
Waterville
Sneem
Castletown Bere
Crookhaven
Goleen
Schull
CLARE
LIMERICK
TIPPERARY
KERRY
CORK
WATERFORD
KILKENNY
CARLOW
WEXFORD
WICKLOW
KILDARE
LAOIS
OFFALY
GALWAY

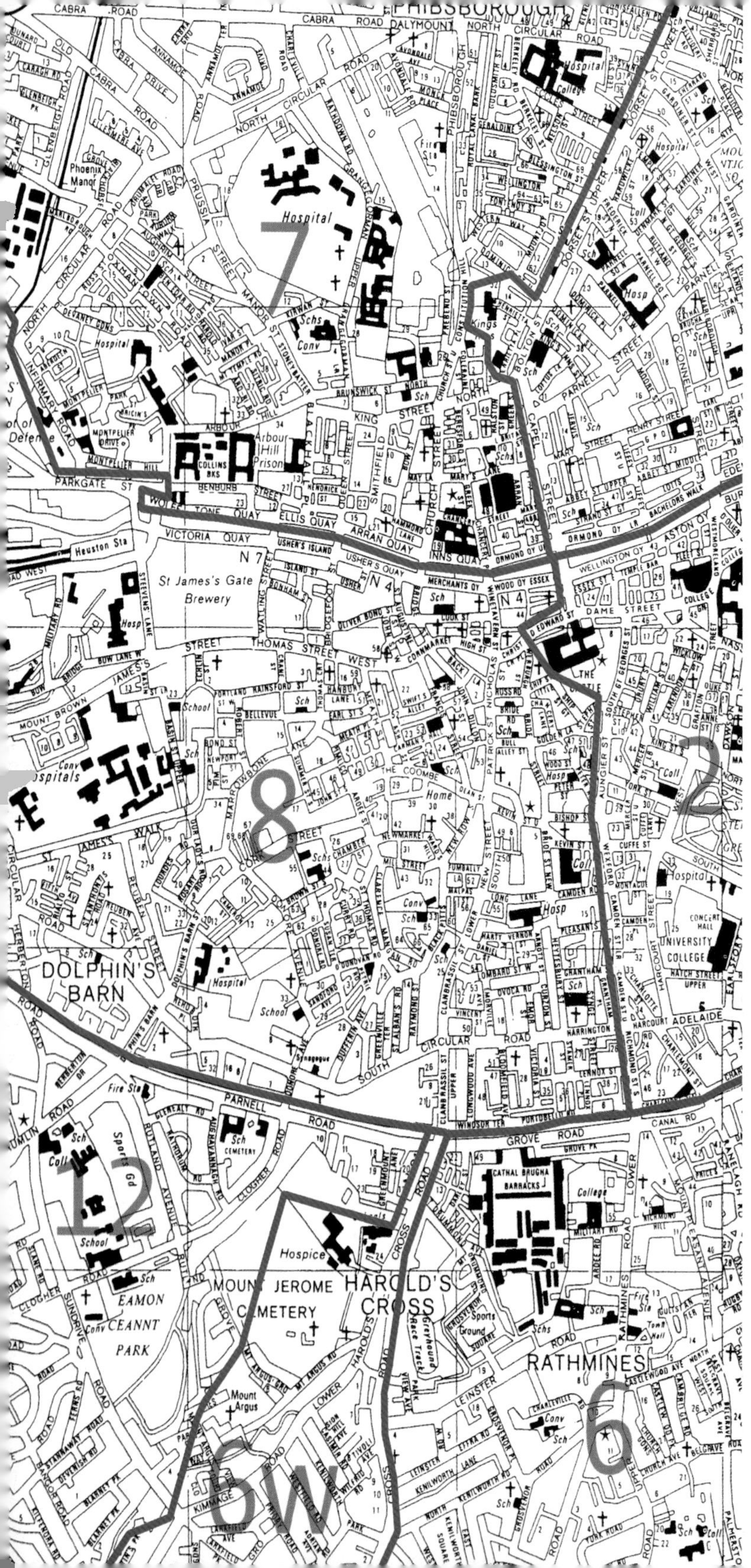

PHIBSBOROUGH
CABRA ROAD
NORTH CIRCULAR ROAD
Phoenix Manor
Hospital
7
PRUSSIA STREET
MANOR ST
STONEYBATTER
Arbour Hill Prison
COLLINS BKS
BENBURB STREET
WOLFE TONE QUAY
ELLIS QUAY
ARRAN QUAY
INNS QUAY
ORMOND QY
PARKGATE ST
VICTORIA QUAY
Heuston Sta
USHER'S ISLAND
USHER'S QUAY
MERCHANTS QY
WOOD QY
ESSEX QY
WELLINGTON QY
ASTON QY
N 7
N 4
St James's Gate Brewery
THOMAS STREET
JAMES'S
MOUNT BROWN
Hospitals
DAME STREET
COLLEGE
THE CASTLE
SMITHFIELD
KING STREET
BRUNSWICK ST NORTH
MARY'S LANE
CAPEL STREET
MARY STREET
HENRY STREET
ABBEY ST UPPER
O'CONNELL STREET
PARNELL
DORSET ST UPPER
DORSET ST LOWER
Kings Inns
8
THE COOMBE
NEW ROW
PATRICK ST
NICHOLAS ST
BRIDE ST
AUNGIER ST
GEORGES ST
2
HARCOURT STREET
UNIVERSITY COLLEGE
CONCERT HALL
DOLPHIN'S BARN
SOUTH CIRCULAR ROAD
PARNELL ROAD
GROVE ROAD
CANAL RD
CATHAL BRUGHA BARRACKS
12
Sports Gd
School
Hospice
MOUNT JEROME CEMETERY
HAROLD'S CROSS
Greyhound Race Track
RATHMINES
6
6W
Mount Argus
EAMON CEANNT PARK
KIMMAGE

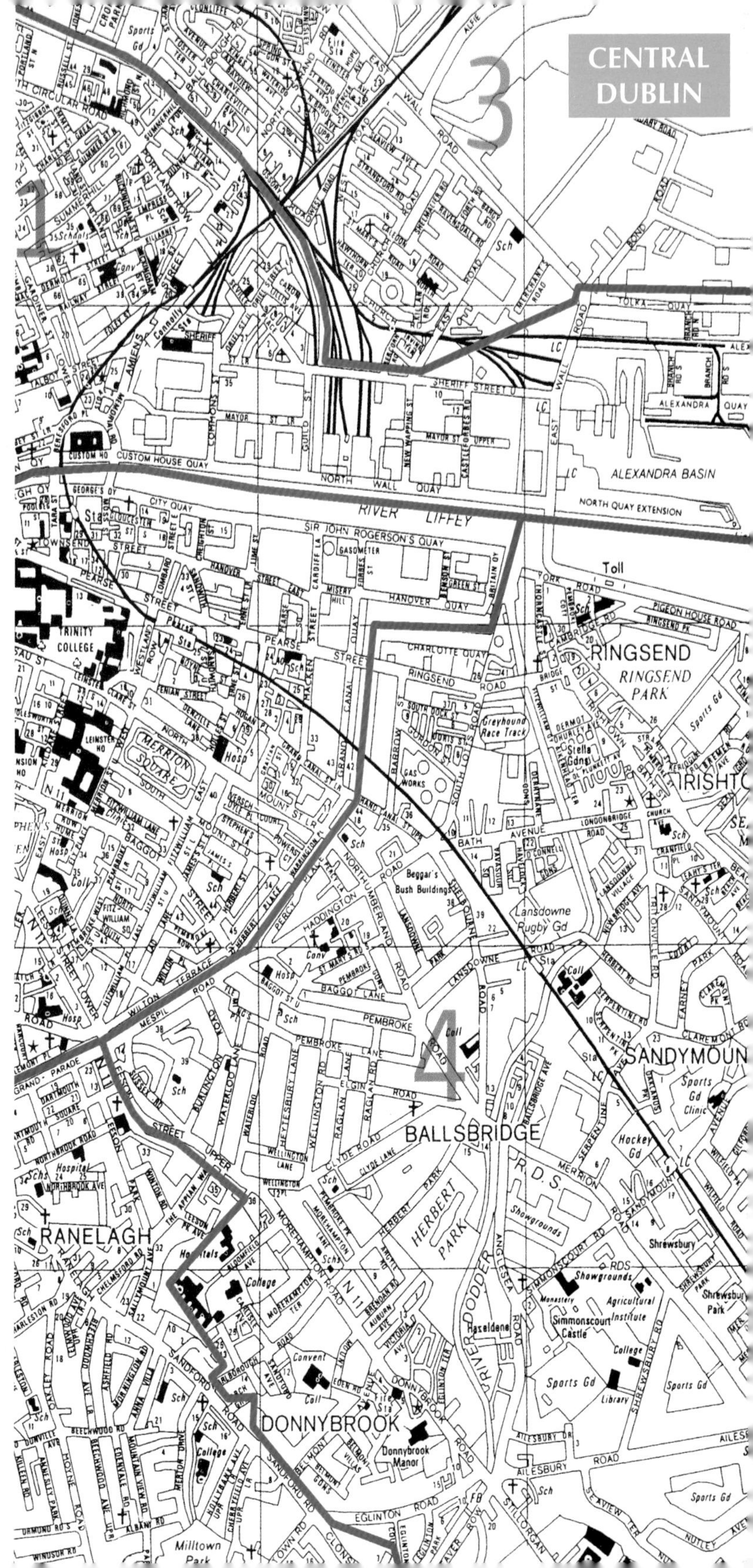

CENTRAL DUBLIN
3
1
4
RINGSEND
RINGSEND PARK
IRISHTOWN
SANDYMOUNT
BALLSBRIDGE
RANELAGH
DONNYBROOK
TRINITY COLLEGE
ALEXANDRA BASIN
NORTH QUAY EXTENSION
RIVER LIFFEY
SIR JOHN ROGERSON'S QUAY
CUSTOM HOUSE QUAY
NORTH WALL QUAY
MERRION SQUARE
HERBERT PARK
R.D.S. Showgrounds
Lansdowne Rugby Gd
Greyhound Race Track
Beggar's Bush Buildings
Simmonscourt Castle
Donnybrook Manor
RIVER DODDER
Toll

DUBLIN CITY

A Town for our Times

Even with the uncertainties of 2002, Dublin continues to be Western Europe's most rapidly expanding economic centre, its creative business and commercial energy matched by the vibrancy of its everyday life and hospitality. For Dublin is a city whose time has come. It's an old town whose many meandering stories have interacted and combined to create today's busy riverside and coastal metropolis. Through a wide variety of circumstances, it has become an entertaining place ideally suited for the civilised enjoyment of life in the 21st Century.

Dubliners tend to wear their city's history lightly, despite having in their environment so much of the past in the way of ancient monuments, historic buildings, gracious squares and fine old urban architecture that still manages to be gloriously alive. They may not quite take it for granted, but nevertheless they have to get on with life. Indeed, these days they've a vigorous appetite for it. So they'll quickly deflate any visitor's excessive enthusiasm about their city's significance with some throwaway line of Dublin wit, or sweep aside highfalutin notions of some figure of established cultural importance by recalling how their grandfathers had the measure of that same character when he was still no more than a pup making a nuisance of himself in the neighbourhood pub.

The origins of the city's name are in keeping with this downbeat approach. From the ancient Irish there came something which derived from a makeshift solution to local inconvenience. Baile Atha Cliath - the official name today - means nothing more exciting than "the townland of the hurdle ford". Ancient Ireland being an open plan sort of place without towns, the future city was no more than a river crossing.

But where the Irish saw inconvenience, the Vikings saw an opportunity. When they brought their longships up the River Liffey, they found a sheltered berth in a place which the locals of the hurdle ford called Dubh Linn - "the black pool". Although the name was to go through many mutations as the Vikings were succeeded by the Normans who in turn were in the business of becoming English, today's name of Dublin is remarkably similar to the one which the Vikings came upon, although the old Irish would have pronounced it as something more like "doo-lin".

The name makes sense, for it was thanks to the existence of the black pool that Dublin became the port and trading base which evolved as the country's natural administrative centre. Thus your Dubliner may well think that the persistent official use of Baile Atha Cliath is an absurdity. But it most empatically isn't the business of any visitor to say so, for although Dublin came into existence almost by accident, it has now been around for a long time, and Dubliners have developed their own attitudes and their own way of doing things, while their seaport - still very much part of the city - has never been busier.

Located by a wide bay with some extraordinarily handsome hills and mountains near at hand, the city has long had as an important part of its makeup the dictates of stylish living, and the need to cater efficiently for individual tastes and requirements. From time to time the facade has been maintained through periods of impoverishment, but even in the earliest mediaeval period this was already a major centre of craftmanship and innovative shop-keeping. Today, the Dublin craftsmen and shop-keepers and their assistants are characterful subjects worthy of respectful academic study. And in an age when "going shopping" has become the world's favourite leisure activity, this old city has reinvented herself in the forefront of international trends.

For Dublin virtually shunned the Industrial Revolution, or at least took some care to ensure that it happened elsewhere. The city's few large enterprises tended to be aimed at personal needs and the consumer market, rather than some aspiration towards heavy industry. Typical of them was Guinness's Brewery, founded in 1759. Today, its work-force may be much slimmed in every sense, but it still creates the black nectar, and if a new mash is under way up at the brewery and the wind is coming damply across Ireland from the west, the aroma of Guinness in the making will be wafted right into the city centre, the moist evocative essence of Anna Livia herself, while the imaginatively renovated Guinness Hopstore provides a visitor centre of international quality

Although some of the vitality of the city faded in the periods when the focus of power had been moved elsewhere, today Dublin thrives as one of Europe's more entertaining capitals, and as a global centre of the computer, communications and financial services industries. While it may be trite to suggest that her history has been a fortuitous preparation for the needs of modern urban life in all its variety of work and relaxation, there is no denying Dublin's remarkable capacity to provide the ideal circumstances for fast-moving people-orientated modern industries, even if those same people find at times that their movement within the city is hampered by weight of traffic. Nevertheless it's a civilised city where the importance of education is a central theme of the strong family ethos, the high level of education making it a place of potent attraction in the age of information technology.

Such a city naturally has much of interest for historians of all kinds, and a vibrant cultural life is available for visitors and Dubliners alike. You can immerse yourself in it all as much or as little as you prefer, for today's Dublin is a city for all times and all tastes, and if you're someone who hopes to enjoy Dublin as we know Dubliners enjoy it, we know you'll find much of value here. And don't forget that there's enjoyment in Dublin well hidden from the familiar tourist trails.

History is well-matched by modernity, or a mixture of both. The glass palaces of the International Financial Services Centre point the way to a maturing new business district which is a pleasure to savour. To the westward, the award-winning transformation of the Smithfield area beside the popular Old Jameson Distillery Visitor centre is another magnet for the discerning visitor who enjoys a sense of the past interacting with the present.

When Dublin was starting to expand to its present size during the mid-20th Century, with people flocking in from all over Ireland to work in the city, it was said that the only "real Dub" was someone who didn't go home to the country for the weekend. Today, with Dublin so popular with visitors, the more cynical citizens might well comment that the surest test of a real Dub is someone who avoids Temple Bar......

But there is much more to this bustling riverside hotbed of musical pubs, ethnic restaurants, cultural events and nightclubs than just a tourist honeypot. After all, in addition to its many places of entertainment and hospitality, Temple Bar is also home to at least 1,300 people. It is also home to many creative enterprises including the dynamic Temple Bar Market on Meeting House Square, where specialist food producers and suppliers gather every Saturday (9-5), setting up stalls selling everything from freshly-baked breads, organic vegetables, farmhouse cheeses and handmade sausages to specialist imports like olives and olive oils. The area has now become such a magnet for foodlovers at weekends that a second market, the Natural Food Fair, opened nearby in Cow's Lane in 2001, selling organic foods and the freshest of produce from land and sea. It's also held on Saturdays (10-6) so you can take in visits to both at the same time.

So there's real life here too. And while, it is Temple Bar which maintains the Dubliner's international reputation as a round-the-clock party animal, the area has settled down and achieved a certain mellowness in its new role: you will definitely meet "real Dubs" here, though in today's very cosmopolitan city, just how we'd define a "real Dub" is a moot point.

Nevertheless, come nightfall and your discerning Dubliner is more likely to be found in a pleasant pub or restaurant in one of the city's many urban villages, delightfully named places such as Ranelagh or Rathmines or Templeogue or Stoneybatter or Phibsborough or Donnybrook or Glasnevin or Ringsend or Dundrum or Clontarf or Drumcondra or Chapelizod, to name only a few. And then there are places like Stepaside or Howth or Glasthule or Foxrock or Dalkey which are at sufficient distance as scarcely to think of themselves as being part of Dublin at all. Yet that's where you'll find today's real Dubs enjoying their fair city every bit as much as city centre folk. Happy is the visitor who is able to savour it all, in and around this town for our times.

Local Attractions & Information

Abbey & Peacock Theatres, Lower Abbey Street	01 878 7222
Andrew's Lane Theatre, off Exchequer Street	01 679 5720
The Ark Arts Centre, Eustace St., Temple Bar D2	01 670 7788
Bank of Ireland (historic), College Green	01 661 5933
Ceol - Irish Traditional Music Centre, Smithfield	01 817 3820
Christchurch Cathedral, Christchurch Place, D8	01 677 8099
City Arts Centre, 23-25 Moss St., D2	01 677 0643
Drimnagh Castle (moat, formal 17c gardens) Longmile Rd 01 4502530	
Dublin Airport	01 814 4222
Dublin Castle, Dame Street	01 677 7129
Dublin Film Festival (April)	01 679 2937
Dublin Garden Festival, RDS (June)	01 490 0600
Dublin International Horse Show, RDS, (August)	01 668 0866

Dublin International Organ & Choral Fest. (June)	01 677 3066
Dublin Theatre Festival (October)	01 677 8439
Dublin Tourism Centre (restored church), Suffolk St.	1850 230 330
Dublin Writer's Museum, Parnell Square	01 872 2077
Dublinia (living history), Christchurch	01 475 8137
Gaiety Theatre, South King Street	01 677 1717
Gate Theatre, Cavendish Row	01 874 4045
Guinness Brewery, St James's Gate	01 453 6700 ext 5155
Guinness Hopstore	01 408 4800
Hugh Lane Municipal Gallery, Parnell Square	01 874 1903
Irish Antique Dealers Fair, RDS (October)	01 285 9294
Irish Film Centre, Eustace Street	01 679 3477
Irish Museum of Modern Art/Royal Hospital Kilmainham	01 671 8666
Irish Music Hall of Fame, Middle Abbey Street	01 878 3345
Irish Tourist Board/Bord Failte, Baggot St Bridge	01 602 4000
Iveagh Gardens, Earlsfort Terrace	01 475 7816
Jameson Distillery, Smithfield, Dublin 7	01 807 2355
Kilmainham Gaol, Kilmainham	01 453 5984
Lansdowne Road Rugby Ground, Ballsbridge	01 668 4601
Mother Redcaps Market nr St Patricks/Christchurch Fri-Sun 10am-5.30pm	
National Botanic Gardens, Glasnevin	01 837 7596
National Concert Hall, Earlsfort Terrace	01 671 1888
National Gallery of Ireland, Merrion Square West	01 661 5133
National Museum of Ireland, Kildare Street	01 677 7444
National Museum of Ireland, Collins Barracks	01 677 7444
Natural History Museum, Merrion Street	01 677 7444
Newman House, St Stephen's Green	01 475 7255
Northern Ireland Tourist Board, Nassau Street	01 679 1977
Number 29 (18c House), Lower Fitzwilliam Street	01 702 6155
Old Jameson Distillery, Smithfield, Dublin 7	01 807 2355
Olympia Theatre, Dame Street	01 677 7744
Point Depot (Concerts & Exhibitions), North Wall Quay	01 836 6000
Powerscourt Townhouse, South William Street	01 679 4144
Pro Cathedral, Marlborough Street	01 287 4292
Project Arts Centre, 39 East Sussex St, D2	01 679 6622
RDS (Royal Dublin Society), Ballsbridge	01 668 0866
Royal Hospital, Kilmainham	01 679 8666
St Michans Church (mummified remains), Dublin 7	01 872 4154
St Patrick's Cathedral, Patrick's Close	01 453 9472
Temple Bar Foodmarket, Saturdays 11am - 4 pm (all year)	
The Dillon Garden, 45 Sandford Rd, Ranelagh, D6	01 497 1308
Tivoli Theatre, Francis Street	01 454 4472
Trinity College (Book of Kells & Dublin Experience)	01 608 2308
War Memorial Gardens (Sir Edwin Lutyens) Islandbridge	01 677 0236
Zoological Gardens, Phoenix Park	01 677 1425

DUBLIN 1

101 Talbot Restaurant

RESTAURANT

101 Talbot Street Dublin 1
Tel: 01 874 5011 Fax: 01 874 5011

Margaret Duffy and Pascal Bradley have created a real buzz around this ground breaking northside restaurant. The nearby Abbey and Gate theatres and the constantly changing art exhibitions in the restaurant have been partly responsible for drawing an interesting artistic/theatrical crowd, but it's essentially their joyfully creative and healthy food that has earned the 101 such a fine reputation. Mediterranean and Middle Eastern influences explain the uniquely enjoyable wholesomeness across the complete range of dishes, always including strong vegetarian options - and dietary requirements are alway willingly met. Children welcome. **Seats 80.** Open 5-11, Tue-Sat. A la carte. No-smoking area. Closed Sun & Mon, Christmas, New Year, bank hols. Amex, Diners, MasterCard, Visa, Laser. **Directions:** 5 minutes walk between Connolloy Station and O'Connell Street.

Bond Restaurant

RESTAURANT 2 Beresford Place Dublin 1 **Tel: 01 855 9244** Fax: 01 888 1612

Overlooking the Customs House and very handy to the IFSC (which makes it busy at lunchtime), this unusual place defies categorisation. Not exactly a restaurant, a bar or even a wine bar, it's really a wine cellar that also offers food. On arrival restaurant guests place their order and are then brought downstairs to the seriously impressive cellar to select from over 140 wines sourced by proprietor Karl Purdy. A reasonable flat-rate corkage charge (€6.35) added to all cellar wine consumed on the premises instead of the usual restaurant percentage system encourages diners to choose better wines - the more expensive the wine, the greater the value. A simple menu offers appetisers (seafood platter, baked mushrooms) alongside salads and pizzas, while main courses (Barbary duck breast topped with plum demi glace and ricotta, spinach stuffed tortellini) are augmented by two daily specials. Finish with classic desserts like chocolate mousse or a tangy raspberry sorbet or match your wine with a well-presented cheese board. In the guide's experience cooking can be inconsistent, but prices are quite modest (mostly under €6 for starters, €19 for main courses) and service is well informed, friendly and accommodating. At the time of going to press there are plans to open the cellar to the public as a wine shop (with a separate entrance) and regular wine tastings are also planned. Not suitable for children. **Seats 100.** Open for coffee from 9.30am Mon-Fri; L&D daily, 12.30-3, 6-10.30. A la carte. No smoking area. Service discretionary. Closed Christmas week. Bond MasterCard, Visa, Laser. **Directors:** Very Bottom of Gardiner Street facing back of Customs House.

Chapter One Restaurant

RESTAURANT 

18/19 Parnell Square Dublin 1
Tel: 01 873 2266 Fax: 01 873 2330
Email: chapter.one.restaurant@oceanfree.net Web: www.adlib.ie

Chef-proprietor Ross Lewis and his partner, restaurant manager Martin Corbett, operate this successful restaurant in the basement beneath the Dublin Writers' Museum and near The Gate Theatre - which you can visit after your main course and return later for dessert and coffee. Ross has built up a well-deserved following for confident, creative cooking which is classic French (chicken velouté with chives & rocket) overlaid with contemporary influences (grilled swordfish with beetroot risotto, fennel purée & chive vinaigrette); menus are always based on first class seasonal ingredients and have a pleasing leaning towards New Irish Cuisine (crepinette of pork with potato confit, glazed apples, cabbage & sage.) Lovely desserts - nougat glacé with mixed berries, perhaps - or an unusual Irish and continental cheese menu to finish. Chapter One was the guide's Restaurant of the Year in 2001, reflecting the consistently memorable dining experience created by great hospitality and service, excellent cooking, an interesting, informative wine list and the characterful atmosphere of this cellar restaurant. Recent changes have seen the introduction of an oyster counter in a spacious new reception area and a wine cave is planned for spring 2002. They also run the coffee shop in the Writers Museum, (10-5 pm daily). Small conferences. Air conditioning. Parking by arrangement with nearby carpark. Children welcome. **Seats 90** (private rooms,14 & 20). L 12.30-2.30 Tue-Sat. D 6-11 Tue-Sat. Set L €25.40. Pre-theatre menu €25.40, 6-7.30. Set D €44.45 & à la carte. House wine €18.42. s.c.10%. Toilets wheelchair accessible. Closed Sun, Mon, 2 wks Xmas, bank hols. Amex, Diners, MasterCard, Visa, Laser. **Directions:** Bottom of O'Connell Street, north side of Parnell Sq, basement of Dublin's Writers Museum.

Clarion Hotel Dublin IFSC

HOTEL/RESTAURANT

International Financial Services Centre Dublin 1
Tel: 01 433 8800 Fax: 01 433 8801
Email: info@clarionhotelifsc.com Web: www.clarionhotelifsc.com

BUSINESS HOTEL OF THE YEAR

This dashing contemporary hotel opened on the river side of the Financial Services Centre in March 2001. It is the first in the area to be built specifically for the mature 'city' district and is meeting the needs of business guests and the financial community admirably. Bright, airy and spacious, it is designed in a style that is refreshingly clean-lined yet comfortable, with lots of gentle neutrals and a somewhat eastern feel that is emphasised by the food philosophy of the hotel - a waft of lemongrass and ginger entices guests through to the Kudos Bar, where Asian wok cooking is served; the more formal restaurant, Sinergie, also features world cuisine, but with more European influences. Early visits to the bar and restaurant indicated a real desire to please - fish cookery and desserts at Sinergie attracted particular praise and service was excellent. Uncluttered bedrooms have many facilities to appeal to the modern traveller, especially when on business: keycard, security eye and security chain are reassuring features and there are many other conveneinces. All rooms have air conditioning, 2 phone lines, with voice mail and ISDN, also a pleasing element of self-containment, with tea/coffee-making, multi-channel TV, ironing facilities, power hairdryer mini-bar and safe. Generous semi-orthopaedic beds, good linen and bright bathrooms with power showers and bath, heated mirror, luxurious towels and top quality toiletries all add to the sense of thoughtful planning that attaches to every aspect of the hotel. There's even a 'Sleep Programme' to help you relax before bed! Leisure facilities, in the basement, are excellent and include an 18m pool and large, well-equipped gym. (Open to membership as well as residents' use). While this is not a place for huge conferences, there is a wide range of rooms for meetings of anything between 8 and 120 people, theatre style, with state-of-the art facilities. 24 hour room service. Leisure centre (indoor swimming pool, gym). Lift. Children welcome (under 12s free in parents' room, cot available free of charge). No pets. **Rooms 147** (17 suites, 70 executive, 75 no smoking). B&B €120pps; room rate available: €203. Kudos Bar & Restaurant open Mon-Fri,12-8.30, Sinergie Restaurant: L Mon-Fri12.15-2.30, D daily, 6-9.45. All à la carte; house wine €18.50. Closed 24-28 Dec. [* Comfort Inn, Talbot Street (Tel: 01-874 9202) is in the same group and offers budget accommodation near the IFSC. Room rate EU64.] Amex, Diners, MasterCard, Visa. **Directions:** From O'Connell Street take left onto Lower Abbey Street (turn after Clerys Store), take the next right at traffic lights. Pass the Abbey Theatre and take a left onto Eden Quay, through the traffic lights onto Custom House Quay taking the left lane. Continue straight through 2 sets of traffic lights, hotel 3rd block on right.

Expresso Bar Café

CAFÉ

Unit 6 Custom House Square I.F.S.C. Dublin 1
Tel: 01 672 1812 Fax: 01 672 1813 Email: expressobar@ireland.com

Following on the great success of the Expresso Bar Café in Ballsbridge - winner of our Bord Bia Bacon Award in 2001 - Ann Marie Nohl and Jane Carthcart have applied the same winning formula to this stylish contemporary restaurant in Dublin's financial heartland. Breakfasts worth getting in early for kick off with freshly squeezed orange juice and lead on to a wonderful menu of temptations, from the best of traditional fries through the likes of pancakes with crispy bacon and syrup or pain au choc. Lunches are in a class of their own too, offering lots of lovely, colourful dishes - cajun salmon with spring onion salsa and lime crème fraîche is typical - all based on the best ingredients. Desserts are given daily on a baord and there's a wide choice of coffees, minerals and a compact, well-selected wine list. Evening opening is planned for 2002. **Seats 62.** Open 7-5 Mon-Fri, 10-5 Sat & Sun. No-smoking area; air-conditioning. Closed 25 Dec-2 Jan. MasterCard, Visa, Laser. **Directions:** New development behind The Clarion Hotel.

The Gresham

HOTEL

23 Upper O'Connell Street Dublin 1
Tel: 01 874 6881 Fax: 01 878 7175

This famous hotel has been at the centre of Dublin society since the early nineteenth century and is one of the city's best business hotels. It's also a favourite meeting place and the lobby lounge is renowned for its traditional afternoon tea, while the Gresham and Toddy's Bars are popular rendezvous for a pint. Business guests especially appreciate the newer air-conditioned bedrooms in the Lavery Wing, which are especially spacious and have ISDN lines and mini-bars, extra large beds and smart bathrooms with separate bath and shower, but others, including six penthouse suites, (one occupied for several months by Elizabeth Taylor and Richard Burton many years ago), offer similar facilities including voicemail and fax/modem points. The hotel prides itself on the quality of its staff Conference/banqueting (300/250). Business centre. Fitness suite. Secretarial services. Video conferencing. Wheelchair access. Own secure multi-storey parking. Not suitable for children. No pets. **Rooms 288** (4 suites, 2 junior suites, 119 executive rooms, 50 no-smoking, 1 for disabled). Lifts. B&B, €146pps, ss €102. Open all year. Amex, Diners, MasterCara, Visa. **Directions:** Situated on Dublins main thoroughfare.

The Harbourmaster Bar & Restaurant

RESTAURANT/PUB

IFSC Dublin 1 **Tel: 01 670 1688** Fax: 01 670 1690

In a waterside setting at Dublin's thriving financial services centre this old Dock Offices building has genuine character and makes a fine restaurant and bar. The bar is very busy at times, but the development has been more towards the restaurant end of the business, now including an impressive contemporary upstairs restaurant, The Greenhouse, in a modern extension which has been designed in sympathy with the original building. Most tables have an interesting (and increasingly attractive) view of the development outside but, as there are now several dining areas, it is wise to ensure you get to the right one on arrival. For fine weather there's also a decked outdoor area overlooking the inner harbour and fountain, with extra seating. The Harbourmaster has that indefinable buzz that comes from being in the financial centre of a capital city and the food is appropriately international and contemporary in style. **The Greenhouse Restaurant:** Mon-Fri L, 12-3. Set L from €28, house wine from €16. Restaurant closed evenings and weekends (except for functions). Bar open Mon-Wed, 12 noon-11.30; Thu-Sat 12 noon-12.30am, Sun 12.30-11. Brasserie food: Mon-Fri, 12-9; Sat 12-10; Sun, 12-7. Closed 25 Dec & Good Fri. Amex, Diners, MasterCard, Visa. **Directions:** Near Connolly train station.

Jurys Custom House Inn

HOTEL *féile bia*

Custom House Quay Dublin 1 **Tel: 01 607 5000** Fax: 01 829 0400

Right beside the Financial Services Centre, overlooking the Liffey and close to train and bus stations, this hotel meets the requirements of business guests with better facilities than is usual in budget hotels. Large bedrooms have all the usual facilities, but also fax/modem lines and a higher standard of finish than earlier sister hotels; fabrics and fittings are better quality and neat bathrooms are more thoughtfully designed, with more generous shelf space - although bath tubs are still tiny. As well as a large bar, there is a full restaurant on site, plus conference facilities for up to 100 and a staffed business centre. No room service. Adjacent multi-storey car park has direct access to the hotel. **Rooms 239** Room Rate €96 (max 3 guests); breakfast from €6. Closed 24-26 Dec. Amex, Diners, MasterCard, Visa.

Morrison Hotel

HOTEL/RESTAURANT

Ormond Quay Dublin 1
Tel: 01 887 2400 Fax: 01 874 4039
Email: sales@morrisonhotel.ie Web: www.morrisonhotel.ie

Located right in the heart of the city close to the new Millennium Bridge over the River Liffey, this stunning contemporary hotel is within walking distance of theatres, the main shopping areas and the financial district. It was a first for Dublin, with dazzling 'east meets west' interiors created by the internationally renowned designer, John Rocha. His simple, cool bedroom design - the essence of orderly thinking - contrasts pleasingly with the dramatic, even flamboyant, style of public areas.

In addition to the more usual facilities, bedrooms have CD players (CD library available), individually controlled air conditioning, modem and mini-bar. Public areas include a range of stylish bars and restaurants catering to the needs of different times - the Café Bar, for example, is ideal for morning coffee or light pre-post-theatre meals, while The Morrison Bar has become the place for cocktails and Lobo is a late night bar (open to 3 am on Friday and Saturday nights). Siting this highly original hotel on the north quays underlines the recent shift of emphasis across the river - this is the area which is already seeing Dublin's most exciting developments as we head into the 21st century. No pets. **Rooms 95** (4 suites, 3 junior suites, 83 executive, 49 no-smoking, 2 for disabled). Lift. B&B €153 pps (Room rate: €318). Closed Dec 25 & 26.

☆ **Halo:** High drama comes into its own in the restaurant, which is on two levels, with angled mirrors giving a sense of unity and acres of curtains - notably a rich purple velvet - falling the full height. Having taken some time to settle in the early days, Jean-Michel Poulot's stylish French and fusion cooking at this fashionable restaurant is now reliably excellent. Fish dishes are a strength - Szechuan peppered rare tuna with green asparagus & bean ragout, chargrilled yellow fin tuna, aioli, mizuna & lambs lettuce salad with aromatic butter sauce is typical - and imaginative vegetarian choices are highlighted on the main menu. Be sure to leave room for original desserts, spectacularly presented. Lunch, at around €25, offers good value. **Seats 96.** No-smoking area. Air conditioning. L& D daily,12:30-2.30 & 7-10:30; house wine €21; sc discretionary. Amex, MasterCard, Visa, Laser. **Directions:** North Quays between Capel Bridge and Millennium Bridge.

Panem

CAFÉ Ha'penny Bridge House 21 Lower Ormand Quay Dublin 1 **Tel: 01 872 8510**

Ann Murphy's little bakery and café has been delighting discerning Dubliners - and providing a refuge from the thundering traffic along the quays outside - since 1996. Athough tiny, it just oozes Italian chic - not surprisingly, perhaps, as Ann's Italian architect husband designed the interior - and was way ahead of its time in seeing potential north of the Liffey. Italian ad French food is prepared on the premises from 3 am each day: melt-in-the-mouth croissants with savoury and sweet fillings, chocolate-filled brioches, traditional and fruit breads, filled foccacia breads are just a few of the temptations on offer. Special deitary needs are considered too - soups, for example, are usually suitable for vegans and handmade biscuits - almond & hazelnut perhaps - for coeliacs. They import their own 100% arabica coffee from Sicily and hot chocolate is a speciality, made with the best Belgian dark chocolate. Simply superb. Open Mon-Fri 8-5, Sat 9-5. Closed Sun & 24 Dec-6 Jan. No Credit Cards. **Directions:** Opposite Millennium Bridge (Northside).

Soup Dragon

CAFÉ 168 Capel Street Dublin 1 **Tel: 01 872 3277** Fax: 01 872 3277

A compact, smart little place with space for just ten bar stools, Soup Dragon offers a stylish way to have a hot meal on a budget.There's no need to book and, surprisingly, there's even a smoking section. A daily choice of soups and stews is available in three different sizes, with a medium portion and a selection of delicious home-made breads and a piece of fruit starting at less than €5. Some change daily, while others stay on the menu for a week or a season. Choose from dahl (Indian lentil), potato & leek or carrot & coriander soup; or opt for something more substantial like beef chilli or a very fine Thai chicken curry from the blackboard menu. In keeping with their healthy philosophy, a range of wholesome and innovative breakfasts is offered, and also a range of freshly squeezed drinks (Red Dragon: strawberry, raspberry and cranberry or home-made lemon & lime lemonade) and smoothies, all made to order so they taste fresh and vibrant. Desserts include old favourites like rice pudding (served with cream) and a range of unusual home-made ice creams. Food to go is also available. **Seats 10.** Open Mon-Fri 8-5.30 & Sat 11-5. Closed Sun, bank hols, Christmas. No Credit Cards. **Directions:** Bridge of Capel Street.

The Winding Stair Bookshop & Café

RESTAURANT 40 Lower Ormond Quay Dublin 1 **Tel: 01 873 3292**

Everybody's favourite place for a wholesome daytime bite and a good browse - window tables at this delightfully higgledy-piggledy cafe beside the Ha'penny Bridge have terrific views across the Liffey. Open 7 days, 10am -5pm (Sun from 1 pm). Amex, MasterCard, Visa.

DUBLIN 2

Acapulco Mexican Restaurant

RESTAURANT 7 South Great Georges St. Dublin 2 **Tel: 01 677 1085**

Reliable Tex-Mex fare at this bright, cheap and notably cheerful place on the edge of Temple Bar.

Mexican staples - nachos with salsa & guacamole, enchiladas, burrito - and good coffee. No smoking area. **Seats 60.** Open 7 days: L 12-3pm, D 6-10.30pm (Fri & Sat 12-4pm & 6-10.45pm, Sun 10am-10.30pm). MasterCard, Visa, Diners.

Alexander Hotel

HOTEL Merrion Square Dublin 2 **Tel: 01 607 3700** Fax: 01 661 5663
Email: alexanderres@ocallaghanhotels.ie Web: www.ocallaghanhotels.ie

Very well situated at the lower end of Merrion Square within a stone's throw of Dail Éireann (Government Buildings), the National Art Gallery and History Museums as well as the city's premier shopping area, this large new hotel is remarkable for classic design that blends into the surrounding Georgian area quite inconspicuously. In contrast to its subdued public face, the interior is strikingly modern and colourful, both in public areas and bedrooms, which are all to executive standard, spacious and unusual. Perhaps its most positive attribute, however, is the exceptionally friendly and helpful attitude of the hotel's staff, who immediately make guests feel at home and take a genuine interest in their comfort during their stay. Conference/banqueting (400/400). Business centre. Secretarial services. Video conferencing. Gym. Children welcome (Under 2s free in parents' room; cots available). No pets. **Rooms 102** (4 suites, 40 no-smoking, 2 for disabled). Lift. B&B €140, ss 120. Room-only rate €240 (max 2 guests). 121/2% s.c. Closed Dec 24-26. Amex, Diners, MasterCard, Visa. **Directions:** Off Merrion Square.

Ar Vicoletto Osteria Romano

RESTAURANT 5 Crow Street Temple Bar Dublin 2 **Tel: 01 670 8662**

Genuine little Italian restaurant, doing authentic, restorative food in a relaxing atmosphere and at very moderate prices. Very friendly helpful staff too - one of the pleasantest spots in Temple Bar. Closed Christmas. Amex, MasterCard, Visa.

Avoca Café

CAFÉ 11-13 Suffolk St. Dublin 2 **Tel: 01 677 4215** Fax: 01 672 6021
Email: info@avoca.ie Web: www.avoca.ie

City sister to the famous craftshop and café who have their flagship store in Kilmacanogue, County Wicklow, this large centrally located shop opened very near the Dublin Tourism office in July 2000 and has already become a favourite daytime dining venue for discerning Dubliners. The restaurant (which is up rather a lot of stairs, where queues of devotees wait patiently at lunchtime) has low-key style and an emphasis on creative, healthy cooking that is common to all the Avoca establishments recommended in the guide. (Avoca Cafés received the Happy Heart Eat Out Award in 2000). Chic little menus speak volumes - together with careful cooking, meticulously sourced ingredients like Woodstock tuna, Hederman mussels, Gubeen bacon and Hicks sausages lift dishes such as smoked fish platter, organic bacon panini and bangers & mash out of the ordinary. All this sits happily alongside the home baking for which Avoca is famous - much of which (along with other specialist produce) can be bought downstairs. Meals daily 10-5, (Sunday 11-5); à la carte. bookings accepted but not required. Amex, Diners, MasterCard, Visa. **Directions:** Turn left into Suffolk St. from the bottom of Grafton St.

Aya @ Brown Thomas

RESTAURANT 49/52 Clarendon Street Dublin 2 **Tel: 01 677 1544** Fax: 01 677 1546
Email: mail@aya.ie Web: www.aya.ie

This dashing contemporary Japanese restaurant was Dublin's first conveyor sushi bar, restaurant and food hall - and was a runaway success from the day it opened, in 1999. Aya is owned by the Hoashi family, who established Dublin's first Japanese restaurant, Ayumi-Ya, where authentic traditional Japanese cuisine was offered from 1983 until closing, just before the guide went to press, in order to build on the success of Aya - an "Aya 2 Go" outlet is about to open in Donnybrook, (Dublin 4), offering all that is currently available from the Aya Deli in Clarendon Street, and a new operation in the IFSC is due to follow shortly. Thus, with its deep-red velvet and beech laminated tables providing wall-to-wall style, the youthful Aya @ Brown Thomas now becomes the parent operation.The dining highlight is a full on-line menu offering a wide range of sushi, all authentically Japanese, and Aya also offers takeaway sushi, fresh and frozen meals and a small selection of Japanese ingredients. The main menu covers all the bases and is impressively wide-ranging, serving everything from well-priced bento boxes at lunchtime to more exotic fare in the evening. Always innovative, promotions like Aya's early week "sushi 55" (55 minutes unlimited sushi for €25.39/£20) and "happy zone" (all plates on the conveyor belt €2 during certain hours) have earned them a loyal following. The service is excellent and, to add to the fun, the staff wear very distinctive grey and red uniforms inspired by "Dr. No", of James Bond fame. Children welcome before 8pm. **Seats 60.** No-smoking area. Air conditioning. Open daily. L 12-4. D 5.30-11 (Sun to 10). Set L €16.90; Set D €29.90. Also à la carte. House wine €16.50. 12.5% sc, evenings only. Closed 25-26 Dec. Amex, Diners, MasterCard, Visa, Laser. **Directions:** Directly behind Brown Thomas off Wicklow Street.

The Bad Ass Café

CAFÉ/RESTAURANT 9-11 Crown Alley Temple Bar Dublin 2 **Tel: 01 671 2596**
Fax: 01 671 2596 Email: bad_ass_@hotmail.com Web: www.badasscafe.com

Original and still the best - the Bad Ass Café has been charming youngsters (and a good few oldsters) with its particular brand of wackiness and good, lively food since 1986, when most people running Temple Bar restaurants were still at school. Kids love the food (the Bad Ass burger is still one of the favourites, and very good too), the warehouse atmosphere, the loopy menu and the cash shuttles (from an old shop) that whizz around the ceiling. Fifteen years after opening, young people still find it cool. Children welcome. **Seats 86.** Open daily, noon-11. Set menu €15.87, all day. A la carte also available. House wine €16.51. No-smoking area. Air conditioning. sc 10%. Closed Dec 25 & 26, Good Fri. The Bad Ass Cafe Amex, MasterCard, Visa, Laser. **Directions:** Behind the Central Bank on the way to the Ha'penny Bridge.

The Bailey

PUB 2-3 Duke Street Dublin 2

Although it's now more of a busy lunchtime spot and after-work watering hole for local business people and shoppers, this famous Victorian pub has a special place in the history of Dublin life - literary, social, political - and attracts many a pilgrim seeking the ghosts of great personalities who have frequented this spot down through the years. Closed 25 Dec & Good Friday.

Belgo Dublin

RESTAURANT 17-19 Sycamore Street Dublin 2 **Tel: 01 672 7555** Fax: 01 672 7550

A Dublin off-shoot of the Belgo restaurants in London and elsewhere, this large, trendy restaurant in Temple Bar offers Belgian specialities, including a huge range of beers and other drinks you're unlikely to come across elsewhere in Ireland. The food goes a lot further than moules & chips -wild boar sausages, for example, and plenty of other seafood. They do a number of specials, otherwise prices may seem a little steep for the informality of the food and service. Children welcome. **Seats 220** (private room, 90). No-smoking area. Air conditioning. Open daily: L 12-3. D 5.30-11 Mon-Thurs (Fri to 12), 12.30-12 Sat (Sun to 10.30). Set menus & à la carte L&D available. SC 12.5%. Toilets wheelchair accessible. Closed 25 & 31 Dec.

Bewley's Oriental Café

CAFÉ Grafton Street Dublin 2 **Tel: 01 635 5470** Fax: 01 6799237

Established in 1840, Bewleys Cafés - and especially the Grafton Street café - have a special place in the affection of Irish people. Bewley's has always been a great meeting place for everyone, whether native Dubliners or visitors to the capital 'up from the country'. Although they have changed hands and undergone renovations in recent years, they have retained a unique atmosphere and it's this - together with some outstanding architechtural features, notably the Harry Clarke stained glass windows in the Grafton Street premises - which makes them special, rather than the food. Full licence. Open daily, from 7.30 am 'until late'. Branches at: Westmoreland Street (Mon-Sat 7.30am-9 pm; Sun 10 am-11 pm) Mary Street, Dublin 1 (Mon-Sat, 7.30 am- 6 pm; closed Sun.) Amex, Diners, MasterCard, Visa.

Bewley's Principal Hotel

HOTEL 19/20 Fleet Street Temple Bar Dublin 2 **Tel: 01 670 8122** Fax: 01 6708103
Email: bewleyshotel@eircom.net Web: bewleysprincipalhotel.com

Conveniently situated in the heart of Temple Bar, within easy walking distance of all the cityís main attractions, this reasonably priced hotel (which is not connected to the other Bewley's hotels) is fairly small, allowing an intimate atmosphere and a welcome emphasis on service. Children welcome (under 10s free in parents' room; cots available). No pets. **Rooms 70** (40 shower only, 35 no-smoking). B&B €84pps, ss €41. (Room-only rate €147). Lift. Closed 24-26 Dec. Amex, Diners, Visa, MasterCard. Heart of Temple Bar, near Fleet Street.

The Bistro

RESTAURANT 4 & 5 Castle Market Dublin 2 **Tel: 01 671 5430** Fax: 01 677 6016

Well located in the pedestrianised walkway between the Powerscourt Centre and George's Street Market, this relaxed, family-run restaurant has attractive warm-toned decor, a friendly atmosphere and good food cooked by co-owner Maire Block. Martin and Robert Block manage and look after front-of-house and it's a formula that brings people back. Expect sound, no-nonsense cooking, including some classics - Tarte Tatin, for example. Daily specials offer especially good value. Open daily 11.30am-11.30pm (Sun to 8pm). Amex, Diners, MasterCard, Visa, Laser.

Brooks Hotel

HOTEL 59-62 Drury Street Dublin 2 **Tel: 01 670 4000** Fax: 01 670 4455
Email: reservations@brookshotel.ie Web: www.sinnotthotels.com

A city sister for the Sinnott family's hotels in Galway - the Connemara Gateway and the Connemara Coast - Brooks is very well located, close to the Drury Street multi-storey car park and just a couple of minutes walk from Grafton Street. Described as a 'designer/boutique' hotel, it's high on style in a comfortable country house-cum-club fashion and has been furnished and decorated with great attention to detail. The whole of the first floor has been designated no-smoking and all rooms have exceptionally good amenities, including well-designed bathrooms with power showers as well as full baths, air conditioning, ISDN lines, teletext TV and many other features. At the time of going to press there are facilities for small conference/private dining (40/30) with back-up business services available on request, but an extension due to be completed during the winter of 2001/2 will include new conference rooms as well as 25 extra bedrooms and a gym. Children welcome (under 3s free in parents' room; cots available). No pets. Lift. **Rooms 75** (3 suites, 30 executive, 62 no-smoking, 3 for disabled). B&B €108, ss €57. Open all year. **Francescas Restaurant** This lower ground floor restaurant has a welcoming ambience, with wooden floors, plaid-covered seating and beautiful book tapestries on the walls creating a pleasant setting for talented head chef Patrick McLarnon's appealing à la carte and set menus. Carefully sourced ingredients (wild salmon, organic chicken, dry aged steak) are used to create well-considered dishes that successfully balance strident and subtle flavours, with a growing emphasis on fish.Thus a classic such as seared foie gras comes with a pear and fennel confit as well as toasted brioche and roasted cod fillet is partnered with razor clams and served with garlic and parsley cream sauce, wilted spinach & noisette potatoes. But dedicated carnivores should not be disappointed here either, with tempting signature dishes such as peat smoked loin of lamb (with fondant potatoes, caramelised shallots, tomato fondue and a caper jus) to choose from. **Seats 70** (private room, 30) No-smoking area. Air conditioning. Early D, 5-7 daily, about €8-15. D 6.30-10 (Sun 7-9.30). Set D from €26.60. A la carte also available. SC discretionary. [*Bar food is served from noon-7pm daily in the Butter Lane Bar.] Amex, Diners, MasterCard, Visa, Laser. **Directions:** Between Grafton and Great St. Georges Streets, 2 mins. from St. Stephen's Green.

Brownes Brasserie and Townhouse

HOTEL/RESTAURANT féile bia 22 St Stephen's Green Dublin 2
Tel: 01 638 3939 Fax: 01 638 3900
Email: info@brownesdublin.com Web: www.brownesdublin.com

BREAKFAST AWARD - DUBLIN

A fine period house on the stretch of St Stephen's Green between Grafton Street and the Shelbourne Hotel has been stylishly converted to create an impressive and exceptionally well-located small hotel and restaurant. The house has something of the atmosphere of a private home about it and includes a front first floor junior suite which can be converted for meetings and private parties, as the bed swings up into the wall. The spacious bedrooms have quality reproduction furniture including generous beds (although not for the very tall, perhaps) and well-finished bathrooms, with quality toiletries and towelling robes. An ironing board is tucked neatly into the wardrobe and there's a CD player as well as TV. Breakfast is a feast worth allowing plenty of time for (and perhaps another hour in bed afterwards to digest it.) The menu is long and tempting, with a choice of coffees and teas, a wide selection of fresh juices and fruits, all sorts of cereals, breads, muffins, croissants and toast - and all this before you get to the cooked breakfast, which includes everything from delicacies like scrambled eggs with smoked salmon, through the Full Monty (an extended version of the traditional fry) to steak served on fried toast with poached eggs. Small conference/banqueting (36/100). Fax/ISDN lines. Lift. Children welcome (Under 12s free in parents' room; cots available). No pets. **Rooms 12** (2 suites, 10 executive). B&B €111 pps, ss €47.74. **Brownes Brasserie** Up a short flight of granite steps, you pass through a reception area and small drawing area furnished with antiques (where aperitifs and digestifs can be served) into the restaurant, which is a long well-appointed split-level room, with big mirrors and plenty of decorative interest to occupy guests between courses. Good-sized tables, comfortable chairs and fresh flowers all create a good impression and well-balanced international menus offer a wide choice - dishes especially enthusiastically received on a recent visit included an excellent shallot tarte tatin (with duck livers sautéed in garlic & rosemary and a cassis jus) and Brownes "lamb trinity", an exceptional main course combining lamb cutlets, char-grilled lambs liver and vine leaves stuffed with minced lamb, served with a dried fruit cous-cous, spinach and a trio of sauces: a true marriage of flavours. Classical desserts (Drambuie bavarois, crème brulée) to finish, or a cheese plate. **Seats 75** (private room, 24). No-smoking area. Air conditioning. L 12.30 - 3, D 6:30-10.30 daily. Set Sun L €34.92, Set D € 47.60. A la carte also available. House wine €18.98. SC discretionary (12.5% on parties of 6+). Closed 24 Dec-4 Jan. Amex, Diners, MasterCard, Visa, Laser, Switch. **Directions:** Stephens Green North,Between Kildare & Dawson Street.

Bruno's - Kildare Street

RESTAURANT féile bia

21 Kildare Street Dublin 2 **Tel: 01 662 4724** Fax: 01 6623856
Email: mail@brunos.ie Web: www.brunos.ie

Bruno Berta's conversion of a characterful cellar under Mitchell's wine shop into a sleek contemporary restaurant dismayed many devotees of the previous establishment which highlighted its old-world charm, but even the style critics admit that it has proved a great success. Head chef Garrett Byrne - whose previous experience includes Nico's in London and The Tea Room and Chapter One in Dublin - sources carefully and is doing an excellent job in the French / modern Irish genre, typically in specialities like blanquette de veau and sauté of foie gras with black pudding & fried egg. Desserts like cherry soup with warm cherry pudding, or crème brulée with apple & raisin spring roll are hard to pass over - but Irish cheeses supplied by Sheridans cheesemongers are also hard to resist. Not suitable for children under 12 after 7 pm. No-smoking area; air-conditioning. **Seats 100.** L 12.30-2.30 & D 6-10.30 Mon-Sat. Set L & early D €18.42; D à la carte. House wine €18.42. SC discretionary. Closed Sun & 25 Dec-3 Jan. Amex, Diners, MasterCard, Visa, Laser. **Directions:** Across the road from side of Shelbourne Hotel.

Bruno's - Temple Bar

RESTAURANT

30 East Essex Street Temple Bar Dublin 2 **Tel: 01 670 6767**
Fax: 01 670 8278 Email: mail@brunos.ie Web: www.brunos.ie

Clean lined lightwood and plain white walls provide a pleasingly simple background for contemporary cooking at Bruno Berta's popular restaurant. Head chef Ciaran Byrne creates seasonal and monthly-changing menus based on the best of Irish ingredients - fish and shellfish come up from up from Castletownbere daily, cheeses from Sheridans cheesemongers and game is offered in season. Pan-fried sea trout with mussel and leek ragout and mushrooom duxelle is a speciality - and a great buzz and value for money complete the winning formula. Not suitable for children under 12 after 7 pm. No-smoking area; air-conditioning. **Seats 60.** L Mon-Fri, 12:30-3 (Fri to 4) D Mon-Sat, 6-10:30. Set L €28.86, also à la carte. House wine €17.78. No-smoking area. Air conditioning. SC discretionary. Closed L Sat, all Sun. Amex, Diners, MasterCard, Visa, Laser. **Directions:** Opposite New Millenium Bridge, Lower Eustace Street.

Buswells Hotel

HOTEL/RESTAURANT féile bia

25 Molesworth Street Dublin 2 **Tel: 01 6146500**
Fax: 01 676 2090 Email: buswells@quinn-hotels.com Web: www.quinnhotels.com

Home from home to Ireland's politicians, this 18th century townhouse close to the Dail (parliament) has been an hotel since 1921 and is held in great affection by Dubliners. Since major refurbishment several years ago, it now offers a fine range of services for conferences, meetings and private dining. Accommodation is comfortable in the traditional style with good amenities for business guests and it's just a few yards from the city's prime shopping and cultural area, making it an ideal base for private visits. The lobby and characterful bar are handy meeting places. Conference/banqueting (85/50). Secretarial services. Video conferencing. Children welcome (Under 3s free in parentsí room; cots available). No pets. **Rooms 69** (2 suites, 17 no-smoking, 1 for disabled). Lift. B&B about

€110pps, ss about €33. Closed 24-26 Dec. **Trumans Restaurant** This elegant well-appointed restaurant has a separate entrance from Kildare Street or access through the hotel. Menus feature lively modern dishes and have the little touches that endear guests to an establishment, such as a tasty amuse-bouche presented before the meal 'compliments of the chef'. Wisely, given the likely clientèle, simpler dishes are always an option - notably roast beef or steaks presented various ways - and vegetarian dishes are creative. Desserts are also interesting (eg, date-stuffed pear in a phyllo crown) or you can finish with Irish cheeses, which attract a small supplement on set menus. No children under 12 after 9pm. **Seats 45** (private room, 12). L 12:30-2 Mon - Fri. D 6-10 Mon - Sat. Set L&D; also à la carte. House wine around €16. SC discretionary. Closed lunch Sat, all Sun, 24-26 Amex, Diners, MasterCard, Visa. **Directions:** Close to Dail Eireann, 5 minutes walk from Grafton Street.

Butlers Chocolate Café

CAFÉ 77 Sir John Rogersons Quay Dublin 2 Tel: 01 671 0599 Fax: 01 671 0480 Email: michelle@butlers.ie Web: www.butlerschocolates.com

Butlers Irish Handmade Chocolates combine coffee-drinking with complimentary chocolates - an over-simplification, as the range of drinks at this stylish little cafe also includes hot chocolate as well as lattes, cappuccinos and mochas and chocolate cakes and croissants are also available. But all drinks do come with a complimentary handmade chocolate on the side - and boxed or personally selected loose chocolates, caramels, fudges and fondants are also available for sale. Branches at: 51 Grafton Street Tel: 01 671 0599); 9 Chatham Street (Tel: 01 672 6333); 18 Nassau Street (Tel: 01 671 0772). Amex, Diners, MasterCard, Visa. 4 city centre locarions.

Café en Seine

CAFÉ/PUB 40 Dawson Street Dublin 2 **Tel: 01 677 4369** Fax: 01 671 7938

The first of the continental style café-bars to open in Dublin, in 1993, the large and lively Café en Seine is still just as fashionable now. It's a most attractive place, too, and offers sustenance as well as drinks at lunchtime (quiches, pasta dishes, smoked salmon salad and roast meats), snacks from late afternoon and coffee and pastries all day. Sunday brunch is popular (1-4 pm). Wheelchair access. No children after 7pm. Bar open 10am-2am daily. Carvery lunch 12-3. Snack menu 4-10. Closed Xmas & Good Fri. Amex, MasterCard, Visa.

Café Mao

RESTAURANT 2 Chatham Row Dublin 2 **Tel: 01 670 4899** Fax: 01 670 4999

In simple but stylish surroundings, Café Mao brings to the Grafton Street area the cuisines of Thailand, Malaysia, Indonesia, Japan and China - about as 'Asian Fusion' as it gets. The atmosphere is bright and very buzzy andinteresting food is based on seasonal ingredients, the standard of cooking is consistently good and so is value for money, although the bill can mount up quickly if you don't watch the number of Asian beers ordered. No reservations. Wheelchair access. Children welcome. **Seats 120.** No smoking area; air conditioning. Open daily. L 12-3. D 5:30-11. Menu à la carte. House wine from €15. SC discretionary (10% parties 6+). Closed Good Fri, 25-26 Dec, 1 Jan. MasterCard, Visa. **Directions:** Just off Grafton St., in the city centre.

Camden Court Hotel

HOTEL Camden Street Dublin 2 **Tel: 01 475 9666** Fax: 01 475 9677 Email: sales@camdencourthotel.com Web: www.camdencourthotel.com

This stylish modern hotel, in a thriving area convenient to St Stephen's Green, has two entrances - one next to the Bleeding Horse pub, the other via an arched passageway through a courtyard. The spacious reception area leads to a smart restaurant, where an enticing breakfast buffet is laid out each morning. Some bedrooms have their own fax machines; all have neat bathrooms, practical fitted furniture and the usual facilities (plus satellite TV, which can show your room bill, speeding check-out). Friendly staff, business and leisure facilities facilities and reasonable rates for the location make this a good city centre base. Conferences (115). Leisure centre (swimming pool, gym, sauna, steam). Children (Under 2s free in parents' room; cots available). No pets. **Rooms 246** (1 suite, 13 no-smoking, 13 for disabled). Lift. B&B €86pps, ss €60; no sc. Closed Christmas & New Year. Amex, Diners, MasterCard, Visa, Laser.

La Cave Wine Bar & Restaurant

RESTAURANT 28 South Anne Street Dublin 2 **Tel: 01 679 4409** Fax: 01 670 5255
Email: lacave@iol.ie Web: www.lacavewinebar.com

Wine bars have not been a noticeable feature of Dublin's hospitality scene until recently, but Margaret and Akim Beskri have run this well-known place just off Grafton Street since 1989. With its traditional bistro atmosphere, classic French cooking and a wide range of wines by the glass, it makes a handy place to take a break from shopping, or for an evening out. A first floor function room has seating for up to 34 - ideal for parties and small functions. No children after 6pm. **Seats 50** (private room, 30) Air conditioning. Open Mon-Sat 12.30-11, Sun 6-11. Set L €19; also à la carte. SC discretionary. Closed 25-26 Dec, Good Fri. Amex, Diners, MasterCard, Visa, Laser. **Directions:** just off Grafton Street.

Central Hotel

HOTEL 1-5 Exchequer Street Dublin 2 **Tel: 01 679 7302** Fax: 01 679 7303
Email: reservations@centralhotel.ie Web: www.centralhotel.ie

Very conveniently located on the corner of South Great George's Street, this hotel is over a hundred years old and is a handy place to stay. It's not unreasonably priced for the city centre and special offers are often available, including weekends. Conference/banqueting (150/100). Children welcome (Under 10s free in parents' room; cots available). Lift. No pets. **Rooms 70** (16 shower only, 1 suite, 1 mini-suite, 4 executive). B&B €95.23, ss €25.39. Closed 24-27 Dec. Amex, Diners, MasterCard, Visa, Laser, Switch. **Directions:** In city centre.

The Chili Club

RESTAURANT 1 Anne's Lane South Annes St Dublin 2 **Tel: 01 677 3721**
Fax: 01 493 8284

This cosy restaurant, in a laneway just off Grafton Street, was Dublin's first authentic Thai restaurant and is still as popular as ever a decade later. It is owned and managed by Patricia Kenna, who supervises a friendly and efficient staff. The head chef, Supot Boonchouy, prepares a fine range of genuine Thai dishes which are not 'tamed' too much to suit Irish tastes. Children welcome. **Seats 42** (private room, 18) L Mon-Sat 12.30-2.30, D daily 6-11.30 (Sun to 11). Set L €14.60. Early D €18.41 (6-7 pm). A la carte L&D available. SC discretionary (10% on parties of 6+). Closed L Sun, 25-27 Dec,1 Jan. Amex, Diners, MasterCard, Visa. **Directions:** off Grafton Street.

The Clarence Hotel

HOTEL/RESTAURANT 6-8 Wellington Quay Dublin 2
Tel: 01 407 0800 Fax: 01 407 0820
Email: reservations@theclarence.ie Web: www.theclarence.ie

Dating back to 1852 this hotel has long had a special place in the hearts of Irish people - especially the clergy and the many who regarded it as a home from home when 'up from the country' for business or shopping in Dublin - largely because of its convenience to Heuston Station. Since the early '90s, however, it has achieved cult status through its owners - Bono and The Edge of U2 and the entrepreneur Harry Crosbie - who have completely refurbished the hotel, creating the coolest of jewels in the crown of Temple Bar. No expense was spared to get the details right, reflecting the hotel's original arts and crafts style whenever possible. Accommodation is a predictably luxurious combination of contemporary comfort and period style, with excellent amenities including mini-bar, private safe, PC/fax connections (fax available on request), remote control satellite television and video and temperature control panels. Public areas include the oak panelled, clublike Octagon Bar, which is a popular Temple Bar meeting place, and The Study, a quieter room with an open fire. Parking in the area is difficult, but there are muti-storey carparks within walking distance. Conference/banqueting (50/70); video-conferencing; secretarial services. Beauty salon. Children welcome (Under 12s free in parents' room). No pets. Lift. **Rooms 50** (5 suites, 45 executive, 3 for disabled). Room rate from €285.

☆ **The Tea Room** The restaurant, which has its own entrance on Essex Street, is a high-ceilinged room furnished in the light oak which is a feature throughout the hotel. Pristine white linen, designer cutlery and glasses, high windows softened by the filtered damson tones of pavement awnings, all combine to create an impressive dining room. Solicitous staff move quietly, quickly offering aperitifs and menus. While putting his own stamp on the (excellent) cooking, head chef Antony Ely, who joined The Clarence last year from The Square in London has continued the hotel's style of fashionably international seasonal menus that offer plenty of choice, including vegetarian options, but are not overlong or overpriced, with lunch menus offering especially good value. Seasonal à la carte dinner menus offer around nine or ten starters and main courses in a modern European/Irish style that is bright and sassy, with strong but not overworked presentation - a brilliant green risotto of broad beans and peas with white truffle oil and deep-fried egg simply presented in a shallow bowl is a good example, enjoyed on a recent visit; signature dishes include a modern Irish starter of deep-fried potato & bacon cakes with buttered savoy cabbage & caper sauce and sautéed John Dory with new potatoe & deep-fried mussels. **Seats 80.** No-smoking area. Air conditioning. L 12.30-2.30 (Sun 11.45-2.30), D 6.30-10.30 daily. Set L from €15.90. A la carte available. House wine from €22. No SC. Food is also served in The Octagon Bar, 11-5.30. Closed 23-27 Dec. Amex, Diners, MasterCard, Visa, Laser, Switch. **Directions:** Located Overlooking the River Liffey at Wellington Quay, Southside.

Clarion Stephen's Hall Hotel & Suites

HOTEL/RESTAURANT

14-17 Lower Leeson Street Dublin 2
Tel: 01 638 1111 Fax: 01 638 1122
Email: stephens@premgroup.com Web: premgroup.ie

Conveniently located just off St Stephen's Green, this 'all-suite' hotel has wooden floors, ISDN lines, voice mail, modem access, fax machines and CD players - and computers. **Rooms 33** (all suites, 9 no-smoking). Wheelchair access. Lift. B&B €125 pps, ss €70.50; room-only rate €243 (max 3 guests). **Romanza** George Sabongi took over this attractive semi-basement adjacent to the hotel in 2001 and with him came the piano bar concept for which he is well-known in Dublin. An enclosed coffee terrace at the back creates a pleasantly summery 'outdoor' atmosphere and, as the restaurant is accessible directly from the hotel and nearby offices, it's a popular lunchtime venue - and very convenient to the National Concert Hall in the evening too. Moderately priced menus include informal Italian fare like quality pizzas and pastas, but there's also a range of antipasti and substantial main courses like charcoal grilled ribeye of beef and barbeque leg of lamb, and Egyptian influence showing in a vegetarian dish such as koushery, which is based on black lentils. You can also just have a drink at the bar (10am-midnight); there's quite an extensive cocktail list and a short bar food menu,10.30-5.30. Live music at weekends.L Mon-Fri, 12.30-3; D Mon-Sat 5-12. A la carte. House wine €16. 10% s.c. on parties of 6+. Closed L Sat, all Sun. Amex, Diners, MasterCard, Visa, Laser. **Directions:** Just off St.Stephen's Green on Lower Leeson Street.

The Commons Café

CAFÉ

The National Concert Hall Earlsfort Terrace Dublin 2 **Tel: 01 475 0060**

This off-shoot of The Commons Restaurant at Newman House on St Stephen's Green is in the main Concert Hall building and makes a good place to drop into before a concert, or just for a meal. The room is lovely - bright and airy room with a large mirrored bar area, blue banquettes and white walls setting off impressive paintings - and friendly staff are anxious to plaease. Menus are quite short and flexible, with no distinction between starters and main courses, but proceed in a fairly logical way from soup and lighter dishes like foccacia and pasta through to more substantial fare. The cooking is good and the quality of carefully sourced ingredients shines through - and it's also good value for money, it this should soon become a popular spot. **Seats 60.** Open Mon-Fri, 8am-10.30pm; Sat 6-10.30. Closed Sun. Amex, Diners, MasterCard, Visa, Laser.

The Commons Restaurant

RESTAURANT ☆

Newman House 85-86 St Stephen's Green Dublin 2
Tel: 01 478 0530 Fax: 01 478 0551
Email: sales@thecommonsrestaurant.ie Web: www.thecommonsrestaurant.ie

Sited on the South of the Green, in the basement of Newman House - considered one of Dublin's finest examples of Georgian splendour - this restaurant was formerly the college dining room of University College Dublin and still evokes literary memories, with several works of modern art dedicated to James Joyce, a scholar at the turn of the last century. Other luminaries associated with the Palladian building are Cardinal John Henry Newman, former rector, and Gerald

Manley Hopkins, professor. The spacious restaurant has French doors opening on to a secluded south-facing terrace (perfect for aperitifs on a warm summer's day), elegantly presented tables and an array of unfailingly polite and professional staff. But it is the skill and imagination of head chef Aiden Byrne - who arrived here in the late summer of 2000 via several highly-esteemed restaurants including Pied à Terre in London - and his use of the highest quality ingredients that make this one of Ireland's finest examples of modern cooking: menus are extensive, but a starter example of terrine of lobster with baby leeks & morels and main course of stuffed pigs trotter with sweetbreads, broad beans and pomme purée convey the style. Wide-ranging à la carte menus do not come cheap, with starters from €19-25 and main courses in the €30-41 range and desserts €13 (making the 10-course Menu Gourmand seem a snip at €76) but the cost is justifed by the quality of food, cooking, service and details (little canapés on arrival, amuse-bouches and the now almost obligatory selection of excellent breads) and, of course, the surroundings. A short 2/3 course 'executive lunch menu' is more accessible (€23/32) and changes every week. Both classic and innovative, it offers simpler but very accomplished dishes like a perfectly executed terrine of rabbit and girolle mushrooms with a carrot and herb salad and roasted saddle of lamb with rosti potato, sweetbreads and garlic. An imaginative dessert menu includes an intriguing "Irish plate" - try it and see. Service, under the supervision of restaurant manager Michael Andrews, is excellent * Cookery demonstrations with lunch included are to be available during 2002. Entrance to the Iveagh Gardens, behind the restaurant, is via Clonmel Street (Admission Free). **Seats 60** (private room 26). No-smoking area. L 12-2.15 Mon-Fri, D 7-10.15 Mon-Sat. Set L €23-32. Gourmet menu € 76. A la carte also available at D. Wines from €22. SC discretionary. Closed L Sat, all Sun, Christmas, bank hols, 2 wks Aug. Amex, Diners, MasterCard, Visa, Laser. **Directions:** Next door to University Church,south side of Stephens Green.

Conrad International

HOTEL

Earlsfort Terrace Dublin 2 **Tel: 01 676 5555** Fax: 01 676 5424
Email: info@conrad-international.ie Web: www.conrad-international.ie

Just a stroll away from the suth-eastern corner of St Stephen's Green and right opposite the National Concert Hall, this fine hotel celebrated its tenth anniversary in 1999 - and was our Business Hotel of the Year in 2001. Service by committed staff is excellent, under the direction of long-serving general manager Michael Governey, and facilities are constantly upgraded. Many of the thoughtfully furnished generously-sized bedrooms enjoy views of the piazza below and across the city, and all offer every comfort for business or leisure guests. Public areas include a raised lounge, two restaurants, the Alexandra and Plurabelle Brasserie (breakfast, lunch and dinner served here), and Alfie Byrne's Pub (serving splendid pub lunches) that opens on to a sheltered terrace Conference/banqueting (300/250). Executive boardroom (12). Business centre; secretarial services. Fax machines & ISDN lines in rooms. Video conferencing. Air conditioning. Hairdresser. Fitness centre. Underground carpark. Children welcome (Under 12s free in parents' room; cots available). No pets. Lift. **Rooms 191** (9 suites, 60 no-smoking, 1 for disabled). Room rate from about €250, SC 15%. Open all year. Plurabelle Brasserie

Cooke's Café

RESTAURANT

14 South William Street Dublin 2 **Tel: 01 679 0536** Fax: 01 679 0546
Email: cookes1@iol.ie Web: www.cookescafe.com

John Cooke has always been ahead of fashions in the Dublin restaurant scene and his stylish café, Cooke's, was among the first of the current wave of trendy café-bistro style places doing Mediterranean and Cal-Ital food. The formula is still working well at Cooke's, where you can be sure of stylish, well cooked food based on the best of ingredients, either in the restaurant or on a heated pavement area with an awning, which is perfect for people-watching. **The Rhino Room**, a first floor restaurant over the cafè, has its own entrance on South William Street. The food is similar - pastas, salads, char-grilled meats and vegetables, all very competently prepared - but it is quieter and suits people who prefer a slightly more formal atmosphere and well-spaced tables. Nearby carpark. No children after 6pm. **Seats 60** (private room, 60). No-smoking area. Air conditioning. L 12.30-2.30 daily (Sun to 3.30). D 6-11 daily (Sun to 10). Set L & Early D about €22 A la carte available. House wine about €19. SC discretionary. Closed bank hols. Amex, Diners, MasterCard, Visa. **Directions:** City centre opposite Powerscourt Town House.

Cornucopia

RESTAURANT 19 Wicklow Street, Dublin 2. **Tel: 01 677 7583**

You don't have to be vegetarian to enjoy this long-established wholefood restaurant and it's very well located for a wholesome re-charge if you're shopping around the Grafton Street area. It was originally a wholefood store with a few tables at the back and, although it has now been a dedicated restaurant for some time, a welcoming waft of that unmistakable aroma remains. The atmosphere is informal, especially during the day (when window seats are well placed for people watching) and people like it for its simple wholesomeness, redolent of good home cooking. In the evening, menus are more ambitious and the cooking moves up a notch or two. Seats 40. Mon-Sat 8.30am-8pm (Thurs to 9pm). All à la carte; wine (1/4 bottles) EUR3. Closed Sun, except Dec. Closed 25-26 Dec & 1 Jan.

Da Pino

RESTAURANT 38-40 Parliament Street Dublin 2 **Tel: 01 671 9308**
Fax: 01 677 3409 Email: m.jimenez@tinet.ie

Just across the road from Dublin Castle, this busy youthful Italian/Spanish restaurant is always full - and no wonder, as they serve cheerful, informal, well cooked food that does not make too many concessions to trendiness and is sold at very reasonable prices. Paella is a speciality and the pizzas, which are especially good, are prepared in full view of customers. Children welcome. No-smoking area. **Seats 80.** Open 12-12 daily. 2-course L Eur 6.22; also à la carte. Wine from €14. Closed 25-26 Dec & Good Fri. Da Pino Amex, Diners, MasterCard, Visa, Laser. **Directions:** Opposite Dublin Castle.

The Davenport Hotel

HOTEL Merrion Square Dublin 2 **Tel: 01 607 3500** Fax: 01 661 5663
Email: davenportres@ocallaghanhotels.ie Web: www.ocallaghanhotels.ie

On Merrion Square, close to the National Gallery, this striking hotel is fronted by the impressive 1863 façade of Merrion Hall, which was restored as part of the hotel building project in the early '90s. Inside, the hotel has been imaginatively designed to be both interesting and comfortable, with a pleasing mixture of old and new influences and was completely refurbished in 2000. Conference/banqueting (390/400). Business centre. Secretarial services. ISDN lines. Video conferencing. Fitness centre. Children welcome (Under 2s free in parents' room; cots available). No pets. Lift. **Rooms 120** (2 suites, 10 junior suites, 60 no-smoking, 2 for disabled). B&B €140 pps, ss €120. Open all year. Amex, Diners, MasterCard, Visa Lower Merrion Street off Merrion Square.

Davy Byrnes

PUB 21 Duke Street Dublin 2 **Tel: 01 677 5217**
Fax: 01 671 7619 Web: www.davybyrnespub.com

Just off Grafton Street, Davy Byrnes is one of Dublin's most famous pubs - references in Joyce's Ulysses mean it is very much on the tourist circuit. Despite all this fame it remains a genuine, well-run place and equally popular with Dubliners, who find it a handy meeting place and also enjoy the bar food. The style is quite traditional, providing 'a good feed' at reasonable prices (most main courses, with hearty vegetables, are under €12). Oysters with brown bread & butter, Irish stew, deep-fried plaice with tartare sauce are typical and there's always a list of daily specials like brown beef stew and sautéed lambs liver with bacon & mushroom sauce - and possibly game in season as well as the regular menu. An outside seating area was added in 2000. No suitable for children under 7. Bar food served daily, 12.30-9. Closed 25-26 Dec & Good Fri. MasterCard, Visa, Laser. **Directions:** 100 yards from Grafton Street.

Diep Le Shaker

RESTAURANT 55 Pembroke Lane Dublin 2 **Tel: 01 661 1829**
Fax: 01 661 5905 Web: www.diep.net

This fashionable two-storey restaurant is elegantly appointed with comfortable high-back chairs, good linen and fine glasses, while sunny yellow walls and a long skylight along one side of the upper floor create a bright, summery atmosphere. The cuisine is mainly Thai, offering a wide range from the famed Tom Yum hot & sour soup with lemon grass and kaffir lime leaves to a selection of the equally typical green and red curries - and, in between, a wide choice including many based on luxurious ingredients like fresh lobster, seabass and black sole. Such is the current popularity of Thai food that Chinese cuisine, which was equally represented when the restaurant first opened in 1999, has now been relegated to a few favourites like sizzling dishes, crispy fried pork and sweet & sour king prawns. Not suitable for children after 8 pm. No smoking area, air conditioning. Jazz Mon & Tue night. **Seats 120.** L Tues-Fri 12.30-2.15, D Mon-Sat 6.30-10.30 (to 11.15 Thu-Sat). Set D €34.28; Gourmet Menu

€44.44. Also à la carte. Wines from €18.41. SC 10%. Closed L Mon & Sat, all Sun. Diep Le Shaker Amex, Diners, MasterCard, Visa, Laser. **Directions:** first lane on left off Pembroke Street.

Dish Restaurant

RESTAURANT 2 Crow Street Temple Bar Dublin 2 **Tel: 01 671 1248** Fax: 01 671 1249 Email: dish@indigo.ie Web: www.dishrestaurant.net

Trevor Browne and Gerard Foote's stylishly spartan restaurant is a cut above most others in the Temple Bar area: global cuisine this may be, but here you you can be sure of substance as well as style. Gerard Foote uses only the best ingredients - organic beef and lamb, free-range chicken and a wide variety of fresh fish daily - to provide the wholesome basis for menus that change regularly to make the most of seasonal produce. Roast fillet of monkfish with savoy cabbage, baby potatoes & cream and organic fillet steak are typical - and cheeses are supplied by Sheridans cheesemongers, of South Anne Street.* Trevor Browne and Gerard Foote have recently opened a second restaurant TriBeCa - see separate entry. Children welcome. **Seats 55.** No-smoking area, air conditioning. Open 12-11 daily. Set L €13.24, Set D from €15.24. L&D also à la carte. House wine €16.19. SC 10% on parties of 6+. Closed 24-28 Dec & Good Fri. Dish Restaurant Amex, Diners, MasterCard, Visa, Laser. **Directions:** off Dame St., beside Central Bank.

Dobbins Wine Bistro

RESTAURANT 15 Stephens Lane Dublin 2 **Tel: 01 661 3321** Fax: 01 661 3331 Email: dobbinswinebistro@eircom.net

Hidden away near Merrion Square, in a 'Nissen hut' between Upper and Lower Mount Street and now something of an institution, this restaurant has operated since 1978 under the close supervision of owner John O'Byrne and manager Patrick Walsh. It has a conservatory area with a sliding roof and a patio at the far end, which is very popular in summer, and a dark intimate atmosphere in the main restaurant. Gary Flynn, head chef since 1979, has attracted a loyal following for consistently good cooking in a style which has not abandoned tradition but incorporates new ideas too. Good details include generous, plain wine glasses and lovely home-baked brown bread. Valet parking. Children welcome. No-smoking area. Air conditioning. **Seats 120** (private room, 40). L Mon-Fri12.30-2.30 .D Tue-Sat 7.30-10.30 Set L €20.95, Set D from €45. A la carte also available. House wine from €19. SC discretionary. Closed L Sat, all Sun, D Mon, bank hols, Christmas week. Amex, Diners, MasterCard, Visa, Laser Between Lower & Upper Mount Street.

Doheny & Nesbitt

PUB 5 Lower Baggot Street Dublin 2 **Tel: 01 676 2945** Fax: 01 676 0655

Only a stone's throw from Toner's (see entry), Doheny & Nesbitt is another great Dublin institution, but there the similarity ends. Just around the corner from the Dail (Irish Parliament), this solid Victorian pub has traditionally attracted a wide spectrum of Dublin society - politicians, economists, lawyers, businss names, political and financial journalists - all with a view to get across or some new scandal to divulge, so a visit here can often be unexpectedly rewarding. Like the Horseshoe Bar at the nearby Shelbourne Hotel which has a similar reputation and shares the clientÈle, half the fun of drinking at Nesbitt's is anticipation of 'someone' arriving or 'something' happening, both more likely than not. Aside from that itÌs an unspoilt, very professionally run bar with an attractive Victorian ambience and a traditional emphasis on drinking. Traditional Irish music on Sunday nights. Closed 25 Dec & Good Fri.

The Dome Restaurant

RESTAURANT/CAFÉ St Stephens Green Shopping Centre St Stephens Green Dublin 2 **Tel: 01 478 1287**

At the top of the shopping centre is this bright and airy daytime restaurant has a lot going for it before you take a bite: beautiful views over St Stephen's Green, a friendly atmosphere, fresh flowers - and even live background music. In the guide's experience hot meals may be hit and miss, but the large salad bar offers a wide-ranging and colourful selection. But the real strength here is the baking - all cakes are home-made, there's a wide choice of desserts and confectionery which would be very hard to beat - and an off sales cake shop too. Service is polite and prompt, with table service for teas and coffees. Children welcome. **Seats 200** No-smoking area. Air conditioning. Open Mon-Sat, 9-5.30. Set L around €8, otherwise à la carte. Wines (1/4 bottles) from €4.13. SC discretionary. Closed Sun, bank hols, Christmas. No Credit Cards. **Directions:** bery top floor of St Stephens Green Shopping Centre.

Dunne & Crescenzi

RESTAURANT 14 South Frederick Street Dublin 2 **Tel: 01 6773 815** Fax: 01 6773 815

This tiny Italian restaurant very near the Nassau Street entrance to Trinity College has delighted Dubliners with its unpretentiousness and the simple good food it offers at reasonable prices. At the time of going to press it's only open during the day, but there are plans to extend opening hours to 10pm shortly, 7 days a week. **Seats 30.** No smoking area; air conditioning. Open 9-7 daily. All à la carte; wine from €10.16 (€3 by the glass). Amex, MasterCard, Visa. **Directions:** off Nassau Street.

Eamonn O'Reilly's One Pico Restaurant

RESTAURANT ☆ féile bia

5-6 Molesworth Place Schoolhouse Lane Dublin 2
Tel: 01 6760300 Fax: 01 6760400
Email: eamonnoreilly@ireland.com Web: www.onepico.com

SOMMELIER OF THE YEAR

Eamonn O'Reilly
Proprietor/Chef

Stylish new two-storey premises in a magical location near St Stephen's Green, nicely tucked in a laneway just a couple of minutes walk from the Dail and Grafton Street, have lifted Eamonn O'Reilly's already highly regarded restaurant into a different league and it is now set to become one of Dublin's most popular restaurants. The cooking is as good as ever - the style distinctly contemporary, with worldwide influences - and sophisticated, technically demanding dishes are executed with confidence and flair. Eamonn has always based his menus on first class ingredients and it is their flavours that stand out, together with the precision of the cooking. Dishes typical of the global-influenced area of his culinary palette include a very beautiful, tightly layered tian of crab and avocado with chilled red pepper & tomato soup and curry crème fraîche and loin of lamb with soft herb crust, red pepper & oregano with scallion & Cheddar cheese potato - on the Guide's visit this was found to be a truly superb dish, with perfectly balanced textures and oodles of flavour. Although not especially impressive visually, roast fillet of seabass with basil crushed potatoes & sauce vierge was also outstanding for its wonderful flavours and simplicity and honey roasted baby vegetables, served in a little copper pan, matched both dishes well. Dishes with Irish influences are less in evidence than formerly, alas, - just a small nod to our own traditions in a starter of black pudding with scallion mash & apple confit - but ask about the tasting of Irish potatoes with organic mushrooms, wild garlic & nettle pesto if it isn't on the menu. Be sure to leave room to sample an innovative and delicious cheese menu and/or beautifully presented desserts that taste as good as they look. Service is solicitous, notably from the charming sommelier, Julien Le Gentil, who is our Sommelier of the Year. He has the great gift of being able to use his knowledge to help guests select the best wine for their choice of food in a way that is not at all daunting and inspires enthusiasm - he will run through a range of possibilities from different regions and in various price brackets, succinctly describing the style and explaining why it will work with, say, a combination of red meat and fish main courses - a great asset to this fine restaurant. Not suitable for young children after 6 pm. **Seats 110** (private room, 20-50) No-smoking area; air conditioning. L 12.30-2.30 daily, (Sun to 7). D 5.30-10.30 Mon-Sat. Set L from €18, Set D €38, Gourmet Menu €63.50. House wine €20. SC 10%. Closed D Sun, bank hols, Dec 25-30. Amex, Diners, MasterCard, Visa, Laser. **Directions:** 2 mins walk off St Stephens Green.

Eden

RESTAURANT

Meeting House Square Temple Bar Dublin 2
Tel: 01 670 5373/2 Fax: 01 670 3330

On Sycamore Street, next to the Irish Film Theatre and opposite Diceman's Corner (The Diceman, Thom McGinty, was a popular Dublin street performer, famous for his costumes), this spacious two-storey restaurant has its own outdoor terrace on the square. Modern, with lots of greenery and hanging baskets, there's an open kitchen which adds to the buzz and provides entertainment if service is slow. Head chef Eleanor Walshe has established a house style which suits the restaurant and has become very popular. Seasonal menus make use of organic produce where possible ands lunch menus change weekly. Salmon tartare with crème fraîche and paprika, spicy lamb meat balls with lemon rice and tomato sauce, sticky toffee pudding with caramel sauce are all typical of the style. Classic desserts could include a caramelised lemon tart served with a scoop of blackcurrant sorbet. A well-balanced and not-too-expensive wine list offers several wines by the glass. Children welcome. **Seats 110** (private room, 12). No-smoking area. Air conditioning. L 12:30-3 daily (Sat & Sun from 12). D 6-10:30 daily. Set L about €17; also à la carte. SC discretionary. Closed Bank Hols, 24-30 Dec. Amex, Diners, MasterCard, Visa.

Elephant & Castle

RESTAURANT 18 Temple Bar Dublin 2 **Tel: 01 679 3121** Fax: 01 679 1399

This buzzy Temple Bar restaurant was one of the first new-wave places in the area and is still doing a consistently good job. Ingredients are carefully sourced and served in a range of big, generous and wholesome salads (their special Caesar salad is renowned), pasta dishes, home made burgers and great big baskets of chicken wings. Service can sometimes be a problem - waiting staff are usually foreign students and, although willing and friendly, it can take longer than anticipated to finish a meal here. Children welcome. No-smoking area. Air conditioning. **Seats 85.** Open Mon-Fri, 8am-11.30pm; Sat, 10.30am-11.30pm, Sun from 12. Toilets wheelchair accessible. Closed 24-26 Dec & Good Fri. Amex, Diners, MasterCard, Visa. **Directions:** Behind Central Bank, Dame Street.

Ely Winebar & Café

RESTAURANT/CAFÉ 22 Ely Place Dublin 2 **Tel: 01 676 8986** Fax: 01 661 7288

Just around the corner from The Shelbourne and a stone's throw from the Merrion Hotel, Erik Robson's wine bar and café occupies the ground floor and basement of an imaginatively renovated Georgian townhouse - polished wooden floors, brick arches and contemporary furnishings are completely at home here, a successful and refreshing blend of old and new. Ely's unusual wine list is the main attraction, offering a huge number of carefully selected wines, with over seventy available by the glass thus providing the opportunity to taste wines which would otherwise be unaffordable to most people. Although not the first restaurant to try this, it is done with great dedication and style at Ely - and the exceptional wine list is backed up by other specialities including a list of premium beers and cigars. On the food side, organic produce, notably meats from the family farm in Co Clare, are a special feature - and not just premium cuts, but also products like black pudding and home-made sausages which make all the difference to simple dishes like sausages and mash. Although food was originally presented more or less as an accompaniment to the exceptional wines it has developed considerably during the first year of operation and quite extensive lunch and evening menus are now offered - including, many visitors will be glad to hear, Kilkee oysters with brown bread and traditional Irish stew made with Burren lamb as well as many contemporary dishes - and wine suggestions are given too. Mature Irish and continental cheeses make the ideal accompaniment to a glass of wine and there's a bar menu of small dishes like mini chicken kebabs with satay sauce, organic beef or lamb meatballs and organic black or white pudding crostini, which you can get in selections of two to four. They also serve great coffee, a perfect accompaniment for their fine selection of handmade Irish chocolates. Open Mon-Sat L 12-3, D 6-10 (Bar open to midnight; tapas menu 7-12). Closed Sun, Christmas week. Amex, Diners, MasterCard, Visa, Laser. **Directions:** Junction of Baggot Street/Merrion Street off St Stephens Green.

Fado Restaurant

RESTAURANT Mansion House Dawson St. Dublin 2 **Tel: 01 676 7200**
Fax: 01 676 7530 Email: info@fado.ie

The Mansion House is the Lord Mayor's residence and it has a delightful restaurant, which is open to the public. The original supper room has been imaginatively renovated - the room itself is of sufficient interest to be worth a look even if you haven't time to eat - and the contemporary food served somehow seems very appropriate to this sparkling restoration. Well-balanced menus, which include a quick 2-course lunch as well as an early dinner, tend to lean towards seafood - specialities include warm oyster vichyssoise, seafood terrine and seabass jardinière. Open all day Mon-Sat 12-10. Set L €14.60, early D (5-7pm) 18.41; also à la carte. Closed Sun, Christmas & Good Fri. Amex, MasterCard, Visa, Laser. **Directions:** Beside the Mansion House Residence Dawson Street.

Fitzers Restaurant

RESTAURANT 51 Dawson Street Dublin 2 **Tel: 01-677 1155**
Fax: 01-670 6575 Email: fitzcat@indigo.ie

Reliable Cal-Ital influenced cooking in a dashing contemporary setting with a heated al fresco dining area on the pavement. Open daily 11.30am-11pm. Closed Dec 25/26, Jan 1, Good Friday. Amex, Diners, MasterCard, Visa. Also at: *Temple Bar Square, Tel: 01-679 0440 (12-11 daily, cl 25 Dec & Good Fri) *National Gallery, Merrion Square Tel: 01-661 4496 (Mon-Sat 10.30-4.30, Sun 2-4.30, closed Gallery Opening days).

The Fitzwilliam Hotel

HOTEL

St Stephens Green Dublin 2 **Tel: 01 478 7000** Fax: 01 4787878
Email: enq@fitzwilliam-hotel.com Web: www.fitzwilliam-hotel.com

This stylish contemporary hotel enjoys a superb location on the north-western corner of St Stephen's Green. Behind its deceptively low-key frontage lies an impressively sleek interior created by Sir Terence Conran's design group CD Partnership. Public areas combine elegant minimalism with luxury fabrics and finishes, notably leather upholstery and a fine pewter counter in the bar, which is a chic place to meet in the Grafton Street area. In addition to the hotels' premier restaurant, Peacock Alley (see below), breakfast, lunch and diner are served daily in the Mezzanine Café. Bedrooms, while quite compact for a luxury hotel, are finished to a high standard with air-conditioning, safe, fax/modem point, stereo CD player and minibar, and care has been lavished on the bathrooms too, down to details such as high quality toiletries. Conference/banqueting (80/60). Secretarial services. Children welcome; (under12s free in parents' room; cots available free of charge). 24 hour room service. Lift. **Rooms 130** (2 suites, 128 executive, 60 no-smoking, 4 for disabled). Room rate €305 (max 2 guests). No service charge. Open all year.

★ **Peacock Alley** This was Dublin's most talked-about restaurant until its controversial proprietor, Conrad Gallagher, turned his attention to a new establishment in London in the summer of 2001, leaving a less flamboyant but very able team to continue in the complex, visually impressive style for which the restaurant is famous. A recent visit by the Guide confirms that this restaurant is on top form - and worth the considerable investment that a visit involves. With a separate entrance from St Stephen's Green, the restaurant is right at the top of the hotel and handy to the roof garden, with a small bar/reception then a large room lightly partitioned into three areas, creating a more intimate atmosphere. Some tables overlook Stephen's Green and/or head chef David Cavalier and his team at work in the open kitchen. It is impeccably appointed, with acres of crisp white linen, fine modern crystal and designer flowers - and remain's one of Dublin's most expensive restaurants. No-smoking area. Air conditioning. **Seats 110** (private room, 60). L daily, 12.30-2.30. D daily, 6.30-10. Set L from €24.06. Early/Late D from €24.06/30.47; Menu Prix Fixe €69.84, Menu Gourmand €82.53. A la carte also available. Sommelier's Selection from €29.20. SC discretionary. Amex, Diners, MasterCard, Visa.

Les Frères Jacques

RESTAURANT

74 Dame Street Dublin 2 **Tel: 01 679 4555** Fax: 01 679 4725
Email: info@lesfreresjacques.com Web: www.esfreresjacques.com

One of the few genuinely French restaurants in Dublin, Les Frères Jacques opened beside the Olympia Theatre in 1986, well before the development of Temple Bar made the area fashionable. Most of the staff are French, the atmosphere is French - and, although the head chef is Irish, the cooking is French in style. Seasonal menus are wide-ranging and well-balanced but - as expected when you notice the lobster tank just beside the door on entering - there is a strong bias towards fish and seafood, all of it from Irish waters; game also features in season. Lunch at Les Frères Jacques is a treat (and good value) but dinner is a feast. The 4-course set dinner offers soup (a langoustine consommé with salmon ravioli perhaps) and three choices on the other courses - crab and roasted bell pepper gateau with gazpacho dressing, braised shank of lamb with lentils and rosemary juices and chocolate millefeuille and orange mousse are all typical examples. The à la carte offers classics such as west coast oysters (native or rock) and grilled lobster, individually priced, and there are also some unsual dishes, like old-fashioned pork shank pie with root vegetables and truffle juices. Finish with cheeses or a classic dessert like warm thin apple tart (baked to order), with a rum & raisin ice cream. The wine list naturally favours France, although there is a little nod to the New World at the end of an extensive selection that makes interesting reading; house wines and a list of "petits vins de bon gout" are good value, also two pages of "recommandations du patron" (en rouge et blanc). Children welcome. No-smoking area. Air conditioning. **Seats 60** (private room, 6-40). L Mon-Fri,12.30-2.30; D Mon-Sat 7-11. Set L€20; Set D €32; D also à la carte. House wine €15.87.SC 12.5%. Closed L Sat, all Sun, Christmas. Amex, Diners, MasterCard, Visa, Laser. **Directions:** next Olympia Theatre.

Good World Chinese Restaurant

RESTAURANT

18 South Great Georges Street Dublin 2
Tel: 01 677 5373 Fax: 01 677 5373

One of a cluster of interesting ethnic restaurants around Wicklow Street and South Great George's Street, the Good World has been owner-managed by Thomas Choi since opening a decade ago. Its large selection of Dim Sum, served daily, has made it a favourite of the local Chinese community. The restaurant also prides itself on an especially full range of other Chinese dishes, suitable for both Chinese and European customers and Thomas Choi makes a welcoming and helpful host. **Seats 95.** Open 12.30pm-3am daily, Set L Mon-Fri 12.30-2.15. Closed 25-26 Dec. Amex, Diners, MasterCard, Visa.

The Gotham Café

RESTAURANT 8 South Anne Street Dublin 2 **Tel: 01 679 5266** Fax: 01 679 5280

A lively, youthful café-restaurant just off Grafton Street, the Gotham does good informal food and is specially noted for its gourmet pizzas - try the Chinatown, for example, which comes with barbecued Peking duck, spring onions, cashew nuts, hoisin sauce & mozzarella cheese. Other specialities include Caesar salad, baby calzoni (two - one with with chèvre, prosciutto, basil & garlic; the other with baby potato, spinach, caramelised red onion, mozzarella & fresh pesto) and Asian chicken noodle salad (satay chicken fillets on a salad of egg noodles tossed in a light basil & crème fraîche dressing). There's plenty for vegetarians too - and it's a great place for brunch on Sundays and bank holidays (11.30-4.15). Children welcome.No-smoking area. Air conditioning. **Seats 65.** Open Mon-Sat 12 -12, Sun L 12-4:30 & D 5-10:30. A la carte. House wine €14.60. SC discretionary (10% on parties of 6+). Closed 2 days Christmas & Good Fri. Amex, Diners, MasterCard, Visa, Laser. **Directions:** just off Grafton Street.

The Grafton Capital

HOTEL Lower Stehens Street Dublin 2 **Tel: 01 475 0888** Fax: 01 475 0908
Email: info@graftoncapital-hotel.com Web: www.capital-hotels.com

In a prime city centre location just a couple of minutes walk from Grafton Street, this attractive hotel offers particularly well furnished rooms and good amenities (including fax/modem) at prices which are not unreasonable for the area. Rooms are also available for small conferences, meetings and interviews. The popular 'Break for the Border' nightclub next door is in common ownership with the hotel, offering guests live entertainment on Wednesday-Saturday nights. Small conference (25). Secretarial services. Wheelchair access. Parking by arrangement with nearby carpark. Children welcome (Under 12s free in parents' room; cots available). No Pets. **Rooms 75** (3 suites, 30 executive rooms, 5 no-smoking, 4 for disabled). B&B €88.90, ss €31.74. Lift. Closed 24-26 Dec. Amex, Diners, MasterCard, Visa, Laser. **Directions:** From Stephen's Green (North), turn left into South King street, take a right and the hotel is on your left.

Harrington Hall

GUESTHOUSE 69/70 Harcourt Street Dublin 2 **Tel: 01 475 3497** Fax: 01 475 4544
Email: harringtonhall@eircom.net Web: www.harringtonhall.com

Conveniently located close to St Stephen's Green, this fine family-run guesthouse was once the home of a former Lord Mayor of Dublin and has been sympathetically and elegantly refurbished, retaining many original features. Echoes of Georgian splendour remain in the ornamental ceilings and fireplaces of the well-proportioned ground and first floor rooms, which include a peaceful drawing room. Bedrooms, which are both comfortable and practical, have neat en-suite bathrooms and have recently had all the windows sound-proofed and ceiling fans installed. All round this is a welcome and considerably cheaper alternative to a city-centre hotel, with the huge advantage of free parking behind the building. Children welcome (under 2s free in parents' room, cot available). Lift. **Rooms 28** (all no-smoking, 2 shower only, 2 junior suites, 6 executive, 2 for disabled). B&B €82.50, ss €45. Closed Dec 23-27. Amex, MasterCard, Visa. **Directions:** Turn right at top of Grafton Street past Stephens Green on left.

Hilton Dublin

HOTEL féile bia Charlemont Place Dublin 2 **Tel: 01 402 9988** Fax: 01 402 9966
Email: reservations_dublin@hilton.com Web: www.dublin.hilton.com

Overlooking the Grand Canal, this fairly new hotel (previously Stakis), is just a few minutes walk from the city centre and caters for all the needs of the modern day guest. Each double-glazed bedroom provides a worktop with modem point, swivel satellite TV, individual heater, tea/coffee-making facilities, trouser press, hairdryer and compact bathroom (club rooms - which include a new floor of 39 rooms upgraded this year - also offer a bathrobe, additional toiletries and chocolates). A buffet-style breakfast is served in the well-appointed Waterfront Restaurant. Conference/banqueting (350/270). Underground carpark. Children welcome (Under 12s free in parents' room; cots available). No pets.Lift. **Rooms 189** (78 no-smoking, 8 for disabled). Room rate €222 (max 2 guests) Closed 23-27 Dec. Amex, MasterCard, Visa.

Hodges Figgis

CAFÉ 56-58 Dawson Street Dublin 2 **Tel: 01 677 4754** Email: books@hodgesfiggis.ie

One of Europe's largest bookshops is also one of the oldest - they've been selling books here since 1768. Always innovative, they were also one of the first to hit on the idea of nourishing the book-hunter's body as well as the mind - their in-store café opened in 1995. As this is the kind of shop where you could easily lose a day, this was one of their best ideas. Café open 9.30-5.30, (Thurs to 7). No Credit Cards.

Il Primo

RESTAURANT 16 Montague Street Dublin 2 **Tel: 01 478 3373** Fax: 01 478 3373
Email: alto.primo@iolfree.ie Web: www.ilprimoireland.com

Dieter Bergman's cheery little two storey restaurant and wine bar between Harcourt Street and Camden Street was way ahead of current fashions when it opened in 1991. It's simple (some would say spartan) but the essentials are right: warm hospitality and excellent, imaginative, freshly cooked modern Italian food that include gourmet pizzas (with smoked salmon & spinach, for example), excellent pastas and lovely salads (try the insalata misto, with mixed leaves, cheese, olives & french beans) The wines are Dieter's special passion: 40 are available by the millilitre - you drink as much or as little as you want and that's the amount you pay for: brilliant. Dieter also organises regular wine tastings and dinners. On the down side, prices can mount alarmingly at dinner resulting in a bill that may seem disproportionate to the simple surroundings. Children welcome. **Seats 30.** No-smoking area. Air conditioning.L & D Mon-Sat, 12.30-3 & 4-11; à la carte. House wine €19 per litre. SC 10%. Closed Sun. Amex, Diners, MasterCard, Visa, Laser. **Directions:** 5 mins from Stephens Green between Harcourt Street & Wexford Street.

Imperial Chinese Restaurant

RESTAURANT 12A Wicklow Street Dublin 2 **Tel: 01 677 2580** Fax: 01 677 9851
Email: imperial@hotmail.com

Mrs Cheung's long-estabished city centre restaurant has enjoyed enduring popularity with Dubliners and has also a clear vote of confidence from the local Chinese community, who appreciate the authenticity of cooking by Chi Hung Lee and Ip Kay Yim. Crispy aromatic duck is a speciality and they are renowned for their Dim Sum on Sundays, when a wide selection of small, typically Chinese dishes is offered. Children welcome. **Seats 180.** Open daily 12.30-11.30 (L12.30-2.10 Mon-Sat). Set L €10.79, Set D €27.94. Also à la carte. House wine €15.17. SC 10%. Closed 25-26 Dec. Amex, MasterCard, Visa, Laser. **Directions:** on Wicklow Street near Brown Thomas.

The International Bar

PUB 23 Wicklow Street Dublin 2

Just a minute's walk from Grafton Street, this unspoilt Victorian bar makes a great meeting place - not a food spot, but good for chat and music. Closed 25 Dec. & Good Friday.

J. Mulligan

PUB 8 Poolbeg Street Dublin 2 **Tel: 01 677 5582**

One of Dublin's oldest and best-loved pubs, Mulligan's 'wine & spirit merchant' is mercifully un-renovated and likely to stay that way - dark, with no decor (as such) and no music, it's just the way so many pubs used to be. The only difference is that it's now so fashionable that it gets very crowded (and noisy) after 6pm - better to drop in during the day and see what it's really like. Closed 25 Dec & Good Fri.

Jacobs Ladder Restaurant

RESTAURANT 4 Nassau Street Dublin 2 **Tel: 01 670 3865** Fax: 01 670 3868
Web: jaladder@gofree.indigo.ie

Adrian and Bernie Roche's smart restaurant overlooks the playing fields of Trinity College and the contemporary decor provides an appropriate backdrop for Adrian's cooking, which is modern Irish with international influences and there's a welcome heartiness to his style. Well-balanced seasonal menus always include some vegetarian dishes - vegetarian and 'healthy eating' dishes are considerately highlighted - and seafood features strongly, typically in a smoked haddock risotto & gratinated free-range egg. Starters might include sautéed lamb kidneys with creamed leeks & coriander and one of about eight main courses on the dinner menu could be roast saddle of rabbit with polenta cake, pea purée cabbage & grain mustard. To finish, choose between Irish farmhouse cheeses and tempting desserts such as a classic lemon tart with raspberry coulis. Children welcome. **Seats 80** (private room, 45) L Tue-Sat 12.30-2.30 (Sat to 2) D 6-10 (Sat from 7) Set D €32. Early D (6-7pm), €24. A la carte also available. House wine €17.14. SC discretionary. Closed Sun & Mon,1 week August, 3 weeks Dec/Jan. Amex, Diners, MasterCard, Visa, Laser. **Directions:** City Centre overlooking Trinity College.

Jaipur

RESTAURANT 41 Great South Georges Street Dublin 2

Tel: 01 677 0999 Fax: 01 677 0979 Email: jaipur@eircom.net Web: www.jaipur.ie

This custom-built restaurant is named after the "Jewel of Rajasthan" and has ambitious aims to offer a different, more contemporay image of ethnic dining. Itís a cool and spacious place, with a large modern spiral staircase leading up to an area that can be used for private parties and the main restaurant below it. Although the modern decor may seem strange, warm colours send the right messages and it is a very pleasing space. Head chef, Kaushik Roy, who is highly regarded in India, is keen to make the most of Irish ingrdinets such as organic lamb, while importing fresh and dried spices directly. Menus offer an attractive combination of traditional and more creative dishes - and Jaipur is the first ethnic restaurant in Ireland to make a serious attempt to devise a wine list suited to spicy foods. Service is attentive and discreet. **Seats 90.** D daily, 5.30-11.30. Set D from €25.40 A la carte. House wine from €15.50. Amex, MasterCard, Visa, Laser, Switch **Directions:** At the corner of Sth Great Georges St. and Lower Stephens St. *Also at: 21 Castle Street Dalkey, Co Dublin. Tel: 01 285 0552

The Joose Bar

CAFÉ 7a, Poolbeg Street Dublin 2 **Tel: 01 679 9611**

Fax: 01 679 9642 Web: www.joosebar.com

Tucked away behind dreary office blocks near Tara Street station, this cheerful café offers a wide variety of excellent drinks, all made to order, in regular and large sizes: Smoothies, made with low fat frozen yoghurt, include The Grind (blueberry, raspberry, banana & apple) and The Squash (blueberry, strawberry and OJ & banana) for example, while Joose Juices include a Stressbuster (orange, lemon, apple & lettuce) and the aptly named The Hair of the Dog (pink grapefruit, lemon, lime and orange) while City Squeezes are combinations of just one or two types of fruit and/or vegetable juice. They also have a soup of the day and a chill cabinet to the side, offering a selection of basic sandwiches, wraps and salads, along with tubs of muesli for the breakfast brigade. Open Mon to Fri. 7.30am-3pm. Closed Sat, Sun & Bank Hols. No credit cards. **Directions:** Beside Mulligans Pub.

Kehoe's

PUB 9 South Anne Street Dublin 2 **Tel: 01 677 8312**

One of Dublin's best, unspoilt traditional pubs, Kehoe's is also one of the busiest in the evening - try it for a quieter daytime pint instead. Closes 25 Dec and Good Friday.

Khyber Tandoori

RESTAURANT 44/45 Sth William St Dublin 2 **Tel: 01 670 4855**

Easily recognised by the doorman, who is colourfully attired in full traditional costume, this large, well-appointed Pakistani restaurant is handy to Grafton Street. Cooking is sound and the menu wide-ranging - the selection offered goes beyond Pakistani specialities, offering a cross-section of popular eastern dishes like tandoori and balti. There's plenty of choice for vegetarians and a nice touch comes as you leave the restaurant and each departing guest is presented with a rose. **Seats 120.** L Mon-Sat, 12 noon-2.15pm, D daily 6-11.30pm. Amex, Diners, MasterCard, Visa.

Kilkenny Restaurant & Café

RESTAURANT/CAFÉ féile bia 5-6 Nassau Street Dublin 2 **Tel: 01 677 7066** Fax: 01 670 7735

Email: info@kilkennyshop.com Web: www.kilkennygroup.com

Situated on the first floor of the shop now known simply as Kilkenny, with a clear view into the grounds of Trinity College, the refurbished Kilkenny Restaurant is one of the most pleasant places in Dublin to have a bite to eat - and the food matches the view. It looks good and the experience generally matches the anticipation. Ingredients are fresh and additive-free (as are all the products on sale in the shopís Food Hall) and food has a home-cooked flavour. Salads, quiches, casseroles, home-baked breads and cakes are the specialities of the Kilkenny Restaurant and they are very good. For quicker bites the shop has a second eating place, Kilkenny Café, where Italian panini and cappuccino are served and the same principles apply. A range of Kilkenny preserves and dressings - all made and labelled on the premises - is available in the shop. Children welcome. **Seats 190.** Open Mon-Fri 8.30-5 (Thu to 7), Sat 9-5, Sun 11-5. L 12-3. A la carte. Licensed. No-smoking area. Air conditioning. Closed 25-26 Dec, 1 Jan. Easter Sun. Amex, Diners, MasterCard, Visa.

L'Ecrivain

RESTAURANT ★

109a Lower Baggot Street Dublin 2
Tel: 01 661 1919 Fax: 01 661 0617
Email: enquiries@lecrivain.com Web: www.lecrivain.com

WINE LIST OF THE YEAR

Derry and Sallyanne Clarke's acclaimed city centre restaurant is light and airy with lots of pale wood and smoky mirrors - since recent renovations, it's on two levels, spacious and very dashing, with lovely formal table settings which promise seriously good food. Derry's cooking style - classic French with contemporary flair and a strong leaning towards modern Irish cooking - remains consistent although new ideas are constantly incorporated and the list of specialities keeps growing. Special treats to try include a wonderful starter of baked rock oysters with York cabbage & crispy cured bacon, with a Guinness sabayon - perhaps followed by a main course speciality of rack of baby Irish lamb (mountain lamb may be used in season), with tomato & mint chutney, fondant potato and rosemary & garlic jus. Menus could also include neglected ingredients like rabbit, which is always appealingly served. Wonderful puddings are presented with panache and might include a hot soufflé or a superb crème brulée with armagnac. Presentation is impressive but not ostentatious and attention to detail - garnishes designed individually to enhance each dish, careful selection of plates, delicious home-made breads and splendid farmhouse cheeses - is excellent.Thoughtful little touches abound - and there are some major ones too, like the policy to add the price of your wine after the 10% service charge has been added to your bill, instead of charging on the total as most restaurants do. Sommelier Martina Delaney aims to achieve an even balance on the wine list, to suit all palates and all pockets; keen to offer a good choice under €40, she lists about twenty imaginatively selected "Suggested Wines", providing for people who want something more challenging than the house wine but prefer somebody else to narrow down the choice a little. The list offers some great classics, but the main selection is wide-ranging and Martina clearly enjoys sourcing lesser-known small producers who tend to sell on quality rather than price, so she can offer "a little gem for under €25". This fine wine list is augmented by a tempting selection of coffees and digestifs - all this, plus excellent service, adds up to a very caring approach and an exceptional restaurant. Seats 101. L Mon-Fri 12.30-2, D Mon-Sat 7-11; Set L €25.31, Set D €44.30. House wine €22.78. SC 10% (on food only). Closed L Sat, all Sun, bank hols. Amex, MasterCard, Visa, Laser. **Directions:** opposite Bank of Ireland headquarters.

La Maison des Gourmets

RESTAURANT

15 Castle Market Dublin 2 **Tel: 01 672 7258** Fax: 01 855 5332
Email: lamaison@indigo.ie Web: www.gourmetmaison.com

La Maison des Gourmets is run by two Frenchmen, Nicolas Boutin and Olivier Quenet, who both had extensive experience as chefs some of Dublin's top restaurants - Guilbaud, Les Frères Jacques - before opening this little place for coffees and patisserie in 1999. The following year they developed the concept to open a bistro-style restaurant, The Tea Rooms, upstairs where (despite the confusing name) rather more substantial fare is served. As well as their own baked goods and charcuterie, the shop stocks Parisian bread, French cheeses and many other specialist foods, some of which find their way upstairs. They also sell vacuum-packed meals, take on-line orders from their menus and provide an outside catering service too.

La Mère Zou

RESTAURANT

22 St Stephen's Green Dublin 2 **Tel: 01 661 6669**
Fax: 01 661 6669 Email: merzou@indigo.ie

Eric Tydgadt's French/Belgian restaurant is situated in a Georgian basement on the north side of the Green. Although there are some concessions to current cuisine (especially on the lunch menu), this establishment's reputation is based on French country cooking, as in terrine of wild rabbit with pistachio nuts (albeit with a raspberry & onion compôte), grilled chicken chasseur (with a mushroom, tomato & white sauce) and specialities such as steamed mussels (various ways) with French fries and even traditional Alsatian sauerkraut with four meats. Prices are reasonable, a policy carried through to the wine list too [* The associated business, Supper's Ready - an enlightened takeaway doing real food like coq au vin - operates from 51, Pleasant Street, Dublin, 8. Tel: 01-475 4556.] **Seats 55** (private room, 8) No-smoking area. L Mon-Fri, 12-2.30. D Mon-Thu, 6-10; Fri & Sat, 6-11; Sun, 6-9.30 Early D available (6-7.15pm), Set L&D available, also à la carte. House wine €13. SC discretionary. Closed L Sat & L Sun, 24 Dec-6 Jan. Amex, Diners, MasterCard, Visa, Laser. **Directions:** beside Shelbourne Hotel.

La Stampa

RESTAURANT/ HOTEL 35 Dawson Street Dublin 2 **Tel: 01 285 4851** Fax: 01 235 2240

Already well-established as a restaurant, major development saw La Stampa open its doors as an hotel in the summer of 2001. There's an exotic lounge bar on the ground floor - to the right of the restaurant entrance - and the reception desk is upstairs, on the first floor. Work was still in progress at the time of the Guide's visit, but some rooms were operational - and very attractive they are too, with sumptuous fabrics, notably velvet, in rich colours echoing the ambience of the restaurant and bar below and neat en-suite bathrooms. No pets. **Rooms 36** (6 suites, 6 junior suites). Room rate €165 **La Stampa:** Reminiscent of a grand French belle époque brasserie, this is one of Ireland's finest dining rooms - high-ceiling, large mirrors, wooden floor, Roman urns, statues, busts, candelabra, Victorian lamps, plants, flowers and various bits of bric-a-brac, the whole noisily complemented by a constant bustle. There's a small bar with a few comfortable seats where you can sip a drink while studying menus that encompass dishes from around the world. Menus are changed fairly often and, although prices can mount rather quickly for the style and quality of food and service, this is a fun and lively place, offering international food in delightful surroundings. No children after 9pm. Smoking unrestricted; air conditioning. **Seats 150** (private room, 60). L 12:30-2:30 Mon-Fri. D 5:30-12am Mon-Fri, 6-12:30am Sat, 6:30-11:30 Sun. Early D 5.30-7, Mon-Fri. L&D à la carte. SC discretionary (10% on parties of 6+). Closed L Sat & L Sun. Amex, Diners, MasterCard, Visa.

Le Meridien Shelbourne

HOTEL
RESTAURANT

27 St Stephen's Green Dublin 2
Tel: 01 663 4500 Fax: 01 661 6006
Email: shelbourneinfo@lemeridien-hotels.com Web: www.shelbourne.ie

The Irish Constitution was drafted here and this opulent 18th-century hotel overlooking St Stephen's Green (Europe's largest garden square) is still central to Dublin life today - officially it may now be called Le Meridien Shelbourne, but to Dubliners it will always remain the dear old 'Shelbourne'. Under the direction of General Manager Jean Ricoux, who joined the hotel in 1997, major renovation has taken place, ensuring its ranking among the worldís great hotels: it has retained all its grandeur, and the entrance creates a strong impression with its magnificent faux-marble entrance hall and Lord Mayor's Lounge, a popular meeting place for afternoon tea. The Shelbourne Bar on Kildare Street is relatively new (food served 12-4 daily includes 'traditional daily specials', some more traditional than others) but the Horseshoe Bar, renowned as a meeting place for local politicians and theatrical society, is nothing short of a Dublin institution. As it is an old building, accommodation varies somewhat. The best rooms and suites are very luxurious, but new rooms have recently been added and 47 of the standard rooms were completely re-designed and refurbished in 2001; all rooms are well-appointed, with good bathrooms, bathrobes, mini-bars and three telephones as standard. The hotel has two restaurants, No 27 The Green (see below) and The Side Door At The Shelbourne (12-11 daily) which has a separate entrance from Kildare Street and, with its striking minimalist decor and Cal-Ital menus, provides a complete contrast to the ultra-traditional atmosphere of the hotel. Conference/banqueting (400/320). Business centre. Fitness centre (indoor swimming pool); hairdressing/beauty salon. Valet Parking. Children welcome. Pets permitted. Lift. **Rooms 190.** B&B from €180pps (Room Only rate €340), SC 15%. Open all year. **No. 27 The Green** This elegant and lofty dining-room offers some very good cooking, combining the best of Irish produce with some traditional/continental flair and expertise. Alongside the daily-changing table d'hôte menus (four choices of starter and main course with dinner providing an additional soup course), there's a substantial à la carte. Specialities, which are strongly seasonal, typically include the best Irish beef in côte de bouef, prime seafood such as Lobster and Dublin Bay prawns and game in season. All in all, this is a well-run restaurant, serving excellent food. Several breads are offered with butter or, as a healthy option, a dish of raw diced vegetables. Service is ultra-professional. **Seats 65.** No-smoking area (no air conditioning). L Sun-Fri,12.30-230; D 6.30-10 Mon-Sat, Sun 6-10. Set menus from €31. L&D also à la carte. House wine from €20.95. SC15%. Closed L Sat. Amex, Diners, MasterCard, Visa. **Directions:** from Trinity College take 3rd right, turn up Kildare Street, Shelbourne on left hand side.

Little Caesar's Palace

RESTAURANT Balfe Street Dublin 2 **Tel: 01 671 8714**

This genuine little pizza place is just a stone's throw from the door of the Westbury Hotel - fresh, tasty and inexpensive pizzas (with good crisp bases) cooked before your very eyes could be the perfect antidote to too much luxury, or too much shopping. Open 12 noon-midnight. Closed 25 Dec & Good Fri. *There's also a Mediterranean food shop & café nearby on Chatham Street and Little Caesar branches at: Rathfarnham (Unit 2, Butterfield, The Orchard Inn. Tel: 01-493 4060); Blackrock, Co Dublin (Main Street. Tel: 01 278 1533). At the time of going to press a new branch is due to open on Harcourt Street, Dublin 2.

The Long Hall Bar

PUB 51 South Great George's Dublin 2 **Tel: 01 475 1590**

A wonderful old pub with magnificent plasterwork ceilings, traditional mahogany bar and Victorian lighting. One of Dublin's finest bars and well worth a visit. Closed 25 Dec & Good Fri.

Longfields Hotel

HOTEL/RESTAURANT Lower Fitzwilliam Street Dublin 2 **Tel: 01 676 1367**
Fax: 01 676 1542 Email: lfields@indigo.ie Web: www.longfields.ie

Located in a Georgian terrace between Fitzwilliam and Merrion Squares, this reasonably priced hotel is more like a well proportioned private house, furnished with antiques in period style - notably in elegant public areas. Comfortable bedrooms are individually furnished although they vary considerably in size as rooms are smaller on the upper floors. Staff are friendly and there is morning coffee and afternoon tea available in the drawing room. 24 hour room service. Children welcome (cots available). No pets. **Rooms 26** (13 shower only, 2 junior suites, 6 executive rooms). B&B €171.45pps, ss €38.40 Lift. Open all year. **Kevin Arundel @ Number 10:** In the basement, with direct access from Longfields Hotel or the street, this excellent restaurant is currently one of Dublin's best-kept secrets. In 2001 Kevin Arundel, previously second chef at L'Ecrivain, took over as chef-patron, refurbished the restaurant and moved the kitchen up into a higher gear. Modern French is the style, seen in starters like a rich, smooth chicken liver parfait served with a Chantilly cream with morels and toasted brioche and a light crab & celeriac remoulade, attractively presented encased in tomato quarters with a wonderful spinach salad on top. Speciality main courses include pot-roast rabbit with spices, saffron risotto, pickled aubergine and caviar and seared fillet of John Dory with crushed new potatoes and niçoise salad. But be sure to leave room for a grand finale of wonderful desserts, such as poached yellow peach with goats cheese ice cream and raspberry coulis, beautifully presented. Efficient service complements the fine food, making this a good venue for lunch and dinner. **Seats 35** (private room, 20). L Mon-Fri, 12.30-2, D daily 6.30-10 (Sun to 9). Set L €21.59, Set D €36.77; house wine 19.68. SC 121/2%. Closed L Sat, L Sun. Amex, Diners, MasterCard, Laser. **Directions:** 200 metres from St Stephens Green.

McDaid's

PUB 3 Harry Street Dublin 2 Tel: 01 679 4395

Established in 1779, McDaids more recently achieved fame as one of the great literary pubs - and its association with Brendan Behan, especially, brings a steady trail of pilgrims from all over the world to this traditional premises just beside the Westbury Hotel. Dubliners, however, tend to be immune to this kind of thing and drink there because it's a good pub - and, although its character is safe, it's not a place set in aspic either, as a younger crowd has been attracted by recent changes. History and character are generally of more interest than food here, but sandwiches are available. Open Mon-Wed,10.30am-11.30pm; Thu-Sat, 10.30am-12.30am; Sun 12.30-11.Closed 25 Dec & Good Fri.

The Mercer Hotel

HOTEL

Lower Mercer Street Dublin 2 **Tel: 01 478 2179** Fax: 01 478 0328
Email: stay@mercerhotel.ie Web: mercerhotel.ie

Tucked away behind the Royal College of Surgeons, this small, intimate hotel is a stone's throw from Stephen's Green and Grafton Street. It aims to create a clubby home-from-home feel; bedrooms have comfortable, undemanding decor and facilities that would be expected of much larger hotels, including air conditioning, CD players, a fridge for your complimentary mineral water and bathrobes as standard. The 'Green Room' makes a good business venue too, for meeting and private dining for 1-120 people.Conference/banqueting (110/80). Business centre. Secretarial services. ISDN lines. Video conferencing. Wheelchair access. Parking. Children welcome (Under 12s free in parentsí room; cots available). No Pets. **Rooms 21** (all executive, 4 no-smoking, 1 for disabled). B&B about €85pps, ss about €44. Lift. Open all year. Amex, Diners, MasterCard, Visa.

The Mermaid Café

RESTAURANT ☆

69-70 Dame Street Dublin 2 **Tel: 01 670 8236** Fax: 01 670 8205
Email: info.@mermaid.ie Web: www.mermaid.ie

Interesting decor and imaginative French and American-inspired cooking are to be found at this restaurant on the edge of Temple Bar. Small, but with every inch of space used with style, owner-chef Ben Gorman's cooking is among the best in the area and his front-of-house partner, Mark Harrell, is a quietly solicitous host. Examples to indicate the style include starters like New England crab cakes with piquant mayonnaise and pork, sage & boiled egg terrine with horseradish cream. Terrific vegetarian main courses such as roast flat mushrooms with coriander egg fried rice and bok choi rub shoulders with 'Giant Atlantic Seafood Casserole', a speciality which changes daily depending on availability, and hearty meat dishes which vary with the seasons but are invariably full of interest. Irish cheeses are imaginatively served and in good condition, while espresso and cappuccino arrive with crystallised pecan nuts. Sunday brunch is not to be missed if you are in the area - kick off with restorative drinks ranging from freshly squeezed juice or home-made lemonade to champagne, then launch into splendid fare like home-made sourdough pancakes and a variety of good things, olive oil bread bruschetta with roast ham, mustard & gratinated Gabriel cheese sauce, West Cork hand smoked haddock & horseradhish with mash - and much else besides. Wines are imported privately and are exclusive to the restaurant. Children welcome. **Seats 55** (private room, 24) No-smoking area. Air conditioning. L 12.30-3 (Sun to 3.30), D 6-11 (Sun to 9.30). Set L €15.24; Set D from €31.74. House wine from €17.71. SC discretionary. Closed Christmas, New Year, Good Fri. * Next door, Gruel (Tel 01 670 7119), is a quality fast-food outlet under the same management. MasterCard, Visa, Laser. **Directions:** Next door to Olympia Theatre.

The Merrion Hotel

HOTEL
RESTAURANT

Upper Merrion Street Dublin 2 **Tel: 01 603 0600** Fax: 01 603 0700
Email: info@merrionhotel.com Web: www.merrionhotel.com

Right in the heart of Georgian Dublin opposite the Government Buildings, the main house of this luxurious hotel comprises four meticulously restored Grade 1 listed townhouses built in the 1760s and now restored to their former glory; behind them, a contemporary garden wing has been added, overlooking two private period and formal landscaped gardens. Inside, Irish fabrics and antiques reflect the architecture and original interiors with rococo plasterwork ceilings and classically proportioned windows - and the hotel has one of the most important private collections of 20th-century art. Public areas include three interconnecting drawing rooms (one is the cocktail bar with a log fire), with French windows giving access to the gardens. Elegant and gracious bedrooms have individually controlled air-conditioning, three telephones, personalised voice-mail with remote access, fax/modem and ISDN lines and video conference facilities, also a mini-bar and safe (VCRs,CD players and tea/coffee making facilities are available on request). Sumptuous Italian marble bathrooms, with a separate walk-in shower, pamper guests to the extreme. The six meeting/private dining rooms combine state-of-the-art technology and Georgian splendour, while the splendid leisure complex, The Tethra Spa, with classical mosaics, is almost Romanesque. Staff, under the excellent direction of General Manager Peter MacCann, are quite exemplary and courteous, suggesting standards of hospitality from a bygone era. Complimentary underground valet parking. Restaurant Patrick Guilbaud (see separate entry) is also on site. Conference/banqueting (50). Secretarial services. Leisure centre; swimming pool.Garden. Children welcome (under 4s free in parents' room, cots available free of charge). No pets.Lift. Valet parking. **Rooms 145** (20 suites, 10 junior suites, 1 shower only, 80 no-smoking, 5 for disabled). Room rate €330.13. Open all year. **Morningtons Brasserie:** The contemporary style of this elegant dining-room is reflected on the plate, where fine Irish ingredients combine with Mediterranean cooking influences. An inexpensive table d'hôte lunch menu contrasts with more choices in the evening, but nonetheless shows off head chef Edward Cooney's competent and precise cooking, backed up by excellent service - and some dishes are usefully highlighted to make an Express Menu, which allows two courses with coffee within 45 minutes. Signature dishes include seared fillet of salmon on olive & dill crushed potatoes with ratatouille dressing and char-grilled sausage of venison, with grain mustard mash, crispy onions and tarragon jus. The wine list is grand, but prices are not over the top for such an illustrious establishment. No-smoking area. Air conditioning. **Seats 66.** L 12:30-2 Mon-Fri, D 6-10 daily. Set L from €20.31 Pre-theatre menu from €21.59, 6-7pm. D also ‡ la carte. House wine from €22.86. Closed L Sat, L Sun. Amex, Diners, MasterCard, Visa. **Directions:** City Centre opposite Government Buildings.

Milano

RESTAURANT 38 Dawson Street Dublin 2 **Tel: 01 670 7744** Fax: 01 679 2717

This stylish contemporary restaurant at the top of Dawson Street is best known for its wide range of excellent pizzas (it's owned by the UK company Pizza Express), but it's more of a restaurant than the description implies. Children are welcome and they run a very popular crèche facility on Sunday afternoons (12-6). Branches also in Temple Bar and on Ormond Quay, north of the Liffey. **Seats 60.** No-smoking area. Air conditioning. Open daily,12 noon-12 midnight (Sun to 11.30). Menu à la carte. House wine €16.39. SC discretionary (10% on parties of 7+). Closed Dec 25 & 26. Milano Amex, MasterCard, Visa, Diners, Laser. **Directions:** Opposite Mansion House, just off Stephens Green.

Moes Restaurant

RESTAURANT 112 Lower Baggot Street Dublin 2 **Tel: 01 676 7610** Fax: 01 676 7606
Email: moesdublin@hotmail.com Web: www.moesdublin.com

Small though the reception area may be - not, perhaps, the most relaxing place to wait for your table in the busy restaurant - do not allow this to spoil your anticipation of the meal to come. The dining-room is in the crisp modern style, with light-wood floors, white walls, interesting prints and excellent lighting; good napery, sparkling crystal glasses and attractive modern cutlery say this as a place to recokon with, yet the pricing is very competitive. Serious reputations have been built in these premises - Derry Clarke, of the highly-acclaimed L'Ecrivain just a few doors away started here, to name but one - and chef/proprietor Ian Connolly is showing every sign of similar talent in his renditions of modern and classical international cooking. menus are not over-long, offering a choice of about eight tempting starters and main courses at dinner, rather less for lunch. A signature dish to look out for is steamed shellfish, which includes a razorfish, with spek bacon and a crabmeat cream - unusual and delicious. Updated versions of traditional Irish themes are to be found in dishes like confit loin ofpork with cider-braised potato, black pudding, cabbage and sage, but vegetarian dishes like sweet potato, red onion & pine nut parcels with couscous & feta fritters and rocket sauce are also tempting enough to lure the most ardent carnivore and the cheeseboard features the best mature Irish farmhouse cheeses from Sheridans cheesemongers, served with organic leaves and apple chutney. **Seats 40.** L Mon-Fri, 12-3; D Mon-Sat, 6-11.SC discretionary. Closed L Sat, all Sun, Dec 24-26, Dec 31-Jan 1. Amex, MasterCard, Laser. **Directions:** Corner Fitzwilliam/Baggot, opposite Larry Murphys.

Mont Clare Hotel

HOTEL Merrion Square Dublin 2 **Tel: 01 607 3800** Fax: 01 661 5663
Email: montclares@ocallaghanhotels.ie Web: www.ocallaghanhotels.ie

A few doors away from the National Gallery, this well-located and reasonably priced hotel is in common ownership with the nearby Davenport and Alexander Hotels. Recent renovations have greatly improved the amenities and the hotel is imaginatively decorated in contemporary style - except the old stained glass and mahogany Gallery Bar, which has retained its original pubby atmosphere. Compact bedrooms are well furnished, comfortable and ideal for business guests with full marbled bathrooms and good amenities, including air conditioning, multi-channel TV with video channel, a personal safe, ISDN lines and fax. There is a business centre and secretarial services, but no on-site leisure facilities; however guests have a complimentary arrangement with a nearby fitness centre. Conference/banqueting (150/120).Video conferencing. Children welcome (Under 2s free in parents' room; cots available free of charge). No pets. Lift. **Rooms 80** (2 junior suites, 40 no-smoking). B&B €107, ss €87; SC 12.5%. Open all year. Amex, Diners, MasterCard, Visa. **Directions:** Corner of Clare St. and Lower Merrion St.

Montys of Kathmandu

RESTAURANT féile bia 28 Eustace Street Temple Bar Dublin 2 **Tel: 01 670 4911** Fax: 01 4944359
Email: montys@tinet.ie Web: www.montys.ie

Wipe-clean tables, black and white interior and a view into the kitchen so that you can get a glimpse of the food being cooked all give this restaurant a fast-food look, but the food here has real character - and at agreeably low prices. The chefs are all from Nepal and although all the familiar dishes are represented there are definite undertones of Nepalese cooking throughout the menu. Friendly staff are more than happy to offer suggestions or choose a well balanced meal for you. Don't skip the appetisers - sheesh kebabs are really good and samosas are well spiced and crisp. Tandoori butter chicken is everything that it should be: moist pieces of tender, tandoori chicken off the bone, cooked in a well balanced creamy masala sauce. Attentive staff foresee problems almost before they arise and sort things out in flash - and they even have their own beer, 'Shiva', brewed exclusively for the restaurant. Children welcome. **Seats 60** (private room, 30) L Mon-Sat, 12-2:30; D daily 6-11:30, (Sun to11). Set L €12.70, Early D €15.17 (6-7pm). L&D à la carte available. House wine from €15. Closed L Sun, 25-26 Dec & Good Fri. Amex, MasterCard, Visa, Laser. **Directions:** opposite the Irish Film Centre.

The Morgan

HOTEL 10 Fleet Street Temple Bar Dublin 2 **Tel: 01 679 3939** Fax: 01 679 3946
Email: sales@themorgan.com Web: www.themorgan.com

In deepest Temple Bar, this unusual boutique hotel is characterised by clean simple lines and uncluttered elegance. Bedrooms have 6í beds in light beech, with classic white cotton bedlinen and natural throws, while standard bedroom facilities include satellite TV and video, CD/hi-fi system, mini-bar, safe, voicemail and internet access. Thereís a residents lounge, fitness room, masseuse and air conditioned meeting room. Strangely, as it seems so much at odds with the cool, reserved style of the rest of the hotel, the All Sports Café next door is part of it. Small conference (20). Wheelchair access. Children welcome (Under 12s free in parents' room; cots available). **Rooms 61.** (2 suites, 7 mini-suites, 20 no-smoking, 1 for disabled). Room rate from about €150 (max 3 guests). Lift. Closed 23-28 Dec. Amex, Diners, MasterCard, Visa. **Directions:** off Wesrmoreland Street.

Neary's

PUB 1 Chatham Street Dublin 2 **Tel: 01 677 7371**

This unspoilt Edwardian pub off Grafton Street is popular at all times of day - handy for lunch or as meeting place in the early evening and full of buzz later when a post-theatre crowd, including actors from the nearby Gaiety theatre, will probably be amongst the late night throng in the downstairs bar. Traditional values assert themslves through gleaming brass, well-polished mahogany and classic like oysters and smoked salmon amongst the bar fare. Closed 25 Dec & Good Fri.

Nude

RESTAURANT 21 Suffolk Street Dublin 2 **Tel: 01 672 5577** Fax: 01 672 5773
Email: nudehq@gofree.indigo.ie

Nude is a new concept in fast food, providing fantastic very fresh food - organic whenever possible -in an ultra-cool environment. Just off Grafton Street it's a great place for a quick snack, with plenty of room to sit down at long canteen-style tables. Queue up, order and pay at the till, then either your food is ready straight away or they'll bring it down to wherever you are sitting. Choose from a selection of soups (seafood chowder, mushroom or Thai chicken) served with freshly baked breads, hot wraps (chicken masala or potato & courgette) and panini (club nude or chicken & cashew) or try the chill cabinet for salads (Caesar, tomato & mozzarella), wraps (hummus, spinach & peppers or Cajun salmon) or soft bread rolls (smoked salmon & cream cheese). They also make freshly squeezed juices and smoothies - a shake-like concoction consisting of fresh fruits, juices and yoghurt blended with ice, with nutritional boostings like ginseng, bee pollen and vitamin C complex to name but a few. charged by the "hit". Winners of the guide's Creative Use of Irish Vegetables Award 2001 - the portions may be small and the prices on the high side, but you'll find yourself returning again and again. **Seats 40.** Open Mon-Sat, 8am-10pm, Sun 11am-8pm. Nude Restaurant MasterCard, Visa, Diners, Laser.

Number 31

GUESTHOUSE 31 Leeson Close Lower Leeson St. Dublin 2 **Tel: 01 676 5011** Fax: 01 676 2929 Email: number31@iol.ie Web: www.number31.ie

Formerly the home of leading architect Sam Stephenson, Noel and Deirdre Comer's 'oasis of tranquillity and greenery' just off St Stephen's Green makes an excellent city centre base, with virtually everything within walking distance in fine weather. Warm hospitality, huge breakfasts and secure parking add greatly to the attraction and rooms have everything you could wish for, including phones, TVs and tea/coffee trays. Rooms in the front of the original Georgian terrace are noisy - ask for one across the garden, adjacent to the interesting sunken sitting room. Not suitable for children under 10. No pets. **Rooms 20** (all en-suite & no smoking). B&B about €85, ss € 19.95. Open all year. Amex, MasterCard, Visa. **Directions:** from St. Stephens Green onto Baggot St., turn right on to Pembroke St. and left on to Leeson St.

O'Donoghue's

PUB 15 Merrion Row Dublin 2 **Tel: 01 676 2807**

O'Donoghues has long been the Dublin mecca for visitors in search of a lively evening with traditional music - live music every night is a major claim to fame - but a visit to this famous pub near the Shelbourne Hotel at quieter times can be rewarding too. Closed 25 Dec & Good Fri.

O'Neill's Pub & Guesthouse

PUB/GUESTHOUSE 37 Pearse Steet Dublin 2 **Tel: 01 677 5213** Fax: 01 8325218

Established in 1885, this centrally located pub on the corner of Pearse Street and Shaw Street is easily recognised by the well-maintained floral baskets that brighten up the street outside.Inside, this cosy bar has kept its Victorian character and charm and serves a good range of reasonably priced home-cooked food - typically soft cheese & garlic stuffed mushrooms, spiced lamb filo parcels and strip loin steak with pepper sauce, all served with french fries and an attractive salad. L 12.30-2, D 5.30-8.45. Accommodation is available in recently renovated rooms and breakfast is served in a pleasant room above the pub. Children welcome. No pets. **Rooms 8** (all en-suite). B&B about €38 pps (about €51 pps at weekends). Closed Christmas & Good Fri. Amex, Diners, MasterCard, Visa.

O'Neill's Public House

PUB 2 Suffolk Street Dublin 2 **Tel: 01 679 3656** Fax: 01 679 0689 Email: mikeon@indigo.ie

A striking pub with its own fine clock over the door and an excellent corner location, it has been in the O'Neill family since 1920 and is popular with Dubliners and visitors alike. Students from Trinity and several other colleges nearby home into O'Neill's for its wide range of reasonably priced bar food, which includes a carvery with a choice of five roasts and an equal number of other dishes (including traditional favourites such as Irish Stew) each day. Wheelchair access. No children after 6pm. Bar food served 12-7 daily (Sun to 8). Closed 25 & 26 Dec, Good Fri. Amex, MasterCard, Visa, Diners. **Directions:** on the corner of Suffolk St and Church Lane, opposite the DublinTourist Centre.

Ocean

RESTAURANT Charlotte Quay Dock Ringsend Dublin 2 **Tel: 01 668 8862**

On a corner of the Grand Canal Basin - a place which has undergone great changes over the last couple of years and is suddenly becoming very chic - this fashionably minimalist bar and restaurant is one of the latest places on a city-centre waterside location. Seafood predominates - oysters, Dublin Bay prawn cocktail, crab salad stylishly presented. Friendly staff who are willing to please, a buzzy cosmopolitan atmosphere and a great location make a pleasing combination. Bars open 12-12.30pm (Fri& Sat to 1.30am). Food all day: L 12-5 pm, D 5-10pm. Amex, Diners, Visa, Laser.

Odessa Lounge & Grill

RESTAURANT/PUB 13/14 Dame Lane Dublin 2 **Tel: 01 670 7643**

Tucked away about 5 minutes from Grafton Street this is a favourite haunt for Dublin's bright young things whose chatter bounces off the walls and high ceiling. It has a long history as a lively place to eat and was one of the first places in Dublin to do brunch. The room downstairs is the perfect place to nurse a hangover with no natural light, subdued lighting, comfy chairs with plenty of room to spread out and read the papers in peace. The food is basic brunch fare but the atmosphere is a major attraction. Eggs Benedict or Florentine, huevos rancheros or a char-grilled steak sandwich (all around €8). The service is relaxed and friendly even when they are very busy there's never a feeling of being rushed. At night is just right for those who want more than a fast-food burger, but who do not want to dress for dinner - and it's also perfect for large groups with something to celebrate. Seats 100. No smoking area. Air conditioning. Sat & Sun open noon-midnight, brunch 12-4. D Mon-Wed 6-11, Thu & Fri 5-12. SC discretionary (10% on parties of 6+). **Directions:** Left off Dame Street onto George's Street, left onto Exchequer Street, then left again.

The Old Mill

RESTAURANT 14 Temple Bar Dublin 2 **Tel: 01 671 9262/01** Fax: 679 6602

Long before this area became trendy Temple Bar, Morrocan chef-patron Lahcen Iouani had a loyal following in the area - since the mid 80s, in fact, when this restaurant delighted discerning Dubliners in an earlier guise as 'Pigalle'. The name change has relevance to local history (you can read all about it on the back of the menu) but other things have thankfully remained the same and Lahcen continues to offer admirably traditional French cooking at refreshingly modest prices. Giving good value to the customer is something he feels strongly about, so you will find most starters like traditional fish soup, salade niçoise and calmar frit in the €5.50 range, with main courses from around €9.50 for vegetarian dishes like lentin & leek gratin, rising to €22 for expensive fish like sole and seabass; in between there are many of the dishes the French always seem to do best, like roast poussin with tarragon jus and saddle of rabbit au poivre. The wine list follows the same admirable philosophy and all desserts (tarte tatin, fresh fruit sabayon) are home-made. **Seats 60.** Air conditioning. Open 4.30-11.30 daily. A la carte. House wine from €15.24. MasterCard, Visa, Laser. **Directions:** behind Central Bank & above Merchants Arch.

The Old Stand

PUB 37 Exchequer Street Dublin 2 **Tel: 01 677 7220** Fax: 01 677 5849

This fine traditional pub, which is a sister establishment to Davy Byrnes, off Grafton Street, occupies a prominent position on the corner of Exchequer Street and St Andrew Street. It has a loyal following amongst the local business community, notably from the 'rag trade' area around South William Street. They offer no-nonsense bar food at reasonable prices and a blackboard at the door proclaims daily specials. Not suitable for children under 7. Bar food served daily 12-9.30. Closed 25-26 Dec & Good Fri. MasterCard, Visa, Laser. **Directions:** off Grafton Street.

The Palace Bar

PUB 21 Fleet Street Dublin 2 **Tel: 01 677 9290**

Just around the corner from the Irish Times offices, The Palace has had strong connections with writers and journalists for many a decade. Its unspoilt frosted glass and mahogany are impressive enough but the special feature is the famous sky-lighted snug, which is really more of a back room. Many would cite The Palace as their favourite Dublin pub. Closed 25 Dec & Good Fri.

Pasta Fresca

RESTAURANT 2-4 Chatham Street Dublin 2 **Tel: 01 679 2402** Fax: 01 668 4563

This long-established Italian wine bar-delicatessen is just off the Grafton Street shopping area and its popular all-day menu is based on good home-made pastas, thin-based crispy pizzas, interesting vegetarian options and a wide range of salads with well-made dressings. Although there are still plenty of fresh pastas on offer, the emphasis is moving towards a broader menu. While other regions and styles are also represented, Tuscan cooking is increasingly favoured in dishes like pollo all Toscana (chargrilled marinated chicken served with Tuscan white beans and salad) and their pasta salad (with Tuscan beans, sweetcorn, fresh vegetables, shaved Parmesan & house dressing). Evening menus offer a wider choice and you can buy Italian groceries, fresh pasta and sauces made on the premises from their deli counter. Children welcome. **Seats 80** (private room, 20). No-smoking area. Air conditioning. Open all day Mon-Sat, 11.30-midnight, Sun 1-10. D from 5.30; à la carte. House wine from €15.24. SC discretionary (10% on tables of 4+). Closed 25-26 Dec. Amex, Diners, MasterCard, Visa, Laser, Switch. **Directions:** off Grafton St., right at A.I.B Bank.

Pearl Brasserie

RESTAURANT 20 Merrion Street Upper Dublin 2 **Tel: 01 661 3572** Fax: 01 661 3629 Email: petitepearl@eircom.net

Just a few doors away from The Merrion Hotel, this stylish basement restaurant with colourful blue banquettes and marble-topped tables was opened in autumn 2000 by Sebastien Masi, previously head chef at The Commons on St Stephen's Green, and his partner Kirstin Batt, who is the restaurant manager. The style is contemporary international, with a classic French base and a pleasing emphasis on clean flavours, highlighting the quality of ingredients. Although fairly balanced, menus show some bias towards seafood, which Sebastien cooks with accuracy and flair. An à la carte lunch menu offering about five choice on each course would come to about €22 for three courses and might include starters of creamy duck liver paté with toasted brioche & onion marmalade and a mildly spicy seafood spring roll with sesame & soya dressing, typically followed by pan-fried cod with asparagus & shallot beurre blanc or lamb cutlet with potato tourte & mint sauce. Dinner menus are also à la carte (around €30 for a 3-course meal)and offer a wider choice and include some luxurious dishes - Asian style crab bisque, pan-fried duck foie-gras with toasted brioche and rhubarb & strawberry compôte, blue fin tuna steak, roasted monkfish in pancetta. Classic desserts such as banana crème brulée with coconut and lemon tart are well-executed and service is charming and well informed. Sunday Brunch is a speciality and there is also a separate bar area called the Oyster Room which serves light snacks, 1-6 daily. **Seats 80** (private areas 12 & 6); no-smoking area; air-conditioning. Open Mon-Sat all day, 12-11; L12-2.30, D6-11; Sun 11-3 &6-10.30. A la carte. House wine €18.41.Closed bank hols, 1st 2 wks Jan. Amex, MasterCard, Visa, Laser. **Directions:** opposite Government Buildings very near Merrion Hotel.

The Pembroke

PUB/RESTAURANT 31/32 Lower Pembroke Street Dublin 2 **Tel: 01 676 2980** Fax: 01 676 6579 Email: crowley brian@ireland.com Web: pembroke.ie

There was consternation amongst traditionalists when this fine old pub was given a complete makeover several years ago, creating the bright and trendy bar that it is now - it even has a cyber café in the basement. But, even if the cosiness of old has now gone for ever, the spacious new bar that has been created has character of its own and, along with some striking design features (notably lighting), the atrium/ conservatory area at the back brings the whole place to life. Meeting the needs of those who get in to work before the traffic builds up, bar food begins with breakfast. **Seats 300.** Food served 7.30am-10.30 pm, Mon-Sat; carvery lunch, 12-2:30. Closed Sun, 25-26 Dec & Good Fri. Amex, MasterCard, Visa, Laser. **Directions:** in Pembroke Street off Baggot near St Stephens Green.

Pizza Stop Restaurant

RESTAURANT 6-10 Chatham House Chatam Lane Dublin 2 **Tel: 01 679 6712** Fax: 01 679 6712

This cheap and cheerful little restaurant has been doing good pizzas and pastas in style since the late '80s. Just the place to meet up with the family for a tasty meal that won't break the bank. **Seats 70.** No-smoking area; air conditioning. Open daily 12-12. MasterCard, Visa. **Directions:** beside Westbury Hotel ,Grafton Street.

The Porterhouse

PUB 16-18 Parliament Street Temple Bar Dublin 2 **Tel: 01 679 8847** Fax: 01 670 9605 Email: porterh.indigo.ie

Dublin's first micro-brewery pub opened in 1996 and, although several others have since set up and are doing an excellent job, The Porterhouse was at the cutting edge. Ten different beers are brewed on the premises and beer connoisseurs can sample a special 'tasting tray' selection of plain porter (a classic light stout), oyster stout (brewed with fresh oysters, the logical development of a perfect partnership), Wrasslers 4X (based on a west Cork recipe from the early 1900s, and said to be Michael Collins' favourite tipple), Porter House Red (an Irish Red Ale with traditional flavour), An Brain Blasta (dangerous to know) and the wittily named Temple Brau. But you don't even have to like beer to love The Porterhouse. The whole concept is an innovative move away from the constraints of the traditional Irish pub and yet it stays in tune with its origins - it is emphatically not just another theme pub. The attention to detail which has gone into the decor and design is a constant source of pleasure to visitors and the food, while definitely not gourmet, is a cut above the usual bar food and, like the pub itself, combines elements of tradition with innovation. This is a real Irish pub in the modern idiom and was a respected winner of our Jameson Pub of the Year award in 1999. No children after 7pm. Bar food served 12:30-9:30 daily. Closed 25 Dec & Good Fri. MasterCard, Visa. [* The original Porterhouse is located on Strand Road on the seafront in Bray, Co Wicklow and, like its sister pub in Temple Bar, it offers bar food daily from 12:30-9:30. No children after 7pm. Closed 25 Dec & Good Fri. MasterCard, Visa. Tel/Fax: 01 286 1839. There is also a brand new Porterhouse in London, located at Covent Garden.]

QV2 Restaurant

RESTAURANT

14-15 St Andrew Street Dublin 2 **Tel: 01 677 3363** Fax: 01 677 3365
Email: frontdesk@qv2restaurant.com Web: www.qv2restaurant.com

Handy to Grafton Street and all the city centre attractions, this popular restaurant accurately describes itself as offering 'International cuisine with an Irish twist'. Eoin McDonnell, head chef since 1991, builds his menus around fresh seasonal produce and hits just the right note on interesting menus that also give good value, especially for lunch and the early bird dinner. Among the international flavours you'll find comforting traditional Irish fare like corned beef with champ, buttered cabbage & parsley cream sauce and house specialities include Eoin's Fish Pie - lots of big chunks of fish in a white wine & parsley sauce, with a crispy filo crust - and Fillet of Lamb Daniel Patrick, with fresh mint mash and a honey & mint mayonnaise. The street level room has more atmosphere, but the basement improves as it fills up. Nice, helpful staff; reasonably priced wine list. Children welcome. **Seats 140** (private room, 40) No-smoking area. Air conditioning. L 12-2.45 Mon-Sat. D 6-10.45 Mon-Sat. A la carte (set menus available for parties of 8+). House wine about €18. SC discretionary (10% on parties of 8+). Closed Sun, Bank Hols, Christmas wk & Good Fri. QV2 Restaurant Amex, Diners, MasterCard, Visa, Laser. **Directions:** just off Dublin Tourism Centre

Rajdoot Tandoori

RESTAURANT

26 -28 Clarendon Street Dublin 2 **Tel: 01 679 4274** Fax: 01 679 4274
Email: info@rajdoottandoori.com Web: www.rajdoottandoori.com

A member of a small UK chain of restaurants specialising in subtle, aromatic North Indian cuisine, this restaurant has had a fine reputation for its food and service since it opened in 1984. Tandoori dishes are the main speciality, based on a wide range of ingredients authentically cooked - this is possibly the only restaurant in Ireland that still uses the traditional charcoal-fired clay ovens rather than gas. Speciality dishes include duck Jaipur (with spring onions, green peppers, mushrooms, garlic & red wine), chicken johl (a spicy Nepalese dish with ginger, garlic, fresh coriander & fenugreek) and king prawn with garlic and chilli. There is also plenty of choice for vegetarians. Set menus include a keenly priced 3-course lunch and pre-theatre dinner. Children over 6 welcome until 7pm. **Seats 120.** No smoking area; air conditioning. L Mon-Sat 12-2.30, Sun 1.30-5.30. D 6-11 daily. Set L €11.35 Set D from €21.59. Early D €20.32(6-7pm). House wine €14.60. No-smoking area. Air conditioning. SC discretionary. Closed 25-26 Dec. Rajdoot Tandoori Amex, Diners, MasterCard, Visa, Switch, Laser. **Directions:** top of Grafton Street, behind westbury Hotel.

Restaurant Patrick Guilbaud

RESTAURANT ★★

21 Upper Merrion Street Dublin 2
Tel: 01 676 4192 Fax: 01 661 0052

The capital's premier French restaurant occupies an elegant ground-floor restaurant in the main house of The Merrion Hotel, opening onto a terrace and landscaped garden (with al fresco eating in fine weather). Although access can also be gained via the hotel, the main entrance is through the original front door to the 1760s Georgian townhouse. Fine works by Irish artists (look out especially for Harry Kernoff's 'Jammet's Restaurant', probably Dublin's finest restaurant in the Sixties) are a major decorative feature, making a very fine setting for one of Ireland's most renowned restaurants. Head chef Guillaume Le Brun presides over a fine kitchen and presents wide-ranging à la carte and set menus - the table d'hôte lunch is a snip at €28 and the €120 menu surprise is just that - you are only told what the dishes are, as they are served. Contemporary French cooking is what you get, albeit with a nod to traditional Irish influences, so the best of Irish ingredients, combined with the precision and talents of a team of gifted chefs, produces dishes of dexterity, appeal and flavour. Desserts are particularly interesting, cheeses come from Philippe Olivier, breads are home-made, and the mostly French wine list includes some great classics, with some reasonably-priced offerings. Service, under the supervision of Stéphane Robin, is immaculate and Patrick Guilbaud himself is almost invariably present to greet guests personally and, discreetly working the tables, he makes a point of having a chat with everyone - whether a resident at the Merrion Hotel, local business person or simply an individual bent on a gastronomic treat in Dublin's most famous restaurant - and making sure that all is well. Children welcome. **Seats 80** (private room, 25) No-smoking area. Air conditioning. L Tue-Sat 12.30-2.15, D 7.30-10.15 Tue-Sat. Set L €28. Menu Surprise €120. L&D à la carte available. House wine from €32. SC discretionary. Closed Sun & Mon, Christmas and 1st week Jan. Amex, Diners, MasterCard, Visa, Laser. **Directions:** opposite Government Buildings.

Saagar Indian Restaurant

RESTAURANT 16 Harcourt Street Dublin 2 **Tel: 01 475 5060/5012** Fax: 01 475 5741
Email: saagar@focus-ireland.com Web: focus-ireland.com/saagar

Meera and Sunil Kumar's highly-respected basement restaurant just off St Stephen's Green offers a wide range of speciality dishes, all prepared from fresh ingredients and thoughtfully coded with a range of one to four stars to indicate the heat level. Thus Malai Kabab is a safe one-star dish, while traditional Lamb Balti and Lamb Aayish (marinated with exotic spices and cooked in a cognac-flavoured sauce) is a three-star and therefore pretty hot. The vegetarian selection is good, as is to be expected of an Indian restaurant, and the side dishes, such as Naan breads which are made to order in the tandoori oven, are excellent. The Kumars also have restaurants in Athlone and Mullingar. **Seats 70.** L 12:30-2:30 Mon-Fri. D 6-11:30 daily. Set L from about €8. Gourmet menu about €50. L&D à la carte available. House wine about €14. Toilets wheelchair accessible. No-smoking area. SC discretionary. Closed Sat & Sun L; 24-27 Dec. Amex, Diners, MasterCard, Visa. **Directions:** opposite Children's Hospital on Harcourt Street (off Stephen's Green).

Saffron 2000

RESTAURANT 18 Merrion Row Dublin 2 **Tel: 01 661 5095**

Caring hospitality is an outstanding feature of this well-appointed owner-managed restaurant near the Shelbourne Hotel. Small and cosy, with traditional Indian decor and a bar at the far end, it attracts a comfortable mixture of regulars and visitors, al of which add up to a pleasantly relaxed atmosphere. An extensive menu offers a wide selection, including classics - lentils soup, onion bhajees, a range of tandoori dishes, a strong selection for vegetarians and even a few European dishes too. L & D. Amex, MasterCard, Laser.

Shalimar Indian Restaurant

RESTAURANT 17 South Great Georges Street Dublin 2 **Tel: 01 671 0738**
Fax: 01 677 3478 Email: anwar@iol.ie

Just across the road from the Central Hotel this welcoming, well-appointed basement restaurant serves generous portions of a wide-range of Indian dishes. Balti dishes are a speciality - diners are invited to mix and match items on the menu to suit individual tastes - and there's also a wide choice of Tandoori and Biryani basmati rice dishes. This is a friendly, relaxing restaurant and prices are reasonable. Wheelchair access. Parking by arrangement with nearby carpark. Children welcome. **Seats 100** (private room, 50) Set L&D & à la carte available. No-smoking area. Air conditioning. SC 10%. Closed Christmas & Good Fri. Amex, Diners, MasterCard, Visa.

Shanahan's on the Green

RESTAURANT 119 St. Stephen's Green Dublin 2 **Tel: 01 407 0939** Fax: 01 407 0940

Located on the west side of the Green, this opulent restaurant is Dublin's first dedicated American style steakhouse - although, as they will be quick to reassure you if required, their wide-ranging menu also offers plenty of other meats, poultry and seafood. However, the big attraction for many of the hungry diners who have headed for Shanahan's in its first year of operation is their certified Irish Angus beef, which is seasoned and cooked in a special broiler, 1600-1800°F, to sear the outside and keep the inside tender and juicy. Their steaks range from a 'petit filet' at a mere 8 oz/225g right up to The Shanahan Steak (24 oz/700g), which is a sight to gladden the heart of many a traditionally-minded Irishman - and many of his trendier young friends too. Strange to think that steak was passé such a short time ago... There is much else to enjoy, of course, but bring a good appetite - and a fat wallet. (Portions tend to be very large, so regulars often order less courses than in other restaurants, which makes for better value.) An American wine waiter will help you choose from a list which, naturally, majors in Californian bottles. Not suitable for children under 12 after 7 pm. **Seats 120.** No smoking area; air conditioning. D only, 6-11 Mon-Sat. A la carte. (SC discretionary, except 15% on parties of 6+). Closed Sun, Christmas week. Amex, Diners, MasterCard, Visa, Laser. **Directions:** on the west side of Stephen's Green.

The Stag's Head

PUB 1 Dame Court Dublin 2 **Tel: 01 679 3701**

In Dame Court, just behind the Adams Trinity Hotel, this impressive establishment has retained its original late-Victorian decor and is one of the city's finest pubs. It can get very busy at times - sometimes dusty and sticky surfaces suggest that the volume of business makes it difficult to keep up with routine housekeeping, but this lovely pub is still worth a visit. Closed 25 Dec & Good Fri.

Stauntons on the Green

GUESTHOUSE 83 St Stephen's Green Dublin 2 **Tel: 01 478 2300**
Fax: 01 487 2263 Email: hotels@indigo.ie

Well-located with views over St Stephen's Green at the front and its own private gardens at the back, this guesthouse - which is in an elegant Georgian terrace on the south of the Green and has fine period reception rooms - offers moderately priced accommodation of a good standard, with all the usual amenities. Itís in the heart of the business and banking district and the Grafton Street shopping area is just a stroll across the Green. Meeting rooms are available, with secretarial facilities on request - and here's private parking. Children welcome. No pets. **Rooms 36** (all en-suite, 20 shower only). B&B about €75 pps, ss about €19. Closed 24-27 Dec. Amex, Diners, MasterCard, Visa.

Stephen's Green Hotel

HOTEL St Stephen's Green Dublin 2 **Tel: 01 607 3600** Fax: 01 661 5663
Email: stephensgreenres@ocallaghanhotels.ie Web: wwwocallaghanhotels.ie

This new hotel on the south-western corner site overlooking St Stephen's Green is the latest in the O'Callaghan Hotels group (Alexander, Davenport, Mont Clare - see entries). Public areas include an impressive foyer and, in memory of the writer George Fitzmaurice who used to live here, 'Pie Dish' restaurant and 'Magic Glasses' bar - both named after titles from his work. Guestrooms have exceptionally good facilities, particularly for business travellers, including air conditioning, writing desk, voice mail and modem line as standard. (Small conference (35). Business centre. Secretarial services. ISDN lines. Video conferencing. Small leisure centre. Children welcome (Under 2s free in parents' room; cots available). No pets. **Rooms 75** (9 suites, 40 no-smoking, 2 for disabled). B&B €144 (Room-only rate €247, max 2 guests). Lift. Open all year. Amex, Diners, MasterCard, Visa. **Directions:** Corner of Harcourt St. and St. Stephen's Green.

Steps of Rome

RESTAURANT Chatham Street Dublin 2 **Tel: 01-670 5630**

For some reason good, inexpensive little Italian places specialising in pizza have clustered around Balfe and Chatham Streets. Each has its following and this authentic little one-room cafe just beside Neary's pub is a favourite lunch spot for many discerning Dubliners. (Branch at Ciao Bella Roma, Parliament St.) Open 12 noon-11pm Mon-Sat, Sun 1-10pm. No Credit Cards.

Tante Zoes

RESTAURANT 1 Crow Street Temple Bar Dublin 2 **Tel: 01 679 4407** Fax: 01 670 7559
Email: robbief@indigo.ie Web: indigo.ie/~robbief/

Tante Zoe's is a dark, relaxing place - dark wood, bamboo and cloth covered tables, with old posters and signs from the deep south on the walls - making it equally suitable for a romantic dinner à deux or a group of pals out for the night. Cajun popcorn - a huge mound of juicy baby shrimps coated in crispy spiced breadcrumbs and served with a Marie Rose-style sauce or crab cakes, Shrimp Creole (spicy tomato sauce with plump jumbo shrimps), blackened chicken with spiced cream sauce are all typical and side dishes include Maque choux (sweetcorn cooked with peppers, onion and tomato). Bread pudding with whiskey sauce could make a great finale on a chilly night.

Genuinely attentive waiting staff contribute to the relaxed atmosphere - and make informed suggestions. Not suitable for children under 10. **Seats 150** (private room, 100) No-smoking area (no air conditioning). Open daily 12 noon-midnight, (Sun 12-4 & 6-12) Set L €11. Early D €15 (6-8pm). Also à la carte, L&D. SC discretionary (12.5% on parties of 6+). Closed 25 Dec & Good Fri. Amex, Diners, MasterCard, Visa, Laser. **Directions:** Temple Bar off Dame Street.

Temple Bar Hotel

HOTEL Fleet Street Temple Bar Dublin 2 **Tel: 01 677 3333** Fax: 01 677 3088 Email: templeb@iol.ie Web: www.towerhotelgroup.ie

This pleasant hotel is handy for both sides of the river. Spacious reception and lounge areas create a good impression and bedrooms are generally larger than average, almost all with a double and single bed and good amenities. Neat, well-lit bathrooms have over-bath showers and marble wash basin units. No parking, but the hotel has an arrangement with a nearby car park. Conference/banqueting (90/80). Wheelchair access. Children welcome. No pets. **Rooms 130** (1 suite, 30 no-smoking, 2 for disabled). B&B about €90pps, ss €45. Lift. Closed 23-27 Dec. Amex, Diners, MasterCard, Visa.

Thomas Read Café

PUB Parliament Street Dublin 2 **Tel: 01 677 1487**

This bustling café-bar was one of the first of its type and it is still one of the best. Attracting a wide variety of customers - including literary types from Trinity College and nearby newspapers - it serves a good cup of coffee, with (or without) light food. Its corner position and large windows looking down to Dame Street make this a fine place to sit and watch the world go by. Closed 25 Dec & Good Fri.

Toners

PUB 139 Lower Baggot Street Dublin 2 **Tel: 01 676 3090** Fax: 01 676 2617

One of the few authentic old pubs left in Dublin, Toners is definitely worth a visit (or two). Among many other claims to fame, it is said to be the only pub ever frequented by the poet W.B. Yeats. Closed 25 Dec & Good Fri.

Trinity Capital Hotel

HOTEL Pearse Street Dublin 2 **Tel: 01 648 1000** Fax: 01 648 1010 Email: info@capital-Hotels.com Web: www.capital-Hotels.com

A stylish new hotel right beside the headquarters of Dublin's city centre fire brigade (inspiring the name 'Fireworks' for its unusual club-style bar) and opposite Trinity college. Very centrally located for business and leisure, the hotel is within easy walking distance of all the main city centre attractions on both sides of the Liffey and the lobby wine and coffee bar is a handy meeting place. Rooms have a safe, interactive TV, phone, data ports, hair dryer, trouser press, tea/coffee trays, comfortable beds and good bathrooms -junior suites suites have jacuzzi powered bath, hi-fi system and mini-bar. Conference/banqueting 40/70. Meeting rooms; business centre; secretarial services. **Rooms 82** (3 suites, 20 no-smoking, 3 for disabled). B&B €89pps, s.c. included. Amex, Diners, MasterCard, Visa. **Directions:** turn left into Towsend Street, cross Tara Street, through traffic lights. Turn right at end right again onto Pearse Street. Hotel 50 mts on right side.

Trinity Lodge

GUESTHOUSE 12 South Frederick Street Dublin 2 **Tel: 01 679 5044** Fax: 01 679 5223 Email: trinitylodge@eircom.net

As centrally located as it is possible to get, owner-run guesthouse offers a high standard of accommodation at a reasonable price just yards away from Trinity College. Air-conditioned rooms have a safe, direct-dial phone, tea/coffee making facilities, multi-channel TV and trouser press, Children welcome (Under 12s free in parents' room; cots available free of charge). No pets. **Rooms 13** (3 suites, 6 executive, 8 no-smoking). B&B €66.67pps, ss €51. Closed 22-29 Dec. Amex, Diners, MasterCard, Visa, Laser, Switch. **Directions:** Just off Nassau Street, near Trinity College.

Unicorn Restaurant

RESTAURANT 12B Merrion Court off Merrion Row Dublin 2 **Tel: 01 676 2182 - 01 662 4752** Fax: 01 662 8584

In a lovely, secluded location just off a busy street near the Shelbourne Hotel, this informal and perennially fashionable restaurant is famous for its buffet hors d'oeuvres selection, piano bar and exceptionally friendly staff. It's particularly charming in summer, as the doors open out onto a terrace which is used for al fresco dining in fine weather - and the Number Five piano bar, which now extends to two floors, is also a great atttraction for after-dinner relaxation with live music (Weds-Sat 9pm-3 am). Good food (regional and modern Italian), efficient service and atmosphere all partially explain The Unicorn's enduring succcess - another element is the constant quest for further improvement. 2001, for example, saw the opening of the "Unicorn Foodstore" Italian delicatessen on Merrion Row as well as the upgrading of Number 5 Piano Bar - and, at the time of going to press, a Unicorn Antipasto/Tapas Bar is planned for December 2001. Many of the Italian wines listed are exclusive to The Unicorn: uniquely, in Ireland, they stock the full collection of Gava wines and the Pio Cesare range will also be exclusive in the near future. Not suitable for children after 9 pm. **Seats 85** (private room 14). No-smoking area; air conditioning. Open Mon-Sat, L12.30-4, D 6-11.15. A la carte. House wine €20. SC discretionary.Closed Sun, 10 days at Christmas Unicorn Amex, Diners, MasterCard, Visa, Laser. **Directions:** near Shelbourne Hotel.

Wagamama

RESTAURANT South King Street Dublin 2 **Tel: 01 478 2152** Fax: 01 478 2154

The Dublin branch of this justly popular London-based noodle bar is full of groovy young things, but thankfully the infamous queue around the block never caught on. The interior is a huge basement canteen, simple and functional, but strikingly designed with high ceilings. The large portions of noodles consist of ramen, udon or soba served in soups or pan-fried, well seasoned and colourfully decorated with South Asian ingredients. There are a few Japanese dishes such as teriyaki (mouth-watering little kebabs) and edamame (freshly steamed geen soya beans, served sprinkled with salt), also an excellent selection of fruit and vegetable juices, some rice dishes and plenty of great vegetarian options. Service is friendly and efficient but all those fashionable bare surfaces make it very noisy. Multi-storey carpark nearby. Children welome. **Seats 130.** No-smoking restaurant; air conditioning. Open daily, 12 noon- about midnight. A la carte. SC discretionary. Amex, Diners, MasterCard, Visa.

Westbury Hotel

HOTEL Grafton Street Dublin 2 **Tel: 01 679 1122** Fax: 01 679 7078
Email: westbury@jurysdoyle.com Web: www.jurysdoyle.com

Possibly the most conveniently situated of all the central Dublin hotels, the Westbury is a very small stone's throw from the city's premier shopping street and has all the benefits of luxury hotels - notably free valet parking - to offset any practical disadvantages of the location. Unashamedly sumptuous, the hotel's public areas drip with chandeliers and have accessories to match - like the grand piano on The Terrace, a popular first floor meeting place for afternoon tea and frequently used for fashion shows. Accommodation is similarly luxurious, with bedrooms that include penthouse suites and a high proportion of suites, junior suites and executive rooms. With conference facilities to match its quality of accommodation and service, the hotel is understandably popular with business guests, but it also makes a luxurious base for a leisure break in the city. Laundry/dry cleaning. Mini-gym. Conference/banqueting (220/200). Business centre. Secretarial services. ISDN lines.Children welcome (Under 12s free in parents' room; cots available). No pets. **Rooms 204** (4 suites, 24 executive rooms, 91 no-smoking, 2 for disabled). Room rate €350 (max 2 guests), SC 15%. Lift. Open all year. **Russell Room** After a drink in one of the hotel's two bars - the first floor Terrace bar and the Sandbank Bistro, an informal seafood restaurant and bar accessible from the back of the building - the Russell Room offers classic French dining, with some global cuisine and modern Irish influences. **Seats 100** (private room, 14) No-smoking area. Air conditioning. SC 15%. L daily,12 30-2.30; D daily 6.30-10.30 (Sun to 9). Set L from €28, D à la carte. House wine €20. Amex, Diners, MasterCard, Visa. **Directions:** The Westbury is approx 11km from the airport near Trinty College & Stephens Green.

The Westin Dublin

HOTEL

College Green Dublin 2 **Tel: 01 6451000**
Fax: 353 1 6451401 Web: www.westin.com

Opening just as we go to press, the Westin Hotel is the latest five star sensation to hit the Dublin hospitality scene; after some delay it finally opened in September 2001. After many months behind scaffolding, Dubliners were curious to see this massive reconstruction of the former mid-nineteenth century AIB and Pearl Buildings emerge. Much of the original was gutted, although part of the former bank has been glassed over to create a dramatic lounging area, The Atrium, which has a huge palm tree feature and bedroom windows giving onto it like a courtyard - very effective. The magnificent Banking Hall has been retained as the main conference and banqueting room and the adjacent Teller Room now makes an unusual circular boardroom, while the vaults have found a new lease of life as The Mint, a bar with its own access from College Street . Other special features of the new hotel include a split-level suite, which has views over Trinity College and includes a living room, board room and private exercise area; the business traveller's Westin Guest Office, designed to combine the efficiency and technology of a modern office with comfort of a luxurious bedroom; and the so-called 'Heavenly Bed' designed by Westin and 'worlds apart from any other bed'. The inner man will also be well looked after - in a 90-seater restaurant, The Exchange, an elegant room in 1930s style which made a promising debut, even in its first week. On the downside, parking is almost non-existent (a select few are allotted valet parking if it is arranged at the time of booking accommodation); it is amazing that planning permission should be granted to any city centre development without integral parking arrangements. **Rooms 163** (13 suites, 5 junior suites, 9 for disabled). Room rate €319 (max 2 guests). Open all year. Amex, Diners, MasterCard, Visa, Laser. **Directions:** on Westmoreland Street beside Trinity College.

Yamamori Noodles

RESTAURANT

71 South Great George's Street Dublin 2 **Tel: 01 475 5001**

Good value speedy cooking with lots of flavour is the secret of Yamamori's success - and atmosphere too. Itís just the kind of buzzy place that young people of all ages like to hang about in - a cool place for family outings. Portions are generous and great value - you can get huge bowls of ramen or plates of yaki-soba plus coffee for a fiver at lunchtime. Evening menus are more extensive. **Seats 110.** Open daily: L 12-5.30, D 5.30-11 (Sun 4-11) Amex, MasterCard, Visa, Laser.

DUBLIN 3

Clontarf Castle Hotel

HOTEL

Castle Avenue Clontarf Dublin 3 **Tel: 01 833 2321** Fax: 01 833 2279
Email: info@clontarfcastle.ie Web: www.clontarfcastle.ie

This historic 17th century castle is convenient to both the airport and city centre. A major refurbishment and extension programme recently added banqueting, conference and business facilities (business centre and secretarial services, same day laundry and dry cleaning and exercise room for guests) as well as major changes to public areas and the addition of 100 rooms. Bedrooms, are furnished to a high standard and well-equipped for business guests with ISDN lines, voicemail and US electrical sockets in addition to the usual amenities; all south-facing rooms have air conditioning and bathrooms are well-designed and finished. The new building has been imaginatively incorporated into the old castle structure, retaining the historic atmosphere - some rooms, such as the restaurant and the original bar, have been left untouched and bedrooms have old-world details to remind guests of their castle surroundings, although it is a pity that so little of the original grounds now remain. Conference/banqueting (550/450). Business centre. Secretarial services. Leisure centre. Children welcome (Under 12s free in parents' room; cots available). No pets.Lift. **Rooms 111** (3 suites, 2 junior suites, 4 executive rooms, 30 no-smoking, 6 for disabled). B&B €143 pps, ss €80. Templars Bistro: D Mon-Sat, 6.30-10.30 (Sun 6-9); L Sun only 1-3. Closed 24-25 Dec. Amex, Diners, MasterCard, Visa, Laser. **Directions:** take coast road from Dublin travelling towards Fairview/Howth, follow signs- 2 miles from City centre.

DUBLIN 4

Aberdeen Lodge

GUESTHOUSE 53 Park Avenue Ballsbridge Dublin 4 **Tel: 01 283 8155** Fax: 01 283 7877
Email: aberdeen@iol.ie Web: www.halpinsprivatehotels.com

Centrally located (close to the Sydney Parade DART station) yet away from the heavy traffic of nearby Merrion Road, this handsome period house offers all the advantages of an hotel at guesthouse prices. Small conferences (50). Garden. Children welcome. No pets. **Rooms 17** (2 suites, 15 executive rooms, 5 no-smoking). B&B€60pps, ss €35 Residents' meals available, D €30 + all-day menu. House wines from €25. 24-hr room service. Open all year. Amex, Diners, MasterCard, Visa. **Directions:** minutes from the city centre by DART or by car, take the Merrion Road towards Sydney Parade DART station and then first left into Park Avenue.

Anglesea Townhouse

GUESTHOUSE féile bia 63 Angelsea Road Ballsbridge Dublin 4
Tel: 01 668 3877 Fax: 01 668 3461

Helen Kirrane's guesthouse brings all the best 'country' house qualities to urban Dublin - a delightful building and pleasant location near Herbert Park, Ballsbridge; comfortable, attractive bedrooms; good housekeeping; a warm, welcoming drawing room with a real period flavour and wonderful breakfasts that prepare guests for the rigours of the most arduous of days. Thoroughly recommended for its creativity and perfectionism in re-defining what a guesthouse can be, Anglesea Townhouse was the winner of our 1999 Irish Breakfast Award. Garden. Children welcome (Under 3s free in parents' room; cots available). No pets. **Rooms 7** (5 shower only, all no-smoking). B&B €65pps, no ss. Closed Christmas and New Year. Amex, MasterCard, Visa, Laser. **Directions:** Located near the Merrion Road South of the city centre.

Baan Thai

RESTAURANT 16 Merrion Road Ballsbridge Dublin 4 **Tel: 01 660 8833**

Delicious aromas and oriental music greet you as you climb the stairs to Lek and Eamon Lancaster's well-appointed first floor restaurant opposite the RDS. Friendly staff, Thai furniture and woodcarvings create an authentic oriental feeling and intimate atmosphere - and many of the staff are Thai. A wide-ranging menu includes various set menus that provide a useful introduction to the cuisine (or speed up choices for groups) as well as an à la carte. The essential fragrance and spiciness of Thai cuisine is very much in evidence throughout and there's Thai beer as well as a fairly extensive wine list. D only, Sun-Thu 6-11, Fri & Sat to 11.30. Amex, Diners, MasterCard, Visa, Laser.

Bella Cuba Restaurant

RESTAURANT 11 Ballsbridge Terrace Dublin 4 **Tel: 01 6605539** Fax: 01 6605539
Email: info@bella-cuba.com Web: www.bella-cuba.com

Authentic Cuban cuisine is presented at its best in this small, intimate restaurant, which demonstrates the Spanish, Caribbean and South American influences on this unique country's cooking, with pork dishes prepared particularly well. Well worth a visit to experience something genuinely different. The wine list, which offers a choice fairly balanced between the old world and the new, includes a pair of Cuban bottles. Not suitable for children after 7pm. **Seats 26.** D only, 5.30-11 daily. A la carte. House wine €17.14 SC discretionary. Closed 25-26 Dec. Amex, MasterCard, Visa, Laser. **Directions:** Near the RDS.

Berkeley Court Hotel

HOTEL féile bia Lansdowne Road Ballsbridge Dublin 4 **Tel: 01 660 1711**
Fax: 01 661 7238 Email: berkeleycourt@jurysdoyle.com Web: www.jurysdoyle.com

Set in its own grounds yet convenient to the city centre, this luxurious hotel is well-known as a haunt of the rich and famous when in Dublin. The tone is set by an impressively spacious chandeliered foyer, which has groups of seating areas arranged around, with bars, restaurants and private conference rooms leading off it. The hotel is famous for its high standards of service and accommodation - bedrooms have a safe, computer modem, mini-bars and extras such as robes and slippers as well as the more usual amenities, and refurbished rooms also have air conditioning. On-site facilities include a health & beauty treatments, a hair salon and gift shop/newsagent. Conference/banqueting (400/380) Video-conferencing, business centre, secretarial services, ISDN lines.Lift. **Rooms 188** (6 suites, 5 junior suites, 24 executive rooms, 25 no-smoking, 6 for disabled). Room rate €300 (max. 2 guests). SC15%. Open all year. Berkeley Room A fine restaurant with very professional staff and some reliable specialities - seafood dishes are especially good and they are renowned for their roast beef. **Seats 60.** No smoking area; air conditioning. L Mon-Fri,12.30-2.15; D Mon-Sat, 6.30-9.15. A la carte. SC 15%.Toilets wheelchair accessible. SC 15%. Restaurant closed L Sat, all Sun (L&D available daily in The Palm Court Café). Amex, Diners, MasterCard, Visa, Laser. **Directions:** Near Lansdowne Road rugby stadium and approx 13 Km from Airport.

Bewley's Hotel, Ballsbridge

HOTEL/RESTAURANT Merrion Road Ballsbridge Dublin 4 **Tel: 01 668 1111** Fax: 01 668 1999 Email: bb@bewleyshotels.com Web: www.bewleyshotels.com

This new hotel has been cleverly built to incorporate a landmark period building next to the RDS (entrance by car is on Simmonscourt Road, via Merrion Road or Anglesea Road; underground carpark). Like its sister hotel at Newlands Cross (see entry), you get a lot of comfort here at a very reasonable cost. ***Restaurant: See O'Connells in Ballsbridge.** Small conferences (30). ISDN lines. Garden. Wheelchair access. Parking. Children welcome. No pets. Lift. **Rooms 220** (80 suites, 100 no-smoking, 20 disabled). Room rate €99 (max 2 adult guests). Closed 6pm 24 Dec - 6pm 26 Dec. Amex, Diners, MasterCard, Visa, Laser. **Directions:** at Junction of Simmonscourt and Merrion.

Blakes Townhouse

GUESTHOUSE 50 Merrion Road Ballsbridge Dublin 4 **Tel: 01 668 8324** Fax: 01 668 4280 Email: blakestownhouse@iol.ie Web: halpinsprivatehotels.com

The latest addition to Pat Halpin's small chain of quality guesthouses, Blakes is very handily situated for anyone attending exhibitions in Dublin, as it's directly opposite the RDS. Drawing room menu available (nice selection of quality wines, from €25) and 24 hour room service . Children welcome. No pets. **Rooms 12** (2 suites, 10 executive, 4 no smoking). B&B €60 pps, ss €35; SC 10%. Open all year. Amex, Diners, MasterCard, Visa. **Directions:** Blakes is opposite the RDS in Ballsbridge.

Burlington Hotel

HOTEL féile bia Upper Leeson Street Dublin 4 **Tel: 01 660 5222** Fax: 01 660 8496 Email: burlington@jurysdoyle.com Web: www.jurysdoyle.com

Ireland's largest hotel, the Burlington has more experience of dealing with very large numbers efficiently and enjoyably than any other in the country. All bedrooms have been recently refurbished and banquets for huge numbers are not only catered for but can have a minimum choice of three main courses on all menus. The Burlington also offers good facilities for business guests; a high proportion of bedrooms are designated executive, with ISDN lines, fax machines and air conditioning. On-site entertainment is provided at Annabelís night club and their bar, Buck Mulliganís, has won numerous awards. Conference/banqueting (1200/1000). Business centre. Secretarial services. Video conferencing. Not suitable for children. No pets.Lift. **Rooms 506** (2 suites, 4 junior suites, 200 executive rooms, 76 no-smoking, 3 for disabled). Room rate €235 (max 2 guests). Open all year. Amex, Diners, MasterCard, Visa, Laser.

Butlers Town House

GUESTHOUSE 44 Lansdowne Road Ballsbridge Dublin 4 **Tel: 01 667 4022** Fax: 01 667 3960 Email: info@butlers-hotel.com Web: butlers-hotel.com

On a corner site in the 'embassy belt' and close to the Lansdowne Road stadium, this large guesthouse has been extensively refurbished and luxuriously decorated in a Victorian country house style. Public rooms include a comfortable drawing room and an attractive conservatory-style dining room where breakfast is served. Rooms are individually decorated and furnished to a high standard, some with four-poster beds. Since a recent change of management there has been some refurbishment and more emphasis on service. Small conferences (20). Wheelchair access. Parking. Children welcome (Under 4s free in parents' room; cots available). No pets. **Rooms 19** (1 shower only, 4 executive rooms, 1 for disabled). B&B about €95, ss about €45. Closed 22 Dec-8 Jan. Amex, Diners, MasterCard, Visa. **Directions:** Corner of Lansdowne Rd and Shelbourne Rd in Ballsbridge.

Cedar Lodge

GUESTHOUSE 98 Merrion Road Ballsbridge Dublin 4 **Tel: 01 668 4410**
Fax: 01 668 4533 Email: info@cedarlodge.ie Web: www.cedarlodge.ie

Conveniently located near the RDS show grounds and conference centre, this recently refurbished guesthouse has spacious rooms, with a full range of amenities. Public rooms are comfortably furnished and there is one room suitable for disabled guests. Children welcome (under 3s free in parents' room; cots available). No pets. **Rooms 15** (all no-smoking, 1 for disabled). B&B €70pps, ss €18. Closed Dec 23-29. Amex, MasterCard, Visa, Laser. **Directions:** directly opposite British Embassy on Merrion Road.

Coopers Café

RESTAURANT Sweepstake Centre Ballsbridge Dublin 4 **Tel: 01 660 1525** Fax: 01 660 1537

The flagship of the Coopers chain of restaurants, Coopers of Ballsbridge is in dashing premises opposite the RDS. Well-situated for the Ballsbridge hotels and exhibition crowds, the Café serves global cuisine - salsa, szechuan, rocket and chilli are the kinds of words that leap off the menu - but it is reassuring to know that, on request, they will also cook a plain steak perfectly and serve it with a simple green salad. Children welcome. **Seats 185.** No-smoking area. Air conditioning. L Mon-Fri & Sun,12:30-3. D 5-11 daily (Sun to 10). Set L menu; à la carte L&D available. House wine about €17. SC discretionary (10% on parties of 8+). Toilets wheelchair accessible. Closed 25-26 Dec & Good Fri. Also at: Lower Leeson Street, Dublin 2 (01 6768615), Greystones (01 2873914). Amex, Diners, MasterCard, Visa. **Directions:** Opposite the RDS.

Ernie's Restaurant

RESTAURANT Mulberry Gardens Donnybrook Dublin 4 **Tel: 01 269 3300** Fax: 01 269 3260

Named after the late Ernie Evans and still owned by the family, the dining-room of this famous restaurant overlooks a pretty courtyard garden, floodlit at night, though its main feature is the fantastic art collection, mostly of Ernie's beloved Kerry, that cover the walls entirely. Both the cooking and service are straightforward and some dishes have real old-fashioned classic sauces - a welcome respite in this era of global cuisine and minimalist restaurants. However, although some old favourites are kept in demand by regular patrons, there is young blood in the kitchen so a hint of modernism and a nod to foreign influences is creeping into a growing number of dishes: starters like Thai beef salad with oriental dressing, warm parcel of goats cheese served with chilli & balsamic vinaigrette and a popular main course of home-made fish cakes on a bed of leaves with a pink peppercorn vinaigrette are typical. Desserts have remained fairly classic however - chocolate marquise with crème anglaise, perhaps - and a selection of teas and coffees is served with petits fours. Good wine list, strong on clarets. Not suitable for children under 12. No-smoking area. Air conditioning. **Seats 60.** Open Mon-Sat, L12.30-2, D 7.30-10. Set L from €16.44, Set D from €30.47 midweek (weekend menus are slightly dearer). A la carte also available. House wine from €17.78. SC 12.5%. Closed Sun & Mon, and 2 weeks at Christmas. Amex, Diners, MasterCard, Visa. **Directions:** from City first left after Victoria Avenue to City right turn opposite Ulster Bank Donnybrook.

Expresso Bar Café

CAFÉ 1 St Mary's Road Ballsbridge Dublin 4 **Tel: 01 660 0585**
Email: expressobar@ireland.com

Ann-Marie Nohl's cool, informal eating place is notable for clean-lined minimalism, and colourful Cal-Ital food and classic brunches: diligently sourced ingredients are well-prepared and carefully presented. The lively breaksfasts for which they have become famous are served all morning and feature many of the best classic dishes, with a twist: thus a simple poached egg on toast comes with crispy bacon (from the renowned pork butcher, Hick's of Sallynoggin and Temple Bar market) and relish, or cooked-to-order pancakes are served with crispy bacon and maple syrup and french toast comes with bacon or winter berries and syrup. Lunch and dinner menus tend to favour an international style, but the same high standards apply: whether it's caesar salad with bacon lardons, parmesan cheese and croûtons (with smoked chicken as an option), char-grilled fillet of beef with red onion marmalade or pan-seared scallops with chilli lime butter and mixed leaves, the concept is simple enough but it's the quality of the ingredients and cooking that make the difference. Saturday and Sunday brunch are a must. Expresso Bar Café was the winner of the Irish Bacon Award in 2001. Not suitable for children under 2 after 6pm. No-smoking area. Air conditioning. **Seats 50.** Open Mon-Fri, 7.30am-9.30pm (L12-5, D 6-9.30), Sat & Sun brunch 10-5. Closed 25-28 Dec. MasterCard, Visa, Laser. **Directions:** opposite Hibernan Hotel off Baggot Street.

The Four Seasons Hotel

HOTEL féile bia

Simmonscourt Road Ballsbridge Dublin 4 **Tel: 01 665 4000**
Fax: 01 665 4099 Web: www.fourseasons.com

Set in its own gardens on a three and a half acre site of the Royal Dublin Society's 42-acre show grounds, this long-awaited international hotel finally opened in 2001. Although its grandiose style and dated decor has met with a mixed reception in Dublin, the site is magnificent, allowing a sense of spaciousness while also being convenient to the city centre - the scale is generous throughout and there are views of the Wicklow Mountains or Dublin Bay from many bedrooms. Public areas are designed to impress, although the cherrywood panelled Lobby Bar was too small from the outset and a second, larger, bar is already planned. Accommodation is very luxurious and, with two-line speaker phones, data port, hi-speed internet access, satellite TV, CD players, bar and safe, the air-conditioned rooms are designed to appeal equally to leisure and business guests. A choice of pillows (down and non allergenic foam) is provided as standard, the large marble bathrooms have separate bath and shower, robes among many desirable features - and there's twice daily housekeeping service, overnight laundry and dry cleaning, one hour pressing and complimentary overnight shoe shine. Meeting planners will appreciate the hotel's state of the art conference and meeting spaces, which can accommodate corporate events, business meetings and parties in groups from 5-500. But the Spa in the lower level of the hotel is perhaps its most outstanding feature, offering: separate men's and women's saunas and steamrooms, a wide range of body and facial treatments, aromatherapy and massage services, plus a gym (with instructors) - and a naturally lit 14m lap pool and adjacent jacuzzi pool, overlooking an outdoor sunken garden. **Rooms 259** (67 suites, 192 executive rooms, 4 floors no-smoking rooms, 12 rooms for disabled). Room rate from €356 (max 2 guests). SC included. Special breaks. Open all year. **Seasons Restaurant:** Executive Head Chef Terry White came to Dublin from the Four Seasons in Toronto and appears committed to sourcing the best Irish ingredients for contemporary international menus - citing, for example, organic produce from a west Cork farm, as well as Irish farmhouse cheeses and other speciality foods. Menus, which include set lunch as well as à la carte choices, considerately highlight dishes which are suitable for vegetarians and "Four Seasons Alternative Cuisine" (dishes lower in sodium, fats, cholesterol and calories). On the Guide's visit shortly after the hotel opened, the restaurant had clearly not settled down and, considering that prices are on a par with Dublin's most respected restaurants, both food and service needed fine-tuning. No-smoking area. Air conditioning. **Seats 90** (private room, 12). Breakfast 7-11 daily, L 12-2.30 daily, D 6.30-10 daily. Set L from €25.39; D à la carte (also available at L). House wine from €21.59. SC 15%, only on parties of 8+.*Less formal dining, including a range of "Irish Home Style Dining" dishes, is available in The Café, open daily 11 am-11pm. Amex, Diners, MasterCard, Visa, Laser. **Directions:** located on the RDS Grounds corner of Merrion and Simmonscourt Road.

Furama Restaurant

RESTAURANT

Eirpage House Donnybrook Dublin 4 **Tel: 01 283 0522**
Fax: 01 668 7623 Email: furama@eircom.net Web: www.adlib.furama.com

In the sleek black interior of Rodney Mak's long-established restaurant Freddie Lee, who has been head chef since the restaurant opened in 1989, produces terrific food with an authenticity which is unusual in Ireland. Even the menu does not read like other Chinese restaurants - dishes aren't numbered, for a start, and they are also presented and described individually. They do offer Set Dinners, which are more predictable - and many traditional Chinese dishes on the à la carte menu - but the option is there to try something different.Service, under the supervision of Rodney Mak and manager Stephen Lee, is friendly and efficient. A Special Chinese Menu can be arranged for banqueting with one week's notice (up to 30 people) and outside catering is also available. Parking. **Seats 100** L Mon-Fri 12.30-2, Sun from 1.30; D daily 6-11.30 (Sun 4-11). Various set menus from €35 pp. A la carte available. House wine from €16.51. No-smoking area. Air conditioning. SC 10%. Closed 24-26 Dec & Good Fri. Amex, Diners, MasterCard, Visa, Laser. **Directions:** Donnybrook opposite Bective rugby ground, near RTE.

Glenogra House

GUESTHOUSE

64 Merrion Road Dublin 4 **Tel: 01 668 3661** Fax: 01 668 3698
Email: glenogra@indigo.ie Web: www.glengora.com

Seamus and Cherry McNamee make a point of providing personal service and good breakfasts at their comfortable Ballsbridge guesthouse. Old and new are carefully combined to create a homelike atmosphere and three new rooms were recently added. Conveniently located for the RDS and within 3 minutes walk of the Sandymount DART station. Children welcome (Under 2s free in parents' room; cots available free of charge). No pets. **Rooms 12** (2 shower only, all no-smoking). B&B €50.15pps, ss €19.69. Closed Christmas & New Year. Amex, MasterCard, Visa, Diners. **Directions:** Opposite 4 Seasons Hotel, RDS.

Herbert Park Hotel

HOTEL/RESTAURANT

Ballsbridge Dublin 4 **Tel: 01 667 2200** Fax: 01 667 2595
Email: reservations@herbertparkhotel.ie Web: www.herbertparkhotel.ie

This large, Irish-owned contemporary hotel is set in an 'urban plaza' near the RDS and the public park after which it is named. It is approached over a little bridge, which leads to an underground carpark and, ultimately, to a chic lower ground foyer and the lift up to the main lobby. Public areas on the ground floor are impressively light and spacious, with excellent light meals and drinks provided by efficient waiting staff. The bright and modern style is also repeated in the bedrooms, which have views over Ballsbridge and Herbert Park and are stylishly designed and well-finished with a high standard of amenities, including air conditioning, individual temperature control, 2 line ISDN phones with voice mail, mini bar, safe, interactive TV with email, internet, PlayStation, in house movies and bill view facility. Suites also have extras like robes, CD player, jacuzzi bath, complimentary mineral water, fruit and chocolates and a daily newspaper. A good choice for the business guest or corporate events, the hotel has a range of meeting rooms and video-conferencing facilities. Conference/banqueting (120/150). Business centre. Secretarial services. Gym. Children under 12 free in parents' room; cots available free of charge. No pets. Lift. **Rooms 153** (3 suites, 1 junior suite, 27 executive rooms, 20 no-smoking, 7 for disabled). B&B from about €130pps, ss€44. No SC. Open all year. **The Pavilion:** In a bright, elegant, contemporary room which is pleasingly devoid of hard-edged minimalism and overlooks a garden terrace (where tables can be set up in fine weather), head chef Aziz Joudar presents fashionable international menus, mainly based on well-sourced Irish ingredients and offering a choice of four dishes on each course on set menus and seven or eight on the à la carte. Irish themes are sometimes introduced - as in stuffed chicken supreme, black pudding & bacon roulade and herb mash - and desserts often include refreshingly simple things like fresh fruit salad with crème fraîche or warm apple pie with vanilla ice cream as well as some more flamboyant dishes. Prices are reasonable, especially when seen in comparison with nearby competition, and the lunch menu offers particularly good value. **Seats 150.** No smoking area; air conditioning. L daily, 12.30-2.30 (to 3 on Sunday); D Mon-Sat, 5.30-9.30. Set L & early D (5.30-7.30) from €19.68; D à la carte. House wine €19. Closed D Sun & D bank hols. *Informal dining is offered at The Terrace, 8am-10pm daily. Amex, Diners, MasterCard, Visa, Laser. **Directions:** from City Centre go straight down Nassau Street, Mount Street, Northumberland Road. Turn right after bridge in Ballsbridge. First on the right.

The Hibernian Hotel

HOTEL/RESTAURANT

Eastmoreland Place Ballsbridge Dublin 4
Tel: 01 668 7666 Fax: 01 660 2655
Email: info@hibernianhotel.com Web: www.hibernianhotel.com

It feels as if it's in a peaceful backwater, yet this splendid Victorian building is only yards from one of Dublin's busiest city centre roads. It's very friendly, with a country house feeling in the size and proportions of its rooms and an elegant decorative style with warm country colours. The names of the rooms evoke a homely atmosphere too - the drawing room, the library and so on. Bedrooms are all individually decorated to a high standard with excellent bathrooms featuring a wide range of amenities. Service is exemplary. Small conference/private parties (20/20). Business centre. Secretarial services. Small garden. Children under 2 free in parents' room; cots available free of charge. No pets. Lift. **Rooms 40** (3 shower only, 10 junior suites, 14 no-smoking, 2 for disabled). Room rate from €190.46 (max 2 guests). Closed Dec 24-26. **The Patrick Kavanagh Room:** In keeping with the rest of the hotel, the restaurant is well-appointed, with elegance and charm. A new head chef, Anthony Duggan, took over the kitchen just as the guide went to press, presenting lunch and dinner menus that change weekly, in addition to an evening à la carte and a separate vegetarian menu. Global influences are certainly at work here, but you will also find more homely themes, such as shank of lamb with champ potato & rosemary jus and simple classics like black sole on the bone with a parsley lemon butter. Desserts tend to be quite traditional - strawberry romanoff with vanilla ice cream, pehaps, or sticky toffee pudding and Irish farmhouse cheeses are an option. Service, under the supervision of restaurant manager Eddie Farrell, is friendly and efficient. **Seats 45** (private room 20). No-smoking area (no air conditrioning). L Mon-Fri 12.30-2.30; D Mon-Sat 6.30-10.(D Sun residents only, 7-9). Set L €22.79 D menu €44.44; D also à la carte. House wine €20.32.SC 12.5%. Closed from Dec 24 D, all Dec 25 & 26. Amex, Diners, MasterCard, Visa, Laser, Switch. **Directions:** turn right from Mespil Rd. into Baggot St. Upper, then left into Eastmoreland Place, the Hibernian is at the end on the left.

Jurys Ballsbridge Hotel

HOTEL 

Pembroke Road Ballsbridge Dublin 4 **Tel: 01 660 5000** Fax: 01 660 5540
Email: ballsbridge@jurysdoyle.com Web: wwwjurysdoyle.com

Centrally located in the Ballsbridge area, always busy, Jurys has the distinction of being both an international hotel providing high levels of service to business and leisure guests, while remaining a popular local hotel for Dubliners. Rooms and service are of a high standard (24 hour room service and laundry and dry cleaning services) and executive rooms also have a modem line, voice mail, mini-bar and 24 hour sports and news channels as well as multi-channel TV. The facilities offered by the hotel generally are excellent - Jurys was for a long time the only Dublin hotel with a swimming pool; the leisure centre currently also has a whirlpool, saunas and gym and there's a health & beauty salon, hairdresser and newsagent on site. There are two restaurants, Raglans and the informal Coffee Dock, and two bars - the larger Dubliner Bar is a great meeting places, especially when matches are played at the nearby Lansdowne Road rugby stadium. Conference/banqueting (850/600). Business centre, secretarial services. Cabaret (May-Oct). No pets. Lifts. **Rooms 303** (3 suites, 300 executive rooms, 150 no-smoking, 2 for disabled). Room rate €270 (max 2 guests). SC 12.5%. Raglans Restaurant **Seats 120.** No-smoking area. Air conditioning. Open for L&D daily. Toilets wheelchair accessible. Open all year. Amex, Diners, MasterCard, Visa, Laser. **Directions:** Hotel Located approx 11km from Airport.

Jurys Ballsbridge The Towers

HOTEL 

Lansdowne Road Dublin 4 **Tel: 01 667 0033** Fax: 01 660 5324
Email: towers@Jurysdoyle.com Web: www.jurysdoyle.com

The Towers is a quieter, more exclusive section of the main Jurys Hotel in Ballsbridge, a hotel within a hotel located to the rear of the main block with its own entrance on Lansdowne Road and a high level of security - entry to the inner foyer and thus to accommodation is by card key. Business and corporate guests are well looked after and constant maintenance and upgrading, plus a high level of service from a committed and well-trained staff, keep this hotel up with the leaders in an increasingly competitive market. The many little extras that make The Towers especially desirable for business guests include complimentary tea, coffee and biscuits, served all day in a seating area known as the hospitality lounge, where a light breakfast (included in the room rate) is also served each morning and complimentary drinks are served, 6-7pm Monday-Thursday. Guests at The Towers also have the benefit of spacious rooms, queen/king size beds, dedicated work desk and lamp, luxurious bathrooms and towelling robes in addition to or of a higher grade than the usual 'executive' extras. There is direct access to the main hotel from The Towers and all its amenities. Lift. **Rooms 105** (4 suites, 101 executive, 50 no-smoking, 2 for disabled). Room rate €320 (max 2 guests), SC 12.5%. Open all year. Amex, Diners, MasterCard, Visa, Laser. **Directions:** Approx 11 Km from the airport.

Jurys Montrose Hotel

HOTEL féile bia

Stillorgan Road Dublin 4 **Tel: 01 269 3311** Fax: 01 269 1164
Email: montrose@jurysdoyle.com Web: www.jurysdoyle.com

This south-city hotel near the University College campus has undergone extensive refurbishment. Removing balconies and rebuilding the whole front has updated the exterior, while interior improvements include the addition of more rooms to executive standard and some wheelchair friendly accommodation. All rooms have quite good facilities (direct dial phone, multi-channel TV, tea/coffee-making facilities and trouser press/iron) and there's 12 hour room service and laundry/dry cleaning services. Executive rooms also have a modem line and complimentary newspaper and business magazines. Although conference facilities are not extensive (max 70 delegates), there's a business centre, seven meeting rooms and free parking, making this an attractive venue for small events. Children welcome (cots available) **Rooms 180** (35 executive). Room rate €149 (max 2 guests); weekend specials available. Open all year. Amex, Diners, MasterCard, Visa. **Directions:** on Stillorgan dual carriageway near RTE studios.

Kites Restaurant

RESTAURANT 15-17 Ballsbridge Terrace Ballsbridge Dublin 4
Tel: 01 660 7415 Fax: 01 660 5978

Lots of natural light with white painted walls, dark wooden fittings and a rich, dark carpet create a good first impression at this split-level Ballsbridge restaurant, and a mix of diners (Chinese and non-Chinese, business and pleasure) tucking into tasty, well prepared food gives the place a nice buzz. The cuisine is combination of Cantonese, Szechuan, peking and Thai and menus range from the standard set meals to a decent list of specials. An excellent house platter of appetisers (€8.89 per person) make a good begining, offering a fine selection of spring rolls, wontons, sesame prawn toasts, spare ribs along with some more unusual additions. Duckling and seafood are sepcialities: half a crispy aromatic duck (€22.86) has well-textured meat and comes with fresh steaming pancakes, while a combination dish of salt & pepper jumbo king prawns and a stir-fry is really mouth-watering - or you could try chicken Szechuan, notable for its well judged spicing. Desserts are not a strong point, but courteous, good humoured and charming service adds considerably to the experience. No-smoking area. Air conditioning. **Seats 100.** L Mon-Sat 12.30-2, D daily 6.30-11.30 (Sun to 11). Set L €18.40, Set D €33. House wine €18.40. SC 10%.Closed 25-26 Dec, Good Fri. Amex, Diners, MasterCard, Visa, Laser. **Directions:** in the heart of Ballsbridge.

Langkawi Malaysian Restaurant

RESTAURANT 46 Upper Baggot Street Dublin 4 **Tel: 01 668 2760**
Fax: 01 668 2760 Email: hosey@indigo.ie

The three main distinct national cuisines that influence Malaysian cuisine - Malay, Chinese and Indian - produce a distinctive culinary range, from hot, fiery dishes through to more subtle flavours; there is an understandable emphasis on Malay dishes since this is the rarer cuisine in Ireland. Satays make a good start for the cautious, while more adventurous diners have plenty to choose from (with clear menu guidance on heat levels). Chef Alex Hosey uses genuine imported ingredients to achieve an authentic Malaysian taste. Wheelchair access. Children welcome. No-smoking area. **Seats 50.** L Mon-Sat 12.30-2, D Mon-Sat 6-11. Set L €16.50, Set D from €25, also à la carte. House wine €15. SC 12.5%. Closed Sun. Amex, Diners, MasterCard, Visa, Laser. **Directions:** beside Searsons Pub.

Lansdowne Manor

GUESTHOUSE 46-48 Lansdowne Road Ballsbridge Dublin 4 **Tel: 01 668 8848**
Fax: 01 668 8873 Email: lansdownemanor@eircom.net Web: www.lansdownemanor.ie

Situated in the heart of 'embassyland', Lansdowne Manor comprises two early Victorian mansions which have been recently refurbished and decorated in period style. It now offers some of the most comfortable guesthouse accommodation in the city, with an elegant period drawing room for guests use and bedrooms - which have specially commissioned furniture reminsicent of 18th century France - with all the amenities usually expected of hotels, including multi-channel TV, trouser press, tea/coffee-making facility and hairdryer; a full laundry and dry cleaning service is also offered.. There are facilities for small conference/private parties (16), with full secretarial services available.. Children welcome (under 8s free in parents' room, cots available free of charge). No pets. **Rooms 22** (9 junior suites, 7 shower only). B&B €70ps, ss €20. Closed 23 Dec-2 Jan. Amex, Diners, MasterCard, Visa, Laser. **Directions:** at corner of Lansdowne/Shelbourne Road.

The Lobster Pot

RESTAURANT 9 Ballsbridge Terrace Ballsbridge Dublin 4 **Tel: 01 660 9170** Fax: 01 668 0025

In a conspicuous position near the Herbert Park Hotel, on the first floor of a redbrick Ballsbridge terrace, this long-established restaurant has lost none of its charm or quality over the years. How good it is to see old favourites like dressed Kilmore crab, home-made chicken liver paté and fresh prawn bisque on the menu, along with fresh prawns Mornay and, that fine old friend, Coq au Vin. All this and wonderfully old-fashioned service too. Long may it last. L 12.30-2.30pm, D 6.45-9.45pm Mon-Sat. Closed Sun, 24 Dec-4 Jan & Good Fri. Amex, Diners, MasterCard, Visa.

Merrion Hall

GUESTHOUSE 54-56 Merrion Road Ballsbridge Dublin 4 **Tel: 01 668 1426** Fax: 01 668 4280 Email: merrionhall@iol.ie Web: www.halpinsprivatehotels.com

This Edwardian style townhouse opposite the RDS is handy to the DART (suburban rail) and makes a good base for business or leisure. Bedrooms are spacious for the location and finished to a good standard, some with four-posters; the suites have air conditioning and whirpool spa baths. There's a comfortable big sitting room and some off-street parking at the back. Small conference/private parties (50/50). Garden. Children welcome (cots available free of charge). No pets. **Rooms 24** (4 suites). B&B €60pps, ss €35. Open all year. Amex, Diners, MasterCard, Visa. **Directions:** located opposite the RDS in the Ballsbridge area of Dublin.

Merrion Inn

PUB 188 Merrion Road Dublin 4 **Tel: 01 269 3816** Fax: 01 269 7669

The McCormacks are a great pub family (see separate entry for their Mounttown establishment) and this attractive contemporary pub on the main road between Dublin and Dun Laoghaire has always had a name for food. At lunchtime there's a good buffet, with a selection of hot main courses as well as a wide range of salads; it's a well-organised operation and details (such as having chilled drinks to hand) are well-planned. In the evening the style moves up a notch or two, with a menu including the likes of warm crispy bacon & croûton salad, pastas and serious main courses such as chargrilled sirloin steak (served with a choice of sauces and salads) as well as some good fish dishes, vegetarian options and thre day's specials. Homely desserts always include homemade apple pie. Bar food served daily 12-10. Closed 25 Dec & Good Fri. Amex, Diners, MasterCard, Visa, Laser. **Directions:** Opposite St. Vincent's Hospital.

The Mespil Hotel

HOTEL Mespil Hotel Mespil Road Dublin 4 **Tel: 01 667 1222** Fax: 01 667 1244 Email: mespil@leehotels.ie

This fine modern hotel enjoys an excellent location in the Georgian district of the city, overlooking the Grand Canal and within easy walking distance of the city centre. Public areas are spacious and elegant in an easy contemporary style and generously-sized bedrooms are comfortably furnished with good amenities; a new wing will shortly add an extra 100 rooms. Dining options include the main 200-seater restaurant 'Glaze Bistro, which is open for lunch and dinner daily and offers a well-balanced choice of traditional and contemporary fare at fair prices (main courses from €11.36), and the Terrace Bar, which has a short but well-chosen slection of dishes including 'The Platter', a tempting main dish selection for two people - potato wedges, spicy chicken strips, vegetarian spring rolls and calamari rings with dipping sauces, all for €12.63. Special breaks offer good value. Small conferences (25). Children welcome (Under 12s free in parents' room; cots available free of charge). No pets. Lift. **Rooms 250** (3 shower only, 68 no-smoking, 12 for disabled). Room rate €135 (max 3 guests). Closed 22-27 Dec. Amex, Diners, MasterCard, Visa, Laser. **Directions:** on the Grand Canal at Baggot St. Bridge.

O'Connells in Ballsbridge

RESTAURANT 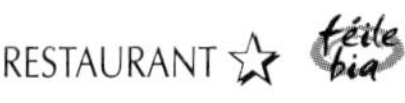

Bewleys Hotel Merrion Road Dublin 4 **Tel: 01 647 3304** Fax: 01 647 3398 Email: info@oconnellsballbridge.com Web: oconnellsballbridge.com

FEILE BIA AWARD

Located in the basement of Bewley's Hotel, with dark wood-panelled walls, crisp white table linen, floor to ceiling windows overlooking a courtyard used for al fresco dining in summer and - this surprising restaurant (which has no connection with the Bewley's café chain) opened in 1999 and has, in true organic fashiom, taken the time naturally required to reach maturity. It's run by Tom O'Connell, previously the general manager of the Berkeley Court Hotel and a brother of Darina Allen (of Ballymaloe Cookery School in County Cork). Although the atmosphere can be a little canteen-like, there is an attractive courtyard to look out on and what you will get here is quality ingredient driven modern Irish cooking - simple food, with natural flavours. Head chef Brian McCarthy, who is from west Cork, joined the team in May 2001 and works closely with Rory O'Connell of Ballymaloe House. His menus, which are arranged by course and price, are extremely reasonable, beginning with soups, paté and sorbet at only €5.02 to a main course maximum of €20.25 (including vegetables). Carefully sourced food is the star here and the menu not only states that beef, eggs and catering supplies are sourced using Bord Bia's Quality Assurance Schemes, but also credits a number of individual producers and suppliers: thus, for example, a starter salad is made with Fingal Ferguson's Gubbeen smoked bacon, from Schull in Co Cork, an East Cork smoked fish plate comprises a selection from Frank Hederman's smokery in Cobh and smoked salmon from Bill Casey at Shanagarry (both Co Cork), a gratin of salmon uses organic fish farmed off Clare Island, Co Mayo and beef comes from the Irish Hereford Prime Beef Society in Glencairn, Co Waterford. A weekly selection of Irish farmhouse cheese, supplied in prime condition by Sheridans cheesemongers, is served with home-made biscuits and excellent classic desserts range from wonderfully wicked warm sticky toffee pudding with butterscotch sauce and pouring cream to a light summer fruit sablé or home-made ice creams. A highly informative wine list, which includes an extensive selection of house wines, reflects the same philosophy and gives details of vintage, region, grape, grower/shipper, merchant, taster's notes, suggested food partnership, bottle size (including some magnums) and price - invariably moderate for the quality offered - for every wine on the list. For wonderful quality and sheer value for money this busy restaurant is a shining example of the direction Irish dining should be taking. **Seats 160** (+ summer courtyard 60). No smoking area. Air conditioning. L daily 12.30-2.30 (Sun to 3). D daily 6-10.30 (Sun to 9.30). Buffet L €16.06, Set Sun €17.33. Early D from €19.05 (6-7pm). Set D from €20.95. A la carte D available. SC discretionary (10% on parties of 6+). Amex, Diners, MasterCard, Visa, Laser. **Directions:** on the junction of Simmonscourt & Merrion Road, next to the RDS in Ballsbridge.

Pembroke Townhouse

GUESTHOUSE — 90 Pembroke Road Ballsbridge Dublin 4

Conveniently located close to the RDS and Lansdowne Road, this luxurious guesthouse has all the amenities usually expected of an hotel, including a lift. There's a drawing room and study for residents' use and individually designed rooms have a safe and fax facilities (on request) for business guests, as well as direct dial phone, cable television, tea/coffee facilities and trouser press. Breakfast is a point of pride (a Gourmet Menu offers dishes like sautéed lambs liver served on a bed of sautéed onions and topped with bacon as well as the traditional cooked breakfast) and guests also have complimentary use of a nearby leisure centre, with indoor swimming pool and gym. Small conferences (12). Children welcome (cots available free of charge). No pets. Lift. **Rooms 48** (7 suites, 41 executive rooms, 2 shower only, 20 no-smoking, 4 for disabled). B&B €108 pps, ss €70. Closed 22 Dec-4 Jan. Diners, MasterCard, Visa.

Raglan Lodge

GUESTHOUSE — 10 Raglan Road Ballsbridge Dublin 4 **Tel: 01 660 6697** Fax: 01 660 6781

Helen Moran's elegant mid 19th-century residence is peacefully situated near the US embassy, yet convenient to the city centre - and reasonably priced too. Well-proportioned, high-ceilinged reception rooms are reminiscent of more leisurely times and the en-suite bedrooms are exceptionally comfortable. Raglan Lodge is renowned for the high level of comfort and service provided, and particularly for outstanding breakfasts: a white-clothed sideboard displays freshly squeezed orange juice, fresh fruits and compôtes, home-made muesli and cereals, creamy porridge, yogurt and cheeses , then you can have a a choice of kippers, scrambled eggs with smoked salmon or a fine traditional breakfast of rashers, sausages, tomatoes and all the trimmings, delivered piping hot under silver domes covers - a great start to the day. (Raglan Lodge was the Dublin winner of our Denny Irish Breakfast awards in 2001).Theatre reservations can be arranged. Children welcome. **Rooms 7** (all en-suite, some shower only 2 no-smoking). B&B €63pps, ss €13. Closed 2 wks Christmas. Amex, Diners, MasterCard, Visa. **Directions:** follow signs for South city to Baggot Street which becomes Pembroke Road, turn right onto Raglan Road, Raglan Lodge is on the left.

Roly's Bistro

RESTAURANT féile bia — 7 Ballsbridge Terrace Ballsbridge Dublin 4 **Tel: 01 668 2611**
Fax: 01 660 8535 Email: rolysbistro Web: rolysbistro.ie

This bustling Ballsbridge bistro has been a smash hit since the day it opened. Chef-patron Colin O'Daly (one of Ireland's most highly regarded chefs) and head chef Paul Cartwright present imaginative, reasonably priced seasonal menus at lunch and an evening à la carte menu. A lively style is based on Colin's classical French training but it also gives more than a passing nod to Irish traditions, world cuisines and contemporary styles. Carefully sourced ingredients are the sound foundation for cooking that never disappoints - Dublin Bay Prawns are always in demand and may be served Newberg (this has become something of a speciality and comes with a tian of mixed long grain and wild rice), or in prawn cocktail, when using fresh Dublin Bay prawns moves that old favourite up into a different class. Chicken stuffed with Clonakilty black pudding - which uses one of Ireland's best-loved contemporary products, made by Edward Twomey in west Cork - is another favourite, but the cooking is always innovative, colourful and appealing. Wholesomely delicious puddings are worth saving a little space for: Pear & Apple Bake with Cinnamon Cream, perhaps, or dark chocolate and apricot slice. Service is generally efficient but discreet. **Seats 140.** No smoking area; air conditioning. L daily 12-3, D daily 6-10 Set L €13.95; also à la carte. SC10%. Amex, Diners, MasterCard, Visa.

Rumm's D4

PUB Shelbourne Road Ballsbridge Dublin 4 **Tel: 01 667 6422** Fax: 01 667 6423 Email: cj@rummsd4.com Web: www.rummsd4.com

Good bar food and comfortable surroundings are a combination that's suprisingly hard to find in Dublin, so this large, well-maintained pub (which is quite handy to the RDS), could be a useful spot to bear in mind. Varied menus and chf's specials lunch and dinner daily. Closed 25 Dec & Good Fri. Amex, MasterCard, Visa. **Directions:** prominent corner position on Shelbourne Road.

The Schoolhouse Hotel

HOTEL 2-8 Northumberland Road Ballsbridge Dublin 4 **Tel: 01 667 5014** Fax: 01 667 5015 Email: school@schoolhousehotel.iol.ie Web: www.schoolhousehotel.ie

Dating back to its opening in 1896 as a school, this building beside Mount Street Bridge has seen many changes lately, culminating in its opening in 1998 as one of Dublin's trendiest small hotels. The Inkwell Bar is always a-buzz with young business people of the area. Rooms are finished to a high standard, with air conditioning, power showers and the usual amenities expected of a quality hotel. Small conference (20). Wheelchair access. Parking. Children welcome (Under 5s free in parents' room; cots available). No pets. Lift. **Rooms 31** (all en-suite, 15 no-smoking, 2 for disabled). B&B about €1209 pps. Closed 24-27 Dec. Amex, Diners, MasterCard, Visa. **Directions:** travelling Southbound from Trinity College at the end of Mount St., adjacent to the Grand Canal.

Waterloo House

GUESTHOUSE 8-10 Waterloo Road Ballsbridge Dublin 4 **Tel: 01 660 1888** Fax: 01 667 1955 Email: waterloohouse@tinet.ie Web: waterloohouse.ie

Evelyn Corcoran has combined two Georgian townhouses to make a luxurious base in a quiet location very convenient to the city centre and also Lansdowne Road (rugby), RDS (equestrian & exhibitions) and several of the city's most famous restaurants. Equally attractive to the business or leisure traveller. ISDN lines. Conservatory & Garden. Wheelchair access. Own parking. Children welcome. No pets.Lift. **Rooms 19** (8 shower only, 1 disabled). B&B about €70pps. Closed Christmas week. MasterCard, Visa. **Directions:** south on Stephens Green on Merrion Row for 1 mile. First turn right after Baggot Street Bridge.

DUBLIN 6

Ashtons

PUB Clonskeagh Dublin 6 **Tel: 01 283 0045**

This famous pub fronts onto a busy road and is built on a steep slope reaching down to the River Dodder. It has an interesting interior and an unexpectedly tranquil atmosphere at the back, where the river view is always full of interest. The range and quality of their lunchtime buffet -a roast, hot dishes including a wide selection of seafood, cold buffet and salads - has earned this pub its enviable reputation. Buffet 12.30-2.30pm, Bar menu 3-9.30pm daily. Closed 25 Dec & Good Friday. MasterCard, Visa, Laser.

Dunville Place

RESTAURANT 25 Dunville Place Ranelagh Dublin 6 **Tel: 01 496 8181** Fax: 01 496 5710

It can be hard to get a table at Mick and Sophie Duignan's fashionable neighbourhood restaurant - and it's particularly popular in summer when the little courtyard at the back can also be used for drinks, or eating out in fine weather. It's a sophisticated place, well-appointed yet informal, and Mick Duignan presents imaginative, contemporary seasonal menus which are carried through with style and include strong vegetarian choices. Asian influences come through quite strongly in the spicing, but Europe is represented too - in, for example, a vegetarian Greek plate with stuffed vine leaves, hummus, tabbouleh and various other little dishes, all served with warm pitta bread. Good desserts might include a classic crème brulée. Sunday brunch is especially popular. D Tues-Fri, 5.30-10.30pm, Sat 6.30-11pm. Sun brunch 11.30-3. Closed Mon; bank hols. Amex, MasterCard, Visa. **Directions:** 5 mins. from St. Stephen's Green.

Ivy Court Restaurant

RESTAURANT — 88 Rathgar Road Dublin 6 **Tel: 01 492 0633**

Swiss chef Josef Frei has been doing a good job at this reliable neighbourhood restaurant for many a year now, and it's greatly to his credit that he has maintained the standard of food - and kept prices to a reasonable level - at a time when the reverse is true in many more fashionable establishments. **Seats 80.** D only, Mon-Sat. Closed Sun, Christmas week. MasterCard, Visa.

Nectar

RESTAURANT — 53 Ranelagh Village Dublin 6
Tel: 01 491 0934 Email: nectarjuice@eircom.net

'Eat Well, Stay Healthy' is the motto at Christopher Keegan's hip juice bar, a compact little place offering freshly squeezed drinks (beetroot, apple, carrot & ginger and passion fruit, orange, kiwi & raspberry) and smoothies eg fruit of the forest. Their wraps and salads can be excellent - the Caesar wrap (spicy chicken on a bed of tomato, leaves and Caesar dressing) is a favourite. At the time of going to press menus are due to be expanded, providing more bistro style food. Nectar has a GM-Free policy. There's also a branch at Exchequer Street, Dublin 2 and also one at the Epicurean Food Hall, Dublin 1. Open daily (Mon-Fri 10am-10pm; Sat 10.30am-8pm, Sun 10.30-6pm). MasterCard, Visa, Laser. **Directions:** Coming out of town, in Ranelagh village on right hand side after triangle.

Poppadom Indian Restaurant

RESTAURANT — 91a Rathgar Road Dublin 6 **Tel: 01 490 2383** Fax: 01 492 3900

Attractively modern, colourful and airy, with deep yellow walls, linen-clad tables and comfortable chairs (and a new bar recently added), this new wave Indian restaurant promises to demonstrate the delicious diversity of Indian cooking and offers some appealingly unusual dishes. Specialities include a starter of Karwari Prawns - deep-fried jumbo prawns marinated in ginger, garlic, yoghurt, garam masala and barbecued in the tandoor, then served with a fresh mint chutney - which is at the top of the €6.35-10.16 range. Of the main courses, which range from €13.97-€19.05, Chicken Avadh is a mild and creamy dish with nuts that was a speciality of the erstwhile Avadh empire of central India while lovers of fiery heat should try Lamb Chettinad, a festive dish of the Chettiyar clan in Tamil Nadu. There's even a house speciality unique to Ireland - this one has to be tried. Vegetarians are spoilt for choice, with seven dishes to choose from, all available as main courses or side orders. Accompaniments like lime rice offer a subtle change from the standard boiled rice and service is excellent. Make a point of trying the masala tea, made with leaf tea and cardamom pods. The wine list helpfully begins with some advice on the styles that partner spicy food well, wisely suggesting Alsace wines, notably Gewurtztraminer as the best all-rounder. Children welcome. **Seats 46.** No-smoking area. Air conditioning. D only, 6-11:45 daily. A la carte. House wine €15.24. SC discretionary. Toilets wheelchair accessible. Closed 25-26 Dec. Amex, MasterCard, Visa, Laser, Switch. **Directions:** a minute away on same side as Colmans Pub- Rathgar.

TriBeCa

RESTAURANT — 65 Ranelagh Village Dublin 6 **Tel: 01 497 4174** Fax: 01 491 1584

Trevor Browne and Gerard Foot, who also who run Dish in Temple Bar, are now serving some of the best fast food to be found in Dublin here in their new New York style restaurant. It has a relaxed, casual feel, with bright and airy decor and wooden floors and tables - just right for carefully sourced burgers (made from 100% organic beef), salads, omelettes and chicken wings, which take their place beside the fusion inspired dishes that keep the more adventurous diners happy. Although not cheap, portions are generous so it works out as good value for money. No reservations, but the turnover is fast. No-smoking area. Air conditioning. **Seats 70.** Open daily from 12-11. Toilets wheelchair accessible. Closed Dec 25, Good Fri. MasterCard, Visa..

Zen Restaurant

RESTAURANT 89 Upper Rathmines Road Dublin 6 **Tel: 01 497 9428** Fax: 01 497 9428

Denis O'Connor's unusual Chinese restaurant in a converted church has a well-earned reputation for authenticity. Staff are sourced in Beijing and, although there are plenty of popular dishes on their menus, this is one of the relatively small number of oriental restaurants in Dublin where more adventurous diners are rewarded with food that is more highly spiced than normal. John Cheung, who has been head chef since 1993, offers a range of menus including one "For A Sichuan Palate" (for a minimum table of four, €34.90 per person) and a speciality "Sichuan Crispy Duck Dinner" for at least two people, which has to be ordered 24 hours in advance (€69.90 for two). D daily, 6-11; L Thurs, Fri & Sun only, 12.30-2.30. Set menus from €26, also à la carte. Amex, Diners, MasterCard, Visa, Laser. **Directions:** Veer left for 750 yards at top of Rathmines Road.

DUBLIN 7

Chief O'Neill's Hotel

HOTEL Smithfield Village Dublin 7 **Tel: 01 817 3838** Fax: 01 817 3839
Email: reservations@chiefoneills.com Web: www.chiefoneills.com

This unusual new hotel is central to the new complex now known as Smithfield Village - and part of a major upgrading of the areas along Dublin's north quays. Accommodation has been designed in a striking modern style which guests will either love or loathe - the bathroom arrangements, for example, are more sculptural than practical - but bedrooms have good facilties, including CD hi-fi systems, ISDN lines, multi-channel TV, while penthouse suites have jacuzzis and rooftop balconies. Lines are simple, colours strong and there's a distinctly youthful air about the place. State of the art conference facilities and meeting roomsattract corporate guests and, for relaxation, Chief O'Neill's Café Bar features live traditional music and a combination of traditional and contemporary Irish food. Unusual attractions incorporated into the hotel complex include The Story of Irish Music, an interactive visitor centre that chronicles Irish musical heritage, with a 180' widescreen auditorium, touch screens and videos - and The Chimney viewing tower, which was once part of the distillery next door and now has two galleries reached by a glass-walled lift. It's open every day and panoramic views over the city can be spectacular on a good day (also available for private parties of up to 50 guests). Video-conferencing. Conference/banqueting (120/150). Children welcome (Under 12s free in parents' room; cots available free of charge). Lift. **Rooms 73** (3 suites, 70 executive rooms, 63 shower only,19 no-smoking, 4 for disabled). B&B €83, ss €83. Amex, MasterCard, Visa, Diners.

The Halfway House

PUB Navan Road Ashtown Dublin 7 **Tel: 01 838 3358** Fax: 01 868 3088

A well-supported local and handy meeting place just off the West-Link motorway, this well-known pub is very large, well-run and offers good quality popular bar food. Wheelchair access. Parking. No children after 7pm. Bar food every day 12-8. Closed 25 Dec & Good Fri. Amex, Diners, MasterCard, Visa.

The Hole in the Wall

PUB Blackhorse Lane Phoenix Park Dublin 7 **Tel: 01 838 9491** Fax: 01 868 5160

PJ McCaffreyís remarkable pub beside the Phoenix Park is named in honour of a tradition which existed here for around a hundred years -the practice of serving drinks through a hole in the wall of Phoenix Park to members of the army garrison stationed nearby. Today the Hole in the Wall also claims to be the longest pub in Ireland - and it is certainly one of the most interesting, best-run and most hospitable. They do good food too - there's a carvery lunch (12.30-3pm) and a bar menu available throughout the day offers a wide choice including traditional Irish dishes like Beef & Guiness Pie, Dublin Coddle and Irish Stew. Wheelchair access. Parking. Children welcome. Pets in certain areas. Bar menu served daily (Mon-Fri 3.30-9.30, Sat 12.30-9.30, Sun 5,30-9.30; Carvery L Mon-Sat 12.30-3, Sun L 12-4.30. Closed 25 Dec & Good Fri. Amex, Diners, MasterCard, Visa, Laser.

Kelly & Ping, Bar & Restaurant

RESTAURANT Smithfield Village Dublin 7 **Tel: 01 817 3840**
Fax: 01 817 3841 Web: www.kellyandping.com

In common ownership with Chief O'Neill's Hotel but with its own separate entrance from Duck Lane, this colourful, glass-fronted two-storey restaurant offers generous portions of keenly priced, mainly Asian, food including a range of Thai curries which can be ordered red (hot), green (medium) or yellow (mild). Other dishes can also be adjusted to taste on request and there's a useful glossary of ingredients and sauces. As well as an inexpensive wine list (nearly all under €26 bar the fizz), there's a good choice of Asian beers. Open daily, noon-11pm (Sun to 6 pm). Closed D Sun, Dec 24-27. Amex, Diners, MasterCard, Visa.

The Old Jameson Distillery

RESTAURANT/PUB/CAFÉ Bow Street Smithfield Dublin 7 **Tel: 01 807 2355**
Fax: 01 807 2369 Email: rdempsey@iol.ie Web: www.whiskeytours.ie

While most visitors to Dublin will visit the recently restored Old Jameson Distillery to do the tour (which is fascinating), it's also a good spot for a bite to eat. There are special menus for groups (including evening functions, when the Distillery is not otherwise open) but The Still Room Restaurant is also open to individuals - light food served all day and lunch, featuring Irish specialities like bacon & cabbage soup and John Jameson casserole - and the standard of cooking is high. Downstairs pub open from 12 noon daily. Conference centre recently opened. Wheelchair access. Children welcome. **Seats 120** Food served daily, 9-5. Ldaily 12.30-2.30. A la carte: carvery main courses from €7. House wine €15.90. No-smoking area. Air conditioning. Closed 25 Dec & Good Fri. Stillroom Restaurant Amex, Diners, MasterCard, Visa, Laser, Switch.

Ta Se Mahogani Gaspipes

RESTAURANT 17 Manor Street Dublin 7 **Tel: 01 679 8138**
Fax: 01 670 5353 Email: mahoganigaspipes@indigo.ie

In a small American-style restaurant in Stoneybatter, a very pleasant neighbourhood of the city in the 'undiscovered' Dublin near Phoenix Park, Drina Kinsley prepares an eclectic menu strong on spicy fare like 'prawns ping do' with crunchy noodles, mangetout, snow peas & black bean sauce and 'Phoenix & Dragon', a dish of chicken, prawns, shallots & scallions in a spicy plum sauce, served in an edible basket, surrounded by basmati rice. Pastas are also there in force and a range of main course salads for lunch and dinner. Sourcing is good at this unusual restaurant - organic meats are supplied by Danny O'Toole, for example, herbs from Eden Not suitable for children after 8 pm.Sunday night opening is under consideration at the time of going to press. **Seats 50.** No-smoking area. L Tue-Fri,12-3; Tue-Sat, D 6-10 (Fri & Sat to midnight). All à la carte. House wine from €13.94 Closed all Sun & Mon, bank hols, Dec 25-26 & 1 month in summer. Diners, MasterCard, Visa. **Directions:** north quays towards O'Connell Street. Left turn on Blackhall Place which becomes Manor Street, half way at North Circlular Road.

DUBLIN 8

Brazen Head

PUB 20 Lower Bridge Street Dublin 8 **Tel: 01 679 5186** Fax: 01 677 9549
Email: info@brazenhead.com

Dublin's (possibly Ireland's) oldest pub was built on the site of a tavern dating back to the 12th century - and it's still going strong. Full of genuine character, this friendly, well-run pub has lots of different levels and dark corners. Food is wholesome and middle-of-the-road at reasonable prices. Live music nightly in the Music Lounge. L & D daily. Closed 25 Dec & Good Fri.

Footplate Brasserie

RESTAURANT féile bia Johns Road Heuston Station Dublin 8 **Tel: 01 7032 250** Fax: 01 6718 969

Conveniently located right beside the platform where the Cork train departs, this is a place to consider for a meeting (could save having to go into town at all), when collecting someone off a train or to ensure due care of the inner man before leaving on a train which may have questionable dining arrangements - it certainly takes the rush out of catching a train and, given the difficulties of estimating journey time in Dublin these day, that in itself is sufficient recommendation. However, although short on atmosphere, the food is far better than might be expected of a railway station and they make a real effort to meet special dietary requirements, with vegetarian, gluten-free dishes and any containing nuts highlighted on the menu and a note to coeliacs to ask about any dish that appeals in case it can be adapted. The style is fairly modern - grilled goats cheese with char-grilled vegetables & red onion marmalade, seared tuna steak with Mediterranean style vegetables - and there's a short sandwich menu if you're in a hurry. Open all day, 11-6.30. A la carte. House wine from €15.17. Closed Dec 25, Jan 1, Sun & bank hols. Visa, Laser. **Directions:** Heuston Station, Platform 2.

Gallic Kitchen

RESTAURANT 49 Francis Street Dublin 8 **Tel: 01 455 4912**

This little spot in Dublin's "antique" district has been delighting locals and visitors alike for the last five years. Patissière Sarah Webb - who also has a stall at the Saturday market in Temple Bar - is renowned for quality baking (quiches, roulades, wraps) and also salads and delicious little numbers to have with coffee. Sourcing is immaculate, cooking skilful and prices reasonable, so you may have to queue. Open Mon-Sat, 9-4.

Havana

PUB Grantham Street Dublin 8 **Tel: 01 476 0046**

This smashing little tapas bar is tucked away on a little street off Camden Street and, although understandably extremely popular with locals and people working in the area, it's otherwise one of Dublin's best kept secrets. prices are very reasonable and lucnch is a real bargain. Home-cooked food freshly made on the premises is the philosophy: Spanish tortilla, Serrano ham, freshly baked breads is the kind of food you'll get, along with tapas like marinated jumbo prawns. Open Mon-Sat 12-10.30 (later Thu-Sat). Closed Sun.

Jurys Christchurch Inn

HOTEL féile bia Christchurch Place Dublin 8 **Tel: 01 454 0000** Fax: 01 454 0012
Email: info@jurys.com

Jurys Christchurch Inn is well placed for both tourist and business travellers, within walking distance of the main city centre areas on both sides of the Liffey and close to attractions in Temple Bar, Dublin Castle and Dublinia (the museum of medieval Dublin). Rooms are comfortable and spacious (though occasionally in need of greater attention to upgrading and maintenance), with large, well positioned work desks and small but practical bathrooms with economy baths and overbath showers. A large multi-storey car park at the rear has convenient access to the hotel. **Rooms 182.** Room rate from €96 (up to 3 adults or 2 adults and 2 children); breakfast from €6. Amex, Diners, MasterCard, Visa. Closed 24-26 Dec

Locks Restaurant

RESTAURANT 1 Windsor Terrace Portobello Dublin 8 **Tel: 01 454 3391**
Fax: 01 453 8352

In an old building with a lovely canalside setting, Locks is furnished and decorated in a warm country house style with soft lighting, open fires and a soothing atmosphere. Short set menus for lunch and dinner offer the kind of food that might be served in a good country house; the seasonal à la carte menu is more ambitious in scale, but offers a similar combination of classic and country French and modern Irish cooking, with a nod towards world cuisine here and there. For example, a starter of Locks fish soup with aïoli & croûtons is a speciality, while main courses include classics like monkfish or lobster thermidor and sole meunière alongside centre loin of lamb with goats cheese ravioli, roasted red peppers, béarnaise & herbs. The cooking is sure, presentation very much in a house style and service professional. The wine list favours France, notably Bordeaux, and offers several house choices (all French) by the glass. Children welcome. **Seats 60** (private room, 30) No-smoking area. L Mon-Fri, 12.15-2.15. D Mon-Sat, 7.15-11. Set L €22.80, Set D €38; L&D à la carte available. House wine €17.45. SC 12.5%. Closed Sat L, all Sun, Bank Hols, Dec 25- Jan 7. Amex, Diners, MasterCard, Visa, Laser. **Directions:** Half way between Portobello and Harolds Cross Bridges.

The Lord Edward

RESTAURANT/PUB 23 Christchurch Place Dublin 8 **Tel: 01 4542 420**
Fax: 01 4542 420 Email: ledward@indigo.ie

Dublin's oldest seafood restaurant is on three floors of a tall, narrow building overlooking Christchurch cathedral. Traditional in a decidedly old-fashioned way, The Lord Edward provides a complete contrast to the current wave of trendy restaurants that has taken over Dublin recently, which is just the way a lot of people seem to like it. There are a few non-seafood options - traditional dishes like Irish stew, perhaps or corned beef and cabbage - and the seafood can be excellent: simplest choices are usually best. Bar food is also available Mon-Fri, 12-2.30. No smoking area. Children welcome. **Seats 40.** L Mon-Fri, 12-3. D 6-10.30 Mon-Sat. Closed Sun, Dec 24 - 6 Jan. Amex, Diners, MasterCard, Visa, Laser. **Directions:** opposite Christchurch Cathedral.

Nancy Hands Restaurant

PUB 30-32 Parkgate Street Dublin 8 **Tel: 01 677 0149** Fax: 01 677 0187

A sister establishment to the Hole in the Wall (see entry), Nancy Hands is new pub based on tradition but far from being a theme pub. It's a characterful place for a drink: the selection stocked is unusually extensive and includes a wide choice of wines (including about 10 by the glass and two wines of the week), also a range of vodkas, whiskies and cocktails. Children welcome. No-smoking area. Air conditioning. Toilets wheelchair accessible. Closed 25 Dec & Good Fri. Amex, Diners, MasterCard, Visa.

The Old Dublin Restaurant

RESTAURANT 90/91 Francis Street Dublin 8 **Tel: 01 454 2028**
Fax: 01 454 1406 Email: olddub@indigo.ie

Eamonn Walsh's oasis of civilised dining is one of Dublin's longest-established fine restaurants. The standard of cooking is high and the food is lively, with new dishes regularly taking their place alongside established favourites. The dining area is in several domestic-sized rooms with special features - a marble fireplace, some very good pictures - creating a cosy old-world atmosphere. While most famous for its Russian and Scandinavian specialities like blini (buckwheat pancake with cured salmon, prawns and herrings), and planked sirloin Hussar, which still feature on the à la carte, recent menus have been noticeably modern. Set lunch and early evening menus are very good value. Hospitable, thoughtful service. Children welcome. **Seats 65** (private room, 32) No-smoking area. L Mon-Fri 12.30-2.30, D Mon-Sat, 6-11. Set L €20, Early D €17; à la carte D available. House wine €17.50. SC discretionary. Closed L Sat, all Sun, bank hols. Amex, Diners, MasterCard, Visa, Laser.

Ryans of Parkgate Street

PUB 28 Parkgate Street Dublin 8 **Tel: 01 671 9352** Fax: 01 671 3590

Ryans is one of Irelandís finest and best-loved original Victorian pubs, with magnificent stained glass, original mahogany bar fixtures and an outstanding collection of antique mirrors all contributing to its unique atmosphere. Good bar food is available at lunch time and in the evening, and there's a separate restaurant upstairs. Closed 25 Dec, Good Fri, first 2 wks Jan & Bank Hols.

Thornton's Restaurant

RESTAURANT ★★ 1 Portobello Road Dublin 8 **Tel: 01 454 9067**
Fax: 01 453 2947 Email: thornton.mdiolfiee.ie

Seriously good cooking in a seriously good restaurant is to be found in this corner premises overlooking the canal. Muriel Thornton and her team of French waiting staff set the tone from the outset, providing a highly professional service to complement Kevin Thornton's superb cooking. There is a small reception bar downstairs (with a view into the kitchen) and, upstairs, a private dining-room and the main dining areas (candle-lit at night) in two rooms. Decor is elegant and understated with heavy silk drapes, 'distressed' painted tiles and a tall vase of flowers catching the eye. Service is impeccable, from the moment a basket of breads (fennel rolls, tomato and basil, walnut etc) arrive to the final presentation of assorted petits fours accompanying coffees and teas. In between, typical offerings might include an amuse-gueule of two plump sautéed prawns in a bisque and truffle sabayon and signature dishes such as sautéed foie gras with scallops and cep sauce served with warm brioche followed by roast suckling pig and trotter with Maxim potato, glazed turnip and a light poitin sauce, finally - another speciality - an iced pyramid, typically of of fruit, with glazed fruits and orange sauce. Alternatively, an entire table can choose the eight-course 'surprise' menu at €92 per person. This is creative cooking of the highest class, utilising first-rate seasonal ingredients, perfectly seasoned and beautifully presented. Chef-patron Kevin Thornton has a perfectionist's eye for detail and a palate to match. Recent visits by the Guide confirm consistently excellent standards at this exceptional restaurant. The wine list, which leads with a menu of champagnes and sparkling wines, is classic as befits the cuisine. There are some very special dessert wines and digestifs, also a fair selection of half bottles. Children welcome. No-smoking area. Air conditioning. **Seats 45** (private room, 14). L Fri only, 12.15-2; D Tue-Sat, 6.30-10.30. Set L €35. Gourmet D €92, L&D also à la carte. House wine from €19.05. SC 12.5%. Closed Sun & Mon, 2 wks Christmas. Amex, Diners, MasterCard, Visa, Laser. **Directions:** Canalside between Rathmines and Harold's Cross Bridges.

DUBLIN 9

Egan's House

GUESTHOUSE 7-9 Iona Park Glasnevin Dublin 9 **Tel: 01 830 3611** Fax: 01 830 3312 Email: eganshouse@eircom.ie

Within walking distance of the Botanic Gardens, this long-established, family-run guesthouse offers comfortable, well-maintained en-suite accommodation and warm hospitality at a reasonable price. Wheelchair access. Parking. Children (Under 3s free in parents' room; cots available). Pets by arrangement. **Rooms 23** (all en-suite, 10 no-smoking). B&B about €42. Closed 24-27 Dec. MasterCard, Visa.

John Kavanagh (GraveDiggers)

PUB 1 Prospect Square Glasnevin Dublin 9 **Tel: 01 8307 978** Email: antokav@gofree.indigo.ie

John Kavanagh's lays claim to being the oldest family pub in Dublin - it was established in 1833 and the current family are the 6th generation in the business. Also known as "The Gravediggers' because of its location next to the Glasnevin cemetery and its attached folk history, this is a genuine Victorian bar, totally unspoilt - and it has a reputation for serving one of the best pints in Dublin. No music, "piped or otherwise".Theme pub owners eat your hearts out. Parking. No children after 7pm. Bar food served weekdays 12-2. Closed Good Fri & Xmas. No credit cards. None Old Glasnevin Cemetery Gate,off BBotanic Road.

DUBLIN 13

Marine Hotel

HOTEL Sutton Cross Dublin 13 **Tel: 01 839 0000** Fax: 01 839 0442 Email: info@marinehotel.ie Web: www.marinehotel.ie

Well-located on the sea side of a busy junction, this attractive hotel has ample car parking in front and a lawn reaching down to the foreshore at the rear. Recently renovated public areas give a good impression: a smart foyer and adjacent bar, an informal conservatory style seating area overlooking the garden and a well-appointed restaurant. Refurbishment of bedrooms, some of which have sea views, is continuing . A popular venue for conferences and social gatherings, especially weddings, the Marine is also the only hotel in this area. providing for the business guest. 24 hour room service. Conference/banqueting (100/180). Indoor swimming pool. Garden. Children welcome (Under 4s free in parents' room; cots available). No pets. **Rooms 48** (4 shower only, 31 executive rooms, 8 no-smoking, 2 for disabled). B&B about €100pps, ss about €24. Lift. Closed 24-27 Dec. Amex, MasterCard, Visa, Diners, Laser. **Directions:** Take coast road towards Howth from city centre, on right at Sutton Cross.

DUBLIN 14

Indian Brasserie

RESTAURANT Main Street Rathfarnham Dublin 14 **Tel: 01 492 0261**

Samir Sapru's Indian Brasserie is just a minute's walk from Rathfarnham Castle, at the Butterfield Avenue end of the village. The restaurant, which is run as a buffet, offers freshly prepared wholesome food, aiming to make it the nearest to home cooking that can be achieved in a restaurant. The selection usually includes around eight starters, five or six salads and seven or eight main courses, with each dish individually prepared from scratch and the selection worked out so that all the dishes complement each other. Breads - which are baked quickly at a very high temperature - are cooked to order. The hospitality is intended to make each guest feel as if they are visiting a private house - customers are encouraged to try a little of everything that has been prepared on the night. Own parking. No children after 7pm. **Seats 50.** No-smoking area. Air conditioning D 5:15-11:30 daily. L Sun only 12:30-3. Set D about €20; early D, 5.30-7.30pm. House wine about €14. SC discretionary. Toilets wheelchair accessible. Closed 25-26 Dec. Amex, Diners, MasterCard, Visa. **Directions:** At the Butterfield Ave. end of Rathfarnham village, under TSB Bank.

The Yellow House

PUB Willbrook Road Rathfarnham Dublin 14 **Tel: 01 493 2994** Fax: 01 494 2441

Named after the unusual shade of the bricks with which it is built, the landmark pub of Rathfarnham makes a perfect rendezvous, with no chance of confusion. The tall and rather forbidding exterior gives little hint of the warmth inside, where pictures and old decorative items relevant to local history repay closer examination. Traditional bar food is served in the lounge and there's a restaurant upstairs serving evening meals and Sunday lunch. Closed 25 Dec & Good Fri. Amex, Diners, MasterCard, Visa.

DUBLIN 15

Ashbrook House

COUNTRY HOUSE River Road Ashtown Castleknock Dublin 15
Tel: 01 838 5660 Fax: 01 838 5660

This beautiful Georgian country house is set in 10 acres of grounds and gardens beside the Phoenix park just 15 minutes from the city and the airport. Large beautifully furnished bedrooms have power showers and two family rooms have a single bed as well as doubles. There are two magnificent drawing rooms, tennis court and walled gardens. Direct dial phones in rooms. B&B from about €32 pps. Single supplement about €10. Closed Christmas/New Year. Amex, MasterCard, Visa

DUBLIN 16

Killakee House Restaurant

RESTAURANT Killakee Road Rathfarnham Dublin 16 **Tel: 01 493 8849**

This famous old house - once the premises of the notorious Hellfire Club - was taken over in 2001 by George Smith, well known for his years as head chef at Kilkea Castle, Co Kildare. A great deal of renovation work was required and, at the time of going to press, the restaurant had only been open a short time and the planned accommodation was not likely to come on stream in the immediate future. An early visit indicated that there was still a considerable amount of settling in to be done although the quality of food was predictably good (George is renowned for his careful sourcing of ingredients). The main difficulty at the time lay with poor presentation, which will surprise anyone familiar with this chef's previous style. However, this is a restaurant with potential: not there yet, perhaps, but one to watch. **Seats 75.** D Tue-Sat 7-10, L Sun 12.30-5. Closed 25 Dec. Amex, MasterCard, Visa, Laser.

DUBLIN 18

Bistro One

RESTAURANT 3 Brighton Road Foxrock Village Dublin 18
Tel: 01 289 7711 Fax: 01 289 9858

This popular first floor neighbourhood restaurant can get very busy but there is a little bar on the way in, where guests are greeted and set up in comfort, and the attitude throughout is laid back but not without care. Tempting menus might include 6 or 8 choices per course, with starters such as seared marinated salmon on a chive potato cake or Bistro One's salad with pancetta, rocket & pine nuts The pasta selection can be starter or main course as preferred - penne with smoked chicken and wild mushroom perhaps. Main courses include classics such as veal alla milanaise and updated club fare like lamb's liver with streaky bacon and puy lentils. There are generous side vegetables and a choice of farmhouse cheese; home made ice creams or classic puddings to finish. Children welcome. **Seats 45** D Tue-Sat 6.45-10.30. A la carte. House wine €21.59. SC 10%. No-smoking area. Closed Sun, Mon and Dec 24-27 & 31. MasterCard, Visa, Laser. **Directions:** First right after Foxrock church travelling South on the N11.

Rodney's Bistro

RESTAURANT Cabinteely Village Dublin 18 **Tel: 01 285 1664**

Busy, buzzy with closely packed tables, great atmosphere - this little restaurant could be described as the definitive bistro. Friendly service and very good cooking explain its great popularity with the locals. Fish is a particularly strong point - monkfish, plaice, cod and even lobster could be among the daily specials and game comes onto the menu in season. An informative wine list is a little short. Not suitable for children. **Seats 38** D 7-10 Tue-Sat. Menu à la carte. House wine 15.87. Air conditioning. SC 10%. Closed Sun & Mon, 2 wks July, 2 wks Jan. Amex, MasterCard, Visa.

DUBLIN 22

Bewley's Hotel at Newlands Cross

HOTEL Newlands Cross Naas Road Dublin 22 **Tel: 01 464 0140** Fax: 01 464 0900
Email: res@bewleyshotels.com Web: www.bewleyshotels.com

The lobby gives a good first impression at this stylish budget hotel just off the N7. Bedrooms will confirm this feeling, especially at the price - a very reasonable room rate offers a large room with double, single and sofa-bed, a decent bathroom and excellent amenities including a trouser press, iron and ironing board and fax/modem lines. Many more expensive hotels might take note of these standards. Good business facilities too (boardrooms for meetings from only €63.49 per day). The adjacent Bewley's Restaurant provides very acceptable food and there is free parking for 200 cars. Small conference (20). Wheelchair access. Parking. Children welcome. (under 16s free in parents' room; cots available). No pets. Lift. **Rooms 260** (5 shower only, 160 no-smoking, 7 for disabled). Room rate about €70. (max 3 adults). Closed Dec 24-26. Amex, Diners, MasterCard, Visa. **Directions:** off N7 - take junction 9 from M50.

Browns Barn

RESTAURANT/PUB Citywest Bridge Naas Road Dublin 22 **Tel: 01 4640903**
Email: info@brownsbarn.ie Web: www.brownsbarn.ie

Prominently located opposite Citywest Business Park, this landmark listed building dates back to the late 17th century and once housed the Royal Garter Stables. It opened as a bar and restaurant early in 2001 and is proving an asset to the area. Imaginative restoration has created a contemporary interior while retaining many of the original features, including the original stone walls which makes such a welcome contrast to new industrial developments along this stretch of road. Especially attractive features include a courtyard that has been transformed into a light-filled bar - and a west-facing walled garden providing summer seating. Bar food is available all day (steak sandwiches, BLT etc) and the restaurant is open for "casual fine dining" at lunch and dinner every day. Menus are in the popular contemporary style - Caesar salad, goats cheese in filo, chargrilled steaks, breast of Barbary duck on potato rösti and an interesting vegetarian choice scuh as vegetable-stuffed courgette with mozarella cheese & deep-fried noodles. Judging by our late summer visit, the cooking, presentation and service are all good - and this, together with a friendly atmosphere, make it good value. Midweek visits might be more enjoyable as it gets very busy at weekends. No smoking area; air conditioning. **Seats 160** (private room, 70). Set L €20.25; D à la carte. House wine €18.98. SC discretionary except 12.5% on parties of 6+. Closed 25 Dec Amex, Diners, MasterCard, Visa, Laser. **Directions:** opposite CityWest Business Park.

Jurys Green Isle Hotel

HOTEL féile bia Naas Road Dublin 22 **Tel: 01 459 3406** Fax: 01 459 2178
Email: greenisle@jurys.com Web: www.jurysdoyle.com

Situated on the Naas Road, close to the major industrial estates, this is a popular hotel for conferences and business. Over half of the bedrooms are executive rooms and there are conference facilities for up to 250 delegates, four meeting rooms for a maximum of 50 each and some business back-up service if required. Laundry/dry cleaning services available. **Rooms 90** (48 executive). Room rate €149 (max 2 guests). Open all year. Visa, MasterCard, Diners, Amex.

Kingswood Country House

RESTAURANT/COUNTRY HOUSE Naas Road Clondalkin Dublin 22
Tel: 01 459 2428 Fax: 01 459 2207 Email: kingswoodcountryhse@eircom.net

Just off the Naas Road and very close to the industrial estates around Newlands Cross, the country house atmosphere of this guesthouse and restaurant comes as a very pleasant surprise. The restaurant has a lovely cosy atmosphere and a loyal following, for service and atmosphere as well as the food. This is an interesting combination of classic French and traditional and new Irish styles. Ingredients are top quality and the policy is to use as much local and free range produce as possible. Private rooms are available for groups and small business meetings. Small conference/private parties (16/30). Garden. Children welcome (under 2s free in parents' room, cots available). **Seats 80** (private room, 30) No-smoking area. L 12:30-2:30 daily. D 6:30-10:30 Mon-Sat. SC 12.5%. Closed D Sun, 25 Dec & Good Fri. Open on bank hols. Amex, Diners, MasterCard, Visa. **Accommodation:** Guest rooms, like the rest of the house, have an old-fashioned charm. **Rooms 7** (all en-suite). **Directions:** 1.5 miles past Newlands Cross heading south on N7.

Red Cow Moran's Hotel

HOTEL Red Cow Complex Naas Road Dublin 22 **Tel: 01 459 3650** Fax: 01 459 1588
Email: info@morangroup.ie Web: www.morangroup.ie

Strategically located close to the motorway and known as a pub for many years, the Red Cow is now an impressive hotel. A grand staircase sweeping up from the marble lobby gives an indication of the style to follow and, although it will also be of interest to private guests, this is definitely a location to check out if you are considering visiting the area on business or wish to organise conferences or meetings. Bedrooms are all of executive standard, with excellent amenities for business guests including voice mail and fax/modem lines. The purpose-built conference centre offers a wide range of facilities and ample car parking. Conference/banqueting (720/550) Secretarial services. Video conferencing. Wheelchair access. Parking. Children welcome (Under 2s free in parents' room; cots available). No pets. **Rooms 123** (3 suites, 6 mini-suites, 44 no-smoking, 5 for disabled). Lift. B&B about €110pps, ss about €24. Closed Christmas. Amex, Diners, MasterCard, Visa.

COUNTY DUBLIN

Inevitably, it is in the countryside and towns in the Greater Dublin Region that some of the pressures of the success of the Irish economy continue to be most evident. For the County Dublin area has been developing so rapidly in recent years that, not surprisingly, its citizens occasionally seem to be undergoing a minor crisis of identity.

They are now - in theory at least - living in three new counties. These are Fingal in the north, South Dublin in the southwest, and Dun Laoghaire-Rathdown in the southeast. But although Dubliners of town and county alike will happily accept that they're part of a thrusting modern city, equally they'll cheerfully adhere to the old Irish saying that when God made time, He made a lot of it. So most folk are allowing themselves all the time in the world to get used to the fact that they are now either Fingallions, or South Dubliners, or - Heaven forbid - Hyphenators out in Dun Laoghaire-Rathdown.

In this approach, they seem to be supported by An Post, the Irish Post Office, which - firmly into the 21st century - still appears to have a sublime disregard for the creation some years ago of these new counties. As far as An Post is concerned, you're still either in Dublin city or Dublin county, and that's that. All of which is good news for the visitor, for it means that if you feel that the frenetic pace of Dublin city is a mite overpowering, you will very quickly find that nearby, in what used to be - and for many folk still is - County Dublin, there continue to be oases of a much more easy-going way of life waiting to be discovered.

Admittedly, the fact that the handsome Dublin Mountains overlook the city in spectacular style means that even up in the nearby hills, you can be well aware of the city's buzz. But if you want to find a vigorous contrast between modern style and classical elegance, you can find it in an unusual form at Dun Laoghaire's remarkable harbour, where one of the world's most modern ferryports is in interesting synergy with one of the world's largest Victorian artificial harbours. Now, a new element has been introduced with the opening of a showcase marina in the harbour, expensively built so that its style matches the harbour's classic elegance.

Should you head northward into Fingal, you'll quickly discover an away from-it-all sort of place of estuary towns, fishing ports, offshore islands alive with seabirds, and an environment of leisurely pace in which it's thought very bad form to hasten over meals in restaurants where portion control is either unknown, or merely in its infancy.

Yet civic pride is a growth industry in Fingal, the pace being set by the attractive modern County Hall in Swords, with the Tidy Town awards of September 2001 seeing the top prizes of Best and Highly Commended for "Dublin County" going respectively to Skerries and Malahide - both of them in Finglas - while the Commended Category award was to Lucan, in South Dublin along the Liffey valley.

Local Attractions and Information

Balbriggan/Skerries Ardgillan Castle	01 849 2212
Donabate Newbridge House, Park & Traditional Farm	01 843 6534
Dun Laoghaire National Maritime Museum, Haigh Terrace	01 280 0969
Dun Laoghaire Tourist Information	01 280 6984/5/6
Lucan Primrose Hill Garden (house attrib. James Gandon)	01 628 0373
Malahide Malahide Castle & Demesne	01 846 2184
Malahide Fry Model Railway (Malahide Castle)	01 846 3779
Malahide Talbot Botanic Gardens (Malahide Castle)	01 872 7530
Sandycove James Joyce Museum (Martello Tower)	01 280 9265
Sandyford Fernhill Gardens (Himalayan species)	01 295 6000
Skerries Skerries Mills - Working Windmills, Craft and Visitor Centre	01 849 5208
Tallaght Community Arts Centre, Old Blessington Rd	01 462 1501

Blackrock

Blueberry's

RESTAURANT 15 Main Street Blackrock Co. Dublin **Tel: 01 2788900** Fax: 01 2788903

This fresh, bright first-floor restaurant has lots of polished wood and classy contemporary table settings - a fitting background for stylish food. The best fresh ingredients provide a sound foundation for confident, creative cooking and well-balanced menus offer plenty of choice: well-made soups, a fine array of tempting starters and main courses that take vegetarian cooking seriously. Seafood is a strong option and there are some modern dishes inspired by tradition. Friendly, efficient service. **Seats 38.** No smoking area. Air conditioning. L 12.30-2.15 (Sun to 2.45), D 5.30-10 (Fri & Sat to 10.30, Sun 6-9). Closed L Sat. Amex, MasterCard, Visa. **Directions:** above Jack O'Rourke's pub on the Main Street Blackrock.

Blackrock

Dali's Restaurant

RESTAURANT 63-65 Main Street Blackrock Co. Dublin
Tel: 01 278 0660 Fax: 01 278 0661

Just across the road from the Library, these premises have been home to several of Dublin's most successful restaurateurs and the present establishment is no exception, having established a loyal local clientèle and a reputation beyond the immediate area. There's a chic little bar just inside the door and a dining area, at a slightly higher level,beyond - all very attractively set up in a style that is contemporary but without hard-edged minimalism. Both the restaurant manager and head chef changed in 2001, but the style has remained consistent - Stewart Hamilton's menus are appealingly light and colourful, including zesty first courses like panfried prawns with a lime, ginger & coriander butter (available as a starter or main course) and salmon fishcakes with a chive beurre blanc, followed by main courses that include several slight variations on old favourites - rack of lamb might come with a salsa verde - and tempting vegetarian dishes such as chargrilled vegetable stack, layered with goats cheese & rocket pesto; prices are moderate , but side dishes are charged extra. Set lunch menus.offer a choice of four or five dishes on each course and are very good value. Children welcome. No smoking area; air conditioning. **Seats 65.** L Tue-Sun, 12-3 D Tue-Sat 6-10.30. Set L €13.90, A la carte L&D available; house wine €17.14, sc discretionary except 10% on parties of 6+. Closed D Sun, all Mon, 25-27 Dec. Amex, Diners, MasterCard, Visa, Laser. **Directions:** ppposite Blackrock Library.

Blackrock

Radisson SAS St Helen's Hotel

HOTEL/RESTAURANT Stillorgan Road Blackrock Co. Dublin **Tel: 01 218 6000**
Fax: 01 218 6030 Email: info.dublin@radissonsas.com Web: www.radissonsas.com

Set in formal gardens just south of Dublin's city centre, with views across Dublin Bay to Howth Head, the fine 18th century house at the heart of this impressive new hotel was once a private residence. Careful restoration and imaginative modernisation have created interesting public areas, including the Orangerie bar and a pillared ballroom with minstrels' gallery and grand piano. Bedrooms, in a new four-storey block adjoining the main building, all have garden views (some of the best rooms also have balconies) and air conditioning and are well-equipped for business guests (with desks and fax machines). Rooms are comfortably furnished to a high standard in contemporary style, although less spacious than might be expected in a new development; small bathrooms with economy baths, especially, fail to live up to the opulence that the old house promises. A fine formal dining room, Le Panto, has views over the garden (D Tue-Sat, L Sun) and offers international fine dining, including a 7-course "Chefs Surprise Menu". There's a less formal Italian restaurant, Talavera, which is in four interconnecting rooms in the lower ground floor; decorated in warm Mediterranean colours, it specialises in dishes from Tuscany and Basilicata (D 7-10 daily). Lighter menus are also offered all day in the Orangerie bar and Ballroom lounge. Conference/banqueting (350/220). Business centre. ISDN lines. Garden, snooker. Ample parking. Children welcome (Under 17s free in parents' room; cots available). No pets. **Rooms 15** (25 suites, 70 no-smoking, 8 for disabled). Room rate €205(max 3 guests). Open all year. Amex, Diners, MasterCard, Visa, Laser. **Directions:** Conveniently located just 3 miles to the City Centre, on N11.

Blackrock

Ristorante da Roberto

RESTAURANT 5 George's Avenue Blackrock Co. Dublin **Tel: 01 278 0759**

First impressions of this popular Italian restaurant are a little confusing - stained glass windows and chandeliers seem at odds with a terracotta-style tiled floor and country kitchen chairs - but the regulars are unfazed. Proprietor-chef Roberto Morsiani offers quite a few house specialities - Prawns Roberto's Way, Greedy Man's Ravioli, Chef's Rustic Veal - plus a wide choice of fish (mostly local), a page of pastas and a vegetarian section and the overall experience provides a contrast to the chic contemporary restaurants nearby. The best tables are in the front section; the back room (where non-smokers tend to end up) is very noisy. **Seats 70.** Air conditioning D Sun-Sat. Closed Mon. Amex, MasterCard, Visa. **Directions:** opposite the Post Office off the Main Street in Blackrock.

Booterstown

La Tavola

RESTAURANT 114 Rock Road Booterstown Co. Dublin **Tel: 01 283 5101**

Kevin Hart and Philip Davis's friendly, informal restaurant has been providing good popular food at customer-friendly prices since 1992. Menus include a range of meat and poultry dishes as well as well-made pizza and pastas - there are vegetarian options. Daily blackboard specials offer fresh fish and some extra meat and poultry dishes. **Seats 42.** No smoking area; D 5-11.15 Tue-Sat (Tue to 10.15); à la carte; house wine about €14; sc discretionary. Closed Sun, Mon. Amex, MasterCard, Visa. **Directions:** Opposite Booterstown Dart Station at bottom of Booterstown Ave. on Rock Road.

Dalkey

Daniel Finnegan

PUB 2 Sorrento Road Dalkey Co. Dublin **Tel: 01 285 8505**

An immaculately maintained pub of great character, much-loved by locals and visitors alike. Itís bright, comfortable and cosy, with wood panelling and traditional Irish seating in 'snugs'. Food is served at lunchtime only - a full hot bar lunch, including starters such as baked Dalkey crab, brie fritters with apple coulis and main courses like roast stuffed pork steak, honey roast half duck and grilled cod steak, followed by traditional desserts like apple pie and lemon cheesecake. The fresh fish (from the harbour nearby) is excellent, the vegetables predictable but tasty and value good. No reservations. - get there early to avoid a long wait. Carpark nearby. Bar food 12.30-3pm Mon-Sat. Closed 25 Dec, Good Fri & & New Year. Amex, Diners, MasterCard, Visa, Laser. **Directions:** Near Dalkey DART station.

Dalkey

Kish Restaurant

RESTAURANT Coliemore Road Dalkey Co. Dublin **Tel: 01 285 0377**
Fax: 01 285 0141 Email: bookekishrestaurant.ie

Purpose-built by the Delaney family, who previously owned the Dalkey Island Hotel, to take advantage of views over Dublin Bay and Dalkey Island, this new restaurant has now settled into its niche as the area's leading fine dining restaurant. Head chef Pat Kiely's experience at top kitchens in Britain and Ireland shows in seasonal menus featuring many special dishes and luxurious ingredients - words like foie gras, lobster and black truffle leap off the choice of nine or so starters, for example, although his own favourite is a relatively modest dish of layers of steamed skate with smoked bacon & parsely, shallot & caper pomme purée. Main courses which follow in a similar style include rather more seafood than meat and there's always a tempting vegetarian dish such as feuillette of garden vegetables with spinach, wild mushrooms & white truffle dressing. Carefully crafted desserts include an assiette of crème brulées (pistachio, coffee, vanilla & passion fruit) with petits biscuits. Besides the main list, the wine selection includes some interesting and moderately priced French country wines (all under €23), and a further 'Petite Cave' list at slightly higher prices. Not suitable for children under 8. Smoking unrestricted; air conditioning. **Seats 55.** L&D Wed-Sun. Set L from €25, Set Sun L€36; L&D also à la carte; house wine €20; 10% s.c. Closed all Mon & Tue, last 3 wks Jan. Amex, Diners, MasterCard, Visa, Laser. **Directions:** 8 miles south of Dublin City just outside Dalkey Village.

Dalkey

RESTAURANT

Munkberrys Restaurant

22 Castle Street Dalkey Co. Dublin **Tel: 01 284 7185**
Email: info@munkberrys.com Web: www.munkberrys.com

This chic, minimalist restaurant in the heart of Dalkey village has earned the support of a local clientèle, who appreciate the stylish cooking and consistently high standard of cooking by head chef Stephen Doris, who has been with the restaurant since it opened in 1999. Specialities such as cod fillet with a Mediterranean crust, putanesca fresca and grilled beef fillet with potato & bacon crèpe and creamed spinach enjoy enduring popularity. Dishes suitable for vegetarians and those containing nuts are thoughtfully highlighted on the menu. Sunday brunch is a speciality, bringing fans from far and wide for good food and live jazz. **Seats 50** D daily: Mon-Sat from 5.30 (early D 5.30-6.45); Sun brunch 12-5.30; Sun D 6-10. Early D €21; Set D €31; also à la carte. House wine from €16.50. Closed 25 Dec, 1 Jan, Good Fri. Amex, Diners, MasterCard, Visa, Laser. **Directions:** located approx 5 miles south of Dublin on the Dart Rail Link.

Dalkey

RESTAURANT

Nosh

111 Coliemore Road Dalkey Co. Dublin **Tel: 01 2840666**
Email: comments@nosh.ie Web: www.nosh.ie

Samantha and Sacha Farrell opened their bright, contemporary restaurant next to the famous Club Bar in December 2000 and, with its clean lines and lightwood furniture, no-nonsense menus, quality ingredients and fair prices, it immediately found a niche in the Dalkey dining scene. Head chef Paul Quinn (previously sous-chef at The Hungry Monk) presents seasonal menus that also change throughout the day. There's brunch (hot dishes, anything from homemade granola with natural yogurt to Thai-style fishcakes with chilli, lime & coriander crème fraîche and a wide range of coffees and other hot and cold drinks) then lunch, where things get a bit more serious, with crab cakes easing to the top of the menu and choices ranging up to the "Posh Nosh" special of the day. In the evening, you might begin with prawn pil-pils in sizzling garlic & chilli oil and proceed to wok-fried monkfish with stir-fried vegetables and noodles topped with crème fraiche (both specialities) or roast marinated chicken with a lime & cashew nut risotto. Top prices (evening main courses) range from around €14 for an imaginative vegetarian dish, to about €19 for beef fillet with spinach, mash and Irish mist sauce, topped with blue cheese. A limited but well-chosen wine list, with a few half bottles, is offered throughout the day. Not suitable for children after 8pm. No smoking area; air conditioning. **Seats 45.** L Tue-Sun, 12-4; D Tue-Sun 6-10(ish). A la carte. House wine €17.71. Closed Mon, all bank hols. MasterCard, Visa, Laser. **Directions:** end of Dalkey Town take left.

Dalkey

PUB/RESTAURANT

The Queen's Bar & Restaurant

12 Castle Street Dalkey Co. Dublin **Tel: 01 285 4569**
Fax: 01 285 8345 Email: queens@clubi.ie

The oldest pub in Dalkey, and also one of the oldest in Ireland, The Queen's was originally licensed to 'dispense liquor' as far back as 1745. Recent renovations and improvements have been done with due respect for the age and character of the premises. There are now two restaurants on the premises - La Romana, which has offered good value Italian/Mediterranean food for some years and the first floor restaurant and piano bar, The Vico, which serves contemporary international food in a more upmarket atmosphere. Good bar food - chowders, casseroles, salads, quiches - is also available every afternoon and can be served to patio areas at the back and front in fine weather. Wheelchair accessible; children welcome at La Romana, up to 7pm; The Vico is not suitable for children under 8. **Restaurants both seat 70.** Vico D only Tue-Sat, 5.30-11 (early D menu, €15.95, 5.30-7); Romana D daily 6-11. Bar menu daily,12-5; limited 'bites' menu Mon-Fri, 5-8pm. Vico closed Sun, Mon & bank hols; establishment closed 25 Dec & Good Fri. La Romana Amex, Diners, MasterCard, Visa, Laser. **Directions:** centre of town,beside Heritage centre.

Dalkey

RESTAURANT

Thai House Restaurant

21 Railway Road Dalkey Co. Dublin **Tel: 01 284 7304**
Fax: 01 284 7304 Email: info@thaihouseireland.com Web: www.thaihouseireland.com

Since 1997, the welcoming atmosphere and authentic, interesting food at Tony Ecock's restaurant has ensured a loyal following - and head chef Wilai Kruekcai has established a reputation for including dishes that are genuinely spicy and do not pander to blander tastes. Begin with the Thai House Special Starter Pack - a tasty sampling plate of six starters: crisp deep-fried dishes like spring rolls, prawns with Thai sauce, marinated skewered pork or chicken satay with sweet and spicy sauce all well-known dishes but spiced and cooked without compromise. From a choice of soups that include the famous Tom Yam Gung (spicy prawn soup with lemon grass and chilli) Tom Yam

Rumit - a spicy soup with prawns, squid, crab and mussels is perhaps the most interesting. Main courses include a range of curries, fried rice dishes and pan-fried dishes such as Bu Paht Pung Galee - delicious crab fried with spring onions, garlic and sugar in special Thai sauce. Vegetarian dishes are listed separately and there are several set menus for two to six people. The wine list includes some Thai beers. Not suitable for children after 8pm. No smoking area. Air conditioning. **Seats 34.** D only, 6-11 daily. Set D €30.48, house wine from €15.88; sc discretionary. Toilets wheelchair accessible. Closed 3 wks late Sep/Oct. Amex, Diners, MasterCard, Visa, Laser. **Directions:** 100 metres from Dalkey DART Station.

Dublin Airport

Great Southern Hotel

HOTEL

Dublin Airport Co. Dublin **Tel: 01 844 6000** Fax: 01 844 6001
Email: res@dubairport.gsh.ie Web: www.greatsouthernhotels.com

This large modern hotel opened in the airport complex in 1998 and is just two minutes drive from the main terminal building (with a coach service available). Rooms are all double-glazed and there's a high proportion of executive rooms (12 of which are designated lady executive). It is a good choice for business guests and, should your flight be delayed, the large bar/bistro on the ground floor could be a welcome place to pass the time. An extension to the hotel under construction at the time of goung to press will provide 82 extra bedrooms. Conference/banqueting (400/240); video conferencing; secretarial services; business centre. Children welcome (Under 2s free in parents' room; cots available free of charge). Lift. **Rooms 147** (2 junior suites, 58 executive rooms, 24 no-smoking, 4 for disabled) Room rate €190 (max 3 guests). Closed 24-26 Dec. Potters Bistro Amex, Diners, MasterCard, Visa, Laser. **Directions:** Situated in airport complex.

Dublin Airport

Posthouse Dublin Airport

HOTEL

Dublin Airport Co. Dublin **Tel: 01 808 0500** Fax: 01 844 6002

This large, comfortable hotel makes an ideal meeting place and guests may use the extensive facilities of the Airport Sports & Leisure complex free of charge. Bedrooms all have TV and pay movies, mini-bar, trouser press and hair dryer; 24 hour room service and 24 hour courtesy bus to and from the airport terminal. Live music in the bar at weekends. Conference/banqueting (130/130) Parking. Children welcome (Under 4s free in parents' room; cots available). Wheelchair accessible. **Rooms 249** (103 executive rooms, 101 no-smoking, 3 for disabled) B&B about €70pps; Closed 24-25 Dec. Amex, Diners, MasterCard, Visa. **Directions:** In airport complex, on the right when entering airport.

Dun Laoghaire

Bistro Vino

RESTAURANT

56 Glasthule Road Dun Laoghaire Co. Dublin
Tel: 01 280 6097 Fax: 01 280 6097

Dermot Baker's small first floor evening restaurant (up steep stairs) is near the seafront at Sandycove. It pre-dates surrounding establishments in this now fashionable area by a long chalk. But it's still a hit with the locals, who appreciate the moderate prices, unpretentious, good food and informal atmosphere. A la carte except for an inexpensive early set menu. D daily, 5-"late". Amex, Diners, MasterCard, Visa. **Directions:** opposite Eagle House pub.

Dun Laoghaire

Brasserie Na Mara

RESTAURANT

1 Harbour Road Dun Laoghaire Co. Dublin **Tel: 01 280 6767**
Fax: 01 284 4649 Email: brasserienamara@irishrail.ie

The old Kingstown terminal building beside the Dun Laoghaire DART station makes a fine location for this harbourside restaurant. The current contemporary decor is stylish - and the bar faces in towards the reception area, so you look out over the harbour while enjoying your aperitif. Interesting menus are in a bright, modern style to suit the decor, include plenty of seafood as one would expect - and prices are not excessive.No smoking area. **Seats 86.** L Mon-Fri 12.30-3, Long L Sun, from 12.30; D Mon-Sat, 6.30-10. Set early D, from €23 (6.30-7.15); Set D €29.15. A la carte available; house wine. SC discretionary except 10% on parties 8+. Closed L Sat , D Sun, bank hols,25 Dec, 1 Jan. Amex, Diners, MasterCard, Visa, Laser. **Directions:** Coast Road, beside Dart, opposite the Pavillion.

Dun Laoghaire

Caviston's Seafood Restaurant

RESTAURANT

59 Glasthule Road Dun Laoghaire Co. Dublin **Tel: 01 280 9120**
Fax: 01 284 4054 Email: caviston@indigo.ie Web: www.cavistons.com

Caviston's of Sandycove has long been a mecca for lovers of good food and was the guide's Happy Heart Eat Out award-winner for 2001. Here you will find everything that is wonderful, from organic vegetables to farmhouse cheeses, cooked meats to specialist oils and other exotic items. But it was always for fish and shellfish that Caviston's were especially renowned - even providing a collection of well-thumbed recipe books for on-the-spot reference. At their little restaurant next door, they serve an imaginative range of healthy seafood dishes influenced by various traditions and all washed down by a glass or two from a very tempting little wine list. Caviston's food is simple, colourful, perfectly cooked - it speaks volumes for how good seafood can be. Children welcome. **Seats 26.** No-smoking restaurant; air conditioning. L only Tues-Sat, 3 sittings: 12-1.30, 1.30-3, 3-5; all à la carte; sc discretionary. Toilets wheelchair accessible. Closed Sun, Mon & Christmas-New Year. Amex, Diners, MasterCard, Visa. **Directions:** Between Dun Laoghaire and Dalkey, 5 mins. walk from Glasthule DART station.

Dun Laoghaire

Cumberland Lodge

GUESTHOUSE

54 York Road Dun Laoghaire Co. Dublin **Tel: 01 280 9665**
Fax: 01 284 3227 Email: cumberlandlodge@tinet.ie

Dating from about 1847, David and Mariea Jameson's handsome regency house convenient to the car ferry has retained its period features throughout. Well-proportioned rooms are furnished with antiques and all bedrooms have direct-dial phones, television and tea/coffee-making. Breakfast is a point of pride, with fresh juice, home-baked breads and hot food cooked to order. **Rooms 6** (5 en suite, 1 with private bathroom), B&B from €44, ss€57. Open all year. Amex, Diners, MasterCard, Visa. **Directions:** right at Cumberland Inn, approaching Dun Laoghaire from Monkstown.

Dun Laoghaire

Duzys Café

RESTAURANT

18 Glasthule Road (over Eagle House Pub) Dun Laoghaire Co. Dublin
Tel: 01 230 0210 Fax: 01 230 0466 Email: duzyscafe@club.ie

On the first floor of the Eagle House pub (see entry) Duzys is a more informal, youthful reinvention of one of Dublin's great success stories, Morels Bistro. It's decorated elegantly in deep reds and blues lightened by creams and plenty of mirrors, with comfortable furniture - and a fish tank clearly indicating what's likely to be on the menu. Niall Hill, previously at Rathsallagh House in Co. Wicklow, took up the reins as head chef in June 2001 so what you can expect is well-sourced seasonal food (some it coming no further than from Caviston's across the road) and contemporary cooking with a classic base. Specialities include an unusual smoked cod and yellow pepper bisque with glazed goats cheese croûton and scallops with couscous and coriander & lime dressing. If you like jazz, go on a Friday or Saturday night. Coffees and light bites available outside meal times. No smoking area. Children welcome. **Seats 80** (private room 35). Open 12.30-10; L Sun-Fri, 12.30-2.45; D daily 6-10. Early D €17.14 (5.30-7); Set D €31.11. House wine €15.24. Closed L Sat, 25-26 Dec, 1 Jan, Good Fri. Diners, Amex, MasterCard, Visa, Laser. **Directions:** 5 minutes from Dun Laoghaire Town Hall, Railway & Port in centre of village over Eagle House Pub.

Dun Laoghaire

Eagle House

PUB

18 Glasthule Road Dun Laoghaire Co. Dublin **Tel: 01 280 4740**

This fine traditional establishment is full of interest and a great local. The interior is dark, but has a fascinating collection of model boats, ships and other nautical bric-à-brac and is arranged in comfortably sized alcoves and 'snugs' on different levels. Bar meals, available at lunchtime and in the evening, can be very good. Bar food daily, from 12.30. Closed 25 Dec & Good Fri. Amex, MasterCard, Visa, Laser. **Directions:** 5 mins walk from Glasthule DART station, opposite Caviston's.

Dun Laoghaire

Gresham Royal Marine Hotel

HOTEL

Marine Road Dun Laoghaire Co. Dublin
Tel: 01 280 1911 Fax: 01 280 1089
Email: info@gresham-royalmarinehotel.com Web: www.gresham-hotels.com

Overlooking Dublin Bay and the ferry port, this grand old Victorian hotel has ample parking and extensive landscaped gardens, yet ití's only a twenty minute DART ride to the centre of Dublin. On entering the marble floored foyer a few steps take you up and through arched columns into the Bay Lounge (popular for afternoon teas) and the Powerscourt Restaurant. Eight bay-windowed suites have four-poster beds and freestanding antique furniture, but most rooms have fitted furniture and standard facilities, including decent bathrooms; those on the executive floor provide extras for business travellers. Conference/banqueting (450/250). No pets. Lift. Garden. **Rooms 103** (8 suites, 2 mini-suites, 60 executive, 2 for disabled). B&B €82.50, sc 15%. Open all year. Amex, Diners, MasterCard, Visa, Laser. **Directions:** Off Marine Road, up from Dun Laoghaire Port.

Dun Laoghaire

Café Mao

BAR The Pavilion Dun Laoghaire Co. Dublin **Tel: 01 2148090**

The large, informal contemporary café-restaurant is a new sister establishment to the popular Café Mao in the city centre. It is run on the same lines with the philsophy of providing simple, quick and healthy food with youthful appeal at a reasonable price. It's a good place for brunch, with tables outside for fine weather. Open 7 days for coffee, lunch & dinner. Bookings accepted.

Dun Laoghaire

McCormacks

PUB 67 Lr Mounttown Dun Laoghaire Co. Dublin **Tel: 01 280 5519**
Fax: 01 280 0145 Email: cormak@iol.ie

This fine pub (and 'emporium') has been run by the McCormack family since 1960. It's one of the neatest pubs around, with a landscaped carpark creating a pleasant outlook for an imaginative conservatory extension at the back of the pub. The main part is full of traditional character and the whole place has a well-run hum about it. Good bar food includes fresh fish available on the day as well as classics like beef hot pot, chicken à la king and lots of salads. Evening menus offer tasty light dishes: moules marinières, warm crispy bacon and croûton salad and steak sandwiches. Main dishes include a fish special, a 10 oz sirloin steak (with mushroom and Irish whiskey sauce perhaps) or pasta dishes with fresh parmesan. No children after 4pm. Bar food daily. Closed 25 Dec, Good Fri; wheelchair accessible. Amex, MasterCard, Visa, Diners. **Directions:** near Dun Laoghaire at Monkstown end.

Dun Laoghaire

Roly @ The Pavilion

RESTAURANT 8 The Pavilion Dun Laoghaire Co. Dublin
Tel: 01 2360 286 Fax: 01 2360 288

Roly Saul has become quite a legend in the Irish hospitality industry and, after a long spell at the eponymous restaurant Rolys Bistro in Ballsbridge, his old fans in Dun Laoghaire are delighted to welcome him back to a place that's never been the same since he sold his famous restaurant Trudi's, which was a home-from-home for many locals. Trudi's was dark, cosy and comforting - his new venture could not be more different: it's full of light, with gleaming contemporary decor balanced by some traditional gilded mirrors and leather upholstery in white and a shade that now looks black but (appropriately enough) will age to a deep burgundy; different levels and a mixture of banquettes and high-back chairs are used to break the area up and give it interest and semi-private areas. Only open a short time before the guide went to press, short menus changed fortnightly were the order of the day, but that may change when the restaurant is fully "run in". Head chef Phil Roberts leads a youthful kitchen team, who relish the international cuisine in starters like rare tuna with ginger risotto spring roll & shitake broth, tian of crabmeat with guacamole & chilled gazpacho and mains of organic salmon, mussels, leek and dicedpotato stew or roast rump of lamb with chilli polenta chips, ratatouille & thyme jus. True to his philosophy of offering an accessible wine list and real value, Roly has managed to keep the (French) house wines - Fox Mountain Chardonnay/Sauvignon Blanc and Jean-Louis Chancel Vin de Pays de Vaucluse - to just €12.70 (£10) and the list has many other good bottles at fair prices. No-smoking area; air conditioning. Not suitable for children under 7 after 7 pm. **Seats 100.** D daily 6-10. (Lunch, 12 -2.30 will be available - phone to inquire; also long Sun L, 12-7.) Closed 25-27 Dec, Good Fri. Amex, MasterCard, Visa, Laser. **Directions:** opposite Railway Station.

Howth

Abbey Tavern

PUB/RESTAURANT Abbey Street Howth Co. Dublin **Tel: 01 839 0307/01 8322006**
Fax: 01 839 0284 Email: info@abbeytavern.ie Web: www.abbeytavern.ie

Just 50 yards up from the harbour, part of this famous pub dates back to the 15th century, when it was built as a seminary for the local monks (as an addition to the 12th century Chapter House next door). Currently owned by James and Eithne Scott-Lennon - James' grandfather bought it in 1945 - the entire establishment was refurbished in 1998 but this well-run and immaculately maintained pub retains features that have always made the Abbey special - open turf fires, original stone walls, flagged floors and gas lights. Bar food such as Howth seafood chowder, smoked salmon with home-made brown bread, and a hot traditional dish such as corned beef and cabbage. A ploughman's salad is available at lunchtime, although recent visits indicate that standards are inconsistent. In 1960 the Abbey started to lay on entertainment and this, more than anything else, has brought the tavern its fame: it can cater for groups of anything between two and 200 and the format, which now runs like clockwork, is a traditional 5-course dinner followed by traditional Irish music. It's on every night but booking is essential, especially in high season. Banqueting for 200. **Abbot Restaurant:** In

1956 a restaurant was opened, quite a novel move in a pub at the time; it is now called The Abbot and has its own separate entrance. Attractively and comfortably refurbished in keeping with the building, with open turf fires at both ends of the main room, it makes a fine setting for food which is generally well-cooked and not over-complicated - despite the fact that the house speciality "Sole Abbey", is an old-fashioned dish of sole fillets stuffed with prawns, mushrooms & herbs, served with a cream hollandaise sauce. Simpler dishes are usually the wisest choice. **Seats 70.** (private room, 40) No smoking area; air conditioning. D only 7-10.30 Mon-Sat, all à la carte, house wine €16. SC discretionary Children welcome; carpark on harbour. Restaurant closed Sun; establishment closed 25-26 Dec & Good Fri. Amex, Diners, MasterCard, Visa. **Directions:** 9 miles from Dublin, Abbey Street, Howth in the centre of Town.

Howth

Aqua Restaurant

RESTAURANT 1 West Pier Howth Co. Dublin **Tel: 01 832 0690** Fax: 01 832 0687
Email: dine@aqua.ie Web: www.aqua.ie

In a stunning sea and harbourside location at the end of the west pier, overlooking the island of Ireland's Eye and with views west towards Malahide, this building was previously a yacht club and has been senstively converted by the current owners to make a fine contemporary restaurant with plenty of window tables. Behind a glass screen, head chef Brian Daly and his team provide entertainment as well as zesty cooking of colourful food that is thoughtfully presented without the overhandling that has beset so many restaurants lately. What was once a snooker room is now a characterful bar - with an open fire and comfortable seating, it has retained a cosy, clubby atmosphere. Brian Daly, who joined the team in June 2001, was previously at Cooke's Café in Dublin (see entry) and has clearly brought that influence with him. His lively modern cooking strongly favours seafood, notably lobster, but dry aged sirloin steak - with grilled peppers, roasted baby potatoes, balsamic vinegar and extra virgin olive oil, perhaps - is also a speciality. The waterside location, well-sourced ingredients, skilful cooking and solicitous service all make dining at Aqua a pleasure, although prices are high (starters begin at €9.50, rising to €14.60 and main courses go from €24.76 to €50.79); vegetables are charged extra (€ 2.48 per portion), which seems an unnecessary small meanness. Well-balanced set menus (early dinner and lunch) offer better value. Plans for 2002 include the installation of a wheelchair lift, new windows and opening a seafood cookery school. **Seats 100.** D Tue-Sat, early D Tue-Fri (5-7 pm), L Sun only, 12.30-6.30. Early D Eur22, Set Sun L €22. A la carte also available. House wine €17. SC discretionary (but 10% on parties 6+). Closed D Sun, all Mon, 25 Dec, bank hols. Amex, MasterCard, Visa, Laser. **Directions:** Left after Howth DART Station.

Howth

The Bloody Stream

PUB/RESTAURANT 14 West Pier Howth Co. Dublin
Tel: 01 839 5076 Restaurant Tel: 01 839 5078

This characterful pub and restaurant is part of Howth DART station, the result of sympathetic and imaginative restoration of areas of the building which had been disused for many years. It's named after a nearby stream, which still occasionally gets out of hand after heavy rain and causes flooding - fortunately the stone floors don't come to much harm. Food is served upstairs in an informal little restaurant and is very acceptable, although the service can be slow. Closed 25 Dec & Good Fri.

Howth

Casa Pasta

RESTAURANT 12 Harbour Road Howth Co. Dublin **Tel: 01 839 3823** Fax: 01 839 3104

Atmosphere in spades is what sets this first floor restaurant overlooking Howth harbour apart, and although this was partly due to its tiny size, doubling it in 1998 didn't diminish its appeal - it's still notoriously hard to get into, especially at weekends. (However ventilation in the new section can be a problem - book into the original room if possible.) The secret of Casa Pasta's success is entertainment - paper tablecloths and crayons provided for budding artists (of all ages), swift young servers and blackboard menus featuring youthful international food (lots of pastas and salads) that is neither over-ambitious nor over-priced - although cooking standards might improve if the choice were reduced. Regulars that locals happily order without even consulting the menu include runny deep-fried brie with spicy chutney, big Caesar salads (possibly with slivers of chicken breast), home-made tagliatelle with mixed seafood in a creamy wine sauce - and desserts like gooey, boozy tiramisu and sticky banoffi pie. Wines are not quite as cheap and cheerful as might be hoped given the style of food and surroundings. Open daily D 6-11, L Sun only 12-6). A la carte, SC discretionary. Children welcome. Open all year. Also at: 55 Clontarf Road, Dublin 3. Tel/Fax: 01 833 1402 Eirpage House, Donnybrook, Dublin 4. Tel: 01 2608108. MasterCard, Visa, Amex. **Directions:** Opposite Howth Yacht Club.

Howth
Deer Park Hotel & Golf Courses
HOTEL/RESTAURANT
Howth Co. Dublin **Tel: 01 832 2624**
Fax: 01 839 2405 Email: sales@deerpark.iol.ie

Set high up on the Hill of Howth, in the midst of Ireland's largest golf complex, the Deerpark Hotel enjoys wonderful views across Howth demesne (of which it is part) to the islands of Ireland's Eye and Lambay - and, on a clear day, right up the coast to the distant Mournes. Golf breaks are a particular attraction, especially in summer, and that guarantees that the hotel is always busy - also, perhaps, why it is so well-worn. However, although far from sumptuous, the hotel makes a comfortable base for anyone visiting the area and rooms have extra large beds, a sofa or armchairs and, in some cases, not just a kettle and tray for making drinks, but a kitchenette with fridge and toaster too. New rooms, an indoor swimming pool, sauna and steam room plus two all-weather tennis courts were recently added. Conference/banqueting (95/100) Parking. Children welcome (under 12s free in parentsí room; cots available). Wheelchair accessible. No pets. **Rooms 80** (all en-suite) B&B about €100. **Restaurant:** The restaurant is situated at the front of the hotel, with sea views and, although somewhat short on atmosphere, is well-appointed with comfortable chairs and white linen. Set 3-course lunch and dinner menus are not adventurous but are based on good ingredients, competently cooked and offer good value - starters can be quite impressive and,although main courses can be spoilt by unimaginative vegetables, steaks are a particularly good bet. * A newer Palm Tree Bistro also offers daytime food. **Seats 75** (private room, 60) L 12-2.30 & D 6-9.30 daily. Set L about €19. Set D about €28; house wine from about €14; sc 12.5%. Toilets wheelchair accessible. Hotel closed 23-27 Dec. Amex, Diners, MasterCard, Visa. **Directions:** Follow coast road from the city centre to Howth, on right before reaching Howth Harbour.

Howth
King Sitric Fish Restaurant & Accommodation
RESTAURANT/ACCOMMODATION
East Pier Howth Co. Dublin
Tel: 01 832 5235 Fax: 01 839 2442
Email: info@kingsitric.ie Web: www.kingsitric.com

Aidan and Joan MacManus' striking harbourside restaurant is named after an 11th century Norse King of Dublin. who had close links with Howth and was a cousin of the legendary Brian Boru. It is one of Dublin's longest established fine dining restaurants - and, from its East Pier site, chef-patron Aidan MacManus can keep an eye on his lobster pots in Balscadden Bay on one side and the fishing boats coming into harbour on the other. Recently completely re-built, this traditional restaurant has blossomed into a fine contemporary space, with first floor dining to take full advantage of the views (notably at lunch, which is especially good value too). Aidan's reputation for cooking seafood (and the excellent sauces that accompany) is of course what brings most people to The King Sitric, and lovers of game also wend their way to the east pier in winter, when it is likely to feature on both lunch and dinner menus. But wine interests Aidan MacManus every bit as much as food and he has long had one of the country's finest wine lists, with an especially fine selection of Chablis, magnificent burgundies and a special love of the wine of Alsace. Hence a very special feature of the newly reconstructed King Sitric: a temperature controlled wine cellar on the ground floor, where tastings are held. This was "Aidan's baby" during the planning of the new restaurant and is cleverly incorporated into the reception area, with only a glass door between them so diners can enjoy the ambience while having aperitifs, or spill over to use stools around the table in the cellar area if the restaurant is very busy. The house wine, Pinot Blanc Cuvée Les Amours Hugel (a special reserve for the King Sitric) is outstanding for both quality and value. The King Sitric received the guide's Wine List of the Year Award in 2001 and the restaurant operates a Food & Wine Club off-season. **Seats 70** (private room, 10/20) No smoking area. Air conditioning. L Mon-Fri,12.30-2.15; D 6.30-10.30 Mon-Sat. Set L from €19.05, set D from €43.18 and à la carte; house wine €18.41; sc discretionary. Toilets wheelchair accessible. Closed Christmas 3/4 days. **Accommodation** There are eight lovely rooms, all with sea views and individually designed bathrooms. **Rooms 8** (2 mini-suites, 1 for disabled, all no-smoking). B&B €60 pps, ss€25.40. Amex, MasterCard, Visa, Laser. **Directions:** All the way across the harbour front, top of the far east pier.

Howth
The Waterside & The Wheelhouse Restaurant
RESTAURANT/PUB Harbour Road Howth Co. Dublin **Tel: 01 839 0555** Fax: 01 839 3632

The ground floor of this attractive premises overlooking the harbourfront is one of the pleasantest bars in the area - well-run, comfortable and full of character. **Wheelhouse Restaurant** On the first floor over the Waterside, this is a friendly and welcoming restaurant, with a cosy ambience and moderately priced middle-of-the-road food. They offer a wide choice on menus that naturally include a large selection of local fish dishes - but they're also known for good steaks and meat dishes; specialities include rack of Kildare lamb with honey & mustard crust, so non-fish eaters will be well looked after too. First courses have been disappointing on recent visits, but main courses remain reliable. **Seats 60.** Air conditioning. D only (in restaurant) 6.30-10 daily. Bar Food served daily 12-8.30. Children welcome. Car parking nearby. Closed 25 Dec. Amex, Diners, MasterCard, Visa. Directions: On the harbour front.

Killiney

Fitzpatrick Castle Dublin

HOTEL

Killiney Co. Dublin **Tel: 01 230 5400** Fax: 01 230 5430
Email: dublin@fitzpatricks.com Web: www.fitzpatricks.com

Half an hour's drive from the city centre (at quiet times), this imposing castellated mansion overlooking Dublin Bay dates back to 1741. It is surrounded by landscaped gardens and, despite its size and grand style, has a relaxed atmosphere. Spacious bedrooms combine old-world charm with modern facilities and have recently been refurbished as part of a major programme that has also seen upgrading of some public areas, function and conference rooms and the leisure centre. The 'Crown Club', on the 5th floor functions as a 'hotel within a hotel', offering pre-arranged private transfer from the airport, private check-in and check-out, private Club lounge and a wide range of facilities for business guests including business support systems, ISDN lines, private email and internet facilities, voice-mail and hands-free phones, interactive digital TV and entertainment system. Five championship golf courses, including Druid's Glen, are nearby. Conferences/banqueting (500/400). Secretarial services. Business centre. Leisure centre; swimming pool. Disco. Children welcome (under 12s free in parents' room; cots available free of charge; crèche), but not in restaurant after 7.30. No pets. Garden. Lift. **Rooms 113** (7 suites, 2 junior suites, 38 executive rooms, 36 no-smoking). B&B €116 pps, ss €58; (room-only rate €160). Closed 24-27 Dec. P.J's Amex, Diners, MasterCard, Visa, Laser. **Directions:** take M50 from the Airport, follow signs for Dun Laoghaire Ferry Port.

Leixlip

Becketts Country House Hotel

HOTEL/RESTAURANT

Cooldrinagh House Leixlip Co. Dublin
Tel: 01 624 7040 Fax: 01 624 7072

A handsome house on the Co Dublin side of the river that divides Leixlip, Becketts is an unusual country house offering a special kind of service aimed specifically at business guests: from the moment you arrive a butler looks after all your needs, whether it be dining, laundry, limousine facilities or specific requirements for meetings or conferences. Imaginatively converted to its present use, luxurious accommodation includes four boardroom suites and six executive suites, all furnished to a high standard in a lively contemporary style. All have a workstation equipped for computers, including modem/internet connection and audio visual equipment, private fax machines etc are also available on request. Public areas, including a bar and a stylish modern restaurant, have a far less business-like atmosphere. Cooldrinagh House overlooks the Eddie Hackett-designed Leixlip golf course, for which golf tee off times may be booked in advance. Conference/banqueting (350/250) Business centre/secretarial services. Wheelchair accessible. No pets. **Rooms 10** (4 suites, 6 executive rooms) B&B about €70. Open all year. Directions: Take N4, turn off at Spa Hotel, next left after Springfield Hotel. Amex, Diners, MasterCard, Visa.

Lucan

Finnstown Country House Hotel

HOTEL

Newcastle Road Lucan Co. Dublin **Tel: 01 601 0700**
Fax: 01 628 1088 Email: manager@finnstown-hotel.ie Web: finnstown-hotel.ie

Very much the hub of local activities, this fine old manor house set in 45 acres of woodland is impressive, but also full of charm. A welcoming open fire in the foyer sets the right tone. All of the large, well-proportioned reception rooms - drawing room, restaurant, bar - are elegantly furnished in a traditional style well-suited to the house. Although quite grand, there is a comfortable lived-in feeling throughout. Bedrooms include studio suites, with a small fridge and toaster in addition to the standard tea/coffee making facilities, and all rooms have good facilities including full bathrooms (with bath and shower). Residential golf breaks are a speciality. Conference/banqueting (80/100) Business centre. Leisure centre. Swimming pool. Tennis, golf (9). Own parking. Wheelchair accessible. Children welcome (Under 3s free in parents' room; cots available). Pets permitted. **Rooms 51** (26 suites, 10 no-smoking, 1 for disabled) B&B about €102. Open all year Amex, Diners, MasterCard, Visa. **Directions:** Off main Dublin-Galway road (N4): take exit for Newcastle off dual carriageway.

Malahide

Beanos

RESTAURANT

On The Green Malahide Co. Dublin **Tel: 01 806 1880** Fax: 01 806 1881

Beanos opened in the late summer of 2001 and, although it may look like an uninspired office block from the road, the split level interior is pleasing - not least, perhaps, due to a good impression created by speedy and welcoming staff, but also because of the warmth given to otherwise sparse decor by a deep red used selectively in lights, carpet and a feature wall. A good few tables have views over the marina - those at the front of the upper level are best - and there's a long bar, with a patio area out at the back for sunny days. Menus are simple enough and appealingly informal, with sections given over to appetizers, salads and pasta, pizzas and grills - and a whole section on burgers - but this doesn't do the food justice: Beano's pizza, for example, is on a thin, crisp base topped with prawn tails, capers, red onion & tomato, while the grills are mainly seared dishes - tuna, salmon, fillet steak, chicken breast - attractively presented with roasted vegetables and interesting salads. Desserts tend towards the rich classics, like crème caramel, or there's an Irish cheeseboard to finish. The restaurant had not been open long when the guide visited, but prices were reasonable for the quality of food and service (average €60 per person for a 3-course meal with wine), making it one to watch. No smoking area; air conditioning. Not suitable for children after 6 pm. **Seats 200.** Open all day (12.30-10.30), L menu 12.30-6, D menu from 6pm. All à la carte. House wine from €16. SC discretionary. Closed 25 Dec. Amex, MasterCard, Visa, Laser. **Directions:** Facing Marina in Malahide Village.

Malahide

Bon Appetit

RESTAURANT

9 St James Terrace Malahide Co. Dublin **Tel: 01 845 0314**
Fax: 01 845 0314 Email: info@bonappetit.ie Web: www.bonappetit.ie

In a Georgian terrace near the marina, Patsy McGuirk's highly-regarded basement restaurant is enhanced by a collection of local watercolours and there's a welcome emphasis on comfort. The style tends to be classic French, sometimes tempered by Mediterranean and modern Irish influences; seafood, mostly from nearby Howth, predominates although steaks, Wicklow lamb, farmyard duckling and ostrich, which is farmed nearby, also feature. Fresh prawn bisque with cognac is a regular and a long-established house speciality is Sole Creation McGuirk (a whole boned black sole, filled with turbot and prawns, in a beurre blanc sauce - now a classic) while simple sole on the bone is presented whole at the table, then re-presented bone-free and neatly reassembled. Roast crispy duckling Grand Marnier on a potato & herb stufing is another speciality, also ostrich, which is farmed nearby. Pretty desserts: fresh strawberries in a crisp filo basket, sliced and sprinkled with Grand Marnier is typical, or there's an Irish cheese platter - and petits fours with your coffee. A fine wine list has its heart in France; there are helpful tasting notes and a special selection, as well as six fairly priced house wines. While not inexpensive, prices have held fairly steady at the Bon Appetit while many new restaurants in the Dublin area have launched at a high point; the set lunch menu is particularly good value. Children welcome. **Seats 60** (private room, 20) No smoking area. Air conditioning. L Mon-Fri12.30-2, D Mon-Sat 7-10.30; Set L €23, Set D €44, also à la carte; house wine from €17; sc discretionary. Closed Sun, bank hols & Christmas week. Amex, Diners, MasterCard, Visa, Laser. **Directions:** coming from Dublin go through the lights and turn left at the Garda Station into James Terrace.

Malahide

Cruzzo Bar & Restaurant

RESTAURANT

The Marina Malahide Co. Dublin **Tel: 01 845 0599**
Fax: 01 845 0602 Email: info@cruzzo.ie Web: www.cruzzo.ie

Built on a platform on columns over the water, this magnificent bar and restaurant is huge and stylish in Florida style, with views over the marina and a general feeling of glamour and pzazz. The interior is dashing, with a bar on the lower floor and a rather grand staircase rising to the main dining areas above, which are comfortable and well-appointed, with well-spaced tables in interesting groupings. Chef Tom Meenaghan, previously executive chef at Conran's Mezzo in London, presents contemporary menus with considerable style. Grilled red mullet with shaved fennel, orange & watercress sald or penne with herbs, cherry tomatoes & parmesan crackling are typical starters (about €6-8.50) while main courses might include a couple of imaginative vegetarian choices, seared tuna with pepper ragoût & basil aioli and fillets teak with black bean sauce, pickled ginger & spring onion salad; prices are in the €12-22 range, but vegetables are extra (from about €3.17 per portion). Service tends to be uneven; beware of having an aperitif in the downstairs bar on arrival - they do not appear to liaise with the restaurant staff and will not add drinks to your bill. **Seats 250.** A la carte L Mon-Fri & Sun,12.30-12.30 (Sun to 4.30); D Mon-Sat 6-10.30. early D Mon-Fri from €15,50 (6-7pm), set D from €23, D also à la carte. (Tue, special musical night, dinner & show €30.47 pp). House wine from €20. SC discretionary. Closed L Sat, L Sun, 25 Dec. Amex, MasterCard, Diners. **Directions:** from Malahide Village through arch into Marina.

Malahide

HOTEL

Grand Hotel

Malahide Co. Dublin **Tel: 01 845 0000**
Fax: 01 845 0987 Email: info@thegrand.ie

Just 8 miles from Dublin airport, and set in six acres of gardens, this large seaside hotel is well-situated for business and pleasure. Many of the bedrooms have sea views, the beach (tidal estuary) is just across the road and there are numerous golf courses nearby. Special breaks offered. Conference/banqueting (700/800) Business centre. Leisure centre (21 metre swimming pool, jacuzzi, gym). Tennis, golf (9/18) and fishing nearby. Own parking. Wheelchair accessible. Children welcome (under 12s free in parents' room; cots available). No pets. Lift. **Rooms 150** (7 suites, 2 mini-suites, 39 executive rooms, 15 shower only, 25 no-smoking, 1 for disabled) B&B about €125 pps. Closed 25-26 Dec. Directions: Centre of Malahide, 10 mins from Dublin Airport and 30 mins from Dublin city centre. Amex, Diners, MasterCard, Visa.

Malahide

RESTAURANT

Le Restaurant 12A

12A New Street Malahide Co. Dublin **Tel: 01 806 1928**
Email: jasonmccabe@ireland.com

This chic little restaurant in the centre of Malahide opened in 2001, a welcome newcomer to the growing cluster of interesting eating places in the town. Although not French-owned, it is in the contemporary French style - clean-lined, with crisp linen and fine modern crystal - with a menu in the window to entice you in. The menu is sensibly limited to a choice of around five to seven dishes on each course; on a late summer visit this included starters of rillette of pork & caramelised apple and marinated brochette of Dublin Bay prawns with a lime & rocket salad (the most expensive listed, at €10.79) and main courses of fresh loin of yellow fin tuna with niçoise salad and chargrilled fillet of beef bourguignonne style (the most expensive main course at €23.49). Vegetables are charged extra (€4.44 for a small selection), which makes the bill mount up rather alarmingly. Tempting desserts (all €6.35) might include a simple crumble like apple & blueberry, with vanilla ice cream or summer puding with fromage frais, or there's a European cheeseboad (€ 8.89). Accurate cooking, attractive presentation and friendly, willing service make for an enjoyable occasion, although the pricing structure makes it quite an expensive outing - a competitively priced early dinner menu would be an attraction. **Seats 46.** D only, Tue-Sun 6-10. A la carte. House wine €16. SC discretionary. Closed Mon, 3 weeks Jan. Amex, MasterCard, Visa, Laser. **Directions:** opposite Gibneys public house, Malahide.

Malahide

RESTAURANT

Les Visages Restaurant

9 Marine Court The Green Malahide Co. Dublin
Tel: 01 8451233 Fax: 01 8460892

Sinead McGowan's pleasant first-floor restaurant overlooks a little of the 'old Malahide' where small boats are beached alongside a couple of old cottages - a glimpse of life as it was here only a few years ago before the massive marina complex (which is inevitably also in view) changed Malahide for ever. Window tables are preferable, of course, but the restaurant is arranged to include convivial booths and all tables seem quite comfortable. A warm welcome and friendly, helpful service make a good start and the food - from menus which are imaginative but not over-ambitious - is generally of an admirably high standard. Air conditioning. **Seats 60.** D Tue-Sat, L Sun only No smoking area. Closed Christmas. **Directions:** Turn left at traffic lights in centre of Malahide, then right at next lights. Restaurant is on right on 1st floor.

Malahide

RESTAURANT

Siam Thai Restaurant

Gas Lane Malahide Co. Dublin **Tel: 01 845 4698**
Fax: 01 845 7178 Email: siames@eircom.net Web: www.siamthai.ie

Handily located in a laneway close to the marina, this large, well-appointed restaurant was well ahead of the wave of global and Pacific Rim restaurants that has hit the Dublin area recently and it is holding its own in the face of growing competition - helped, perhaps, by the presence of a Thai band 'Tropical Trio', which plays seven nights a week. Suracheto Yoodsang, head chef since 1996, presents menus that offer many of the Thai classics on an extensive à la carte as well as the set menus. Although perhaps blanded down a bit for local tastes, the balance of ingredients is 'true Thai' and there's a willingness to vary the spiciness according to personal preference. Siam Combination Appetizers (including chicken satay, spring rolls, special coated prawns, marinated pork ribs, prawns wrapped in ham and bags of golden wonton with plum sauce) make a good beginning, followed by main courses like Ghung Phad Phong Garee (Tiger prawns with scallions, mushrooms and basil leaves and a spicy sauce) and Ped Makham (succulent boneless crisp-skinned duck with crispy noodles and plum sauce). No monosodium glutamate is used. A sister restaurant, Siam Thai Restaurant, Monkstown, Co Dublin (Tel: 01 284 3308) is run on identical lines. Children welcome.No-smoking area; air conditioning. **Seats 96.** D 6-12 daily, Sun 5-10. Set D from €24.85; à la carte available, house wine €16.95, SC 10%. Closed 25-26 Dec & Good Fri . Amex, Diners, MasterCard, Visa, Laser. **Directions:** Turn left at Church to end of road.

Malahide

Silks

RESTAURANT

5 The Mall Malahide Co. Dublin **Tel: 01 845 3331**

This smart Chinese restaurant is spacious, modern and airy, with cheerful mustard seed yellow walls and staff who are friendly and helpful to match. Although the long menu offers no major surprises, but the food is well above average and shows some real imagination and flair. Sizzlers and sweet & sours are there, but they are expertly done using highest quality ingredients, especially the seafood. Excellent crispy Peking duck with pancakes or a light, delicately spiced chicken and mushroom broth make good starters followed, perhaps, by fresh-flavoured main courses of crunchy salt & chilli squid and prawns with ginger and spring onions. Cantonese-style chicken is a speciality dish worth looking out for: meltingly tender slices of chicken in a light, fruit-based sauce with just a hint of spiciness. Desserts are unsurprising but good - banana fritters with an above average vanilla ice cream, perhaps, or a simple bowl of lychees. Reservations are essential as this restaurant has a loyal following and they are busy every night of the week. **Seats 90.** Private room 20. No-smoking area. Air conditioning. D only, Mon-Sat 6-12.30; Sun 5-11.

Monkstown

Empress Restaurant

RESTAURANT

Clifton Avenue Monkstown Co. Dublin
Tel: 01 284 3200 Fax: 01 284 3188

Since opening in 1992 owner-chef Burt Tsang has built up a strong local following for this first-floor restaurant just off Monkstown Crescent. He offers regional Chinese dishes - Sichuan, Shandong and Beijing - plus Thai and Vietnamese cuisine, in set dinners for varying numbers in addition to an à la carte. Specialities include Beijing duck, carved at the table and served with fresh vegetables and hoi sin sauce on pancakes, which requires 24 hours notice. A good choice of vegetarian options is always available; typically Thai vegetable curries. Charming service. D 6-12 Mon-Sat; Sun open from 3pm. Directions: Just off the Crescent.

Monkstown

The Purty Kitchen

PUB/RESTAURANT

Old Dunleary Road Monkstown Co. Dublin **Tel: 01 284 3576**
Fax: 01 284 3576 Email: c-cm@iol.ie Web: purtykitchen.com

Established in 1728 - making it the second oldest pub in Dublin (after The Brazen Head) and the oldest in Dun Laoghaire - this attractive old pub has seen some changes recently, but its essential character remains and it's well set up for enjoyment of the bar food for which it has earned a good reputation. Ballymaloe-trained chef Sheenagh Toal took over as head chef in January 2001 so, although the old favourites like the famous Purty Kitchen seafood chowder and Purty fishcakes with tartare sauce are still there, there's been a move towards a fresher style in contemporary cooking that includes the likes of chargrilled ciabatta with melted mozzarelle & pesto dressing and prawns in crispy filo pastry with tomato & chilli mayonnaise alongside the more traditional dishes. More substantial dishes include 'all day breakfast', home-made beef burgers and baked black sole, on or off the bone, all at reasonable prices. Bar food 12.30-9.30pm daily. Amex, Diners, MasterCard, Visa, Laser.

Monkstown

Siam Thai

RESTAURANT

The Cresent Monkstown Co. Dublin **Tel: 01 284 3308**

See entry for Siam Thai, Malahide, North County Dublin.

Portmarnock
HOTEL

Portmarnock Hotel & Golf Links

Strand Road Portmarnock Co. Dublin **Tel: 01 846 0611**
Fax: 01 846 2442 Email: marketing@portmarnock.com Web: www.portmarnock.com

Originally owned by the Jameson family, Portmarnock Hotel and Golf Links enjoys a wonderful beachside position overlooking the islands of Lambay and Ireland's Eye. Very close to the airport, and only eleven miles from Dublin city centre, the hotel seems to offer the best of every world - the peace and convenience of the location and a magnificent 18 hole Bernhard Langer-designed links course. Public areas, including an impressive foyer, are bright and spacious, with elegant modern decor and a relaxed atmosphere. The Jameson Bar, in the old house, has character and there's also an informal Links Bar and Restaurant next to the golf shop (open 12-10 daily). Accommodation is particularly imaginative, designed so that all rooms have sea or golf course views. Sixty rooms have recently been refurbished and all - including some in the original house which are furnished with antiques, two suites with four-posters and private sitting rooms and executive rooms with balconies or bay windows - are furnished to a very high standard of comfort and have excellent bathrooms. Conference/banqueting (250/220) Business centre. Golf (18); garden. Children welcome, cots available. No pets. Lift. **Rooms 103** (2 suites, 14 executive, 6 no-smoking, 4 for disabled). B&B €140pps, ss €70. Open all year.

☆ **The Osborne Restaurant** Named after the artist Walter Osborne, who painted many of his most famous pictures in the area including the view from the Jameson house, the restaurant has been a major addition to the north Dublin dining scene since the hotel opened in 1996. The guide visited shortly after Stefan Matz, previously chef and co-owner of the highly-regarded Erriseask House Hotel in Connemara, joined the hotel as executive chef in May 2001 and, although not completely settled in at the time, his arrival is a great asset to the hotel. Signature dishes brought from Connemara, such as saddle of mountain lamb with roast garlic and fines herbes and fillet of beef freshly smoked on turf, enhance menus that make full use of local ingredients - especially seafood from the nearby fishing port of Howth - and a tempting 7-course Tasting Menu is cleverly devised to reduce to a 4-course Table'd'Hote. Luscious desserts include hot soufflés - dark chocolate and orange, perhaps, with vanilla ice cream - and an irresistible Dessert Suprise. Restaurant manager Martin Meade is a Powers Irish Coffee champion and enjoys laying on the spectacle that will finish your meal off with a flourish. No smoking area; air conditioning. **Seats 110** (private room, 20). D only Tues-Sat, 7-10.15. Set D €44.50, Tasting Menu €69.90. A la carte available; house wine from €18.73; no sc. Closed Sun, Mon. Amex, Diners, MasterCard, Visa, Laser. **Directions:** On the coast in Portmarnock.

Saggart
HOTEL

Citywest Hotel Conference Leisure & Golf Resort

Saggart Co. Dublin **Tel: 01 4010 500**
Fax: 01 4588 565 Email: info@citywesthotel.com Web: www.citywesthotel.com

Only about 25 minutes from the city centre and Dublin airport (traffic permitting), this large hotel was planned with the needs of the rapidly expanding western edge of the capital in mind and provides excellent conference and leisure facilities. It is set in its own estate, which includes two 18-hole Christy O'Connor Jnr. designed championship golf courses and a comprehensive leisure centre with a large deck level swimming pool and a wide range of health and beauty facilities. The other big attraction is the hotel's banqueting, conference and meeting facilities, which include a new state of the art convention centre catering for 4,000 delegates, making Citywest one of the largest venues in the country. All this, plus committed staff, a high standard of accommodation and a steady hand in the kitchen (head chef Derek McLoughlin has been with the hotel since 1995) make the hotel a fine amenity for west Dublin. Conference/banqueting (6,500/2,200); secretarial services, video-conferencing. Golf. Hairdressing/beauty salon. Children welcome (under 6s free in parents' room, cots available free of charge). Lift. **Rooms 332** (14 suites, 11 junior suites, 316 executive rooms). B&B €85pps. Closed 25 Dec. Amex, MasterCard, Visa, Laser. **Directions:** off Naas Road - N7.

Skerries

The Red Bank Restaurant & Lodge

RESTAURANT/GUESTHOUSE

7 Church Street Skerries Co. Dublin
Tel: 01 849 1005 Fax: 01 849 1598
Email: redbank@eircom.net Web: www.redbank.ie

There's a double-entendre to the name of Terry and Margaret McCoy's restaurant - there is a sandbank of the same name nearby, but it's also in a converted banking premises, which makes a restaurant of character and practicality - even the old vault had its uses: as a wine cellar. Margaret provides a warm welcome, serving aperitifs and crudités in an elegantly furnished bar/reception area and overseeing service in the comfortable, traditional restaurant (where smoking is only allowed if a private party takes over a room). One of the great characters of contemporary Irish cooking, Terry is an avid supporter of local produce and suppliers and fresh seafood from Skerries harbour provides the backbone of his menus, but without limiting the vision - this is a man who goes out at dawn with a bucket to gather young nettles for soup. Dishes conceived and cooked with generosity have names of local relevance - thus, for example, grilled goats cheese St Patrick is a reminder that the saint once lived on Church Island off Skerries. The dessert trolley is legendary (perhaps the traditional adjective 'groaning' should apply to the diners - a large space should be left if pudding is to be part of your meal). Should the sauces and accompaniments prove too much, plainly cooked food is gladly provided and dishes suitable for vegetarians are marked on the menu. No smoking area. **Seats 50.** D daily, 7-9.45; L Sun only, 12.30-4.30.Set D from €38, Set Sun L €24. A la carte also available. House wine €20; sc discretionary. Children welcome. Closed 24-25 Dec **Accommodation** As well as comfortably furnished bedrooms, there are facilities for meetings/small conferences. Gourmet golf breaks are a speciality. Children under 4 free in parents' room (cots available free of charge). **Rooms 12** (8 shower only, 7 no-smoking, 1 for disabled). B&B €47 pps, ss €13. Amex, Diners, MasterCard, Visa, Laser. **Directions:** opposite AIB Bank in Skerries.

Stillorgan

China-Sichuan Restaurant

RESTAURANT

4 Lower Kilmacud Road Stillorgan Co. Dublin
Tel: 01 288 4817 Fax: 01 288 0882

David and Julie Hui's unique restaurant runs in co-operation with the cultural exchange programme of the state-run China Sichuan Catering Service Company, which supplies chefs and special spices direct from Sichuan province. They have gained well-earned recognition for authentic oriental food and a refusal to 'bland-down' the style to suit local tastes. Spicy and chilli-hot dishes are identified on menus: 'Bon Bon Chicken' for example, is a dish of cold chicken shreds in a hot and spicy sauce, but spicing can be varied to suit individual tastes. While set menus are relatively limited (especially at lunch time), the à la carte offers plenty to tempt the most jaded palate. Children welcome before 8 pm. **Seats 60.** Air conditioning. L Mon-Fri 12.30-2.15, L Sun 1-2.30. D daily 6-11. Set L about €11, Set D about €26, à la carte available; house wine about €15; sc 10%. Toilets wheelchair accessible. Closed L Sat, 25-27 Dec & Good Fri. Directions: 5 miles south from city, through Stillorgan main road, turn right from Lower Kilmacud Road. Amex, MasterCard, Visa.

Stillorgan

Stillorgan Park Hotel

HOTEL/RESTAURANT

Stillorgan Road Stillorgan Co. Dublin
Tel: 01 288 1621 Fax: 01 283 1610
Email: sales@stillorganpark.com Web: www.stillorganpark.com

This hotel is notable for great improvements made in recent years and is furnished in a dashing modern style throughout. Public areas include the stylish reception and lounge areas and bedrooms - some with views of Dublin Bay - are spacious, attractively decorated in a contemporary style, with well-finished bathrooms. Ample parking is an attraction and facilities for business guests include work space and fax/modem lines in rooms. Conference/banqueting (600/420), video-conferencing, business centre, secretarial services. Children welcome (cots available). Pets by arrangement. **Rooms 135** (4 suites, 2 junior suites, 119 executive rooms, 20 no-smoking, 4 for disabled) Lift. B&B €97.50 pps, ss €72.50. SC incl. **The Purple Sage Restaurant** An attractive, informal restaurant with seating in several areas, the stylishly decorated Purple Sage certainly doesn't have that 'hotel dining room' atmosphere. Staff are welcoming and charming and menus are imaginative and appealing in the contemporary global style. Vegetarian dishes are especially tempting and the hotel regularly runs special themed dining weeks, including one when 'healthy options' are highlighted on the menu. The cooking is good and the real effort made to please and interest customers is commendable. Children welcome. **Seats 50.** No smoking area. Air conditioning. L & D daily, 12-2.30 & 5.45-9.30. Set L €23, Set D from €35; à la carte D available; house wine €18.50; sc discretionary. Amex, Diners, MasterCard, Visa, Laser. **Directions:** situated on main N11 Dual Carriageway.

Swords

Lukas Restaurant

RESTAURANT River Mall Main Street Swords Co. Dublin **Tel: 01 8409080/8409081**
Fax: 01 8409080 Email: bookings@lukas-swords.com Web: www.lukas-swords.com

Kate Gibbons' informal first-floor restaurant is an atmospheric little place serving youthful food, well cooked, attractively presented and at fairly reasonable prices. Ecelectic menus include quite a few pasta dishes, spicy ones - quesadillas, for instance, or chicken wings Tex-Mex style, and there are several Mexican/Cajun main courses as well as steaks and a list of daily blackboard specials. Popular desserts like tiramisu, banoffi and profiteroles are home-made and enjoyable. D daily 5.30-10.30 (Sun 5-10). A la carte. House wine €14.60. Closed 24-26 Dec & 1 Jan. MasterCard, Visa, Laser. **Directions:** just off Main Street on the river side.

Swords

The Old Schoolhouse

RESTAURANT Church Road Swords Co. Dublin **Tel: 01 840 2846**
Fax: 01 840 5060 Email: sinclair@gofree.indigo.ie

In a quiet riverside site close to the Northern Cross motorway, and only a short drive from the airport, this 18th century stone school building has been restored by the Sinclair family to make a attractive country-style restaurant. Major renovations recently saw the dining room restored to its original 20' height, and the garden and conservatory upgraded for al fresco dining. Personal service and good home cooking are the aims; all ingredients are locally sourced and fresh every day, which allows for a seasonal à la carte and table d'hôtet menus (plus daily blackboard specials which include a lot of seafood). A la carte menus offer starters such as Westport mussels with garlic, shallots and white wine and an unusual Old Schoolhouse-style chowder, with big chunks of fish, whole crab claws and generous juices rather than soup. Main courses include classics such as black sole on the bone meunière (faithfully rendered) and less usual options like wild boar with figs. Children welcome. **Seats 80** (private room, 10/20). No smoking area. Air conditioning. L daily 12.30-2.30 (Sun 1-3.30), D Mon-Sat 6.30-10.30. Set L €19 (Set Sun L €26). Early D €25 (Mon-Fri, 6.30-7.30); Set D €41; à la carte also available; house wine €210; sc discretionary. Closed D Sun, Christmas/New Year,bank hols. *Paparazzi Café (Tel 01 890 4233), on the main street in Swords, is a contemporary sister restaurant, offering modern menus all day (Sun-Wed 9.30am-10pm, Thu-Sat to 11.30). Amex, Diners, MasterCard, Visa, Laser. **Directions:** Coming from Dublin turn left after Lord Mayor's Pub.

CARLOW

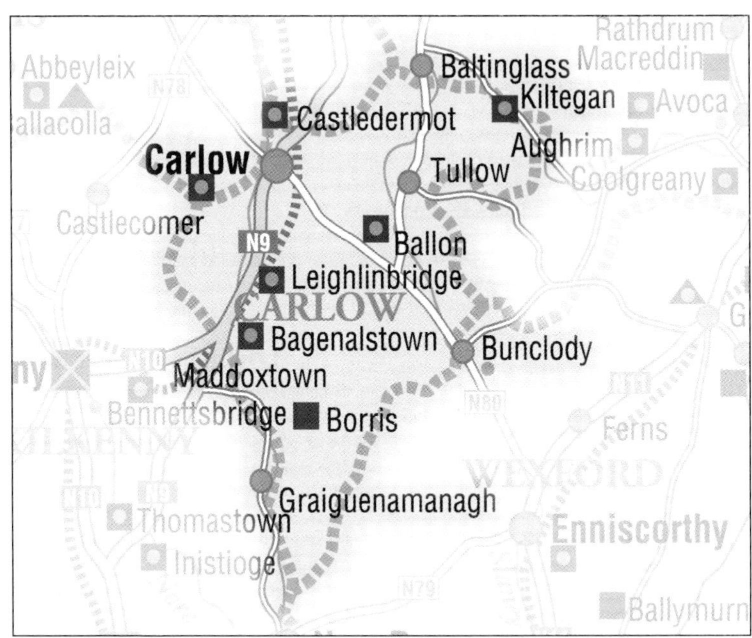

Surrounded by counties as famous as Kildare, Wicklow, Wexford and Kilkenny, Carlow is punching above its weight - and then some - in 2002. Although it is Ireland's second smallest county, it confidently incorporates such wonderful varieties of scenery that it has been memorably commented that the Creator was in fine form when He made this enchanting place. Whether you're lingering along the gentle meanderings of the waterway of the River Barrow, or enjoying the upper valley of the River Slaney while savouring the soaring lines of the Blackstairs Mountains as they sweep upwards to the 793 m peak of Mount Leinster, this gallant little area will soon have you in thrall.

There's history a-plenty if you wish to seek it out. But for those who prefer to live in the present, the county town of Carlow itself buzzes with student life and the energetic trade of a market centre, while a more leisurely pace can be enjoyed at riverside villages such as Leighlinbridge and Bagenalstown. The award-winning Leighlinbridge is the Gold Medallist for 2002 in the Entente Florale, the European floral decorations competition, and it's also Carlow's top-scoring community in the national Tidy Towns contest, so perhaps it's as well to know it's pronounced 'Lochlinbridge'. The neat little towns of Borris and Bagenalstown are charmers, yet they're among Ireland's better kept secrets - typical, in fact, of Carlow county, a place cherished by those who know it well.

Local Attractions and Information

Carlow town Tourist Information 0503 31554
Carlow county Carlow Rural Tourism 0503 30411/30446
Carlow Micro-brewery 0503 34356
Tullow Altamont Gardens 0503 59128

Bagenalstown

COUNTRY HOUSE

Kilgraney House

Bagenalstown Co Carlow **Tel: 053 75283** Fax: 0503 75595
Email: kilgraney@indigo.ie Web: www.kilgraneyhouse.com

Halfway between Carlow and Kikenny, Bryan Leech and Martin Marley's charming late Georgian house - which (encouragingly) takes its name from the Irish 'cill greíne', meaning 'sunny hill or wood' - is in a lovely site overlooking the Barrow Valley. Set in extensive wooded grounds that feature - amongst many other delights - a croquet lawn, fine cut-stone outbuildings (currently under renovation) and the kitchen garden that provides much that Bryan and Martin will transform into delicious dinners, in a contemporary style that also makes good use of other local and artisan produce. A typical summer menu might include baked St Tola goats cheese with a sun-dried tomato and basil pesto crust served with a mixed leaf garden salad, pea soup with fresh mint, baked breast of corn-fed chicken with leek and white carrot & tarragon wine sauce, a seasonal dessert and farmhouse cheeses - and your breakfast next morning will be worth allowing time to enjoy. But it is for the sheer sense of style pervading the house that it is most famous - the enjoyment that Bryan and Martin have derived from their dedication to its restoration and furnishing is abundantly clear: elegant, yes, but with a great sense of fun too. Dinner is normally served at a communal table; private dining on request. Self-catering accommodation is also available, in two courtyard suites and the gate lodge. Not suitable for small children. **Rooms 8** (2 suites, 3 shower only, all no smoking). No dogs. B&B €57.50, ss €20. Residents' D, 8 pm. Set 6-course D, €40. (Vegetarian meals on request.) Wine from about €20. Closed 1 Nov-1 Mar. Amex, MasterCard, Visa. **Directions:** Just off the R705,halfway between Bagenalstown and Borris.

Bagenalstown

Lorum Old Rectory

COUNTRY HOUSE

Kilgreaney Bagenalstown Co. Carlow **Tel: 0503 75282**
Fax: 0503 75455 Email: lorum@lorum.com Web: www.lorum.com

This historic country house is close to many places of interest, including medieval Kilkenny, Altamont Gardens, New Ross (where river cruises are available), Kildare's National Stud and Japanese Gardens. Also close by is Gowran Park racecourse and activities such as golf and a riding school (offering both outdoor and indoor tuition). Elegant, spacious and very comfortable accommodation includes a lovely drawing room for guests and a bedroom with a four-poster; all rooms have phones and tea/coffee trays. But it is Don and Bobbie Smith's hospitality that keeps bringing guests back. Euro-Toques member Bobbie prepares good home cooking based mainly on organic ingredients and dinner for residents is served at a long mahogany table (book by 3 pm). This relaxed place was the guide's Pet Friendly Establishment for 2000 and there are many interesting resident animals - so it is hardly surprising that this is a place where guests are welcome to bring their own dogs too, by arrangement. Not suitable for children. Private parties/small conferences (10). Own parking. **Rooms 5** (all en-suite). B&B €55 pps, ss €15. Dinner available for residents (except Sunday). Closed 15 Dec-1 Jan. MasterCard, Visa, Laser. **Directions:** 6 Km from Bagenalstown on the R705.

Ballon

Ballykealey Country House

HOTEL

Ballon Co. Carlow **Tel: 0503 59288**
Fax: 0503 59297 Email: bh@iol.ie Web: www.ballykealeyhouse.com

Seat of the Lecky family for three centuries, the present house was designed by Thomas A Cobden (designer of Carlow cathedral) and built in the 1830s as a wedding present. Gothic arches and Tudor chimney stacks take you back to the architectural oddities of the time, but the house is set in well-maintained grounds and has recently been extensively refurbished. Large, comfortably furnished reception rooms have a friendly atmosphere and quite impressive individually designed rooms are in keeping with the character of the house but with the necessary modern amenities, including direct-dial phones, tea/coffee trays and multi-channel TV. Small conferences (35), secretarial service; banqueting (200). No wheelchair access; not suitable for children under 12. No pets. **Rooms 12** (all non-smoking). B&B about €58pps, ss €25 +10% sc. Brontës Restaurant **Seats 38** (private room 25/30). D Tue-Sun. Closed 23 Dec-7 Feb. Amex, Diners, MasterCard, Visa. **Directions:** N80 South of Carlow, 10 miles on right.

Ballon

Sherwood Park House

COUNTRY HOUSE

Kilbride Ballon Co.Carlow **Tel: 0503 59117**
Fax: 0503 59355 Email: info@sherwoodparkhouse.ie Web: www.sherwoodparkhse.ie

Patrick and Maureen Owens, who have run this delightful Georgian farmhouse next to the famous Altamont Gardens since 1970, accurately describe it as "an accessible country retreat for anyone who enjoys candle lit dinners, brass and canopy beds and the relaxing experience of eating out while staying in". Spacious accommodation is furnished in period style and thoughtful in the details that count - and Maureen takes pride in offering guests real home cooking based on the best of local produce. Cots are available without charge and children under 3 may stay free in their parents' room. Dinner for residents is served at 8 pm and guests are welcome to bring their own wine. There's a lovely garden, and it's a good area for walking - and fishing the Slaney. Golf nearby. Private parties (max 14). (**Rooms 4**, all en-suite & no-smoking. B&B €40, ss €10. Open all year. Amex, MasterCard, Visa. **Directions:** Drive to junction N80/N81. Signed from there.

Borris

ACCOMMODATION

The Step House

66 Main Street Borris Co. Carlow
Tel: 0503 73209 Fax: 0503 73395

Cait Coady's attractive old house has undergone extensive renovation and has been stylishly decorated and furnished in period style, with antiques throughout. Well-proportioned reception rooms include a fine dining room (used for breakfast); a matching drawing room that overlooks the back garden (which is still being developed) and a putting green. Comfortable, elegant bedrooms are furnished to a high standard and have TV and tea/coffee facilities. A great deal of commitment is evident in the ongoing renovation and upgrading of this fine old house, including the recent conversion of the whole of the lower ground floor making a magnificently characterful kitchen and living room area with direct access to the garden. The Coadys also own the bar next door and also one of Ireland's finest classic pubs, Tynans Bridge Bar, in Kilkenny city. NB - there are several flights of stairs, including steps up to the front door. Not suitable for children. Pets permitted in some areas by arrangement. **Rooms 5** (all no-smoking, 4 shower only). B&B about €32pps. Closed 20 Dec-16 Mar. MasterCard, Visa. **Directions:** From main Carlow-Kilkenny road, take turning to Bagnelstown.

Carlow

GUESTHOUSE

Barrowville Townhouse

Kilkenny Road Carlow Town Co. Carlow **Tel: 0503 43324**
Fax: 0503 41953 Web: www.barrowvillehouse.com

Ex-hoteliers Marie and Randal Dempsey have run this exceptionally comfortable and well-managed guesthouse just a few minutes walk from the town centre for ten years. Although immaculately maintained the house is old, so bedrooms vary in size and character, but all are comfortable and attractively furnished with a mixture of antiques and fitted furniture, plus direct dial phones, tea/coffee trays and TV. Good housekeeping and generous, thoughtfully designed and well-finished bathrooms contribute greatly to a generally high standard of comfort. Marie Dempsey is renowned for excellent breakfasts served in a handsome conservatory (complete with a large vine) overlooking the lovely back garden. There is also a particularly pleasant and comfortable residents' drawing room, with an open fire, grand piano and plenty to read. Barrowville was the guide's Guesthouse of the Year for 2000. Private parking. Not suitable for childen under 15. No pets. **Rooms 7** (2 shower only, all no-smoking). B&B €35pps, ss €10. Open all year. Amex, MasterCard, Visa. **Directions:** Southside of Carlow Town on the N9.

Carlow

RESTAURANT

The Beams Restaurant

59 Dublin Street Carlow Co Carlow **Tel: 0503 31824**

Originally a coaching inn, this characterful building was restored by Betty and Peter O'Gorman, who opened it as a restaurant in 1986. Massive wooden beams create a warm atmosphere and are a reminder of the building's long history (it has held a full licence since 1760) and, although there are some eccentricities about the restaurant and the way it is run, the essentials are right and many of the country's trendy young restaurateurs would do well to come and learn some basics here. Classic French cuisine is the speciality of French chef Romain Chall, who has been at The Beams since it opened and was deservedly described by the late Peter O'Gorman as a "master craftsman". He has established a reputation for fine fare, including game in season and fish cooked with admirable simplicity; house specialities include filled pancakes (a favourite starter), a terrine based on local black pudding and home-made ice creams.Vegetarian dishes regularly feature on the menu (seasonal vegetables, many of them home grown, are a delight) and any special dietary requirements can be met at a day's notice. **Seats 40**, D only Tue-Sat 7.30-9.30 pm (Sat to 10 pm); D about €32; no s.c. Closed Sun & Mon, bank hols, Christmas wk & 1 wk July. MasterCard, Visa. **Directions:** Town centre, on main street.

Carlow

PUB/CAFÉ

Lennon's Café Bar

121 Tullow Street Carlow Co. Carlow **Tel: 0503 31575**

Sinead O'Byrne, who previously worked at Bord Bia's Food Centre, opened this attractive modern café-bar with her husband in the summer of 2000 and its stylish contemporary design and good, reasonably priced food has clearly been a hit with the local student population. In a manner reminiscent of that great Kerry speciality, the pub that gradually develops into a restaurant at the back without actually having a dedicated restaurant area, the design of the bar - which has striking metal spiral staircase at the back - helps the atmosphere to shift into café gear as you move through it. Simple, uncluttered tables and speedy service of jugs of iced water bode well for menus that include well-made soups, open sandwiches (on good home-made bread) ciabattas and wraps, some very tempting salads and a range of hot specials like baked cod with pesto crust served with basil mash & salad or roasted vegetable tart with tossed salad. Vegetarian dishes are highlighted on the menu, some local sources are credited, food is fresh and well-presented and, with main courses averaging around €7, prices are very accessible: a winning formula. Leave room for delicious desserts - hazelnut meringue roulade with raspberry sauce, perhaps, or chocolate cake with chocolate sauce. Food available Mon-Fri,12-3 & Sat 12-4.

Leighlinbridge

The Lord Bagenal Inn

PUB/HOTEL/RESTAURANT Main Street Leighlinbridge Co. Carlow **Tel: 0503 21668**
Fax: 0503 22629 Email: info@lordbagenal.com Web: www.lordbagenal.com

The Lord Bagenal is beautifully situated on the River Barrow and it's a useful place to break a journey or, now that accommodation has been added, as a base for exploring this fascinating area - there's a very pleasant riverside walk nearby and recent developments include a new harbour right beside the inn. Although now more of an hotel than the pub that is fondly remembered by many regular patrons, proprietors James and Mary Kehoe have taken care to retain some of the best features of the old building - notably the old end bar, with its open fire and comfortably traditional air and the restaurant section beside it - while incorporating many interesting new ideas. (The most novel is a supervised indoor playroom, which is in the bar but behind glass so that, in time-honoured fashion, offspring can be seen and not heard.) The new bar arrangement includes a lunchtime carvery/buffet which has been disappointing on several recent visits and nowhere near the quality that earned the Lord Bagenal a fine reputation over the past 20 years. (A second carvery is due to be completed shortly after publication and an 'all day breakfast' is available on Sundays from 8am.) However, choices from afternoon and evening bar menus (available 3-6pm and 6-10pm) may be better. But it is the restaurant that draws serious diners, from a wide area, notably anyone with an interest in wine, as James Kehoe's dedication and flair have resulted in a list that is renowned throughout the country. Well-balanced seasonal dinner and à la carte menus offered each evening are based on well-sourced produce such as Dunmore East seafood and local farmhouse cheeses; the style is fairly robust modern Irish, interpreted with due regard for country appetites. The spacious new bedrooms are comfortably furnished in a neutral "hotel" style with phones, TV and tea/coffee facilities and there is growing emphasis on meetings and conferences. There are several golf courses within a short drive (including Mount Juliet), and a nearby equestrian centre (Carlow Farmers Hunt meets weekly in season and hire of horses can be aranged); fishing boats also for hire. Marina (30 berths). Conferences/ banqueting 250. Garden, fishing, walking, playroom. Children welcome; no perts. **Rooms 12** (all en-suite, 1 for disabled) B&B from £40 pps, ss £12. Meals avilable from 8 am, L 12-2.30, D 6-9.30/10pm; à l carte. House wine £12.95. Bar food 10 am-9.30/10 pm daily, carvery 12-2.30 pm daily. Closed 25/26 Dec. Amex, Diners, MasterCard, Visa, Laser. **Directions:** Just off the main N9 Dublin/Waterford Road in Leighlinbridge. 8 miles Carlow/20 miles Kilkenny.

CAVAN

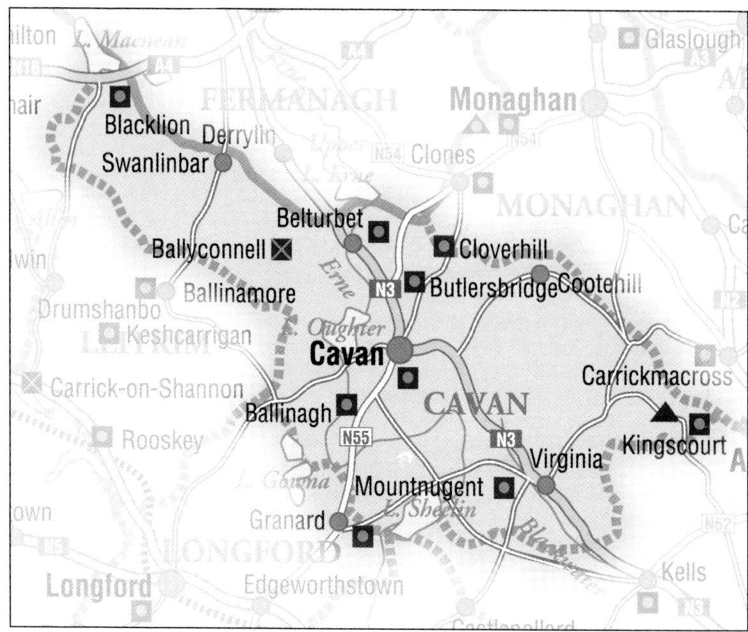

In its quiet way, lake-studded Cavan is one of Ireland's most watery counties. And as the county's main roads have naturally followed the easiest routes through the least resistant territory along the lake shores, most visitors have an abiding impression of Cavan as a place of low-lying rounded little hills, intertwined with many lakes and rivers. Certainly much of the county is classic drumlin country, almost with more water than they know what to do with.

But the very fact that the meandering waterways restrict the roads means that much of Cavan is hidden. In 2002, this is a virtue. It is a place best discovered by the discerning visitor. Much of it has quiet and utterly rural charm, seemingly remote - yet it isn't so very far from Dublin.

So if you take your time wandering through this green and silver land - particularly if travelling at the leisurely pace of the deservedly renowned Shannon-Erne Waterway which has joined Ireland's two greatest lake and river systems - then you'll become aware that this is a place of rewardingly gentle pleasures. And you'll have time to discover that it does have its own mountain, or at least it shares the 667 m peak of Cuilcagh with neighbouring Fermanagh.

In fact, Cavan is much more extensive than is popularly imagined, for in the northeast it has Shercock with its own miniature lake district, while in its southeast it takes in all of Lough Ramor at the charming lakeside village of Virginia. It also shares Lough Sheelin, that place of legend for the angler, with Westmeath and Meath, and always throughout its drumlin heartlands you can find many little Cavan lakes which, should the fancy take you, can be called your own at least for the day that's in it.

Local Attractions and Information

Bailieboro, Tourism Information	042 9666666
Ballyjamesduff, Cavan County Museum	049 8544070
Ballyjamesduff, International Pork Festival (June)	049 8544242
Belturbet, Tourist Office	049 9522044
Cavan town, Cavan Crystal	049 4331800
Cavan town, Tourist Information	049 4331942
Cootehill, Maudabawn Cultural Centre	049 5559504
Killykeen, Equestrian Centre	049 4361707

Ballinagh
GUESTHOUSE

Lacken Mill House & Gardens

Lacken Lower Ballinagh Co Cavan **Tel: 049 4337 592 - 049 4367 933**
Fax: 049 4337 592 - 049 4367 933
Email: info@lackenmillhouse.com Web: www.lackenmillhouse.com

A reader's email led us to this restored Victorian millhouse set in gloriously unspoilt rolling countryside in a little known area about seven miles from Cavan town. To say that the restoration of the house - and, even more so perhaps, the gardens and woodland areas alongside the river - has been a labour of love for Dubliners Eamon O'Donoghue and Naoimi Brennan since they purchased the derelict property several years ago is, if anything, an understatement. Their achievement is remarkable, especially as they not only remain sane but are relaxed and hospitable hosts to those lucky enough to find their home. Welcoming log fires are a feature of this warm and comfortable house (fuel is not in short supply) and the dining room, where both breakfast and evening meals are served, opens onto a patio and gardens: magic in fine weather. Spacious individually decorated bedrooms have well-finished shower rooms (there is also a luxurious bathroom, which any guest may use) tea/coffee trays, direct dial phones and TV (fax facility and iron available on request). Behind the house, the ruins of a corn and flax mill are still standing and awaiting restoration, but extensive areas of woodland have already been cleared to make long walks (there are even hammocks dotted around, should you feel the need of a rest) and the river and its wildlife provide endless interest. Many guests never feel the need to wander, but restless souls will find plenty of other activities nearby, including fishing, golf and horseriding. Children welcome (under 2s free in parents' room, cot available without charge). Dogs allowed in some areas. **Rooms 5** (all shower only); room service avalable on request. B&B €38pps, ss €7. Closed 19-28 Dec. MasterCard, Visa. **Directions:** N3 to Cavan, N55 to Ballinagh & follow signs 2.5 miles.

Ballyconnell
PUB/RESTAURANT/ACCOMMODATION

Angler's Rest

Main Street Ballyconnell Co. Cavan
Tel: 049 952 6391 Email: bycl@iol.ie

Golf, fishing, walking and cycling are among the pursuits that attract visitors to this lovely lakeland area and Francis McGoldrick's characterful pub makes an inexpensive and welcoming base for a relaxing stay. Modest accommodation is comfortable, staff hospitable and the bar has spirit - a real inn, in fact. There's a pleasantly informal restaurant at the back of the bar and, as the proprietor is also the chef, you can be sure of consistency in the kitchen. Live music some evenings (inquire for further details.) Children welcome; under 6s free in parents' room, cot available free of charge. Garden. **Rooms 8** (all with en-suite shower) B&B €30 pps, ss €10. Bar Food served 6-9 daily, L Sun 12.30-2.30 pm. Closed 25 Dec & Good Fri. MasterCard, Visa. **Directions:** on N3 Main Street in Ballyconnell village.

Ballyconnell
RESTAURANT

Polo D Restaurant

Main Street Ballyconnell Co. Cavan **Tel: 049 952 6228**

Owner-chef Paul O'Dowd's cottagey little restaurant consists of two small rooms on two floors with the country character of stripped pine, old brick and stonework - all of which suit its daytime persona, when informal light meals are served. But Paul's talents really come into play at dinner time, when he presents imaginative contemporary menus - typically a trio of seafood with prawn & vermouth sauce, crispy duck with mango & peach sauce and an accomplished dessert selection - all cooked with a flair and confidence. Low-key surroundings (quite a squeeze and cutlery wrapped in paper napkins) are more than offset by reasonable prices, and friendly, helpful service, making this a very welcome addition to dining options in the area. Children welcome. Wheelchair accessible. **Seats 40.** Light meals all day; L 12-3pm, D 6-10pm Mon-Sat. Set D about €32, early menu about €20 (5-7pm), also à la carte; house wine about €16. Closed Sun. MasterCard, Visa.

Ballyconnell
HOTEL

Slieve Russell Hotel & Country Club

Ballyconnell Co Cavan **Tel: 049 952 6444**
Fax: 049 9526474 Email: slieve-russell@quinn-hotels.com

Close to the attractive town of Ballyconnell, this striking flagship of the Sean Quinn Group is named after a nearby mountain and set amongst 300 acres of landscaped gardens and grounds, including 50 acres of lakes. Everything is on a generous scale - and it's very much the social and business centre of the area. In the foyer, generous seating areas are arranged around the marble colonnades and a grand central staircase, flanked by a large bar on one side and two restaurants at the other. All bedrooms have pleasant country views, extra large beds and spacious marble bathrooms as well as the usual amenities (direct dial, phone tea/coffee tray,TV, trouser press). Excellent conference and business facilities are matched by leisure facilities in the Golf and Country Club - the championship golf course, which opened in 1992, has become one of the top golfing venues in Ireland and there's a putting green, practice area and nine hole, par 3 course. Off-season value breaks. Children under 3 free in parents' room, cot available free of charge; crèche.Conference/banqueting (800/500); video-conferencing. Leisure centre. Golf, tennis, snooker, garden. Hairdresser. No pets. Lift. **Rooms 151** (10 suites, 3 mini-suites, 3 for disabled) B&B from about €100 pps, ss about €25. Open all year. Amex, Diners MasterCard, Visa. **Directions:** take N3 from Dublin to Cavan, go to Belturbet and Ballyconnell.

Belturbet

Erne Bistro

RESTAURANT/PUB

The Lawn Belturbet Co Cavan **Tel: 049 952 2443**

This well established restaurant and lounge bar is near the bridge over the River Erne and handy to the Emerald Star marina. Past a welcoming reception area with fresh flowers, there's a door to the comfortable bar and another takes you through to the restaurant, which is in two connecting rooms. Busy decor and friendly staff give it a warm ambience and it's an idea to order an aperitif quickly to allow the time required to consider an exceptionally long à la carte menu reminiscent of the '70s and early '80s, which may send out warning signals as short menus tend to be a good sign. But this is the exception that proves the rule, as everything is very well done in classic style - for example, a random choice from a selection of no less than seven soups offered showed that the basics are in place, and good home-made bread is served with it. Salads are well-dressed, with generous quantities of crab, prawns, or whatever and home-made paté arrives with both warm toast and brown bread. Ingredients are well-sourced and main course specialities include old favourites - tournedos chasseur, darne of salmon on a bed of fresh spinach, roast duckling and black sole are all typical. Christmas Day Luncheon (2 sittings) and New Year Gala Dinner are much in demand. Special menus are available for private parties. Taxi service available. Live music (occasional). No-smoking restaurant. Not suitable for children after 8pm. **Seats 80** (private room, 40). D daily in summer, 7-11(Sun to 10), L Sun only 1-3. All à la carte. Closed Mon off-season (Oct-Mar). MasterCard, Visa, Laser. **Directions:** at Bottom of Bridge Street Belturbet.

Belturbet

International Fishing Centre

RESTAURANT/GUESTHOUSE

Loughdooley Belturbet Co. Cavan **Tel: 049 952 2616**

Fax: 049 952 2616 Email: michelneuville@eircom.net Web: www.angling.holidays.com

At this lovely waterside location, Michel and Yvette Neuville offer residential fishing holidays, mainly for continental guests although B&B is available when there is room and there's also a restaurant which is open to non-residents. The centre is like a little corner of France, with all signage in French, and neatly manicured lawns sweeping down to the river where, in typical French style, the menu is clearly displayed. When the weather allows, tables are set out on the terrace. Not suitable for children under 10. As well as attracting local diners, the restaurant provides an excellent facility for holidaymakers on river cruises, as there are pontoons at the bottom of the garden. A very French set menu is accompanied by a much longer wine selection (in French francs at the time of going to press, although it will presumably be in Euros in 2002) - and a refreshingly reasonable bill. **Restaurant: Seats 80** Max preferred table size 8, (Private Room, 30). Set D 6-10pm daily, about €19. **Accommodation: Rooms 16** (all en-suite). No pets. €30.09 pps, svce incl; no ss. Open all year. MasterCard, Visa.

Blacklion

MacNean House & Bistro

RESTAURANT ☆ féile bia
ACCOMMODATION

Main Street Blacklion Co. Cavan
Tel: 072 53022 Fax: 072 53404

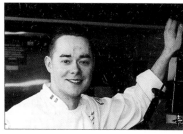

Nearby attractions include Marble Arch Caves and Florence Court, golf, fishing and hill walking - but it is Neven Maguire's cooking that has put this little border town firmly on the culinary map. Since winning the Baileys Euro-Toques Young Chef competition in 1994 - with a prize giving him experience in a famous Luxembourg restaurant - Neven's cooking moved into the international class, culminating in his selection to represent Ireland at the world's most prestigious (although, perhaps, dated) cooking competition, the Bocuse d'Or, in 2001. Here, in a small and distinctly low-key family restaurant, this delightful and utterly dedicated young chef sources the best local produce and prepares menus that reflect international trends rather than local preferences. Local lamb, beef, duck, guinea fowl, quail, scallops, langoustine ("Dublin Bay Prawns"), cod, halibut and organic produce from nearby Eden Plants are typical and the choice is extraordinarily wide (and perhaps sometimes over-ambitious) for a small establishment. The range of menus offered is amazing: in addition to a fine table d'hôte at and an extensive à la carte, Neven offers a number of others including a fish tasting menu, a 6-course 'surprise' menu and a vegetarian menu. His dedication comes through in cooking of the highest order, although presentation is sometimes a little over-worked - reflecting, perhaps, the demands of competitions. Desserts have always been a particular passion for Neven and it's a must to leave a little room for one of his skilfully crafted confections - the grand finale is just that in this case. Sunday lunch somehow combines elements of the traditional meal with more adventurous choices - and very good value at €21. Friendly service, by family members, has become much more professional recently and, as we go to press (autumn 2001), there are plans to re-style the dining room. This could make a big difference to the dining experience, as the setting has seemed increasingly at odds with Neven's exceptional cooking. Not suitable for children after 8 pm. No-smoking restaurant. **Seats 40.** D Wed/Thu-Sun 6-10pm (Sun to9.30); L Sun only, 12.30-3.30. Set D, €44, Vegetarian Menu €32; other menus available, also à la carte. House wine from €16. Service discretionary. **Accommodation: Rooms 5** (all en-suite, 2 shower only). €33 pps, s.€36. Direct-dial phone, tea/coffee tray & TV in all rooms. Children under 3 free in parents' room; cot available free of charge. No pets. Closed Mon, Tue in Summer, also Wed in winter, 1 week Christmas, 1 week Oct. Mac Nean Bistro MasterCard, Visa. **Directions:** on N17, main Belfast-Sligo Road.

Cavan

Hotel Kilmore

HOTEL féile bia

Dublin Road Cavan Co. Cavan **Tel: 049 433 2288**
Fax: 049 433 2458 Email: kilmore@quinn-hotels.com Web: www.quinnhotels.com

The leading hotel of the area, the Kilmore has an impressive foyer and spacious public rooms and it's the focal point of local business and social activities - also a pleasant place to break a journey. Bedrooms, which include a bridal suite, have been recently refurbished and are well-equipped with direct dial phones, TV, tea/coffee trays and trouser press. Business centre, secretarial services, video conferencing. Garden. Leisure activities nearby include golf, fishing and horse-riding. Conference/banqueting (600/500) Children welcome (under 2s free in parents' room, cot available without charge). No pets. **Rooms 39** (2 mini-suites, 37 executive, 2 rooms for disabled). Open all year. B&B €55pps, ss €16. Amex, Diners MasterCard, Visa. **Directions:** on N3,3km outside Cavan town.

Cavan

Lifeforce Mill

CAFÉ/RESTAURANT

Mill Rock Cavan Co. Cavan **Tel: 049 436 2722** Fax: 049 436 2923

The Lifeforce Mill dates back to 1846 and, although the commercial milling operation closed down in the 1950s, it is now enjoying a new lease of life welcoming visitors and producing Lifeforce Stoneground Wholemeal Flour. All of the original machinery has been restored to working order, including what is believed to be the only working McAdam Water Turbine. Designed by Belfast engineer Robert McAdam, the turbine was used to harness the power of the Kennypottle River and drive the great stone wheels instead of the usual, but slower and less efficient, water wheel. The innovative mill tour allows visitors to experience the end result as well as learning about the workings of the mill itself: each visitor makes a loaf of traditional soda bread with the stoneground flour produced by the mill at the beginning of the tour and collects it, hot from the ovens of the coffee shop, on leaving. Wholesome fare is served in the coffee shop/restaurant - which also has a tale to tell. Although Victorian, it is not part of the original mill site - it was transported from Drogheda to avoid demolition during road improvements, then re-erected beside the mill. Not suitable for very small children (under 2). **Restaurant Seats 65,** Tue-Sat all day, 9-5. Toilets wheelchair accessible. Closed Mon & 24 Dec-7 Jan. MasterCard, Visa. **Directions:** signed in the centre of Cavan town.

Cloverhill

The Olde Post Inn

RESTAURANT/PUB/ACCOMMODATION

Cloverhill Cavan Cloverhill Co. Cavan
Tel: 047 55555 Fax: 047 55111 Email: oldepostinn@eircom.ie

This old stone building in a neatly landscaped garden served as a post office until 1974 and now makes an attractive inn. There's a proper bar to enjoy your pre/post-prandial drinks and the restaurant is furnished in an appropriately old-world style, with bare walls and beams, country furniture - comfortably rustic. Friendly, efficient service, imaginative menus and sound cooking, in a contemporary Irish style, make for an enjoyable dining experience. Local produce features strongly - typically locally farmed venison and duckling (a speciality - maple-roasted with potato & thyme stuffing and a wild berry sauce, perhaps). Accommodation is reasonably comfortable, although not as luxurious as the brochure implies. Ample parking. Wheelchair access (restaurant/ground floor only). Children welcome. **Restaurant Seats 70** Private room (25); no smoking area. D 6.30-9.30 (daily Mar-Sep) Set D about €35; also à la carte. L Sun only, from 12.30. **Rooms 6** (all en-suite, 2 shower only), B&B about €40 pps, ss about €6.50. 1 family room; children free in parents' room up to 12. No pets. Closed D Sun, all Mon & 2 wks Feb. MasterCard, Visa. **Directions:** 5 miles North of Cavan town, on M54 to Monaghan.

Kingscourt

HOTEL

Cabra Castle Hotel & Golf Club

Kingscourt Co. Cavan **Tel: 042 966 7030**
Fax: 042 966 7039 Email: cabrach@iol.ie Web: www.cabracastle.com

Formerly known as Cormey Castle and renamed Cabra Castle in the early 19th century, this impressive hotel is set amidst 100 acres of garden and parkland, with lovely views over the Cavan countryside, famous for its lakes and fine fishing. (The nearby Dun A Ri Forest has many walks and nature trails on land once part of the Cabra estate.) Although initially imposing, with its large public rooms and antique furnishings, the atmosphere at Cabra Castle is relaxing. Due to the age of the building, the bedrooms vary in size and outlook, but all are comfortable and individually decorated. Accommodation includes some ground floor rooms suitable for less able guests and, in addition to rooms in the main building, the newer rooms in an extension are particularly suitable for families. There are also some romantic beamed rooms, in a courtyard that has been converted to provide modern comforts without sacrificing character. The combination of formal background and easy ambience make this a good venue for private and business functions; it is popular for both weddings and conferences. Conferences/banqueting (200/350). Garden, golf (9), fishing. Off-season value breaks. Children welcome (under 3s free in parents' room, cots available without charge); pets permitted by arrangement. **Rooms 80** (2 suites, 2 junior suites, 8 executive rooms, 2 for disabled). B&B €89pps, ss €19. Closed 24-26 Dec. Amex, MasterCard, Visa, Laser. **Directions:** Dublin - N2 - Navan - R162 - Kingscourt.

Kingscourt

PUB

Gartlans Pub

Main Street Kingscourt Co Cavan **Tel: 042 966 7003**

This pretty thatched pub is a delightfully unspoilt example of the kind of grocery/pub that used to be so typical of Ireland, especially in country areas. Few enough of them remain, now that the theme pub has moved in, but this one is real, with plenty of local news items around the walls, a serving hatch where simple groceries can be bought, all served with genuine warmth and hospitality. The Gartlans have been here since 1911 and they have achieved the remarkable feat of appearing to make time stand still. Closed 25 Dec & Good Fri.

Mountnugent

COUNTRY HOUSE

Ross House & Castle

Mountnugent Co. Cavan
Tel: 049 854 0218 Fax: 049 854 0218
Email: rosshouse@eircom.net Web: www.ross-house.com

In mature grounds on the shores of Lough Sheelin, Peter and Ulla Harkort's old manor house enjoys a very lovely location and offers a good standard of accommodation at a modest price. Bedrooms, which are distinctly continental in style, have telephone, TV and tea/coffee trays and some unusual features: three have their own conservatories, four have fireplaces (help yourself to logs from the shed) and most have unusual continental style showers. Peace and relaxation are the great attraction, and there's a fine choice of activities at hand: a pier offers boats (and engines) for fishermen to explore the lake, there's safe bathing from a sandy beach, tennis and a sauna. At the castle nearby, Peter and Ulla's daughter Viola Harkort provides most unusual accommodation (it is a very real castle) and organises pony trekking and horse-riding. Ulla cooks for everyone, making packed lunches, sandwiches and High Tea (€4/14)) and a 4-course dinner (€20). Equestrian, fishing, tennis. Sauna, jacuzzi. Children and pets welcome. **Rooms 6** (all en-suite, 5 shower only). B&B from €35 pps, ss €13. Open all year. MasterCard, Visa. **Directions:** 5km from Mountnugent, well signposted.

COUNTY CLARE

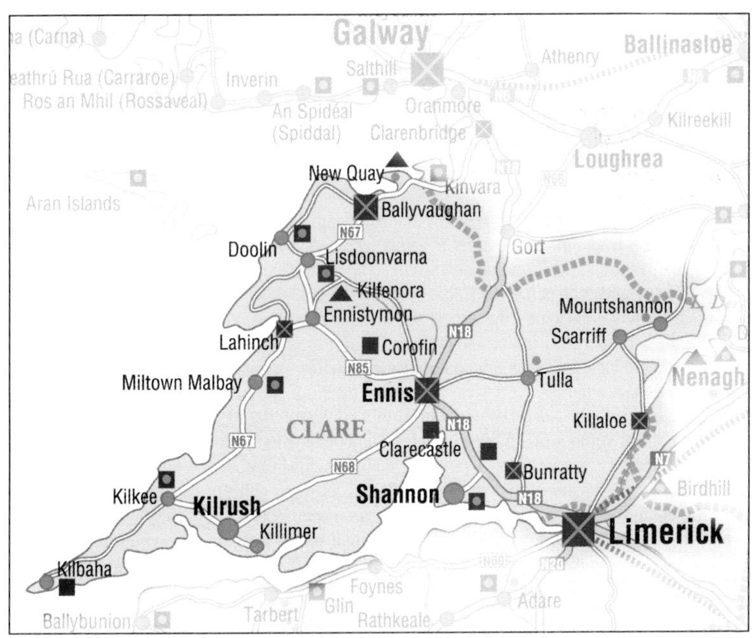

Clare is a larger-than-life county which is bounded by the Atlantic to the west, Galway Bay to the north, the Shannon and Lough Derg to the east, and the Shannon Estuary to the south. And it's typical of Clare that, even with its boundaries marked on such a grand scale, there is always something extra added. Thus the Atlantic coasts include not only the astonishing and majestic Cliffs of Moher, but also one of Ireland's greatest surfing beaches at Lahinch on Liscannor Bay. As for that Galway Bay coastline, it is where The Burren, the fantastical North Clare moonscape of limestone which is home to so much unexpectedly exotic flora, comes plunging spectacularly towards the sea around the attractive village of Ballyvaughan.

To the eastward, Lough Derg is one of Ireland's most handsome lakes, but even amidst its generous beauty, we find that Clare has claimed one of the most scenic lake coastlines of all. As for the Shannon Estuary, well, Ireland may have many estuaries, but needless to say the lordly Shannon has far and away the biggest estuary of all.

A mixture of old and new adds to Clare's attraction. As 2002 gets into its stride, the county town of Ennis continues to celebrate the announcment in September 2001 that it had been adjudged Ireland's tidiest large town, while at the same time continuing its development as Ireland's leading IT urban centre. Yet - particularly in the northwest of the county - Clare is also a great stronghold of traditional Irish music. Add to that its reputation as "The Banner County" of sporting legend. Then, too, in recent years Clare has become the leading county for the study of dolphin life - the hundred-plus colony of bottle-nose dolphins which make the Shannon Estuary their summer home are monitored from the increasingly busy recreational port of Kilrush, while Doolin in the north of the county has its own exceptionally friendly dolphin.

Other places like Ennistimon, Milltown Malbay, Corofin and Mountshannon - they all have a very human and friendly dimension. For this is a county where the human spirit defines itself as being very human indeed, in the midst of scenic effects which at times seem to border on the supernatural.

Local Attractions and Information

Ballyvaughan Aillwee Cave	065 707 7036
Bunratty Bunratty Castle & Folk Park	061 360788
Cliffs of Moher Tourist Information	065 708 1171
Corofin Clare Heritage Centre	065 683 7955
Ennis Tourist Centre	065 682 8366
Killimer Killimer-Tarbert Ferry	065 53124
Kilrush Kilrush Heritage Centre	065 905 1577
Kilrush Scattery Island Interpretive Centre	065 905 2139
Quin Craggaunowen (Celts & Living Past)	061 360788
Shannon Airport Tourist Information	061 471664

Ballyvaughan

Aillwee Cave

CAFÉ

Ballyvaughan Co. Clare **Tel: 065 707 7036**
Fax: 065 707 7107 Email: aillwee@eircom.net Web: www.aillweecave.ie

Visitors to this 2-million-year-old cave will see more than the amazing illuminated tunnels and waterfalls, for there is much of interest to foodlovers as well. Driving up to the entrance, look out for the sign to the cheese-making demonstrations - for it is here that the local Burren Gold cheese is made. Even if the process is in a quiet phase at the time of a visit, there is still plenty to see - and buy - as the cheesemaking takes place alongside a well-stocked food shop. Just inside the entrance to the cave there is a souvenir shop with a good book section (including travel and cookery books of Irish interest) and a themed potato bar café serving inexpensive, wholesome fare - typically baked potatoes with Burren Gold cheese. Fast food (coffee, paninis etc) also available outside - and a new mountain trail "guaranteed to work up an appetite" is planned for 2002.* The Liscannor Rock Shop is a sister enterprise - and it also provides wholesome, inexpensive food in its little café (and goodies, such as home-made preserves, to take home too). Children welcome. Cafe **Seats 80.** No-smoking area. Meals all day Mon-Sun (9.30-6.30). Closed 22-27 Dec. MasterCard, Visa. **Directions:** 2 miles south of Ballyvaughan.

Ballyvaughan

An Fear Gorta (Tea & Garden Rooms)

RESTAURANT

Ballyvaughan Co. Clare **Tel: 065 707 7157**
Fax: 065 7077127 Email: kadonoghue@ireland.com

Approached from the harbourfront through a lovely front garden, Katherine O'Donoghue's delightful old stone restaurant dates back to 1790, when it was built as a residence for 'coast security officers'. Having been rebuilt by the present owners in 1981, it is now just the spot for a light bite to eat. In fine weather the beautiful back garden or the conservatory can be idyllic; otherwise the homely dining room offers comfort and shelter, with its informal arrangement of old furniture and a tempting display of home-baked fare. This is the speciality of the house - all laid out on an old cast-iron range and very reasonably priced - beginning at only €1.15 for scone, butter & home-made jam. Speciality teas are available as well as savoury choices including farmhouse cheeses, home-baked ham and Tea Room Specials including Open Smoked Salmon Sandwich on Brown Bread. 2-3 course lunch specials are available at around €8 and there's home-made jam and marmalade to take away. Open 11-5.30 (L 12-4.30.) Mon-Sat June-Sept; Closed Oct-May. No Credit Cards. **Directions:** on the harbour front in Ballyvaughan, beside Monks pub.

Ballyvaughan

Gregans Castle Hotel

COUNTRY HOUSE
RESTAURANT

Ballyvaughan Co. Clare **Tel: 065 707 7005**
Fax: 065 707 7111 Email: res@gregans.ie Web: www.gregans.ie

Gregans Castle has a long and interesting history, going back to a tower house, or small castle, which was built by the O'Loughlen clan (the region's principal tribe) between the 10th and 17th centuries and is still intact. The present house dates from the late 18th century and has been continuously added to, up to the present day. The present owners, Peter and Moira Haden, opened Gregans Castle as a country house hotel in 1976 and (true to the traditions of the house)

have continued to develop and improve it, recently with their son Simon-Peter who is now Manager. The exterior is grey and stark, in keeping with the lunar landscape of the surrounding Burren, serving only to heighten the contrast between first impressions and the warmth, comfort and hospitality to be found within. Spacious accommodation, which includes four suites and two mini-suites, is furnished to a very high standard and rooms all have excellent bathrooms and lovely countryside views. Peace and quiet are the dominant themes - the otherwise luxurious rooms are deliberately left without the worldly interference of television. Yet this luxurious hotel is not too formal or at all intimidating; non-residents are welcome to drop in for lunch or afternoon tea in the Corkscrew Bar - named after a nearby hill which, incidentally, provides the most scenic approach to Ballyvaughan. In fine weather guests can sit out beside the Celtic Cross rose garden and watch patches of sun and shade chasing across the hills. In the morning, allow time to enjoy an excellent breakfast. Children welcome (no concessions, but cot available @ €12). No pets. All day room service. **Rooms 22** (4 suites, 2 junior suites, 10 executive) B&B €98 pps; ss€78. No service charge. **The Dining Room** The restaurant, which was greatly improved by a recently added bay window area, is decorated in a rich country house style and elegantly furnished in keeping with the rest of the house. Most tables have lovely views over the Burren (which on fine summer evenings enjoys very special light effects as the sun sets over Galway Bay) and dinner is often gently accompanied by a pianist or harpist. Head chef Regis Herviaux cooks confidently in the modern Irish style with some French influence and offers a wide choice of dishes based on the best of local produce, including organic vegetables. There is always a selection of local cheeses, with homemade biscuits. **Seats 50** (Private Room, 30). No smoking area. Children welcome (not under 10 after 7.30). Toilets wheelchair accessible. D 7-8.30, 5-course D €50, any 2 courses €33. House wines from €20. Service discretionary. Short à la carte lunch is available in the Corkscrew Bar, 12-3 daily. Hotel closed 23 Dec-14 Feb (open weekends only 15 Oct-22 Dec; special rates available). Amex, MasterCard, Visa. **Directions:** on N67, 3.5 miles South of Ballyvaughan.

Ballyvaughan

Hyland's Hotel

HOTEL

The Square Ballyvaughan Co. Clare **Tel: 065 707 7037**
Fax: 065 7077131 Email: hylands@tinet.ie

Open fires, comfortable well-crafted furniture and sympathetic lighting create a welcoming atmosphere that is carried through into all areas of this well-loved hotel, which dates back to the 18th century. New bedrooms were recently added and all are very comfortable, with good amenities (direct dial phone, tea/coffee tray, TV). Restaurant meals are available in the evening and an extensive bar menu, which includes a range of dishes based on local seafood, is offered all day (12.30-9). **Rooms 30.** B&B €57 pps, ss€19. Closed Dec&Jan. * The hotel has been on the market for some time (after eight generations in the Hyland family) but, judging by recent visits, it remains reassuringly unchanged. Amex, Diners, MasterCard, Visa, Laser. **Directions:** in centre of Ballyvaughan, beside the harbour.

Ballyvaughan

Monks Bar & Restaurant

PUB/RESTAURANT

The Quay Ballyvaughan Co. Clare
Tel: 065 707 7059 Fax: 065 707 0330

This famous pub has been drawing people along to the pier at Ballyvaughan since 1981. It's an informal, cottagey kind of a place with several small bars, open fires and a reputation for informal service of fresh seafood, especially crab. This it still does since changing hands in 2000, although prices have gone up and standards have tended to be inconsistent. However, on the guide's most recent visit (late summer 2001), this attractive place seemed to be its old self again. Live music (Tue traditional, Sat modern). **Seats 80.** No smoking area. Toilets wheelchair accessible. Food served 12 noon-8 pm daily. A la carte. Closed 25 Dec, Good Fri. MasterCard, Visa. **Directions:** in Ballyvaughan Village, beside the pier.

Ballyvaughan

Rusheen Lodge

ACCOMODATION/GUESTHOUSE

Knocknagrough Ballyvaughan Co. Clare
Tel: 065 707 7092 Fax: 065 707 7151
Email: rusheen@iol.ie Web: rwww.rusheenlodge.com

Karen McGann took over the reins at Rusheen Lodge in 2001 and is determined to maintain the reputation for hospitality earned by her uncle and aunt John and Rita McGann - who are not far away, should occasional help be required, as they swapped houses with Karen and live next door. Fresh flowers in both the house and garden create a riot of colour in contrast to the overall green-greyness of the surrounding Burren, suggesting an oasis in a wilderness - which is just what Rusheen Lodge provides. Generously proportioned, well-appointed bedrooms have phones, tea/coffee trays,

TV, trouser press and good bathrooms and there are spacious public rooms, making this a very comfortable place to stay. All this, plus good food and warm hospitality, make Rusheen Lodge (which was the guide's Guesthouse of the Year for 2001) outstanding. While evening meals are not provided, the pubs and restaurants of Ballyvaughan are only a few minutes walk and breakfast - whether traditional Irish or continental - is a major feature of a stay. It was John McGann's father, Jacko McGann, who discovered the Aillwee Cave, an immense network of caverns and waterfalls under the Burren which is now a major attraction in the area. Children welcome, under 3s free in parents' room (cot avaialble without charge). No pets. **Rooms 8** (2 suites, 6 executive rooms, 1 for disabled, all no-smoking). B&B €45pps, ss€18. Closed Nov-Feb. MasterCard, Visa, Laser. **Directions:** 3/4 Km from village on the N67.

Ballyvaughan

Whitethorn Restaurant

RESTAURANT

Ballyvaughan Co. Clare **Tel: 065 707 7044**

Fax: 065 707 7155 Email: whitethorne@eircom.net Web: thewhitethorn.com

Sarah and John McDonnell's restaurant is beautifully located on the sea side of the road and they also run a fine craft shop and a visitor centre, "Burren Exposure", where visitors learn about the formation of the Burren rockscape, its history and the amazing diversity of flora which brings so many visitors to the region in early summer. The restaurant has magnificent sea views and offers excellent home-made self-service fare throughout the day (which visitors can take indoors or out depending on the weather and inclination): home-made soups including chowder and a daily special - tomato & basil perhaps, smoked salmon and potato tart and aubergine charlotte are typical and all modestly priced. Friday and Saturday evenings in July and August bring a more formal dining arrangement, offering the same good cooking and excellent value in imaginative menus based on local produce. Tempting vegetarian dishes, nice homely desserts - and wine suggestions to partner each dish, taken from an especially interesting wine list which earned the Guide's 2000 award for Wine List of the Year. John operates the Australian Wine Bureau in Ireland, but the restaurant wine list travels much further afield. His helpfulness is relaxed and unaffected and his sheer enthusiasm is infectious. Self-service Meals 9.30-6 daily, average main course €8. **Restaurant, Seats 120.** A la carte dinner served "on certain evenings" - a phone call for details is advised. House wine €15.17. Closed Nov-Mar. MasterCard, Visa, Laser. **Directions:** main Galway Road from Ballyvaughan 1 km.

Bunratty

Bunratty Castle Hotel

HOTEL

Bunratty Co. Clare **Tel: 061 707034**

Fax: 061 364891 Email: info@bunrattycastlehotel.iol.ie

This modern hotel on a rise just beside Bunratty Castle has been quite attractively designed to reflect its Georgian origins. Public seating areas are spacious and comfortable, traditionally furnished rooms have all the modern comforts, including air conditioning and bathrooms with both (tiny) bath and good overbath shower. The hotel's restaurant food is somewhat limited (pizzas, pasta, steaks) but it's within easy walking distance of all the pubs and restaurants in Bunratty. Ample parking. Children welcome; pets allowed in some areas. **Rooms 59.** B&B about €65pps. Closed 25 Dec. Amex, Diners, MasterCard, Visa. **Directions:** in Bunratty village, opposite the castle (nr Bunratty Village Mills).

Bunratty

Bunratty Manor Hotel

HOTEL/RESTAURANT

Bunratty Co. Clare **Tel: 061 707984**

Fax: 061 360 588 Email: bunrattymanor@eircom.net Web: www.bunrattymanor.net

Despite having a name which implies considerable age, this small hotel in Bunratty village is newly built - which may be disappointing if character and antiquity are high priorities, but there are advantages in the convenience of modern shower rooms, double glazing and comfortable orthopaedic beds. Prices are more reasonable than the bigger hotels and there's a good restaurant on-site as well as pubs and other eating places nearby. Conference/banqueting (25/60).Children welcome (under 2s fee in parents' room, cots available without charge). No Pets. garden. **Rooms 14** (shower only). B&B €59 pps, ss €20 **Ristorante Ponte Vecchio:** Head chef David Hughes offers traditional Italian cuisine in a pleasingly well-appointed dining room, which opens onto a terrace (where barbecues are held in fine weather). Seafood is a speciality and is delivered from Kenmare three times a week, but the menu offers much else besides, including vegetarian dishes. Lunch and dinner (3-course menus from €19) can be arrranged for groups, who can bring wine at very reasonable corkage charges. **Seats 48.** D only, Tue-Sun 6-9.30. Set D €22.75, house wine €15.75. Closed D Mon, 25 Dec, Jan-Feb. Amex, Diners, MasterCard, Visa, Laser. **Directions:** turn off main road into Bunratty first buildings on right.

Bunratty

Durty Nelly's

RESTAURANT/PUB

Bunratty Co. Clare **Tel: 061 364861**

Although often seriously over-crowded with tourists in summer, this famous and genuinely characterful old pub in the shadow of Bunratty Castle somehow manages to provide cheerful service and above-average food to the great numbers who pass through its doors. All-day fare is served downstairs in the Oyster Restaurant daily, upstairs there is a more exclusive restaurant, The Loft, open in the evening only (Mon-Sat, 6-10). Both areas offer à la carte menus. Closed 25 Dec, Good Fri. Amex, Diners, MasterCard, Visa. **Directions:** just off the N18 Limerick-Galway road, beside Bunratty Castle.

Bunratty

Fitzpatrick Bunratty Hotel

HOTEL

Bunratty Co. Clare **Tel: 061 361177**

Fax: 061 471252 Email: info@fitzpatricks.com Web: fitzpatrickhotels.com

Conveniently located just ten minutes from both Shannon International Airport and Limerick city, Fitzpatrick Bunratty is in wooded grounds beside Bunratty Castle and Folk Park and offers good facilities for business and leisure guests. The style of the building is typical of many hotels established in the 1960s and is still a disadvantage, making the hotel seem dated in some areas, although the Fitzpatrick Hotel Group have been energetic in their efforts to upgrade facilities. Public areas are quite impressive, as are recent additions, including a new gallery lounge and PJ's restaurant as well as a fine fitness centre with 20 metre swimming pool and an excellent conference & banqueting centre with state-of-the-art facilities. Thirty new bedrooms have recently been added but, although the older ones have been refurbished, they still seem dated; however they are well-equipped, with the usual facilities. Off season breaks offer good value. Conference/banqueting (1000/500); video-conferencing; business centre; secretarial services. Leisure centre. Hairdresser. Garden. Children under 2 free in parents room; cots available. No pets. Wheelchair accessible. **Rooms 115** (6 suites, 11 mini-suites, 13 executive rooms, 4 no-smoking rooms). B&B about €85 pps, ss About €32. Closed 24-26 Dec. Amex, Diners, MasterCard, Visa. **Directions:** just off N18 Limerick-Galway road, beside Bunratty Castle.

Bunratty

Muses Restaurant

RESTAURANT

Bunratty House Mews Bunratty Co.Clare **Tel: 061 364 082**

Fax: 061 364 350 Email: muses@oceanfree.net Web: www.musesrestaurant.com

Disregard any off-putting first impressions as you approach Aidan McGrath's basement restaurant at the back of the Bunratty estate - once inside, all is warmth and welcome. A small hall leads to a lovely bar area overlooking Bunratty Park and castle, with a proper counter and deep sofa to relax in while enjoying a promptly served aperitif and consulting helpful staff about the menu, a well-balanced offering that promises well, especially in unusually imaginative use of vegetables which are planned as an integral part of each dish and make mouth-watering reading. Seafood and local organic produce are much in evidence, also wild game in season. The dining rooms consists of three small rooms, with well-appointed tables and lovely flowers, prints and bric-à-brac creating a soothing, restful atmosphere. High quality ingredients, skilful cooking and caring service should make for a memorable experience here. Each main dish has its own complementary vegetable garnish: a starter of lobster ravioli comes with creamed York cabbage & basil butter, or there's an organic leaf salad tossed with marinated feta cheese, black olives and air-dried ham while a main course of seared breast of duck is served with roast apricots, braised kohlrabi and apricot jus; a platter of more unusual vegetables is also served as a side dish, without extra charge - and, at an average of €20 for a main course, prices are quite reasonable for the quality offered. A well-chosen, fairly priced wine list will also add to the pleasure. Private parties and small weddings can be catered for. Not suitable for children under 10 after 7.30 pm. No smoking area. **Seats 45.** D Tue-Sat,last orders 9.30; à la carte. House wines from about €18; sc discretionary. Closed Christmas, all Jan. MasterCard, Visa, Laser. **Directions:** bearing left at the village green, turn sharp left up the hill road for100 metres, restaurant's spaces are on the right hand side.

Clarecastle

Carnelly House

COUNTRY HOUSE

Clarecastle Co. Clare **Tel: 065 6828442**

Fax: 065 6829222 Email: info@carnelly_house.com Web: www.carnelly_house.com

Conveniently located for Shannon airport and for touring the west of Ireland, Dermott and Rosemarie Gleeson's fine redbrick Georgian house is set on 100 acres of farm and woodland and offers discerning guests very special accommodation. Reception rooms include an impressive drawing room with Corinthian pillars, Francini ceiling, grand piano and a striking panelled dining room where communal dinners are taken at 7.30 pm. (Residents only, except groups for lunch or dinner by arrangement.) Bedrooms are large and furnished to a high standard, with antiques, canopied king size or twin beds and luxurious private bathrooms. Yet the grandeur is not at all daunting and Carnelly - which is well-placed for a wide range of country pursuits, including many of the country's most famous hunts - has been described as "one of the warmest, friendliest and most entertaining houses in Ireland". Children welcome (under 3s free in parents' room, cot available free of charge). There is also a gate lodge, which is available by the night, week or month. Conferences/baqueting (25/25). Pets permitted by arrangement. Garden, walks. **Rooms 5** (all executive, 1 no -smoking) €115 pps, ss€75.50. Open all year. Amex, Diners, MasterCard, Visa, Laser. **Directions:** one mile south of Clarecastle on Limerick Road.

Corofin

Clifden House

COUNTRY HOUSE

Corofin Co. Clare **Tel: 065 683 7692**
Fax: 065 6837692 Email: clifdenhousecountyclare@eircom.net

This unusual early Georgian manor on the shore of Lough Inchiquin was found "slipping gracefully into ruin" 25 years ago by Jim and Bernadette Robson who, while conceding that "the work is not yet finished nor will it be twenty years hence", have gone a considerable way towards restoration "following the criteria of respecting its tradition of hospitality and the comfort of our friends and guests". Bedrooms are highly individualistic (one bathroom in particular even more so), stylish and comfortable - do not be concerned that certain areas are only partially restored. Hospitality is king here and the Robsons enjoy their food, in every sense of the word - organic meats come from a nearby farm, fish and game are also local and vegetables and fruit from their own walled garden - Bernadette enjoys cooking (ask to see her collection of old cookery books) and everybody enjoys the results. There is a short wine list and guests are also welcome to bring their own. Accommodation is also offered in two 3- and 4-bedroom holiday houses in a stable wing, with cobbled yard and riverside lawn; they can be either self-catering or serviced. Gardens, walking, fishing (boats available). Children welcome (cot available, no charge). No pets. **Rooms 4** (1 shower only). €60 pps (no ss). Communal dinner at 8 pm, €32. Closed early Nov-mid Mar. Amex, MasterCard, Visa. **Directions:** going north out of Corofin turn left at Grotto take 2nd right then 1st right.

Corofin

Fergus View

FARMHOUSE

Kilnaboy Corofin Co. Clare **Tel: 065 683 7606**
Fax: 065 683 7192 Email: deckell@indigo.ie

Mary Kelleher runs a very hospitable house and the care taken to ensure guests enjoy their visit to the full is shown in details like the the information packs on the area compiled by her and left in each bedroom - and an interesting breakfast menu that includes home-made yogurt, freshly squeezed juice, home-made muesli, local cheese and a wide range of teas as well as cooked breakfasts with free range eggs. Rooms are comfortable although a little on the small side, as often happens when family homes are converted to include en-suite facilities. But refurbishment is an ongoing business - recent improvements include the installation of traditional wooden windows throughout the house and a new entrance conservatory, which opens onto the garden and has extensive views. Every time the guide visits there is something else in progress: the latest plan is replacement of all interior doors with solid pine doors and installation of a new sitting room fireplace in keeping with the period of the house - and all the bedrooms will be re-carpeted and freshly painted too. There's is also a lovely stone cottage next door, Tigh Eamon, which has been charmingly converted for self-catering accommodation. Children welcome (cot available). No pets. **Rooms 6** (5 en-suite, all shower only and no-smoking). B&B €32pps (€29.20 without shower); ss €15 (€10 without shower). D 6.30 Mon-Thu €22.86; wine licence. No D Fri-Sun; closed 1 October-Easter. **Directions:** 2 miles north of Corofin on Kilfenora road, first house on the left after Kilnaboy Medieval Church at Kilnaboy.

Cratloe

Bunratty View

ACCOMMODATION

Cratloe Bunratty Co. Clare **Tel: 061 357352**
Fax: 061 357491 Email: bunrattyview@eircom.net

Joe and Maura Brodie provide comfortable, spacious accommodation at their modern house conveniently close to Bunratty Castle and Shannon Airport. Rooms have double and single beds, phone, tea/coffee facilities, satellite TV, hairdryers and there's a comfortable residents' lounge with an open fire and bright dining room, where good breakfasts are served. **Rooms 6** (4 shower only, all no-smoking, 2 suitable for less able guests); B&B €32 pps, ss €7. Closed Dec-Jan. MasterCard, Visa. **Directions:** signed off the N18 (1st left after Bunratty Castle, coming from the airport).

Doolin

Aran View House Hotel

HOTEL/RESTAURANT

Coast Road Doolin Co. Clare **Tel: 065 707 4061**

Fax: 065 707 4540 Email: bookings@aranview.com Web: www.aranview.com

Just outside Doolin, and commanding dramatic sea views across to the islands, the Linnane's family-run hotel makes a good base for a family holiday - it is only a mile to a good beach, there is sea-angling and golf nearby and, of course, there is the traditional music for which Doolin is world famous. Public rooms include a comfortable bar for all weathers - it has a sea view and an open fire. Bedrooms vary considerably in size and outlook due to the age and nature of the building: rooms at the front are most desirable - several at the back have no view, but are otherwise pleasant. There are two extra large ones and two singles; all have phones, tea/coffee trays and TV (local stations) Children are welcome - outdoor play area and children's menu provided. There is a restaurant (open to non-residents) with very reasonably priced set menus (lunch,£10; dinner, £20) available as well as an à la carte offering local produce, including lobster. **Rooms 19** (some shower only, 6 no smoking, 2 for disabled); B&B €50.79 pps, ss €12.70 . Closed Nov-April. Amex, Diners, MasterCard, Visa. **Directions:** N67 exit off near Lisdoonvarna to Doolin.

Doolin

Ballinalacken Castle

HOTEL/RESTAURANT

Doolin Co Clare

Tel: 065 707 4025 Fax: 065 707 4025

Email: ballinalackencastle@eircom.net Web: ballinalackencastle.com

Well away from the bustle of Lisdoonvarna, and with wonderful views of the Atlantic, Aran Islands, Cliffs of Moher and the distant hills of Connemara, Ballinalacken is easily identified by the 15th century castle still standing beside the hotel. In the O'Callaghan family ownership since opening in 1940, and currently managed by Marian O'Callaghan, Ballinalacken has retained a Victorian country house atmosphere with its welcoming fire in the hall and well-proportioned public rooms comfortably furnished with antiques. Public rooms and some bedrooms enjoy magnificent views and additions and renovations are undertaken on an on-going basis; many improvements were noted on the guide's most recent visit. Bedrooms are all en-suite, varying according to age and location in the building - some have double and single beds, some are shower only; the best are large with seating areas and sea views. Dated decor should be improved and greater comfort achieved by a major renovation and redecoration programme to be completed over the winter of 2001/2. The grounds - which include a lovely big field as well as planted areas nearer the house - are also to be upgraded, over a 3-year period. Children welcome (under 2s free in parents' room). Pets permitted by arrangement. **Rooms 13** (all en-suite, 3 shower only; 10 no-smoking). B&B €50pps, ss€30. **Restaurant:** The restaurant offers lovely views from window tables and provides a fitting setting for Frank Sheedy's confident new Irish cooking, which is based firmly on the best local produce. Good home-made breads - traditional brown, walnut, tomato - set the tone and a choice of half a dozen starters might include local seafood, a well-made terrine (game, pine nut and pork, perhaps), two soups and a vegetarian option such as a tartlet of local goat cheese. Well-balanced flavours and accurate cooking are evident throughout, typically in a delicate seafood dish like scallops with oriental cabbage and red pepper sauce, which could easily disappoint. Confit of duck, lobster and Burren lamb are specialities, side vegetables are varied and generous, desserts delicious and the cheeseboard impressive. Good coffee, served at the table or in the drawing room, rounds off the evening nicely and refills are automatically offered. Open to non-residents. D daily, 6.45-9. A la carte. Service discretionary. Closed end Oct-mid Apr. Amex, MasterCard, Visa. **Directions:** coast road, R477 North of Doolin village.

Doolin

Cullinans Restaurant & Guesthouse

RESTAURANT/GUESTHOUSE

Doolin Co Clare **Tel: 065 707 4183**

Fax: 065 707 4239 Email: cullinans@eircom.net Web: www.cullinansdoolin.com

Music may be Doolin's major attraction, but people also travel here specially to eat at Cullinans. James Cullinan is the chef and Carol looks after service in an unpretentious, comfortable dining room overlooking the little river at the back of the house. Menus include a very nice early dinner, with three or four choices on each course (including vegetarian dishes) and an à la carte which is available at any time from opening. Local produce - including Burren smoked salmon, Inagh goats cheese, Doolin crabmeat and Aran scallops - is credited on the menu, providing a sound base for fairly modern Irish cooking with some French influence, as in specialities like tian of Doolin crab, Inagh cheese with basil house pesto and, of course, loin of Burren lamb, perhaps stuffed with local black pudding and served with a shallot jus. Tempting desserts - home-churned ice creams perhaps - or farmhouse cheeses to finish. Children welcome. No smoking restaurant. **Seats 25** D Thu-Tue,

6-9.30. A la carte; early D €23 (6-7pm). House wine 15.87.Closed Wed & Oct-Easter. **Accommodation** Warm hospitality, comfortable beds and a good breakfast make this a good place to stay. Cheerful modern rooms have all the necessities, including phones and tea/coffee trays - at a reasonable price. Rooms at the back are quieter and have a pleasant outlook over the garden and river. Children welcome (under 3s free in parents' room, cot available without charge). No pets. **Rooms 6** (all shower only & no-smoking, 1 for disabled). B&B €35 ss €25. MasterCard, Visa, Laser. **Directions:** centre of Doolin between McGanns & O'Connors pub.

Doolin

Doolin Crafts Gallery

RESTAURANT Ballyvoe Doolin Co. Clare **Tel: 065 7074309** Fax: 065 7074511

Matthew O'Connell and Mary Gray's delightful shop could keep you happily occupied for longer than you think: it's jam-packed with terrific, quality crafts and clothing - some of them exclusively available here - and the Flagship Restaurant will tempt you to linger over what is, with unusual accuracy, described as "simple home cooking, using local produce, and home baking": grilled local goats cheese with pesto on garden salad, Lisdoonvarna smoked salmon plate, fresh salmon mayonnaise on brown bread, Kerry apple pie. The garden is quite charming too, and very typical of Clare. **Seats 40** (+ 20 in garden) No-smoking restaurant. Open 10-6 daily. Closed 1 Oct-Good Fri. A la carte. Wine licence. Service charge discretionary. **Directions:** Beside the cemetery, just outside Doolin.

Ennis

Newpark House

FARMHOUSE Newpark House Ennis Co. Clare **Tel: 065 6821233**
Email: newparkhouse.ennis@eircom.net Web: http//homepagetinet.ie/~newparkhouse/

Strange as it may seem to find a genuine farmhouse in a country setting within easy walking distance of the pubs and restaurants of Ennis, the Barron family home is the exception that defies easy description. It's an old house of great historic interest with large homely rooms, furnished with old family furniture and an hospitable, relaxing atmosphere. Bedrooms vary in size and character, as old houses do, but are comfortable and full of interest. Children welcome (under 3s free in parents' room, cot available); pets permitted by arrangment. Communal dinner €22 at 6.30, please book by 3 pm. Bring your own wine. **Rooms 6** (all en-suite; 4 triple rooms, 1 family room). B&B about €38pps, ss €6. **Directions:** R352, turn right at Roselevan Arms.

Ennis

Old Ground Hotel

HOTEL/RESTAURANT/PUB O'Connell Street Ennis Co. Clare **Tel: 065 6828127**
Fax: 065 6828112 Email: oghotel@iol.ie Web: www.oldground.ennis.ie

This ivy-clad former manor house dates back to the 18th century and, set in its own gardens, creates an oasis of calm in the centre of Ennis. One of the country's best-loved hotels, the Old Ground was bought by the Flynn family in 1995 and has been imaginatively extended and renovated by them in a way that is commendably sensitive to the age and importance of the building. Despite the difficulties of dealing with very thick walls in an old building, major improvements were made to existing banqueting/conference facilities in the mid '90s, then an extra storey was added to provide new rooms. Again, this has been a sensitive development and, as the famous ivy-clad frontage continues to thrive, the external changes are barely noticeable to the casual observer. Major refurbishment has also taken place throughout the interior of the hotel, including all bedrooms - which have good amenities and well-designed bathrooms - the O'Brien Room restaurant and a traditional style bar, Poet's Corner (bar menu 12.30-9) features traditional music on some nights.* Town Hall Café, an informal contemporary restaurant in an historic building adjacent to the hotel, opened in 2001. Children welcome (free cot available). Conference/banqueting (max 200). **Rooms 83** (7 mini-suites, 20 executive rooms, 5 no-smoking) B&B about €75pps; ss about €40. Closed 25-26 Dec. **O'Brien Room Restaurant:** The hotel's formal dining room is at the front of the hotel and has great character. Head chef Gerry Walsh, who has been with the hotel since 1977, takes pride in using local produce in imaginatively presented dishes such as roast rack of Burren lamb with apricot & almond stuffing or a trio of local seafood. O'Brien Room **Seats 65** (private room, 70) L12.30-3. D 6.30-9.30 daily. Amex, Diners, MasterCard, Visa. **Directions:** situated in the town centre.

Ennis

Quality Auburn Lodge Hotel

HOTEL Galway Road Ennis Co. Clare **Tel: 065 6821247**
Fax: 065 6821232 Email: auburnlodgehotel@eircom.net Web: www.choicehotelsireland.com

This pleasant modern hotel just 20 minutes from Shannon airport is built around a central courtyard containing a soothing garden, creating a peaceful atmosphere throughout the building. With six championship golf courses nearby and the major attractions of County Clare within easy reach, it makes a good just-out-of-town base for business or pleasure. Quite spacious rooms have good facilities (phone, tea/coffee tray, TV, trouser press/ironing board) and include some larger executive suites and a pretty bridal suite. Children welcome (under 12s free in parents' room, cots available free of charge). Lakeside walks nearby. Business centre; secretarial services. Conference/banqueting (500/400). **Rooms 95** (2 suites, 14 no smoking). B&B €70 pps, ss €20. Amex, MasterCard, Visa, Laser. **Directions:** Galway end of Ennis Town (N18).

Ennis

Temple Gate Hotel

HOTEL féile bia

The Square Ennis Co. Clare **Tel: 065 682 3300**

Fax: 065 682 3322 Email: info@templegatehotel.com Web: wwwtemplegatehotel.com

Built in the centre of Ennis town, to a clever design that makes the best possible use of the site, this family-owned hotel opened to some acclaim in 1996. While retaining the older features (including a church which was first used as a pub and is now the Great Hall Banqueting/Conference room), existing Gothic themes have also been successfully blended into the new, creating a striking modern building which has relevance to its surroundings in the heart of a medieval town. Since then it has succeeded in providing the comfort and convenience expected by today's travellers at a reasonable price. In 1998, 40 new deluxe rooms and state-of-the-art syndicate/conference rooms for up to 100 people were added and the newer "Preachers Bar" replaced the original one in the church. The restaurant has since been extended and redesigned to the same theme as Preachers Bar. Conference/banqueting (220/265); business centre, secretarial services, ISDN lines. Children under 10 free in parents' room; cot available without charge. No pets. Garden. **Rooms 70** (2 suites, 2 junior suites, 11 non-smoking, 1 for disabled). B&B €70 pps, ss€28. Closed 25 Dec. Amex, Diners, MasterCard, Visa, Laser, Switch. **Directions:** Ennis, follow signs to tourist office hotel, hotel situated beside it.

Ennis

Town Hall Café

CAFÉ

O'Connell Street Ennis Co. Clare **Tel: 065 682 8112**

Adjacent to (and part of) The Old Ground Hotel, the Town Hall Café has a separate street entrance and this contemporary space in no way feels like a 'hotel restaurant'. The old town hall has been well restored and the restaurant is in an impressive high-ceilinged room with sensitively spare decor - large art works which will be loved or loathed, big pots and simple table settings allow the room to speak for itself. Daytime menus are limited but varied, a mixture of modern bistro-style dishes (eg chargrilled tandoori chicken salad with homemade hazelnut dressing), daily specials, and tea-room fare - just what people need to re-charge during a day's shopping it seems, as the cooking is good, service swift and value excellent. In the evening it all moves up a notch or two, when a shortish à la carte menu comes on stream, offering about half a dozen choice per course. Starters (average €6) might include country style terrine with spicy Indian chutney and classic Meditrerranean fish soup with garlic bread, followed by main courses (average €17) like butterbaked tranche of salmon with a citrus jus or prime 10oz sirloin steak with a grain mustard & Irish whiskey sauce. Desserts from a daily selection. Not fine dining, but great at the price. **Seats 80.** Open 10-5 (coffee 10-12, L 12-4, teas 4-5) & D 6-10. Amex, Diners, MasterCard, Visa. **Directions:** Town centre.

Ennis

West County Conference & Leisure Hotel

HOTEL

Clare Road Ennis Co. Clare **Tel: 065 6828421**

Fax: 065 6828801 Email: cro@lynchotels.com Web: www.lynchhotels.com

Recently extended and refurbished, this modern hotel 5 minutes walk from the centre of Ennis town is not only a well-located and comfortable base for holidaymakers but also renowned for its exceptional business and conference facilities, earning Lynch Hotels the guide's 2000 Business Hotel Award. The hotel's Island Convention Centre can seat 1,650 delegates in a range of four conference rooms and five meeting rooms that are almost infinitely variable. There is also video-conferencing, full business/office support services and an impressive Health and Leisure Club in which to wind down or shape up. Bedrooms include interconnecting rooms, mini-suites, family rooms and 43 recently added Premier standard rooms with ISDN lines. Off-season value breaks. Children under 3 years free in parents' room; cots available free of charge. No pets. Lift. **Rooms 152** (1 executive, 29 non-smoking, 1 for disabled). B&B €82.53 pps, ss €25.40. Open all year. Amex, Diners, MasterCard, Visa. **Directions:** N18 main Limerick-Galway road. Five minutes walk from Ennis Town.

Ennis

HOTEL

Woodstock Hotel & Golf Club

Shanaway Road Ennis Co. Clare
Tel: 065 684 6600 Fax: 065 684 6611
Email: info@woodstockhotel.com Web: www.woodstockhotel.com

This sister hotel to the Hibernian Hotel, Dublin and McCausland Hotel, Belfast is built around a 19th century manor house on around 200 acres, now mostly utilised by the golf course. It opened in May 2000 and, although it has settled down somewhat since opening, initial impressions may still be mixed, but generous parking space, an impressive foyer and a welcoming fire burning in the grate create a more positive mood. Spacious public areas are furnished with style and large, luxurious bedrooms have equally luxurious bathrooms and also ISDN lines in addition to the more usual amenities. Golf is the major attraction (championship course on site, residents' rates available) and there's a health and fitness club on the premises, also an equestrian centre half a mile away. Children are welcome (free in parents' room up to 2; cots available free of charge). Conferences/banqueting (200/180); business centre, secretarial services; video conferencing on request. Golf (18); leisure centre (gym, swimming pool, sauna, jacuzzi). Lift. **Rooms 65.** (2 junior suites, 47 no-smoking, 3 for disabled). B&B from €107.93 pps, single from ss €31.74. **Spikes Brasserie:** High-ceilinged, with cool blue-grey decor (a little too) reminiscent of the Clare skies and stylish classic table settings, with white linen and fresh flowers, the dining room has a formal atmosphere at odds with its title. Head chef Chris King's moderately priced table d'hôte and à la carte menus are, perhaps, designed with golfers in mind and offer quite substantial fare alongside contemporary dishes. Local seafood, such as scallops and Atlantic prawns, feature - panfried, perhaps, and served with tomato & chilli dressing and a basil & lemon salad - and Angus beef, typically a fillet steak chargrilled and served with a red onion tartlet & thyme jus. Desserts tend to be classical - try the warm apple & jameson tart with fresh cream. **Seats 100.** D 7-10pm daily, L Sun only, 12.30-2.30pm. Set D from €25.33, Set Sun L €18.98. House wine from €17.71.(* Bar food also available 12.30-7.30 daily, in Spikes Bar). Closed L Mon-Sat; 24-25 Dec. Amex, Diners, MasterCard, Visa, Laser, Switch. **Directions:** from Ennis, take main N18; at the first roundabout take N85 to Lahinch for 1 km, then turn left and continue 1 km to hotel.

Ennistymon

RESTAURANT/ACCOMMODATION

Byrne's Restaurant & Townhouse

Main Street Ennistymon Co.Clare
Tel: 065 707 1080 Fax: 065 707 2103
Email: byrnesennistymon@eircom.net

Located in a fine period house at the top of this old market town, Byrne's has views of Ennistymon's famous cascading river from the restaurant and terrace at the back of the building. Contemporary style, immaculate cleanliness, genuine hospitality and ambitious standards of food and cooking are the hallmarks. Menus are in the modern mode - prawns in filo with spiced tomato chutney & crisp salad, baked goats cheese, roast crispy duckling with sage & fig stuffing, smoked garlic jus, pan-seared scallops, crème brûlée, home-made ices - pleasing cooking, caring service and good valuetoo. Head chef Vivienne Kelly came from O'Grady's in Clifden and, together with owners Richard and Mary Byrne, is determined to achieve high standards, so this is a place that's earning recognition in the area. No smoking area; air conditioning. Not suitable for children after 8 pm. **Seats 55.** D only, Mon-Sat 6.30-9.30pm; à la carte; early D, Mon-Fri 6.30-7, €24.10. House wines from €17.75. Closed Sun. * Please call the restaurant to check opening times in winter (Nov-Feb). **Accommodation** 2002 will see the opening of six superior rooms with full bathrooms (including power showers), king-sized beds, TV/radio, coffee/tea making facilities and complimentar fresh fruit & Irish spring water. Amex, Diners, MasterCard, Visa, Laser. **Directions:** large prominent building overlooking Main Street.

Kilbaha

Anvil Farm Guesthouse

ACCOMODATION Kilbaha Loop Head Co Clare **Tel: 065 905 8018** Fax: 065 905 8331

In a house beside the family's clifftop farm at the end of the Loop Head peninsula, Maura Keating provides comfortable accommodation in one of the country's most remote and unspoilt areas. Rugged cliff scenery, angling, diving, bird watching and walking are some of the attractions that bring visitors to this wild and windblown beauty spot - the perfect antidote to city life. There is plenty to visit in the area too - Maura has all the details for her guests - and good local food for dinner, including Aberdeen Angus beef from their own farm, locally caught Atlantic salmon and local Inagh and Cratloe cheeses. Visitors may also visit the farm, which has a variety of animals and a special interest in Irish sport horse breeding. **Rooms 5** (all en-suite, 4 shower-only) B&B about €25, ss about €7. D for residents by arrangement. Closed Nov-Mar. **Directions:** take Loop Head road from Kilkee; Anvil Farm is 2 miles after Cross village.

Kilfenora

Vaughan's Pub

PUB Kilfenora Co Clare **Tel: 065 708 8004**

Fax: 065 708 80144 Email: vaughanspub@vaughanspub.com Web: vaughanspub.com

One of the most famous music centres in the west of Ireland, traditional Irish music and set dancing at Vaughan's pub and (previously thatched) barn attract visitors from all over the world. In the family since about 1800, John and Kay Vaughan have worked hard since the mid-70s to ensure that visitors to this attractive old pub have the best possible time and it is now being taken over by Mark and Orla Vaughan and moving into a new generation. The pub is warm and homely, with an open fire in the front bar and a garden set up with tables at the back. Kay still personally supervises the food, which has become an important part of the operation over the years: traditional Irish menus (bacon & cabbage, beef & Guinness casserole) are based on good local ingredients, including organic meats, seafood and North Clare cheese. **Seats 50** food served 12-9 daily,Closed 25 Dec & Good Fri. Visa, MasterCard. **Directions:** 18 miles from Ennis on the main street of Kilfenora, next to the church.

Kilkee

Halpins Townhouse Hotel

HOTEL Erin Street Kilkee Co. Clare **Tel: 065 9056032**

Fax: 065 9056317 Email: halpins@iol.ie Web: www.halpinsprivatehotels.com

Adapting the original Victorian building of the Halpin family's small townhouse hotel to provide en-suite bathrooms has meant that bedrooms are neat rather than spacious, but they are comfortable and well-appointed with direct-dial phone, TV, hospitality tray with mineral water as well as tea/coffee-making facilities and a laundry service. There's a characterful basement bar with an open fire where visitors, including the many who come to play the adjacent Kilkee Golf Course get together after dinner at the hotel's restaurant, Vittles. In common ownership with Aberdeen Lodge and Merrion Hall (see Dublin entries.) Conference/banqueting (50), secretarial service. Own parking. Off-season value breaks. Children welcome (cots available). **Rooms 12** (2 suites, 10 executive, 4 non-smoking) B&B €45 pps, ss €25 Closed 15 Nov-15 March. Vittles Amex, Diners, MasterCard, Visa. **Directions:** centre of Kilkee.

Kilkee

Ocean Cove Golf & Leisure Hotel

HOTEL Kilkee Bay Kilkee Co. Clare **Tel: 065 9083111**

Fax: 065 9083123 Email: cro@lynchhotels.com Web: www.lynchhotels.com

Despite the name, this well-located hotel with views over Kilkee Bay has a wide range of facilities for business that are lacking in the area and should thus prove an asset to this traditional family holiday and golfing area. Bedrooms have ISDN lines in addition to the more usual facilities and there's a business centre, secretarial services and video-conferencing. Kilkee Golf Club is adjacent to the hotel (preferential rates). Conference/banqueting (50); Off season value breaks. Children welcome (under 3s free in parents' room, cots available free of charge); children's playroom. Equestrian activities, diving, tennis and cycling all available nearby. Gym. No pets. **Rooms 50** (13 non-smoking) B&B €82.53pps, ss €25.39 (Room rate only available, €75, max 2 adults, 2 children). Lift. 24 hr room service. Amex, Diners, MasterCard, Visa. **Directions:** N67 Kilkee Bay, located in Kilkee town, 40 minutes drive from Ennis town.

Killaloe

Cherry Tree Restaurant

RESTAURANT Lakeside Ballina Killaloe Co.Clare **Tel: 061 375 688** Fax: 061 375 689

This new restaurant beside the Lakeside Hotel was purpose-built over the winter of 1999/2000 by proprietor/chef Harry McKeogh - after almost a decade as head chef at the renowned Cooke's Cafe in Dublin - and was, quite rightly, an immediate hit. It makes the most of its lovely waterside location and this impressive modern building - specifically its striking interior - makes a fine setting for Harry's cool contemporary cooking. Carefully sourced ingredients provide the basis for a wide range of admirably simple dishes, including great salads, based on locally grown organic produce. Specialities include warm asparagus bundles with truffle oil, fresh Castletownbere crab salad with bay leaves, avocado mango salsa & crisp spring roll, roast magret of Soulard farm duck with wilted organic leaves, crispy chicken wontons and honey ginger soy sauce - and superb dry-aged sirloin of beef (supplied by Pat Hunt in Carrick-on-Suir and aged further by hanging on the premises), which is cut to order and cooked as requested then served with a classic béarnaise sauce and thickly sliced, golden brown potato crisps. It's wonderful meat, served in an admirably simple dish - and was a very worthy winner of the guide's Irish Beef Award in 2001. **Seats 60** (private room, 12) No smoking area. D 6-10 Tues-Sat, all à la carte. House wine about €17.14. Closed Sun, Mon; 24-26 Dec; Jan 20-5 Feb. Amex, Diners, MasterCard, Visa, Laser. **Directions:** at Molly's Pub in Ballina turn down towards the Lakeside Hotel, you will find The Cherry Tree restaurant by The Lakeside Hotel.

Killaloe

Goosers

PUB/RESTAURANT/ Ballina Killaloe Co. Tipperary **Tel: 061 376 791** Fax: 061 376 244

Just across the road from the river and close to the bridge that links Tipperary and Clare, this attractive almost-riverside pub offers good food on blackboard specials (soups with freshly baked brown bread, oysters, mussels, Irish stew and bacon and cabbage are typical), but it is understandably popular and can be uncomfortably crowded, especially weekends, so midweek or off-season visits might be most enjoyable. The restaurant is at the back with a separate side entrance and they do a good Sunday lunch (booking advised). Outdoor seating. No music. Wheelchair accessible (including toilets). **Seats 70** (private room, 10). No smoking area. Air conditioning. Barfood served daily, 12.30pm-10pm. Restaurant: 6.30-10pm daily and Sun L 12.30-2.30 all year; Set L about €21; à la carte available; house wine about €15; sc discretionary. Children (not under 4) welcome before 8pm. No car park. Closed 25 Dec & Good Fri. Amex, Diners, MasterCard, Visa. **Directions:** riverside Ballina.

Killaloe

Waterman's Lodge Hotel

HOTEL/RESTAURANT Ballina Killaloe Co Clare **Tel: 061 376 333**
Fax: 061 375445 Email: info@watermanslodge.ie Web: www.watermanslodge.com

Views down to Killaloe and across the Shannon are among the pleasant features of this appealing country house hotel. It changed hands late in 1998 and has since been undergoing systematic refurbishment. Head chef Chris Bray, who has been with the hotel since 2000, presents wide-ranging modern menus including some less usual ingredients (swordfish, kangaroo) alongside the more familiar (deep fried Cooleeney cheese, Ballina beef) and symbols on the menu considerately indicate dishes suitable for vegetarians, pescatarians and vegans and any unsuitable for coeliacs. Bar food is available, 12.30-7.30 daily. Golf, fishing, horse riding and pony trekking are all available nearby. Children welcome (under7s free in parents' room, cots available without charge). No pets. **Rooms 10** (1 shower only) B&B €76.18, ss €32. **Seats 40** D 6.30-9.30 daily. Set D from €32; à la carte available; house wine €17.71; sc discretionary. Closed 24-25 Dec. Amex, Diners, MasterCard, Visa, Laser. **Directions:** N7 to Birdhill turn left 500yds after the bridge.

Lahinch

Barrtra Seafood Restaurant

RESTAURANT Lahinch Co. Clare **Tel: 065 7081280**

SEAFOOD RESTAURANT OF THE YEAR

Paul and Theresa O'Brien have been providing fine food and hospitality at their traditional, whitewashed restaurant on the cliffs just outside Lahinch for over a decade. A conservatory added to the side of the original cottagey building made it lighter and brighter, opening up the whole area to make a more spacious atmosphere. Reception is the weak point of this otherwise admirable restaurant - the room itself is small and inadequate and it is sometimes necessary to wait there for an uncomfortably long time before being seated. Once into the restaurant itself, however, things immediately take a turn for the better and the sound of lots of people enjoying their meals and having a good time is infectious. The decor is appealingly simple and the views of Liscannor Bay - which can be magic from window tables on a fine evening - are the visual highlight. But local seafood is the star attraction and Theresa's excellent, unfussy cooking makes the most of a wide range of fish, while also offering a choice for those with other preferences, including a vegetarian menu. Paul, meanwhile, provides warm and easy hospitality and maintains good service. Main courses include lobster, when available, as well as the day's selection of other local seafood - and all at the kind of prices that many restaurants claim to be "impossible" these days. Richly flavoured chowders, glorious crab salads with home-made mayonnaise and breads, perfectly cooked fish with excellent sauces (cod with orange and ginger atttracted particular praise on a recent visit, also Thai spiced angler tails); exact timing and perfect judgment of flavourings enhances while always allowing the fish to be "itself". Vegetables are also a strong point, served on a platter which might include beautiful Clare potatoes, wilted spinach, flavoursome flaked carrot - and some warm ratatouille as well. An interesting and keenly priced wine list, good cheeseboard, home-baked breads and aromatic cafetière coffee show an attention to detail in tune with an overall high standard which we have found consistently enjoyable over the years. Children welcome. **Seats 32** D only Tue-Sun 5-10, Set D €33; Early D 5-6.30, €19; also à la carte. House wines from €13.50. s.c. discretionary. Closed Nov-Feb & Mon except Jul-Aug. Amex, MasterCard, Visa, Laser. **Directions:** 2.5 miles on Miltown Malbray road from Lahinch.

Lahinch

COUNTRY HOUSE

Moy House

Moy House Lahinch Co Clare
Tel: 065 708 2800 Fax: 065 7082500
Email: moyhouse@eircom.net Web: www.moyhouse.com

On a 15 acre site on the river Moy which also includes areas of mature woodland, Moy House enjoys a commanding position overlooking Liscannor Bay. Set on a hill, with unimpeded coastal views, the house has recently been renovated and decorated to an exceptionally high standard: combining the best materials with an inspired sense of design has created one of Ireland's most appealing (and luxurious) country houses and manager Bernie Merry runs it with genuine hospitality and great attention to detail. Although it appears to be quite a small, low building as you approach, the scale is larger than at first appears and its hillside position allows for a lower floor on the sea side - there is a side entrance below with direct access to the dining room and lower bedrooms (useful for anyone who might have difficulty with the narrow spiral staircase which joins the two floors internally). On the main entrance level there are four bedrooms and also a large, elegant drawing room with an open fire and honesty bar, where guests are free to enjoy aperitifs before going down to dine, or to relax with coffee (or tea or herbal/fruit tea) and petits fours after dinner. The decor throughout is in rich country house tones, with rugs and beautiful heavy fabrics used to great advantage - antique furniture is lovely but it is the inspired use of fabrics which is memorable. Bedrooms, which all have sea views, are wonderfully spacious and luxuriously appointed, as are the bathrooms (with underfloor heating so tiles are always warm on bare feet). Dinner - which is mainly for residents, although bookings may be taken from non-residents if there is room - and breakfast are served at separate tables in a dining room which is elegant yet also cosy, which would be reassuring in wild weather. The 4-course dinner menu offers three or four choices on each course: steamed mussels in garlic butter, cream of cauliflower & cheese soup, honey roast duckling with courgette & herb stuffing & orange sauce and fruit of the forest tart with plum compôte are all typical; farmhouse cheeses are also offered and there's a short but interesting wine list (house wines are from New Zealand, but Europe is also well-represented). All round, this lovely house offers a unique experience and is worth a special trip. **Rooms 8** (2 shower only) B&B €108 pps, ss€44. D7-8.15, €38. House wine €22. Closed Christmas & New Year. Amex, MasterCard, Visa. **Directions:** on the sea side of the Miltown Malbay road outside Lahinch.

Lahinch

HOTEL

Quality Aberdeen Arms Hotel

Main St Lahinch Co. Clare **Tel: 065 7081100**
Fax: 065 7081228 Email: aberdeenarms@eircom.net Web: aberdeenarms.ie

The Aberdeen Arms is the oldest golf links hotel in Ireland, with a history going back to 1850. A major refurbishment and extension programme has recently been completed, including the construction of a health centre, renovation of public areas and the addition of banqueting and conference facilities. Public areas are spacious and comfortably furnished, including the lively Klondyke Bar (named after Lahinch's famous 5th hole) and an all-day grill room. Bedrooms are generously sized with good bathrooms and quality furniture. Most have views of the golf links and the long sandy beach which brings large numbers of keen surfers to ride the waves. Children welcome (under 5s free in parents' room). No pets. **Rooms 55.** B&B €69.50pps, ss €12.70. Closed Jan & Feb. Amex, Diners, MasterCard, Visa, Laser. **Directions:** 20 miles northwest of Ennis, centre of town.

Liscannor

RESTAURANT

The Conch Shell

Liscanner Co Clare **Tel: 065 708 1888**

Approached by a staircase up the outside of a building on the main street, this new restaurant was opened in 2001 by husband and wife team Gordon (front of house) and Suzanne (the chef) Lightbourne. The reception area is comfortably furnished with a sofa and armchairs - and it's worth noting that it's the only place where smoking is allowed, so some may prefer to have coffee here after dinner. Over an aperitif, select from a shortish menu that favours seafood, but also offers other popular dishes, notably steak, and a couple of vegetarian dishes before moving into a large open-plan (and rather dimly lit) dining area that's quite plain - a little gloomy even - early in the evening, but brightens as it fills and a buzz develops. Ingredients in dishes such as queen scallop salad with lemon & sorrel sauce, turbot with rösti crust are clearly well-sourced, very fresh and well cooked - and main courses come with a generous vegetable platter, including delicious local potatoes. Desserts include refreshing seasonal fruit - in a strawbery & rhubarb compôte, perhaps, and home-made icecreams. Children welcome. No smoking in main restaurant. **Seats 40.** D Tue-Sun, 6.30-10. A la carte. House wine about €18. No s.c. Closed Mon (Sun-Thu off-season). MasterCard, Visa. **Directions:** centre of Liscanner village.

Lisdoonvarna

Sheedy's Country House Hotel

HOTEL
RESTAURANT

Lisdoonvarna Co. Clare
Tel: 065 707 4026 Fax: 065 707 4555
Email: enquries@sheedyscountryhouse.com Web: www.sheedyscountryhouse.com

If there were an award for "most improved establishment", Sheedy's would most definitely be the recipient. Although it has always been characterised by a high standard of maintenance indoors and out, with attractive furnishings, warm ambience (in every sense - the sunny foyer has a comfortable seating area and an open fire for chillier days) and friendly hands-on management, all of which made Sheedy's one of the west of Ireland's best loved small hotels - the old building presented insurmountable difficulties when major upgrading of bedrooms became necessary. So, over the winter of 2000/1, John and Martina Sheedy took the bull by the horns and embarked on a reconstruction programme that has seen this lovable duckling emerge as a lovely swan. All the bedrooms are now spacious and individually designed to a high standard with quality materials and elegant, quietly soothing colours; comfort is the priority, so bathrooms have power showers as well as full baths and there are CD music systems in addition to TV and the usual room facilities. Good food and warm hospitality remain constant qualities however. No pets. **Rooms 11** (1 suite, 2 junior suites, all no-smoking, 1 for disabled). B&B €50.80pps, ss 31.75. Closed 10 Oct-Easter. **Sheedys Restaurant:** The restaurant - and, specifically, John Sheedy's cooking - is a major attraction and, in the setting of a stylishly subdued olive-grey, curtainless dining room with plain candle-lit tables, he presents confident modern Irish cooking. On menus that assure diners of the traceability of ingredients, prawns in spring rolls with chilli jam and goats cheese & onion tart are typical starters, while seared salmon with a stew of peas and baby onions with crispy bacon and chives and rump of Burren lamb with a casserole of butter beans and rosemary, both perfectly cooked and served with a generous platter of equally perfect vegetables, give a fair indication of the style. Hospitality and service are also exemplary and prices reasonable for the high standard offered, making this a regular treat for a growing number of devotees. No smoking restaurant. **Seats 27.** D only 6.30-8.30. A la carte. House wine €16.50. Closed 1 Oct -Easter. MasterCard, Visa, Laser. **Directions:** 200 metres from square of town on road to Sulphur Wells.

Miltown Malbay

Berry Lodge

COUNTRY HOUSE/RESTAURANT

Annagh Miltown Malbay Co. Clare **Tel: 065 87022**
Fax: 065 87011 Email: rita.meade@esatclear.ie

Near the coast of west Clare, between Kilkee and Lahinch, this Victorian country house is the family home of Rita Meade, who has run it as a restaurant with accommodation since 1994 and cookery classes - given by Rita in her own kitchen - are a special feature of Berry Lodge. (Information, including a short breaks brochure, is available on request.) On the down side, the house can seem a little bleak and uninviting on arrival, an impression which is reinforced by the fact that there is no real reception area. However the restaurant - which is set up in an informal country style with pine furniture - has been considerably extended recently, to include a new conservatory area at the back of the house, overlooking the garden. Menus are interesting, food quality is very high and the cooking is sound - a combination which makes for an enjoyable dining experience. Meats, from a local butcher, are exceptional and, in the hands of a good cook, a dish like roast best end of lamb with swede and sweet potato crumble and rosemary & redcurrant flavoured sauce can be memorable. **Seats 45.** D6.30-9.30 (daily in high season), L Sun only, 1-3 pm. Set D about €32, Set

Sun L about €18. House wine about €15, s.c. discretionary. In winter, the restaurant is open only Sat D & Sun L, except for group bookings. **Accommodation** Bedrooms are on the small side (shower rooms even more so) but furnished with an attractive mixture of old and new, including Irish craft items. Children welcome. No pets. **Rooms 5** (all shower only,1 suitable for disabled guests). B&B about €28 pps, ss about €13. MasterCard, Visa. **Directions:** on the N67, between Quilty and Miltown Malbay.

Mountshannon

An Cupán Caifé

RESTAURANT

Main Street Mountshannon Co Clare **Tel: 061 927275**
Fax: 061 927275 Email: dagmarhilty@eircom.net

Dagmar Hilty's little restaurant on the main street only seats about 20, but there are also tables for nearly as many again outside in fine weather. Better still, perhaps, there's a welcoming fire on cold days - and a range of about a dozen wines on the mantlepiece for perusal, with a short description hanging from the bottle neck: a novel idea that adds to the atmosphere - and you're also welcome to bring your own. Brief lunchtime menus go on a blackboard, while more extensive evening choices are displayed in a rather dashing menu. Specialities include excellent side salads, lovely home-made cakes and a wide range of drinks & beverages. Open 12-9 Fri -Mon & Tues, also D Thurs, 5-9. Closed L Thurs, all Wed. MasterCard, Visa, Laser. **Directions:** on Main Street Mountshannon Village.

New Quay

Linnane's Lobster Bar

PUB

New Quay The Burren Co Clare **Tel: 065 707 8120**

Right on the rocks - with sliding doors opening up in summer, the better to enjoy views clear across Galway Bay - the Linnane family's unpretentious pub has a great reputation for good pints of stout and seafood, especially lobster. In winter there's a cosy turf fire and a more limited selection of food - chowder and homebaked bread perhaps, or crab salad. Building work, including an extension and new toilets, was in progress at the time of our last visit (spring 2001). A phone call is advised to check times of opening and whether food is available off-season. Meals 12-8 daily (weekends only Oct-Easter). MasterCard, Visa. **Directions:** halfway between Kinvara and Ballyvaughan.

Newmarket-on-Fergus

Carrygerry Country House

COUNTRY HOUSE

Newmarket-on-Fergus Co Clare
Tel: 061 363739 Fax: 061 363823

Only 10 minutes from Shannon airport and in a beautiful rural setting, Carrygerry is a lovely residence dating back to 1793. It overlooks the Shannon and Fergus estuaries and, peacefully surrounded by woodlands, gardens and pastures, seems very distant from an international airport. Reception rooms are elegantly furnished with antiques and are very comfortable, with open fires. Bedrooms are all non-smoking and include three suitable for disabled guests. Rooms in the main house are spacious and furnished to a high standard in period style, with all the amenities and those in the coachyard are also comfortably furnished, although with rather less style. Children under 12s free in parents' room. Pets permitted. * Carrygerry has been run as a country house hotel by Marinus and Angela van Kooyk since 1996 although, as the guide went to press, it seemed likely that the hotel may soon change hands. **Rooms 12** (4 shower-only; 3 suitable for disabled guests; all no-smoking.) B&B about €63 pp, ss about €14. Closed Jan & Feb. Amex, Diners, MasterCard, Visa. **Directions:** very close to Shannon airport; after Shannon Aerospace, turn right, hotel at the end of that road.

Newmarket-on-Fergus

Clare Inn Golf & Leisure Hotel

HOTEL

Dromoland Newmarket-on-Fergus Co Clare **Tel: 061 368161**
Fax: 061 368622 Email: cro@lynchotels.com Web: www.lynchhotels.com

Built in the grounds of Dromoland Castle, this 1960s hotel overlooks the Shannon estuary and shares the Castle's golf course. Like the other Lynch hotels (group recipients of the guide's Business Hotel Award in 2000), facilities for conferences and business guests are good, with back-up secretarial services, a business centre and video-conferencing. As well as golf, there's a leisure centre with 17-metre pool, gymnasium and sauna, so the combination of business and leisure facilities make this a popular conference venue. However, the hotel is also a favourite destination for families and the management seem unable to keep up with the resulting wear and tear. Maintenance in public areas left a lot to be desired on a recent visit and, although bedrooms are generally quite large and well-appointed, including some extra features including free movies, ISDN lines and an in-room safe, here too maintenance was poor and refurbishment required. Breakfast, although adequate, is a depressing experience, served in a large canteen-like room. However, staff are pleasant and helpful and rates are reasonable for the area. Children welcome (under 3s free in parents' room, cot available; playroom, crèche). No pets. Lift. **Rooms 183** (1 suite, 22 executive rooms, 4 no-smoking). B&B €82.53pps, ss€25.39. Room-only €74.91 (max 3). Open all year. Amex, Diners, MasterCard, Visa. **Directions:** located on the Dromoland Estate, 10 minutes drive from Ennis Town & Shannon Airport.

Newmarket-on-Fergus
HOTEL

Dromoland Castle Hotel

Newmarket-on-Fergus Co Clare **Tel: 061 368144**
Fax: 061 363355 Email: sales@dromoland.ie Web: www.dromoland.ie

Dromoland is one of Ireland's grandest hotels, and also one of the best-loved. The ancestral home of the O'Briens, barons of Inchiquin and direct descendants of Brian Boru, High King of Ireland, it is one of the few Irish estates tracing its history back to Gaelic royal families. Today, the visitor is keenly aware of this sense of history, but will not find it daunting. Under the warm and thoughtful management of Mark Nolan, who has been General Manager since 1989, Dromoland is a very relaxing hotel, where the grandeur of the surroundings - the castle itself, its lakes and parkland and magnificent furnishings - does not overpower but rather enhances the pleasure for guests. It is an enchanting place, where wide corridors lined with oak panelling are hung with ancient portraits and scented with the haunting aroma of woodsmoke. Public areas are very grand, with all the crystal chandeliers and massive antiques to be expected in a real Irish Castle, but the atmosphere suggests that a lot of fun is to be had here too. Bedrooms are all furnished to a very high standard, with luxurious bathrooms. The Brian Boru International Centre brought a new dimension to the Castle's activities a few years ago and can accommodate almost any type of business gathering, including exhibitions, conferences and banquets. A new wing, built to blend in with the castle, was recently completed. Child under 12 free in parents' room (cot available free of charge). No pets. Lift. **Rooms 100** (6 suites, 15 junior suites), Room only, €352 (max 2 guests.)

★ **Earl of Thomond Restaurant:** The most beautiful room in the castle, the Earl of Thomond Dining Room is magnificent, with crystal, gilding and rich fabrics - and has a lovely view over the lake and golf course. Guests ease into the experience of dinner with an aperitif in the Library Bar, overlooking the eighth green, before moving through to beautifully presented tables and gentle background music provided by a traditional Irish harpist. In the evening a wide choice includes a table d'hôte menu, vegetarian menu and an à la carte beginning with Head Chef David McCann's Dromoland signature dish, a "New Irish Cuisine" spectacular of traditional black pudding and buttermilk pancake topped with pan-fried foie gras and glazed apple; a superb dish and well worth trying. The à la carte continues in similar vein, offering a wonderful selection of luxurious dishes. The table d'hôte is more down-to-earth - a little less glamorous than the carte but with the same quality of ingredients and cooking - and possibly more Irish in tone. David McCann bases his menus on the best of local produce, all the little niceties of a very special meal are observed and service, under restaurant manager Tony Frisby, is excellent. Briefer lunch menus offer a shortened à la carte and a Chef's Suggested Lunch with a choice of three on each course. The wine list - about 250 wines, predominantly French - is under the constant review of sommelier Pascal Playon, winner of our Sommelier of the Year Award in 2000, who is not only knowledgable, but an exceptionally thoughtful and helpful wine host. (House wines from €23). A 15% service charge is added to all prices. Non-smoking Restaurant. D daily, 7-10, L Sun only 12.30-1.30; L&D set menus offered, à la carte also available.* Beside the castle, the Dromoland Golf and Country Club incorporates an 18-hole parkland course, a gym, a Health Clinic offering specialist treatments, also the Green Room Bar and Fig Tree Restaurant, which provide informal alternatives to facilities in the castle, including excellent food. Open all year. Amex, Diners, MasterCard, Visa. **Directions:** located on N18, 17 miles from Limerick, 8 miles from Shannon.

Rineen
RESTAURANT

Black Oak Restaurant

Rineen Miltown Malbay Co. Clare **Tel: 065 708 4408**

Set on a hillside with views over Liscannor Bay, this large modern house may not look like a restaurant (and the sign at the gate is small, although it is well-signed from Lahinch), but it is well-established and very comfortable, with plenty of sofas and chairs in a smallish reception area - a policy of seating guests quickly and taking orders from the table prevents overcrowding. The dining room is decorated in warm tones, with well-spaced, well-appointed tables - fresh flowers, good linen and glasses, comfortable chairs - setting a positive tone ahead of the meal. While not especially innovative, moderately priced menus offer a very fair choice, with starters like St Tola goat cheese, crab in filo pastry and mussels in wine then main courses such as rack of lamb and Seafood Pot (a house speciality - a generous and perfectly cooked selection of fish cooked in a tomato, leek, saffron & garlic sauce and served in its own pot), well-presented with a selection of side vegetables. Desserts tend towards the classics - lemon tarte, variations on crème brûlée. This restaurant delivers what it promises: good fresh food, with a high level of comfort and service at reasonable prices. Air conditioning. Seats 65 (Max table size, 10). D Wed-Mon, 5.30-9.30 pm.; early D 5.30-6pm about €20; Set D about €28 from 6.30pm. House wines from about €13. Closed Tue & Christmas-April. MasterCard, Visa. **Directions:** 7 km outside Lahinch village on the Miltown road.

Shannon

Oakwood Arms Hotel

HOTEL

Shannon Co Clare **Tel: 061 361500**

Fax: 061 361414 Email: manager@oakwoodarms.com Web: www.oakwoodarms.com

John and Josephine O'Sullivan opened this mock-Tudor red brick hotel in 1991 and it created a good impression from the start, with its high standard of maintenance and neatly laid-out flower beds. The lounge bar and function room both have aviation themes: the bar honours the memory of the pioneer female pilot Sophie Pearse, who came from the area, and the restaurant is named after The Spruce Goose, Howard Hughes' famous flying boat. Public areas are quite spacious and comfortably furnished and there is ample evidence of a well-run establishment. Each visit sees exemplary routine refurbishment, improvements and developments - this year, a new fitness centre has just been completed and Sophie's lounge has been refurbished. Although not individually decorated, rooms have all the necessary comforts and are double-glazed with air conditioning, ISDN lines, hospitality trays, ironing facilities and TV. Conference/banqueting (300/250) facilities are good, with video-conferencing and back-up secretarial services available. The attractive Spruce Goose restaurant is moderately priced, and serves fresh, homely food. Under 5s free in parents' room; cots available. No pets. **Rooms 101** (4 suites, 4 junior suites, 23 executive rooms, 37 no-smoking) €62 pps, ss €33. No s.c. Closed 24-26 Dec. Amex, Diners, MasterCard, Visa, Laser. **Directions:** located on the N19, 2 kms from Shannon Airport.

Shannon

Quality Hotel Shannon

HOTEL

Ballycasey Shannon Co Clare **Tel: 061 364 588**

Fax: 061 364 045 Email: sales@qualityshannon.com Web: www.choicehotelsireland.ie

A recent addition to the choice of accommodation at Shannon airport, the Quality Hotel offers modern comforts at a reasonable price. Rooms all have multi-channel TV and modem points and the hotel is geared for the convenience of guests who are meeting or seeing off relatives, or want somewhere for a quick business meeting before heading off to another destination. Wholesome fare is served in the informal hotel restaurant, Lannigans. Conferences/banqueting (20/60). Lift. Ample parking.Children under 12 free in parents' room. No pets. **Rooms 54** (10 no-smoking, 3 for disabled). B&B €63.45 pps, s.s.€19.05. Amex, MasterCard, Visa. **Directions:** on N19 coming to Shannon Town.

Shannon

Shannon Great Southern Hotel

HOTEL féile bia

Shannon Airport Shannon Co Clare **Tel: 061 471122**

Fax: 061 471982 Email: res@shannon.gsh.ie Web: www.greatsouthernhotels.com

Just two minutes walk from the main terminal building at Shannon Airport, the Shannon Great Southern is in an unexpectedly lovely location overlooking the estuary and, with its views and rather gracious atmosphere, it retains a little of the old romance of flight. On the practical side it also offers unbeatable convenience for travellers recovering from or preparing for international flights. The hotel is fully sound-proofed and bedrooms, all of which have been recently refurbished and upgraded, are spacious and comfortable, with all the amenities expected of a good modern hotel, including ISDN lines. Activities available include snooker and a mini-gym for residents, and there is golf and horseriding nearby. Day trips can be arranged to local sites, such as the Cliffs of Moher or the Aillwee Caves, including admission and full day transport. The hotel also has good conference facilities for groups of 12 to 200 (banqueting 140), backed up by a private business centre with full secretarial services. **Rooms 115.** (1 suite, 56 executive rooms, 29 no-smoking rooms. Room Rate €130 (up to 3 guests) Closed 24-26 Dec. Amex, Diners, MasterCard, Visa, Laser. **Directions:** at Shannon Airport, 2 minutes walk from terminal building.

Tulla

RESTAURANT

Flappers Restaurant

Tulla Co Clare **Tel: 065 683 5711**

Jim and Patricia McInerney's simple little split-level restaurant (the lower part is non-smoking) is refreshingly free of decoration, except for a pair of striking pictures and fresh flowers on the tables. Lunchtime sees the emphasis on fairly hearty food and good value but, although the menu is limited, you can easily work up to a rather smart 3-course meal if you wish: organic mixed greens with honey mustard dressing to start, perhaps, lemon peppered chicken (breast of chicken grilled with a light lemon pepper sauce) and a home-made dessert such as fresh fruit meringues with banana cream. In the evening the mood changes and, in addition to a set 2 or 3-course menu, there's a more ambitious à la carte offering the likes of spicy crab cakes with basil aioli and leek and wild mushroom puff pastry tartlet, followed by main courses like roast rack of lamb with creamy flageolet beans and redcurrant sauce or grilled salmon on a bed of roasted peppers and courgettes with lemon & chive cream sauce. Vegetarian options are imaginative and desserts like flourless chocolate cake with frangelico ice cream are equally tempting. There's a well-chosen and very fairly priced wine list too- and even a take-away service, which must be a boon for holidaymakers self-catering in the area as well as locals. Not suitable for children after 8pm. **Seats 40** No-smoking area; air conditioning. Wheelchair access to toilets. L 12-3, D 7-10. (Shorter hours in winter - please phone for details) A la carte. House wine €15.17. SC discretionary (except 10% on groups of 8+). Closed all Sun, D Mon, bank hols and first 2 weeks Nov. MasterCard, Visa, Laser. **Directions:** Main St. Tulla village, 10 miles from Ennis.

COUNTY CORK

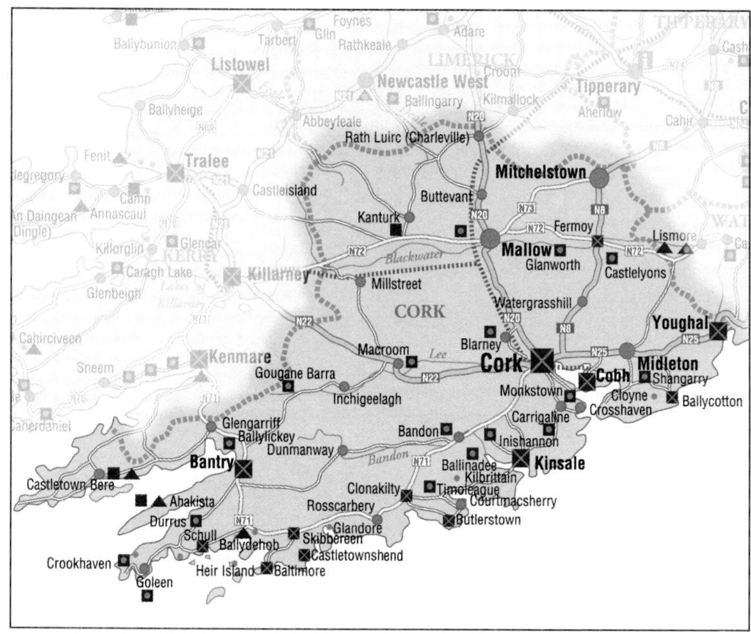

Cork City

It is Cork, of all Ireland's cities, which most warmly gives the impression of being a place at comfort with itself through being set in the midst of a land flowing in milk and honey. Cork is all about the good things in life. While it may be stretching things a little to assert that the southern capital has a Mediterranean atmosphere, there's no doubting its Continental and cosmpolitan flavour, and the Cork people's relaxed enjoyment of it all.

There is now a specific pride in this Continental emphasis, with the announcement - in October 2001 - that Cork will be the European City of Culture in 2005. The buildup to this highlight in civic and cultural life will take all the time available, and during it Cork will benefit as the world outside increases its awareness of Cork's special qualities, and its appreciation of the pleasant commodities of life.

Trading in such commodities has always been what Cork and its famous "merchant princes" are all about. At one time, the city was known as "the butter capital of Europe". The way in which sea and land intertwine throughout the wonderfully sheltered natural harbour, and through the lively old city itself, has encouraged waterborne trade in farm produce and a sea-minded outlook. Thus today Cork is at the heart of Ireland's most dynamically nautical area, a place world-renowned for its energetic interaction with the sea, whether for business or pleasure.

It's an area noted, too, for the entertaining and individualistic quality of its branded products. Just eastward of the city is Midleton, home to the Jameson Heritage Centre, and home as well to Irish Distillers manufacturing headquarters where they create products as various as Jameson, Powers and Paddy whiskey - to name only three of their whiskey brands - as well as Huzzar Vodka and Cork Dry Gin.

In the city itself, we find two Irish stouts being brewed - Murphy's and Beamish. Each has its own distinctive flavour, each in turn is different from Dublin's Guinness, and it is one of life's pleasures in one of Cork's characterful pubs to discuss and compare their merits. If the thought of that leaves you speechless, you can always head northwest of the city, where the Blarney Stone in Blarney Castle is just waiting to make you eloquent and able to take on the Cork people's delightful line in deflationary and quirky humour.

Local Attractions and Information

Cork Airport	021 4313031
Cork Arts Society	021 4277749
Cork City Gaol	021 4305022
Cork Tourist Information	021 4273251
Guinness Cork Jazz Festival (late October)	021 4278979
Cork International Choral Festival (April/May)	021 4308308
Cork International Film Festival (October)	021 4271711
Cork Public Museum	021 4270679
Crawford Gallery, Emmett Place	021 4273377
English Market (covered, speciality food stalls Mon-Sat), corner between Grand Parade & Patrick Street	
Firkin Crane Dance Centre, Shandon	021 4507487
Opera House	021 4270022
Railway Station	021 4504888
Triskel Arts Centre, Tobin St off Sth Main St	021 4272022

Amicus

RESTAURANT 14A French Church Street Cork **Tel: 021 427 6455** Fax: 021 422 3547

Tucked into a small space in Cork's Huguenot district, Ursula and Robert Hales' newly opened restaurant is already filling a gap on the Cork circuit. Outside you'll find a few tables for street dining while indoors you can enjoy Robert's well-prepared food in a bistro-style environment. This tiny restaurant, almost cramped with tables, comprises one small, bustling room, which has been fitted out with cool creams, wood, large mirrors and a few choice canvasses. Starters include fresh, flavoursome salads (typically including Parma ham with peach & mint leaves and roasted peppers salad). Main courses offer a choice of gourmet hamburgers as well as seafood, pasta and chargrilled chicken. Service, under Ursula's direction is smart and friendly, with children made especially welcome. But the main attraction is the availability of real food at affordable prices. A short, but well chosen wine list complements the uncomplicated food, which Robert presents with flair. If early signs are anything to go by there's no reason why Amicus can't become a firm favourite with Cork's casual diners. **Seats 38.** Open Mon-Sat: Breakfast 8.15-12, L 12-6, D6-10.30. A la carte; house wine about €13.90. MasterCard, Visa. MasterCard, Visa, Laser.

The Barn Restaurant

RESTAURANT Glanmire Cork **Tel: 021 4866211** Fax: 021 4866525

At Glanmire, on the edge of the city on the old Youghal road, this long-established neighbourhood restaurant has earned a devoted local clientèle for its good French/Irish cooking and professional service. It is comfortably old-fashioned, with uniformed waiters and food with a real home-cooked flavour. Dinner menus offer a wide choice on all courses - roast fillet of local salmon with sorrel sauce indicates the style and everything is cooked to order. Vegetarians are well looked after, saucing is good and accompaniments are carefully selected. Finish with Irish cheeses or something from the traditional dessert trolley. Sunday lunch is very popular and menus are similar in style. Car park. D daily, 6.30-9.30, L Sun only 12-2.30. Set D €35.55, Set Sun L €20.33. Closed Ash Wed & Good Fri. MasterCard, Visa, Amex.

Bully's Restaurant

RESTAURANT 40 Paul Street Cork **Tel: 021 4273555**

A small, buzzy and inexpensive restaurant in one of the busiest little shopping streets in the city centre, Bully's has built up a strong reputation over the years for good food at reasonable prices. A speciality is pizzas, which had ultra light, crisp bases long before they began to show up in fashionable restaurants; the dough is made on the premises every day using Italian flour. But their No.10 pizza (€10.73) is a Cork Special, with ham, sausage, black and white pudding as well as tomatoes and mozzarella. They serve lots of other things too - freshly made burgers, steaks, omelettes, chicken dishes and pasta - and there's a short, reasonably priced wine list. Pavement seating outside the restaurant has eased the crush a bit of late and there are plans to open up extra seating upstairs, to cater for larger groups. No smoking restaurant. **Seats 35.** Open Mon-Sat 8am-11.15, Sun 9am-11pm (Open for breakfast in Paul Street only.) A la carte. House wine €15.20

Closed 25-26 Dec & 1 Jan. Also at: 7 Douglas Village East, Douglas, Cork (021-4892415) Mon-Sat, 12-11, Sun 1-10; Open 1 Jan in Douglas only. Amex, MasterCard, Visa, Laser. **Directions:** In Cork city centre, next to Paul Street Shopping centre.

Café Gusto

CAFÉ

3 Washington Street Cork **Tel: 021 4254446** Fax: 021 4254446
Email: info@cafegusto.com Web: www.cafegusto.com

Big ideas are evident in this little designer coffee bar near Singer's Corner, which specialises in gourmet rolls, wraps and salads, either to go or eat on the premises. The brainchild of Marianne Delaney, previous manager of The Exchange on George's Quay, and her Ballymaloe-trained partner Denis O'Mullane, Café Gusto came to our attention when a reader praised their "exemplary sourcing" - and small is indeed beautiful here, where coffee is made by baristas trained to master standard, using 100% arabica beans from the Java Roasting Company. The same philosophy applies throughout this tiny café, which was transformed by local designers and craftsmen to provide the perfect space for discerning customers to enjoy zestful international flavours in a short menu ranging from Simply Cheddar (freshly baked Italian bread filled with with beef tomato, white onion & relish) to The Flying Bacon (filled with chicken, bacon, Emmenthal, honey Dijon, lettuce & tomato). Food prices range from €3.10 to €4.14 (not much more than supermarket sandwiches) and the extensive selection of coffees, teas, herbal teas etc are good value, starting at only €1.15. No smoking area; air conditioning. **Seats 20.** Open Mon-Sat, 11 am-5pm. **Directions:** across from Capitol Cinema.

Café Paradiso

RESTAURANT ☆

16 Lancaster Quay Western Road Cork **Tel: 021 4277 939**
Fax: 021 4274973 Email: dpcotter@eircom.net Web: www.cafeparadiso.ie

Café Paradiso was a well-deserved success from the moment it opened its doors in 1993, but the fan club has grown immeasurably with the success of the lovely Café Paradiso Cookbook - which enabled the philosophy of this mould-breaking vegetarian restaurant to reach a far wider public. The book includes (amongst many other culinary gems) the recipe for goats' cheese, pinenut and oven-roasted tomato charlotte, served with wilted greens and puy lentils in basil oil - which is a house speciality and selected as the guide's Vegetarian Dish of the Year in 2000; it's an excellent example of the exciting mainstream cooking at this colourful little restaurant, where even the most committed carnivores love every mouthful. It's a lively place with a busy atmosphere and the staff, under the direction of Bridget Healy, are not only friendly and helpful but obviously enthusiastic about their work. Seasonal menus based on the best organic produce available are topped up by daily specials, might include a modish starter like vegetable sushi with tempura of courgette & cauliflower, pickled ginger, wasabi and a dipping sauce and a summer gratin of courgettes, broad beans & new potatoes with a tangy Gabriel cheese crust, basil cream, roasted baby beetroots and fresh peas. Irresistible desserts too - gooseberry and almond tartlet with amaretto custard, perhaps, or strawberry baked alaska with summer berry sauce - and some organic wines on a well-priced global list. Café Paradiso may be tiny, but optimum use is made of the space and this is inspired and beautifully cooked food, served with charm. Significantly, in this era of "cheffy" food and big egos, the creator of this wonderful food decribes himself simply as "owner cook". **Seats 45.** No Smoking area. Open Tues-Sat: L12.30-3, D 6.30-10.30. A la carte. House wines from €15.24. Service discretionary. Closed Sun, Mon, Christmas, last 2 weeks Aug. Visa, MasterCard, Diners, Laser. **Directions:** On Western Road, opposite Jurys Hotel.

Coal Quay Café

CAFÉ

Cornmarket Street Cork Tel: 021 4272880 Fax: 021 4272897
Email: bodega@indigo.ie

Cork's coolest eating place is attached to the youthful Bodega bar, which is very beautiful but can get very noisy with its stone walls and wooden floors accentuating loud music and conversation - in contrast to the Café, which has its own entrance and (in the guide's experience) a surprisingly quiet atmosphere. Housed in an old limestone warehouse building, the spacious restaurant is informal in the best contemporary style, with carefully selected simple, clean-lined furnishings (comfortable chairs, quality table settings) and artwork by local artists, changed monthly. Sourcing of quality local foods is a high priority, although menus are international: expect starters like onion, mozzarella & roasted tomato tartlet and spicy chicken cakes with courgette & pepper salsa, plenty of salads, pastas, grills (spicy lamb kebab with couscous, tzatziki & pitta bread perhaps) and seafood (typically seared scallop salad, with crispy snow peas & tangy hazelnut dressing) - and lovely desserts, like lemon tart with raspberry sorbet for example. The place has great style, staff are attentive, friendly and very professional, cooking is excellent - and it's good value for the high standard of food and service (starters average €5, main courses €15). A shortish wine list includes a cocktail menu as well as a limited selection of international wines. Menu available in Bodega at other times. Parking in the area is not difficult after 6.30pm. No smoking area. **Seats 120** (private room, 50). L Wed-Sat, 12-3.30, (Sun 12.30-3), D Wed-Sat 5.30-10.30, Sun 5.30-9. A la carte. House wine €18.41. SC discretionary (12/5% on parties of 6+). Closed 25 Dec. Amex, MasterCard, Visa, Laser. **Directions:** Travelling west from Patricks Bridge, turn left in Cornmarket Street from Coal Quay/Lavitt's Quay.

Crawford Gallery Café

RESTAURANT

Emmet Place Cork **Tel: 021 274415** Fax: 021 4652021
Web: www.ballymaloe.ie

This fine 1724 building houses an excellent collection of 18th- and 19th-century landscapes and has recently has a large new extension added. It is also home to the Crawford Gallery Café, one of Cork city's favourite informal eating places, which is managed by Fern Allen, daughter of Ivan and Myrtle Allen, who founded the world famous Ballymaloe House at Shanagarry in the mid '60s - and, by a remarkable coincidence, Fern is also the great grand-daughter of Arthur Hill, architect of a previous extension to the gallery, completed in 1884. The menu reflects the Ballymaloe philosophy that food is precious and should be handled carefully, that meals should be happy and convivial and that cooking is an art, so the gallery Café serves freshly prepared dishes made from natural local ingredients and offers Ballymaloe breads and many of the other dishes familiar to Ballymaloe fans. The menu changes weekly, but the style - a judicious mixture of timeless country house fare and contemporary international dishes featuring carefully sourced meats, fish from Ballycotton and the freshest of seasonal vegetables - remains reassuringly constant. Home-made pickles, relishes, chutenys and preserves are delicious details. A short well-balanced wine list offers a good choice of half and quarter bottles. **Seats 70.** No smoking area. Mon-Sat, L 12.30-2.30 (Sat to 3). Set L €16.50; also à la carte. House wine €16.50. Service discretionary. Closed Sun, 24 Dec (after lunch)- early Jan. MasterCard, Visa, Laser. **Directions:** In the Crawford Municipal Gallery, next to the Cork Opera House.

The Crow's Nest Bar & Restaurant

PUB/RESTAURANT

Victoria Cross Cork **Tel: 021 454 3330**
Email: thecrowsnestbarandrestaurant@eircom.net

Pleasant, friendly and enormously popular in the locality, this large, recently refurbished pub is clearly a much-needed addition to the facilities of the area. (A large free carpark on the Carrigrohane Road, directly opposite, no doubt adds to the attraction.) Both the bar and upstairs restaurant are bright and colourful in a contemporary (but emphatically not minimalist) style and the selection of past awards collected by the proprietor-chef indicates an encouraging level of commitment to good food. The restaurant menu is imaginative, with the provenance of some ingredients given, which is confidence-inspiring: steaks are a speciality, for example, and the local butcher who supplies them is credited on the menu. However, the longish menus (plus blackboard specials) might be somewhat over-ambitious: while the standard of food and cooking is certainly above average, service slows noticeably as the pub downstairs fills up with the evening rush. An informative, well-priced wine list includes some lesser-known choices and a fair number of half bottles. Not suitable for children after 7 pm. Bar meals 12.30-9 daily (carvery lunch & short à la carte afternoon menu). Restaurant **Seats 40.** Air conditioning. D 6-10pm daily (Sun to 9), à la carte; s.c. discretionary. House wine €12.65.Closed 25-26 Dec & Good Fri. Amex, MasterCard, Visa, Diners, Laser. **Directions:** one mile from City Centre via Western road.

Dan Lowrey's Tavern

PUB

13 MacCurtain Street Cork **Tel: 021 505071**

This characterful pub just across the road from Isaacs was established in 1875 and has been run by Anthony and Catherine O'Riordan since 1995. Long before the arrival of the "theme pub", Lowrey's was famous for having windows which originated from Kilkenny Cathedral, but it also has many of its own original features, including a fine mahogany bar. Catherine O'Riordan herself oversees the kitchen, so it's a good place for an inexpensive home-cooked meal - popular dishes like home-made quiche or lasagne served with salad or fries, for example, or Kinsale seafood pie, filled with salmon, monkfish & cod, topped with creamed potatoes and toasted breadcrumbs. There's also a nice little quarter-bottle wine list representing Chile, California, Italy and Portugal, all at €3.62 Meals 12.30-3 daily. Closed 25 Dec & Good Fri. **Directions:** Next to Everyman Palace Theatre.

The Douglas Hide

PUB 63 Douglas Street Cork **Tel: 021 4315695** Email: douflashide@eircom.net

Tadhg and Aoife O'Donovan's narrow little bar is bright and cheerful, with two smallish dining areas behind it, making for a friendly, informal ambience. Despite its small size, it's quite comfortable, with wooden bench seats running along the walls and a young clientele creating a lively atmoshere. Some modern paintings and background music (not too obtrusive) complete the scene, but it's the food that makes this a destination bar. Sensibly short menus change as the day progresses - imaginative soups, sandwiches, pastas and lightish bites for lunch include some tempting vegetarian options (brie and homemade chutney on ciabatta or Greek salad, for example) while more substantial dinner menus offer tasty starters like dressed crab timbale or smoked haddock potato cake with fromage frais & mustard sauce, and mains like chicken in a spicy Moroccan sauce with couscous or fish specials (based on market availability). Specialities include O'Flynn's spicy handmade sausages and mash; there's also a Sunday Brunch menu. Outside meal times, it operates as a normal pub, with pub opening times. The standard of food and cooking is high, the service friendly and attentive - and 2002 should see an extension of the exisiting dining area, with provision for a no-smoking area. **Seats 45**, L12-3pm (Sun 12.30-4pm), D 5-9 pm daily; all à la carte; house wines from €15.87. S.c. discretionary. Closed 25 Dec & Good Fri. MasterCard, Visa, Laser. **Directions:** opposite South Presentation Convent on Douglas Street.

ECO Douglas

RESTAURANT 1 Eastville Douglas Village Cork **Tel: 021 4892522**
Fax: 021-4895354 Email: mail@eco.ie Web: www.eco.ie

This busy, contemporary restaurant is understandably popular, as it combines interesting menus with good cooking and reasonable prices - a winning formula by any standards, so booking ahead is wise. Space is limited and the decor on the dark side, but the lively buzz compensates for lack of natural light and tables are reasonably spaced, although the small reception area can be a problem if your table isn't ready on arrival: service is usually friendly and helpful, but delays do occur. Perhaps the choice offered - on an interesting international menu with vegetarian dishes considerately highlighted in green - is a bit over-ambitious and it might be wise to opt for specialities such as cajun salmon or stir fries at busy times. Good wine list - over 80 reasonably priced wines from all over the world, including Argentina and Uruguay. Children welcome. Parking can be difficult. **Seats 75.** No-smoking area; air conditioning. Open Mon-Sat 12-11, Sun & bank hols D only, 5-11pm . Evening menu from 5 pm. A la carte. House wine £10.95. Service discretionary except on parties over 7 (10%). Closed Good Fri, 25-26 Dec. Amex, MasterCard, Visa. **Directions:** In Douglas village - 3 miles out from city centre, 1 mile from airport.

The Exchange Bar

PUB 1 Buckingham Place Georges Quay Cork **Tel: 021 431 1786**
Fax: 021 489 3391 Web: www.theexchangebar.com

Gary & Katie O'Donovan breathed new life into this fine old quayside building when they opened it as a wine bar ("Cork's first wine focused licensed premises"). You'll find oodles of wines by the glass (or bottle) and Ballymaloe-trained chef Mary-Clare Horgan offers a range of wholesome lunchtime food: in addition to daily specials and desserts from a board, a compact menu offers informal fare like home-made soup served with health loaf or olive and tomato bread; salads - typically chicken with roasted peppers, spring onion, balsamic vinaigrette with roasted pinenuts & parmesan shavings - and gourmet sandwiches. Vegetarian dishes are highlighted and there's a range of coffees, teas and hot chocolate (also available in the morning). Unnecessarily loud music can make conversation difficult. **Seats 70.** Bar Food served Mon-Sat 10.30-3 1(Sat 11-3), L menu 12-3. No food serve on Sun. Wine by the glass, from €3.49. MasterCard, Visa, Laser. **Directions:** Waterfront, City Centre.

Farmgate Café

RESTAURANT/CAFÉ Old English Market Princes Street Cork
Tel: 021 427 8134 Fax: 021 463 2771

A sister restaurant to the Farmgate Country Store and Restaurant in Midleton, Kay Harte's Farmgate Café shares the same commitment to serving fresh food - and, as it is located above the English Market, where ingredients are purchased daily, it doesn't come much fresher than this. They serve traditional food, including some famous old Cork dishes with a special market connection - tripe & drisheen and corned beef & champ with green cabbage. Another speciality is "the freshest of fish". All this and home-baked cakes and breads too. Moderately priced meals daytime Mon-Sat. Diners, MasterCard.

Fenns Quay Restaurant

RESTAURANT féile bia 5 Fenns Quay Sheares Street Cork **Tel: 021 427 9527** Fax: 021 4279526

Partially in a 250-year old listed building (the entrance and front part of the restaurant are in an extension), this is a bright, busy restaurant with a welcoming atmosphere and simple decor enlivened by striking modern paintings. Both lunch and dinner menus offer plenty of interesting choices, with several vegetarian options and daily specials, including seafood from the nearby English Market. Carefully sourced ingredients are local where posssible (including meat from the owners' own business, which is a point of pride) presented in a contemporary style based on classical cooking; typical examples include warm chicken brochettes with chapatis, spiced tomato dip and salad (from a range available as starters or main courses) and fillet steak "Welly style" with sauté potatoes, which is a house speciality. Lunch menus include some informal food, like open sandwich of the day and desserts are all coeliac friendly. The wine list, while not extensive, offers variety at reasonable prices, with a good range by the glass - good value is a feature of both food and drink. Despite recent refurbishment, the age of the building has made it difficult to provide wheelchair access. Children welcome. On street parking can be difficult. No-smoking area; air conditioning. **Seats 46.** Open all day Mon-Sat 10-10; L 12.30-3, D 6.30-10. Set L €14.60, Short D €19.05, Set D from €25.39. Also à la carte. House wine €15.87. Service discretionary. Closed Sun, 25 Dec. Amex, MasterCard, Visa, Laser. **Directions:** Central city - 2 minutes from the Courthouse.

Flemings

RESTAURANT/ACCOMMODATION Silver Grange House Tivoli Cork
Tel: 021 482 1621 Fax: 021 482 1178

Clearly signed off the main Cork-Dublin road, this large Georgian family house is set in well-maintained grounds, including a kitchen garden which provides most of the fruit, vegetables and herbs required for the restaurant during the summer. The light, airy double dining room is decorated in an elegant low-key style that highlights its fine proportions, while well-appointed linen-clad tables provide a fine setting for Michael Fleming's classical cooking. Seasonal table d'hôte and à la carte menus offer a good selection of classics, slightly influenced by current international trends - a vegetarian dish of crispy vegetable wontons with tossed leaf salad, Atlantic prawns & scallops with grilled polenta & a sweet pepper jus - but the main thrust of the cooking style is classical French. Vegetables are imaginative in selection and presentation, while desserts may include a beautiful tasting plate. Lunch and dinner are served every day. **Accommodation:** There are four spacious en-suite rooms, comfortably furnished in a style appropriate to the age of the house (approx.€40 pps/, ss€20). Closed 25-27 Dec. Amex, Diners, MasterCard, Visa. **Directions:** Next to Lotamore House; well-signed up to the left off Cork-Dublin road as you are leaving the city.

G's

RESTAURANT Grafton Mall Grand Parade Cork **Tel: 021 4276430**

Gina Casey's informal café-style restaurant is open through the day and its situation in the Grafton shopping Mall (beside the multi-storey carpark) makes it an ideal meeting place. Gina - whose previous experience includes working at Longueville House and with Michael Clifford - sources ingredients with care and offers a concise menu that varies through the day, beginning with breakfast (from 9 am) and finishing with teas in the afternoon. A sensibly limited range of hot dishes includes a fish of the day, regular main courses might include a tasty vegetarian dish like warm char-grilled salad served on a basil potato cake and topped with vegetable crisps & balsamic dressing - and there's a warning that hot food takes 15-20 minutes to prepare, which is reassuring if you value freshly cooked food. 'Special sambos' like bacon, cheese & tomato melt with relish in a pitta pocket are quicker and old favourites like meringue roulade and chocolate biscuit cake with caramel sauce are equally good as a snack with tea or coffee. A short wine list includes a couple of quarter bottles, but no halves. Children welcome. **Seats 107.** No smoking area; air conditioning. Open Mon-Sat, 9-4.30; L 12-3.30, (average main course €8.85). House wine €17.71. Closed Sun, bank hols, Christmas. MasterCard, Visa, Laser.

Great Southern Hotel

HOTEL

Cork Airport Hotel Cork **Tel: 021 4947500** Fax: 021 4947501
Email: res@corkairport.gsh.ie Web: www.greatsouthernhotels.com

This brand new hotel opened in spring 2001 and is very handily located, within walking distance of the terminal. Ideal for a first or last night's stay, it's also a useful meeting place and is well equipped for business guests. Rooms have voice mail, fax/modem lines, desk space and TV with in-house movie channel as well as more usual facilities like radio, hair dryer, tea/coffee trays and trouser press. There's a business centre with secretarial services and extensive conference/banqueting facilities. Gym, jacuzzi, sauna. Ample free parking. **Rooms 81.** Room rate about €140. Open all year. Amex, Diners, MasterCard, Visa, Laser. **Directions:** Situated in Airport Complex.

Hayfield Manor Hotel

HOTEL
RESTAURANT

Perrott Avenue College Road Cork **Tel: 021 484 5900**
Fax: 021 431 6839 Web: www.hayfieldmanor.ie

Set in two acres of gardens next door to University College Cork, Hayfield Manor Hotel provides every comfort and a remarkable level of privacy and seclusion just a mile from the city centre. Although recently built - it only opened in 1996 - it has the genuine feel of a large period house. Conference rooms of varying sizes include a library/boardroom beside the drawing room that doubles as a private dining room. Spacious bedrooms vary in decor, are beautifully furnished to a very high standard with antiques and have generous marbled bathrooms with individual tiling, heated towel rails and quality toiletries. Conference facilities for up to 120 delegates; secretarial services. Tennis, golf and fishing nearby. Beauty and massage therapies by arrangement. Under 5s free in parents' room (cots available). No pets. **Rooms 87** (5 suites, 12 junior suites, 70 executive rooms; 15 no-smoking, 6 for disabled). B&B €172 pps, ss €76. Open all year.

The Manor Room: There is no dedicated reception area or cocktail bar attached to the restaurant, which means aperitifs must be taken in the bar (which can be noisy), at the table - or, perhaps, in the lobby - which is not an ideal way to begin a fine dining experience. However, once inside this well-appointed, traditional dining room, the view over the walled garden at the back of the hotel is soothing, giving it the quiet, serene atmosphere that head chef Robert Cowley's fine cooking deserves. He has been with the hotel since 1997, and makes good use of local produce, often with a contemporary twist - steamed Bantry Bay mussels may be flavoured with lemongrass and ginger - and even a little drama: try a speciality starter of table-side pan-seared foie gras, for example, one of a range of about eight starters on a luxurious evening menu. A main course speciality from a similar number of choices is prawn & mussel crusted monkfish tail, which may sound like too much of a good thing but the cooking is in confident hands and dishes are not over complicated. Well-judged combinations and skilful cooking are impressive - as in details like complimentary amuse-bouches, and well-made sauces and dressings - although, on a recent visit, service failed to match the high standard of the food. Ensure that you are offered the full wine list if taking an aperitif in the bar, as the bar list is very limited. **Seats 90.** L12.30-2, D 7-10 (Sun to 9.30). Set L €28.50. Set D €51; à la carte also available. House wine €32 Service discretionary (10% on parties of 8+) *Informal meals are also available in the bar, 11am-8pm daily. Amex, Diners, MasterCard, Visa, Laser.

Hotel Isaacs

HOTEL

48 MacCurtain Street Cork **Tel: 021 450 0011** Fax: 021 450 6355
Email: cork@isaacs.ie Web: www.isaacs.ie/cork

Opposite the theatre and approached through a cobbled courtyard, this attractive hotel offers comfort in spacious rooms at a reasonable price. The bedrooms have attractive polished stripped wood floor, free-standing pine furniture and the usual amenities; some rooms over the street could be noisy. Car park nearby. Lift. **Rooms 36** (all en-suite, some shower-only, some no-smoking, 2 for disabled) B&B about €60pps. Closed 3 days Christmas. **Greene's Restaurant** Despite being next door to the well-known Isaacs restaurant (with the confusion of the hotel's similar name). Greene's Restaurant has established itself successfully and is clearly prospering. The atmosphere is more like an independent restaurant than an hotel dining room and the style lively and international; prices are quite reasonable. **Seats 100.** Food served from 7.30 am.Closed 24 Dec(from 3pm) - 28 Dec. Diners, MasterCard, Visa. **Directions:** Halfway along MacCurtain Street, opposite Dan Lowrey's Pub.

Imperial Hotel

HOTEL South Mall Cork **Tel: 021 427 4040** Fax: 021 427 4040
Email: info@imperialhotelcork.ie Web: www.imperialhotelcork.ie

This thriving hotel in Cork's main commercial and banking centre was taken over by the Flynn family in 1998. It dates back to 1813 and has a colourful history - Michael Collins spent his last night here, no less, and that suite now bears his name. However, it's the convenient location, near the river and just a couple of minutes walk from the Patrick Street shopping area - that makes this hotel so popular for business and pleasure - also the free car parking available for residents. Rooms are all en-suite, with a mixture of furnishings, and there are attractive weekend and off-season rates. Conference/banqueting (300). Private car park. Children welcome; under 12s free in parents' room, cots available. No pets. **Rooms 88** (all en-suite, 5 shower-only). Room rate €106.31(max 3 guests) Closed 24-27 Dec. Amex, Diners, MasterCard, Visa, Laser. **Directions:** City centre Location.

Isaacs Restaurant

RESTAURANT 48 MacCurtain Street Cork **Tel: 021 450 3805**
Fax: 021 455 1348 Email: isaacs@iol.ie

This large, atmospheric modern restaurant in an 18th-century warehouse has been one of the great restaurant success stories, not just in Cork but throughout the country. The co-owners, Michael and Catherine Ryan together with partner/head chef Canice Sharkey, make a great team. Canice cooks tempting, colourful dishes which cleverly combine sunny Mediterranean influences and reassuring Irish traditions - a comforting potato and leek soup might sit easily on the menu alongside tempura of prawns with soya and ginger and a traditional seafood chowder may come with garlic croûtons. Although it has been done in a quiet, low-key way, this restaurant has played a leading role in the culinary revolution that has been overtaking Ireland. Isaacs' exciting blend of Irish and international themes, together with a policy of providing great food and good value in an informal, relaxed ambience has proved irresistible since they day they opened and was way ahead of the current fashion. Michael Ryan received the Bord Bia New Irish Cuisine Award in our 2000 edition. The term describes updated traditional Irish food, seen in dishes that have their roots in the past and their heads in the present, utilising traditional and native ingredients in a colourful, contemporary style. **Seats 120.** L Mon-Sat 12.30-2.30, D daily 6.30-10.30 (Sun to 9). Short à la carte and daily blackboard specials; vegetarian dishes highlighted. House wine from €15.87. Service discretionary (10% on parties of 8+). Closed Christmas week. Amex, Diners, MasterCard, Visa, Laser. **Directions:** opposite Dan Lowrey's Pub.

The Ivory Tower

RESTAURANT Exchange Princes Street Cork **Tel: 021 427 4665**

Seamus O'Connell, one of Ireland's most original culinary talents, runs this unusual restaurant upstairs in an early Victorian commercial building. Very best quality ingredients (all local and organic or wild, including game in season), creative menus and excellent details like delicious home-baked breads, imaginative presentation are the hallmarks of The Ivory Tower - and vegetarian dishes interesting enough to tempt hardened carnivores are always a feature. Menus start off with a "surprise taster" to set the mood and examples from a high summer menu that show the style include a starter of Roquefort soufflé baked in a globe artichoke & served with truffle beurre blanc, which might be followed by a little granita, then, from a choice of about nine dishes, perhaps wild salmon hot smoked to order over oak, with saffron apple sauce. Desserts are equally unconventional, so why not finish with aphrodisiac of tropical fruits? A shortish wine list includes a number of rare treats, including some organic wines. Children welcome (by prior arangement). **Seats 35** D Thu-Sun, 6.30-9.30. Set menus €44.44 & €63.49; also à la carte. House wine €19.05. SC discretionary. *A cookery school is due to open in spring 2002: 3 day courses once monthly and a children's course in summer. Amex, Diners, MasterCard, Visa, Laser, Switch. **Directions:** corner of Princes/Oliver Plunkett street. City Centre. Upstairs - Red Door- Metal Angel.

Jacobs on the Mall

RESTAURANT ☆

30A South Mall Cork **Tel: 021 4251530** Fax: 021 4251531

Its location in the former Turkish baths has created a highly unusual and atmospheric contemporary dining space for what is now established as one of Cork's leading restaurants (possibly the leader; the hierarchy in Cork city has never been the same since Declan Ryan moved out of the restaurant business). Mercy Fenton returned from abroad to take up the position of head chef here when the restaurant opened in 1998 and she is doing a superb job. Modern European cooking is the promise and, with close attention to sourcing the best ingredients allied to outstanding cooking skills, the results are commendably simple and never less than exceptional in terms of balance and flavour. Lunch and dinner menus change daily and are sensibly brief - offering a choice of around five to seven dishes on each course, notably creative vegetarian dishes and lovely fish - taste the freshness in a dish like cod with champ and green beans. Creativity with deliciously wholesome and colourful ingredients, accurate cooking, stylish presentation and efficient yet relaxed service all add up to a memorable dining experience. Finish on a high note - with a Jacobs Dessert plate, perhaps. Farmhouse cheeses, always so good in Cork, are served with digestive biscuits and oatcakes. Children welcome. **Seats 130** (Private room, 25, with own bar). No smoking area; air conditioning. Toilets wheelchair accessible. L Mon-Sat 12.30-2.30, D Mon-Sat 6.30-10pm. A la carte. House wines €17.14; s.c.10% . Closed Sun and 25-26 Dec. Amex, Diners, MasterCard, Visa, Laser, Switch. **Directions:** beside Bank of Ireland, at the Grand Parade end of the South Mall.

Jacques Restaurant

RESTAURANT ☆

Phoenix Street Cork **Tel: 021 427 7387**
Fax: 021 427 0634 Email: jacquesrestaurant@eircom.net

An integral part of Cork life since 1982, sisters Eithne and Jacqueline Barry's delightful restaurant has changed with the years, evolving from quite a traditional place to the dashing Mediterranean-toned bistro it is today. There is always a personal welcome and, together with Eileen Carey, who has been head chef since 1986, they are known for putting a high value on the provenance and quality of the food that provides the basic building blocks for their delicious meals. Menus have always been based on carefully sourced ingredients from a network of suppliers built up over many years and this care, together with skill and judgment in the kitchen, shows particularly in having the confidence to keep things simple and allow the food to speak for itself. Menus are refreshingly short, allowing this skilled team to concentrate on the delicious cooking that is their forte - in sun-filled starters such as Spanish salad of chick peas, roast tomatoes & Serrano ham and main courses including an updated classic of traditional roast duck with potato & apricot mash & apricot & tamarind sauce with roast vegetables, which is a speciality. Desserts could be lemon tart or almond cake with plums in red wine & mascarpone cheese. Consistently good cooking in stylish, relaxed surroundings and service which is unfailingly helpful and attentive have led to Jacques' present position as one of Cork's leading restaurants - and it's excellent value too, especially the early dinner. **Seats 50.** No-smoking area; air conditioning. An interesting, fairly priced wine list includes some organic wines and about ten half bottles. L Mon-Sat 12-3, D Tue-Sat 6-10. Set L €15.10, Set D from €29.07; early D 6-7, €16.30. Also à la carte. House wine €16.30. Service discretionary. Closed D Sun & D Mon, bank hols & 24-28 Dec. Amex, MasterCard, Visa, Laser. **Directions:** rear of GPO, off Pembroke Street.

Jurys Cork Hotel

HOTEL

Western Road Cork **Tel: 021 427 6622** Fax: 021 427 4477
Email: cork@jurysdoyle.com Web: www.jurysdoyle.com

Consistently popular with both business and leisure guests since it opened in 1972, this comfortable hotel has a relaxed atmosphere and is in an attractive riverside setting half a mile from the city centre. It's a good base for business guests; bedrooms include some designated lady executive and all rooms are a good size with both double and single beds. The foyer and bedrooms have recently been upgraded in a programme of regular refurbishment that is an admirable feature of the hotel. Lunch and dinner are served in the main dining room, the Glandore Restaurant, and bar food is available in the Library Lounge, 7.30am-6 pm daily. Children welcome (under 12s free in parents' room, cot available withou charge; playroom,crèche). Pets permitted by arrangement. Garden. Conference/banqueting 700/500. Business centre, secretarial services, video-conferencing. Leisure centre, swimming pool. **Rooms 122** (1 suite, 2 junior suites,41 executive, 68 no-smoking, 20 disabled). Room rate €197 (max 2 guests). SC 12.5%. Closed 25 Dec. Amex, Diners, MasterCard, Visa, Laser. **Directions:** Hotel located near city centre .

Jurys Cork Inn

HOTEL Anderson's Quay Cork **Tel: 021 427 6444** Fax: 021 427 6144
Email: julieann_brennan@jurysdoyle.com Web: www.jurysdoyle.com

In a fine central riverside site, this budget hotel has all the features that Jurys Inns have now become well known for: room prices include accommodation for up to four (including a sofa bed) and there is space for a cot (which can be supplied by arrangement). No room service. Limited parking (22 spaces), plus arrangement with nearby car park. **Rooms 133** (7 suitable for disabled guests). Room rate Sun-Thu €75 Fri-Sat €84 (max 3 guests).Café/restaurant 7-10am, 6-9.30pm. The Inn Pub bar serves lunch every day and there's a late bar (residents only) every night. (Bar closed on Good Friday). Closed 25 Dec. Amex, Diners, MasterCard, Visa.

The Kingsley Hotel

HOTEL/RESTAURANT Victoria Cross Cork **Tel: 021 480 0500** Fax: 021 480 0527
Email: res@kingsleyhotel.com Web: www.kingsleyhotel.com

Conveniently situated in an attractive location alongside the River Lee, just minutes from both Cork airport and the city centre, this new hotel has proved a valuable addition to the accommodation scene in Cork, especially for business visitors. The large, comfortably furnished foyer and an informal restaurant area a few steps up from it (and overlooking the weir) make good meeting places and accommodation is of a high standard. Spacious rooms offer traditional comfort and are designed with care: air conditioning, desk space, ISDN lines, interactive TV with message facilities, safes, trouser press with ironing board and same day laundry service all increase the hotel's appeal for business guests - and these details are matched by excellent conference, business and leisure facilities as well as a dining-in option which is well above average hotel fare. Private dining facilities are also available, in rooms catering for 16-80 guests.Conference/banqueting (90/80); 24 hour business centre, secretarial services; video-conferencing on request. Lift. Leisure centre, swimming pool. Children welcome (under 12s free in parents' room, cot available). Garden. No pets. **Rooms 69** (2 suites, 4 junior suites, 2 executive, 25 no-smoking, 4 for disabled). B&B £100, ss £35.

Otters at the Kingsley: Set up in contemporary bistro style, with darkwood furniture, comfortable upholstered chairs and uncluttered table settings, this restaurant appeals to non-residents as well as hotel guests. Head chef John Dillon presents international menus that offer plenty of choice without being overlong, typically including Bandon smoked salmon with horesradish cream and 'The Kingsley crispy duck', served on colcannon, with a coriander & mustard seed sauce, or pan-fried West Corl sirloin steak, with Lyonnaise potatoes and a thyme & red wine sauce. Service is friendly and professional. **Seats 100** (function room 140). L daily12.30-2.30, D 6-10 (Sun from 6.30). Set L from €20. Also à la carte. House wine €17. SC discretionary. Amex, Diners, MasterCard, Visa. **Directions:** on main N22 Kilkenny road.

Lancaster Lodge

GUESTHOUSE Lancaster Quay, Western Road Cork **Tel: 021 425 1125**
Fax: 021 425 1126 Email: info@lancasterlodge.com Web: lancasterlodge.com

Robert White's guesthouse opened in 1999 and it was built with vision and finished with care, to offer hotel quality accommodation with personal supervision at a moderate price. Spacious rooms are furnished to a high standard (with ISDN lines and safes as well as the more usual facilities) and well-designed bathrooms. Excellent breakfasts are served in a contemporary dining room. Children welcome (under 5s free in parents' room, cot available). Lift. Parking. 24 hr reception. **Rooms 39** (3 shower only, 2 junior suites, 2 for disabled). B&B about €75 pps. Closed 24-25 Dec. Amex, Diners, MasterCard, Visa. **Directions:** located alongside Jury's Hotel on Cork's Western Road.

Lotamore House

ACCOMMODATION

Tivoli Cork **Tel: 021 482 2344**
Fax: 021 482 2219 Email: lotamore@iol.ie

This large period house is set in mature gardens and, although not grand, it was built on a generous scale. Big, airy rooms have air conditioning, phones, TV and trouser press (tea/coffee trays on request), and they're comfortably furnished to sleep three, with room for an extra bed or cot and full bathrooms. A large drawing room has plenty of armchairs and an open fire and, although only breakfast and light meals are offered, Fleming's Restaurant (see entry) is next door. Children welcome (Under 5s free in parents' room, cots available, baby-sitting by arrangement). Wheelchair access. Own parking. **Rooms 20** (5 no-smoking, 1 for disabled). Garden. Pets permitted. B&B €45, ss €10. Closed Christmas week. Amex, Diners, MasterCard, Visa. **Directions:** on N8, 5 minutes drive from City Centre.

Lovetts Restaurant & Brasserie

RESTAURANT

Churchyard Lane off Well Road Douglas Cork **Tel: 021 429 4909**
Fax: 021 429 4024 Email: lovetts@indigo.ie

Home to both the restaurant and the Lovett family since 1977, this fine restaurant is in a late Georgian house situated in mature grounds. Management is now in the capable hands of Niamh Lovett and head chef is Marie Harding, a talented and creative cook committed to serious cooking, using the best of fresh, free range and local products. There's a fully licensed bar (the extensive wine list is Niamh's father Dermod Lovett's particular passion) and private dining is available in the 'Wine Geese' Room. Marie's dinner menus are consistently interesting and always offer a separate vegetarian menu. **Seats 60.** (Private room 8-24). No-smoking restaurant. D à la carte. House wine about €18. Service discretionary. DTue-Sat, 5.30-9.30. Closed Sun, Mon, bank hols, Christmas week, 1st week Aug. Amex, Diners, MasterCard, Visa, Laser. **Directions:** close to south Cork city; from Douglas Road take turning to Mahon and Blackrock and go through a roundabout. Take the fourth turn on the left, Wells Road; Lovetts is off it in Churchyard Lane.

Maryborough House Hotel

HOTEL/RESTAURANT

Maryborough Hill Douglas Cork
Tel: 021 436 5555 Fax: 021 436 5662
Email: maryboro@indigo.ie Web: www.maryborough.com

The Maryborough House Hotel has at its heart a fine country house set in its own grounds and gardens and has been developed with sensitivity. The original house, which is beautifully proportioned, has many fine features, restored with care and furnished in period style with antiques. The main entrance is via the original flight of steps up to the old front door and, although there is no conventional reception area, guests receive a warm welcome at the desk just inside the front door. The new section of the hotel is modern and blends comfortably with the trees and gardens surrounding it. The new part (which had an extra 22 rooms added, less than two years after opening) includes excellent leisure facilities and accommodation which is exceptionally good in terms of design - simple, modern, bright, utilising Irish crafts. Rooms are generously-sized, with a pleasant outlook, good amenities and extras including complimentary mineral water. Bathrooms are well-finished and well-lit, with plenty of marbled shelf space, generous towels and a robe; they have environmentally friendly toiletries and suggestions on saving water by avoiding unnecessary laundry. Two new meeting rooms have recently been added and a second conference room is planned for 2002. Conference/banqueting (500/350). Leisure centre. Children welcome (under 2s free in parents room, cots available). No pets. **Rooms 79** (2 suites, 3 junior suites, 74 executive rooms, 17 no-smoking, 8 for disabled). Lift. B&B €70, ss €25. Closed 24-26 Dec.

Zings: The hotel's design-led dining area is now more logically located next to the bar, which was recently moved up from its original position on the lower ground floor. Gerry Allen, who has been head chef since the hotel opened in 1997, offers European cuisine with traditional and Mediterranean flavours - a speciality that sums up the style neatly is spiced pot-roasted lamb shank with olive mash. International influences dominate, but local produce is also in evidence, as in a starter quiche of sundried tomato, basil & smoked Gubbeen cheese and main courses like sliced

Skegamore duck breast with a balsamic & orange jus, which makes a nice contemporary interpretation of the classic partnership. Pretty desserts include some good ices - real vanilla, for example, and passion fruit parfait. Not suitable for children after 7pm. **Seats 140.** No smoking area; air conditioning. L daily 12.30-2.30, D 6.30-10. set L €21.50, Set D from €32. House wine €20. SC discretionary. * Bar meals also available every day, 9.30am-9pm. Amex, Diners, MasterCard, Visa, Laser.

Metropole Ryan Hotel & Leisure Centre

HOTEL

MacCurtain Street Cork **Tel: 021 450 8122**
Fax: 021 450 6450 Email: enq@metropoleh.com

This imposing city-centre hotel next door to the Everyman Palace and backing on to the River Lee, celebrated its centenary in 1998. Many of the original features remain, such as the marble facade, outside carved stonework and plaster ceilings inside. Always popular with those connected with the arts and entertainment industry, there are many displays (photos and press cuttings) of stars past and present in the public areas and the atmospheric, traditionally-styled Met Tavern. The hotel has recently completed a refurbishment programme, noticeably in the bedrooms, most of which now combine a period feel with modern facilities. Unusually for an old city-centre hotel, there's a splendid leisure club with a large (and unconventionally shaped) indoor swimming pool, overlooked by the Waterside Café (where breakfast is served) and also a gym. Extensive conference facilities (for up to 350). Children under 2 free in parents' room, cots available. No pets. **Rooms 113** (3 junior suites, 30 executive rooms, 10 no-smoking, 1 for disabled). B&B about €110. Open all year. Amex, Diners, MasterCard, Visa.

Nakon Thai Restaurant

RESTAURANT

Tramway House Douglas Cork **Tel: 021 436 9900** Fax: 021 488 8002
Email: nakonthai@eircom.net Web: www.nakonthai.com

Efficient reception gets guest off to a good start at this smart new restaurant in Douglas village. Authenticity is to be expected as the chef, Samai Singkham, was previously head chef at the Dusit Thani in Bangkok and the aim is to provide traditional Thai cuisine in a relaxed and friendly atmosphere, although the flavours typical of Thai cuisine - coriander, lime, chilli, saltiness - seem to have been tamed somewhat, presumably to meet local demand. There are some Chinese and Japanese dishes on the menu and Vietnamese food may be added in 2002. Several set menus are offered and an à la carte that may seem overlong, but there is considerable overlap between dishes that are basically similar and everything is freshly cooked, without any artificial flavourings or MSG. If in doubt try some of the house specialities such as hot & sour prawn soup and steamed red snapper in lemon sauce, or a sizzling dish of fried beef with chilli, onion, pepper, garlic & spring onions. A limited dessert selection includes exotic Thai fruit salad for a refreshing finish. Informative fairly priced wine list. Not suitable for children after 7pm. **Seats 42.** No smoking area. D daily 5.30-11. Set menus from €21; à la carte also available. House wine from €14.60. SC discretionary (10% on parties of 8+). Closed 5 days Christmas. Amex, Diners, MasterCard, Visa, Laser. **Directions:** Douglas east, from Douglas village.

Pí Restaurant

RESTAURANT

Courthouse Chambers Washington Street Cork
Tel: 021 4222 860 Fax: 021 4273 727

Most of the produce is local and comes from the nearby English Market, but contemporary international food for all is the aim at this large, bright modern restaurant, which appeals to all age groups and is especially popular with families. Reception is friendly and there's seating at the bar as well as a sizable seating area to have a drink and wait comfortably for your table. Pizzas (€7-11.50) are the main speciality and there's a 'create your own pizza' menu as well as an extensive list of regulars offering every imaginable combination of toppings from a simple margarita (tomato sauce, basil, mozzarella & beef tomato) to Pi in the Sky (parma ham, artichokes, porcini dusted mushrooms & rocket). But there's also a shortish à la carte of more 'grown-up' dishes - about ten on each course, typically starting with salad of blackened chicken with pineapple/chilli salsa & toasted pistachio nuts or duck confit salad and progressing to dishes including a perfectly cooked fillet steak with 3-peppercorn & wild mushroom sauce, or tapenade roast hake, with spring onion & basil beurre blanc. Vegetarian dishes are marked up and there are lots of gooey desserts and icecreams (yes, including 'Pi Scream') alongside some welcome refreshment in, say, citrus parfait with orange & grapefruit fillets. An extensive, unusual and wide-ranging wine list includes a large selection available by the glass. Good cooking, good service and good value in a fun atmosphere keep people coming back for more. Children welcome.

Seats 100+. Unrestricted smoking; air conditioning. Open daily 12-11: L 12-5, D 6-11. A la carte. House wine €18 (glass, €4.44). SC discretionary. Amex, MasterCard, Visa, Laser. **Directions:** across the courthouse on Washington Street.

Proby's Bistro

RESTAURANT/ACCOMMODATION

Proby's Quay Crosses Green Cork
Tel: 021 431 6531 Fax: 021 4975882

This restaurant, which was extensively refurbished in late summer 1999, is handier to the city centre than it first appears and is a pleasant spot for a bite to eat during the day (tables outside for fine weather) as well as in the evening, when a piano bar is an added attraction. The style - established before the current wave and competently executed - is global cuisine, with an emphasis on things Mediterranean. Menus offer lively fare with an international tone yet plenty of local produce; pork & pigeon terrine is an unusual speciality, served with onion confit & cinnamon toast and West Cork black pudding is another favourite starter, served with grainy mustard sauce & scallion mash. Main courses specilalities include baked fresh seafood with roast red pepper beurre blanc, braised fennel in white wine & Dubliner cheese & chive potatoes. Specials change daily and there's a short fast lunch menu (€ 6.35). Seasonal accommodation is available next door, when rooms occupied by students at the adjacent Deanshall during the academic year become available for visitors in summer, when Proby's is open for breakfast (June to September). Children welcome. **Seats 120** (private room 40). Air conditioning, no-smoking area. Open Mon-Sat, 10 am - midnight: L 12-6, D 6-10 (Fri & Sat to 11). A la carte, also early D 6-7.30, €12.60; s.c. discretionary. House wine €15.24. Closed Sun & 3-4 days at Christmas. Amex, MasterCard, Visa, Laser. **Directions:** Between St. Finbarre's Cathedral and Beamish & Crawford brewery.

Rochestown Park Hotel

HOTEL

Rochestown Road Douglas Cork **Tel: 021 489 2233** Fax: 021 489 2178
Email: info@rochestownpark.com Web: www.rochestownpark.com

Formerly a home of the Lord Mayors of Cork, this attractive hotel stands in lovely grounds and the original parts of the building feature gracious, well-proportioned public rooms. Facilities include excellent conference/banqueting facilities (recently extended up to 700/450 respectively; video-conferencing available) and a fine leisure centre with a Roman style 20-metre swimming pool and a Thalasso Therapy Centre. Rooms are furnished to a high standard with all the comforts, including air conditioning, ISDN lines, fax and safe as well as the more usual conveniences like tea/coffee trays, multi-channel TV and trouser, all of which make this a popular base for business guests, who are well looked after in an executive wing. Conerence and meeting facilities are amongst the best in the country and there's a business centre and secretarial services available to guests. Since opening in 1989 the hotel has seen many changes under the watchful eye of General Manager Liam Lally and the latest improvement is the addition of another 48 rooms and eight executive houses. Children welcome (under 5s free in parents' room; cots available). Leisure centre, indoor swimming pool, creche, hairdresser. Garden. No pets. **Rooms 162** (1 suite, 5 junior suites, 92 executive rooms, 3 for disabled). Lift. B&B from €51pps, ss €22.86. Open all year. **Gallery Restaurant:** The restaurant is in a pleasant position overlooking the hotel gardens; the ambience and service are both good and head chef Gerry Kirwin ensures that the food goes beyond the expectations of a hotel dining room, making dining-in a positive option for residents. Menus, which change monthly, are well-balanced and always include some strong vegetarian options in starters like seasonal salad with walnuts & beetroot chips or a main course of tagliatelle with black olives, sundried tomatoes & fresh Parmesan shavings; prime Irish beef is a speciality and there's always a choice of local seafood. Set menus are good value. L&D daily. SC 12.5%. Amex, Diners, MasterCard, Visa, Laser. **Directions:** Adjacent to South ring road which links all main routes into Cork city.

Seven North Mall

GUESTHOUSE

7 North Mall Cork **Tel: 021 4397191**
Fax: 021 4300811 Email: sevennorthmall@eircom.net

Angela Hegarty runs one of the city's most pleasant guesthouses, on a tree-lined south-facing mall overlooking the River Lee. Rooms in this 1750s townhouse are all spacious, individually furnished in keeping with the house (with bathrooms skilfully built in) and good amenities. Some rooms have river views and there is a ground floor room specially designed for disabled guests. Excellent breakfasts. Many of the city's best restaurants, pubs, museums, galleries and theatres are within a short walk. Not suitable for children under 12. **Rooms 7** (2 shower only,1 for disabled). B&B €60 pps, ss€15. Closed 16 Dec-6 Jan. MasterCard, Visa, Laser. **Directions:** near North Gate Bridge, City Centre.

Silver Springs Moran Hotel

HOTEL Féile bia — Tivoli Cork **Tel: 021 450 7533** Fax: 021 450 7641

This well-known hotel situated in 25 acres of landscaped gardens about five minutes drive from the city centre is a modern tower block overlooking the River Lee and has an eye-catching external glass lift; spacious bedrooms are furnished to a high standard, with good bathrooms and some of them share the view. Self-contained conference/banqueting suites can each accommodate up to 700 guests & there's a business centre. A well-equipped leisure centre has indoor tennis and squash, as well as a 25-metre pool, and there's a 9-hole golf course on site. **Rooms 109** (3 suites, 2 mini-suites, 29 executive rooms, 16 no-smoking rooms and 5 for disabled). B&B about €90 pps. Amex, Diners, MasterCard, Visa. **Directions:** at the Tivoli flyover above the main Cork/Dublin road and clearly signed off it. (From Cork, take first left then right at the flyover.)

Cork City

Taste of Thailand

RESTAURANT — 8 Bridge Street Cork Co. Cork **Tel: 021 4505404**

This authentic Thai restaurant has earned a strong following, giving it a lively atmosphere, even early in the week. Wide-ranging menus offer plenty of choice, including vegetarian options and the familiar set menus ('banquets') for groups of various sizes, as well as an à la carte which has a more interesting selection of dishes. Except for some of the exotics, ingredients are mostly fresh and the cooking is sound; dishes have good flavour and are attractively presented. Good food, service and value explain this restaurant's popularity: booking is advisable and, if you are not having the early menu it might be wise to allow plenty of time for the first sitting to finish, as arrivals for the popular 8 o'clock slot may have to wait for tables and there is nowhere to do so in comfort. **Seats 60** (private room 12). D daily, 6-11; Early D about €16 (6-7 pm), otherwise à la carte. House wine about €13 (BYO also allowed). **Directions:** Near the city centre, just across St Patrick's Bridge.

Travelodge

HOTEL — Frankfield Road South Ring Road Cork **Tel: 021 431 0722**

Well-maintained budget accommodation - generous sized bedrooms, with an extra sofabed, TV and decent bathrooms. No service, but tea/coffee-making in the room and breakfast available at the adjacent Little Chef. Room rate about €65. **Directions:** Just over a mile from Cork city centre and a mile from Cork airport on the main airport road.

The Wine Vault

PUB — Lancaster Quay Western Road Cork **Tel: 021 427 5751**

Situated just across the road from the entrance to Jurys Hotel, Reidy's Wine Vault makes a convenient meeting place and can be a good choice for a quick bite to eat. Originally a wine warehouse, it has been imaginatively converted to its present use, with a high vaulted ceiling and an attractive mixture of old and new fixtures and furnishings. Noelle Reidy supervises the food personally and early visitors will be greeted by the aroma of bread baking at the back, shortly followed by soups, pies and casseroles (shepherd's pie, Irish stew) for lunch, all marked up on the blackboard as they come on stream; don't overlook the home-cooked Cork spiced beef, which is a local speciality. Closed 25 Dec, Good Fri. Amex, Diners, MasterCard, Visa.

CORK COUNTY

Cork seems like a miniature country in its own right, as you'd expect of Ireland's largest county. Its highly individualistic people will happily go along with this distinction as they reflect on the variety of their large territory, which ranges from the rich farmlands of East Cork, away westward to the handsome coastline of West Cork where the mighty light of the famous Fastnet Rock swings across tumbling ocean and spray-tossed headland.

While the people of the county have a proprietorial attitude towards their own city, in recent years there has been a significant upsurge in civic pride in the county's islands, villages and towns, the old town of Clonakilty in West Cork being a byword for urban regeneration. Having been the overall winner of the Tidy Towns award in 1999, it took Cork county's top award at the end of 2000, and in September 2001 was still comfortably in the Highly Commended section

Midleton in East Cork is home to the Jameson Heritage Centre, where the fascinating story of whiskey is entertainingly told in a town which is also the locality for Irish Distillers' manufacturing headquarters, producing Jameson, Power's and Paddy whiskey together with many variants, as well as Huzzar Vodka and Cork Dry Gin.

At the far end of East Cork, the by-pass it at last a-building around the ancient port of Youghal, an intriguing place which will re-discover itself once the blight of excessive through traffic has been removed. The spectacularly located township of Cobh facing south over Cork Harbour is also asserting its own identity, with a renewed sense of its remarkable maritime heritage being expressed through events such as a Sea Shanty Festival, while the town's direct link with the Titanic is celebrated in many ways.

The county is a repository of the good things of life, a treasure chest of the finest farm produce, and the very best of seafood, brought to market by skilled specialists. But it isn't all work by any means. As Ireland's most southerly county, Cork enjoys the mildest climate of all, and it's a place where they work to live, rather than live to work. The arts of living, in fact, are probably seen at their most skilled in County Cork, and they are practised in a huge territory of such variety that it is difficult to grasp it all, even if you devote your entire vacation to this one county.

But when you remember that your mind has to absorb the varieties of experience offered by, for instance, the stylish sophistication of Kinsale as set against the lively little ports further west, or the bustle of Youghal as matched with the remote and peaceful mountains above Gougane Barra in the northwest of the county, then you really do begin to wonder that so much can be crammed into this one place called County Cork.

Local Attractions and Information

Ballydehob Nature Art Centre	028 37323
Bantry Bantry House	027 50047
Bantry Murphy's International Mussel Fair (May)	027 50360
Bantry Tourism Information	027 50229
Blarney Blarney Castle	021 438 5252
Cape Clear Island International Storytelling Festival (early September)	028 39157
Carrigtwohill Fota Estate (Wildlife Park, Arboretum)	021 481 2728
Castletownroche Annes Grove (gardens)	022 26145
Cobh The Queenstown Story	021 4813591
Cobh Sirius Arts Centre	021 4813790
Cork Airport	021 431 3131
Crosshaven Ford Cork Week July 2002 R. Cork YC	021 483 1023
Glengarriff Garinish Island	027 63040
	Kinsale Gourmet Festival (October)
Kinsale Charles Fort	021 477 2263
Kinsale Desmond Castle	021 477 4855
Kinsale Tourism Information	021 477 2234
Macroom Brierly Gap Cultural Centre	026 42421
Mallow Cork Racecourse	022 50207
Midleton Jameson Heritage Centre	021 461 3594
Millstreet Country Park	029 71810
Mizen Head Mizen Vision Signal Station	028 35591

Shanagarry Ballymaloe Cookery School Gardens	021 464 6785
Skibbereen Creagh Gardens	028 22121
Skibbereen Tourism Information	028 21766
Skibbereen West Cork Arts Centre	028 22090
Youghal Myrtle Grove	024 92274

Ahakista

Ahakista Bar

PUB

Durrus Nr Bantry Ahakista Co. Cork **Tel: 027 67203**

Anthony and Margaret Whooley run one of the most relaxed bars in the country: known affectionately as "the tin pub" because of its corrugated iron roof, it has a lovely rambling country garden going down to the water at the back, where children are very welcome to burn off excess energy. It's been in the family for two generations now and, although finally succumbing to the telephone after years of resistance, it's a place that just doesn't change. Normal pub hours don't apply in this part of the world, but they're open from 12 noon and evenings all year, except 25 Dec & Good Fri. **Directions:** Sheeps Head from Durrus.

Ahakista

Hillcrest House

FARMHOUSE

Ahakista Durrus nr Bantry Ahakista Co. Cork **Tel: 027 67045**
Email: agneshegarty@oceanfree.net Web: www.ahakista.com

Agnes Hegarty's traditional farmhouse attracts many types of visitor, including walkers, who revel in the 55 mile "Sheep's Head Way" - and hospitality comes first at this working farm overlooking Dunmanus Bay, where guests are welcomed with a cup of tea and home-baked scones on arrival. Families are particularly well catered for as there's a large games room, swing and a donkey on the farm - and comfortably furnished rooms are big enough for an extra child's bed. There is also a ground-floor room suitable for less able guests, with parking at the door and direct access to the dining room, where moderately priced evening meals and fine cooked-to-order breakfasts are served. Hillcrest House was the guide's Farmhouse of the Year for 2001. **Rooms 4** (3 en-suite & no-smoking, 2 shower only) B&B €25.50 pps (en-suite €28) (Under 2s free in parents' room, cot available without charge.) High tea £12, or evening meals by arrangement (7 pm; €20.50); light meals also available. Closed 1 Nov-1 Apr. Visa. **Directions:** 25km after Ahakista on Sheeps Head Peninsula.

Ballinadee

Glebe House

COUNTRY HOUSE

Ballinadee nr Kinsale Bandon Co. Cork **Tel: 021 477 8294**
Fax: 021 477 8456 Email: glebehse@indigo.ie Web: http:/indigo.ie/~glebehse/

Church records provide interesting detail about this charming old rectory near Kinsale which dates back to 1690 (when it was built for £250; repairs and alterations followed at various dates, and records show completion of the present house in 1857 at a cost of £1,160). More recently, under the hospitable ownership of Gill Good, this classically proportioned house has been providing a restful retreat for guests since 1989. The house, which is set in beautiful, well-tended gardens (including a productive kitchen garden) has spacious reception rooms and large, stylishly decorated bedrooms with phone and tea/coffee making facilities. The Rose Room is on the ground floor, with french doors to the garden. A 4-course candle-lit dinner for residents, much of it supplied by the garden, is served at a communal table (please book by noon). Although unlicensed, guests are encouraged to bring their own wine. The whole house may be rented by parties by arrangement and several self-catering apartments are also available. Children welcome (under 5s free in parents' room, cots available). Pets permitted. **Rooms 4** (2 shower only, all no-smoking), B&B €45 pps, ss €12. Residents' D €30, at 8 pm. Closed Christmas & New Year. Diners, MasterCard, Visa. **Directions:** take N71 west from Cork to Innishannon bridge, go over bridge and take a sharp left. Travel 5 miles. After village sign,1st on right.

Ballycotton

Bayview Hotel

HOTEL/RESTAURANT

Ballycotton Co. Cork **Tel: 021 464 6746**
Fax: 021 464 6075 Email: info@bayviewhotel.net Web: www.bayviewhotel.net

Overlooking Ballycotton Harbour, Bayview Hotel enjoys a magnificent location on the sea side of the road, with a path to the beach through its own gardens. Since 1971 the hotel has been owned by John and Carmel O'Brien, who completely rebuilt it - fairly low, and sympathetic to the traditional style and scale of the surrounding buildings and harbour - in the early 1990s.

Comfortable, homely public areas are complemented by spacious well-furnished bedrooms with good bathrooms; they open on to small balconies and include two corner suites (with jacuzzi) and some particularly cosy top floor rooms. Small conferences/banqueting (80). Children under 12 free in parents' room. No pets. **Rooms 35** (2 suites, 3 no-smoking rooms, 5 wheelchair accessible) B&B €96pps, ss €30. Closed 28 Oct-31 Mar. **Capricho at the Bayview:** Head chef Ciaran Scully has been at the Bayview since 1995 and his creative daily menus are modern Irish, developed from a classic French base with contemporary international overtones. This talented chef promises an interesting and satisfying dining experience, especially when complemented by an elegantly appointed restaurant with lovely sea and harbour views and good service. His menus offer less usual dishes such as roast saddle of rabbit and game in season, in addition to a predictably wide selection of local seafood, meats and interestin vegetarian dishes such as a terrine of roast vegetables and feta cheese with mustard aioli and toasted pinenuts. Finish with a classic dessert like tangy lemon tart, served with poached rhubarb & vanilla ice cream, or a farmhouse cheese selection. In fine weather, light meals may be served in the garden. An extensive wine list that tends to favour France includessome special bottles; abov average choice of half bottles. Not suitable for children under 12. No smoking area. **Seats 65** (private room 36) D 7-9 daily, L Sun only, 12.30-6. Set D €43, Set Sun L €21. A la carte also offered. Wine selection from about €23. (Bar meals available 12.30-5.30 daily). Amex, Diners, MasterCard, Visa, Laser. **Directions:** at Castlemarty on the N25 turn onto the R632 in the direction of Garryroe.

Ballycotton

Spanish Point Seafood Restaurant

RESTAURANT/ACCOMODATION/GUESTHOUSE Ballycotton Co. Cork

Tel: 021 4646177 Fax: 021 4646179 Email: spanish@indigo.ie

Halfway through the village of Ballycotton you suddenly come upon the entrance to Spanish Point, an attractive old building on the seaward side of the road with a clear view across the bay. John and Mary Tattan have been running this relaxed seafood restaurant since 1991 and have built up a considerable reputation locally. The Tattans take pride in using local produce, especially fish from the family's two trawlers, and the arrival of head chef Frederic Desormeaux in 1999 has eased Mary's work in the kitchen and introduced new dishes to menus that are interesting without being over complicated: dishes like goujons of lemon sole with a basil & lime mayonnaise, or panfried monkfish on a hot smoked Gubbeen cheese risotto with crispy parma ham & sundried tomato pesto are typical of the new style. In a little lounge/bar at the back or the sun lounge recently added for residents and diners, aperitifs are served and orders taken; menus change weekly and offer a good choice - majoring on local seafood, of course, but also offering meat and poultry dishes; vegetarian options are usually available - ask if this is not mentioned on the menu. The restaurant is in two rooms (one a conservatory) overlooking the harbour - a fitting setting for good food, cooked and presented with care, and with service to match. A sun deck has recently been added so, when weather permits, outside dining is a special treat. The wine list includes an interesting house selection. Small conferences/banqueting (60) by arrangement. **Seats 60.** No smoking area. Open daily, 8am-9.30pm, L 12.30-3, D 6.30-9.30; Set L €19, Set D €35.50. House wine €16.50. A la carte also offered. Service discretionary. Low season open weekends only - phone for details. Accommodation: Comfortable, well-furnished bedrooms all have sea views and good amenities including phone, TV and tea/coffee trays. Children welcome (under 3s free in parents' room, cot available without charge). Pets permitted. **Rooms 5** (all shower only & no smoking) B&B €38 pps, ss 6.45. Closed Sun before Christmas-14 Feb. MasterCard, Visa, Laser. **Directions:** off the N25.

Ballydehob

Annie's Restaurant

RESTAURANT Main Street Ballydehob Co. Cork **Tel: 028 37292**

Anne and Dano Barrie have been running their cottagey restaurant since 1983 - and, for many, a visit to West Cork is unthinkable without a meal here. During 2001 they extended into the building next door, almost doubling the number of covers and upgrading the whole restaurant so all facilities, including disabled, are on the ground floor. But you needn't worry that it's all been changed, as the fundamentals are thankfully intact and it's not at all designerish or minimalist - pretty much the same Annie's, just a bit bigger. Annie makes a great host, welcoming everybody personally, handing out menus - and then sending guests over to Levis' pub across the road for an aperitif. Then comes over, takes orders and returns to collect people when their meals are ready - Annie's does have a wine licence but there has never been room for waiting around until tables are ready, so this famous arrangement works extremely well. As to the food at Annie's, everything is freshly made on the day, using local ingredients - fish is delivered every night, meat comes from the local butcher (who kills his own meat), farmhouse cheeses are local (including one of Ireland's most renowned cheeses, Gubeen, which is made by Annie's sister-in-law Giana Ferguson) and all the breads, ice creams and desserts for the restaurant - and for 'Clara' (see below) - are made on the premises. As for Dano's cooking, it is simple and wholesome, the nearest to really good home cooking you could ever hope to find in a restaurant. Dano cooks fish like a dream. This place is still magic. Children welcome, but not after 9 pm. Street parking only. **Seats 40.** D Tue-Sat 7-9.30, Set D from about €30, à la carte also offered. House wine about €16. Service discretionary. Closed Sun & Mon, all Oct-Nov & 24-26 Dec. **Café Clara:** Annie's sister restaurant up the road is a cafe/bookshop and is, in Annie's own true words: "Cheep & cheerful - honest to god soups, sandwiches and daily specials". **Seats 26.** Open 10.30-5.30 Mon-Sat. MasterCard, Visa.

Ballydehob

Levis' Bar

PUB Corner House Main Street Ballydehob Co. Cork **Tel: 028 37118**

Julia and Nell Levis have run this 150-year-old bar and grocery for as long as anyone can remember. It is a characterful and delightfully friendly place, whether you are just in for a casual drink or using the pub as the unofficial 'reception' area for Annie's restaurant across the road (see entry for Annie's above). Closed 25 Dec & Good Fri.

Ballylickey

Ballylickey Manor House

COUNTRY HOUSE/RESTAURANT Ballylickey Bantry Bay Co. Cork **Tel: 027 50071**
Fax: 027 50124 Email: ballymh@eircom.net Web: homepage.eircomnet/~ballymh

Built some 300 years ago by Lord Kenmare as a shooting lodge and home to the Franco-Irish Graves family for four generations, Ballylickey Manor enjoys a stunning, romantic setting overlooking Bantry Bay, with moors and hills behind. There are ten acres of gardens, through which the Ouvane river (trout and salmon fishing) flows. Choose between the elegant and grand bedrooms in the Manor, all lavishly furnished, or more rustic accommodation in the garden - cottages and chalets, some grouped around the outside swimming pool. Dinner for residents is served in a lovely period dining room. Garden, outdoor heated swimming pool. Family accommodation "on application" (cot available, about €25) No pets. Private parking. **Rooms 12** (7 suites, 5 en-suite) B&B about €127 pps. Closed Nov-Mar. Amex, Diners, MasterCard, Visa. **Directions:** on N71 between Bantry & Glengariff.

Ballylickey

Larchwood House Restaurant

RESTAURANT/ACCOMODATION Pearsons Bridge nr Bantry Ballylickey Co. Cork
Tel: 027 66181

The gardens are a special point of interest here, complementing the restaurant, which is in a relatively modern house with both the traditionally-furnished lounge (where afternoon tea and scones are served) and dining room enjoying lovely views. Sheila Vaughan, a Euro-Toques chef, presents accomplished dinner menus priced according to the choice of main course, with a typical selection being smoked salmon with citrus salad, an unusual soup such as carrot & peach, pear and melon cocktail, loin of lamb with lemon and mint, and carrageen with blackcurrant coulis - wonderful food in very generous quantities, all the more enjoyable for the garden setting -there are acres to explore, river boulders to cross and nothing prettier than the wild bluebell wood in spring. **Seats 25.** D 7-9.30 Mon-Sat, about €33. House wine about €16. Service discretionary. Closed Sun & Christmas week. Accommodation: Comfortable en-suite bedrooms vary in situation and outlook: there are two upstairs, two in an adjacent building; those at the back overlook the garden. Excellent breakfasts offer a wide choice, including several fish options and a local cheese plate. **Rooms 4** (all en-suite) B&B about €36pps. Amex, Diners, MasterCard, Visa. **Directions:** Take the Kealkil Road off N71 at Ballylickey; after 2 miles signed just before the bridge.

Ballylickey

Sea View House Hotel

HOTEL/RESTAURANT Ballylickey Bantry Co. Cork
Tel: 027 50462/50073 Fax: 027 51555
Email: seaviewhousehotel@eircom.net Web: www.cnmvhotels.com

Personal supervision and warmth of welcome are the hallmarks of Kathleen O'Sullivan's restorative country house hotel close to Ballylickey Bridge. Spacious, well-proportioned public rooms include a graciously decorated drawing room, a library, cocktail bar and television room, while generously-sized bedrooms - some in a brand new wing and many with sea views - are all individually decorated, with good bathrooms. Family furniture and antiques enhance the hotel and standards of maintenance and housekeeping are consistently high. Children welcome (free in parents' room under 4, cot available without charge). Pets permittedin some areas by arrangement. **Rooms 25** (some junior suites, 1 shower-only; 1 ground floor room suitable for less able guests.) B&B about

€65pps, ssabout€26. Restaurant: Overlooking the garden, with views over Bantry Bay, the restaurant is elegant and well-appointed with antiques, fresh flowers and plenty of privacy. Set five-course dinner menus change daily and offer a wide choice on all courses, with the emphasis firmly on local produce, especially seafood, in dishes like simple Irish oak smoked salmon, blackberry sorbet, brill in a light wine sauce or roast rack of lamb with rosemary. Choose from classic desserts - Baileys cream mousse, strawberry shortcake - or local cheeses to finish. Tea or coffee and petits fours may be served out of doors on fine summer evenings. **Seats 50.** No-smoking restaurant. Toilets wheelchair accessible. D 6.45-9 daily, L Sun only 12.45-2; Set D about €32, Set Sun L about €20. House wines from £about €15.50.10% sc. Hotel closed mid Nov-mid Mar. Amex, Diners, MasterCard, Visa, Laser. **Directions:** On N71, 3 miles from Bantry, 8 miles from Glengarriff.

Baltimore

Baltimore Bay Guest House & La Jolie Brise

RESTAURANT/ACCOMODATION/GUESTHOUSE The Waterfront Baltimore Co. Cork **Tel: 028 20600** Fax: 028 20495 Email: youenjacob@youenjacob.com Web: baltimorebay@youenjacob.com

It is hard to say whether this is a restaurant with rooms, or a guesthouse serving food. Taking the accommodation first, the Jacobs have eight very attractive, well-equipped bedrooms in their guesthouse overlooking the harbour. Everything in it is big - the rooms, the beds, the bathrooms. Amenities are good - direct-dial phones, tea/coffee-making facilities, TV with Video. Furniture is modern, with a light sprinkling of Georgian and Victorian pieces and, in addition to a good sitting area in each room, there's a comfortable residents' lounge. Children up to 4 free in parents' room (cot available). Pets permitted. No private parking. **Rooms 8** (7 en-suite,1 shower only for wheelchairs). B&B €44.44pps, ss €12.70. Open all year. **La Jolie Brise:** Just along from Bushe's Bar, La Jolie Brise has brought a breath of fresh air to eating out in Baltimore. Run by Youen Jacob the younger, this cheerful continental-style café spills out on to the pavement and provides holiday-makers with good, inexpensive meals to be washed down with moderately priced wines. Breakfast menus include regular continental and full Irish breakfast and several fish choices, including hot smoked salmon, plus a range of drinks including hot chocolate. Generous, well-made pizzas (also available to take away) and pastas are available and for lunch and dinner there are "European & Irish" specialities like traditional mussels & chips and char-grilled sirloin steaks with salad & chips: all youthful, contemporary use of local ingredients. The only downside to ths great little place is that it can get very crowded in summer and it's hard to keep pristine. **Seats 50.** Smoking unrestricted. Open 8am-11 pm daily; à la carte & special menus. House wine €12.06. Service discretionary. Amex, MasterCard, Visa, Diners, Laser. **Directions:** The Square, Baltimore.

Baltimore

Baltimore Harbour Resort Hotel & Leisure Centre

HOTEL Baltimore Co. Cork **Tel: 028 20361** Fax: 028 20466 Email: info@bhrhotel.ie

Since the Cullinane family took over this old hotel, they have done a prodigious amount of work, beginning with the complete refurbishment of the original building prior to re-opening in 1995. Most recently, they added on a block of suites (incorporating the traditional arch which now leads through to the carpark) and a new leisure centre, which has a wide range of facilities including a 16-metre swimming pool and gymnasium. The hotel enjoys a lovely position overlooking Roaring Water Bay and is well located for deep sea fishing and visits to nearby islands, including Sherkin and Cape Clear. Modern furnishings, with plenty of light wood and pastel colours, create a sense of space in public areas and the accommodation includes family rooms, junior suites and the new luxury suites. All rooms are comfortably furnished, with neat bathrooms and sea views, and the larger ones have double and single beds. Public areas include a bar that can be reversed to serve the Sherkin Room (banqueting/conferences for 140) and a bright semi-conservatory Garden Room for informal meals and drinks. Children are well looked after - there's a playroom, a children's club in school holidays and under 3s are free in parents' room (cots available). Off-season breaks are good value. No pets. Lift. **Rooms 64** (12 suites, 1 mini-suite). B&B about €70pps, ss about €23. Closed early Jan—mid Feb. Amex, Diners, MasterCard, Visa. **Directions:** signposted on the right as you enter Baltimore on the R595 from Skibbereen.

Baltimore

Bushe's Bar

PUB /ACCOMMODATION

The Square Baltimore Co. Cork
Tel: 028 20125 Fax: 028 20596
Email: tombushe@eircom.net Web: http://homepage.eircom.net/~bushesbar

Everyone, especially visiting and local sailors, feels at home in this famous old bar. It's choc-a-bloc with genuine maritime artefacts such as charts, tide tables, ships' clocks, compasses, lanterns, pennants et al - but it's the Bushe family's hospitality that makes it really special. Since Richard and Eileen took on the bar in 1973 it's been "home from home" for regular visitors to Baltimore, for whom a late morning call is de rigeur (in order to collect the ordered newspapers that are rolled up and stacked in the bar window each day). Now there's a new generation of Bushes involved with the business, so all is humming nicely. Simple, homely bar food starts early in the day with tea and coffee from 9.30, moving on to home-made soups and a range of sandwiches including home-cooked meats (ham, roast beef, corned beef), salmon, smoked mackerel or - the most popular by far - open crab sandwiches, served with home-baked brown bread. And all at around a fiver or less. This is a terrific pub, at any time of year, and was a very worthy recipient of our Jameson Pub of the Year Award in 2000. Bar food served 9.30am-9pm daily. Accommodation: Over the bar, there are some big, comfortable bedrooms, all with a double and single bed, bath & shower, TV and a kitchenette with all that is needed to make your own continental breakfast. There are also showers provided for the use of sailors and fishermen. **Rooms 3.** B&B €23 pps, ss €9.50. Bar closed 25 Dec & Good Fri. Amex, MasterCard, Visa, Laser. **Directions:** in the middle of Baltimore, on the square overlooking the harbour.

Baltimore

Casey's of Baltimore

HOTEL/RESTAURANT

Baltimore Co. Cork **Tel: 028 20197** Fax: 028 20509
Email: caseys@eircom.net Web: www.caseysofbaltimore.com

With dramatic views over Roaring Water Bay to the islands beyond, this attractively developed hotel has grown from the immaculately maintained bar/restaurant that the Caseys had run for twenty years. The old back bar and restaurant have been ingeniously developed to extend the ground floor public areas and make best use of the view, and bedrooms are spacious and well-furnished, with good facilities (phone, TV, tea/coffee tray, trouser press) neat bathrooms and views. The staff are always friendly and helpful, there's a relaxed atmosphere and there are well-organised outdoor eating areas for bar food in fine weather. On less favoured days, the open fires are very welcome - and there's traditional music at weekends. Children are welcome (cots available, €7), but not in public areas after 7 pm. No pets. **Rooms 14** (13 en-suite,1 shower only) B&B €66 pps, ss €25. Bar meals daily 12.30-2.30 & 6.30-7.30.Closed 2-8 Mar, 5-18 Oct, 21-27 Dec. **Restaurant:** A comfortable informal dining room overlooking the bay provides just the setting for good, unpretentious food. Baltimore seafood naturally takes pride of place - crab and lobster are specialities and there will always be other fish of the day on the blackboard. Dinner menus may well begin with the local version of smokies (creamed smoked mackerel, topped with cheese and served hot) and soups will certainly include the Casey's chowder - and Roaring Water Bay mussels are served as a main course, steamed in the shell with white wine, garlic and onion. Steaks (served with pepper sauce or garlic butter) are almost as popular and there's always a vegetarian option, such as a vegetable stir-fry. Friendly, relaxed service adds to the enjoyment. **Seats 65**: L 12.30-2.30, D 6.30-9.30 daily. Set L (Sun) €17, Set D €32. House wine from €15.24; à la carte also available; service discretionary. Amex, Diners, MasterCard, Visa, Switch. **Directions:** from Cork take the N71 to Skibbereen & then R595 to Baltimore.

Baltimore

Chez Youen

RESTAURANT

Baltimore Co. Cork **Tel: 028 20136** Fax: 028 20495
Email: chezyouen@youenjacob.com Web: www.youenjacob.com

Since 1979, Youen Jacob's Breton restaurant has been a major feature in Baltimore. Although other eating places have sprung up around him, Youen is still doing what he does best: simple but dramatic presentation of seafood in the shell. Lobster is very much a speciality and available all year round. The Shellfish Platter is a sight to behold: a complete meal of Dublin Bay Prawns, crab and often velvet crab as well as lobster - all served in shell. Only minor concessions are made to non-fish eaters - starters of leek and potato soup or melon with port and, correspondingly, half a duck with wild mushroom sauce or steak with green peppercorn sauce for main course, although vegetarians are willingly catered for. **Seats 40.** No smoking area. D daily 6-10. Set D from €29.83; Shellfish Platter €40.52; à la carte also offered. House wine from €18.41. Service 10%. Closed Nov & Feb. Amex, Diners, MasterCard, Visa, Laser. **Directions:** The Square,Baltimore.

Baltimore

RESTAURANT ☆

Customs House Restaurant

Baltimore Co. Cork **Tel: 028 20200**

Susan Holland and Ian Parr's uncluttered contemporary restaurant has made a lot of friends over the last few years and it's easy to see why. They don't take credit cards, do Sunday lunch or allow young children. But they do use only the freshest of local produce in season and they do great daily menus - blackboard menus that highlight local seafood, especially, which is cooked by Susan with flair, served by Ian with unflappability - and give outstanding value for money. The couple, who are Australian, have been running the Customs House as a seasonal restaurant since 1995, then - and this seems to be the secret of the restaurant's dramatic improvement in a few short seasons - use the winter months to travel and gain experience in some very distinguished kitchens indeed. Superb ingredients, presented with deceptive simplicity in classic French and Italian dishes, are often given the lightest of twists to freshen familiar themes: specialities include brandade de morue, confit of tuna and sole meunière, all served with organic salads, or simple, perfectly cooked organic side vegetables - new potatoes and spinach, perhaps. Then those unbeatable timeless desserts - hazelnut meringue with strawberries and crème anglaise, tarte tatin with house vanilla ice cream, or (very) local cheese - Cooleeney, Gubbeen, Carraig goat - in perfect condition. All this is complemented by an interesting, highly informative and keenly-priced wine list and Ian Parr's efficient, refreshingly low-key service. **Seats 30.** No smoking area. D Wed-Sat (sometimes Sun), 7-9.30; Set D €20 (3-course, no choice) & €30 (choice of five on each course); house wines €13. Vegetarian dishes on request; not suitable for children under 12. (Cheques, incl sterling cheques, accepted). No Credit Cards. Closed Mon, Tue. Some Sundays; Oct-Apr. **Directions:** beside the Garda Station 50 Metres from Pier.

Baltimore

RESTAURANT

The Mews Baltimore

Baltimore Co. Cork **Tel: 028 20390** Fax: 028 20390

Owner-chef Lucia Carey runs this well-appointed restaurant on the ground floor and adjacent conservatory of an attractive stone building. Menus are contemporary and the cooking combines the admirable qualities of generosity and lightness. Meals start off with freshly-baked breads and tapenade and prompt service means that starters like baked goats cheese or prawn, crab and coriander filo parcels will not be far behind. Main courses could include a variation on traditional themes such as rack of lamb served on olive potatoes and drizzled with home-made mint pesto while a typical vegetarian dish might be filo tartlet filled with seasonal vegetables in a blue cheese sauce, all served with imaginative and well-cooked vegetables. Good home-made ices are likely desserts, or you could finish with a local cheese plate and freshly brewed coffee. A short wine list is expensive when compared with the good value available locally. **Seats 30.** No smoking area. D Tues-Sun, 6-10; à la carte (average main course €21); house wine €19. No Credit Cards. Closed Mon & Oct-May. **Directions:** in village of Baltimore.

Baltimore

B&B

The Slipway

The Cove Baltimore Co. Cork

Tel: 028 20134 Fax: 028 20134

Email: theslipway@hotmail.com Web: www.theslipway.com

Quietly located just beyond the bustle around the square, Wilmie Owen's delightful house has uninterrupted views of the harbour and distant seascape from all the bedrooms and the lovely first floor breakfast room, which has a balcony. This unusual and imaginatively designed house now also has a charming oyster bar in a converted outbuilding; very much intended for residents, it is only open when Wilmie's husband Dave Owen is not away fishing. Not suitable for children; no pets. **Rooms 4** (all shower only & no-smoking). B&B €32 pps, ss €13. No. Credit Cards. Closed Nov-Mar officially, but phone to check. **Directions:** through Baltimore village, 500 metres in the Beacon direction.

Bandon

The Munster Arms Hotel

HOTEL

Oliver Plunkett Street Bandon Co. Cork **Tel: 023 41562**
Fax: 023 41562 Email: info@kingsleyhotels.com

This substantial town-centre hotel has spacious public areas and, unlike many of the hotels in the area, is as popular with business guests and locals as it is with holiday-makers. It is well-situated for touring the area and there is plenty to do, including angling and riding (there is an equestrian centre nearby). Bedrooms are generally quite big and well-furnished with generous beds and stylish, well-fitted bathrooms (four of the older ones are shower only), providing a good standard of comfort and amenities at a reasonable rate. Conference/banqueting (300/240) with secretarial services available. No private parking, but safe street parking is available beside the hotel. Children free in parents' room up to 12; cot available. Pets permitted by arrangement. **Rooms 30** (all en-suite, 5 no-smoking) B&B about €44.44. Closed 25-26 Dec. Amex, Diners, MasterCard, Visa. **Directions:** In the centre of Bandon town; coming from Cork, turn left at the bridge and left again into Oliver Plunkett Street.

Bantry

O'Connor's Seafood Restaurant

RESTAURANT

The Square Bantry Co. Cork **Tel: 027 50221**
Fax: 027 50221 Email: oconnorseafood@yahoo.com Web: www.oconnorseafood.com

O'Connor's long-established seafood restaurant is right on the main square (site of the annual early-May mussel festival) and, after 34 years in the family, the business is now in the capable hands of Matt & Ann's son, Mark, with Simon Wood as head chef. A lobster and oyster fish tank by the entrance sends all the right messages and, beyond the front room, there are booths and a seated bar (full bar facilities include beers on draft) in the back, all decorated in a nautical theme. Bantry Bay mussels, cooked all ways, are a speciality - a starter of them grilled with herbs and lemon butter fits the bill perfectly, followed perhaps by fresh scallops and salmon mornay in shells, served with an abundance of vegetables, or else mussels marinière with a fish pie as a main course. There are some non-fish dishes available, all using local produce - fillet steak is another speciality. At lunchtime you can have soup and a sandwich in the bar or daily-changing dishes off the blackboard. No children after 6.30 pm. **Seats 46.** No smoking area; air conditioning. Open 12.15-9.30 daily, L 12.30-3, D6-9.30. Set L from €6.98, Set D from €25.39. A la carte. House wine €15.24, sc discretionary. Telephone to confirm opening times off-season. MasterCard, Visa, Laser. **Directions:** Town Centre. Promient location on square.

Bantry

The Westlodge Hotel

HOTEL

Bantry Co. Cork **Tel: 027 50360** Fax: 027 50438

Easily spotted on an elevated site above the main road into Bantry, the Westlodge Hotel seems to have thought of all the possible requirements to make a family holiday successful, regardless of weather conditions. A wide range of outdoor activities can be organised, including golf, water sports, horse riding and pony trekking. But - and this is the hotel's greatest strength - there's also plenty to keep energetic youngsters happy if the weather should disappoint, including a 16m swimming pool in the leisure centre. Bedrooms have all been fairly recently refurbished and there is 24-hour room service. The restaurant is well-positioned to take advantage of the view of the bay. Banqueting/conference facilities (300) with back-up secretarial services and video-conferencing available on request. **Rooms 95** (3 suites, 4 disabled). Lift. B&B €76ps, ss€12. Closed 23-18 Dec. Amex, Diners, MasterCard, Visa, Laser. **Directions:** On the edge of town, on the main Cork-Bantry road.

Blarney

Blairs Inn

PUB/RESTAURANT

Cloghroe Blarney Co. Cork
Tel: 021 4381470 Fax: 021 43 82353
Email: blair@eircom.net Web: www.homepage.eircom.net/~blair

John and Anne Blair's delightful riverside pub is in a quiet, wooded setting just outside Blarney yet, sitting in the garden in summer, you might see trout rising in the Owennageara river (or see a heron out fishing), while winter offers welcoming open fires in this comfortingly traditional country pub. It's a lovely place to drop into for a drink or a session - there's traditional music on Monday nights from April to October - and they have built up a special reputation for their food. Anne supervises the kitchen personally, and care and commitment are evident in menus offering a wide (but not over-extensive) range of interesting but fairly traditional dishes including seafood (from Kenmare and Dingle); old favourites like corned beef with champ & cabbage & parsley sauce, casserole of beef & stout and Irish stew sit easily alongside some fancier fare and make a pleasing change from the international menus that have taken the country over lately; there's always a vegetarian dish on, and game in season too. Children welcome, but not after 7 pm. **Seats 40/50** (restaurant/bar) & **60** in garden. No-smoking area. Bar menu 12.30-9.30 daily. Restaurant L 12.30-3, D 6.30-9.30. A la carte. House wine about €16. Service discretionary. Closed 25 Dec & Good Fri. Amex, Diners, MasterCard, Visa, Laser. **Directions:** 5 minutes from Blarney village, on the R579.

Blarney

Blarney Park Hotel

HOTEL

Blarney Co. Cork **Tel: 021 438 5281**
Fax: 021 438 1506 Email: info@blarneypark.com Web: www.blarneypark.com

Blarney may be best known for its castle (and the famous Blarney Stone) but for many people this modern hotel is the reason for the visit. There is always something going on at Blarney Park and its excellent facilities for both conferences and leisure are put to full use. Close proximity to Cork city (just half an hour on the Limerick road) makes this a very convenient location for business. The leisure centre has a 40-metre water slide and 20-metre pool among its attractions and there are two all-weather tennis courts on site. Conference/banqueting (270/250); business centre, secretarial services, video-conferencing. **Rooms 91** (11 shower only; 1 junior suite, 14 executive rooms, 2 no-smoking, 2 disabled). Lift. B&B about €88.88 pps, ss about €25. Open all year. Amex, Diners, MasterCard, Visa. **Directions:** in centre of Blarney, on left on entering town from Cork.

Butlerstown

Atlantic Sunset

ACCOMODATION/COUNTRY HOUSE

Dunworley Butlerstown Bandon Co. Cork
Tel: 023 40115

Mary Holland provides comfortable accommodation and a genuinely warm welcome in her neat modern house with views down to the sea at Dunworley. The house is wheelchair accessible and the ground floor rooms are suitable for less able guests. The breakfast room and some bedroom windows have sea views and, weather permitting, the sight of the sun setting over the Atlantic can indeed be magnificent. Sandy beaches and coastal walk nearby. **Rooms 4** (2 en-suite, shower only). B&B about €22pps (about€24 en-suite). Closed 20 Dec-1 Jan. **Directions:** from Bandon road R602 to Timoleague, then Butlerstown village, Atlantic Sunset 1 km.

Butlerstown

Butlerstown House

ACCOMODATION/COUNTRY HOUSE

Butlerstown Bandon Co. Cork
Tel: 023 40137 Fax: 023 40137
Email: mail@butlerstownhouse.com Web: www.butlerstownhouse.com

Elisabeth Jones' classic late eighteenth century house is set in ten acres of private grounds with long views over the rolling west Cork countryside to the Dunmanway Mountains. Guests are welcomed on arrival with tea in the drawing room, allowing a little time to wind down to the pace appropriate to a house characterised by peace and tranquillity. Elegant reception rooms are comfortably furnished in period style; the drawing room opens on to south facing gardens, and if the weather should disappoint there are open fires throughout. The staircase is a fine example of Georgian craftsmanship, leading to four bedrooms that include a master bedroom with four-poster bed. Breakfast is a major event and is taken in style at the "Butlerstown Table" in the dining room. Full catering facilities are available for house parties and small conferences, ie parties of up to 10 people for 2-3 nights. Self-catering accommodation available by the week all year. Not suitable for children under 12. Pets permitted by arrangement. **Rooms 4** (3 en-suite, 1 shower only, 1 with private bathroom, all no-smoking) B&B €60pps, ss £10. Closed 1 Nov-end Feb. MasterCard, Visa.

Butlerstown

Otto's Creative Catering

RESTAURANT/B&B

Dunworley Butlerstown Bandon Co Cork **Tel: 023 40461**
Email: ottokunze@eircom.net Web: www.creativecookery.com

NATURAL FOOD AWARD

With the help of their talented son who lives nearby and is a creative and practical woodworker, Hilde and Otto Kunze have created a dream of a place here, very close to the spot where they originally started the famous Dunworley Cottage restaurant many years ago. The house is a little unusual from the outside, but only reveals its true personality once you are inside; words cannot do it justice, so you must go and see it for yourself. Deeply committed to the organic philosophy, their vegetable gardens provide a beautiful and satisfying view from the dining room, where meals of wonderful simplicity cooked by Otto are presented by Hilde. Take time to marvel at the sheer originality and ingenuity of their home over a drink (brought with you, as they have no licence) in the sitting room, while also pondering a dinner menu that offers several choices on each course. Typically you will start with a vegetarian salad platter, with organic leaves and several dips or, perhaps, a fish plate of Anthony Cresswell's smoked wild salmon and Frank Hederman's eel and mussels, again with organic leaves. Freshly baked breads and butter will be left temptingly close by on the table - try to resist trying everything as there are still marvellous soups (most likely based on whatever vegetable is most prolific at the time), before you even reach main courses of, perhaps, wild salmon caught off the Seven Heads, panfried and served with a dill & white wine cream or a Swedish speciality such as 'Cheap', of lean minced lamb, spiced with paprika, pepper and garlic, fried and served with a garlic cream. A magnificent selection of vegetables, with potatoes and rice, accompanies the main course. Then there are desserts - apfelstrudel with vanilla ice cream, perhaps, or home-grown strawberries with cream. Or, if you are very lucky, there might be freshly picked top fruit, warm from the trees in the growing tunnels - cherries, plums, apricots, white peaches.....This wonderful food needs no embellishment, it is extraordinarily good value for the quality given - and it clearly gives Otto and Hilde great satisfaction to see their guests' appreciation. This place is a must for any food lover travelling in west Cork. Organic farm; cookery school (please inquire for details). **Seats 30** (max table size 12). Smoking unrestricted. D €45, by reservation (24 hours notice if possible), also Sun L, 1 pm. Bring your own wine (no corkage). Accommodation: Two more bedrooms (and a wheelchair accessible toilet) remained to be built at the time of our visit, but the two completed bedrooms have also the fresh originality of the rest of the house and are furnished in a simple Scandinavian style which, like the cleverly designed shower rooms, is intensely practical. And, of course, you will wake up in a most beautiful place - and have more of that superb food to look forward to, at a breakfast that counts home-made sausages and home-produced rashers among its gems. MasterCard, Visa. **Directions:** Bandon to Timoleague to Barryroe to Dunworley.

Butlerstown

O'Neill's

PUB

Butlerstown Bandon Co. Cork **Tel: 023 40228**

Butlerstown is a pretty pastel-painted village, with lovely views across farmland to Dunworley and the sea beyond. Dermot and Mary O'Neill's unspoilt pub is as pleasant and hospitable a place as could be found to enjoy the view - or to admire the traditional mahogany bar and pictures that make old pubs like this such a pleasure to be in. O'Neill's is now a popular stopping off point for the newly opened "Seven Heads Millennium Coastal Walk" so it may be useful to know that children (and well-behaved pets) are welcome. Closed 25 Dec & Good Fri. **Directions:** Courtmacsherry - Clonakilty Coast Road.

Butlerstown

Sea Court

COUNTRY HOUSE

Butlerstown Bandon Co. Cork

Tel: 023 40151 / 023 40218 / US 513 961 3537 Fax: 513 7215109 (U.S)

Email: seacourt-inn@yahoo.com Web: www.tourismresources.ie/cht/seacort.htm

Set in 10 acres of beautiful parkland, Sea Court is at the heart of an unspoilt wonderland for bird-watchers and walkers - and a restful retreat for any discerning traveller. For sixteen years David Elder - an American academic who spends his summers in Ireland - has devoted his energies to restoring this gracious Georgian mansion and, while the task is nowhere near completion, the achievement is remarkable - and ongoing. The grounds and exterior generally were a credit to him on our recent visit and, while it is wise not to expect too much luxury, what Sea Court has to offer guests is comfortable and very reasonably priced accommodation in a real and much-loved country house; bedrooms are, for the most part, elegantly proportioned with bathrooms that are already very adequate and gradually being upgraded. Breakfast, cooked by David himself, is served at a long dining table; dinner is also available by reservation - and there is a drawing room with an open fire. The house is also available for small conferences (12-16 people) and for rental off-season. **Rooms 4** (all with en-suite or private bathrooms). B&B €35, no s.s. D €30 (by arrangement - min 4 persons). Closed 21 Aug-7 June. **Directions:** Butlerstown is signposted from Timoleague.

Carrigaline

Carrigaline Court Hotel

HOTEL

Main Street Carrigaline Co. Cork **Tel: 021 485 2100**

Fax: 021 437 1103 Email: carrigcourt@eircom.net Web: www.carrigcourt.com

The spacious foyer of this new hotel creates a good first impression and it has attractive features throughout, with interesting contemporary furniture in both public areas and bedrooms, which are stylishly decorated and well-equipped with work desks and ISDN lines. All rooms have king size beds as well as all the more usual amenities, and marbled bathrooms are quite luxurious, with good quality toiletries. Friendly staff are very pleasant and helpful. Conference/banqueting facilities (300), also smaller meeting rooms and secretarial services. Leisure centre; swimming pool. Children welcome (under 12s free in parents' room, cot available). Off-season budget breaks. No pets. **Rooms 52** (2 suites, 50 executive, 2 for disabled). Lift. B&B about €88.88 pps, ss about €20. Closed 25 Dec. Kingfisher Restaurant Amex, MasterCard, Visa, Diners, Laser. **Directions:** follow signs Ringaskiddy (Car Ferry)/Carrigaline.

Carrigaline

Glenwood House

GUESTHOUSE

Ballinrea Road Carrigaline Co. Cork **Tel: 021 4373 878**
Fax: 021 4373 878 Email: glenwoodhouse@eircom.net Web: glenwoodhotel.ie

This well-respected guesthouse is in purpose-built premises, very conveniently located for Cork Airport and the ferry and set in gardens, where guests can relax in fine weather. Comfortable, well-furnished rooms (including one designed for disabled guests) have all the amenities normally expected of hotels, including ISDN lines, TV with video channel, trouser press/iron, tea/coffee facilities and well-designed bathrooms. Breakfast has always been a strong point - fresh fruits and juices, cheeses, home-made breads and preserves as well as hot dishes (available from 7am for business guests, until 10 am for those taking a leisurely break). A guest sitting room with open fire makes a cosy retreat on dark winter evenings. At the time of going to press four new bedrooms were under construction. Under 10s free in parents' room. **Rooms, 16** (all en-suite). B&B about €45pps, ss about €13. Closed 25-31 Dec. Diners, MasterCard, Visa, Laser. **Directions:** follow signs to Ringaskiddy car ferry. Entering Carrigaline, turn right at roundabout; the guesthouse is signed on the right.

Carrigaline

Gregory's Restaurant

RESTAURANT

Main Street Carrigaline Co. Cork **Tel: 021 437 1512**

Owner-chef Gregory Dawson and his partner and restaurant manager Rachelle Harley opened here in 1994 and it's bright, comfortable and friendly, with plenty of buzz. Sensibly short à la carte menus based on local produce change monthly and the cooking style is fairly classical, sometimes with a modern twist. Dishes like mildly spiced home-made lamb sausage with aubergine sauce, or seared breast of chicken with butterbeans, tomato, chilli & garlic are typical and there's always an Irish cheese plate as well as a selection of classic desserts. Good details include home-baked breads and delicious coffee and service is friendly and helpful. **Seats 40.** No-smoking area. Air conditioning. Toilets wheelchair accessible. D Wed-Sat 6.30-10, L Sun only 12.30-3; D à la carte, Sun L €19. House wine €16.50. Closed D Sun, all MonTue, bank hols, 2 weeks Oct, 25-27 Dec,1 wk spring. Amex, Diners, MasterCard, Visa. **Directions:** on Main Street, opposite Bank of Ireland.

Castlelyons

Ballyvolane House

COUNTRY HOUSE

Castlelyons Co. Cork **Tel: 025 36349**
Fax: 025 36781 Email: ballyvol@iol.ie Web: ballyvolanehouse.ie

Jeremy and Merrie Greene's gracious mansion is surrounded by its own farmland, magnificent wooded grounds, a recently restored trout lake and formal terraced gardens, all carefully managed and maintained to a high standard - a major replanting of 400 rhododendrons, azaleas and specimen trees is the current project. The Italianate style of the present house - including a remarkable pillared hall with a baby grand piano and open fire - dates from the mid 19th century when modifications were made to the original house of 1728. This is a very lovely house, elegantly furnished and extremely comfortable, with central heating and big log fires; bedrooms are varied, but all are roomy and, like the rest of the house, are furnished with family antiques and look out over attractive gardens and grounds. Ballyvolane has private salmon fishing on 8km of the renowned River Blackwater, with a wide variety of spring and summer beats. Fishing is Merrie's special enthusiasm (a brochure is available outlining the fishing services she provides) and she's also a great cook, providing guests with delicious country house dinners which are served in style around a long mahogany table (no smoking in the dining room). There is much of interest in the area - the beautiful Blackwater Valley is well worth exploring, with its many gardens and historic sites, and Lismore, the Rock of Cashel and Waterford Crystal are among the many interesting places which can easily be visited nearby.

The standard of hospitality, comfort and food at Ballyvolane are all exceptional, making this an excellent base for a peaceful and very relaxing break. French is spoken. Children welcome (cot available, €7). No pets. Garden; fishing; walking. **Rooms 6** (1 shower only, 1 for disabled). B&B €75pps ss €20. Residents D about €34 at 8pm, book by 10am (no-smoking dining room); menu changes daily. House wine about €18. Closed 23-31 Dec. Amex, MasterCard, Visa. **Directions:** from Cork, turn right off N8 onto R628. Follow signs house.

Castlemartyr

Old Parochial House

COUNTRY HOUSE

Castlemartyr Midleton Co. Cork
Tel: 021 466 7454 Fax: 021 466 7429
Email: enquiries@oldparochial.com Web: www.oldparochial.com

Kathy Sheehy will have tea and home-made scones for you on arrival at this warm and welcoming period house in the village of Castlemartyr. Conveniently situated for many activities and places of interest, including the Jameson Heritage Centre, Fota Wildlife Park & Arboretum, golf, beaches and wonderful cliff and woodland walks, this lovely house would make a perfect base for a restful and interesting break. Fresh flowers throughout the house set a caring tone, not only in the fine well-proportioned drawing room and dining rooms (which both have log fires) but also in bedrooms that are elegantly furnished with antiques and have bathrooms cleverly designed to maintain the architectural harmony of the old house. Unexpected little luxuries include a turn down service at night and home-made biscuits and Irish chocolates in each bedroom, as well as the convenience of tea/coffee trays, trouser press and TV. There's even a complimentary drink offered by the fire each evening before retiring - a truly hospitable touch. Children welcome (under 5s free in parents' room, cot available free of charge). Garden. No pets. **Rooms 3** (1 shower only, all no smoking). B&B €41.55, no ss. Closed 1 Nov-31 Jan. MasterCard, Visa. **Directions:** take N25 to Castlemartyr. At bridge turn for Garryroe & Shangarry. House first on left hand side.

Castletownbere

MacCarthy's

PUB

The Square Castletownbere Co. Cork **Tel: 027 70014**

Dating back to the 1870s, and currently run by Adrienne MacCarthy, this famous old pub and grocery store really is the genuine article. Fortunately, it shows no signs of changing. Atmosphere and live traditional music are the most obvious attractions, but the grocery is real and provisions the local fishing boats. Simple bar food - seafood chowder, open seafood sandwiches - is available all day. Closed 25 Dec & Good Fri. No Credit Cards. **Directions:** in town centre, near the ferry slip.

Castletownbere

The Old Presbytery

ACCOMODATION/B&B

Brandy Hall House Castletownbere Co. Cork **Tel: 027 70424**
Fax: 027 70420 Email: marywrigley@eircom.net Web: www.midnet.ie/oldpresbytery/index.htm

On the edge of Castletownbere and well-signposted from the road, this very pleasant old house on 4 acres is in a magnificent position - on a little point with the sea on two sides and clear views of Berehaven Harbour. The house dates back to the late 1700s and has been sensitively restored by the current owners, David and Mary Wrigley. The five bedrooms vary in size and outlook but all have phone, tea/coffee tray and TV and are furnished to a high standard, in keeping with the character of the house. Breakfast - which includes a vegetarian menu - is served in a pleasant conservatory overlooking the sea. Children welcome (under 5s free in parents' room, cot available); pets permitted by arrangement. **Rooms 5** (all en-suite, 4 shower only). B&B about €32, ss about €13. MasterCard, Visa. **Directions:** turn left as the road narrows by Brandy Hall bridge and follow the sign.

Castletownshend

Bow Hall

ACCOMODATION

Main Street Castletownshend Co. Cork **Tel: 028 36114**

Castletownshend is one of west Cork's prettiest villages and this very comfortable 17th century house on the hill is a wonderful place to stay. With a pleasant outlook over beautiful well-tended gardens to the sea, excellent home-cooking and a warm welcome by enthusiastic hosts, Dick and Barbara Vickery, a visit to this lovely home is a memorable experience. The house is full of interest but its most outstanding feature is perhaps the food, which is not only imaginative but much of it is home-grown too. Residents' dinner is available by reservation and this treat will be a truly seasonal menu, based on their own produce fresh from the garden - potatoes, courgettes, swiss chard, salads, fresh herbs and fruit - picked just before serving with other local specialities such as fresh crab or salmon. Menus change daily and breakfasts are also a highlight, with home-baked breads and muffins, home-made sausages, home-made preserves among the delights. Non-smoking house. No pets. **Rooms 3** (1 en-suite, 2 with private bathrooms), B&B €44.44, ss €6.35; min 2 night stay preferred. Advance bookings essential, especially in winter; D 8 pm, by reservation; €32 (no wine licence). Closed Christmas week. **Directions:** Main Street of Castletownend.

Castletownshend
PUB /RESTAURANT

Mary Ann's Bar & Restaurant

Castletownshend Co. Cork **Tel: 028 36146**
Fax: 028 36377 Email: maryanns@eircom.net

Mention Castletownshend and the chances are that the next words will be 'Mary Ann's', as this welcoming landmark has been the source of happy memories for many a visitor to this picturesque west Cork village over the years. (For those who have come up the hill with a real sailor's appetite from the little quay, the sight of its gleaming bar seen through the open door is one to treasure.) The pub is as old as it looks, going back to 1846, and has been in the energetic and hospitable ownership of Fergus and Patricia O'Mahony since 1988. Any refurbishments at Mary Ann's have left its original character intact. The O'Mahonys have built up a great reputation for food at the bar and in the restaurant, which is split between an upstairs dining room and The Vine Room at the back, which can be used for private parties. Seafood is the star, of course, and comes in many guises, usually along with some of the lovely home-baked brown bread which is one of the house specialities. Another is the Platter of Castlehaven Bay Shellfish and Seafood - a sight to behold, and usually including langoustine, crab meat, crab claws, and both fresh and smoked salmon. Much of the menu depends on the catch of the day, although there are also good steaks and roasts, served with delicious local potatoes and seasonal vegetables. Desserts are good too, but local West Cork cheeses are an excellent option.* A Wine Club was started at Mary Ann's in September 2001 and conference facilities are planned for spring 2002, catering for meetings of up to 40/private dining for 30. Bar food 12-2.30 & 6-9 daily. Restaurant **Seats 30.** Set D €33; L Sun only in winter, 12-2.30. House wine €15.17. Service discretionary. Closed 25 Dec, Good Fri & last 3 weeks Jan. MasterCard, Visa, Laser. **Directions:** five miles from Skibbereen.

Clonakilty
RESTAURANT/PUB

An Sugan

41 Wolfe Tone Street Clonakilty Co. Cork **Tel: 023 33498**

The O'Crowley family has owned An Sugan since 1980 and they have done a great job: it's always been a really friendly, well-run place and their reputation for good food is well-deserved. This year saw major changes, with a new extension now providing a contemporary café bar (with outside seating in a sheltered courtyard at the back), in contrast to the traditional atmosphere of the original bar and restaurant. Food served in the new area is lighter and more modern, but the older bar and restaurant remain equally popular and have kept their character. Menus changes daily and remain very strong on seafood - fish specials could include a choice of ten, ranging from cod on a bed of champ to lobster salad. The family is building a small hotel nearby, which should be the ideal complement to An Sugan. No private parking. Restaurant seats 48.Food served 12.30-9.30 daily . A la carte. House wine €15.24. Service discretionary. Closed 25-26 Dec & Good Fri. MasterCard, Visa, Laser. **Directions:** from Cork on the left hand side as you enter Clonakilty.

Clonakilty
HOTEL

Dunmore House Hotel

Muckross Clonakilty Co. Cork
Tel: 023 33352 Fax: 023 34686
Email: dunmorehousehotel@eircom.net Web: www.dunmorehotel.com

The magnificent coastal location of Jeremiah and Mary O'Donovan's family-owned and managed hotel has been used to advantage to provide sea views for all bedrooms and to allow guests access to their own stretch of foreshore. Comfortable public areas include a bar and lounges; bedrooms are furnished to a high standard and the numerous leisure activities in the area include angling and golf - green fees are free to residents on the hotel's own (highly scenic) nine hole golf course - cycling, horse-riding and watersports; packed lunches are provided on request. Conference/banqueting 250. Wheelchair accessible. Children welcome (under 4s free in parents' room; cot available). Pets permitted by arrangement. **Rooms 23** (2 junior suites,1 room for disabled). B&B €69.95pps, ss€12.70. Closed 23-27 Dec and 20 Jan- 8 Mar. Amex, Diners, MasterCard, Visa, Laser. **Directions:** 3 miles outside Clonakilty Town, well signed.

Clonakilty

HOTEL/RESTAURANT

Emmet Hotel

Emmet Square Clonakilty Co. Cork
Tel: 023 33394 Fax: 023 35058
Email: emmethotel@eircom.ie Web: emmethotel.com

The Emmet Hotel is hidden away in the centre of Clonakilty on a lovely serene Georgian square that contrasts unexpectedly with the hustle and bustle of the nearby streets; it's a most attractive location, although parking is likely to be difficult. The standard of furnishing and comfort is high throughout, with management in the capable hands of Tony and Marie O'Keeffe (who run a separate restaurant next door, see below). Conference/banqueting for 150. Children welcome (under 2s free; cots available). Pets permitted by arrangement. **Rooms 20** (2 executive) B&B about €57.14pps, ss about €12.70. Open all year. **O'Keeffe's of Clonakilty:** O'Keeffe's is located in separate premises next door, but the restaurant also has direct access from the hotel and bookings are made through the hotel. Overlooking Emmet Square, the restaurant is creatively decorated in a colourful style that is most unexpected in an old house and allows a complete change of atmosphere. Marie O'Keeffe's cooking is based on the best of seasonal local produce, much of it organic, and her reputation for creative modern cooking was already well known, so the restaurant is proving a great success. A short, moderately priced à la carte menu offers four or five choices on each course plus half a dozen specials. Typical starters might include pesto cakes with Union Hall smoked salmon, crème fraîche and roasted pine nuts or prawns in garlic butter, followed by main courses like Castletownbere cod with with a herb crust and garlic mayonnaise or Asian style chicken on soy noodles. D 6.30-9.30 daily (L available in the hotel); à la carte, sc discretionary. Restaurant closed 25-26 Dec. Amex, Diners, MasterCard, Visa, Laser, Switch. **Directions:** in the centre of Clonakilty - turn left into Emmet Square at the Catholic Church.

Clonakilty

RESTAURANT

Fionnuala's Little Italian Restaurant

30 Ashe Street Clonakilty Co. Cork
Tel: 023 34355 Email: timtra@eircom.net

Fionnuala Harkin's charmingly higgledy-piggledy restaurant celebrated 10 years in business last summer and, despite recent extensions that provided an extra two dining rooms and a small wine bar, it's still packed out all the time. The reasons for its popularity are simple: good home-cooked food (organic whenever possible), reasonable prices and friendly service. Pizza made with Clonakilty black pudding is one of the most popular dishes, and other favourites include Pollo alla Cacciatora (chicken in red wine, tomatoes, garlic & herbs, served with pasta or potatoes roasted with olive oil, garlic & rosemary) and spinach & cream lasagne. Local speciality foods such as Ummera smoked chicken and Union Hall smoked fish also feature regularly and vegetarian dishes are always on the regular menu. Children welcome. **Seats 50** (private room, 20). No smoking area. D only 5.30-10 daily . A la carte (average D from about €18). House wine €12.50. Closed 24-26 Dec & Mon-Tue in winter. MasterCard, Visa, Laser. **Directions:** in Clonakilty town centre - on the left as you enter the town through Ashe St.

Clonakilty

HOTEL/RESTAURANT

The Lodge & Spa at Inchydoney Island

Inchydoney Island Clonakilty Co. Cork
Tel: 023 33143 Fax: 023 35229
Email: administration@inchydoneyisland.com Web: www.inchydoneyisland.com

A determined programme of landscaping has ensured that the exterior of this luxurious but architecturally uninspired hotel has softened somewhat since its opening in 1998 - and even the large car park, which is unfortunately located between any hotel and the sea, is gradually being broken up as planted areas become established. Other design features - such as keeping the function area quite separate from the rest of the hotel - are clearly sensible and, once inside the hotel (as opposed to the Dunes Pub, which has a more down to earth atmosphere) that pampered feeling soon takes over. Public areas are spacious and impressive, notably a large, comfortably furnished first-floor residents' lounge and library, with a piano and extensive sea views. Bedrooms, all furnished and decorated in an uncluttered contemporary style, have ISDN lines, safes - and most have wonderful views. Outstanding health and leisure facilities include a superb Thalassotherapy Spa, which offers a range of special treatments. However, even without taking up any of the these amenities, there is something in the air that makes this a very relaxing place. Special breaks are a major attraction - fishing, equestrian, golf, therapies or simply an off-season weekend away. Conferences/banqueting (300/200); secretarial service, video-conferencing (by arrangement). Thalassotherapy spa (24 treatment rooms/beauty treatments); leisure centre, swimming pool; equestrian; snooker. Children welcome (under 12s free in parents' room; cots available, €12). Pets permitted in some areas. **Rooms 67** (4 suites, 63 executive rooms; 17 non-smoking; 2 for disabled). Room rate €285. SC10%. Closed 25-26 Dec. **Gulfstream Restaurant:** Located on the first floor, with panoramic sea views from the (rather few) window tables, this elegant restaurant offers fine dining in a broadly Mediterranean style, utilising organic produce where possible. Menus change monthly, include vegetarian options and willingly cater for special dietary requirements. **Seats 80** Private rooms (70) No smoking area. D daily 7.30-10, Set D €50. House wine €19. SC10%. [*Informal bar meals also available 12-9 daily.]. Amex, Diners, MasterCard, Visa. **Directions:** N71 from Cork to Clonakilty causeway to Inchydoney .

Cloyne

Barnabrow Country House

COUNTRY HOUSE/RESTAURANT

Cloyne Midleton Cloyne Co. Cork
Tel: 021 4652 534 Fax: 021 4652 534
Email: barnabrow@eircom.net Web: www.barnabrowhouse.com

John and Geraldine O'Brien's sensitive conversion of an imposing seventeenth century house makes good use of its stunning views of Ballycotton, and the decoration is commendably restrained. Innovative African wooden furniture (among items for sale in an on-site shop) is a point of interest and spacious bedrooms are stylishly decorated and comfortable (although only two have a bath). Some bedrooms are in converted buildings at the back of the house, but (good) breakfasts are served in the main dining room, at a communal table. Recent developments have increased the dining capacity at Barnabrow, so they can now cater for weddings and other functions (up to 150) as well as normal private dining . Head chef Eamon Harty is Ballymaloe trained and brings to Barnabrow's **Trinity Rooms Restaurant** and catering operations the philosophy and cooking style that has earned such acclaim. Children welcome (cots available, £5). Pets permitted by arrangement. **Rooms 19** (all en-suite & no-smoking; 17 shower only). B&B €55pps, ss €13. D 7-9 Tue-Sat, L Sun Only 12.30-3; D à la carte; Set Sun L €19. House wine €15.87; service discretionary. Closed 24-28 Dec. Trinity Rooms Diners, MasterCard, Visa. **Directions:** from Cork, turn right off N25 at Midleton roundabout for Cloyne, Cloyne, 2 miles on Ballycotton road.

Cloyne

The Cross of Cloyne

PUB

Cloyne Co. Cork **Tel: 021 465 2401**

Imaginatively refurbished in the modern idiom without losing its character, this long narrow room has an open fire at the far end for colder times, interesting music some nights - and Colm Falvey's food too. What more could you ask of a country pub? Closed 25 Dec & Good Fri.

Cobh

Mansworth's Bar (Est 1895)

PUB

Cobh Co. Cork **Tel: 021 481 1965** Fax: 021 481 4905

Cobh's oldest established family-owned bar dates back to at least 1895 and is currently in the capable hands of John Mansworth, who is a great promoter of the town and a knowledgeable provider of local information. Bar snacks are available but it's really as a character pub that Mansworth's is most appealing. It's a bit of a climb up the hill to reach it but well worth the effort, especially for anyone with an interest in the history of Cobh as a naval port - the photographs and memorabilia on display here will provide hours of pleasure. Not suitable for children after 7 pm. Pets permitted. Open from 10.30 am. Closed 25 Dec & Good Fri. **Directions:** Top of town, above St. Colman's Cathedral.

Cobh

Robin Hill House & Restaurant

GUESTHOUSE/RESTAURANT

Lake Road Rushbrooke Cobh Co. Cork
Tel: 021 481 1395 Fax: 021 481 4680
Email: robinhillhouse@eircom.net Web: www.robinhillhouse.com

A neat driveway leads up to Colin and Teresa Pielow's freshly-painted Victorian rectory and the whole interior has also been renovated since they came here in 1999. The dining operation is so central to this house that it feels like a restaurant with rooms. There's a comfortable reception area (with a real fire) and, alongside it, a stylishly bright restaurant with high-back chairs and handsomely-laid tables in the modern idiom with very fine glasses - all overlooking a terrace and gardens to the sea beyond. Well-made freshly-baked breads, bowls of butter and jugs of iced water arrive immediately, along with an exceptional wine list. (Colin has also set up a tasting room in his wine cellar). Seasonal menus offer about four choices on each course plus daily specials and include some especially tempting and unusual dishes, including game in season. Starters like home cured gravadlax from wild Irish salmon, with a dill vinaigrette or Pielows rustic game terrine with a bitter onion compôte might be followed by pan-fried saddle of rabbit with a creamy whole-grain mustard sauce or a chargrilled selection of seafood. Desserts include classics like fresh raspberry sablé and there's an Irish & continental cheese selection. Some dishes - daily specials and the cheeseboard, for example - attract a supplement. **Seats 50** Not suitable for children under 12. D Tue-sat, 7.30-9.30; L Sun only 12.45-2.15. Set D €35.55,Set Sun L €20.95. House wines from €15.87; s.c. discretionary. Restaurant closed D Sun, all Mon. **Accommodation:** En-suite accommodation is offered in rooms imaginatively furnished in a somewhat minimalist style; they have specially made furniture in different woods - hence the Beech Room, the Sycamore Room, the Cherry Room and so forth. (The same craftsman also made a magnificent cigar humidor which is an exceptional piece of work.) Rooms all have phones, TV and tea/coffee-making facilities. Garden. **Rooms 6** (all en-suite & no smoking) B&B €50.80, ss€19.05. Establishment closed 25-27 Dec & 7 Jan -7 Feb. MasterCard, Visa, Laser. **Directions:** Over the bridge past Fota, take right turn right for Cobh 4 miles past the Statoil garage, next turn left, 300 yardson the left.

Cobh

WatersEdge Hotel

HOTEL

Cobh Co. Cork **Tel: 021 481 5566**

Fax: 021 481 2011 Email: watersedge@eircom.net Web: www.watersedgehotel.ie

The name says it all at Michael and Margaret Whelan's enterprising new hotel, which is neatly slotted between the road and the harbour, taking full advantage of its unique waterside setting. There's a carpark underneath the hotel and public areas include an impressive foyer, while the spacious bedrooms - some of which have French windows opening onto a verandah, most have a sea view - include a suite which is designed to be used for small conferences as well as accommodation. Children welcome (under 2s free in parents' room, cot available without charge). Pets permitted by arrangement. **Rooms 19** (1 suite, 1 for disabled, 5 no-smoking). B&B €76pps, ss €26. Open all year. **Jacob's Ladder** Michael Whelan has been in the tugboat business for many years (there may well be a tug berthed alongside the hotel when you visit) and the restaurant name has particular maritime relevance. The restaurant is well-located within the hotel, with large windows affording views across the harbour and well-appointed tables are arranged brasserie style, creating a light, bright atmosphere. Beni McGrath, previously head chef at The Wine Vault in Waterford, took over the kitchen early in 2001 and his style is a combination of traditional Irish, French and contemporary fusion cooking. Local seafood is, of course, the star here - including Rossmore oysters and Shanagarry smoked salmon as well as seafish landed nearby, but vegetarians are not overlooked (smoked cheese & ratatouille parcels or spinach & ricotta tortellini with pesto cream sauce & parmesan shavings would be typical) and red meats (including Wicklow lamb), duck and pigeon feature regularly too. Finish with updated classic desserts or cheeses served with home-made chutney & toast. Informative, fairly priced wine list. L daily, 12.30-3, D daily, 6.30-9; à la carte (Average main course: L,€10; D,€ 20). House wine €16.44; sc discretionary. Amex, Diners, MasterCard, Visa, Laser. **Directions:** R624 off the N25. Follow signs for Cobh Heritage Centre.

Crookhaven

O'Sullivans

PUB

Crookhaven Skibbereen Co. Cork **Tel: 028 35319** Fax: 028 35319

This long-established family-run bar is in an attractive location right on the harbour at Crookhaven, with tables beside the water - when it's not too busy, it can be heaven on a sunny day. Angela O'Sullivan personally supervises all the food served in the bar - home-made soups and chowders, shrimps, open sandwiches, home-baked bread, scones and desserts - all good homely fare. Bar food daily 10.30-9 (Sun to 8 pm). Closed 25 Dec & Good Fri. MasterCard, Visa, **Directions:** from Cork, take the N71 and turn left on to the R591 just before Bantry.

Durrus

Blairs Cove House

RESTAURANT/ACCOMMODATION

Durrus Co. Cork **Tel: 027 61127**

Fax: 027 61487 Email: blairscove@eircom.net

At the head of Dunmanus Bay, Blairs Cove enjoys a stunning waterside location. Although additions over the years have enlarged the restaurant considerably - and include the option of enjoying the view from an elegant conservatory while you dine - the original room at this remarkable restaurant is lofty, stone-walled and black-beamed: but, although characterful, any tendency to rusticity is immediately offset by the choice of a magnificent chandelier as a central feature, gilt-framed family portraits on the walls and the superb insouciance of using their famous grand piano to display an irresistible array of desserts. They have things down to a fine art at Blairs Cove - and what a formula: an enormous central buffet groans under the weight of the legendary hors d'oeuvre display, a speciality that is unrivalled in Ireland. Main course specialities of local seafood or the best of meat and poultry are char-grilled at a special wood-fired grill right in the restaurant and, in addition to those desserts, full justice is done to the ever-growing selection of local farmhouse cheese for which

West Cork is rightly renowned. This place is truly an original. Banqueting (50). **Seats 85.** D 7.15-9.30 Tue-Sat. Set D €44; service discretionary. Closed Sun/Mon (Sun only in Jul & Aug) & Nov-Mar. Accommodation: 3 Suites. Three small apartments, offered for self-catering or B&B, are furnished in very different but equally dashing styles and there is also a cottage in the grounds. Children welcome, cot available; pets permitted by arrangement. B&B €95 pps, ss€19; no service charge. Diners, MasterCard, Visa. **Directions:** 1.5 miles outside Durrus on 591N,on right hand side

---

Fermoy

Castlehyde Hotel

HOTEL/RESTAURANT

Castlehyde Fermoy Co. Cork **Tel: 025 31865**
Fax: 025 31485 Email: cashyde@iol.ie Web: castlehydehotel.com

In a lovely unspoilt area only a short drive from Cork, this would make a soothing base for exploring north Cork. Erik Speekenbrink's delightful hotel is retained within the original buildings of a beautifully restored 18th century courtyard building, with all the original features preserved. Warm hospitality, gracious surroundings, open fires and a high level of comfort combined with the character of the old buildings and courtyard make this an unusually appealing hotel. Bedrooms, which are individually furnished to a high standard with antiques, have a great style and the feeling of a private home; ground floor rooms along a courtyard verandah are more suitable for guests with limited mobility. Small conferences (35). Heated outdoor swimming pool. Children welcome (under 10s free in parents' room, cot available free of charge). No pets. **Rooms 24** (5 cottage suites, 10 no-smoking , 1 for disabled). B&B about €95pps, ss about €35. **Mermaids Restaurant** A conservatory extension helps make the most of the restaurant's pleasant situation, overlooking a lawn and mature woodland. Lunch and dinner menus in a creative Irish international style offer some unusual choices - a wild boar terrine with toast brioche perhaps - and, given the lengthy descriptions on many current menus, are refreshingly brief and to the point. **Seats 65.** (Private room, 14). L only 12.30-2.30 (Sun to 3), D 6.30-9; Set Sun L about €20, D à la carte. House wine about €18. Service discretionary; air conditioning. Toilets wheelchair accessible. *Light meals also available during the day, 11-5. Amex, Diners, MasterCard, Visa. **Directions:** at Fermoy, turn off the N8 and take the N72 (Mallow direction) for about 2 miles.

Fermoy

La Bigoudenne

RESTAURANT

28 MacCurtain Street Fermoy Co. Cork **Tel: 025 32832**

At this little piece of France in the main street of a County Cork town, Noelle and Rodolphe Semeria's hospitality is matched only by their food, which specialises in Breton dishes, especially crèpes - both savoury (made with buckwheat flour) and sweet (with wheat flour). They run a special pancake evening once a month or so, on a Saturday night. But they do all sorts of other things too, like salads that you only seem to get in France, soup of the day served with 1/4 baguette & butter, a plat du jour and lovely French pastries. Even the bill is a pleasant surprise. As we go to press the Semerias are expecting to return to the premises after a temporary absence for structural repairs to the building but, except that they will no longer be serving lunch, there should be no major changes. **Seats 18.** D Tues-Sun,5.45-10. Early D Tue-Thu €16.44 (5.45-7.15), Set D € 24.06; Fri, Sat Gourmet Menu €32; Sun Set D €24.06, also à la carte. House Wine €15.17. Closed Mon & Jan. Amex, MasterCard, Visa. **Directions:** on the main street, opposite ESB.

Glandore

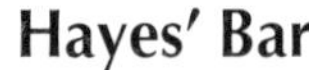

Hayes' Bar

PUB

The Square Glandore Co. Cork
Tel: 028 33214 Email: dchayes@tinet.ie

Hayes Bar overlooks the harbour, has outdoor tables - and Ada Hayes' famous bar food. The soup reminds you of the kind your granny used to make and the sandwiches are stupendous. Everything that goes to make Hayes' special - including the wines and crockery collected on Declan and Ada's frequent trips to France (which also affect the menu, inspiring the likes of Croque Monsieur) - has to be seen to be believed. Order a simple cup of coffee and see what you get for about €1.50. Wine is Declan's particular passion and Hayes' offers some unexpected treats, by the glass as well as the bottle, at refreshingly reasonable prices. Great reading too, including a lot of background on the wines in stock - and you can now see some of Declan's pictures exhibited, from June to August. By any standards, Hayes' is an outstanding bar. Meals 12-6, Jun-Aug; weekends only off-season. Closed weekdays Sep-May except Christmas & Easter.

Glanworth
ACCOMODATION

Glanworth Mill Country Inn

Glanworth Co. Cork
Tel: 025 38555 Fax: 025 38560
Email: glanworth@iol.ie Web: www.glanworthmill.com

Beside a Norman castle on the banks of the River Funcheon, this imaginatively converted old stone mill - complete with the old mill wheel which has been restored, encased in glass and worked into the interior design - makes an unusual place to stay. The whole restoration programme has been undertaken with commendable vision and to a high standard throughout, including landscaping of the riverside garden area. Public areas include a restful sitting room and the Mill Tea Rooms, where informal meals are served (12 noon-9.30 pm). Bedrooms - styled on the era and taste of the writer each is named after, including Anthony Trollope, Elizabeth Bowen and William Trevor - all have good en-suite bathrooms, phones, complimentary water and fruit. Small conferences/private parties(46). No pets. **Rooms 10** (1 junior suite,all no-smoking). B&B about €65pps, ss about €13. Children under 2 free in parents' room. More formal meals are served in the Fleece'n'Loom Restaurant, which includes a conservatory area. [*It is possible that the inn may change hands during 2002, although there is no definite information available at the time of going to press.] **Seats 50** D Mon-Sat 7-9.30 & L Sun, à la carte.House wine about €15, sc 10%. Closed Christmas/New Year & Good Fri. Amex, Diners, MasterCard, Visa, Laser. **Directions:** take N8 between Mitchelstown and Fermoy, signposted 5 miles to Glanworth Mill.

Goleen
FARMHOUSE

Fortview House

Gurtyowen Toormore Goleen Co.Cork **Tel: 028 35324**
Fax: 028 35324 Email: Web: www.westcorkueb.ie/fortview

Violet & Richard Connell's remarkable farmhouse in the hills behind Goleen is immaculate. It is beautifully furnished, with country pine and antiques, brass and iron beds in en-suite bedrooms (that are all individually decorated) and with all sorts of thoughtful little details to surprise and delight. Richard is a magic man when it comes to building - his latest creation is a lovely conservatory dining room that he has completed with great attention to detail. For her part, Violet loves cooking, and provides guests with a great choice at breakfast - including Tom & Giana Ferguson's Gubbeen cheese, made down the road - and she provides residents' dinners, to the great delight of her guests. **Rooms 5** (all en-suite). B&B €32-40pps. Set D served at 8pm, €25. book by noon.Closed 1 Nov-1 Mar. **Directions:** 2 km from Toormore on main Durrus-Bantry road (R591).

Goleen
RESTAURANT/ACCOMMODATION

The Heron's Cove

Harbour Road Goleen Harbour Co. Cork
Tel: 028 35225 Fax: 028 35422
Email: suehill@eircom.net Web: www.heronscove.com

When the tide is in and the sun is out there can be few prettier locations than Sue Hill's restaurant overlooking Goleen harbour. She does tasty, inexpensive day-time food - which can be served on a sunny balcony - like hearty soups and home-baked bread, home-cooked ham, farmhouse cheeses and seafood specials. Delicious desserts - tangy lemon tart or a wicked chocolate gateau - are also available with afternoon tea or freshly brewed coffee. The Heron's Cove philosophy is to use only the best of fresh, local ingredients - typically in wholesome starters like fisherman's broth or warm duckling salad and main courses such as Goleen lamb cutlets with a redcurrant sauce. Lobster and Rossmore oysters are available fresh from a tank and prices are refreshingly reasonable. Children welcome at discretion of the management. **Seats 30** Open all day, 12-9.30, L 12-3 (Sun L 1.30-3), D 5.30-9.30. Set L €16.50; D à la carte. Closed Christmas & New Year. Accommodation Good-sized en-suite rooms have bathrooms, satellite TV, phones, tea/coffee-making facilities and hair dryers. The three doubles have private balconies with sea views and two smaller rooms have a woodland view. Garden. Accommodation not suitable for children. **Rooms 5** (all en-suite & no smoking). B&B €35pps, ss €8. Open for dinner, bed & breakfast all year except Christmas week, but it is always advisable to book, especially off-season. Amex, Diners, MasterCard, Visa, Laser. **Directions:** turn left in Goleen Village down 300 m to harbour

---

Gougane Barra
HOTEL

Gougane Barra Hotel

Gougane Barra Macroom Co. Cork **Tel: 026 47069** Fax: 026 47226
Email: gouganebarrahotel@eircom.com Web: gouganebarra.com

In one of the most peaceful and beautiful locations in Ireland, this delightfully old-fashioned family-run hotel is set in a Forest Park overlooking Gougane Barra Lake (famous for its monastic settlements). The Lucey family has run the hotel since 1937, offering simple, comfortable accommodation as a restful base for walking holidays. Rooms are comfortable but not over-modernised, all looking out on to the lake or mountain. There are quiet public rooms where guests often like to read; breakfast is served in the lakeside dining room. No weddings or other functions are accepted. Children welcome (under 11s free in parents' room.) No pets. **Rooms 27** (all en-suite). B&B €56pps, ss €19. Closed mid-Oct-mid Apr. Amex, Diners, MasterCard, Visa, Laser. **Directions:** situated in Gougane Barra National Forest, well signposted.

Heir Island

Island Cottage

RESTAURANT

Heir Island Skibbereen Co. Cork **Tel: 028 38102**
Fax: 028 38102 Email: ellmaryislandcottage.com Web: islandcottage.com

Just a short ferry ride from the mainland yet light years away from the "real" world, this place is unique. Hardly a likely location for a restaurant run by two people who have trained and worked in some of Europe's most prestigious establishments - but, since 1990, that is exactly what John Desmond and Ellmary Fenton have been doing at Island Cottage. Everything about it is different from other restaurants, including the booking policy: a basic advance booking for at least six people must be in place before other smaller groups of 2 to 4 can be accepted - not later than 3pm on the day; changes to group numbers require 24 hours notice and a booking deposit of €6.50 per head is required to reserve a table. The no-choice 5-course menu (€25) depends on the availability of the fresh local, organic (where possible) and wild island ingredients of that day. A vegetarian dish can be accommodated with advance notice. An early autumn menu will give an idea of his attachment to the island and the kind of meal to expect: roast duck legs on a bed of turnip with duck jus (using hand-reared ducks "of exceptional quality" from Ballydehob), Cape Clear turbot with shrimp sauce on a bed of sea beet or spinach (the turbot is farmed on Cape Clear Island and the shrimp is caught by local fishermen; sea beet is a wild foreshore vegetable, rather like spinach) and a classic terrine of vanilla ice cream with meringue served with a blackberry sauce, using berries picked by children holidaying on the island. Cookery courses and demonstrations can be arranged, also private dinner parties (October-May). Details of cottages for rent also available from the restaurant. **Seats 24** (max table size 10; be prepared to share a table). D €25 approx. Wed-Sun, 8.15-11.45 pm; one sitting served at group pace. L by arrangement only, off-season: groups of 8-24. Closed Mon & Tues and mid Sep-mid May. No credit cards. **Directions:** From Skibbereen, on Ballydehob road, turn left at Church Cross, signposted Hare island and Cunnamore. Narrow winding road, past school, church, Minihan's Bar. Continue to end of road, Cunnamore car park. Ferry departs Cunnamore pier at 7.55 returns at 11.55 (journey: 4 minutes.)

Innishannon

Innishannon House Hotel

HOTEL/RESTAURANT

Innishannon Co. Cork **Tel: 021 775121**
Fax: 021 775609 Email: inishannon@tinet.ie

This lovely house was built in 1720 in the 'petit chateau' style and both it and the riverside location and gardens have great charm. Public rooms include a residents' bar and sitting room, and bedrooms vary in shape and character; the best rooms have river views, while others overlook the lovely gardens and all have original wooden shutters.After many years as a family-run business, the hotel changed hands in 2001 and is currently operated by a consortium, who have plans for major upgrading and a new bedroom block. So far everything seems much the same, but changes are probably inevitable in the near future. Garden, fishing, boating. **Rooms 13** (1 suite). B&B about €90.

Kanturk

Assolas Country House

COUNTRY HOUSE

Kanturk Co. Cork **Tel: 029 50015** Fax: 029 50795
Email: assolas@eircom.net Web: www.assolas.com

Home to the Bourke family for generations and currently managed by Joe and Hazel Bourke, this gracious 17th century manor house is famous for generous, thoughtful hospitality, impeccable housekeeping and wonderful food.Hazel was the winner of the guide's Euro-Toques Natural Food Award in 2000 and very deservedly so - she is a Euro-Toques chef and renowned for imaginative and skilled use of organic produce from their own garden and the surrounding area, offered in a daily residents' dinner menu which documents in detail the produce used in their kitchen and the people who supply it. Memorable dinners are served in a lovely dining room - high-ceilinged and elegantly proportioned with deep red walls, antique furniture and crisp white linen - which is not over-decorated, providing an appropriate setting for food that is refreshingly natural in style as well as substance. Bedrooms vary according to their position in this lovely old house - some are very spacious and overlook the garden and river, and there are some courtyard rooms which are especially suitable for families. A lovingly maintained walled kitchen garden, a little river with tame swans and a couple of boats for guests to potter about in all add to the charm - even boots kept beside the front door for the use of anyone who may feel like looking up the local otters at dusk. The wine list concentrates on European wine, notably Maison Guigal, which has supplied the house wines since 1983. The famous Blackwater Valley Reichensteiner, made locally by Dr Billy Christopher, is also listed. Rooms 9 (all en-suite). B&B EUR90 pps, ss EUR15. Dining room Seats 20 (max table size 14). Residents' D EUR45, 7-8 pm; house wine EUR20. Service is included in prices and tipping is discouraged. Closed Nov-Mar. MasterCard, Visa, Laser. **Directions:** Signposted off N72, 8 miles West of Mallow.

Kanturk

The Vintage

PUB

O'Brien Street Kanturk Co Cork
Tel: 029 50549 Fax: 029 51209

Stephen Bowles has been running this fine pub since 1985, and it's a consistently well-run establishment: the attractive, well-maintained exterior draws people in and, once through the door, the comfortable, pleasingly traditional interior keeps them there. Be sure to stay for a pint or a quick bite of bar food, even if it's only a bowl of home-made soup. Other regulars include steaks done various ways, fish of the day, eg fillet of lemon sole with tartare sauce and something special for vegetarians, as well as freshly prepared sandwiches. Meals 12.30-9.30 Mon-Sat, 6-10 Sun. Closed 25 Dec & Good Fri. MasterCard, Visa. Directions: In a terrace of houses alongside the river in Kanturk village.

Killeagh *- Ballymackeigh House & Brownes Restaurant, see Youghal.*

Kilbrittain

Casino House

RESTAURANT ☆

Coolmain Bay Kilbrittain Nr Kinsale Co.Cork **Tel: 023 49944**
Fax: 023 49945 Email: chouse@eircom.net

While Kerrin and Michael Relja's delightful restaurant is just a few miles west of Kinsale, it has been one of the country's best kept secrets for a long time and is only recently beginning to get the recognition it deserves. The couple's cool continental style makes a pleasing contrast to their lovely old house, and the warmth of Kerrin's hospitality is consistently matched by the excellence of Michael's food. Michael cooks with verve and confidence, in starters such as quail & duck roulade served on a red wine & onion confit or pan-fried oysters in a wholegrain mustard sabayon with white wine cababge. Well-balanced main course choices lead off with a vegetarian dish - vegetable cous-cous tartlet on a baby spinach salad, topped with a red paprika dressing perhaps - and include less usual dishes like saddle of rabbit with a pistachio nut & chicken stuffing wrapped in prosciutto ham & served with forest mushrooms and its own jus. Meats are treated equally creatively, Ballydehob duck is a speciality and nightly specials will include imaginative seafood dishes which depend on availability but all come with their own vegetable garnish and deliciously simple seasonal side vegetables. The Reljas attention to detail is outstanding and their perfectionism in every aspect of the restaurant is admirable. Local cheeses are handled with particular respect, earning the restaurant this guide's Farmhouse Cheese Award in 1999. **Seats 35** (private room 22). D Mon-Tues/Thurs-Sun 7-9, L Sun only,1-3; all à la carte; house wine about €17; sc discretionary. Closed 1 Jan-17 Mar & Wed except Jul-Aug. MasterCard, Visa. **Directions:** on R600 between Kinsale and Clonakilty.

Kinsale

Actons Hotel

HOTEL *féile bia*

Pier Road Kinsale Co. Cork **Tel: 021 4772135**
Fax: 021 4772231 Email: actons@indigo.ie

Overlooking the harbour and standing in its own grounds, this attractive quayside establishment is Kinsale's most famous hotel, dating back to 1946 when it was created from several substantial period houses. It has recently undergone extensive renovations. The leisure facilities are excellent and there are also good conference/banqueting facilities for up to 300. Bar food available daily, 12-9. Swimming pool, sauna, gym, solarium. Children welcome (under 12s free in parents' room, cots available.) No pets. Wheelchair access. Lift. **Rooms 76** (3 mini-suites,2 for disabled). B&B about €85pps, ss about €32 (midweek breaks available). Open all year. Amex, Diners, MasterCard, Visa, **Directions:** on the waterfront, short walk from town centre.

Kinsale
GUESTHOUSE

Blindgate House

Blindgate Kinsale Co Cork
Tel: 021 4777858 Fax: 021 4777868
Email: info@blindgatehouse.com Web: www.blindgatehouse.com

Maeve Coakley's newly purpose-built guesthouse is set in its own developing garden high up over the town and has brought a new element to the range of accommodation offered in Kinsale. With spacious rooms, uncluttered lines and a generally modern, bright and airy atmosphere, Blindgate makes a refreshing contrast to the more traditional styles that prevail locally. All bedrooms are carefully furnished with elegant modern simplicity, have full en-suite bathrooms and good facilities including fax/modem sockets as well as phones, satellite TV, tea/coffee trays and trouser press. Maeve is a hospitable host - and well-known in Kinsale for her skills in the kitchen, so breakfast here is a high priority: there's a buffet displaying all sorts of good things including organic muesli, fresh fruits and juices, famhouse cheese and yogurts, as well as a menu of hot dishes featuring, of course, the full Irish Breakfast alongside catch of the day and other specialities - so make sure you allow time to enjoy this treat to the full. **Rooms, 11.** B&B €63.50pps. Closed 23 Dec-1 Mar. Amex, Diners, MasterCard, Visa, Laser. **Directions:** 200m after St Multose Church on left hand side.

Kinsale
HOTEL

The Blue Haven Hotel

3/4 Pearse Street Kinsale Co. Cork **Tel: 021 477 2209**
Fax: 021 4774268 Email: bluhaven@iol.ie

Due to the nature of the building, public areas in this attractive hotel at the heart of Kinsale are quite compact, but the lounge/lobby and the bar areas are well-planned and comfortable. A major refurbishment programme and the addition of eight deluxe bedrooms was recently completed, so all the bedrooms are new or redone, with double glazing offsetting the street noise that is inevitable in a central location. However, although both the well-appointed rooms and their neat bathrooms make up in thoughtful planning anything they lack in spaciousness, there are plans to reduce the number of rooms in order to create more space. Not very suitable for children, but unders 4s free in parents' room, cots available. No pets. Street parking. **Rooms 17** (4 shower only). B&B about €110pps, ss about €30. Restaurant: **Seats 60** (private room, 22) D 7-9.30 daily, Set D about €40, à la carte available,. House wine from €20; sc 10%. Closed 24-26 Dec. Amex, Diners, MasterCard, Visa, Laser, Switch. **Directions:** in the centre of town.

Kinsale
RESTAURANT/PUB

The Bulman

Summercove Kinsale Co.Cork **Tel: 021 477 2131** Fax: 021 477 3359

The Bulman bar is characterful and maritime (though this is definitely not a theme pub) and a great place to be in fine weather, when you can wander out to the seafront and sit on the wall beside the carpark.The first floor restaurant specialises in locally caught seafood. Wheelchair access. Own carpark. **Seats 50.** (Phone for food service times). Closed 25 Dec & Good Fri. MasterCard, Visa, **Directions:** beside Charles Fort, short distance from Kinsale.

Kinsale
B&B

Chart House

6 Denis Quay Kinsale Co. Cork
Tel: 021 477 4568 Fax: 021477 7907
Email: charthouse@eircom.net Web: www.charthouse-kinsale.com

Billy and Mary O'Connor took over this delightful 200 year old house in 1999 and completely renovated it with commendable attention to period details, opening their luxurious accommodation in spring 2000. Beautifully furnished bedrooms have orthopaedic mattresses, phone, TV, hair dryer and a trouser press with iron; tea and coffee are served by the fire in a cosy reception/sitting room. An imaginative breakfast menu is served communally on a fine William IV dining room suite. Not suitable for children. No pets. **Rooms, 4.** (2 suites with jacuzzi baths, 2 shower only, all no-smoking). B&B €76, ss €38. Closed Christmas week. Amex, MasterCard, Visa, Laser. **Directions:** on Pier road between Actons and Trident hotels, turn right after Actons, last house on right.

Kinsale
RESTAURANT

Crackpots Restaurant

3 Cork Street Kinsale Co. Cork **Tel: 021 477 2847**
Fax: 021 477 3517 Email: crackpots@iol.ie Web: www.dragnet-systems.ie/dira/crackpots

This attractive and unusual restaurant has a lot going for it - not only can you drop in for a glass of wine at the bar as well as the usual meals but all the pottery used in the restaurant is made on the premises so, if you take a fancy to the tableware, you can buy that too. Menus are imaginative and considerate, with plenty for vegetarians and, although there is no shortage of fish, the range of dishes offered provides some contrast in an area that naturally specialises heavily in seafood. International influences are at work - Moroccan meatballs, tostada, thai chicken might all be on the same menu - and that's all part of the fun. An interesting wine list features some "Wine Geese" labels (a visit to nearby Desmond Castle will tell you all about this) and some organic wines. Children welcome. **Seats 50.** No smoking area; air conditioning. D daily 6-10.30, Sun L 1-3, Early D €18.41 (6-8pm); also à la carte, house wine €15.24. Closed Nov. Amex, MasterCard, Visa, Switch. **Directions:** between Garda Station and Wine Museum, in the centre of town.

Kinsale

Fishy Fishy Café & The Gourmet Store

RESTAURANT Guardwell Kinsale Co. Cork **Tel: 021 477 4453**

This delightful fish shop, delicatessen and restaurant is a mecca for gourmets in and around Kinsale and was our Seafood Restaurant of the Year in 2001. The café, which has tables both indoors, alongside the shop, and outside under an awning, sports trendy little aluminium chairs and an agreeably continental air. Although all sorts of other delicacies are on offer, seafood is the serious business here - and, as well as the range of dishes offered on the menu & specials board, you can ask to have any of the fresh fish on display cooked to your liking. Not that you'd feel the need to stray beyond the menu, in fact, as it makes up in interest and quality anything it might lack in length - and you can have anything you like from seafood chowder or smoked salmon sandwich to grilled whole prawns with lemon garlic & sweet chilli sauce or fresh lobster, crayfish or crab. No smoking restaurant. Not suitable for children under 7. **Seats 36.** L daily 12-3.45 (Mon-Sat only off season); à la carte; house wines from €17.71. Closed Sun from Oct to Apr. MasterCard, Visa, Laser, Switch. **Directions:** opposite St Multose church, beside the Garda station.

Kinsale

Harbour Lodge

GUESTHOUSE Scilly Kinsale Co. Cork **Tel: 021 477 2376**

Fax: 021 4772675 Email: relax@harbourlodge.com Web: www.harbourlodge.com

At the time of going to press, Roaul and Seiko de Gendre had just finished renovating this newly-acquired property (previously The Moorings) and opened for business. Everything has been refurbished, with new carpets, top of the range beds and bedding and upgraded bathrooms, which are now luxurious, with the largest, thickest possible towels and bathrobes - and in-house laundry to take care of them. The position, away from the bustle of the town centre is lovely and peaceful; some bedrooms have balconies and there's a large conservatory "orangerie" (where breakfast is served). for the leisurely observation of comings and goings in the harbour and a sitting room with an open fire for chilly days. A high level of personal attention and service is the aim, including the arrangement of transport to and from The Vintage for guests wishing to dine there. **Rooms 8** (1 suite, 1 wheelchair accessible, all no smoking). B&B €80 pps, ss €50.79 (child or other 3rd person sharing room €44). Open all year. Amex, Diners, MasterCard, Visa, Laser. **Directions:** 0.5 mile from Town Centre, beside the Spinnaker.

Kinsale

Jean Marc's Chow House

RESTAURANT 7 Pearse Street Kinsale Co Cork **Tel: 021 4777117** Fax: 021 4778929

Jean-Marc Tsai is no stranger to Kinsale - many will remember his exquisite combination of classical French and Chinese cooking in his previous restaurant, Chez Jean Marc. But this little place is something different; very Asian and very accessible with average prices for a meal only around €26. It opened shortly before we went to press last year and Jean Marc's new combination of Chinese, Thai and Vietnamese cuisines has gone down a treat with the area's discerning diners, who now cite the Chow House as a favourite evening destination. It's bright and modern, with comfortable seating and a lively atmosphere - a patio at the back has been used for outside seating in fine weather but it's ingeniously being turned into a covered 'Monsoon Garden', which increases the seating significantly. Although specialist ingredients must obviously be imported, Jean-Marc uses a lot of fresh local produce and everything is very authentic, colourful, attractively presented and fresh-flavoured - all this with friendly, helpful service and terrific value for money makes for a throughly enjoyable experience - truly a winning combination. No dessert menu (desserts are bought in and vary according to availability.) Not suitable for children after 8.30. **Seats 48** (max table size 14). No smoking area. D daily, 7-10 (Sat to 10.30). House wine €15.24. Closed early Jan-17 Mar. MasterCard, Visa, Laser. **Directions:** next door to A.I.B. Bank.

Kinsale

Man Friday

RESTAURANT Scilly Kinsale Co. Cork **Tel: 021 477 2260** Fax: 021 477 2262

High up over the harbour, Philip Horgan's popular, characterful restaurant is housed in a series of rooms. It has a garden terrace which makes a nice spot for drinks and coffee in fine weather. Abdu LeMarti, who has been head chef since 1985, presents seasonal à la carte menus that major on seafood but offer plenty else besides, including several vegetarian choices and duck, steak and lamb. While geared to fairly traditional tastes, the cooking is sound and can include imaginative ideas. Simple, well-made desserts include good ice creams. Service is cheerful and efficient. **Seats 100** (private room, 50) No smoking area; air conditioning. Toilets wheelchair accessible. D Mon-Sat; à la carte, house wine about€17; sc discretionary. Closed Sun, Dec 24-26. Amex, Diners, MasterCard, Visa. **Directions:** 10 minutes walk from town centre, overlooking harbour at Scilly near the Spaniard Pub.

Kinsale

Max's Wine Bar

RESTAURANT 48 Main St. Kinsale Co. Cork **Tel: 021 477 2443**

Max's is run by a young couple, Anne Marie Galvin, who supervises front of house, and chef-owner Olivier Queva. Taking over from one of Kinsale's most highly regarded restaurateurs, Wendy Tisdall, in 1999 cannot have been easy but Anne Marie and Olivier have been doing a good job and have now taken their place as one of the best restaurants in Kinsale. It's a characterful little place with stone walls at the bar end, varnished wooden tables and an attractive conservatory area at the back. They offer a light snack lunch and a short menu that's available at lunch or in the early evening, as well as the main dinner menu. Olivier's seasonal menus change regularly and offer a balance of meats and poultry - fillet of lamb with shallots & mushroom-stuffed raviolis, grilled poussin with chestnut & potato cake, beef fillet with Guinness sauce - as well as the seafood from the pier - langoustines, oysters, mussels, black sole, salmon, ray and so on - which is always so much in demand. Imaginative vegetarian dishes, like pasta with cherry tomatoes, Gabriel cheese, courgettes & basil pesto are always offered too. A wide selection of wines is now available by the glass. Not suitable for children under 5 after 8pm. **Seats 32.** No smoking area. L 12.30-3 Mon-Sat, Sun L 1-3, D 6.30-10.30 daily, Set L/Early D £12.50 (6.30-7.30 daily), à la carte available; house wine £11.50, sc discretionary. Closed 1 Nov-1 Mar. Amex, MasterCard, Visa, Laser, Switch. **Directions:** street behind the petrol station on pier.

Kinsale

The Old Bank House

ACCOMMODATION/GUESTHOUSE féile bia

11 Pearse St. Kinsale Co. Cork
Tel: 021 477 4075 Fax: 021 477 4296
Web: www.oldbankhousekinsale.ie

Marie and Michael Riese's townhouse in the middle of Kinsale has earned a high reputation for quality of accommodation and service - it has an elegant residents' sitting room, a well-appointed breakfast room and comfortable country house-style bedrooms with good amenities, antiques and quality materials. In 1999, the Old Bank House expanded into the Post Office next door, to include a further seven bedrooms and - this is a major improvement - they now have a lift. All rooms are furnished and decorated to the same high standard, with lovely bathrooms, phone, TV and 24 rooms service for coffee, tea, wine, mineral water etc (which may also be served in the sitting room) ISDN line and safe available at reception. No smoking in public areas. Not suitable for children. Small dogs allowed by arrangement. Lift. **Rooms 17** (4 junior suites). B&B €70pps, ss €44. Closed 5-27 Dec. Amex, MasterCard, Visa, Laser. **Directions:** next to the post office.

Kinsale

The Old Presbytery

ACCOMMODATION 43 Cork Street Kinsale Co. **Tel: 021 477 2027**
Fax: 021 477 2166 Email: info@oldpres.com Web: www.oldpres.com

This old house in the centre of the town has provided excellent accommodation for many years and the current owners, Philip and Noreen McEvoy, have added three new self-catering suites, each with two en-suite bedrooms, sitting room, kitchenette and an extra bathroom. The new rooms are well-proportioned and furnished in the same style and to the same high standard as the original refurbished bedrooms (with stripped pine country furniture and antique beds); they can be taken on a nightly basis, sleeping up to six adults. The top suite has an additional lounge area leading from a spiral staircase, with magnificent views over the town and harbour **Rooms 6** (3 suites, 3 shower only, all no-smoking). B&B €44.40pps, ss €19. Closed Dec & Jan. Amex, MasterCard, Visa, Laser. **Directions:** follow signs for Desmond Castle - same Street.

Kinsale

Perryville House

ACCOMODATION

Long Quay Kinsale Co. Cork **Tel: 021 477 2731**
Fax: 021 477 2298 Email: sales@perryville.iol.ie

One of the prettiest houses in Kinsale, Laura Corcoran's characterful house on the harbour front has been renovated to a high standard and provides excellent accommodation. Gracious public rooms are beautifully furnished, as if for a private home. Spacious, individually decorated bedrooms vary in size and outlook (ones at the front are most appealing, but the back is quieter) and all have extra large beds and thoughtful extras such as fresh flowers, complimentary mineral water, quality toiletries, robes and slippers. The suites have exceptionally well-appointed bathrooms, although some rooms have shower only. Breakfasts include home-baked breads and local cheeses. Morning coffee and afternoon tea are available to residents in the drawing room and there is a wine licence. No smoking establishment. Own parking. Not suitable for children under 13. No pets. **Rooms 22** (7 junior suites, 4 shower only, all no-smoking). B&B about €90 pps, sc discretionary. Closed 1 Nov-1Apr. Amex, Diners, MasterCard, Visa. **Directions:** central location, on right as you enter Kinsale from Cork, overlooking marina.

Kinsale

Sovereign House

ACCOMODATION

Newman's Mall Kinsale Co.Cork Kinsale Co. Cork **Tel: 021 477 2850**
Fax: 021 477 4723 Email: sovereignhouse@eircom.net Web: sovereignhouse.com

In the heart of old Kinsale, the McKeown family's Queen Anne townhouse dates from 1708. It offers a high level of comfort in elegant and fascinating surroundings. Fourposter beds are at home in this historic house, but so too are the modern amenities - good bathrooms, direct dial phones and tea & coffee trays. The house also has a reading room and a full size snooker room. **Rooms 4** (1 suite, all en-suite & no-smoking). No pets. B&B about €90pps. Closed Nov-end Feb. MasterCard, Visa. **Directions:** turn left at White House, take second right at roundabout, take second right at Desmond Castle, then turn left.

Kinsale

The Spaniard Inn

PUB

Scilly Kinsale Co Cork **Tel: 021 4772436**
Fax: 021 4773303 Web: www.dragnet-systems.ie/dira/spaniard.htm

Who could fail to be charmed by The Spaniard, that characterful and friendly old pub perched high up above Scilly? Although probably best known for music (nightly), it offers bar food all year round and there's a restaurant in season. The Spaniard changed hands just before the guide went to press, but menus are expected to remain similar, with fairly traditional fare served informally in the bar and a wider choice of popular dishes (traditional bacon & cabbage, roast duckling, rack of lamb, catch of the day) in the restaurant in summer. Closed 25 Dec & Good Fri. Amex, MasterCard, Visa, Laser.

Kinsale

Toddies

Restaurant/Guesthouse

Eastern Road Kinsale Co. Cork **Tel: 021 477 7769**
Email: toddies@eircom.net Web: www.toddieskinsale.com

Pearse O'Sullivan, is the son of Conal and Vera O'Sullivan - until recently proprietors of the lovely Innishannon House Hotel - and grandson of the legendary hotelier Toddy O'Sullivan, hence the name. It's one of the best locations in the area - easy to find yet secluded, with views across the water from the restaurant. Commitment, hard work - and that magic ingredient of great delight - have clearly gone into converting the house and furnishing it in a pleasingly personal contemporary style enhanced by interesting art. Aperitifs are served and ambitious menus presented in a cosy little sitting room at the back, while the well-appointed restaurant has harbour views and a lively atmosphere. A wide choice of starters range from soup (cream of potato and watercress, perhaps) to sophisticated dishes like terrine of foie gras with creamed black truffle vinaigrette and an organic salad, while main courses start range from an imaginative vegetarian dish (a strudel of spinach, wild mushrooms and ricotta with asparagus spears, pine nuts & a roasted pepper coulis, perhaps) to prime fish like Dover sole (typically a baked parcel with sautéed spinach & asparagus with a clam & saffron vinaigrette (also available meunière). Seafood, including lobster, is dominant and other choices include a choice of steaks (sirloin, fillet and entrecôte) with various sauces. Finish with mainly classic desserts, or farmhouse cheeses. A wide-ranging and informative wine list includes an interesting Sommelier's Choice selection. This is clearly a significant addition to the dining options in Kinsale although pricing is high for a restaurant that has yet to prove its worth. Banqueting (50). Children welcome. D Wed-Mon, 7-10. A la carte. (Starters about EUR6-15; main courses about EUR20-30.50.) House wine EUR18.41. SC discretionary. Closed Tue & 1 Jan-13 Feb. **Accommodation** Although the accommodation offered is in three lovely generous guest rooms, rather than suites as described, they have luxurious bathrooms and harbour views. Amenities include phone/ISDN line,TV & tea/coffee-making facilities, with secretarial services available on request. Pets permitted by arrangement. Garden.

Rooms, 3. B&B €85.71pps, ss €41.27, (Room only rate €171.40, max 2 guests). Amex, MasterCard, Visa, Laser. **Directions:** 4th house on left hand side past Texaco Station as you enter Kinsale.

Kinsale

HOTEL/RESTAURANT

Trident Hotel

World's End Kinsale Co. Cork

Tel: 021 477 2301 Fax: 021 477 4173

Email: info@tridenthotel.com Web: www.tridenthotel.com

This blocky, concrete-and-glass 1960s waterfront building enjoys one of Kinsale's finest locations and, under the excellent management of Hal McElroy, is a well-run, hospitable and comfortable place to stay. The genuinely pubby **Wharf Tavern** is a good meeting place and Gerry O'Connor, head chef for the main restaurant, also has responsibility for the bar food (12-9 daily). Bedrooms include two suites, with private balconies directly overlooking the harbour and all bedrooms are spacious and comfortable, with phone, TV and tea/coffee trays (iron and board available on request). Conference/banqueting (220); secretarial services, video-conferencing on request. Children welcome. No pets. Lift. **Rooms 58** (2 suites, 2 wheelchair accessible). B&B €92 pps, ss €33. **Savannah Waterfront Restaurant** While it is difficult for a hotel restaurant to compete with the exceptional number and variety of restaurants in Kinsale, the Savannah - which is named after the first steam-powered vessel to cross the Atlantic from west to east - does a good job. The restaurant, well-located on the first floor with views over the harbour - which also makes it an exceptionally pleasant room for breakfast - has plenty of atmosphere. The food is good and especially welcome in winter, when many of the smaller restaurants are closed **Seats 80.** D daily, 7- 10 (Sun to 9.30), L Sun only 12.30-2. Set L from €19; Set D €35, D also à la carte. House wine from €18.40. SC discretionary. Toilets wheelchair accessible. Amex, MasterCard, Visa, Laser. **Directions:** take the R600 from Cork to Kinsale - the hotel is at the end of the Pier Road.

Kinsale

RESTAURANT/ACCOMMODATION

Vintage Restaurant

50 Main Street Kinsale Co. Cork

Tel: 021 477 2502 Fax: 021 477 4828

Email: info@vintagerestaurant.ie Web: www.vintagerestaurant.ie

Raoul and Seiko de Gendre have been running the cottagey Vintage restaurant successfully since 1994 . Frederic Pastorino, who has been head chef since January 2000, has the kitchen running sweetly and specialises in 'continental cuisine with an Irish accent'.The best of Irish ingredients are used in dishes that tend towards the classical and wide-ranging à la carte menus are especially strong on seafood in summer and game in the winter - examples that indicate the style include a speciality horse d'oeuvre of home-smoked wild fish and seafood from Irish waters, terrine of white and black pudding, foie gras and pork; many of the main course choices are luxurious: Dublin lawyer (lobster), scallops, sole, turbot and game (venison, wild duck) all feature in season. Details are good - tasty little amuse-bouches are served with aperitifs, tables are beautifully appointed, service professional. Wine appreciation evenings and other special events are held regularly off-season (i.e. mid-Feb-Easter and mid Oct-early Jan). Private dining room available (25).No-smoking area; air conditioning **Seats 56.** D Tues-Sat 6.30-10 all à la carte, house wine £16.50, sc discretionary. Open 7 days Easter-15 Oct; closed 2 Jan-13 Feb, also Sun & Mon off season except for festive Sundays. Accommodation Roaul and Seiko de Gendre have recently acquired Harbour Lodge (previously The Moorings), a well-located guesthouse in the Scilly area of Kinsale, which overlooks the marina. Amex, Diners, MasterCard, Visa, Laser, Switch. **Directions:** from the post office, turn left at the Bank of Ireland - restaurant is on the right.

Macroom

HOTEL

The Castle Hotel & Leisure Centre

Main Street Macroom Co. Cork **Tel: 026 41074** Fax: 026 41505

Email: castlehotel@eircom.net Web: www.castlehotel.ie

The neat frontage of this hotel conceals major changes that have been taking place recently. In the ownership of the Buckley family since 1952, it is currently under the management of Don and Gerard Buckley, who are maximising its potential; first through gradual refurbishment and, more recently, through thoughtfully planned reconstruction. (By April 2002 the hotel plans to open 30 new bedrooms, a conference and banqueting centre seating, a new restaurant & bar, reception and café). Meanwhile, existing public areas gleam welcomingly, and the bar and dining room, especially, are most attractive. Original bedrooms are on the small side but all have been refurbished recently; there are slight variations - some older rooms are shower-only, newer ones have trouser presses - but all have phone, TV and tea/coffee trays. An impressive 2-storey extension at the back has a new leisure centre on the ground floor (with fine swimming pool, updated gym and adjacent carpark) and new bedrooms above it. Conferences/banqueting (60). Off-season value breaks. Children welcome (under 4s free in parents' room, cots available). No pets. **Rooms 42** (all en-suite,12 shower only; 16 executive rooms). B&B €66 pps, ss €20. Closed 24-28 Dec. Amex, Diners, MasterCard, Visa, Laser. **Directions:** on N22, midway between Cork & Killarney.

The Mills Inn

Macroom
PUB/ACCOMODATION

Ballyvourney Macroom Co. Cork **Tel: 026 45237**
Fax: 026 45454 Email: info@millinn.ie

One of Ireland's oldest inns, The Mills Inn is in a Gaeltacht (Irish-speaking) area and dates back to 1755. It was traditionally used to break the journey from Cork to Killarney - and still makes a great stopping place as the food is good and freshly cooked all day - but is now clearly popular with locals as well as travellers. It has old-world charm (despite the regrettable conversion of real fires to gas) and there is a genuine sense of hospitality. Toilets wheelchair accessible. L&D daily. Closed 25 Dec. Accommodation: Rooms vary considerably due to the age of the building, but all are comfortably furnished with neat bathrooms and good amenities. Superior rooms have jacuzzi baths, and there is a large, well-planned ground-floor room suitable for less able guests (who can use the residents' car park right at the door - in a courtyard shared with a vintage car and an agricultural museum). Full room service is available for drinks and meals. Small conferences/banqueting (20/60), secretarial services. Off season value breaks. Children are welcome (under 12s free in parents' room, cots available). Pets permitted. **Rooms 13** (7 executive rooms, 3 shower only, 1 for disabled). B&B about €45pps. Wheelchair access. Diners, MasterCard, Visa. **Directions:** on N22, 20 minutes from Killarney.

Longueville House Hotel

Mallow
HOTEL/RESTAURANT 🏛★

Mallow Co. Cork **Tel: 022 47156** Fax: 022 47459
Email: info@longuevillehouse.ie Web: longuevillehouse.ie

When Longueville House opened its doors to guests in 1967, it was one of the first Irish country houses to do so. Its history is wonderfully romantic, "the history of Ireland in miniature", and it is a story with a happy ending. Having lost their lands in the Cromwellian Confiscation (1652-57), the O'Callaghans took up ownership again some 300 years later. The present house, a particularly elegant Georgian mansion of pleasingly human proportions, dates from 1720, (with wings added in 1800 and the lovely Turner conservatory - which is still in good order and due shortly to take on a new lease of life as an extension to the dining room - in 1862) overlooks the ruins of their original home, Dromineen Castle. Longueville was the our Hotel of the Year in 2000 and many things make it special, most importantly the warm, informal hospitality and charm of the O'Callaghans themselves - Michael and Jane, their son (and talented chef) William and his wife Aisling. The location, overlooking the famous River Blackwater, is lovely. The river, farm and garden supply fresh salmon in season, the famous Longueville lamb and all the fruit and vegetables. In years when the weather is kind, the estate's crowning glory (and Michael O'Callaghan's great enthusiasm) is their own house wine, a light refreshing white fittingly named "Coisreal Longueville". Graciously proportioned reception rooms include a bar and drawing room both elegantly furnished in country house style. Accommodation is equally sumptuous and bedrooms are spacious, superbly comfortable and stylishly decorated to the highest standards (under the personal supervision of Jane O'Callaghan). As well as being one of the finest leisure destinations in the country, this all adds up to a good venue for small conferences and business meetings and the large cellar/basement area of the house has now been deveopled as a new conference centre. A range of back-up services is available to business guests. Conference/banqueting (65/80). Children welcome (under 4s free in parents' room, cots available). Pets permitted in some areas. **Rooms 22.** (1 suite, 5 junior suites, 15 executive rooms, 6 no-smoking). B&B €90pps. Closed mid-Dec-early Mar (but may open for groups of 20+ excl. Christmas/New Year. Shooting weekends available Nov, Dec, Jan; telephone for details).

Presidents' Restaurant Named after the family collection of specially commissioned portraits of all Ireland's past presidents, which made for a seriously masculine collection until Ireland's first woman president, Mary Robinson, broke the pattern, this is the main dining room and opens into the conservatory - and there is a smaller room for those who wish to smoke. William O'Callaghan's well-balanced dinner menus offer a sensibly limited choice of four or five dishes on each course, plus an intriguing Tasting Menu for complete parties. Local ingredients star, in a starter of house smoked salmon with a garden salad, for example, followed by rack of Longueville lamb or home reared pork loin. Home produce influences the dessert menu too, as in gooseberry tart with elderflower ice cream (a magic combination) and it is hard to resist the local farmhouse cheeses. Home-made chocolates and petits fours come with the coffee and service, under Jane or Aisling O'Callaghan's direction, is excellent. A fine wine list includes many wines imported directly by Michael O'Callaghan **Seats 40** D daily, 6.30-9, Set D €47, Bar Food 1-5 daily, house wine about €18, sc discretionary (10% on parties of 8+). Annual closures as above. Amex, Diners, MasterCard, Visa, Laser.

Midleton

The Farmgate

RESTAURANT Coolbawn Midleton Co. Cork **Tel: 021 463 2771** Fax: 021 463 2771

This unique shop and restaurant has been drawing people to Midleton in growing numbers since 1985 and it's a great credit to sisters Marog O'Brien and Kay Harte. Kay now runs the younger version at the English Market in Cork while Marog looks after Midleton. The shop at the front is full of wonderful local produce - organic fruit and vegetables, cheeses, honey - and their own super home baking, while the evocatively decorated, comfortable restaurant at the back, with its old pine furniture and modern sculpture, is regularly transformed from bustling daytime café to sophisticated evening restaurant (on Friday and Saturday) complete with string quartet. Marog O'Brien is a founder and stallholder of the recently established Midleton Farmers Market, which is held on Saturday mornings. Meals all day Mon-Sat, D Fri & Sat. Closed Bank Hols. MasterCard, Visa.

Midleton

Finins

PUB 75 Main Street Midleton Co. Cork **Tel: : 021 463 1878** Fax: 021 463 3847

Finin O'Sullivan's thriving bar in the centre of the town has long been a popular place for locals to meet for a drink and to eat some good wholesome food. An attractive, no-nonsense sort of a place. L & D daily. Closed 25-26 Dec. Amex, Diners, MasterCard, Visa.

Midleton

Glenview House

COUNTRY HOUSE Midleton Co. Cork **Tel: 021 463 1680** Fax: 021 463 4680
Email: glenviewhouse@esatclear.ie Web: dragnet-systems.ie/dira/glenview

When Ken & Beth Sherrard acquired their lovely Georgian house near Midleton in 1963 it was virtually derelict. Two years later, Ken bought the entire contents of the Dublin Georgian buildings infamously demolished to make way for the new ESB offices - and today this well-tended, comfortable and elegantly furnished house is the richer for that act of courage. Now, with a welcoming fire in the hall and two well-proportioned reception rooms on either side, it's hard to imagine it any other way. Except for one adapted for wheelchair users, bedrooms are all comfortably furnished (one has an old bath with a highly original - and practical - shower arrangement built in), hair dryers and tea/coffee-making facilities. The latest phase of restoration has created some delightful self-catering accommodation in converted outbuildings - with the agreeable arrangement of dinner in the main house as an option. Dinner is cooked by Beth and served at a communal table (8pm, usually residents only; book by noon). There is much to do in the area: the heritage sites at Cobh and Midleton are nearby, also Fota Wildlife Park, Arboretum & Golf, wonderful walks and much else besides. Midleton Market (every Saturday) is a must for foodlovers. Garden, terrace, croquet, lawn tennis, forest walks. Children welcome. **Rooms 7** (4 in main house, 3 in converted coach house, 4 shower-only 1 fully wheelchair accessible). B&B about €50pps, ss about€10. Open all year. Amex, MasterCard, Visa, **Directions:** take L35 from Midleton to Fermoy for 2.5 miles, take left for Watergrasshill and then immediately right. Glenview is signposted from the road.

Midleton

Loughcarrig House

COUNTRY HOUSE Midleton Co. Cork **Tel: 021 463 1952**
Fax: 021 461 3707 Email: info@loughcarrig.com Web: www.loughcarrig.com

Bird-watching and sea angling are major interests at this relaxed and quietly situated country house, which is in a beautiful shoreside location. Small conferences (20; max capacity sitdown meal 10).Children welcome (free in parents' room under 2, cot available without charge). **Rooms 4** (all en-suite). Closed Christmas/New Year. B&B €30 pps, ss €9. **Directions:** take N25 from Cork road to Whitegate, 2 miles from roundabout. See sign.

Midleton

Midleton Park Hotel

HOTEL féile bia Old Cork Road Midleton Co. Cork **Tel: 021 463 1767**
Fax: 021 463 1605 Email: info@midletonparkhotel.ie

This pleasant hotel close to the Old Midleton Distillery is roomy with good business facilities. Recently refurbished bedrooms - which are all en-suite with tea/coffee facilities, TV, video, phone, hair dryer and trouser press - include some suitable for disabled guests and some non-smoking rooms as well as a 'presidential suite' for VIP guests. Although it is used a lot by the business community, the hotel also makes a good base for touring east Cork - Fota Island wildlife park, Cobh harbour (last port of call for the Titanic) are nearby and golf packages are arranged. Banqueting/conferences 400/350. Secretarial services. Children welcome. No pets.Wheelchair access. Ample parking. **Rooms 40.** B&B about €65pps. Closed 25 Dec. Amex, Diners, MasterCard, Visa. **Directions:** 12 miles east of Cork city, off N25.

Midleton

Old Midleton Distillery

CAFÉ/PUB

Midleton, Co. Cork **Tel: 021 461 3594** Fax: 021 461 3642
Email: amcenery@idl.ie Web: irish-whiskey-trail.com

The Old Midleton Distillery is a fascinating place to visit - that such visiting can be thirsty work is acknowledged at the door (a whiskey tasting is part of the tour) but it can also be hungry work. Sensibly, the Centre has a pleasant restaurant where you can get a wide range of dishes, including simple fare like Irish stew, shepherd's pie and lasagne - and there's always a good selection of home-made cakes. Food available 10-5 daily. Closed Christmas period & Good Fri. Toilets wheelchair accessible. MasterCard, Visa. **Directions:** 15 miles east of Cork on main Waterford (N25) road.

Midleton

Rathcoursey House

RESTAURANT/ACCOMMODATION

Ballinacurra, Nr. Middleton, Co. Cork
Tel: 021 461 3418 Fax: 021 461 3393
Email: beth@rathcoursey.com Web: rathcoursey.com

Set in 35 acres of woodland above an inlet of Cork Harbour, this peaceful small Georgian manor was opened to guests in 1999 by the food writer and former restaurateur Beth Hallinan - since moving here she has not only renovated the whole house, but planted 2,000 trees, a herb garden and also a children's garden. Beth's renowned 4-course dinner is available for residents, by arrangement - book well ahead, as this has become a favourite destination for discerning travellers in the know. Children welcome (children's garden with sandpit & stage; babies free in parents' room, cot available); pets permitted by arrangement. **Rooms 6** (1 junior suite, 1 shower only, 1 suitable for disabled guests). B&B about €65pps, ss about€13. Residents' dinnerabout €32, house wine about €13. Open all year. MasterCard, Visa. **Directions:** at Midleton roundabout take Whitegate road. After 4km turn right for East Ferry, then small village of Rathcoursey and follow green arrows to the left.

Mitchelstown

O'Callaghans Café

CAFÉ

19-20 Lr Cork Street Mitchelstown Co. Cork
Tel: 025 24657 Email: ocalhansdeli@eircom.net

The ideal place to break a journey, O'Callaghans have lovely deli and bakery as well as tasty fare for a snack or full meal in the café. If you're going home to an empty house, this is the place to stock up with delicious home-baked breads and cakes, home-made jams and chutneys - and, best of all perhaps, there's a range of home-made frozen meals. The only down-side to this life-saving stopping place is that it's closed on Sundays. To avoid the busy main street, park around the corner on the road to the creamery. Restaurant **seats 120.** Food served 8.30 am-5.30 pm Mon-Sat. Closed Sun.

Monkstown

The Bosun

RESTAURANT/PUB /ACCOMMODATION

The Pier Monkstown Co. Cork
Tel: 021 484 2172 Fax: 021 484 2008

PUB OF THE YEAR

Nicky and Patricia Moynihan's waterside establishment close to the Cobh car ferry, has grown a lot over the years, with the restaurant and accommodation growing fast and becoming an increasingly important part of the enterprise. Bar food is still taken seriously, however; seafood takes pride of place and the afternoon/evening bar menu includes everything from chowder or garlic mussels through to real scampi and chips, although serious main courses for carnivores such as rack of lamb and beef stroganoff are also available. Next to the bar, a well-appointed restaurant provides a more formal setting for wide-ranging dinner and à la carte menus - and also Sunday lunch, which is especially popular. Again seafood is the speciality, ranging from popular starters such as crab claws or oysters worked into imaginative dishes, and main courses that include steaks and local duckling as well as seafood every which way, from grilled sole on the bone to medallions of marinated monkfish or a cold seafood platter. There's always a choice for vegetarians and vegetables are generous and carefully cooked. Finish with home-made ices, perhaps, or a selection of Irish farmhouse cheeses. Restaurant **Seats 80** (max table size 12). No-smoking area; air conditioning. D daily 6.30-9.30, L Sun 12-2.30, Set D €33.65, à la carte also available; house wine €17.14, sc discretionary. Bar food available 12-9.30 daily. **Accommodation:** Bedrooms are quite simple but have everything required (phone, TV, tea/coffee trays); those at the front have harbour views but are shower only, while those at the back have the advantage of a full bathroom and are quieter. Guests tend to be working in the area and resident all week, with weekends bringing more leisure visitors. **Rooms 15** (9 shower only). Lift. B&B €44.44pps, ss €6.35. Children welcome (under 5s free in parents' room, cot available without charge). Closed 24-26 Dec. Amex, Diners, MasterCard, Visa, Laser. **Directions:** on sea front, beside the Cobh ferry.

Oysterhaven

Finders Inn

RESTAURANT Nohoval Oysterhaven Co. Cork **Tel: 021 477 0737** Fax: 021 477 0737

Very popular with local people (but perhaps harder for visitors to find) the McDonnell family's characterful restaurant is in a row of traditional cottages above Oysterhaven, en route from Crosshaven to Kinsale. It is a very charming place, packed with antiques and, because of the nature of the building, broken up naturally into a number of dining areas (which gives it an air of mystery). Seafood stars, of course - smoked salmon, Oysterhaven oysters, bisques, chowders, scallops and lobster are all here, but there are a few other specialities too, including steaks, lamb and lovely tender crisp-skinned duckling with an orange-sage sauce. Good desserts, charming service and a great atmosphere. Well worth taking the trouble to find. Not suitable for children under 8 after 8 pm. **Seats 90** (private room, 70). D Mon-Sat 7-9.30, sc discretionary. Toilets wheelchair accessible. Closed Xmas week. MasterCard, Visa, Diners. **Directions:** from Cork, take Kinsale road, turn left at The Huntsman roadhouse, follow Oysterhaven road and, at crossroads, go straight ahead towards the water.

Oysterhaven

Oz-Haven

RESTAURANT Oysterhaven Co Cork **Tel: 021 477 0974**

In a delightful waterside location at the head of Oysterhaven creek, Australian Paul Greer has transformed what was once a cosy cottage restaurant into something very different. The stone walls and open fires are still there, but the whole place has been done over in a highly idiosyncratic, colourful modern style - there's a great sense of fun about the whole approach and, despite its modernism, it works suprisingly well with the old building. Well-spaced tables in three separate areas have comfortable high-back carver chairs and are simply laid in quality contemporary style, with generous wine glasses and white plates decorated only with the restaurant logo. Interesting, quite ambitious weekly-changing menus offer world cuisine through a choice of six starters and main courses ; typical examples include a special of lobster offers lobster done four ways; Thai red curry with tiger prawns & squid flavoured with "all the tastes from the east"; and satay chicken strips coated in "the rich peanut flavours of the orient". Whatever about the hype, this is a promising restaurant, delivering interesting, well-cooked and attractively presented (if quite expensive) food and friendly attentive service in entertaining surroundings. Let's hope the format will work in this rural area.* Oz Cork Café Bistro, 73 Grand Parade, Cork city, is under the same management (Tel:021-427 2711). Amex, MasterCard, Visa, Laser. **Directions:** 30 min. from Cork City, turn for Oysterhaven just before Kinsale.

Rosscarbery

Celtic Ross Hotel, Conference and Leisure Centre

HOTEL Rosscarbery Co. Cork **Tel: 023 48722**
Fax: 023 48723 Email: info@celticrosshotel.com

Opened in 1997, this contemporary hotel is close to the sea, overlooking Rosscarbery Bay (although not on the sea side of the road). It's an attractive modern building with an unusual tower feature containing a bog oak, which is quite dramatic. Well placed as a base for touring west Cork, the facilities in the leisure centre offer alternative activities if the weather should disappoint. Public areas are spacious, the restaurant looks over the road to the sea, as do many of the bedrooms, which are well-equipped with phones, tea/coffee trays and TV. Shortage of accommodation in the area means this hotel is always busy and recent visits indicate that the necessary care and maintenance systems may not be adequate. Children welcome (under 3s free in their parents' room; cots available). Conference/banqueting (250/220). **Rooms 67** (3 suites, 3 for disabled). Wheelchair access. Lift. B&B about€96pps, ss about€20. Open all year. Amex, Diners, MasterCard, Visa. **Directions:** take N71 from Cork to Inishannon to Bandon to Clonakilty and then Rosscarbery.

Rosscarbery

O'Callaghan-Walshe

RESTAURANT

The Square Rosscarbery Co. Cork **Tel: 023 48125**
Fax: 023 48125 Email: funfish@indigo.ie

This unique restaurant on the square of the old village (well off the busy main West Cork road) has a previous commercial history that's almost tangible - and the atmosphere is well-matched by both proprietor-host Sean Kearney's larger-than-life personality and the exceptional freshness and quality of the seafood, although steaks share the billing. Menus change weekly but specialities to look out for include a superb Fruits de Mer platter (available as small or large but, in the Guide's experience, the small one is very large indeed with an exceptional range and quality of fish and shellfish included). The famous Rosscarbery Pacific oysters feature, of course, char-grilled prime fish such as turbot, steamed lobster with lemon butter. Ultra-freshness, attention to detail in breads and accompaniments, all add up to make this place a delight. Not suitable for children after 8 pm.Smoking unrestricted. **Seats 40** D 6.30-9Tue-Sun, all à la carte, house wine €24, sc discretionary. Closed Sun; phone ahead to check opening times in winter. MasterCard, Visa, Laser. **Directions:** main square in Rosscarbery.

Schull

Adèle's

RESTAURANT/CAFÉ

Main St. Schull Co. Cork **Tel: 028 28459**
Fax: 028 28865 Email: adeles@oceanfree.net Web: www.adelesrestaurant.com

Adèle Connor's bakery and coffee shop in Schull works like a magnet - if you happen to be in Schull early in the morning, you'll find it hard to squeeze in to buy some of her wonderful home bakes, never mind trying to find a table for a cup of coffee and a home-baked scone. There are delicious savoury things too, such as ciabatta specials served with small tossed salads - traditional and smoked Gubbeen with chutney perhaps - or an omelette with roasted red pepper and garlic. In the evening Simon Connor presents a different kind of menu in the first floor restaurant; a set menu might include a scallop soup and a smooth duck liver mousse then main courses like a bowl of mussels with a spicy tomato & lime sauce tossed salad or whole prawns with butter and garlic, with saffron potatoes followed by petit pot au chocolat or blueberry muffin with vanilla ice cream, perhaps. Times of opening vary according to the season; bookings advised. Children welcome. No wheelchair access. **Seats 40.** Open daily from 9.30, D 7.30-10.30, Sun L 11-5, Set L about €9, Set D about €22, à la carte available, house wine about €14, sc discretionary. Closed Nov-Christmas/Jan-Easter. Amex, MasterCard, Visa. **Directions:** turn off N71 at Ballydehob for Schull - in town centre.

Schull

Corthna Lodge

GUESTHOUSE

Schull Co. Cork **Tel: 028 28517** Fax: 028 28032

Situated up the hill from Schull, commanding countryside and sea views, Loretta Davitt's roomy modern house has been one of the best places to stay in the area since opening in 1991. All the bedrooms are very comfortable with good amenities, the atmosphere is hospitable and easy-going there's plenty of space for guests to sit around and relax (both indoors, in a pleasant and comfortably furnished sitting room and outdoors, on a terrace overlooking the lovely garden towards the islands of Roaring Water Bay). Children welcome (cots available, €12.70). Pets permitted by arrangement. **Rooms 9** (1 suite, 7 shower only, 4 for disabled and 4 no-smoking). B&B €32pps, ss €12.70. Open all year. Visa. **Directions:** through village, up hill, first left first right - house is signposted.

Schull

Grove House

GUESTHOUSE

Colla Road Schull Co. Cork **Tel: 028 28067**
Fax: 028 28069 Email: billyoshea@yahoo.com

Overlooking Schull Harbour, just a few minutes walk from the main street, this beautifully restored period house is a much-needed addition to the accommodation in the area. Many period features have been retained and the large bedrooms have individual character; the outlook from them has improved greatly over the last year as landscaping is beginning to mature. A lovely dining room is used for breakfast - featuring local foods such as Gubbeen smoked bacon or Sally Barnes smoked fish - and there's a guest sitting room and panelled reading room. **Rooms 5** (4 shower only, all no smoking); B&B €52.50, ss €17.50. Closed Christmas; limited opening Nov-Feb (bookings only). Amex, MasterCard, Visa, Laser. **Directions:** on right beyond C/Ireland Colla Road, 4 mins walk - village.

Schull

La Coquille

RESTAURANT

Main Street Schull Co. Cork **Tel: 028 28642**

Jean-Michel Cahier's little restaurant, like its menu, appears to have remained more or less the same since it opened. This is perhaps unsurprising as competently handled classics are the main feature, typically duck paté, onion soup, half roast duck with orange sauce and scallops with a brandy cream. It offers more red meats and poultry than most places in the area but the menu in the window doesn't do it justice as there is also a blackboard brought to the table with the day's specials (mostly fish). Desserts, also classic, usually include tarte tatin and meringue suisse. **Seats 35.** No smoking area. D 7-9.30. Set D from about €32, also à la carte. House wine from about €14. Service 10%. Opening hours appear to be erratic, a phone call to check would be wise, especially off-season. Amex, Diners, MasterCard, Visa. **Directions:** in the village, across from the church.

Schull

Lasair Choille

B&B

Ardmanagh Schull Co. Cork **Tel: 028 27982**
Email: venita@gofree.indigo.ie Web: www.cork-guide.ie

A mile or so outside Schull, at the foot of Mount Gabriel, Venita and David Galvin's newly-built guesthouse offers modern, clean-lined accommodation in an area of natural beauty. It's furnished to a high standard in contemporary style, with a large lounge with communal tea/coffee making facilities and television and spruce en-suite bedrooms. It would make a good base for the many activity holidays in the area - or simply touring the area. Packed lunches available (€5), also residents' dinner on request, based on local foods and organic produce from the garden. (€15). Children welcome (unders 2s free in parents' room but no cot available). Small conferences (10). No pets. Garden. B&B €32, ss €6.35. **Directions:** left at Bank on Main Street, right at T-junction.

Schull

Stanley House

ACCOMMODATION

Schull Co. Cork **Tel: 028 28425**
Fax: 028 27887 Email: stanleyhouse@eircom.net

Nancy Brosnan's modern guesthouse provides a west Cork home from home for her many returning guests. Compact bedrooms are comfortably furnished with tea/coffee making facilities and there's a pleasant conservatory running along the back of the house, with wonderful sea views over a field where guests can watch Nancy's growing herd of deer and sometimes see foxes come out to play at dusk. Good breakfasts too. Children welcome (under 3s free in parents' room, cots available without charge). No pets. **Rooms 4** (all shower only, all no-smoking). B&B €26 pps, ss€7. Closed 31 Oct- 28 Feb. MasterCard, Visa. **Directions:** turn left at top of town. Turn right at graveyard, next left.

Schull

T J Newman's

PUB

Corner House Pier Road Schull Co. Cork **Tel: 028 28090**

Just up the hill from the harbour, this characterful and delightfully old-fashioned little pub has been a special home-from-home for regular visitors, especially sailors up from the harbour, as long as anyone can remember. The premises was sold in 2000 but, although Kitty Newman is missed, there is very little obvious change. Closed 25 Dec & Good Fri. MasterCard, Visa, Laser, Switch.

Shanagarry

Ballymaloe House

COUNTRY HOUSE/RESTAURANT ★ féile bia

Shanagarry Midleton Co. Cork
Tel: 021 465 2531 Fax: 021 465 2021
Email: res@ballymaloe.com Web: www.ballymaloe.ie

CHEF OF THE YEAR

Ireland's most famous country house hotel, Ballymaloe was one of the first country houses to open its doors to guests when Myrtle and her husband, the late Ivan Allen, opened The Yeats Room restaurant in 1964. Accommodation followed in 1967 and since then a unique network of family enterprises has developed around Ballymaloe House - including not only the farmlands and gardens that supply so much of the kitchen produce, but also a craft and kitchenware shop, a company producing chutneys and sauce, the Crawford Gallery Café in Cork city and, of course, Tim and Darina Allen's internationally acclaimed Cookery School. Yet, despite the fame, Ballymaloe is still most remarkable for its unspoilt charm: Myrtle - now rightly receiving international recognition for a lifetime's work "recapturing forgotten flavours, and preserving those that may soon die"- is ably assisted by her children and now their families too. The house, modestly described in its Blue Book (Irish Country House & Restaurants Association) entry as "a large family farmhouse" is in the middle of the family's 400 acre farm, but the description fails to do justice to the gracious nature of the original house, or the sensitively designed later additions. The intensely restorative atmosphere of Ballymaloe is still as strong as ever; there are few greater pleasures than a fine Ballymaloe dinner followed by the relaxed comforts provided by a delightful, thoughtfully furnished (but not over decorated) country bedroom. Groundfloor courtyard rooms are suitable for wheelchairs. Children welcome. Special winter breaks offered. **Rooms 33.** B&B from€100pps, ss€20. Service discretionary.

Restaurant: The restaurant - which has recently been extended and now allows more pre-dining space - is in a series of domestic-sized dining rooms (some for non-smokers) and guests are called to their tables from the conservatory or drawing room, where aperitifs are served. A food philosophy centred on using only the highest quality ingredients is central to everything done at Ballymaloe, where much of the produce comes from their own farm and gardens. The rest, including seafood from Ballycotton and Kenmare, and meats from the trusted local butcher, comes from leading local producers. Rory O'Connell (who is Darina Allen's brother) has been head chef at Ballymaloe since 1995 and presents a daily 7-course dinner menu, with vegetarian dishes given a leaf symbol. He is doing an inspired job in the kitchen, creating generous, beautiful, daringly simple meals: Ballymaloe brown bread, crudités with garlic mayonnaise, paté de campagne with pickles, superb roast rib of Cloyne beef with three sauces (horseradish cream, béarnaise & garlic mayonaise), Irish farmhouse cheeses with home-made biscuits and a dessert trolley that included rhubarb compôte and vanilla ice cream ware typical of the truly impressive yet homely dishes that leave us lost in admiration - and, as if a 7-course dinner isn't enough, they even offer second helpings of the main course! The teamwork at Ballymaloe is a sight to behold: this is, quite simply, as good as it gets. Finish with coffee or tea and home-made petits fours, served in the drawing room - and perhaps a drink from the small bar before retiring contentedly to bed. Children welcome at lunchtime, but the restaurant is not suitable for children under 10 after 7pm. (Children's high tea is erved at 5.30.) Buffet meals only on Sundays. **Seats 100.** L daily 1-1.30, D daily 7-9.30; Set D €55. House wine from €20.32. Service discretionary. Reservations essential. House closed 23-27 Dec. Amex, Diners, MasterCard, Visa, Laser. **Directions:** take signs to Ballycotton from N25. Situated between Cloyne & Shanagarry.

Skibbereen
RESTAURANT

Kalbo's Bistro

48 North Street Skibbereen Co. Cork
Tel: 028 21515 Email: kalbos@eircom.ie

Siobhan O'Callaghan and Anthony Boyle are doing a great job at this bright, buzzy town-centre restaurant. It's informal but there has always been an air of quality about it - staff are quick and helpful and Siobhan's simple food is wholesome and flavoursome in a light contemporary style - good soups, pastas, baguettes, tortillas and salads at lunchtime and more serious dishes of local seafood, rack of lamb, steaks and so on in the evening. Home-made burgers come with a choice of toppings and vegetarian options (highlighted on the menu) are imaginative. **Seats 45.** Open daily, L 11.30-4.30 (Sun 12-2.30), D 6.30-9.30. A la carte; house wine €13.90, sc discretionary. Closed 24-27 Dec & Good Fri. Amex, Diners, MasterCard, Visa. **Directions:** in town centre.

Skibbereen
HOTEL

Liss Ard Lake Lodge

Skibbereen Co. Cork **Tel: 028 40000**
Fax: 028 40001 Email: lissardresort@eircom.net

This Victorian lodge opened in 1994 as a most unusual small luxury hotel. It has gone through a turbulent phases but is re-opening for the 2002 season for groups (not necessarily large numbers - three or four couples would be enough) and weddings. It is set in extensive gardens (which are open to the public) and has been designed and renovated with oriental simplicity, thereby enhancing the garden and water views framed by every window. Rooms - all suites except 1 double - combine clean-lined simplicity with unexpected amenities: mini-bars, TV units with video, and hi-fi. Equally unusual bathrooms are finished to a very high standard. Telephone for further details. Amex, Diners, MasterCard, Visa.

Skibbereen
RESTAURANT

Ty Ar Mor Seafood Restaurant

46 Bridge Street Skibbereen Co. Cork **Tel: 028 22100**
Email: tyarmor@iol.ie Web: www.tyarmor.com

Chef Michel Philippot and front-of-house manager Rosaleen O'Shea's delightful little Breton restaurant in the centre of Skibbereen has a lively atmosphere and gives an exceptionally high quality of ingredients, cooking and service - and all at very moderate prices. The Menu Gastronomique offers great value at just €37.50, with solitary supplements of just €8.25/€17.15 respectively for lobster starters and main courses and choices of eight starter and main courses within the Table d'Hôte price. Begin, perhaps, with a traditional Breton fish soup with rouille and croûtons, half a dozen Rossmore oysters with shallot sauce and lemon or an cassolette of prawns & squid in lobster & Armagnac sauce. Outstanding main courses might include classics like black sole on the bone with garlic butter and grilled fillet of turbot beurre blanc alongside more contemporary renditions such as fillet of John Dory with lime & ginger and carnivorous choices like chargrilled rack of spring lamb with grain mustard sauce or chargrilled fillet steak sauce poivrade. And desserts will not disappoint: for those who crave it, gateau maison is made with chocolate and Grand Marnier, while other classics such as îsle flottante, pears poached in red wine & cinnamon or even a wonderful caramelised tarte tatin provide a memorable - and lighter - end to a magnificent meal. For those with the appetite to appreciate them, local cheeses are beautifully presented, French style, with a walnut salad. The value for money is exceptional and very professional service, from mostly French staff, matches the food: this place is a gem. Not suitable for children under 12. **Seats 30** (Max table size, 12). D only, 6.30-9.15 Wed-Mon (D daily in Jul-Aug, closed Mon-Tue in winter and Tue in spring & autumn.) Restaurant closed end Oct-mid Dec & 2 weeks Feb/Mar.) Set D from €35, Menu Gastronomique €37.50; s.c 10%. House wine €17.75. Closed Nov. MasterCard, Visa, Laser. **Directions:** Skibereen town centre, towards Schull.

Skibbereen
HOTEL

West Cork Hotel

Ilen Street Skibereen Co. Cork **Tel: 028 21277**
Fax: 028 22333 Email: info@westcorkhotel.com Web: www.westcorkhotel.com

This family-owned hotel enjoys a riverside site beside the bridge, on the western side of the town, and has recently undergone major refurbishment to both public areas and accommodation. Bedrooms are not especially large, but they are now comfortably furnished in a gently contemporary style and have all the necessary amenities (phone, tea/coffee tray, TV) and neat, well-designed en-suite bathrooms. Rooms at the back are quieter and have a pleasant outlook over trees and river. Conference/banqueting (250). Children welcome. Pets permitted by arrangement. Garden. **Rooms 30.** (3 suites, 4 junior suites, 23 executive rooms). B&B €76, ss 14. Closed 22-27 Dec. Amex, Diners, MasterCard, Visa, Laser. **Directions:** follow the N71 west through Skibereen.

Timoleague
RESTAURANT

Dillon's

Mill Street Timoleague Co. Cork **Tel: 023 46390**

On the main road to West Cork, Dillons was one of the first café-bars and has always laid the emphasis on good food. Although still very much involved, times have changed since Isabelle Dillon did all of the cooking herself - she now has a creative American chef, so you're less likely to find dishes inspired by her native Brittany than vibrant international food, on menus that change daily. All à la carte; average main course around €18. Open daily in summer, 6.30-9.30; closed Mon in Oct; closed Mon &Tue, Nov-17 Mar. No bookings. No Credit Cards. **Directions:** on main street of village. On N71.

Timoleague
ACCOMODATION

Lettercollum House

Country House Timoleague Co. Cork
Tel: 023 46251 Fax: 023 46251
Email: info@lettercollum.ie Web: www.lettercollum.ie

Con McLoughlin and Karen Austin no longer run the famous restaurant in the Chapel of their Victorian house but they still offer accommodation. The very roomy bedrooms are furnished and decorated in a homely way which is ideal for families - who will have great fun at Lettercollum. Any food served is based on carefully sourced ingredients including organic produce from their own walled garden as well as the best of local meats and seafood. Television. Computer room available.

Children up to 3 are free in parents' room; cots available. No pets. The best bedroom has the only bath. **Rooms 9** (8 shower only). B&B €40pps, ss €10 MasterCard, Visa. **Directions:** N71 from Cork to Bandon, R602 to Timoleague.

Union Hall

Dinty's Bar

RESTAURANT/PUB

Union Hall Co. Cork **Tel: 028 33373**

For those in the know Dinty and Marion Collins' traditional pub has long been the best place in the area for good, unpretentious bar meals. Seafood dominates the menus, but there's plenty else besides - if you don't feel like seafood chowder, fresh crab salad, Bantry Bay mussels, Union Hall smoked salmon or mackerel, real scampi (made with Ballycotton prawns) or a big seafood platter - how about a fine big steak with garlic butter, onions, mushrooms and fries, or proper chicken goujons, made with strips of chicken breast and served with honey & mustard sauce? All this and much besides is cooked for you by Marion and served in a comfortably set-up dining area and an enjoyably relaxed atmosphere. Children welcome. Bar food served daily in summer, weekends in winter: L12.30-2.30, D 5-9.A la carte: average starter around €6.50, average main courses, around €11.50. Seafood Platter (house sepciality) €21.59. House wine € 13.97. Diners, MasterCard, Visa, **Directions:** just off main Leap to Skib road.

Union Hall

Shearwater

ACCOMMODATION

Keelbeg Pier Union Hall Co. Cork **Tel: 028 33178**
Fax: 028 34020 Email: shearwater@esatclear.ie

Adela Nugent's B&B is located close to Keelbeg pier, on an elevated site overlooking Glandore harbour and the surrounding countryside. All bedrooms are good-sized and comfortably furnished with en-suite facilities (only one with bath); most rooms overlook the harbour. The breakfast room and TV room also have views, and there's a patio for guests' use in fine weather. Children welcome (under 2s free in parents' room). No pets. **Rooms 4** (3 shower only; all no smoking). B&B about26pps, ss about €12.70. Closed 31 Oct-1 Apr. None Amex, Diners, MasterCard, Visa, **Directions:** Off N71 between Clonakilty and Skibbereen.

Youghal

Aherne's Seafood Restaurant & Accommodation

ACCOMMODATION
RESTAURANT

163 North Main St Youghal Co. Cork
Tel: 024 92424 Fax: 024 93633
Email: ahernes@eircom.net Web: www.ahernes.com

Now in its third generation of family ownership, one of the most remarkable features of Aherne's is the warmth of the FitzGibbon family's hospitality and their enormous enthusiasm for the business which, since 1993, has included seriously luxurious accommodation. It is for its food - and, especially, the ultra-fresh seafood that comes straight from the fishing boats in Youghal harbour - that Aherne's is best known, however. While John FitzGibbon supervises the front of house, his brother David reigns over a busy kitchen. Bar food (daily 12-7) tends towards simplicity - oysters, chowder, smoked salmon (all served with the renowned moist dark brown yeast bread) - its sheer freshness tells the story. Restaurant meals are naturally more ambitious and include some token meat dishes - rack of lamb with a rosemary jus, char-grilled fillet steak with mushrooms and shallot jus - although seafood is still the undisputed star of the show and David is not afraid of simplicity when it is merited. Specialities like prawns cooked in garlic butter or fresh crab salad can make memorable starters, for example, and hot buttered Youghal Bay lobster are all, in a sense, simple dishes yet they have plenty of glamour too. Nage of prawns and monkfish with vermouth & vegetables is a more complex speciality, and equally tempting. A wine list strong on classic French regions offers a fair selection of half bottles and half a dozen champagnes. **Seats 65.** No smoking area; air conditioning. Live music on Sat evenings. D 6.30-9.30 daily, L Sun only,12.30-2, Set Sun L about €22, Set D about €40; also à la carte ; house wine from about€17, sc discretionary. Toilets wheelchair accessible. **Accommodation:** The stylish rooms at Aherne's are generously sized and individually decorated to a very high standard; all are furnished with antiques and have luxurious, beautifully finished bathrooms. Housekeeping is exemplary and excellent breakfasts are served in a warm and elegantly furnished residents' dining room. Rooms more recently added are equipped to give the option of self-catering if required. Children under 2 free in parents' room. No pets. **Rooms 12** (5 junior suites, 7 executive rooms, 1 for disabled, all no-smoking) B&B about €85pps, ss about €26. Wheelchair access. Closed Xmas 5 days. Amex, Diners, MasterCard, Visa. **Directions:** on N25, main route from Cork-Waterford.

Youghal

Ballymakeigh House & Brownes Restaurant

FARMHOUSE/RESTAURANT

Killeagh Youghal Co. Cork **Tel: 024 91373**
Fax: 024 95370 Email: ballymakeigh@eircom.net

Winner of our Farmhouse of the Year Award in1999, Ballymakeigh House provides a high standard of comfort, food and hospitality in one of the most outstanding establishments of its type in Ireland. Set at the heart of an east Cork dairy farm, this attractive old house is immaculately maintained and run by Margaret Browne, who is a Euro-Toques chef and author of a successful cookery book. The house is warm and homely with plenty of space for guests, who are welcome to use the garden and visit the farmyard. The individually decorated bedrooms are full of character and equally comfortable and Margaret's hospitality is matched only by her energetic pursuit of excellence - ongoing improvements and developments are a constant characteristic of Ballymakeigh. Equestrian centre, tennis, garden, children's playground. Off-season value breaks. Children welcome (under 3s free in parents' room, cots available). No pets. **Rooms 6** (all en-suite, 2 no smoking). B&B €45pps, ss €15. House closed Nov-Apr. **Brownes Restaurant:** Margaret and her team have earned an excellent reputation at Ballymakeigh House over the years, for a personal blend of traditional and new Irish cuisine with international influences, all based on the very best of fresh local ingredients. So, when the Brownes planned an equestrian centre nearby, it was natural to build on that success by incorporating a restaurant into the new development - hence the fine big country-style restaurant just along the road, which they now operate during the day and for evenings, six days a week. Good home cooking of local ingredients is a speciality - crisp honey roast duck, baked ham with Jameson whiskey sauce - and home baking is also a strong point. Children welcome; vegetarian menu available. **Seats 90** (private room, 90) L Wed-Sun,12-4 (Sun from 12.30), D Wed-Sun 6-9.30 (Sun to 9), Set Sun L€22; early D EUr25 (5-7pm); Set D from €27. House wine€15, sc discretionary. Closed Mon & Tue. MasterCard, Visa. **Directions:** Located on N25 20 miles east of Cork City.

Youghal

The Old Imperial Hotel with Coachhouse, Bar & Restaurant

HOTEL/RESTAURANT/PUB

27 Main Street Youghal Co. Cork
Tel: 024 92435 Fax: 024 90268

James and Mary Browne's new hotel presents an attractive, sprucely-painted face to the world and provides a badly-needed addition to the limited choice of quality accommodation and food in the town. There's a separate entrance to the hotel off the street, but it would be a pity to miss the downstairs bar, which incorporates the wonderful old-world bar listed in the guide last year as D. McCarthy ("A lovely little low-ceilinged bar of great character with an open fire and a long history to tell....") as well as the much larger new bar area which has just been added. The limitations of the site have resulted in a shortage of space in the hotel, which is on three rather steep floors, with no lift and no space for a residents' sitting room or separate reception area for the first-floor restaurant (where breakfast is also served). Bedrooms also tend to be on the small side, although there are two quite impressive junior suites and all rooms are furnished and fitted to a high standard with all the usual amenities including trouser press with steam iron. **Restaurant** Ballymaloe-trained chef Patrick Kennedy offers menus that show individuality and an impressive freshness of approach. Seven starters on the à la carte dinner menu might include a warm salad of farmhouse cheese with garlic croûtons, pine nuts and walnut oil dressing or sautéed wild mushrooms on a rosemary & garlic potato cake with truffle cream sauce - and a choice of eight or nine courses will include several dishes featuring local seafood well-balanced by a fair selection of meats and poultry - and at least one imaginative vegetarian dish. Carefully sourced ingredients, confident, accurate cooking and simple, attractive presentation add up to a very satisfying dining experience. Service is friendly although, if the guide's experience is typical, better training is required to bring this side of the operation into line with the high quality of food and cooking. **Seats 40.** No smoking area; air conditioing. D daily, 6.15-9.15. * Bar meals served daily, 12.30-9; L12.30-3.30 (Sat 1-2.30); D 6.30-9. Diners, MasterCard, Visa, Laser. **Directions:** On the N25 - 30 miles from Cork Airport.

COUNTY DONEGAL

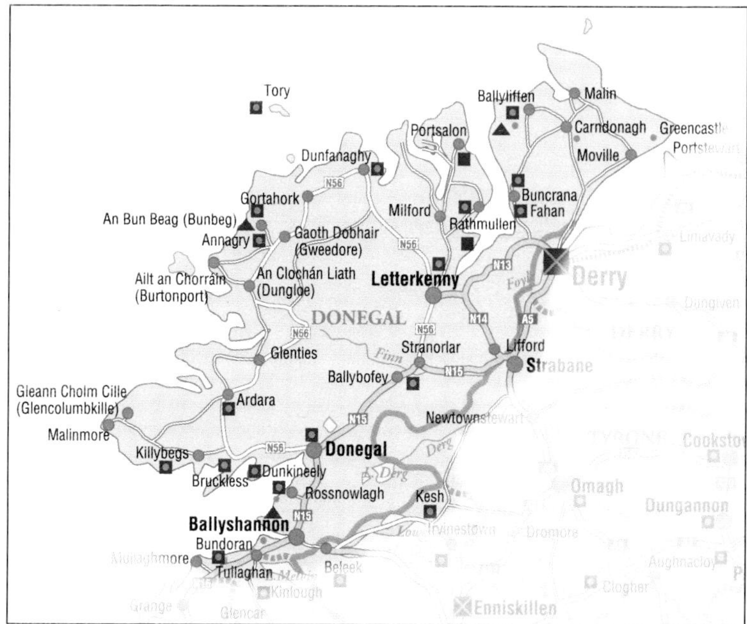

Donegal is big country. It may not have Ireland's highest mountains, nor is it Ireland's biggest county. But nevertheless there's a largeness of spirit about this northwesterly corner which lingers fondly in the recollection of those who visit it, their memories reinforced by visions of a magnificent coastline with some of Ireland's finest beaches.

In 2002, Donegal is literally taking flight. The spectacular Glenveagh National Park in the northern part of the county has been selected as the location for the re-introduction of the golden eagle to Ireland. Almost a century after the species became extinct, the first six golden eagle chicks were released at Glenveagh in June 2001. Over a five year period, 50 birds will be released, and there are high expectations of success for the programme.

In the far north of Donegal, Ireland's most northerly township is the spick and span village of Malin, a place of legendary neatness which, in September 2001, was Donegal's highest-placed award winner in the Tidy Towns competition, and for good measure, it was also the top award winner in the entire northwest. The County's Highly Commended award went to Glenties, while the Commended winner was Letterkenny.

For many folk, particularly those from Northern Ireland, Donegal is the holiday county par excellence. But in recent years, despite the international fluctuations of trading conditions, there has been development of modern industries and the strengthening of the fishing, particularly at the hugely busy harbour of Killybegs, home port of the world's largest fishing vessel, the Atlantic Dawn.

This entrepreneurial spirit has led to a more balanced economy, with the pace being set by the county town of Letterkenny, where the population has increased by 50% since 1991. In 2002, another town which is being regenerated is Buncrana on the eastern shore of the large and handsome Lough Swilly, "The Lake of Shadows". With a new car ferry across Lough Swilly to Rathmullan from Buncrana's developing harbour - where a marina is on the way - there's a growing sense of loughside community and vitality. And vitality at this level makes Donegal a more attractive place for today's visitor.

But much and all as Donegal county is increasingly a place where people live and make a living, nevertheless it is still a place of nature on the grand scale, a place assaulted by the winds and weather of the Atlantic Ocean if it is given the slighest chance. Yet at places like Bundoran and Rossnowlagh, where splendid beaches face straight into the Atlantic, enthusiastic surfers have demonstrated that even the most demanding weather can have its sporting uses. Bundoran in

September 2001 was the spectacular setting for the World Masters Surfing Championship - in truly epic conditions, Mark Richards from Australia won his fifth world title.

For most folk, however, it is the contrast between raw nature and homely comfort which is central to Donegal's enduring attraction. For here, in some of Ireland's most rugged territory, you will find many sheltered and hospitable places whose amenities are emphasised by the challenging nature of their broader environment. And needless to say, that environment is simply startlingly utterly beautiful as well.

Local Attractions and Information

Arranmore Ferry Burtonport-Arranmore	075 20532
Ballintra Ballymagroarty Heritage Centre	073 34966
Buncrana National Knitting Centre	077 62355
Bundoran Tourism Information	072 41350
Burt Grianan of Aileach	077 68000
Churchill Glebe House & Gallery (Derek Hill)	074 37071
Donegal Airport Carrickfin	075 48232
Donegal Highlands Hillwalking/Irish language (adults)	073 30248
Donegal town Donegal Castle	073 22405
Donegal town Tourism information	073 21148
Donegal town Waterbus Cruises	073 21148
Dunfanaghy Workhouse Visitor Centre	074 36504
Dungloe Mary from Dungloe Int. Festival (July/August)	
Dungloe Tourism Information	075 21297
Glencolumbcille Folk Museum	
Glencolumbcille Tourism Information	073 30017
Glenties Patrick Mac Gill Summer School (August)	
Glenveagh National Park (Castle, gardens, parkland)	074 37088
Greencastle Maritime Museum	077 81363
Letterkenny An Grianan Theatre	074 20777
Letterkenny Arts Centre	074 29186
Letterkenny County Museum	074 24613
Letterkenny Newmills watermill	074 25115
Letterkenny North West Tourism	074 21160
Lifford Cavanacor Historic House	074 41143
Tory Island Ferry	075 31320

Annagry

Danny Minnie's Restaurant

RESTAURANT

Annagry Co. Donegal **Tel: 075 48201** Fax: 075 48201

The O'Donnell family has run Danny Minnie's since 1962, and a visit is always a special treat. There's nothing about the exterior as seen from the road to prepare first-time visitors for the atmosphere of this remarkable restaurant: hidden behind a frontage of overgrown creepers a surprise awaits when, after a warm welcome from Terri O'Donnell, guests are suddenly surrounded by antiques and elegantly appointed candle-lit tables. The menu is presented in both Irish and English and Brian O'Donnell's cooking is a good match for the surroundings - fine, with imaginative saucing, but not at all pompous. On a wide-ranging à la carte menu, seafood stars in the main courses - lobster and other shellfish, availability permitting - and there is also a strong selection of meats including Donegal mountain lamb, typically served with caramelized onions, blackcurrant & mint jus and Donegal beef, served various ways including classic Beef Wellington. Vegetables are a strength and gorgeous desserts such as crêpes suzette with orange and Grand Marnier can be relied on to create an appropriately dramatic finale. Under Terri's direction, helpful service from attentive waitresses is another bonus. Danny Minnie's was a deserving winner of the guide's Atmospheric Restaurant of the Year in 2000. **Seats 80** (private room, 30). No smoking area; air conditioning. D daily in summer, 6.30-9.30. Bar food 12-12 daily high season, Set D €32, also à la carte, house wine €15.24; sc10%. (Phone ahead to check opening hours, especially for lunch, off peak season) Closed Christmas & Sun/Mon off season. [Accommodation is also offered in eight non-smoking rooms, five of them en-suite and one suitable for disabled guests]. Diners, MasterCard, Visa. **Directions:** R259 off N56 - follow Airport signs.

Ardara

The Green Gate

B&B

Ardvally Ardara Co.Donegal **Tel: 075 41546**

Paul Chatenoud's amazing little B&B is a one-off. Above Ardara, up a steep and twisting boreen that will reward you with a stunning view on arrival, Paul offers simple but comfortable accommodation in his unspoilt traditional cottage and converted outbuildings. It's a far cry from the Parisian bookshop he once ran, but this little place is magic. In the morning (or whenever you wake up - he will be working around his lovely garden and is happy to stop at any time it suits his guests), he cooks up breakfast while you take in the laid-back homeliness of his cosy cottage sitting room. Just be glad you found it, because he's probably right - it may well be "the most beautiful place anywhere in Ireland". Children welcome (Under 10s free in parents' room, cot available). Pets permitted. **Rooms 4** (all en-suite). B&B €30pps, ss €10. Open all year. No Credit Cards. **Directions:** off Donegal Road, one mile from Ardara, on the hill.

Ardara

Nancy's Bar

PUB

Front Street Ardara Co Donegal **Tel: 075 41187**

This famous pub, in the village renowned for its tweeds and handknits, is a cosy, welcoming place, with five or six small rooms packed with bric à brac and plenty of tables and chairs for the comfortable consumption of good home-made food, especially seafood. Famous for their chowder - maybe try it with a "Louis Armstrong" (smoked salmon on brown bread topped with grilled cheese) and finish with an Irish coffee. Live music too. Bar food served daily 12-9.30, from Easter to September. Wheelchair access. Closed 25 Dec & Good Fri. No Credit Cards. **Directions:** Centre of Ardara.

Ardara

Woodhill House

RESTAURANT/COUNTRY HOUSE/PUB

Ardara Co.Donegal **Tel: 075 41112**
Fax: 075 41516 Email: yates@iol.ie Web: woodhillhouse.com

Formerly the home of Ireland's last commercial whaling family, John and Nancy Yates' large country house is set in its own grounds overlooking the Donegal Highlands and the hard restoration work they have put in over more than a decade is now bearing fruit. This hospitable house has a full bar where light lunches are served and unusual accommodation in the main house and nearby converted outbuildings - rooms are all en-suite but vary greatly in position, size and character so it is worth spending a few minutes discussing your preferences when booking. There's also a restaurant (booking recommended as it's very popular locally) offering quite traditional food based on local ingredients at reasonable prices: specialities include oysters, Donegal mountain lamb, duck off the bone and carrageen pudding. Gradually restoring the garden is perhaps Nancy's greatest challenge and it's turning out beautifully, not only on the kitchen garden side but as a pleasure garden too. Renovations, on both the main house and some fine outbuildings, continue on an ongoing basis. Small conferences (15). Children welcome (free in parents' room up to 6). Pets permitted in some areas. **Rooms 9** (all en-suite, 7 shower-only). B&B about €50 pps, ss about €30. Closed 24-27 Dec. **Restaurant: Seats 40** (private room, 15). No smoking area. D 6.30-10 daily, Set D £25, house wine about €13.; sc discretionary. * Bar lunch available 12-2 pm daily. Closed 20-27 Dec. Amex, Diners, MasterCard, Visa. **Directions:** 1/4 mile from Ardara and well signed.

Ballybofey

Jackson's Hotel

HOTEL

Ballybofey Co.Donegal **Tel: 074 31021**
Fax: 074 31096 Email: bjackson@iol.ie

Although it has a town centre location, this attractive family-run hotel is set in its own gardens and enjoys a tranquil position alongside the River Finn. The spacious, elegantly furnished foyer creates a good first impression and this is followed through in other public areas including the restaurant, which overlooks the garden. Bedrooms, all recently refurbished to a high standard, are very comfortable with direct-dial phones, tea/coffee trays and TV with video channel, and the best have river views. Conference/banqueting (400/600); business centre, ISDN lines, secretarial services. Leisure centre (22m pool). Children welcome (under 2s free in parents' room, cots available). Bank Holiday Special Breaks throughout the year offer particularly good value. Horse-riding, golf, fishing and bike hire all nearby. Pets permitted in some areas. **Rooms 88** (2 suites, 4 executive rooms). B&B about €60 pps, ss about€20 Wheelchair access. Lift. Open all year. Amex, Diners, MasterCard, Visa. **Directions:** beside the river, in the centre of town.

Ballybofey

Kee's Hotel

HOTEL/RESTAURANT Stranorlar Ballybofey Co.Donegal **Tel: 074 31018** Fax: 074 31917 Email: info@keeshotel.ie Web: www.keeshotel.ie

This centrally located, all-year hotel has an unusually long line of continuous family ownership, having been in the Kee family since 1892. Public areas have recently undergone radical renovations, including a new foyer, meeting rooms and a lift. Bedrooms are regularly refurbished and most are very comfortable with good bathrooms; those at the back of the hotel, with views of the Blue Stack Mountains, are most desirable and avoid the problems caused by through traffic which may be disturbing at the front. Residents have direct access from their rooms to the hotel's excellent leisure facilities. Golf and fishing nearby. Conference/banqueting (150/250). Children welcome, under 3s free in their parents' room; cots and high chairs available, crèche at certain times in the leisure centre. Special breaks offered by the hotel include a novel "Post Christmas Recovery Break". **Rooms 53** (1 junior suite, 31 executive rooms,1 for disabled). B&B €74pps, ss €13. Lift. Open all year. **The Looking Glass** Hand-worked tapestries decorate this pleasant warm-toned restaurant, which is in two areas with plenty of alcoves for privacy. Head chef Frank Pasquier's daily menus offer a choice of four starters and main courses on 3- and 4-course Table d'Hôte, in addition to quite an ambitious à la carte. A typical menu might include roast goats cheese on a bed of Mediterranean terrine with split tomato dressing, a soup (smoked haddock chowder perhaps) and main courses like best end of lamb with red cabbage confit and garlic cream or pan-fried cod with courgette & sweet potato mousseline and saffron butter. Vegetarian dishes are included on the main menus. Dessert specialities include warm apple tart (cooked to order) and there's an Irish farmhouse cheese trolley. No smoking area. **Seats 74** (private room, 60). D 6.30-10.30 daily, Sun L 12.30-3, Set Sun L about €18; Set D €34, à la carte available; house wine €15.50. sc discretionary. [Informal meals also available in the Old Gallery, 12.30-3 and 5.30-9.30 daily.] Amex, Diners, MasterCard, Visa, Laser. **Directions:** On the Main Street in the village of Stranorlar.

Ballyliffin

Rossaor House

ACCOMMODATION Ballyliffin Inishowen Co. Donegal **Tel: 077 76498** Fax: 077 76498

Brian and Anne Harkin's very pleasant and hospitable house is in a beautiful area that deserves to be better known and it has amazing views down over two golf courses to Pollen Strand and Malin Head. Bedrooms are furnished to a high standard (generous beds, direct dial phone, tea/coffee facilities and TV) and luxuriously decorated - an aspect of the business in which Anne clearly takes particular pleasure. Spacious, comfortably furnished public rooms include a large sitting room, which takes full advantage of the view, and a conservatory (considerately situated overlooking the lovely garden and away from the full blast of morning sunshine) where excellent breakfasts are served with commendable efficiency. There is also self-catering accommodation on the property - details from the Harkins. Children welcome (cot available). No pets. **Rooms 4** (all en-suite). B&B about €32pps, ss about €6.50. Closed Christmas. MasterCard, Visa. **Directions:** N2 Dublin to Aughnacloy, A5 to Derry Cross bridge as you enter Derry. Take signs to Buncrana, then Clonmany. Ballyliffin is 1 mile to the right.

Bruckless

Bruckless House

FARMHOUSE Bruckless Co. Donegal **Tel: 073 37071** Fax: 073 37070 Email: bruc@bruckless.com Web: www.iol.ie/-bruc/bruckless.html

Clive and Joan Evans' lovely 18th-century house and Connemara pony stud farm is set in 19 acres of woodland and gardens overlooking Bruckless Bay - an ideal place for people who enjoy quiet countryside and pursuits like walking, horse-riding and fishing. Family furniture collected through a Hong Kong connection add an unexpected dimension to the elegant reception rooms and generous, comfortably furnished bedrooms. Bedrooms include two single rooms and there is a shared bathroom. Pets permitted by arrangement. **Rooms 5** (2 en-suite, 1 shower only, all no-smoking) B&B €38-45pps, no ss. Closed Oct-Mar. Amex, MasterCard, Visa. **Directions:** On N56, 12 miles West of Donegal town.

Bunbeg

Ostan Gweedore Hotel & Leisure Centre

HOTEL Bunbeg Co.Donegal **Tel: 075 31177** Fax: 075 31726 Email: ostangweedore@ireland.com Web: ostangweedore.com

Although its architectural style may not be to today's taste, Ostan Gweedore was built to make the most of the view - and this it does very well. Most of the comfortable if rather dated bedrooms (plus three suites) and all the public areas, including the recently refurbished restaurant and the Library

Bar ("the most westerly reading room on the Atlantic seaboard") have superb views over the shoreline and Mount Errigal. It's ideal for families, with its wonderful beach and outdoor activities, including tennis, pitch & putt and day visits to nearby Tory Island. Wet days are looked after too, with indoor leisure facilities, including a 19-metre swimming pool, jacuzzi and gym, all supervised by qualified staff. (A spa and beauty & health centre is also to open in April 2002). Fishing and golf (9 hole) available locally. This romantic setting means weddings are popular (conferences/banqueting up to 300) and the hotel offers an imaginative "Flybreak", including a return flight Dublin to Donegal, overnight stay and dinner 'on the edge of a continent', at a very competitive rate. Check for latest offers. Under 5s free in parents' room (cot available, free of charge). Pets permitted by arrangement. **Rooms 39** (3 suites). B&B about €76pps. Closed Nov-Feb. Ocean Restaurant Amex, MasterCard, Visa, Laser, Switch. **Directions:** 45 minutes from Letterkenny,close to Carrickfinn Airport.

Bundoran

Le Chateaubrianne

RESTAURANT — Sligo Road Bundoran Co. Donegal **Tel: 072 42160** Fax: 072 42160

Since opening here in 1993, Brian and Anne Loughlin have established this welcoming and very professionally run establishment as the leading restaurant in the area. Brian's cooking is classic French with modern Irish and international overtones and he is a strong supporter of local produce. Imaginative dinner menus offer a well-balanced selection with local seafood well represented (crab profiteroles are a typical starter), also game in season, with interesting vegetarian options available. Sunday lunch provides something for everyone by offering a clever combination of traditional roasts and more adventurous fare; the same high standard of cooking applies and the meal will be nicely finished off with coffee and petits fours. **Seats 56** (private room, 20). No-smoking restaurant. D 6.30-9.30 Tues-Sat, L Sun only 12.30-3, Set Sun L €20.32, Set D from €29.85; house wine €16.51 sc discretionary. Closed Mon, 24-25 Dec, 3 wks Jan & bank hols. Amex, MasterCard, Visa. **Directions:** on Left entering Bundoran from Sligo.

Carndonagh

Corncrake Restaurant

RESTAURANT — Malin Street Carndonagh Co. Donegal **Tel: 077 74534**

It is difficult to describe Brid McCartney and Noreen Lynch's restaurant adequately because, although it is just the front room of a fairly ordinary house on the main street of a small town, that is where any sense of being "ordinary" ends. The room is not large, but it has a confident, professional air and its low-key decor creates an unlikely spaciousness. Tables are well-appointed, with gleaming glasses and quality cutlery giving a hint to the philosophy at work in the kitchen. It is significant that Brid and Noreen have made a conscious decision to live and work in this lovely (and, so far, unspoilt) part of the country, that they relish it and take pleasure in the produce of the area - and in their work. This is perhaps best seen through their decision to run off-season residential cookery courses at the restaurant, together with Rossaor House (see entry) who provide the accommodation element. Back at the restaurant, local produce appears typically in mussels in a tarragon cream or main courses (about €14-16) like roast rack of Donegal mountain lamb with rosemary & redcurrant gravy - and all main dishes are served with their own variation on a wonderful northern speciality, lovage champ. No children after 8 pm. **Seats 26** No smoking area. D 6-10 (Sun to 9), à la carte only, house wine about €14; sc discretionary. Open 7 nights June-Sept, Fri/Sat in Mar-May & Oct-Dec, Closed Christmas-17 Mar.*From 17th March 2002, The Corncrake will be in new premises in Carndonagh (the phone number will remain unchanged). No Credit Cards.

Clonmany

Glen House

B&B — Straid Cloneny Inishowen Co. Donegal **Tel: 077 76745**

Doris Russo's charming period house is beautifully located and would make a most comfortable and hospitable base for any of the many activities that this lovely area offers - including visiting the near-by waterfall, which has recently been opened to the public. Rooms are appealingly decorated in an unpretentious country style which will take many guests back to their childhood. MasterCard, Visa.

Culdaff

McGrory's of Culdaff

PUB/RESTAURANT/ACCOMMODATION — Culdaff Co. Donegal **Tel: 077 79104** Fax: 077 79235 Email: mcgr@eircom.net Web: www.mcgrorys.ie

In an area that has so much to offer, in terms of natural beauty and activities like golf, angling and walking, McGrory's would make an ideal base. An inn in the true sense of the word, offering rest and refreshment to travellers, this northwestern institution was established in 1924 and remains in the active care of the McGrory family. It has recently undergone a major makeover, resulting in a pleasing combination of old and new which is easy on the eye and includes a new restaurant as well as an overhaul of the whole premises. Comfortable bedrooms vary in size and outlook but are attractively furnished in a classic contemporary style that is both practical and appropriate; all have well-planned bathrooms and all the necessary amenities (phone, tea/coffee tray, TV). For anyone touring the Inishowen peninsula it's a logical place to take a break, as popular bar food is available throughout the day. But it is probably for music that McGrory's is most famous - as well as traditional sessions in The Front Bar on Tuesday and Friday nights, Mac's Backroom Bar (constructed on the site of the old outhouses of McGrory's shop) is a major venue for live shows featuring international names. (Live music Wednesday and Saturday; events listings on the web.) Conference/banqueting (100).Special interest/off season breaks. **Rooms 10** (all with full en-suite bathrooms). Children welcome (under 12s free in parents' room; cot available free of charge). No pets. B&B €44.44, ss €12.70. **Restaurant:** D Sun-Sat, L Sun. Bar meals daily, 12.30-8. Closed 24-28 Dec. Amex, MasterCard, Visa, Laser.

Donegal

St. Ernan's House Hotel

COUNTRY HOUSE/HOTEL

Donegal Co. Donegal
Tel: 073 21065 Fax: 073 22098
Email: info@sainternans.com Web: www.sainternans.com

Set on its own wooded island connected to the mainland by a causeway, tranquillity is the main characteristic of Brian and Carmel O'Dowd's unique country house hotel. Spacious public rooms have log fires and antique furniture and, while they vary in size and outlook, the individually decorated bedrooms are furnished to a high standard and have good amenities including (surprisingly perhaps) television, while most also have lovely views. Children under 6 not catered for. No pets. **Rooms 12** (2 suites, 3 executive, 1 shower only) B&B €125pps, ss on request. **Restaurant** The dining room is mainly for resident guests, but reservations may be taken from non-residents if there is room. Daily 5-course country house-style dinner menus based on local produce; vegetarian dishes on request. No smoking restaurant. **Seats 25.** D 6.30-8.30 daily, D from about €22 (semi-à la carte, priced by course); house wine from €19. Closed end Oct-Easter. MasterCard, Visa, Laser. **Directions:** One mile south of Donegal Town on its own tidal island.

Dunfanaghy

The Mill Restaurant & Accomodation

RESTAURANT/B&B

Figart Dunfanaghy Co. Donegal **Tel: 074 36985**
Fax: 074 36985 Email: themillrestaurant@oceanfree.net

Beautifully located on the shore of the New Lake, which is a special area of conservation, the mill was the home of Susan Alcorn's grandfather and, as they are a family of accomplished painters, the walls are hung with wonderful watercolours. Susan and her husband Derek, who is the chef, have run this remarkable place as a restaurant with rooms since March 2000 and, not surprisingly, it has already acquired a dedicated following as the location is superb, the welcome warm and the cooking both imaginative and assured. The dining room is on two levels, with plenty of windows framing the views, fresh flowers on the tables, soft lighting and some well-placed antiques - a room of character and atmosphere. Menus are based firmly on local ingredients and offer about half a dozen choices on each course and change every 6 weeks. House specialities include a starter of salmon & crab terrine, upside down fish pie with lobster & scallops and local meats like Donegal lamb and Glenties pork - which might typically be smoked, cooked with a herbed crust and served with grilled apple and savoy cabbage. There's always at least one vegetarian option (which is encouragingly placed well up the menu rather than just being tagged on as an afterthought as vegetarian options so often are) and a classic sweet menu (offering treats such as a delectable rhubarb trifle with ginger ice cream) is nicely rounded off with a selection of farmhouse cheeses. Menus for Sunday lunch (only on the first Sunday of the month) are a little simpler and shorter, but similar in style to the cooking at dinner. No-smoking restaurant; air conditioning. Children welcome. **Seats 45.** D Tue-Sat 7-9pm, L 1st Sun of the month only 12.30-2pm. Set D €34.50; Sun L €18.98. House wine €13.50; sc discretionary. Closed Mon, mid-week after Hallowe'en & Jan-Feb). Accommodation is available in six individually decorated rooms, which have opened gradually as they have been finished. The decor is simple but stylish, with good new beds and some lovely antique pieces, and there's also a lovely little sitting room off the dining room, with comfy big chairs and sofas to relax in. Children welcome (under 5s free in parents' room, cot available without charge). **Rooms 6** (all en-suite & no-smoking, 4 shower only). B&B €38 pps, ss €7. Closed Jan-Feb. MasterCard, Visa, Laser. **Directions:** Take N56 from Letterkenny to Dunfanaghy. 1/2 mile outside Dunfanaghy on Falcarragh Rd on right hand side of the lake.

Dunkineely

Castle Murray House Hotel

HOTEL/RESTAURANT St. John's Point Dunkineely Co.Donegal **Tel: 073 37022**
Fax: 073 37330 Email: castlemurray@eircom.net Web: www.castlemurray.com

Thierry and Claire Delcros' beautifully located clifftop hotel has wonderful sea and coastal views over the ruined castle after which it is named. Since they opened in 1991, the Delcros have made numerous improvements, including the addition of a little bar and a residents' sitting room and a large verandah complete with awning where summer meals can be served. Bedrooms have been recently refurbished and individually decorated with a mixture of modern and antique pieces that give each room its own character; most have sea views and all are quite large with a double and single bed, good bathrooms and facilities including digital TV as well as phone and tea/coffee trays. A new sun area on the sheltered flat roof at the back of the building has direct access from some bedrooms. Good breakfasts are served in in the restaurant, or in bedrooms on request. Banqueting (60). Pets permitted. Children welcome; extra beds and cots available. Off-season value breaks. **Rooms 10** (all en-suite). B&B €62.22pps, ss €22.85. Closed 25-26 Dec, 31 Dec, mid Jan-mid Feb. **Restaurant** The restaurant is on the seaward corner of the hotel and maximises the impact of the dramatic view, including the castle (which is floodlit at night). Tweed curtains and an open fire make for real warmth in this exposed location, even in winter. Owner-chef Thierry Delcros' multi-choice menus (basically 3-course, plus options of soup and sorbet), are sensibly priced according to the choice of main course and offer a wide selection, including vegetarian dishes. Seafood is the speciality of the house in the summer months; in winter there are more red meats, poultry and game. **Seats 50.** No smoking restaurant. D daily 7-9.30, (Sun 6.30-8) L Sun only 1.30-4; D from €31.74 (depending on choice of main course); Set Sun L €18.41; house wine about €15.87; no sc. Closed 25-26 Dec, 31 Dec, mid Jan-mid Feb as above but phone to check restaurant opening in low season, which varies according to demand. MasterCard, Visa, Laser. **Directions:** Situated on the N56, 8km from Killybegs, 20km Donegal Town on the coast road to St Johns Point. Take first left outside Dunkineely Village.

Fahan

St. John's Country House & Restaurant

RESTAURANT/COUNTRY HOUSE Inishowen Fahan Co.Donegal
Tel: 077 60289 Fax: 077 60612
Email: stjohnsrestaurant@eircom.net Web: eircom.net/~stjohnscountryhouse

In this substantial period house overlooking Lough Swilly, Reggie Ryan and Phil McAfee have run Restaurant St John's to growing acclaim since 1980. It's one of the most hospitable houses in Ireland - Reggie has a way with guests (and there's many an international figure among them) which must be pretty well unrivalled, making each one feel especially welcome so the whole occasion is relaxed and fun (for which special talent he received our Host of the Year Award in 2000). A conservatory extension has allowed for lough views in addition to the original cosy inside rooms, all a fit setting for Phil's cooking, which combines a respect for tradition and an understanding of the value of simplicity with a willingness to experiment, ensuring that the many guests who regularly return always have a meal that is both stimulating and relaxing. Given the location, seafood is very popular (a delicious house speciality is baked turbot on a creamy casserole of butterbeans sweetcorn, smoked bacon & chives) but Phil's table d'hôte and à la carte menus are based on a wide range of local ingredients, including game in winter. Donegal mountain lamb, which she cooks in many different ways is an established favourite (earning Restaurant St John's the Guide's Irish Lamb Award in 1999 for another excellent speciality of "Rack of Donegal Mountain Lamb with Rosemary and Mascarpone Risotto"), but the crispy roast duckling is also a real treat. Vegetarian dishes on regular menu; vegetarian menu available. A carefully selected wine list includes nine house wines, a special seasonal selection and a good choice of half bottles. **Seats 75** (private room, 25) No smoking restaurant; air conditioning. D Tue-Sun 7.30-9.30, Set D €35.55; L Sun only 1-3pm, €15.24 house wines from €18.41; SC discretionary. Restaurant closed Mon. **Accommodation:** Stylish, comfortable rooms are furnished with antiques. Children welcome (under 3s free in parents' room, cot available). No pets. **Rooms 5** (1 suite, 2 shower only, all no-smoking) B&B €44.44 pps, ss €4.44. Establishment closed Jan-Feb. Amex, MasterCard, Visa, Laser, Switch. **Directions:** In Fahan village on R238 Derry-Buncrana road.

Greencastle
RESTAURANT

Kealys Seafood Bar

The Harbour Greencastle Co. Donegal **Tel: 077 81010**
Fax: 077 81010 Email: kealys@iol.ie

CREATIVE USE OF SEAFOOD AWARD

Under-stated quality seems a fair description of the tone of James and Tricia Kealy's excellent seafood restaurant, which has always valued simplicity. Since 1989 the restaurant has been a key establishment in a major fishing port and still retains the original bar at its heart. Lunch menus are shortish and the dishes offered simple; however the choice is very adequate and the quality of food and cooking consistently good. Dinner is more ambitious and, in addition to a wide selection of ultra-fresh seafood, James includes a fair selection of meat and poultry - steaks, Inishowen lamb, duck - as well as vegetarian dishes. Unlike many seafood restaurants, where the emphasis on menus tends to be solely on the main ingredient (often with a very rich sauce), James takes a more creative and balanced approach to this precious resource, presenting it as a component in complete dishes which are modern in tone but also often echo traditional Irish themes. House specialities demonstrating this healthy and (ecologically sound) philosophy include a starter of spinach wrapped seafood terrine with a tomato and chilli coulis and main courses like pan fried fillet of cod with parsley sauce on a chive and garlic champ and baked Atlantic salmon with a wholgrain mustard crust served on Irish spring cabbage and bacon. James is now developing dishes using lesser known fish , including the "new" deep sea varieties- panfried fillet of orange roughty with vegetable brunoise and vermouth sauce is now an established favourite, for example. He also bakes a variety of breads and uses local organic vegetables and farmhouse cheeses - typically Gubbeen, St Killian, Boilie and Cashel Blue. Not suitable for children after 8 pm. **Seats 60.** No smoking area. L 12.30-3pm (Sun from 1-3, D 7-9.30 (Sun to 8.30); Set D €28.57, also à la carte, house wine about €11.43. Closed Mon, 2 wks Nov-Dec. Amex, MasterCard, Visa. **Directions:** on the harbour at Greencastle. 20 miles north of Derry City.

Killybegs
HOTEL

Bay View Hotel

Main Street Killybegs Co Donegal **Tel: 073 31950**
Fax: 073 31856 Email: bvhotel@iol.ie Web: www.bayviewhotel@iol.ie

This friendly new hotel on the harbourfront is a great addition to the accommodation and facilities of the area, for leisure and business. Public areas include a cocktail bar adjacent to the first floor restaurant as well as the main Wheel House Bar at street level and good leisure facilities will appeal to business guests and make this a fine 'weather proof' base for a family holiday - there's a 16 metre swimming pool, plus sauna, jacuzzi, steam room and gym. Comfortable bedrooms have full bathrooms and all the necessary facilties (phone, TV, tea/coffee tray and trouser press), while executive rooms also have mini-bar, fax/modem line and access to a lounge with boardroom table; many overlook the harbour, although those at the back may be quieter, especially at weekends when there is live music in the main bar. Leisure centre, swimming pool. Conference/banqueting (300/280). Children welcome, cot available free of charge. **Rooms 37** (3 executive, 6 no smoking, 3 for disabled).Lift. B&B €120, ss €25. Closed 24-28 Dec. Captain's Table Amex, MasterCard, Visa, Laser. **Directions:** 25 km from Donegal Town.

Killybegs
PUB/RESTAURANT/ACCOMODATION

The Fleet Inn

Bridge Street Killybegs Co. Donegal
Tel: 073 31518 Fax: 073 31664

Marguerite Howley's pleasant establishment just off the main thoroughfare is an inn in the real sense, offering food, drink and shelter - although, admittedly, bar food is not part of the package which might sometimes be disappointing to visitors. Rooms are a mixture of sizes, ranging from singles to family rooms, all cheerfully decorated, with direct dial phones and TV. Not very suitable for children. No pets. **Rooms 10** (all en-suite, 5 no-smoking). B&B about €32 pps. **Restaurant** The upstairs restaurant is open in the evening only and offers a short but appealing menu. It's predictably strong on seafood - Donegal Bay prawns tossed in garlic butter, seared scallops with fresh herb risotto and garlic & tomato sauce - but offers a vegetarian choice such as leek & red pepper tartlet and a few meat dishes, including chargrilled steak and, perhaps, venison served roast garlic, braised red cabbage & port jus. **Seats 40** (private dining area, 12). No smoking area. D only, 7-10 daily in summer (Nov-Feb closed Mon & Tue). A la carte; house wine about €13; sc discretionary. NB: Data not confirmed at time of going to press; a phone call ahead is advised. **Directions:** In the centre of Killybegs - a right turn just after the harbour.

Kincasslagh

Iggy's Bar

PUB

Kincasslagh Co.Donegal **Tel: 075 43112**

Just a short walk up from the harbour - it's also called the Atlantic Bar - Ann and Iggy Murray have run this delightfully unspoilt pub since 1986 and it's an all year home-from-home for many a visitor. The television isn't usually on unless there's a match and Ann makes lovely simple food for the bar, mainly seafood - home-made soups, delicious crab sandwiches and Rombouts coffee. No children after 7 pm. Light food available 10.30-12.30 Mon-Sat. Closed 25 Dec & Good Friday. No Credit Cards. **Directions:** On the corner of the Main Street, where the road turns off to the harbour.

Laghey

Coxtown Manor

RESTAURANT/COUNTRY HOUSE

Laghey Co Donegal
Tel: 073 34575 Fax: 073 34576
Email: coxtownmanor@oceanfree.net Web: www.coxtownmanor.com

Just a short drive from the county town, this late Georgian house set in its own parkland is in a lovely, peaceful area close to Donegal Bay. It's an exceptionally friendly, welcoming place and Belgian proprietor, Edward Dewael - who fell for the property a year or two ago and is still in the process of upgrading it - personally ensures that everything possible is done to make guests feel at home. Public areas include a very pleasant wood-panelled bar with an open fire - well-stocked, notably with Belgian beers and a great selection of digestifs to accompany your after dinner coffee - and an elegant period dining room, which is the heart of the operation and, like the style of food presentation, attractive without being too formal. Dining at Coxtown is a very pleasant experience indeed, not least because of the positive, relaxing tone of staff who settle guests in with the prompt offer of aperitifs and presentation of menus which are sensibly priced for any two or three courses; there are a few supplements but pricing overall is moderate. Among the choice of seven starters you'll find a good home-made soup of the day or bisque and probably mussels of some sort and duck liver paté with toast and onion marmalade (€3 supplement), while typical main courses from a choice of nine would be veal escalopes with mushrooms, muscat & honey sauce and John Dory a la'Ostendaise (pan fried and served with prawns). The aim is to serve (mostly) local produce in a Belgian way and they're offering a different experience from other dining options in the area, with a high standard of cooking and good value. Belgian chocolate features every which way on the dessert menu (Dame blanche, a speciality of home-made vanilla ice cream with hot chocolate sauce and cream is worth leaving room for) but fresh fruit salad (with or without champagne mousse) is a refreshing option. Banqueting (55). Not suitable for children after 8pm. **Seats 55** (private room 24). No smoking area. D 7-9 (daily in summer), L Sun only 12.30-5. Set Sun L €21.46, Set D from €24.76. House wine €17.14. Restaurant closed Mon-Tue off season. **Accommodation** The atmosphere is more restaurant with rooms than country house: bedrooms, while large, well-proportioned and comfortable (some with countryside views and open fireplaces), perhaps need more attention before reaching the standard now expected of an Irish country house, although this is fairly reflected in the pricing. Breakfast buffet 8-10am; cooked options include delicious Fermanagh dry-cured black bacon. Children welcome (under 5s free in parents'room, cot available without charge). **Rooms 5** (4 en-suite, 1 with private bathroom). B&B €50 pps, ss €19. Establishment closed 18 Feb-21 Mar. MasterCard, Visa, Laser. **Directions:** main sign on N15 between Ballyshannon & Donegal Town.

Letterkenny

Castle Grove Country House

COUNTRY HOUSE/RESTAURANT

Ballymaleel Letterkenny Co.Donegal
Tel: 074 51118 Fax: 074 51384
Email: marytsweeney@hotmail.com Web: www.castlegrove.com

Parkland designed by "Capability" Brown in the mid 18th-century creates a wonderful setting for Raymond and Mary Sweeney's lovely period house overlooking the lough, which is undoubtedly the first choice for discerning visitors to the area, especially executives with business in Letterkenny. The last few years have seen major changes, including a new conservatory, a larger new restaurant and, most recently, the adjoining coach house has been developed to make seven lovely new bedrooms - all carefully designed and furnished with antiques to feel like part of the main house - and a small conference room (max 30). The original walled garden is also under restoration as part of an ongoing development of the gardens which is expected to continue for several years. Bedrooms are generally spacious and elegantly furnished to a high standard, although several of the older rooms have shower only. Good breakfasts include a choice of fish as well as traditional Irish breakfast, home-made breads and preserves. There is a high standard of maintenance and housekeeping and staff are friendly and helpful. Two boats belonging to the house are available for fishing on Lough Swilly and there is a special arrangment with three nearby golf clubs. Conference/banqueting (30/50). No pets. **Rooms 15** (1 suite, 2 executive rooms, 4 shower only, all no-smoking) B&B from about €57.14, ss €12.70. **Restaurant** Pascal Desnet has been head chef at Castle Grove since 1998. He offers several menus - table'd'hôte, à la carte and vegetarian - at dinner, plus 2 or 3-course set lunch menus. The style is a combination of classic French and modern Irish with international overtones and menus are based on local ingredients, including home grown herbs, vegetables and soft fruit, as well as local seafood including wild salmon and Swilly oysters. Not suitable for children after 8pm. No smoking restaurant. **Seats 50** (private room, 20) L 12.30-2 Mon-Sat, D 6.30-9 daily (early D 6.30-7.30 €25.39), Set L from €13.33, Set D €36.19, also à la carte; house wine from €12.70; sc discretionary. Closed 25-26 Dec. (Restaurant also closed Sun off-season) Amex, Diners, MasterCard, Visa, Laser. **Directions:** Ramelton Rd 3 miles from Letterkenny.

Letterkenny

Letterkenny Court Quality Hotel

HOTEL

Main Street Letterkenny Co. Donegal **Tel: 074 22977**
Web: choicehotelsireland.com

This modern hotel offers a comfortable, reasonably priced base for business, or for touring the area. Bedrooms are attractively furnished in a contemporary style, with the usual facilities, including tea/coffee trays and cable TV. Conference/banqueting (80/50), secretarial services. There are two bars and an informal restaurant (Paddy Garibaldi's).Children welcome (under 10s free in parents' room). Wheelchair access. **Rooms 80** (includes 30 suites, 20 no smoking rooms and 5 for disabled). B&B from about €50. Amex, Diners, MasterCard, Visa. **Directions:** Main Street Letterkenny.

Letterkenny

Metropolitan Bar & Restaurant

RESTAURANT/PUB

106 Lr Main St Letterkenny Co. Donegal **Tel: 074 20800** Fax: 074 20803

The Gallagher family's contemporary Bar and Restaurant is designed on a grand scale and has brought a new style of cosmopolitan hospitality to Letterkenny. **Seats 120.**

Lough Eske

Ardnamona House

COUNTRY HOUSE

Lough Eske Co. Donegal **Tel: 073 22650**
Fax: 073 22819 Email: ardnamona@gofree Web: ardnamona.com

The glorious gardens, which were first planted by Sir Arthur Wallace in the 1880s, are central to the special atmosphere of Kieran and Annabel Clarke's secluded Victorian house overlooking Lough Eske and it's hard to credit that it's only a few miles from Donegal town. It's a gentle, hospitable house and draws people who value its peace and beauty. Front rooms have lovely views over the Lough to the mountains beyond, but all are individualistic with private bathrooms (and a peaceful outlook through rhododendrons and azaleas which have received international acclaim). Gardeners will enjoy doing the garden trail (guide leaflet provided and all plants labelled) and special interest groups are welcome to visit the gardens by arrangement. There are also miles of walks through ancient oak forests full of mosses and ferns and private boating and fishing on the Lough. Except on Sun & Mon, communal dinner is available for residents, by reservation, at 8.30pm. (€25.40; wine licence). Children welcome; dogs allowed by arrangement. **Rooms 6** (all with en-suite or private bathrooms). B&B €60, ss €12.70. Amex, MasterCard, Visa. **Directions:** from Donegal, follow signs to Harveys Point Country Hotel, then pick up sign to Ardnamona.

Lough Eske

Harvey's Point Country Hotel

HOTEL

Lough Eske Co.Donegal **Tel: 073 22208**
Fax: 073 22352 Email: reservations@harveyspoint.com

In a stunning location on the shores of Lough Eske, this unusual hotel has a distinctly Alpine atmosphere, with chalet-style buildings, pergolas and covered walkways joining the residential area to the main bars and restaurant. Maintenance is immaculate and the atmosphere can be deeply peaceful. Rooms, which are based on a Swiss design with show-wood furniture and four-posters, have all been refurbished recently; generally they have good amenities and direct access to verandah and gardens, although some are shower-only (and of continental design, ie without shower cubicle, which can get messy). Conferences/banqueting (200/350). Dinner dances and special breaks are often offered; telephone for details. Not suitable for children. Pets permitted. **Rooms 20** (4 executive rooms, all en-suite, some shower only). B&B €76.18 pps, ss €19.05. Nov-Mar: open Wed-Sun L only. **Restaurant** The restaurant has recently been extended right down to the shores of Lough Eske, taking advantage of the beautiful view and Marc Gysling's cooking - which reflects Swiss training, with Irish influences - should not disappoint. Menus are imaginative but not over-fussy, local produce is used to good effect, the saucing is good and so are details - for example Irish and French cheeses, which are served plated, come with a delicious home-made nut bread as well as grapes and crackers. Service is attentive and professional. The wine list includes a range of 'everyday easy drinking' wines (all under €25) and a good selection of half bottles. **Seats 120** (private room, 80). No smoking restaurant; air conditioning. Toilets wheelchair accessible. D 6-9.30 daily in summer (Nov-Mar: open only Wed D-Sun L)), Sun L 12.30-4.30; Set D €41.90, Set Sun L €18.98; house wine from €18.41; no sc. Amex, Diners, MasterCard, Visa, Laser. **Directions:** 6km from Donegal town - well signed.

Lough Eske

B&B

Rhu Gorse

Lough Eske Co. Donegal **Tel: 073 21685**
Fax: 073 21685 Email: rhugorse@iol.ie

Beautifully located, with stunning views over Lough Eske (and windows built to take full advantage of them), Grainne McGettigan's modern house may not be architecturally outstanding but it has some very special attributes, notably the warmth and hospitality of Grainne herself. Bedrooms and bathrooms are all ship-shape and residents can have afternoon tea as well as breakfast, although not evening meals (however Harveys Point is very close, see entry, and Donegal town also nearby). Animals are central to Rhu Gorse, which is named after a much-loved pedigree dog bred by Grainne's father-in-law (a descendant now follows her around everywhere), and one of her special interests is breeding horses: not your average B&B, but a comfortable, hospitable and very interesting base for a walking holiday or touring the area. **Rooms 3** (2 en-suite, 1 shower only); B&B €38, ss €13. Closed 1 Nov-Easter. Visa. **Directions:** take N15 /N56 from Donegal Town. Take signs for Lough Eske & Harveys Point Hotel. Pick up signs for Rhu-Gorse.

Portsalon

ACCOMMODATION

Croaghross

Portsalon Co. Donegal
Tel: 074 59548 Fax: 074 59548
Email: jkdeane@croaghross.com Web: www.croaghross.com

John and Kay Deane's new single-storey house was purpose built and this latter-day country house enjoys a lovely location on the Fanad peninsula, overlooking Lough Swilly. It's within 5 minutes walk of a great beach - and the renowned 100-year old Portsalon Golf Course - and very convenient to Glenveagh National Park. Three bedrooms open onto a sun terrace, while the two side rooms overlook a landscaped rock garden - one is especially suitable for wheelchair users, who can park beside it. Residents' dinner is, like breakfast, based on local ingredients and good home cooking, with home-made breads and farmhouse cheeses always available (please book ahead; very reasonably priced short wine list offered). Barbecues are sometimes arranged when the weather is favourable and, although officially closed in winter, bookings can be made by arrangement. This is an attractive option for a group, as the house is centrally heated throughout and the living room has a big open fire. The Deanes also have a 3-bedroom self-catering cottage available nearby. Children welcome (under 5s free in parents' room, cot available). Pets permitted. **Rooms 5** (1 for disabled). B&B from €30pps, ss €6.50. Residents D 7.30 pm, from €16.80; wines from €11. Closed 15 Dec-15 Jan. MasterCard, Visa, Laser. **Directions:** Letterkenny - Ramelton- R246 (Milford Direction) through Kerrykeel to Portsalon; opposite golf course turn up hill.

Ramelton

B&B

Ardeen

Ramelton Co Donegal **Tel: 074 51243**
Fax: 074 51243 Email: ardeenbandb@eircom.net Web: www.ardeenhouse.com

Overlooking Lough Swilly, set in its own grounds on the edge of the characterful town of Ramelton and well-located for touring Donegal and Glenveagh National Park, Anne Campbell's mid-nineteenth century house is not too grand and has the comfortable atmosphere of a family home. Individually decorated bedrooms with views over the Lough or nearby hills all have their own character and are charmingly furnished (Anne is very handy with a sewing machine and time available in the winter is well used for guests' comfort). The drawing room and dining room are both furnished with antiques and have open fires, making this a very warm and comfortable place to return to after a day out. No dinners, but there are some good pubs and restaurants nearby (within walking distance in fine weather). Children welcome (cots available free of charge). Pets by arrangement. Garden, tennis. Self-catering cottage also available. **Rooms 5** (4 en-suite, 1 with private bathroom, all no smoking). B&B €30-35. Open all year (Oct-Easter by prior arrangement only). MasterCard, Visa. **Directions:** Entering Ramelton from Letterkenny turn right follow river to Town Hall, turn right 1st house on right.

Ramelton
B&B

Frewin Country House

Ramelton Co Donegal
Tel: 074 51246 Fax: 074 51246
Email: flaxmill@indigo.ie Web: accommodationdonegal.net

Thomas and Regina Coyle have restored this unspoilt Victorian house with the greatest attention to period detail and guests have the opportunity to drink in the atmosphere on arrival while having a cup of tea in the little book-lined library, where the old parish safe is still set in the wall. Beautifully furnished bedrooms have snowy white bedlinen and a robe provided in case of night-time forays along the corridor and a delicious breakfast, including freshly baked breads warm from the oven, is taken communally at a long polished table - at night lit only by candlelight. This beautiful house is most unusual, notably because Thomas Coyle specialises in restoring old buildings and is a collector by nature - much of his collection finds a place in the house, some is for sale in an outbuilding at the back. No dogs. No smoking except in sitting room & library. **Rooms 4** (3 en-suite, 1 with private bath). B&B €45, ss €13. D €25.40 (by arrangement). Closed 25 Dec. MasterCard, Visa. **Directions:** take right turn on approach road from Letterkenny. Located 300 yards on right.

Rathmullan
HOTEL

Fort Royal Hotel

Rathmullan Co.Donegal **Tel: 074 58100**
Fax: 074 58103 Email: fortroyal@eircom.net Web: www.fortroyalhotel.com

Overlooking the sea, and with direct access to a sandy beach, the Fletcher family's attractive Victorian hotel is set in 19 acres of lawn and woodland on the shores of Lough Swilly. It's a good base for family holidays or visiting places of local interest, including Glenveagh National Park and Glebe House, the artist Derek Hill's former home, which has a museum and gallery next door. Public rooms, which include a recently refurbished bar, are spacious, well-proportioned and comfortably furnished in country house style, with big armchairs and open fires. Well-appointed bedrooms (all en-suite, most with bath and shower, a few bath only) are designed for relaxation and enjoy a pleasant outlook over wooded grounds. Croquet, tennis, golf and pitch & putt are available on the premises and activities such as riding and fishing nearby. Special interest breaks offered. Children welcome (under 8s free in parents' room, cot available without charge). Pets permitted. **Rooms 15** (4 executive rooms, all en-suite). B&B €80pps, ss €25. Closed 1 Nov-1 Apr. **Restaurant** This attractive traditional dining room overlooking lawns and woodland is well-appointed with crisp white linen and fresh flowers - just the right setting for good country house cooking. Much of the food at Fort Royal comes from the hotel's own walled gardens and is cooked by Robin and Ann Fletcher's son, Timothy, who has been head chef since 1995. He is establishing a growing reputation for good food at this delightful hotel and offers nightly dinner menus with about five choices on each course and considerately priced with two- or three-course options. Typical examples from a summer menu include a starter of tomato, mozarella & basil; cream of potato & parsley soup; grilled fillets of brill with brill & chive hollandaise (and vegetable selection) and panna cotta with summer fruit compôte. Tea or coffee is served in the lounge afterwards - or, on fine evenings, you could take it outside and enjoy the view down over the lough. **Seats 50.** No smoking restaurant; not suitable for children after 8pm. D daily, 7.30-8.30 (last orders). Set D from €29. *Light lunches are also served in the bar or at tables in the garden. Phone ahead to check availability. Amex, Diners, MasterCard, Visa, Laser. **Directions:** R247 from Letterkenny, through Ramelton - hotel signposted on entry to Rathmullan village.

Rathmullan
COUNTRY HOUSE/RESTAURANT

Rathmullan House

Rathmullan Co.Donegal
Tel: 074 58188 Fax: 074 58200
Email: info@rathhouse.com Web: www.rathmullanhouse.com

IRISH BREAKFAST AWARD - ULSTER

Built as a summer house by the Batt banking family of Belfast in the 1800s, Rathmullan has been run as a country house hotel since 1961 by Bob and Robin Wheeler who have now semi-retired and it's currently managed by their sons William and Mark and daughter-in-law Mary. Set in lovely gardens on the shores of Lough Swilly, this gracious early nineteenth century house is fairly grand with public areas which include three elegant drawing rooms, but it's not too formal - and there's a cellar bar which can be very relaxed. Bedrooms vary in decor, facilities and cost to suit different requirements and budgets - there are luxurious garden suites (close to the swimming pool and leisure facilities) as well as the unpretentious old-fashioned comforts of family rooms at the top of the house, which many guests like best. Donegal has an other-worldliness that is increasingly hard to capture in the traditional family holiday areas, and the laid-back charm of Rathmullan House - albeit given invisible backbone by the professionalism of the Wheeler family and their staff - somehow symbolises that special sense of place. Small conferences (20). Swimming pool, steam room, tennis. Children welcome; cot €12. Pets permitted by arrangment. **Rooms 24** (11 suites, 1 room for disabled). B&B €90pps, ss €25. **Pavilion Dinning Room** The dining room with its unusual tented ceiling makes the most of the garden outlook and provides a fine setting for Seamus Douglas's country house cooking as well as the tremendous breakfasts for which Rathmullan is justly famous. Each morning, a tremendous buffet is laid out, offering a huge variety of juices, fresh and poached fruits with yogurt and carrageen pudding to go with them, cooked ham, smoked salmon and farmhouse cheeses, plus home-baked breads, scones and preserves from the garden - and all this before anything from the menu of hot dishes is even contemplated. Great variety and consistent exellence make Rathmullan a worthy winner of the Denny Irish Breakfast Awards for the Ulster region. **Seats 70.** No smoking restaurant. daily D 7.30-8.45, Set D €42.50; house wine from €13.50; sc 10% Toilets wheelchair accessible.[*A less formal Cellar Restaurant is open 1-4pm, in summer; bar food is also available,1-4 pm daily] Closed 6 weeks from 2 Jan. Amex, MasterCard, Visa, Diners, Laser. **Directions:** Letterkenny to Ramelton - turn right to Rathmullan at the bridge, through village and turn right to hotel.

Rossnowlagh

HOTEL/RESTAURANT

Sand House Hotel

Rossnowlagh Co. Donegal
Tel: 072 51777 Fax: 072 52100
Email: info@sandhouse-hotel.ie Web: www.sandhouse-hotel.ie

Mary and Brian Britton's famous crenellated hotel is perched on the edge of a stunning sandy beach two miles long. The wonderful sea views and easy access to the beach are great attractions of the Sand House. Many of the bedrooms have a superb outlook and all are very comfortable, with good bathrooms - and everyone can enjoy the view from the sun lounge (known as the Atlantic Conservatory). Immaculate maintenance and a high standard of furnishing have always been a special feature, and a major refurbishment of the ground floor, including reception, bars and lounges was recently completed, as well as the addition of a new entrance and lounge areas along the front of the hotel. But it is nevertheless the hospitality of the Britton family and staff (not to mention Mary Britton's reputation for exceptional housekeeping) which is the real appeal of this remarkable hotel. Golf, horse riding, boating and walking available nearby. Conference/banqueting (50). Children welcome (under 2s free in parents' room; cots available). Pets permitted by arrangement. **Rooms 45** (1 suite, 4 shower only, all no-smoking). B&B €85pps, ss €25. Closed Dec-Jan.

Restaurant: The restaurant is rather unexpectedly at the front of the hotel (and therefore faces inland) but is well-appointed, in keeping with the rest of the hotel. Sid Davis, Head Chef since 1994, presents 5-course dinner menus that change daily. It is wholesome fare and simplest choices are usually the wisest; meals finish well with a choice of Irish cheeses or desserts that include very good fruit pies. **Seats 100.** No smoking restaurant. D daily 7-8.45 (Sun to 9), L Sun only. 1-2.30. Amex, Diners, MasterCard, Visa. **Directions:** coast road from Ballyshannon to Donegal Town.

Rossnowlagh

PUB/RESTAURANT/B&B

Smugglers Creek Inn

Rossnowlagh Co.Donegal **Tel: 072 52366**
Fax: 072 22000 Email: smugglerscreek@eircom.net

High up on the cliffs, overlooking Donegal Bay and the Blue Stack Mountains, this inn actually dates back to 1845 although most of what you see today is due to the efforts of the present owner, Conor Britton, who has undertaken a major refurbishment and extension programme since he took over in 1991. Developments to date have been very sympathetically done, with stonework, stone-flagged floors and open fires providing both atmosphere and comfort. The inn has a reputation for traditional bar food - chowder, home-baked bread, garlic mussels - although the standard has been less consistent on recent visits than previously. Many dishes offered on the bar menu - moules marinières, home-made pâté with hot toast - are also on the restaurant menu which majors on seafood (such as Donegal Bay seafood platter) but also provides a wider choice, including vegetarian options. No children after 9 pm. **Seats 60** (private room, 28). Food available daily in summer, 12.30-9, mainly à la carte; house wine €13.97; sc discretionary. Closed Mon & Tues, Oct-Easter. MasterCard, Visa. **Directions:** 6 miles north of Ballyshannon on coast road, 10 miles south of Donegal town.

Tory Island
HOTEL

Ostan Thoraig (Hotel Tory)

West End Tory Island Co. Donegal **Tel: 074 35920**
Fax: 074 35613 Email: hoteltory@tinet.ie

The Gaeltacht (Irish-speaking) island of Tory lies eight miles off the north-west corner of Donegal and, in spite of its exposed position, has been inhabited for four thousand years. Perhaps not surprisingly, this other-worldly island managed quite well without an hotel until recently, but once Patrick and Berney Doohan's Ostan Thoraig was built in 1994 it quickly became the centre of the island's social activities - or, to be more precise, The People's Bar in the hotel quickly became the centre. The hotel is beside the little harbour where the ferries bring in visitors from mainland ports. Although simple, it provides comfortable en-suite accommodation with telephone and television. A special feature of the island is its 'school' of primitive art (founded with the support of well-known artist Derek Hill of nearby Glebe House and Gallery, Church Hill). It even has a king as a founder member: the present King of the Tory is Patsy Dan Rogers, who has exhibited his colourful primitive paintings of the island throughout the Ireland, Britain and America. A tiny gallery on Tory provides exhibition space for the current group of island artists. Small conferences. Children welcome (cot available, small charge). Pets permitted by arrangement. **Rooms 14** (1 for disabled) B&B about €40pps, ss about €13. Wheelchair access. Closed Oct-Easter. [NB: Current data not confirmed at time of going to press; a phone call ahead is strongly advised.] MasterCard, Visa, **Directions:** Tory is accessible by ferry (subject to weather conditions) from several mainland ports: telephone 075-31320 for details, or ask at the hotel.

COUNTY GALWAY

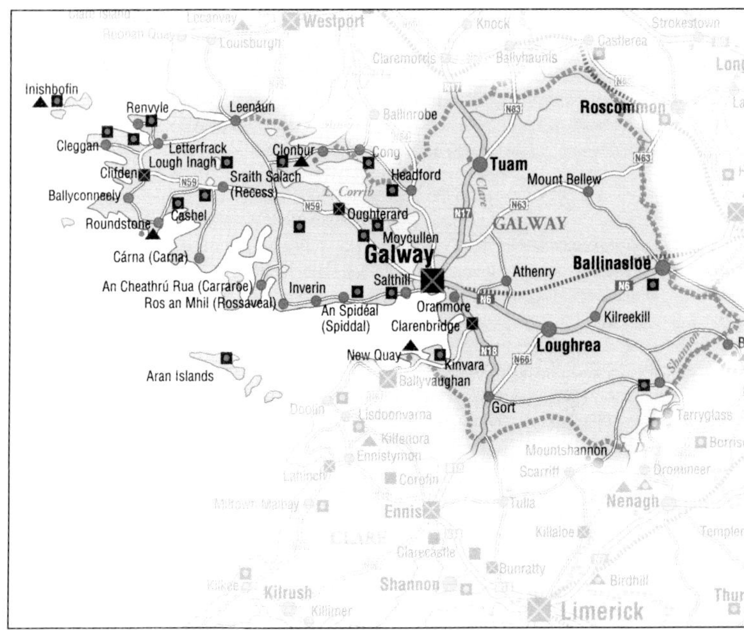

Gaway is buoyant in 2002, borne along on the feelgood factor created by winning the All-Ireland Gaelic Football Final in Croke Park in Dublin on September 23rd 2001. Victory at the end of the longest football season in history is all the sweeter because Galway was one of the counties which fell at an early hurdle. But they then re-entered through the new back door of the repechage system, and eventually got to the final via "the scenic route".

Very appropriate, as it happens, for Galway can match any other Irish county for the variety and charm of its many scenic routes. But it also has more to offer than any other Irish county in the way of slightly offbeat expeditions, in addition to all the usual visual attractions of Ireland's Atlantic seaboard. Visiting the Aran Islands, for instance, can be done by air as well as by sea. Then, too, there are many coastal boat trips, including an informative seaborne tour from Killary Harbour, Ireland's only genuine fjord, while Lough Corrib is also served by miniature cruise liners. As for sport ashore, the Galway Races at the end of July have developed into a six day meeting which is firmly established as Ireland's premier summer horse racing event, while the Ballinasloe International Horse Fair at the end of October is simply unique.

This has to be Ireland's most generous county, for in effect you get two counties for the price of one. They're neatly divided by the handsome sweep of island-studded Lough Corrib, with the big country of many mountains to the west, and rolling farmland to the east. As a bonus, where the Corrib tumbles into Galway Bay, we find one of Ireland's - indeed, one of Europe's - most vibrant cities. Galway city is a bustling place which cheerfully sees itself as being linked to Spain and the great world beyond the Atlantic.

The theme of double value asserts itself in other ways. As Autumn ripeness makes its presence felt, the county and city provide not one, but two, Oyster Festivals. Once September has ushered in the traditional oyster season, Galway's long and distinguished connection with the splendid bivalve mollusc is celebrated first with the Clarenbridge Oyster Festival on the southeast shore of Galway Bay, and then a week or so later with the Galway Oyster Festival itself, right in the heart of the city

However much the Spanish links may have been romanticised as they filter through the mists of time, the fact is that today Galway city is a place confident of itself. Its strength in the west, when seen in the national context, is a welcome counterbalance to the inevitable domination of the Greater Dublin area on the east coast. For though Galway city's population is only a fraction of

Dublin's total, nevertheless the western capital is more than ready to stand fair square for the pride of Connacht and a positive assertion of the qualities of life beyond the Pale and west of the Shannon. It does so with pride and pleasure in its cultural riches and the diversity of its territory.

Lough Corrib is both a geographical and psychological divide. East of it, there's flatter country, home to hunting packs of mythic lore. West of the Corrib - which used itself to be a major throughfare, and is now as ever a place of angling renown - you're very quickly into the high ground and moorland which sweep up to the Twelve Bens and other splendid peaks, wonderful mountains which enthusiasts would claim as the most beautiful in all Ireland.

Their heavily indented coastline means this region is Connemara, the Land of the Sea, where earth, rock and ocean intermix in one of Ireland's most extraordindary landscapes. Beyond, to the south, the Aran Islands are a place apart, yet they too are part of the Galway mix in this fantastical county which has its own magical light coming in over the sea. And yet all its extraordinary variety happens within very manageable distances. For instance, in the western part of Galway city, the mature and leafy suburb of Taylor's Hill speaks eloquently of a quietly comfortable way of life which has been established for well over a century. But much less than an hour's drive away, whether along the shores of Galway Bay, or taking the Corrib route via Oughterard, you'll quickly find yourself in the rugged heart of Connemara, where the scatter of cottages bespeaks a different style, an austere way of life which is every bit as significant an element in that remarkable Galway tapestry which enchants Galwegians and visitors alike.

Local Attractions and Information

GALWAY CITY

Arts Centre 47 Dominick St	091 565886
Galway Airport	091 752874
Galway Arts Festival (July)	091 565886
Galway Crystal Heritage Centre	091 757311
Galway Market (specialist foods), Saturday mornings	
Galway Races (late July/early August, Sept & Oct)	091 753870
Galway Oyster Festival (late September)	091 527282/522066
Kenny's Bookshops & Art Galleries High Street	091 562739
O'Brien Shipping (Aran Island Ferries)	091 563081
Tourist Information	091 563081
Town Hall Theatre	091 569755

COUNTY GALWAY

Aran Islands Heritage Centre	099 61355
Aran Islands Ferries from Rossaveal	091 568903/561767
Aran Islands Flights from Inverin Airport	091 593034
Aughrim Battle of Aughrim Centre	0905 73939
Ballinasloe International Horse Fair (early October)	0905 43453
Clarenbridge Oyster Festival (September)	091 796342
Clifden Connemara Pony Show (mid August)	095 21863
Clifden Connemara Safari - Walking & Islands	095 21071
Gort Thoor Ballylee (Yeats' Tower)	091 631436
Inishbofin Arts Festival (Biennial, September)	095 45909
Inishbofin Ferries (Cleggan)	095 44642
Inisheer Duchas Inis Oirr (Arts Centre)	099 735576
Killary Cruises on Connemara Lady	091 566736
Letterfrack Connemara Bog Week (May)	095 43443
Letterfrack Connemara Sea Week (October)	095 43443
Letterfrack Kylemore Abbey & Gardens	095 41146
Roundstone Roundstone Arts Week (July)	095 35834
Roundstone Traditional bodhran makers	095 35808
Tuam Little Mill (last intact cornmill in area)	093 25486

Galway
RESTAURANT ☆

Archway Restaurant

Victoria Place Galway Co.Galway **Tel: 091 563 693**
Fax: 091 563 074 Email: archway@indigo.ie Web: www. archway.ie

Every inch of space has been used with ingenuity and style at this immaculate little French restaurant - there's a delightful reception area which somehow finds room for a sofa and comfy armchairs and, upstairs, a room of character which promises good things to come and simply oozes professionalism. Now well established as Galway's leading restaurant, tempting menus carry through to excellent cooking and attention to detail - and all at very acceptable prices for the high quality provided. Specialities that give a fair impression of the style include irresistible starters like panfried foie gras with crispy galette of potato and elderberry sauce and main courses which are balanced but understandably strong on seafood, like seared fillet of seabass with herb risotto, beignet of tapenade and bouillabaisse sauce or roast fillet of brill with Jerusalem artichoke, vanilla & cider vinegar sauce. Game is also available in season and vegetarian dishes are imaginative. Classic desserts are worth waiting for and there's a good cheese plate (served in exemplary style with water biscuits, walnuts and a well-dressed salad) as well as delicious petits fours with your tea or coffee, so some forward planning may be required. Very professional service. Children welcome. **Seats 30** (no smoking area; air conditioning). L&D Tue-Sat: 12.30-1.45; 7-9.45. Set L €19.60; D Prestige Menu €38.09; à la carte also available, L&D; house wines from €25. Service discretionary. Closed Sun (except bank hol weekends), Mon & 22 Dec-10 Jan. Amex, Diners, MasterCard, Visa. **Directions:** off Eyre Square.

Galway
ACCOMODATION/GUESTHOUSE

Ardawn House

College Road Galway Co. Galway **Tel: 091 568 833**
Fax: 091 563 454 Email: ardawn@iol.ie Web: www.galway.net/pages/ardawn-house/

Mike and Breda Guilfoyle's hospitable guesthouse is easily found, just a few minutes walk from Eyre Square. Accommodation is all en-suite and rooms are comfortably furnished, with good amenities. But it's Mike and Breda who make Ardawn House special - they take great pride in every aspect of the business, (including an extensive breakfast) and also help guests to get the very best out of their visit to Galway. Children welcome. Pets permitted by arrangement. **Rooms 8** (all shower only & no-smoking). B&B €57pps, ss €32. Closed 22-26 Dec. Amex, MasterCard, Visa, Laser. **Directions:** off N6, take city last exit; follow signs to city centre. First house on right after greyhound track.

Galway
HOTEL

Ardilaun House Hotel

Taylors Hill Galway Co. Galway **Tel: 091 521 433**
Fax: 091 521 546 Email: ardilaun@iol.ie Web: www.ardilaunhousehotel.ie

Although Ardilaun House Hotel is convenient to the city, its wooded grounds give it a country feeling. Friendly, helpful staff make a good impression on arrival and everything about the hotel - which has recently been extensively renovated, extended and refurbished - confirms the feeling of a well-run establishment. Public areas are spacious, elegantly furnished and some - notably the dining room - overlook gardens at the back. Bedrooms are furnished to a high standard (and have modem lines as well as the usual amenities) and in-house leisure facilities include snooker and a new leisure centre with indoor swimming pool, gym, solarium, beauty salon and treatment rooms. Purpose-built conference facilities offer a wide range of options for large and small groups (max 400), with back-up business services, including video conferencing on request. An attractive banqueting room is especially suitable for weddings (up to 270 guests). Children welcome (under 3s free in parents' room, cots available without charge). Pets permitted. **Rooms 89** (1 suite, 2 junior suites, 9 executive rooms, 6 shower only, 8 no-smoking, 3 for disabled). Lift. B&B €101.58 pps, ss €25.39. Closed 23-28 Dec. Amex, Diners, MasterCard, Visa, Laser. **Directions:** 1 mile from city centre, take signposts for Salthill.

Galway
HOTEL

Brennan's Yard Hotel

Lower Merchants Galway Co. Galway **Tel: 091 568 166**
Fax: 091 568 262 Email: info@brennansyardhotel.com Web: brennansyardhotel.com

In an old stone building close to Spanish Arch, this hotel first opened in 1992 - all rooms were individually designed with country pine antiques and Irish craft items, giving the hotel special character. A major expansion and renovation programme saw 25 new rooms added in 1999; original rooms were refurbished to the same standard, the restaurant was also redecorated, a new bar built and, finally, a long-promised new reception and lobby area completed. Providing maintenance programmes are kept up, this will remain an interesting choice for city centre accommodation. Children welcome; cots available. **Rooms 45** (10 no-smoking). Lift. B&B €66.50 pps, ss €16.50. Closed 24-28 Dec. Amex, Diners, MasterCard, Visa, Laser. **Directions:** in Galway city centre, beside Spanish Arch.

Galway

Corrib Great Southern Hotel

HOTEL

Renmore Galway Co. Galway **Tel: 091 755 281**
Fax: 091 751 390 Email: res@corrib.gsh.ie Web: www.greatsouthernhotels.com

This large modern hotel overlooks Galway Bay and has good facilities for business guests and family holidays (ask about their Weekend Specials). Public areas include O'Malleys Pub, which has sea views, and a quieter residents' lounge; in summer evening entertainment and crèche facilities are laid on. Bedrooms vary considerably; the best are spacious and well-planned, with stylish bathrooms but all have good facilities including TV with video channel, phone with modem line, tea/coffee suitable for groups of 8 to 750, with video-conferencing and back-up facilities available; banqueting for up to 550. Children welcome; under 2s free in parents' room, cots available without charge, children's teas (5-6pm); playroom, crèche. Leisure centre; swimming pool. No pets. **Rooms 180** (4 suites, 46 executive, 20 no-smoking, 2 disabled). B&B €123 pps, ss €30. Lift. Closed 24-26 Dec. Amex, Diners, MasterCard, Visa, Laser. **Directions:** on main Dublin Road into Galway city.

Galway

Devondell

B&B

47 Devon Park, Lr. Salthill Galway Co. Galway **Tel: 091 528 306**
Email: devondel@iol.ie Web: www.devondell.com

Although quite unremarkable from the road, Berna Kelly's immaculate house has won many admirers and it's easy to see why: a warm welcome, pretty bedrooms with crisp white linen and many homely touches and Berna's special breakfasts served in a fine dining room overlooking the back garden, are just a few of the reasons guests keep coming back. It's a little difficult to find on the first visit, but well worth the effort. **Rooms 4** (all en-suite & no smoking, 3 shower only). B&B €38 pps. Closed Nov-Mar. No Credit Cards. **Directions:** Fr Griffin Road to T-Junction - take left after 400 - 500 yds, take right at Devon Park House, go to fork 100 yds up, take left and sharp left.

Galway

Galway Bay Hotel, Conference & Leisure Centre

HOTEL

The Promenade Salthill Galway Co. Galway **Tel: 091 520 520**
Fax: 091 520 530 Email: info@galwaybayhotel.net Web: www.galwaybayhotel.net

Like its sister hotel the Hodson Bay (see entry), the Galway Bay is designed to take full advantage of its fine location: thus the entrance and carpark are very sensibly located at the back of the site, allowing unimpeded views over the bay to the distant hills of County Clare from public rooms on the ground floor as well as many of the spacious, well-equipped bedrooms. Excellent facilities for both business and leisure make this a valuable addition to the Galway hospitality scene. Conference/banqueting (1000/600), video-conferencing, business centre. Leisure centre, swimming pool. Children welcome (free in parents room under 2, cot available). Playroom. Garden. No pets. **Rooms 153** (4 suites, 5 executive, 24 no smoking, 9 for disabled). Lifts. B&B €101.58 pps, ss €32. Open all year. Amex, Diners, MasterCard, Visa. **Directions:** located on Salthill Road beside Leisureland overlooking Galway Bay.

Galway

Glenlo Abbey Hotel

HOTEL

Bushypark Galway Co. Galway **Tel: 091 526 666**
Fax: 091 527 800 Email: glenlo@iol.ie Web: www.glenlo.com

Originally an eighteenth century residence, Glenlo Abbey is just two and a half miles from Galway city yet offers all the advantages of the country - the hotel is on a 138-acre estate, with its own golf course and Pavilion. It enjoys views over Lough Corrib and the surrounding countryside. The scale of the hotel is generous throughout, public rooms are impressive and bedrooms are well-furnished with good amenities and marbled bathrooms. The old Abbey has been restored to provide privacy for meetings and private dining, and there is a fully equipped business service bureau to back up seminars, conferences and presentations; (conference/banqueting 250/170). For indoor relaxation there's the Oak Cellar bar (where light food is served) and, in addition to the classical River Room restaurant, the hotel operates an historic Pullman train carriage as a restaurant in the hotel grounds - it's in beautiful order, has a great atmosphere and, needless to say, makes a meal here a memorable event. No pets. Own parking. **Rooms 46** (4 suites, 17 no-smoking, 2 for disabled). Wheelchair access, Lift. Room rate about €300. Open all year. Amex, Diners, MasterCard, Visa. **Directions:** 2.5 miles from Galway on N59 in the direction of Clifden.

Galway

Goya's

CAFÉ 2/3 Kirwans Lane Galway Co. Galway **Tel: 091 567010**
Email: goyas@eircom.net Web: www.goyas.ie

If only for a cup of cappuccino or hot chocolate and a wedge of chocolate cake or a slice of quiche, a restorative visit to this delightful contemporary bakery and café is a must on any visit to Galway. There's something very promising about the cardboard cake boxes stacked up in preparation near the door, the staff are super, there's a great buzz and the food is simply terrific. What's more, you don't even have to be in Galway to enjoy Emer Murray's terrific baking - contact Goya's for her seasonal mail-order catalogues "Fabulous Festive Fancies"(Christmas cakes, plum pudding, mince pies etc) and "Easter Delights" (simnel cake and others); wedding cakes also available. Open all day Mon-Sat. MasterCard, Visa, Laser. **Directions:** on the corner of Kirwan's Lane, between Sheridans Cheesemongers and Kirwan's Lane Restaurant.

Galway

Great Southern Hotel

HOTEL Eyre Square Galway Co. Galway **Tel: 091 564 041**
Fax: 091 566 704 Email: res@galway.gsh.ie Web: www.greatsouthernhotels.com

Overlooking Eyre Square right in the heart of Galway, this historic railway hotel was built in 1845 and has retained many of its original features and old-world charm which mixes easily with modern facilities. Public rooms - notably the foyer - are quite grand. There's a country style bar, O'Flahertys Pub, down in the basement (with access from the Square or the hotel) in addition to the hotel cocktail lounge. Bedrooms, which which have been recently upgraded, are traditionally furnished with dark mahogany and brass light fittings. Conference/banqueting (350/300); back-up business facilities and video-conferencing. Indoor swimming pool. Children under 2 free in parents' room, cots available. No pets. Arrangement with nearby carpark. **Rooms 108** (11 suites, 30 executive, 21 no-smoking, 2 for disabled). Lift. B&B €128 pps, ss €30 (Room only rate: €115). Closed 24-26 Dec. Amex, Diners, MasterCard, Visa, Laser. **Directions:** in centre of city overlooking Eyre Square.

Galway

Jurys Galway Inn

HOTEL féile bia Quay St. Galway Co.Galway **Tel: 091 566 444** Fax: 091 568 415

Jurys Galway Inn is magnificently sited to make the most of both the river - which rushes past almost all the bedroom windows - and the great buzz of the Spanish Arch area of the city (just outside the door). Like the other Jurys room-only 'inns', the hotel offers a fair standard of basic accommodation without frills. Rooms are large (sleeping up to four people) and well finished, with everything required for comfort and convenience - ample well-lit work/shelf space, neat en-suite bathroom, TV, phone - but no extras. Beds are generous, with good-quality bedding, and open wardrobes are more than adequate. Neat tea/coffee-making facilities are built into the design, but there is no room service. Public areas include an impressive, well-designed foyer with seating areas, a pubby bar with good atmosphere and self-service cafeteria. Arrangement with next door car park. **Rooms 128.** Room Rate €94 (max 3 adults; 2 rooms for disabled). Closed 24-26 Dec. Amex, Diners, MasterCard, Visa. **Directions:** city centre, beside Spanish Arch, overlooking the bridge.

Galway

K C Blakes

RESTAURANT 10 Quay Street Galway Co. Galway **Tel: 091 561826** Fax: 091 561829

K C Blakes is named after a stone Tower House, of a type built sometime between 1440 and 1640, which stands as a typical example of the medieval stone architecture of the ancient city of Galway. The Caseys' restaurant, with all its sleek black designer style and contemporary chic could not present a stronger contrast to such a building. Proprietor-chef John Casey sources ingredients for K C Blakes with care and cooks with skill to produce dishes ranging from traditional Irish (beef and Guinness stew), modern Irish (black pudding croquettes with pear & cranberry sauce), classical French (sole meunière) to global cuisine (a huge choice here - let's say chicken fajita) and creative dishes based on the new deep-sea varieties of fish such as siki shark. It's a remarkable operation, aimed at a wide market and keenly priced. Closed 25 Dec. Amex, MasterCard, Visa.

Galway

COUNTRY HOUSE

Killeen House

Bushy Park Galway Co. Galway
Tel: 091 524 179 Fax: 091 528 065
Email: killeenhouse@ireland.com Web: www.killeenhousegalway.com

Catherine Doyle's delightful house really has the best of both worlds. It's on the Clifden road just on the edge of Galway city yet, with 25 acres of private grounds and gardens reaching down to the shores of Lough Corrib, offers all the advantages of the country, too. The house was built in 1840 and has all the features of a more leisurely era, when space was plentiful - not only in the reception rooms, which include an elegant dining room overlooking the gardens (where delicious breakfasts are served in style), but also the bedrooms. These are luxuriously and individually furnished, each in a different period, e.g. Regency, Edwardian and (most fun this one) Art Nouveau. Not suitable for children under 12. Garden. No pets. **Rooms 5** (1 shower only). Lift. B&B €70pps, ss €30. Closed 23-27 Dec. Amex, Diners, MasterCard, Visa. **Directions:** on N59 between Galway city and Moycullen village.

Galway

Kirbys of Cross Street

RESTAURANT Cross Street Galway Co. Galway **Tel: 091 569404** Fax: 091 569403

One of a trio of establishments situated on the corner of Cross Street and Kirwan's Lane (the others are two of Galway's leading pubs, Busker Browne's and The Slate House), this dashingly informal two-storey restaurant offers contemporary cuisine in specialities like grilled black & white seafood pudding on a seafood vegetable salad. No-smoking area; air conditioning. Children over 7 welcome. No parking. **Seats 80.** L&D daily. Closed 25 Dec. Amex, Diners, MasterCard, Visa. **Directions:** city centre - on corner of Cross street and Kirwan's Lane.

Galway

Kirwan's Lane Restaurant

RESTAURANT Kirwans Lane Galway Co. Galway **Tel: 091 568 266** Fax: 091 561645

Clifden man Michael O'Grady is the chef-proprietor at this classy contemporary restaurant in a laneway just beside the Hotel Spanish Arch. It opened in 1996, was an immediate success and extended to double the capacity less than three years later. Recent visits confirm that it remains one of the most interesting restaurants in the city. Menus offer a wide choice of international dishes based on local ingredients - the style is light and fresh, with lots of seafood, vibrant salads and vegetables, typically seen in a dish of seared fresh scallops with citrus tagliatelle, leek ribbons, cherry tomatoes & black bean butter. The style at lunch and dinner is similar; evening menus are slightly more formal, but not overlong. Live piano playing sometimes adds to the atmosphere. Not suitable for children under 7. No parking (multi-storey carpark nearby). **Seats 100.** No smoking area; air conditioning. L 12.30-2.30, D 6-10 Mon-Sat, all à la carte, house wine about €18; sc discretionary. Toilets wheelchair accessible. Closed Sun & 24-30 Dec. Amex, MasterCard, Visa, Laser. **Directions:** just off Cross St and Quay St.

Galway

The Malt House

RESTAURANT Old Malt Shopping Mall High St Galway Co. Galway **Tel: 091 567 866**
Fax: 091 563 993 Email: info@malt-house.com Web: www.malt-house.com

The Cunningham's welcoming old restaurant and bar in a quiet cul-de-sac laneway off High Street has great character and a friendly attitude. There's a lunchtime bar menu with soups and salads, served with good home-made bread, popular hot seafood dishes - baked garlic mussels, panfried crab claws - steaks and vegetarian dishes. Dinner menus are more formal but the emphasis is still on fairly traditional dishes - and none the worse for that. No parking. **Seats 50.** No smoking restaurant; air conditioning. Mon-Sat: L 12.30-2.30, D 6.30-10.30. also Bar Food. Set L€20.95, Set D €32, à la carte available, house wine €17.14; no sc. Closed Sun & 25 Dec-3 Jan. Amex, Diners, MasterCard, Visa, Laser. **Directions:** city centre location beside The Kings Head Pub.

McDonagh's Seafood House

Galway
RESTAURANT

22 Quay Street Galway Co. Galway **Tel: 091 565 001**
Fax: 091 562 246 Email: mcdonagh@tinet.ie

This unusual restaurant is a fish shop during the day - they buy whole catches from local fishermen and have it on sale in the shop within a couple of hours of leaving the boat. Buying the whole catch guarantees the wide variety that has made the shop famous. Then, when it comes to the cooking, there's the fish & chips operation - select your variety and see it cooked in front of you. On the other side of the shop is the Seafood Bar, a more formal restaurant where an extensive range of dishes is offered. They even do their own smoking on the premises and fish caught by anglers can be brought in and smoked to take home - and they do party food, too. The Bill of Fare is informative on the characteristics and eating quality of mainstream fish and shellfish - variety and good value are the key points here. The family also owns the Hotel Spanish Arch (091 569600) nearby and a wine bar across the street. Carpark nearby. **Seats 42.** No smoking area; air conditioning. L 12-2.30 daily, D 5-10 Mon-Sat, Set L about €12, Set D from about €20, à la carte available, house wine about €13; sc discretionary. Closed 24-25 Dec & 1 Jan. Amex, Diners, MasterCard, Visa, Laser. **Directions:** at bottom of Quay Sreet, near Jury's Inn and The Spanish Arch.

Norman Villa

Galway
ACCOMMODATION

86 Lower Salthill Galway Co. Galway **Tel: 091 521131**
Fax: 091 521131 Email: normanvilla@oceanfree.net

Dee and Mark Keogh's guesthouse is exquisite. It's a lovely old house, immaculately maintained and imaginatively converted to make the most of every inch, ensuring guest comfort without spoiling the interior proportions. It's dashingly decorated, with lovely rich colours. A great collection of modern paintings looks especially magnificent juxtaposed with antique furniture. Dee and Mark are dedicated hosts, too. Bedrooms have neat shower rooms ingeniously fitted into tiny spaces and also phones and tea/coffee-making facilities. A converted coach house in the garden also provides a self-contained suite. Garden. No pets. **Rooms 6** (all shower only & no-smoking) B&B €51 pps, ss €12. Closed 30 Nov- 1 Feb. MasterCard, Visa. **Directions:** follow signs from Galway city centre to Salthill, then Lower Salthill - house is beside P.J. Flaherty's Pub.

Park House Hotel

Galway
HOTEL

Forster St. Eyre Square Galway Co. Galway **Tel: 091 564 924**
Fax: 091 569 219 Email: parkhousehotel@eircom.net Web: www.parkhousehotel.ie

This attractive, owner-run hotel just off Eyre Square is furnished to a high standard and warmly decorated throughout. Providing a high level of personal service is a particular point of pride, making this an especially comfortable base for visitors on business or leisure. There are facilities for small conferences and banqueting (40/50) and one of the hotel's greatest assets in this busy city is a private residents' car park. Children welcome (under 12s free in parents' room, cots available). No pets. **Rooms 57** (all en-suite, 1 for disabled). Lift. B&B €120pps, ss €120. Closed 24-26 Dec. Amex, Diners, MasterCard, Visa, Laser. **Directions:** city centre, off Eyre Square.

Radisson SAS Hotel

Galway
HOTEL

Lough Atalia Road Galway Co. Galway
Tel: 091 538300 Fax: 091 538380
Email: salesgalway@radissonsas.com Web: www.radissonsas.com

People coming out of the new Radisson SAS tend to have a smile on their faces - it's that kind of place. From the minute you step into the high, airy foyer with its satellite reception desk, unusual sculptures and audacious greenery you feel this is a place designed to make people feel good. The feeling is confirmed by the atmosphere in adjacent public areas, including a very pleasant big lounge area a few steps up, in a sunny position looking over the (not quite finished) leisure centre to Lough Atalia and a bar in a cosier position towards the front of the hotel. The big, bright colourful Marina restaurant has great appeal in the modern idiom and its design works equally well for formal dining and as an encouraging place start to the day with the famous Scandinavian buffet breakfast. Bedrooms are designed in three distinct styles - Scandinavian, Maritime or Classic - all equally appealing in their way and furnished to a high standard, with exellent bathrooms and facilities (air conditioning, phone/ voice mail & modem, safe, TV with video channel as well as the more mundane but necessary tea/coffee making and trouser press); all of this plus 3-hour express laundry and 24 hour room service make this the ideal business accommodation. Business centre, secretarial services, video-conferencing. Conference/banqueting (660/480). Leisure centre (indoor swimming pool); children's golf. Children welcome (under 10s free in parents' room, cot available without charge). **Rooms 204** (3 suites, 10 junior suites, 138 no smoking, 10 for disabled.) Lift. B&B €95, ss €51. Amex, Diners, MasterCard, Visa, Laser. **Directions:** by lake Lough Atalia, 200m from Bus & Train Station.

Galway

Tigh Neachtain

PUB

Cross Street Galway Co. Galway **Tel: 091 568820**

Tigh Neachtain is one of Galway's oldest pubs - the origins of the building are medieval - and it has been in the same family for a century. Quite unspoilt, it has great charm and a friendly atmosphere - the pint is good and there's bar food. But perhaps the nicest thing of all is the way an impromptu traditional music session can get going at the drop of a hat. The River God Café restaurant is on the first floor. Closed 25 Dec & Good Fri. No credit cards.

Galway

Westwood House Hotel

HOTEL

Dangan Upper Newcastle Galway Co. Galway **Tel: 091 521 442** Fax: 091 521 400
Email: westwoodreservations@eircom.net Web: www.westwoodhousehotel.com

This new hotel is in the same group as the Schoolhouse Hotel in Dublin and the Station House Hotel, Clifden (see entries). Well located, on the edge of Galway and convenient to both the city and Connemara, it's set well back from the road and offers a high standard of accommodation for business and leisure at fairly reasonable prices. Air-conditioned throughout, the hotel has good conference/banqueting facilities (350/275) with back-up services and fax/ISDN lines in bedrooms. A range of 2-3 night leisure breaks offers particularly good value and head chef Brenadan Scannell, who has been with the hotel since it opened in 1999, has established an excellent reputation for the hotel's Meridian Restaurant. No pets. **Rooms 58** (6 junior suites, 8 executive, 17 no smoking, 3 for disabled). Lift. B&B €99.50pps, ss €25. Closed 24-25 Dec. Amex, Diners, MasterCard, Visa, Laser. **Directions:** on edge of Galway city, take the N59 for Clifden Road.

Aran Islands

Kilmurvey House

Kilronan Inishmore Co. Galway **Tel: 091 961 218**
Fax: 099 61397 Email: kilmurveyhouse@eircom.net Web: www.kilmurveyhouse.com

Right at the foot of the island's most famous attraction, Dun Aengus fort (and beside the visitor centre), this 150 year old stone house is near Kilronan harbour and within walking distance of beaches, pubs and restaurants. It has been extended to provide extra en-suite accommodation, but that is completely in line with the habit of organic development in a family home that includes furnishings accumulated from the early 20th century (or beyond), to this day - an interesting record of changing interior fashions through a century or more. But it's the scrupulous cleanliness and Treasa Joyce's warm and chatty personality that make this an ideal place to stay for a cycling or walking holiday, or just to relax. Children welcome (unders 5s free in parents' room) **Rooms 12** (all en-suite and no smoking), B&B €35, ss €15. Closed 31 Oct-1 Apr. MasterCard, Visa, Laser.

Aran Islands

Man Of Aran Cottages

RESTAURANT/B&B

Kilmurvey Inishmore Co. Galway
Tel: 099 6130 Fax: 099 61324
Email: manofaran@eircom.net

Despite its fame - this is where the film Man of Aran was made - Joe and Maura Wolfe make visiting their home a genuine and personal experience. The cottage is right beside the sea, surrounded by wild flowers, and Joe has somehow managed to create a successful organic garden in this exposed location, so their meals may include his vegetables (even artichokes and asparagus), salads, nasturtium flowers and young nettle leaves as well as Maura's home-made soups, stews and freshly-baked bread and cakes. They're open for lunch in summer and you can eat in the little restaurant or, on fine days, take your food out to benches in the garden with stunning views across the sea towards the mountains. Packed lunches are available too. Maura and Joe also cook almost every night during the summer; occasionally, they make arrangements for guests staying with them to go to Teach Nan Phaidi (5 minutes walk, see separate entry). **Seats 40.** L 12.30-3 (soups, sandwiches, desserts); D 7.30. Set D from €22; house wine from €16. **Accommodation** The three little bedrooms are basic but full of quaint, cottagey charm and they're very comfortable, although only one is en-suite. Breakfast will probably be a well cooked full-Irish - made special by Joe's beautifully sweet home-grown cherry tomatoes if you are lucky - although they'll do something different if you like. No pets. **Rooms 3** (1 en-suite). B&B €28-32, ss €9. Closed Nov-Mar. **Directions:** mini bus or cycle from Kilronan.

Aran Islands
RESTAURANT/GUESTHOUSE

Pier House Restaurant & Guest House

Kilronan Inishmore Co. Galway
Tel: 099 61417 Fax: 099 61122 Email: pierhouse@iol.ie

In a new building, right on the pier where the boats arrive, Maura & Padraig Joyce's house incorporates a restaurant where Ballymaloe-trained Aine Maguire cooks. The accommodation is smartly decorated and comfortable, with more facilities than most island accommodation - there's a large residents lounge and bedrooms (which all have views) have TV and phones as well as communal tea/coffee making facilities downstairs to use at any time. It is perhaps less characterful than some of the older houses, but very comfortable and well-run. Self-catering cottage also available. **Rooms 12** (all en-suite & no smoking). B&B €34.28, ss €16.51. **Restaurant** Aine Maguire has brought the Ballymaloe philosophy to Kilronan and is serving wonderful food, with the emphasis on good ingredients and clean, modern cooking. Lots of local seaweeds gathered from the shores are used as other cooks use herbs, especially in pasta sauces. Other house specialities include clam chowder, local fish, such as ray with herbed yogurt & caramelised butter and monkfish with smoked butter hollandaise & salsa verde - butter is smoked by the same local smoker, Gearoid de Brun, who does other produce, including smoked salmon and tuna. Seafood tends to dominate, but they also do great steaks and sometimes get organic beef from Inis Oirr - where possible Aine uses organic and free range products, including local eggs. A wide selection of yeast, sourdough and soda breads is served, also home-made ices. It's quite an expensive restaurant and if there is a criticism, it would be that pricing seems inconsistent (eg stuffed mackerel is not much less than steak at €17.27/17.43 respectively), but to find food of this quality on an island is a blessing in itself so it seems churlish to be critical. Gourmet pizza night, Tue. **Seats 46.** No smoking restaurant. Children welcome (from 6-7.30). D Tue-Sun, 6-10. A la carte. House wine €15.24, sc discretionary. Closed Nov-Mar. MasterCard, Visa, Laser. **Directions:** Galway to Rossaveal then ferry, 30 minutes to Island.

Aran Islands
RESTAURANT

Teach Nan Phaidai

Chill Mhiurbhigh Kilmurvey Inishmore Co. Galway
Tel: 099 61330 Fax: 099 61330

Just around the corner from Man of Aran Cottage, this quaint little thatched restaurant is whitewashed in traditional fashion with cheerful yellow windows. Inside, it's clean and fresh with a huge open fireplace providing ventilation as well as warmth - a charming setting for good food, which is served all day. Snacks are available morning and afternoon, while the lunch menu offers more substantial fare - Teach nan Phaidi chowder, whiskey cured Aran smoked salmon to start, perhaps, then pan fried fillet of hake, a small sirloin steak or vegetable korma and a selection of desserts. Evening menus overlap with lunch but are more formal and offer a wider choice, including roast crispy half duckling with a honey citrus sauce, perhaps, and seared king scallops with bacon and a white wine and butter sauce - served with island-grown, seaweed nurtured potatoes. Desserts include lovely home-made ice cream. It's popular with locals as well as visitors, as there's a great buzz, the cooking's good (chefs tend to change at island restaurants, but the standard here seems to be consistent) and service, by charming well-informed staff, is excellent. An efficient bus-service will collect and drop-off people from all B&B's throughout the island. **Seats 60.** Children welcome. Open 11 am-9pm daily; L 11-3.30, D 7-9. Average main course about €19; house wine about €18. Closed Christmas week. MasterCard, Visa.

Ballinasloe
HOTEL

Haydens Gateway Business & Leisure Hotel

Dunlo Street Ballinasloe Co.Galway **Tel: 0905 42347**
Fax: 0905 42895 Email: cro@lynchhotels.com Web: www.lynchhotels.com

Now in the ownership of the Lynch family (who have hotels in Ennis, Limerick, Kilkee and Galway), this long-established hotel is the centre of local activities in and around Ballinasloe - conference facilities are good and there's a pleasant banqueting room overlooking the courtyard garden at the back. As it's about halfway between Dublin and Galway, with refreshments available all day, it's a handy place to break the journey although, on recent visits, the standard of tidiness in public areas has been less than satisfactory. Conference/banqueting (300/350), Special breaks (golf etc). Children welcome. No pets. **Rooms 48** (7 executive rooms, 2 no-smoking, 1 for disabled). Lift. B&B €82.53pps, ss €25.39 (room-only rate: €74.91). Bar Food 12.30-10 daily; buffet. Open all year. Amex, Diners, MasterCard, Visa. **Directions:** N6 Galway-Dublin road, on main street of town.

Ballinasloe

RESTAURANT/PUB

Tohers Restaurant & Bar

18 Dunlo Street Ballinasloe Co Galway
Tel: 0905 44848 Fax: 0905 44844

This family-run pub on the main street is very attractive, with a traditional style bar on the ground floor and the restaurant in three separate dining rooms upstairs. A tempting bar lunch menu offers simple but tasty fare: a choice of soups with home-baked bread, a range of freshly-baked baguettes with various fillings (roast marinated chicken breast with curry mayonnaise, for example, or BLT), smoked salomon & cream cheese bagel or chicken salad - plus daily hot specials like home-made burger and chicken fajitas. If you can hit Ballinasloe at lunch time, this is the spot to be and it's only a short walk up from the new marina too. Restaurant meals are, of course, more formal and offer more choice. Bar meals Mon-Sat, 12-3. Restaurant: Tue-Sat D 6.30-10. Set D €32 (on request, for parties only), otherwise à la carte; house wine €17.14. SC discretionary. Restaurant closed Sun, Mon. Establishments closed 2 weeks mid Oct. MasterCard, Visa, Laser. **Directions:** town centre.

Barna

O'Grady's on the Pier

RESTAURANT Sea Point Barna Co. Galway **Tel: 091 592223** Fax: 091 590677

In a stunning position, with views over the harbour and beach to distant mountains, Michael O'Grady's latest venture opened in 2000 and has attracted a loyal clientèle. Some of the elements of the stream-lined contemporary wine bar are there (notably on the first floor) but tradition has also been allowed its place - the old fireplace has been kept, for example, which bodes well for cosy sessions in wild weather - and Michael's aim is for his seafood to be "simply prepared and very fresh as my father did it years ago". This he is doing very well, although fans of the sister restaurants (notably Kirwans in Galway city, which is probably the most fashion-conscious of the group) should not be disappointed as world cuisine is certainly allowed a little space here too, notably among the daily blackboard specials. Always innovative, Michael was one of the first chefs to pay serious atttention to the new deep-sea varieties of fish, which are becoming increasingly important as traditional fish stocks decline - and he was the worthy joint winner of the 2001 Creative Seafood Dish Award (together with Cathal Reynolds of Cré-na-Cille, Tuam). Children welcome. **Seats 85** (max table size 10, private room 22). No smoking area, air-conditioning. Open Sat & Sun 12-3; D daily 6-10.Set L €19, also à la carte L&D; house wine€16. Closed 23 Dec-3 Jan. MasterCard, Visa, Amex, Laser, Switch. **Directions:** Galway City - Salthill - Barna village, down to pier, 4 miles from city.

Cashel

COUNTRY HOUSE
RESTAURANT

Cashel House Hotel

Cashel Connemmara Co. Galway
Tel: 095 31001 Fax: 095 31077
Email: info@cashel-house-hotel.com Web: www.cashel-house-hotel.com

Dermot and Kay McEvilly were among the pioneers of the Irish country house movement when, as founder members of the Irish Country Houses and Restaurants Association (now known as The Blue Book) they opened Cashel House as an hotel in 1968. The following year General and Madame de Gaulle chose to stay for two weeks, an historic visit of which the McEvilly's are justly proud - look out for the photographs and other memorabilia in the hall. The de Gaulle visit meant immediate recognition for the hotel, but it did even more for Ireland by putting the Gallic seal of approval on Irish hospitality and food. Comfort abounds here, even luxury, yet it's tempered by common sense, a love of gardening and the genuine sense of hospitality that ensures each guest will benefit as much as possible from their stay. The gardens, which run down to their own private beach, contribute greatly to the atmosphere, and the accommodation includes especially comfortable ground floor garden suites, which are also suitable for less able guests (wheelchair accessible but no special grab rails etc in bathrooms). Relaxed hospitality combined with professionalism have earned an international reputation for this outstanding hotel and its qualities are perhaps best seen in details - log fires that burn throughout the year, day rooms furnished with antiques and filled with fresh flowers from the garden, rooms that are individually decorated with many thoughtful touches. Service (with all day room service, including all meals) is impeccable and superb breakfasts include a wonderful buffet display of home-made and local produce, including everything from soda bread and marmalade to black pudding in addition to hot dishes cooked from the breakfast menu. (Cashel House was winner of the 2001 Denny Breakfast Award for Connaught.) Not very suitable for children, but cots are available (€12.70). Pets permitted by arrangement. **Rooms 32** (13 suites, 9 superior rooms, 1 shower only, 16 no-smoking). B&B €110pps, no ss; sc 12.5%. **Restaurant** A large conservatory extension (completely revamped in 2001) enhances this well-appointed split-level restaurant. Although assisted by head chef Eileen Joyce since 1999, Dermot McEvilly has overseen the kitchen personally since the hotel opened, providing a rare consistency of style in five-course dinners that make imaginative use of local produce and seafood - lobster, oysters, fresh and home-smoked wild salmon, mussels, turbot, monkfish - is a great strength. Connemara lamb regularly stars and another, more unusual, speciality is roast stuffed crown of pork. Garden produce is also much in evidence throughout, in soups, salads, side dishes, fine vegetarian dishes and desserts, such as rhubarb tart or strawberries and cream. Farmhouse cheeses come with home-baked biscuits and a choice of coffees and infusions is offered to finish. Service, under the personal supervision of Kay McEvilly and restaurant manager Ray Doorley, is excellent. An interesting wine list includes four House Wines (€21.50). Lunch and afternoon tea are served daily in the bar (2-5). **Seats 70.** No smoking restaurant. D daily 7.30-8.30, Set D €44.44; à la carte bar L available (1-2pm). 12.5% s.c. added to bills. Closed 10 Jan-10 Feb. Amex, MasterCard, Visa, Laser. **Directions:** south off N59 (Galway-Clifden road) 1 mile west of recess.

Cashel

Zetland Country House Hotel

HOTEL/RESTAURANT — Cashel Bay Cashel Co. Galway **Tel: 095 31111**
Fax: 095 31117 Email: zetland@iol.ie Web: www.connemara.net/zetland/

On an elevated site, with views over Cashel Bay, Zetland House Hotel was originally built as a sporting lodge in the early 19th century - and still makes a good base for fishing holidays. This is a charming house, with a light and airy atmosphere and an elegance bordering on luxury, in both its spacious antique-furnished public areas and bedrooms. The latter are individually decorated in a relaxed country house style. The gardens surrounding the house are very lovely too, greatly enhancing the peaceful atmosphere of the house. Incidentally, the origin of the name goes back to the time when the Shetland Islands were under Norwegian rule and known as the Zetlands - the Earl of Zetland (Lord Viceroy 1888-1890) was a frequent visitor here, hence the name. Small conferences/banqueting (60). Special breaks. Garden, tennis, billiards. Children welcome (under 4s free in parents' room; cot available: €12.70). Pets permitted by arrangement in some areas. **Rooms 19** (6 executive rooms, 1 shower only). B&B about €80 pps, ss about €35; 12.5% s.c. added to bills. Wheelchair access. **Restaurant** Like the rest of this lovely hotel, the dining room is bright, spacious and elegant. Decorated in soft, pretty shades of pale yellow and peach that contrast well with antique furniture - including a fine sideboard where plates and silver are displayed - the restaurant is in a prime position for taking full advantage of the view and makes awonderful place to watch the light fading over the mountains and the sea. A warm welcome and quietly efficient service from staff who are clearly happy in their work greatly ehances the pleasure of dining - and the quality of food and head chef Paul Meehan's cooking (in an apppropriate country house style) are both very high. Excellent breakfasts are also served in the restaurant - home-made preserves are an especially delicious feature. Children welcome. **Seats 60.** No smoking restaurant. L 12.30-2, D 7.30-8.30. Set D about €40; house wine about €23. Closed Nov-Apr. Amex, Diners, MasterCard, Visa. **Directions:** N59 from Galway. Turn left after Recess.

Clarenbridge

Oyster Manor Hotel

HOTEL — Clarenbridge Co. Galway **Tel: 091 796777**
Fax: 091 796770 Email: reservations@oystermanorhotel.com Web: oystermanorhotel.com

Family-owned by Ned and Julianne Forde, this modern hotel on the edge of Clarenbridge is popular for conferences and family celebrations (800/350 respectively) and the large bar at the back makes a focal point, with live music most nights. Rooms have all the necessary amenities and are comfortably furnished with modern facilities. Children free in parents' room up to 10; cot available without charge. No pets. **Rooms 26** (1 suite, 3 executive rooms, 3 no-smoking). B&B about €90pps. Wheelchair access. Closed 24-26 Dec. Amex, Diners, MasterCard, Visa. Directions: Main Limerick Road, South East of Galway City. Amex, Diners, MasterCard, Visa. **Directions:** main Limerick road, South East of Galway city.

Clarenbridge

Paddy Burkes

PUB/RESTAURANT — Clarenbridge Co. Galway **Tel: 091 796226** Fax: 091 796016

Established in 1650 and still going strong, Paddy Burkes' internationally famous pub and seafood bar has been home to the Clarenbridge Oyster Festival for nearly half a century. Extensive renovations have recently brought many improvements. Although most famous for its seafood, this characterful old pub serves much else besides, including stir-fries, curries, steaks and vegetarian dishes, both on the regular bar menu and as daily specials. The visitors book reads like a Who's Who - an unbelievable array of the rich and famous. And that's not including the ones who "prefer not to be named". * The pub changed hands in 2000, but no significant changes have so far been made by the new owners. Bar Meals 12.30-10 daily no smoking area; air conditioning; wheelchair access. Closed 24-25 Dec & Good Fri. Amex, Diners, MasterCard, Visa. **Directions:** seven miles south of Galway city on Limerick Road.

Clifden

HOTEL

Abbeyglen Castle

Sky Road Clifden Co. Galway **Tel: 095 21201**
Fax: 095 21797 Email: info@abbeyglen.ie Web: abbeyglen.ie

Set romantically in its own parkland valley overlooking Clifden and the sea, Abbeyglen is family-owned and run in a very hands-on fashion by Paul and Brian Hughes. It's a place that has won a lot of friends over the years and it's easy to see why: it's big and comfortable and laid-back - and there's a generosity of spirit about the place which is very charming. Public areas include a spacious drawing room for residents and a relaxing, pubby bar with open peat fire. Bedrooms (all with good bathrooms) are quite big and have been recently refurbished, as part of an ongoing improvement programme. Helipad. Garden. Pitch & putt. Snooker. Outdoor swimming pool. Pets permitted. Not suitable for children. Wheelchair accessible. **Rooms 29** (9 superior, 20 standard, all en-suite) Lift. B&B about €90pps, ss about €30. Closed 10 Jan-1 Feb. Amex, Diners, MasterCard, Visa. **Directions:** about 300 yards out of Clifden on the Sky road, on the left.

Clifden

HOTEL

Ardagh Hotel & Restaurant

Ballyconneely Road Clifden Co. Galway
Tel: 095 21384 Fax: 095 21314
Email: ardaghhotel@eircom.net Web: www.commerce.ie/ardaghhotel

Beautifully located, overlooking Ardbear Bay, Stephane and Monique Bauvet's family-run hotel is well known for hospitality, comfort and good food. Public areas have style, too, in a gentle sort of way - not "decorated" but furnished in a homely style with good fabrics and classic country colours. Turf fires, comfortable armchairs and a plant-filled conservatory area upstairs all indicate that peaceful relaxation is the aim here. Bedrooms vary according to their position but they are all well-furnished, with all the amenities required for a comfortable stay. (Not all have sea views - single rooms are at the back with a pleasant countryside outlook, and have shower only). Bedrooms include some extra large rooms, especially suitable for families. Children welcome (under 5s free in parents' room, cot available without charge); pets permitted by arrangement. **Rooms 21** (3 suites, 4 shower only). B&B €90pps, ss €40. **Restaurant** The well-appointed restaurant is on the first floor and set up to take full advantage of the view, providing a fitting setting for Monique's fine cooking, which specialises in local seafood. She makes imaginative use of local ingredients, including organic vegetables, in nightly 5-course dinner menu offering plenty of choice - typically in a house speciality such as mussels with roast monkfish tail on baby spinach with saffron, or roast rack of Connemara lamb with a Mediterranean vegetable tart , on a tomato & thyme jus. The dinner menu is good value, offering a wide choice with lobster available at a reasonable supplement. **Seats 55.** No smoking area. (Light bar food, 11-5 daily. D 7.15-9.30 daily, Set D €44.50, à la carte also available; house wine €17.75; sc discretionary. Closed Nov-Mar. Amex, Diners, MasterCard, Visa, Laser. **Directions:** 2 km south of Clifden on Ballyconneely-Roundstone road, on left hand side.

Clifden

COUNTRY HOUSE

Dolphin Beach Country House

Lower Sky Road Clifden Co. Galway
Tel: 095 21204 Fax: 095 22935
Email: dolphinbeach@iolfree.ie Web: www.connemara.net/dolphinbeachhouse

Billy and Barbara Foyle's stunning beachside house is set in 14 acres of wilderness, which only serves to emphasise the style and luxury within. It started as an early 19th century farmhouse, now totally renovated and extended to include new bedrooms. Those familiar with the old Foyle magic will find it much in evidence here: Billy is brother to Paddy, of The Quay House and Eddie, who has been running the original family hotel in Clifden for many years and recently acquired Rosleague House at Letterfrack from their sister

Anne... Something they have in common is a talent for creating original interiors and, in this case, an example is Billy's unusual woodwork - bedheads, mirror frames, anything that takes his fancy - which is an important characteristic of the fresh style at Dolphin Beach. They have also spared no cost to ensure that the best materials are used throughout which creates a wonderful feeling of quality: bedrooms are finished to a very high standard, with antique furniture, pristine bedlinen, lovely bathrooms and underfloor heating. They grow their own organic vegetables too, and these, together with other local produce, notably seafood and Connemara lamb, are used for residents' dinners which are served each evening in a dining room overlooking the beach (reservations required when booking your room). Breakfast follows the same philosophy - you can even collect your own free-range eggs for breakfast. Not suitable for children. No pets. **Rooms 8** (all en suite, some shower only). B&B €44.44 pps, ss €12.70. Resdidents dinner €29.21 (booking essential). Visa, Laser. **Directions:** take Sky Road from Clifden, approx 3 miles.

Clifden

Fire and Ice

RESTAURANT Station House Courtyard Clifden Co. Galway **Tel: 095 22946**
Email: fireandice@eircom.net

Although located at The Station House Hotel, this special place is independently run by Gary Masterson and Winnie Lynch, and, not only does it emphatically have its own personality, but it has quietly taken its place as the leading restaurant in the area. Both are experienced and well-travelled chefs, so the world cuisine offered in this pleasing contemporary restaurant is especially appropriate and the cooking has a ring of authenticity not always found in Irish restaurants following this style. The restaurant is very attractive - high-ceilinged, with big windows, lots of warm wood tones and colourful high-backed chairs - providing a stylish backdrop for what they accurately call "fine dining without the formality and pretentiousness". Carefully sourced, accurately cooked dishes reflect a wide range of influences, in dishes like mussels with chilli, ginger, lemongrass, coconut & coriander; crispy duck with stirfry noodles, plum jus and sweet chilli sauce, monkfish & black pudding, onion & leek marmalade with rösti potatoes & pancetta dressing. Presentation seems effortlessly stylish, flavours are clear and well-combined, service is well-informed and friendly - and it's great value. Not suitable for children under 10 after 8 pm. **Seats 45.** No smoking restaurant; air conditioning. D Tue-Sat (also Sun in Aug), Sun Brunch 11.30-3.30. A la carte (average starter €7, average main course €18.50). House wine from €15. SC discretionary. Closed Sun (except Aug), Mon. MasterCard, Visa. **Directions:** main Galway-Clifden road, in Station House Courtyard. 2 minutes walk from Clifden town centre.

Clifden

Mitchell's Restaurant

RESTAURANT Market Street Clifden Co. Galway **Tel: 095 21867** Fax: 095 21770

This unpretentious family-run restaurant offers efficient, welcoming service and very agreeable "good home cooking" all day, every day throughout a long season. The international flavours are there (in snacks like Cajun chicken pannini and Thai chicken wrap, for example) but how refreshing it is to find old friends like deep-fried Gubbeen cheese, steamed mussels in garlic and bacon & cabbage there amongst the home-made spicy fishcakes and fresh crab salad with home-made brown bread. There's some overlap onto the à la carte menu, which offers a judicious selection from the snack menu but a wider choice of main dishes, including traditional Irish stew and a range of seafood. This is a very fair place, offering honest food at honest prices: half dozen local oysters €7.55, for example, and whole sole on the bone with lemon butter at €21.52. **Seats 74.** No smoking area; air conditioning. Not suitable for children after 6 pm. Open daily, 12-10; L 12-6, D 6-10. A la carte. House wine €16.51. Closed 7 Nov-9 Mar. Amex, MasterCard, Visa, Laser. **Directions:** next to SuperValu supermarket.

Clifden

O'Grady's Seafood Restaurant

RESTAURANT Market Street Clifden Co. Galway **Tel: 095 21450**

O'Grady's was the first place to create a reputation for Clifden as a good food town. In season they're open for lunch and dinner and they certainly know how to cook seafood. Although the more traditional dishes are still there on the Seafood bar menu, the restaurant menu has undergone some modernisation of late, possibly to bring the style more into line with its trendier sister restaurants Kirwan's Lane (Galway city), Kirwan's on the Mall (Westport) and, most recently, O'Grady's on the Pier, at Barna. Baked whole seabass in Cajun spices is a speciality of the house, for example. Desserts remain traditional - pear & almond tarte tatin with cinnamon whipped cream, perhaps - or you can finish with a selection of farmhouse cheeses, imaginatively served with crispy fried apples, port soaked walnuts & biscuits. Not suitable for children under 7 after 6 pm. **Seats 48** (private room,

8) No smoking area. L&D Tue-Sun, L 12-2.30, D 6.30-10; all à la carte, house wine €15.87; sc discretionary. Closed Mon & Oct-Apr. Amex, MasterCard, Visa, Laser. **Directions:** on one-way street around town. Right in the centre of Clifden.

Clifden
ACCOMMODATION

The Quay House

Beach Road Clifden Co. Galway
Tel: 095 21369 Fax: 095 21608
Email: thequay@iol.ie Web: www.thequayhouse.com

In a lovely location - the house is right on the harbour, with pretty water views when the tide is in - The Quay House was built around 1820. It has the distinction of being the oldest building in Clifden and has also had a surprisingly varied usage: it was originally the harbourmaster's house, then a convent, then a monastery, was converted into a hotel at the turn of the century and finally, since 1993, has been enjoying its most recent incarnation as specialist accommodation in the incomparable hands of long-time hoteliers, Paddy and Julia Foyle. Airy, wittily decorated and sumptuously comfortable rooms include not only two wheelchair-friendly rooms but a whole new development alongside the original house - seven stunning studio rooms with small fitted kitchens and balconies overlooking the harbour. As in the older rooms, excellent bathrooms all have full bath and shower. Breakfast, including delicious freshly-baked breads and scones straight from the Aga, is served in the conservatory. Although officially closed in winter it is always worth inquiring. Children under 12 free in parents' room (cots available). No pets. **Rooms 14** (all with full bathrooms, 2 for disabled). B&B€63pps, ss €19. Closed 7 Nov-12 Mar. MasterCard, Visa, Laser. **Directions:** 2 minutes from town centre, overlooking Clifden harbour - follow signs to the beach road.

Clifden
HOTEL/RESTAURANT

Rock Glen Country House Hotel

Clifden Co. Galway **Tel: 095 21035**
Fax: 095 21737 Email: rockglen@iol.ie Web: connemara-net/rockglen-hotel

Built in 1815 as a shooting lodge for Clifden Castle, Rock Glen is now run by the Roche family as a delightful hotel - beautifully situated in quiet grounds well away from the road, it enjoys views over a sheltered anchorage. The public rooms and some of the bedrooms have the full advantage of the view, but the whole hotel is very restful and comfortable, with a pleasing outlook from all windows. Rooms are furnished in country house style, with good bathrooms (all have a full bath and over-bath shower) and amenities - some, such as tea/coffee trays, are not in the rooms but available on request. In addition to local activities - fishing, pony trekking, golf - there's a putting green on site, also all-weather tennis and croquet; indoors there are plenty of places to read quietly and a full size snooker table. Children welcome - under 4s free in parents' room, cots available. Pets permitted by arrangement, in some areas. **Rooms 27** (1 suite, 2 mini-suites). Wheelchair access. Lift. B&B about €90pps, ss about €45; sc 12.5%. **Restaurant** Five-course dinner menus are considerately also available as individually priced courses (ie semi à la carte); local ingredients, especially seafood, play a major role in an updated country house style and dishes like herb crusted roast rack of Connemara lamb with garlic flan, spring cabbage & minted paloise or seared fresh king scallop with chunky kale & smoky pancetta tartlet, red onion jam and vanilla & orange dressing are typical. Finish with tempting desserts - biscotti of poached nectarine, perhaps, with mascarpone cream & glazed meringue - or Irish farmhouse cheese & biscuits. Service is friendly and efficient and an excellent breakfast is served in the restaurant. **Seats 60.** No-smoking restaurant. D 7-9 daily, à la carte; house wine about €18; sc 12.5%. Toilets wheelchair accessible. Closed end Nov-mid Mar. Amex, Diners, MasterCard, Visa. **Directions:** N57 from Galway, 1.5 miles from Clifden on Ballyconneely road.

Clifden
B&B

Seaview House

Clifden Co. Galway **Tel: 095 21441**
Email: rodteck@eircom.net Web: www.connemara.net/seaview

Sheila Griffin offers stylish and comfortable accommodation in her attractive house, which she has recently renovated to retain its character while adding modern comforts. At the time of going to press it is expected that a conservatory on the front of the house will be completed by Easter 2002.

Rooms 6 (all shower only & no-smoking). B&B €42pps, ss €8. Closed Christmas week. MasterCard, Visa. **Directions:** beside Bank of Ireland - left at square and a little down on right.

Clifden

HOTEL

Station House Hotel

Clifden Co. Galway **Tel: 095 21699**

Fax: 095 21667 Email: info@stationhousehotel.com Web: stationhousehotel.com

Built on the site of the late lamented railway station this large new hotel comes complete with leisure centre and conference/banqueting facilities 250/150). Public areas are impressively spacious and modern, while bedrooms are a good size, contemporary in style and comfortably furnished with ISDN lines as well as more usual amenities such as direct-dial phones, tea/coffee making and TV. The old Station House has become a themed bar and restaurant, run separately (see below) and the complex includes a wide range of shops and boutiques. Leisure centre, indoor swimming pool, beauty salon. Fishing, walking, cycling. Children welcome (under 2s free in parents' room; cots available without charge); playroom. No pets. **Rooms 78** (2 junior suites, 8 executive, 48 no-smoking, 4 for disabled) B&B €101.58pps, ss €19.05. Closed 25 Dec. Restaurant - see separate entry: Fire & Ice. Amex, Diners, MasterCard, Visa, Laser. **Directions:** follow N59 from Galway city. 70 km.

Clifden

ACCOMODATION/GUESTHOUSE

Sunnybank House

Clifden Co. Galway **Tel: 095 21437**

Fax: 095 21976 Email: info@sunnybankhouse.com Web: www.sunnybankhouse.com

Set in its own mature gardens, with panoramic views, Sunnybank is owned and run by the O'Grady family, of O'Grady's restaurant. At a reasonable price they offer very comfortably appointed en-suite bedrooms with good facilities (phone, tea/coffee-making, iron/trouser press and TV) and day rooms for guests' use. Ongoing renovations and improvements include the recent addition of a porch and refurbishment in both public areas and bathrooms. There is also a heated swimming pool, sauna and tennis court. Not suitable for children under 7; no pets. **Rooms 8** (1 suite, 5 shower only, all no-smoking). B&B €57 pps, ss 12.70. Closed 1 Nov-1 Apr. MasterCard, Visa, Laser. **Directions:** N59 - right at Esso station & first left, house 200m on right.

Clonbur

ACCOMMODATION

Ballykine House

Clonbur Co. Galway

Tel: 092 46150 Fax: 092 46150

Email: ballykine@eircom.net Web: www.olirl.com/galway/ballykinehouse.htm

Comfortable accommodation and Ann Lambe's warm hospitality make this an appealing base for a peaceful holiday. There are guided forest walks from the house, angling on Lough Corrib, an equestrian centre (at nearby Ashford Castle) and bikes for hire locally. It's also well-placed for touring Connemara. Rooms have TV, tea/coffee making facilities and hairdryers. No evening meals but the pubs and restaurants of Clunbur - including Burke's pub (Tel: 092-46175), which is renowned for its food (and music) - are all within walking distance. There's plenty of comfortable seating in the sitting room and conservatory for lounging and chatting, also a pool table - and a drying room for anglers is planned shortly. Garden. **Rooms 5** (4 with en-suite shower; 1 with private bath, restricted use), B&B €26, ss €10. Closed 1 Nov-31 Mar.

Costello

COUNTRY HOUSE

Fermoyle Lodge

Costello Co. Galway

Tel: 091 786 111 Fax: 091 786 154

Email: fermoylelodge@eircom.net Web: www.fermoylelodge.com

One of Ireland's best-kept secrets, Nicola Stronach's delightful sporting lodge seems to enjoy the best of all possible worlds. Although only 29 miles from Galway (and six miles from the ferry to the Aran Islands), it's hidden from the road in one of the wildest and most remote parts of Connemara. Protected by mature woodland and shrubs, it has stunning lake and mountain views, with both salmon and sea trout fishing on the doorstep. All this and creature comforts too. The spacious, well-proportioned house has been sensitively renovated and beautifully furnished and decorated. Nicola has used the best of materials wisely, in a warm, low-key style that allows for every comfort without detracting from the wonderful setting that is its greatest attribute. Bedrooms are all very comfortable, with private bathrooms - and Nicola has yet another ace up her sleeve in the form of her French husband, who's a wizard in the kitchen as well as on the lough. A set dinner (€35), changed nightly, is served for residents at 7pm - 24 hour notice is required and any particular dislikes or allergies should be mentioned on booking. Not suitable for children. Pets permitted in certain areas. **Rooms 6** (all en-suite & no smoking). B&B €75pps, ss €25. No sc. Closed Nov-Mar. MasterCard, Visa. **Directions:** from Galway, take N59 to Clifden. At Oughterard turn left just before the bridge signed Costello - Lodge is 11 miles along this road on right.

Craughwell
PUB

Raftery's, The Blazers Bar

Craughwell Co. Galway **Tel: 091 846004** Fax: 091 846004
Email: rafterys@eircom.net

Donald and Theresa Raftery's famous family-run establishment is on the main Galway-Dublin road and is the meeting place for the well-known Galway Blazers Hunt, who are kennelled close by. It was completely refurbished in 2000 - and can make a handy stopping place: popular bar food is served every day - house specialities are seafood chowder, smoked salmon and home-made brown bread, bacon & cabbage. Bar Food: 10.30-7 daily. Closed 25 Dec & Good Fri. MasterCard, Visa. **Directions:** on N6 between Loughrea and Galway.

Craughwell
COUNTRY HOUSE
RESTAURANT ☆

St. Clerans

Craughwell Co. Galway
Tel: 091 846 555 Fax: 091 846 600
Email: stclerans@iol.ie Web: www.merv.com/stclerans

COUNTRY HOUSE OF THE YEAR

Once the home of John Huston, St Clerans is a magnificent manor house beautifully located in rolling countryside. It has been carefully restored by the current owner, the American entertainer Merv Griffin, and decorated with no expense spared to make a sumptuous, hedonistically luxurious country retreat, operating under the management of Seamus Dooley. The decor, which is for the most part elegant, with some regard for period tastes, does occasionally go right over the top - as evidenced in the carpets in the hall and drawing room. But there's a great sense of fun about the furnishing and everything is of the highest quality. Each room is individually decorated and most are done in what might best be described as an upbeat country house style. Others - particularly those on the lower ground floor, including John Huston's own favourite room, which opens out onto a terrace with steps up to the garden - are restrained, almost subdued, in atmosphere. All are spacious, with luxuriously appointed bathrooms (one has its original shower only) and a wonderful away-from-it-all feeling. Putting green, driving range, horse-riding, clay pigeon shooting, fishing & croquet all on site. Small conferences/private parties (230/28). Children under 12 free in parents' room (cot available without charge). No pets. **Rooms 12** (all en-suite) Room rate about €450 (for two , with breakfast). Wheelchair access. **Restaurant** The restaurant, which is open to non-residents by reservation, provides a sumptuous setting for excellent cooking by Japanese head chef Hisashi Kumagai. However, despite the glamorous surroundings, thoughtful service by well-informed and friendly staff create a surprisingly relaxed atmosphere that adds greatly to the pleasure of dining - and watching floodlighting gradually brighten on a huge tree in the meadow as the evening shadows deepen is a memorable experience. All this - and wonderful food too. Menus change daily but the style - an unusual mixture of Japanese and international cuisine - is seen in specialities such as millefeuille of panfried shark with risotto, sundried tomato citrus beurre blanc & sevruga caviar, while local ingredients like farmed venison might typically be used in a noisette of venison with woodland mushroom ragoût and madeira sauce. The cooking is exellent, presentation attractive without being over-wrought and service well-judged. Restaurant not suitable for children. **Seats 24** (private room, 24). D 7-9. daily, Set D about €60, house wine about €21; sc discretionary. Open all year. Amex, MasterCard, Visa. **Directions:** 5 minutes off main Dublin- Galway road (N6) just outside village of Craughwell.

Furbo

HOTEL

Connemara Coast Hotel

Furbo Co. Galway **Tel: 091 592 108**
Fax: 091 592 065 Email: sinnott@iol.ie Web: www.sinnotthotels.com

Like the other Sinnott hotels - Connemara Gateway and Brooks Hotel in Dublin - this beautifully located hotel is an attractive building which makes the best possible use of the site without intruding on the surroundings. Set on the sea side of the road, in its own extensive grounds, it is hard to credit that Galway city is only a 10 minute drive away. An impressive foyer decorated with fresh flowers sets the tone on entering, public areas are spacious and facilities are particularly good - a fine bar, two restaurants, a children's playroom and a leisure centre (which has a Canadian hot tub) among them. A policy of constant refurbishment and upgrading of facilities ensures that the hotel has a warm, well-cared for atmosphere. Conference/banqueting facilities (450/400)with secretarial back-up. A range of special breaks is available. Children under 3 free in parents' room; cots available. No pets. **Rooms 112** (1 suite, 9 executive rooms). B&B €101.60pps, ss €32. Restaurant open 7-9.15 pm; bar food also available. Closed 24-26 Dec. Amex, Diners, MasterCard, Visa, Laser. **Directions:** 6 miles from Galway city on Spiddal Road.

Headford

COUNTRY HOUSE

Lisdonagh House

Caherlistrane Headford Co.Galway **Tel: 093 31163**
Fax: 093 31528 Email: cooke@lisdonagh.com Web: lisdonagh.com

Situated about 15 minutes drive north of Galway city in the heart of hunting and fishing country, Lisdonagh House is on an elevated site with beautiful views overlooking Lake Hackett. It is a lovely property, with large well-proportioned reception rooms, a fine staircase and luxurious bedrooms, furnished with antiques and decorated in period style, with marbled bathrooms to match. A 4-course residents' dinner (choice limited to one of two main courses), about €40, is served between 8 and 9. House wine about €16. Small conferences/private parties for up to 30. Children welcome (under 2s free in parents' room, cots available). Pets permitted in some areas. **Rooms 10** (7 executive rooms, 3 shower only, 5 no-smoking, 3 for disabled) B&B about €115 pps, ss about €40. Wheelchair access. Closed mid Nov-mid Mar. Amex, MasterCard, Visa, **Directions:** from Oranmore roundabout, through Claregalway on to N17 for 16 miles, turn off at R333 through Belclare to Caherlistrane.

Inishbofin

HOTEL

Day's Inishbofin House Hotel

Cregboy Claregalway Inishbofin Co. Galway
Tel: 095 45809/091 798635 Fax: 095 45803

This modest, but hospitable family-run hotel beside the harbour has been first (and last) port of call for many visitors to the island over the years. There are plans to upgrade the hotel substantially and add a leisure centre, hopefully in time for the 2002 season. Off-season, inquire about the availability of food and drink on the island. No pets. **Rooms 14** (8 en-suite). B&B €44.44pps, no ss. Wheelchair access. Closed Sep-Apr. For ferry bookings and enquiries, phone: 095 44642 or 095 21520. Credit card bookings are accepted. Also details of Inishbofin Ferry from P O'Halloran, on Inishbofin: 095 45806. Visa, Laser. **Directions:** Ferries to the island run regularly from Cleggan, with ticket offices in Clifden (regular buses between Clifden and Cleggan) and also at Kings of Cleggan. For bookings and enquiries, phone: 095 44642 or 095 21520. Credit card bookings are accepted.

Inishbofin

RESTAURANT

The Dolphin Restaurant

Middle Quarter Inishbofin Co. Galway **Tel: 095 45991**
Fax: 045 45992 Email: inishshark@hotmail.com

Menus change throughout the day at Pat and Catherine Coyne's versatile little island restaurant, which opened in the summer of 2000 and is a great asset to the island. At lunchtime - which considerately runs all afternoon - there's a range of drinks to comfort or refresh, depending on the weather, home-bakes (including hot waffles with maple syrup and cream) and made to order sandwiches or tuna melts as well as tempting salads (smoked salmon, or local crabmeat perhaps) and simple hot meals, some with special child appeal. Evening menus are more substantial - Connemara lamb chops on a bed of game chips with a basil pesto sauce, perhaps, or poached wild salmon with lemon & herb butter. **Seats 43.** No smoking restaurant. L Fri-Sun 12.30-5; D daily, 7-9.30. A la carte. Wines from €16.50. No sc. Closed Oct-May. MasterCard, Visa. **Directions:** boat from Cleggan Pier to Inishbofin Island.

Kilcolgan
RESTAURANT/PUB

Moran's Oyster Cottage

The Weir Kilcolgan Co. Galway
Tel: 091 796 113 Fax: 091 796 503

This is just the kind of Irish pub that people everywhere dream about. It's as pretty as a picture, with a well-kept thatched roof and a lovely waterside location (with plenty of seats outside where you can while away the time and watch the swans floating by). It's also brilliantly well-run by the Moran family - and so it should be, after all they've had six generations to practise. They're famed throughout the country for their wonderful local seafood, including lobster, but especially the native oysters (from their own oyster beds) which are in season from September to April. Willie Moran is an ace oyster opener, a regular champion in the famous annual competitions held in the locality. Farmed Gigas oysters are on the menu all year. Then there's chowder and smoked salmon and seafood cocktail and mussels - and, perhaps best of all, delicious crab sandwiches and salads. An extension recently completed includes a private conference room. Morans was the Guide's 1999 Seafood Pub of the Year. **Seats 170.** Meals 12 noon -10pm daily. House wine about €14. Closed 25 Dec & Good Fri. Amex, MasterCard, Visa. **Directions:** just off the Galway-Limerick road, signed between Clarenbridge and Kilcolgan.

Kinvara
PUB/RESTAURANT

The Pier Head Bar & Restaurant

The Quay Kinvara Co. Galway **Tel: 091 638188**

Mike Burke took over this well-known harbourside establishment in the picturesque village of Kinvara in 2000 and, with the help of an excellent Belgian chef Philippe de la Roux, has rapidly built up a reputation for serving the best food in the area. Seafood is, of course, the main speciality - especially lobster - served in the shell with garlic butter and a side salad it makes a meal for €33 - and the other thing they take pride in doing well is top of the range steak, using local beef (totally traceable) which is salughtered and butchered specially. As well as good food, there's also traditional music, on Wednesday nights, all year round. Children welcome. **Seats 100** (private room 50). No smoking area. Food served daily in summer, 5-10 (Sun 12-8); off-season 5-8 (end Oct-May). A la carte.Closed 25 Dec & good Fri. Diners, MasterCard, Visa, Laser.

Kinvara
PUB

Tully's

Kinvara Co. Galway **Tel: 091 637146**

Definitely a spot for traditional music, this is a real local pub in the old tradition, with a little grocery shop at the front and stone-floored bar at the back. Tully's has a fine old stove in the bar for cosy winter sessions, which is always a good sign (They also have a small enclosed garden with a few parasoled tables for fine weather). Not a food place, although sandwiches, teas and coffees are always available. Normal pub hours. Closed 25 Dec & Good Fri. No credit cards.

Kylemore
RESTAURANT

Kylemore Abbey Restaurant and Tea House

Kylemore Co. Galway **Tel: 095 41146**
Fax: 095 41368 Email: info@kylemoreabbey.com Web: www.kylemoreabbey.com

Kylemore Abbey, with its stunning mountain and waterside setting, would make a dramatic location for any enterprise. But what the Benedictine nuns are doing here is truly astonishing. The abbey is not only home for the nuns but is also run as an international girls' boarding school. In addition, the nuns run a farm and a restored walled garden, which is open to the public. A short walk further along the wooded shore leads to the Gothic church, a miniature replica of Norwich cathedral. In a neat modern building beside the carpark is one of the country's best craft shops - and an excellent restaurant. Everything at this daytime self-service restaurant is made on the premises, and the range of wholesome offerings includes a good selection of hot and cold savoury dishes, including traditional beef & Guinness casserole, Irish stew and several vegetarian options - typically black eye bean casserole or vegetarian lasagne. Home baking is a special strength and big bowls of the nuns' renowned home-made jams are set up at the till, for visitors to help themselves. Beside them are neatly labelled jars to buy and take home. **Seats 240.** Meals daily 9.30-5.30. Closed Christmas week & Good Fri. (The Garden Tea House, in the restored walled garden, is now open Easter-Hallowe'en, 10.30-5, using produce from the garden.) MasterCard, Visa, Amex, Laser. **Directions:** 2 miles from Letterfrack, on the N59 from Galway.

Leeanne

Blackberry Café & Coffee Shop

CAFÉ

Leeanne Co. Galway **Tel: 095 42240**

Sean and Mary Hamilton's lovely little restaurant is just what the weary traveller hopes to happen on when touring or walking in this beautiful area. They're open through the afternoon and evening every day during the summer, serving home-made soups and chowders (from about €3) with home-baked bread, substantial snacks such as fish cakes and mussels (from about €8.75-€11.50) and delicious desserts like rhubarb tart and lemon meringue pie with cream (all €3.75). Extra dishes like hot smoked trout and a chicken main course might be added to the menu in the evening, but the secret of the Blackberry Café's appeal is that they don't try to do too much at once and everything is freshly made each day. **Seats 40.** Open 12-9 daily in high season. A la carte. House wine €13.97 (also 1/4 bottles, €3.75). Closed Tue in shoulder seasons. Closed 30 Sep-Good Fri. MasterCard, Visa, Laser. **Directions:** on main street, opposite car park.

Leenane

Delphi Lodge

COUNTRY HOUSE

Leenane Co. Galway **Tel: 095 42222**
Fax: 095 42296 Email: delphilodge.ie Web: www.delphilodge.ie

One of Ireland's most famous sporting lodges, Delphi Lodge was built in the early 19th-century by the Marquis of Sligo. It is beautifully located in an unspoilt valley, surrounded by the region's highest mountains (with the high rainfall dear to fisherfolk). Owned since 1986 by Peter Mantle - who has restored and extended the original building in period style - the lodge is large and impressive in an informal, understated way, with antiques, fishing gear and a catholic selection of reading matter creating a stylish yet relaxed atmosphere. The dozen guest rooms are all quite different, but they are en-suite (with proper baths) and very comfortably furnished (with lovely lake and mountain views). Dinner, for residents only, is taken at a long oak table. It is cooked by Cliodhna Prendergast, who has "a range of dishes that is vast and eclectic" - some traditional, some 'nouveau', some oriental. (To illustrate the point; home made game sausages are a speciality, also nephrops from Killary Bay, with warmed rocket butter.) The famous Delphi Fishery is the main attraction, but people come for other country pursuits, painting, or just peace and quiet. A billiard table, the library and a serious wine list (great bottles at a very modest mark-up) can get visitors through a lot of wet days. Just across the road, four restored cottages offer self-catering accommodation. Small conferences/banqueting (20/28). Not suitable for children. No pets. Garden, fishing, walking. **Rooms 12** (all executive standard). B&B €90 pps, ss €45. Meals 1 pm and 8pm. Residents L €15, D € 45; House wine €19. Closed 20 Dec-10 Jan. MasterCard, Visa. **Directions:** 8 miles northwest of Leenane on the Louisburgh road.

Leenane

Killary Lodge

ACCOMODATION/GUESTHOUSE

Leenane Co. Galway **Tel: 095 42276**
Fax: 095 42314 Email: lodge@killary.com Web: www.killary.com

Situated on the shores of Killary harbour, Jamie and Mary Young's former hunting lodge has been renovated in a relaxed modern style and now offers a very comfortable place to stay in a beautiful location, six miles from their famous Little Killary Adventure Centre. Those with an interest in outdooor pursuits will get particular enjoyment from the many activities operating from here and Little Killary, but it also makes an excellent base for touring Connemara. Friendly staff, an informal atmosphere and home cooked evening meals are all part of the attraction and there is plenty of walking - and other activities such as water-skiing and kayaking, available on site - for the energetic. Conferences and corporate training are among the many programmes offered at this unusual establishment - contact the manager, Kathy Evans, for further details. Garden, tennis, walking, cycling. **Rooms 21** (12 shower only, 2 for disabled). B&B €50 pps, no ss. Residents D €25; house wine €12.70. Closed Dec-Jan. MasterCard, Visa, Laser. **Directions:** 3 miles outside Leenane on Clifden Road (N59).

Leenane

Portfinn Lodge

RESTAURANT/ACCOMMODATION

Leenane Co. Galway
Tel: 095 42265 Fax: 095 42315
Email: rorydaly@anu.ie Web: www.anu.ie/portfinn

There are few views in Ireland to beat the sight of the sun sinking behind the mountains over Killary harbour. On a good evening that's something you can look forward to at Rory and Brid Daly's seafood restaurant, Portfinn Lodge. The dining area is in a room of the main house and an adjoining conservatory. The lobster tank at the entrance bodes well for a good meal - 90% of the menu will be seafood: prawns, salmon, brill, turbot and many of their cousins make a nightly appearance.

There is plenty else to choose from, however, including local lamb in various guises and at least one vegetarian dish daily. Good brown bread comes with country butter, which is quite a feature in these parts, and there's always an Irish cheeseboard. Not suitable for children under 12. **Seats 35.** No smoking area. D 6.30-9 daily, Set D €30, house wine from €15.24; sc 10%. Closed 1 Nov- 31 Mar. **Accommodation** Modest but comfortable accommodation is offered in eight neat purpose-built en-suite rooms, all sleeping three and one with four beds; one room has wheelchair access. Pets permitted by arrangement. Fishing, walking. **Rooms 8** (all en-suite). B&B €32pps, ss €25, 10% sc. MasterCard, Visa. **Directions:** midway between Westport and Clifden.

Letterfrack

Rosleague Manor

COUNTRY HOUSE/RESTAURANT Letterfrack Co. Galway **Tel: 095 41101**
Fax: 095 41168 Email: rosleaguemanor@eircom.net Web: www.rosleague.com

A lovely pink-washed Regency house of gracious proportions and sensitively handled modernisation, Rosleague looks out over a tidal inlet through gardens planted with rare shrubs and plants. Although the area offers plenty of activity for the energetic, there is a deep sense of peace and it's hard to imagine anywhere better to recharge the soul. The hotel recently changed hands within the Foyle family and is now run by Anne Foyle's nephew, Mark Foyle; considerable refurbishment was completed before the hotel re-opened in spring 2001 and renovations are continuing on an ongoing basis. Garden, tennis, fishing, walking. **Rooms 20** (4 junior suites). B&B €95.23pps, ss €25.39. D 7.30-9.30 daily; Set D €40.63. House wine €17.14. Wheelchair access. Closed Nov-Mar. Amex, MasterCard, Visa, Laser. **Directions:** on N59 Main Road, 7 miles north of Clifden.

Milltown

Finns Bar & Restaurant

RESTAURANT féile bia Milltown Tuam Co. Galway **Tel: 093 51327** Email: jonfin.indigo.ie

John and Lucy Finn's restaurant is on the river, in a charming little award-wining tidy town a few miles north of Tuam - a welcome sight for hungry travellers between Galway and Sligo. John cooks an eclectic mix of international (Caesar salad, chicken korma, tagliatelle house style) and traditional (prawn cocktail, steaks, honey roasted duck) dishes - reasonably priced and served in a relaxed atmosphere. The cooking is sound, it's good value for money and the small village setting - where everyone seems to know someone at another table - makes a welcome change from busy towns. Children welcome, but not after 7 pm. **Seats 60** (Private room 24); no smoking area, air conditioning. DTue-Sun, 5-9pm. A la carte, house wines from €13.33. Service discretionary. Closed Mon, 25 Dec & Good Fri. Children welcome. Visa, Laser. **Directions:** 8 miles from Tuam, main N17 to Sligo.

Moyard

Garranbaun House

COUNTRY HOUSE Moyard Co. Galway
Tel: 095 41649 Fax: **095 41649**

In a spectacular position overlooking Ballynakill Bay, the Finnegans' imposing 19th century Georgian-style manor has wonderful views of the Twelve Bens, Diamond Hill and the Maam Turks - and there is a trout lake, Lough Garraunbaun, attached to the estate. Delia Finnegan is a most hospitable host, keeping her beautifully furnished house immaculate without spoiling the relaxed atmosphere. Books, turf fires and a grand piano say a lot about the things that bring people here and, alongside Connemara lamb and local seafood, the organic garden, free range chicken and eggs provide an excellent base for Delia's dinners. Cheeses served are all Irish and baking of bread and scones is a daily event. Not suitable for children under 14. No pets. **Rooms 3** (2 en-suite, 1 with private bathroom, all no-smoking). B&B about €45pps, no ss.Residents dinner by arrangement. Open all year. Visa. **Directions:** from Clifden take Westport road - 6 miles on there's a sign on the left.

Moyard

Rose Cottage

FARMHOUSE/B&B Rockfield Moyard Co. Galway **Tel: 095 41082**

This long-established farmhouse is situated on a working farm in a scenic location surrounded by the Twelve Bens mountains. Patricia O'Toole took over management from her mother Mary in 1997 and was already well prepared for the job, as the family has always helped here. Simple comfortable accommodation and farmhouse cooking are what's on offer. There's a sitting room with an open turf fire (and television), a dining room for guests (separate tables) and bedrooms have tea/coffee making trays and hair dryers. Nearby attractions include sandy beaches, scenic walks, fishing, island trips, traditional Irish music, horse riding and golf. No pets.* It is possible that Rose Cottage may change hands during the coming year, although the family anticipate operating normally during the 2002 season. **Rooms 8** (6 shower only). B&B €25.29pps, no ss. Closed Oct-Mar. MasterCard, Visa. **Directions:** 6 miles from Clifden, 2.5 from Letterfrack.

Moycullen

Moycullen Country House & Restaurant

COUNTRY HOUSE/RESTAURANT

Moycullen Co. Galway
Tel: 091 555 621 Fax: 091 555 566
Email: info@moycullen.com Web: www.moycullen.com

Overlooking Lough Corrib, and set peacefully in 30 acres of rhododendrons and azaleas, Moycullen House was built as a sporting lodge in the arts and crafts style at the beginning of the century and has been run as a country house for some years by the Casburn family. When Richard and Louise Casburn decided to open this very professionally run restaurant in the house in 1998, they added a new name to the list of must-visits in the area. A great deal of thought and work went into getting the changes right, and the effort has paid off handsomely. Louise looks after front-of-house beautifully and Richard is the chef - his menus are ambitious but he offers a sensibly short à la carte with daily extras, including seafood. Having worked with Gerry Galvin at nearby Drimcong House in its heyday and been influenced by its philosophy, Richard seeks out quality ingredients, which he treats with due respect and very pleasing results. The style is fairly modern but based on classics. A well-balanced and fairly priced Table d'Hôte menu could include starters of baked oysters with a herb & garlic crust and sautéed lambs' kidneys & smoked bacon salad with a honey & mustard dressing while typical main courses could include turbot as one of the daily specials and, from the carte, roast loin of Connemara lamb with roasted shallots, spinach and potato - simply delicious. (Moycullen was selected for the Bord Bia Irish Lamb Award in 2001). Presentation is not overworked and cooking is excellent. Banqueting (45). garden, walking. **Seats 40.** D Thurs-Tues 6.30-9.30; L Sun only, 4-5 pm. Set D €45, also à la carte; Set Sun L from €21. House wine €18. sc discretionary. Closed Wed. Accommodation Large bedrooms furnished with antiques all have private baths and there's a spacious residents' sitting room with an open log fire. Children welcome; under 5s free in parents' room, cot/extra bed available without charge; baby-sitting by arrangement. No pets. **Rooms 3** (1 superior room, all no-smoking). B&B €72 pps, ss€8. House closed Christmas & 8 Jan-10 Mar Amex, MasterCard, Visa, Laser. **Directions:** N59 Galway to Moycullen; at Cross Roads, take left turn onto Spiddal Road, signed on left after about 1.5km.

Moycullen

White Gables Restaurant

RESTAURANT

Moycullen Village Moycullen Co. Galway **Tel: 091 555 744**
Fax: 091 556 004 Email: wgables@indigo.ie Web: whitegables.com

Kevin and Ann Dunne have been running this attractive cottagey restaurant on the main street of Moycullen since 1991 and it's now on many a regular diner's list of favourites. Open stonework, low lighting and candlelight (even at lunch time) create a soothing away-from-it-all atmosphere. Kevin sources ingredients with care and offers weekly-changing dinner and à la carte menus and a set Sunday lunch (which is enormously popular and has two sittings). Cooking is consistently good in a refreshingly traditional style and, while there is much else to choose from - roast half duckling with orange sauce is one of their most popular dishes - fresh fish is the main speciality, including lobster (served thermidor, perhaps) from their own tank and other classics like sole on the bone, scallops mornay, monkfish panfried in garlic butter and poached turbot in martini sauce. Well-cooked seasonal vegetables are always particularly enjoyable at this fine restaurant and their roast beef, as served for Sunday lunch, is like no other. Good desserts, including home-made ices, and friendly, efficient service all help make this one of the area's finest restaurants. **Seats 45.** Children welcome. No smoking area; air conditioning. D 7-10 (daily in high season), L Sun only, 12.30 & 2.30. Set D €33, Set Sun L €19.68. House wine €17.14; sc discretionary. Closed Mon except mid-Jul-mid-Aug & 23 Dec-14 Feb. Amex, MasterCard, Visa, Laser. **Directions:** on N59 in Moycullen village, 8 km from Galway city.

Oranmore

Galway Bay Golf & Country Club Hotel

HOTEL

Oranmore Co. Galway **Tel: 091 790 500**
Fax: 091 790 510 Email: cro@lynchotels.com Web: www.lynchotels.com

This rather handsome modern hotel, just eight miles from Galway city, looks out over an 18-hole championship golf course (designed by Christy O'Connor Jnr.) towards Galway Bay and has recently been acquired by the Lynch Hotel Group. The location is lovely, it has a wide range of facilities for both business and leisure and is potentially one of the pleasantest hotels in the area. Public areas include an impressively spacious lobby, large bar and a well-appointed restaurant with imaginative decor - all have views. Generous-sized bedrooms, which include six for wheelchair users and a high proportion of executive suites, are comfortably furnished with all the necessary facilities and many have lovely views across the bay, although a recent visit suggests that maintenance and routine refurbishment have been allowed to lapse. The hotel offers a number of special packages, giving good value on both golf and non-golfing breaks. Conference/banqueting (275); business centre, secretarial services. Children welcome. No pets. **Rooms 92** (53 suites, 6 rooms for disabled). Golf (18), gym, garden, walking. Closed 25 Dec. B&B £65 pps, ss £20. Amex, Diners, MasterCard, Visa. **Directions:** turn left at Oranmore off main Galway - Limerick road (N18). Hotel is signposted.

Oranmore

Quality Hotel & Leisure Centre, Galway

HOTEL

Oranmore Co. Galway **Tel: 091 792 244**
Fax: 091 792 246 Email: qualityhotelgalway@eircom.net Web: qualityhotelgalway.com

This large new hotel is easy to find (a big plus for business locations) and offers a high standard of accommodation. Excellent leisure facilities include a 20-metre pool - and there's a selection of meeting rooms including a fine one on the top floor, overlooking the pool. **Rooms 93** (20 no-smoking, 3 for disabled). Room rate about €140. Closed 24-26 Dec. Amex, Diners, MasterCard, Visa. **Directions:** at the Oranmore roundabout on the main (N6) road.

Oughterard

Connemara Gateway Hotel

HOTEL

Oughterard Co. Galway **Tel: 091 552328**
Fax: 091 552332 Email: gateway@iol.ie Web: www.sinnotthotels.com

An attractive building set well back from the road, this low, neatly designed hotel creates a good impression from the outset. The large foyer has lots of comfortable seating in country-look chintz fabrics. Open turf fires are welcoming and an abundance of flower arrangements bring colour and add interest throughout, as does the work of local artists and sculptors. The hotel offers a number of off-season and special interest breaks which make it an attractive base for an activity breaks (golf, fishing, walking, equestrian) or visiting the many attractions nearby, including the Victorian gardens at Kylemore. Bedrooms are variable (reflecting the hotel's origins as a 1960s motel) but all are comfortable, with considerate details (like a little washing line in the bathroom) and some have access to the garden at the back. No rooms designed for wheelchairs, but all are ground floor. There's quite a characterful public bar, used by locals as well as residents, a good leisure centre and a children's games room. Children under 2 free in parents' room; cots available. Pets permitted in some areas. **Rooms 62.** (all en-suite, 1 mini-suite). B&B€76, ss €32. Closed Dec & Jan, excl New Year. Amex, Diners, MasterCard, Visa, Laser. **Directions:** take N59 from Galway towards Maam Cross - Hotel is at Oughterard 25 km from Galway City.

Oughterard

Corrib Wave Guesthouse

GUESTHOUSE

Portacarron Oughterard Co. Galway **Tel: 091 552 147**
Fax: 091 552 736 Web: www.corribwave.com

A fisherman's dream, Michael and Maria Healy's unpretentious waterside guesthouse offers warm family hospitality, comfortable accommodation, an open turf fire to relax by and real home cooking. All rooms have phone, tea/coffee-making, TV, radio and a double and single bed; some are suitable for families. Best of all at Corrib Wave is the location - utter peace and tranquillity. Golf and horseriding nearby and everything to do with fishing organised for you. **Rooms 10** (all en-suite). B&B €35. Closed 20 dec-2 Jan. MasterCard, Visa. **Directions:** from Galway, signed from N59, 1km before Oughterard.

Oughterard

Currarevagh House

COUNTRY HOUSE

Oughterard Co. Galway **Tel: 091 552 312**
Fax: 091 552 731 Email: currarevagh@ireland.com

Tranquillity, trout and tea in the drawing room - these are the things that draw guests back to the Hodgson family's gracious, but not luxurious early Victorian manor overlooking Lough Corrib. Built in 1846, with 150 acres of woodlands and gardens and sporting rights over 5,000 acres, Currarevagh has been open to guests for over half a century. The present owners, Harry and June Hodgson, are founder members of the Irish Country Houses and Restaurants Association (known as the Blue Book). Yet, while the emphasis is on old-fashioned service and hospitality, they are adamant that the atmosphere should be more like a private house party than a hotel, and their restful rituals underline the differences: the day begins with a breakfast worthy of its Edwardian origins, laid out on the sideboard in the dining room; lunch may be one of the renowned picnic hampers required by sporting folk. Then there's afternoon tea, followed by a leisurely dinner. Fishing is the ruling passion, of course - notably brown trout, pike, perch and salmon - but there are plenty of other country pursuits to assist in building up an appetite for June's simple cooking, all based on fresh local produce. Not suitable for children. Pets permitted by arrangement. Garden, tennis. **Rooms 15** (all en-suite). B&B about €85, ss about €25. 10% sc. Closed late Oct-1 Apr. MasterCard, Visa. **Directions:** take N59 to Oughterard. Turn right in village square and follow Gann Road for 4 miles.

Oughterard

River Run Lodge

RESTAURANT/GUESTHOUSE

Glann Road Oughterard Co. Galway **Tel: 091 552697**
Fax: 091 55669 Email: riverrun@indigo.ie

Tom and Anne Little's modern guesthouse and restaurant is quietly located in landscaped gardens just outside the village of Oughterard, on the banks of the Owenriff River. Warm wood tones and a welcoming fire in the reception area sets a caring note that is evident throughout the house, especially in the thoughtful planning of spacious bedrooms which all have exceptional facilities including minibar, hospitality tray, satellite television, radio, trouser press with iron and writing desk - there's even a suite, The Corrib: overlooking the back garden, it has a double and single bed, comfortable chairs, a separate dressing room and separate bath and shower. A ground floor room beside the front door has less privacy than others. **Rooms 8** (some shower only). B&B about €50pps. Open all year. **Restaurant** The well-appointed restaurant is in the prime spot, towards the back of the house and overlooking maturing gardens and the little river - and dinner is likely to be the highlight of your visit. Ingredients are carefully sourced and everything is freshly prepared and cooked to order. There's a shortish à la carte menu, with half a dozen choices on each course and the style is modern international. Delicious starters typically include Thai spiced crab cakes with beautifully dressed leaves and goats cheese with a hazelnut crust on a bed of poached pears, followed perhaps by baked kassler (smoked pork) with garlic mash and apple cider sauce or baked fillet of cod with an oriental crust - which, considerately, is also offered as plain baked cod with lemon & herb butter. Not surprisingly this little gem is popular with locals as well as resident guests, so booking is required. **Seats about 30.** Set D about €26; house wine about €18. Amex, MasterCard, Visa. **Directions:** in Oughterard village take turning for Glann Road - its a few hundred yards down on the right.

Oughterard

Sweeney's Oughterard House

HOTEL

Oughterard Co. Galway **Tel: 091 552207**

The Higgins family have owned and run this attractive creeper-clad old hotel for several generations. Prettily situated opposite the river and surrounded by mature trees (on the Clifden side of the town), it is genuinely old-fashioned with comfortable, cottagey public rooms furnished with antiques - a very pleasant place to break a journey. (Very acceptable light food is served in the bar during the day.) Bedrooms vary considerably - some have four-posters. Fishing is the main attraction, but there are plenty of other outdoor pursuits including the gentle pleasure of taking tea on the lawn. Closed 22 Dec-mid-Jan.

Portumna area

Red Oak Restaurant

RESTAURANT

Clonmoylan Portumna Co. Galway
Tel: 0509 49347 (after 3 pm) / 0509 49339 / 087 7974079

Anne Hilty's pretty little cottage restaurant near the marina at Clonmoylan has earned itself a fine reputation and attracts many regular visitors. Aside from printed menus that include diverse dishes ranging from oak smoked salmon to spaghetti bolognese, samosas and apple pie with cream, dinner menus offer seafood platters, loin of lamb and fillet of beef - and, given adequate notice, you can have virtually anything you like. Half portions are available at half price too, which many guests appreciate. What you get here is honest home cooking, with everything made from scratch using fresh ingredients - and people love it. Open from 4-11 pm (last orders 9pm) any day there are bookings, which usually means weekends off season and most evenings in summer. Dinner officially starts at 7pm, but can be earlier by arrangement (eg for a family); teas are available in the afternoon and there's a full bar available to guests who are dining. No credit cards, but foreign currency is accepted as well as cash and cheques. **Directions:** On the west shore of Lough Derg, six miles from Portumna.

Portumna

Shannon Oaks Hotel & Country Club

HOTEL

St. Josephs Rd Portumna Co. Galway **Tel: 0509 41777**
Fax: 0509 41357 Email: sales@shannonoaks.ie Web: www.shannonoaks.ie

Situated near the shores of Lough Derg, this attractive, privately-owned hotel opened in 1997. The interior is spacious and the large lobby is quite impressive, with polished wooden floor, faux-marble pillaring featuring a winter treescape and ample (if clearly well-used) seating in contemporary style.

Public rooms include a warm-toned restaurant, which can be opened out in summer, and a cosy, pub-like bar. It's a good choice for business and corporate events - bedrooms have air conditioning and fax/modem lines as standard, conference and meeting facilities are designed for groups of all sizes, with full back-up services. Off-duty delegates will find plenty to do too, a fine leisure centre on-site has an air-conditioned gymnasium as well as a swimming pool and ancillary services and nearby activities include river cruising, fishing, golf, horseriding, cycling and clay pigeon shooting. Conference/banqueting(600/350). Children welcome (under 5s free in parents' room). No pets. **Rooms 63** (3 suites, 4 no smoking, 2 for disabled). B&B €73.64 pps ss €25.39. Open all year. Amex, Diners, MasterCard, Visa, Laser. **Directions:** situated on St Joseph Road, Portuma.

Recess

Ballynahinch Castle Hotel

HOTEL/RESTAURANT

Recess Co. Galway **Tel: 095 31006**

Fax: 095 31085 Email: bhinch@iol.ie Web: www.ballynahinch-castle.com

IRISH BREAKFAST AWARD - CONNAUGHT

This crenellated Victorian mansion enjoys a most romantic position in ancient woodland on the banks of the Ballynahinch River. Renowned as a fishing hotel, it is impressive in scale and relaxed in atmosphere. This magic combination, plus a high level of comfort and friendliness (and an invigorating mixture of residents and locals in the bar at night) all combine to bring people back. Renovations and extensions have recently been undertaken, with great attention to period detail, a policy also carried through successfully in furnishing both public areas and bedrooms. Most bedrooms and some reception rooms - notably the dining room - have lovely views over the river. **Restaurant:** It's a lovely setting for head chef Robert Webster's fine meals based on the produce of the area - specialities include panfried wild Atlantic salmon with savoy cabbage, smoked bacon & trumpet mushrooms and oven-roasted rack of Connemara lamb with crusty local black pudding. It's also a wonderful place to start the day with an excellent breakfast to give you a good start ahead of a day's fishing or touring the area: a host of good things are displayed on the buffet - fresh juices, fruits, freshly-baked breads and much more - and a wide range of hot dishes cooked to order including, of course, that delicious black pudding and rashers, from McGeough's famous butchers shop in Oughterard. The bar food is good too. Facilities for small conferences (24); Fishing, cycling, walking; garden, tennis. Children welcome (under 3s free in parents' room; cots available without charge). No pets. **Rooms 40** (3 suites, 4 no smoking). B&B €95 pps, ss €25.36. Restaurant open daily, D only 6.30-9 (Set D €42). Bar meals 12.30-3 & 6.30-9.30 daily. 10% sc added to bills. Closed Christmas & Feb. Amex, Diners, MasterCard, Visa, Laser. **Directions:** N59 to Clifden 2nd left after Recess, to Ballynahinch to Roundstone, 4km.

Recess

Lough Inagh Lodge

HOTEL

Recess Co. Galway **Tel: 095 34706**

Fax: 095 3470 Email: inagh@iol.ie Web: www.commerce.ie/inagh

Maire O'Connor's former sporting lodge on the shores of Lough Inagh makes a delightful small hotel with a country house atmosphere. It has large, well-proportioned rooms, interesting period detail and lovely fireplaces with welcoming log fires, plus all the modern comforts. Public areas include two drawing rooms, each with an open fire, a lovely dining room (the Finnisglen Room) with deep green walls and graceful spoonback Victorian mahogany chairs (non-residents welcome when there is room) and a very appealing bar (with a big turf fire and its own back door and tiled floor for wet fishing gear). Bedrooms, some with four-posters, are all well-appointed and unusually spacious, with views of lake and countryside. Walk-in dressing rooms lead to well-planned bathrooms and tea/coffee-making facilities are available in rooms on request. While it has special appeal to sportsmen, Lough Inagh is only 42 miles from Galway and makes a good base for touring Connemara. Walking, cycling, golf and pony trekking all nearby; garden. Off-season breaks offer especially good value. Small conferences (15). Children welcome (under 3s free in parents' room, cots available without charge). Pets permitted. **Rooms 12** (5 junior suites, 7 executive); B&B €95 pps, ss €32. Restaurant open daily 7-8.45 (reservations required); Bar meals 12.30-4 & 7-9 daily. Closed mid Dec-mid Mar. Amex, Diners, MasterCard, Visa. **Directions:** from Galway city travel on N59 for 40 miles.Take Right N344 in recess Right for Lough Inagh Lodge.

Renvyle

HOTEL

Renvyle House Hotel

Renvyle Co. Galway **Tel: 095 43511**
Fax: 095 43515 Email: renvyle@iol.ie Web: www.renvyle.com

In one of the country's most appealingly remote and beautiful areas, this famous Lutyens-esque house has a romantic and fascinating history, having been home to people as diverse as a Gaelic chieftan and Oliver St John Gogarty - and becoming one of Ireland's earliest country house hotels in 1883. Although it was in a state of decline for some time, recent (and continuing) investment is gradually bringing this magic place back to its old self. It is approached via a stunning scenic drive along a mountain road with views down into a blue-green sea of unparallelled clarity. However, once reached, the hotel seems to be snuggling down for shelter and has only limited views. This sheltered feeling is reinforced by the cosy atmosphere of the original building, with its dark beams, rug strewn floors and open fires - and a snug conservatory where guests can survey the garden and landscape beyond from a comfortable vantage point. Photographs and mementoes recording visits from the many famous people who have stayed here - Augustus John, Lady Gregory, Yeats and Churchill among them - keep guests happily occupied for hours, but there is plenty to distract you from this enjoyable activity. There's a heated outdoor swimming pool and other on-site activities include tennis, trout fishing, golf (9 hole) and croquet - while the surrounding area offers more challenging activities. Just loafing around is perhaps what guests are best at here, however, and there's little need to do much else. Head chef Tim O'Sullivan looks after the inner man admirably in lovely dinners featuring local seafood and Connemara produce, including lamb and game - and the hotel's bar food is also excellent. All this, plus the scent of a turf fire and a comfortable armchair, can be magic. Continuing refurbishment and improvements will bring all bedrooms up to a high standard by March 2002, when three new suites are also due for completion. Special breaks; excellent conference venue. (conference/banqueting 150/180); business centre, secretarial services. Children welcome (cots available; crèche, playroom, children's playground, children's tea). **Rooms 65** (3 suites, 1 junior suite, 4 for disabled). B&B €92, ss €32. Restaurant open 7-9.30 daily. Bar lunch, 12-3. Closed 6 Jan-1 Mar. Amex, Diners, MasterCard, Visa. **Directions:** 12 miles from Clifden.

Roundstone

O'Dowd's

PUB Roundstone Co. Galway **Tel: 095 35809** Fax: 095 35907 Email: odowds@indigo.ie

The O'Dowd family have been welcoming visitors to this much-loved pub overlooking the harbour for longer than most people care to remember - and, although there are some new developments from time to time, the old bar is always the same. It's one of those simple places, with the comfort of an open fire and good pint, where people congregate in total relaxation. A reasonably priced bar menu majoring in seafood offers sustenance or, for more formal meals, the restaurant next door does the honours. All day food also available at the adjacent family-run coffee shop. Own parking. Meals 11.30-9.30 daily. Closed 25 Dec, 3-6pm in winter & some Bank Hols. Amex, MasterCard, Visa. **Directions:** On harbour front in Roundstone village.

Tuam

RESTAURANT

Cré-na-Cille

High Street Tuam Co. Galway **Tel: 093 28232**
Fax: 093 28232 Email: crenacille@eircom.net

Cathal and Sally Reynolds' consistently excellent restaurant in Tuam makes a fine stopping place en-route to Galway city or Connemara but, as it is deservedly popular with the locals both at lunchtime and in the evening, booking is strongly advised. Evenings are a little more formal and the setting softer, but the common link is Euro-Toques chef Cathal Reynolds' confident use of local ingredients in generous food at remarkably keen prices. From wide-ranging menus - set lunch, early evening special, set dinner and à la carte - offering a wide range of seafood, meats, poultry and game in season come starters like John Begley's black pudding with apple and onion in a balsamic sauce, main courses like herb-crusted rack of Connemara mountain lamb in red wine jus or a vegetarian dish of the day - a vegetarian crumble perhaps. Always an inventive chef, Cathal was the worthy joint winner of the 2001 Creative Seafood Dish Award (together with Mike O'Grady of O'Grady's on the Pier, Barna). His winning dish "Siki Shark Cais Bán", is totally different from a dish created by Michael O'Grady with the same fish, a useful demonstration of its versatility: Cathal's "cutlet" of deep sea siki shark was stuffed with a local cheese and pan-fried, then served in an excellent basil, tomato & white wine sauce. Another nice feature of the restaurant is a customer-friendly wine list, which has a special €14 cellar. Arrangement with nearby carpark. Children welcome to 8 pm. **Seats 47** + private room, seats 32, recently refurbished). No-smoking area; air conditioning. L&D Mon-Sat, Early D (6-7pm). À la carte available at L&D. House wine from about €15 SC discretionary. Closed Sun, 25-26 Dec & all bank hols. Amex, Diners, MasterCard, Visa. **Directions:** in the town centre - take the N17 direction from the square; about 100 yards down on the right.p

COUNTY KERRY

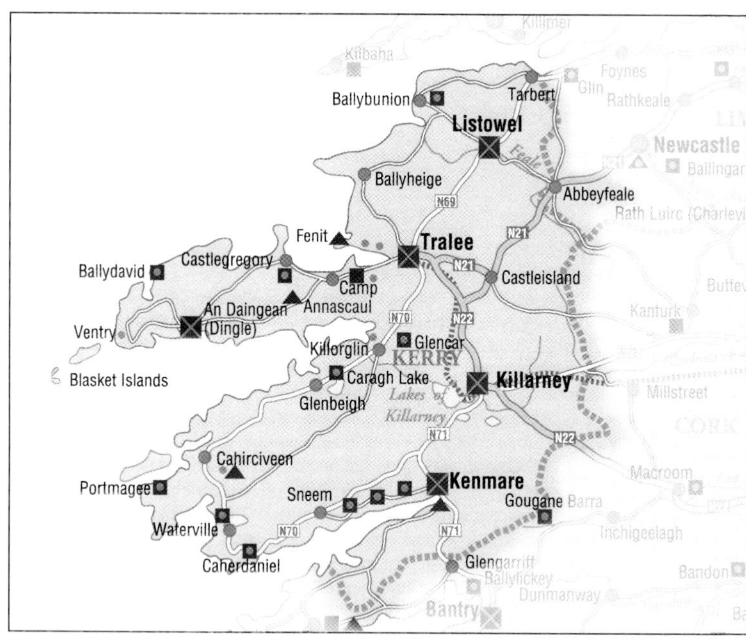

This large and splendid county in the far southwest is Ireland's longest-established tourism area. So it's quite a challenge simply being Kerry. Thus, from time to time, the Kingdom - as everyone knows it - has to re-invent itself in order to meet new market demands, while still retaining its traditional attractions.

It has high standards to maintain. Kenmare in south Kerry, already a gastronomic honeypot, is regularly among the towns which are tops for tidiness in all Ireland. And the main focal point for visitors in large numbers, the bustling town of Killarney, likewise gets a good rating in the current Tidy Towns Awards, as too does the village of Sneem, westward in the famous Ring of Kerry. Perhaps more importantly, for 2002 Killarney is a Silver Medallist in the Entente Floral, the pan-European contest, with the commendation from the judges particularly praising the way the town is gradually resolving the inevitable planning tensions between the built-up centre and the periphery.

Such things are very much of our time, yet there's a continuing timelessness about Kerry that gives it a unique quality. What can we say about this splendid place that the Kerrymen (and women) haven't said already? And we can only agree that it's all absolutely true. This magnificent county really is the Kingdom of Kerry. Everything is king size. For not only has Kerry mountains galore - more than anywhere else in Ireland - but the Kingdom also has the highest of all, in Carrantuohill.

By international standards, this loftiest peak of MacGillicuddy's Reeks (try pronouncing it "mackil-cuddy") may not seem notable at just 1038 m. But when you sense its mysterious heights in the clouds above a countryside of astonishing beauty, its relative elevation is definitely world league. And that beauty of the lower countryside sweeps out into Kerry's fabulous coastline, and up into Kerry's mountains as well. They're beautiful, and remarkably varied with it. So, in the upland stakes, Kerry has quantity and quality. Thus it's no surprise to find that, when the enthusiastically visiting Victorians were grading scenery in the early days of tourism, Kerry frequently merited the "sublime" rating. This meant that the county, and particularly the area around Killarney, became a visitors' mecca.

At one stage, this was a distinct drawback, with some truth to accusations of tackiness. But in modern times, the entire tourism business in Kerry has put itself through a bootstraps operation, so that by and large they now have - if you'll excuse the expression - a very classy product. And through it all, the Kingdom has a timeless glory which suits man and beast alike. For the folk in Kerry are renowned for their longevity, particularly in the area along the coast from Kenmare.

Down there, along towards Sneem, you'll hear of Big Bertha, the world's longest-lived cow. She lived productively to the remarkable age, in bovine terms, of 37. She was a great milker, and ancestress in her own lifetime of a veritable herd of progeny. Don't doubt her existence even for a nano-second. Because, as with everthing else in Kerry, it's all absolutely true and then some.

Local Attractions and Information

Beaufort Hotel Dunloe Castle Gardens	064 44583
Castleisland Crag Cave	066 41244
Dingle Ocean World	066 52111
Dunquin Great Blasket Centre	066 915 6444/915 6371
Glencar Into the Wilderness Walking Tours (May-Sep)	066 60104
Kenmare Walking Festivals	064 41034
Kenmare Heritage Centre	064 41233
Killarney Muckross House, Gardens & Traditional Farm	064 31440
Killarney Tourism Information	064 31633
Killorglin Kerry Woollen Mills	064 44122
Killorglin Puck Fair (ancient festival), mid-August	066 976 2366
Lauragh Dereen Gardens	064 83103
Listowel St John's Art Centre	068 22566
Listowel Writers' Week (June)	068 21074
Tralee Kerry the Kingdom- multi-image audiovisual	066 712 7777
Tralee Rose of Tralee Festival (late August)	066 712 3227
Tralee Siamsa Tire Arts Centre	066 712 3055
Valentia Island The Skellig Experience	066 947 6306

Annascaul

The South Pole Inn

PUB

Annascaul Co. Kerry **Tel: 066 57388 /57477**

Annascaul, on the Dingle peninsula, is one of the most-photographed villages in Ireland – mainly because of the brilliantly colourful and humorous frontage painted onto his pub by the late Dan Foley (which appeared on the front cover of at least three international guidebooks last year.) It is still a fine pub, although its theatrical owner is much missed since he passed on to the greater stage. Nearby, The South Pole, which is down at the lower end of the street is equally interesting - the name becomes clear when you realise there is a connection with the great Irish explorer Sir Ernest Shackleton. As well as being a delightful, well-run pub, The South Pole is full of fascinating Shackleton memorabilia. Closed 25 Dec & Good Fri.

Ballydavid

Gorman's Clifftop House & Restaurant

GUESTHOUSE/RESTAURANT

Glaise Bheag Balldavid Dingle Peninsula Co. Kerry
Tel: 066 915 5162 Fax: 066 915 5162
Email: gormans@eircom.net

GUESTHOUSE OF THE YEAR

Beautifully situated near Smerwick Harbour on the Slea Head scenic drive and Dingle way walking route, Sile and Vincent Gorman's guesthouse is, as they say themselves "just a great place to relax and unwind". It's also a very comfortable place to do this, as the whole premises has recently been virtually rebuilt and upgraded to a high standard. Natural materials and warm colours are a feature throughout the house and open fires, newspapers and books in two generous lounging areas (and a lot of pottery from the nearby Louis Mulcahy workshops) create a welcoming laid-back atmosphere. Bedrooms, which include some on the ground floor with easy access from the parking area, are not luxurious but very comfortable and attractively furnished in country style with thoughtfully finished bathrooms as well as phones and TV. The Gormans are knowledgeable and helpful hosts too, giving personal advice where it's needed in addition to the interesting information about the area provided at reception. Breakfast - an excellent buffet with home-baked breads, freshly squeezed juices, fruits, cheeses and cold meats as well as hot dishes cooked to order - is a treat and will set you up well for the day. Children welcome (under 2s free in parents' room, cot available free of charge). No pets. Garden, tennis, fishing, cycling, walking. **Rooms 9** (all en-suite & no smoking, 2 superior, 1 for disabled, shower only). B&B €50 pps, ss€25. **Restaurant:** The restaurant - which is open to non-residents - is on the sea side of the house, with large windows commanding superb sea views and, on fine evenings, spectacular sunsets. Vincent Gorman is the chef and Sile, who is a warm and solicitous host, supervises front of house; it's a good team, ensuring service that is both friendly and efficient. Vincent offers a couple of soups - fresh salmon chowder or carrot & courgette, perhaps - and four or five other starters, such as potato cake & black pudding sandwich with mushroom & bacon sauce (attractively presented and lighter than it sounds) and a pretty smoked Irish salmon with cream cheese & chives. Well-balanced main courses include several seafood dishes and the ever-popular sirloin steak (with mushroom & brandy sauce perhaps); vegetarian choices are always given - a main course of Mediterranean style vegetable parcels with tomato fondue is typical - and copious dishes of delicious vegetables are left on the table. But don't forget to leave a little room, as desserts are a strong point: home-made ice creams, profiteroles with chocolate sauce, orange treacle tartlets and passionfruit panna cotta are just a few of the temptations on offer, or you can finish with a cheese plate. Tea or coffee can be served in the lounge, which smokers will prefer as the dining room is no smoking. **Seats 35.** D daily, 6-9. Set D €32. Housewine from €14. Closed 24-25 Dec & 10 Jan -1 Mar. MasterCard, Visa, Laser. **Directions:** 8 miles west of Dingle - Sign posted An Fheothanach. Keep left at V,5 miles out.

Ballybunion

Harty-Costello Townhouse Bar & Restaurant

GUESTHOUSE/RESTAURANT

Main St. Ballybunion Co. Kerry **Tel: 068 27129**
Fax: 068 27489 Email: hartycostello@eircom.net

Although styled a townhouse in the contemporary mode, Davnet and Jackie Hourigan's welcoming town centre establishment is really an inn, encompassing all the elements of hospitality within its neatly painted and flower bedecked yellow walls, albeit at different times of day. Spacious, well-maintained bedrooms have not only television, direct dial phones, tea & coffee-making facilities and hair dryer, but also comfortable chairs and curtains thoughtfully fitted with blackout linings to keep out intrusively early summer light. There's also a pleasant lounging area between the accommodation and the evening restaurant (also on the first floor) and a choice of no less than three bars in which to unwind. Seafood is the speciality in the restaurant, where both table d'hôte and à la carte menus are offered, complemented by an extensive wine list. It all adds up to a relaxing and hospitable base for a golfing holiday, or for touring the south-west. Children welcome (under 12s free in parents' room). No pets. **Rooms 8** (all en-suite & no-smoking). B&B €57pps, ss €6.50. Closed Oct-Apr. Amex, MasterCard, Visa, Laser.

Ballybunion

Iragh Ti Connor

HOTEL

Main St Ballybunion Co. Kerry **Tel: 068 27112** Fax: 068 27787
Email: iraghticonnor@eircom.net Web: www.golfballybunion.com

The name, which translates as "the inheritance of O'Connor", says it all: what John and Joan and Joan O'Connor inherited was a 19th century pub with potential and, thanks to their scrupulous attention to detail when planning and sourcing materials like real slates and wooden windows for its transformation, their inheritance has now been transformed into a fine establishment with exceptionally large, comfortable bedrooms. All rooms have been carefully refurbished and furnished with antiques to complement the convenience of satellite television, direct dial phones and generous bathrooms with cast-iron tubs and power showers - and many rooms even have working fireplaces, where fires can be lit on request. Public areas, which include the original public bar, a lounge bar and a fine dining restaurant with a baby grand to add to the atmosphere, are also generous in scale, and furnished with style and individuality. Golfing holidays are a serious attraction here and Iragh Tí Connor is fast establishing a reputation as one of the best places to stay on the discerning golfers' circuits. **Rooms 17** (3 junior suites, 14 superior rooms). B&B €80 pps, ss €35. Closed 24-25 Dec. Amex, MasterCard, Visa. **Directions:** on the left as you come into the Main Street from Listowel.

Ballybunion
GUESTHOUSE

Teach de Broc Countryhouse

Links Rd Ballybunion Co. Kerry **Tel: 068 27581** Fax: 068 27919
Email: teachdebroc@eircom.net Web: www.ballybuniongolf.com

You don't have to play golf to appreciate this highly popular guesthouse, but it certainly must help as it is almost within the boundaries of the famous Ballybunion links. Aoife and Seamus Brock offer a high standard of comfort, with direct dial phones, TV and tea/coffee-making in all rooms and not only have recent extensions and refurbishments resulted in a new dining room and an extra four deluxe rooms, plus the upgrading of existing rooms, but the commitment to constant upgrading and improvement continues. But, however comfortable and well-located this exceptional guesthouse may be, it's the laid-back and genuinely hospitable atmosphere that really gets them coming back for more. Own parking. Not suitable for children. No pets. Wine licence. **Rooms 10** (all en-suite & no-smoking, 6 executive,1 for disabled). B&B €63.47pps, ss €25.39. Closed Dec-Feb. MasterCard, Visa, Laser. **Directions:** directly opposite Ballybunion golf club.

Ballyferriter
RESTAURANT

Tigh an Tobair

Ballyferriter Co. Kerry **Tel: 066 915 6404** Fax: 066 915 6526
Email: tighantobair@eircom.net Web: htt://homepage.eircom.net/~antobair

Way out on the Dingle peninsula near the famous Louis Mulcahy pottery, Tigh an Tobair ("the house of the well") is named after its most unusual feature: the well in the middle of the room around which it is, quite literally, arranged - glass-topped for safety, but clearly visible. Laura Meiland took over this well-known little place in 1999 and head chef Stephen Mahon - who joined her in spring 2000 - enjoys producing food that is "honest, robust, inventive and tasty". It's a good place to plan a break when touring or walking in the area - informal lunchtime menus include unusual specialities like Dutch pancakes as well as a wide range of other hot dishes and sanwiches; dinner menus are quite wide ranging and moderately priced.There are always vegetarian options (most also suitable for coeliacs) and they have occasional theme nights with entertainment, including Hallowe'en, St Valentine's Day and Lughnasa (August). Not suitable for children after 7 pm. Live music (inquire for details). **Seats 50.** L&D daily in summer, L12-4, D 6-9.30 (Sun to 9). A la carte (average D main course €10); house wine €15.87. Closed Jan-Feb, & Wed during off-season. MasterCard, Visa, Laser. **Directions:** on the main Slea Head drive,15 minutes from Dingle, in the centre of Ballyferriter.

Beaufort
PUB/RESTAURANT féile bia

The Beaufort Bar & Restaurant

Beaufort Killarney Co. Kerry
Tel: 064 44032 Fax: 064 44390

In the fourth generation of family ownership, Padraig O'Sullivan's immaculate establishment near the Gap of Dunloe is an absolute delight. Recent major renovations have seen the old tree at the front left safely in place which, together with features like the stonework and an open fire in the bar for winter, all contribute to the genuine character that can easily be lost in refurbishments. The pride taken by the family in running this fine pub is palpable and the upstairs restaurant (which can be reached through the bar or by a separate entrance from the carpark) is a logical extension of the existing business. Head chef Tim Brosnan, who joined the team in 1999, presents quite extensive, well-balanced à la carte dinner menus with a generous, traditional tone (seafood cocktail, chilled galia melon with a seasonal fruits & a strawberry sorbet, chicken liver paté; roast rack of Kerry lamb or duckling, sole meunière) plus a few more international dishes. There's a pleasingly local feel to some dishes - Aghadoe black pudding is singled out for mention; finish with classic desserts or farmhouse cheeses. Pricing is fairly moderate (main courses about €11-22) and Sunday lunch especially good value. Children welcome. Restaurant seats 56. No smoking area. D Tue-Sat, 6.30-9.30, à la carte; L Sun only, 12.30-2.30; set Sun L €16.51. House wine €16.51. SC discretionary. Closed Sun D, all Mon. Establishment closed 2 wks late Nov & early spring. MasterCard, Visa. **Directions:** follow the N72 to Kilorglin. Turn left at Beaufort bridge. It is the first stone village on the left in the village.

Beaufort
HOTEL

Hotel Dunloe Castle

Beaufort Killarney Co. Kerry **Tel: 064 44111** Fax: 064 44583 Web: www.iol.ie/khl

Sister hotel to the Hotel Europe (Fossa) and Ard-na-Sidhe (Caragh Lake), Dunloe Castle has many features in common with the larger Europe: the style of the building is similar, the same priorities apply – generous space is allowed for all areas throughout, the quality of furnishing is exceptionally high and both maintenance and housekeeping are superb. The original castle is still part of the development, but the hotel is mainly modern and, like the Europe, the atmosphere is distinctly continental. Everything is on a large scale, with wide corridors leading to spacious bedrooms, some with dining areas and all with magnificent views, satellite TV & in-house video, airconditioning and ironing facilities. Major improvements have been made recently, including a re-styling of the exterior to include a new entrance and foyer, a lobby bar, terrrace and a new caé. The park around the hotel, is internationally renowned for its unique botanical collection, which includes many rare plants. As well as an equestrian centre, the hotel also has its own fishing rights on the River Laune (fishing free of charge to residents; ghillie available on request). Conference/banqueting (150/180). Leisure centre, swimming pool. Snooker, pool table. Garden, fishing, walking, tennis, equestrian. Children welcome (under 2s free in parents' room, cot available without charge; playroom, playground). No pets. **Rooms 110** (1 suite, 40 no smoking). Lift. B&B from €228 (room rate with breakfast, max 2 guests). Closed 1 Oct-mid April. Amex, Diners, MasterCard, Visa. **Directions:** off main Ring of Kerry road.

Caherciveen
RESTAURANT

Brennan's Restaurant

12 Main St Caherciveen Co. Kerry **Tel: 066 947 2021**
Fax: 066 947 2914 Email: brenrest@iol.ie

Conor and Teresa Brennan run a professional operation here, serving a deservedly popular early evening menu and a later wider-ranging à la carte every day. Conor takes pride in using the best of local ingredients and serving them imaginatively but without overdressing so you may expect plenty of seafood - prawns, crabmeat, salmon, hake, turbot - and meats. including local mountain lamb, to be given contemporary treatment (Caherciveen black pudding might come with caramelised shallots & balsamic vinegar, for example) without being slavishly fashionable. A good cheese plate and well-made desserts, notably ices **Seats 68** (private room, 30). D 5.30 -10 daily. Early evening menu (5.30-7 pm) A la carte also available. House wine from about €15. Children welcome. Arrangement with local carpark. Closed Mon &Tue from Nov-Mar; 24-26 Dec. Amex, Diners, MasterCard, Visa. **Directions:** On the right in Main Street as approaching from Killarney.

Caherciveen
PUB

O'Neills "The Point Bar"

Renard Point Caherciveen Co. Kerry
Tel: 066 947 2165 Fax: 066 947 2165

In the same family for 150 years, Michael and Bridie O'Neill's pub, The Point Bar, is beside the Valentia Island car ferry. Renovated in true character by the present owners, it's always neat and makes an appealing place to drop into for a quick one while you're waiting for the ferry – but even better to stay awhile and make the most of their super fresh seafood, served during the summer. The menu covers everything from a whole range of salads and open sandwiches on brown bread – fresh and smoked wild salmon, smoked mackerel, crabmeat, crab claws – to hot dishes like deep-fried squid and a couple of hake and monkfish dishes with garlic and olive oil. Not very suitable for children. The Valentia Island ferry runs continuously – i.e. not to a time table – from April-September inclusive. L Mon-Sat, D daily. Food available only from April to October. No credit cards.

Caherciveen
PUB/RESTAURANT

QC's Bar & Restaurant

3 Main St. Caherciveen Co. Kerry **Tel: 066 947 2244**
Fax: 066 947 2244 Email: acooke@oceanfree.net Web: www.qcbar.com

Kate and Andrew Cooke renovated this old building with style and sensitivity - introducing a pleasingly continental tone (Spanish to be precise) while retaining interesting and characterful features such as the original stone wall and a big fireplace that must be a great draw on cold winter days. The bar counter is also over a century old and there are numerous nautical antiques and pictures of local interest. Local meats and fish feature - the fish is supplied by the family company, Quinlan's Kerry Fish at Renard's Point - and, as a charcoal grill from the Basque region is a major feature in the kitchen, chargrills, with lots of olive oil and garlic, are typical of the style. Spanish omelette is, of course, another speciality (and very good it is too) and the wine list is almost exclusively Spanish. Children welcome. **Seats 36** L Mon-Sat 12.30-3, D daily 6.30-9.30 (Sun from 5.30). Closed L Sun, 25 Dec, Good Fri. MasterCard, Visa (min transaction €25). MasterCard, Visa, Laser. **Directions:** In the centre of town.

Cahirciveen

The Quarry Restaurant

RESTAURANT Kells Post Office Cahirciveen Co. Kerry **Tel: 066 9477601**
Fax: 066 9477660 Email: patscraftshop@eircom.net Web: www.patscraftshop.com

Pat Golden's family-run "one stop shop" on the Ring of Kerry is extremely useful to know about - not only will you get good home cooking here, but there's a post office and foodstore, filling station, tourist information point and bureau de change. Aside from these practical points, there are more interesting aspects to this many-sided venture as it also includes a fine craft shop, with quality Irish clothing and gift items and a unique attraction in the shape of 'The Golden Mile Nature Walk' up behind the quarry, which is just the place to walk off your lunch. The restaurant is on the first floor with large windows to take advantage of panoramic views over Kells Bay to the Dingle Peninsula and - another surprise - the cooking style includes genuine Mediterranean influences as well as Irish dishes as head chef Elena Stavri is a Greek Cypriot and "cooks with the heart". So you'll find real home-made Greek food like moussaka, hummous, tzatziki and baklava sitting happily alongside Irish stew and wild Dingle Bay salmon.The pricing is reasonable (most main courses around €9; top price, for sirloin steak, about €16) and, best of all perhaps, this is somewhere you can get a decent bite to eat during the day on a Sunday, when most of our recommendations in the are closed. * On alternate Friday nights in July & August Greek mezza style banquets are held - ring the restaurant for information and booking. **Seats 86.** No smoking area; air conditioning. Children welcome. Open daily 9am-6pm, Easter-Oct. A la carte; house wine about €13.50. Closed Nov-Easter. Amex, Diners, MasterCard, Visa, Laser, Switch. **Directions:** Midway between Glenbeigh & Cahirciveen.

Caherdaniel

Derrynane Hotel

HOTEL/RESTAURANT Caherdaniel Co. Kerry
Tel: 066 947 5136 Fax: 066 947 5160
Email: info@derrynane.com Web: www.derrynane.com

If only for its superb location – on the seaward side of the Ring of Kerry road – this unassuming 1960s-style hotel would be well worth a visit, but there is much more to it than the view, or even its waterside position. The accommodation is quite modest but very comfortable, the food is good and, under the excellent management of Mary O'Connor and her well-trained staff, this hospitable, family-friendly place provides a welcome home from home for many a contented guest. Activity holidays are a big draw - there are beautiful beaches, excellent fishing with local fisherman Michael Fenton (who supplies all necessary equipment and has a fully licensed boat), Waterville Golf Course offers special rates at certain times - and the hotel has published its own walking brochure. Don't leave the area without visiting Daniel O'Connell's beautiful house at Derrynane – or the amazing Ballinskelligs chocolate factory. Children welcome (under 4s free in parents' room, cots available without charge; playroom) Heated outdoor swimming pool, tennis, pool table. Well-behaved small dogs with their own beds may stay with their owners. Garden. **Rooms 74** (all en-suite, 10 no smoking). B&B €70pps, ss €20. **Restaurant:** Beautifully located, overlooking the heated outdoor swimming pool and the hotel's gardens (which reach down to the shore), the restaurant enjoys stunning sea views on a good day and the best of local ingredients are used in imaginative, very fairly priced four-course dinner menus. **Seats 50** (private room, 20) D 7-9 daily, Set D €32, sc discretionary. House wine about €15. Non smoking restaurant; air conditioning. Hotel closed Oct-Easter. Amex, Diners, MasterCard, Visa, Laser. **Directions:** Midway between Sneem and Waterville on the ring of Kerry.

Caherdaniel

Iskeroon

ACCOMMODATION Bunvalia Caherdaniel Co. Kerry **Tel: 066 947 5119** Fax: 066 947 5488
Email: info@iskeroon.com Web: www.iskeroon.com

Geraldine and David Hare's beautiful old house is in a secluded position overlooking Derrynane Harbour. The effort taken to get there makes it all the more restful once settled in. All three of the comfortable and interestingly decorated bedrooms overlook the harbour – and the islands of Deenish and Scarriff – and each has its own private bathroom just across a corridor. The private pier at the bottom of the garden joins an old Mass Path which, by a happy chance, leads not only to the beach but also to Keating's pub (known as Bridie's) where a bit of banter and some good seafood is also to be had in the evenings, although it's wise to check on this beforehand. Unsuitable for children. No pets. **Rooms 3,** all with private bathrooms. B&B approx €100pps, ss€20. Closed 30 Sep-1 May. MasterCard, Visa. **Directions:** Between Caherdaniel and Waterville (N70), turn off at the Scariff Inn, signed to Bunavalla Pier. Bearing left at each bend, go to the pier and left through "private" gate; cross beach and enter through white gate posts.

Camp

Barnagh Bridge Country House

GUESTHOUSE

Cappaclough East Camp Co. Kerry **Tel: 066 713 0145**
Fax: 066 713 0299 Email: bbguest@eircom.net Web: www.barnaghbridge.com

Snuggled into the hillside overlooking Tralee Bay, Heather Williams' unusual architect-designed guesthouse is in extensive grounds between the mountains and the sea. Attractive and comfortable, it was purpose-built, with five individually furnished guest bedrooms (decor themed on local wild flowers), all with en-suite shower rooms. In the dining room guests can drink in the view of Tralee Bay while doing justice to Heather's breakfasts – fresh juices, newly baked breads and scones, locally made preserves, and Dingle smoked salmon and scrambled eggs or a traditional fry (in addition to daily specials such as kippers or French toast). The stylishly decorated guest drawing room opens onto a patio overlooking the Maharees islands and their spectacular sunsets, and the latest improvement is a conservatory, which extends the reception area and dining room - and maximises still further on the wonderful view. Garden, fishing, walking. Not suitable for children under 10. No pets. **Rooms 5** (all en-suite & non-smoking). B&B €35 pps, ss €12. Closed 31 Oct-1 March. Amex, MasterCard, Visa. **Directions:** Take N86 Dingle Road from Tralee; after 9 miles, take Connor Pass/Castlegregory road (R560); guesthouse is 1 mile on the left.

Camp

The Cottage Restaurant

RESTAURANT

Camp Co. Kerry **Tel: 066 713 0022**
Web: www.kerryview.com

Frank & Gretta Wyles opened their bright, airy restaurant in September 1999 and, although newly built, both design and materials are in the local idiom so it fits in remarkably well and is already maturing gracefully. It's a welcome addition to the local dining scene, especially because it's an all-year enterprise. Local ingredients feature in wholesome, quite traditional fare (west coast chowder, rack of lamb with roasted vegetables, herb mash). Seafood is a speciality (daily specials) and also steaks, various ways; vegetarian dishes - typically tagliatelle with basil, wild mushrooms & fresh vegetables in a cream & wine reductionare always on the main menu. Pleasant service and reasonable prices too. Ample parking; children welcome. **Seats 60.** (private room, 14). D 6-10 daily, L Sun only 12-3.30; à la carte; house wine from € 13.50; sc discretionary. Amex, MasterCard, Visa, Laser. **Directions:** On the Tralee-Castlegregory-Conor Pass-Dingle road (10 miles from Tralee).

Camp

James Ashe

PUB/RESTAURANT

Camp Tralee Co. Kerry **Tel: 066 413 0133**

This fine old pub just off the Tralee-Dingle road has been in the family for 200 years and the present owners Rory and Gertie Duffin, intend to keep things pretty much the way they've been, at least in the recent past. It's a delightful place, full of genuine character and hospitality. Seafood (typically in monkfish, crab & salmon gratin) and local lamb and beef feature in generous wholesome food with the emphasis on flavour. Daytime food available 12.30-7 (Sun to 8); D 6-10; à la carte; house wine about €10.50. Closed 25 Dec & Good Fri. Phone ahead to check opening times off season. Amex, Diners, MasterCard, Visa. **Directions:** On the main Tralee-Dingle road, 10 miles from Tralee.

Camp

Suan Na Mara

B&B

Castlegregory Rd Camp Co. Kerry **Tel: 066 7139258** Fax: 066 7139258
Email: suanmara@eircom.net Web: www.kerryweb.ie/suanmara

Fionnula Fitzgerald's welcoming modern B&B near the sea is set well back from the road in spacious grounds and even has its own pitch & putt course in an adjoining field. It's a relaxed and very pleasant place to stay, with a comfortable sitting rooms for guests and bedrooms that are a little on the small side but well-equipped, with hair dryer, TV, radio and tea/coffee making facilities and neat bathrooms. Maintenance is immaculate, hospitality genuine - and breakfast will be a treat. Garden, pitch & putt, tennis, walking. **Rooms 7** (all en-suite & no smoking). B&B €31 pps, ss€29. Children welcome (cot available, €6.35). Closed 3 Nov-1 Apr. MasterCard, Visa. **Directions:** Take N86 to Camp Junction and then R560 for approx 5 Km.

Caragh Lake
COUNTRY HOUSE/
RESTAURANT

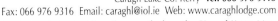

Caragh Lodge

Caragh Lake Co. Kerry **Tel: 066 976 9115**
Fax: 066 976 9316 Email: caraghl@iol.ie Web: www.caraghlodge.com

Less than a mile from the Ring of Kerry, Mary Gaunt's lovely Victorian house and gardens nestling on the shores of the startlingly beautiful Caragh Lake is an idyllic place, with views of Ireland's highest mountains, the McGillicuddy Reeks. The house – which is elegantly furnished with antiques but not too formal – makes a cool, restful retreat. Bedrooms include some recently added garden rooms with wonderful views, their own entrance and sitting room (complete with open log fire), and are all sumptuously furnished with lovely bathrooms. Salmon and trout fishing, boating and swimming are all available at the bottom of the garden and there's tennis too. Not suitable for children under 12. No pets. **Rooms 15** (all en-suite, 8 junior suites, 6 superior). B&B €80, ss €30. **Restaurant:** In the elegant dining room overlooking the lake (open to non-residents by reservation), Mary's real love of cooking shines through. Local produce (such as freshly caught seafood, often including wild salmon from Caragh Lake, Kerry lamb and home-grown vegetables) takes pride of place. Wide-ranging menus tempt with starters like warm potato pancakes with home-cured salmon & chive cream and parmesan gratinated oysters, followed by soup or sorbet of the day and main courses including specialities such as crispy half duck with an orange duck jus and confit of wild salmon on a bed of spinach with lemon butter sauce. Baking is a particular strength, not only in delicious home-baked breads, but also baked desserts and treats for afternoon tea - including recipes handed down by Mary's family through the generations. D 7-8.30; €38 (average, à la carte). House wine €18. sc discretionary. Establishment closed mid Oct-mid April. Amex, Diners, MasterCard, Visa. **Directions:** From Killorglin on N70, Glenbeigh direction, take second road signed Caragh Lake; at end of road go left again. The house is on the right.

Caragh Lake

Carrig House Country House & Restaurant

COUNTRY HOUSE/RESTAURANT
Caragh Lake Co. Kerry **Tel: 066 976 9100**
Fax: 066 976 9166 Email: info@carrighouse.com Web: www.carrighouse.com

At the heart of Frank and Mary Slattery's sensitively extended Victorian house lies a hunting lodge once owned by Lord Brocket - and he chose well, as it is very atttractive and handsomely set in fine gardens with the lake and mountains providing a dramatic backdrop. The house is welcoming and well-maintained, with friendly staff (Frank himself carries the luggage to your room) and a very relaxed atmosphere, notably in a series of sitting rooms where you can chat beside the fire or have a drink before dinner. Individually decorated bedrooms furnished with antiques (some with their own patio) are large, high-ceilinged and airy, with generous, well-designed bathrooms. The gardens are extensive and a laminated map is available, naming the various areas - Waterfall Garden , Pond Garden, Rock Walk etc - and the main plantings in each; a more detailed list is available on request. Not suitable for children under 8 except small babies (under 1 free of charge, cot available). Dogs allowed in some areas. Swimming (lake), fishing (ghilly & boat available), walking, garden, croquet. **Rooms 16** (1 suite, 1 junior suite, 12 superior, 2 no smoking) B&B €75pps, ss€31. **Restaurant:** Situated in a prime position overlooking the lake, the restaurant is open to non-residents (booking essential). An extensive à carte menu based on local ingredients is offered - notably seafood and Kerry lamb - with organic vegetables, herbs and fruit supplied by their own walled kitchen garden. Vegetarian dishes are always available. **Seats 50.** No smoking restaurant. D daily, 6.30-9. A la carte. House wine €21.50. SC discretionary. Establishment closed 1 Dec-1 Mar. MasterCard, Visa, Laser, Switch. **Directions:** Left after 2.5 miles on Killorglin/Glenbeigh Road N70 (Ring of Kerry).

Caragh Lake
HOTEL

Hotel Ard-na-Sidhe

Caragh Lake Co. Kerry **Tel: 066 976 9105** Fax: 066 976 9282
Email: sales@kih.liebherr.com Web: www.iol.ie/khl

Set in woodland and among award-winning gardens, this peaceful Victorian retreat is in a beautiful mountain location overlooking Caragh Lake. Decorated throughout in a soothing country house style, very comfortable antique-filled day rooms provide plenty of lounging space for quiet indoor relaxation and a terrace for fine weather – all with wonderful views. Bedrooms – shared between the main house and some with private patios in the garden house – are spacious and elegantly furnished in traditional style, with excellent en-suite bathrooms. This is a sister hotel to the Hotel Europe and Dunloe Castle (see entries), whose leisure facilities are also available to guests. Dooks, Waterville, Killeen and Mahony's Point golf courses are all within easy reach. Not very suitable for children, although concessions are given (under 12s free in parents' room; cots available). No pets. **Rooms 19** (5 no smoking). B&B Room Rate €228 (max 2 guests) sc included. 24 hr room service. Closed 1 Oct-1 May. Amex, Diners, MasterCard, Visa, Laser. **Directions:** Off N70 Ring of Kerry road, signed 5 km west of Killorglin.

Castlegregory

Spillanes

PUB

Fahamore Maharees Castlegregory Co. Kerry **Tel: 066 713 9125** Fax: 066 713 9538

It's a long way down from the main road to reach the Maharees, but well worth it for many reasons, not least a visit to Marilyn and Michael Spillane's great traditional pub - they work hard at both the food and hospitality and have earned a well-deserved loyal following as a result. There's a tempting display of salads and desserts to choose from and seafood stars on the menu - mussels grilled with garlic breadcrumbs, crabclaws served in shell with brown bread and a cocktail dipping sauce, fresh and wild salmon in salads and open sandwiches, scampi made from Dingle prawns. There's plenty for meat-lovers, such as chargrilled steaks, several chicken dishes (in the evening), some vegetarian dishes and some with child-appeal too. Meals daily in high season (Jun-Sep), 12.30 to 9.30 (Sun 2-9). No food Nov-mid March. MasterCard, Visa, Laser. **Directions:** Dingle Peninsula, 3.5 miles north of Castlegregory, between Brandon and Tralee bays.

Dingle

Bambury's Guesthouse

GUESTHOUSE

Mail Road Dingle Co. Kerry **Tel: 066 915 1244** Fax: 066 915 1786
Email: info@bamburysguesthouse.com Web: www.dbamburysguesthouse.com

Just a couple of minutes walk from the centre of Dingle, Jimmy and Bernie Bambury's well-run, purpose-built guesthouse has spacious rooms (including three suitable for disabled guests) with tea/coffee trays, phone, satellite TV, hair dryer and complimentary mineral water. Bernie Bambury's breakfasts include griddle cakes with fresh fruit and honey – a house speciality – and vegetarian breakfasts are offered by arrangement. Not suitable for children under 4; no pets. Own parking. **Rooms 12** (all shower only & no smoking) B&B €46, ss €16. Open all year. MasterCard, Visa. **Directions:** On N86, on the left after the Shell garage, on entering Dingle.

Dingle

Beginish Restaurant

RESTAURANT

Green Street Dingle Co. Kerry **Tel: 066 915 1321** Fax: 066 915 1321
Email: dunlavin@gofree.indigo.ie

Ronan and Denise Kane have been running this famous restaurant since March 2000 - and, not only do both the food and service continue to please devotees of the previous régime, but they have been steadily earning their own reputation independent of the establishment's illustrious past. Unusually for cottagey Dingle, the restaurant is high-ceilinged and elegant, with a conservatory at the back overlooking the garden – lovely at night, when it is floodlit. Seafood is naturally very much in evidence, but Ronan's well-balanced menus offer a wide choice, including Kerry mountain lamb and a vegetarian dish of the day. The style includes classics alongside contemporary dishes: Glenbeigh oysters served on a bed of ice, crispy seafood springroll with a balsamic & ginger sauce, poached Dingle Bay lobster (Thermidor, or served simply with garlic or melted butter) and honey glazed duck breast & leg conift with apple & Calvados sauce are all typical. Classic desserts or Irish cheeses with a glass of port to finish. Caring service from staff who really want guests to enjoy their visit. **Seats 52.** D only, Tues-Sun, 6-10; Set D €26.03, also à la carte. House wine €17.14; sc discretionary. Closed Mon &15 Dec-early Feb. MasterCard, Visa, Laser. **Directions:** Below the Catholic Church, on the opposite side of the street.

Dingle

Benners Hotel

HOTEL

Main Street Dingle Co.Kerry **Tel: 066 915 1638** Fax: 066 915 1412
Email: benners@eircom.net Web: www.bennershotel.com

Major refurbishment and the addition of spacious new rooms at the back have greatly improved this centrally-located hotel. Public areas include a streetside bar which has more character than expected of an hotel (food available 6.30-9.30 daily) and a large, bright, dining room towards the back of the building. Bedrooms in the older part of the hotel have more character (some have four-posters), but the new back bedrooms are quieter. Private parking. Children welcome (under 4s free in parents' room, cot available without charge). Pets by arrangement. **Rooms 52** (4 junior suites, disabled 2) Lift. B&B about €95 pps, ss about €20. Closed 25-26 Dec. Amex, Diners, MasterCard, Visa. **Directions:** In centre of town, beside The Lord Baker's.

Dingle

Captains House

GUESTHOUSE The Mall Dingle Co. Kerry **Tel: 066 915 1531** Fax: 066 915 1079

When Jim, a retired sea captain, and Mary Milhench bought this guesthouse in the late 80s they were renewing a seafaring tradition going back to the original captain, Tom Williams, who first took lodgers here in 1886. Today this charming house is as relaxed and hospitable a place as could be wished for: approached via a little bridge over the Mall river then through a lovely garden, it has been renovated and furnished with the antiques and curios collected by Jim on his voyages. The age and nature of the building - which extends into the next door premises - has created a higgledy-piggledy arrangement of rooms that adds to the charm; rooms vary considerably, as would be expected, but all have comfort (orthodpaedic beds, phones, satelllite TV, hospitality trays, plenty of hot water) as well as character. A welcoming turf fire in the reception area encourages guests to linger over tea, or with a book, and breakfast - which is a very special feature of a stay here - is served in the conservatory. Not suitable for children. No pets. **Rooms 9** (1 suite, 7 shower only, all no smoking). B&B €45pps, ss €5. Closed 1 Dec-16 Mar. Amex, MasterCard, Visa. **Directions:** Turn right at town entrance roundabout and Captains House is 100 metres up on left.

Dingle

The Chart House

RESTAURANT The Mall Dingle Co. Kerry **Tel: 066 915 2255** Fax: 066 9152255
Email: charthouse@iol.ie Web: www.charthousedingle.com

Informal in furnishing style and general approach, Jim McCarthy's purpose-built restaurant brought a new element to Dingle's dining scene when it opened in 1997 and it quickly became established as one of the leading restaurants in an area exceptionally well-endowed with good eating places. While based mainly on local ingredients, notably seafood, head chef Gary Fitzgerald's menus are international in tone - a speciality starter of Annascaul black pudding, for example, is accompanied by gingered apples then wrapped in filo pastry and served with a bacon jus and, similarly, a main course of pan-fried John Dory comes with citrus couscous, slow roasted tomatoes & basil pesto. Prices are fairly moderate (starters around €7.50, main courses average €20). But there are some themes from closer to home too: char grilled fillet steak comes with bubble & squeak, glazed pearl onions and rosemary jus, for instance. Meat- and fish-free dishes - probably two or more on each course - offer mainstream contemporary cooking and are equally appealing to non-vegetarians. Desserts include some classics like a basket of home-made ice creams or warm cherry and almond tart with mascarpone cream– and Irish cheeses are cannily offered, at €10.80, with a glass of vintage port. The wine list has helpful tasting notes as well as a clear layout of country of origin as well as vintages - and, of course, there's always a Chateau MacCarthy in stock. **Seats 45.** No smoking area, air conditioning. D Wed-Mon, 6.30-10; à la carte. House wine €16.18. Closed Tues & 7 Jan -13 Feb. MasterCard, Visa. **Directions:** On the roundabout as you enter the town.

Dingle

Cleevaun House

GUESTHOUSE Ladys Cross Dingle Co.Kerry **Tel: 066 915 1108** Fax: 066 915 2228
Email: cleevaun@iol.ie Web: www.cleevaun.com

A cup of tea or coffee and a slice of home-made porter cake welcomes guests to Charlotte and Sean Cluskey's well-run, recently renovated guesthouse just outside the town. Set in an acre of landscaped gardens overlooking Dingle Bay, it's near enough to Dingle to be handy and far enough away to enjoy the peace that the peninsula promises. Furnishing throughout is in a pleasant country pine style: bedrooms are all non-smoking, have good facilities and are well organised, with quality beds, quilted bedspreads and well-finished en-suite bathrooms; one bedroom has a separate dressing room. Charlotte's breakfasts – served in a large south-facing dining room overlooking Dingle Bay – are quite a speciality. **Rooms 9.** B&B €44, ss €19. Closed 15-Nov-15-Mar. MasterCard, Visa, Laser. **Directions:** Just outside the town, on the Slea Head/Ventry scenic route R559.

Dingle

Dick Mack's

PUB Green Lane Dingle Co. Kerry **Tel: 066 915 1960**

Once a cobbler's, this old shop-bar still sells an eclectic mixture of modern leather items, wellington boots and patent hangover cures. It's run by Dick's son, Oliver J MacDonnell, who has had the wisdom to leave well alone. Seating is basic, there's an old gas fire for cold evenings and the cashier's booth is put to good use as a snug. Definitely not a food place but open over lunchtime (12-2.30) and evenings (4-11). **Directions:** A few doors up the street from the Beginish restaurant.

Dingle Skellig Hotel

Dingle
HOTEL

Dingle Co. Kerry **Tel: 066 915 0200** Fax: 066 915 1501
Email: dsk@iol.ie Web: www.dingleskellig.com

Although modest-looking from the road, this 1960s hotel enjoys a shoreside location on the edge of the town and has won many friends over the years. It is a particularly well-run, family-friendly hotel, with organised entertainment for children and an excellent leisure centre. Roomy public areas are comfortably furnished with a fair degree of style. Good use is made of sea views throughout, especially in the conservatory restaurant, which has special anti-glare glass. Bedrooms are reasonably large, have been recently refurbished and have small but neat bathrooms. It is best known as a holiday destination, but the Dingle Skellig also has excellent conference and business meeting facilities, with back-up services including French and German translation on request. Conference/banqueting 250/230); business centre, secretarial services. Children under 3 free in parents' bedrooms; cots available free of charge; all year crèche, playroom, children's playground. **Rooms 112** (3 suites, 38 executive & 10 no-smoking bedrooms.) Leisure centre, swimming pool. Fishing, garden. Closed 20-27 Dec & all Jan. Amex, Diners, MasterCard, Visa, Laser. **Directions:** On the sea side of the road as you approach Dingle from Tralee & Killarney.

Doyle's Seafood Restaurant & Townhouse

Dingle
RESTAURANT/ACCOMMODATION

John Street Dingle Co. Kerry
Tel: 066 915 1174 Fax: 066 915 1816
Email: cdoyles@iol.ie Web: www.doylesofdingle.com

In the good hands of Sean Cluskey and his wife Charlotte (who runs Cleevaun guesthouse), flagstone floors and old furniture give this restaurant lots of character. Local seafood is the main attraction - nightly specials depend on the day's landings - and lobster, selected from a tank in the bar, is a speciality. There are, however, concessions to non-seafood eaters – eg duo of Kerry mountain lamb (roast rack and leg with braised puy lentils, roast garlic & thyme jus) and traditional beef & Guinness stew - and vegetarian dishes such as crispy provencal strudel with basil, olives and tomato butter sauce. Puddings are nice and traditional or there's a plated selection of farmhouse cheeses from the Munster region to finish. **Seats 45.** No-smoking area; air conditioning. D only, Mon-Sat 6-10. A la carte; house wine €17.75; sc 10%. Closed Sun. **Accommodation:** High quality accommodation includes a residents' sitting room as well as eight spacious bedrooms with well-designed en-suite bathrooms. B&B €60 pps. Establishment closed mid Nov-mid Feb. Amex, Diners, MasterCard, Visa, Laser. **Directions:** On entering Dingle, take third exit from roundabout into The Mall; turn right into John Street.

Emlagh House

Dingle
COUNTRY HOUSE

Dingle Co. Kerry **Tel: 066 915 2345** Fax 066 915 2369
Email: info@ emlaghhouse.com Web: www.emlaghhouse.com

This luxurious country house style guesthouse is tucked into a site just behind the Dingle Skellig Hotel, on the sea side of the road and, although the surroundings are still a little raw, it has been built with exceptional attention to detail and will age gracefully as soon as the landscaping has matured. Proprietors Michael and Marion Kavanagh have assembled quite a team around them and are particularly fortunate to have Stella Doyle (previously proprietor-chef at Doyle's Seafood Restaurant) as Manager - aside from specific skills and experience, she is an especially warm and hospitable hostess. The style throughout the house is gracious, in large, well-proportioned rooms furnished in traditional country house style but with a contemporary streak that gives it a great lightness of touch. Bedrooms (most of which have harbour views) are elegant and extremely comfortable, with features including individually controlled heating/air conditioning, trouser press with iron, direct dial phone with modem, satellite TV, video, radio & CD - the latter wired to lovely marbled bathrooms with underfloor heating, separate shower and bath, double basins, heated mirror and towel rails and thick bathrobes. Some interconnecting rooms are available to provide private accomodation for groups. Breakfast is served in a stylish dining room with contemporary influences in the decor alongside the antiques - Stella cooks delicious things to start the day on the right note and it comes as no surprise that light evening meals are to be offered here in due course. Many activities (golf, fishing, sailing, equestrian) available nearby. Not suitable for children under 8. No pets. **Rooms 12** (11 superior, 1 for disabled). B&B €102, ss €31. Closed mid Dec-mid Feb. MasterCard, Visa, Laser. **Directions:** N86 fro Tralee. Turn left at Skelligs Hotel sign.

Dingle
ACCOMMODATION

Greenmount House

Upper John St. Dingle Co. Kerry
Tel: 066 915 1414 Fax: 066 915 1974
Email: mary@greenmounthouse.com Web: greenmounthouse.com

Just five minutes walk from the centre of Dingle, John and Mary Curran have run one of Ireland's finest guesthouses since the mid-70s. It's an exceptionally comfortable place to stay, quietly located on the hillside, with private parking and uninterrupted views across the town and harbour to the mountains across the bay. The well-appointed bedrooms (all of which are non-smoking) fall into two groups – half are in the original house and, although smaller than the newer ones, are also furnished to a very high standard. The others are junior suites with generous seating areas and good amenities, including fridges as well as tea/coffee-making trays, phone and TV (and their own entrance and balcony). There's also a comfortable residents' sitting room and a conservatory overlooking the harbour, where breakfast - which has always been a special feature of Greenmount and won our Denny Breakfast Award (Munster Region) in 2001 - is served. The buffet - laden down with all kinds of fresh and poached fruits, juices, yogurts, cheeses, freshly baked breads - is augmented by an extensive choice of hot dishes, including the traditional full Irish breakfast. Home baking is a speciality and all the preserves are home-made too - the wonder is that anyone ever leaves this place of a morning at all. Not suitable for children under 8. No pets. **Rooms 12** (7 superior, all en-suite & no smoking); Room rate €125 (2 guests). Closed 10-27 Dec. MasterCard, Visa. **Directions:** Turn right and right again on entering Dingle.

Dingle
RESTAURANT

The Half Door

John St. Dingle Co. Kerry **Tel: 066 915 1600** Fax: 066 915 1883
Web: www.halfdoor@iol.ie

Since 1991 chef-proprietor Denis O'Connor and his team have been preparing great seafood at the cottagey Dingle restaurant he runs with his wife Teresa. Menus go with the seasons but whatever is available is perfectly cooked and generously served without over-presentation. An outstanding speciality of the house is the seafood platter, available hot or cold as either a starter or main course with (depending on availability of individual items) lobster, oysters, Dublin Bay prawns, scallops, crab claws and mussels (attractively presented with garlic or lemon butter). Good traditional puddings or Irish farmhouse cheeses to follow. **Seats 50.** No smoking area; air conditioning. D Mon-Sat, 6-10.Early D 6-6.30 only; later, à la carte. Closed Sun; 24-26 Dec. Amex, MasterCard, Visa. **Directions:** on entering Dingle, turn right onto The Mall at roundabout, then right onto John St.

Dingle
GUESTHOUSE

Heatons House

The Wood Dingle Co. Kerry **Tel: 066 915 2288** Fax: 066 915 2324
Email: heatons@iol.ie Web: www.heatonsdingle.com

Cameron and Nuala Heaton's fine purpose-built guesthouse is set in well-mainytained gardens just across the road from the water and, although convenient to the town, it's beyond the hustle and bustle of the busy streets. An impressive foyer-lounge area sets the tone on arrival and spacious bedrooms confirm first impressions: all have bathrooms finished to a very high standard and phones, TV and hospitality trays - and the two new junior suites and three superior rooms added this year are not only luxurious but very stylish in a refreshingly contemporary idiom. Getting guests off to a good start each day is a point of honour and breakfast includes an extensive buffet (everything from fresh juices to cold meats and Irish cheeses) as well as a full hot breakfast menu. **Rooms 16** (2 junior suites, 3 superior, all no smoking). B&B €55 pps, ss€40. Closed 23-26 Dec. MasterCard, Visa. **Directions:** Approximately 600 metres beyond the marina on the west side of town.

Dingle
PUB

James Flahive

The Quay Dingle Co. Kerry **Tel: 066 915 1634**

They don't make them like this any more - James Flahive's welcoming, friendly old pub has been a home from home for many a regular visitor for over 30 years. It's hard to imagine any call for a tailor's shop in Dingle these days, but that's how it started off in the 1890s; more recently it's long been a special favourite of sailing people and has had some very distinguished visitors and photos of many of them adorn the walls - along with several of Dingle's best-loved resident, Fungie the dolphin. No food, but a good pint and good company. Opening hours are irregular.

Dingle

Lord Baker's Seafood Restaurant & Bar

PUB/RESTAURANT Dingle Co. Kerry **Tel: 066 915 1277** Fax: 066 915 2174

Believed to be the oldest pub in Dingle, this business was established in 1890 by a Tom Baker. A popular businessman in the area, a colourful orator, member of Kerry County Council and a director of the Tralee-Dingle Railway, he was known locally as "Lord Baker" and as such is now immortalised in John Moriarty's excellent pub and restaurant in the centre of Dingle. A welcoming turf fire burns in the front bar, where bar food such as chowder and home-baked bread or crab claws in garlic butter is served. At the back, there's a much more sophisticated dining set-up in the restaurant proper (and, beyond it, a walled garden). Seafood (notably lobster from their own tank) stars, of course, but there's also a good choice of other dishes – local lamb (roast rack or braised shank, perhaps), also Kerry beef, chicken and local duckling – all well-cooked and served in an atmosphere of great hospitality. In addition to the main menu there are chef's specials each evening - and an unusual house speciality features on the dessert menu: traditional plum pudding with brandy sauce! Sunday lunch in the restaurant is a particularly popular event and very well done (booking strongly advised); on other days the lunchtime bar menu, plus one or two daily specials such as a roast, can be taken in the restaurant. The wine list includes a Connoisseur's Selection of ten wines, including some new classics as well as friends from the old world. **Seats 120.** L Fri-Wed12.30-2; D Fri-Wed, 6-9.45. Set menus & à la carte. No smoking area. Closed 24-25 Dec & Good Fri. **Directions:** Town centre.

Dingle

Milltown House

ACCOMMODATION Milltown House Dingle Co.Kerry **Tel: 066 915 1372**
Fax: 066 915 1095 Email: milltown@indigo.ie Web: www.indigo.ie/~milltown/

This attractive guesthouse on the western side of Dingle, is set in immaculate gardens running down to the water's edge and enjoys beautiful views of the harbour and distant mountains. Day rooms include an informal reception room, a comfortably furnished sitting room and a conservatory breakfast room overlooking the garden - breakfast is quite an event, offering everything from fresh juices and fruit, through cold meats and cheeses, freshly baked breads and an extensive cooked breakfast menu. The bedrooms – all very comfortable and thoughtfully furnished with phone, TV with video channel, tea/coffee making facilities and iron/trouser press - include two with private patios. Constant upgrading is the policy here: a number of rooms have recently been increased in size and a new lounge, with sea and mountain views, has been added to the front of the house. Some room service available. Garden. Not suitable for children under 10. No pets. Garden. **Rooms 10** (1 disabled). Closed Dec & Jan. Amex, MasterCard, Visa. **Directions:** West through Dingle town, 0.75 miles from town centre.

Dingle

Pax Guest House

ACCOMMODATION Upper John St. Dingle Co. Kerry **Tel: 066 915 1518** Fax: 066 915 2461
Email: paxhouse@iol.ie Web: www.pax-house.com

Just half a mile out of Dingle, this modern house enjoys what may well be the finest view in the area – and, thanks to the exceptional hospitality and high standards of the owners, Joan Brosnan and Ron Wright, is also one of the most comfortable and relaxing places to stay. The furnishing style is daringly bright and fresh and thoughtfully furnished bedrooms have every amenitiy (including little fridges as well as phone, TV, tea/coffee making facilties and iron/trouser press) and well-finished bathrooms, most with full bath. Two suites have their own terraces where guests can lounge around and enjoy that stupendous view. Breakfast is a major event, featuring fresh Dingle Bay seafood as well as an exceptional range of meats and cheeses. Garden. Children welcome (under 2s free in parents' room; cots available, €7). Pets permitted by arrangement. **Rooms 13** (all en-suite & no-smoking, 2 suites, 1 executive, 3 shower only). B&B 60 pps, ss €10. Wine licence. Closed Dec & Jan. MasterCard, Visa, Laser. **Directions:** Turn off at sign on N86.

Dingle

Tigh Mhaire de Barra

PUB The Pier Head Dingle Co. Kerry **Tel: 066 915 1215**

Real hospitality, good food and music are the attractions of Mhaire de Barra and Pat Leahy's harbourside pub. In unpretentious and comfortable surroundings they serve good things like home-made soups with freshly-baked bread, local seafood specials, traditional dishes like boiled bacon and cabbage and Kerry porter cake at lunchtime. Evening meals include an additional range of hot main courses. Dingle Pies, for which the pub is famous, are included in the menu off-season (Oct-March), when the rush of the tourist season has died down. (Like many high-volume establishments in holiday areas, this is a place that is at its best off-season anyway; the bar has been disappointingly untidy on recent visits in high season) Self-catering accommodation has recently been added to the back of the pub, in a quiet garden setting. Meals daily, 12.30-9 (Sun closed 2.30-4 pm). Closed 25 Dec & Good Fri. MasterCard, Visa. **Directions:** On harbour front in Dingle town.

Fenit

The Tankard

PUB/RESTAURANT

Kilfenora Fenit Tralee **Tel: 066 713 6164** Fax: 066 713 6516
Email: sulladn@compuserve.com Web: www.adlib.ie.eaterie/tankard

Easily spotted on the seaward side of the road from Tralee, this bright yellow pub and restaurant has built up a great reputation, especially for seafood. An imaginative bar menu is available from lunchtime to late evening (1-9) serving the likes of "smokeys" and boxty, warm chicken salad and vegetarian choices like mushroom & mozzarella salad. **Restaurant:** Except on Sunday this is an evening restaurant, although lunch is available by arrangement. A phone call is worthwhile to get the best of seafood cooking, which can be exceptional: although bar menus give a passing nod to current trends, the restaurant style is quite traditional and beyond fashion - simple well-cooked food, based on the finest of local ingredients with excellent saucing and unfussy presentation makes a refreshing change from the ubiquitous 'world cuisine'. Beyond seafood there's quite a wide choice, especially steaks in various guises, duckling, Kerry lamb and some strong vegetarian options. There are sea and mountain views from the restaurant, which has recently been extended and opened out to make the most of its location, with a patio area and a path down to the sea. **Seats 100.** D daily 6-10, à la carte; L Sun only 12.30-2, Set Sun L about €17 House wines from about €16; sc discretionary Closed 25 Dec & Good Fri. Amex, Diners, MasterCard, Visa. **Directions:** From Tralee, 5 miles out on the Fenit road, beyond the Spa.

Fenit

West End Bar

PUB/RESTAURANT/B&B

Fenit Tralee Co. Kerry
Tel: 066 713 6246 Fax: 066 713 6599

The O'Keeffes' family-run pub is exactly seven minutes walk from the marina. Good food is available in both the bar and the restaurant, which has earned a sound reputation in the area and has recently been extended to include a conservatory. Head chef Bryan O'Keeffe's style is "classic French with Irish popular cuisine", with seafood and meats billed equally as specialities. Expect starters ranging from Atlantic fisherman's chowder with brown bread, through local 'Cromane' mussels with bayleaves, garlic & cream, to egg mayonnaise and deep-fried 'Roulet Brie' pieces. Main courses include old favourites - sirloin steak, half roast duckling, rack of lamb - and a range of seafood dishes including sole on the bone (with lemon butter) and turbot ((steambaked, with a leek & martini sauce) at very reasonable prices. Simple, inexpensive accommodation is offered in ten en-suite rooms (B&B about €26, no ss.) Bar/restaurant Meals 5.30-9.30 daily. A la carte; house wine about €13. Phone ahead to check food service off-season. Bar closed 25 Dec & Good Fri. MasterCard, Visa. **Directions:** 8 miles from Tralee; on corner as you turn down to the marina.

Glencar

The Climbers' Inn

ACCOMMODATION

Glencar Killarney Co Kerry **Tel: 066 976 0101**
Fax: 066 976 0104 Email: climbers@iol.ie

Established in 1875 and in family ownership for four generations, the current owners of the oldest established walking and climbing inn in Ireland are Johnny and Anne Walsh, an energetic young couple who have made big improvements since they took over in 1995. They specialise in walking holidays and short breaks, with or without guides, and offer every comfort for the traveller, whether arriving on foot, on horseback or, more prosaically, by car. (It may sound less exciting but, whether approaching from Killarney or Sneem, the drives are spectacular.) Accommodation comprises budget (hostel) and bed & breakfast (rooms with en-suite showers) and has all been recently refurbished. Rooms are simple, functional and spotlessly clean. Home-cooked dinners are served in the dining area of a bar reminiscent of alpine inns, furnished with old church furniture. A guest chef is invited from a different country each season, so the style of cooking varies accordingly. It will, however, be based on local ingredients, often wild, and will aim to satisfy hearty mountain appetites with big soups, home-baked brown bread and main courses which include Kerry mountain lamb, wild venison or salmon (with plenty of wholesome vegetables and a good pudding). Bar food is also available daily from 12 noon – 6 pm in the summer season. "Into the Wilderness" tours are organised from the inn – details from Johnny Walsh, or any tourist office. Not suitable for children under 10. Pets permitted. **Rooms 8** (all en-suite, shower only & no-smoking). B&B about €32 pps, ss about €7. D about €20 House wine about €16; sc 10%. Closed Nov-Mar. Amex, Diners, MasterCard, Visa. **Directions:** Glencar valley near foot of Carrauntoohill.

Kenmare

An Leath Phingin

RESTAURANT

35 Main Street Kenmare Co. Kerry **Tel: 064 41559**

As the ground floor is cosy in a traditional Irish way, visitors may be surprised to find that Cornelius Guerin's long-established restaurant specialises in northern Italian food. All is revealed as soon as the menu appears, however, or when going up to the first floor which is more stylish and arty, with Italian posters. Cornelius takes pride in sourcing the best of local ingredients - organic green salads from Billy Clifford, Kenmare smoked salmon for risotto, meats from the local "A Taste of Kerry" butcher - and interpreting Italian dishes with a certain amount of artistic chef's licence, which should not be seen as a criticism, as this is passionate cooking, well-executed and none the worse for some untraditional twists. Choices range from old favourites like salad Caprese, through home-made pork sausages flavoured with fennel and bruschetta, to a range of interesting home-made pastas (tortellini, perhaps, with spinach, ricotta and parmesan), risotto (typically with smoked salmon) and half a dozen pizzas. Reasonable prices (main courses in the €13-17 region) and friendly, helpful service add to the enduring appeal of this attractive restaurant.D only Thur-Mon. A la crte. House wine about €14. Closed Wed; 15 Nov-15 Dec. MasterCard, Visa. **Directions:** Town centre, next to "Treats" food & wine shop.

Kenmare area

Avoca Handweavers

CAFÉ

Moll's Gap Kenmare Co. Kerry **Tel: 064 34720** Fax: 064 35742
Email: info@avoca.ie Web: www.avoca.ie

High up at a famous viewing point on the Ring of Kerry, this outpost of the County Wicklow weaving company sells its fine range of clothing and crafts - and offers wholesome, home-made fare to sustain the weary sightseer. Restaurant seats 80. No-smoking area. Food service all day 10-5. Closed 20 Nov -10 Mar. Amex, Diners, MasterCard, Visa. **Directions:** On Ring of Kerry, 14 miles from Killarney, 6 from Kenmare at famous panoramic crossroads.

Kenmare

Ceann Mara

B&B

Kenmare Co. Kerry **Tel: 066 441220** Email: ceann.mara@eircom.net

In a peaceful location just outside Kenmare, Thérese Hayes's pleasing modern house is set in lovely gardens that run down to the water. Interesting, comfortable reception rooms are full of family antiques and mementoes and the four bedrooms are all very different, but thoughtfully furnished. Very good breakfasts are served in a lovely dining room overlooking the garden. Dogs allowed by arrangement in some areas. **Rooms 4** (3 en-suite, 1 private, 2 non-smoking). B&B about €28 pps. Closed Oct-May. **Directions:** Off Cork road R569, about a mile from Kenmare.

Kenmare

d'Arcy's

RESTAURANT/B&B

Main St. Kenmare Co. Kerry
Tel: 064 41589 Email: info@darcyskenmare.com

Formerly a bank – you can still make out where the vault used to be – Pat Gath has been running this well-known restaurant with rooms since 1998. Head chef Brendan Byrne joined the team in 2001 bringing with him experience in some fine establishments including Tinakilly House, Co Wicklow, The Tea Room at The Clarence Hotel in Dublin and Sheen Falls Lodge, just across the river here in Kenmare. He is already putting his mark on the cooking through well-balanced contemporary menus which also work with the established house style, where seasonal local ingredients are integrated in dishes with a global flavour. Start, perhaps, with Kenmare Bay Mussels in a saffron broth or home made beef sausages with glazed apples and move on to seared scallops with herb risotto, fresh green asparagus & squid ink sauce or an unusual dish of roast loin of lamb with grilled liver, bacon, onion and capers with aubergine confit & rosemary jus. Finish with farmhouse cheeses (with an optional glass of vintage port) or delicious desserts such as warm pear, chocolate and almond tart with Baileys ice cream. A good wine list, home-made breads, and pleasant service all add to the appeal of this pleasantly cosmopolitan restaurant. No smoking area. No children after 8 pm. **Seats 50.** D daily in summer, 6-10 (phone to check opening off season); Set D from €21, also à la carte. House wine €15.87; sc discretionary. Closed Christmas & mid-Jan/Feb. **Accommodation:** The five bedrooms are all pleasantly decorated with neat new shower rooms and further upgrading is planned shortly. B&B €29; ss €7. MasterCard, Visa, Laser, Switch. **Directions:** At the top of town near The Park Hotel.

Kenmare

Dromquinna Manor Hotel

HOTEL Blackwater Bridge PO Kenmare Co. Kerry **Tel: 064 41657** Fax: 064 41791

Built in 1850 in an idyllic location – the hotel is set in 42 acres of wooded grounds and has three quarters of a mile of sheltered south-facing sea frontage – Dromquinna Manor has a number of unusual features including a romantic tree house (a 2-bedroom suite with four-poster and balcony, 15ft up a tree), a safe little sandy beach (beside the informal Boat House Bistro) and a 34ft Nelson Sport Angler with professional skipper for fishing parties and scenic cruises. The interior of the house features an original oak-panelled Great Hall, a traditional drawing room complete with concert grand piano, a panelled bar, pool room and table tennis room. Bedrooms are all individually decorated to specific themes, with good bathrooms; a new ground floor suite is wheelchair friendly. The hotel is popular for weddings. Conference/banqueting (40/150). Children welcome (playroom, playground).Garden. Walking. Tennis. Boating. Pets permitted. **Rooms 48** (1 suite, 2 mini-suites, 2 shower only) B&B about €60 pps, ss about €26. Closed 31 Oct-1 Mar. Amex, Diners, MasterCard, Visa. **Directions:** 3 miles outside Kenmare on the Sneem Road.

Kenmare

The Horseshoe

PUB/RESTAURANT 3 Main St. Kenmare Co. Kerry **Tel: 064 41553** Fax: 064 42502

Chef-proprietor Irma & Richard Zovich's pleasingly old-fashioned bar and restaurant is cosy and well-run – and the good home cooking she offers in the informal oil-cloth-tabled restaurant at the back, with its open fire and original cattle stall divisions, is unpretentious and wholesome. Soups, chowders, chicken goujons, burgers and pies will all be home-made, as will the chips (a rare enough event these days). Seafood and steaks are the key players on evening menus, but there's plenty else to choose from, including strong vegetarian options. Classic puddings – apple pie, chocolate tart – and a short but adequate wine list. No children after 8.30. **Seats 45.** L Mon-Sat 12-4, D daily 5-10.30 (Sun to 11.30); à la carte. House wine €16; sc dicretionary. Closed L Sun, 25 Dec, Good Fri. Open weekends only Jan-Mar. MasterCard, Visa, Laser. **Directions:** Centre of Kenmare.

Kenmare

Jam

CAFÉ 6 Henry Street Kenmare Co. Kerry **Tel: 064 41591**

James Mulchrone - previously head chef at D'Arcy's Restaurant - opened this delightful bakery and café-restaurant in March 2001 and, unlikely as this may seem in the town that has the highest concentration of good eating places in Ireland, it has brought something new. Affordable prices, friendly service and an in-house bakery are proving a winning combination; everything is made on the premises using the best of local produce and you can pop into the self-service café for a bite at any time all day. To give a little flavour of the wide range offered, lovely main course choices include salmon baked in pastry with spinach, smoked Gubbeen & bacon quiche or, for vegetarians, hot roast vegetable & goats cheese tart. This is the place to visit if you are planning a fine day out as they have all you could want for a delicious picnic, including a wide range of sandwiches and salads, home-made sausage rolls and all sorts of irresistible cakes and bisuits. The café menu changes daily and vegetarian dishes always offered. **Seats 50.** No smoking area; air conditioning. Open daily in summer, 8am-6pm. Closed Sun in winter & 3 days Christmas week. No Credit cards.

Kenmare

The Lime Tree Restaurant

RESTAURANT ☆ Shelburne St. Kenmare Co. Kerry **Tel: 064 41225** Fax: 064 41839 Email: benchmark@iol.ie

Built in 1832, Tony and Alex Daly's restaurant is an attractive cut stone building set well back from the road. An open log fire, exposed stone walls, original wall panelling and a minstrels' gallery (which provides an upper eating area) all give character to the interior and, once it fills up, there's always a real buzz. Menus change with the seasons, and there are always daily specials, including several imaginative vegetarian options such as a starter of home-made ravioli of potato & blue cheese with Parmigianno reggiano cheese and main courses like millefeuille of goat's cheese with spicy crumble & rocket salad. Cooking is very sound and local produce – Sneem black pudding, local free-range duck and Kerry lamb (oven-roasted, with sweet mint pesto perhaps) – is highly valued; local seafood such as Killmakillogue mussels appear in delicious specialities like seafood potpourri "en papillotte". Finish, perhaps, with a traditional pudding like warm blackberry and pear fruit crumble. Warm hospitality and excellent service add greatly to the enjoyment of the dining experience - and you can have more than a good meal here too, as part of the first floor has been given over to an impressive contemporary art gallery (open daily from 4pm until the restaurant closes). It might be wise to budget a little extra for dinner here - you could be taking home a modern masterpiece. Wheelchair accessible. No-smoking area; air conditioning. Not suitable for children after 7 pm. **Seats 60.** D daily 6.30-10; à la carte (average main course about €18). House wine €17; sc discretionary. Closed-Nov-Apr. MasterCard, Visa. **Directions:** Next to the Park Hotel.

Kenmare

The Lodge

GUESTHOUSE

Kilgarvan Rd. Kenmare Co. Kerry **Tel: 064 41512**
Fax: 064 42724 Email: thelodgekenmare@eircom.net

In a town where good accommodation can be hard to find at short notice, this large, purpose-built guesthouse just 3 minutes walk from the centre, is a welcome addition. It offers hotel-style accommodation - in spacious rooms which are a little impersonal but have everything needed - including phone, TV, safe, iron/trouser press and tea/coffee facilities, as well as well-finished bathrooms - at guesthouse prices. Children welcome (under 2s free, cot available without charge). No pets. Garden. **Rooms 11** (all en-suite & no smoking, 1 disabled). B&B €52 pps, ss€38. Closed 7 Nov-17 Mar. Amex, MasterCard, Visa. **Directions:** On the Cork road opposite the golf course.

Kenmare

Mulcahys Restaurant

RESTAURANT

16 Henry Street Kenmare Co.Kerry
Tel: 064 42383 Mobile: 087 236 4449

The decor at Bruce Mulcahy's wacky restaurant is definitely different, with all sorts of influences jumbled up (including the useless holes in walls that seem to have invaded contemporary interior design of late); it's a bit weird but warm, fairly comfortable and sympathetically lit - and it certainly gives people something to talk about while waiting to eat. The cooking style is "modern Irish with Asian influences", so menus offer fashionable fare such as a starter of sushi & sashimi (Japanese nori sheets filled with local seafood and served with wasabi, pickled ginger & mirin dip) and main courses like pan-fried scallops seasoned with tea and scampi oil, served on a bed of baby leeks & grapes, with a cardamom & orange jus. Vegetarians might be offfered an upbeat organic homemade pasta and there are some fairly traditional dishes in disguise - such as cep & pistachio crusted loin of Kerry lamb with trufled potato salad, spinach & thyme cream. All a bit wordy on the menu, but there's genuine enthusiasm here both in the cooking and front of house. A mainly youthful clientèle makes for an enjoyably lively atmosphere. Children welcome. Smoking unrestricted. **Seats 30.** D Wed-Mon, 6-10 . A la carte. Early D(6-8pm) €21.59; Set D €38.09, also à la carte. House wines from €16.38.SC discretionary. Closed Tue &10 Jan-25 Mar. Diners, Visa, Laser. **Directions:** Halfway down Henry Street, on the left hand side heading away from the bridge.

Kenmare

Muxnaw Lodge

COUNTRY HOUSE

Castletownbere Road Kenmare Co. Kerry **Tel: 064 41252**

Within walking distance from town (first right past the double-arched bridge towards Bantry), Hannah Boland's wonderfully cosy and homely house was built in 1801 and enjoys spectacular views across Kenmare Bay. Disregard any imperfections in the rather steep driveway or cobwebs around the door - this is very much a home where you can relax in the TV lounge or outside in the sloping gardens (you can even play tennis on the all-weather court). Bedrooms are tranquil, all en suite and with cleverly hidden tea/coffee-making facilities, and are individually furnished with free-standing period pieces and pleasant fabrics. Notice is required by noon if you would like dinner – a typical meal cooked in and on the Aga might be carrot soup, oven-baked salmon and apple pie, but guests are always asked beforehand what they like. **Rooms 5.** (all en-suite & no-smoking). B&B €32. Residents D €19. Closed 25 Dec. Visa. **Directions:** Within walking distance of town.

Kenmare

The New Delight

RESTAURANT/CAFÉ

18 Henry St. Kenmare Co. Kerry **Tel: 064 42350**

This well-named vegetarian café and restaurant serves almost wholly organic food and offers an array of eclectic dishes (with a more Asian slant in the evening). Typically, you could have a celery soup, a warm Mediterranean salad, and lemon tart – everything is home-made (bread, scones, carrot cake etc). Enclosed tea garden. **Seats 40.** Open all day; L & D daily. Closed Dec-mid Mar. No Credit Cards. **Directions:** In the town centre.

Kenmare
RESTAURANT ☆

Packie's

Henry St. Kenmare Co. Kerry
Tel: 064 41508 Fax: 064 42135

Tom and Maura Foley's buzzy little restaurant is stylish but unpretentious, with small tables and a big heart. Great local ingredients, especially organic produce and seafood, mingle with imports from sunnier climes and, in Maura's skilful hands, result in imaginative Ireland-meets-the-Med food that is memorable for its simplicity and intense flavouring. First impressions are of world cuisine and there's a clear awareness of international trends, but the cooking here is far above the influence of fashion. Maura modestly describes her food as "simple, with an emphasis on local ingredients" but what makes it special is her sure judgment of complementary food combinations. Many of these are traditional and that is why they have lasted - crab cake with tartare sauce, rack of lamb with rosemary and garlic sauce for example. Red onion and caper salsa may sound like an exotic accompaniment for wild smoked salmon, but it's actually a long-established partnership. Close examination of menus will probably reveal more dishes that have stood the test of time than new ones, but the important factor here is the sheer quality of both food – especially local seafood – and cooking, also that new flavours will only be introduced because they make genuinely good partnerships. Puddings include good ices and a nice variation on bread and butter pudding – Moriarty's barm brack and butter pudding with rum – or there are Irish farmhouse cheeses to finish. Interesting and well-priced wine list. **Seats 35.** D only Tues-Sat, 5.30-10; à la carte. House wine about €14.60; sc discretionary. Closed Sun & Mon and 1 Nov-30 Mar. MasterCard, Visa. **Directions:** Town centre.

Kenmare
HOTEL
RESTAURANT ★

Park Hotel Kenmare

Kenmare Co. Kerry **Tel: 064 41200** Fax: 064 41402
Email: info@parkkenmare.com Web: parkkenmare.com

In a lovely location adjoining Kenmare town, with views over sloping gardens to the ever-changing mountains across the bay, this renowned hotel was built in 1897 by the Great Southern and Western Railway Company as an overnight stop for passengers travelling to Parknasilla, 17 miles away. Since 1985, when Francis Brennan became proprietor, Park Hotel Kenmare has earned international acclaim for exceptional standards of service, comfort and cuisine. Once inside the granite Victorian building, a warm welcome and the ever-burning fire in the hall begin weaving the Park's special magic: any tendency to formality in the antique furnishings is offset by amusing quirks of taste and, despite the constant quest for perfection, it is surprisingly relaxed. Public rooms are not overpoweringly grand and several open onto a verandah overlooking river and gardens. Luxurious bedrooms are spacious, with excellent bathrooms and are furnished to exceptional standards of comfort with all the traditional extras expected of top hotels – fresh flowers, robes, mineral water, quality toiletries – and some newer ones, such as hi-fi systems. A constant programme of renovation and upgrading ensures that accomodation is always of the highest international standard. But the most outstanding feature of the Park Hotel is its staff. The exceptional standard of training overseen by Francis Brennan through the years has had a very significant effect on standards not only in the hotel, but also throughout the country (and beyond) as those trained under his management have moved on to other positions. For this contribution, the Guide awarded Francis Brennan a Skills Development Award in 2000. **Rooms 49** (9 suites, 6 junior suites, 27 superior, 4 no smoking, 1 for disabled). Children welcome (under 4s free in parents' room, cots available without charge). Pets permitted in some areas; kennels available nearby. B&B €214pps, (single occupancy €224). **Restaurant:** Service in this elegant dining room is unfailingly outstanding and the views from window tables are simply lovely – a fitting setting for very fine food. A stylishly restrained classicism has characterised this distinguished kitchen under several famous head chefs. Joe Ryan, who has been head chef since 1999, offers seasonal à la carte and daily set dinner menus - and has clearly been on top form on the Guide's most recent visits.There is an understandable leaning towards local seafood, including lobster, but Kerry lamb and local Skeaghanore duck are also specialities and there are interesting vegetarian dishes. Joe Ryan's disciplined dinner menus offer three dishes on each course, making up in quality and flavour anything they lack in length. Superb attention to detail - from the first trio of nibbles offered with aperitifs in the bar, through an intriguing amuse-bouche served at the table (a tiny brandade of salt cod with beetroot perhaps), well-made breads, punctilious wine service and finally the theatrical little Irish coffee ritual and petits fours at the end of the meal - all this contributes to a dining experience that is exceptional. Dishes attracting special praise on a spring visit include a pretty, seasonal terrine of dill-marinated salmon with leeks, asparagus and a gravalax dressing (seafood terrines are a speciality), a delicious main course of pan-fried John Dory, served on a base of caramelised onions with smoked aubergine and a pavé of Mediterranean vegetables, and an irresistible dark chocolate torte served on a crispy base with an orange sorbet. The wine list, although geared towards the deep-pocketed guest, offers a fair selection in the €26-40 bracket and includes a wine suitable for diabetics. Service, under the direction of restaurant manager John O'Sullivan, is immaculate. A short à la carte lounge menu is available, 11am-6pm. Not suitable for children under 8 after 8 pm. No smoking area. **Seats 80** (private room, 40). D only, 7-9 daily; 5-course D €58 (2 courses €41), also à la carte. House wine from €20; sc discretionary. Hotel closed 2 Jan-19 April & 28 Oct-23 Dec. Amex, Diners, MasterCard, Visa. **Directions:** Top of town.

Kenmare

The Purple Heather

PUB/RESTAURANT

Henry Street Kenmare Co. Kerry **Tel: 064 41016**

Daytime sister restaurant to Packie's, Grainne O'Connell's traditional darkwood and burgundy bar gradually develops into an informal restaurant at the rear. Run by the O'Connell family since the mid-1970s, The Purple Heather was among the first to establish a reputation for good food in Kenmare. What they aim for – and achieve, with commendable consistency – is good, simple, home-cooked food. Start with refreshing freshly squeezed orange juice, well-made soups that come with home-baked breads or salad made of organic greens with balsamic dressing. Main courses include a number of seafood salads, vegetarian salads (cold and warm), pâtés – including a delicious smoked salmon pâté– plus a range of omelettes, sandwiches and open sandwiches (Cashel Blue cheese and walut, perhaps, or crabmet with salad) or Irish farmhouse cheeses (with a glass of L.B.V Offley port if you like). **Seats 40.** Bar open 10.45-7; food served Mon-Sat, 11.45-5. Closed Sun, Christmas, Good Fri. No Credit cards. **Directions:** Town centre.

Kenmare

The Rosegarden

GUESTHOUSE/RESTAURANT

Gortamullen Kenmare Co. Kerry
Tel: 064 42288 Fax: 064 42305
Email: rosegard@iol.ie Web: www.euroka.com/rosegarden

Peter and Ingrid Ringlever's guesthouse is set back from the road, with an immaculate garden and pond at the front and a distinctly continental feel about the whole house (the couple are Dutch). Everything is spotlessly clean and the centrally-heated bedrooms, all with good showers, offer guests satellite TV, tea/coffee-making facilities and biscuits. **Rooms 8** (all shower only & no-smoking). **Restaurant:** Dinner (quite an extensive à la carte or nightly-changing table d'hôte) combines local produce with some international touches: Kenmare Bay shrimps in a classic cocktail sauce, lobster & crab bisque, loin of pork with a mild pepper sauce, several ways with steak and Indonesian chicken are all typical and desserts include temptations like old-fashioned hot apple cake with vanilla ice cream and specia;ity pancakes. Nice little wine list, at reasonable prices. 3- and 7-day specials are offered, with dinner included. Restaurant **Seats 26.** D daily ,6.30-9; Set D €19, also à la carte; house wine €15.SC discretionary Closed Nov-Mar. Amex, Diners, MasterCard, Visa, Laser. **Directions:** Just out of town at the start of the Ring of Kerry road.

Kenmare

Sallyport House

COUNTRY HOUSE

Kenmare Co. Kerry **Tel: 064 42066** Fax: 064 42067
Email: port@iol.ie Web: www.sallyporthouse.com

The Arthur family's renovated country house on the edge of Kenmare is in a quiet and convenient location overlooking the harbour, with fine garden and mountain views at the rear. It is spacious throughout, from the large entrance hall (with welcoming fire) to bedrooms that are thoughtfully furnished with a mixture of antique and good quality reproduction furniture, plus orthopaedic beds, TV, phone and (unusual enough to merit mention) lights and mirrors correctly placed for their function. All rooms have practical, fully-tiled bathrooms with powerful over-bath showers and built-in hair dryers. Under Janie Arthur's eagle eye, housekeeping is outstanding - and delicious breakfasts are served in a sunny dining room overlooking the garden. Not suitable for children. No dogs. **Rooms 5** (all en-suite & no-smoking). B&B €63.49, ss €31.74. Closed Nov-Mar. No credit cards. **Directions:** South of town on N71, between town and bridge.

Kenmare
HOTEL
RESTAURANT ★

Sheen Falls Lodge

Kenmare Co. Kerry **Tel: 064 41600** Fax: 064 41386
Email: info@sheenfallslodge.ie Web: www.sheenfallslodge.com

Set in a 300-acre estate just across the river from Kenmare town, this stunning hotel made an immediate impact from the day it opened in April 1991; it has continued to develop and mature most impressively since - and was the Guide's Hotel of the Year in 1999. The waterside location is beautiful and welcoming fires always burn in the elegant foyer and in several of the spacious, elegantly furnished reception rooms, including a lounge bar area overlooking the tumbling waterfall. Luxurious suites and bedrooms all have superb amenities, marbled bathrooms and views of the cascading river or Kenmare Bay. Exceptional facilities for business and private guests include state-of-the-art conference facilities, a fine library, an equestrian centre and The Queen's Walk (named after Queen Victoria), which takes you through lush woodland on the estate. There's also a Health Spa with a pretty indoor plunge pool and, beside it, an informal evening bar and bistro, "Oscars", which has its own separate entrance as well as direct access from the hotel. But it is the staff, under the guidance of the exceptionally warm and hospitable General Manager, Adriaan Bartels, who make this luxurious and stylish international hotel the home from home that it quickly becomes for each new guest. Two luxuriously appointed self-contained two-bedroomed thatched cottages, Little Hay Cottage and the recently completed Garden Cottage, are also available to rent, singly or together. Conference/banqueting (120). Leisure centre (swimming pool, jacuzzi, sauna, steam room, massage), snooker, equestrian, walking, fishing, gardens, tennis, cycling. **Rooms 61** (9 suites, 8 junior suites, 44 executive rooms, 10 no-smoking bedrooms, 1 disabled). Room rate €380 (1 or 2 guests).

La Cascade Restaurant: This beautifully appointed restaurant is arranged in tiers to take full advantage of the waterfalls – floodlit at night and providing a dramatic backdrop for Chris Farrell's modern Irish cooking, with the backing of faultless service under restaurant manager Johnny Le Poel. A sensibly limited daily table d'hôte and a short vegetarian menu are offered, with a leaning towards seafood, although the overall choice is balanced with three meat or poultry dishes on a main course selection of six. Variations on a number of specialities include starters of tian of crab (with mango salsa, avocado cream & muscat dressing perhaps), fresh salmon smoked at the Lodge (with horseradish cream & a salad of herbs) and roast loin of rabbit (with apple purée, poultry juice and black truffle). Main courses are in a similar vein – Kerry lamb is a speciality, of course, and predictably delicious - typically it might be roast loin, with onion mousseline, fricassée of chanterelles, confit of shallot & truffle jus. Speciality desserts include updated classics like hot soufflés (mango with lime sabayon sauce, perhaps) and farmhouse cheeses, served with scrumptious parmesan biscuits. The wine cellar is a particular point of pride and guests can choose their own bottle from nearly 500 wines - and port can also be served in the cellar after dinner. The hotel's Chef du Sommelier, Alain Bras, was the Guide's Sommelier of the Year for 2001 and has seemingly limitless knowledge of wines from all over the world. Like other exceptional sommeliers, Alain wears his knowledge lightly and is supremely accessible and warmly enthusiastic in his manner when assisting guests towards the best wine for their menu choices. Annual tastings, with a panel of invited guests, help him make an objective selection for the hotel's wine list: price and quality are equally important and his motto is 'to cover every possible taste and choice at the right price.' *Light lunches (smoked salmon, club sandwiches etc) and afternoon tea are available in the sun lounge, 12-6 daily and the informal Oscar's Bistro offers an extensive à la carte dinner menu every night, 6-10pm. Restaurant **Seats 120** (private room, 20). D only 7-9.30. Set D €60 House wines from €26. SC discretionary. Hotel closed Jan. Amex, Diners, MasterCard, Visa, Laser. **Directions:** Take N71to Glengariff, take 1st left after suspension bridge.

Kenmare
ACCOMMODATION

Shelburne Lodge

Cork Road Kenmare Co. Kerry
Tel: 064 41013 Fax: 064 42135

Shelburne Lodge is the oldest house in Kenmare and has all the style and attention to detail that would be expected from Tom and Maura Foley, proprietors of the dashing Kenmare restaurant, Packies. A fine stone house on the edge of the town, the lodge is set back from the road in its own grounds and lovely gardens. Spacious day rooms include an elegant, comfortable drawing room and a large, well-appointed dining room where excellent breakfasts are served. Accommodation, in seven rooms individually decorated to a high standard, is extremely comfortable and everything (especially beds and bedding) is of the highest quality; individual decoration extends to the excellent bathrooms – all with full bath except the more informal conversion at the back of the house, which is especially suitable for families and has neat shower rooms. No evening meals are served, but residents are directed to the family's restaurant, Packies. Garden, tennis. Own parking. No pets. **Rooms 9** (2 shower-only). B&B €57, ss €19. Closed 1 Dec- 28 Feb. MasterCard, Visa. **Directions:** 500 yards from town centre, on the Cork road R569.

Killarney
HOTEL/RESTAURANT

Aghadoe Heights Hotel

Killarney Co. Kerry **Tel: 064 31766** Fax: 064 31345
Email: info@aghadoeheights.com Web: www.aghadoeheights.com

A few miles out of town and well-signposted off the N22 road (both directions: Tralee and Cork), this famous low-rise hotel, built in the '60s, enjoys stunning views of the lakes and the mountains beyond and also overlooks Killarney's two 18-hole championship golf courses. Major refurbishment of the hotel was undertaken in the winter of 1999/2000 and, while the exterior was still undergoing modifications in summer 2001, the renovation of the interior is complete and the new bedrooms, especially, are undoubtedly a huge improvement. The new rooms - junior suites and a Presidential Suite - have superb views and balconies and are equipped and furnished to a high standard in a contemporary style. The whole hotel is luxuriously furnished and decorated, with lots of marble, antiques and good paintings, and the famous first-floor restaurant, Fredrick's, has been extended and incorporated into an open-plan lounge area, where traditional Afternoon Tea is served (2-5.30pm). Conference/banqueting facilities have also been increased and upgraded (150/80); business centre. Leisure centre, swimming pool, beauty salon, garden, tennis. Children welcome (Under 2s free in parents' room; cot available, €19). No pets. Garden. **Rooms 75** (2 suites, 7 junior suites, 36 superior rooms, 2 for disabled). Lift. B&B €199 pps, ss€45. Closed Jan-Feb. **Fredrick's:** The restaurant itself may have changed somewhat - while still on the first floor it is now part of an open plan area - but the same team is still in place: head chef Robin Suter has been with the hotel since 1990 and restaurant manager John Doyle's history goes back even further, to 1986 - and the classic style of food and service for which the hotel is famous remains the same. A la carte menus (considerately priced by course for those not requiring the full five-course dinner) offer updated variations on well-loved dishes - fresh seafood cakes may come with a tomato chilli salsa, for example, and roast loin of lamb with girolles & rôsti potatoes - but there's no messing about with the great classics like grilled chateaubriand sauce béarnaise and sole meunière. Piano 7-11pm. Not suitable for children under 10 after 7 pm. **Seats 120** (private room 40). D daily, 6.30-9.30; L Sun only 12.30-2. Set D €52 (also semi-à la carte); house wine from €24.75, sc discretionary. Amex, Diners, MasterCard, Visa, Laser. **Directions:** Two miles west of Killarney. Signposted off N22.

Killarney
HOTEL

Arbutus Hotel

College St. Killarney Co. Kerry **Tel: 064 31037** Fax: 064 34033
Email: arbutushotel@eircom.ie

In the Buckley family since 1926, this old hotel has charm and personality that most newer ones lack. Since Sean Buckley took on the mantle in 1986, some major refurbishment has taken place - notably in 1997, when major work was done to 20 bedrooms, the foyer, restaurant and the lift. In addition to ongoing maintenance and further refurbishment, Sean is gradually replacing the antiques which were discarded when the previous generation modernised the hotel. Live music in the bar is a particular feature. Children welcome (under 3s free in parents' room; cot available).

Rooms 35 (4 junior suites, 3 shower only). B&B about €85 pps, ss about €32. Closed 17-30 Dec. Amex, Diners, MasterCard, Visa. **Directions:** Killarney town centre.

Killarney

Bricín

RESTAURANT

26 High Street Killarney Co Kerry
Tel: 064 34902 Fax: 064 39030

Paddy & Johnny McGuire's delightful country-style restaurant is on the first floor over an excellent craft shop which stocks an outstanding range of Irish pottery. Bricín has been restoring weary shoppers since 1990 and its large area is broken up into "rooms", which creates a surprisingly intimate atmosphere. The country mood suits head chef Maighread Forde's wholesome cooking: soups, salads and sandwiches are available all day and the lunch menu offers great value and good cooking in dishes like chicken pancakes with salad or chips, baked salmon in a white wine sauce with vegetables and potatoes and a vegetarian dish such as leek & lentil bake. Dinner menus move up a few gears, in starters like mussels in white wine sauce and main courses including rack of Kerry lamb, chargrilled fillet beef and the house speciality, Boxty, which comes with a variety of fillings and a mixed salad. Wine licence.No smoking area; air conditioning. Children welcome. Open Mon-Sat, 10-4.30; L 12.30-4.30; D 6-9.30 (early menu 6-7). Closed Sun, bank holidays; evenings Nov-Mar. Amex, Diners, MasterCard, Visa. **Directions:** Central Killarney; continuation of Main Street.

Killarney

Castlerosse Hotel

HOTEL

Killarney Co. Kerry **Tel: 064 31144** Fax: 064 31031
Email: castler@iol.ie

This low rise modern hotel enjoys a lakeside setting with superb lake and mountain views from back rooms, including the restaurant and bar. Major developments, which have transformed it in recent years, include an impressive leisure centre and a well-appointed new wing; older rooms were also refurbished and upgraded to match the new standard at the time. Corridors to some rooms are long, but luggage can be delivered to back rooms by car - and that all have easy access to well-maintained grounds and the hotel's 9-hole golf course. Conferences / Banqueting (180) Leisure centre, swimming pool; Golf (9), tennis, fishing, cycling, fishing. Garden. Children welcome (under 2s free in parents room; cots available). No Pets. **Rooms 121** (1 suite, 15 no smoking, 2 for disabled). B&B £50 pps, ss £15. Closed Nov-March. Amex, Diners, MasterCard, Visa. **Directions:** 2km from Killarney on Killorglin Rd., Adjoins Killarney Golf Club.

Killarney

The Cooperage

RESTAURANT

Old Market Lane Killarney Co. Kerry **Tel: 064 37716**
Fax: 064 37716 Email: chezmart@iol.ie

In an excellent location, in a pedestrianised laneway just off the Glebe public carpark, Mo Stafford and head chef Martin McCormack's striking contemporary restaurant brought a new element of choice to the Killarney dining scene when it opened in 2000. A lot of thought went into the decor, which is more than just eye-catching and (unlike many contemporary restaurants) the dining space is comfortable as well as visually impressive - even more so since the recently addition of a lounge area where you can have a relaxing aperitif or after dinner drink. Moody background jazz, played just loud enough for appreciation without interfering with conversation helps make this a restaurant with lots of atmosphere, which is unusual in the modern genre and even more at lunch time as well as evening settings. Better still, the food and service live up to the surroundings: a friendly welcome sets the tone from the outset, followed through by contemporary menus which suggest an element of simplicity and recognition of seasonality and provenance of ingredients as well as eye appeal. Lunch menu are shortish, plus blackboard specials, with more choice in the evening, including game in season (typically cooked in Irish cream liqueur and game stock and served in its own sauce with fried apple and game chips) and there's always a list of specials, including several fish dishes. Desserts range from wholesome (apple & mixed berry crumble) to indulgent (rich dark chocolate cake). Apart from a lively atmosphere, what you get here is imaginative good food, well prepared and at reasonable prices (average evening main course €16). Shortish fairly priced wine list. ***Seats 80.** No-smoking area; air conditioning. L Mon-Sat 12.30-2.45, D 6-10 daily. A la Carte. House wine €15.17. Closed L Sun; 25 Dec. MasterCard, Visa, Laser. **Directions:** Located in the centre of Killarney, under the arch at Market Cross, Killarney Main St.

Courtney's Restaurant

Killarney

RESTAURANT 24 Plunkett St. Killarney Co. Kerry **Tel: 064 32689** Fax: 064 32689

This restaurant previously achieved national fame as The Strawberry Tree (now relocated to Macreddin Village, Co Wicklow) but both the first-floor restaurant and the characterful olde-worlde pub downstairs have changed remarkably little since it took on its new name and owners - and one of the main reasons for this is that Eileen O'Brien, who was The Strawberry Tree's head chef for six years, remains the power in the kitchen. Menus no longer carry the renowned "charter" of commitment to wild, organic and free-range, but Eileen is maintaining the policy as far as possible, with the eventual aim of being 100% organic - and the high standard of cooking remains, of course, the same. The provenenace of some ingredients is given - 'old fashioned farmed duck', for example, comes from Dennis Barry's farm - and others are specified as free-range or wild. Menus are as exciting as ever: starters might include a salad of Darjeeling tea cured salmon and a warm salad of Guinness-battered black pudding over a mixed salad with warm apple dressing while main courses are strong on game (in summer this might be rabbit, pigeon and venison) and organic Kerry beef, with oven-roast tomato, basil mash and wild garlic sauce, perhaps. Delicious, wittily conceived desserts - or the cheeseboard - are always worth saving room for. *Limited bar food 12.30-8. **Seats 28.** Not suitable for children under 12. D Mon-Sat, 6.30-10. Closed Sun. MasterCard, Visa. **Directions:** Centrally located in Plunkett Street, in the heart of Killarney.

Dromhall Hotel

Killarney

HOTEL Muckross Rd. Killarney Co. Kerry **Tel: 064 31431** Fax: 064 34242
Email: info@dromhall.com Web: dromhall.com

A sister hotel to Randles Hotel next door, this completely re-built establishment opened in summer 2000 and includes a leisure centre situated between the two hotels, for their common use. An impressive reception area establishes a positive tone which is confirmed by well-appointed public areas - including Kayne's bar and restaurant where very acceptable contemporary food is served - and unsually spacious bedrooms which are furnished to a high standard, with well-designed bathrooms. Ample parking. Lift. **Rooms 70** (3 junior suites, 2 executive, 3 for disabled). B&B about €69.84 pps, ss about €25. Closed 23-29 Dec. Diners, MasterCard, Visa. **Directions:** On right going out of Killarney on the Muckross road, beside Randles Hotel.

Earls Court House

Killarney

GUESTHOUSE Woodlawn Junction Muckross Rd. Killarney Co. Kerry **Tel: 064 34009**
Fax: 064 34366 Email: earls@eircom.net Web: killarney-earlscourt.ie

Roy and Emer Moynihan's purpose-built guesthouse is quite near the town centre and provides owner-run hotel-type accommodation at a fairly moderate price. The scale is generous: a large foyer has comfortable seating and spacious, well-planned bedrooms all have double and single beds, good bathrooms, phone and satellite TV; tea/coffee-making facilities are available on request. Breakfast is served in a pleasant dining and limited room service also available. Children welcome (under 2s free, cot available without charge). No pets. **Rooms 11.** B&B €63 pps, ss €37. Closed Nov-Feb. MasterCard, Visa. **Directions:** On the N71 from Killarney to Kenmare, take the first left after the filling station on the left, then 3rd entrance on the left.

Fuchsia House

Killarney

ACCOMMODATION Fuchsia House Muckross Road Killarney Co. Kerry **Tel: 064 33743**
Fax: 064 36588 Email: fuchsiahouse@eircom.net Web: www.fuchsiahouse.com

A short walk from the town centre, this purpose-built guesthouse is set well back from the road, with ample car parking in the front. Arriving guests are greeted with tea and home-made cake in the drawing room, a prelude to an outstanding breakfast the next morning, with many fresh goodies on show. Spacious bedrooms, luxuriously furnished with smart co-ordinating fabrics and top quality beds and bedding, offer facilities more usually associated with expensive hotels, from remote-control satellite TV and direct-dial telephone to a professional hairdryer and power shower in the well-equipped bathrooms. Hosts Tom and Mary Treacy are part of a family of well-known and dedicated Killarney hoteliers (Killarney Lodge, Killarney Park and Ross Hotels), ensuring the house is immaculately run and maintained. A large conservatory for guests' use overlooks the well-maintained rear garden. Children welcome (under 10s free in parents room; cots available; childrens' playground.) No Pets. **Rooms 10** (all en-suite & no smoking, 1 for disabled). B&B €46pps, ss €25.39. Closed Nov-mid Mar. Diners, MasterCard, Visa. **Directions:** Located on N71, .75 km from town on the right hand side.

Killarney

Gaby's Seafood Restaurant

RESTAURANT 27 High St. Killarney Co.Kerry **Tel: 064 32519** Fax: 064 32747

One of Ireland's longest established seafood restaurants, Gaby's has a cosy little bar beside an open fire just inside the door, then several steps lead up to the main dining area, which is cleverly broken up into several sections and has a pleasantly informal atmosphere. Chef-proprietor Gert Maes offers well designed seasonal à la carte menus in classic French style – and in three languages. Absolute freshness is clearly the priority – a note on the menu reminds that availability depends on daily landings – but there's always plenty else to choose from, with steaks and local lamb as back-up. Specialities include wild Atlantic salmon, with chive & lemon cream and red onion marmalade, Atlantic prawns on a bed of tagliatelle in a light garlic sauce and lobster "Gaby": fresh lobster, cognac, wine, cream and spices - cooked to a secret recipe! Lovely desserts include "my mother's recipe" - an old-fashioned apple & raspberry crumble with warm wild honey scented berries, sauce anglaise and caramel ice cream - or you can finish with an Irish cheese selection and freshly brewed coffee. Toilets wheelchair accessible. **Seats 75.** D only, Mon-Sat 6-10pm; à la carte; house wine about €22; sc discretionary. Closed Sun, Christmas/New Year & mid Feb-mid Mar. Amex, Diners, MasterCard, Visa. **Directions:** On the Main Street.

Killarney

Great Southern Hotel Killarney

HOTEL/RESTAURANT Killarney Co. Kerry **Tel: 064 31262** Fax: 064 31642
Email: res@killarney.gsh.ie Web: www.greatsouthernhotels.com

This classic railway hotel was established in 1854 and its pillared entrance and ivy-clad facade still convey a sense of occasion. Recent refurbishment has greatly improved all aspects of the hotel - and has been completed with due respect for the age and history of the building; the spacious foyer, especially, has retained a high level of grandeur and all the public areas - which include a homely residents' drawing room and a fine bar - are elegant, high-ceilinged rooms with a soothing atmosphere. Belying its central position, the hotel is set in 36 acres of landscaped gardens, providing peace and relaxation on the premises. Facilities added over the years include two tennis courts and a leisure centre and further major improvements, due for completion by May 2002, will provide new suites, and refurbishment of the conference centre and main restaurant. Conference/banqueting (800/700); business centre; secretarial services; video conferencing. Leisure centre, swimming pool. Garden. Tennis. Children welcome (under 2s free in parents room; cots available, crèche, playground; children's tea 5.30-6). Pets permitted by arrangement. **Rooms 175** (32 suites, 20 superior rooms, 6 for disabled). B&B €142 pps, ss €30 (room-only rate also available: €127, max 3 guests); sc 12.5%. Open all year (off-season breaks available). *The moderately priced Torc Great Southern Hotel, is a sister hotel; it makes a good base for a family holiday and for Killarney's championship golf courses - special breaks available. Tel: 064 31611 Fax: 064 31824 email: res@torc.gsh.ie. **Peppers at the Southern:** This lovely new bistro-style restaurant opened in the summer of 2000. Situated quietly in a corner position behind the bar and overlooking the gardens, it has been dashingly decorated in the modern idiom, with high-back chairs, an elegant black, brown and beige/gold colour scheme and (in common with other areas of the hotel) fine paintings. The ambience, professional service and head chef José Caro's imaginative menus and sound cooking have made it an immediate success and - unusually for an hotel restaurant - it is now established as one of Killarney's leading eating places. **Seats 60.** D only, Mon-Sat 6.30-9.30. Amex, Diners, MasterCard, Visa, Laser. **Directions:** In the heart of Killarney town.

Killarney

Hotel Europe

HOTEL Fossa Killarney Co. Kerry **Tel: 064 31900** Fax: 064 32118
Email: receptioneurope@kih.liebherr.com Web: www.iol.ie/khl

Although now around thirty years old, the Europe was exceptionally well built and has been so well maintained through the years that it still outshines many a new top level hotel. A facelift to the front façade is the only obvious recent change but maintenance has always been excellent. Public areas are very large and impressive, furnished to the highest standards and make full use of the hotel's wonderful location. Bedrooms follow a similar pattern, with lots of space, quality furnishings, beautiful views and balconies all along the lake side of the hotel. Leisure facilities include a 25-metre swimming pool, fitness suite and sauna; the hotel adjoins the three Killarney golf clubs - Killeen, Mahony's Point and Lackabane and the two nine hole courses, Dunloe and Ross, are nearby. The hotel's continental connections show clearly in the style throughout but especially, perhaps, when it comes to food - breakfast, for example, is an impressive hot and cold buffet. Excellent conference and meeting facilities include a 450-seat auditorium with built-in microphones and translation system. Given the high standards and facilities offered, rates are reasonable, and it is also worth inquiring about special breaks. Leisure centre, swimming pool, beauty and hair salons. Equestrian, fishing, (indoor) tennis, snooker. Children welcome (under 12s free in parents room, cot available without charge; playroom, playground). No pets. Lift. **Rooms 204** (8 suites, 60 no smoking, 154 twin rooms). Room Rate from €228 (max 2 guests), sc incl. **Panorama Restaurant:** Aptly-named, this beautifully situated and elegantly appointed restaurant has views over the Lakes of Killarney with the mountains beyond providing a haunting backdrop - a fine setting for head chef Willie Steinbeck's classic European cooking, which makes full use of local produce like Kerry lamb and salmon through wide-ranging international menus. Table d'hôte and à la carte menus are accurately descriptive (which is unusual at the moment) and offer something to please everyone, including vegetarians. Lovely breads are made in-house - and there's a very extensive range offered at breakfast. Starters might include a seasonal soup (a well-flavoured carrot & courgette with dainty baby carrot pioeces in it, perhaps) and Westphalian ham (presumable from the ecellent german butchers shop across the road, which is well worth a visit) appropriately served with a freshly-made coleslaw. This might be followed by a sorbet, or maybe marinated local salmon with rösti & hrseradish cream - a well-conceived dish with all the elements well-balanced. Main courses might include meltingly tender suckling pig in caraway jus, or duck breast in Madeira sauce, served with well-matched vegetables. Delicious desserts - chocolate marquise with redcruurants, maybe, or cherry clafoutis with Black Forest ice cream - then a slow coffee as you watch the light fading behind the mountains...Service is pleasant and very efficient. [*A separate informal restaurant, The Brasserie, offers popular all day food, 11am-11pm daily.] **Seats 450.** D daily, 7-9.30. Set 4-course D €54. House wine €25. Hotel closed 10 Nov-15 Mar. Amex, Diners, MasterCard, Visa, Laser. **Directions:** on main Ring of Kerry road.

Killarney

GUESTHOUSE

Kathleen's Country House

Tralee Rd. Killarney Co. Kerry **Tel: 064 32810** Fax: 064 32340
Email: info@kathleens.net Web: www.kathleens.net

Long before the new wave of purpose-built guesthouses, Kathleen O'Regan Sheppard was offering hotel standard accommodation at guesthouse prices, and this family-run business continues to offer good value, hospitality and comfort in a quiet location – in gardens just a mile from the town centre. All of the individually decorated rooms are non-smoking and furnished to a high standard, with orthopaedic beds, phone, TV, tea/coffee-making facilities and each fully tiled bathroom has both bath and shower. An ongoing programme of maintenance and refurbishment ensures that everything is immaculate, including spacious public areas that provide plenty of room for relaxing - there are several sitting areas and even a library. Excellent breakfasts are served in a spacious dining room overlooking the garden, setting you up for a day that's as energetic or as relaxing as you chose to make it: Kathleen's is well situated for a wide range of outdoor pursuits (golf, fishing, pony-trekking, horse riding, walking, cycling and tennis are all nearby) and for some of the country's most beautful scenic drives. Everything served at breakfast is based on the finest produce, local where possible, and beautifully presented - a speciality fresh fruit plate, for example, is as pretty as a picture and, like many other things around the house, reflects Kathleen's love of art. Special rates are offered off-season. Not suitable for very young children (over 5s welcome). **Rooms 17** (all no smoking, 2 for disabled). B&B €57.14 pps, ss €44.44. Closed 1 Nov-10 Mar. Amex, MasterCard, Visa. **Directions:** 1 mile north of Killarney Town off N22 (Tralee road).

Killarney

HOTEL

Killarney Lake Hotel

Muckross Road Killarney Co. Kerry **Tel: 064 31035**
Fax: 064 31902 Email: lakehotel@eircom.net

Coming into town from Kenmare on the N71, this beautifully located hotel is set well back from the road right on the lake shore, with the ruins of McCarthy Mor Castle within the grounds. The hotel was built in 1820 and visited by Queen Victoria when she came to Ireland in 1861 - the hotel still has the original horse-drawn carriage in which she travelled and the spacious high-ceilinged lounges with open log fires also date back to the nineteenth century and give the central area of the hotel real period character. Recent developments include the addition of 24 new junior suites, with jacuzzis and private balconies overlooking the lakes and three Roman and Medieval themed "fantasy suites". All bedrooms are comfortably furnished and have the usual modern amenities, although the decor in some rooms may seem a little dated. Conference/banqueting 60/40. Own fishing, tennis, garden, walking. Children welcome (under 3s free in parents room; cots available without charge, playroom). No Pets. Lift. **Rooms 70** (3 theme suites, 27 junior suites). B&B €89 pps, ss from €22. Closed 18 Dec-19 Feb. MasterCard, Visa, Laser. **Directions:** 1.5 miles from Killarney town.

Killarney
ACCOMMODATION

Killarney Lodge

Countess Rd. Killarney Co. Kerry **Tel: 064 36499**
Fax: 064 31070 Email: klylodge@iol.ie Web: www.killarneylodge.net

Catherine Treacy's fine purpose-built guesthouse is set in private walled gardens just a two minute walk from the town centre. It has large en-suite air-conditioned bedrooms with all the amenities expected of an hotel room, including direct dial phone and TV, and large public rooms to relax in. Garden. Parking. Children welcome (under 10s free in parents room; cots available without charge). Wheelchair accessible. No pets. **Rooms 16** (all no smoking, 2 junior suites, 14 superior, 1 shower only, 1 for disabled). B&B €60 pps, ss€40; no sc. Closed 15 Nov-15 Feb. Amex, Diners, MasterCard, Visa, Laser. **Directions:** 2 minutes walk from town centre off Muckross Road.

Killarney
HOTEL
RESTAURANT
HOTEL OF THE YEAR

Killarney Park Hotel

Kenmare Place Killarney Co. Kerry **Tel: 064 35555** Fax: 064 35266
Email: info@killarneyparkhotel.ie Web: www.killarneyparkhotel.ie

Situated in its own grounds, a short stroll from the town centre, the Treacy family's luxurious, well run hotel is deceptively modern - despite its classical good looks, it will celebrate its first decade in March 2002. However it has already undergone a transformation, with the refurbishment of all public areas and the leisure centre, the addition of two penthouse suites, several new junior suites and a state-of-the-art conference room. Indeed, constant improvement is so much a theme here that it is hard to keep up with developments as they occur: an interesting forward-looking aspect of the current changes is that (in common with a number of other forward-looking Irish hotels), redesign of existing rooms is resulting in a smaller number of more spacious ones - here, for example, superior rooms are currently being redesigned as junior suites. Public areas have an elegant Victorian feel, enhanced by the sweeping staircase that leads to bedrooms that are furnished in contemporary country house style, with great attention to detail. The Killarney Park has become a benchmark of quality development in the hotel industry and the observant traveller will recognise many of its finer features and design details in numerous other caringly developed hotels around the country. Housekeeping is immaculate and luxurious suites and deluxe rooms are spacious, with air conditioning, a private entrance hall and a sitting area with fireplace creating a real home from home feeling - and all rooms have been thoughtfully and individually designed, with well-planned bathrooms, judicously selected antiques and the many small details that make a hotel room really comfortable - a decent hair dryer, iron as well as trouser press, bathrobes & slippers, multi music system as well as satellite TV, and the security of an in-room safe. Beautiful fabrics and warm, soothing colour schemes are an important aspect of the hotel throughout - it's the first thing that strikes you as you pass through Reception into a series of seating areas, with fires and invitingly grouped sofas and armchairs. The same sense of comfort characterises the Garden Bar (which has a sheltered terrace for fine days) and also the quiet Library, which provides a relaxing haven. Most importantly, of course, the staff at this family-run hotel are committed to looking after guests with warmth and discretion, making it an ideal choice for both business and pleasure: a worthy winner of our Hotel of the Year Award for 2002. (The much older Ross Hotel, nearby, is a sister hotel and equally delightful in its way). Conference/banqueting (150); business centre; secretarial services, video conferencing (on request). Leisure centre, swimming pool, sauna, plunge pool, jacuzzi pool; treatment rooms. Library; billiard room. Garden, walking, cycling. Children welcome (under 2s free in parents room; cots available without charge, playroom). No Pets. **Rooms 73** (3 suites, 20 junior suites, 30 no-smoking, 1 for disabled). Lift. 24 Hour room service. Room rate, with breakfast, €335 (max 2 guests); no sc. **Restaurant:** It is hard to credit that this large and opulent room with its ornate ceiling, heavy drapes and grand paintings is only ten years old. Unashamedly designed in the style of the grand hotel dining rooms of yesteryear, the restaurant underlines this hotel's respect for the best of traditional hospitality and it is appropriate that head chef Odran Lucey (who joined the hotel in 1999) should have come here from The Merrion Hotel, Dublin, where the same values are upheld. A lengthy à la carte menu is available in high season, otherwise a table d'hôte with several choices is is offered. To indicate the style, an escalope of foie gras, for example, is served with Clonakilty black pudding, apple compôte and deep-fried celeriac, creating a nicely-judged combination of old and new traditions. Similarly a main course of roast duckling (a very popular choice in the south-west of Ireland), which is accompanied by champ mash and an elderberry and whiskey jus. A mood of gentle formality pervades, enhanced by courteous service and the presence of a pianist who plays throughout dinner. The wide-ranging wine list includes many of the classics and, not only a fair choice of half bottles, but also a sommelier's choice of the week, offering half a dozen good wines by the glass. An interesting feature of the restaurant is an open wine cellar which guests are free to browse Restaurant seats 150 (private room,40). No smoking area; air conditioning. D daily 7-9.30; L Sun only,12.30-2. Set D €45. House wines from €24. SC discretionary. Amex, Diners, MasterCard, Visa, Laser. **Directions:** Located in Killarney town - all access routes lead to town centre.

Killarney

Killarney Royal

HOTEL

College St. Killarney Co. Kerry **Tel: 064 31853** Fax: 064 34001
Email: royalhot@iol.ie Web: www.killarneyroyal.ie

This older sister to the luxurious Hayfield Manor Hotel in Cork city (see entry) has recently completed a major refurbishment programme and the results, in an elegant period style that is totally appropriate to the age and design of the building, are very impressive. No expense has been spared to ensure the highest quality of materials and workmanship, air conditioning has been installed throughout the hotel and rooms have been individually designed, all with marble bathrooms and sitting areas. Wheelchair accessible. Arrangement with nearby carpark. Children welcome (under 7s free in parents room; cots available). No pets. **Rooms 29** (5 suites, 5 no-smoking). B&B about €115 pps, ss about €60. Closed 22-28 Dec. Amex, Diners, MasterCard, Visa. **Directions:** Town centre of Killarney on College Street off the N22.

Killarney

Killeen House Hotel

HOTEL

Aghadoe Killarney Co. Kerry **Tel: 064 31711** Fax: 064 31811
Email: charming@indigo.ie Web: www.killeenhousehotel.com

Just 10 minutes drive from Killarney town centre and 5 minutes from Killeen and Mahoney's Point golf courses, this early nineteenth century rectory has become Michael and Geraldine Rosney's "charming little hotel". You don't have to be a golfer to stay here but it must help, specially in the pubby little bar, which is run as an "honour" bar with guest's golf balls accepted as tender. Most visitors clearly relish the bonhomie, which includes addressing guests by first names. Rooms vary in size but all have full bathrooms (one with jacuzzi) and are freshly-decorated, with phone and satellite TV. There's a comfortable traditional drawing room with an open fire for guests, furnished with a mixture of antiques and newer furniture. The hotel is popular with business guests as well as golfers; secretarial services are available, also all day room service. The dining room is open to non-residents. Children welcome (under 12s free in parents' room; cots available without charge). Pets permitted by arrangement. Garden. **Rooms 23** (all en-suite). B&B €67.50 pps, ss €42.50; sc10%. D daily, 7-10; Set D €40, house wine €19.05., restaurant sc discretionary. Closed 1 Nov - 1 Easter. Amex, Diners, MasterCard, Visa. **Directions:** 4 miles from Killarney - just off Dingle Road.

Killarney

Panis Angelicus

CAFÉ

15 New Street Killarney Co. Kerry **Tel: 064 39648**

New Street is just the place for this stylish contemporary café and breadshop - the tempting display of freshly baked breads, scones and gateaux will draw you in and then you'll be hooked by the aroma of freshly brewed Italian coffee - which is served with homemade biscuits or Belgian chocolates. No matter what time you drop in there will be plenty to tempt, even if it's just homemade soup with a gourmet sandwich (homebaked Limerick ham with wholegrain Irish mustard, perhaps) or a hot Irish potato cake with garlic butter, green salad and crusty bread. Outside of meal times you can just have that cup of tea or coffee - and maybe take some goodies home for later. Dinner menus are more ambitious and offer a wide choice while retaining a fresh, youthful approach. Unusually, Panis Angelicus not only offers interesting vegetarian food but also specialises in gluten free breads, soups, sauces and desserts. **Seats 35.** No smoking area. Children welcome. Open daily from 9.30am; L 12-4, D Wed-Mon 6.30-9.45. House wine from €14.60. Amex, MasterCard, Visa, Laser. **Directions:** Opposite the Credit Union.

Killarney

Randles Court Clarion Hotel

HOTEL

Muckross Rd. Killarney Co. Kerry **Tel: 064 35333** Fax: 064 35206
Email: randles@iol.ie Web: www.randleshotels.com

Within easy walking distance of the town centre, but also convenient to attractions such as Muckross House and Killarney National Park, this attractive house was originally built in 1906 as a family residence and underwent extensive refurbishment before opening as an hotel in 1991.

Although it has grown a little since then it has retained the domesticity and warmth of the family home. Period features, including fireplaces and stained glass windows, have been retained and comfortably furnished public rooms include a small bar, a large drawing room with log fire, tapestries and antiques and an elegant restaurant opening onto a sheltered patio. Spacious bedrooms are furnished to a high standard, with direct dial telephones, satellite television, radio, hair dryers and well-appointed bathrooms. Leisure facilities at the neighbouring sister hotel, Dromhall, are available to guests at Randles. Own parking. No pets. **Rooms 50** (2 suites, 12 mini-suites, 1 for disabled). B&B about €105 pps. Closed 20-28 Dec. Amex, Diners, MasterCard, Visa.

Killorglin

Nick's Seafood Restaurant & Piano Bar

RESTAURANT

Lr Bridge St. Killorglin Co. Kerry **Tel: 066 976 1219** Fax: 066 976 1233

Nick Foley's cooking – classic French with an Irish accent– has earned a particular reputation for his way with local seafood, although there are always other choices, notably prime Kerry beef and lamb. Moules marinière or provençale, lobster thermidor, shellfish mornay and peppered steak in brandy cream sauce are all typical of his classic style. Vegetarians aren't forgotten either – there's a choice of three dishes on the regular menu. Dessert choices are changed daily and there's a good cheeseboard. Aside from providing excellent food, Nick's is also renowned for its music and great atmosphere. Children welcome. **Seats 80** (private room,30). No-smoking area; air conditioning. D Wed-Sun 6.30-10 in winter, daily in summer. Set D about €37. Extensive wine list; house wine about €17; sc discretionary. Closed all Nov, Mon-Tue in Dec-Mar & 24-25 Dec. Amex, Diners, MasterCard, Visa. **Directions:** On the Ring Road of Kerry, 20 km from Killarney.

Listowel

Allo's Bar & Bistro

PUB/RESTAURANT/ACCOMMODATION

41 Church St. Listowel Co. Kerry
Tel: 068 22880 Fax: 068 22803

Named after the previous owner ("Alphonsus, aka Allo"), Armel Whyte and Helen Mullane's café-bar seems much older than it is – they reconstructed the whole interior with salvaged materials (the flooring was once in the London Stock Exchange). It is convincingly done with the long, narrow bar divided up in the traditional way, although the restaurant has since been extended into the house next door. Armel's cooking is well-known for lively combinations of traditional and new Irish cooking with some international influences, all based on the most carefully sourced ingredients, local as far as possible. An imaginative bar menu which offers everything from home-made soups and sandwiches to a range of main courses changed daily, includes a tempting 'Tasty Bits' listing of little dishes to try by the pair instead of a main course. Evening à la carte menus are naturally more ambitious, offering about five choices one each course - typically including starters of Allos beef herb & cheeese meatballs with Mexican salsa, a main course of roasted John Dory fillets on garlic mash with a white wine & chive beurre blanc and finishing, perhaps, with an unusual buttermilk & vanilla ice cream with poached peaches and shortbread biscuits. presentation is not over-worked and the food is delicious. **Seats 50** (private room, 20). No smoking area. Open Tue-Sat, L12-7, D 7-9.15. L & D à la carte; House wine €17.78. Accommodation: When the restaurant was extended in summer 1999, Armel and Helen also added three beautiful guest bedrooms. Spacious and stylishly furnished with antiques, they have four-poster beds and luxurious Connemara marbled bathrooms. **Rooms 3** (1 shower only), B&B €57.14, ss €19.05. Establishment closed Sun, Mon; 25 Dec & Good Fri. Amex, MasterCard, Visa, Laser. **Directions:** Coming into Listowel on the N69, located half way down Church Street on the right hand side.

Listowel

Listowel Arms Hotel

HOTEL

The Square Listowel Co. Kerry
Tel: 068 21500 Fax: 068 22524 Email: listowelarms@ireland.com

This much-loved old hotel is rich in history and especially famous as the main venue for the annual Listowel Writers Week. Since 1996 the hotel has been blessed with the energetic and discerning ownership of Kevin O'Callaghan, who has overseen a major extension and overhaul of the whole premises during the last few years. The extension has provided a new restaurant, kitchen, banqueting area and new bedrooms, all overlooking the River Feale - and a further block of 18 new suites is to be ready for the 2002 season. Improvements previously made to the existing building have all been done with great sensitivity, so greater comfort has been gained throughout the hotel without loss of character. Private car parking is also planned, to the rear of the hotel, which will be a great convenience to guests, as on-street parking can be difficult. Non-residents will find this a great place to drop into, as bar food is available all day (10am-9pm) and they serve lovely traditional dishes like braised beef & stout casserole. Conference/banqueting (500/400); video-conferencing, secretarial services, ISDN lines. Wheelchair accessible. Lift. Children welcome (under 5s free in parents' room, cots available without charge). Pets permitted by arrangement. **Rooms 37** (all en-suite). B&B €51 pps, ss €19. (Higher rates apply to Festival weeks, incl Murphys Irish Open & Listowel Race Week.) MasterCard, Visa. **Directions:** In the corner of the historic old square in Listowel town centre.

Portmagee

The Moorings

GUESTHOUSE/PUB/RESTAURANT

Portmagee Co. Kerry **Tel: 066 947 7108** Fax: 066 947 7220 Email: moorings@iol.ie Web: www.moorings.ie

Gerard & Patricia Kennedy's fine guesthouse overlooks the harbour and many bedrooms - which are comfortably furnished with phone, TV, tea/coffee making facilities and full bathrooms - have a sea view. Children welcome (unders 3s free in parents' room, cot available without charge). No pets. **Rooms 14** (all en-suite) B&B €44.44 pps, ss €10.56. Food is available daily in the bar (12-8) and restaurant (D Tue-Sun 6-10,), all à la carte. Seafood stars and the style is fairly traditional - chowder, seafood selection, deep-fried brie for starters; main courses of seafood platter, poached salmon, steaks - and lobster, which is quite moderately priced. House wine €15.23. Restaurant closed Mon except bank hols. Establishment closed 1 Nov-15 Mar. MasterCard, Visa, Laser. **Directions:** Turn right 3 miles outside Caherciveen on the Waterville Road.

Sneem

Great Southern Hotel Parknasilla

HOTEL

Parknasilla Sneem Co. Kerry **Tel: 064 45122** Fax: 064 45323 Email: res@parknasilla.gsh.ie

Overlooking Kenmare Bay, set in 300 acres of sub-tropical parkland, this classic Victorian hotel is blessed with one of the most beautiful locations in Ireland. The spacious foyer with its antiques and fresh flowers sets a tone of quiet luxury, enhanced by the hotel's collection of original art (currently being catalogued). Whether activity or relaxation is required there are excellent amenities at hand – including an outdoor swimming pool and Canadian hot tub - and an abundance of comfortable places (including a no-smoking drawing room) for a quiet read or afternoon tea. Public rooms include an impressive restaurant and a library (added in 1995 for the hotel's centenary and available for the use of all guests, although also ideal for meetings and small conferences). Bedrooms vary in size and outlook but all have en-suite bathrooms with bath and shower, tea/coffee making facilities, direct-dial telephone, radio, TV with in-house movie channel, trouser press and hair dryer. Afternoon tea at Parknasilla is a relaxing affair, served in the spacious interconnecting lounges along the front of the hotel. Leisure centre, swimming pool. Golf, tennis, snooker, fishing, equestrian, walking. Children welcome (under 2s free in parents room; cots available without harge; children's tea 5.30-6). No Pets. **Rooms 84** (1 suite, 8 junior suites, 13 superior rooms, 1 for disabled).Lift. B&B €159, ss €30. No sc. 24 housr room service. Amex, Diners, MasterCard, Visa, Laser. **Directions:** 30 miles outside Killarney, past Kenmare en route to Sneem.

Tahilla

Tahilla Cove Country House

COUNTRY HOUSE

Tahilla Near Sneem Co. Kerry **Tel: 064 45204** Fax: 064 45104 Email: tahillacove@eircom.net Web: www.tahillacove.com

This family-run guesthouse feels more like a small hotel – it has a proper bar, for example, with its own entrance (which is used by locals as well as residents). This is a low-key place, with an old country house in there somewhere (which has been much added to) and there is a blocky annexe in the garden. It has two very special features, however: the location, which is genuinely waterside, is really lovely and away-from-it-all; and the owners, James and Deirdre Waterhouse. Tahilla Cove has been in the family since 1948, and run since 1987 by James and Deirdre – who have the wisdom to understand why their many regulars love it just the way it is and, apart from regular maintenance (and some recent major refurbishment) little is allowed to change. Comfort and relaxation are the priorities. All the public rooms have sea views, including the dining room and a large sitting room, with plenty of armchairs and sofas, which opens onto a terrace (where there are patio tables and chairs overlooking the garden and the cove with its little stone jetty). Accommodation is divided between the main house and another close by; rooms vary considerably but all except two have sea views, many have private balconies and all are en-suite, with bathrooms of varying sizes and appointments (only one single is shower-only). All rooms have phone, TV, hair-dryer and individually controlled heating. Food is prepared personally by the proprietors and, although the dining room is mainly intended for residents, others are welcome when there is room – simple 4-course country house style menus change daily – and bar food is available from noon to 7 pm. (It's a lovely place to drop into for a cup of tea overloking the little harbour). Garden. Walking. Fishing. Wheelchair accessible. Children welcome. Pets permitted.

Rooms 9 (1 shower only). B&B €55 pps, ss €20. Closed 15 Oct-29 Mar. Amex, Diners, MasterCard, Visa. **Directions:** On the northern side of Kenmare Bay (route N70). Ring of Kerry 11 miles west of Kenmare and 5 miles east of Sneem.

Tralee

Abbey Gate Hotel

HOTEL

Maine Street Tralee Co. Kerry **Tel: 066 712 9888** Fax: 066 712 9821 Email: abbeygat@iol.ie Web: www.abbeygatehotel.com

Situated in a relatively quiet corner in the centre of Tralee, this big modern hotel has a large marble-floored foyer with ample seating space; other public areas include the main Vineyard Restaurant and an enormous traditional-style Market Place pub, where bar food is served all day. Bedrooms are a good size, comfortably furnished in a modern style with usual amenities including phone, satellite TV, tea/coffee-making facilities and well-finished en-suite bathrooms (all with bath and shower). The facilities give it corporate appeal but it also makes a good base for a family break as it's moderately priced and children are welcome – there's an outdoor playground, informal meals at the Market Place buffet and Tralee's famous Aquadome is nearby. Off-season & special breaks available. Conferences / Banqueting (350/280); secretarial services; video conferencing. Children under 2 free in parents room; cots available without charge. No pets. **Rooms 100** (14 no-smoking, 8 for disabled). B&B €76.95 pps, ss €40. Closed 25 Dec. Amex, Diners, MasterCard, Visa, Laser, Switch. **Directions:** Town centre.

Tralee

Ballygarry House Hotel

HOTEL

Killarney Road Tralee Co.Kerry **Tel: 066 712 3322** Fax: 066 712 3322 Email: ballygarry@eircom.net Web: www.ballygarry.com

Recently renovated and upgraded to a high standard, this pleasant roadside hotel presents a neat face to arriving guests and also has extensive landscaped gardens. The furnishing style is traditional with occasional contemporary twists; warm colours, notably in oriental rugs used on wooden floors, create a welcoming atmosphere in public areas and darkwood furniture in bedrooms is used to effect against contrasting furnishings and pale walls. This is an appealing hotel and moderately priced. Conference/banqueting 150/450.Children welcome (free in parents' room under 6, cot available without charge).garden. No pets. **Rooms 30** (1 for disabled). Lift. B&B about €85pps, ss about €50, sc 12.5%. Special breaks available. Closed 22-26 Dec. Amex, MasterCard, Visa. **Directions:** 1 mile outside Tralee town on the Killarney road.

Tralee

Barrow Guest House

GUESTHOUSE

West Ardfert Tralee Co. Kerry **Tel: 066 713 6437** Fax: 066 713 6402 Email: info@barrowhouse.com Web: www.barrowhouse.com

In a stunning shoreside position on Barrow Harbour, this recently renovated guesthouse dates back to 1723 and was once home to the Knight of Kerry. Despite occasional reminders of the modern world from a nearby road, the house has largely retained its unique tranquil setting - and the front bedrooms and public rooms, which include a period drawing room and a breakfast room, where both buffet and hot breakfasts are served, all have wonderful views across water to the Slieve Mish Mountains and Dingle peninsula. Bedrooms are spacious and extremely comfortable, with orthopaedic beds, phone/ISDN lines, satelllite TV, tea/coffee facilities and lovely bathrooms, some with jacuzzi baths; everything has has been completed to a very high standard, albeit with a hint of the hotel about some of the furnishings. Angling and golf are major attractions - the Arnold Palmer designed Tralee Golf Club is next door and Killarney, Ballybunion and Waterville are within range - and a new helicopter service has made travelling to neighbouring golf courses easier. There are plans for a health spa and seaweed baths. No dinner, but good restaurants nearby (see entries under Fenit and Tralee) Some rooms are in an adjacent courtyard. **Rooms 9** (1 suite, 3 superior rooms, all no-smoking). B&B €45 pps, ss €32. MasterCard, Visa, Laser. **Directions:** R558 - follow signs for Tralee Golf Club.

Tralee

The Brandon Hotel

HOTEL Princes Street Tralee Co. Kerry **Tel: 066 712 3333** Fax: 066 712 5019

Overlooking a park and the famous Siamsa Tire folk theatre, and close to the Aquadome, Tralee's largest hotel is at the heart of activities throughout the area. Spacious public areas are quite impressive, and while some bedrooms are on the small side, all have been recently refurbished and have direct-dial phone, radio and TV (no tea/coffee-making facilities) and tiled bathrooms. There's a well-equipped leisure centre and good banqueting/conference facilities. B&B about €90 pps. Closed 22-29 Dec. Amex, Diners, MasterCard, Visa.

Tralee

Brook Manor Lodge

GUESTHOUSE Fenit Road Tralee Co. Kerry **Tel: 066 712 0406**
Fax: 066 712 7552 Email: brookmanor@eircom.net

Set back from the road, in 3.5 acres of grounds, Vincent and Margaret O'Sullivan's large purpose-built guesthouse offers immaculate accommodation and warm hospitality. Public rooms and bedrooms are spacious and very comfortably furnished - bedrooms have generous beds and all the usual modern facilities - TV, phone, trouser press, tea/coffee making, hair dryer and radio/alarm - everything, in short, that the traveller (and, specifically, the golfing traveller) could need. Breakfast is a special point of pride, cooked to order from an extensive menu. Not very suitable for children, but concessions are given (under 8s free in parents' room, cot available free of charge.). No pets. **Rooms 8** (all no smoking, 1 suite, 1 junior suite, 2 superior rooms, 2 shower only, 1 for disabled.) B&B €57.14, ss €12.70. Amex, MasterCard, Visa. **Directions:** 2Km from Town Centre on Fenit road.

Tralee

Castlemorris House

ACCOMMODATION Ballymullen Tralee Co. Kerry **Tel: 066 718 0060**
Fax: 066 712 8007 Email: castlemorris@eircom.net

Mary and Paddy Barry's attractive creeper-clad Victorian house makes a lovely place to stay, with good home baking (complimentary afternoon tea in front of the drawing room fire on arrival) and the friendly atmosphere of a family home. Bedrooms are spacious and well-furnished for comfort with style. Breakfast is a speciality and dinner is available by arrangement. Garden. Children welcome (cot available). Pets allowed by arrangement. **Rooms 6** (4 shower only). B&B €52 pps, no ss. Open all year. Amex, MasterCard, Visa. **Directions:** On the edge of Tralee town (Dingle side).

Tralee

Meadowlands Hotel

HOTEL Oakpark Tralee Co Kerry
Tel: 066 718 0444 Fax 066 718 0964 Email: meadowlands@iol.ie

This fine hotel set quietly in landscaped gardensis just two years old and, already the high quality of design, materials and workmanship, together with caring service from well-trained staff, is ensuring its position as one of Tralee's leading hotels. Stylish, well-designed bedrooms are spacious and comfortable, with striking decor; suites have jacuzzis and queen size beds, one a four-poster. All have individually controlled air conditioning and heating, multi-channel television, direct dial phones, tea/coffee-making facilities and trouser press with ironing board. The proprietor, Paddy O'Mahony, operates his own fishing boats, ensuring that seafood served in the restaurant "An Pota Stoir", is on the plate within hours of landing; head chef John O'Leary has earned a reputation for imaginative menus and sound cooking, especially seafood - and the decor is appropriately nautical. The hotel bar, "Johnny Franks", offers informal fare such as home-made fish cakes and Dingle seafood platter, 12.30-9pm daily - and regularly features live music. Children welcome (cots available, free of charge). Wheelchair accessible. No pets. **Rooms 27** (3 suites, 24 superior rooms, 1 for disabled). Lift. 24 hour room service. B&B €76.18 pps, ss €19.05. Closed 24-26 Dec.

Tralee

Oyster Tavern

PUB/RESTAURANT The Spa Tralee Co. Kerry
Tel: 066 7136102 Fax: 066 7136047

This well-maintained roadside bar and restaurant has achieved high standards of food and service over a long period of time, earning a loyal local following. Menus are well-balanced and moderately priced; seafood is a speciality. Sunday lunch is especially good value and very popular. **Seats 140.** Open 10.30am -11pm, L&D daily. Closed 25 Dec, Good Fri. Diners, MasterCard, Visa. **Directions:** 4 miles outside Tralee, on the Fenit road.

Tralee

Quality Hotel Tralee

HOTEL

Castle Street Tralee Co. Kerry **Tel: 066 712 1877** Fax: 066 712 2278

This historic hotel was once the famous Benners Hotel. It has gone through several name changes recently and was completely refurbished by new owners in the late 1990s, so that it now offers accommodation that is well-priced if you need to be in the centre of the town. Air conditioning, safes and details like trouser press with iron and ironing board in all rooms, as well as the more usual phone, TV, tea/coffee facilities. No private parking. No pets. **Rooms 45** (5 no smoking). Wheelchair accessible. Lift. B&B €70pps, ss €15. Closed 24-26 Dec. Amex, MasterCard, Visa, Laser. **Directions:** In town centre.

Tralee

Restaurant David Norris

RESTAURANT ☆

Ivy Terrace Tralee Co. Kerry **Tel: 066 718 5654**

Although located on the first floor of an unprepossessing modern building, things look up as you enter proprietor-chef David Norris's new restaurant, which has a nice little reception area with a sofa and stools at a small bar and simple, tasteful decor with lots of plates on the walls and lightwood furniture in the Charles Rennie Macintosh style. Well-spaced tables are dressed with quality linen, plain glasses and white china, relieved by fresh flowers. David Norris's pedigree is impressive - before opening here he was head chef at several esteemed establishments including the late lamented Drimcong House in Co. Galway, Marlfield House Co Wexford and, most recently, The Mustard Seed at Echo Lodge, Co. Limerick. With this background in mind, it comes as no surprise that his sourcing should be immaculate: ingredients are organic wherever possible and everything served is handmade on the premises (breads, pasta, ice creams). The emphasis is on taste, and presentation that is beautiful but without over-elaboration - and the aim is to offer the best of food at reasonable prices. Everything conveys a sense of excitement and energy (he even offers a "Stress Free" early menu for people "too tired to cook" in summer) and menus, while promising in the extreme, are not over-ambitious in extent. A tasty little amuse-bouche arrives with your aperitif, setting the tone for an evening full of thoughtful detail. A typical starter, of wild mushroom ravioli on a bed of garlic croûtons on a cream sauce, will be memorable for its intensity of flavour and presented with stunning simplicity; fish of the day might be gurnard - a perfectly cooked seared fillet, drizzled with a smidgeon of pesto-style herb dressing (made of chervil, dill and wild garlic leaves) and presented on a bed of sliced waxy potatoes with a wholegrain mustard sauce: deliciously simple. Desserts will probably include a chocolate tasting plate, but home-made ice creams are a speciality, served in a crisp pastry tuile, with fresh fruit and a butterscotch sauce. The details are immaculate right to the end, when your tea or coffee is served with home made fudge. Excellent cooking, professional service, an informative but sensibly limited wine list and excellent value for money should all win this fine new restaurant many friends - it certainly deserves to succeed. **Seats 40.** No smoking area. D Tue-Sat, 5.30-7.30. Set D €26-33; à la carte also available. House wine €17.70; sc discretionary, except 10% on parties of 10+. Closed Sun, Mon. (Annual closures not confirmed at time of going to press.) Amex, MasterCard, Visa, Switch. **Directions:** Facing Siamsa Tire.

Tralee

Restaurant Uno

RESTAURANT

14 Princes St. Tralee Co. Kerry
Tel: 066 718 1950 Fax: 066 718 1951

Maeve Duff has built up a great following since she took over these premises just across the road from the town park in 1999. The restaurant is in several areas: a cosy front room doubles as reception and opens into a second high-ceilinged room which is brightly lit and more modern in style, with extra seating also in a balcony area above it. Menus favour the contemporary side of the restaurant's psyche, with a leaning toward Cal-Ital and global influences plus a seasoning of more traditional dishes - thus starters like oriental duck spring roll with raspberry dip and fettucine with chicken and a mushroom, roast pepper & pesto cream alongside soup of the day and deep fried breaded mushrooms with seasonal leaves and garlic mayonnaise. Similarly, main courses range from Thai red chicken or vegetable curry with coconut rice & poppadums to honey roast duckling and steaks, all under €20. Desserts are quite traditional - crème brûlée, hot apple pie with cream - and the wine list is short (on choice and information) but well-balanced and includes four house wines. All round this buzzy place is offering a fair deal. Not suitable for children after 8 pm. **Seats 65** (private room 25). No smoking area. L Mon-Sat 12.30-2.15, D daily 5.30-9.45 (Sun from 4); à la carte. House wine €12.70. Closed L Sun, Mon Oct-early Jun & 1 week Jan. Amex, Diners, MasterCard, Visa. **Directions:** Beside Brendan Hotel.

Tralee

Val's Bar & Bistro

PUB/RESTAURANT féile bia — Bridge Street Tralee Co. Kerry **Tel: 066 712 1559**

A major makeover has taken place at this, the happening place for informal dining and music, where there's traditional music every Monday, Tuesday and Thursday night. Very stylish, designer-driven, this place is all of a piece with tinted windows, very dark woods and very dark leather on seats and bar stools. Differing floor heights are cleverly exploited too, and a distinctive feature is a mammoth area at the bottom of the stairs up to the bistro, which looks like an enormous three-sided sofa which would seat about 10 people. Although gloomy if you come in out of bright sunlight, the lighting is subtle but effective once your eyes adjust.They have maintained consistent standards here, of both bar and the upstairs bistro food, even when there have been changes of personnel, so the policy of providing quality and good value is likely to continue. Bistro **Seats 50.** Air conditioning. L Mon-Sat,12.30-2.30; D daily 6-10. Closed Sun L, 3 days Christmas, Good Fri. MasterCard, Visa. **Directions:** Town centre, beside Abbey carpark.

Ventry

The Skipper

RESTAURANT — Ventry Co. Kerry **Tel: 066 915 9900** Fax: 066 915 9994

Genuine French cooking and charming service at realistic prices are hardly to be expected in this remote area, so Michel and Cathy Chauvet's smashing little two-storey restaurant on the Slea Head drive is all the more welcome. Seafood stars - traditional Breton seafood soup with croûtons and crabmeat gratin are mouthwatering examples, and there is much else beside including lobster - good value and unusually priced at about €5 per 100g/1/4 lb, which is practical. Or what about an omelette as only the French can make them? Other French classics like confit of duck Périgord style sit easily alongside more dishes more familiar to Irish tastes, like steaks and Irish stew. It's worth venturing out of Dingle, or planning your trip to Slea Head around mealtimes here if you can. Don't be afraid of very French specials, like whole fish with their heads and all, though. Children welcome. **Seats 50** (private room 10). Open 12-10 daily.L12-3, early D 5-7.30, D 6-9.30; Early D £€12.70 (5-7.30 only) later à la carte. House wine €15.87. Closed Nov & 1 week Jan-Feb. MasterCard, Visa, Laser. **Directions:** After Dingle, 5 miles on Slea Hd. road.

Waterville

Butler Arms Hotel

HOTEL/RESTAURANT — Waterville Co.Kerry **Tel: 066 947 4144** Fax: 066 947 4520
Email: reservations@butlerarms.com Web: www.butlerarms.com

One of Ireland's best-known hotels – it is one of several to have strong links with Charlie Chaplin – Peter and Mary Huggards' Butler Arms Hotel dominates the seafront at Waterville. Like many hotels which have been owner-run for several generations it has established a special reputation for its homely atmosphere and good service. Improvements are constantly being made and public areas, including two sitting rooms, a sun lounge and a cocktail bar, are spacious and comfortably furnished, while the beamed Fisherman's Bar (which also has a separate entrance from the street) provides a livelier atmosphere. Bedrooms vary from distinctly non-standard rooms in the old part of the hotel (which many regular guests request) to smartly decorated, spacious rooms with neat en-suite bathrooms and uninterrupted sea views in a wing constructed in the early '90s and 12 junior suites just completed for the 2002 season. Off season value breaks; shooting (woodcock, snipe) Nov-Jan. Garden; fishing; tennis. Snooker. Wheelchair accessible. Own parking. Children welcome. Lift. **Rooms 30** (2 suites). B&B about €100 pps, ss €32 No sc. Closed 20 Oct.-11 April. Amex, Diners, MasterCard, Visa.

Waterville

The Huntsman

RESTAURANT — Waterville Co. Kerry **Tel: 066 947 4124** Fax: 066 947 4560

Raymond and Deirdre Hunt's landmark restaurant has been providing a warm and restoring stop on the Ring of Kerry since 1978. There's always a welcoming turf fire in the bar and tables are set up in both bar and restaurant to maximise some of Kerry's finest sea and mountain views. Raymond specialises in classic French seafood cookery and, although the bar menu is quite extensive and includes popular dishes such as deep-fried fish and fries, Irish stew, omelettes and pasta, as well as classics – grilled black sole and shellfish in garlic butter - the full à la carte menu is also available for bar meals. (Mixing choices from the two menus is also allowed.) No smoking area.

Bar/Restaurant **Seats 90** (private room,18). Food service all day, 8-10pm. L from 11.30 & D 6-9.30 daily. Set L €20.25, Set D €33. À la Carte available. House wine from €15.50. SC discretionary. Advisable to call ahead for reservations off season. Closed 3 days Christmas; Mon-Thu off-season (Nov-Feb). Amex, MasterCard, Visa, Laser. **Directions:** As you enter the village on seaside opposite Church of Ireland.

Waterville

PUB/RESTAURANT/ACCOMMODATION

The Smuggler's Inn

Cliff Road Waterville Co. Kerry
Tel: 066 947 4330 Fax: 066 947 4422

Harry and Lucille Hunt's famous clifftop pub enjoys a remarkable location right beside the world famous championship Waterville Golf Course (and overlooking a mile of sandy beach to the sea and mountain views beyond). It's a real inn, providing food, drink and shelter. A good place to take a break from the Ring of Kerry on a good day – there are garden tables overlooking the beach for fine summer days. Local ingredients provide the base for fairly traditional cooking by Harry and son Henry, who is also a chef - with seafood (including lobster from their own tank) being the speciality. Non seafood-lovers have plenty of other choices, including Kerry lamb and beef, of course, and there's a separate vegetarian menu available. Restaurant/Bar **Seats 85.** Air conditioning. Food served 8am-9.30pm daily; L12-5, D 6-10 (snack menu only 3-6 pm). Set L €20, Set D from about €23. House wine about €17.50 Accommodation is offered in modest but pleasantly decorated rooms which vary in size, outlook and facilities (one has a balcony) and price, but all are comfortably furnished. There's a first-floor residents' sitting room with sofas and armchairs, books, television – and magnificent sea views. Children welcome (under 6s free in parents' room, cots available without charge). Pets by arrangement. **Rooms 17** (all en-suite). B&B €38, ss €20. Closed 1 Nov -1 Mar. Amex, Diners, MasterCard, Visa, Laser. **Directions:** Next to Waterville Golf Club.

COUNTY KILDARE

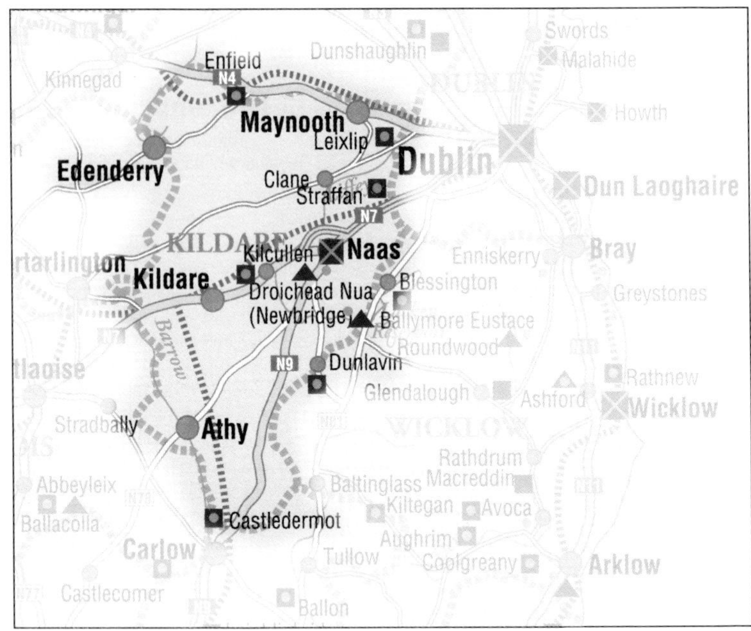

As you'd expect from a place which includes the famed racecourses of The Curragh, Punchestown and Naas among its many amenities, Kildare is the horse county par excellence. The horse is so central and natural a part of Irish life that you'll find significant stud farms in a surprisingly large number of counties. But it is in Kildare that they reach their greatest concentration in the ultimate equine county. Thus it's ironic that, a mere 400 million years ago, Kildare was just a salty ocean where the only creatures remotely equine were the extremely primitive ancestors of sea horses.

However, things have been looking up for the horse in County Kildare ever since, and today the lush pastures of the gently sloping Liffey and Barrow valleys provide ideal country for nurturing and training champions. Apart from many famous private farms, the Irish National Stud in Kildare town just beyond the legendary gallops of The Curragh is open for visitors, and it also includes a remarkable Japanese garden, reckoned the best Japanese rock garden in Europe, as well as the Museum of the Horse.

Once you get away from the busy main roads, Kildare is full of surprises. In fact, getting off the main roads is what enjoyment of life in Kildare is all about - it's significant in 2002 that Kildare's three top award holders in the Tidy Towns competition - Kill, Rathangan and Johnstown - include two places, Kill and Johnstown, which have succeeded in getting themselves by-passed, while the Highly Commended award - to Rathangan - is held by a neat rural township which so enjoys being off the beaten track that it's astonishing to think it's only 30 miles from the heart of Dublin.

In the northwest of the county, you enter the awe-inspiring Bog of Allen, the largest in Ireland, across whose wide open spaces the early engineers struggled to progress the Grand Canal on its route from the east coast towards the Shannon. Such needs of national transport are intertwined through the county's history. Today, Kildare is inevitably under commuter pressure from Dublin, and the fact that it is on the main route from the capital to the south and southwest means that at first it seems to have more miles of motorway per square mile of county than anywhere else.

Yet the underlying quality of the land is such that only the shortest diversion from the arterial roads is all that is required to find total rural peace in a lovely place of gentle waterways, fertile meadows, and quiet woodland.

Local Attractions and Information

Carbury Ballindoolin House & Garden 0405 31430
Clane Kildare Failte 045 892307
Celbridge Castletown House 01 628 8252
Curragh The Curragh Racecourse 045 441205
Kilcock Larchill Arcadian Gardens (follies) 01 628 7354
Kildare (Tully) Irish National Stud 045 21617
Kildare (Tully) Japanese Gardens 045 21251
Kildare Tourism Information 045 522696
Kill Goff's Bloodstock Sales (frequent) 045 886600
Naas Naas Racecourse 045 897391
Newbridge Riverbank Arts Centre 045 433480
Punchestown Punchestown Racecourse 045 897704
Straffan Steam Museum 01 627 3155

Athy

Coursetown Country House

COUNTRY HOUSE Stradbally Road Athy Co Kildare **Tel: 0507 31101** Fax: 0507 32740

Although situated just off the Stradbally road, Jim and Iris Fox's fine 200 year old house is attached to a large arable farm. The house is large, welcoming, immaculately maintained and very comfortable, with some unusual attributes, including Jim's natural history library (where guests are welcome to browse) and extensive, well-tended gardens stocked with many interesting plants, including a number of rare fruit trees. Bedrooms vary according to their position in the house, but all are thoughtfully furnished in a pleasantly homely country house style and have direct dial phones, tea/coffee facilities and hair dryers. Iris takes pride in ensuring that her guests have the comfort of the very best beds and bedding - and the standard of details in the pristine shower rooms is equally high, with lots of lovely towels and quality toiletries. (A bathroom is also available for anyone who prefers to have a good soak in a tub.) Another special feature is a ground floor room near the front door which has been specially designed for wheelchair users, with everything completed to the same high standard as the rest of the house. Then there is breakfast - again, nothing is too much trouble and the emphasis is on delicious helathy eating. The wide selection offered includes fresh juices and fruit salad, poached seasonal fruit (eg plums from the garden) pancakes, French toast with banana & maple syrup, Irish farmhouse cheeses, home-made bread and preserves - and the traditional cooked breakfast includes lovely rashers specially vacuum-packed for Iris by Shiel's butchers, in Abbeyleix. Small weddings catered for (20). Not suitable for children under 8. **Rooms 5** (all with en-suite shower, all no smoking, 1 for disabled). B&B €50, ss €10 Amex, MasterCard, Visa. **Directions:** just outside Athy, on Stradbally Road. Well signposted.

Athy

Tonlegee House

COUNTRY HOUSE/RESTAURANT Athy Co. Kildare **Tel: 0507 31473**
Fax: 0507 31473 Email: marjorie@tonlegeehouse.com Web: www.tonlegeehouse.com

Marjorie Molloy's elegant country house just outside Athy was built in 1790 and now combines modern comfort with a pleasing element of old-fashioned style. The individually decorated en-suite bedrooms include one single room and all are comfortably furnished to a high standard with phones, TV and complimentary mineral water and well-finished bathrooms. Children welcome. Pets permitted by arrangement. **Rooms 12** (5 superior, 2 shower only). B&B €55 pps, ss €20; sc discretionary. **Restaurant:** Hugh Johnston has been head chef since 1998 and his seasonal menus are in a modern European style, based on home-grown and local produce. Over an aperitif in the drawing room, imaginative menus make good reading and offer a balanced choice, including house specialities such as a starter of quail & wild mushroom pie with Madeira sauce. Local Kildare lamb is an especially strong option - roast rack with a herb crust, perhaps, served with celeriac purée and roasted garlic - and also vegetarian dishes like mille feuille of aubergine and courgette with rocket & basil sauce. Tempting desserts might include a thin apple tart with cinnamon cream (cooked to order) or home made ice creams - or make the most of a good Irish farmhouse cheeseboard. **Seats 40.** D only 7-9.30pm (Sun &Mon residents only). Set D €26-34, also à la carte. house wine from 15.80; sc discretionary.Closed 24 Dec-8 Jan. Amex, MasterCard, Visa, Laser. **Directions:** from Dublin, take M7, then onto M9 to N78, through Athy, across 2 bridges, passing by the canal take 1st left after Tegral factory.

Ballymore Eustace
RESTAURANT/PUB

Ballymore Inn

Ballymore Eustace Co. Kildare **Tel: 045 864 585**
Fax: 045 864 747 Email: theballymoreinn@hotmail.com

It's the food that draws people to the O'Sullivan family's pub and it's wise to book well ahead to get a taste of the wonderful things this country kitchen has to offer, especially at weekends. The outside of the Ballymore Inn gives little away, although the blackboard menu at the door is a hint of what's to come. Inside, the clues begin to add up, especially if you turn right into the more 'foodie' side. Unusual craft furniture, imaginative use of colour and striking fresh flowers and plants all add up to the kind of place where details count so the menu, when it arrives, fits into the pattern. There's plenty to choose from, such as delicious soups, Caesar salad with crispy bacon, excellent meats - Kildare sandwich with baked ham, farmhouse cheese & apricot chutney, for example, or sirloin steak with herb butter or grilled Ardrahan cheese, served with sauté potatoes or champ or grilled pork cutlet with tomato & black olive dressing - pasta dishes (with chicken and chilli perhaps) and delicious, homely desserts. Creative modern pizzas that marry artisan Irish food products with traditional methods are a house speciality and their special pizza oven has turned out to be a marvel for all sorts of other dishes too. Pizzas have wonderfully light, thin and crisply cooked bases and every ingredient is in tip-top condition; their Grilled Fennel, Roasted Peppers, Basil and Ardrahan Cheese Pizza one was the winner of our Vegetarian Dish of the Year for 1999. Currently, the menu invites you to construct your own pizza, starting with a choice of five bases (tomato plus a range of cheeses, costing €4.44-7.62 depending on size and selected base) and select from ten toppings (mushrooms, olives, anchovy, grilled peppers, bacon etc), costing 32-95 cents each. Evening menus for the restaurant overlap with the café-bar menu to some extent, but are more structured and offer a much wider choice of dishes. Children welcome. **Seats 50.** No smoking area; air conditioning. L&D Mon-Sat: L 12.30-3 (Fri & Sat to 6) & D 6-9 (Fri & Sat to 10); house wine €12.87; sc discretionary. Closed 3-6pm Mon-Thu; no food on Sun. Closed bank hols, 25 Dec & Good Fri. Amex, MasterCard, Visa, Laser. **Directions:** turn right 2.5 miles after Blessington on Baltinglass Road.

Castledermot
HOTEL/RESTAURANT

Kilkea Castle

Kilkea Castledermot Co. Kildare **Tel: 0503 45156**
Fax: 0503 45187 Email: kilkea@iol.ie

The oldest inhabited castle in Ireland, Kilkea dates back to the twelfth century and has been sensitively renovated and converted into a hotel without loss of elegance and grandeur. Rooms, many with lovely views over the formal gardens and surrounding countryside, are splendidly furnished to incorporate modern comforts. Public areas include a hall complete with knights in armour and two pleasant ground floor bars - a cosy back one and a larger one that opens onto a terrace overlooking gardens and a golf course. Some of the bedrooms in the main castle are very romantic - as indeed is the whole setting - making it understandably popular for weddings. The adjoining (architecturally discreet) leisure centre, offers state-of-the-art facilities: indoor swimming pool, saunas, jacuzzi, steamroom, well-equipped exercise room and sunbed. Outdoor sports include clay pigeon shooting, archery, tennis and fishing. An 18-hole championship golf course, which has views of the castle from every fairway, uses the River Greese flowing through the grounds as a natural hazard and a couple of extra lakes were added to increase the challenge still further; informal meals are served in the golf club. Special weekend breaks at the castle are good value. Conferences/banqueting (300/500); secretarial services. Leisure Centre, swimming pool. Garden. Tennis, Golf (18), fishing. Children welcome. No pets. **Rooms 36** (1 suite, 9 mini-suites, 8 exec, 3 shower only). B&B about €165 pps, ss about €45.

De Lacy's Restaurant: Named after Hugh de Lacy, who built Kilkea Castle in 1180, this beautiful first-floor restaurant has a real 'castle' atmosphere and magnificent views over the countryside. It also overlooks the delightful formal kitchen garden (source of much that appears on the table in summer) and has a bright, airy atmosphere. Guests may take coffee on the terrace in summer and wander around to see the old fruit trees, vegetables and herbs. Both cooking and service are consistently excellent at this very special venue. Restaurant seats 60 (40 private). L daily 12.30-2.00, Sun to 2.30, D 7.00-9.30. Set L about €24. Set D about €40. House wine about €18; sc 12.5%. Toilets wheelchair accessible. Closed 23-27 Dec. Amex, Diners, MasterCard, Visa. **Directions:** signed from Castledermot village.

Curragh

Martinstown House

COUNTRY HOUSE

The Curragh Co. Kildare **Tel: 045 441 269** Fax: 045 441 208
Email: info@martinstown.com Web: www.martinstownhouse.com

Just on the edge of the Curragh, near Punchestown, Naas and The Curragh race courses, this delightful 200 year old 'Strawberry Hill' gothic style house is on a farm, set in 170 acres of beautifully wooded land, with free range hens, sheep, cattle and horses and a well-maintained walled kitchen garden that provides vegetables, fruit and flowers for the house in season. Meryl Long welcomes guests to this idyllic setting, aiming to offer them 'a way of life which I knew as a child (but with better bathrooms!), a warm welcome, real fires and good food.' It is a lovely family house, with very nicely proportioned rooms - gracious but not too grand - open fires downstairs, and bedrooms that are all different, very comfortably furnished with fresh flowers and each with its own special character. A stay here is sure to be enjoyable, with the help of a truly hospitable hostess who believes that holidays should be fun, full of interest and with an easy-going atmosphere. Golf and equestrian activities nearby. Not suitable of children. **Rooms 4** (2 en-suite, 2 with private bathrooms, 1 shower only) B&B €95pps, ss €15 Closed 12 Dec -10 Jan. Amex, MasterCard, Visa. **Directions:** Kilcullen exit off M9 then N78 towards Athy. Sign at 1st crossroads.

Kilcullen

Berneys Bar & Restaurant

PUB/RESTAURANT

Main St. Kilcullen Co. Kildare **Tel: 045 481 260**
Fax: 045 481 877 Email: berneys@indigo.ie

This welcoming bar on the main street is a real local, with its own character, a beer garden for summer and a log fire that's a welcome sight on cold days. The cooking is a mixture of Irish and country French and, in addition to a good choice of sandwiches and salads, there's a short bar menu offering several soups, hot dishes and puddings, changed daily. Guests arriving for evening meals go to the bar, where menus are considered over a drink, before going into the adjacent restaurant, a large L-shaped room decorated in warm colours and with interesting pictures. Recent refurbishment has improved the it considerably, with a new carpet and white linen tablecloths and napkins not only visually attractive, but also practical, as introducing sound-absorbing fabrics has reduced the noise level and made the room more relaxing. The menu is based on good ingredients - local lamb, steaks and duck, fresh fish - and is not adventurous, but well-cooked and attractively presented; it rarely changes as the clientèle is made up mainly of regulars who like things the way they are - and accept prices that are a little high for the area because it is reliably good. Service is friendly - most guests are known to long-term, efficient staff. Not suitable for children after 7pm. Restaurant: **Seats 80** (private room, 40). No-smoking area; air conditioning. D Mon-Sat 7-10 (Sun to 9) Set D about €45. A la carte also available. House wine about €16; sc discretionary. Bar Food Mon-Sat noon -11pm. Toilets wheelchair accessible. Parking. Closed Sun, 25 Dec & Good Fri. Amex, Diners, MasterCard, Visa. **Directions:** south of Naas continue on M9, turn right into Kilcullen, in town over the bridge.

Leixlip

Leixlip House Hotel

HOTEL/RESTAURANT

Captains Hill Leixlip Co. Kildare **Tel: 01 624 2268**
Fax: 01 624 4177 Email: info@leixliphouse.com Web: www.leixliphouse.com

Up on a hill overlooking Leixlip village, this lovely Georgian house is just eight miles from Dublin city centre. Having undergone extensive renovation (it has been furnished and decorated to a high standard in period style) it opened as a hotel in 1996. Gleaming antique furniture and gilt-framed mirrors enhance thick carpeted public rooms in soft country colours, all creating an atmosphere of discreet opulence. Bedrooms include two suites furnished with traditional mahogany furniture; the strong, simple decor particularly pleases the many business guests who stay here. Hotel guests have complimentary use of a nearby gym. Conference/banqueting (70/140). Secretarial services. Children welcome (under 12s free in parents' room, cots available without charge). No pets. **Rooms 15** (9 shower only). B&B about €95 pps, ss about €40. **The Bradaun Restaurant:** The commitment to quality evident in the hotel as a whole is continued in the restaurant, a bright, high-ceilinged, formally appointed dining room. Sean Hicks, wo has been head chef since the hotel opened, offers consistently good modern Irish cooking; his imaginative, wide-ranging menus are based on fresh seasonal produce and well executed with admirable attention to detail. Set menus offer particularly good value for money. An extensive, informative and carefully chosen wine list includes an interesting and well-balanced Recommended Wines of the Month selection within an accessible price range and a fair selection of half bottles. Not suitable for children after 8pm. **Seats 45.** L 12.30-3 (Sun to 4.30) & D 7-10 (Sun to 8.30); early D €23.50, 7-8.30. Set L €22.22 (incl Sun). Set D €23; à la carte also available. House wine from €23; sc discretionary. Hotel closed 25 Dec. Amex, Diners, MasterCard, Visa, Laser. **Directions:** Leixlip exit off M4 motorway. Take right in Leixlip village at traffic lights.

Maynooth
HOTEL

Glenroyal Hotel & Leisure Club

Straffan Rd. Maynooth Co. Kildare **Tel: 01 629 0909**
Fax: 01 629 0919 Email: hotel@glenroyal.ie Web: www.glenroyal.ie

Situated on the outskirts of the university town of Maynooth, and only 20 minutes from Dublin city centre, this large hotel meets local demand for essential facilities covering a wide range of events - conferences, corporate events and weddings - and provides extensive leisure facilities, including a dramatically designed 20 metre pool (with underwater loungers, whirlpool and children's splashpool), a gymnasium and much else besides. Bedrooms are all comfortably furnished - mostly in contemporary style - with all the amenities of a good modern hotel and neat en-suite bathrooms. Conferences/Banqueting (400/275); secretarial services. Video conferencing. Leisure centre. Children welcome (under 4s free in parents room; cots available). No Pets. **Rooms 57** (10 executive , 7 shower only, 1 for disabled). B&B about €75 pps, ss about €20. Lift. Wheelchair accessible. Closed 25 Dec. Amex, Diners, MasterCard, Visa. Directions: From Dublin, M4 to Maynooth turn right off slip road to Maynooth. Amex, Diners, MasterCard, Visa. **Directions:** from Dublin, M4 to Maynooth turn right off sliproad for Maynooth.

Maynooth
COUNTRY HOUSE
RESTAURANT

Moyglare Manor

Maynooth Co. Kildare
Tel: 01 628 6351 Fax: 01 628 5405
Email: info@moyglaremanor.ie Web: www.moyglaremanor.ie

Country hedges and workaday farmland give way to neatly manicured hedging, rolling parkland then beautifully tended gardens as one approaches this imposing classical Georgian manor - and it comes as no surprise to find that the owner, Norah Devlin, lavishes her love of beautiful things on the place, with a passion for antiques that has become legendary. Gilt-framed mirrors and portraits are everywhere, shown to advantage against deep-shaded damask walls. The remarkable abundance of chairs and sofas of every pedigree ensures comfortable seating, even when the restaurant is fully booked with large parties milling around before and after dining. First-time visitors sometimes describe it as 'like being in an antique shop' but, after recovering from the stunning effect of its contents, guests invariably reflect on the immaculate maintenance and comfort of the place under the careful stewardship of long-time manager Shay Curran. Spacious bedrooms are also lavishly furnished in period style, some with four-posters or half testers, and include a ground-floor suite; all have well-appointed bathrooms with quality appointments and good attention to detail. All rooms have recently been upgraded to a very high standard and, despite a longstanding aim for peacefulness, the modern world seem to have caught up with Moyglare and televisions have been installed in bedrooms. Golf nearby (four courses within 10 miles), also tennis and horseriding nearby. Small conferences/banqueting (40); secretarial services. Not suitable for children under 12. No Pets. Garden; walking. **Rooms 16** (1 suite, 4 executive, 2 rooms for disabled). B&B €115 pps, ss €25. **Restaurant:** Hotel manager Shay Curran personally supervises the formally-appointed restaurant, which is in several interconnecting rooms; the middle ones nice and cosy for winter, those overlooking the garden and countryside pleasant in fine weather. Grand and romantic, it's just the place for a special occasion and there's a pianist playing background music in the evening. Lunch and dinner menus offer a nicely balanced combination of traditional favourites and sophisticated fare, attractively presented, with a vegetarian option always available. There is an emphasis on seafood and game in season - roast pheasant, perhaps, hung long enough to give it a gamey flavour, perfectly cooked and served off the bone accompanied by a nice little serving of green-flecked champ as well as game chips and Cumberland sauce. Lunch menus offer less choice than dinner, but are nevertheless quite formal and convey a sense of occasion. Fine meals are complemented by an exceptional wine list of special interest to the connoisseur (Moyglare Manor was the winner of our 1999 Wine List of the Year Award). Not suitable for children under 12. Restaurant seats 40 (private room, 25). No smoking area. L Sun-Fri 12.30-2; D daily 7-9. Set L €28.50, Set Sun €31.50. D à la carte . House wine €20.25; sc 12.5%. Closed 24-27 Dec. Amex, Diners, MasterCard, Visa, Laser. **Directions:** from Dublin to West on N4. Take exit for Maynooth keep right at Catholic church, 2 miles on, turn left at Moyglare crossroads, next right.

Naas

Killashee House Hotel

HOTEL

Naas Co. Kildare **Tel: 045 879277** Fax: 045 879266
Email: reservations@killasheehouse.com Web: www.killasheehouse.com

Set in 27 acres of gardens and woodland just outside Naas town, this recently opened hotel was once a boarding school and has provided a great boost to the facilities of the area in its new guise. Approached along a driveway just long enough to give a sense of scale and setting (although spoilt a little by the car parking arrangements in front of the building), the entrance and lobby areas are impressive - the latter overlooks a fine inner courtyard planted with Virginia creeper, which will be very attractive when mature. A large traditionally furnished lounge area on the first floor, with views of the grounds and courtyard, is approached by a rather grand staircase (not quite finished on the guide's visit); furnished with attractively grouped seating areas, this is a pleasant place for afternoon tea and informal socialising - there is a pianist at certain times. Conference and business events are well catered for, with 20 conference rooms of various sizes designed to anticipate requirements. Bedrooms, which have been designed with both luxury and practical requirements in mind, include a number of suites and some with four-poster beds; all rooms have multi-line phones, data ports, voicemail, fax (on request), and safe as well as the more usual amenities. Formal dining is offered at the elegant main restaurant, Turners (where a harpist plays at weekends), and informal food is available in other areas. Already a popular venue for weddings, the hotel is also well located for many of the county's sporting activities including horseracing (four courses nearby), golf (five clubs nearby), car racing (Mondello Park) and attractions such as the Wicklow Mountains, The Japanese Gardens and The National Irish Stud. On site facilities include archery, cycling and woodland walks; a leisure centre and spa will open during 2002. Conference/banqueting 1600/660. Secretarial services; video conferencing. Children welcome (under 2s free in parents' room, cot available without charge). Pets allowed in some areas. Garden, walking. **Rooms 84** (6 suites, 9 junior suites, 75 superior, 28 no smoking, 2 for disabled). Lift. B&B €105 pps, ss €45. Closed 25-26 Dec. Amex, MasterCard, Visa, Laser. **Directions:** 30 minutes from Dublin on N7 to Naas, then 1 mile along R448, Kilcullen road.

Naas

Les Olives Restaurant

RESTAURANT

10 South Main Street Naas Co. Kildare **Tel: 045 894788**
Email: lesolive@indigo.ie

Olivier Pauloin-Valory is the proprietor chef of this successful little restaurant on on the first floor over Kavanagh's pub, in the centre of Naas. Prior to re-opening with a new name in the summer of 2001 (it was previously known as Joe Olives), the restaurant was closed for six months and underwent major refurbishment. Regulars are drawn from a wide area around the town - seafood is a particular attraction, in specialities such as prawn kebabs Les Olives, or lobster salad with a lemon or chive butter sauce, but squid, scallops & John Dory are all likely to feature too, also game in season. Daily fish specials are shown on blackboard, where you you'll usually also find some less likely soulmates, such as ostrich (which is farmed nearby) and kangaroo (which is not). Good cooking (including vegetables, which is less usual than it should be) and friendly efficient service go a long way towards an enjoyable night out - helped along by M. Pauloin-Valory's new wine cave, which offers an extensive range of wines, including champagnes and rare vintages. Not suitable for children under 10. **Seats 45.** D only 7-10 Tue-Sun; à la carte. House wine WUR13; sc discretionary. Closed Mon; Christmas, Good Fri. MasterCard, Visa, Laser. **Directions:** town centre.

Naas

Thomas Fletcher

PUB

Main Street Naas Co. Kildare **Tel: 045 897 328** Fax: 045 897 328

This great old pub goes back well into the 1800s and has been in the Fletcher family since Tom Fletcher's father ran it in the 1930s. It's the kind of place that puts Irish theme pubs to shame, with its simple wooden floor and long, plain mahogany bar broken up in the traditional way with mahogany dividers and stained glass panels. They did up the back lounge recently, but there's no need to worry - it shouldn't need more work for another couple of hundred years. Closed 25 Dec, Good Fri & Bank Hols. **Directions:** Main street Naas beside Superquinn.

Narraghmore

The Pond House

COUNTRY HOUSE

Narraghmore Co. Kildare **Tel: 045 485 456** Fax: 045 485 456

No need to explain the name of Nuala Clarke's unusual guesthouse, which will become obvious as soon as you reach it. Although it's in a different county, The Pond House is handy enough to Rathsallagh (see entry, Dunlavin, Co Wicklow) to be a regular recipient of overflow custom, a system which pleases all concerned - word has got around and some very interesting people stay here. The house is quietly located and spacious with a large patio area at the back, the atmosphere is distinctly laid back and, unusually for a guesthouse, it even has a proper bar where race-goers and wedding guests can enjoy a small one or two before heading upstairs. Bedrooms are pleasant in a country pine way, but by no means luxurious (no phone or TV and they're all shower only.) Nuala is a natural hostess and clearly enjoys making people feel at home. Chilkdren welcome (under 4s free in parents' room, cots available without charge). Garden, fishing , walking. Pets allowed by arrangement. **Rooms 5** (all shower only). B&B €38.09pps, ss €12.70. Open all year. MasterCard, Visa. **Directions:** 1.2 miles off main Dublin Carlow road to Narraghmore, next right; sign-posted.

Newbridge

Keadeen Hotel

HOTEL

Newbridge Co. Kildare **Tel: 045 431 666** Fax: 045 434 402
Email: keadeen@iol.ie Web: www.keadeenhotel.kildare.ie

Centrally located and easily accessible off the M7 motorway, this family-owned hotel is set in eight acres of fine landscaped gardens just south of the town (and quite near the Curragh racecourse). Accommodation is generously sized and furnished to a high standard. A fine romanesque Health & Fitness Club has an 18-metre swimming pool and scented aromatherapy room among its attractions, plus a staffed gymnasium with specialist equipment imported from America. Extensive conference and banqueting facilities (800/600); secretarial services. Video conferencing can be arranged. Leisure centre, swimming pool. Garden. Parking. No Pets. Children welcome (under 3s free in parents rooms; cots available). **Rooms 55** (1 suite, 3 junior suites, 20 executive, 1 for disabled) Room rate about €135. Closed 24 Dec-2 Jan. Amex, Diners, MasterCard, Visa. **Directions:** from Dublin take N7 off M50, take sliproad sign posted Curragh race course & follow signs for Newbridge.

Newbridge

The Red House Inn

HOTEL/RESTAURANT

Newbridge Co. Kildare **Tel: 045 431 516**
Fax: 045 431 934 Email: info@redhouse.ie

Proprietor-manager Brian Fallon runs a tidy ship at this cosy inn just off the motorway. It has a very relaxed atmosphere, especially in the characterful bar and the restful conservatory and garden at the back, and bedrooms all have good amenities. Conference/Banqueting (400/300); secretarial services. Garden. Children under 5 free in parents' room; cots available. **Rooms 12** (1 suite, 1 junior suite, 2 no-smoking rooms, 1 for disabled). B&B about €60 pps, ss abour €13. No sc. Restaurant: The dining room is well appointed in a classic style, very suitable for the mainly traditional home-cooked food for which The Red House is known, especially prime beef and Kildare lamb although vegetarian options are always given too. Children welcome. **Seats 75** (private room, 25). No smoking area; air conditioning. L& D daily 12.30-3, 6.30-10. Toilets wheelchair accessible. Closed 3 days Christmas, early Jan & Good Fri. Amex, Diners, MasterCard, Visa. **Directions:** on the N7 between Naas and Newbridge.

Straffan

Barberstown Castle

COUNTRY HOUSE
RESTAURANT

Straffan Co. Kildare
Tel: 01 628 8157 Fax: 01 627 7027
Email: castleir@iol.ie Web: www.barberstowncastle.com

Barberstown Castle is fascinating; steeped in history through three very different historical periods, it's one of the few houses in the area to have been occupied continuously for over 400 years. The oldest part is very much a real castle - the original keep in the middle section of the building, which includes the atmospheric cellar restaurant, was built by Nicholas Barby in the early 13th century. A more domestic Elizabethan house was added in the second half of the 16th century and Hugh Barton (also associated with nearby Straffan House, now the Kildare Hotel & Country Club, with whom it shares golf and leisure facilities) then built the 'new' Victorian wing in the 1830s. Most recently, in the current ownership of Kenneth Healy, the property has been thoroughly renovated and appropriately refurbished, in keeping with its age and style, to offer a high standard of modern comfort. Very comfortable accommodation is provided in well-appointed, individually decorated en-suite rooms - some are in the oldest section, the Castle Keep, others are more recent, but most are stylish and spacious. Public areas, including two drawing rooms and an elegant bar, have been renovated with the same care, and there are big log fires everywhere. Conferences/Banqueting (60/150); Children welcome (under 6s free in parents'room; cot available without charge). Garden. No pets. **Rooms 22** (1 suite, 5 mini-suites, 17 executive, 1 shower only, 1 for disabled). B&B €109 pps, ss EU31; sc inc.. The Castle Restaurant: The restaurant is in a series of whitewashed rooms in the semi-basement of the old Castle Keep, which gives it great atmosphere, heightened by fires and candles in alcoves. Head chef Ciaran Woods, who joined the castle in 1999, presents a six-course Tasting Menu (served to complete parties only) and a seasonal à la carte with about seven choices on each course. Game is offered in season - in a starter of roast mallard with coco bean salad & truffle dressing, for example, or roast pheasant with puy lentils and pot-au-fea of vegetables. There will also be several prime fish dishes and local lamb and beef also feature of course. Desserts may include a hot soufflé (pistachio, for example, served with praline ice cream) and there's a good selection of Irish farmhouse cheeses and home-baked breads. **Seats 75** (private rooms 20/32)). No-smoking restaurant. D only 7.30-9.30. Tasting Menu €48.88; à la carte also available. House wine €23; sc discretionary (10% on parties of 7+) Toilets wheelchair accessible. Closed 24-26 Dec & 6 Jan-6 Feb. Amex, Diners, MasterCard, Visa. **Directions:** west N4 - turn for Straffan exit; South N7 - Kill exit.

Straffan

The K Club

HOTEL

RESTAURANT ★ féile bia

Straffan Co. Kildare **Tel: 01 601 7200** Fax: 01 601 7299
Email: sales@kclub.ie Web: www.kclub.ie

The origins of Straffan House go back a long way - the history is known as far back as 550 AD - but it was the arrival of the Barton wine family in 1831 that established the tone of today's magnificent building, by giving it a distinctively French elegance. It was bought by the Smurfit Group in 1988 and, after extensive renovations, opened as an hotel in 1991. Set in lush countryside, and overlooking its own golf course, the hotel boasts unrivalled opulence. The interior is magnificent, with superb furnishings and a wonderful collection of original paintings by well-known artists, including William Orpen, Louis le Brocqy, Sir John Lavery and Jack B.Yeats, who has a room devoted to his work. (Catalogue available from Reception). All bedrooms and bathrooms are individually designed in the grand style, with superb amenities and great attention to detail. Under the guidance of Ray Carroll, who has been with the hotel from the outset and was general manager before becoming Chief Executive of the Resort, it is run with apparently effortless perfection. The hotel and golf course are in the midst of major developments in preparation for the Ryder Cup, which the K Club will host in 2005; these include a new bedroom extension and an extension to the Byerley Turk Restaurant, which both opened in 2001, and a second 18-hole golf course which is due for completion in 2002. However, the hotel is never too busy for training and, with the support of the state training agency CERT, the K Club pioneered a 4-year in-hotel Food and Beverage Course in 1998 to attract the high calibre staff required for top hotels. To highlight this innovative programme, a special Skills Development Award was awarded to Ray Carroll and his team at the K Club by the Guide in 2001, for their initiative and foresight in instigating such a far-reaching scheme. Although most famous for its golf, the hotel also offers river fishing for salmon and trout and coarse fishing with a choice of five stocked lakes (equipment bait and tackle provided; tuition available). For guests interested in horticulture there is a mapped garden walk, with planting details. Conferences/ Banqueting (120/180); secretarial services. Leisure centre, swimming pool; specialist therapies; beauty salon. Golf (18), tennis, garden, walking, fishing, cycling, equestrian. Snooker, pool table. Pets permitted in some areas by arrangement. Children welcome (cots available, €60). Lift. 24 hour concierge, 24 hour room service, twice daily housekeeping. **Rooms 105** (7 suites, 5 junior suites, 60 executive rooms, 10 garden suites, 10 no smoking, 10 for disabled). Room rate from €270. No sc. **The Byerley Turk** Dramatically draped tall windows, marble columns, paintings of racehorses, tables laden with crested china, monogrammed white linen, gleaming modern crystal and silver - these all create an impressive background for the hotel's fine food. While the style has not changed noticeably since the restaurant was extended in 2001, the room is now a more interesting shape (enabling one end to be closed off for private parties without affecting normal dining arrangements) and as the old trompe l'oeil cocktail bar has been seamlessly absorbed into the entrance to the new accommodation, a larger bar has been created, with dark green walls creating a pleasingly clubby atmosphere and - the stroke of genius that is the making of this extension - it opens onto an elegant terrace with a distinctly French tone, thus reflecting the changes made in the Barton years. Here, on fine summer evenings, guests consider menus over an aperitif and admire the new golf course taking shape across the river. Executive chef Michel Flamme, who has been with the hotel since it opened, bases his cooking on classical French cuisine, using the best of local and estate-grown produce; his Menu du Jour (€65) is concise, with just three choices on each course but all the little touches - a complimentary amuse-bouche, home-made petits fours with the coffee - that make a special dining experience memorable will be in place. A seasonal à la carte is also offered, and a surprise "Tasting Menu" (€120), for complete parties. All menus are luxurious and notable for a growing number of specialities, which include crispy wontons of Dublin Bay prawns, with basil, pine kernels and olive oil, and some dishes with a definite Irish flavour such as braised loin of organic bacon with Savoy cabbage, onion & parsley cream, also a range of hot soufflés (€20). Service, under the direction of restaurant manager Jimmy Redmond (who has also been with the hotel since it opened) is friendly and professional. Given the intertwined history of Straffan House and the Barton family, it is appropriate that the Bordeaux Reserve from Barton and Guestier should be the label chosen for the hotel's house wine. Children welcome. **Seats 115** (private room 14). No smoking area; air conditioning. D only 7.30-10 daily. Set D €65; Gourmet Menu €120; also à la carte. House Wine from €25; sc discretionary. * A less formal dining option is available at The Legends Restaurant at the golf club (12.30-11 daily). Amex, Diners, MasterCard, Visa, Laser. **Directions:** 30 mins south west of Dublin airport and city (M50 - N4).

COUNTY KILKENNY

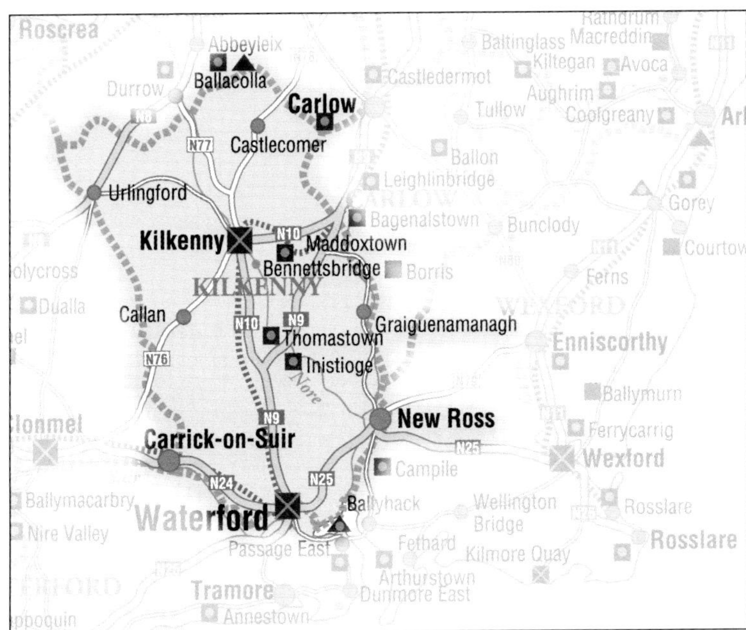

Kilkenny is a land of achingly beautiful valleys where elegant rivers weave their way through a rich countryside spiced by handsome hills. So naturally it's a place whose people care passionately about their county, and the miniature city at its heart. For Kilkenny - the Marble City - is one of Ireland's oldest cities, and proud of it. Its selection of ancient buildings is unrivalled. But, by today's standards of population, this gem of a place is scarcely a city at all. Yet it's a city in every other way. Thus 2002 will undoubtedly see a continuation of the campaign to maintain the time-hallowed city status, while at the same time developing Kilkenny's image as "The Creative Heart of Ireland".

Civic pride is at the heart of it, and Kilkenny city's enthusiasm received national recognition in September 2001 when, yet again, it became the county's leading award winner in the Tidy Towns contest. Enjoying its reputation as a major centre for civilisation and culture for well over 1500 years, Kilkenny thrives on a diverse mixture of public debates about conservation, arts festivals, and - believe it or not - a comedy festival of international standing.

Rivers are the key to the county. Almost the entire eastern border is marked by the Barrow, which becomes ever more spectacularly lovely as it rolls gently through the beautiful Graiguenamanagh, then thrusts towards the sea at the tiny river port of St Mullins. The southern border is marked by the broad tidal sweep of the Suir, and this fine county is divided diagonally by the meandering of the most beautiful river of all, the Nore. Invaders inevitably progressed up its tree-lined course past what is now the lovely river village of Inistioge towards the ancient site of Kilkenny city itself. They quickly became Kilkenny folk in the process, for this is a land to call home. The monastic and later mediaeval city lent itself so naturally to being an administrative centre that at times it appeared set to become the capital of Ireland.

Today, it seems odd at first that this miniature city doesn't have its own university, and in 2002 moves are afoot to establish a Third Level College. But after you've enjoyed Kilkenny's mellow streets and old buildings, you'll soon realise that, with its plethora of festivals featuring artistic, theatrical and comedy themes, Kilkenny has its own individual buzz of creativity and energy which many an arid modern unversity campus might well envy.

Local Attractions and Information

Callan Edmund Rice House	056 25993
Gowran Gowran Park Racecourse	056 26225
Kilkenny Kilkenny Castle	056 21450
Kilkenny Cat Laughs Comedy Festival (May)	056 63416
Kilkenny Rothe House (16c house, exhibitions)	056 22893
Kilkenny City Tourist Information	056 51510
Thomastown Jerpoint Abbey	056 24623
Thomastown Kilfane Glen & Waterfall	056 24558
Thomastown Mount Juliet (parkland surrounding hotel)	056 24455
Tullaroan Kilkenny GAA Museum	056 69202

Bennettsbridge

Calabash Bistro

RESTAURANT

Chapel Street Bennettsbridge Co. Kilkenny **Tel: 056 27850**
Email: calabash@eircom.net

Brian Kelly (front of house) and Jack Moylan (the chef) have been running this appealing restaurant and the adjacent Calabar coffee shop in the centre of Bennettsbridge village since 1999 and it is a good place to build into visits on the "Kilkenny Craft Trail" as many of the workshops are in and around the village. Although not large, it has a comfortable little reception area and the restaurant is full of interest (pictures, unusual objects, a rather mysterious stairase and balcony) and doors opening onto a garden patio area at the back give the room a light and spacious feeling. Menus are refreshingly straightforward, with no wordy descriptions and hardly an exotic reference to be found. What you get here is real food and everything is based on fresh ingredients - locally produced beef, fish from Castletownbere - and cooked to order. Shortish à la carte menus include good soups (with home-baked bread) and starters like deep-fried brie with real Cumberland sauce or warm savoury tart with smoked salmon & leek (a choice of seven, all under €10), while main courses range from the perennially popular sirloin steak with garlic & herb butter (the most expensive at €19.05) to vegetarian dish of the day (a pasta bake, perhaps). Everything has that real home-made flavour and, be warned, portions are very generous. A shortish wine list is generally informative (although, oddly, most vintages are not given) and includes four half bottles; a half dozen Selected French Wines includes some interesting bottles. Private parties and buffets for large groups can be arranged. **Seats 26** (private room 14). No smoking area. Children welcome early evening, but not suitable after 8 pm. D Thu-Mon, 6-9.30. A la carte except early D 6-7pm Jun-Aug only, €18.99. Housewine €14.40. Closed Tue, Wed; 1st fortnight Nov, Christmas & mid-Feb-mid Mar. (Open all bank hols except Christmas.) Amex, MasterCard, Visa. **Directions:** 7km outside Kilkenny on Wexford Road.

Bennettsbridge

Nicholas Mosse Irish Country Shop

CAFÉ

Bennettsbridge Co. Kilkenny **Tel: 056 27505**
Fax: 056 27491 Email: sales@irishcountryshop.com Web: www.irishcountryshop.com

One of the best reasons to go just outside Kilkenny city to Bennettsbridge is to visit the Nicholas Mosse Pottery. They have recently moved the whole operation over to the old riverside mill, which now has a new shop and visitor centre where you can see the full range - including handblown glass and table linens as well as acres of the famous spongeware. Their informal little tea shop is on the first floor, overlooking the river, and offers reasonably priced wholesome fare - including, of course, delicious home-baked scones made with the local Mosse's flour. **Seats 28.** Children welcome. No smoking area. Open Mon-Sat 9-6, Sun 1.30-5. Closed 25/26 Dec & 1 Jan. Amex, Diners, MasterCard, Visa. Directions: 4 miles south of Kilkenny. Turn off just before bridge. Amex, Diners, MasterCard, Visa, Laser. **Directions:** 4 miles south of Kilkenny, just before bridge turn off.

Graiguenamanagh

Waterside

RESTAURANT/GUESTHOUSE

Graiguenamanagh Co. Kilkenny **Tel: 0503 24246**
Fax: 0503 24733 Email: info@waterside.iol.ie Web: www.watersideguesthouse.com

Brian and Brigid Roberts operate a restaurant with accommodation at this attractive old stone warehouse on the quayside, which was converted some years ago. The restaurant is well-appointed and offers modern European food on varied and enticing menus - in very pleasant waterside surroundings. A la carte dinner menus offer about half a dozen dishes on ecah course, using fresh local produce wherever possible, typically in a starter of Graiguenamanagh smoked eel with side salad & horseradish sauce. (The eel fishery at Graiguenamanagh dates back to the Cistercian monks who built the town and weirs on the river and is now active again) Game might be offered in season and vegetarian choices, such as a pancake with fennel, spinach & tomato, are always included. Finish with a nice homely dessert such as apple, sultana & cinnamon tart with home-made vanilla ice cream, or an Irish cheese plate (choice of half a dozen ports to accompany, if you wish). Sunday lunch menus are more restricted, but similar in style. An eclectic but not overlong wine list is fairly priced and under constant review (announcements of New Arrivals give it a sense of excitement). **Seats 35.** Smoking unrestricted. D 6.45-8.30 daily; L Sun only 12.30-2.30. A la carte menus. **Guesthouse** The accommodation is quite simple but comfortable, with direct dial phones, tea/coffee making facilities and TV in all rooms. Some rooms at the top of the building are especially spacious and overlook the river. (No lift.) **Rooms 10** (all shower only) B&B €50pps, ss €15. Closed Christmas period. MasterCard, Visa, Laser. **Directions:** 17 miles south east of Kilkenny on banks of the River Barrow.

Inistioge

COUNTRY HOUSE

Berryhill

Berryhill Inistioge Co. Kilkenny
Tel: 056 58434 Fax: 056 58434
Email: info@berryhillhouse.com Web: www.berryhillhouse.com

George and Belinda Dyer's delightful country house was built by George's family in 1780 - it has been immaculately maintained by successive generations and stands high above a valley, on the family's 250 acre farm, proudly overlooking the River Nore. Handsomely covered with virginia creeper, it is comfortably big rather than grand, with a homely hall and well-proportioned reception rooms full of lovely old family things. Bedrooms are very spacious - junior suites really, with a dressing/sitting area and room to make tea and coffee; each has an animal theme and one has access to a private balcony. No dinner, but there are good restaurants nearby. Breakfast is a speciality - fresh fruits, Nore smoked salmon & scrambled egg and 'anything the heart desires' taken at the dining room table in front of a log fire. Not suitable for children under 8. No pets. **Rooms 3** (all junior suites, all no smoking) Minimum stay 2 nights. B&B €57.14 ss €12.70; no service charge. Closed 1 Nov-30 Apr. MasterCard, Visa. **Directions:** R700 from Thomastown to Inistigoe, through square bear right over bridge, 1st left, 1st right and 2nd on left.

Inistioge

RESTAURANT

The Motte Restaurant

Plass Newyd Lodge Inistioge Co. Kilkenny **Tel: 056 58655**
Email: atmotte@gofree.indigo.ie

HOST OF THE YEAR

On the edge of the picturesque village of Inistioge, with views of extensive parklands and the River Nore, The Motte is situated in the classically proportioned Plas Newydd Lodge, named in honour of the ladies of Llangollen, who eloped from Inistioge in the late 18th century. Although small in size, this unique country restaurant is big on personality - of the host, the irrepressible Tom Reade-Duncan, who makes every guest feel as welcome as the flowers in spring and greatly adds to the enjoyment of the occasion with his offbeat humour and helpful way with local knowledge, and of the chef, Alan Walton, as conveyed through his imaginative menus and distinctive style of cooking. The pair of them combine a special blend of classical style and wacky artistic inspiration. Menus are sensibly limited to five or six choices on each course - starters might include crab and seaweed terrine, for example, or gnocchi with red pesto and pine nuts, while main courses range from variations on local beef - Thai marinated sirloin steak, perhaps, to an unconventional dish with middle eastern flavours like apricot glazed boned poussin in almond & raisin sauce. Vegetarians are always catered for, side vegetables invariably imaginative and perfectly cooked and desserts - toffee ice cream 'spring rolls' with butterscotch sauce perhaps - delicious. A private dining room has recently been added and small weddings or parties can be catered for. No smoking area; air conditioning. **Seats 40** (Private room, 16). D only,Tues-Sat 7-9.30 (also Sun, 7-9, on bank hol weekends only). Set D €31.50. House wine €15; sc discretionary (except 10% on groups of 6+). Closed Sun (except bank hol weekends), Mon; Christmas week. MasterCard, Visa. **Directions:** oposite village "name sign" on Kilkenny side of village.

Kilkenny
GUESTHOUSE

Butler House

16 Patrick Street Kilkenny Co. Kilkenny **Tel: 056 65707**
Fax: 056 65626 Email: res@butler.ie Web: www.butler.ie

Located close to Kilkenny Castle, this elegant Georgian townhouse was restored by the Irish State Design Agency in the 1970s. The resulting combination of what was at the time contemporary design and period architecture leads to some interesting discussions. However bedrooms are very spacious and the accommodation is very adequate, with all the amenities now expected of good 3-star guesthouse accommodation (although bathrooms are curiously utilitarian and only have showers, even though there is plenty of space for more comfort). The garden has recently been landscaped and all bathrooms and the dining room are to be upgraded and decorated "soon". Conferences (120). **Rooms 14** (1 suite, 3 superior, 12 shower only) B&B €75, ss €25, sc discretionary. Closed 23-29 Dec. Amex, Diners, MasterCard, Visa, Laser. **Directions:** city centre opposite Kilkenny Castle.

Kilkenny
RESTAURANT

Café Sol

William Street Kilkenny Co. Kilkenny **Tel: 056 64987**

Eavan Kenny and Gail Johnson opened this fun café-restaurant just off the High Street in 1995 and have recently given it a complete refurbishment, which has made the restaurant much more comfortable and cosy, especially for the evening. Good home-cooked all-day food has made their reputation: soups with freshly baked scones, imaginative sandwiches, great vegetarian dishes like Mediterranean salad with goats cheese, sundried tomatoes, roast peppers & olives, light fish dishes like sautéd mackerel with mushrooms & herbs, gorgeous salads - local Lavistown sausages with creamy mashed potato, grainy mustard mayonnaise and salad. Lots of nice bakes, too - and a good range of drinks to wash them down. Evening menus are more formal, but the same sound principles apply. A concise, well-selected wine list offers some interesting choices and good value. **Seats 60.** No smoking area; air conditioning. Open all day Mon-Sat, 10-5, & (Jun-Aug only) D 6.30-10. Eavan and Gail also offer outside catering and freezer cooking and they can open in the evening for private functions in winter. Set L from €15.24; Set D €24, à la carte menu also available. House wine €14.60. Children welcome in the daytime; not suitable for children under 10 after 6.30pm. Closed Sun, bank hols in winter & 25-29 Dec. MasterCard, Visa, Laser. **Directions:** coming from castle - up High St. - 2nd turn left opposite Town Hall.

Kilkenny
HOTEL

The Hibernian Hotel

1 Ormonde Street Kilkenny Co. Kilkenny **Tel: 056 71888** Fax: 056 71877
Email: info@hibernian.iol.ie Web: www.kilkennyhibernianhotel.com

Formerly the Hibernian Bank, this Georgian building has been restored to its former glory to become The Hibernian Hotel. The nine older rooms at the front are particularly spacious and furnished to a very high standard in keeping with the character of the building, but the new accommodation which has been built to blend in achieves this quite well. New rooms are also generous and impressively furnished in an upbeat cross between traditional and contemporary styles; they have good amenities, well-planned bathrooms - and the advantage of a quieter situation away from the street. Of the public areas, the old banking hall makes an impressive traditional style bar, the Hibernian Bar, set up with comfortable chairs and tables for informal eating; there is also a restaurant, Jacob's Cottage, which has been built and decorated to avoid feeling like a hotel dining room and has its own entrance from the street. Similarly, in contrast to the Hibernian Bar, Morrisons Bar is the cool place to hang out at night. Conference suites (max 80). **Rooms 40** (3 suites, 4 junior suites, 35 superior, 4 no-smoking) B&B €100.30 pps, ss €25.39. Lift . Closed Dec. 24-25. Amex, Diners, MasterCard, Visa, Laser. **Directions:** in the centre of Kilkenny.

Kilkenny
HOTEL

Hotel Kilkenny

College Road Kilkenny Co. Kilkenny **Tel: 056 62000** Fax: 056 65984
Email: kilkenny@griffingroup.ie Web: www.griffingroup.ie

This sister hotel to the Ferrycarrig Hotel near Wexford (see entry) is set in landscaped gardens on the edge of the city, and has recently completed a major development and refurbishment programme. These include an impressive 5-star health & fitness club with 20 metre swimming pool and a wide range of facilities including special beauty, relaxation and massage treatments and even a hairdressing salon. A new stone conservatory style bar enhances the hotel entrance considerably, 24 deluxe rooms were added and all the older bedrooms have ben refurbished. Bedrooms have been done in an unusual modern classic style, using specially commissioned Irish-made furniture, and the result is comfortable, interesting and and very pleasing to the eye. A stylish modern restaurant, Brooms Bistro, was ahead of the current fashion when it opened several years ago and has proved a great success. Informal meals are also available in the Rosehill bar every day (12.30-8.30). Conference/banqueting 400/380. Children welcome (under 2s free in parents' room; cots available without charge). No pets. **Rooms 103** (all en-suite, 24 executive rooms). B&B €95. Amex, Diners, MasterCard, Visa. **Directions:** on ring road at Clonmel roundabout exit.

Kilkenny

Kilkenny Design Centre

RESTAURANT féile bia Castle Yard Kilkenny Co. Kilkenny **Tel: 056 22118** Fax: 056 65905

Situated in what was once the stables and dairy of Kilkenny Castle - and overlooking the craft courtyard, this first floor self-service restaurant (above the temptations of a different sort on display in the famous craft shop below) is deservedly popular. The premises underwent an extension and major refurbishment in 2000 and now has a lift and disabled toilets as well as a much larger and more comfortable restaurant. Wholesome, healthy and absolutely delicious fare is consistently provided at very reasonable prices here, and the new layout allows for a much more attractive and accessible display of their wonderful food. Everything is freshly prepared every day, home baking is a strong point and salads are always colourful and full of life. It is good to see local ingredients used in well cooked traditional Irish dishes like beef in Kilkenny beer, local Lavistown sausages with caramelised onion & mustard mash - and classic Irish stew. **Seats 180.** No smoking area. Meals Mon-Sat 9-5. Self service. Closed Sun, bank hols, 5 Jan-9 April. Amex, Visa, Laser. **Directions:** opposite Kilkenny Castle.

Kilkenny

Kilkenny Ormonde Hotel

HOTEL/RESTAURANT Ormonde St. Kilkenny Co. Kilkenny

Tel: 056 23900 Fax: 056 23977

Email: info@kilkennyormaonde.com Web: www.kilkennyormonde.com

Sister establishment to the famous Aghadoe Heights Hotel, Killarney (see entry), this brand new hotel enjoys an outstandingly convenient central location for both business and leisure guests, beside (but not adjacent to) a multi-storey carpark and within walking distance of the whole city. Spacious public areas include an impressive foyer, Earls Bistro - where sassy international cooking is available at lunch and dinner daily - and an elegant dining room, Fredricks (see below). Generously large bedrooms are furnished to a high standard in a pleasing contemporary style, with ISDN lines and safes in addition to the more usual amenities, and both business/conference and on-site leisure facilities are excellent. Friendly, well-motivated and efficent staff ensure a pleasant stay or well-run business event. Conference/banqueting (500/400). Busines centre, video conferencing. Leisure centre, swimming pool. **Rooms 118** (6 suites, 5 junior suites, 12 superior rooms, 70 no smoking, 6 for disabled) B&B €120.63pps, ss €31.74. Children welcome (under12s free in parents' room, cots available without charge). Closed 25 Dec **Fredricks Fine Dining** Restaurant The restaurant bears the same name as the Killarney restaurant that has earned such a high reputation for Aghadoe Heights over the years. Head chef Will Fitzgerald (previously at the Morrison Hotel, Dublin) has been with the hotel since opening and is also responsible for the food at Earls Bistro (see above); he presents lively international menus based mainly on carefully sourced local produce, cooking is accurate and service, as in other areas of the hotel, a strong point. The restaurant, which is also used for breakfast, was too small from the outset and was due to be extended on the guide's most recent visit (summer 2001). **Seats 68.** No smoking area; air conditioning. Open D Tues-Sat 6-9 & L Sun 12.30-2.30. Set D €35.59. House wine about €19. sc discretionary. Closed Sun, Mon. Amex, Diners, MasterCard, Visa. **Directions:** Kilkenny city centre off Patrick Street junction.

Kilkenny

Kilkenny River Court Hotel

HOTEL féile bia The Bridge John St Kilkenny Co. Kilkenny

Tel: 056 23388 Fax: 056 23389

Email: reservations@kilrivercourt.com Web: www.kilrivercourt.com

In common ownership with the lovely Barrow House near Tralee (see entry), this hotel is beautifully situated in a courtyard just off the narrow, bustling streets of the city centre, with only the River Nore separating it from Kilkenny Castle. Although equally attractive for business or leisure - bedrooms and public areas are all finished to a high standard and the Health & Leisure Club provides excellent facilities for health, fitness and beauty treatments - the hotel has already established a special reputation for conferences and incentive programmes, with state-of-the-art facilities for groups of varying numbers and plenty to do when off duty in the city, as well as outdoor pursuits - golf, fishing, equestrian - nearby. Conference/Banqueting (210/160). Leisure centre, indoor swimming pool. Wheelchair access. Children under 3 free in parents' room. Private parking (access can be a little difficult). **Rooms 90** (2 suites, 41 executive, 19 no smoking, 4 for disabled). B&B €70pps, ss €40. Closed 25-26 Dec. Amex, MasterCard, Visa. **Directions:** follow city centre signs, directly opposite Kilkenny Castle, two archways on the Dublin side Bridge - use the castle as a landmark.

Kilkenny
RESTAURANT/GUESTHOUSE

Lacken House

Dublin Road Kilkenny Co. Kilkenny
Tel: 056 61085 Fax: 056 62435
Email: info@lackenhouse.ie Web: www.lackenhouse.ie

This period house on the edge of Kilkenny city has been home to the leading restaurant in the area for over 15 years. It was taken over by Jackie and Trevor Toner in 2001 and they have achieved their intention to run it in the same way and to maintain the high standards for which it was well- known. The existing staff were retained, including chef Nicola O'Brien, who had been head chef for two years previously and continues her practice of using the best local produce and mainly organic vegetables and fruit. The style is a combination of traditional and modern cooking - and there is a willingness to maintain a flexible approach and accede to any special requests wherever possible, whether for dietary reasons or simply preference. Private parties and functions are also catered for. **Seats 45.** (Private room, 20). DTue-Sat, 7-10; Set D from €32; house wine €16.50. Closed Sun (except bank hol weekends), Mon; 7-21 Jan. **Accommodation:** Nine en-suite guest bedrooms are offered; they vary in size and outlook but all have phone TV, tea/coffee-making trays. Excellent breakfasts are served in the restaurant. B&B €50pps, ss €15. Closed 24-28 Dec. MasterCard, Visa. **Directions:** on the Dublin/Carlow road into Kilkenny.

Kilkenny
RESTAURANT

Lautrecs Brasserie

9 St. Kieran Street Kilkenny Co. Kilkenny **Tel: 056 62720**
Fax: 056 58799 Web: www.restaurantskilkenny.com

This cheerful, informal restaurant is just around the corner from the Tourist Information Office. First appearances are deceptive, as it seems to be very small on first entering, via doors that open out onto the pavement, with some tables semi-alfresco, which is an attractive feature on hot summer evenings. However, most of the restaurant is hidden from view and it is actually quite large. Menus match the informality of the decor, with quite a few pastas and pizzas as well as more substantial bistro fare, like steaks - typically with sun-dried tomato & anchovy butter - and fish dishes such as seared fillet of salmon with tapenade. This is a place to have fun; service can be slow at times, but prices are reasonable. **Seats 66.** D Sun-Thu 6-10, Fri & Sat 6-11. Set D €19, also à la carte; house wine €16.50. MasterCard, Visa. **Directions:** next to Dunnes Stores in city centre.

Kilkenny
PUB/RESTAURANT

Marble City Bar

66 High Street Kilkenny Co. Kilkenny **Tel: 056 61143**
Email: langtons@oceanfree.net

A recent change of ownership brought this historic bar into the well-known local Langton Group of publicans, which should have had predictable enough consequences. So the citizens of Kilkenny were in for quite a shock when the cutting edge international designer David Collins was brought in to cast his highly original eye over the premises with a view to a total re-vamp. The results are fascinating - and, of course, controversial (especially the ultra-modern stained glass window which now graces the otherwise traditional frontage), but it is a wonderful space to be in and attracts a varied clientèle, ranging from the merely curious to fans of all ages and many walks of life who are there to enjoy the vibrant atmosphere - and make the most of their excellent contemporary European bar food. Food service begins with breakfast, from 10am daily; main menus from 12 noon-8.30 pm. Not suitable for children under 5 after 8pm. Closed 25 Dec & Good Fri. Amex, Diners, MasterCard, Visa, Laser, Switch.

Kilkenny
HOTEL féile bia

Newpark Hotel

Castlecomer Road Kilkenny Co. Kilkenny
Tel: 056 22122 Fax: 056 61111

Very much at the heart of local activities, this 1960s hotel on the N77 recently completed a huge extension and renovation programme and the makeover - symbolised by an impressive circular foyer which is really striking from the road and even more so on entering - is a revelation. The whole job has been done with great flair and attention to detail but, when viewing the older bedrooms - which are too small for comfort by today's standards and, in many cases, have only a small shower room en-suite - it is clear that some challenges regarding the constrictions of the original building still remain to be met. However, the project to date is praiseworthy and the foyer and atrium features, conference and meeting rooms have been particularly imaginatively handled. The Scott Dove Bar & Bistro and banqueting suites have entrances from the hotel and carpark and there's an elegant formal restaurant in clean-lined contemporary style, Damask Restaurant, in a quiet position at the back of the hotel overlooking the gardens. Conference/banqueting (500/350). Children welcome. No pets. **Rooms 111.** (16 shower only, 10 no-smoking, 2 for disabled). Wheel chair access. Lift. B&B about €90, ss about €20. Open all year. Amex, Diners, MasterCard, Visa.

Kilkenny

Rinuccini Restaurant

RESTAURANT/B&B

No 1. The Parade Kilkenny Co. Kilkenny **Tel: 056 61575**
Fax: 056 51288 Email: info@rinuccini.com Web: www.rinuccini.com

Antonio and Marion Cavaliere's well-established Italian restaurant is in a semi-basement in the impressive terrace opposite Kilkenny Castle and the closely packed tables are an indication of its popularity. When empty it looks a little bleak, but the room quickly fills up with a healthy mixture of locals (who clearly have their preferred tables) and tourists. The cooking style is mainly classic Italian, with quite an extensive à la carte evening menu and a much shorter one at lunchtime. Service is prompt, from the time fresh bread and butter is delivered speedily with the menu. Food is characterised by freshness of ingredients and a high standard of cooking: excellent minestrone (a classic test), delicious seafood and memorable pasta. The simple things are right, which is always a good sign - but that doesn't necessarily preclude luxury: spaghettini with fresh lobster is one of the house specialities. **Seats 56.** L&D daily 12-2.30, D 6-10.30 (Sun 12-2 & 6-9.30); à la carte. House wine €17.71. **Accommodation:** The Cavalieres opened seven newly renovated rooms in July 2000: all are large and en-suite (all shower-only, 4 no-smoking) with air conditioning, TV, tea/coffee facilities and trouser press with iron. A DIY breakfast is supplied, for you to make up your own continental breakfast in the room. Room rate €45 (max 4 guests). Amex, Diners, MasterCard, Visa. **Directions:** opposite Kilkenny Castle.

Kilkenny

Zuni

HOTEL/RESTAURANT

26 Patrick St Kilkenny Co. Kilkenny **Tel: 056 23999**
Fax: 056 56400 Email: info@zuni.ie Web: www.zuni.ie

Another very centrally located new hotel, Zuni is a few doors up the street from the Hibernian and offers a lighter, brighter more youthful style of accommodation than other comparable establishments - some guests may find the minimalist approach rather stark, others will love it. Everything is pristine and there are phones (& ISDN lines) and TV, although no tea/coffee-making facilities. Breakfast is served in the restaurant (see below). Booking advised. Children welcome (under 3s free in parents' room; cot available, €20.) No pets. Lift. **Rooms 13** (1 suite, 8 shower only, 5 no smoking, 1 for disabled) B&B €70ps, no ss. Hotel closed 23-26 Dec. **Restaurant:** In a large airy room overlooking a courtyard at the back of the hotel and with a separate entrance on the side of the building, the restaurant is an oasis of contemporary chic in this bustling city. Head chef Maria Raftery, who joined the hotel in spring 2001, offers eclectic menus at lunch and dinner and cooks colourful, attractively presented food that is clearly popular with locals as well as visitors. Restaurant **Seats 60.** L Tues-Sat 12.30-2.30, D 6.30-10. A la carte & Set Sun L, £16.95. House wine £12.95. Restaurant closed Mon. Amex, MasterCard, Visa Laser Switch Directions: 200 yards from Kilkenny castle.

Maddoxtown

Blanchville House

COUNTRY HOUSE

Dunbell Maddoxtown Co. Kilkenny **Tel: 056 27197**
Fax: 056 27636 Email: info@blanchville.ie Web: www.blanchville.ie

Tim and Monica Phelan's elegant Georgian house is just 5 miles out of Kilkenny city, surrounded by its own farmland and gardens. It's easy to spot - there's a folly in its grounds. It's a very friendly, welcoming place and the house has an airy atmosphere, with matching well-proportioned dining and drawing rooms on either side of the hall and the pleasant, comfortably furnished bedrooms in period style all overlook attractive countryside. Dinner is available to residents (bookings required before noon) and, like the next morning's excellent breakfast, is taken at the communal mahogany dining table. No wine licence but guests are welcome to bring their own. Not suitable for children under 10. Well-behaved dogs are permitted by arrangement. The Coach House has been renovated to make three self-catering apartments. garden, tennis; snooker, pool table; playroom. **Rooms 6** (5 en-suite, 1 with private bathroom, 1 shower only, all non-smoking) B&B €55pps, ss €15. Closed 1 Nov-1 Mar. MasterCard, Visa, Laser. **Directions:** N10 from Kilkenny to Carlow/Dublin 2 miles; first right after Pike Pub, a mile to crossroads (Connolly's Pub), take left, go one mile.

Thomastown

Mount Juliet Estate

HOTEL
RESTAURANT

Thomastown Co. Kilkenny **Tel: 056 73000** Fax: 056 73019
Email: info@mountjuliet.ie Web: mountjuliet.com

Built over 200 years ago by the Earl of Carrick, and named in honour of his wife, Mount Juliet House is one of Ireland's finest Georgian houses. Lying amidst 1500 acres of unspoilt woodland, pasture and formal gardens beside the River Nore, it is one of Europe's greatest country estates, with world class sporting amenities and conference facilities. It retains an aura of eighteenth century grandeur. The original elegance has been painstakingly preserved, so that the hand-carved Adam fireplaces, walls and ceilings decorated with intricate stucco work and many other original features can still be enjoyed today. Bedrooms have period decor with all the comfort of modern facilities and, as well as the main house, additional rooms on the estate are in The Club, and the Rose Garden two-bedroom suites. The Jack Nicklaus-designed golf course on the estate went straight into the list of top-ranking courses when it opened in 1991; it hosted the Irish Open for three years consecutively (from 1993 to 1995). Conference/banqueting (200/140). Children welcome. No pets. **Rooms 59** (2 suites, 2 junior suites, 3 no smoking, 1 for disabled). Room rate from about €200. Open all year. **Lady Helen Dining Room** Although grand, this graceful high-ceilinged room, softly decorated in pastel shades and with sweeping views over the grounds, is not forbidding and has a pleasant atmosphere. To match these beautiful surroundings, classic daily dinner menus based on local ingredients are served, including wild salmon from the River Nore, vegetables and herbs from the Mount Juliet garden and regional Irish farmhouse cheese. Service is efficient and friendly. **Seats 60.** D only 7-9.30. Set D about €50. House wine about €21. It can be difficult to get a reservation at the Lady Helen Dining Room, especially for non-residents, so booking well ahead is advised, otherwise opt for one of the other dining choices on the estate. *Informal dining is available in The Club, Presidents Bar and also a newer contemporary restaurant, Kendals, open for breakfast & dinner daily. Amex, Diners, MasterCard, Visa. **Directions:** M7 from Dublin, then M9 towards Waterford, arriving at Thomastown on the N9 via Carlow and Gowran.

Thomastown

Silks

RESTAURANT

Marshes St. Thomastown Co. Kilkenny **Tel: 056 54400**
Fax: 056 58799 Web: www.restaurantskilkenny.com

This rather dashing contemporary restaurant in a converted schoolhouse on the edge of the town has brought Mediterranean cuisine to Thomastown with a vengeance and it's become the place to be seen. There are two rooms - the back one, which overlooks garden and pond, would be pleasant on a summer evening or for Sunday lunch. There is a bar, but it is more likely that you will be shown straight to have a drink and consider the menu at your table. There's a choice of menus but the style is fairly consistent: Mediterranean/global plus some local specialities, such as Lavistown cheese tartlet. Typical starters might include sesame crab toast with leaves of smoked salmon, a coriander relish and chilli jam and a typical main course is breast of duck with crushed peppercorns and honey, with cassis sauce. The set lunch offers good value. There's also an outdoor eating area in a walled garden, where there are tables set up with parasols. **Seats 70** (private room, 40). L 12-2 (Sun -3); Set L €17.75. D 6.30-9.30, Set D from €17.75 (most à la carte main courses cost more than the dinner menu). House wine about €16. Closed Mon & 1st two weeks Jan. Wheelchair access. Public car park adjacent. MasterCard, Visa. **Directions:** along Mount Juliet Road, Thomastown.

COUNTY LAOIS

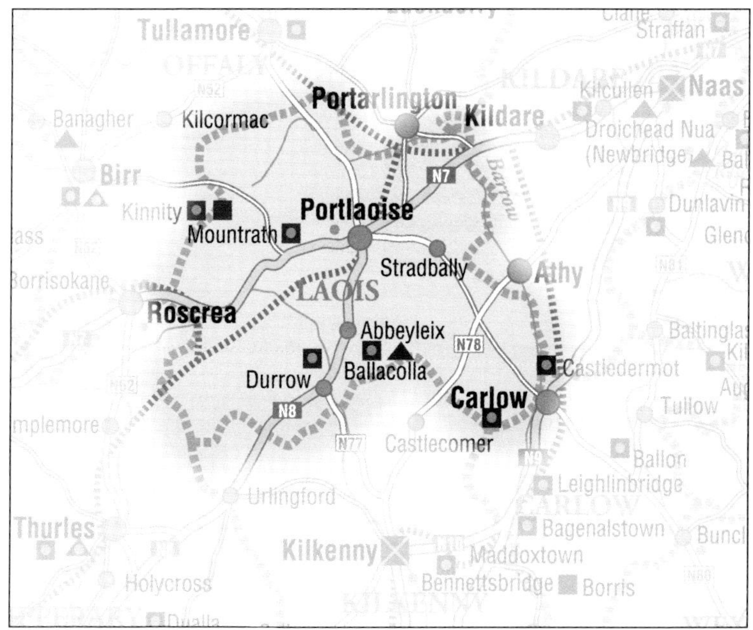

Laois, the quintessential midlands county, has a special position at the heart of Ireland's rural life. For in the midst of it is Ballacolla, the setting in early October for the National Ploughing Contest, a very special celebration of the conclusion of harvesting, and of Ireland's vibrant farm life. A well-kept little place, Ballacolla also features regularly in the Tidy Towns awards, though the most recent listings - in September 2001 - saw the award for the best-kept village in all Ireland going to Castletown in west Laois, a neat place above the upper reaches of the River Nore.

With its territory traversed by the rail and road links from Dublin to Cork and Limerick, Laois is often glimpsed only fleetingly by inter-city travellers. But as with any Irish county, it is a wonderfully rewarding place to visit as soon as you move off the main roads. And a salutary place to visit as well. For, in the eastern part, between Stradbally and Portlaois, there's the Rock of Dunamase, that fabulous natural fortress which many occupiers inevitably assumed to be impregnable. Dunamase's remarkably long history of fortifications and defences and sieges and eventual captures has a relevance and a resonance for all times and all peoples and all places.

But there's much more to Laois than mournful musings on the ultimate vanity of human ambitions. With its border shared with Carlow along the River Barrow, eastern Laois comfortably reflects Carlow's quiet beauty. To the northwest, we find that Offaly bids strongly to have the Slieve Bloom Mountains thought of as an Offaly hill range, but in fact there's more of the Slieve Blooms in Laois than Offaly, and lovely hills they are too. And though the River Nore may be thought of as quintessential Kilkenny, long before it gets anywhere near Kilkenny it is quietly building as it meanders across much of Laois, gathering strength from the weirdly-named Delour, Tonet, Gully, Erskina and Goul rivers on the way.

The Erskina and Goul rivers become one in Laois's own Curragh, a mysterious place of wide open spaces and marshy territory northwest of Durrow which, in marked contrast, was created as a planned estate township by the Duke of Ormond. To the northeast, there is planning afoot for Portlaois itself. With improving links to Dublin, Portlaois - which had a population of 9,500 in 1996 - expects to have 35,000 citizens and a much improved infrastructure by 2020.

Local Attractions and Information

Abbeyleix Abbeyleix Heritage House	0502 31653
Abbeyleix Sensory Gardens	0502 31325
Ballacolla National Ploughing Contest (October)	0507 25125
Ballinakill Heywood (Lutyens gardens)	0502 33563
Donaghmore Castletown House Open Farm	0505 46415
Emo Emo Court (Gandon house & gardens)	0502 26573
Portlaois Dunamaise Theatre & Arts Centre	0502 63356
Portlaois Tourist Information	0502 21178
Slieve Bloom Slieve Bloom Rural Development Assoc.	0509 37299
Stradbally National Steam Traction Rally (August)	0502 25444

Abbeyleix

Morrissey's

PUB

Main Street Abbeyleix Co. Laois **Tel: 0502 31281**

One of Ireland's finest and best-loved pubs, Morrissey's is a handsome building on the wide main street of this attractive little town. It's a great place to lift the spirits while taking a break between Dublin and Cork – food is not its strength but a quick cup of coffee and enjoyment of the atmosphere is sometimes all that's needed. Morrissey's has been in the same family since it first opened as a grocery in 1775, when it started life as a thatched one-storey house. In 1880 it was rebuilt as the lofty two-storey premises we see today, with high shelf-lined walls and a pot belly stove to gather round on cold days. The present owner, Patrick Mulhall, is rightly proud of this special place, which is unique in so many ways. They have a list of people who have served their time at Morrissey's since 1850 – and, true to the old tradition, television, cards and singing are not allowed. No children after 7 pm. Closed 25 Dec & Good Fri. **Directions:** in the village, on the right heading south.

Abbeyleix

Preston House

RESTAURANT/ACCOMMODATION

Main Street Abbeyleix Co. Laois
Tel: 0502 31432 Fax: 0502 31432

HAPPY HEART EAT OUT AWARD

A sign on the pavement outside Michael and Allison Dowling's attractive creeper-clad house welcomes people to their friendly and informal country-style restaurant. Allison's good home cooking starts off with delicious scones, served with tea or coffee and home-made preserves before lunch, at which time the choice widens to a short but tempting à la carte – typically including starters like smoked haddock chowder with freshly-baked brown bread or grilled goat's cheese and side salad followed, perhaps, by fish of the day or a speciality such as stirfry beef with roast vegetables. Vegetarians do very well here too, so if you're in a meat-free mood you can look forward to colourful, zesty dishes such as ratatouille or spinach crèpe with salad. Delicious desserts include sophisticated classics like crème brûlée but there are always simple, wholesome options too, like apple crumble. Dinner menus are also à la carte and, although more formal and offering a wider choice, the same philosophy applies: this is deliciously healthy, well-balanced food with the emphasis on freshness and making best use of local produce - and thanks to the long opening hours and reasonable prices, it is exceptionally accessible. A first-floor ballroom runs across the whole width of the building and, with a library area up a few stairs at one end providing comfortable seating for non-participants and a minstrels' gallery at the other, it makes a superb venue for local events. Not suitable for children after 6 pm. **Seats 50.** No smoking restaurant. 10am-9pm: L Tue-Sun,12.30-3 (Sun from 1); D Thu-Sat 6-9. A la carte available. House wine €13.97; sc discretionary (10% on parties of 6+). Closed D Sun-Wed, all Mon, 10 days Christmas. **Accommodation** The four large, high-ceilinged bedrooms are interestingly furnished with antiques and unusual en-suite facilities have been cleverly incorporated without spoiling the proportions of these fine rooms – by hiding them in what appears to be a long wardrobe but which opens up to reveal a row of individual facilities – shower, WC etc. Children welcome (under 4 free in parents' room). Pets permitted. **Rooms 4** (all shower only & no-smoking). B&B €44.44, ss €6.35. MasterCard, Visa. **Directions:** in the village, a few doors down from Morrisey's.

Ballacolla

Foxrock Inn

PUB/B&B

Clough Ballacolla Co. Laois **Tel: 0502 38637**
Fax: 0502 38637 Email: foxrockinn@eircom.net Web: www.foxrockinn.com

Sean and Marian Hyland run a very friendly, relaxed little place here for lovers of the country life. Hill walking, fishing (coarse and game), golf and pitch & putt are all in the neighbourhood (golf and fishing packages are a speciality) and they'll make packed lunches to see you through the day. Evening meals, an open fire and traditional music (Tuesdays, May-September) make the pub a welcoming place to come back to and there is accommodation just up the stairs, in six modest but comfortable rooms (5 en-suite, all no smoking). Two new en-suite family rooms will be available for the 2002 season. B&B €32 pps, ss €6.70. Closed 25 Dec & Good Fri. Visa. **Directions:** follow signs from Abbeyleix to Borris-in-Ossory (N7).

Mountrath

Roundwood House

COUNTRY HOUSE

Mountrath Co. Laois **Tel: 0502 32120**
Fax: 0502 32711 Email: roundwood@eircom.net
Web: hidden-ireland.com/roundwood

Just a couple of miles off the main Dublin-Limerick road, Frank and Rosemarie Kennan's unspoilt early Georgian house lies secluded in mature woods of lime, beech and chestnut. A sense of history and an appreciation of genuine hospitality are all that is needed to make the most of a stay here – forget about co-ordinated decor and immaculate maintenance, just relax and share the immense pleasure and satisfaction that Frank and Rosemarie derive from the years of renovation work they have put into this wonderful property. Although unconventional in some ways, the house is extremely comfortable and well-heated (with central heating as well as log fires) and all the bathrooms have been recently renovated (all have full bath). The Kennans also have several beautifully converted rooms at the back and further outbuildings, Coach House and Forge Cottage, available for self-catering. An extraordinary (and historically unique) barn is the next stage; this enterprise defies description, but don't leave Roundwood without seeing it. Children, who always love the unusual animals and their young in the back yard, are very welcome and Rosemarie does a separate tea for them. Residents dinner (8 pm) is based on the best local and seasonal ingredients (notably locally reared beef and lamb); Rosemarie's food suits the house perfectly – good interesting cooking without unnecessary frills – and Frank is an excellent host. Children welcome (under 3s free in parents' room, cot available without charge; playroom). Garden, walking. Pets allowed in some areas. **Rooms 10** (all en-suite & 4 no-smoking). B&B £47 pps, ss €20. No sc. Dinner for residents €27.55 – please book by noon. Closed 25 Dec & Jan. Amex, Diners, MasterCard, Visa, Laser. **Directions:** on the left, 3 miles from Mountrath, on R440.

Portlaoise

Ivyleigh House

GUESTHOUSE

Bank Place Portlaoise Co. Louth **Tel: 0502 22081**
Fax: 0502 63343 Email: info@ivyleigh.com Web: www.ivyleigh.com

IRISH BREAKFAST AWARD - LEINSTER

A reader's letter led us to this lovely early Georgian house, which is set back from the road only by a tiny neatly box-hedged formal garden, but has a coachyard (with parking), outhouses and a substantial lawned garden at the back. It is a listed building and has clearly fallen into good hands as the present owners, Dinah and Jerry Campion, have restored it immaculately and furnished it beautifully in a style that successfully blends period elements with bold contemporary strokes, which gives it great life. Two lovely sitting rooms (one with television) are always available to guests and there's a fine dining room with a large communal table and a smaller one at the window. Bedrooms are the essence of comfort, spacious, elegant, with working sash windows and everything absolutely top of the range including pocket-sprung mattresses and even real linen sheets and pillowcases. Large shower rooms have many excellent details and terrific power showers (and, unusually, the space to make the most of them) although those who would give anything for a bath to soak in will be disappointed. But it is perhaps at breakfast that this superb guesthouse is at its best. An extensive menu shows a commitment to using quality local produce that turns out to be even better than anticipated: imaginative, perfectly cooked and beautifully presented. Fruits and yogurts include natural yogurt with geranium jelly and (on a late summer visit) poached plums; 'pefect porridge' comes with cream - or you can have cereals, including home-made muesli - and hot dishes include wondefully creamy baked free range eggs with cream & cheese, and Cashel Blue cheesecakes - light and delicious, like fritters - come with mushrooms and tomatoes. There is also, of course, the option of a Full Irish Breakfast and - very unusually - there's a vegetarian variation on the great traditional fry. The details that count - freshly-baked brown bread, leaf tea or freshly brewed coffee, smooth, friendly service and meticulous timing of hot dishes - all add up to an exceptional experience. And through it all Dinah Campion (who must rise at dawn to bake the bread) is charming, efficient and hospitable. This is one of the best guest houses in Ireland and is well placed for touring the midlands, to break a journey, or for a short break from Dublin. No evening meals, but the Campions direct guests to good restaurants nearby. Not suitable for children under 8. **Rooms 6** (all shower only & no smoking); phone, tea/coffee facilities; television on request. B&B€52.50, ss €17.50. Closed 22 Dec-4 Jan. MasterCard, Visa. **Directions:** Centre of town follow signs for multi storey car park, 30 metres from carpark.

Portlaoise

Kingfisher

RESTAURANT Old AIB Bank Portlaoise Co. Laois **Tel: 0502 62500** Fax: 0502 62700

Situated in the centre of Portlaoise in the old AIB bank, this highly regarded Indian restaurant specialises in Punjabi cuisine and has the great advantage of being open every night. You enter into a very large, high-ceilinged room (the former banking hall), with a reception area off it where you are greeted by immaculately attired and genuinely friendly staff. The decor is unusual, using pale washes to portay the crumbling sandstone walls of an ancient Indian temple, including disintegrating murals with some entertainingly mischievous details. The relaxed ambience and people of all ages enjoying themselves makes for a very atmospheric room. Simple table presentation and enormously long menus may send out warning signals, but there are poppadums with dipping sauces to see you through the decision-making phases and, once food appears, it is clearly accomplished cooking, without recourse to elaborate presentation but well-flavoured with the fresh flavours of individal ingredients and authentic spicing creating satisfying combinations, in dishes that vary from creamy styles with almonds, to very spicy dishes with 'angry' green peppers. Tandoori, balti, biryani, 'exquisite' dishes and 'old favourite' dishes like korma, rogan josh, do piaza are all there, but they are well executed, served with professionalism and charm, and very reasonably priced (average main course well under €10). **Seats about 75.** L Wed-Fr, 12-2, D daily, 5.30-11 (early D Mon-Fri 5.30-7). Amex, MasterCard, Visa. Laser. **Directions:** town centre.

Portlaoise

The Kitchen & Foodhall

RESTAURANT Hynds Square Portlaoise Co. Laois **Tel: 0502 62061** Fax: 0502 62075

Jim Tynan's smashing restaurant and food shop is definitely worth a little detour. Delicious home-made food, an open fire, relaxed atmosphere - a perfect place to break a journey or for a special visit. Lovely home-bakes, ready meals, speciality foods and wines in the shop. **Seats 200** (daytime)/50 (evening). Open all day, 9-5.15, Mon-Sat; L from 12.30. D Thur-Sat, 7-9.30. Set L from about €7. D à la carte. House wine €13.90. Wheelchair access. Closed 24 Dec-3 Jan. MasterCard, Visa. **Directions:** in the centre of Portlaoise, beside the Courthouse.

COUNTY LEITRIM

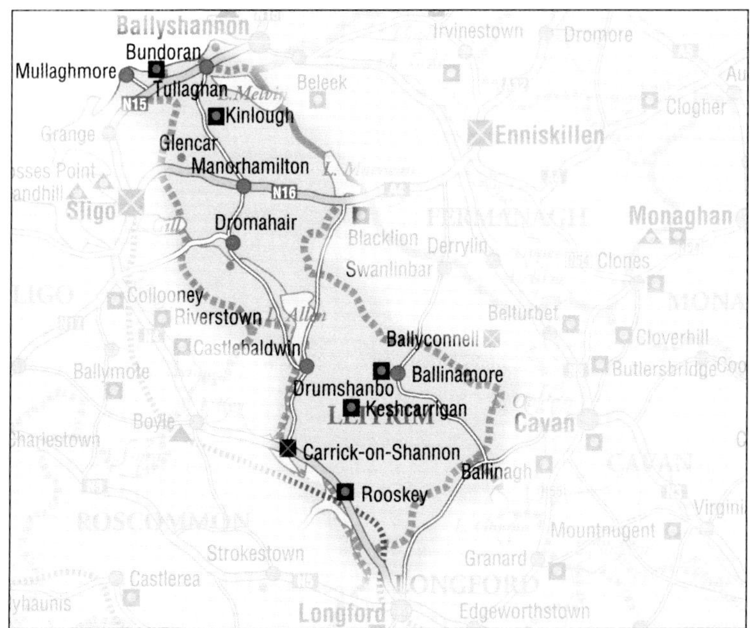

Leitrim is increasingly seen as a pleasantly away-from-it-all sort of place which has many attractions for the determined connoisseur. So with some of Ireland's better known holiday areas suffering if anything from an excess of popularity, the true trail-blazers may well find the remoteness they seek in Leitrim.

And in this age of detailed statistical analysis, it's intriguing to find that, of all Ireland's counties, it is Leitrim which has to try hardest. That's official. Because, according to government data, it is Leitrim which has the doubtful distinction of having the poorest soil in the entire country. It's a covering of such low fertility, so we're told, that it is barely capable in some places of growing even the scrubbiest trees.

Yet the very fact that Leitrim is thus categorised in the official statistics shows that such general overviews can easily become excessively blunt instruments of analysis. For there is at least one pocket of fertility in in the north of the county that has been so intensively nurtured that one of Ireland's leading organic horticulture firms is able to grow superb produce here - and its associated enterprise, The Organic Centre at Rossinver, is a "must visit" destination for any food lover visiting the area. And as for Leitrim lacking in glamorous tourist attractions other than the obvious one of the magnificent inland waterways, well, even that is largely a matter of perception.

For Leitrim shares the shores of Lough Gill with Sligo, so much so that Yeat's Lake Isle of Innisfree is within an ace of being in Leitrim rather than Sligo of Yeatsian fame. To the northward, we find that more than half of lovely Glencar, popularly perceived as being one of Sligo's finest jewels, is in fact in Leitrim. As for the notion of Leitrim being the ultimate inland and rural county - not so. Leitrim has an Atlantic coastline, albeit of only four kilometres, around Tullaghan.

It's said this administrative quirk is a throwback to the time when the all-powerful bishops of the early church aspired to have ways of travelling to Rome without having to cross the territory of neighbouring clerics. Whatever the reason, it's one of Leitrim's many surprises, which are such that it often happens that when you're touring in the area and find yourself in a beautiful bit of country, a reference to the map produces the unexpected information that you're in Leitrim. So forget about those gloomy soil facts - this is a county of hidden quality which deserves to be better known, not least in that the river ports of Dromod and Carrick-on-Shannon rated highly in the most recent Tidy Town Awards.

And for anyone who seeks the essential Ireland, it's worth noting that the ancient Irish system of bar licences results in Leitrim having more pubs per head of population than any other county -148 souls per licence, which barely stands comparison with the Dublin figure of 1,119. This means the Leitrim pubs, like the county itself, have to try harder with all sorts of quaint ancillary trades in order to stay in business, and they're all the better for that.

Local Attractions and Information

Ballinamore Shannon-Erne Waterway	078 44855
Ballinamore Slieve an Arain Riverbus Cruises	078 44079
Carrick-on-Shannon Moonriver Cruises	078-21777
Carrick-on-Shannon Tourism Information	078 20170
Dromahair Parke's Castle (restored 17c fortified hse)	071 64149
Drumshanbo Sliabh an Iarainn Visitor Centre	078 41522
Manorhamilton Glens Arts Centre	072 55833
Mohill Lough Rynn House and Gardens	078 31427
Rossinver Eden Plants & The Organic Centre	072 54122

Ballinamore

Glenview House

GUESTHOUSE/RESTAURANT

Aghoo Ballinamore Co. Leitrim **Tel: 078 44157**
Fax: 078 44814 Email: glenvhse@iol.ie

Teresa Kennedy's farm guesthouse beside the Shannon-Erne Waterway is a great place for a family holiday as there's lots to do in the area, and there's a tennis court and outdoor play area as well as an indoor games room with a pool table and table tennis. She also runs a restaurant that attracts a balanced mixture of locals and holidaymakers; guests for dinner gather in the bar - a long room with a fire and many chairs indicating the numbers she sometimes expects; here menus and drinks are dispatched in rapid succession before diners are brought to formally-laid tables in the large dining room. A piano in the corner suggests that parties can get going in here, but the immediate business is more serious: your 5-course dinner might start with crab claws in garlic buttter or a mixed leaf salad, then a soup or sorbet before a hearty main course - sirloin steak, perhaps, breast of chicken or even ostrich. Finish with fairly traditional desserts and coffee before heading back to the bar or upstairs to bed. Children welcome (under 2s free in parents' room, cot available without charge; baby sitting available). No pets. **Rooms 6** (all en-suite & no smoking) B&B €38.09 pps, ss €6.35. **Restaurant: Seats 50** (private room 25). Non-smoking restaurant. D daily, 6-8.30 pm. Set D from €19.05 (Gourmet Menu €29.20). House wine €15.24. Reservations advised. MasterCard, Visa.

Carrick-on-Shannon

Bush Hotel

HOTEL

Carrick-on-Shannon Co. Leitrim **Tel: 078 20014**
Fax: 078 21180 Email: info@bushhotel.com Web: www.bushhotel.com

One of Ireland's oldest hotels, the Bush has undergone considerable refurbishment in recent years and, while rooms will vary in size and comfort, all are en-suite (most with full bath) and have TV, tea/coffee making facilities, trouser press and phones - and this is an hotel that makes up in personality anything it may lack in contemporary style and finish. Public areas, including a very pleasant restaurant (open for lunch and dinner as well as serving a good breakfast) and two bars, have character and a pleasing sense of history. Staff are exceptionally pleasant and helpful and there's direct access to the carpark at the back of the hotel off the N4 bypass. Informal meals are available all day at the self-service coffee shop/carvery (8am-6pm) and there's bar food too (6-9.30). Conference/banqueting (400); secretarial services available. Children welcome; pets allowed in some areas. The hotel has a gift shop, tourist information point and bureau de change and can arrange car , bicycle and boat hire and supply fishing tackle and golf clubs. Golf nearby. Tennis; garden. **Rooms 28** (1 suite, 20 superior rooms, 8 shower only). B&B €57pps, ss €6. Closed 24-31 Dec. Amex, MasterCard, Visa, Laser. **Directions:** town centre.

Carrick-on-Shannon

Hollywell Country House

COUNTRY HOUSE

Liberty Hill Cortober Carrick-on-Shannon Co. Leitrim
Tel: 078 21124 Fax: 078 21124 Email: hollywell@esatbiz.com

After many years as hoteliers in the town (and a family tradition of inn-keeping that goes back 200 years), Tom and Rosaleen Maher moved some years ago to this delightful period house on a rise over the bridge, with beautiful views over the Shannon and its own river frontage. It's a lovely, graciously proportioned house, with a relaxed family atmosphere. Tom and Rosaleen have an easy hospitality (not surprisingly, perhaps, as their name derives from the Gaelic "Meachar" meaning hospitable), making guests feel at home very quickly and this, as much as the comfort of the house and its tranquil surroundings, is what makes Hollywell special. Bedrooms are all individually furnished in period style and it's worth getting up in good time for delicious breakfasts, with freshly-baked bread and home-made preserves. No evening meals, but Tom and Rosaleen advise guests on the best local choices and there's a comfortable guests' sitting room with an open fire to gather around on your return. Garden. Fishing (coarse). Not suitable for children under 12. No pets. **Rooms 4** (all en-suite). B&B from €38.50pps, ss from €6.13. Closed 10 days Christmas-New Year. Amex, MasterCard, Visa. **Directions:** from Dublin, cross bridge on N4, keep left at Gings pub. Hollywell entrance is on left up the hill.

Carrick-on-Shannon

The Landmark Hotel

HOTEL Dublin Road Carrick-on-Shannon Co. Leitrim **Tel: 078 22222**
Fax: 078 22233 Email: landmarkhotel@eircom.net Web: thelandmarkhotel.com

This very large almost-riverside hotel is aptly named and brings much-needed business and leisure facilities to the area. Public areas are impressive - notably a dramatic lobby with a large marble and granite fountain feature and imposing cast iron staircase. Bedrooms, many of which have views over the Shannon, are spacious and comfortable, with individual temperature control as well as the more usual amenities (direct dial phone, TV, tea/coffee facilities, trouser press) and well-finished bathrooms. There are two restaurants, Ferrari's (open every night) and La Gondola, where a real effort is made to provide an experience more personal than expected in an hotel dining room, but opening hours are restricted to Friday & Saturday night and Sunday lunch. La Gondola is elegantly appointed and head chef Dave Fitzgibbon (previously at the SAS Radisson in Co Londonderry and with the Rankins in Belfast) sources local organic and seasonal produce for continental style cooking which favours Italy; Ferrari's is less formal, with a contemporary menu. Excellent leisure facilities include a 20m swimming pool with separate children's pool, jacuzzi, sauna, steamroom, gym and health & beauty salon. Conference/banqueting (400/350); secretarial services; business centre; video conferencing available. Leisure centre. Golf nearby (9). Off-season breaks. Children welcome (under 4s free in parents' room; cots available without charge). No pets. **Rooms 60** (4 suites, 4 for disabled). Lift. B&B €122 pps. La Gondola: Fri & Sat D 7-10, L Sun; à la carte. Ferrari's D daily, 6-10. House wine €12.06. SC discretionary. Hotel closed Christmas. Amex, Diners, MasterCard, Visa. **Directions:** on N4, 2 hours from Dublin.

Carrick-on-Shannon

The Pyramids

RESTAURANT Carrick-on-Shannon Co. Leitrim **Tel: 078 20333**

Unlikely as it may be in a town like Carrick-on-Shannon, proprietor-chef Milad Serhan runs a successful Lebanese restaurant here and the menu offers plenty of authentic dishes, bringing a genuine middle Eastern flavour to the western edge of Europe. **Seats 35.** L Wed-Mon, 12-2.30 D Sun, Mon & Wed 5.30-11.30, Thurs-Sat 5.30-12. Closed Tue. MasterCard, Visa, Laser. **Directions:** town centre.

Cootehall

Cootehall Bridge Restaurant & Coffee House

RESTAURANT/CAFÉ Cootehall Co. Leitrim **Tel: 079 67173**

Cootehall is one of those places which can't decide which county it is in but, whether it is in Roscomon or Leitrim, Manfred Kan's seasonal restaurant provides a very complete service once it gets going. A substantial à la carte dinner menu is offered, (typically including French onion soup, steaks, Wiener Schnitzel and a separate vegetarian menu) and Manfred's good cooking and great value for money send many a customer happy into the night. There's also a children's menu, varied desserts and waffles and a range of novelty ice cream dishes. Open Tuesday-Sunday from 12.30-10 pm.(Lunch to 3.30, then teas, ices etc; Dinner 6-10pm). Dinner reservations recommended. MasterCard, Visa. **Directions:** right of the bridge as you approach the village.

Cootehall

M J Henry's

PUB Cootehall Co. Leitrim **Tel: 079 67030**

The more theme pubs and superpubs there are, the better everyone likes James Henry's bar, which hasn't changed in at least 30 years. A visit to Cootehall would be unthinkable without checking on this little gem They don't make them like this any more, alas, but this delightful old pub - complete with formica from the most recent renovation - is a gem. Get in beside the fire with a hot whiskey and the world will do you no harm. Closed 25 Dec & Good Fri. **Directions:** 2 miles off Sligo-Dublin road.

Keshcarrigan — Canal View House & Restaurant

ACCOMMODATION/RESTAURANT

Keshcarrigan Co. Leitrim **Tel: 078 42056**
Fax: 078 42261 Email: canalviewcountryhome@eircom.net

A fireside cup of tea and home-baked scones or biscuits in the comfortable residents' lounge (with views of the cruisers passing) welcomes guests on arrival at Jeanette Conefry's immaculate guesthouse and restaurant overlooking the Shannon-Erne Waterway. Bedrooms – some with water views, all with a pleasant outlook – are individually furnished to a high standard, with direct-dial telephones and neat en-suite shower rooms. Peace and quiet are an attraction here, but television is available in bedrooms on request. Families are welcome and well looked after. Pets permitted by arrangement. **Rooms 6.** B&B about €32 pps, ss about €6.50. Closed Christmas week. **Restaurant:** At this well-established restaurant overlooking the Shannon-Erne Waterway, chef Michael Flaherty offers traditional cooking in the classical style: typical menus could include deep-fried mushrooms with a light garlic sauce, steaks various ways, roast half duckling with orange & Cointreau sauce and salmon bonne femme. Vegetarian dishes are available on request. There are private mooring facilities so that restaurant guests on boats can stay there overnight. **Seats 40.** (private room, 12).D Mon-Sat, 6-9, Sun 6.30-8; L Sun only 1-3; Set D about €29. House wine about €12.50; sc discretionary. Wheelchair accessible. Open all year. Amex, MasterCard, Visa. **Directions:** R209 from Carrick-on-Shannon to Keshcarrigan village; 4th house on right after village.

Kilclare — The Sheermore/Lynch's Bar

PUB

Kilclare Co. Leitrim **Tel: 078 41029**

Known from the road as "The Sheermore", this friendly bar, grocery and hardware shop presents its much more attractive side to the water and you can sit outside at the back in fine weather, or choose between a conservatory overlooking the bridge or a move right into the bar if the weather dictates. Food isn't elaborate here, but Mrs Lynch makes home-made soup every day and cuts sandwiches freshly to order - just the right thing, in the right place. Children welcome. Pets allowed in certain areas. Bar Food served daily, 12-9 (Sun 12-2 & 5-9). Closed 25 Dec, Good Fri. MasterCard, Visa, Laser. **Directions:** On Carrick-on-Shannon to Ballinamore road.

Kinlough — Courthouse Restaurant

RESTAURANT/B&B

Main Street Kinlough Co. Leitrim
Tel: 072 42391 Fax: 072 42824 Email: thecourthouserest@eircom.net

In the old courthouse of the attractive village of Kinlough, Piero and Sandra Melis's stylish little restaurant is a particularly welcoming place and offers good contemporary cooking in the Mediterranean style with some more down to earth local influences, especially at lunchtime. A wide ranging menu includes specialities like turbot with squid ink risotto and free range duck with spinach and wild mushrooms and there are always daily specials. Other typical dishes include starters like Caprese salad (buffalo mozzerella with sliced tomato, fresh basil & home-made pesto), main course salmon alla marinara (grilled salmon steak with spinach pancake & spicy tomato sauce), seafood risotto and pasta dishes such as the tasty vegetarian penne four cheeses (tube pasta cooked in a creamy gorgonzola, cheddar, parmesan and smoked cheese sauce, served with a side salad. Traditional desserts include an irresistible panna cotta with home-made chocolate sauce and boozy fruits! Everything is freshly made on the premises - and good food, good value and the helpful attitude of the staff all encourage return visits. Not suitable for children after 8 pm. * A sister restaurant "Tamarindo Blu" recently opened at Astoria Wharf, on the seafront in Bundoran. Operated by chef/partner Bruno Boe, it specialises in home-made pizzas and pasta specialities. **Seats 30** (private room 10). D Wed-Mon, 6.30-10, L Sun only 12.30-2.30. D à la carte; Set Sun L €17.78. House wine €15.24; sc discretionary. No-smoking area. Closed Tue & Nov-Feb. Accommodation: Neat, freshly decorated bedrooms offer comfortable accommodation at a very reasonable price. **Rooms 4** (all shower only). B&B €32 pps, ss €6.35. MasterCard, Visa, Laser. **Directions:** off main Donegal-Sligo road (N15), 5 km towards Sligo from Bundoran. Take turning directly opposite Tullaghan House.

Leitrim — The Barge Steakhouse

RESTAURANT\PUB

Leitrim Village Carrick-on-Shannon Co. Leitrim **Tel: 078 20807**

This attractive stone building on the main street has been extensively renovated and gradually developed under the current ownership of John and Rose Pierce, so that it now offers a restaurant as well as the characterful bar which was open last season. A conservatory is under construction at the time of going to press and will provide more space for the 2002 season. Rose Pierce provides a daytime bar menu as well as an à la carte for the restaurant. Cooking is reliable and menus are quite traditional; typical starters include deepfried mushrooms, prawn cocktail and egg mayonnaise and, as the name implies, steaks are the speciality of the house - however, good as they may be, there is plenty else to choose from, including crispy duck and several pasta dishes. There's a little children's menu too, and a short list of popular wines. Open 12.30-10 daily, L 12.30-6, D 6-9. **Seats 21.** Non smoking restaurant. Closed 25 Dec & Good Fri. Amex, Diners, MasterCard, Visa, Laser. **Directions:** Drumshambo road out of Carrick-on-Shannon.

Tullaghan

COUNTRY HOUSE/B&B

Tullaghan House

Tullaghan Co. Leitrim **Tel: 072 41515/ 42055**
Fax: 072 41515 Email: emmccanney@hotmail.com

This delightfully unspoilt Georgian residence is set back from the road in its own garden (entrance usually from a slip road at the back although, on a recent visit, this was blocked by construction work). It's run by the (equally delightful) McCanney sisters: Elizabeth, Cathleen, Suzanne and Rosa, who took over the house in the spring of 1998 and are gradually making improvements, in a gentle way so as not to lose the charming family home atmosphere that is one of its main attributes. The bedrooms are all individually furnished, with very different characters, and public rooms are spacious and comfortable, with old family furniture. No evening meals but the Courthouse Restaurant at Kinlough (see entry) is nearby. Children welcome (under 6s free in parents' room). Pets permitted in some areas. **Rooms 6** (all en-suite). B&B about €32.35, ss about €13. Closed 23 Dec-5 Jan. MasterCard, Visa. **Directions:** on main Dublin-Sligo road (N15), 1 mile towards Sligo from Bundoran, on right hand side.

COUNTY LIMERICK

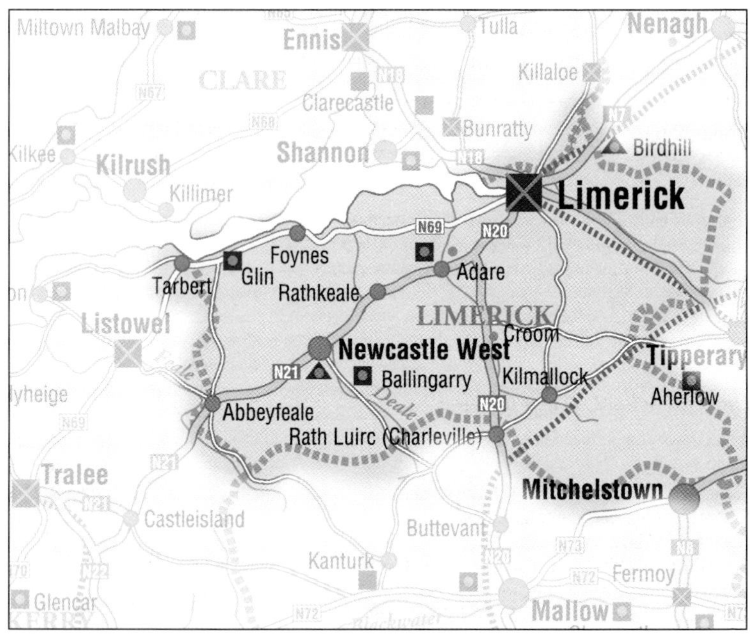

The story of Limerick city and county is in many ways the story of the Shannon Estuary, for in times past it was the total access and ready availability of the transport provided by Ireland's largest estuary - it is 60 miles long - which dictated the development of life along its southern shore and into the River Shannon. Today, the area's focal point for national and global transport is of course Shannon International Airport, which is actually located in south County Clare, but is very much a part of the shores of the Shannon Estuary, the region's dominant geographical feature.

The summer of 2001 saw the opening of improved waterway links through the heart of Limerick itself, the welcome regeneration of the old city continuing in tandem with it. But significant and all as this is, there's more to Limerick county than waterways. As we move inland from the river, the very richness of the countryside soon begins to develop its own dynamic. After all, eastern Limerick is verging into Tipperary's Golden Vale, and the eastern county's Slieve Felim hills, rising to Cullaun at 462 m, reflect the nearby style of Tipperary's Silvermine Mountains.

Southwest of Limerick city, the splendid hunting country and utterly rural atmosphere of the area around the beautiful village of Adare - Limerick's top award winner in the most recent tidy towns contest - makes it a real effort of imagination to visualise the muddy salt waters of the Shannon Estuary just a few miles away down the meandering River Maigue, yet the Estuary is there nevertheless. Equally, although the former flying boat port of Foynes and the nearby jetty at Aughinish may be expanding to accommodate the most modern large ships, just a few miles inland we find ourselves in areas totally remote from the sea in countryside which lent itself so well to mixed farming that the price of pigs in Dromcolliher (a.k.a. Drumcolligher) on the edge of the Mullaghareirk Mountains reputedly used to set the price of pigs throughout Ireland.

This rural emphasis south of the Estuary received a boost on October 14th 2001, when horse racing was re-started at the completely re-built Limerick Racecourse at Greenmount Park at Patrickswell, between Adare and Limerick City, "right in the heart of National Hunt country...." The first new Grade One track in Ireland for 50 years, it is part of a modern complex which is "a racecourse for 15 days of the year, and a multi-purpose event and exhibition centre for 350 days of the year".

Limerick city may have come to international attention in the late 1990s through the popular success of Frank McCourt's moving book Angela's Ashes, but by the time it appeared the picture it conveyed was long since out of date. Nobody would deny that Limerick can be a gritty place with its own spin on the human condition, but in recent years the growth of the computer industry in concert with the rapid expansion of the remarkably vibrant University has given Limerick a completely new place in Irish life, and the city's energy and urban renewal makes it an entertaining place to visit, while the eclectic collection on stunning display in the unique Hunt Museum in its handsome waterside setting has a style which other areas of Limerick life are keen to match.

With newfound confidence, Limerick has been paying greater attention to its remarkable heritage of Georgian architecture, and October 6th 2001 saw the official opening by Limerick Civic Trust of the restored Georgian house and garden at 2 Pery Square. It will act as the focal point for an area of classic urban architecture which deserves to be better known.

That said, Limerick still keeps its feet firmly on the ground, and connoisseurs are firmly of the opinion that the best pint of Guinness in all Ireland is to be had in this no-nonsense city, where they insist on being able to choose the temperature of their drink, and refuse to have any truck with modern fads which would attempt to chill the rich multi-flavoured black pint into a state of near-freezing tastelessness aimed at immature palates.

Local Attractions and Information

Adare Heritage Centre	061 396666
Adare May Fair	061 396894
Bruree Heritage Centre and de Valera Museum	063 91300
Croom Waterwheel and Heritage Centre	061 397130
Foynes Flying Boat Museum	069 65416
Glin Glin Castle Pleasure Grounds & Walled Garden	068 34364
Limerick Belltable Arts Centre, 69 O'Connell St	061 319866
Limerick Georgian House & Garden, 2 Pery Square	061 314130
Limerick Hunt Museum, Customs House, Rutland St	061 312833
Limerick King John's Castle	061 360788
Limerick Limerick City Art Gallery, Pery Square	061 310633
Limerick Limerick Museum, John's Square	061 417826
Limerick Tourism Information	061 317522
Limerick University of Limerick	061 333644
Lough Gur Interpretive centre, 3000BC to present	061 360788
Patrickswell Limerick Racecourse (Greenmount Park)	061 355055

Limerick
PUB/RESTAURANT

Aubars Bar & Restaurant

49-50 Thomas Street Limerick Co. Limerick
Tel: 061 317799 Fax: 061 317572

Padraic Frawley's new look city centre bar and restaurant typifies the renewal of Limerick itself - a university city with a youthful population and city, it is said, with more cafés, pubs and restaurants than any other in Ireland. Padraic, a hotel management graduate who trained at the highly respected catering college nearby in Shannon, returned to his home city at the grand old age of 27 bursting with ideas collected during experience abroad and proceeded to transform an old pub into a dashing new bar and restaurant (and nightclub) that has achieved national recognition. The layout is on several levels with no hard divisions and a mixture of seating in various areas, which can lead to confusion between customers coming in to eat rather than have a drink, although watchful staff soon have new arrivals sorted. While the style is uncompromisingly modern, down to the designer crockery, the solid traditional values of good training and supervsion prevail - and the emphasis is on providing consistently excellent contemporary cooking, professional service and value for money. Well-balanced menus (inspired by the Gary Rhodes' style: 'dishes that are simple to make, tasty and look great') change monthly - and offer clean-lined modern cooking in a range of hot dishes, several salds, low-fat options: seafood crêpes, Caesar salad with char-grilled chicken (presented in a filo basket), roast fillet of salmon on potato & celeriac purée and home-made pork & herb sausages with champ & onion gravy are all typical - and nice old-fashioned desserts that even include apple pie made by Padraic's octogenarian grandmother. A short well-selected wine list includes weekly specials by the glass. Food available 8 am-9pm daily. Amex, Diners, MasterCard, Visa, Laser.

Limerick

Brulées Restaurant

RESTAURANT

Corner of Henry St & Mallow Street Limerick Co. Limerick
Tel: 061 319 931

Just a stroll across from Jurys Limerick Inn, Donal Cooper and Teresa Murphy's well-appointed corner restaurant has achieved recognition as the leading fine dining restaurant in Limerick and is a first choice destination for discerning diners visiting the city. Dining areas on serveral levels break groups up nicely and are elegantly furnished in a simple classic style that makes the most of limited space. A soothing ambience and welcoming details - olives and freshly baked breads to nibble -get guests off to a good start while reading Teresa's appealing menus. She takes pride in using the finest of ingredients, both local and imported, in imaginative, colourful modern Irish cooking, which is as good as it sounds - mixed green salad leaves with bacon, crunchy potato curls & basil oil make a tasty starter, or a vegetarian dish like baked filo parcels of oriental style shredded vegetables on peanut tofu and black bean sauce can be a tempting option. Main courses also offer a balanced combination of international influences and dishes with their hearts closer to home such as Irish beef fillet serves on black pudding mash, with field mushrooms and a bacon & mustard cream. Seafood specialities include a lovely dish of mussels, clams and crab claws, steamed with julienne vegetables, garlic cream and saffron and there is always a daily special. Cooking is accurate, presentation attractive without being fussy and, with main courses averaging around €20, this is good value for the quality. Simple, attractively prepared and carefully cooked side vegetables are another plus point - and gorgeous puddings include (what else) a classic crème brûlée, served with crunchy shortbread and warm berry compôte. **Seats 30.** No smoking area. L Tue-Fri, 12.30-2.30; D Tue-Sat, 6.30-9.30. A La carte. House wine €15.87; sc discretionary. Closed Sun, Mon; 24-25 Dec. Amex, Diners, MasterCard, Visa, Laser. **Directions:** On the corner of Henry St.and Lower Mallow Street, near Jury's Inn roundabout.

Limerick

Castleroy Park Hotel & Conference Centre

HOTEL/RESTAURANT

Dublin Road Limerick Co. Limerick
Tel: 061 335 566 Fax: 061 331 117
Email: sales@castletroy-park.ie Web: www.castletroy-park.ie

Although far from enticing from the road, this blocky redbrick hotel has mellowed a little with time and has a warm and welcoming atmosphere in the large foyer and all the public areas. While not individually decorated, rooms (regularly refurbished, the latest phase to be completed by early 2002) are thoughtfully furnished with special attention to the needs of the business traveller (good desk space, second phone, fax and computer points). The hotel is much sought after as a conference venue and, after work, The Merry Pedlar pub offers a change of scene. Conferences / Banqueting (450-250); secretarial services. Business centre. Garden. Leisure/fitness centre, swimming pool. Children welcome (under 12s free in parents room, cot available without charge). **Rooms 107** (2 suites, 5 junior suites, 25 executive, 50 no-smoking, 1 for disabled). Lift. B&B €110 pps, ss €85. Hotel closed 24-26 Dec. **McLaughlin's Restaurant:** The hotels' fine dining restaurant has recently been refurbished and provides a comfortable formal setting for head chef Tom Flavin's inernational cuisine. In additon to table d'hôte menu, a wide-range à la carte ensures that guests staying in the hotel for several nights are spoilt for choice. About ten starters include several soups and specialities like Bluebell Falls organic goats cheese terrine with a spiced guacomole dressing, while main courses offer about fourteen dishes, almost equally balanced between meat/poutry, seafood and vegetarian dishes. Some are quite unusual - ballotine of goose, for example, studded with foie gras and served with red cabbage & rosemary scented jus, but there are plenty of simpler choices too. Desserts range from the pretty (selection of cie creams with sails of raspberry tuile) to the homely (indivdual apple pie). Professional service; quite an extensive wine list tends to favour France. **Seats 75.** No smoking area; air conditioning. D Tue-Sat, 5.30-10. Set D €38; also à la carte. House wine, €18.50. Restaurant closed Sun & Mon. Amex, Diners, MasterCard, Visa, Laser. **Directions:** On main Dublin-Limerick road (N7); 3 miles from Limerick city, 25 minutes from Shannon airport.

Limerick

DuCartes at the Hunt Museum

RESTAURANT

Hunt Museum Old Custom House Rutland Street Limerick Co. Limerick
Tel: 061 312662 Fax: 061 417929

This delightful modern café/restaurant is at the back of the museum, overlooking the river, with tables outside on the terrace in fine weather. As well as providing an appropriately elegant space to restore visitors to the museum, it is a popular lunchtime venue for locals. All ingredients are sourced locally and prepared daily: attractively presented and healthy home-cooked food in the modern idiom should not disappoint, although it may be a little short on personality. [D, for groups only by arrangement] **Seats 70.** No smoking area; air conditioning. Meals daily 5-5 (Sun 2-5), L 12-3. Set L €15.24. House wine about €14. Closed Sun am, 25 Dec. MasterCard, Visa.

Limerick

Eastern Tandoori

RESTAURANT

2-3 Steamboat Quay Limerick Co. Limerick
Tel: 061 311575 Fax: 061 311578

This luxuriously furnished richly-coloured glass-fronted waterside restaurant looks especially enticing from the outside at night and, by a lucky chance, has parking at the door, where the white-coated proprietor greets arriving gests personally. Well-appointed tables reflect the decorative themes and are enhanced by lovely lighting, altogether creating an exceptionally pleasant ambience. Menus in the familar Indian style are arranged by category and descriptive, with clear pride taken in regional specialities. Cooking is excellent and service is very professional and formal: waiters in regional costume present dishes in the traditional Indian way, with serving dishes on hotplates and accompaniments served separately. There's a good range of beers to complement the food. Prices are very reasonable and, together with reliably enjoyable food and good service, this is a restaurant that deserves more recognition. **Seats 80.** No smoking area; airconditioning. Toilets wheelchair accessible. L daily,12-2.30; D daily 6-11.30. A la carte. Amex, Diners, MasterCard, Visa, Laser.

Limerick

Finn's Bar & The Milestone

PUB

62 William Street Limerick Co. Limerick **Tel: 061 313495** Fax: 061 313496
Email: info@finnsbar.ie Web: www.finnsbar.ie

Seamus and Liam Flannery have recently taken on this city centre family business from their father, Michael Flannery, who has been in charge since 1960. It still has a traditional pub front but the new generation decided that the building, which is over 200 years old, needed a complete makeover - and it's now uncompromisingly 21st century. But the design is both striking and warm - modern but comfortable was the brief . A dramatic sculptural chandelier makes an unusual focal point in the high-ceilinged front bar, which also has a gallery around it, creating interesting spatial relationships which can be studied from above as well as below. Clean lines are emphasised by another feature which is unusual, possibly unqiue, in Irish pubs: a total absence of advertising; the only branding allowed is their own and their swirling black and gold logo appears on everything. Providing a comfortable place where quality food and drink is served by friendly staff is the aim, and it is achieved with commendable consistency at The Milestone. After breakfast (fresh orange juice, toasted bagel & cream cheese etc), then a lunch menu offering a tasty selection of soups, sandwiches and salads; hot dishes are cooked to order and attractively presented; seafood is quite prominent everything is home-made, including a speciality chowder, scones and desserts of the day. (Average main course about €7, seafood a little more). Service is pleasant and informal - and speciality coffees come with complimentary chocolates. DJ music on weekend evenings - the more traditional Milestone bar downstairs is quieter. **Seats 45.** Food available Mon-Sat, 9.30-3.30; L11.30-3.10. (No food on Sun). House wine about €16.44). Closed 25 Dec & Good Fri. Amex, MasterCard, Visa, Laser. **Directions:** 100 metres off Wiliam Street/O'Connell Street Junction.

Limerick

Greenhills Hotel

HOTEL Ennis Road Limerick Co. Limerick **Tel: 061 453033** Fax: 061 453307

Owner-managed by the Greene family since 1969, this friendly hotel is conveniently located just 5 minutes from the city and 20 minutes from Shannon airport. As well as providing a convenient base for touring the west, the hotel makes a useful business location and offers good conference facilities for up to 400 delegates (with back-up business services including French and German translation). Bedrooms include 11 executive rooms, 15 for non-smokers and ten rooms suitable for disabled guests - an unusually high proportion. Bedrooms are comfortably furnished in contemporary style and have full en-suite bathrooms (bath and shower). Good health and leisure facilities are a major attraction. **Rooms 57.** B&B about €70. Closed 25 Dec. Amex, Diners, MasterCard, Visa. **Directions:** On the edge of Limerick city, in the Ennis direction.

Limerick

Jurys Inn Limerick

HOTEL féile bia

Lower Mallow Street Limerick Co. Limerick **Tel: 061 207000**
Fax: 061 400966 Email: jurys_inn@jurysdoyle.com

Like other Jurys Inns, this budget hotel enjoys a prime city centre location and has carparking available in an adjacent multi-storey carpark. Rooms are large, comfortable and furnished to a high standard, especially considering the moderate cost, although maintenance may not always be up to the high standard required of relatively spartan budget accommodation. Bathrooms are fairly basic but have everything required including a proper (if budget-sized) bath as well as overbath shower. Don't expect high levels of service - that's what keeps the costs down - but there is a restaurant and pub-like bar as part of the development. Traffic noise can be disturbing in front rooms, as the trucks head to and from the west all night. Room rate €75 (max 3 guests). Closed 25 Dec. Amex, Diners, MasterCard, Visa.

Limerick

Jury's Limerick Hotel

HOTEL féile bia

Ennis Road Co. Limerick **Tel: 061 327 777** Fax: 061 326400
Email: limerick@jurysdoyle.com Web: www.jurysdoyle.com

Set in a garden site on the banks of the Shannon, the hotel is just two minutes walk from the city centre, 15 minutes drive from Shannon airport and within a short drive of many of the west's most dramatic scenic attractions. Good-sized rooms are decorated to a high standard with plenty of workspace for business guests and neat, well-lit bathrooms. Unusually for a city centre hotel, Jurys has a good leisure centre and also an outdoor tennis court. Children welcome (cots available). Conference/banqueting 200/160. Garden. **Rooms 95** (1 suite, 12 executive) Lift; 24 hour room service. Room rate €184 (max 2 guests). Closed 24 & 25 Dec. Amex, Diners, MasterCard, Visa. **Directions:** Approx 24 km from Shannon Airport.

Limerick

Limerick Inn Hotel

HOTEL

Ennis Road Limerick Co. Limerick **Tel: 061 326 666** Fax: 061 326 281
Email: limerick-inn@limerick-inn.ie Web: limerick-inn.com

This large low-rise modern hotel a few miles out of town on the Shannon Airport road is well-placed as a base for touring, although its main strength is as a conference venue - the largest of five conference rooms can accommodate 600 delegates and there are smaller meeting rooms for groups of up to 30; backup secretarial services are available. Bedrooms, all of which have full en-suite bathrooms (bath and shower), include four suites and 30 executive rooms, and there is a fine health and leisure centre.Hairdresser. Tennis; walking; garden. Children welcome (under 12s free in parents room; cots available). No Pets. **Rooms 153** (20 no-smoking). B&B about €100. Closed Dec 24-26 Amex, Diners, MasterCard, Visa. **Directions:** 2 miles north of Limerick on N18, from Shannon/Galway south on N18.

Limerick

The Locke Bar & Restaurant

PUB/RESTAURANT

3 Georges Quay Limerick Co. Limerick **Tel: 061 413733**
Fax: 061 413733 Email: lock@eircom.net Web: www.lockebar.com

Right beside the pontoons on George's Quay, this atmospheric 18th century pub has open fires in winter and a riverside beer garden in summer. There's a carvery lunch in the bar every day (and traditional Irish music on Sunday, Monday & Tuesday evenings) and the first floor restaurant provides a more formal setting for à la carte dining by candle light - and a balcony for fine weather, overlooking the Abbey river . Fresh local produce is used in traditional dishes with modern touches, such as Limerick bacon & cabbage with colcannon & mustard sauce; seafood is a speciality, including oysters and lobster from their own fish tank, and vegtarian dishes are always available. Food available daily, 10-5; L12-3, D 5-10. Set L €16.44 (Set Sun L €17.71); Early menu € 16.44 (5-7pm), Set D from €21, also à la carte. House wine €17.71. No sc. Closed 25 Dec, Good Fri. Amex, Diners, MasterCard, Visa, Laser. **Directions:** City Centre beside St Mary's Cathederal.

Limerick

Manna

RESTAURANT

Unit C2 Cornmarket Square Robert Street Limerick Co. Limerick
Tel: 061 318317 Fax: 061 318231

Pale walls decorated with striking modern pictures, light wood floor and tables, good lighting, lovely flowers and stylish, comfortable high-back chairs all create a good impression at this pleasing contemporary restaurant. On the whole it's a calm and relaxing place to be and it's clearly a hit with well-heeled locals - although tightly-packed tables and loud music may make communication difficult. Lively modern international menus are quite extensive and cooking can be impressive. Unusual side orders include herbed couscous and basmati rice and there are tempting desserts, such as pannacotta with fresh fruits - all at reasonable prices. The wine list is also moderate by the bottle, although less so by the glass. No private parking. **Seats 60.** D Tue-Sun, 6-10.45. A la carte. Closed Mon. Amex, Diners, MasterCard, Visa. **Directions:** In Limerick's newly modernised markets area, on city side of the Dublin road.

Limerick

RESTAURANT

Paul's Restaurant

59 O'Connell Street Limerick Co. Limerick **Tel: 061 316600**
Fax: 061 316600

This professionally operated restaurant on Limerick's main thoroughfare has been run by Paul Fox and Julie Ptashnick since 1997. The decor, which is colourful and modern but with due respect paid to the more traditional essentials of dining (comfortable high back chairs, tablecloths), creates a pleasing balance between formality and the relaxed ambience which is now an expected aspect of dining out. Paul uses local produce and other speciality Irish foods on international menus that cleverly integrate many of the old favourites (sirloin steak with choice of sauces) along with global influences (bruschetta, crostini, mussels with mild curry, coconut, lime & ginger sauce). Carefully sources ingredients, accurate cooking and good value, together with a pleasant ambience and professional service under the direction of Julie Ptashnick make for an appealing package, which has earned the restaurant a well-deserved reputation as one of the city's best restaurants. **Seats 46.** No smoking area. Not suitable for children after 7pm. D Mon-Sat, 5.30-10.Early D €14.50 (5.30-7); house wine €15.90. No sc (except 10% on parties of 6+). Closed Sun & 23 Dec-7 Jan. Amex, Diners, MasterCard, Visa, Laser. **Directions:** City Centre on main Throughfare.

Limerick

HOTEL

South Court Business & Leisure Centre

Adare Road Limerick Co. Limerick **Tel: 061 487 487** Fax: 061 487499
Email: cro@lynchotels.com Web: www.lynchotels.com

Ideally located for Shannon Airport and the Raheen Industrial Estate, the South Court Hotel presents a somewhat daunting exterior, but once inside visitors soon discover that it caters especially well for business guests, both on and off-duty - hence the Guide's Business Hotel Award to Lynch Hotels in 2000; since then, these facilities have seen major improvement with the opening of a 1,250 seater International Convention Centre. In addition to excellent conference and meeting facilities, comfortable bedrooms are impressively spacious and well equipped, with generous desk areas and the latest technology, including fax/modem/ISDN points, in every room. Executive bedrooms have a separate work area providing a 'mini-office' with a leather desk chair and private fax machine - and 67 new 'lifestyle suites' with in-room gym, designed by the internationally renowned Irish designer Paul Costelloe, were launched in 2001. Leisure facilities are to be improved dramatically in 2002 with the opening of a 'Polo Lifestyle Club', designed with international rugby player (and local hero) Keith Wood. Conference/banqueting (1250/850); business centre; secretarial services, video conferencing. Leisure centre, hairdressing. Children welcome (under 3s free in parents' room, cot available without charge, playroom, children's playground). No Pets. **Rooms 127** (1 suite, 15 junior suites, 55 executive, 14 no-smoking). B&B €82.53 pps, ss €74.91; room-only rate also available:€74.91 (max 3 guests). Amex, Diners, MasterCard, Visa. **Directions:** Located onthe main N20 Cork/Killarney road, 20 minutes from Shannon Airport.

Limerick

RESTAURANT

Tiger Lilies Bistro

9B Ellew Street Limerick Co. Limerick
Tel: 061 317484 Fax: 061 317868

The black beams, exposed stone walls and wooden floors of an old bonded warehouse in a redevelopment area provide a characterful setting for this terrific informal restaurant. Pleasant lighting, fresh flowers, light background jazz and changing art displays by local artists all add up to a very pleasing ambience. It's attractive from the outside too, with plants and tables for al fresco dining in fine weather although, unfortunately, it faces a carpark (although this does have its compensations). The upbeat tone of the interior is reflected in stylish table settings - even if ordinary paper napkins do seem a bit out of place - and modern menus (very colourfully presented) with fashionable global influences offer some more down to earth dishestoo, like venison sausage with champ potato (albeit with chilli jam). Strong fish options include less usual choices like whole sea bass (with braised chicory and caper & citrus butter) and vegetarian dishes are imaginative. Prices seem high for the casual ambience (evening main courses rise to as much as €25) but this is above average bistro food, based on fresh local produce, accurately cooked and complemented by well-trained service. Well selected, interesting wine list. **Seats 95.** No smoking area. Open 10am-10/11pm; L Mon-Sat 12-4, D Tue-Sat 6.30-10/11. A la carte. House wine €17.14. Closed all Sun, D Mon, bank hols, 24-28 Dec. MasterCard, Visa, Laser. **Directions:** Between Cruises Street and the Gateway.

Adare
HOTEL
RESTAURANT

Adare Manor Hotel & Golf Club

Limerick Co. Limerick **Tel: 061 396566** Fax: 061 396124
Email: reservations@adaremanor.com

The former home of the Earls of Dunraven, this magnificent neo-Gothic mansion is set in 900 acres on the banks of the River Maigue. Its splendid chandeliered drawing room and the glazed cloister of the dining room look over formal box-hedged gardens towards the Robert Trent Jones golf course. Other grand public areas include the gallery, named after the Palace of Versailles, with its unique 15th century choir stalls and fine stained glass windows. Luxurious bedrooms have individual hand carved fireplaces, fine locally-made mahogany furniture, cut-glass table lamps and impressive marble bathrooms with strong showers over huge bathtubs. A new clubhouse and 25 townhouses were recently completed in the grounds. Conference/banqueting (250/200). Leisure centre, Golf (18), Equestrian. Walking. Garden. Fishing. Children welcome. Rooms 63 (staterooms 13; some rooms for disabled). Wheelchair access. Lift. B&B about €320. Open all year. **Oak Room Restaurant:** Local produce, including vegetables from the estate's own gardens, is included on seasonal menus which change weekly, and although based on classical French cuisine, the style includes some modern Irish food, as in roast lamb cutlets on colcannon, for example. A separate vegetarian menu is offered. Seats 70 L&D daily; sc15%. *Meals also available from the Clubhouse Bar & Restaurant, 7am-10 pm daily. Open all year. Amex, Diners, MasterCard, Visa. **Directions:** On N21 in Limerick.

Adare
GUESTHOUSE

Carrabawn Guesthouse

Killarney Road Adare Co. Limerick **Tel: 061 396 067**
Email: carrabaw@indigo.ie Web: www.carrabawnhouseadare.com

In an area known for high standards, with prices to match, this immaculate owner-run establishment set in large mature gardens provides a good alternative to the local luxury accommodation. Bernard and Bridget Lohan have been welcoming guests here since 1984 - and many of them return on an annual basis because of the high level of comfort and friendly service provided. Bedrooms are very well maintained with all the amenities required. In addition to seeing guests off with a good Irish breakfast, light evening meals can be provided by arrangement. Children welcome (under 2s free in parents' room). Pets permitted. **Rooms 8** (all shower only & no smoking). B&B €42 pps, ss€18. Closed 23-30 Dec. Amex, MasterCard, Visa, Laser, Switch. **Directions:** On N21 in Adare.

Adare
HOTEL
RESTAURANT

Dunraven Arms Hotel

Adare Co. Limerick **Tel: 061 396 633**
Fax: 061 396 541 Web: www.dunravenhotel.com

Established in 1792, and set in one of Ireland's most picturesque villages, the Dunraven Arms has seen many changes over the last few years and is now a large hotel. Yet, under the personal management of Bryan and Louis Murphy, it somehow manages to retain the comfortable ambience of a country inn. A very luxurious inn nevertheless: the furnishing standard is superb throughout, with antiques, private dressing rooms and luxurious bathrooms, plus excellent amenities for private and business guests, all complemented by an outstanding standard of housekeeping. It's an excellent base for sporting activities - equestrian holidays are a speciality and both golf and fishing are available nearby - and also extremely popular for both conferences and private functions, which are held beside the main hotel (with separate catering facilities). Leisure centre, indoor swimming pool. **Rooms 76** (6 suites, 12 junior suites, 66 executive rooms). Room rate €178 +12.5% sc. Hotel closed 25 Dec. **Maigue Restaurant:** Named after the River Maigue, which flows through the village of Adare, the restaurant is delightfully old fashioned - more akin to eating in a large country house than in an hotel. Sandra Earl, who has been head chef since 1998, takes pride in using the best of local produce in meals that combine the traditions of the area with influences from around the world on menus that offered a balanced selection of about half a dozen dishes on each course. Although particularly renowned for their roast rib of beef (carved from a trolley), other specialities like River Maigue salmon and local game in season, especially pheasant, are very popular. **Seats 80.** Open daily, D 7.30-10, Set D about €35 à la carte also available; L Sun only 12.30-2.30, about €18 House wine about €14.60, sc 12.5%. [*The Inn Between, across the road in one of the traditional thatched cottages, is an informal restaurant in common ownership with the Dunraven Arms; D only, 6-9.30. Amex, Diners, MasterCard, Visa, Laser. **Directions:** First building on RHS as enter the village coming from Limerick (approx. 11 miles).

Adare

HOTEL

Fitzgeralds Woodlands House Hotel

Knockanes Adare Co. Limerick **Tel: 061 605 100** Fax: 061 396 073
Email: dfitzgerald@woodlands-hotel.ie Web: www.woodlands-hotel.ie

Just outside Adare, the Fitzgerald family's hotel has grown dramatically since it opened in 1983 and management has now moved into the next generation. The whole hotel has been systematically upgraded and developed over the years - the low, grey-tiled building is set in well-kept gardens and presents a neat and welcoming appearance from the road. It has always been a popular venue for weddings and is particularly well suited to large gatherings, with spacious public areas throughout, including two bars, and a restaurant and banqueting suite overlooking gardens and countryside. New and upgraded bedrooms have significantly raised the standard of accommodation. A new leisure centre, with 20 metre pool, jacuzzi, sauna, steamroom and gym was recently added, also a a barbecue garden area with thatched cottage feature Conferences/Banqueting (350/330); secretarial services. Leisure centre, swimming pool; hairdresser; beauty salon. Children welcome (under 4s free in parents' room; cots available without charge, playroom). Garden. **Rooms 94** (5 junior suites, 45 executive, 10 shower only. 2 for disabled). B&B €75 pps, ss €19. Closed 24-25 Dec. Amex, Diners, MasterCard, Visa, Laser. **Directions:** Take N21 from Limerick, turn left at roundabout before Adare.

Adare

RESTAURANT

The Wild Geese Restaurant

Rose Cottage Adare Co. Limerick **Tel: 061 396451**
Fax: 061 396451 Email: wildgeese@indigo.ie

David Foley and Julie Randles' restaurant is in one of the prettiest cottages in the prettiest village in Ireland - and a charming atmosphere, caring service and good cooking all add up to an irresistible package. Dinner menus are considerately priced by course, so you're not tied into the full meal, and offer about half a dozen choices for starters and main courses. Terrine of smoked bacon, chicken liver and duck foie gras on toasted brioche & redcurrant dressing and steamed mussels with a lemon butter sauce are typical starters, and examples from the main course selection might include panfried fillets of monkfish served on celeiac purée with asparagus and a tapenade & pinenut sauce, rounded off with an interesting choice of desserts including a hot soufflé (pear, perhaps, complemented by a pear ice cream), or you can conclude with Irish cheeses, served with treacle bread and water biscuits. Not suitable for children after 7 pm. **Seats 45.** No-smoking area. L Tue-Sat 12.30-2.30, D Tue-Sat 6.30-10; L à la carte, Set D from €35.43. House wine €20.32. Closed Sun, Mon, 24-26 Dec & 3 weeks Jan. Amex, Diners, MasterCard, Visa, Laser. **Directions:** From Limerick, at top of Adare village, opposite Dunraven Arms Hotel.

Ballingarry

COUNTRY HOUSE
RESTAURANT

The Mustard Seed at Echo Lodge

Ballingarry Co. Limerick
Tel: 069 68508 Fax: 069 68511
Email: mustard@indigo.ie

One of the country's prettiest and most characterful restaurants, Dan Mullane's famous Mustard Seed started life in Adare in 1985. Having celebrated its first decade it began the next one by moving just ten minutes drive away to Echo Lodge, a spacious Victorian country residence set on seven acres, with mature trees, shrubberies, kitchen garden and orchard - and very luxurious accommodation. Elegance, comfort and generosity are the key features - seen through decor and furnishings which bear the mark of a seasoned traveller whose eye has found much to delight in while wandering the world. The main house and garden having been put in order, Dan's next project was the conversion of an old schoolhouse in the garden, to provide four new superior suites, a new residents' lounge and a small leisure centre with sauna and massage room. This was completed in 2001 and is already in great demand from regulars who make Echo Lodge their base for golf and fishing holidays. Small conferences (20). Garden. **Rooms 17** (3 suites, 4 shower only, 1 for disabled). B&B €82.50 pps, ss €32. Special winter breaks offered, depending on availability. **Restaurant:** Food and hospitality are at the heart of Echo Lodge and it is in ensuring an enjoyable dining experience, most of all, that Dan Mullane's great qualities as a host emerge (he was the Guide's Host of the Year in 2001). The evening gets off to an auspicious start when aperitifs, served in the Library, come with a tasty amuse-bouche, and it is evident that attention to detail is the hallmark here - an impression confirmed when you go in to the beautiful dining room to find fresh flowers on each table, carefully selected to suit the decor. Head chef Tony Schwartz - whose previous experience includes working in the renowned kitchens of Drimcong House in Co Galway (now much missed as it no operates as a restaurant) - cooks in what he describes as "interesting Irish" style. The kitchen gardens supply much of the produce for the restaurant, other ingredients are carefully sourced from organic farms and artisan food producers. Menus are wide-ranging and very seasonal - the components of a delicious tossed salad (with chorizo sausage, garlic croûtons & parmesan shavings, with soya & balsamic dressing, pehaps) will be dictated by the leaves and herbs in season and the soup course - typically a creamy leek & potato - may also be influenced by garden produce. Main courses are based on the best local meats (typically, grilled loin of pork with a wild mushroom risotto and apple &thyme sauce), seafood just up from the south-western fishing ports and game, in season - and, with so such an abundance of garden produce, vegetarians need no fear of being overlooked. Using the best Irish farmhouse cheeses at their peak of perfection is another point of honour - or you can finish with gorgeous puddings, which are also likely to be inspired by garden produce. Finally, irresistible home-made petits fours are served with tea or coffee, at the table or in the Library. All absolutely delicious - and the hospitality element is truly exceptional. Not suitable for children. **Seats 50.** Non-smoking restaurant. D 7-9.30pm, Set D €45. House wines from €19. Closed Sun & Mon in low season; house closed 24-26 Dec, all Feb. Amex, MasterCard, Visa, Laser. **Directions:** From top of Adare village take first turn to left, follow signs to Ballingarry - 8 miles.

Castleconnell

Castle Oaks House Hotel

HOTEL/RESTAURANT

Castleconnell Co. Limerick **Tel: 061 377666** Fax: 061 377717
Email: info@castle-oaks.com Web: www.castle-oaks.com

Set quietly in 26 acres of wooded countryside on the banks of the Shannon, this attractive hotel is in an idyllic location on the edge of the picturesque village of Castleconnell, just a few miles on the Dublin side of Limerick. The old part of the hotel is a Georgian mansion, with the gracious proportions and elegance that implies, although a new wing provides extra accommodation which makes up in comfort and convenience anything it might lack in character. (One bedroom is designed for asthmatics, with hard surfaces and specially chosen fabrics.) Private fishing is a particular attraction, and the hotel also offers an unusual venue for conferences and weddings in a converted chapel. Nice, helpful staff and a family-friendly attitude make this a pleasant hotel. Conference/banqueting (200/250); business centre; secretarial services. Leisure centre (15-metre pool). Fishing, tennis, cycling, walking. Garden. Children welcome (under 4s free in parents room; cots available without charge). No Pets. **Rooms 20** (2 suites, 2 executive, 2 shower only, 1 no-smoking room). B&B €65 pps, ss €13. **Acorn Restaurant** A gracious room with river views, the restaurant is pleasantly furnished with chintz, velvet and flowers giving it a nice country house feeling. Well-appointed tables look promising, with crisp linen and polished glasses and, (although it may not be obvious from reading menus which fail to do justice to the food), quality local produce is the foundation on which quite impersonal-sounding dishes are based. Simple, freshly-cooked dishes will impress through their attention to the essentials of accurate cooking and good flavour - the qualitites that make or break dishes like chicken liver paté with Cumberland sauce or baked fillet of seabass with roasted peppers, cherry tomatoes & basil dressing. Staff are keen to please and service, under the direction of restaurant manager Niall Dooley, is friendly and efficient. Amex, Diners, MasterCard, Visa, Laser. **Directions:** N7 from Limerick left for Castleconnell, on left as you enter village.

Croom

Mill Race

RESTAURANT

Croom Mills Croom Co. Limerick **Tel: 061 397130** Fax: 061 397199
Email: croommills@eircom.net Web: www.croommills.com

One of the most imaginatively handled restorations of its type, a visit to Croom Mills shows the whole traditional corn milling process from beginning to end - including a sample of freshly baked bread hot from the oven. Many other exhibits illustrate related operations and crafts - the blacksmith, for instance, in his 19th century forge - and several primary power sources are to be seen in action, including the giant 16 foot cast iron waterwheel, built in Cork in 1852. The tour takes about an hour, but there are other attractions here too, notably one of the country's best craft and gift shops and the Mill Race Restaurant. Major improvements have recently been completed, which has added to the comfort - but the food has been excellent from the word go, and would be hard to better. Vegetarians are well looked after and there's an outdoor eating area overlooking the millrace. This is good home cooking served in very pleasing surroundings. * During the winter of 2001/2 further improvements will enable the Mill to open a fully licensed fine dining restaurant, serving evening meals. **Seats 150.** No-smoking area. Food served daily 9-5.30. Sun to 6pm. Set L €13.90; à la carte also available. Wine licence. Closed 25-30 Dec, Good Fri. Amex, MasterCard, Visa, Laser.

Glin

COUNTRY HOUSE

Glin Castle

Glin Co. Limerick **Tel: 068 34173** Fax: 068 34364
Email: knight@iol.ie Web: www.glincastle.com

The Fitzgeralds, hereditary Knights of Glin, have lived in Glin Castle for 700 years and it is now the home of the 29th Knight and his wife Madame Fitzgerald. The interior is stunning, with beautiful interiors enhanced by decorative plasterwork and collections of Irish furniture and paintings. Guests are magnificently looked after by manager Bob Duff. Accommodation was originally all in suites - huge and luxurious, but not at all intimidating because of the lived-in atmosphere that characterises the whole castle - but additional rooms ("small, friendly, with a family atmosphere") have recently been opened. Furnished and decorated in traditional country house style (there was no need for this family to haunt the auctions in order to furnish the new rooms), everything has been done just right and every room feels as if it has always been that way. When the Knight is at home he will take visitors on a tour of the house and show them all his pictures and old furniture. Not to be missed while in Glin is O'Shaughnessy's pub, just outside the castle walls; one of the finest pubs in Ireland, it is now in its sixth generation of family ownership and precious little has changed in the last hundred years. The garden and house are open to the public at certain times. Small conferences/private parties (15/30). Garden. Walking. Tennis. Children over 10 welcome. Pets by arrangement. **Rooms 15** (3 suites, all no-smoking). Room rate €242. Dinner is available by reservation. Dining Room **Seats 30.** Non-smoking. D 7-9.30, Set D €41.90 House wine from about €15; sc discretionary. Closed 5 Nov-1 Apr. Amex, Diners, MasterCard, Visa, Laser. **Directions:** 32 miles west of Limerick on N69, 4 miles east Tarbert Car Ferry.

Newcastlewest

PUB /RESTAURANT

Arrabrook Bar & Restaurant

Killeline Newcastlewest Co. Limerick **Tel: 069 61600**
Fax: 069 77428 Email: arrabrook@eircom.net Web: www.arrabrook.com

Just off the N21, this is a useful place to bear in mind to break a journey and well worth the short detour required. The proprietor is Conleth Roche, well known in the area as a previous joint-owner of the lovely Wine Geese Restaurant in Adare village, and although only open since January 2001, his latest venture is already making a national impact. It's an attractive half-timbered building with a spacious, airy high-ceilinged interior well broken up into bar and brasserie areas, and comfortably furnished to ensure the maximum enjoyment of food which is both imaginative and beautifully cooked. Head chef Niall Ennis's limited but exceptionally enticing bar menu offers a dozen or so savoury choices ranging through soups, sandwiches and substantial hot dishes like shank of lamb with root vegetables, buttermilk mash & onion gravy or panfried venison sausages on colcannon with caramelised onions & a red wine jus. Something for everyone in fact. Freshly made pasta is delicious with an oven-roasted plum tomato sauce, smoked bacon, black olives and parmesan cheese shavings, for example, and open Italian style sandwiches are made with home-made ciabatta and various fillings - such as perfect slices of smoked chicken breast topped with generous amount of Gubbeen cheese (in perfect condition) and a deliciously fruity chutney. Limerick gammon with mature cheddar is another option, served hot with pickled vegetables and mustard mayonnaise, and desserts like warm wild berry and almond pie with fresh cream or dark chocolate mousse cake with a red berry coulis are equally moreish. This is bar food with a difference. Restaurant meals offer a much wider choice and dishes are more complex, but the same chef is responsible for both areas, so the same high standard may be expected. Bar meals Mon-Sat 12-6, L 12-2.30; Sun 12-4; Set L €18.98; no smoking area. Restaurant **Seats 70** (private room 8-25); no smoking restaurant. D Mon-Sat, 6-10. Restaurant closed D Sun. Amex, MasterCard, Visa, Laser. **Directions:** Signposted N21 turn left just before entering Newcastlewest situated on R522 500 yards from cross.

COUNTY LONGFORD

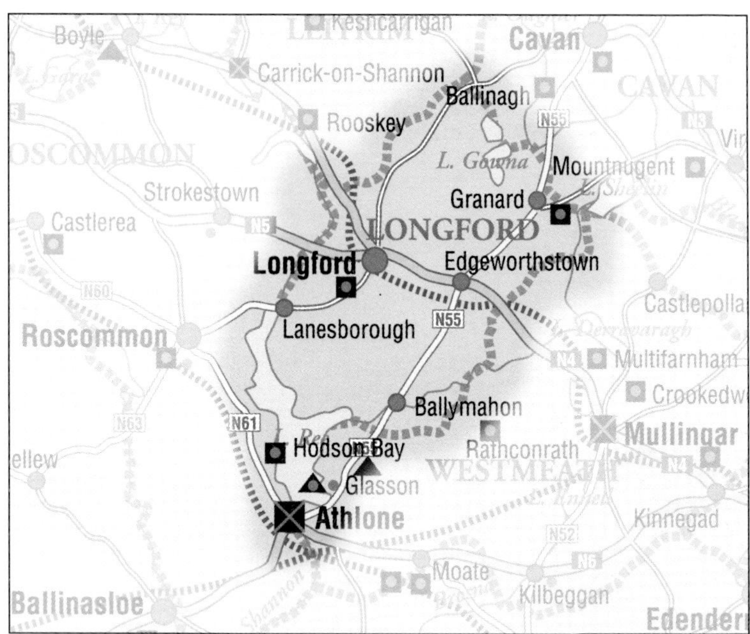

The people of Longford have become so accustomed to seeing their county dismissed by speed-through travel guides as "the least interesting territory in all Ireland" that they've adopted a sensibly wry attitude to the whole business. Thus they get on with life in a style appropriate to a quietly prosperous and unpretentious county which nevertheless can spring some surprises,

These are not, however, to be found in the scenery, for Longford is mostly either gently undulating farming country, or bogland. The higher ground in the north of the county up towards the intricate Lough Gowna rises to no more than 276m in an eminence which romantics might call Carn Clonhugh, but usually it's more prosaically known as Corn Hill. Yet this is an area which arouses passionate patriotism. A few miles to the north is Ballinamuck, scene of the last battle in the Rising of 1798, in a part of Longford renowned for its rebellions against foreign rule.

Over to the east, where there's more high ground, there is even less pulling of the punches in the name of the little market town in its midst, for Granard - which sounds rather elegant - can actually be translated as "Ugly Height". Yet this suggests a pleasure in words for their own sake, which is appropriate, for Longford produced the novelist Maria Edgeworth from Edgeworthstown, a.k.a Mostrim, while along towards that fine place Ballymahon and the south of its territory on the Westmeath border, Longford takes in part of the Goldsmith country.

Goldsmith himself would be charmed to know that, six kilometres south of the road between Longford and Edgeworthstown, there's the tiny village of Ardagh, a place of just 75 citizens which is so immaculately maintained that it has been the winner of the Tidiest Village in the Tidy Towns awards three times during the past ten years.

In fact, Longford does rather well in the Tidy Towns competition - the national holder in 2001 of the Tidiest Village category was Newtowncashel, which is also the county's top scorer in all categories in 2002. Newtowncashel is in the southwest of the county, atop a hill immediately eastward of Elfeet Bay on northern Lough Ree, where the scenery becomes more varied as County Longford has a lengthy shoreline along the Shannon's middle lake.

It also has pretty Richmond Harbour west of Longford town at Clondra, where the Royal Canal - gradually being restored along its meandering track from Dublin - finally gets to the Shannon. And as for Longford town itself, they're working on it, including a revival of the town's old canal harbour, and some day the rest of Ireland will wake up to find that there's life a-plenty going on there, if you just know where to look for it.

Local Attractions and Information

Ardagh Heritage Centre	043 75277
Ballinamuck 1798 Memorial & Visitor Centre	043 24848
Ballymahon Bog Lane Theatre	0902 32252
Kenagh Corlea Trackway (Bog Road) Visitor Centre	043 22386
Longford Backstage Theatre & Arts Centre	043 47885
Longford Carriglass Manor (Gandon stableyard, lace museum)	043 41026
Longford Tourism Information	043 46566
Newtowncashel Heritage Centre	043 25021

Granard

Toberphelim House

FARMHOUSE

Granard Co. Longford **Tel: 043 86568**
Email: tober2@eircom.net Web: www.toberphelimhouse.com

Dan and Mary Smyth's Georgian farmhouse is about half a mile off the road, on a rise that provides a lovely view of the surrounding countryside. Very much a working farm – cows, beef cattle and sheep plus an assortment of domestic animals and hens - it is a hospitable, easy-going place. Guests are welcome to wander around and walk the fields. ("Rubber boots are a must"). There's a guests' sitting room with television; two bedrooms have a single and double bed in each and one twin room has a separate private bathroom. All are comfortably furnished and well-maintained, but don't expect amenities like phones and TV in the rooms. Families are welcome - and light meals and snacks can usually be arranged as long as notice is given before 12 noon. Children welcome. **Rooms 3** (2 shower only, 1 private). B&B €40pps, ss €6. Closed 21 Sep-1 May. MasterCard, Visa. **Directions:** take the N55 at the Cavan end of Granard, turn off at the Statoil station making a right at the next junction. The house is situated about half a mile towards Abbeylara, to the left.

Longford

Aubergine Gallery Café

CAFÉ Ballymahon Street Longford Co. Longford **Tel: 043 48633** Web: themarketbar.com

Stephen and Linda Devlin have run this restaurant overlooking the market square since 1998 and it draws customers from a wide area. It's up a steep staircase from the Market Bar, in an L-shaped room with chunky wooden furniture, an unusual display of local art (an interesting distraction between courses) and a long service bar along one side. Large candles all around the room make for an atmospheric space after dark - during daylight, by contrast, the eye is drawn to a window table that opens onto a plant-filled balcony over the square. Stephen's menus are Irish/Mediterranean - a house speciality is (of course) char-grilled aubergine, feta cheese, basil & tomato bruschetta - and it summarises the style quite well. Which is not to say that the wider picture is ignored: a good steak is de rigeur in these parts, for example - here it may be a 10 oz aged sirloin steak with whiskey and pepper cream - and there will be poultry (crispy duck leg confit perhaps). Seafood nage - monkfish, salmon, haddock & mussels in tarragon, tomato & leek beurre blanc sauce - is an elegant and well-flavoured dish. Desserts include a welcome amount of fruit, in a delicious deep apple pie with custard sauce perhaps. Service, under the direction of Linda Devlin, is friendly and helpful. **Seats 35.** No smoking area. Children welcome. L Tue-Sun, 12-2.30 (Sun to 3); D Wed-Sat, 6.30-9.30. Set L about €15, Set Sun L €19, D à la carte. House wine €16. Closed D Sun, all Mon, D Tue, 4 weeks holidays each year (month not confirmed at time of going to press). MasterCard, Visa, Laser. **Directions:** right side of market square over Market Bar.

Longford

Longford Arms Hotel

HOTEL

Main Street Longford Co. Longford **Tel: 043 46296**
Fax: 043 46244 Email: longfordarms@eircom.net

Located right in the heart of the midlands, this comfortable family-run hotel has recently been renovated to a high standard. The hotel presents a neat face to the street and public areas give a good impression on arrival. Bedrooms are comfortably furnished and particularly convenient for business guests as they have adequate desk space and the amenities required for this type of travel (including trouser presses and irons). All bedrooms have good bathrooms (with both bath and shower). The coffee shop provides wholesome casual daytime food and they do all their baking in-house – a good place to take a break. (Bar/coffee shop food is open all day, 12-8). Conference/banqueting (500/550); video-conferencing; business centre; secretarial services. Children welcome (under 3s free in parents' room; cots available). Wheelchair accessible. Pets by arrangement. **Rooms 66.** (20 no-smoking; ISDN lines available). B&B about €60 pps, no ss. Own parking. Closed 25-26 Dec. Amex, Diners, MasterCard, Visa. **Directions:** centre of Longford town.

COUNTY LOUTH

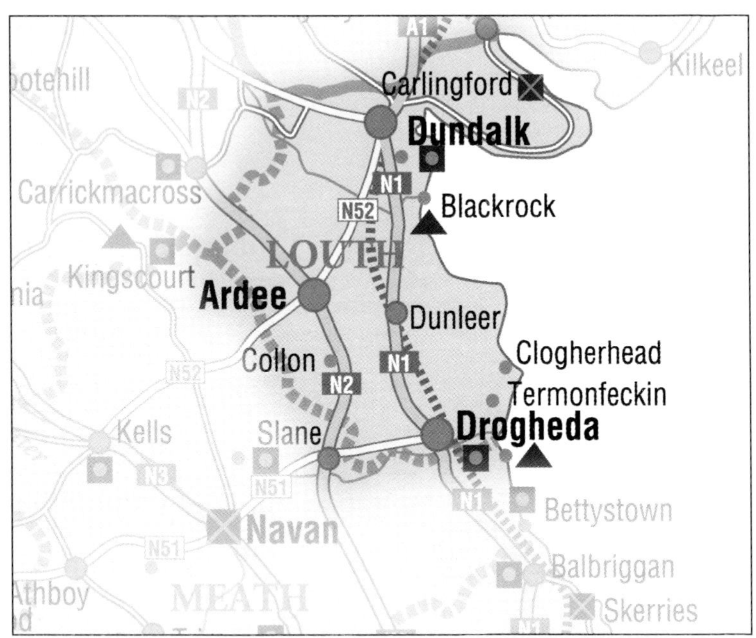

Major infrastructural improvements in Louth include one of the pleasantest stretches of motorway known to the Guide....... Yes, motorways can be a pleasure in themselves - the section in question is the M1 between Dundalk and Monasterboice. With traffic pressure thus removed from other roads, Louth begins to find itself. And though it may be Ireland's smallest county at only 317 square miles, it still manages to be two or even three counties in one.

Much of Louth is fine farmland, which is at its best in the area west of the extensive wildfowl paradise of Dundalk Bay, on whose shores we find the attractive village of Blackrock, one of Ireland's better kept secrets. But as well there are the distinctive uplands in the southwest, whose name of Oriel recalls an ancient princedom. And in the north of the county, the Cooley Mountains sweep upwards in a style which well matches their better-known neighbours, the Mountains of Mourne, on the other side of the handsome inlet of Carlingford Lough.

Its name might suggest that this is a genuine fjord, but it isn't. However, its beauty is such that there's more than enough to be going along with, and on its Louth shore the ancient little port of Carlingford town used to be a best-kept secret. It was a quiet little place imbued with history, but today it is happily prospering both as a recreational harbour for the Dundalk and Newry area, and as a bustling visitor attraction in its own right.

The county's three main townships of Ardee, Dundalk and Drogheda each have their own distinctive style, and all three have been coming vibrantly to life in recent years. The historic borough of Drogheda is the main commercial port while Dundalk is the county town, and the evocatively-named Port Oriel at Clogher Head is Louth's most active fishing harbour. In the current Tidy Town listings, Tallanstown north of Ardee is the top scorer, with Knockbridge - just five miles away - taking the Highly Commended award, while the ferry port of Greenore at the entrance to Carlingford Lough is third, in the Commended slot.

Local Attractions and Information

Ardee (Tallanstown) Knockabbey Castle & Gardens	042 937 4690
Carlingford Heritage Trust, Tourism Information	042 937 3888
Carlingford Carlingford Adventure Centre	042 937 3100
Carlingford Carlingford Sea School	042 937 3879
Drogheda Droichead Arts Centre	041 983 3946
Drogheda Millmount Museum	041 983 3097
Drogheda (Tullyallen) Old Mellifont Abbey	041 982 6459
Drugheda Tourism Information	041 983 7070
Dundalk County Museum	042 932 7056
Dundalk Tourism Information	042 933 5484
Dunleer White River Mills: working flour mill	041 985 1141
Termonfeckin Irish Countrywomens Assoc. College	041 982 2119

Blackrock

The Brake

PUB/RESTAURANT

Main Street Blackrock Co. Louth

Tel: 042 932 1393 Fax: 042 932 2568

Although it may not look especially inviting from the outside, first-time visitors are always amazed by the warmth and country charm of The Brake once they get inside the door – all old pine and rural bric-à-brac, it has open fires and friendly staff. It's a great place to stop just for a cup of tea, but even better if you're hungry – it has a well-deserved reputation for good bar meals, with a wide range offered – not just the usual pub staples, but home-made chicken kiev, for example and seafood such as smoked mussels, wild salmon in season, jumbo prawns and even lobster. There are lots of meat dishes, too, especially steaks with a range of sauces and creamy dishes that come with rice, such as prawns provençal, beef stroganoff and pork à la crème. Salads and accompaniments are particularly good, all arranged buffet style. Beware of the unusual opening hours though – this is a late afternoon into evening place. No children under 12. **Seats 130.** No smoking area; air conditioning. D daily 6.30-10.30 (Sun to 9.30). A la carte; house wine €13.97; sc discretionary. Closed 24-25 Dec, 31 Dec & Good Fri. MasterCard, Visa, Laser. **Directions:** Turn off the main Dublin-Belfast road 3 miles south of Dundalk. It is situated on the seafrontin the village.

Blackrock

Clermont Arms

PUB/RESTAURANT

Main Street Blackrock Co. Louth

Tel: 042 932 2666 Fax: 042 932 2568

Sister establishment to The Brake, next door, the Clermont Arms has been developed with the same blend of charm and practicality, making it a characterful and relaxing place for a drink or good food. Also like its older sister, The Clermont is open only from late afternoon into evening (from 4pm). For summer, there's a large paved area at the back, sheltered and away from the road. Not suitable for children under 12. **Seats 110.** No smoking area; air-conditioning. D 6-10 daily (Sun to 9). A la carte. House wine about €14, sc discretionary. Closed 25 Dec, 31 Dec & Good Fri. MasterCard, Visa, Laser. **Directions:** Turn off the main Dublin-Belfast road 3 miles south of Dundalk. Pub is situated on the seafront in Blackrock village.

Carlingford

Beaufort House

GUESTHOUSE

Carlingford Co. Louth

Tel: 042 937 3879 Fax: 042 937 3878

Email: michaelcaine@beauforthouse.net Web: www.beauforthouse.net

Michael and Glynnis Caine's immaculate property is well-placed to maximise on the attractions of a quiet and beautiful waterside position with wonderful sea and mountain views, while also being just a few minutes walk from Carlingford village. All areas are spacious and furnished to high specifications: hotel standard bedrooms have phone, TV with video channel and tea/coffee making facilities. The Caines were previously restaurateurs and dinner is available by arrangement for parties of eight or more. (Set D €32). There's a tennis court on-site and associated activities include a sailing school and yacht charter - corporate sailing events (team building and corporate hospitality), including match racing in Carligford Lough, are a speciality. Golf nearby. Helipad; ample car parking. Small conference/banqueting (20/30). Children welcome (under 2s free in parents' room). Pets by arrangement. Garden. **Rooms 5** (all en-suite & no-smoking, 2 shower only). B&Babout €40 pps, no ss. MasterCard, Visa. **Directions:** Located on shore of Carlingford Lough south of the east pier of Carlingford Harbour. Well sign posted.

Carlingford

Georgina's Tearooms

CAFÉ Castle Hill Carlingford Co. Louth **Tel: 042 937 3346** Email: teaf@eircom.net

Although not the handiest place to find, Georgina Finegan's little daytime restaurant high up in the web of small roads above King John's Castle is well worth seeking out. It is a (relatively) recent addition to a 20-year old small bakery specialising in meringues and desserts and, since opening in 1997, has built up a loyal customer base including "people who return on a daily, weekly or even annual base for the good food and friendly tea room setting." They come from Belfast, Dublin and "places in between", they're local, and they're visitors from all over the world - the fact is that there is something for everyone at this unpretentious café. Although a recently added conservatory has brought some extra space, the original café is really quite small, but it's cosy and seems just right for simple fare like soup of the day with a traditional sandwich like egg, tomato & parsley, or open sandwiches like ham & apple salad or ploughman's cheese platter, made with home-made wholemeal or white soda bread. Fashion has crept in too, in the shape of tortilla wraps (smoked salmon & cream cheese, for example) and pastrami & gouda on toast, with sweet beetroot. But many people just drop in for a wedge of lemon meringue pie or Austrian apple pie, or maybe a slice of carrot cake and a cup of tea - after all, that's where it all started. **Seats 35.** Children welcome. Open daily, 10.30-6. Closed 1 week Sep, Christmas, 1 week Jan. No Credit Cards. **Directions:** Opposite King Johns Castle.

Carlingford

Ghan House

COUNTRY HOUSE/RESTAURANT Carlingford Co. Louth **Tel: 042 937 3682**
Fax: 042 937 3772 Email: ghanhouse@eircom.net Web: www.ghanhouse.com

This 18th century house is attractively located in its own walled grounds on the edge of Carlingford village. It is of interest both for its accommodation and, more unusually, because the Carroll family run a cookery school on the premises. The accommodation is in four very different country rooms in the main house, each with sea or mountain views (three with well-finished en-suite bathrooms), and eight new bedrooms, which have been finished to a high standard in a separate building. In addition to the cookery school (contact Paul Carroll for the 2002 programme), Ghan House is also an increasingly popular venue for small conferences and meetings, including team development and corporate hospitality; details of services and rates available on request. Conference/banqueting (55). Garden; walking. Children welcome (under 5s free in parents' room; cots available). Pets permitted by arrangement. **Rooms 12** (all en-suite, 1 shower only, all no-smoking) B&B €60pps, ss €10. **Restaurant:** Dinner is, of course, a high priority at Ghan House – the style is contemporary, based mainly on quality local produce, notably seafood; oysters are synonymous with Carlingford (in corn and parmesan crusted oysters with smoked chilli butter, perhaps) smoked salmon and crab (the latter typically served in a salad with fennel) come from nearby Annagassan. A set dinner menu with about five choice on each course is also priced by course, allowing considerable flexibility without having a separate à la carte. Typical dishes on a summer menu might include crispy duck confit with Asian potato salad, roast hake with prawn orzo & basil cream and red goosberry cheesecake with blackcurrant cream Interesting, fairly priced wine list. Non-residents welcome (bookings advised). **Seats 54.** No smoking restaurant. D only, Fri & Sat 7-9.30; Set D from €40, gourmet menu €60 (when available); house wine €17; sc discretionary. Children welcome. Closed Sun-Thur, except for groups by arrangement. House closed 23 Dec-10 Jan. Amex, MasterCard, Visa, Laser. **Directions:** 15 minutes from main Dublin - Belfast Road N1.10 metres after 30 mph on left hand side after entering Carlingford from Dundalk direction.

Carlingford

Kingfisher Bistro

RESTAURANT Darcy MaGee Court Dundalk Road Carlingford Co. Louth
Tel: 042 937 3716

Mark and Clare Woods took over this little restaurant at the heritage centre in 1998 and it's already built up a great following. Although tiny, it packs quite a punch; it's amazing how much variety Mark manages to create a kitchen with very limited space and how well Claire manages the service. To give the gist, modern menus begin with a "something soup" and a selection of eight starters (risotto of ham and pea with basil oil & fresh parmesan and smoked fish cakes with olive tapenade & crème fraîche are typical), while a similar number of main courses offers dressed up old favourites like sirloin steak (with potato rösti, garlic & parsley butter and onion sauce) alongside ideas from further afeld like Thai spiced pork with sticky rice, curry oil, sweet soy & Asian salad. There are quite a few vegetarian dishes (including a house special). Desserts are not a particular priority (choice of four, possibly including apple strudel) but the wine list is another suprise for such a tiny place - not long by some standards, but interesting and fairly priced. Pricing generally is very reasonable and the minimum charge given on the menu is fair.

Not suitable for children. **Seats 26.** D Tue-Sun 6.30-9.30 (Sun 5.30-8.30). A la carte (minimum charge €15.17 per person). House wine €20.95. MasterCard, Visa. **Directions:** Dundalk Road, Carlingford.

Carlingford

O'Hares

PUB

Carlingford Co. Louth **Tel: 042 73106**

This renowned pub changed hands yet again in 2000 - and again, thankfully, there has been little noticeable change. It's one of those lovely places with a grocery at the front and an unspoilt hard-floored pub with an open fire at the back. Loos (always clean) are in the yard and the food is simple but good. You can have soup and sandwiches if you like, but the speciality is Carlingford oysters – with a pint of stout of course. Live music: traditional on Thursday nights, jazz on Sunday afternoons. Closed 25 Dec & Good Fri. **Directions:** In centre of village.

Carlingford

The Oystercatcher Lodge & Bistro

RESTAURANT/ACCOMODATION

Market Square Carlingford Co. Louth
Tel: 042 937 3922 Fax: 042 937 3987
Email: bmckev@eircom.net Web: www. oystercatchercarlingford.com

Brian and Denise McKevitt's popular little restaurant with rooms has been doing great business on the square in Carlingford village since summer 1998. Seafood is the main offering – Carlingford oysters, of course (several ways), crab puffs and Carlingford Lough mussels with a leek, saffron and wine sauce are all typical first courses. There are half a dozen seafood main courses to match, but carnivores do well too, with local lamb, steaks, duck and pork done in various ways. There are also some vegetarian choices and excellent range of salads and vegetables which are laid out for self-service with the main course. Not suitable for children under 7 after 8 pm. **Seats 40** (private room, 18) No smoking area D 6-10 daily (Thu-Sun only off-season) Set D €30.47. House wines €16.19; sc discretionary (except 10% on groups of 6+). Closed Mon, Tue & Wed in Oct-Mar; Christmas week. Accommodation Guest rooms are bright, spacious and very clean, with polished floors. **Rooms 8** (all shower only) B&B about €38.09 pps, ss about €19.05. Children welcome (under 3s free in parents' room; cots available, €3.81. MasterCard, Visa, Laser. **Directions:** In the Village centre.

Clogherhead

Little Strand Restaurant

RESTAURANT

Strand Street Clogherhead Co. Louth
Tel: 041 988 1061 Fax: 041 988 1062

This delightful part of the country remains largely unknown, so there is a great sense of discovery when you find somewhere for a good meal in atttractive villages like Clogherhead and Termonfeckin. Catherine Whelahan's neat new building, on the righthand side as you go down to the beach, is set back a little from the road, with steps up to the front door.The fairly large ground floor restaurant is surprisingly formally appointed for the location and, upstairs, there's an impressive lounge area, used for aperitifs and coffee at busy times. You don't have to be a fish-lover to enjoy a meal here - menus offer a range of meat and vegetarian dishes including, intriguingly, Skipper's Choice (a 12 oz sirloin steak topped with Clogherhead prawns) but local seafood, brought in to the nearby fishing harbour of Port Oriel, is of course the speciality and very good it is too. House specialities include crab claws in garlic/lemon butter, lobster thermidor and sole on the bone with lemon, lime and dill butter; an exceptional dish is Clogherhead scampi, cooked and served the traditional way with sauce tartare - and very good value at about €15.20. The restaurant has only been open since late in 1999 and has now settled down nicely - the proprietor, Catherine Whelahan, continues to work hard to get the details right. **Seats 60** (Private room 12-16). No-smoking area; air conditioning. D Wed-Sun, 7-"late" (Sun from 5); à la carte; also autumn & spring special menus, about €19; house wine about €15, sc discretionary. Closed Mon, Tue, bank hols. MasterCard, Visa. **Directions:** 7 miles from Drogheda, 3 miles from Termonfeckin village.

Collon

Forge Gallery Restaurant

RESTAURANT

Guesthouse Church St Collon Co. Louth **Tel: 041 982 6272**
Fax: 041 982 6584 Email: forgegallery@eircom.net

For the best part of fifteen years this charming two-storey restaurant has been providing consistently excellent food, hospitality and service. It has earned a great reputation and a devoted following along the way. It's a most attractive place – the building itself is unusual and has been furnished and decorated with flair, providing a fine setting for food that never disappoints. Weekly menus combine country French and New Irish styles, with a few other influences along the way – notably Thai. Everything is based on the best possible seasonal produce, much of it local – seafood, game in season, vegetables, fruit – and great home-made breads - white yeast bread, scones or brown bread with thyme perhaps. Typical main courses include a special vegetarian dish such as pillows of filo with leeks and roquefort as well as local meat, such as rack of tender Cooley lamb, and seafood such as the 'Forge Rendezvous' of prawns and scallops in chablis & cream. *Accommodation is planned for 2002 - contact the restaurant for details. **Seats 60.** No smoking area; air conditioning. D only Tue-Sat, 7-10. Set D from €38.09; à l carte also available. House wine from €19.05; sc discretionary). Closed Sun & Mon; 23-26 Dec & 7-21 Amex, Diners, MasterCard, Visa, Laser. **Directions:** On N2, 35 miles from Dublin due north, midway between Slane and Ardee, in centre of village.

Drogheda

PUB

Black Bull Inn

Dublin Road Drogheda Co. Louth
Tel: 041 983 7139 Fax: 041 9836854

This attractive roadside pub is on the left of the hill, just as you leave Drogheda in the Dublin direction. It has built up a reputation for food over the years and has an interesting shop/delicatessen next door. Not suitable for children after 7pm. Food available all day. Closed 25 Dec & Good Fri. Amex, MasterCard, Diners, Visa, Laser. **Directions:** On N1, on southern edge of town.

Drogheda

HOTEL

Boyne Valley Hotel & Country Club

Drogheda Co. Louth **Tel: 041 983 7737**
Email: reservations@boynevalleyhotel.ie Web: www.boynevalleyhotel.ie

At the heart of this substantial hotel, set in large gardens just on the Dublin side of Drogheda town, lies an 18th century mansion. It is not as obvious as it used to be since developments created a completely new entrance, but it is still there and provides some unspoilt, graciously proportioned rooms that contrast well with the later additions. Owner-run by Michael and Rosemary McNamara since 1992, it has the personal touch unique to hands-on personal management and is popular with locals, for business and pleasure, as well as a base for visitors touring the historic sites of the area. While rooms in the old building have more character, the new ones are finished to a high standard. A new conference room and excellent leisure centre add greatly to the hotel's facilities. Conference/banqueting (400/300); secretarial services. Leisure centre, indoor swimming pool. All weather tennis; pitch & putt; garden. Pets allowed in some areas. **Rooms 38** (10 shower only, 9 no-smoking). B&B €76.50 pps, ss €30.47. Open all year. Amex, Diners, MasterCard, Visa, Laser. **Directions:** On southern edge of Drogheda town, on N1.

Dundalk

HOTEL

Ballymascanlon House

Dundalk Co. Louth **Tel: 042 9371124**
Fax: 042 9371598 Email: info@ballymascanlon.com

Set in 130 acres of parkland, this hotel just north of Dundalk has developed around a large Victorian house. Although it has been in the same family ownership since 1948, major improvements have been made over the last few of years. This has been done with great style, and lifted the hotel into a completely different class. Corporate facilities include three versatile meeting rooms and there are back-up business services available. The new leisure facilities, which include a 20 metre deck level pool and tennis courts, are impressive. Conference/banqueting (250/250); secretarial services. Leisure centre. tennis, golf (18), garden, walking. Children welcome (under 2s free in parents' room; cots available). **Rooms 74** (3 suites, 2 mini-suites, 54 executive rooms, 1 for disabled) B&B about €70pps. Wheelchair accessible. Lift. Closed 24-27 Dec. Amex, Diners, MasterCard, Visa. **Directions:** N1 from Dublin, 3 miles north of Dundalk.

Dundalk

PUB/RESTAURANT

Fitzpatrick's Bar & Restaurant

Jenkinstown Rockmarshal Dundalk Co. Louth
Tel: 042 937 6193 Fax: 042 937 6193

Flowers and a neat frontage with fresh paintwork will draw attention to this attractive and well-run establishment. It has plenty of parking and is well organised for the informal but comfortable consumption of food in a series of bar/dining rooms, all with character and much of local interest in pictures and artefacts. Prompt reception, friendly service and unpretentious home-cooked food at resonable prices all add up to an appealing package and its obvious popularity with locals is well deserved. **Seats 70** (private room 40). Smoking unrestricted; air conditioning. Recent extensions include a new public bar, to be open for the 2002 season, and it is hoped 10 bedrooms will come on stream in 2002. Open Tue-Sun 12 noon -10pm, L from 12.30, D 6-10. A la carte menus. Closed Mon, Good Fri, 25 Dec. MasterCard, Visa. **Directions:** Just north of Dundalk town, take Carlingford road off main Dublin-Belfast road.

Dundalk

RESTAURANT féile bia

Quaglino's

88 Clanbrassil Street Dundalk Co. Louth
Tel: 042 933 8567 Fax: 042 932 8598

Quaglino's is a long-established and highly regarded restaurant in Dundalk. Here owner-chef Pat Kerley takes great pride in the active promotion of Irish cuisine and uses as much local produce as possible. The restaurant is run on traditional lines, with good service a priority. As in most Louth restaurants, generosity is the keynote. Children welcome. **Seats 60.** No smoking area; air conditioning. D Mon-Sat, 6.30-11. Set D about €24-32, à la carte available; sc discretionary. Closed Sun. Amex, Diners, MasterCard, Visa. **Directions:** Town centre, upstairs restaurant.

Termonfeckin

RESTAURANT

Triple House Restaurant

Termonfeckin Drogheda Co. Louth
Tel: 041 982 2616 Fax: 041 982 2616

The pretty village of Termonfeckin provides a fine setting for Pat Fox's popular restaurant, which is in a 200-year-old converted farmhouse in landscaped gardens surrounded by mature trees. The decor may feel distinctly dated now, but that's quickly forgotten in front of a log fire in the reception area on cold evenings (an alternative to the conservatory used for aperitifs in summer) when pondering the menu over a glass of wine. Committed to using the best of local produce, Pat offers wide-ranging menus and daily blackboard seafood extras from nearby Clogherhead – fresh Clogherhead prawns, Annagassan crab, and a dish he entitles, intriguingly, Port Oriel Pot-Pourri. But locally-reared meats feature too, in rack of local lamb with a herb crust, for example. Specialities include lovely spinach-filled crêpes and, for dessert, a dacquoise that varies with the season's fruits. Plated farmhouse cheeses typically include Cashel Blue, Cooleeney and Wexford Cheddar. The wine list reflects Pat's particular interests and special evenings are sometimes held for enthusiasts off-season. Children welcome. **Seats 40.** No smoking area. D Tue-Sat 6.30-9.30, L Sun only 1-6.30; Set D about €25, à la carte available; early D about €18, 6.30-7.30 only; Set L about €18. House wine bout €17; sc discretionary.T oilets wheelchair accessible. Closed Mon Sep-May, 26-28 Dec. MasterCard, Visa. **Directions:** 5 miles north east of Drogheda.

COUNTY MAYO

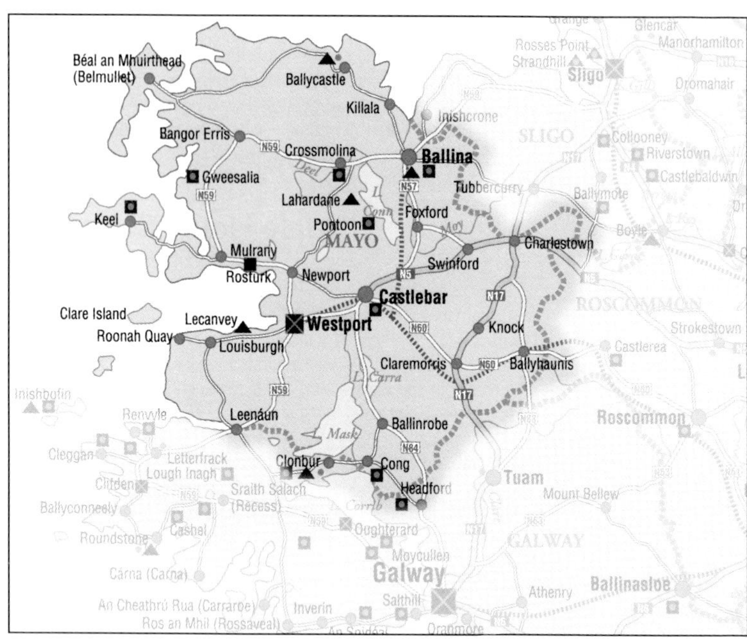

Mayo is the happening county in 2002. Its prettiest township, Westport on Clew Bay, is the current national holder of Ireland's cherished Tidiest Town award. And at Turlough, five kilometres east of the county town of Castlebar, an exciting new museum development will have its first complete year in 2002. This is the Museum of Country Life at Turlough Park House, the first fully-fledged department of the National Museum to be located anywhere outside Dublin. Officially opened in September 2001, it celebrates Irish country life as it was lived between 1850 and 1960 with a remarkable display of artefacts which were in regular everyday use, yet now seem almost exotic.

It is a vibrant and extraordinary display which makes full use of the most modern museum techniques, housed in an attractive setting with all facilities for visitors. The very fact of its existence tells us much about the spirit of Mayo, for it was back in 1991, before the years of economic growth, that Mayo County Council bought the Victorian mansion of Turlough House at the suggestion of County Manager Des Mahon, who felt it would lend itself to a development of national importance if the powers that be could be persuaded. Ten years down the line, his dream came true, and Mayo now has a focal point of international historic interest.

Which is only as it should be, for Mayo is magnificent. All Ireland's counties have their devotees, but enthusiasts for Mayo have a devotion which is pure passion. In their heart of hearts, they feel that this austerely majestic Atlantic-battered territory is somehow more truly Irish than anywhere else. And who could argue with them after experiencing the glories of scenery, sea and sky which this western rampart of Ireland puts on ever-changing display?

Yet among Mayo's many splendid mountain ranges we find substantial pockets of fertile land, through which there tumble fish-filled streams and rivers. And in the west of the county, the rolling hills of the drumlin country, which run in a virtually continuous band right across Ireland from Strangford Lough, meet the sea again in the island studded wonder of Clew Bay. At its head the delightful town of Westport is a cosmopolitan jewel of civilisation set in dramatic country with the holy mountain of Croagh Patrick (762 m) soaring above the bay.

Along Mayo's rugged north coast, turf cutting at Ceide Fields near Ballycastle has revealed the oldest intact field and farm system in existence, preserved through being covered in blanket bog 5,000 years ago. An award-winning interpretive centre has been created at the site, and even the most jaded visitor will find fascination and inspiration in the clear view which it provides into Ireland's distant past.

As a contemporary contrast, only a few miles to the southeast the lively town of Ballina is where the salmon-rich River Moy meets the sea in the broad sweep of Killala Bay. It takes a leap of the imagination to appreciate that the sheltered Moy Valley is in the same county as the spectacularly rugged cliffs of Achill Island. But leaps of the imagination is what Mayo inspires.

Local Attractions and Information

Ballina Street Festival/Arts Week (July)	096 70905
Ballina Tourism Information	096 70848
Castlebar Linenhall Arts Centre	094 23733
Castlebar Tourism Information	094 21207
Castlebar Turlough House (see entry under Turlough)	094 31589
Ceide Fields Interpretive Centre	096 43325
Clare Island Ferries	098 27685
Crossmolina, Enniscoe House Restored Gardens & Agricultural Museum	096 31112
Foxford Woollen Mills Visitor Centre	094 56756
Inishkea Island Tours Belmullet	097 85741
Inishturk Island Ferries	098 45520 / 45541
Killasser (Swinford) Traditional Farm Heritage Centre	094 52505
Kiltimagh Glore Mill Follain Arts Centre	094 82184
Knock Interational Airport	094 67222
Mayo North Family History Research Centre	096 31809
Moy Valley Holidays	096 70905
Turlough Turlough Park House. Museum of Country Life. Open Tuesday to Saturday 10am to 5pm, Sundays 2pm to 5pm, closed Mondays	094 31589
Westport Westport House & Children's Zoo	098 25430/27766
Westport Tourism Information	098 25711

Achill Island

The Beehive

CAFÉ/RESTAURANT

Keel Achill Island Co.Mayo
Tel: 098 43134/43018 Fax: 098 43018

At their informal restaurant and attractive craft shop in Keel, husband and wife team Patricia and Michael Joyce take pride in the careful preparation and presentation of the best of Achill produce, especially local seafood such as fresh and smoked salmon, mussels, oysters and crab. Since opening in 1991, they have extended both the menu and the premises and now offer all-day self-service food, which you can have indoors or take out to a patio overlooking Keel beach in fine weather Everything is homemade, and they specialise in soups such as cheddar & onion, courgette & onion, leek & mussel, seafood chowder and traditional nettle soup (brotchán neantóg) all served with homemade brown scones. Baking is a speciality, so there's always a tempting selection of cakes, bracks, teabreads, fruit tarts, baked desserts and scones with home-made preserves or you can simply have a toasted sandwich, or an Irish farmhouse cheese plate (with a glass of wine perhaps). Further improvements due for 2002 include the addition of a wheelchair toilet and a new seating area. * The family also has accommodation on the island; details from the restaurant. **Seats 60** (private room, 20) No smoking area. Children welcome. Meals, 10-6 daily, Easter-early Nov; à la carte; wine licence, house wine €12.70 (1/4 bottle list, all €3.75). Amex, MasterCard, Visa, Laser. **Directions:** Situated in the centre of Keel overlooking beach and Minuan cliffs.

Achill Island

The Boley House Restaurant

RESTAURANT

Keel Achill Island Co. Mayo **Tel: 098 43147** Fax: 098 43427

Noreen McNamara Cooney has run this picturesque, immaculately maintained cottage restaurant for 30 years and there is no sign of its popularity diminishing. Local seafood is of course the star - and this, together with the unique atmosphere, is what keeps bringing people back. Children welcome. **Seats 60.** No smoking restaurant. D only, 6.30-9.15 daily; Set D about €26; à la carte also available; house wine about €17; sc discretionary. Toilets wheelchair accessible. Open all year. MasterCard, Visa. **Directions:** 10 miles from Achill Sound.

Achill Island
GUESTHOUSE

Gray's Guest House

Dugort Achill Island Co. Mayo
Tel: 098 43244 Fax: 098 43315

Vi McDowell has been running this legendary guesthouse in the attractive village of Dugort since 1979, and nobody understands better the qualities of peace, quiet and gentle hospitality that have been bringing guests here for the last hundred years. It is an unusual establishment, occupying a series of houses, and each area has a slightly different appeal. There's a large, traditionally furnished sitting room with an open fire and several conservatories for quiet reading. Bedrooms and bathrooms vary considerably due to the age and nature of the premises, but the emphasis is on old-fashioned comfort; they all have tea & coffee-making trays and there are extra shared bathrooms in addition to en-suite facilities. Children are welcome and there's an indoor playroom and safe outdoor play area plus pool and table tennis for older children. Dogs are allowed by arrangement. It's a nice place to drop into for coffee, light lunch or afternoon tea (which is served in the garden in fine weather) and the dining room is open to non-residents for evening meals by arrangement (7pm). Packed lunches supplied. Pets permitted by arrangement. Children welcome before 8pm; (under 3s free in parents' room). Garden, walking, pool table. **Rooms 15** (all en-suite). B&B €40pps, ss €6. Set D €26, house wine €12.70. Closed 25 Dec. Personal cheques accepted. **Directions:** Castlebar/Westport, Newport, Achill Sound, Dugort.

Ballina
PUB

Gaughans

O'Rahilly Street Ballina Co. Mayo **Tel: 096 70096**
Email: gaughan@indigo.ie Web: www.gaughans.hypermart.net

This is one of the great old pubs of Ireland and has a gentle way of drawing you in, with the menu up in the window and a display of local pottery to arouse the curiosity. Michael Gaughan opened the pub in November 1936 and his son, Edward, took over in 1972. Edward's wife Mary is a great cook and, once they started doing food in 1983 they never looked back. Everybody loves the way they run the place and Mary still does all the cooking. Her specialities (all good home cooking) include chicken fillet in cream sauce, cod in breadcrumbs & mushrooms, smoked haddock vol-au-vent meat loaf, shepherd's pie and good old-fashioned roasts - lamb, pork, chicken, turkey and beef are all regulars. There's always a daily special (€6.67) and old favourites like lemon meringue pie and pineapple upside down pudding for dessert. There are lighter options on the menu too, like open smoked salmon or crab sandwich, quiche lorraine with salad, ploughman's lunch. Great wholesome fare. And, charmingly listed along with the Bewley's tea and coffee, the wine and Irish coffee "Glass of spring water: Free." Now that's style. Pets permitted. Children welcome. Bo smoking area. Bar food served Mon-Sat, 11am-6pm. Closed 25 Dec & Good Fri. MasterCard, Visa, Laser. **Directions:** Ballina town centre near the post office.

Bangor Erris
HOTEL/PUB/RESTAURANT

Teach Iorrais Hotel

Geesala Bangor Erris Co Mayo **Tel: 097 86888**
Fax: 097 86855 Email: teachior@iol.ie Web: www.teachiorrais.com

This new hotel in the Gaeltacht has brought much needed facilities to this remote and fascinating area. It's a great place to drop into during the day for a bite to eat or just a cup of tea - there's always a welcoming fire in the bar (which has character, although the hotel is modern) and staff are very friendly. Bedrooms are comfortably furnished, with neat en-suite bathrooms, direct dial phone, tea/coffee facilities and television with video channel. Off-season breaks offer especially good value and there are many activites nearby, including golf, horse riding, walking, boating and fishing (there's a drying room for tackle and bait). Teach Iorrais is a popular place for weddings and would also be an interesting choice for conferences and corporate events. Conference/banqueting (400/325); secretarial services. No pets. Children welcome (under 10s free in parents' room; cots available). Garden. **Rooms 31** (all en-suite,1 suite, 10 no-smoking, 1 for disabled). B&B €60.95 pps, ss €12.70. Bar food 1-5pm daily. Open all year. MasterCard. **Directions:** At Bangor Ellis take first left approx 8 miles.

Ballycastle
RESTAURANT

Mary's Bakery & Tea Rooms

Main Street Ballycastle Co. Mayo **Tel: 096 43361**

Mary Munnelly's homely little restaurant is the perfect place to stop for some good home cooking. Baking is the speciality but she does "real meals" as well - home-made soups like mushroom or smoked bacon & potato, wild salmon various ways and free range chicken dishes. And, if you strike a chilly day, it's very pleasant to get tucked in beside a real fire too. **Seats 30.** No smoking area. Toilets wheelchair accessible. Open 10am-late in summer (shorter hours off season); Closed Sun

Oct-Easter & first 3 weeks Jan. No Credit Cards. **Directions:** From Ballina - Killala - main road to Ballycastle, on way to Ceide Fields.

Ballycastle

Polke's

PUB

Main Street Ballycastle Co. Mayo **Tel: 096 43016**

This lovely old general merchants and traditional pub is just across the road from Mary's Bakery and well worth a visit. The long, narrow bar behind the shop is completely unspoilt, friendly and a joy to find yourself in. The whole place is immaculate too (including the outside loo in a whitewashed yard at the back), giving the lie to the widely-held view that "character" pubs are, by definition, scruffy. Closed 25 Dec & Good Fri.

Castlebar

Breaffy House Hotel

HOTEL

Breaffy Rd Castlebar Co. Mayo **Tel: 094 22033** Fax: 094 22276
Email: cro@lynchhotels.com Web: www.lynchhotels.com

This handsome hotel set in its own grounds just outside Castlebar town dates back to 1890 and retains some of the original country house atmosphere. It has undergone major renovation and refurbishments over the last few years and, since a change of ownership in 2000, the restaurant and some of the bedrooms have been refurbished. Sixty new bedrooms and a leisure complex (with swimming pool) are due to open during 2002. Conference/banqueting (500); business centre; secretarial services; video conferencing on request. Preferential local golf rates. Garden. Off season value breaks. Children welcome (cots available without charge). **Rooms 60** (2 junior suites). Lift. B&B €82.53pps, ss €25.39. (Room only rate also available: €75, max 3 guests). No s.c. Closed 24-26 Dec. Amex, Diners, MasterCard, Visa. **Directions:** Approx. 4 km outside Castlebar on Claremorris Road (N60).

Cong

Ashford Castle

HOTEL
RESTAURANT ☆

Cong Co. Mayo **Tel: 092 46003** Fax: 092 46260
Email: ashford@ashford.ie Web: www.ashford.ie

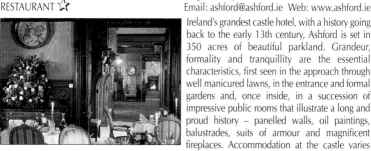

Ireland's grandest castle hotel, with a history going back to the early 13th century, Ashford is set in 350 acres of beautiful parkland. Grandeur, formality and tranquillity are the essential characteristics, first seen in the approach through well manicured lawns, in the entrance and formal gardens and, once inside, in a succession of impressive public rooms that illustrate a long and proud history – panelled walls, oil paintings, balustrades, suits of armour and magnificent fireplaces. Accommodation at the castle varies considerably due to the size and age of the building, and each room in some way reflects the special qualities of this unique hotel. The best bedrooms and the luxurious suites at the top of the castle - many with magnificent views of Lough Corrib, the River Cong and wooded parkland - are elegantly furnished with period furniture, some with enormous and beautifully appointed bathrooms, others with remarkable architectural features, such as a panelled wooden ceiling recently discovered behind plasterwork in one of the suites (and now fully restored). A bijou fitness centre has computerised exercise equipment; steam room; sauna and whirlpool, all strikingly designed in neo-classical style. A specialist team backs up impressive conference facilities. The hotel's general manager, Rory Murphy, brings his own natural and easy charm to the job of making guests from all over the world feel comfortable and relaxed in what might seem rather awesome surroundings, while at the same time managing to ensure that the appropriate standards are continually maintained at this great hotel; in recognition he was presented with the Guide's International Hospitality Award for 2001. The hotel's exceptional amenities and sports facilities are detailed in a very handy little pocket book; in it you'll find everything you need to know about the equestrian centre, falconry, hunting, clay target shooting, archery, cycling, pony & trap tours, golf (resident instructor & equipment hire), tennis, lake & river fishing, lake cruising, jogging, guided walking & cycling tours on the estate - and a guide to scenic routes and attractions in Mayo and Galway - this little book is a gem. Conference/banqueting (110/75); business centre; secretarial services; video conferencing on request. Fitness centre. Equestrian centre, falconry, tennis, golf (9), fishing, cycling, walking, snooker. No pets. **Rooms 83** (4 suites, 2 junior suites, 5 executive). Lift. 24 hour room service. Room rate: €394 (max 2 guests); s.c.15%. **The Connaught Room** This small room is the jewel in Ashford Castle's culinary crown and one of Ireland's most impressive restaurants. Denis Lenihan, who has been Executive Chef at the castle since 1975, oversees the cooking for both this and the George V Dining Room. The style is classical French using the best of local ingredients – Atlantic prawns, Galway Bay sole, Cleggan lobster, Connemara lamb – in sophisticated dishes that will please the most discerning diner. Irish farmhouse cheeses and warm soufflés are among the tempting endings for luxurious meals, which are greatly enhanced by meticulous attention to detail. Service is discreet and extremely professional. An extensive wine list includes a special selection of Wines of the Month, of varying styles and from several regions, at friendly prices. **Seats 25** D only, 7-9.15 (usually residents only). **George V Dining Room** Lunch and dinner are served in this much larger but almost equally opulent dining room, and an all-day snack menu is also available. A five-course dinner menu is offered and although the standard of cooking and service equals that of The Connaught Room, there is a more down to earth tone about the menus, which are in English, with a choice of about eight on the first and middle courses.Local smoked salmon cared at your table and tails of Cleggan lobster in a rich Newburg sauce with spaghetti of vegetables are typical of menus that major in seafood but have plenty of other options to choose from. A separate vegetarian menu has less choice but is more modern and includes some tempting suggestions. If at least two people (preferably a whole party) are agreed, a 7-course Menu Surprise tasting menu is available - and after dinner you will be presented with a souvenir copy of the Menu Surprise: a wonderful way to commemorate a special occasion. Lunch offers a shortened and somewhat simplified version of the dinner menu, but the same high standards apply. **Seats 150.** No smoking restaurant. L 1-2.15, D 7-9.15. Set L €36, Set D €56. A la carte D also available; house wine €25. s.c.15%. Amex, Diners, MasterCard, Visa. **Directions:** 1/2 hour drive from Galway City (on R345).

Crossmolina

Enniscoe House

COUNTRY HOUSE

Castle Hill Nr Crossmolina Ballina Co. Mayo **Tel: 096 31112**
Fax: 096 31773 Email: mail@enniscoe.com Web: www.enniscoe.com

In parkland and mature woods on the shores of Lough Conn, Enniscoe is stern and gaunt, as Georgian mansions in the north-west of Ireland tend to be, but any intimidating impressions of "the last great house of North Mayo" are quickly dispelled once inside this fascinating old place. Built by ancestors of the present owner, Susan Kellett, (they settled here in the 1660s), Enniscoe attracts anglers and visitors with a natural empathy for the untamed wildness of this little known area - the house has great charm and makes a lovely place to come back to after a day in the rugged countryside. Family portraits, antique furniture and crackling log fires all complement Susan's warm hospitality and deliciously simple, wholesome dinners, which non-residents are welcome to share by reservation. It is the activities at the back of the house that have attracted special interest lately however: in the old farm buildings, the local Historical Society operates a genealogy centre, The Mayo North Family History Research Centre (096 31809) that researches names and families of Mayo origin. Alongside there's a small but growing agricultural museum that houses a display of old farm machinery, and there's a small conference centre in the courtyard along with three delightful self-catering units. Perhaps the most exciting developments are in the gardens and woodlands, however; a network of paths has made much of the beautiful woodland area around the house more accessible to guests and major renovations have recently taken place in the walled gardens, which are now open to the public and have tearooms. Another garden produces organically grown vegetables, herbs and fruit for the house. There is brown trout fishing on Logh Conn and other trout and salmon fishing nearby; boats, ghilllies, tuition and hire of equipment can be arranged. Children are welcome and dogs are also allowed by arrangement. Closed 14 Oct-1 Apr. Amex, MasterCard, Visa. Small conference (30); P €35.55, 8pm - non residents welcome by reservation; house wines €12.70. **Rooms 6** (2 no-smoking). B&B €76.18pps, ss €12.70. **Directions:** 2 miles south of Crossmolina on R315. Amex, MasterCard, Visa. **Directions:** 2 miles south of Crossmolina on R315.

Foxford

Healy's Hotel

HOTEL

Pontoon Foxford Co. Mayo
Tel: 094 56443 Fax: 094 56572
Email: healyspontoon@eircom.net Web: www.irelandmayohotel.com

This famous old hotel, loved by fisherfolk, landscape artists and many others who seek peace and tranquillity, changed hands in 1998, and there has since been considerable renovation and refurbishment, without spoiling the old-fashioned qualities that have earned this hotel its special reputation: just a good bit of painting and decorating, some overdue refurbishment in the bar and a general tidy up around the front. At the back, overgrowth has been cleared to re-establish old gardens (500 new roses have been planted), and also develop a beer garden. Accommodation is modest but comfortable - and also very moderately priced. There's a great feeling of people happy in what they're doing around here (notably the fisherfolk); it's all very relaxed and the hotel has lots of information on things to do in the area - including golf at around a dozen courses within an hour's drive. Small banqueting facilities (60); garden, fishing. Packed lunches available. Children welcome (under 3s free in parents' room; cots available). Pets permitted by arrangement. The restaurant is open for dinner every evening and lunch on Sunday. **Rooms 14** (all shower only). B&B €39pps, ss €11.* Bar food 12.30-9.30 daily. Closed 25 Dec. Amex, Diners, MasterCard, Visa, Laser. **Directions:** From Dublin take the N4 to Longford, swithching to the N5. 3 miles from Foxord.

Lahardane

Leonard's

PUB

Lahardane Ballina Co. Mayo **Tel: 096 51003**

This unspoilt roadside traditional pub & grocery shop was established in 1897 and the original owners would be proud of it today. If you get hungry, there's the makings of a picnic on the shelves. Closed 25 Dec & Good Fri.

Lecanvey

T. Staunton

PUB

Lecanvey Westport Co. Mayo **Tel: 098 64850/64891**

Therese Staunton runs this great little pub near the beginning of the ascent to Croagh Patrick - genuinely traditional, with an open fire it has the feeling of a real 'local'. Not really a food place, but home-made soup and sandwiches or plated salads are available every day until 9pm. Occasional traditional music sessions - and frequent impromptu sing-songs. Closed 25 Dec & Good Fri. No Credit Cards. **Directions:** 8 miles from Westport on Louisburgh Road.

Mulrany

Rosturk Woods

ACCOMMODATION

Mulrany Co. Mayo
Tel: 098 36264 Fax: 098 36264
Email: stoney@iol.ie Web: www.rosturk-woods.com

Beautifully located in secluded mature woodland, with direct access to the sandy seashore of Clew Bay, Louisa and Alan Stoney's delightful family home is between Westport and Achill Island, with fishing, swimming, sailing, walking, riding and golf all nearby. It is a lovely, informal house; the three guest bedrooms are all en-suite and very comfortably furnished. Louisa Stoney enjoys cooking for guests, but please book dinner 24 hours in advance. There is also self-catering accommodation available. Garden. Pets allowed by arrangement. **Rooms 3** (all en-suite & no-smoking). B&B €45pps, ss €15.75. Residents' D €32, 7-8pm (24 hours notice). Closed Christmas. No Credit Cards. **Directions:** 7 miles from Newport on Mulrany Achill Island Road.

Newport

Newport House

COUNTRY HOUSE
RESTAURANT

Newport Co. Mayo
Tel: 098 41222 Fax: 098 41613

To its many visitors, a stay at Newport House symbolises all that is best about the Irish country house, which was the Guide's Country House of the Year in 1999. Currently in the caring hands of Kieran and Thelma Thompson, Newport has been especially close to the hearts of fishing people for many years, but the comfort and warm hospitality of this wonderful house is accessible to all its guests – not least in shared enjoyment of the club-fender cosiness of the little back bar. The house has a beautiful central hall, sweeping staircase and gracious drawing room, while bedrooms, like the rest of the house, are furnished in style with antiques and fine paintings. The day's catch is weighed and displayed in the hall and the cosy fisherman's bar provides the perfect venue for a reconstruction of the day's sport. **Restaurant:** John Gavin, who has been head chef since 1983, presents interesting five course menus. Not surprisingly, perhaps, fresh fish is a speciality – not only freshwater fish caught on local lakes and rivers, but also a wide variety of sea fish from nearby Achill. An outstanding wine list includes a great collection of classic French wines – 170 clarets from 1961-1990 vintages, a great collection of white and red burgundies, excellent Rhones – and a good New World collection too. Fishing, garden, walking, snooker. Children welcome (under 2s free in parents' room; cots available). Wheelchair accessible. Pets allowed in some areas. **Rooms 18** (2 shower only, 2 private, 16 en-suite) B&B about €110, ss about €23, no s.c. Restaurant **Seats 38.** No smoking restaurant; air conditioning. D daily 7-9.30; Set D €43; house wine about €17. Toilets wheelchair accessible Non-residents welcome by reservation. **Directions:** In town of Newport.

Westport
HOTEL

Atlantic Coast Hotel

The Quay Westport Co. Mayo **Tel: 098 29000** Fax: 098 29111
Email: achotel@iol.ie Web: www.atlanticcoasthotel.com

Behind the traditional stone façade of an old mill on Westport harbour, this bright and interesting modern hotel has many pleasant surprises in store. Spacious public areas are designed and furnished in a very pleasing combination of traditional and contemporary themes and materials and the tone is continued through to bedrooms, which are spacious, with stylish Italian bathrooms; direct dial phone, hairdryers, satellite TV, tea/coffee tray and trouser press are standard in all rooms; fax/modem ports available on request. The Blue Wave restaurant is situated right up at the top of the building - a good idea, although the view is somewhat restricted by sloping roof windows and the room can become very hot in summer. Conferences/banqueting (160/145). Children welcome (under 4s free in parents' room, cots available without charge). Leisure centre, swimming pool; fishing; discount at local golf club. **Rooms 85** (3 suites, 2 for disabled). Lift. B&B 76.20pps, ss €19.05; s.c.12.5%. Closed 24-26 Dec. **Directions:** Located at Westport harbour, 1 mile from town centre on main Louisburgh and coast road.

Westport
RESTAURANT

The Creel

The Harbour Westport Co. Mayo
Tel: 098 26174 Email: bennett@gofree.indigo.ie

Frank and Julie Bennett opened this attractive daytime restaurant on the harbourfront in the summer of 2000 and it has gone down a treat. It's a pleasant, cottagey place with pine furniture and warm tones in the terracotta tiled floor, nautical bric-a-brac and traditional baskets used for display. There's some comfortable seating too, and magazines lying around - the idea is to make it a homely place where people can lounge about and relax awhile. An imaginative blackboard menu offers a range of hot dishes and snacks, all under €10 - typically hot meals like beef & mushroom pie with red wine (served with potatoes and vegetables) and chef's chicken & coconut korma (served with basmati rice), lighter dishes such as smoked salmon tart with salad and light bites like toasted paninis (with goats cheese & tomato relish for example). Home-made desserts are temptingly displayed at the counter (where you'll also find well-priced wines alongside the juices and mineral waters). Tasty, lively food well-cooked, pleasant service and surroundings - and good value - make this the pefect place for a daytime meal. **Seats 50.** Open daily, 11-6 (Sat to 7, Sun to 5). Closed Mon & Tues off-season (Sep-Mar) and 2 weeks in winter. MasterCard, Visa.

Westport
HOTEL féile bia

Hotel Westport

The Demesne Newport Rd Westport Co. Mayo **Tel: 098 25122**
Fax: 098 26739 Email: sales@hotelwestport.ie Web: www.hotelwestport.ie

Just a short stroll from Westport town centre this large modern hotel is set in its own grounds and offers excellent facilities for both leisure and business guests. It makes a good base for a holiday in this lovely area and numerous short breaks are offered, including family breaks at times when special children's entertainment is available (June-August). The conference and business centre provide a fine venue for corporate events of all kinds, including incentive breaks, and the hotel and surrounding area provide all the activities and amenities necessary for off-duty delegates. Bedrooms, which include some with four-poster beds, are well-appointed, with phone/ISDN lines, TV/video, tea/coffee facilities and trouser press. The whole hotel is unsually wheelchair-friendly, without steps or obstacles. Conference/banqueting (500/350); video conferencing; business centre; secretarial services. Leisure centre, swimming pool. Garden. Children welcome (under 3s free in parents' room; cots available without charge.) **Rooms 129** (6 suites, 7 wheelchair friendly rooms) Wheelchair accessible. Lift. B&B €102 pps, ss €19, sc discretionary. Open all year. Amex, Diners, MasterCard, Visa, Laser. **Directions:** On Castlebar road, turn right onto north mall, then turn onto Newport Road, 1st left and at the end of the road.

Westport
HOTEL

Knockranny House Hotel

Westport Co Mayo **Tel: 098 28600**
Fax: 098 28611 Email: info@khh.ie Web: www.khh.ie

Set in landscaped grounds on an elevated site overlooking the town, this purpose-built hotel opened in 1997 and still looks a little raw. However, once inside the door, the spacious foyer, friendly staff and the sight of a welcoming fire create an agreeably contrasting warm atmosphere. The foyer sets the tone for a hotel which has been built on a generous scale and is full of contrasts, with spacious public areas balanced by smaller ones - notably the library and drawing room - where guests can relax in more homely surroundings. Bedrooms are also large - the suites have four poster beds and sunken seating areas with views and all rooms are very comfortable with high quality furnishings, television, tea/coffee-making facilities and trouser press; some have jacuzzi baths and phones with ISDN. The hotel dining room, La Fougère Restaurant ("the fern") is at the front of the hotel, with views across the town. Guests have use of a nearby leisure centre. **Rooms 57** (3 suites, 9 superior, 3 shower only, 4 no smoking, 2 for disabled.) B&B €115, ss €60. Closed 24-27 Dec. Amex, MasterCard, Visa, Laser. **Directions:** Take N5/N60 from Castlebar. Hotel is on the left before entering Westport.

Westport

The Lemon Peel

RESTAURANT

The Octagon Westport Co Mayo **Tel: 098 26929** Fax: 098 26965
Email: robbie@lemonpeel.ie Web: www.lemonpeel.ie

Proprietor-chef Robbie McMenamin's simply-furnished little restaurant just off The Octagon has been a favourite with locals and visitors alike ever since it opened in 1998 - and, despite the arrival of more restaurants in the area, it remains the most popular restaurant in town. The atmosphere is buzzy and friendly and the food interesting. Robbie sources ingredients with care and his cooking is creative and accurate. Starters like honey baked goat's cheese with black olive tapenade and crab duglère (a house special topped with light cheddar), typically followed by cajun crusted salmon with fruit salsa, lemon & basil cream or a more traditional dish of lamb fillet roasted with rosemary & garlic and served with wholegrain mustard sauce keep tempting people back for more. Specials change on a weekly basis and everything comes with a choice of mashed potatoes - plain, basil, champ, garlic, or olive olive - in addition to the vegetables of the day. Lovely homely puddings like rhubarb & apple crumble and gorgeous chocolate mousse and freshly brewed coffee to finish. Good food, good service - good place. Not suitable for children under 12. **Seats 32.** No smoking area; air conditioning. D only 6-9.30 (Sun 6-9). Early menu €19 (6-7 only), Also à la carte. House wine €15; sc discretionary. Closed Mon & Feb. (Telephone off season to check opening times.) MasterCard, Visa, Laser. **Directions:** Westport Town Centre.

Westport

Matt Molloy's Bar

PUB

Bridge Street Westport Co. Mayo **Tel: 098 26655**

If you had to pick one pub in this pretty town, this soothingly dark atmospheric one would do very nicely – not least because it is owned by Matt Molloy of The Chieftains, a man who clearly has respect for the real pub: no TV (and no children after 9 pm). Musical memorabilia add to the interest, but there's also the real thing as traditional music is a major feature in the back room or out at the back in fine weather. It's worth noting that normal pub hours don't apply – this is an afternoon into evening place, not somewhere for morning coffee. Closed 25 Dec & Good Fri. No Credit Cards.

Westport

The Olde Railway Hotel

HOTEL

The Mall Westport Co. Mayo **Tel: 098 25166**
Fax: 098 25090 Email: railway@anu.ie Web: www.anu.ie/railwayhotel

Once described by William Thackeray as 'one of the prettiest, comfortablest hotels in Ireland', The Olde Railway Hotel was built in 1780 as a coaching inn for guests of Lord Sligo. Attractively situated along the tree-lined Carrowbeg River, on the Mall in the centre of Westport, it remains a hotel of character, well known for its antique furniture and a slightly eccentric atmosphere. Warm, friendly reception and a complimentary cup of tea on arrival (and at any other time during your stay) immediately makes guests feel welcome - and certain concessions have been made to the demands of modern travellers, including en-suite bathrooms, satellite television and private car parking. There's a conservatory dining room quietly situated at the back of the hotel and several very spacious ground floor rooms with en-suite showers were recently added. The large bar, which is the public face of an otherwise quite private hotel, serves very acceptable bar food - a private garden now supplies organic herbs and vegetables for the hotel. Own parking. Garden, fishing, cycling (bicycles provided without charge). Children welcome (cots available). No pets. **Rooms 26** (12 superior rooms, some shower only, all no-smoking). 24 hour room service. B&B €57.15 pps, ss €25.40. Open all year. Amex, MasterCard, Visa, Laser. **Directions:** Entering Westport from N5 (Dublin-Westport) road, turn right just before bridge. Hotel is on the mall overlooking the river.

Westport

RESTAURANT

Quay Cottage

The Harbour Westport Co. Mayo **Tel: 098 26412** Fax: 098 28120
Email: kirsten@oceanfree.net Web: www.quaycottage.com

Kirstin and Peter MacDonagh have been running this charming stone quayside restaurant since 1984, and it never fails to delight. It's cosy and informal, with scrubbed pine tables and an appropriate maritime decor, which is also reflected in the menu (although there is also much else of interest, including mountain lamb, steaks and imaginative vegetarian options). But seafood really stars, typically in starters chowder, of calamari and prawns baked in garlic butter or baked crab au gratin and main courses like herb crusted fillet of cod with pesto butter an a red pepper balsamic syrup - or grilled fillet of turbot with a white wine & prawn sauce. There are nice homely desserts – or a plated farmhouse cheese selection such as Cashel Blue, smoked Gubbeen and an Irish brie – and freshly-brewed coffee by the cup. Service, supervised by Kirstin, is generally friendly and efficient, although it slowed noticeably towards the end of the Guide's most recent visit. Children welcome. **Seats 80** (private room, 40) No smoking area; air conditioning. D 6-10 daily. Set D from €32; also à la carte; house wine €14.60; sc discretionary. Toilets wheelchair accessible. Closed 24-26 Dec, 2 weeks Jan/Feb. Amex, MasterCard, Visa, Laser. **Directions:** On the harbour front, at gates to Westport House.

COUNTY MEATH

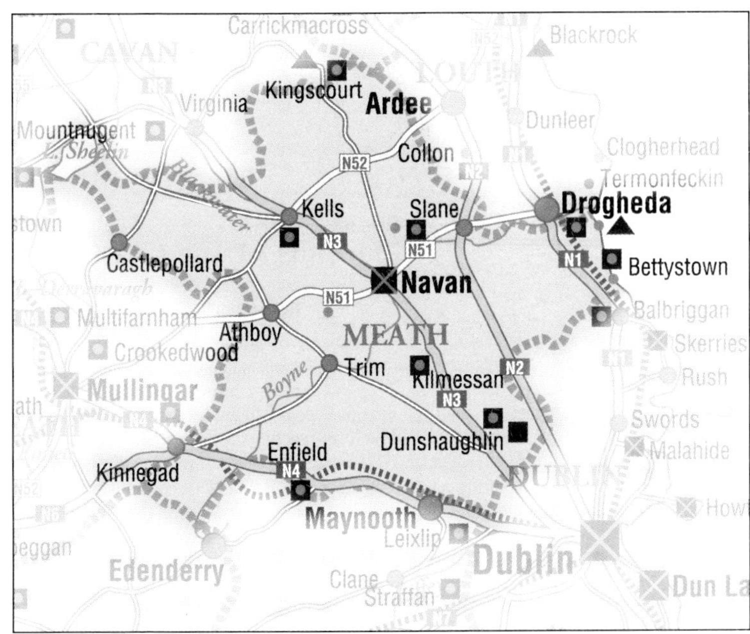

Meath in 2002 is a county which finds itself living in interesting times. Pressures of prosperity and population pose problems. There is talk - and it is more than just talk - of the county town of Navan entering a development phase which, by 2015, will find it has become a riverside city of some 80,000 citizens.

Nevertheless such changes - and the need to find ways through the county for new major roads - are projects which you feel Meath can absorb. Royal Meath; Meath of the Pastures... the word associations which spring so readily to mind perfectly evoke a county which is comfortable and confident with itself, and rightly so. That said, so many people wish to live here that Meath County Council is one of the Irish local authorities which, at the end of 2001, was looking seriously at the possibility of positive discrimination in favour of the county's own people when it came to matters of planning and building new houses.

Despite such problems, people already living in Meath get on with the business of improving their locality, and the current holder of the county's top award in the national Tidy Towns competition is the charming village of Moynalty. Hidden away beside a stream on the road between Kells and Kingscourt, Moynalty is even better known for its annual steam threshing festival.

The evidence of an affluent history is everywhere in Meath. But it's a history which sits gently on a county which is enjoying its own contemporary prosperity at a pace which belies the bustle of Dublin just down the road. That said, anyone with an interest in the past will find paradise in Meath, for along the Boyne Valley the neolithic tumuli at Knowth, Newgrange and Dowth are awe-inspiring, Newgrange in particular having its remarkable central chamber which is reached by the rays of sun at dawn at the winter solstice.

Just 16 kilometres to the southwest is another place of fascination, the Hill of Tara. Royal Tara was for centuries the cultural and religious capital of pre-Christian Ireland. Its fortunes began to wane with the coming of Christianity, which gradually moved the religious focal point to Armagh, but nevertheless Tara was a place of national significance until it was finally abandoned in 1022 AD.

Little now remains of the ancient structures, but it is a magical place, for the approach by the road on its eastern flank gives little indication of the wonderful view of the central plain which the hill suddenly provides. It is truly inspiring, and many Irish people reckon the year is inccomplete without a visit to Tara, where the view is to eternity and infinity, and the imagination takes flight.

Local Attractions and Information

Laytown Sonairte (National Ecology Centre)	041 982 7572
Navan Tourism Information	046 73442
Newgrange (inc Dowth & Knowth)	041 988 0300 / 982 4488
Oldcastle Loughcrew Passage Tombs (3000BC)	049 854 2009
Tara Interpretive Centre	046 25903
Trim Tourism Information	046 37111
Trim Trim Castle (restored Norman stronghold)	046 38619

Bettystown

RESTAURANT

Bacchus At The Coastgaurd

Bayview Bettystown Co. Meath
Tel: 041 982 8257 Fax: 041 982 8236

Kieran Greenway and Anne Hardy's fine seafood restaurant is right beside the beach, with views over Bettystown Bay where, even at night, it is interesting to see the lights of the ships waiting in the bay to go up the river to the port at Drogheda. The entrance is from the road side (actually the back of the building, as the sea is at the front) and the door opens into a cosy bar where aperitifs are served. The menu majors in seafood, supplied by local fishermen and from the west coast – in starters like deep fried prawns in filo with mango salsa and citrus sauce, perhaps, and main courses such as roast fillet of salmon with boxty cake & lemon beurre blanc. But the choice is far from being restricted to seafood; vegetarian options are included - parcel of stir fry vegetables set on ginger butter sauce, perhaps - and there's a good selection of poultry and red meats. This is an excellent restaurant with creative, accurately-cooked food, a cosy ambience and friendly, efficient service. Not suitable for children after 7pm. **Seats 70** (private room, 20). No smoking area. D Tue-Sat, 6-10; Sun L, 12.30-3. D à la carte; early D €27.93 (6-7.30 only); house wine €16.51; sc discretionary. Closed D Sun, all Mon Sep-June; closed all bank hols. Amex, MasterCard, Visa, Laser. **Directions:** N1 to Julianstown Co Meath. Coast road to Bettystown.

Bettystown

HOTEL/RESTAURANT

Neptune Beach Hotel

Bettystown Co. Meath **Tel: 041 982 7107** Fax: 041 982 7412
Email: info@neptunebeach.ie

In a great location overlooking the famous long sandy beach at Bettystown and adjacent to a golf links, this striking modern hotel also has excellent in-house leisure facilties, notably a leisure club with 20m swimming pool. Spacious public areas include a large bar with sea views and a characterful traditonal lounge bar on the road side of the building plus a large lounge area designed around a well feature and a second bar overlooking the beach. Bedrooms are generous and have all the usual modern amenities (best ones at the front have the view). Restaurant meals are well above the standard expected of an hotel - both for Sunday lunch (a jazz buffet, served in a funtion room overlooking the beach) and dinner, in Le Pressage restaurant. **Rooms 38.** B&B from about €70 pps. Restaurant: D daily 6-10.15 (Sat to 10.30, Sun to 9.30); L Sun only. Open all year. Amex, MasterCard, Visa. **Directions:** N1 to Julianstown follow coast road through Laytown to Bettystown.

Castletown

COUNTRY HOUSE

Mountainstown House

Castletown Kilpatrick Navan Co. Meath
Tel: 046 54154 Fax: 046 54154 Email: pollock@oceanfree.net

Set on a 750-acre farm amidst unspoilt rolling countryside, John and Diana Pollocks' home is a huge house of great character. It was bought by the Pollock family in 1796, from Samuel Gibbons who ran it as a sporting estate. The front door is approached up seriously impressive steps, which give some inkling of what is to come - not only does this magnificent place have the grandly proportioned reception rooms and large countryhouse bedrooms that might be expected, but there's a wonderful 18th century courtyard at the back, complete with a spring well and original carriagewash. Peacocks and all kinds of poultry stroll around this amazing place with measured insouciance... It's a marvellously romantic venue for a wedding reception (max 80). **Rooms 6** (1 suite, 3 with private bathrooms, all no smoking). B&B about €60pps, ss about €13. Residents' D at 8 pm, about €26 (24 hrs notice required). Children welcome (under 3s free in parents' room, cots available). Pets by arrangement. Own parking. No credit cards. Closed 22 Dec-2 Jan. **Directions:** from Dublin on N3, turn right at 3rd traffic lights in Navan for Kingscourt/Nobber/Wilkinstown.

Dunshaughlin
FARMHOUSE

Gaulstown House

Dunshaughlin Co. Meath **Tel: 01 825 9147**
Fax: 01 825 9147 Web: irishfarmholidays.com

Built in 1829, this fine farmhouse is surrounded by mature trees and set on a working farm. It also overlooks a golf course and is within a short walk of Dunshaughlin village. Spacious en-suite accommodation has all the necessary amenities and good home cooking is Kathryn Delaney's particular interest – be it a really good breakfast to set guests up for the day, afternoon tea on the lawn or – the speciality of the house – dinner for residents, which is served at 6.30pm if booked in advance. Home-reared lamb, local sausages, home-grown vegetables, free range eggs and local honey are all used in everyday cooking. All baking is done in the farm kitchen and an Irish farmhouse cheeseboard is offered at dinner. Traditional dishes like Irish stew and bacon and cabbage are served with pride and there are country puddings such as apple pie. Garden. Children over 12 welcome. No pets. **Rooms 3** (all en-suite & no-smoking) B&B about €26 pps. * There are also some self-catering apartments in converted courtyard stables. Closed Oct-Mar. MasterCard, Visa. **Directions:** 2 km off R125, opposite golf club.

Dunshaughlin
GUESTHOUSE

The Old Workhouse

Dunshaughlin Co. Meath **Tel: 01 825 9251**
Fax: 01 825 9251 Email: comfort@a-vip.com

It's hard to imagine that this striking cut-stone listed building was once a workhouse – it has now been restored by Niamh and Dermod Colgan to make a beautiful old house of great character and charm, with highly individual bedrooms, one of which has a kingsize four-poster bed. Each has been furnished and decorated with great attention to detail, using carefully sourced antiques and an ever-growing collection of old plates. Of the five rooms, three are officially shower-only but the Colgans have got around the problem of space with ingenuity by installing half-baths instead of shower trays. More power to them for their thoughtfulness (others please take note). Niamh is an enthusiastic cook and lavishes attention on breakfast, sourcing ingredients with great care. Wheelchair accessible. Not suitable for children. **Rooms 5** (1 junior suite, 1 with four-poster, 1 for disabled, all no-smoking). B&B €63.49pps, ss €25.39. Closed 1 Dec-1 Feb. MasterCard, Visa. **Directions:** on N3 1 mile south of Dunshaughlin village.

Enfield
HOTEL/RESTAURANT

Johnstown House Hotel & Spa

Enfield Co. Meath **Tel: 01 405 4000** Fax: 01 405 4001
Email: info@johnstownhouse.com Web: www.johnstownhouse.com

This new hotel opened in August 2001 and has a considerable amount of development to complete in the coming year or so to bring it up to its eventual size (124 bedrooms and suites are planned in due course) and to complete the Spa which is a central theme. Well-located in 80 acres of woods and parkland only about half an hour's drive from Dublin's western suburbs (traffic permitting), it has at its heart a mid 18th century house which has been carefully restored. Although the original house is only a small part of the hotel it is the focal point and the main entrance; large wings extend either side of it in classical style, where the building's original ones once were, to provide a large banqueting area on one side and the spa and leisure centre (due to open in 2002) on the other. An unusually fine feature of the old house is a drawing room with a plasterwork ceiling designed by the renowned Francini brothers, who were responsible for some of Ireland's finest plasterwork in great houses of the time; as the house was not of comparable importance with others they worked on, there is a theory that they did it in return for a favour, such as free use of a hunting lodge on the estate. This is a promising venture and its proximity to Dublin should help ensure its success. Conference/banqueting 800/500; secretarial services; video conferencing. Children welcome (under 2s free in parents' bedroom, cots available without charge. **Rooms 17** (3 for disabled). Lift. 24 hr room service. Room rate €250 (max 2 guests). **Restaurant:** All accommodation is in new areas, but a fine dining restaurant, The Pavilion, and a private dining room are among the rooms in the old building. The executive head chef is Eric Faussurier, well known from the Portmarnock Hotel & Country Club, in Co Dublin, where he previously held the same position; he presents à la carte menus based on classical French cuisine, with a contemporary tone. (Luxurious signature dishes include a starter of ravioli of langoustine tail and scallops with a sweet ginger and saffron nage and a main course of aiguillette of beef fillet on a bed of wild mushrooms and pommes maxim, served with a foie gras and truffle sauce.) M. Faussurier is also responsible for the Atrium Brasserie, where less formal dining is available, and his lively popular menus offer good value. For further relaxation, there's a Coach House Bar, a traditional bar with a mezzanine Whiskey and Cigar lounge. Amex, Diners, MasterCard, Visa, Laser. **Directions:** from Dublin Airport,- M50 to N4, take left in Enfield village.

Kells

Boltown House

FARMHOUSE/COUNTRY HOUSE

Kells Co. Meath
Tel: 046 43605 Fax: 046 43036
Email: boltown@eircom.net Web: hiddenireland.com/boltown

FARMHOUSE OF THE YEAR

Jean and Susan Wilson's family home is a lovely eighteenth century farmhouse four miles from Kells, set amongst gently rolling countryside with immaculately kept lawns and herbaceous borders. The house is spacious, with well-proportioned rooms furnished with a mixture of heirlooms and other well-loved pieces, and new upholstery finding its place alongside beautifully faded fabrics in true organic fashion. Fresh flowers are everywhere, together with books, country magazines and pictures collected over several generations. There are endless things to do in the area - traditional country pursuits - hunting, fishing, golfing - are all nearby, major historic sites to see and several exceptionally interesting gardens within a short drive. But the main attraction to this lovely place is the Wilsons' exceptional hospitality and wonderful home-cooked food. Scones appear straight from the Aga when guests arrive and are served with homemade jam and tea from beautiful china cups. Guests have a drink in front of the drawing room fire before dinner, which is served in a traditional dining room with family silver and crystal on the sideboard. Susan, a chef with some impressive experience, uses the best local ingredients (many of them home-grown) in meals that are memorable for simple, fresh-flavoured style: typically, a starter salad made with well-dressed cos, tiny bacon lardoons, pine kernels, chopped avocado and oven-dried tomatoe; a main course of salmon with a perfect hollandaise accompanied by simply boiled country potatoes, home-grown chard and courgettes cooked to perfection. And for dessert: little lemon curd-filled pancakes with cream, perhaps. Breakfast is a feast - of plums stewed with orange zest, maybe, home-made brown bread, free range eggs – every mouthful delicious. Accommodation is in light and airy bedrooms with electric blankets, crisp white sheets and recently renovated bathrooms with lots of towels and toiletries. Just delightful. Garden. Pets permitted. **Rooms 3** (all en-suite) B&B €50pps; ss €10. Residents D €30.47, at 7.30pm (book by noon). Closed Christmas & New Year. Amex, MasterCard, Visa. **Directions:** take Oldcastle road from Kells, after Top petrol station on right, take 2nd left signed Kilskyre 3km. Boltown House 3/4 mile on right. Name on Gate.

Kells

The Ground Floor Restaurant

RESTAURANT Bective Square Kells Co. Meath **Tel: 046 49688** Fax: 046 28347

A bright and attractive contemporary restaurant near the centre of Kells, The Ground Floor is a younger sister of The Loft in Navan and has much in common with it: wacky pictures and a youthful buzzy atmosphere, plus interesting, colourful food at accessible prices - the most expensive dish on the regular menu is a 16oz T-Bone steak at about €20, but most main courses are well under €12.70. Popular dishes from around the world abound in starters like kofta kebabs, spicy buffalo wings and crostini and main courses ranging from Greek and caesar salads, through home-made burgers to steaks, pastas and pizzas. Interesting daily blackboard specials are often a good bet. Exceptionally pleasant and helpful staff add greatly to the relaxed ambience. **Seats 60.** Air conditioning, no smoking area. D 5.30-10.30 daily. A la carte menus. House wine €16.44. 10% sc added to parties of 4+. MasterCard, Visa, Laser. **Directions:** near centre of Kells/Athboy/Mullingar road.

Kells

White Gables

B&B

Headfort Place Kells Co. Meath **Tel: 046 40322**
Fax: 046 49672 Email: kelltic@eircom.net

Just across the road from the Heritage Centre, Joe and Penny Magowan's delightful old house is on a slip road, with trees and a little park sheltering it from the main road. It has a restful garden at the back - overlooked by the residents' sitting room and dining room - for guests' use and the comfortable, cottagey bedrooms have all been recently refurbished. Penny is a Cordon Bleu cook and previously ran a restaurant in the town: breakfasts are extensive and evening meals are available by arrangment for groups of eight or more. "Kelltic Walking Holidays" operates from White Gables, so a range of information on the locality is available for guests. **Rooms 4** (3 en-suite, 1 with private bathroom & all no smoking). B&B €30 pps, ss €8. Children welcome, cots available. Open all year. No Credit Cards. **Directions:** on the outskirts of Kells, within walking distance of all amenities.

Kilmessan

The Station House

RESTAURANT

Kilmessan Co. Meath **Tel: 046 25239** Fax: 046 25588
Email: stnhouse@indigo.ie Web: www.thestationhousehotel.com

Chris and Thelma Slattery's unique establishment is an old railway junction and all the various buildings have been converted to a new use.The restaurant is a comfortable, homely place with the reception area and restaurant spread over several rooms, lots of antiques and a welcoming open fire in the bar. Daily set dinner menus and an à la carte that take both traditional tastes and current food trends into account are offered, and there is always an imaginative vegetarian choice. Home-made duck liver paté with Cumberland sauce and fingers of toast, rack of Kilmessan lamb (with mushroom & leek confit, rosemary & redcurrant jus perhaps) and farmhouse cheeses or desserts such as chocolate and orange parfait or warm lemon tart are all typical. Live music (mandolin/piano) give a sense of occasion to dinner on Saturday night. Sunday lunch is extremely popular and justifies two sittings - staff somehow remain calm and cheerful throughout. *While the restaurant has had a well-earned reputation for good food for many years, major renovations involving accommodation and other facilities have recently been completed and are now open for business, but not yet viewed by the Guide. (B&B €44.44 pps, ss €12.70. Conferences, weddings, special breaks.) Restaurant: **Seats 90.** Children welcome. No smoking area. L 12.30-2.30 (Sun to 4.30), D 7-10.30 (Sun to 9.30), Set L €20.26. Set Sun L €16.45; D à la carte; house wine €15.11; sc discretionary. Amex, Diners, MasterCard, Visa, Switch. **Directions:** from Dublin N3 to Dunshaughlin turn left; after half a mile, turn right at fork, following signs.

Navan

Ardboyne Hotel

HOTEL

Dublin Road Navan Co. Meath **Tel: 046 23119** Fax: 046 22355
Email: ardboyne@quinn-hotels.com Web: quinn-hotels.com

Standing in its own grounds on the outskirts of town, this modern hotel has a thriving conference and function trade. The entrance and all public areas give a good first impression, although bedrooms are on the small side and could be more comfortable with a little more attention to detail. Restaurant: As has been the case for a number of years, the restaurant is above average for a country hotel. The atmosphere may leave a lot to be desired but friendly, helpful staff and an interesting, well-balanced menu are plus points and the cooking is sound and generous. Conference/banqueting (600/400). Parking. Children under 2 free in parents' room; cots available. Wheelchair accessible. **Rooms 29** (2 suites, 27 executive, all en-suite). B&B about €60ps, ss about €20. Children welcome. **Seats 80.** No smoking area; air conditioning. L 12.30-3 & D 6-10 daily. Set L about €16; Set Sun L about €17, Set D about €27, also à la carte, house wine about €16, sc discretionary. Toilets wheelchair accessible.Closed 24-26 Dec. Amex, Diners, MasterCard, Visa. **Directions:** from Dublin, N3 to Navan, hotel on left approaching town.

Navan

Hudson's Bistro

RESTAURANT

30 Railway Street Navan Co. Meath **Tel: 046 29231** Fax: 046 73382

Since Richard and Tricia Hudson's stylish, informal bistro opened in 1991 it has built up a strong following and is now established as a leading restaurant in the area. Richard's menus include an exciting à la carte based on wide-ranging influences – Cal-Ital, Mexican, Thai, French and modern Italian. Appealing vegetarian and healthy options are a feature – and, traditionalists will be pleased to hear, the ever-popular sirloin steak has not been overlooked. There are Irish cheeses and/or some very tempting puddings to finish. The wine list echoes the global cooking and is keenly priced. Children welcome. **Seats 54.** No smoking area. D Tue-Sun 6-9.30/10. D from about €26.50, à la carte also available; early menu €16.20 (6-7 pm only). House wine €14.60; sc 10%. Closed Mon, 24-25 Dec & 1 Jan. Amex, MasterCard, Visa, Laser. **Directions:** follow directions to town centre, on left hand side, 5 houses down from roundabout.

Navan

Killyon House

GUESTHOUSE

Dublin Road Navan Co. Meath **Tel: 046 71224**
Fax: 046 72766 Email: killyonguesthousenavan@eircom.net

Just across the road from the Ardboyne Hotel, Michael and Sheila Fogarty's modern guesthouse immediately attracts attention, with its striking array of colourful flowers and hanging baskets. The house is furnished with interesting antiques, and made comfortable by modern double-glazing which reduces traffic noise. The back of the house, which leads down to the banks of the Boyne, is unexpectedly tranquil, however, and the dining room overlooks the river, giving guests the added interest of spotting wildlife, sometimes including otters and stoats, along the bank from the window. The Fogartys are extremely hospitable hosts and nothing (even preparing a very early breakfast) is too much trouble. The house is very well run and rooms are all en-suite and comfortable. There's also a separate guests' sitting room and, although they are too close to the restaurants of Navan to make evening meals a viable option, they do a very good breakfast. Own parking. Children under 5 free in parents' room; cots available without charge. Garden; fishing. 6 rooms (all en-suite, 4 shower only). B&B about 32pps, ss about €6.35. Closed 24-25 Dec. MasterCard, Visa. **Directions:** on N3, opposite Ardboyne Hotel on river Boyne.

Navan

The Loft Restaurant

RESTAURANT

26 Trimgate St. Navan Co. Meath **Tel: 046 71755**
Fax: 046 28347 Email: theloft@tgavigan.com

Older sister to The Ground Floor in Kells, this thriving two-storey restaurant has much in common with it, notably strong modern decor (including some interesting original paintings by the Northern Ireland artist Terry Bradley), exceptionally pleasant, helpful staff and a lively global menu at reasonable prices that lays the emphasis on accessibility: this is a place for all ages and every (or no particular) occasion. The menu is similar to The Ground Floor (see entry), also with daily blackboard specials - typically a main course of poached supreme of Boyne salmon with a light yogurt & prawn sauce and desserts like bread & butter pudding, served fashionably stacked, surrounded by strawberry coulis. Children welcome. **Seats 70.** Air conditioning, no smoking area. D daily: Mon-Thu 5.30-10.30, Fri & Sat 6-11.30, Sun 5-10. Early D €15.17 (Mon-Fri 5.30-7.30 only), otherwise à la carte. House wine €16.44. 10% sc added to tables of 4+. Closed 25 Dec, 1 Jan. MasterCard, Visa, Laser. **Directions:** centre of Navan, corner of Main street and Railway st.

Navan

Ryan's Bar

PUB

22 Trimgate Street Navan Co. Meath **Tel: 046 21154** Fax: 046 78333

This very pleasantly refurbished pub makes a good meeting place for a drink or lunch, when contemporary light meals are offered - soups, hot panini bread (stuffed with smoked salmon, cream cheese & tomato perhaps, or chicken with a satay sauce), wraps (including a vegetarian one filled with grated cheese, apple, carrot and a chive mayonnaise) and toasties (honey baked ham, perhaps, with a salad garnish). Apple pie and cream may be predictable but it's delicious nonetheless - and there's always a dessert among the daily specials. It's good value too - there's nothing on the menu over €5 .The lovely airy bar makes for a comfortable atmosphere and staff are friendly and efficient. Disc parking.Open from 11.30 am; L Mon-Fri. 12.30-2.30. Closed 25 Dec & Good Fri. MasterCard, Visa, Laser. **Directions:** Main Street, Navan.

Navan

Shahi Tandoori

RESTAURANT

19 Watergate Street Navan Co. Meath **Tel: 046 28762**

Mahammad Kahlid's attractive, well-maintained and conveniently restaurant is situated beside a carpark in the main street. Once inside, the traditional Indian decor, with dim lighting, red and green napiery, oriental candle holders and lots of Indian artefacts is welcoming - and hospitable staff promptly offer the menu and wine list. An extensive menu includes a couple of set dinners and an à la carte that offers many dishes not usually encountered in Irish/Indian restaurant - and also some simple western dishes - steak and chips, roast chicken - providing an alternative if someone in a group wants the choice. It is clear that they know and love Indian food: after a complimentary starter of poppadoms and various dips, appetising main dishes are served Indian style, with silver dishes on table heaters, with dips and excellent breads to accompany. This well-run establishment offers good food and service at very fair prices (main courses from around €11). An otherwise fairly standard wine list includes several especially suited to spicy food. Open from 5.30pm daily. MasterCard, Visa.

Navan

Southbank Bistro

RESTAURANT

1 Ludlow St Navan Co. Meath **Tel: 046 72406** Fax: 046 76824
Email: dine@southbankbistro.com Web: www.southbankbistro.com

A few paces uphill from Bermingham's, a fine old character pub (the perfect place for an aperitif), the enticing little frontage of the Southbank Bistro beckons with its promising low-key contemporary design and twinkling candles. Prompt, friendly reception, pleasant surroundings - deep rusty red walls and a fairly contemporary style make for an informal atmosphere, lots of candles give added intimacy. The restaurant is made up of two rooms, with a service bar at the back (and a private dining room upstairs about to open as we go to press). The à la carte menu is quite extensive and can be adapted to suit particular dietary requirements, such as coeliac or vegan; smoked bacon potato cake with cabbage crisps & plum chutney and cod terrine with sun-dried tomato wrapped in spinach & served on mixed lettuce are typical starters and main courses might include rack of Meath lamb on mushroom & red onion creamed potatoes with red wine jus. Pasta and vegetarian choices are imaginatively handled, with pasta dishes also available as starters. To finish, look no further than crème brûlee, which is a house speciality: raspberry, perhaps, served with cantuccini biscuit & chocolate hazelnut truffle. A concise wine list is rather uninformative but offers an interesting selection. **Seats 45.** No smoking area. D: Mon-Fri 5-11, Sat 5-11.30, Sun 4-9. Early menu €17.75 (5-7 only); D a la carte. House wine €15. 10% sc. Closed 25-26 Dec, Good Fri. Amex, MasterCard, Visa, Laser. **Directions:** take N3 from Dublin, turn left at Meath Chronicle on by-pass, left at T-junction, 6 doors on the left.

Navan

The Willows Restaurant

RESTAURANT — Old Bridge Inn Navan Co. Meath **Tel: 046 22682**

A warm welcome, good cooking and a sprinkling of less usual dishes are all part of the appeal of this attractive Chinese restaurant on the edge of Navan town. A long menu offers a mixture of cantonese and Szechuan dishes, with a few western ones as well. A starter platter of house specials immediately indicates a confident cook at work and service details, such as the hot towels provided with finger foods and a big pottery bowl with a lid to keep the rice warm, are authentic and pleasing. The standard set meals are available but the more unusual dishes may be a better bet. Carpark (entrance via a side road). D daily, Sun all day (12.30-9.30 pm). Set menus & à la carte. MasterCard, Visa. **Directions:** on Dublin-Navan road, on left after the bridge as you approach the town.

Oldcastle

The Fincourt

PUB/RESTAURANT/ACCOMMODATION — Oliver Plunkett Street Oldcastle Co. Meath

Garry and Jackie O'Neill are running a fine inn in this small country town near the Loughcrew Hill passage graves and historic gardens. The pub has plenty of character and an open fire, their coffee shop is open all day Monday-Saturday, then Robert's Restaurant (which also has an open fire in winter and can be reached through the bar or its own street entrance) serves dinner on Friday and Saturday (6-10) and the restaurant is open all day on Sunday from noon-10pm. Menus are not over-ambitious (Sunday lunch is a blackboard menu) and the cooking is wholesome and generous. Accommodation is to a high standard - the rooms are more like hotel bedrooms than B&B, with phone, multi-channel TV, hair dryer and tea/coffee facilities. Fax, photocopy and email also available on request. Self catering accommodation also offered. **Rooms 5** (all en-suite). B&B about €40. Open all year. Amex, Diners, MasterCard, Visa. **Directions:** in the centre of Oldcastle, near the Diamond.

Skryne

O'Connell's

PUB — Skryne nr Tara Co Meath **Tel: 046 25122**

Three generations of O'Connells have been caretakers of this wonderfully unspoilt country pub. The present owner, Mary O'Connell, has been delighting customers old and new for over ten years now. It's all beautifully simple – two little bars with no fancy bits, lots of items of local interest, and a welcoming fire in the grate. What more could anyone want? **As for directions:** – just head for the tower beside the pub, which is visible for miles around. Closed 25 Dec & Good Fri.

Slane

Boyle's Licensed Tea Rooms

CAFÉ — Main St. Slane Co. Meath **Tel: 041 982 4195** Email: info@meathtourism

Boyle's has been run for over a decade by Josephine Boyle, the third generation of the family to do so. The tea rooms lie behind a superb traditional black shopfront with gold lettering, with an interior that has barely changed since the 1940s. Visitors from all over the world come here, often after visiting nearby Newgrange – hence the unlikely facility of menus in 12 languages! Traditional afternoon tea (Devon style, with scones, jam and cream) is perhaps the main event, although soup and sandwiches are available for those with more savoury tastes. But the food – which is plainly cooked and, true to the era evoked, includes bought-in cakes and shop jam – is not really the point here, as people come for the character. Theoretically, at least, there's food service all day 11-11 (Sun from 12.30), but this is a place where they decide for themselves when to close the door - if you're going specially, a phone call might be wise. Closed Tues, 25 Dec & Good Fri. MasterCard, Visa. **Directions:** turn left at square in Slane village from Dublin 2nd business house.

Slane

Conynghan Arms Hotel

HOTEL

Slane Co. Meath **Tel: 041 988 4444** Fax: 041 982 4205

This attractive stone hotel creates a good impression with its lovely signage and twin bay trees at the main entrance. Chintzy fabrics and wood panelling make for a cosy country feeling in the restaurant and bar areas; the self-service counter in the bar serves traditional home-made food all day (12 noon -8 pm) – roast chicken with stuffing, bacon and cabbage, delicious apple tart – and is good value. All the bedrooms have recently been refurbished and are comfortably furnished in appropriate traditional style; some have four poster beds, all have direct line phones and tea/coffee-making facilities and iron & ironing boards are available on request. The hotel is understandably popular for weddings, but it is also well placed as a base to visit the great historic sites of Newgrange, Knowth and Dowth, the site of the Battle of the Boyne, and the Hill of Tara. Golf nearby. **Rooms 15** (1 suite, all en-suite). B&B €47 pps. Children welcome (cots available without charge). Closed 23-27 Dec. MasterCard, Visa. **Directions:** Centre of Slane in Navan direction.

COUNTY MONAGHAN

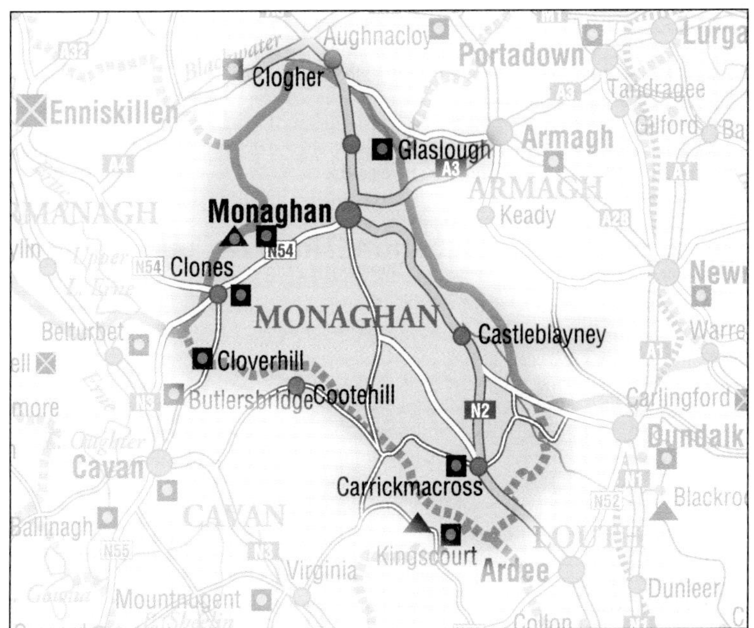

Of all Ireland's counties, it is Monaghan which is most centrally placed in the drumlin belt, that strip of rounded glacial hills which runs right across the country from Strangford Lough in County Down to Clew Bay in far Mayo.. Monaghan, in fact, is all hills. But as very few of them are over 300 metres above sea level, the county takes its name from Muineachain - "Little Hills".

Inevitably, the actively farmed undulating country of the little hils encloses many lakes, and Monaghan in its quiet way is a coarse angler's paradise. Also looking to water sports is the line of the old Ulster Canal, much of which is in Monaghan. Once upon a time, it connected Lough Erne to Lough Neagh. It has been derelict for a very long time, but with the success of the restored Shannon-Erne Waterway along the line of the old Ballinamore-Ballyconnell Canal bringing new life to counties Leitrim, Cavan and Fermanagh, the even more ambitious notion of restoring the Ulster Canal is being given serious consideration in 2002, providing us with the vision of cruisers chugging through Monaghan on a fascinating inland voyage all the way from from Waterford on the south coast to Coleraine on the north coast, and in particular bringing fresh interest to the Counties of Monaghan, Armagh and Tyrone along the line of the Ulster Canal.

Vision of a different sort is the theme at Annaghmakerrig House near the Quaker-named village of Newbliss in west Monaghan. The former home of theatrical producer Tyrone Guthrie, it is now a busy centre for writers and artists who can stay there to complete 'work in progress'. In the east of the county at Castleblayney, there's a particularly attractive lake district with forest park and adventure centre around Lough Mucko. Southwards of Castleblayney, we come to the bustling town of Carrickmacross, still famous for its lace, but in 2002 it is being feted as Mnaghan's top award winner in the Tidy Towns competition.

In northeast Monaghan at Clontibret, there's gold in them thar little hills. Whether or not its in sufficient quantities to merit mining is a continuing matter of commercial debate, but the fact that it's there at all is another of Monaghan's more intriguing secrets.

Local Attractions and Information

Carrickmacross Carrickmacross Lace Gallery	042 966 2506
Carrickmacross (Kingscourt Rd) Dun a Ri Forest Park	042 966 7320
Castleblayney Lough Muckno Leisure Park	042 974 6356
Clones Clones Lace Exhibits	047 51051
Glaslough Castle Leslie Gardens	047 88109
Monaghan town Tourism Information	047 81122
Monaghan town Monaghan County Museum	047 82928
Monaghan town (Newbliss Rd.) Rossmore Forest Park	047 81968

Carrickmacross

Nuremore Hotel & Country House

HOTEL/RESTAURANT

Carrickmacross Co. Monaghan **Tel: 042 966 1438** Fax: 042 966 1853 Email: nuremore@eircom.net Web: nuremore-hotel.ie

This fine, well-managed country hotel has prospered and developed over the years and is now an impressive establishment by any standards. Set in a parkland estate with its own 18-hole golf course, the hotel serves the sporting, leisure and business requirements of a wide area very well. As you go over the little bridge ("Beware - ducks crossing") and the immaculately maintained hotel and golf club open up before you, worldly cares seem to recede - this is a place you can get fond of. The hotel gives a very good impression on arrival and this sense of care and maintenance is continued throughout all the elegantly public spacious areas and generous, attractively furnished bedrooms which are very comfortably set up and regularly refurbished. It would make an excellent base to explore this little known area - and there is plenty to do on site. The superb country club has a full leisure centre with swimming pool and a good range of related facilities (including a recently added gymnasium and beauty treatment rooms) and there's a conference centre with state-of-the-art audio-visual equipment. Conference/banqueting (500/300); secretarial services, business centre. Leisure centre, swimming pool, beauty salon; golf (18), fishing, tennis, garden; snooker. Children welcome (cots available, €13; playroom). No pets. **Rooms 72** (7 junior suites, 11 executive, 1 for disabled, 18 no smoking). B&B €110 pps, ss €50. **The Restaurant at Nuremore** The restaurant is well-appointed in a fairly formal country house style, with generous white-clothed tables and a couple of steps dividing the window area and inner tables, allowing everybody to enjoy the view over golf course and woodland. Good food has always been a high priority at the Nuremore, which is well established as the leading restaurant in the area, and recent changes promise some exciting developments over the next year or two. Raymond McArdle, previously head chef at Deane's Brasserie in Belfast has taken over as head chef at The Nuremore and his ambitious plans for the restaurant have the full backing of proprietress Julie Gilhooly. Raymond sources ingredients meticulously, using local produce as much as possible in top rank daily set lunch and dinner menus and an evening à la carte. Examples from an early autumn lunch menu offering a choice of four on each course indicate the style: to start, terrine of duck, braised ham & foie gras pressé, with pickled girolles, quail eggs and balsamic jus, followed by fillet of Irish Angus beef (a speciality), with parsnip gratin, ceps and truffle butter, then classic desserts like pear & almont tart with fresh cream. Evening menus are in a similar style, but are more luxurious and offer a wider choice, including fresh foie gras and lobster. Smartly uniformed, well-trained waiting staff are pleasant and efficient. **Seats 100** (private room, 50). No smoking area; air conditioning. L daily, 12.30-2.30; D daily 6.30-9.30 (Sun to 9). Set L €23 (Set Sun L €25); Set D €40, also à la carte. House wine €19; sc discretionary. Open all year. Amex, Diners, MasterCard, Visa, Laser. **Directions:** On N2, 55 miles from Dublin.

Clones

Hilton Park

COUNTRY HOUSE

Clones Co. Monaghan **Tel: 047 56007** Fax: 047 56033 Email: jm@hiltonpark.ie Web: www.hiltonpark.ie

Hilton Park, Johnny and Lucy Madden's wonderful 18th century mansion, has been described as a "capsule of social history" because of their collection of family portraits and memorabilia going back 250 years or more. In beautiful countryside, amidst 200 acres of woodland and farmland (home to Johnny's sheep) with lakes, Pleasure Grounds and a Lovers' Walk to set the right tone, the house is magnificent in every sense, and the experience of visiting it a rare treat. Johnny and Lucy are natural hosts and, as the house and its contents go back for so many generations, there is a strong feeling of being a privileged family guest as you wander through grandly-proportioned, beautifully furnished rooms. Four-posters and all the unselfconscious comforts that make for a very special country house stay are part of the charm, but as visitors from all over the world have found, it's the warmth of Johnny and Lucy's welcome that lends that extra magic. Lucy, an enthusiastic organic gardener and excellent cook, supplies freshly harvested produce for meals in the house and other ingredients are carefully sourced from trusted suppliers of organic and free-range products. This is exceptional hospitality, with an Irish flavour – and, in recognition, Hilton Park was presented with the Guide's International Hospitality Award in 1999. The Maddens offer special weekend breaks and discounts for 2-night stays; they also have a picturesque gate lodge available for self-catering (sleeps 4). Not suitable for children under 8 (except babies, free in parents' room, cot available). No pets. **Rooms 6** (all en-suite & no smoking). B&B €110 pps, ss €30. Residents D €35 at 8 pm; (please give 24 hours notice). House wine €20. No sc. Closed Oct-Mar. MasterCard, Visa. **Directions:** 3 miles south of Clones on Scotshouse road.

Glaslough

COUNTRY HOUSE/RESTAURANT

Castle Leslie

Glaslough Co. Monaghan

Tel: 047 88109 Fax: 047 88256

Email: ultan@castleleslie.ie Web: www.castleleslie.com

Castle Leslie is an extraordinary place, with a long and fascinating history to intrigue guests. Suffice it to say that it is set in a 1,000 acre estate, has been in the Leslie family for over 300 years and has changed very little in that time. There is no reception desk, just a welcoming oak-panelled hall (and afternoon tea in the drawing room), and there are no phones, television sets or clocks in the rooms, although concessions to the 20th century have been made in the form of generous heating and plentiful hot water. The fourteen bedrooms are all different, furnished and decorated around a particular era, with en-suite bathrooms a feature in their own right with huge baths, wacky showers and outrageous toilets, all done in a tongue-in-cheek style, reflecting the family's eccentric history and the wonders of Victorian plumbing. In a charming reverse of circumstances, the family lives in the servants' wing, so guests can enjoy the magnificence of the castle to the full – it has all the original furniture and family portraits. The estate has wonderful walks, and pike fishing, boating and picnic lunches on the estate are available by arrangement. Due to the nature of the castle (and the fact that the Leslies see it as a wonderful refuge from the outside world for adults) this is not a suitable place to bring children. Conferences/banqueting (100/90) **Rooms 14** (3 suites, 13 en-suite, 5 shower only, 1 with private bathroom, all no smoking). B&B €88, ss €25. **Restaurant** Good food is an important element of any visit to Castle Leslie. Non-residents are welcome to come for dinner, by arrangement, and it is all done in fine old style with pre-dinner drinks in the drawing room (or the Fountain Garden in summer) and dinner served in the original dining room (which has remained unchanged for over a century); the waitresses even wear Victorian uniforms. Many entertaining wine and food events are held during the year - contact the Castle for details. Seats 75. No smoking area. D daily 7-9.30; Set D €43 (Gourmet Menu with wine €76). House wine about €20. MasterCard, Visa. **Directions:** 10 mins from Monaghan Town.

Monaghan

PUB/RESTAURANT

Andy's Bar and Restaurant

12 Market Street Monaghan Co. Monaghan

Tel: 047 82277 Fax: 047 84195

The Redmond family's well-run bar and restaurant in the centre of Monaghan has a strong local following, and it is easy to see why. The high-ceilinged bar is furnished and decorated in traditional Victorian style, with a lot of fine mahogany, stained glass and mirrors. Everything is gleaming clean and arranged well for comfort, with high-backed bar seats and plenty of alcoves set up with tables for the comfortable consumption of their good bar food. Substantial bar meals include a range of mid-day specials on a blackboard as well as a concise written menu. A different, slightly more sophisticated range is offered in the evening, as well as a short children's menu. The upstairs restaurant (which is undergoing total refurbishment at the time of going to press) offers a much more extensive range of popular dishes, including a good choice of prime fish and steaks various ways - specialities include garlic Monaghan mushrooms and steak with whiskey & beer sauce. Traditional desserts like pavlova, lemon cheesecake, fresh fruit salad and home-made ices are served from a trolley, and there might be something comforting like a hot treacle sponge pudding in cold weather. Bar meals Mon-Sat, 12-3, & 6-10.15; Sun 4-9.30. Restaurant D Tue-Sat, 6-10.15, Sun 6-9.30. Set D €25.39; house wine €14.60. Closed Sun L, Mon D, 25 Dec, Good Fri & 1-14 July. MasterCard, Visa, Laser. **Directions:** Opposite Market House.

Monaghan
HOTEL

Hillgrove Hotel

Old Armagh Road Monaghan,Co. Monaghan
Tel: 047 81288 Fax: 047 84951
Email: hillgrove@quinnhotels.com Web: quinnhotels.com

The appropriately named Hillgrove is the leading hotel in the area, overlooking the town from a fine hillside location. It is impressively well-run and has good conference and banqueting facilities (1000/600). Garden. Children welcome (free in parents' room to 3, cots available). No pets. **Rooms 44** (2 suites, 2 junior suites, 2 for disabled). B&B about €65 pps, ss about €20. Open all year. Amex, Diners, MasterCard, Visa. **Directions:** Take N2 from Dublin to Monaghan town.

COUNTY OFFALY

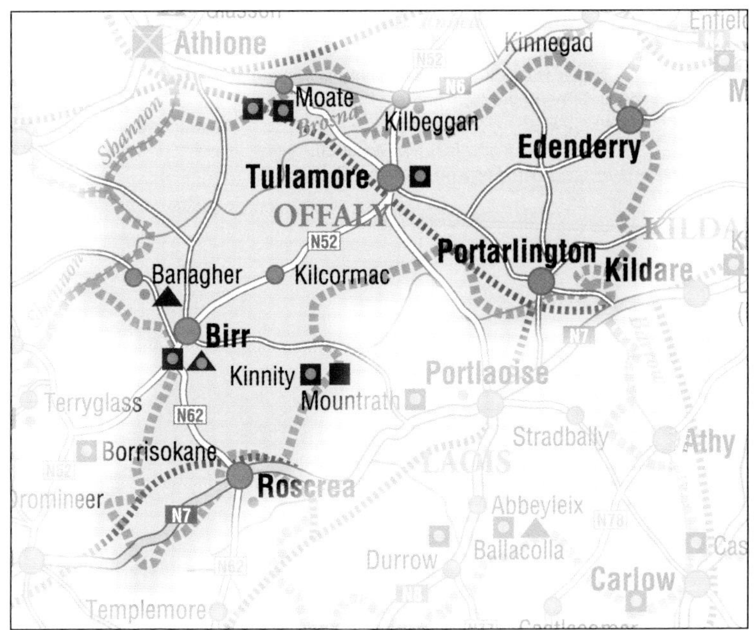

Offaly enters 2002 with a distinction which may well stand it in good stead in these turbulent times. In April 2001 it was announced that, as a result of a very detailed analysis by the Central Statistics Office, it had been found that the good people of Offaly had on average the lowest personal disposable income of all the counties in the Republic of Ireland. Yet when the national media dispatched investigators down to Offaly to report on this state of affairs, the reports coming back indicated that Offaly people were unfazed by the news, and did not seem to be totally reliant on money to enjoy life. For they live in a quietly beautiful place whose values are not dependent on the excesses of the consumer society.

At the heart of the old Ely O'Carroll territory, Offaly is Ireland's most sky-minded county. At Birr Castle, there's the Parsons family's famous restored 1845-vintage 1.83 m astronomical telescope, through which the 3rd Earl of Rosse observed his discovery of the spiral nebulae. And in Tullamore, there's a thriving amateur Astronomical Society whose members point out that the wide clear skies of Offaly have encouraged the regular observation of heavenly bodies since at least 1057 AD, when astronomy was the province of moon-minded monks.

Back in Birr meanwhile, the restored gardens of Birr Castle are an added attraction, but still the sky calls, and the annual Irish Hot Air Balloon Meeting has been run with increasing success since 1970. It attracts serious international balloonists who welcome the opportunity for participation in a relaxed fun event where everyone wins a prize, and is equally suitable for beginners, as Offaly's bogs provide a soft landing - "there's a bit of give in a bog".

Offaly is also historic hunting country. It is home to the Ormonde, which may not be Ireland's largest or richest hunt, "but it's the oldest and undoubtedly the best." Once upon a time, they invited the neighbouring County Galway Hunt for a shared meet, and afterwards the carousing in Dooley's Hotel in Birr reached such a hectic pitch that the hotel was joyously torched by the visitors. Dooley's was rebuilt to fulfill its central role in Birr, and the hunt from across the Shannon has been known as the Galway Blazers ever since.

The Grand Canal finally reaches the great river at Shannon Harbour in Offaly, after crossing Ireland from Dublin, and on the river itself, waterborne travellers find that Offaly affords the opportunity of visiting Clonmacnoise, where the remains of an ancient monastic university city give pause for thought. In the south of the county, the Slieve Bloom Mountains rise attractively above Offaly's farmland and bogs. These are modest heights, as they attain just 526 m on the peak of Arderin. However, it is their understated charms which particularly appeal, and in the Slieve Blooms we find

Ireland's first organised system of gites, the French concept whereby unused farmhouses have been restored to a comfortable standard for self-catering visitor accommodation.

Nestling in a valley of the Slieve Blooms is the unspoilt village of Kinnitty, where Offaly's quality of life is most in evidence. And in the far east of the county, where Offaly marches with Kildare, we find Clonbulloge, top title holder in Offaly in the current Tidy Towns awards, a pretty place on the banks of the stream known as the Figile River.

Local Attractions and Information

Banagher Cloghan Castle (15C Tower House)	0509 51650
Birr Castle Demesne & Historic Science Centre	0509 20336 / 22154
Birr Tourism Information	0509 20110
Clonmacnoise Visitor & Interpretive Centre	0905 74195
Edenderry Canal Festival (June)	0405 32071
Shannonbridge Clonmacnoise & West Offaly Railway	0905 74114
Slieve Bloom Rural Development Society	0509 37299
Tullamore Offaly Historical Society	0506 21421
Tullamore Offaly Tourist Council	0506 52566
Tullamore Tullamore Dew Whiskey Heritage Centre	0506 25015
Tullamore Tourism Information	0506 52617

Banagher

J.J. Hough's

PUB

Main St Banagher Co. Offaly **Tel: 0509 51893**

Hidden behind a thriving vine, which threatens to take over in summer, this charming 250-year old pub is soothingly dark inside – making a fine contrast to the cheerful eccentricity of the current owner, Michael Hough. Very much a local, it's also popular with people from the river cruisers, who come up from the harbour for the pints and the craic. Traditional music every night (weekends only off-season). Children and pets welcome. Closed 25 Dec & Good Fri. **Directions:** on Shannon just off Athlone Limerick road.

Banagher

The Shannon Hotel

HOTEL

West End Banagher Co. Offaly **Tel: 0509 51306** Fax: 0509 51941

A charming place dating back the to the 17th century, this hotel was once the home of Anthony Trollope. Having recently moved into the energetic ownership of Joseph and Patricia Moran, it has welcoming fires, a real sense of hospitality and live music (traditional and contemporary) at weekends. The bar is a very pleasant place to be at any time of day, whether for a quiet cup of coffee in the morning or something more substantial, like traditional lamb stew, later on. Simple en-suite bedrooms have all been recently refurbished with phone, multi-channel TV, hairdryers & tea/coffee facilities. Bar food available 8am-10pm daily. Own parking. **Rooms 12** (all en-suite) B&B €38.09, ss 6.35. Closed 25 Dec. MasterCard, Visa, Laser. **Directions:** at the bottom of the main street, near the harbour.

Banagher

The Vine House

PUB/RESTAURANT

Banagher Co. Offaly **Tel: 0509 51463** Fax: 0509 51463

This atmospheric bar and restaurant is the perfect haven for boating people - head chef Adam Ashton has been sending guests happy into the night for 10 years now. Music nightly May-August (bands at weekends, weekdays ballads & traditional); Saturday nights only off-season. Food served: 12 noon - 3.30 pm and 7-9.30 pm daily from Easter-late September/early October; off-season: evenings only, closed Mondays. MasterCard, Visa. **Directions:** at the bottom of the village, very close to the harbour.

Birr

Dooly's Hotel

HOTEL

Emmet Square Birr Co Offaly
Tel: 0509 20032 Fax: 0509 21332
Email: doolyhotel@esatclear.ie Web: www.dooleyshotel.com

A good holiday centre with plenty to do locally – Birr Castle gardens are very near, also golfing, fishing, riding and river excursions. This attractive, old-fashioned hotel is one of Ireland's oldest coaching inns, dating back to 1747 and is right on Emmet Square, the centre of Georgian Birr. Public rooms, including two characterful bars, are traditional in furnishing style but have all been refurbished recently. Bedrooms have been upgraded and now include a junior suite and an executive room; all are en-suite with full bathrooms (bath and shower). When there's a function on, the hotel tries to allocate quiet rooms if possible. Coffee shop/bistro open 8.30am-9.30pm daily; bar meals available; brasserie (light food) 11am-7pm. 12.30-9.15 pm daily. B&B about €50pps. Closed 25 Dec. Amex, Diners, MasterCard, Visa, Laser. **Directions:** On main square, centre of town.

Birr

Spinners Town House & Bistro

RESTAURANT/GUESTHOUSE

Castle Street Birr Co. Offaly
Tel: 0509 21673 Fax: 0509 21672
Email: spinners@indigo.ie Web: www.spinners-townhouse.com

Taken over by Tim Darragh, Liam Maloney and Seamus Merrigan in February 2000, this unusual establishment in the centre of Birr runs through five Georgian townhouses, restored and refurbished throughout in a simple contemporary style. The new owners first added four spacious new rooms (similar in style but "with a hint of the baronial gothic") and then refurbished the bistro, making the central courtyard garden and its surrounding arches a major feature. Stylish, thoughtfully designed bedrooms include family rooms, doubles and twins, all with en-suite or private bathrooms - and a further three bedrooms are to come onstream by April 2002. In addition to their own sitting room and a breakfast room, where a traditional hot Irish breakfast based on organic bacon and sausages is served, guests have the use of the enclosed courtyard garden. **Rooms 13.** B&B €32pps, ss €6.35. **Spinners Bistro** Everything is based on fresh ingredients, local wherever possible, with fish and seafood the main speciality, accounting for about four starters (try their house special of wild salmon, potato & herb cakes, served with chervil mayonnaise) and a similar number of main courses. But there is plenty else to choose from too, including interesting vegetarian alternatives (a starter mushroom bruschette with sundried tomato & mozzarella and main course tagliatelle with mushrooms & sundried tomatoes are typical). Hereford prime Irish beef is another speciality - a 12 oz sirloin, perhaps, with a choice of sauces - and it is good to see pork featuring in a dish like Somerset pork, where the fillet is cooked in a creamy cider & apple sauce. Desserts tend to be old favourites, like banoffi pie and home-made icea creams. Open to non-residents. Seats 42 D Tue-Sun, 5-10 à la carte; sc discretionary; licensed. Closed Mon. Amex, Diners, MasterCard, Visa, Laser. **Directions:** next door to Birr Castle Demense.

Birr

The Stables Restaurant & Townhouse

RESTAURANT/ACCOMMODATION

Oxmantown Mall Birr Co. Offaly
Tel: 0509 20263 Fax: 0509 21677
Email: cboyd@indigo.ie Web: www.thestablesrestaurant.com

The Boyd family's characterful establishment is in a lovely old Georgian house overlooking the tree-lined mall. It has a strong local following. The restaurant is in the converted stables and coach house and has lots of atmosphere, with attractive exposed bricks and stonework, arches and an open fire in the period drawing room (which is used as a bar and reception area). The cooking style is quite traditional – a blend of Cordon Bleu and traditional Irish, but with some unexpectedly adventurous options like pan-fried ostrich and more seafood than might be expected in the midlands – and hearty country portions are the norm. Children welcome. Banqueting (90). Seats 65 D Tue-Sat, 5.30-9.30 (also Sun 6.30 -8.30 Jun-Sep) L Sun only, 12.30-3. Set D €33, à la carte also available; Set Sun L €19; house wine €15.24; sc discretionary. No smoking area; air conditioning. Closed all Mon, also D Sun Oct-May, Ash Wednesday, Good Fri. **Accommodation** Old world en-suite bedrooms overlooking the mall or the courtyard include two large new rooms added in 2000. **Rooms 8.** B&B €32pps, ss €6.35. Amex, Diners, MasterCard, Visa, Laser, Switch. **Directions:** town centre, opposite original gates of Birr castle.

Crinkle

The Thatch Bar & Restaurant

PUB/RESTAURANT

Crinkle Birr Co Offaly
Tel: 0509 20682 Fax: 0509 21847

This characterful little thatched pub and restaurant just outside Birr shows just how good a genuine, well-run country pub with imaginative, freshly cooked food can be. Since 1991, the energetic owner Des Connole has worked tirelessly to improve standards with the help of head chef Brian Maher. Five-course dinner menus change weekly and include a mixture of traditional dishes such as sirloin steaks with mushrooms in garlic and more interesting things – a lot of seafood, exotics like ostrich (which is farmed in Ireland) and kangaroo; local produce is there as well, of course, in pigeon and rabbit terrines, for example, and roast duck with vegetable stir-fry, loin of pork with a rhubarb compôte. Good food and warm hospitality make this one of the best eating places in the area. Children welcome. Parking. **Seats 50** (private room, 15-20). D 6.30-9.30 daily, à la carte; L Sun-12.30 & 2.30; Set Sun L EUR19.05; early evening bar menu Mon-Sat 5.30-7.30, à la carte; house wine €16.51; sc discretionary. Bar food 12.30-2 Mon-Sat. Early D 5-7.30 (à la carte, in bar). No smoking area; air conditioning. Toilets wheelchair accessible. Closed 25 Dec, Good Fri. Diners, MasterCard, Visa. **Directions:** 1 mile from Birr (Roscrea side).

Kinnitty

Ardmore House

B&B

The Walk Kinnitty Co. Offaly **Tel: 0509 37009**
Email: ardmorehouse@eircom.net Web: www.kinnitty.net

Christina Byrne's stone-built Victorian house is set back from the road in its own garden and offers old-fashioned comforts: brass beds, turf fires and home-baked bread for breakfast. Bedrooms are deliberately left without amenities, in order to make a visit to Ardmore a real country house experience and encourage guests to spend less time in their rooms and mix with each other - tea is available downstairs at any time. Two new rooms were added in 2001 - one with jacuzzi bath and the other a wheelchair friendly ground floor room. Children welcome (under 2s free in parents' room, cot available); pets allowed in certain areas. **Rooms 5** (4 en-suite, 3 shower only, 1 with private bathroom, all no smoking). B&B €32pps, ss €11. Closed 25 Dec. **Directions:** in village of Kinnity, 9 miles from Birr.

Kinnitty

The Glendine Bistro

RESTAURANT/B&B

Kinnitty Birr Co. Offaly **Tel: 0509 37973** Fax: 0509 37975

The clean-lined simplicity of Percy and Phil Clendennan's attractive contemporary restaurant provides a welcome contrast to other, more traditional, dining options nearby, giving visitors to this unspoilt area a choice of styles. Head chef Jamie Owens offers wide-ranging menus that suit the surroundings: this is steak country and prime Hereford beef features in steaks various ways, but there are also many more international dishes like barbecued tiger prawns & king scallops with chargrilled peppers or Irish ostrich on a bed of pesto courgettes, with balsamic dressing - and sound cooking is backed up by friendly service. Vegetarian options, typically stir frys and fresh pasta dishes, are always available. Seats 60 (private room 30). No smoking area; air conditioning. D Wed-Sat, 6.30-9.30. L Sun only, 1-4. D à la carte; Set Sun L €16.80. House wine €15.24. Closed D Sun, all Mon &Tue. **Accommodation** Five bright, comfortably furnished en-suite bedrooms are offered, all with direct dial phones, TV and tea/coffee-making facilities. Children under 6 free in parents' room; cot available. **Rooms 5** (all shower-only & no smoking). Open all year. MasterCard, Visa, Laser. **Directions:** in centre of Kinnitty village.

Kinnitty

Kinnity Castle

HOTEL/RESTAURANT

Kinnitty Co. Offaly
Tel: 0509 37318 Fax: 0509 37284
Email: kinnittycastle@eircom.net Web: kinnittycastle.com

Furnished in keeping with its dramatic history and theatrical character, this luxurious Gothic Revival castle in the foothills of the Slieve Bloom Mountains is at the centre of a very large estate (accessible for horse-riding and walking) with 650 acres of parkland and formal gardens. Public areas – a library bar, Georgian style dining room, Louis XV drawing room and an atmospheric Dungeon Bar where there is traditional music on Friday nights all year – are mainly furnished in the style expected of a castle hotel. The accommodation, however, is slightly different: bedrooms are all interesting and comfortable but vary considerably according to their position in the castle: the best are big and romantic, with stunning views over the estate (and sumptuous, dramatically styled bathrooms). A further 42 bedrooms, conference centre and leisure centre are due to open in 2003. Currently there are medieval-style banqueting/conference facilities for up to 180/220 in a courtyard at the back of the castle, which are new but atmospheric, and a small leisure centre (no swimming pool as yet). Tennis, fishing, equestrian, garden. Children welcome (Under 12s free in parents' room; cots available). No pets. **Rooms 37** (10 suites, 11 mini-suites, 16 executive rooms, 1 shower only). No lift (long corridors and a lot of stairs). B&B €115pps, ss €20;.s.c.121/2%. Open all year. **Sli Dhala Restaurant** The dining room is quite grand as befits a castle, but the atmosphere is very relaxed and the emphasis is on enjoyment. Well-balanced table d'hote menus have plenty of choice, offering six or seven dishes on each course. A typical winter meal might include starters like a winter terrine of wild game with bacon & apricot on a cider mustard dressing, smoked salmon (predictable but generous and nicely presented with capers and a citrus vinaigrette) and grilled goats cheese on a brown bread croûton with sun-dried tomato pesto and apple chutney, then soup or sorbet; main courses may well include two fish choices (panfried monkfish on gingered leeks with a salsa and puy lentils is typical) and probably fillet steak (with a shallot and girolle and essence, perhaps) along with some more seasonal choices. Finish with a classic dessert such as creamy Baileys cheesecake with physalis or a lovely chocolate & chestnut roulade with armagnac - or a farmhouse cheese plate. Restaurant manager Desmond O'Connor is an excellent host: genuine hospitality and good cooking combined with atmospheric surroundings make the dining experience at Kinnitty quite special. **Seats 45** (private rooms 10 & 50); smoking unrestricted; children welcome. D daily, 7-9.30; L Sun only, from 12.30. Set menus and à la carte. sc 12.5%. Amex, Diners, MasterCard, Visa, Laser. **Directions:** in Kinnitty village.

Shannonbridge

The Village Tavern

PUB

Main Street Shannonbridge Co. Offaly **Tel: 0905 74112**

At J.J. Killeen's wonderful pub weary travellers can be restored, particularly by the house special of hot rum and chocolate, perfect after a damp day on the river. Meanwhile you can also top up on groceries, fishing bait and gas. Music nightly May-September; weekends only off-season. **Directions:** on the main street of Shannonbridge, between Ballinasloe and Cloghan.

Tullamore

Annaharvey Farm

FARMHOUSE

Annaharvey Tullamore Co. Offaly
Tel: 0506 43544 Fax: 0506 43766

Henry and Lynda Deverell's restored grain barn, with pitch pine floors and beams, open fires and comfortable accommodation, provides a good base for a holiday offering all the pleasures of the outdoor life. Equestrian activities are the main attraction (including tuition in indoor and outdoor arenas), but walking, cycling and golfing also lay their claims - and, for the rest days, major sights including Clonmacnoise and Birr Castle are nearby. Conference/banqueting (50/50).Golf, equestrian, walking, garden, snooker, clay pigeon shooting. D 7-9.30; set residents' dinner about €25; house wine about €15; toilets wheelchair accessible. Children welcome (under 3s free in parents' room; cots available without charge). No pets. **Rooms 5** (all en-suite & no-smoking). B&B about €32pps, ss €6.35. Closed mid Dec-mid Feb. MasterCard, Visa, Laser. **Directions:** from Tullamore R420.

Tullamore

Tullamore Court Hotel Conference & Leisure Centre

HOTEL

Tullamore Co. Offaly
Tel: 0506 46666 Fax: 0506 46677
Email: info@tullamorecourt.hotel.ie Web: www.tullamorecourthotel.ie

An attractive building, set back from the road a little and softened by trees, this large modern hotel has an extensive foyer and public areas are bright and cheerful. It serves the local community well, with fine conference and banqueting facilities (750/550 respectively) and an excellent leisure centre and it's an ideal base for business or pleasure. Bedrooms are very pleasantly decorated in an easy modern style, using warm colours and unfussy fabrics and the staff are exceptionally friendly and helpful. There are interesting things to do in the area - Clonmacnoise and Birr Castle are both quite near, golf and horseriding are available nearby and walkers will love the unspoilt Slieve Bloom Mountains. The hotel has been building up a reputation for good food and could make a refreshing place to break a journey, as there's an interesting bar menu available all day and the restaurant is open for both lunch and dinner. Leisure centre, swimming pool, crechè, garden. Children welcome (Under 4s free in parents' room; cots available). Pets permitted by arrangement. **Rooms 72** (3 junior suites, 9 executive rooms, 10 no smoking, 4 for disabled). Lift. B&B €135 pps, ss €20. Closed 25 Dec & L 26 Dec. Amex, Diners, MasterCard, Visa, Laser. **Directions:** South end of town.

COUNTY ROSCOMMON

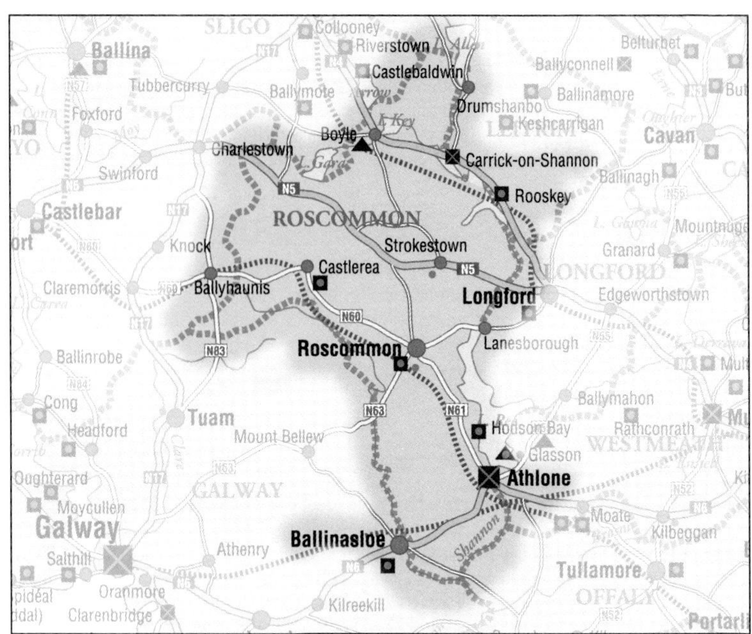

Roscommon is one of those counties which deserve gentle and detailed exploration. It rewards with quiet surprises. Right at its heart, the ancient episcopal "city" of Elphin has perhaps the oldest restored working windmill in Ireland. And hidden away in the north of the county is the village of Keadue, long a star in the Tidy Towns contest - in 2002, Keadue is Roscommon's top scorer for neatness yet again.

It could be said that Roscommon has been a county much put upon by the counties about it. Or, put another way, to the casual visitor it seemed that just as Roscommon was on the verge of becoming interesting, it became somewhere else. In one notable example - the hotel complex at Hodson's Bay on the western shores of Lough Ree - the location is actually in Roscommon, yet the exigencies of the postal service have given it to Athlone and thereby Westmeath.

But Roscommon is a giving sort of county, for it gave Ireland her first President, Gaelic scholar Douglas Hyde (1860-1949), it was also the birthplace of Oscar Wilde's father, and as well the inimitable songwriter Percy French was a Roscommon man. Like everywhere else in the western half of Ireland, Roscommon suffered grieviously from the Great Famine of the late 1840s, and at Strokestown, the handsome market town serving the eastern part of the county, Strokestown Park House has been sympathetically restored to include a Famine Museum. A visit to it will certainly add a thoughtful element to your meal in the restaurant.

Roscommon town itself has a population of barely 1,500, but the presence of extensive castle ruins and a former gaol tell of a more important past. The gaol was once noted for having a female hangman, today it has shops and a restaurant. Northwestward at Castlerea, we find Clonalis House, ancestral home of the O'Conor Don, and final resting place of O'Carolan's Harp. In the north of the county, the town of Boyle near lovely Lough Key with its forest park is a substantial centre, with a population nearing the 2,000 mark. Boyle is thriving, and symbolic of this is the restored King House, a masterpiece from 1730. Reckoned to have been the most important provincial town house in Ireland, it is today filled with exhibits which eloquently evoke the past.

Lough Key is of course on one of the upper reaches of the inland waterways system, and a beautiful part it is too. In fact, all of Roscommon's eastern boundary is defined by the Shannon and its lakes, but as the towns along it tend to identify themselves with the counties across the river, Roscommon is left looking very thin on facilities. But it has much to intrigue the enquiring visitor. For instance, along the Roscommon shore of Lough Ree near the tiny village of Lecarrow, the remains of a miniature city going back to mediaeval times and beyond can be dimly discerned among the trees down towards Rindown Point.

These hints of of an active past serve to emphasise the fact that today, Roscommon moves at a gentler pace than the rest of Ireland - something which is reflected in its pubs to people ratio. It is second only to Leitrim on this scale, as Leitrim has just 148 people for every pub licence, while Roscommon has 170. Slainte!

Local Attractions and Information

Boyle Boyle Abbey (12th C Monastery)	079 62604
Boyle Frybrook House (18thC town hse)	079 62513
Boyle King House (500 years of Irish life)	079 63242
Boyle Lough Key Forest Park	079 62363
Boyle Tourism Information	079 62145
Elphin Restored windmill	078 35181
Frenchpark Dr Douglas Hyde Interpretive Centre	0907 70016
Roscommon town County Museum	
Roscommon Town Race Course	903 26231
Roscommon town Tourism Information	0903 26342
Roscrea Clonalis, Ancestral Home of the O'Conors	0907 20014
Strokestown Park House, Garden & Famine Museum	078 33013
Strokestown Roscommon County Heritage Centre	078 33380

Boyle

Kate Lavin's Bar

PUB St Patricks Street Boyle Co. Roscommon **Tel: 079 62855**

Although established in 1889, the survival of Marie Harvey's characterful pub is nothing less than a miracle, as it has been left virtually untouched ever since and closed for around twenty years. The two old ladies who lived here got tired of running it and simply shut the door until a younger relative took up the challenge in the late '80s – and had the wisdom to leave well alone. It's one of those magic places with an open fire in the sitting room and the old range in the kitchen -- it's lit on St Patrick's Day every year, when a couple of big pots of stew are cooked on it and, believe it or not, served free of charge. Traditional music on Wednesday nights. Open Mon-Wed 8pm; Thu-Sun 6pm. Children welcome. Pets permitted by arrangement. Closed 25 Dec & Good Fri. No credit cards. **Directions:** centre of town.

Carrick-on-Shannon

Glencarne

COUNTRY HOUSE/FARMHOUSE Ardcarne Carrick-on-Shannon Co. Roscommon
Tel: 079 67013 Fax: 079 67013

On the border between Leitrim and Roscommon - Glencarne House is physically in Leitrim, but the postal address is Roscommon - the Harrington family's large Georgian house is set well back from the road, with a large garden in front and farmland behind, so it is easy to find, yet without interference from traffic. Spacious and elegantly furnished with antiques, this is very much a family home and Agnes Harrington has won lots of awards for hospitality and home-cooked food based on their own farm produce. Garden. Children welcome; pets permitted by arrangement. **Rooms 4** (all en-suite & no smoking). B&B €35pps, ss €6.35. Set D €25.50, 7.30pm (book by 6pm); wine licence. Closed 15 Oct-1 Mar. No Credit Cards. **Directions:** on the N4, halfway between Carrick-on-Shannon and Boyle.

Castlerea

Clonalis House

COUNTRY HOUSE Castlerea Co. Roscommon **Tel: 0907 20014**
Fax: 0907 20014 Email: clonalis@iol.ie

Although the exterior may be daunting, this 45-roomed Victorian Italianate mansion is magic. It stands on land that has been home of the O'Conors of Connacht for 1,500 years and the hospitable owners Pyers and Marguerite O'Conor-Nash enjoy sharing their rich and varied history with guests, who are welcome to browse through their fascinating archive. Amazing heirlooms include a copy of the last Brehon Law judgment (handed down about 1580) and also Carolan's Harp. Everything is on a huge scale: reception rooms are all very spacious, with lovely old furnishings and many interesting historic details, bedrooms have massive four poster and half tester beds and bathrooms to match and the dining room is particularly impressive, with a richly decorated table to enhance

Marguerite's home cooking. A reduction is offered for stays of three or more nights. Horse riding, fishing, shooting and golf (9) are all nearby. Unsuitable for children. No pets. B&B €73 pps, ss €10. Set Residents D €30.48 (24 hours notice necessary; not available Sun or Mon.) Closed 1 Oct-mid Apr. Amex, MasterCard, Visa.

Knockvicar

The Harbour Lights Café

RESTAURANT

Cootehall Road Knockvicar Co. Roscommon **Tel: 079 67788**

The interior of this marina-side building is well-designed on two levels to take full advantage of the beautiful location, and enhanced by dashing decor which is colourful, comfortable and stylishly appointed in the current idiom - fashionable high-back chairs, classy tableware, fine glasses - an unusually cosmopolitan approach for the area. The seasonal nature of the business means that a change of chef is always possible but, on the guide's most recent visit (early summer 2001), a French chef was offering interesting no-choice menus based on French regional specialities - an unusual concept, especially in this area. At the time of going to press the restaurant is open only on Friday and Saturday evenings ("7 until late") but a phone call to check opening times is advised. Amex, Diners, MasterCard, Visa. **Directions:** about 2.5 miles from the N4, near Knockvicar P.O.

Rooskey

Shannon Key West Hotel

HOTEL

Rooskey Co. Roscommon **Tel: 078 38800**
Fax: 078 38811 Web: keywest.firebird.net

This large riverside hotel on the Leitrim/Roscommon border has brought valuable facilities to the area and is open all year (except Christmas), making it a particularly good venue for off-season short breaks, meetings and conferences. On-site amenities include a gym, jacuzzi, solarium and steam room (but no swimming pool) and there is plenty to do and see in the area. Reliable bar food also makes this a useful place to bear in mind for breaking a journey. Conference/banqueting (250/220); business centre; video conferencing and back-up secretarial services. Leisure centre. Children welcome (under 4s free in parents' room, cots available). **Rooms 39,** all en-suite. B&B about €63 pps, ss €7.62. Closed 24/25 Dec. Amex, MasterCard, Visa, Laser. **Directions:** on N4, main Dublin-Sligo route, midway between Longford and Carrick-on-Shannon.

Roscommon

The Abbey Hotel

HOTEL/RESTAURANT

Roscommon Co. Roscommon **Tel: 0903 26240** Fax: 0903 26021

The heart of this pleasant town centre hotel is an old manor house and, although there are more recent extensions - and plans for a leisure centre and new rooms - the atmosphere of the original building prevails. Most bedrooms are modern with the usual facilities - phone, tea/coffee-making, multi-channel TV, and there's a romantic honeymoon suite with a four-poster in the old house. Banqueting (70). Garden. Children welcome (under 10s free in parents' room; cots available). Wheelchair accessible. **Rooms 25** (all en-suite). B&B about €65 pps, ss €12.40

Restaurant: A fairly recent addition, the restaurant is designed on two levels in a semi-brasserie style and makes a popular meeting place, where friendly, helpful staff serve unpretentious wholesome fare. **Seats 70** (private room, 50). L 12.45-2.30 daily. D 7-9.30 daily. Set L about €19; Set Sun L about €21.50; à la carte available. House wine about €14. No smoking area. Toilets wheelchair accessible. Hotel closed 24-25 Dec. Diners, MasterCard, Visa. **Directions:** edge of town, on the main Galway road.

Strokestown

Strokestown Park Restaurant

RESTAURANT

Strokestown Co. Roscommon **Tel: 078 33013**
Fax: 078 33712 Email: info@strokestownpark.ie

Strokestown House, the famine museum, gardens and parkland have much of interest to offer the visitor and it would be easy to spend a whole day there - fortunately, wholesome fare is available from the restaurant at the house, which is open all day. Pets allowed (on a lead) in gardens and parklands. Own parking. Closed 1 Nov-31 Mar. MasterCard, Visa. **Directions:** 144km fro Dublin on N5.

COUNTY SLIGO

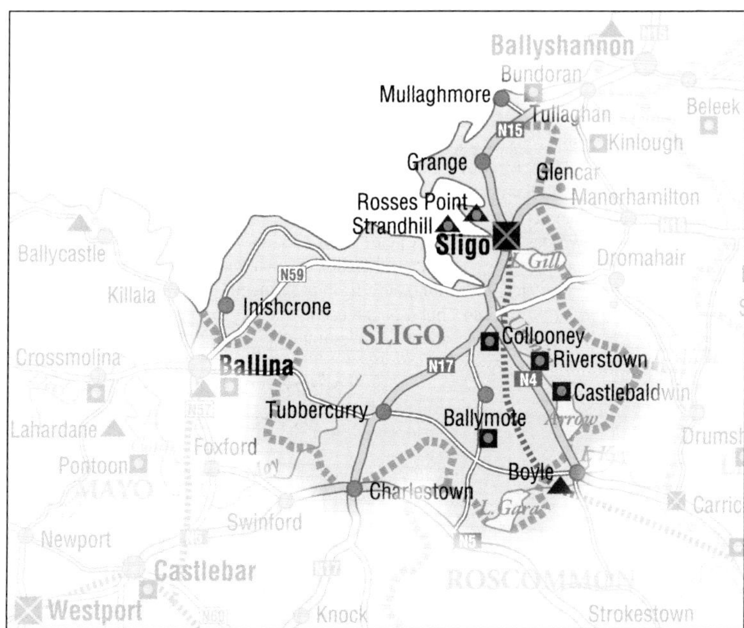

Not now, nor at any time, would you think that Sligo is one of Ireland's smallest counties. Yet such is the case. But there's a stylish confidence to Sligo which belies its small area. Perhaps it's because they know that their place and their way of life have been immortalised through association with two of the outstanding creative talents of modern Ireland, W.B.Yeats and his painter brother Jack. The former's greatness is beyond question, while the latter's star was never higher than it is today.

But whatever the reason for Sligo's special quality, there's certainly something about it that encourages repeat visits. The town of Sligo itself is a fine place, big enough to be reassuring, yet small enough to be comfortable. Sligo moves into 2002 with fresh confidence and new or restored architecture - the Town Hall has been refurbished as the City Hall, the Courthouse has been restored, and the Model School on The Mall has been enlarged and reborn as the Model Arts and Niland Gallery.

The county in which it is set is an area in which nature has been profligate in her gifts. The mountains, with unique Ben Bulben setting the standard, are simply astonishing. The sea is vividly omnipresent, and the beaches are magnificent.

Mankind has been living here with enthusiasm for a very long time indeed, for in recent years it has been demonstrated that some of County Sligo's ancient monuments are amongst the oldest in northwest Europe. Lakes abound, and there are tumbling rivers a-plenty. Yet if you wish to get away from the bustle of the regular tourist haunts, Sligo can look after your needs in this as well, for the western part of the county down through the Ox Mountains towards Mayo is an uncrowded region of wide vistas and clear roads.

Local Attractions and Information

Carrowmore Largest Megalithic Cemetry in Ireland	071 61534
Drumcliff Drumcliffe Church & Visitor Centre (Yeats)	071 44956
Drumcliff Lissadell House	071 63150
Inniscrone Seaweed Bath House	096 36238
Sligo Discover Sligo Tours	071 47488
Sligo Model Arts & Niland Gallery	071 41405
Sligo Sligo Abbey (13thC Dominican Friary)	071 46406
Sligo Sligo Airport, Strandhill	071 68280
Sligo Sligo Art Gallery	071 45847
Sligo Tourism Information	071 61201
Sligo Yeats Memorial Building, Hyde Bridge	071 42693
Strandhill Seaweed Baths, Maritime House	071 68686

Ballymote

Temple House

COUNTRY HOUSE

Ballymote Co. Sligo **Tel: 071 83329** Fax: 071 83808
Email: guests@templehouse.ie Web: www.templehouse.ie

One of Ireland's most unspoilt old houses, this is a unique place – a Georgian Mansion situated in 1,000 acres of farm and woodland, overlooking the original lakeside castle which was built by the Knights Templar in 1200 A.D. The Percevals have lived here since 1665 and the house was redesigned and refurbished in 1864 – some of the furnishings date back to that major revamp. The whole of the house has retained its old atmosphere, and in addition to central heating has log fires to cheer the enormous rooms. Spacious bedrooms are all furnished with old family furniture and guests have the use of an elegant sitting room with open fires. Deb Perceval's evening meals are served in the very beautiful dining room and are a treat to look forward to – she is a Euro-Toques chef and takes pride in preparing fine meals based on produce from the estate and other local suppliers. A typically delicious menu might include: leek & brie puff pastry tarlet with homegrown salads, salmon cutlet with lime & coriander, mocha ice cream gateau and and Irish cheeseboard. NB: Sandy Perceval is seriously allergic to scented products, so guests are asked to avoid all perfumes, aftershave and aerosols. Children welcome (under 2s free in parents' room; cots available). No pets. **Rooms 6** (4 en-suite, 2 shower only). B&B €65pps. Residents D€30, 7.30pm (book by 1pm); house wine €9. Children's tea 6.30pm; sc discretionary. Closed Nov 30-Apr 1. Amex, MasterCard, Visa, Laser. **Directions:** signposted on N17 south of Ballinacarnow village.

Castlebaldwin

Cromleach Lodge

HOTEL
RESTAURANT ★

Castlebaldwin via Boyle Castlebaldwin Co. Sligo **Tel: 071 65155**
Fax: 071 65455 Email: info@cromleach.com Web: www.cromleach.com

Set in the hills just above Lough Arrow, Cromleach Lodge enjoys one of the finest views in Ireland. The building, which is uncompromisingly modern in style and occupies a prominent position, has been the source of some controversy – however proprietors Moira and Christy Tighe wanted to maximise the view from both restaurant and rooms and find that their design has served them very well. But it is not architecture that brings people to Cromleach, rather the drive and dedication of Christy and Moira, which translates into high standards of both food and accommodation. Most importantly, they have the magic ingredient of genuine hospitality, doing everything possible to ensure comfort and relaxation for their guests. Spacious bedrooms are thoughtfully furnished with king-size and single beds, excellent bathrooms and every comfort to please the most fastidious of guests. Like the style of the building itself, the slightly fussy decor is a subject of some controversy but that is a matter of personal preference; this is a supremely comfortable place and everything is of the highest quality. Housekeeping is outstanding (it is one of the few places to provide not only a mini-bar but, more importantly, a jug of fresh milk in the fridge for your tea and coffee). Other extras include a complimentary basket of fruit. Small conferences (14); off-season cookery-class breaks. Children welcome (under 5s free in parents' room; cots available) without charge. Pets permitted by arrangement. **Rooms 10** (5 junior suites, 2 executive, 5 no-smoking) B&B €135 pps, ss€40. Restaurant The restaurant (which is totally non-smoking) is arranged as a series of rooms, creating a number of individual dining areas for varying numbers of people – a system which works better for groups than couples dining alone. Immaculate maintenance and lovely simple table settings – crisp linen, modern silver and crystal, fine, understated china and fresh seasonal flowers – provide a fit setting for dinner, the high point of every guest's visit to Cromleach. Moira Tighe and her personally trained all-female kitchen team work superbly well together, producing some memorable cooking. A growing number of specialities are in constant demand (many developed by pastry chef Sheila Sharpe) so menus have to include these as a base, with new dishes added as appropriate. The cooking style is modern (without being slavishly fashionable) but it's Moira's scrupulously careful sourcing of ingredients, pride in local produce and consistently excellent cooking that makes this restaurant so special. Menus offered include an 8-course Gourmet Tasting Menu (for residents only, included in the dinner bed & breakfast rate) and a 5-course table d'hôte (€55). Specialities include simple starters like warm smoked salmon on creamed organic spinach and a sophisticated tasting selection of award-winning desserts. The wine list leads with 26 accessible house wines from around the world, in the €23-38 bracket, and the dessert menu comes with helpful suggestions of dessert wines and ports. Moira is an exceptional chef and was a very worthy recipient our Chef of the Year Award in 2000. Well-trained, friendly staff provide excellent service to complement the high standards pf the kitchen. The consistent achievement of excellence in all areas at Cromleach - food, hospitality, accommodation - is truly exceptional. **Seats 50** (private rooms, 4-24).D only, 6.30-9 daily (Sun to 8) Set D €55, also à la carte; house wines from €23; sc discretionary. No smoking restaurant. Toilets wheelchair accessible. Closed Nov-Jan. Amex, MasterCard, Visa. **Directions:** signposted from Castlebaldwin on the N4.

Cliffoney

La Vecchia Posta

RESTAURANT

Cliffoney Co. Sligo **Tel: 071 76777** Fax 071 76788

After thirty years in Italy the Donlevy family returned to their native Sligo to open an Italian restaurant in this neat stone-faced house, with views towards Classiebawn Castle and Mullaghmore headland in the distance. Guests are greeted with the offer of an aperitif, in a spacious seating area, where old funiture lends atmosphere, or at your table in a big high-ceilinged room with large uncurtained windows and high light fittings - it can seem a little chilly on a gloomy evening (candles on the tables would help a lot). The atmosphere is transformed on Friday nights, when they have jazz dinners. Promptly presented menus are in Italian, with English translations and especially strong on antipasti (some of which are suitable as light main courses); Italian-speaking staff are happy to explain head chef Francesco Lachini's dishes. Authentic Italian cooking is the strength of the restaurant, as seen in good pasta dishes - tortelli toscani (parcels with a potato & onion stuffing and mushrooms sauce), for example, or delicious ravioloni (filled with ricotta and spinach in a rosemary sauce). Fish, delivered from Killybegs, is a speciality - sole, salmon and crab are all in regular dishes, and there may be some not mentioned on the menu, so it's worth asking. Attractive meat dishes include grilled sirloin steak strips drizzled with extra virgin olive oil and sprinkled with rosemary and more unusual choices like rabbit, cooked in a tomato sauce with onions and herbs. Desserts - a choice of five including fresh fruit salad - are a weak point (it would be nice to see some really good Italian ice creams) but Italian coffees are predictably good. Children welcome. **Seats 60.** No smoking area; air conditioning. D Tue-Sun, 6-10, L Sun only, from 12.30. Set D €25.39, also à la carte; Set Sun L €17.14. House wine €17.14; s.c. discretionary. Closed Mon (inc bank hols), all Feb. MasterCard, Visa, Laser. **Directions:** on side of main Sligo/Bundoran/Donegal road in the village of Cliffoney.

Collooney

Glebe House

COUNTRY HOUSE

Collooney Co. Sligo **Tel: 071 67787**
Fax: 071 30438 Email: glebehouse@esatbiz.com

Brid and Marc Torrades have decided to scale down their renowned restaurant with rooms just outside Collooney village (which they have been running since 1990) and it will now be operated as a country house with meals for residents only. Brid, who is an enthusiastic Euro-Toques chef, was the winner of the Guide's Natural Food Award last year and is a great example to the many chefs and restaurateurs who source their ingredients impeccably but may fail to pass this information on to their guests. Not only does Brid take great pride in sourcing the best of local ingredients for her cooking - which is imaginative without being fussy - but she also presents guests with a detailed list of the items used on each night's menu and their provenance. Thus, for example, salads, herbs, garden vegetables and soft fruits are grown in their own walled garden and tended by Gordon Ryan, who grows them without chemicals and uses organic seed. Listed cheeses may be from Corleggy

Farm, Co Cavan, Cliffoney Farm, Co Sligo, West Cork natural Cheese Co, Knockalara Cheese, Co Wexford, Cashel Blue Cheese, Co Tipperary and Cooleeney Cheese, Co Tipperary. Salmon is from the Ballisadare River, rod fished by local fishermen. Sea fish are landed at Killybegs; beef and lamb come from local co Sligo farms, ducks from Thornhill Poultry, Co Cavan. Brid's delicious dinner menus are changed daily and always include strong vegetarian choices. Garden & fishing. Children welcome (under 3s free in parents' room; cots available). **Rooms 3** (all en-suite). B&B €38 pps, ss €12. Residents' D Tue-Sun 6.30-9,30; Set D €32; house wine €16; no sc. No smoking area. Closed Nov-Mar. Amex, Diners, MasterCard, Visa, Laser. **Directions:** leave the N4 at the Collooney exit; at Colooney roundabout, take the first right; 400 yards, turn left; 400 yards to top of lane.

Collooney

Markree Castle

HOTEL/RESTAURANT

Collooney Co. Sligo **Tel: 071 67800** Fax: 071 67840
Email: markree@iol.ie Web: markreecastle.ie

Sligo's oldest inhabited house has been home to the Cooper family for 350 years. Set in magnificent park and farmland, this is a proper castle, with a huge portico leading to a covered stone stairway that sweeps up to an impressive hall, where an enormous log fire always burns. Everything is on a very large scale, and it is greatly to the credit of the present owners, Charles and Mary Cooper, that they have achieved the present level of renovation and comfort since they took it on in a sad state of disrepair in 1989 - and they have always been generous with the heating. Ground floor reception areas include a very comfortably furnished double drawing room with two fireplaces (where light food – including their famous afternoon tea – is served). There is a lift and also disabled toilets, but the layout of the castle makes it difficult for elderly people or wheelchair users to get around; a phone call ahead to ensure the (very willing) staff are available to help would be wise. Conferences/banqueting (50/150). Children welcome (under 4s free in parents' room; cots available). Pets permitted. **Rooms 30** (all en-suite, 5 executive rooms, 1 for disabled). Lift. B&B about €80 pps, ss about €10. **Restaurant** There is a beautiful dining room, where head chef Tom Joyce has been serving very good food since 1993. Apart from small quibbles (wilted flowers on the table), a recent visit confirmed that standards of food and service here have remained high - and the surroundings alone make dining here a memorable occasion. Non-residents are welcome. (Reservations recommended). **Seats 80** (private room, 40) D 7.30-9.30 daily;L 1-2.30 Sun only. Set D about €30, Set Sun L about €18; house wine about €14; no sc. No smoking restaurant. Hotel closed 24-26 Dec. Amex, Diners, MasterCard, Visa. **Directions:** just off the N4, take the Dromohair exit at Collooney roundabout.

Mullaghmore

Eithna's Seafood Restaurant

RESTAURANT

The Harbour Mullaghmore Co. Sligo **Tel: 071 66407**
Email: eithnasrestaurant@eircom.net Web: www.eithnasseafood.com

Situated right on the harbour at Mullaghmore, Philipe and Eithna Huel's atmospheric seafood restaurant specialises in fish and shellfish caught by local fishermen in Donegal Bay. Since opening in 1990 they have gradually built up a reputation that now extends far beyond the local population - those in the know now travel specially for Eithna's cooking, particularly lobster (served various ways) and the seafood platter, which is extremely good value at €28.57. For this you get a cold half lobster, prawns, crab, crab claws, razor fish, mussels and clams; all served in the shell - the exact ingredients may vary a little according to availability but it will balance out. The platter is attractively served and comes with tossed organic salad greens, mayonnaise, fresh lemon, a bread basket and a dish of potatoes (quite probably from Normandy). There are some options other than seafood offered, including starters like pan-fried pigeon breast, also vegetarian dishes - and tempting desserts might include iced chocolate mousses, home-made ice cream with merinugue & fruit sauce, and a refreshing choice like rhubarb with strawberries. **Seats 50.** No smoking area. Children welcome. D Wed-Mon in high season, 6.30-9.30. (Opening variable Sep-Easter; phone for information). Set D from €32. House wine €15.17. MasterCard, Visa, Laser. **Directions:** 16 miles from Sligo on N15 to Donegal turn at Cliffoney.

Riverstown

Coopershill House

COUNTRY HOUSE

Riverstown Co. Sligo **Tel: 071 65108** Fax: 071 65466
Email: ohara@coopershill.com Web: www.coopershill.com

Undoubtedly one of the most delightful and superbly comfortable Georgian houses in Ireland, this sturdy granite mansion was built to withstand the rigours of a Sligo winter – but numerous chimneys suggest there is warmth to be found within its stern grey walls. Peacocks wander elegantly on the croquet lawns (and roost in the splendid trees around the house at night) making this lovely place, home of the O'Hara family since it was built in 1774, a particularly perfect country house. Nothing escapes Brian O'Hara's disciplined eye: in immaculate order from top to bottom, the house not only has the original 18th century furniture but also some fascinating features – notably an unusual Victorian free-standing rolltop bath complete with fully integrated cast-iron shower 'cubicle' and original brass rail and fittings, all in full working order. Luxurious rooms are wonderfully comfortable and have phones and tea/coffee making facilities. Lindy runs the house and kitchen with the seamless hospitality born of long experience, and creates deliciously wholesome, unpretentious food which is served in their lovely dining room (where the family silver is used with magnificent insouciance – even at breakfast). Tennis, boating, fishing, garden, croquet; snooker room. Children welcome (under 2s, free in parents' room; cots available, €6.35. No pets. **Rooms 8** (7 en-suite, 1 shower only, 1 private). B&B €87.61 pps, ss €19.05. Dining Room **Seats 16-20.** Residents' D 8.30 daily; Set D €38.09-€43.17, house wines from €13.97; sc discretionary. No smoking restaurant. Closed 1 Nov-31 Mar (off season house parties of 12-16 people welcome.) Amex, Diners, MasterCard, Visa, Laser, Switch. **Directions:** signposted from N4 at Drumfin crossroads.

Rosses Point

Austie's

PUB/RESTAURANT

Rosses Point Co. Sligo **Tel: 071 77111/087 2634216**

This 200 year-old pub overlooking Sligo Bay has always been associated with a seafaring family and is full of fascinating nautical memorabilia. It has a very nice ship-shape feeling about it and friendly people behind the bar. The sea stars on the simple bar menu too, with local seafood in dishes like garlic mussels, seafood chowder and in open sandwiches or salads made with crab, prawns and salmon - although there are other choices, including ever-popular steaks. Not a daytime pub (except in high summer the usual opening time is 4 pm). If you're going out to Rosses Point specially, it's wise to ring ahead and check opening times off-season. No smoking area. Bar food served 12.30-9.45 in summer, evenings only off-season (Sept-Mar). A la carte menu; house wine from €13.33; sc discretionary. No food available Mon &Tue off season. Closed 25 Dec & Good Fri. MasterCard, Visa, Laser. **Directions:** drive up village promenade, can't miss.

Sligo

Bistro Bianconi

RESTAURANT

44 O'Connell St. Sligo Co. Sligo **Tel: 071 41744**

This informal restaurant is gentle on the eye, with its terracottas and soft sandy tones, gentle wall lights and large leafy plants. It has never been a restaurant with pretensions but it's a good family-friendly place with food to please all age groups and table service. The idea was based on Italian restaurants in Liège, Belgium, and when they first opened in 1993 menus were strictly Italian – a wide range of pizzas and good pastas and salads – but recent menus are designed towards suiting the modern Irish palate. The menu is now more global – still mainly Italian but also featuring spicier cuisines. **Seats 75.** D 5.30-11.30 daily, Set D from about €16; house wines about €14 (full licence); sc discretionary(10% on groups of 9+). No smoking area; air conditioning. Toilets wheelchair accessible. Street parking only. Closed 25-26 Dec & Good Fri. Amex, Diners, MasterCard, Visa. **Directions:** situated on main street.

Sligo

Coach Lane Restaurant @ Donaghy's Bar

RESTAURANT/PUB

1-2 Lord Edward Street Sligo Co. Sligo
Tel: 071 62417 Fax: 071 71935

The restaurant over Orla and Andy Donaghy's pub is approached by an attractive side alley, with a menu board dislayed on the street. It's a long narrow room, furnished in a comfortable mixture of traditional and contemporary styles, with well-appointed white-clothed tables, soft lighting and neatly uniformed waitresses in black polo shirts and trousers with white aprons all creating a good impression. On the down side background music can be intrusively loud and service slow to get started, but Andy's menus are lively and attractive - and the cooking is confident, making this a significant arrival on the Sligo scene. Specialities using local produce include a porterhouse steak (marinated in herbs and chargrilled), fresh whole lobster and Sligo Bay salmon. There's also a wide choice of salads, pasta dishes and chicken - and the cooking style ranges from traditional (steak with home-made fries, crispy onion rings & HP sauce) to spicy (cajun chicken with a fresh fruit salsa). **Seats 65** (plus 40 on a new outside terrace, weather permitting). Air conditioning. Toilets wheelchair accessible. D daily 6.30-10, Set D €32, also à la carte; L Sun 12-4. House wine €14.60; service discretionary except 10% on parties of 8+.Closed 25 Dec & Good Fri. Amex, MasterCard, Visa, Laser. **Directions:** N4 to Sligo, left at Adelaide St. make a right into Lord Edward St.

Sligo

Garavogue Bar & Restaurant

PUB

Rear 15/16 Stephens Street Sligo Co. Sligo **Tel: 071 40100**
Fax: 071 40104 Email: garavogue@hotmail.com

Named after the Garavogue river which flows past the wide paved area outside the front door, this dashing restaurant opened in 1999 to a rapturous welcome from locals who know their food and relish the sheer style of the place. It's in a particularly attractive new building that maximises the natural advantages of the site - town centre yet with space, light and water around it - and also has a cleverly designed interior, with height and loads of drama giving visual impact. A central bar takes pride of place on the ground floor and is the initial focal point, before the eye is drawn up towards the first floor restaurant area. Snazzy bar food - nachos with salsa, sour cream, melted cheddar & guacamole; crispy chicken strips with creamy curry dip - is served here, while main meals are available upstairs and maintain a similar tone. Window tables on the first floor are especially desirable. Outside seating. No children after 8 pm. Smoking unrestricted; air conditioning. Lift. **Seats 150** (private room 12). Open daily 12-9 (L12-3, evening menu 3-9; Sun brunch 12-3.). House wine from about €16. sc discretionary. Open all year. MasterCard, Laser. **Directions:** located on Bank of Garavogue River access through rear Bank of Ireland carpark.

Sligo

Hargadon Bros.

PUB

O'Connell St. Sligo Co. Sligo **Tel: 071 70993**

Unquestionably one of Ireland's greatest old pubs, the best time to see Hargadon's properly is early in the day when it's quiet – they'll give you good coffee (and a newspaper to go with it) and you can relax and take in the detail of this remarkable old place. It still has the shelves which used to hold the groceries when it was a traditional grocer-bar, the snugs and the old pot belly stove – and it's still owner-run and unspoilt. Later in the day it gets very busy, especially at weekends – but by then it's time for a bit of craic anyway. **Seats 100.** Light food available in the morning; meals served Mon-Sat, 12-4. No smoking area; air conditioning. Toilets wheelchair accessible. Closed 25 Dec & Good Fri. **Directions:** in town centre on the main street.

Sligo

Montmartre

RESTAURANT

Market Yard Sligo Co. Sligo **Tel: 071 69901** Fax: 071 40065
Email: montmartre@eircom.net Web: www.dinequick.com

French run and staffed, this restaurant has been thriving since opening in December 1999 and bookings are strongly advised, especially at weekends. Although not big, it has a light and airy feel and a restful atmosphere enhanced by strategically placed potted palms and a lack of clutter. A small bar area doubles as reception, staff are smartly uniformed and the restaurant is well-appointed in the French style, with comfortable chairs and white crockery. Proprietor-chef Stephane Magaud presents varied menus offering imaginative French cuisine in a light, colourful style, matched by sound cooking and attractive presentation. Local produce feaures in some dishes, especially seafood - Lissadell oysters and mussels, for example, also lobster and wild salmon; there may also be game in season. From a wide selection of dishes on several menus (including the early dinner, which is exceptional value), typical examples are hot smoked salmon with white wine and herb glaze and a speciality main course dish of braised quail à l'échalote with basil mash. Finish with classic desserts - white & dark chocolate bavarois, tarte à l'orange et aux amandes - or a cheese plate. The wine list is mostly French, with a token gesture to the New World, and includes ten wines available by the glass. **Seats 50.** Air conditioning, no smoking area. Toilets wheelchair accessible. D Tues-Sun, 5-11. A la carte. Early D €20.37. House wine from about €16. Closed Mon, 23-28 Dec. Amex, MasterCard, Visa, Laser. **Directions:** 150 yards from theatre towards Market Yard.

Sligo

Sligo Park Hotel

HOTEL

Pearse Road Sligo Co. Sligo **Tel: 071 60291** Fax: 071 69556
Email: sligopk@leehotels.ie Web: www.leehotels

Set in landscaped gardens and parkland on the edge of Sligo town, this contemporary hotel provides a warm welcome and excellent leisure, conference and banqueting facilities. An impressively refurbished foyer with a water feature is the latest in an ongoing programme of renovation and refurbishment. The hotel operates a number of special breaks, including very reasonable "Golden Years" 3-night packages, and they also offer Christmas and New Year programmes; aside from activities and facilities in the hotel, there is plenty to do in the area. Leisure centre, tennis, garden, snooker. Children welcome (under 4s free in parents' room; cots available). **Rooms 110** (48 executive rooms, 2 shower only, 6 no-smoking, 2 for disabled). B&B about €70 pps, ss about €16. Closed 23-26 Dec & Good Fri. Amex, Diners, MasterCard, Visa, Laser. **Directions:** on the N4, 1 mile from Sligo.

Sligo

Tower Hotel Sligo

HOTEL/RESTAURANT/PUB

Quay Street Sligo Co. Sligo **Tel: 071 44000**
Fax: 071 46888 Email: towsl@iol.ie Web: www.towershotelgroup.ie

This neat redbrick hotel is very centrally located and makes a comfortable base for business or leisure. First impressions in the spacious, colourful lobby area are good and the standard of interior design throughout the hotel is high. Conference/banqueting (200/160). Children welcome (under 5s free in parents' room; cots available). No pets. **Rooms 60** (3 suites, 3 executive, some no smoking, 1 for disabled). Lift. B&B €67.50 pps, ss €19. Closed 25-26 Dec. Amex, Diners, MasterCard, Visa. **Directions:** located next door to city hall in the centre of Sligo.

Strandhill

Strand House Bar & Restaurant

RESTAURANT/PUB

Strandhill Co. Sligo **Tel: 071 68140** Fax: 071 68593

Just ten minutes drive from Sligo, close to the airport and one of Europe's most magnificent surfing beaches, this well-known bar has a big welcoming turf fire, cosy snugs and friendly staff. No children after 9pm. Bar meals served all day (12-3pm). [A restaurant was due to open late autumn 2001.] Toilets wheelchair accessible. Air conditioning. Closed 25 Dec & Good Fri. No Credit Cards. **Directions:** follow signs to Sligo airport (Strandhill). Strand House is situated at the end near the beach.

COUNTY TIPPERARY

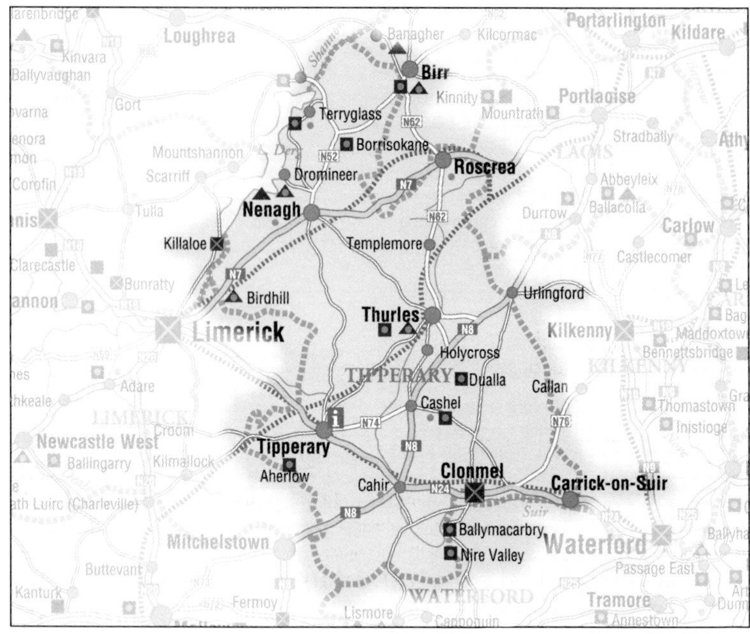

Until September 2002, Tipperary are the All-Ireland Hurling Champions. They may well retain the title this Autumn, but as we move into 2002, it is enough to know that the county which saw the foundation of the Gaelic Athletic Association (in Thurles) is currently the title-holder in what is arguably the most Gaelic of all games.

The cup of life is overflowing in Tipperary. In this wondrously fertile region, there's an air of fulfilment, a happy awareness of the world in harmony. And the placenames reinforce this sense of natural bounty. Across the middle of the county, there's the Golden Vale, with prosperous lands along the wide valley of the River Suir and its many tributaries, and westwards towards County Limerick across a watershed around Donohill.

The county's largest town, down in the far south under the Comeragh Mountains, is the handsome borough of Clonmel - its name translates as "Honey Meadow". Yet although there are many meadows of all kinds in Tipperary, there's much more to this largest inland county in Ireland than farmland, for it is graced with some of the most elegant mountains in the country. The Comeraghs may be in Waterford, but Tipperary gets the benefit of their view. Totally in southeast Tipperary is Slievenamon (719 m) the "Mountain of the Women". Along the south of the county, the Knockmealdowns soar. Across the valley, the lovely Galtees reach 919 m on Galtymore, and on their northern flank, the Glen of Aherlow is a place of enchantment.

North of the Golden Vale, the Silvermine Mountains rise to 694 m on Keeper Hill, and beyond them the farming countryside rolls on in glorious profusion to Tipperary's own "sea coast", the beautiful eastern shore of Lough Derg. Inevitably, history and historic monuments abound in such country, with the fabulous Rock of Cashel and its dramatic remains of ancient ecclesiastical buildings setting a very high standard for evoking the past. But Tipperary lends itself every bit as well to enjoyment of the here and now. Tipperary is all about living life to the full, and they do it with style in a place of abundance.

Local Attractions and Information

Aherlow, Glen of Glenbrook Trout Farm	062 56214
Birdhill Tipperary Crystal Visitor Centre	061 379066
Cahir Cahir Castle	052 41011
Carrick-on-Suir Ormond Castle	051 640787
Carrick-on-Suir Tipperary Crystal Visitor Centre	051 641188
Cashel Bru Boru Culture Centre	062 61122
Cashel Rock of Cashel	062 61437
Cashel Tourism Information	062 61333
Clonmel Clonmel Racecourse	052 23422
Clonmel Tourism Information	052 22960
Nenagh Heritage Centre	067 32633
Nenagh Tourism Information	067 31610
Roscrea Roscrea Heritage - Castle & Damer House	0505 21850
Thurles Race Course	0504 21040
Tipperary Race Course (Limerick Junction)	062 51357
Tipperary town Tourism Information	062 51457

Ardfinnan

Kilmaneen Farmhouse

FARMHOUSE B&B — Newcastle Ardfinnan Co. Tipperary **Tel: 052 36231** Fax: 052 36231
Email: kilmaneen@eircom.net Web: www.kilmaneen.com

As neat as a new pin, Kevin & Ber O'Donnell's delightfully situated farmhouse is on a working dairy farm, surrounded by three mountain ranges - the Comeraghs, the Knockmealdowns and the Galtees - and close to the river Suir and the Tar, making it an ideal base for walking and fishing holidays. It's an old house but well restored to combine old furniture with modern comforts. Bedrooms are not especially big, but they are very thoughtfully furnished (including tea/coffeee facilties and iron/trouser press) and, like the rest of the house, immaculate. There's a big garden, where guests can relax and enjoy the peaceful setting and Ber's dinners are based on fresh farm produce. Fishing, walking. **Rooms 3** (all en-suite & no smoking). B&B €32.50 pps, ss €6.50. Children welcome (under 3s free in parents' room, cots available). Dining room seats 12; no-smoking. D from 7pm (book in advance) Set D €22.50. No sc. Closed Nov-Mar. MasterCard, Visa. **Directions:** take R665 or R670 to Ardfinnan. Signposted from "Hill Bar" in Ardfinnan village.

Ballinderry

Brocka-on-the-Water Restaurant

RESTAURANT — Kilgarvan Quay Ballinderry Nenagh Co. Tipperary **Tel: 067 22038**

Anthony and Anne Gernon's almost-waterside restaurant has attracted a following disproportionate to its size over the years and, although it has recently been extended to include a new high-ceilinged conservatory style room at the back, which opens onto a garden patio, it is still basically carved out of the lower half of a family home that is by no means huge. The atmosphere is very much a "proper restaurant" - yet with all the warmth of welcome that the family situation implies. There's a reception room with an open fire, comfy chairs, interesting things to read and look at (Anthony's a dab hand at wood carving) - and aperitifs served in generous wine glasses, while you read a menu that promises good things to come in the adjoining dining room and conservatory. Guests arriving in daylight will notice hens clucking around a garden well-stocked with fruit and vegetables - promising the best of all possible beginnings for your dinner. Seasonal menus depend on availability of course, but there are always some specialities retained by popular demand, including deep-fried Cooleeney cheese with home-made chutney and Gaelic steak with home-grown vegetables. (Cooleeney is one of Ireland's finest cheeses, made by Breda Maher on the family farm near Thurles.) **Seats 50** (private room, 30). Air conditioning. Toilets wheelchair accessible. Booking essential. D 7-9.30 Mon-Sat in summer (call to check opening times off season). Set D €38.09, also à la carte. Sc discretionary. House wine €21.59. Closed Sun. No Credit Cards. **Directions:** Lough Derg drive, half way between Nenagh and Portumna.

Birdhill

Matt The Thresher

PUB — Birdhill Co. Tipperary **Tel: 061 379227** Fax: 061 379219

Ted and Kay Moynihan's large roadside pub never ceases to amaze – every year it seems to get bigger and develop more additions to the core business. But it's all done with such style and confidence, it's kept so scrupulously clean and the new parts are integrated into the older ones so successfully that you can't help but admire it – even if you really prefer smaller, less energetic pubs. The bar food is very acceptable too – interesting but not too adventurous, based on freshly cooked quality ingredients and varied without offering an over-long menu. Soups, home-made breads, seafood – fresh and smoked salmon, crab claws, mussels – and a good range of sandwiches. There are more substantial main meals – steaks and lamb cutlets, for example – in the evenings. Children welcome. Bar Food Mon-Sat 10am -9.45pm, Sun 11am-8.45. Wheelchair accessible. Closed 25 Dec & Good Fri. Amex, Diners, MasterCard, Visa. **Directions:** N7, halfway between Nenagh-Limerick.

Borrisokane

Ballycormac House

COUNTRY HOUSE

Aglish Co. Tipperary **Tel: 067 21129**
Fax: 067 21200 Email: ballyc@indigo.ie

John and Cherylynn Lang's farmhouse is a charming, cottagey place, delightfully furnished and very comfortable in a laid-back way – and one of the five bedrooms is a romantic suite with its own fireplace. Country pursuits are the big attraction here, esepcially equestrian activities - the Langs have up to 30 horses and ponies on site so there's something to suit everyone, from the novice to the experienced rider. They are approved by A.I.R.E. (Irish Association of Riding Establishments) and offer trail riding and cross country riding in spring and summer, also fox hunting breaks in winter. Golf, fishing, watersports and rough shooting can also be arranged. Cherylynn cooks a country house style dinner for guests, based on fresh local ingredients (including produce from their own garden). Non-residents are welcome for dinner by reservation, if there is room, also Sunday lunch. Mention any special dietary requests (including vegetarian meals) when booking. Children and well-behaved pets welcome (children under 2 free in parents' room; cot available). **Rooms 5** (1 suite, 1 with private bathroom, all no smoking). B&B €32, no ss). Dining Room **Seats 12** (no smoking). Set D €28; Set L €15.24. House wine €15.24. 8pm (book by 12). Open all year. MasterCard, Visa. **Directions:** take N54 towards Portumna. Turn right once through Borrisokane, signposted all the way in.

Borrisokane

Dancer Cottage

B&B

Curraghmore Borrisokane Co. Tipperary **Tel: 067 27414**
Fax: 067 27414 Email: dcr@eircom.net Web: www.dancercottage.cjb.net

A neat well planned garden and plenty of parking make a good impression at Carmen and Wolfgang Roedder's modern tudor style house nera Borrisokane. An extensive array of tourist literature in the big hall guarantees that no guest here will ever be short of things to do in the area and there's a comfortable L shaped sitting/dining room to relax in when you get back, with a wood-burning stove and lots of books. Bedrooms include two recently purpose-built ones with wheelchair access and a family room with an extra bed; all are comfortably furnished with some lovely pieces of antique German furniture, immaculate bathrooms and tea/coffee facilities. Extensive breakfast menus include several home-baked breads, speciality porridge, stuffed pancakes and French toast as well as the traditional Irish fry - and, like the evening meals, breakfast is served at a communal table overlooking the lovely back garden, which has furniture for guests' use. Children welcome (under 2s free in parents' room, cot available without charge, small children's playground). Pets allowed by arrangement. Garden, cycling. **Rooms 4** (all with shower & no smoking, 2 for disabled). Residents D €21.50 (when boooked in advance). B&B €25.50, ss €6.50. Amex, MasterCard, Visa. **Directions:** N 52 from Nenagh or Birr to Borrisokane, in town road signs.

Cahir

Clifford's at The Bell

RESTAURANT ☆

2 Pearce Street Cahir Co. Tipperary **Tel: 052 43232**

A pleasant pub in the centre of Cahir became, somewhat unexpectedly perhaps, the location of one the country's finest centres of culinary excellence when Michael and Deirdre Clifford opened here in 2000. On two floors over the pub (with well-appointed loos on the ground floor and upstairs), the restaurant has lots of character, with the Cliffords' collection of original art (lining the stone walls alongside many well-earned accolades),well-planned lighting, crisp linen and - a trademark dating back to the original Cliffords in Cork city - a single flower floating in a huge glass of water. Michael sources his ingredients with care: meats come from two butchers - Kennedy's of Cahir and O'Dwyers of Cashel - the weekly Cahir country market is a source of local vegetables and flowers and Deirdre's father also supplies home-grown garden produce. Over a tasty amuse-bouche, the early dinner menu tempts with exceptional value and the carte offers a great choice: eight starters include Michael's nettle soup, his famous gateau of Clonakilty Black Pudding and a stylish cassolette of lamb's kidneys and liver in a grape & port jus. Typical main courses might include a superb loin of Tipperary lamb with kebab of roasted vegetable served with pear and thyme jus (the saucing is invariably excellent) and daily specials like roast monkfish with chilli & tomato - accompanied by exceptionally imaginative vegetables. Finish, perhaps, with homely rhubarb crumble with vanilla ice cream, or the cheeseboard - typically Ardrahan, St Tola, Milleens, Carrigbyrne and Cashel Blue, all in perfect condition, with crackers and grapes, then aromatic dark-roasted coffee and a plate of scrumptious petits fours. There are no gimmicks here, just delightful, thoughtfully organised surroundings; warm hospitality and professsional service; superb ingredients and a truly great chef with the maturity to "faites simple". Just remember that this is farming country and appetites come big. Children welcome. **Seats 50.** No smoking area. D Tue-Sun 6.30-10.30. D à la carte (early D, 6.30-8 Apr-Aug only, €18). House wines about €18. MasterCard, Visa. **Directions:** in centre of Cahir, just off square.

Cashel

Carron House

FARMHOUSE

Carron Cashel Co. Tipperary **Tel: 052 62142**
Fax: 052 62168 Email: hallyfamily@eircom.net

Mary Hally's farmhouse is on an award-winning dairy farm, up a long well-maintained drive off the main road. First impressions are very encouraging, as there's a lovely garden in front of the large, modern house - and separate entrances for the house and farm. Good-sized bedrooms include one on the ground floor with wheelchair access and all are very comfortably furnished, with generous beds, television, tea/coffee facilities, hair dryers and neat en-suite shower rooms. Housekeeping throughout is immaculate and there's a guest sitting room (with books) and a large sun room/dining room overlooking the garden which are both always available to guests. Mary, who is a friendly, attentive and informative hostess, gives guests a good send-off in the morning, with a generous, well-cooked and nicely presented breakfast. **Rooms 4** (all with en-suite shower & all no smoking). B&B €30.47 pps,. ss €12.70. Closed 1 Nov-1 Apr. MasterCard, Visa. **Directions:** take N8 for 2 miles. Sign posted at left of crossroads, follow signs.

Cashel

Cashel Palace Hotel

HOTEL

Main Street Cashel Co. Tipperary **Tel: 062 62707** Fax: 062 61521
Email: reception@cashel-palace.ie Web: www.cashel-palace.ie

One of Ireland's most famous hotels, and originally a bishop's residence, Cashel Palace is a large, graciously proportioned Queen Anne style house (dating from 1730) set well back from the road in the centre of Cashel town. The beautiful reception rooms and some of the spacious, elegantly furnished bedrooms overlook the gardens, and the Rock of Cashel at the rear. The present owners, Patrick and Susan Murphy, took over the hotel in 1998 and, although much remains to be done, they are gradually renovating and refurbishing public areas and bedrooms to a high standard - the most recent improvement involved the renovation and conversion of the old coach house, to make 10 new deluxe rooms. Conference/banqueting (90/100). Secretarial services. Garden. Children welcome (under 8s free in parents' room; cots available). No pets. **Rooms 23** (5 suites). Lift. B&B€111pps, ss €45. Bar food: Mon-Thu, 10.30-8; Fri-Sun, 10.30-6). **Buttery Restaurant:** L, 12.30-2.30; D, 6-9.30 (Sat to 10). A la carte: starters about €11, main courses about €23. Closed 24-26 Dec. Amex, Diners, MasterCard, Visa, Laser. **Directions:** Situated just off main road in Cashel.

Cashel

Chez Hans

RESTAURANT

Rockside Cashel Co. Tipperary **Tel: 062 61177**

Hans-Peter Matthia's dramatically converted Wesleyan chapel is tucked behind the town right under the Rock of Cashel. Although many others have since followed suit, the idea of opening a restaurant in a church was highly original when he established it in 1968. The atmosphere and scale – indeed the whole style of the place – is superb and provides an excellent setting for the fine food which Hans-Peter and his son Jason prepare for appreciative diners (some of whom travel great distances for the treat). The wide choice of starters ranges from a simple soup, through luxurious choices such as pâté of chicken liver and foie gras or oak smoked wild Irish salmon with pickled cucumber and crème fraîche. Main courses offer an equally wide choice, always including rack of Tipperary lamb, cassoulet of seafood – a selection of half a dozen varieties of fish and shellfish with a delicate chive veloute sauce – and roast duckling with honey and thyme roasted shallots and soy and ginger sauce. This restaurant is always very busy (there may be several sittings on some nights) and service can be off-hand, spoiling an otherwise enjoyable experience. Booking ahead is essential. D only, Mon-Sat (good value early dinner menu available every evening). Closed 25 Dec, Good Fri, 3 weeks Jan. (Prices and opening times not confirmed at the time of going to press; please phone to check.) MasterCard, Visa.

Cashel

Dualla House

COUNTRY HOUSE

Dualla Cashel Co. Tipperary **Tel: 062 61487** Fax: 062 61487
Email: duallahse@eircom.net Web: www.tipp.ie/dulla-house.htm

Set in 300 acres of of rolling Tipperary farmland in the "Golden Vale" , Martin and Mairead Power's fine Georgian manor house faces south towards the Slievenamon, Comeragh, Knockmealdown and Galtee Mountains. Just 3 miles from the Rock of Cashel, this is a convenient base for exploring the area but its special appeal is peace and tranquillity which, together with comfortable accommodation in large airy bedrooms, great hospitality and Mairead's home cooking, keep guests coming back time and again. An extensive breakfast menu includes local apple juice as well as other fresh fruits and juices, farmhouse cheeses, porridge with local honey, also free-range eggs and sausages from the local butcher in the traditional cooked breakfast - and home-made bread and preserves. Children welcome. **Rooms 4.** (3 en-suite, 1 with private bathroom, all no smoking). B&B €40 pps, ss €10. Open all year. MasterCard, Visa. **Directions:** 3 miles from Cashel on Dualla (R691) road, coming from Dublin. Signed from N8 on left after Horse & Jockey.

Cashel

Legends Townhouse & Restaurant

GUESTHOUSE/RESTAURANT

The Kiln Cashel Co. Tipperary **Tel: 062 61292**
Email: info@legendsguesthouse.com

Tucked just under the Rock of Cashel (and with direct access from the Bru Boru carpark at the back), Rosemary and Michael O'Neill's neat purpose-built guesthouse offers comfortable accommodation and makes an hospitable base for visiting the area's many sites. Although the building is fairly new, open fires and old furniture give the house a pleasingly old-world feeling and, as Michael is an experienced chef, food is an important part of the visit. He offers shortish but well-balanced menus based on carefully sourced ingredients and including familiar dishes: starters like warm black pudding and apple salad or Cashel Blue in filo pastry with a walnut salad, are typical and main courses are likely to include Tipperary lamb, typically a roast rack in a herb crust. Cheerful, efficient serving staff under Rosemary's supervision enhance the enjoyment of a visit here. D Tue-Sat and Sun L, open to non-residents. **Rooms 7** (3 shower only), B&B about €32 pps. ss about €13. Amex, MasterCard, Visa.

Cashel

The Spearman

RESTAURANT

97 Main Street Cashel Co. Tipperary **Tel: 062 61143**

As we go to press David and Louise Spearman's highly respected restaurant is about to take a major change of direction and will re-open in late autumn 2001 as a home-bakery and tea rooms. Details have not been confirmed, but it will be open throughut the day. **Directions:** opposite turn for Clonmel road on the main street.

Clonmel

Angela's Restaurant

RESTAURANT

14 Abbey Street Clonmel Co. Tipperary **Tel: 052 26899**

A great little daytime meeting place in the centre of town, Angela's is renowned for delicious, wholesome food - and wholefoods. Baking is a speciality and seasonal and organic produce goes into savoury flans - with Cooleeney or Cashel Blue and fresh herbs, perhaps - and sausage rolls made from fresh minced beef and pork. Fish of the day might come with a fresh basil and sun-dried tomato crust and you can get specials like bruschetta with mixed leaves or lime marinated chicken with tossed salad. Desserts lean towards the comforting - bread & butter pudding, plum & almond tart - and they're open all day for tea, coffeee and sandwiches. A cuppa with one of their special oaten Anzac biscuits is just ace. Takeaway service also available. **Seats 60.** No smoking area. Children welcome. L 12.30-3 Mon-Sat. All à la carte. Closed bank holidays. No Credit Cards. **Directions:** near Friary Church on river Suir.

Clonmel

Clonmel Arms Hotel

HOTEL

Sarsfield Street Clonmel Co. Tipperary **Tel: 052 21233** Fax: 052 21526
Email: theclonmelarms@eircom.net Web: http://www.tipp.ie/clonmelarms.htm

This pleasant old town centre hotel has plenty of atmosphere, a welcoming open fire, a characterful bar and comfortable, reasonably priced accommodation. Recently refurbished rooms have all the usual amenities - phone, TV, tea/coffee making - and full bathrooms. A useful base for business visitors: secretarial service are available and there's a carpark nearby. Conferences/banqueting (300); secretarial services available. Lift. 24 hr room service. Children welcome (under 6s free in parents' room, cot available without charge). Pets permitted by arrangement. **Rooms 30** (2 executive). B&B €57 pps, ss €12.70 (Room-only rate also available, €50.79; max 3 guests). Bar food available 3.30-9.30 daily; L&D served daily in the Old Bank restaurant. Open all year. Amex, Diners, MasterCard, Visa, Laser. **Directions:** town centre.

Clonmel

HOTEL

Hotel Minella

Clonmel Co. Tipperary **Tel: 052 22388**
Fax: 052 24381 Email: hotelminella@eircom.net

Just on the edge of Clonmel, in its own grounds overlooking the River Suir, the original part of this hotel was built in 1863 as a private residence and, since the early 1960s, has been owner-run as an hotel by by Jack and Elizabeth Nallen. The Nallen family are great racing enthusiasts and have stables nearby, where their Minella horses are trained and the racing theme is carried throughout the hotel. They've expanded the hotel over the years, to provide extensive banqueting and conference facilities and high quality accommodation. Public areas in the old house, including a cocktail bar, restaurant and lounge areas, have a lovely view over well-kept lawns and the river. Bedrooms, which include three suites with steam rooms, five junior suites with jacuzzis, ten executive rooms and one suitable for disabled guests, are all furnished to a high standard with well-finished bathrooms (three are shower-only) and housekeeping is exemplary. Excellent facilities and the romantic situation make the hotel especially popular for weddings. Leisure centre with 20 metre swimming pool. **Rooms 70.** B&B about €100pps, ss about €26. Closed 23-28 Dec. Amex, Diners, MasterCard, Visa.

Clonmel

RESTAURANT

Mr. Bumbles

Kickham St. Clonmel Co. Tipperary **Tel: 052 29188** Fax: 052 29380

Declan Gavigan's large bistro-style restaurant in the centre of town caters for a changing clientèle throughout the day and evening, seven days a week. With a stylish seating area at reception, attractively laid tables and plenty of plants, the atmosphere is relaxed and informal. The menus – a light morning and afternoon menu, a fairly short à la carte lunch menu and a choice of à la carte or set dinner in the evening – offer straightforward, popular dishes with an international tone as well as the hearty steaks (char-grilled with green peppercorn sauce) and Tipperary lamb (herb marinated, served with cream & garlic potato gratin and its ratatouille sauce) for which the area is renowned. Lunchtime main courses include home-made burgers, skewered marinated chicken breast Tandoori style (with pilaf rice, mango and coriander yogurt) and a roast of the day with hot vegetables. Consistently high standards, friendly service, fair pricing - and long opening hours - make this cheerful restaurant a great asset to the area. **Seats 60.** No smoking area. L 12.30-2.30 daily (Sun to 3); D 6-10 daily (Sun to 9.30). A la carte; house wine about €13.50; sc discretionary. Closed 25-26 Dec. MasterCard, Visa. **Directions:** situated beside Superquinn car-park, opposite the Omniplex cinema.

Clonmel

PUB

Sean Tierney

13 O'Connell Street Clonmel Co. Tipperary **Tel: 052 24467**

What an amazing place this tall, narrow pub is. Warm, welcoming and spotlessly clean in spite of the huge amount of memorabilia and bric a brac filling every conceivable space. No "characterful" dust here; every bit of brass or copper, every glass and bottle glints and gleams to an almost unbelievable degree. The front bar, especially, is seriously packed with "artefacts of bygone days – in short a mini-museum". A giant screen is discreetly hidden around the corner, for watching matches. Upstairs (and there are a lot of them – this is a four storey building) there's a relaxed traditional family-style restaurant. Food starts with breakfast at 10.30 and there are all sorts of menus for different times and occasions. Expect popular, good value food like potato wedges, mushrooms with garlic, steaks and grills rather than gourmet fare, although the evening restaurant menus are more ambitious. Toilets are at the very top, but grand when you get there. Children welcome before 8 pm. Food served daily: Mon-Sat,10.30-9.30 (Sun to 8.30); L 12.30-3, D 7-9.30 (Sun to 8.30). No smoking area. Closed 25 Dec, Good Fri, Easter Sun. MasterCard, Visa, Laser. **Directions:** Town centre, opposite Dunnes Stores.

Cloughjordan
COUNTRY HOUSE

Charlie Swan Equestrian Centre

Modreeny Cloughjordan Co.Tipperary
Tel: 0505 42221 Fax: 0505 42128 Email: cswan@iol.ie

The famous national hunt champion jockey, Charlie Swan, runs an equestrian centre on this 200-acre estate and the house, an impressive Georgian mansion, has been renovated by his parents Captain Donald and Theresa Swan, who now offer accommodation here. Built on the historic site of the ruined Elizabethan Castle of Modreeney, it's a magnificent house overlooking beautiful parkland and rolling countryside. Everything is on a grand scale - classically proportioned reception rooms, generous high-ceilinged bedrooms (not en-suite, but this is a real country experience) and even a cellar restaurant. A good base for exploring the area, or more active pursuits: golf, fishing, shooting, sailing nearby. Horse-riding instruction, show jumping, country riding, hunting (Nov-Mar) on site. Swimming pool (outdoor), garden, games room. Pets permitted. Children welcome (under 5s free in parents' room, cots available without charge). Rooms 4. B&B €40 pps, ss €6.35. Closed 20 Dec-5 Jan. MasterCard, Visa. **Directions:** 9 miles from Nenagh on Golf Course road.

Dromineer
PUB

The Whiskey Still

Dromineer Nenagh Co. Tipperary **Tel: 067 24129**

Dromineer is one of the Shannon's most-visited places, popular with cruisers, anglers, sailing folk (and even walkers) alike. Declan Collison and Fiona Neilan took over The Whiskey Still in 1999 and have already made great improvements to the building - and established a well-deserved reputation for good food. It's a characterful old place just up from the harbour, with a stove in the bar for cold days and table service to wherever you're sitting. The cooking style is lovely - the kind of thing a good home cook would make when not too pressured for time but with a some professional flair in the presentation. Baked garlic mussels, poached chicken breast in a lovely spring onion cream and a generous smoked haddock bake are all typical, followed by a well-made lemon meringue pie, perhaps, or apple cobbler with fresh cream. Just the job for boating folk. Food served all year: Monday-Saturday12.30-9.30 pm, Sundays & bank holidays 12.30-9pm. Closed 25 Dec & Good Fri.

Garrykennedy
PUB

Ciss Ryan's Pub

Garrykennedy Portroe Nenagh Co. Tipperary **Tel: 067 23364**

Garykennedy is a charming little harbour about six miles from Nenagh, but it's really in a world of its own. Ciss Ryan's is a lovely old traditional pub and it's well-run - and spotlessly clean. Live music (modern) on Saturday nights. Wheelchair accessible. No Pets. Children welcome before 9 pm. Own parking. Closed 25 Dec & Good Fri. MasterCard, Visa. **Directions:** 8 miles from Killaloe; turn left at Portroe cross.

Garrykennedy
PUB/RESTAURANT

Larkins

Garrykennedy Portroe Nenagh Co. Tipperary
Tel: 067 23232 Fax: 067 23264

Although much newer than its neighbouring hostelry, Larkins is a delightfully spic-and-span cottage style thatched building with traditional white walls and red paintwork. They serve traditional bar food daily 12-9.30 pm (Sun to 9pm) and there's music too - ballads on Wednesdays and traditional music Wednesday, Friday & Saturday night and Sunday all day & evening. **Seats 40** (+ 25 upstairs). Air conditioning. Food available 11am-9.30 pm daily. Sun L 12.30-6, evening menu 6-10. A la carte menus. House wine about €13.50. Children welcome. Pets allowed in some areas. MasterCard, Visa. **Directions:** 7 miles from Nenagh.

Glen of Aherlow
HOTEL

Aherlow House Hotel

Glen of Aherlow Co. Tipperary **Tel: 062 56153** Fax: 062 56212
Email: aherlow@iol.ie Web: www.aherlowhouse.ie

Originally a hunting lodge, the hotel is romantically located in a forest on the slopes of this famous glen and enjoys stunning views of the surrounding mountains and countryside. The old house is lovely, with well-proportioned rooms furnished in an appealing country house style. The drawing room, bar and dining room are all well-placed to take advantage of the view, and there is a large terrace for fine weather. The bedrooms in the original house also reflect the gracious style, while those recently added have less character, but are comfortably furnished and have all the modern conveniences. 1999 saw the construction of fourteen self-catering houses - which unfortunately dominate the site but are quite appealing in a "mountain lodge" style. Most recently, a private dining room has ben added. Conference/banqueting (400/300); secretarial services. Children welcome (under 5s free in parents' room). No Pets. **Rooms 29** (all en-suite). B&B €82pps, ss €15.50. Open all year. Amex, Diners, MasterCard, Visa, Laser. **Directions:** from Tipperary town take the R664 road. Signposted to the right after 4 miles.

Nenagh

Country Choice Delicatessen & Coffee Bar

CAFÉ

25 Kenyon Street Nenagh Co. Tipperary **Tel: 067 32596**
Fax: 067 32596 Email: peter@countrychoices.com Web: www.countrychoice.ie

This magic place is a mecca for food-lovers from all over the country, who make sure of building in a visit to Peter and Mary Ward's unique shop when planning a journey anywhere near Nenagh. Old hands head for the little café at the back first, fortifying themselves with the superb, simple home-cooked food that reflects a policy of seasonality – if the range is small at a particular time of year, so be it. Meats, milk, cream, eggs, butter and flour: "The economy of Tipperary is agricultural and we intend to demonstrate this with a finished product of tantalising smells and tastes." Specialities developed over the years include Cashel Blue and broccoli soup – served with their magnificent home-baked breads (made with local flours) – savoury and sweet pastry dishes (quiches, fruit tarts) and tender, gently-cooked meat dishes like lamb ragout and beef and Guinness casserole. The shop carries a very wide range of the finest Irish artisan produce, plus a smaller selection of specialist products from further afield, such as olive oil and an unusual range of quality glacé fruits that are in great demand for Christmas baking (they probably make Ireland's best Christmas puddings for sale in the shop too). Several specialities deserve special mention: there's a great terrine, made from the family's saddleback pigs; the preserves - jam (Mary Ward makes 12000 pots a year!) and home-made marmalade, based on oranges left to caramelise in the Aga overnight, producing a runny but richly flavoured preserve; then there is Peter's passion for cheese. He is one of the country's best suppliers of Irish farmhouse cheeses, which he minds like babies as they ripen and, unlike most shops, only puts on display when they are mature: do not leave without buying cheese. As well as all this, they run regular art exhibtions in the shop - and they're introducing wine and food courses shortly. Definitely worth a detour. **Seats 40.** No smoking area. Open all day (9-5.30); L 12-3.30 daily, à la carte; house wine from € 31. Children welcome. Closed Sundays, bank hols & Good Fri. **Directions:** enter Nenagh from Dublin. Down main street, left for Thurles, on left half way down.

Terryglass

The Derg Inn

PUB /RESTAURANT

Terryglass Co. Tipperary **Tel: 067 22037**
Fax: 067 22297 Email: derginn@eircom.net

The Derg Inn's crackling fire is a welcome sight on a cold day and this, plus tables set up for the comfortable enjoyment of a good meal, will quickly get hungry guests into a relaxed mood (especially boating visitors, after the walk up from the harbour). This is one of the country's best pubs for food and - ironically, as head chef Rob Oosterbaan is from Holland - traditional Irish dishes like bacon & cabbage and beef & Guinness pie are really exceptional. Rob sources everything with great care, using the best of local produce including organic food when possible. Evening menus are quite wide-ranging and a choice of five or six on each course might include delicious home-made paté with Derg Inn mango chutney & garlic bread, fillet steak with wholegrain mustard sauce (Lakeshore mustard is made nearby, at Ballinderry) and more-ish desserts like praline parfait with cinnamon syrup. Sunday lunch is also quite a speciality, but you don't have to eat at the Derg - there's an interesting little wine list to enjoy with or without food and a very pleasant bar. Music in summer - sometimes Friday nights and usually Saturday, various styles; Sunday night is the one for traditional music enthusiasts. **Seats 130** (private function room, 70). No smoking area. Toilets wheelchair accessible. Open all day. Bar food throughout the day. L 12-6 daily. D 6-10 daily. A la carte. House wine €14. Sc discretionary. Closed Good Fri, 25 Dec. MasterCard, Visa, Laser. **Directions:** in the heart of Terryglass village.

Terryglass

Kylenoe

COUNTRY HOUSE

Terryglass Nenagh Co. Tipperary **Tel: 067 22015** Fax: 067 22275

Virginia Moeran's lovely old stone house on 150 acres of farm and woodland offers homely comfort and real country pleasures close to Lough Derg. The farm is home to an international stud and the woodlands provide a haven for an abundance of wildlife, including deer, red squirrel, badgers, rabbits and foxes. With beautiful walks, riding (with or without tuition), golf and water sports available on the premises or close by, this is a real rural retreat. Spacious, airy bedrooms are furnished in gentle country house style, with antiques and family belongings, and overlook beautiful rolling countryside. Downstairs there's a delightful guests' sitting room and plenty of interesting reading. Virginia enjoys cooking – her breakfasts are a speciality – and dinner is available to residents by arrangement. Importantly for people who like to travel with their dogs, this is a place where man's best friend is also made welcome – and Kylenoe was the recipient of our Pet Friendly Establishment Award in 1999. Children welcome (under 2s free in parents' room; cot available) **Rooms 4** (2 en-suite, all no-smoking) B&B €45pps, ss €6.35. Residents D 8pm, €34 (book by noon). Closed 21-30 Dec. MasterCard, Visa. **Directions:** Nenagh - Borrisokane - through Terryglass, 1.5 miles out on left hand side on the Ballinderry road.

Thurles

Dwan Brew Pub & Restaurant

PUB/RESTAURANT féile bia

The Mall Thurles Co. Tipperary
Tel: 0504 26007 Fax: 0504 26060

This trendy bar and microbrewery opened in the centre of Thurles in 1998 - it's an old building which has been given the contemporary design treatment and this, together with the entertainment value of the in-house brews, means it is understandably popular with a young crowd who like their music very loud. The staff are friendly and helpful, the food style is world cuisine - panfried tiger prawns, cajun chicken are typical, also the ubiquitous steak - and adequately executed. Ground floor wheelchair accessible. Children welcome before 9 pm, Barfood served 10.30am-9.30pm (Mon-Sat). Parking nearby. Closed 25 Dec & Good Fri. MasterCard, Visa. **Directions:** off Liberty Square.

Thurles

Inch House Country House & Restaurant

RESTAURANT/COUNTRY HOUSE féile bia

Bouladuff Thurles Co. Tipperary
Tel: 0504 51348/51261 Fax: 0504 51754
Email: inchhse@iol.ie Web: www.tipp.ie/inch-house.htm

Built in 1720 by John Ryan, one of the few landed Catholic gentlemen in Tipperary, this magnificent Georgian house managed to survive some of the most turbulent periods in Irish history and to remain in the Ryan family for almost 300 years. John and Norah Egan, who farm the surrounding 250 acres, took it over in a state of dereliction in 1985 and began the major restoration work which has resulted in the handsome, comfortably furnished period house which guests enjoy today. Reception rooms on either side of a welcoming hallway include an unusual William Morris-style drawing room with a tall stained glass window, a magnificent plasterwork ceiling (and adjoining library bar) and a fine dining room which is used for residents' breakfasts and is transformed into a restaurant at night. Both rooms have period fireplaces with big log fires. The five bedrooms are quite individual and are furnished with antiques. Children welcome (under 5s free in parents' room; cot available). No Pets. **Rooms 5** (all en-suite, 1 shower only). B&B €50.19 pps, ss €6.35. Restaurant Polished wood floors, classic country house decor and tables laid with crisp white linen and fresh flowers provide a fine setting for dinner, especially when the atmosphere is softened by firelight and candles. Menus are changed weekly and offer a well-balanced choice in a fairly traditional style that combines French country cooking and Irish influences. Specialities that indicate the style include local Cooleeney cheese fritters with pear coulis; herb crêpe filled with chicken & mushroom, in cream sauce; and entrecôte steak with oyster mushroom sauce. Anyone with special dietary needs, including vegetarians, should mention this on booking to allow for preparation of extra dishes. Banqueting (45). Not suitable for children under 10 after 7 pm. **Seats 45.** No smoking restaurant. D Tue-Sat 7-9.30; Set D from €34.28; house wine €16.50; sc discretionary. Closed Sun & Mon, 23-29 Dec. MasterCard, Visa. **Directions:** from Thurles town, take the Nenagh road, drive for 4 miles and it is situated on the left.

COUNTY WATERFORD

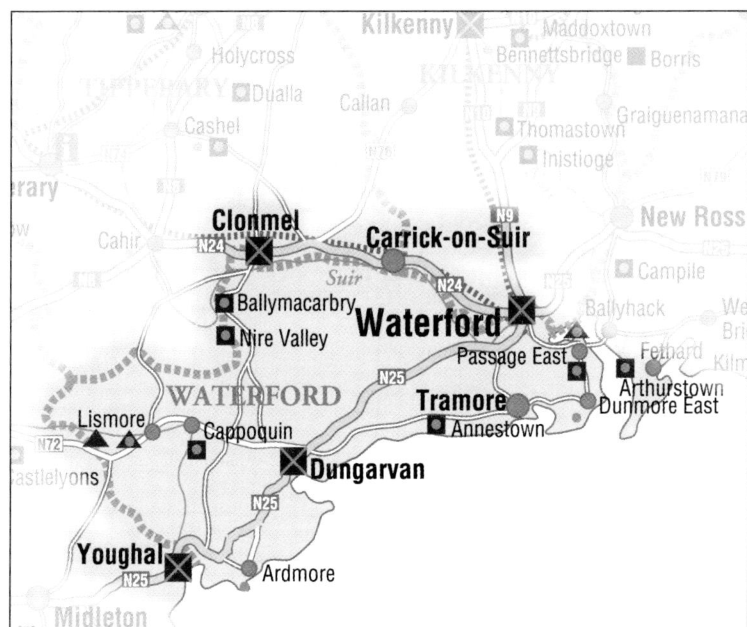

The campaign to establish the main campus of a new university of the southeast in Waterford city will be gathering momentum during 2002. For although this old riverside town is developing in many ways, there's no doubt that the focus of a university would add a welcome extra dimension to life in the region and a city which is best known globally for its creation of the world-famous crystal glass.

On the quays of Waterford, we are witness to a trading and seafaring tradition which goes back at least 1,149 years. But this sense of history also looks to the future, as Waterford has been selected as the assembly port for the Tall Ships of all nations at the beginning of their European sail training programme in July 2005. Today's larger commercial ships may be berthed downstream on the other side of the river at Belview, but the old quays retain a nautical flavour which is accentuated by very useful marina berthing facilities in the heart of town.

This fine city port of Waterford was founded in 853 AD when the Vikings - Danes for the most part - established the trading settlement of Vadrefjord. Its strategic location in a sheltered spot at the head of the estuary near the confluence of the Suir and Barrow rivers guaranteed its continuing success under different administrators, particularly the Normans, so much so that it tended to overshadow the county of Waterford, almost all of which is actually to the west of the port.

But for many years now, the county town has been Dungarvan, which is two-thirds of the way westward along Waterford's extensive south coast, which includes the attractive Copper Coast - between Fenor and Stradbally - in its midst. This spreading of the administrative centres of gravity has to some extent balanced the life of the Waterford region. But even so, the extreme west of the county is still one of Ireland's best kept secrets, a place of remarkable beauty between the Knockmealdown, Comeragh and Monavullagh mountains, where fish-filled rivers such as the Bride, the Blackwater, and the Nire make their way seawards at different speeds through valleys of remarkable variety and beauty.

West Waterford is a place of surprises. For instance, around the delightful coastal village of Ardmore, ancient monuments suggest that the local holy man, St Declan, introduced Christianity to the area quite a few years before St Patrick went to work in the rest of Ireland. And across the bay from Ardmore, the Ring neighbourhood is a Gaeltacht (Irish-speaking) area with its own bustling fishing port at Helvick.

Dungarvan itself is in the midst of an attractive revival. It has relinquished its role as a commercial port, but is enthusiastically taking to recreational boating and harbourside regeneration instead. Along the bluff south coast, secret coves gave smugglers and others access to charming villages like Stradbally and Bunmahon - the former is Waterford county's current top scorer in the national Tidy Towns competition. Further east, the increased tempo of the presence of Waterford city is felt both at the traditional resort of Tramore, and around the fishing/sailing harbour of Dunmore East, which devotees would claim as the Number One Enjoyment Centre in all Ireland.

Local Attractions and Information

Ballymacarbry Nire Valley & Comeraghs on Horseback	052 36147
Cappoquin Mount Melleray Activity Centre	058 54322
Cappoquin Tourism Information	058 53333
Dungarvan Tourism Information	058 41741
Kilmeaden Old School House Craft Centre	051 853567
Lismore Lismore Castle & Gardens	058 54424
Passage East Car Ferry (to Ballyhack, Co Wexford)	051 382480
Waterford Airport	051 875589
Waterford Christ Church Cathedral (18c Neoclassical)	051 858958
Waterford Waterford Crystal Glass Centre	051 332500
Waterford Heritage Museum	051 871227
Waterford Int. Festival of Light Opera (Sept)	051 375437
Waterford Reginald's Tower 13th C Circular Tower	051 304220
Waterford Theatre Royal	051 874402
Waterford Tourism Information	051 875823
Waterford Waterford Treasures at the Granary	051 304500

Annestown

Annestown House

COUNTRY HOUSE

Annestown Co. Waterford **Tel: 051 396 160**

Fax: 051 396 474 Email: relax@annestown.com Web: www.annestown.com

Half way up the hill on the Tramore-Dungarvan road, John and Pippa Galloway's comfortable home overlooks a small bay, with a private path leading to the beach below. In front of the house are manicured lawns – one for croquet, one for tennis – while inside there are several lounges with log-burning fires and a billiard room with full-size table. Everywhere you look there are books – a catholic collection ranging from classics to thrillers. For the evening meal there will be, typically, dishes such as mushroom soup, roast duck and rhubarb crumble. Annestown also has a wine licence. In the morning, a hearty Irish breakfast (with excellent breads) will set you up for the day ahead. All the centrally-heated bedrooms are en suite with direct-dial telephone and tea-making facilities (and hot water bottles are thoughtfully provided for those who still feel cold). **Rooms 5** (all en-suite & no-smoking), B&B about €51 pps, ss about €44. Residents' D Mon-Sat about €29, 7.45pm; house wine about €20 (book by noon). Closed 1 Nov-14 Feb. Amex, MasterCard, Visa. **Directions:** midway between Tramore and Bunmahon on coast road R675.

Ardmore

White Horses Restaurant

RESTAURANT

Ardmore Co. Waterford **Tel: 024 94040**

Christine Power's delightfully bright and breezy café-restaurant on the main street of this famous little seaside town is one of those places that changes its character through the day but always has style. They're open for all the little lifts that visitors need through the day - morning coffee, afternoon tea - as well as imaginative lunches (plus their traditional Sunday lunch, which runs all afternoon) and a more ambitious à la carte evening menu. Vegetarian dishes feature on both menus - a noodle stir-fry during the day perhaps, and Ardsallagh goat's cheese with sesame seed salad in the evening - and there's a good balance between traditional favourites like steaks and more adventurous fare: the daytime fish could be deep-fried plaice with tartare sauce, for example, while its evening counterpart might be Helvick salmon with a crust of cousous, served with a sauce verte. Attractive and pleasant to be in - the use of local Ardmore pottery is a big plus on the presentation side - this is a friendly, well-run place and equally good for a cuppa and a gateau or pastry from the home-made selection on display, or a full meal. **Seats 60.** No smoking area; air conditioning. In summer (1 May-end Sep) open: Tue-Sun 11am-"late" (around 11pm); L 11-4, D 6-11; (also open Mon in Aug). In winter (Oct-Apr) open weekends only: Fri from 6 pm, Sat 11 am-late & Sun 12-4. A la carte except Sun Set L, €17.14. Licensed; sc discretionary. Closed Mon all year, except Aug. MasterCard, Visa. **Directions:** in centre of Main Street.

Ballymacarbry

Melody's Nire View Bar

PUB

Ballymacarbry Co. Waterford **Tel: 052 36147**

This well-known pony-trekking and horse riding centre in the upper reaches of the Nire Valley has been in the family for over a hundred years - and it's a great place to take a break if you're walking or simply touring the area. When something simple but good is needed, Melody's is just the spot for a bowl of Carmel's home-made soup served with freshly baked brown bread, or a freshly-cut sandwich and a bit of crisp-crusted apple tart. The soup might be mulligatawny, mixed vegetable, simple mushroom or carrot & tomato, but it will certainly be made from fresh ingredients that morning and the sandwiches - typically turkey, ham, cheese or salad - are freshly made up to order. Recent renovations and extensions have made the pub brighter and more comfortable without losing its atmosphere and its most important features - genuine hospitality, real open fires and simple good food - remain unchanged. There's live music on Tuesdays, Wednesdays & (usually) Sundays in summer too. Maps are available for a number of walks taking from 11/2-4 hours. Light meals.Closed 25 Dec & Good Fri. No credit cards. **Directions:** on Nire Valley scenic route, R671, between Clonmel and main Dungarvan-Lismore road (N72).

Ballymacarby

Glasha Farmhouse

FARMHOUSE

Glasha Ballymacarby Co. Waterford **Tel: 052 36108**
Fax: 052 36108 Email: glasha@eircom.net Web: www.glashafarmhouse.com

Paddy and Olive O'Gorman's spacious farmhouse is set in its own grounds high up in the hills and provides a very comfortable base for a relaxed rural break. Fishing is a major attraction (the Nire runs beside the farmhouse and permits are available locally), also walking (Glasha links the Comeragh and Knockmealdown sections of the famous Munster Way), pony trekking (see Melody's Nire View Bar, above), golf (available locally) and painting this beautiful area. Olive thinks of everything that will help guests feel at home and bedrooms have lots of little extras including TV/radio, hair dryers, electric blankets, tea/coffee-making, spring water and magazines; all rooms are en-suite and the newer ones have lovely bathrooms with jacuzzi baths. There's plenty of comfortable lounging room for guests' use, including a conservatory - and the nearest pub is just 3 minutes' walk from the house. Children welcome, cots available. **Rooms 9** (4 with jacuzzi, 5 shower only, all no-smoking). B&B about €40 pps, ss about €8. Closed Christmas. **Directions:** off 671 road between Clonmel and Dungarvan.

Ballymacarbry

Hanora's Cottage

GUESTHOUSE
RESTAURANT

Ballymacarbry Nire Valley Co. Waterford
Tel: 052 36134 Fax: 052 36540
Email: hanorascottage@eircom.net Web: www.hanorascottage.com

IRISH BREAKFAST AWARD - MUNSTER & NATIONAL WINNER

Major renovations and extensions were completed at the Wall family's large modern guesthouse in the spring of 1999, but Hanora's still nurtures the spirit of the ancestral home around which it is built. The Walls are caring and hospitable hosts and this, plus the luxurious accommodation and good food they provide, makes Hanora's a very special place - and especially wonderful for foot-weary walkers. Spacious, thoughtfully furnished rooms are now all new or recently refurbished, most have jacuzzi baths and there are three especially romantic ones for honeymooners. There's also a new conservatory with a spa tub, overlooking the garden with views of the mountains. Overnight guests have the privilege of starting the day with Hanora's legendary breakfast buffet, which is the Munster and National Winner the Denny Irish Breakfast Awards; it takes some time to get the measure of this feast, so make sure you get up in time to make the most of it. Local produce and an amazing variety of exotics (some of which you may not previously have encountered) jostle for space on the beautifully arranged buffet: the menu begins in orderly fashion with freshly squeezed orange and grapefruit juice and luscious Crinnaghtaun Apple Juice from Lismore, moves on to Seamus Wall's homemade muesli and Mary's Nire Valley Porridge then launches into an amazing list of more fresh fruits before reaching the bread section...Seamus is the baker, beginning at 6am every day so that, when guests come down for breakfast, he'll have an incredible dozen or more types of bread, scones, muffins and buns ready, including organic and gluten free varieties. Alongside the breads you'll find local farmhouse cheeses, smoked salmon and home made jams - and, while that rounds off the buffet, the cooked breakfast options are yet to come: for your hot dish you can have Syl Murray's home-made sausages, Clonakilty black & white ouddings, Biddy Cooney's free-range eggs (various ways) and much else besides. This is truly a gargantuan feast, designed to see you many miles along the hills before stop for a little packed lunch (based on Seamus's delicious freshly-baked breads) and ultimately return for dinner.*NB: Special offers will be available at Hanora's throughout the coming year. **Rooms 11** (3 junior suites, all no smoking). Not suitable for children. No pets.B&B €85 pps. Closed 22-27 Dec. **Restaurant:** A completely new restaurant and kitchen emerged from the recent extension of Hanora's Cottage, to the delight of chefs Eoin and Judith Wall. Dinner visitors travel from far and wide to mingle with residents at the fireside in the spacious, warmly furnished seating areas which now extend into the old dining room. Here you can have an aperitif and ponder on Eoin and Judith's imaginative, well-balanced menus, before moving through to the restaurant, which overlooks a new garden and the riverside woodland. Enthusiastic supporters of small suppliers, Eoin and Judith use local produce whenever possible and credit them on the menu - fresh fish from Dunmore East, free range chickens from Stradbally and local cheeses, for example. There's a separate vegetarian dinner menu on request (€31) as well as an à la carte which offers a choice of six or seven dishes on each course, usually including some vegetarian options. Dishes recently enjoyed include starters of sautéed lambs kidneys with wholegrain mustard mash and mushroom paté on crostini with mixed salad. Lamb is abundant locally, so roast rack of lamb makes an excellent main course choice (served, perhaps, with a delicious mint hollandaise), while oven-baked cod with cheese and chutney crust is also typical; the fish doesn't have far to travel and is beautifully fresh and accurately cooked. Desserts tend to be quite classical, including home-made ice creams, and are often fruit based. Not suitable for children under 12. D Mon-Sat, à la carte. House wine €14.60. Closed 22-27 Dec. MasterCard, Visa, Laser. **Directions:** From Clonmel or Dungarvan via Ballymacarbry.

Cappoquin

COUNTRY HOUSE/RESTAURANT

Richmond House

Cappoquin Co. Waterford
Tel: 058 54278 Fax: 058 54988
Email: info@richmondhouse.net Web: www.richmondhouse.net

Set in private parkland just outside Cappoquin, the Deevy family's fine 18th century country house and restaurant offers a winning combination of genuine hospitality, high standards of comfort, thoughtful service and excellent food. Approaching through well-tended grounds, a good impression is made from the outset, a feeling confirmed by the welcoming hall, which has a wood-burning stove and well-proportioned, elegantly furnished reception rooms opening off it. Nine individually decorated en-suite bedrooms vary in size and appointments, as is the way with old houses, but all are comfortably furnished in country house style with full bathrooms. Children welcome; cots available without charge. **Rooms 9** (all en-suite & no smoking). B&B €76pps, ss €13. Closed 23 Dec-20 Jan. Restaurant The restaurant is the most important single element at Richmond House, and non-residents regularly make up a high proportion of the guests. Warm and friendly service begins at the front door, then menus are presented over aperitifs, in front of the drawing room fire or in a conservatory overlooking the garden. Herbs, fruit and vegetables are grown on the premises for use in the kitchen and Paul is an ardent supporter of local produce, buying seafood from Dunmore East and Dungarvan, beef, lamb, bacon and sausages from his trusted local butcher, and extra organic produce grown nearby. Paul constantly seeks ways to improve the range and style offered and there is a sureness of touch in his kitchen, seen in stimulating menus that always include imaginative vegetarian choices and offer a balance between traditional country house cooking and more adventurous dishes inspired by the current trend towards global cuisine. Dinner menus offering about five choices on each course are changed daily (although based on a core of speciality dishes, such as roast rack of West Waterford lamb on garlic scented mushrooms, with home-made mint jelly and rosemary jus); a slightly shorter separate vegetarian menu is also offered - and one or two local specialities such as Crinnaghtaun apple juice will always feature. Under Claire's direction, service is excellent and admirably discreet care continues throughout. A carefully selected and fairly priced wine list includes interesting house wines and a dozen half bottles. Children welcome (under 3s free in parents' room). Restaurant **Seats 40.** No smoking area. D 7-9 daily; Set D €43, à la carte also available; house wine €16.50; sc discretionary. Amex, Diners, MasterCard, Visa, Laser. **Directions:** half a mile outside Cappoquin on N72.

Cappagh
FARMHOUSE

Castle Farm Country House

Cappagh Millstreet Dungarvan Co. Waterford
Tel: 058 68049 Fax: 058 68099
Email: castlefm@iol.ie Web: www.waterfordfarms.com/castlefarm/

Set in 1.5 acres of recently landscaped gardens overlooking the River Finisk, the Nugent family's unusual farmhouse is in the 18th century wing of a 15th century castle. Although most of the house seems quite normal inside, it blends into the original building in places - so, for example, the dining room has walls five feet deep and an original castle archway. Spacious, comfortably appointed rooms have king size beds, television, tea/coffee facilities and neat shower rooms; (there is also a a full bathroom available for any guest who prefers a bath). Meticulous housekeeping, a very pleasant guests' sitting room and fresh flowers everywhere all add up to a very appealing farmhouse indeed, and Joan uses their own produce - fruit, vegetables, meats and herbs - in her cooking. Children welcome (under 2s free in parents' room; cots available). Pets in certain areas. **Rooms 5** (all en-suite). B&B €35pps, ss €7. Dining Room **Seats 20.** Closed 1 Nov-1 Mar. Amex, Visa, Laser. **Directions:** off N72 on R671, Nire Valley scenic route.

Cheekpoint
RESTAURANT

McAlpin's Suir Inn

Cheekpoint Co. Waterford **Tel: 051 382 220**
Email: cheekpoint@eircom.net Web: www.mcalpins.com

This immaculately maintained black-and-white painted inn is 300 years old and has been run by the McAlpin family since 1972. During that time they have earned an enviable reputation for hospitality and good food served at a moderate price, notably local seafood. It's a characterful, country style place with rustic furniture, cottagey plates and old prints decorating the walls. Seasonal menus offer a choice of about six starters (nearly all seafood and under €6.50) and ten main courses, including three cold dishes and two vegetarian ones, again all moderately priced - specialities include a generous seafood platter and home-made seafood pie. All meals come with brown soda bread, butter and a side salad – and there's a nice little wine list including a special selection of eight good New World wines, "The €14 Cellar". Own parking. No children after 8 pm **Seats 36.** No smoking area; air conditioning. D 6-9.45 Mon-Sat; à la carte; sc discretionary. Closed Sun, Christmas-mid Jan. MasterCard, Visa, Laser. **Directions:** 7 miles east of Waterford.

Dungarvan
FARMHOUSE/B&B

Gortnadiha House

Ring Dungarvan Co. Waterford
Tel: 058 46142 Email: ringcheese@tinet.ie

Eileen Harty's home is on a working dairy farm in a lovely setting, with woodland gardens and sea views. In addition to the normal farming activities, this one has a special claim to fame, as they're producers of the characterful Ring Farmhouse Cheese, which is made on the premises. Accommodation in the family home is comfortable, hospitality is warm and breakfasts offer a very wide selection of local and home produce, including fresh fish in season - and, of course, farmhouse cheese. Children welcome. Pets by arrangement. **Rooms 3** (2 shower only). B&B €35 pps, ss €7. Closed Nov-Mar. Visa. **Directions:** N25 Rosslare to Cork. 3km from Dungarvin, follow the sea.

Dungarvan
RESTAURANT/CAFÉ

King John's Patisserie

Harbour Mill Davitt's Quay Dungarvan Co. Waterford
Tel: 058 45756 Fax: 058 45854

This little place may be elusive if you're looking for a name but, come coffee time, cruise along the quayside and keep an eye out for the bright blue awning. Just the place for a coffee any-which-way you like it, this light and airy modern café just exudes quality and style with its beech tables and flooring, peppermint green and indigo blue seating, lots of chrome and a selection of newspapers to browse while you sip. A range of fatly-packed freshly-cut sandwiches will catch your eye just inside the door, and the main display offers all kinds of tempting pastries and gateaux - including specialities like "chocolate squidgy cake" - all explained with admirable interest and patience by friendly staff. They also do hearty breakfasts, there's a blackboard menu offering home-made hot dishes at lunchtime (with a glass of wine if you like) and a take-away service. Wheelchair accessible. Children welcome. **Seats 40.** No smoking area; air conditioning. Open all day (8am-9pm); all à la carte; licensed; sc discretionary. Closed Sun, 24 Dec (10 days) & Good Fri. MasterCard, Visa. **Directions:** off main N25 Waterford-Cork road, waterside position on harbour.

Dungarvan
HOTEL

The Park Hotel

Dungarvan Co. Waterford **Tel: 058 42899** Fax: 058 42969
Email: photel@indigo.ie Web: www.parkhotel.ie

This attractive hotel on the outskirts of Dungarvan is owner-run by the Flynn family, who have many years of experience in the hotel business It has views over the Colligan River estuary and fits comfortably into its surroundings, with mature trees softening the approach. Public areas include a cosy traditional bar with panelled walls and a spacious, elegantly appointed dining room. Bedrooms are furnished and decorated to a high standard, with well-finished bathrooms (full bath with shower), phone, multi-channel TV, tea/coffee-making facilities and trouser press - and generous desk space as well as easy chairs. In addition to the many outdoor activities in the area – including tennis, fishing, windsurfing, walking, horse-riding, pony-trekking as well as shooting and hunting in season – there's an aqua and fitness centre with 20-metre pool, separate children's pool and many other features. Exceptionally friendly and helpful staff ensure an enjoyable stay at this relaxing hotel. Conference/banqueting (300/300). Own parking. Leisure centre. Children welcome (under 4s free in parents' room; cots available without charge, baby sitting avilable). Pets allowed in some areas. **Rooms 45** (3 shower only). B&B €60.95pps, ss €19.05. Closed Christmas. Amex, Diners, MasterCard, Visa, Laser. **Directions:** outskirts of Dungarvan.

Dungarvan
GUESTHOUSE/RESTAURANT

Powersfield House

Ballinamuck West Dungarvan Co. Waterford
Tel: 058 45594 Fax: 058 45550
Email: powersfieldhouse@cablesurf.com

Edmund and Eunice Power's brand new guesthouse opened in 2001 and is a very welcome addition to the limited amount of quality accommodation in this lovely area. Although new, it has been furnished in traditional country house style with antiques and interesting fabrics creating a soothing and relaxing atmosphere. Each bedroom has been individually decorated and finished to a high standard, with all the necessary comforts including phones (with ISDN & fax facilities), TV and tea/coffee trays. Children are welcome (under 4s free in parents' room; cot availabe without charge; children's playground). Eunice also runs a small restaurant at the house several nights a week, offering a set menu based on local produce such as Helvic seafood, local organic vegetables and Knocklara cheese. Although the surroundings were still a little raw at the time of the Guide's visit, new planting should mature enough to soften the setting a little for the 2002 season. **Rooms 6** (all en-suite and no smoking). B&B €45 pps, ss €12. Restaurant not suitable for children under 12. **Seats 18.** D Thu-Sat, 7-10. Set D €34.29; house wine €17.78; sc discretionary. MasterCard, Visa Laser, Switch. **Directions:** 1 mile from Dungarvan on Cork road.

Dungarvan
RESTAURANT ☆

Tannery Restaurant

10 Quay Street Dungarvan Co. Waterford
Tel: 058 45420 Fax: 058 45118

The best-known cutting edge establishment in the south-east is located in this old leather tannery which was imaginatively converted a few years ago to make a stylish contemporary restaurant for Paul and Maire Flynn. The kitchen is open to view as guests go upstairs to the first-floor dining area and the tannery theme is echoed throughout the light, clean-lined interior, creating a sense of history that, along with dramatic paintings and fresh flowers, adds greatly to the atmosphere. Colourful, modish dishes are equally contemporary and wide-ranging menus inspired by global trends are based mainly on local ingredients, which Paul supports avidly and souces with care: local seafood features in a successful modern rendition of bouillabaisse, in a saffron broth and main courses such as salt cod cakes with egg & spring onion cream and rocket salad. Dashing desserts are (very) tempting - lovely simple dishes like compôte of blackberries witrh vanilla cream or pannacotta with oranges are hard to resist, but don't miss the cheese, which won the Guide's Farmhouse Cheese Award in 2000: a selection of four farmhouse cheeses is presented in perfect condition: Mine Gabhar fresh goat's cheese may be offered in season (April-October), a ripe Cashel Blue will often be included and a Durrus or Milleens, perhaps, or if you are lucky the West Cork Cheese Company's wonderful mature Gabriel, Desmond or Mizen - all served with biscuits, celery, walnuts and some luscious fruit. The à la carte is fairly priced for food of this quality, but interesting and frequently changed lunch and early evening menus are especially good value. Toilets wheelchair accessible. Children welcome before 8.30pm. **Seats 52** (private room up to 30). No smoking area. L Tue-Sun, 12.30-2.30; D Tue-Sat (also Sun in Jul & Aug), 6.30-9.30. Early D €22.22 (Tue-Fri, 6.30-7.30 only); Set Sun L €20.95; house wine €17.14; sc discretionary. Closed 3 weeks end Jan-Feb. Amex, Diners, MasterCard, Visa. **Directions:** down laneway to right of old library.

Dunmore East

The Ship

RESTAURANT Dunmore East Co. Waterford **Tel: 051 383 141** Fax: 051 383 144

The Prendivilles' well-known bar and restaurant is in a Victorian corner house, with a patio on the harbour side which is used mainly for casual lunches in summer. Inside, an atmospheric bar and informal restaurant are designed around a nautical theme - and, although concessions are made to non-seafood eaters, seafood is emphatically the star. Starters might feature an imaginative creation such as cured fillets of monkfish with chervil and dill, served with a sorbet "bloody mary style". Soups will usually include a good bisque and main courses range from simple pan-fried fish of the day to luxurious dishes such as poached fillets of dover sole and prawns with a lobster and brandy sauce (which has been known to be garnished rather surprisingly with a goat's cheese lasagne). Tempting desserts tend to be variations on classic themes and there's always an Irish farmhouse cheeseboard. Set Sunday lunch menus, offered in spring and autumn only, are shorter and simpler, but also major on seafood. Children welcome before 9 pm. **Seats 75.** No smoking area; air conditioning. L daily Jun-Aug, 12.30-2; otherwise L Sun only in Apr-May & Sep-Oct. D 7-10 daily. Set Sun L €18.41; D à la carte; house wine €17.14; sc discretionary. Closed 25 Dec & Good Fri. Amex, Diners, MasterCard, Visa. **Directions:** 11 miles from Waterford on the Dunmore road.

Faithlegg

Faithlegg House Hotel

HOTEL Faithlegg Co. Waterford **Tel: 051 382000** Fax: 051 382010
Email: faithlegg@iol.ie Web: wwwtowerhotelgroup.ie

This lovely 18th century house is set in wooded landscape with magnificent views over its own golf course and the Suir estuary. The house has been sensitively developed as a luxury hotel - the tone is set in the reception area, with its original stone floor, classic fireplace and Waterford Crystal chandelier and a similar sensitivity to the essentials of conversion is evident throughout. Public areas are spacious and elegant and bedrooms, in both the old house and a discreetly positioned new wing, are furnished to a high standard with excellent facilities, including ISDN lines; large, graciously proportioned rooms and suites in the old house are really lovely, while those in the new wing are more practical. Somewhere along the line, an architectural sense of humour has been at work too, as visitors to the snooker room will discover. Numerous health, fitness and beauty treatments are available in the new leisure centre, which has a 17 m swimming pool. Self-catering accommodation is also offered in the grounds. Conference/banqueting (180/150); secretarial services. Ample parking. Golf (18), fishing, gardens, walking; leisure centre, swimming pool; snooker. Children welcome (under 3s free in parents' room; cots available without charge). No pets. **Rooms 82** (14 suites, 14 executive, 10 no-smoking, 6 for disabled). Lift. B&B €117.50pps, ss €25. Closed 23-27 Dec &3 Jan-8 Feb. **Roseville Room** You can have an aperitif and consider menus in the bar, which is quite large and comfortably furnished in a clubby style; orders may be taken here and you will be called through when your table is ready. Chef de Cuisine Eric Thèze's classic French menus change daily, which is ideal for residents staying for several nights, and there is also a separate vegetarian menu (it may not be offered, but should be available on request). A balanced choice of about four starters and main courses is offered, with a soup or sorbet and perhaps three desserts. Salad of smoked salmon with endive, black olives & citrus vinaigrette; broccoli & blue cheese soup (or raspberry & vodka sorbet); pan seared medallions of venison with a red berry & cranberry sauce; and poached pear and pineapple with kirsch syrup & honey ice cream give a fair indication of the style. The restaurant is shared between two lovely classical, formally appointed dining rooms (guests in the other room seemed to be getting better service and having more fun on the Guide's visit, but perhaps that's just human nature). Reliable rather than inspired cooking and rather plain presentation (which makes a change from perilously stacked food) are perfectly acceptable considering the reasonable price of a 5-course dinner in this lovely dining room; in the Guide's experience, service may be a little uneven - probably because tables may be turned around several times on busy nights. **Seats 85** (private room 40). No smoking area; air conditioning. Not suitable for children after 7.30. D daily, 6.30-9.30; L Sun 12.30-2.30. Amex, Diners, MasterCard, Visa, Laser. **Directions:** off Dunmore East road; 6 miles outside Waterford city.

Lismore
HOTEL/RESTAURANT

Ballyrafter Country House Hotel

Lismore Co.Waterford **Tel: 058 54002** Fax: 058 53050
Email: info@waterfordhotel.com Web: ballyrafter@waterfordhotel.com

Fishing is a big draw to Joe & Noreen Willoughby's welcoming country house hotel, but a relaxing atmosphere, log fires and good home cooking appeal to a growing number of people who simply enjoy the area and have come to see the unpretentious comforts of Ballyrafter as a home from home. The bar, where informal meals are served, is lined with photographs of happy fisherfolk - if you are dining in the restaurant, you can have an aperitif here while looking at the menu, or beside the fire in the drawing room next door. Bedrooms in the main house are simple and comfortable and one side of the the courtyard area at the back of the hotel has been thoughtfully developed to provide five new executive bedrooms, all very carefully designed to replicate the older ones. (New PVC windows were installed for practical reasons, but even these were carefully sourced to provide the correct sliding mechanism); there is also large new first floor room which could be used as a boardroom or for small functions and, on the ground floor, the existing function area overlooking the yard has been completely rebuilt as a conservatory, which allows light through to the bar and transforms that section of the hotel. **Rooms 14** (5 shower only). B&B about €51 pps, ss abou t€20. Restaurant An open fire, family antiques and flowers from the garden create a caring atmosphere in the restaurant and the Duke of Devonshire's fairytale castle looks magical from window tables when floodlit at night. Appetising home-cooked meals are based on local ingredients including, of course, fresh and smoked Blackwater salmon, along with home-produced honey and local cheeses like Knockanore and Ring, and service is friendly and helpful. **Seats 30.** No Smoking Restaurant. D 7.30-9.30 daily (Mon residents only); Set D about €31; L Sun only 1-3 pm, Set L about €16. House Wine: about €13; 10% sc. Bar Meals 12-6.30 daily, L 1-2.30. Closed Dec-Mar. Amex, Diners, MasterCard, Visa. **Directions:** on the edge of Lismore town, from Cappoquin direction.

Lismore
PUB /RESTAURANT/B&B

Buggy's Glencairn Inn

Glencairn, nr Lismore Tallow Co. Waterford
Tel: 058 56323 Fax: 058 56232
Email: buggysglencairninn@eircom.net Web: www.lismore.com

This is Ken and Kathleen Buggy's dream of a country pub - and reassuring notices beside the cheerfully painted door ease visitors into the little fire-lit bar. Ken's artlessly rustic food is the main attraction, however, and everything in this miniscule pub is based on fresh ingredients and "made on the day" so be prepared for limited choice, especially towards the end of service. The menu offers around four to six dishes per course, served in the bar as well as two little dining rooms charmingly set up with a stylish country informality. Starters like wild duck liver paté or a freshly made soup of the day (with home-made brown soda bread), may be followed by fish as available on the day - cooked simply in butter, olive oil and lemon juice - or casserole of rabbit or chicken provençale, all served with crisp little chips, vegetable of the day and a side salad. Finish up with something like blackberry & apple crumble (with home-made ice cream), or farmhouse cheeses, then cafetière coffee or an Irish coffee. Upstairs there are four delightful en-suite rooms (€50.79 pps, ss €12.70. Not suitable for children under 9 after 6pm. **Seats 20.** No smoking area. D & Bar Food daily in summer, 7.30-8.45 (Sun 7-8.30), Wed-Sun in winter; all à la carte; house wine €16.51; sc 10%. Closed Mon & Tue off season, Christmas period & occasionally throughout the year. (A phone call ahead is wise; dinner reservations advised). MasterCard, Visa, Laser. **Directions:** between Tallow and Lismore, turn left at Hornibrooks and travel 2 miles, pink building.

Tallowbridge
PUB/RESTAURANT

The Brideview Bar & Restaurant

Tallow Co. Waterford **Tel: 058 56522** Fax: 058 56729

This attractive bar and restaurant is beautifully located just outside Tallow, beside an old stone bridge over the River Bride and with parking space in a yard beside the pub. Recent extensions and renovations have kept some character in the older bar - which is along the road side of the building and has an open fire - while creating a fine informal dining space with large windows maximising on views over the river and a large garden which is well away from the road, with picnic tables set up for sunny days. Menus are not over-ambitious and change weekly (plus daily blackboard specials); the emphasis is on providing home-cooked food and good value. Wild mushroom & pork paté with mini-toast & salad garnish, poached fillet of salmon with teriyaki sauce & crispy noodles and brandy snap baskets with raspberries are all typical of the evening Bistro menu, while Sunday lunch balances traditional and less predictable dishes rather well. Home-cooked bar food is available all day, making this a useful place to know if you are touring or walking in the area. Children welcome. Restaurant seats 42. L 12.30-3, D 6-9. 12.30 and 9.30. Set Sun L €16.44, otherwise à la carte. House wine €15.17. Closed 25-26 Dec & Good Fri. Amex, MasterCard, Visa Laser. **Directions:** near Tallow on N72 12 miles Fermoy - 3 Lismore.

Tramore

Rockett's "The Metal Man"

PUB

Westown Tramore Co. Waterford **Tel: 051 381496**

Open fires and a friendly, welcoming atmosphere will always draw you into this unusual pub but it's the speciality of the house, Crubeens (pig's trotters) which has earned it fame throughout the land. Crubeens (cruibíns) were once the staple bar food in pubs everywhere but, as they've been supplanted by crisps, peanuts and lasagne & chips, Rockett's is one of the few places to keep up the old tradition. Two bars are set up with tables for the comfortable consumption of these porcine treats - and you can forget about finger bowls here: the back room even has a sink in the corner for rinsing sticky fingers! Food served Wed-Sat 7-9 pm & Sun 1-6 (weekends only in winter). Phone ahead to check times. Closed 25 Dec & Good Fri.

Waterford

Chez K's Steak & Seafood Restaurant

RESTAURANT

26-31 Johns Street Waterford Co. Waterford **Tel: 051 844180**
Fax: 051 856925 Email: muldoons@iol.ie

First impressions of this restaurant may be off-putting, as it's self-service, with non-existent decor, poor lighting and very basic table settings. But, once you get past the block, you'll find that lots of young local people have discovered what good food and value for money are offered here - and a cheerful young crowd enjoying themselves creates atmosphere, so eating here might be more enjoyable than anticipated. A wide choice of food is displayed in chilled cabinets around the cooking area and the quality is there for all to see; cutting costs on the frills clearly pays off, as they are able to offer, for example, black (Dover) sole at a mere €20.32. (Black sole has become the benchmark for pricing in east coast restaurants recently and there are some who would cheerfully charge twice that and get away with it.) It comes perfectly cooked, served simply with a lemon beurre blanc - and a full complement of vegetables, including boiled new potatoes (in season). On the steak side, a carpaccio of beef, for example, comes with rocket, roasted beetroot and Parmesan shavings: surprising - and simply delicious. D daily 6-10pm. Diners, MasterCard, Visa, Laser. **Directions:** head for the junction at Parnell street; restaurant is on the left.

Waterford

Dwyer's Restaurant

RESTAURANT

8 Mary Street Waterford Co. Waterford
Tel: 051 877478 Fax: 051 877480

Quietly located in an elegantly converted old barracks, chef-proprietor Martin Dwyer and his wife Sile have been running this highly regarded restaurant since 1989, and Clive Nunn designed refurbishments have recently introduced a classy contemporary tone to the decor. Without show or fuss, they consistently provide excellence: low-key presentation of some of the country's finest food is accompanied by discreet, thoughtful service. Martin carefully sources the best seasonal local produce which he prepares in a style that is basically classic French, with some country French and modern Irish influences. He sums up his philosophy with admirable simplicity: "We feel that the basis of good food is taste rather than presentation or fashion". Menus change monthly and main courses lean towards seafood – seared turbot on a bed of fennel, with fennel cream sauce and roast fillet of hake with prawn vinaigrette would both be typical – but there are strong choices for carnivores and vegetarians too. Classic desserts are well worth leaving room for, and there's always an Irish cheese plate. Espresso and herbal teas are offered as well as regular cafetière coffee and tea. Like the cooking, the wine list favours France, although Spain, Italy, Germany and the New World are also represented. The early evening menu is particularly good value. Children welcome before 8 pm. **Seats 32** (private room, 8). No smoking area. D 6-10 Mon-Sat, Set D, early evening menu, 6-7 pm only; à la carte also available; house wine about €14; sc discretionary. No private parking. Toilets wheelchair accessible Closed Sun, Christmas week & bank hols. Amex, Diners, MasterCard, Visa. **Directions:** 50 yards south of Bridge, turn right – 100 yards down road on right.

Waterford

Foxmount Farm & Country House

COUNTRY HOUSE/FARMHOUSE

Passage East Rd. Waterford Co. Waterford
Tel: 051 874 308 Fax: 051 854 906
Email: foxmount@iol.ie Web: www.iol.ie/tipp/foxmount.htm

Foxmount Farm, the Kent family's 17th century country house and working dairy farm, is just 15 minutes drive from the centre of Waterford city. The house is lovely, with classically proportioned reception rooms and it is a haven of peace and tranquillity. Margaret Kent's home-cooked food is one of the main reasons guests keep returning to Foxmount - dinner, prepared by her personally and based on the farm's own produce, is available for residents by arrangement; vegetarian or other special dietary requirements can be built into menus if mentioned on booking. Margaret is a great baker, as guests quickly discover when she serves afternoon tea in the drawing room (or in the morning, when freshly-baked breads are presented at breakfast). Five very different rooms are all thoughtfully furnished, and include some family rooms, but bear in mind that peace and relaxation are the aim at Foxmount, so don't expect phones or TVs in bedrooms or a very early breakfast. There is a hard tennis court on the premises (plus table tennis). Children welcome, pets by arrangement. **Rooms 5** (all en-suite & no-smoking). B&B €44.44pps, ss 12.70. Residents' D €25.39 at 7pm (book by noon) BYO wine. Closed Nov-Mar. No credit cards. **Directions:** from Waterford city, take Dunmore Road - after 4 km, take passage east road for 1 mile.

Waterford

Gatchell's Restaurant

RESTAURANT

Waterford Crystal Visitor Centre Kilbarry Waterford Co. Waterford
Tel: 051 854815 Fax: 051 332561

If you intend visiting the Waterford Crystal Visitor Centre it might be useful to know that a tasty bite to eat can be part of the plan. Well-known Waterford restaurateurs, Paula and Peter Prendiville are operating this all-day restaurant here. Although it's self-service, they provide interesting, wholesome fare like savoury pork & pasta au gratin, crab & mushroom bake and coronation chicken salad - and visitors who despair of ever finding traditional Irish food in the current tidal wave of global cooking will be pleased to see dishes with a respect for tradition here, such as beef, Guinnness & orange casserole (beef marinated in stout and cooked with vegetables, herbs and orange). **Seats 160.** No smoking restaurant. Children welcome. Open daily 8.30am-5.30 (in winter 9-5). A la carte (average main course about €8.85). MasterCard, Visa, Laser. **Directions:** At Waterford Crystal Visitor Centre.

Waterford

The Gingerman Bar

PUB

7 Arundel Lane Waterford Co. Waterford **Tel: 051 879522** Fax: 051 879522

Michael Tierney's recently renovated pub is in the old Norman area of the city, in a pedestrianised lane just off Broad Street. It's a very pleasant place, with welcoming open fires in several bars, and has already earned reputation for good food. Carefully sourced ingredients come from trusted local suppliers and the emphasis is on fresh, home-made and healthy. (They don't serve chips and don't even have a deep fryer in the kitchen). The style is mainly modern, with an all day menu offering snacks like hot sandwiches, paninis and filled baked potatoes (the latter popular as an alternative to sandwiches for people on a gluten-free diet) and there are four hot specials, changed daily. One of the favourites is pasta with chicken & smokey bacon on a white wine & garlic sauce, served with a panini - and there are more traditional choices too, like beef & Guinness stew, served with home-made soda bread and bacon ribs with colcannon & parsley sauce. Good cooking is complemented by efficient service, provided by keen, friendly young staff. Open 10am-11.30pm. Food served Mon-Sat, 12-6. A la carte (average snack €6.30; hot specials about €8.85). No food on Sun. MasterCard, Visa, Laser, Switch. **Directions:** opposite city square.

Waterford

Goose's Barbecue Restaurant & Wine House

RESTAURANT

19 Henrietta Street Waterford Co. Waterford
Tel: 051 858426 Fax: 051 858426

Waterford people seem to have taken to self-service in a big way recently - this one is a little different from the other listed, but the same principles of high quality and good value apply. Here, in a historic site (the details of which are given on the menu), they have a self-service salad buffet and all the main meals are freshly prepared when you order them and cooked in view of customers. There are little starters like cajun chicken wings and saucy sausages and main dishes like boozy beef steaks and medallions of lamb barbecued with rosemary & herbs, served with jacket potato. Vegetarians can have mixed veg & tofu skewers and there's a blackboard giving the fish of the night and desserts. Not suitable for children after 7pm. **Seats 40.** D Tue-Sat, 5.30-10.30. A la carte (average main course €16). House wine €18. Closed Sun, Mon.

Waterford
HOTEL

Granville Hotel

The Quay Waterford Co. Waterford
Tel: 051 305 555 Fax: 051 305 566
Email: stay@granville-hotel.ie Web: www.granville.hotel.ie

One of the country's oldest hotels, this much-loved quayside establishment in the centre of Waterford has many historical connections – with Bianconi, for example, who established Ireland's earliest transport system, and also Charles Stuart Parnell, who made many a rousing speech here. Since 1979, it's been owner-run by the Cusack family, who have overseen significant restoration and major refurbishment. It's a large hotel – bigger than it looks perhaps – with fine public areas and well-appointed bedrooms (all with well-designed bathrooms with both bath and shower). This is a good choice for business guests and would also make a comfortable base for touring the area or participating in the many activities available locally, including boating, fishing, golf, walking and horse riding. Off season value breaks available. Conference/banqueting (200/200), video conferencing, secretarial services. Parking nearby. Children welcome (under 3s free in parents' room; cots available without charge). No pets. **Rooms 98** (4 suites, 94 executive rooms, 20 no-smoking). Lift. B&B €90 pps, ss €20. Closed 25-26 Dec. Amex, Diners, MasterCard, Visa, Laser. **Directions:** in city centre, on the quays, opposite clock tower.

Waterford
PUB

Henry Downes

8-10 Thomas St. Waterford Co. Waterford **Tel: 051 874 118**

Established in 1759, and in the same (eccentric) family for six generations, John de Bromhead's unusual pub is one of the few remaining houses to bottle its own whiskey. Although not the easiest of places to find, once visited it certainly will not be forgotten. Large, dark and cavernous – with a squash court on the premises as well as the more predictable billiards and snooker – it consists of a series of bars of differing character, each with its own particular following. It achieves with natural grace what so-called Irish theme pubs would dearly love to capture (and can't). Friendly, humorous bar staff enjoy filling customers in on the pub's proud history – and will gladly sell you a bottle of Henry Downes No.9 to take away. Wine about €9 (to drink in pub). Open from 4.30pm to normal closing time. Closed 25 Dec & Good Fri. No credit cards. **Directions:** second right after Bridge Hotel, halfway up Thomas street on right.

Waterford
RESTAURANT

O'Grady's

Cork Road Waterford Co. Waterford **Tel: 051 378 851**
Fax: 051 374 062 Email: info@ogradyshotel.com Web: www.ogradys.ie

Off-road parking and a warm reception from the proprietors get guests off to a good start at Sue and Cornelius O'Grady's restaurant in a restored Gothic lodge on the main Cork road. The dining area is well-situated at the rear of the building, away from the road and, while this has always been a reliable restaurant, the Guide's most recent visit was most impressive. Menus change weekly and include 2/3 course lunch menus and an interesting, well-balanced à la carte; they always offer tempting vegetarian dishes - a starter of wild mushrooms risotto, perhaps, and main courses like Mediterranean vegetable millefeuille with parmesan cream sauce. The best of local seafood features in starters like home-cured gravad lax with dill potatoes, straightforward oysters or a well-made chowder - while main courses offer a well-balanced selection ranging from sauté of lambs kidneys in a Dijon mustard sauce and fillet of cod with roast pepper salsa to pork fillet with apples and cider - also luxurious lobster and ever-popular choices like steaks. Finish with a classic dessert like hazelnut & praline parfait or raspberry pavlova, or farmhouse cheeses, perhaps, which are served plated. Children welcome. **Seats 60** (private room, 12). No smoking area. L 12.30-2.15 & D 6.30-9.30 daily. Set L €18, Set D €35; house wine €17; sc 10%. [There are also 9 en-suite bedrooms, €50 pps.] Closed Xmas, Good Fri. Amex, Diners, MasterCard, Visa, Switch, Laser. **Directions:** on main Cork road, 1 mile from city centre.

Waterford
HOTEL

Tower Hotel Waterford

The Mall Waterford Co. Waterford **Tel: 051 875 801** Fax: 051 870 129
Email: tower@iol.ie Web: www.towerhotelgroup.ie

A central location, within easy walking distance of everything in the city, ample private parking, large conference/banqueting capacity and excellent on-site leisure facilities are major attractions at this big hotel. Considerable investment over the last few years has seen an improvement in standards throughout the hotel: an impressive new bistro and carvery restaurants were almost complete at the time of the Guide's last visit and a new state of the art conference centre was also installed in 2001. The lobby and reception area is due for a revamp in time for the 2002 season, but some bedrooms may not yet have been refurbished: it is worth checking on this when making a reservation as there is a big difference between old and new rooms. Conference/banqueting facilities (650/400), Leisure Centre, indoor swimming pool, Children welcome (under 3s free in parents' room). Own parking. No pets. **Rooms 140** (3 suites, 3 executive, 3 for disabled) B&B €83.80 pps, ss €19. Closed 24-26 Dec. Amex, Diners, MasterCard, Visa, Laser. **Directions:** Waterford city centre overlooking marine.

Waterford

HOTEL

Waterford Castle Hotel & Golf Club

The Island Ballinakill Waterford Co. Waterford
Tel: 051 878 203 Fax: 051 879 316
Email: info@waterfordcastle.com Web: www.waterfordcastle.com

This beautiful hotel dates back to the 15th century. It is uniquely situated on its own 310 acre wooded island (complete with 18-hole golf course) and is reached by a private ferry. The hotel combines the elegance of earlier times with modern comfort, service and convenience - and the location is uniquely serene. Its quietness (and the golf facility for off-duty relaxation) makes the castle a good venue for small conferences and business meetings, but it is also a highly romantic location and perfect for small weddings. All guestrooms have recently been refurbished and, although they inevitably vary in size and outlook, all are very comfortably furnished in a luxurious country house style. Dinner is served daily in the Munster Dining Room: Michael Quinn, head chef since 1997, was Ballymaloe trained and has experience in a number of respected restaurants; he cooks in a classical style with modern influence. Conference/banqueting (30/70). Golf, fishing, tennis, walking. Children welcome (under 4s free in parents' room; cots available). No Pets. **Rooms 19** (5 suites, 14 en-suite) Lift. Room rate about €400 (2 guests). Amex, Diners, MasterCard, Visa, Laser. **Directions:** outskirts of Waterford city just off Dunmore East.

Waterford

RESTAURANT

The Wine Vault

High Street Waterford Co. Waterford
Tel: 051 853 444 Fax: 051 853 444
Email: info@waterfordwinevault.com Web: www.waterfordwinevault.com

Situated in the medieval part of the city, in an 18th century bonded warehouse with the remains of a 15th century tower house, David Dennison's informal little wine bar and restaurant includes a vaulted wine merchant's premises and has great atmosphere. Head chef Fergal Phelan's informal, bistro-style menus are international in tone and strong on vegetarian choices and local produce, notably seafood - as seen in specialities like Wine Vault gravadlax, seared scallops with puff pastry shell with wilted spinach and a chive beurre blanc and hot seafood platter. Other carefully sourced ingredients include local beef, pork, eggs and poultry; organic vegetables and farmhouse cheeses. A special gourmet tasting menu has wines specifically chosen by wine-man David to complement each course. Lunchtime specials and early evening menu (5.30-7) are especially good value. Exceptional wine list. Toilets wheelchair accessible. Children welcome **Seats 50** (private room 50). No smoking area; air conditioning. L 12.30-2.30 & D 5.30-10.30 Mon-Sat. A la carte; early evening menu from €20.32 (5.30-7.30 only); house wine €21.59. sc discretionary. Closed Sun (excep bank hol weekends), 25 Dec. Amex, MasterCard, Visa, Laser. **Directions:** take right turn off quay - city square car park. Take next left to High street.

COUNTY WESTMEATH

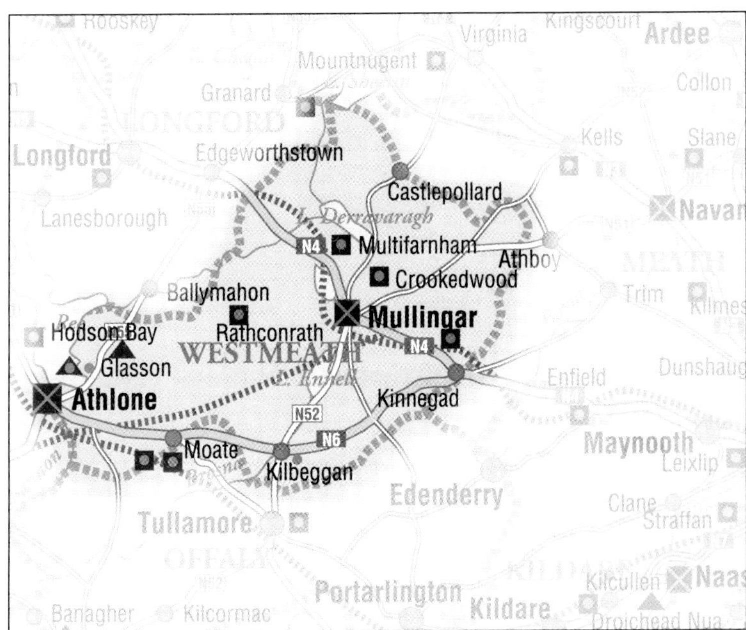

The movement to recognise Athlone's growing significance by designating it a city will accelerate during 2002, because for quite some time now, Athlone has been re-inventing itself as the cosmopolitan capital of the Shannon inland waterway, while building on its strength at the geographical centre of Ireland. But there's more to Westmeath than Athlone, for Mullingar to the east provides its own vitality and prosperity, giving Westmeath a healthy balance.

As its name suggests, in the distant past Westmeath tended to be ruled by whoever held Meath. But today, Westmeath is a county so cheerfully and successfully developing its own identity that perhaps they should find a completely new name for the place. For this is somewhere that makes the very best of what it has to hand.

Its highest "peak" is only the modest Mullaghmeen of 258 m, 10 kilometres north of Castlepollard. But this is in an area where hills of ordinary height have impressive shapes which make them appear like miniature mountains around the spectacularly beautiful Lough Derravaragh, famed for its association with the legend of the Children of Lir, who were turned into swans by their wicked stepmother Aoife, and remained as swans for 900 years until saved by the coming of Christianity.

Westmeath abounds in lakes to complement Derravaragh, such as the handsome expanses of Lough Owel and Lough Ennell on either side of the fine county town of Mullingar, where they've been making life even more watery in recent years with schemes to speed the restoration of the Royal Canal on its way through town from Dublin to the north Shannon.

Meanwhile, Athlone has, like Mullingar, greatly benefited from having a by-pass built to remove through traffic bound for the west coast. Thus Athlone is confidently developing as Ireland's main inland river town, its Shannonside prosperity growing on a useful mixture of electronics, pharmaceuticals and the healthcare industry.

Despite such modern trends, this remains a very rural place - immediately south of the town, you can still hear the haunting call of the corncrake coming across the callows (water meadows). But Athlone itself has a real buzz, particularly in the compact area around the old castle by the west bank quayside. And north of it, there's Lough Ree in all its glory, wonderful for boating in an area where, near the delightful village of Glasson, the Goldsmith country verges towards County Longford, and they have a monument to mark what some enthusiasts reckon to be the true geographical centre of all Ireland. You really can't get more utterly rural than that.

Local Attractions and Information

Athlone All Ireland Amateur Drama Festival (May)	0902 73358
Athlone Athlone Castle Visitor Centre	0902 92912
Athlone River Festivals	0902 94981
Athlone Tourism Information	0902 94630
Ballykeeran MV Goldsmith Lake & River Cruises	0902 85163
Glasson Glasson Rose Festival (August)	0902 85677
Kilbegggan Locke's Distillery Museum	0506 32134
Kilbeggan Race Course	0506 32176
Moate Dun na Si Folk Park	0902 81183
Mullingar Tourism Information	044 48761
Mullingar Westmeath Tourism Council	044 48571
Mullingar Belvedere House, Gardens & Park	044 49060

Athlone

Gertie Brownes & Hatters' Lane Bistro

PUB/RESTAURANT

9 Custume Place Athlone Co. Westmeath
Tel: 0902 74848 Fax: 0902 73233

Gertie Brownes and Hatters restaurant make a good twosome. The pub is characterful olde-worlde and graced by a big open fire, although the crowd is youngish (loud music, smoke) and it's hard to tell what's old and what's themed. Traditional music on Mondays, all year. Downstairs, in the cottagey Hatters restaurant - which can be reached from inside the pub or by a separate entrance around the corner in the laneway - cheerful checked tablecloths, an open fire and candles on the tables provide an appropriate setting for enjoyable informal food. Children welcome up to 7pm. Restaurant **Seats 45.** Air conditioning. L Mon-Fri; DMon-Sat, 6-10. All à la carte. Closed Sun & bank hols. Amex, MasterCard, Visa. **Directions:** close to the bridge, east of the river in central Athlone.

Athlone

Higgins'

PUB/B&B

2 Pearse Street Athlone Co. Westmeath **Tel: 0902 92519**

The Higgins' well-run, hospitable pub is near the castle and provides comfortable inexpensive accommodation in a very central location. Bedrooms range from a single room to a large family room, all with hairdryer, TV and access to tea and coffee-making facilities in the breakfast room. Bedrooms have secondary glazing to reduce the possibility of disturbance at night and there's a residents' lounge, also with television. The pub only does light bar food, but there are several good restaurants nearby including some suitable for inexpensive family meals. Children welcome. No pets. **Rooms 4** (all en-suite, shower-only & no-smoking). B&B about €28 pps, ss about €6.35. No private parking. Closed 25 Dec & Good Fri. MasterCard, Visa. **Directions:** town centre, near the main Post Office and castle.

Athlone

Hodson Bay Hotel

HOTEL féile bia

Hodson Bay Athlone Co. Westmeath
Tel: 0902 80500 Fax: 0902 80520
Email: info@hodsonbayhotel.com Web: www.hodsonbayhotel.com

Very much the centre of local activities, this well-located modern hotel adjoins Athlone Golf Club on the shores of Lough Ree, just four miles outside Athlone town. With lovely lake and island views and a wide range of leisure activities on site – including boating and fishing and a fine leisure centre – it's in great demand as a venue for both business and social occasions. It is the only establishment providing such facilities in the locality and attracts large numbers from a wide area; to meet these demands it has grown considerably since opening in 1992 - the Waterfront Bar & Buttery were recently extended and refurbished and 20 new bedrooms, a children's playroom and the Garden Restaurant breakfast room have also been added. Bedrooms are bright and comfortable, with contemporary decor, well-finished en-suite bathrooms and double and single beds in most rooms. Phone, TV, hairdryer, trouser press and tea/coffee trays are standard. If there is a downside, it is that the hotel is almost always so busy that it is difficult for maintenance and routine refurbishment to keep pace with ongoing wear and tear, especially in public areas - and, similarly, keeping food standards up to the high quality to which the hotel clearly aspires is a challenge which is difficult to meet. Excellent banqueting/conference facilities (700/500); secretarial services, business centre; video conferencing available. Helipad. Leisure centre, swimming pool. Golf (18), fishing, equestrian, tennis, walking, garden. Children welcome (under 2s free in parents' room; cots available without charge. playroom, children's playground). No pets. **Rooms 133** (7suites, 29 executive rooms, 1 for disabled). 2 Lifts. Limited room service.B&B €78 pps, ss €52. **L'Escale Restaurant** The restaurant is on the lake side of the hotel, well-appointed in traditional style. Head chef Tony Hanevy has been at the hotel since 1992 and food is generally above the usual expectation for hotels. In addition to the basic à la carte, daily set menus ensure variety for residents. While not adventurous, the quality of ingredients, cooking, presentation and service all ensure an acceptable meal. Expect popular dishes: steaks may be predictable but this is great beef country and they are well-cooked, with a choice of sauces. The seafood selection sometimes includes lobster, along with several fish. There is a short vegetarian menu and farmhouse cheese is always available in addition to traditional desserts. **Seats 150.** No smoking area; air conditioning. L 12.30-2.30 & D 7-9.30 daily. Set L €17, (Sun L €20), Set D €32, à la carte available, house wines from €17; sc discretionary. [Bar food available 10-9 daily). Open all year. Amex, Diners, MasterCard, Visa, Laser. **Directions:** located off the Roscommon road, just 5 minutes from Athlone town.

Athlone

The Left Bank Bistro

RESTAURANT

Fry Place Athlone Co. Westmeath **Tel: 0902 94446**
Fax: 0902 94509 Email: leftbank@isite.ie Web: www.leftbankbistro.com

Athlone has alway been a great place to break the journey if you're travelling across the country, but it has recently become much more than a handy stopover: now recognised as the culinary capital of the inland waterways, it has become a destination town for discerning travellers, whether by car or by boat. Annie McNamara and Mary McCullough's wacky little Left Bank Bistro was one of the cornerstones of that reputation - and it has now left its bohemian image behind and moved into a new era, in elegant and spacious new premises nearer the river. Here architectural salvage materials and interesting, subtle colours combine well with contemporary wooden furniture and a gently minimalist style to create a space which is both impressive and relaxing. Bare tables and paper napkins convey an informal atmosphere that suits Annie's lively food which, thankfully, has not changed noticeably since the move. Short, keenly-priced lunch menus - plus several extra lunch-time savoury dishes chalked up on a blackboard - offer a wide range of delicious-sounding dishes with the multi-cultural stamp which, together with carefully sourced ingredients and good cooking, earned the previous restaurant an enviable reputation in just a few years. Foccacia bread features a lot - in sandwiches, Tandoori Chicken Breast (on foccacia, with garlic mayonnaise, mixed leaf salad & sauté potatoes) and in Marinaded Steak Sandwich (with sauté onions, sauté potatoes & mixed leaves) - fresh fish dishes are listed separately, and vegetarians can choose between blackboard specials and regular dishes from the menu, including Greek salad, Left Bank Salad (with a wedge of foccacia) and Vegetable Spring Rolls (or samosas). Dinner menus are more extensive and tend to be based on more expensive ingredients, but the style is similar and, here again, vegetarian dishes are especially attractive. After a choice of delicious desserts or farmhouse cheeses, dip into a nice little drinks menu that offers a range of coffees, teas and hot chocolate. **Seats 70.** No smoking area; air conditioning. Open 10.30-9.30. L 12-5 & D 6-9.30 Tue-Sat; all à la carte main courses from about €7.50 (L) , €12.50 (D); house wine €15.17. Closed Sun, Mon, bank hols & Christmas. Amex, MasterCard, Visa, Laser. **Directions:** behind Athlone Castle on west side of Shannon.

Athlone

Manifesto

RESTAURANT

Custume Place Athlone Co. Westmeath **Tel: 0902 73241**

Up a flight of wide, carpeted stairs reminiscent of 1950s cinemas, this stylish new restaurant just east of the bridge offers classical French food in chic minimalist surroundings inspired by cocktail bars of the '60s, and is finding a niche in a local market exceptionally well-served by good eating places. Quality materials - marble, leather, fine woods - and bare tables graced by white linen napkins and a single long-stemmed rose set the tone. Head chef Philippe Got's seasonal menus are backed up by professional, helpful service under the supervision of the Irish-Italian Maître d', Felicity Magliocco. **Seats 75.** Open Wed-Sun, 5.30-10.30: early menu 5.30-7, D 7-10.30. L Sun only. Closed Mon & Tue. MasterCard, Visa. **Directions:** heading west through town, the restaurant is on the right just before the bridge.

Athlone

The Olive Grove

RESTAURANT

Bridge St. Custume Place Athlone Co. Westmeath
Tel: 0902 76946 Fax: 0902 71248

Garry Hughes and Gael Bradbury opened their charming little restaurant in the autumn of 1997 and it has quickly built up a following for its pleasant, informal atmosphere (seasoned with a good dash of style), excellent home-cooked food from noon until late (light food in the afternoon), good value and a great willingness to do anything which will ensure a good time being had by all. The style is vaguely Mediterranean and youthful – as seen in starters such as bruschetta and vegetarian specials like Greek salad – but this is beef country and the speciality of the house is chargrilled steaks. Children welcome. Parking nearby. **Seats 50.** No smoking area. Open from L 12-4 & D 5.30-10 Tues-Sun (Sun 12-5.30); à la carte (average main course about €7.50 (L); €15 (D); house wines €14.60, sc discretionary. Closed Mon, 25 Dec, 1 Jan, bank hols. Amex, MasterCard, Visa, Laser. **Directions:** travelling from Dublin, take the left before the bridge in Athlone town centre.

Athlone

Restaurant Le Chateau

RESTAURANT

St. Peter's Port The Docks Athlone Co. Westmeath
Tel: 0902 94517 Fax: 0902 93040
Email: lechateau@eircom.net Web: www.r-l-c.net

Steven and Martina Linehan's atmospheric quayside restaurant is in a converted Presbyterian Church just west of the bridge. The church, which was closed in the early 1970s, has been magnificently transformed into a two-storey restaurant of great character which complements the couple's well-earned reputation for excellent food and hospitality. Designed around the joint themes of church and river, the upstairs section has raised floors at each end, like the deck of a galleon, while the church theme is reflected in the windows – notably an original "Star of David" at the back of the restaurant – and the general ambience, which is extremely atmospheric. Candles are used generously to create a relaxed, romantic atmosphere, notably during their renowned Candlelight Dinners. Le Chateau was the Guide's Atmospheric Restaurant of the Year in 1999. Children welcome. **Seats 100** (private room, 18). No smoking area; air conditioning. L & D daily, 12.30-3. & 5.30-10); Early D €20.32 (5.30-6.45 pm only); other menus à la carte; house wines from €17.14; sc discretionary, except 10% on parties of 6+. Full bar. Amex, MasterCard, Visa, Laser. **Directions:** heading west through Athlone, over Shannon and left at castle, left again and onto bank of Shannon.

Athlone

Sean's Bar

PUB

13 Main Street Athlone Co. Westmeath **Tel: 0902 92358**

West of the river, in the interesting old town near the Norman castle (which has a particularly good visitors' centre for history and information on the area, including flora and fauna of the Shannon), Sean Fitzsimons' seriously historic bar lays claim to being the pub with the longest continuous use in Ireland – all owners since 900 AD are on record. (It has actually been certified by the National Museum as the oldest pub in Britain and Ireland - and the all-Europe title is currently under investigation.) Dimly-lit, with a fine mahogany bar, mirrored shelving and an enormous settle bed, the bar has become popular with the local student population and is very handy for visitors cruising the Shannon (who have direct access to the river through the back bar and beer garden). The sloping floor is a particularly interesting feature, cleverly constructed to ensure that flood water drained back down to the river as the waters subsided (it still works). A glass case containing a section of old wattle wall original to the building highlights the age of the bar, but it's far from being a museum piece. Food is restricted to sandwiches (Mon-Sat), but the proper priorities are observed and they serve a good pint. Closed 25 Dec & Good Fri. **Directions:** on the west quayside, just in front of the castle.

Glasson

Glasson Village Restaurant

RESTAURANT

Glasson Co. Westmeath **Tel: 0902 85001**

In an attractive stone building which formerly served as an RIC barracks, chef-proprietor Michael Brooks opened the Village Restaurant in 1986, making his mark as a culinary pioneer in the area. On the edge of the village, there's a real country atmosphere about the place, enhanced by old pine furniture and a conservatory which is particularly pleasant for Sunday lunch. As has been the case since they opened, fresh fish features strongly on the menu – Michael takes pride in having introduced fresh seafood at a time when it wasn't popular locally, and aims to maintain the special reputation earned for fresh fish (including shellfish in season and freshwater fish like Lough Ree eel). The cooking style is imaginative and fairly traditional – country French meets modern Irish perhaps. A la carte menus change with the seasons, set menus daily and there are always a couple of vegetarian dishes. Parking. Children welcome. **Seats 50** (private room, 18). No smoking area. D Tue -Sat 6-9.30 (also Sun on bank hol w/e); L Sun only 12.30-2.30. Set D €29.84; Set Sun L €18.41; early D €20.95 (6-7pm only); D also à la carte available; house wines from €14.92; sc discretionary. D Sun, all Mon, 3 weeks from mid Oct and 24-26 Dec. Amex, Diners, MasterCard, Visa, Laser. **Directions:** 5 miles from Athlone on Longford/Cavan road (N55).

Glasson

Grogan's Pub

PUB/RESTAURANT Glasson Athlone Co. Westmeath **Tel: 0902 85158**

It's hard to cross the Midlands without being drawn into at least a short visit to this magic pub in the "village of the roses". It's one of those proudly-run, traditional places with two little bars at the front (one with a welcome open fire in winter) and everything gleaming; it was established in 1750 and feels as if the fundamentals haven't changed too much since then. There's traditional music on Wednesday nights, when three generations of the same family play and visiting musicians are also welcome. At the back, in a very pleasant informal bar/restaurant known as "Nannie Murph's", Anne Casey offers light (and some more substantial) meals in a colourful contemporary style. Nannie Murph's open: Mon-Sat, 12 noon-4 pm & 5.30-9pm, Sun 4-8 pm. Cards: Mastercard, Visa, Laser. Nannie Murph's closed 24-26 Dec, 31 Dec, 1 Jan. & Good Fri. **Directions:** in centre of Glasson village.

Glasson

The Three Jolly Pigeons

PUB Glasson Co. Westmeath **Tel: 0902 85162**

McCormack's "Three Jolly Pigeons"is an unspoilt country pub, with an open fire and a friendly welcome - but its special claim to fame is that Oliver Goldsmith (1728-1774) was reared nearby at Lissoy parsonage - and the area inspired some of his most famous work, including the poem "The Deserted Village" - and The Three Jolly Pigeons is actually named in the play "She Stoops to Conquer" (1773). Closed 25 Dec & Good Fri. **Directions:** outside Glasson on the N55, halfway between Glasson & Ballymahon.

Athlone

Wineport Lodge

RESTAURANT/ACCOMMODATION féile bia

Glasson Athlone Co. Westmeath
Tel: 0902 85466 Fax: 0902 85471
Email: lodge@wineport.ie Web: www.wineport.ie

Since opening Wineport, their wonderful lakeside restaurant in 1993, Ray Byrne and Jane English have worked tirelessly on improvements – the restaurant is now much bigger and includes a private dining room, The Chart Room. Wineport is almost a second home to many of their regulars. Its stunning location and exceptional hospitality draw guests back time and again – guests who return with additions to the now famous Wineport collections (nauticalia, cats) and find the combination of the view, the company and a good meal irresistible. Head chef Feargal O'Donnell is a member of Euro-Toques and presents strongly seasonal menus based on local ingredients including game in season, eels, home-grown herbs, free range eggs and wild mushrooms. However, the style is international, with an occasional nod to traditional Irish themes: Typical starters include potted liver parfait with cornichons & fresh brioche and prawn &ginger spring roll with lime & sesame jam.and, while main courses will always include a dish using certified Irish Angus beef, (rib-eye or fillet with a choice of sauces) interesting vegetarian dishes such as panfried piquillas peppers with grilled aubergine, mozzarella & rosemary foccacia, are always offered and an Irish cheeseboard, often including boilie, smoked Gubbeen and Cooleeney camembert and Cashel Blue. Ray and Jane were the Guide's Hosts of the Year in 1999. **Seats 100** (private room, 50). No smoking area; air conditioning. Children welcome. D daily 6-10 (Sun to 9); L 1-3.30 (Sun 12.45-3.45), Set Sun L €25; Set D €40; à la carte L&D available; house wine €18; sc discretionary. Closed 24-26 Dec. **Accommodation:** Ten bedrooms, furnished to the highest standards and with balconies overlooking the lake, are due to open in January 2002 and will provide a luxurious alternative to hotel accommodation, with a cosy lounge, board room facilities and high-tech TV/phone/ internet access. Extra large bathrooms and air conditioning are special features. Ray and Jane have decided to build on the history of the townland of Wineport by naming each room after a wine or a region famous for its wine; this will be accompanied by some interesting related artefacts - and a little taste of that particular wine to enjoy in your room overlooking the Shannon - with your hosts' compliments! **Rooms 10** (all no smoking, 1 for disabled). Business centre; garden, fishing, walking. Children welcome (under 10s free in parents' room, cots available without charge). Conference/banqueting (40/100). B&B €100 pps, ss €100; sc discretionary. Amex, Diners, MasterCard, Visa, Laser. **Directions:** midway between Dublin and Galway take the Longford/Cavan exit off the Athlone relief road; fork left after 2.5 miles at the Dog & Duck; 1 mile, on the left.

Kinnegad

The Cottage

RESTAURANT Kinnegad Village Kinnegad Co. Westmeath **Tel: 044 75284**

In the village of Kinnegad, just at the point where the Galway road forks to the left, this delightful homely cottage restaurant is one of Ireland's best-loved stopping places, with comfy traditional armchairs and real home-made food – anything from proper meals with a glass of wine at given times to snacks at any time and a really great afternoon tea. Baking is a speciality, with scones and home-made preserves, a wide variety of cakes and irresistible cookies always available. Home-made soups, hot dishes like poached salmon, quiches and omelettes served with a salad are all typical, along with desserts such as apple pie or gateaux. The only sad thing is that they're closed at weekends, when so many people are travelling between Dublin and the west coast. Children welcome. **Seats 35.** No smoking restaurant. Open Mon-Fri, 8am-6pm; à la carte. Closed Sat, Sun, bank hol Mons & Jan-Feb. No Credit Cards. **Directions:** on the N4, Dublin - Galway/Sligo road.

Moate

P. Egan

PUB Main St. Moate Co. Westmeath **Tel: 0902 82014** Email: peganspub@eircom.net

Easy to recognise with its bright red and black paintwork and the bikes outside, this cheerful traditional pub in the centre of Moate has a turf range in the back bar and it's a friendly place to drop in for a drink and some low-down on the area. Traditional Irish music is a speciality. Own parking. Children welcome up to 6pm. Pets allowed by arrangement. Visa. Directions: Directly beside Bank of Ireland on Main Street. Visa. **Directions:** directly beside the Bank of Ireland on the Main Street.

Moate

Temple Country House & Spa

COUNTRY HOUSE Horseleap Moate Co. Westmeath **Tel: 0506 35118**
Fax: 0506 35008 Web: spiders.ie/templespa

Relaxation is the essence of Declan and Bernadette Fagan's philosophy at Temple, their charming and immaculately maintained 200 year-old farmhouse in the unspoilt Westmeath countryside. On its own farmland – where guests are welcome to walk – close to peat bogs, lakes and historical sites, outdoor activities such as walking, cycling and riding are all at hand. There are three lovely country style en-suite rooms in the house and a further five in the courtyard. Relaxation programmes and healthy eating have always been available at Temple, but the new Spa has moved this side of the operation into a new phase, offering yoga, hydrotherapy, massage, reflexology and specialist treatments such as Yon-Ka spa facial and seaweed body contour wraps. Temple is a member of the Health Farms of Ireland Association, which means that Bernadette gives special attention to healthy eating guidelines (and caters for vegetarian, vegan and other special diets). She uses the best of local produce – lamb from the farm, their own garden vegetables, best midland beef, cheese and yogurts – in good home cooking. And, although the Spa is a major attraction, you do not have to be a Spa guest to enjoy a stay at Temple. Garden, cycling, sauna, steam room, children's playground. **Rooms 8** (all en-suite, 5 no-smoking) B&B about €65 pps, ss about €25 (min 2-night stay at weekends). Spa weekends from about €275 pps (ss about €40). Residents' D Tue-Sat, about €26 (book by 10 am; no D Sun, Mon). Wine licence. Closed Christmas-New Year. Amex, MasterCard, Visa. **Directions:** just off N6, 1 mile west of Horseleap.

Mullingar

The Belfry Restaurant

RESTAURANT Ballynegall Mullingar Co. Westmeath **Tel: 044 42488**
Fax: 044 40094 Email: belfryrestaurant@eircom.net

ATMOSPHERIC RESTAURANT OF THE YEAR

The tall spire will lead you to tthe Murphy family's new restaurant in a magnificently converted church near Mullingar.The design is brilliant, with (excellent) toilets near the entrance, perfect for a quick freshen up before heading up thickly carpeted stairs to a mezzanine lounge which is luxuriously furnished with big lounge-around leather sofas, striking lamps and fresh flowers. Everything has been done to the very highest specifications, colours schemes are subtle and elegant - and the whole setup is highly atmsopheric. Head chef Thérèse Gilsenan, who has already made her mark on several places around Westmeath, has a very down to earth approach to cooking, sourcing ingredients well and working in a style that is refreshingly unselfconscious - professionally presented but never over the top, with more elements of good home cooking than cheffy stuff. Menus are carefully constructed to offer a good balance of ingredients and styles, to suit big country appetites and also more sophisticated urban tastes. Sunday lunch menus, for example, include dressed up traditional dishes (like roast loin of crackling pork with fruit stuffing served with fresh apple & lemon purée) alongside modern dishes like tempura of cod with lime & coriander tartare sauce and a vegetarian pasta dish of penne with wild forest mushrooms. Younger guests also get special choices like fresh mini pizza with tomato bacon & fresh mozzarella - a good way to introduce children to quality dining. A second staircase descends to the dining area, which is very striking and extremely atmospheric, especially when seen in candlight with a room full of people enjoying themselves, with background music from the grand piano where the altar used to be.Well-made breads and soups, cooking everything freshly to order - the details are right. Delicious desserts might include a fresh strawberry & orange cassis trifle, (an ingenious variation of the classic trifle) and there's a choice of coffees. Charming, helpful and well-timed service adds greatly to the enjoyment of the visit. 'Wines from the Crypt' are listed - and you are invited to browse. * There are plans to open a cookery school here "in the near furture". **Seats 68** (private room 24). No smoking area; air conditioning. Children welcome. D Wed-Sat, 6-10, L Sun Only 2-7. D à la carte, Set Sun L €24.06; house wine €16.44. Closed D Sun, all Mon & Tue, & 12-30 Jan. MasterCard, Visa, Laser. **Directions:** Castlepollard road, off the Mullingar by-pass.

Mullingar
PUB/RESTAURANT

Canton Casey & Fat Cats Brasserie

Market Square Mullingar Co. Westmeath
Tel: 044 40193 (Restaurant: Tel 044 49969) Fax: 044 84208

Canton Casey's pub is a lovely old-fashioned place, a real traditional pub with friendly staff and a welcoming fire in winter - a pleasant place to read the paper over a pint at quiet times, although it has become fashionable with a youthful crowd and can be very busy in the evenings. Over the pub, there's an informal brasserie serving contemporary food in a high-ceilinged room on the first floor. It has a slightly French atmosphere, with its tall softly draped windows and oil-clothed tables and - predictably enough - the decor is distinctly feline. L Tue-Fri,12.30-2.30; D Tue-Sun, 6-late. Closed L Sat-Sun, all Mon. MasterCard, Visa. **Directions:** town centre.

Mullingar
RESTAURANT/ACCOMMODATION

Crookedwood House

Crookedwood Mullingar Co. Westmeath
Tel: 044 72165 Fax: 044 72166
Email: cwoodhse@iol.ie Web: iol.ie/~cwoodhse

Noel Kenny's former rectory is set in a lovely area of lush rolling farmland right in the centre of Ireland, with fine views over Lough Derravaragh - the lake that inspired one of Ireland's great legends, the Children of Lir. The original house, which is almost two centuries old, includes the whitewashed cellars which provide a characterful setting for a restaurant that has a well-earned reputation for excellence. Noel bases his strong, distinctive cooking on local ingredients such as beef and venison as well as the seafood that has become a hallmark of the best Irish restaurants, all to be found in punchy, colourful dishes that are gimmick-free and unselfconsciously wholesome - and naturally there's a speciality swan dessert in honour of the Children of Lir. Restaurant **Seats 70** (private room, 35). No smoking restaurant. D 6.30-10 (except Sun), L Sun only 12.30-2.30. Set D about €34.28, also à la carte; sc discretionary. Toilets wheelchair accessible. Closed D Sun, Mon & 4 days Christmas. **Accommodation:** There are eight spacious, thoughtfully planned bedrooms. Children welcome (under 4s free in parents' room; cots available). Wheelchair accessible. Pets permitted by arrangement. **Rooms 8** (all en-suite, 5 no smoking). B&B about €66.66, ss about €12.70. Amex, Diners, MasterCard, Visa. **Directions:** from Dublin take the third exit on the Mullingar Bypass, (signalled Castlepollard). In Crookedwood village turn right at the Wood pub; about a mile on the right.

Mullingar
CAFÉ

Gallery 29 Café

16 Oliver Plunkett St. Mullingar Co. Westmeath **Tel: 044 49449**
Fax: 044 49449 Email: corbetstown@eircom.net

Ann & Emily Gray ran their great little restaurant across the road (at number 29) in premises so tiny that you couldn't swing a Manx kitten in them, but they are moving to larger new premises just across the street, where they will have a wine licence and possibly a function room. They're great bakers and the food to date has reflected that - freshly baked breads, scones, muffins, baked puddings, tarts and gateaux are all displayed near the door to tempt you in - but there's much else beside, including good soups, "tailor-made" sandwiches, fashionable focaccia with every imaginable filling and hot main courses, like lasagne, curry and pies. Everything is home-made and it's a good place for any time of day, including breakfast (with freshly squeezed juice) and afternoon tea. Outside catering and freshly made dishes for home freezing are also offered. **Seats 50.** No smoking area. Open Mon-Sat, 9.30-5.30 (late opening with a bistro menu is planned for Thu-Fri evenings). All a la carte. No credit cards. Closed Sun. 24 Dec-7 Jan. **Directions:** from Dublin through traffic lights at Market Square in town centre. About 60 - 70m on right hand side.

Mullingar

Greville Arms Hotel

HOTEL Pearse St. Mullingar Co. Westmeath **Tel: 044 48563** Fax: 044 48052

Right at the heart of Mullingar's shopping area, this privately owned hotel is old-fashioned in the best sense of the word – well-maintained and well-run, with a strong sense of pride, friendly staff and a good deal of natural charm. Renovation and refurbishment have been undertaken on an ongoing basis over the years and housekeeping is of a high standard throughout. Public areas are in excellent order, including a lovely garden (with William Turner athenaeum) and, since 1998, a rooftop garden and conservatory. Bedrooms are comfortably furnished with good amenities and are well organised for the hotel's many business guests; all have full en-suite bathrooms. An attractive, well-run carvery and food bar is open all day, making it a good place to break a journey. Conference/banqueting (200/400).Video conferencing; secretarial services. Business centre.Garden.Children welcome (under 8s free in parents' room; cots available). No Pets. **Rooms 40** (2 suites, all en-suite). B&B about €70pps; no sc. Own parking. Open all year. Amex, Diners, MasterCard, Visa. **Directions:** town centre, on the main street.

Mullingar

Woodville House

RESTAURANT/ACCOMMODATION

Gaybrook Mullingar Co. Westmeath
Tel: 044 43694 Fax: 044 42941
Email: woodvillehouse@eircom.net

About five miles outside Mullingar, this early 19th century two-storey over-basement house makes a fine setting for a restaurant of character. On the ground floor there's a welcoming fire in the drawing room/reception area, a proper little bar and, down in the semi-basement, arched ceilings and open stone walls create a great atmosphere in several dining areas - but there are also windows, so it isn't gloomy or oppressive. Eunan Gallagher has been head chef since 1996 - his menus change weekly, but house specialities include a starter of Corbetstown goats cheese, served with a hazelnut crust on a compôte of pears and local beef - in roast sirloin for Sunday lunch, perhaps, with a cognac & pink peppercorn cream sauce. Well-appointed tables, efficient friendly service and interesting, well-cooked food in generous country portions all add up to an appealing package and it's easy to see why this restaurant has earned a loyal following. Banqueting - weddings & special occasions (30). Restaurant seats 80. (private room, 10). No smoking area. Children welcome. D 6.30-10 Tues-Sat, L Sun only 12.30-3, Set Sun L €19.68. Set D from €19.68 (2-course)-€38.09; early D €22.22,(6.30-7.30); Closed D Sun, Mon, 23-26 Dec, Good Fri. **Accommodation:** There are six en-suite rooms in a converted coachhouse behind the restaurant. B&B €44.44 pps, ss €6.35. Children welcome (under 8 free in parents' room, cots available without charge). Amex, MasterCard, Visa, Laser. **Directions:** 6 miles Mullingar; 3 miles Miltown Pass.

Multyfarnham

Mornington House

COUNTRY HOUSE Mornington Multyfarnham Co. Westmeath **Tel: 044 72191**
Fax: 044 72338 Email: info@mornington.ie Web: www.mornington.ie

Warwick and Anne O'Hara's gracious Victorian house is surrounded by mature trees and is just a meadow's walk away from Lough Derravarragh where the mythical Children of Lir spent 300 years of their 900 year exile. The Lough is now occupied by a pleasing population of brown trout, pike, eels and other coarse fish. It has been the O'Hara family home since 1858 and is still furnished with much of the original furniture and family portraits and, although centrally heated, log fires remain an essential feature. Bedrooms are typical of this kind of country house – spacious and well-appointed, with old furniture (three have brass beds) – but with comfortable modern mattresses. Anne (a Euro-Toque member) cooks proper country breakfasts and country house dinners for residents and Warwick does the honours front-of-house. Pets allowed by arrangement. Garden; fishing. **Rooms 5** (2 en-suite, all no smoking). B&B €60 pps, ss €10. Set residents D €32, at 8pm (book by 2pm). Closed Nov-Mar. Amex, MasterCard, Visa. **Directions:** exit N4 for Castlepollard.

COUNTY WEXFORD

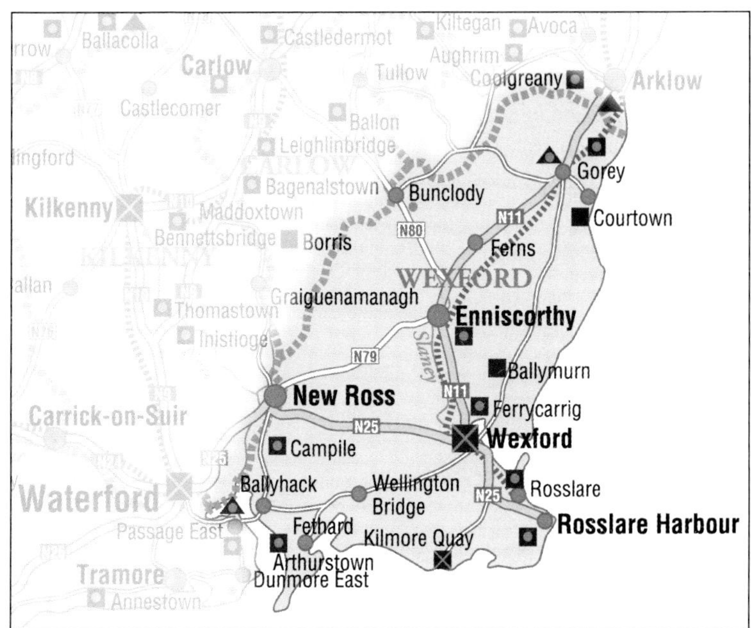

For many people coming to Ireland in 2002, Wexford county is their introduction, as the international ferry terminal of Rosslare is one of our busiest busiest passenger ports. But for those of us already in Ireland, when we think of Wexford, the thoughts are of beaches, sunshine and opera. The longest continuous beach in all Ireland runs along Wexford's east coast, an astonishing 27 kilometres from Cahore Point south to Raven Point, which marks the northern side of the entrance to Wexford's shallow harbour.

As for sunshine, while areas further north along the east coast may record marginally less rainfall, in the very maritime climate of the "Sunny Southeast" around Wexford, the clouds seem to clear more quickly, so the chances of seeing the elusive orb are much improved. As for opera, well, the annual Wexford Opera Festival every October is a byword for entertaining eccentricity - as international enthusiasts put it, "we go to Wexford town in the Autumn to take in operas written by people we've never heard of, and we have ourselves a thoroughly good time."

All of which is fine and dandy, but there's much more to the intriguing county of Wexford than sun, sand and singing. Wexford itself is but one of three substantial towns in it, the other two being the market town of Enniscorthy, and the river port of New Ross. While much of the county is low-lying, to the northwest it rises towards the handsome Blackstairs Mountains, where the 793m peak of Mount Leinster may be just over the boundary in Carlow, but one of the most attractive little hill towns in all Ireland, Bunclody, is most definitely in Wexford. In the north of the county, Gorey is a pleasant and prosperous place, and for connoisseurs of coastlines, the entire south coast of Wexford is a fascinating area of living history, shellfish-filled shallow estuaries, and an excellent little harbour at the much-thatched village of Kilmore Quay inside the Saltee Islands.

Round the corner beyond the impressive Hook Head, home to Ireland's oldest lighthouse, Wexford County faces west across its own shoreline along the beauties of Waterford estuary. Here, thee's another fine beach, at Duncannon, while nearby other sheltered little ports of west Wexford - Arthurstown and Ballyhack - move at their own sweet and gentle pace, though developments in the pipeline may make land and estuary more accessible to each other.

This is already happening in New Ross, where the authentic re-creation of a 19th Century emigrant ship - the impressive Dunbrody - is proving to be a very effective focal point for the revival of the picturesque waterfront, a fitting place for the lovely River Barrow to meet ships in from sea in an area historically linked with President John F Kennedy

Eventually, though, all roads lead to Wexford town itself, revitalised with a restored waterfront and quayside at the heart of the historic town. It's a working harbour for the famous Wexford mussel boats, but combined with it is an area for relaxation and taking the air in this extraordinary opera town.

Local Attractions and Information

Ballygarrett Shrule Deer Farm	055 27277
Ballyhack Ballyhack Castle	051 389468
Campile Kilmokea Gardens	051 388109
Coolgreany Ram House Gardens ("garden rooms")	0402 37238
Dunbrody Abbey & Visitor Centre	051 388603
Duncannon Duncannon Fort	051 388603
Enniscorthy National 1798 Visitor Centre	054 37596
Enniscorthy Tourism Information	054 34699
Enniscorthy Wexford County Museum	054 46506
Ferrycarrig National Heritage Park	053 20733
Hook Head Hook Head Lighthouse	051 397055
Johnstown Castle Demesne & Agricultural Museum	053 42888
Kilmore Quay Saltee Island Ferries	053 29684
New Ross Dunbrody - re-creation of 19th C ship	051 425239
New Ross Galley River Cruises	051 421723
New Ross John F Kennedy Arboretum	051 388171
New Ross John F Kennedy Homestead, Dunganstown	051 388264
New Ross Tourism Information	051 421857
Rosslare Ferry Terminal	053 33622
Saltmills (nr Fethard-on-Sea) Tintern Abbey	051 562650
Wexford North Slobs Wildfowl Reserve	053 23129
Wexford Opera Festival (October)	053 22144
Wexford Tourism Information	053 23111

Arthurstown
HOTEL
RESTAURANT ☆

Dunbrody Country House

Arthurstown Co. Wexford
Tel: 051 389 600 Fax: 051 389 601
Email: dunbrody@indigo.ie Web: www.dunbrodyhouse.com

Catherine and Kevin Dundon have created something very special at their elegant Georgian manor. Set in twenty acres of parkland and gardens on the Hook Peninsula, just across the estuary from Waterford city, this was the ancestral home of the Chichester family and the long tradition of hospitality at this tranquil and luxurious retreat is very much alive and well. Catherine and Kevin are thoughtful and caring hosts and there is a feeling of true welcome here - beginning, perhaps, with a gentle greeting from their affectionate dogs (who look out for newcomers from their vantage point on the granite steps at the front door). Well-proportioned public rooms, which include an impressive entrance hall and gracious drawing room, are all beautifully furnished and decorated with stunning flower arrangements and the occasional unexpectedly modern piece that brings life to a fine collection of antiques. Spacious bedrooms, including those in a new wing which blends admirably with the original building, have superb bathrooms and offer all the comforts expected of such a house - and fine views over the gardens. An exceptional breakfast offers a magnificent buffet - fresh juices, fruit compôtes, cheeses - as well as hot dishes from a tempting menu. While Dunbrody provides a wonderfully relaxing place for a leisure break, they also cater for business meetings, small conferences, product launches and incentive programmes (full details available on request). Conference/banqueting (60/110). Business centre, secretarial services. Garden, walking. Children welcome (cot available without charge). No pets. Dunbrody was the Guide's Country House of the Year in 2001. **Rooms 20** (6 suites, 6 junior suites, 4 executive, 3 no-smoking,1 disabled). B&B €112 pps; ss €25. Closed

23-26 Dec. **The Harvest Room:** The restaurant looks out onto a pleasure garden and, beyond, to an organic vegetable and fruit garden. A well-proportioned, elegant room with an open fire in winter, it presents a striking blend of classic and contemporary style - bold choices which bring life to the room include some beautiful modern rugs, specially commissioned from Ceadogan Rugs at Wellington Bridge. Likewise, chef/proprietor Kevin offers tempting à la carte and set menus that succeed unusually well in combining classical and international influences with local produce and Irish themes: specialities of the house include, for example, roast loin of bacon with a clove and Irish Mist, served on a bed of braised cabbage leaves & potato cake, a dish which brilliantly marries traditional and contemporary tastes. (In recognition it was selected for the Guide's Irish Bacon Award in 2000.) Rack of Wexford lamb with caramelised kumquats, served on a basil pomme purée is another such dish and, while beautifully presented, this is not ostenatious cooking - Kevin's creations are outstanding for flavour before all else. Catherine leads a well-trained and efficient dining room staff with the charm and panache that typifies all aspects of the hospitality at this exceptional country house. **Seats 70.** No-smoking area. Toilets wheelchair accessible. D Mon-Sat 6.30-9.15. L Sun only 1.15-2.30 pm. Set Sun L €35. Set D €50. House wines €19. sc discretionary. Not suitable for children after 8pm. Closed 23 Dec -31 Jan. Amex, Diners, MasterCard, Visa, Laser. **Directions:** N11 from Dublin, R733 from Wexford to Arthurstown.

Bunclody

Chantry Restaurant

RESTAURANT

Bunclody Co. Wexford **Tel: 054 77482** Fax: 054 76130

Beautifully located on the River Slaney, at the foot of the Blackstairs Mountains, Bunclody is an attractive little town - and The Chantry is especially beautifully located within it. The fine old house, which was originally a Wesleyan chapel, enjoys a position of unexpected serenity above its own lovely waterside gardens, where guests can relax and enjoy the lovely trees and plants, including many rare species. The restaurant - which is lined with fascinating old pictures relating to local history - is in a high room with a little gallery (just the right size for a grand piano) but, with its deep red walls and chandeliers, it doesn't feel too churchy. Menus offered vary considerably depending on the time of day - all day food tends to be casual, with a carvery lunch from 12.30, but evening service is more formal. At dinner, the self-service buffet is removed and an à la carte menu with table service is offered instead. Typical dishes from the carte might include a first course salad of smoked chicken with cherry tomato, scallions & balsamic vinaigrette while main courses include a speciality of traditional honey-glazed baked Chantry ham, with fresh parsley sauce and vegetarian dishes like tofu & vegetable stirfry. Early bird specials are especially good value - and what all the various menus have in common is good home cooking at reasonable prices. **Seats 50** (private room, 14). No smoking area. Children welcome. Toilets wheelchair accessible. Own parking. Pets in certain areas. Open 9am-9pm Mon-Sat, 10-4 Sun. Sun L 12.30-4pm. House wine about €15.87. All a la carte menus. SC discretionary. Open all year. MasterCard, Visa. **Directions:** in town centre.

Campile

Kilmokea Country Manor & Gardens

COUNTRY HOUSE

Great Island Campile Co. Wexford **Tel: 051 388 109**
Fax: 051 388 776 Email: kilmokea@indigo.ie Web: www.kilmokea.com

This most peaceful and relaxing late Georgian country house is set in 7 acres of Heritage Gardens, including formal walled gardens (open to the public, 9-5; cream teas, for guests and garden visitors, are served in a Georgian conservatory). The house is tastefully and comfortably furnished, with a drawing room overlooking the Italian Loggia, an honesty library bar, and an elegant dining room. The individually-designed and immaculately maintained bedrooms command lovely views over the gardens and towards the estuary beyond. They have no television to disturb the tranquillity (though there is one in the drawing room. Owner Emma Hewlett (husband Mark helps out at weekends) does practically everything herself, from preparing and cooking the evening meal on the trusty Aga (a typical dinner might include asparagus hollandaise, honeyed trout, rhubarb compôte with home-made orange biscuits and Irish farmhouse cheeses) to offering aromatherapy treatments (for which she holds several qualifications) during the day. A billiards room (where smoking is allowed), some new rooms and self-catering suites in an adjoining coach house were opened in 2000; they have a separate entrance and lighter, more contemporary atmosphere than the main house. To avoid disappointment, discuss your preferences when booking. Banqueting (40). Garden, fishing, walking; games room - billiards, table tennis. Children welcome (under 3s free in parents' room, cots available without charge). Pets allowed by arrangement. * A tennis court, indoor swimming pool, jacuzzi and gym are due for completion in autumn 2002. **Rooms 6** (1 suite, 6 en-suite, 2 shower only, 1 private, 2 for disabled, all no-smoking). B&B €80 pps; ss €20. Residents D €35.56; book by noon.Closed 5 Nov-1 Mar. MasterCard, Visa, Laser, Switch. **Directions:** off R733 from New Ross to Ballyhack, follow signs to Kilmokea Gardens.

Carne

The Lobster Pot

PUB/RESTAURANT Ballyfane Carne Co. Wexford **Tel: 053 31110** Fax: 053 31401

Near Carnsore Point and just over 5 miles from Rosslare ferry port, Ciaran and Anne Hearne's good-looking country pub – in elegant dark green with lots of well-maintained plants – is a welcome sight indeed. Inside the long, low building several interconnecting bar areas are furnished in simple, practical style, with sturdy furniture designed for comfortable eating. For fine summer days there are picnic tables outside at the front. One room is a slightly more formal restaurant, but the atmosphere throughout is very relaxed and the emphasis is on putting local seafood to good use, providing good value and efficient service. Daily deliveries ensure fresh fish supplies and the catch dictates daily specials. Simple seafood meals are served all day in the bar, including excellent seafood chowder and a wild Irish smoked salmon platter. A more comprehensive evening menu offers River Rush oysters and lobsters from the tank, crab mornay and, for a change of mood, crispy duckling and various steaks. No reservations, so avoid busy times or you could be in for a long wait. **Seats 100.** Wheelchair access. Children welcome, but not after 7pm. Open daily, 12-9.30. Closed 25 Dec & Good Fri. Amex, MasterCard, Visa.

Courtown

Harbour House Guesthouse

GUESTHOUSE Courtown Gorey Co. Wexford **Tel: 055 25197** Fax: 055 25117
Email: stay@harbourhouseguesthouse.com Web: www.harbourhouseguesthouse.com

Donal and Margaret O'Gorman's spick-and-span guesthouse is situated a stone's throw from the harbour and a few minutes from the resort's sandy beaches. Comfortable bedrooms, including two new ones added in 2001, all offer TV, tea-making facilities and hairdryer, and there's a well-appointed residents' lounge. Start the day with a traditional breakfast with all the trimmings from Irish soda bread to black pudding. Garden; children's playground. Children under 3 free in parents' room; cots available without charge). Pets allowed by arrangement. **Rooms 15** (all en-suite & no-smoking). B&B €32pps; ss €7. Closed 1 Nov-17 Mar. MasterCard, Visa. **Directions:** centre of Courttown Harbour.

Enniscorthy

Ballinkeele House

COUNTRY HOUSE Ballymurn Enniscorthy Co. Wexford **Tel: 053 38105**
Fax: 053 38468 Email: info@ballinkeele.com Web: www.ballinkeele.com

Set in 350 acres of parkland, game-filled woods and farmland, this historic house is a listed building; designed by Daniel Robertson, it has been the Maher family home since it was built in 1840 and remains at the centre of their working farm. It is a grand house, with a lovely old cut stone stable yard at the back and some wonderful features, including a lofty columned hall with a big open fire in the colder months, beautifully proportioned reception rooms with fine ceilings and furnishings which have changed very little since the house was built. Nevertheless, it is essentially a family house and has a refreshingly hospitable and down-to-earth atmosphere. Large bedrooms are furnished with antiques and have wonderful countryside views; central heating has recently been installed in the upstairs rooms and is due for completion on the ground floor for the 2002 season. Margaret Maher is a keen amateur painter and runs small art workshops at Ballinkeele with Patricia Jorgensen, who is well-known for her botanical paintings. Croquet and bicycles are availabe for guests' use and horse riding, fishing and golf can be organised nearby. Garden. Children are welcome, but there are no concessions; cot available, €15). No pets. **Rooms 5** (all en-suite, 2 superior, 2 shower only, all no-smoking). B&B €63 pps; ss 19. Residents Set D €35 at 7:30 (book by noon; no D on Mon); house wine €14. Private parties up to 14. Closed 12 Nov-28 Feb. MasterCard, Visa, Laser. **Directions:** from Wexford N11 north to Oilgate village, turn right at signpost.

Enniscorthy

Monfin House

COUNTRY HOUSE St. Johns Enniscorthy Co. Wexford
Tel: 054 38582 Fax: 054 38583
Email: info@monfinhouse.com Web: www.monfinhouse.com

This classic Georgian house just outside Enniscorthy was built in 1823 and has all the simplicity and elegance of that period. Having carried out major refurbishment, Chris and Avril Stewart opened their house to guests in 2001, with the aim of providing a quiet and relaxing haven, with the emphasis on comfort, personal service and, particularly, the joys of food and wine. This they do very well: guests are free to stroll around the grounds and see the walled garden (which is destined for restoration to its original design and purpose) and your bedroom will provide a tranquil sanctuary - spacious and very comfortably furnished with a whirpool or antique bath, although kept without the worldly intrusion of amenities like television (phone and modem connection are available on request however). Avril sources food carefully, using local and organic produce wherever possible in her country house style cooking. A candlelit dining room with an open fire provides a soothing setting for a 5-course no choice dinner, and there is an interesting wine list with refreshingly low mark-up prices. (Chris has a "day job" in the wine business.) A typical dinner might start with a warm salad of cherry tomatoes with balsamic dressing, then a seasonal soup such as mushroom & lettuce or pea & coriander; there might be roast duck for the main course, served with a raspberry sauce, buttered leeks and peppers and courgette gratin, then a classic dessert like orange soufflé. This is not the end, however, as there is still a cheese plate to come - and chocolates with your coffee, which is served in front of another fire, in the drawing room. Breakfast is to the same high standards - and you may well need a walk afterwards. Not suitable for children under 12. **Rooms 4** (all en-suite & no smoking). B&B about €65 pps, ss €19.05. Residents' D €31.75; wine from €15.87 Private Dinning at Country House. **Directions:** from Enniscorthy take New Ross road - turn left after Grain Mill. 0.5 mile upon right hand side.

Enniscorthy

HOTEL

Riverside Park Hotel

The Promenade Enniscorthy Co. Wexford
Tel: 054 37800 Fax: 054 37900
Email: riversideparkhotel@eircom.net Web: www.riversideparkhotel.com

This new riverside hotel opened in 1998 and, while it may be visually at odds with the pleasing traditional style of the area, it has brought welcome amenities to the town. Public areas are quite impressive of their type, rooms are comfortably furnished in a moderate contemporary style and there are good facilities for conferences and functions. Off-season and special interest breaks are offered and there is plenty to do in this beautiful area, including fishing, golf and horse riding. There is a pleasant riverside path in a linear park beside the hotel and this can be a useful place to break a journey to stretch the legs and have a bite to eat. Conference/banqueting facilities (700/450), secretarial services. Own parking. No pets. Children welcome (cots available without charge). **Rooms 60** (1 suite, all no smoking, 4 for disabled). Lift. B&B €89 pps. Hotel closed 25-26 Dec. Moorings Restaurant In the Guide's experience, food and ambience are both above the standard expected of a country hotel. David Anderson, who has been head chef since the hotel opened. His seasonal à la carte and daily set menus successfully marry the demands for both traditional and contemporary dishes and the cooking is sound. There is also an informal Tex-Mex restaurant in the hotel and bar food is available 12.30-7.30 daily. L 12.30-2.30, D 7-9. Set Sun €18.50, Set D from €29; à la carte also available L&D. Diners, MasterCard, Visa. **Directions:** 0.5 from the new bridge, centre Enniscorthy Town. Just off N11 Dublin - Rosslare road.

Ferrycarrig Bridge

HOTEL féile bia

Ferrycarrig Hotel

Ferrycarrig Bridge Co. Wexford **Tel: 053 20999** Fax: 053 20982
Email: ferrycarrig@griffingroup.ie Web: www.griffingroup.ie

Although very close to the main Rosslare road - steeply sloping gardens have steps from the main entrance up to the car park which is almost adjacent to the road - this modern hotel is in a lovely location overlooking the Slaney estuary and has excellent amenities, including a superb health and fitness club with 20 metre swimming pool and state-of-the-art facilities for conferences and business meetings. Neatly uniformed staff are exceptionally welcoming and friendly (although not every guest will relish being on first name terms as soon as the receptionist has checked it on the computer); service generally is caring without being intrusive. All bedrooms, including original ones recently upgraded as well as 13 new bedroom and suites, have splendid views across the water and some have balconies with wooden loungers; in-room facilties are good, including a safe (which uses the room key card) and an iron/trouser press unit as well as the usual phone, television, tea/coffee tray, although some power points and cables are inconveniently positioned. Housekeeping is of a high standard and generous bathrooms have a phone extension and large baths with good showers. Special interest and off-season value breaks are offered. Conference/banqueting (400/350). Leisure centre. Garden. Children welcome (cots available, €6.35; playroom). No pets. **Rooms 103** (4 suites, 5 junior suites, 35 no smoking, 2 for disabled). Lift. B&B €108 pps; ss €32. Hotel open all year. **Tides Gourmet Restaurant:** The smaller of the hotel's two restaurants, Tides offers discerning guests modern French cuisine in the atmosphere of an independent restaurant rather than an hotel dining room. It has its own reception/bar area and is formally appointed with linen cloths and napkins, quality tableware, fresh flowers and chilled water in in-house stoppered bottles. Tony Carty, who has been head chef since 1999, presents imaginative and well-balanced à la carte menus offering a selection of about eight on each course, including strong vegetarian options. There is an understandable leaning towards seafood but plenty of other choice, usually including beef, pork and poultry dishes. Tables are set up to maximise on the waterside position and most have a lovely view. Dishes enjoyed on a recent visit include Kilmore crabmeat spring roll with Asian greens & hoi sin sauce, which was judiciously sauced and worked very well; fillet of beef with mushroom duxelle, sweet potato & garlic café au lait was outstanding for excellent meat, perfectly cooked in a well-judged combination (the 'café au lait' was a well-flavoured brown jus with puréed garlic). Cheeses were disappointing (not at room temperature), but desserts included an exquisitely light chocolate truffle tart and home-made chocolates came with coffees that included a superb Moroccan triple expresso. Food presentation is fashionable but not over the top and service is pleasant and professional. **Seats 45.** No-smoking area. Air conditioning. D Tue-Sat 7-9:15 (limited opening in winter). A la carte. House wines from €16. sc discretionary. No children.*The 150-seater Boathouse Bistro, serves modern Irish cooking B, L & D daily. *Bar food is also available daily: Mon-Thu, 12:30-8.30; Fri-Sun 12.30-6. Amex, Diners, MasterCard, Visa, Laser. **Directions:** located on N11, 3 miles north of Wexford town.

Gorey

COUNTRY HOUSE/RESTAURANT

Marlfield House

Courtown Rd Gorey Co. Wexford
Tel: 055 21124 Fax: 055 21572
Email: info@marlfieldhouse.ie Web: www.marlfieldhouse.com

The Bowe family's Marlfield House is the luxury country house hotel par excellence. This is no ordinary hotel, but an example of how to transform a fine 19th-century house into an elegant oasis of unashamed luxury, where guests are cosseted and pampered in surroundings that can only be described as sumptuous. You enter the wooded drive through imposing gates, observing the enclosed wildfowl reserve with its own island and lake; to the rear of the house are further well-maintained gardens and manicured lawns, including a fine kitchen garden that provides much of the produce used in the restaurant. The interior features marble fireplaces, antiques, notable paintings, glittering chandeliers and fine fabrics. The hand of Mary Bowe is very much in evidence, perhaps even more noticeable in the bedrooms (including four-posters and half-testers), six of which are on the ground floor. These are 'State Rooms', larger and even more grand than those upstairs. All offer fine bedding and exquisite furnishings, plus every conceivable amenity, from fresh flowers and fruit to books and magazines. Bathrooms, many in marble, some with separate walk-in shower and spa tub, are equally luxurious and well-appointed, naturally providing bathrobes and top-quality toiletries. Housekeeping is immaculate throughout, service from committed staff thoughtful and unobtrusive. Although Mary and Ray Bowe are still very much involved, the house is now under the direction of daughter Margaret Bowe, continuing the family tradition. Conference/banqueting (20/20). Tennis. Dogs and children are welcome by prior arrangement. (Children under 2 free in parents' room, cots available without charge). **Rooms 20** (6 staterooms, 14 superior, all no smoking). B&B €120pps. Closed 17 Dec-1 Feb. **Restaurant:** The graceful dining-room and resplendent conservatory merge into one, allowing views out across the gardens. The conservatory, with its hanging baskets, plants and fresh flowers (not to mention the odd stone statue), is one of the most romantic spots in the whole of Ireland, further enhanced at night by candlelight – a wonderful setting in which to enjoy chef Henry Stone's accomplished cooking. Henry sources ingredients with care and a lot of the fruit, vegetables and herbs are grown in their own gardens, ensuring a strongly seasonal dimension to menus which are always interesting and attractive without being slavishly fashionable. The main emphasis is on flavour and this fine chef has a down to earth quality which is most refreshing in a fine dining restaurant. Typical examples that indicate the style include chicken liver parfait with a salad of asparagus, served with a beetroot and balsamic reduction and toasted brioche; pan-seared scallops with rocket & fennel cream; cream of celeriac soup and (a somewhat unlikely speciality but a superb dish that has captured the hearts of regular diners for its flavoursome succulence) roast belly of pork with potato galette, home-grown buttered spinach, roast garlic and shallots. Vegetarian choices are always offered - oyster and shitake mushroom wonton raviolis with creamed leeks and roast cherry tomato, perhaps - and an Irish cheesboard which is temptingly displayed on a side table. Elegant desserts might include a dashing high-rise banana gratin with Malibu sabayon topped with a ball of superb dark chocolate sorbet, then it's off to the drawing room for coffee and petits fours to round off the feast. An extensive wine list, long on burgundies and clarets, is informative. **Seats 65** (private room, 20). No-smoking restaurant. Air conditioning. D daily, 7-9; L Sun only 12.30-1:45. D à la carte; Set Sun L €33. House wine €24. SC discretionary. Light à la carte lunches are served daily in Library. Amex, Diners, MasterCard, Visa, Laser. **Directions:** 1 mile outside Gorey on Courtown Road (R742).

Gorey

Pooles Porterhouse

PUB

78 Main Street Gorey Co. Wexford **Tel: 055 21271** Fax: 055 80856

The three Poole brothers, Eric, Colin and Brian, are the driving force behind the renewed success of their substantial town-centre pub. With its traditional darkwood decor and open fires, it looks and feels as if it has always been a pub - and in fact it has been in the family for three generations and was run as a restaurant for some years by the brothers' parents before seeing a more recent change of use. But then along came these three energetic and far-sighted young men, who did up the building, obtained a licence and re-opened it as a pub and restaurant. Eric, a chef with wide-ranging experience beginning nearby at Marlfield House where the foundation stone of his "no short cuts" philosophy was laid, and culminating as head chef at a demanding Dublin pub, started the food side of the Porterhouse himself while Colin and Brian looked after other aspects of the business. Before long their reputation for good food has created such demand that Eric now has two other chefs working with him - and everyone shares responsibility for menus which are very impressive. Daytime fare tends to be light and snacky (but classy too - try the quenelles of duck liver paté with fruit coulis and home-made brown bread, for example), augmented by daily main course specials on the blackboard. Evening menus are more formal, offering a choice of about eight starters and a dozen or so main courses ranging from updated versions of the traditional meat and poultry dishes popular in rural areas to some sophisticated seafood (typically a duo of scallops & smoked haddock with creamy white wine & chive sauce, one of the most expensive main courses at €20.25) and vegetarian options. Home-made desserts are also a speciality - this is the place to break a journey if you can. **Seats 60.** No smoking area; air conditioning. Children welcome (but not after 8 pm). Food available daily, 12.30-8: L 12-2.30; Bar menu 2.30-9 (Sat & Sun to 8); D 4-9. Set Sun L €14.60, otherwise à la carte. House wine €15.17. Amex, MasterCard, Visa, Laser. **Directions:** centre Main street, beside pedestrian crossing.

Kilmore Quay

Kehoe's Pub & Maritime Heritage Centre

PUB

Kilmore Quay Co. Wexford **Tel: 053 29830** Fax: 053 29820
Email: info@kehoe.iol.ie Web: www.kehoes.com

Recent harbour developments, and especially the new marina, have brought an extra surge of activity to this thriving fishing village – and well-informed visitors all head straight for Kehoe's. It has been family-owned for generations – James and Eleanor Kehoe have been running it since 1987 - and, among the changes made over the years, the most challenging was in 1994 when they decided to do a really good refurbishment job, to enhance the pub's traditional ambience – everything was done correctly, from the roof slates to the old pitch pine flooring (and ceiling in the Parlour). At the same time, the interior was used to display a huge range of maritime artefacts, some of them recovered from local wrecks by James and his diving colleagues. They have created what amounts to a maritime museum; even the beer garden at the back of the pub is constructed from a mast and boom discarded by local trawlers - it now also has patio heaters to encourage people to eat outdoors on summer evenings. The other major change has been to the food side of the business, which has crept up on Kehoe's gradually: a few years ago they did little more than soup and sandwiches but now the pub has an established reputation for the quality and range of its bar meals – seafood, such as Ocean Pie (a selection of locally caught fish, topped with sauce and baked) - as well as vegetarian dishes and other main courses such as lasagne and stuffed chicken breasts wrapped in bacon. There's a short but very adequate wine list in addition to normal bar drinks. Kehoe's was the Guide's Pub of the Year Award for 2001. Children welcome. Wheelchair access. Open daily for food 12.30-8. Closed 25 Dec, Good Fri. Visa. **Directions:** In the village.

Kilmore Quay

Quay House

GUESTHOUSE/RESTAURANT

Kilmore Quay Co. Wexford **Tel: 053 29988**
Fax: 053 29808 Web: www.quayhouseguesthouse.com

Siobhan and Pat McDonnell's pristine guesthouse is centrally located in the village (not on the quay as might be expected) and is especially famous for its support of sea angling and diving – they have an annexe especially geared for anglers with drying/storage room, fridges and freezers, live bait and tackle sales. They can also provide packed lunches as well as evening meals. The whole place is ship shape, with attractive, slightly nautical bedrooms ("a place for everything and everything in its place"), practical pine floors and neat en-suite facilities (most shower only). The breakfast room and restaurant, Quay Plaice, has been extended into an existing patio - overlooking the village's pretty thatched cottages, the sea and beach - which has now been covered to provide extra seating as the restaurant side of the business has expanded: a full à la carte menu is offered, in a contemporary style, majoring in seafood. Children welcome (infants free in parents' room, cots available without charge). Pets by arrangement. Garden. **Rooms 7** (all en-suite, 4 no smoking) .B&B €36 pps; ss €2. Restaurant: D daily in summer, 6-9.30 pm Set D €45, also à la carte; house wine €14.60. Accommodation open all year; restaurant closed Mon & Tue in winter. MasterCard, Visa, Laser. **Directions:** Wexford 14 miles, Rosslare Ferry route.

Kilmore Quay

The Silver Fox

RESTAURANT — Kilmore Quay Co. Wexford **Tel: 053 29888**

Absolute freshness is the key to chef Nicky Cullen's reputation at this middle-market seafood restaurant close to the harbour, where popular dishes and more ambitious seafood creations appear unselfconsciously side by side. Menus at The Silver Fox are wide-ranging and offer some poultry and meat dishes (also vegetarian dishes, by arrangement) as well as the wide choice of seafood for which they have become famous; in the Guide's experience, simplest choices have always been wisest. Harbour developments at Kilmore Quay, including a marina, have been done with an admirable regard for the size and character of the village, but the growing number of visitors means booking is strongly advised, especially in summer. Children welcome. **Seats 130** (private room, 35). No-smoking area. Air conditioning. Toilets wheelchair accessible. Open Mon-Sat, L 12:30-6, D 6-9:30. Sun L 12:30-2:30, Sun D 6-9. Set Sun L about €13. L&D à la carte available. House wines about €13; sc discretionary. Closed 24-26 Dec, Jan 10 days. MasterCard, Visa. **Directions:** 20 min. drive from Rosslare ferry, Wexford town and Ballyhack ferry.

Rosslare Harbour

Great Southern Hotel

HOTEL — Rosslare Harbour Co. Wexford **Tel: 053 33233** Fax: 053 33543
Email: res@rosslare.gsh.ie Web: www.greatsouthernhotels.com

A popular family venue, this 1960s' hotel is perched on a clifftop overlooking the harbour – very handy for the port and a useful place to get a fortifying breakfast if you're coming off an overnight ferry, or if there are delays. It has good facilities and recent refurbishment has included the exterior, all public areas, most of the bedrooms, the restaurant, function rooms and the Maritime Bar (which has an extensive collection of memorabilia covering the history of shipping in the area). Conference/banqueting (200/150). Bedrooms are well-equipped, with phone, TV with video channel, tea/coffee making facilities and trouser press. Bar food is available every day and there's an evening restaurant. Leisure centre, indoor swimming pool. Tennis. Snooker. Parking. Children welcome (under 2s free in parents' room, cots available without charge; children's playground, playroom, crèche.). No pets. **Rooms 100** (8 no-smoking, 1 for disabled). Lift. B&B €87 pps; ss €30. Closed Jan. Amex, Diners, MasterCard, Visa, Laser. **Directions:** overlooking Rosslare Harbour and ferry terminal.

Rosslare

Kelly's Resort Hotel

HOTEL/RESTAURANT — Rosslare Co. Wexford **Tel: 053 32114** Fax: 053 32222
Email: kellyhot@iol.ie Web: www.kellys.ie

Constant renovating, refurbishing and building work each winter keep raising standards ever higher at this renowned hotel. Quite simply, the hotel has everything, for both individuals and families, many of whom return year after year (the number of children is limited at any one time, so as not to create an imbalance). The many public rooms range from a quiet reading room and the snooker room to a supervised crèche and gallery lounge: pictures (mostly modern) throughout the hotel form an outstanding art collection. Many of the bedrooms have sea views, some with balconies; housekeeping throughout is immaculate. Leisure facilities are second to none, including a therapeutic spa and beauty centre, two indoor swimming pools, indoor tennis, and, a bit of fun for francophiles, boules. Outside the summer holiday season (end June-early Sept), ask about special breaks, when rates are reduced. Banqueting (40). Leisure centre, swimming pools. Tennis. Fishing (sea). Snooker. Hairdresser. Playroom. Children's playground. Garden. Parking. No pets. **Rooms 99** (all superior, 1 for disabled). Lift. B&B €97 pps, ss €6. **Main Dining Room:** This L shaped room, which is exceptionally well run under the eagle eye of Pat Doyle, features wonderful examples from the hotel's renowned art collection and is cleverly designed to have an intimate atmosphere. The Chef de cuisine Jim Ahearne and his team provide excellent value for money and continue to satisfy literally hundreds of guests daily. Menus reflect the value placed on fresh local produce: Rosslare mackerel, Slaney salmon and locally sourced vegetables are used in daily-changing menus offering fairly traditional cooking in starters like chicken liver pate maison with Cumberland sauce and leek, bacon & Cheddar quiche with tossed greens; followed by char-grilled lamb burgers with sautéed onions & mushrooms and pan grilled lemon sole fillets with sauce tartare. Finish with desserts like bread & butter pudding & cream or banoffie pie with vanilla custard. The hotel's renowned wine list is meticulously sourced and excellent value. **Seats 250** (private room 40); no smoking area, air conditioning. L 1-2.15 D 7.30-9 (Sat from 7); Set L €18; Set D €34. House wine €18; s.c. discretionary.

☆ **La Marine Bistro:** This cool contemporary restaurant adjacent to the hotel complements the main restaurant perfectly and has its own separate entrance. A stunning zinc bar imported from France is the focal point of a lovely area where you can have an aperitif in comfort (although the turnover is brisk and you will be encouraged to go directly to your table if it is ready). Offering the perfect informal dining option, La Marine is the place to see and be seen - and it can be hard to get a table, especially for dinner at weekends. The atmosphere can be electric, although comfort is not a top priority; fashionably sparse tables have fresh flowers, good quality cutlery and paper napkins, but space is at a premium so be prepared for a bit of a squeeze. Head chef Eugene Callaghan has been intrumental in the development of the restaurant from the outset and a recent visit confirmed consistent improvement and a greater degree of confidence, seen in menus that have become more ambitious and are excellently executed. Ingredients are carefully sourced, using local seasonal produce as much as possible and a finely judged balancing act between traditional and fusion fare is achieved, thus starters like creamy seafood chowder find themselves alongside a melt-in-the mouth salt & pepper squid with chilli, soy & coriander dip and down to earth main courses like grilled fillet of Wexford beef with gratin dauphinois & béarnaise sauce rub shoulders with crispy duck confit with egg noodles, honey & ginger sauce. Desserts are deliciously classic - baked rhubarb pastry slice with aricot & cointreau glaze, perhaps, or there's a selection of Irish cheese.Wines (a selection off the main restaurant list), reflecting the style of food, are fairly priced. Service is swift and friendly. Sunday lunch is more traditional and may feature upbeat versions of traditional roasts. A light snack menu is also available every afternoon, 3-6pm. **Seats 60** L daily 12.30-2.15; D 6.30-9.30. Amex, Diners, MasterCard, Visa, Laser. **Directions:** take the signs for Wexford. Situated outside Rosslare town.

Tagoat

COUNTRY HOUSE

Churchtown House

Tagoat Rosslare Co. Wexford
Tel: 053 32555 Fax: 053 32577
Email: churchtown.rosslare@indigo.ie Web: churchtown-rosslare.com

Patricia and Austin Cody's Georgian house is set in about eight and a half acres of wooded gardens and dates back as far as 1703. It has been completely renovated and elegantly furnished to make a comfortable country house restreat for discerning guests and is extremely handy for the Rosslare ferryport, about four miles away. The Codys are renowned for their hospitality and, if you're lucky enough to arrive at this well-run house at around teatime, you'll be served delicious home-made cake and tea in the drawing room. Good food is an important feature here and a fine Irish breakfast is served in the bright dining room, where dinner is also available for residents by arrangement. Spacious en-suite bedrooms decorated in country house style have phones and TV. Garden. Not suitable for children under 10. Pets by arrangement. **Rooms 12** (2 junior suites, 4 shower only, 1 for disabled, all no-smoking). B&B €95 pps; ss €15. Residents' D 7.30-8pm, Set D €35, book by noon. Licensed. Closed 30 Nov-1 Mar. Amex, MasterCard, Visa, Laser. **Directions:** on R736 half mile from N25, at Tagoat.

Wexford

RESTAURANT

Forde's Restaurant

Crescent Quay Wexford Co. Wexford **Tel: 053 23832 /22816**
Fax: 053 23832 /22816

In a recently renovated building near the Ballast Office, proprietor-chef Liam Forde's bistro-style first-floor restaurant overlooking the harbour has great atmosphere - created by many happy customers and excellent use of lighting, with mirrors reflecting lots of candles. Tables are quite well-spaced and comfortable and the varied seasonal à la carte menus offer a wide choice, with vegetarian (and vegan) options prominently listed amd a leaning towards seafood. From a dozen or so starters, try button mushrooms filled with brie & garlic then deep-fried in an almond coating (a nice little twist on the old favourite) or a delicious salad of marinated seared scallops, with mini crab spring rolls and a lemon dressing. Main courses might include a fish special trio of salmon, scallops & turbot in a light cream sauce (a well-judged dish, perfectly cooked) and rack of local lamb with rosemary and raspberry jus and accompanying vegetables (small buttered steamed potatoes in their jackets, a mixture of julienne courgette, finely sliced onion & broccoli florets, stir fried briefly in butter and spring rolls filled with mashed potato). Everything is made on the premises - stocks, pastas, ice creams - the cooking is spot on and details excellent. Interesting , informative wine list. The early evening menus is particularly good value. There are plans to open a rather different kind of restaurant for the 2002 season - details from Liam Forde. **Seats 50.** No smoking area, air conditioning. Children welcome. D Mon-Sat, 5.30-10. Early D, €19 (5-6pm only). D menu à la carte. House wine about €20; s.c.discretionary. Closed Sun (except during Opera Festival), 24-26 Dec. Diners, MasterCard, Visa, Laser. **Directions:** the quay front.

Wexford

La Dolce Vita

RESTAURANT

Westgate Wexford Co. Wexford
Tel: 053 23935 Fax: 053 23935

Chef-proprietor Roberto Pons greets guest personally to his restaurant, which has earned a strong local following since he moved here in 1998. The exterior of the building is promising and perhaps leads first-time guests to expect more character - and, unusually for an Italian restaurant, the ambience tends to be rather quiet. A committed Euro-Toques chef, Roberto cooks in traditional Italian style - risotto, osso bucco, rombo in salsa verde - and, except for necessary Italian imports, everything is based on the freshest and best of local Irish produce. In line with this style of restaurant, presentation is rather plain (no bad thing perhaps), but the cooking is generally reliable. Dishes that merited special praise on a recent visit include meltingly tender lambs liver with butter & sage, which came with excellent side vegetables, and a perfect pannacotta but, surprisingly, a scampi risotto was spoilt by overcooked rice. **Seats 60.** No-smoking area. Wheelchair access. D daily 6-10; à la carte. House wines €14.60. Children welcome. Closed 2 weeks Feb. MasterCard, Laser. **Directions:** opposite county hall, 200m on left.

Wexford

La Riva

RESTAURANT

Crescent Quay Wexford Co. Wexford **Tel: 053 24330**

Just off the quays, Frank and Anne Chamberlaine's first floor restaurant has been doing a good job since 1991. It's up a steep flight of stairs – which do not give a very good first impression – however, once inside, a warm welcome offsets any negative feelings. The restaurant itself is delightful in a bright, informal way, with views through to the kitchen. A blackboard menu offers tempting specials, notably seafood - roast monkfish and parmesan, prawns with garlic & chilli sauce, scallops with rosemary & orange. Pasta dishes can be starters or main courses, and there are more serious main courses also, like rack of lamb (with roast shallots and garlic, perhaps). **Seats 42.** No-smoking area. Air conditioning. D daily 6-10:30. A la carte menu. House wines £10.95; sc discretionary. Children welcome. Closed 2 weeks Jan. MasterCard, Visa.

Wexford

Mange 2

RESTAURANT

100 South Main St. Wexford Co. Wexford **Tel: 053 44033**

Mange 2 retains its reputation as one of Wexford's most exciting restaurants and continues to offer creative cooking which is also good value for money. But the room is pretty basic - farmhouse-style pine tables, plastic flowers and terracotta red painted walls - and does not do justice to the food, although it does have views through to the kitchen. However, it is a warm and welcoming place; tables are cleared very promptly and everything possible is done to ensure guests enjoy the food. Head chef Richie Trappe's menus are ambitious and vegetarians are well looked after - and there are blackboard specials daily in addition to à la carte menus. Expect colourful starters like roast red pepper, potato & fennel seed samosa with baby beets & yogurt dressing or grilled praws with garlic chill butter, on crispy carrot & endive, tomato & basil dressing. Typical main dishes might be roast saddle of venison with parmentier potatoes, swiss chard & coarse mustard glaze or house smoked monkfish fillet with char-grilled aubergine, provençal sauce and parmesan snaps. There really is something here to please everyone - and speedy service too. **Seats 40.** Wheelchair access. Air conditioning. D 6-11.30 daily, Sun 6-10. A la carte. House wines about €12.50 SC discretionary. Children welcome. Closed Mon & 3 weeks in Jan. Amex, MasterCard, Visa. **Directions:** Wexford town centre near Talbot Hotel.

Wexford

McMenamin's Townhouse

B&B

3 Auburn Terrace Wexford Co.Wexford **Tel: 053 46442**
Fax: 053 46442 Email: mcmem@indigo.ie Web: www.wexford-bedandbreakfast.com

Seamus and Kay McMenamin's redbrick end-of-terrace Victorian house is within walking distance of the town centre and has been one of the most highly-regarded places to stay in this area for some years. It is useful for first or last night overnight stops for travellers on the Rosslare ferry, as a base for the Wexford Opera or for a short break in this undervalued corner of Ireland. Bedrooms are on the small side, with neat shower rooms, and the decor is perhaps a little tired, but they take pride in providing top quality beds and rooms have everything required including TV and tea/coffee-making facilities. The McMenamins' extensive local knowledge is generously passed on to guests and this, together with a good breakfast - quite extensive menus include home-made yogurt old-fashioned treats like kippers and lambs' kidneys in sherry sauce, served with freshly baked breads and home-made preserves - gets you off to a good start and helps to make the most of every day. Children welcome (under 2s free in parents' room, cots available without charge). No pets. **Rooms 5** (all shower only & no-smoking). B&B €35 pps; ss €10. Closed 20-30 Dec. Amex, MasterCard, Visa. **Directions:** central near bus/rail station opposite cineplex.

Wexford

The Sky & The Ground

PUB

112/113 South Main Street Wexford Co. Wexford
Tel: 053 21273 Fax: 053 21832
Email: skyandg@gofree.indigo.ie Web: www.skyandtheground.com

Candle light, framed old advertisements, basic tables and chairs and a worn wooden floor create the atmospheric drinking space at the Sky & the Ground, a genuine old-style pub that frequently features traditional Irish music sessions. A short bar menu is displayed on a daily changing blackboard; starters are usually restricted to soup, with around five main courses to choose from. Typically, dishes like lemon sole with orange & dill and farmhouse style chicken with garlic & brie cheese come with hefty portions of mashed potatoes and bowls of stir-fried vegetables and desserts might include a freshly-made apple & almond flan, served with a drizzle of lemon syrup. There is also a patio garden around at the back where they serve food, weather permitting. There is also no segregation of drinkers from customers who are eating, which can sometimes make the service a bit erratic. Upstairs there's an evening restaurant "Heavens Above" which is also a place with lots of character - more formal than the setup down below but a place where you could let your hair down a bit. The appropriately named "Next Door" off-licence is also under the same management; it stocks over 300 wines from all over the world and an unusually wide range of bottled beers from different countries (all available to customers in the bar or restaurant). Pub seats 50. Food served Mon-Sat: L 12-3 Limited snack menu 3-6. Restaurant: Mon-Sat, D 6-10; closed Sun. MasterCard, Visa, Laser. **Directions:** on the south end of Wexford's main street.

Wexford

Talbot Hotel

HOTEL

Trinity St. Wexford Co. Wexford **Tel: 053 22566**
Fax: 053 23377 Email: talbotwx@eircom.net Web: talbothotel.ie

Sister hotel to the Stillorgan Park Hotel in Dublin, this 1960s hotel actually dates back to 1905. It is well-located on the harbour-front location and also convenient to the town centre - indeed, so many activities revolve around it that many would say the Talbot is the town centre. A warm welcome from friendly staff, plus the contented crowd that always seems to be milling around the foyer, immediately sets arriving guests at ease - and one is immediately struck by the range and quality of original paintings, which is a feature of great interest throughout the hotel. Bedrooms are inevitably somewhat limited by their age and the style of the building, but quite pleasant and comfortable, with phone, TV and tea/coffee trays as standard. The basement leisure centre is an unexpectedly characterful area, confirming the feeling that the Talbot will always spring a few surprises - one of which is that 'The Slaney Gourmet Club' meet at the hotel on the last Tuesday of each month for 'a taste of the exotic'; there's also live jazz in the Trinity every Thursday night in summer and weekend entertainment all year. Conference/banqueting facilities (300/350). Leisure centre, indoor swimming pool. Children welcome (under 14s free in parents' room). Wheelchair access. Lift. Own parking. No pets. **Rooms 99** (all en-suite, 2 for disabled) B&B about €70 pps, ss about €20. Open all year. Amex, MasterCard, Visa.

Wexford

CAFÉ

Wexford Arts Centre Café

Cornemarket Wexford Co. Wexford
Tel: 053 23764 Fax: 053 24544

'Good affordable food should be in everyone's hands' is the motto of this daytime cafe housed in the Wexford Arts Centre. Inside, the decor is pretty basic but don't let that put you off, as it's run by Tess Smyth whose speciality is all things sweet and her exceptional tarts, cakes and biscuits are always on offer. Breakfast is served from 8.30 and includes high-quality fry-ups and bacon sandwiches; toasted muesli and a banana malt and honey smoothie are available as the more healthier options. A brief menu for snacks and lunch starts at 12 and is complemented by daily soups and pasta specials listed on a blackboard. Otherwise, expect fresh vibrant salads which are definitely a strength and foccacia breads filled with bacon, brie, tomato and mayo or goats cheese, pesto, spinach and grilled vegetables and fat chips with sour cream and chilli sauce. Large helpings at low prices ensure the loyalty of local fans. This is also a perfect place for some reviving afternoon tea. **Seats 45.** Open Mon-Sat 8.30-6. SC discretionary. Closed bank hols.

Wexford

HOTEL

White's Hotel

Georges Street Wexford Co.Wexford **Tel: 053 22311**
Fax: 053 45000 Email: info@whiteshotel.iol.ie Web: wexfordirl.com

From the outside this famous hotel looks relatively modern, certainly when approached from the car park, but the reality is that there was a hostelry on this site in the late 18th century, which is more apparent when viewed from George Street. Older bedrooms have been modernised and there's a health and fitness club (but no swimming pool) in the basement. 40 new bedrooms are planned shortly, along with major improvements to the reception, bar, restaurant and conference rooms. Conference/banqueting (400/350). Secretarial services. Parking. Children welcome (under 3s free in parents' room, cots available). Pets by arrangement. Lift. **Rooms 82** (all en-suite). B&B about €60 pps; ss about €20. Open all year. Amex, Diners, MasterCard, Visa. **Directions:** follow signs when leaving N25 or N11.

COUNTY WICKLOW

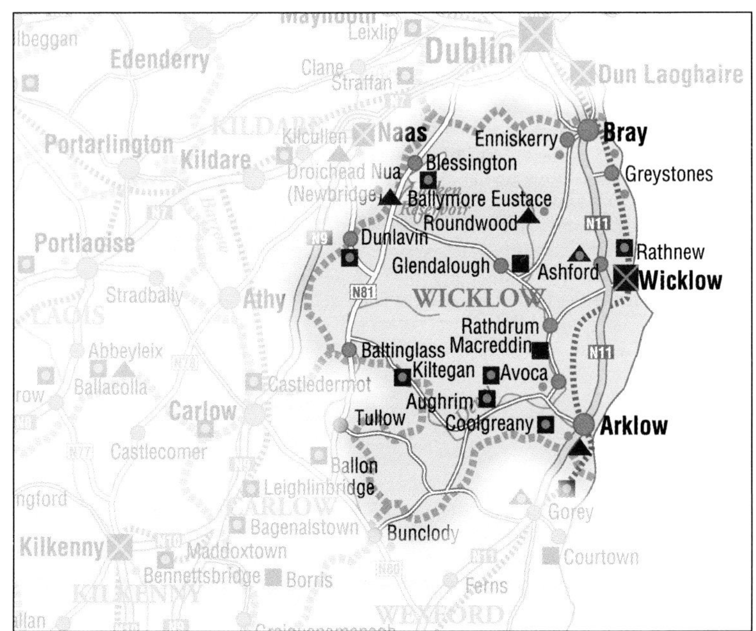

Although there are at least three Irish counties looking at possible ways of practising positive discrimination in population and planning matters in favour of their own citizens as we head into 2002, it is Wicklow County Council's moves in this direction which seem to have attracted most attention. But then, Wicklow is right beside Dublin - in fact, thanks to its famous hills and mountains, it is the only other county which can be seen from the heart of the Capital.

Although the booming presence of Dublin is right next door, this sublimely and spectacularly lovely county is very much its own place, a totally away-from-it-all world of moorland and mountain, farmland and garden, forest and lake, seashore and river. It's all right there, just over the nearest hill, yet it all seems so gloriously different. Known as "The Garden of Ireland" , this horticulturally diverse county is renowned for the variety of famous gardens open to the public (some with fine houses which may also be visited). One of the county's most appealing attractions is the annual Wicklow Gardens Festival, held through May, June and July. At this time many private gardens, not normally open to the opublic, may also be seen - full details are available from Wicklow Tourism.

In times past, Wicklow may have been recorded - by those who kept the official histories - as a mountain stronghold where rebels and hermits alike could keep their distance from the capital. But modern Wicklow has no need to be in a state of rebellion, for it is an invigorating and inspiring place which captivates everyone who lives there, so much so that while many of its citizens inevitably work in Dublin, they're Wicklow people a very long way first and associate Dubs - if at all - an extremely long way down the line.

Their attitude is easily understood, for even with today's traffic, it is still only a very short drive to transform your world from the crowded city streets right into the heart of some of the most heart-stoppingly beautiful scenery in all Ireland. Such scenery generates its own strong loyalties and sense of identity, and Wicklow folk are rightly and proudly a race apart. Drawing strength from their wonderful environment, they have a vigorous local life which keeps metropolitan blandness well at bay.

And though being in a place so beautiful is almost sufficient reason for existence in itself, they're busy people too, with sheep farming and forestry and all sorts of light industries, while down in the workaday harbour of Arklow in the south of the county - a port with a long and splendid maritime history - they've been so successful in organising their own seagoing fleet of freighters that there are now more ships registered in Arklow than any other Irish port. Also in the south of the county is the neat village of Aughrim, Wicklow's top scorer in the current Tidy Town awards. In such a beautiful county, it's an achievement of real distinction.

Local Attractions and Information

Arklow Tourism Information	0402 32484
Ashford Mount Usher Gardens	0404 40116
Avoca Tourism Information	0402 35788
Blessington Russborough House & Gardens	045 865239
Bray Kilruddery House & Gardens	01 286 3405
Bray National Sealife Centre	01 286 6939
Derrynamuck Dwyer McAllister Traditional Cottage	0404 45325
Enniskerry Powerscourt Gardens	01 204 6000
Glendalough Tourism Information	0404 45688
Glendalough Visitor Centre	0404 45325
Rathdrum Avondale House	0404 46111
Rathdrum Kilmacurragh Arboretum	01 647 3000
Wicklow County Gardens Festival (May-July)	0404 66058
Wicklow Mountains National Park	0404 45425
Wicklow Town Wicklow Historic Gaol	0404 61599
Wicklow Town Tourism Information	0404 69117

Arklow

Christy's

PUB

38 Main St. Arklow Co. Wicklow **Tel: 0402 32145**

Swift, friendly service on arrival will immediately endear new customers to Michael Murray's attractively renovated town centre bar. Promptly presented menus and the offer of a drink gets hungry guests off to a good start and positive feelings are reinforced by appetising food at neighbouring tables and an interesting menu which nicely balances the traditional and the contemporary. House specials, for example, range from Mexican beef wrap or chargrilled supreme of chicken with stir-fried vegetables and sauté potatoes or egg noodles to Christy's fish & chips (which comes with a choice of traditional tartare sauce, salsa or lemon & dill mayo) or joint of the day. Cooking and presentation both live up to the promise of the menu, making a place people will return to. Wine choice restricted to a small selection of quarter bottles. Live music at weekends. Children welcome up to 7pm. Own parking at rear. Food served 12.30-6pm daily. Closed Good Fri, 25 Dec. MasterCard, Visa. **Directions:** Directly on Main Street, Parking at rear.

Arklow

Kitty's of Arklow

PUB/RESTAURANT

56 Main Street Arklow Co. Wicklow
Tel: 0402 31669 Fax: 0402 31553

Kitty's is something of an institution in Arklow and, since changing hands in 2000, has been renovated and "relaunched" with a strong emphasis on food. It's a big blue double-fronted building in the centre of town, with large and airy bar areas on the ground floor decorated in a sort of retro 50s style (with big comfortable chairs and old-fashioned radiators) and a first floor bistro restaurant, which is divided into a non-smoking section along the front of the building and a long, narrow area for smokers at the back. It's very popular with locals ranging from young commuters to large family groups, who like the informal atmosphere and modern food at affordable prices - the early evening menu is especially good value.There's no reception area downstairs, but greeting and seating (at uncovered wooden tables with good, simple appointments) is efficiently handled on arrival at the top and menus, offering about nine choices on each course, are promptly produced. Descriptions aren't too fussy and everything sounds appetising: typical starters include a mixed antipasto plate (mixed plate of Italian marinated vegetables with cold meat, cheese & homemade grissini) and Thai fish cakes (with a lime dressing and pepper jam), while main courses might include several fish dishes, such as grilled coconut & chilli turbot on a bed of stir-fried bok choi and an intriguing 'tempura of toleppio' with a mango salsa. Good quality ingredients are used although cooking can be inconsistent, with some dishes well executed and others disappointing. But it's a place you could find yourself going back to, not least because notably friendly, efficient and professional staff make sure everyone's happy - and what's more, they are happy to let you have one course if you like (min charge €15.24). Not suitable for children after 7 pm. **Seats 110** (private room 24). No smoking area; air conditioning. D daily 6-10pm. Early D €22.86 (6-7pm only). Set D €20.20. House wine €15.17. A la carte also available. Bar food daily: 10.30 am-5 pm; à la carte.Closed 25 Dec & Good Fri. Amex, Diners, MasterCard, Visa, Laser. **Directions:** Town Centre.

Arklow
COUNTRY HOUSE

Plattenstown House

Coolgreaney Road Arklow Co. Wicklow
Tel: 0402 37822 Fax: 0402 37822
Email: mcdpr@indigo.ie Web: www.wicklow.ie/farm/f-plattn.htm

Margaret McDowell describes her period farmhouse well as having "the soft charm typical of the mid 19th century houses built in scenic Wicklow". About halfway between Dublin and Rosslare (each about an hour's drive away) and overlooking parkland, this quiet, peaceful place is set in 50 acres of land amidst its own lovely gardens close to the sea. There is plenty to do in the area, with golf, riding stables and forest walks all nearby, as well as the sea. There's a traditional drawing room overlooking the front garden, a TV lounge (where smoking is allowed) available for guests' use and a dining room. Breakfast is served in a lovely dining room, where evening meals are also served by arrangement. Bedrooms vary in size and outlook according to their position in the house and have very different characters, but all are comfortably furnished. Garden. Children welcome (under 3s free in parents' room). No pets. **Rooms 4** (3 en-suite with shower only, 1 with private bathroom, all no-smoking). B&B about €36.82 pps, ss €8.89. Closed at Christmas. MasterCard, Visa. **Directions:** Top of Arklow town,small roundabout,straight on to Coolgreaney Road.2.5 miles on left.

Arklow
HOTEL

Woodenbridge Hotel

Vale of Avoca Arklow Co. Wicklow
Tel: 0402 35146 Fax: 0402 35573
Email: wbhotel@iol.ie Web: www.woodenbridgehotel.com

This pleasant country hotel lays claim to the title of Ireland's oldest hotel, with a history going back to 1608, when it was first licensed as a coaching inn on the old Dublin-Wexford highway - and later came to great prominence when gold and copper were mined in the locality. Michael Collins stayed at the hotel during secret meetings with senior British Army officers in February 1922 (the room he stayed in can be booked, subject to availability) and Eamon and Sinead De Valera spent their honeymoon here. Today it is still very popular for weddings and makes a friendly and relaxing base for a visit to this beautiful part of County Wicklow. The many other historical associations in the area include the home of Charles Stewart Parnell, nearby at Avondale. Bedrooms - many of them overlooking Woodenbridge golf course - are comfortably furnished, with phone, TV and tea/coffee trays. As well as a more formal restaurant, there's wholesome food to be had in the lively bar. Children welcome (under 4s free in parents' room; cots available without charge). **Rooms 23** (5 no smoking, 1 for disabled). B&B €70pps, ss €24. No pets. Closed 25 Dec. Amex, MasterCard, Visa, Switch. **Directions:** Turn off N11 Arklow (N4).

Ashford
PUB

Ashford House

Inchanappa Lodge Ashford Co. Wicklow
Tel: 0404 40481 Fax: 0404 40990
Email: info@ashfordhouse.ie Web: www.ashfordhouse.iol.ie

Under the energetic ownership of Thomas Murphy since 1998, this large pub in the centre of Ashford village has undergone a major transformation. Welcoming open fires, plenty of natural materials and friendly staff create a warm tone and a number of carefully planned areas with completely different styles and atmospheres seem to provide something for every taste and time of day. The main bar, while far from olde worlde, is traditional enough to please those who enjoy a classic Irish pub and, behind it, there's an informal, high-ceilinged bistro (also with an open fire); daytime food can be served in either area. There's also a separate restaurant (currently oriental) and even a contemporary nightclub, Club Aqua, with full bar, separate seating and dance floor. Bar menu all day, 12.30-9.30. House wine from €15.25. Children welcome up to 8pm. Toilets wheelchair accessible. Amex, MasterCard, Visa. **Directions:** Dublin-Wexford road (N11); off roundabout on Main St.

Ashford
FARMHOUSE/GUESTHOUSE

Ballyknocken House

Ashford Co. Wicklow **Tel: 0404 44627**
Email: cfulvio@ballyknocken.com Web: www.ballyknocken.com

Perfectly placed for walking holidays in the Wicklow Hills, playing golf, or simply for touring the area, Catherine Fulvio's charming Victorian farmhouse provides comfort, cosiness, good food and hospitality. Catherine took over this family business in 1999, after a period working at nearby Tinakilly House, and she has since refurbished it throughout in old country style - not only the bedrooms, but also the dining room, parlour and sitting room have had the makeover and her energetic quest for perfection also extends to the garden, where new fruit tree, roses and herbs are now settling in. Comfort and style aside, splendid dinners (with wine list), extensive breakfasts and relaxing atmosphere ensure guests keep coming back for more. **Rooms 7** (1 shower only & no smoking) B&B €45 pps, ss €25. D Tue-Sat for residents, Set D €26.50. Closed 1 Dec-28 Feb. MasterCard, Visa. **Directions:** Turn right after Texaco Petrol Station in Ashford. Continue for 3 miles. House on right.

Aughrim
HOTEL

Lawless Hotel

Aughrim Co. Wicklow **Tel: 0402 36146** Fax: 0402 36384
Email: lawhotel@iol.ie Web: www.lawhotel.com

Picturesquely situated beside the river in the lovely village of Aughrim, the O'Toole family's delightful hotel dates back to 1787 and recent renovations and extensions have, on the whole, been undertaken with respect for the character of the original building although, unfortunately it has been somewhat dwarfed by the adjacent development of holiday homes. Bedrooms are cosily decorated, in character with a country inn, although on the small side which has limited bathroom design. The "Thirsty Trout" bar and the "Snug" lounge are appealing and there's a lovely dining room overlooking the river. A paved area at the back beside the river is used for informal summer food and makes a romantic spot for wedding photographs. Conference/banqueting (250/250). Secretarial services. Fishing. Garden. Parking. Children welcome (under 2s free in parents' room). No pets. **Rooms 14** (all en-suite, 5 no-smoking). B&B about €60 pps, ss about €25. Wheelchair access (ground floor only). Closed 24-26 Dec. Diners, MasterCard, Visa. **Directions:** Follow signs for 8 miles from roundabout at Arklow's Upper Main Street.

Avoca Village
CAFÉ

Avoca Handweavers

Avoca Handweavers Avoca Village Co. Wicklow
Tel: 0402 35105 Fax: 0402 35446
Email: info@avoca.ie Web: www.avoca.ie

Avoca handweavers, established in 1723, is Ireland's oldest business. It's a family owned craft design company which now has half a dozen branches throughout Ireland (most of which feature in this Guide) and the business originated here, at Avoca village, where you can watch the hand weavers who produce the lovely woven woollen rugs and fabrics which became the hallmark of the company. Today the appeal of Avoca shops is threefold: the high standard of crafts sold, their beautiful locations, and restaurants that have built up a well-deserved reputation for imaginative, wholesome home-cooked food. Garden. Parking. Children welcome. Pets allowed in some areas. **Seats 75.** Open all day (10-5) Mon-Sun. House wine about €12.50. No-smoking area. No service charge. Wheelchair access. Closed 25-26 Dec. Amex, Diners, MasterCard, Visa, Laser. **Directions:** Leave N11 at Rathnew and follow signs for Avoca.

Blessington
HOTEL féile bia

Downshire House Hotel

Blessington Co. Wicklow
Tel: 045 865 199 Fax: 045 865 335
Email: info@downshirehouse.com Web: www.downshirehouse.com

Situated just 18 miles from Dublin on the N81, in the tree-lined main street of Blessington, this friendly village hotel offers unpretentious comfort which is very winning. Blessington is an attractive village in an area of great natural beauty and archaeological interest – and it's also very close to Ireland's great Palladian mansion, Russborough House, home of the world-famous Beit art collection. The present owner, Rhoda Byrne, has run the hotel since 1959 and instigated many improvements, including conference facilities for up to 200 and refurbishment of public areas. Simply furnished bedrooms, which include two single rooms, all have en-suite bathrooms with full bath and shower. Conference/banqueting (200/250). Garden, walking. Children welcome; cots available (€8). **Rooms 25** (all with full en-suite bathrooms). B&B €69pps; ss€8. Closed 22 Dec-10 Jan. MasterCard, Visa, Switch. **Directions:** 18 miles from Dublin on the N81.

Bray
RESTAURANT

The Tree of Idleness Restaurant

Seafront Bray Co. Wicklow
Tel: 01 286 3498 Fax: 01 282 8183

This much-loved seafront restaurant opened in 1979 when the owners, Akis and Susan Courtellas, arrived from Cyprus bringing with them the name of their previous restaurant (now in Turkish-held north Cyprus). A collection of photographs of old Cyprus in the reception area establishes the traditional Mediterranean atmosphere of the restaurant – and the menu cover bears a drawing of the original Tree of Idleness. Since Akis' death some years ago, Susan has run the restaurant herself with the help of Tom Monaghan, restaurant manager since 1980 and, since 2001, Derek Cooling (who was previously second chef) has assumed the mantle of head chef, so it is he who now offers modern Greek Cypriot/Mediterranean menus based on the style which has made this restaurant famous - and the most remarkable feature of the Tree of Idleness is its consistency, in maintaining both high standards and the unique house style. Alongside the classics – tzatziki, humus, taramosalata, Greek salad, dolmades, moussaka (including a vegetarian variation), souvlaki – there are some specialities which have had the world beating a path to the door for 20 years. First, there is the suckling pig: boned and filled with apple and apricot stuffing, it is served crisp-skinned and tender, with a wonderful wine and wild mushroom sauce. Then there is the dessert trolley, which is nothing less than temptation on wheels: it always carries a range of fresh and exotic fruits, baklava, home-made ice creams, several chocolate desserts, Greek yogurt mousse and much else besides. Service is excellent and the wine list includes some rare vintages, including wines from the Russian Massandra Collection, which go back to 1923. No children under 10 after 8 pm. **Seats 50.** No-smoking area. D Tue-Sun, 7.30-10.30. Set D €34.28, à la carte also available. House wines from €£19.05. 10% SC. Closed Mondays, Christmas & 2 weeks Sep. Amex, MasterCard, Visa, Laser. **Directions:** On seafront towards Bray Head.

Dunlavin

Rathsallagh House, Golf & Country Club

COUNTRY HOUSE
RESTAURANT

Dunlavin Co. Wicklow
Tel: 045 403 112 Fax: 045 403 343
Email: info@rathsallagh.com Web: www.rathsallagh.com

This large, rambling country house is just an hour from Dublin, but it could be in a different world. Although it's very professionally operated, the O'Flynn family insist it is not an hotel and - despite the relatively recent addition of an 18-hole golf course with clubhouse in the grounds - the gentle rhythms of life around the country house and gardens ensure that the atmosphere is kept decidedly low-key. Day rooms are elegantly furnished in country house style, with lots of comfortable seating areas and open fires. Accommodation includes beautiful big rooms with luxurious bathrooms in a new block, built discreetly behind the main courtyard in materials which will age gracefully to match the older buildings while, as in all old houses, the original rooms do vary; some are very spacious with lovely country views while other smaller, simpler rooms in the stable yard have a special cottagey charm. Rathsallagh is renowned for its magnificent Edwardian breakfast buffet, which was recognised in 2001 through selection as National Winner of the Guide's Denny Irish Breakfast Awards. Breakfast at Rathsallagh offers every conceivable good thing: not only fresh juices, fresh and stewed fruits, dried fruit compôtes, home-made muesli, Irish farmhouse cheeses, smoked salmon and kedgeree but also a whole ham on the bone and silver chafing dishes full of reminders of yesteryear - liver, lambs kidneys wrapped in bacon, kidneys and juicy field mushrooms as well as the more usual rashers, sausages, black and white pudding tomatoes - the list goes on and on - and there's more to come from the kitchen too, as eggs to accompany this feast are cooked to order and, of course, there's a selection of home-made breads, croissants and toast, local honey and home-made jams and chutney. It's a sight to gladden the heart of any guest and a few rounds of golf or a good walk in the hills will definitely be needed afterwards. Good food, warm hospitality and surroundings that are quiet or romantic to suit the mood of the day make Rathsallagh an ideal venue for conferences and small weddings. **Restaurant:** Head chef John Luke creates interesting menus based on local produce, much of it from Rathsallagh's own farm and walled garden. A drink in the old kitchen bar is recommended while reading the 4-course menu - country house with world influences - then guests can settle down in the graciously furnished dining room overlooking the gardens and the golf course. Roast local beef is a speciality, as is Wicklow lamb. Leave some room for some Irish farmhouse cheese served from a traditional trolley, or delicious desserts which are often based on fruit from the garden. * Food served all day at Rathsallagh Golf Club (Closed Jan). Amex, Diners, MasterCard, Visa, Laser. **Directions:** 15 miles south of Naas off Carlow Road, take Kilcullen Bypass (M9), turn left 2 miles south of Priory Inn, follow signposts.

Enniskerry

RESTAURANT/CAFÉ

Powerscourt Terrace Café

Powerscourt House Enniskerry Co. Wicklow
Tel: 01 204 6070 Fax: 01 204 6072
Email: simon@avoca.ie Web: www.avoca.ie

Situated in a stunning location overlooking the famous gardens and fountains of Powerscourt House, the Pratt family of Avoca Handweavers opened this self-service restaurant in the summer of 1997. It is a delightfully relaxed space, with a large outdoor eating area as well as the 160-seater café, and the style and standard of food is similar to the original Avoca restaurant at Kilmacanogue. So head chef Eimer Rainsford ensures that everything is freshly made, using as many local ingredients as possible – including organic herbs and vegetables – with lots of healthy food. Avoca cafés are renowned for interesting salads, home-bakes and good pastries, and also excellent vegetarian dishes many of which, such as oven-roasted vegetable and goat's cheese tart, have become specialities. A new room in the east Wing was opened in 2001, providing a private rooms for groups of 20-90 people. Parking (some distance from the house). Children welcome. **Seats 160** (indoor), additional 140 outside terrace (private room 20-90). No-smoking area. Toilets wheelchair accessible. Open daily 10 -5 (Sun to 5.30). House wine €12.63. Closed 25-26 Dec. Amex, Diners, MasterCard, Visa, Laser. **Directions:** 2 miles from Enniskerry Village.

Enniskerry

RESTAURANT

Wingfields Bistro

Church Hill Enniskerry Village Co. Wicklow **Tel: 01 204 2854**

Although windows and a door (often left open in summer) overlook the street and may mislead first-time visitors, the entrance to this attractive restaurant is up an alley on the side of the building. Once you're inside and through a small reception area, you find yourself in an attractive, well-lit dining room with well-appointed linen-clad tables and lots of original modern paintings. Proprietor/manager Toni Sinnott and head chef Martin Cuddihy opened here in autumn 2000 and they seem to be doing an excellent job. Martin's menus are not over-long, offering a well-balanced choice of about half a dozen starters and slightly more on the main course selection; local seafood features strongly and, of course, the lamb which is virtually synonymous with the county - specialities include Dublin Bay prawns with a roast garlic & cherry tomato dressing and rack of Wicklow lamb served on a bed of pea purée with a rosemary jus. Cooking is accurate and food attractively presented in an admirably simple house style (no towering culinary architecture here), with the emphasis on sound combinations and flavour. deatils, like home-baked bread and freshly cooked vegetables are good and service is professional, unobtrusive and relaxed. A shortish, carefully chosen wine list includes a range of house wines (about €15-20) and a few half bottles.*There are plans to extend the restaurant for the 2002 season, which will increase the seating capacity to 60; a full bar and daytime opening is also planned. **Seats 46.** No smoking area; air condirioning. D Mon-Sat, 7-9, L Sun only 1-7.30. D à la carte, Set Sun L €21.59. House wine €15.24. Closed D Sun. MasterCard, Visa, Laser, Switch. **Directions:** Into Village from Monument, head uphill towards Powerscourt Demense. 50 yards up on the right.

Glen O' The Downs

HOTEL

Glenview Hotel

Glen O' The Downs Co. Wicklow **Tel: 01 2873399**
Fax: 01 2877511 Email: glenview@iol.ie Web: www.glenviewhotel.ie

Famous for its views over the Glen O'The Downs, this well-located hotel has all the advantages of a beautiful rural location, yet is just a half hour's drive from Dublin. Major renovations and additions have recently been completed, resulting in a dramatic improvement of all facilities. Landscaping and upgrading of the exterior and a new reception area gives a favourable impression on arrival. The hotel's conference area offers state-of-the-art facilities and there's an excellent Health and Leisure Club, and 74 new bedrooms include a penthouse suite. Bedrooms, which are attractively furnished in warm colours and a gently modern style, have good facilities including TV and radio, safe, phone with computer terminal, trouser press, tea/coffee making facilities and hairdryer. All this, together with special breaks (golf, health and fitness, riding) offering good value, make the hotel a valuable asset to the area. Conference/banqueting (250/180). Business centre, secretarial services, executive room, ISDN lines, video conferencing. Leisure centre (indoor swimming pool). Garden. Children welcome before 7pm. Pets by arrangement. **Rooms 74** (2 suites, 19 executive rooms, 35 no-smoking rooms, 1 for disabled). Lift. B&B €114.27, ss € 38.09. Hotel closed 25 Dec. **Woodlands Restaurant:** The restaurant has a great natural asset in forest views over the Glen-O'-the Downs although it can otherwise be somewhat short on atmosphere. The presence of head chef Derek Dunne, a well-known successful competitor in the Irish Culinary Team, puts the food on a more ambitious level than most hotel dining rooms. He presents interesting table d'hôte and à la carte menus based on local ingredients - quite a lot of seafood, Wicklow lamb, venison - and mainly classical French in style. Cooking is competent but may not always live up to the promise of the menu. **Seats 80.** No-smoking area; air conditioning. D daily, 6.30-9.30; L Sun only, 12.30-2.30. Set D €43.17, à la carte also available; Set Sun L €22.85. House wines from €18. No s.c. Closed 25 Dec, bank hols. Amex, Diners, MasterCard, Visa, Laser. **Directions:** On N11, turn left 2 miles after Kilmacanogue.

Glendalough

Derrymore House

B&B Lake Road Glendalough Co. Wicklow **Tel: 0404 45493** Fax: 0404 45517
Email: patkelleher@eircom.net Web: http://homepage.eircom.net/~derrymore/

Very close to Glendalough, on a six-acre site of natural mountain woodland, Pat and Penny Kelleher's friendly B&B is in an unique position in the valley of Glendalough, overlooking the Lower Lake. It makes a quiet base for the outdoor pursuits which can be so enjoyable in the area - notably walking, fishing and horseriding - and seems like an oasis of calm when there are too many visitors around for comfort. Bedrooms are appropriately furnished in a fresh country style with antique furiture and neat en-suite shower rooms. A guests' sitting room has multi-channel TV/VCR and a library of videos and, in fine weather, it is very pleasant to have a private garden to sit in. Home-baked bread for breakfast. Not suitable for children under 8. No pets. **Rooms 5** (all no-smoking). B&B €28 pps; ss €8. Closed Nov-Mar. **Directions:** Dublin, Kilmacanoge, Roundwood, Annamoe, Glendalough (N11).

Greystones

The Hungry Monk

RESTAURANT Church Road Greystones Co. Wicklow **Tel: 01 287 5759** Fax: 01 287 7183

Well-known wine buff Pat Keown has run this hospitable first floor restaurant on the main street since 1988. Pat is a great and enthusiastic host; his love of wine is infectious and the place is spick and span – and the monk-related decor is a bit of fun. A combination of hospitality and interesting good quality food at affordable prices are at the heart of this restaurant's success – sheer generosity of spirit ensures value for money as well as a good meal. Seasonal menus offered include a well-priced all-day Sunday lunch and an evening à la carte menu. Menus are well-balanced to include traditional dishes – rack of Wicklow lamb with minted gravy and redcurrant jelly, steak with garlic & chive butter – and several vegetarian dishes. Blackboard specials include the day's seafood dishes and also any special wine offers; the outstanding wine list includes a wide range of half bottles and wines by the glass. *In 2001 The Hungry Monk Wine Bar opened downstairs, offering a short well-chosen menu of about eight varied dishes and a carefully selected mini-wine list. Children welcome. Restaurant: **Seats 50.** No-smoking area; air conditioning. D Tue -Sat 7-11; L Sun only, 12.30-8. D à la carte; Set Sun L €21.56. House wine €16.51. s.c.10%. *Wine Bar open Tue-Sat, 5pm-midnight, Sun 4-10 Closed Mon, 24-26 Dec. Amex, MasterCard, Visa, Laser. **Directions:** Centre of Greystones village beside DART.

Greystones

Vino Pasta

RESTAURANT Church Road Greystones Co. Wicklow **Tel: 01 287 4807** Fax: 01 287 4827

Attractive awnings and clear signage make a good start at this popular neighbourhood restaurant and, once past the tiny bar/reception area, teracotta walls, ethnic bric-à-brac and a crowd of happy diners create a warm atmosphere. Tables settings are bistro-style - paper cloths & napkins - and the menu is moderately priced, majoring in pastas and pizzas, with daily fish specials on a blackboard menu. Prompt, friendly service, sound cooking and generous portions add up to a good deal.**Seats 50.** No smoking area. Air conditioning. Children welcome up to 7pm. D 5-10.30 daily (Sun 3-9). A la carte. House wine about €14. 10% sc on parties of 6+. Closed 2 wks Jul, 25 Dec. Amex, MasterCard, Visa.

Kilmacanogue

Avoca Café

CAFÉ Avoca Handweavers Kilmacanogue Co. Wicklow **Tel: 01 286 7466**
Fax: 01 286 2367 Web: www.avoca.ie

CREATIVE USE OF VEGETABLES AWARD

Avoca Handweavers is one of the country's most famous craft shops but it is also well worth allowing time for a meal when you visit. Head chef Leylie Hayes has been supervising the production of the famously wholesome home-cooked food at Avoca Handweavers Restaurant since 1990 and people come here from miles around to tuck into fare which is as healthy as it is delicious - the Guide's Happy Heart Eat Out Award in 2000 was in recognition of this and this year they have done it again, this time for their Creative Use of Vegetables. While tarts and quiches are always popular, they also offer lots of healthy dishes bursting with vitamins, including a wide range of salads. Hot food includes traditional dishes such as beef and Guinness casserole and vegetarians are especially well catered for, both in special dishes – nut loaf, vegetable-based soups – and the many that just happen to be meatless. Although traditional home cooking is the overall theme, many dishes, such as Mediterranean vegetable & chèvre tart, roasted vegetable & chicken pancake stack and green bean and coconut soup, have a welcome contemporary twist. Farmhouse cheeses are another strong point, as is the baking – typical breads made daily include traditional brown soda, cheese bread and a popular multigrain loaf. There is also a wide range of excellent delicatessen fare for sale in the shop - and you can make many of their dishes at home too, using recipes given in the beautiful Avoca Café Cookbook. Children welcome. **Seats 20.** No-smoking area; air conditioning. Open daily, 10-5. House wine about €12.50. No s.c. Closed 25-26 Dec. Amex, Diners, MasterCard, Visa, Laser. **Directions:** On N11 sign posted before Kilmacanogue Village.

Kiltegan
COUNTRY HOUSE

Barraderry Country House

Barraderry Kiltegan Co. Wicklow
Tel: 0508 73209 Fax: 0508 73209
Email: jo.hobson@oceanfree.net Web: www.barraderrycountryhouse.com

Olive and John Hobson's delightful Georgian house is in a quiet rural area close to the Wicklow Mountains and, now that their family has grown up, the whole house has undergone extensive refurbishment and alteration for the comfort of guests. Big bedrooms with country views are beautifully furnished with old family furniture and have well-finished bathrooms and there's a spacious sitting room for guests' use too. Barraderry would make a good base for touring the lovely counties of Wicklow, Kildare, Carlow and Wexford and there's plenty to do nearby, with six golf courses within a half hour drive, several hunts and equestrian centres within easy reach and also Punchestown, Curragh and Naas racecourses - and, of course, walking in the lovely Wicklow Mountains. Garden. Children welcome (under 3s free in parents room). Pets allowed in some areas. **Rooms 4** (all en-suite, all no-smoking). B&B about €32 pps; ss about €6.35. Closed 15 Dec-15 Jan. **Directions:** 7 km from Baltinglass on R747, 1 km Kiltegan. No Credit Cards.

Kiltegan
HOTEL

Humewood Castle

Kiltegan Co. Wicklow **Tel: 0508 73215** Fax: 0508 73382
Email: humewood@iol.ie Web: www.huumewood.com

Humewood was the Guide's Romantic Hideaway of the Year in 1999 and it's easy to see why. You arrive on a perfectly ordinary Irish country road, stop at a large (but not especially impressive) gate and press the intercom button, as instructed. Slowly the gate creaks open – and you are transported into a world of make-believe. It's impossible to imagine anywhere more romantic to stay than Humewood Castle. A fairytale 19th-century Gothic Revival castle in private ownership set in beautiful parkland in the Wicklow Hills, it has been extensively renovated and stunningly decorated. While the castle is very large by any standards, many of the rooms are of surprisingly human proportions. Thus, for example, while the main dining room provides a fine setting for some two dozen guests, there are more intimate rooms suitable for smaller numbers. Similarly, the luxuriously appointed bedrooms and bathrooms, while indisputably grand, are also very comfortable. Country pursuits are an important part of life at Humewood too - horseriding, fishing and shooting can all be arranged - but even if you do nothing more energetic than just relaxing beside the fire, this is a really special place for a break. Conference/banqueting (120/100). Business centre, secretarial services. Snooker. Garden, tennis, walking, cycling. Parking. Children welcome. Pets by arrangement. **Rooms 14** (4 en-suite, 1 shower only, all no-smoking). Room rate with breakfast, about €350 high season. Residents' D about €55; house wine about €22; s.c.15%. Closed 1 Feb-31 Amex, Diners, MasterCard, Visa. **Directions:** On M81 Blessington - Baltinglass, Kiltegan.

Macreddin Village

HOTEL/RESTAURANT

The BrookLodge Hotel

Macreddin Village Co. Wicklow **Tel: 0402 36444** Fax: 0402 36580
Email: brooklodge@macreddin.ie

Built on the site of a deserted village, this completely new venture is an extraordinary food, drink and leisure complex built as a village in a Wicklow valley. The driving force is Evan Doyle, who proved himself at The Strawberry Tree in Killarney, a fine restaurant outstanding for its commitment to using wild, free-range and organic produce long before these became buzz words among a wider public. Now this new village has an hotel and restaurant already receiving national recognition for taking a position on organic food, and the little "street" alongside has an olde-worlde pub (Actons), a brewery and gift shops selling home-made produce etc related to the enterprise. Organic food markets, held on the first Sunday of the month (first and third in summer) are a great attraction here. The hotel looks a little bleak on arrival, but the interior is spacious and wecloming, with elegant country house furnishings, open fires and plenty of places to sit quietly or meet for a sociable drink. (There's a choice of two bars in the hotel, plus Actons pub). There's a large, bright conference room overlooking the garden and bedrooms are furnished and decorated to a high standard in an old-world style with lots of country furniture. Midweek, weekend and low season special offers are good value. Conference/banqueting (250/150). Business centre, video conferencing. Equestrian centre. Garden, walking, cycling. Snooker. Children welcome (under 3s free in parents' room, cots available). Pets by arrangement. **Rooms 40** (1 suite). Lift. B&B €105 pps; ss €40.63. Closed 24-25 Dec. **The Strawberry Tree:** Wisely, Evan Doyle's famous Strawberry Tree restaurant was relocated at Macreddin and co-owner Freda Wolfe, who made her name at Dublin's Eden Restaurant, jointly oversees the food side of the operation with Evan. It is an unusual room, with a mirrored ceiling - quite unlike the rest of the hotel. The original philosophy prevails here: farmhouse cheeses are from Sheridans Cheesemongers, meat from Hugh Robson's organic farm in Co Clare, smoked fish from Frank Hederman in Cobh, Co Cork and organic vegetables from Denis Healy - although, when their own walled organic garden is fully established, much of the produce used will be grown just outside the kitchen. Menus are not too long and, given the quality of ingredients used and the standard of cooking, both lunch and dinner represent very good value. **Seats 70** (private room, 28). No-smoking area. Toilets wheelchair accessible. Air conditioning. D 7-10 daily. Sun L 1-7. Set Sun L €28. Set D €41.90. House wines €19. SC discretionary. *William Actons Pub - Bar food daily, 12.30-9; barbecue on Sundays in summer, 1-7 pm.

Rathdrum

GUESTHOUSE

Avonbrae Guesthouse

Rathdrum Co .Wicklow **Tel: 0404 46198** Fax: 0404 46198
Email: avonbrae@gofree.indigo.ie Web: www.avonbrae.com

Paddy Geoghegan's hospitable guesthouse makes a comfortable and relaxed base for a visit and is especially popular with lovers of the outdoor life - walking, cycling, riding, pony-trekking, golf and fishing are major attractions to this beautiful area, but it's also ideal just for a quiet break. (Paddy offers weekly and weekend rates and off-season breaks which are very reasonable.) Simply furnished bedrooms vary in size and outlook but all have tea and coffee trays and en-suite facilities (only the smallest room has a bath). There are open fires as well as central heating and a comfortable guest sitting room. For fine weather, there's a tennis court in the well-kept garden, and although this sounds grander than it is, there is even a nice little indoor swimming pool. Children welcome (free in parent's room under 12 months, cot available). Pets permitted by arrangment. **Rooms 7** (6 shower only, 1 with private bathroom). B&B €33 pps; ss €8. Evening meals €20 at 6.30pm; packed lunches available by arrangemen (€4.50). Closed 1 Dec-31 Mar. Amex, MasterCard, Visa, Laser. **Directions:** About 500 yrds outside Rathdrum on Glendalough Road.

Rathnew

HOTEL/RESTAURANT

Hunter's Hotel

Newrath Bridge Rathnew Co. Wicklow
Tel: 0404 40106 Fax: 0404 40338
Email: reception@hunters.ie Web: www.hunters.ie

A rambling old coaching inn set in lovely gardens alongside the River Vartry, this much-loved hotel has a long and fascinating history – it's one of Ireland's oldest coaching inns, with records indicating that it was built around 1720. In the same family now for five generations, the colourful Mrs Maureen Gelletlie takes pride in running the place on traditional lines with her son Richard, who is the manager. This means old-fashioned comfort and food based on local and home-grown produce – with the emphasis very much on 'old fashioned' – which is where its character lies. There's a proper little bar, with chintzy loose-covered furniture and an open fire, a traditional dining room with fresh flowers – from the riverside garden where their famous afternoon tea is served in summer - and comfortable country bedrooms. Conference (30). Garden. Parking. Children welcome. No pets. **Rooms 16** (1 junior suite, 1 shower only, 1 disabled).Wheelchair access. B&B €88.90 pps, ss €19.10. **Restaurant:** In tune with the spirit of the hotel, the style is traditional country house cooking: simple food with a real home-made feeling about it - no mean achievement in a restaurant and much to be applauded. Seasonal lunch and dinner menus change daily, but you can expect classics such as chicken liver pâté with melba toast, soups based on fish or garden produce, traditional roasts – rib beef, with Yorkshire pudding or old-fashioned roast stuffed chicken with bacon – and probably several fish dishes, possibly including poached salmon with hollandaise and chive sauce. Desserts are often based on what the garden has to offer, and baking is good, so fresh raspberries and cream or baked apple and rhubarb tart could be wise choices. **Seats 50.** Non-smoking restaurant. Toilets wheelchair accessible. L daily, 1-2.30 (Sun 2 sittings: 12.45 & 2.30). D daily 7.30-9. Set D €34.28. Set L €23.50. No s.c. House wine €15,90. Closed 24-26 Dec. Amex, Diners, MasterCard, Visa. **Directions:** Off N11 at Ashford or Rathnew.

Rathnew

COUNTRY HOUSE
RESTAURANT

Tinakilly Country House & Restaurant

Rathnew Co. Wicklow
Tel: 0404 69274 Fax: 0404 67806
Email: reservations@tinakilly.ie Web: www.tinakilly.ie

Josephine and Raymond Power have been running this fine hotel since January 2000 and it is greatly to their credit that they have retained all the things which Raymond's parents, William and Bee Power achieved to earn its reputation, while also bringing a youthful enthusiasm and energy which has contributed a new liveliness of atmosphere. It first opened for guests in 1983, after completion of a sensitive restoration programme and the first of many extensions, all carefully designed to harmonise with the original building. Since then, caring owner-management and steadily improving amenities have combined to make it a favourite destination for both business and leisure. It's a place of great local significance, having been built in the 1870s for Captain Robert Halpin, a local man who became Commander of The Great Eastern, which laid the first telegraph cable linking Europe and America. Now, there's always a welcoming fire burning in the lofty entrance hall, where a fascinating collection of Halpin memorabilia is of special interest and an original chandelier takes pride of place among many fine antiques. Tinakilly is one of the country's top business and corporate venues, but there is also a romantic side to its nature as bedrooms all have views across a bird sanctuary to the sea, and there are also period rooms, some with four-posters. To all this, add personal supervision by caring owners, friendly, well-trained staff, lovely grounds and a very fine kitchen and the recipe for success is complete. Tinakilly House was the Guide's Hotel of the Year in 2001. Conference/banqueting (65). Secretarial services. Fitness suite. Garden, walking, tennis. Children welcome (under 2s free in parents' room, cots available without charge). No pets. **Rooms 52** (6 suites, 33 junior suites, 12 executive, 1 for disabled). Lift. B&B €119 pps; ss €61. **Brunel Dining Room:** This panelled split level restaurant is in the west wing of the house, which catches the evening sunlight, and it has a relaxed, intimate atmosphere. Head chef Chris Daly presents a range of menus including a seasonal à la carte and a daily table d'hôte. The kitchen garden produces an abundance of fruit, vegetables and herbs for most of the year and this, plus local meats – notably Wicklow lamb and venison – and seafood, provides the basis for his cooking. While also putting his personal stamp on the kitchen, Chris Daly is very successfully maintaining Tinakilly's house style of sophisticated country house cooking with the main influence – classic French – showing in well-made sauces and elegant presentation. Signature dishes include local lobster salad with orange segments and raspberry vinaigrette, loin of Wicklow lamb with fondant potatoes, ratatouille & thyme and caramel roast pineapple with coconut Malibu ice cream. **Seats 80** (private room, 30). No smoking restaurant. Air conditioning. D Mon-Sat 7.30-9, Sun 6.30-8.30. Set D €57. House wine from €. SC discretionary. Open all year. Amex, Diners, MasterCard, Visa, Laser. **Directions:** From N11/M11 main Dublin - Wexford Road to Rathnew Village, Tinakilly is 500 metres from village on R750 to Wicklow Town.

Roundwood

PUB

RESTAURANT

Roundwood Inn

Roundwood Co. Wicklow

Tel: 01 281 8107

Jurgen and Aine Schwalm have owned this 17th century inn in the highest village in the Wicklow Hills since 1985. There's a public bar at one end, with a snug and an open fire, and in the middle of the building the main bar food area, furnished in traditional style with wooden floors and big sturdy tables. The style that the Schwalms and head chef Paul Taube have developed over the years is their own unique blend of Irish and German influences. Excellent bar food includes substantial soups, specialities such as Galway oysters, smoked Wicklow trout, smoked salmon and hearty hot meals such as the house variation on Irish stew. Blackboard specials often include home-made gravad lachs, lobster salad and a speciality dessert, Triple Liqueur Parfait. The food at Roundwood has always had a special character, which together with the place itself and a consistently high standard of hospitality, has earned it an enviable reputation with hillwalkers, Dubliners out for the day and visitors alike. Bar meals 12-9.30 daily. **Restaurant:** The restaurant is in the same style and only slightly more formal than the main bar, with fires at each end of the room (now converted to gas, alas) and is available by reservation. Restaurant menus offer a different choice, leaning towards more substantial dishes such as rack of Wicklow lamb, roast wild Wicklow venison, venison ragout and other game in season - and they do a wonderful dish of roast suckling pig, which is not to be missed when available. German influences are again evident in long-established specialities such as smoked Westphalian ham and wiener schnitzel and a feather-light Baileys Cream gateau which is also a must. An interesting mainly European wine list favours France and Germany, with many special bottles from Germany unlikely to be found elsewhere. Not suitable for children after 6.30. **Seats 70** (private room, 32). L Sun only,1 pm, D Fri & Sat, 7.30-9.30; à la carte. House wine from about €16; SC discretionary; reservations advised. Restaurant closed L Mon-Sat, D Sun-Thur. Bar closed 25 Dec & Good Fri. Amex, MasterCard, Visa. **Directions:** In the centre of Roundwood village.

Wicklow

RESTAURANT

The Bakery Restaurant & Café

Church Street Wicklow Co. Wicklow

Tel: 0404 66770 Fax: 0404 66717

Sally Stevens' lovely restaurant has great character – the fine stone building has retained some of its old bakery artefacts, including the original ovens in the café downstairs. Lots of candles in the reception area and restaurant set a warm tone which is then complemented by an admirably restrained theme – stone walls and beams provide a dark background for quite austere table settings which work wonderfully well in this room, and earned The Bakery the Guide's Table Presentation of the Year award in 1999. Imaginative menus change monthly and cover a wide range of tastes, from traditional to adventurous - to indicate the styles, specialities include: rack of Wicklow lamb with potato galette, roast garlic & thyme jus and pan fried seabass with lemongrass & coconut risotto and mango chilli salsa. Vegetables are highly valued - a seasonal selection is served in a big dish to help yourselves and a separate vegetarian menu is available. To finish, a classic dessert like panna cotta with raspberry & lime compôte, perhaps, or plated farmhouse cheeses. Good coffee and friendly service. Children welcome. **Seats 80** (private room, 36). No-smoking area. D daily, 6-10 (Fri & Sat to 11, Sun to 9); Early D €19.04 (6-7.30 only); Set D from €24.12, otherwise à la carte. House wine €15.19. SC discretionary. Closed D Sun in winter, 23-27 Dec, Good Fri. MasterCard, Visa, Laser. **Directions:** Centre of Wicklow town.

Wicklow

HOTEL

The Grand Hotel

Abbey Street Wicklow Co. Wicklow **Tel: 0404 67337**

Fax: 0404 69607 Email: grandhotel@eircom.net Web: www.grandhotel.ie

At the centre of local activities, this friendly hotel has large public areas including the Glebe Bar, which is very popular for bar meals (especially the lunchtime carvery). The conference/banqueting facilities for up to 300/260 are in constant use, especially for weddings. Pleasant, comfortably furnished bedrooms are all en-suite and warm, with all the necessary amenities. Wheelchair access. Open all year. No pets. Children welcome (under 5s free in parents' room). **Rooms 33** (all en-suite, 3 executive). Amex, MasterCard, Visa, Laser. **Directions:** Travelling from Dublin first hotel in town.

Wicklow — The Old Forge

PUB Abbey Hill Wicklow Co. Wicklow **Tel: 0404 66778 / 67032**

On a corner site, with tables outside, a real effort is being made at this pub to make the most of the location, both by planting outside and an interior makeover to a somewhat minimalist style which can lack atmosphere when the bar is quiet. But a speedy welcome and quite a tempting menu will cheer hungry visitors up: there are small snacks, large snacks, square meals and desserts, offering everything from home-made soup or potato skins through warm BBQ beef baguette or ciabatta roll with brie & ham, to pasta specials or roast of the day (plus desserts on a blackboard menu). Good quality ingredients, sound cooking and generous portions add up to a fair deal, making this unpretentious pub a useful place to know. Food served daily, 12.30-6; dining room open L Sun-Fri, 12.30-2.30. Dining room closed Sat. No private parking. **Directions:** N11 to Rathnew then R750 to Wicklow.

NORTHERN IRELAND

BELFAST

With its architecture very much in the distinctive contemporary "Belfast style", the Odyssey Centre on the east bank of the River Lagan is now so much a part of life in Belfast and Northern Ireland that it takes an effort to remember it only opened for business as recently as 2001. The setting for events as diverse as ice hockey tournaments, rock concerts and other mass gatherings, this impressive arts and entertainment complex in its turn reflects the look of the successful Waterfront Hall on the Lagan's west bank. Yet Belfast is home to several distinctive architectural styles, and there's a growing awareness of the quieter 18th Century architecture which preceded the exuberance of the city's very rapid 19th Century Victorian expansion.

In terms of urban significance, the cities of Ireland tend to be relatively recent developments which often started as Viking trading settlements that later "had manners put on them" by the Normans. But Belfast is even newer than that. When the Vikings in the 9th century raided what is now known as Belfast Lough, their target was the wealthy monastery at Bangor, and thus their bases were at Ballyholme and Groomsport further east. Then, when the Normans held sway in the 13th Century, their main stronghold was at Carrickfergus on the northern shore of the commodious inlet known for several centuries as Carrickfergus Bay.

At the head of that inlet beside the shallow River Lagan, the tiny settlement of beal feirste - the 'mouth of the Farset or the sandspit' - wasn't named on maps at all until the late 15th Century. But Belfast proved to be the perfect greenfield site for rapid development as the Industrial Revolution got under way. Its rocketing growth began with linen manufacture in the 17th Century, and this was accelerated by the arrival of skilled Huguenot refugees in 1685.

There was also scope for ship-building on the shorelines in the valleymouth between the high peaks crowding in on the Antrim side on the northwest, and the Holywood Hills to the southeast, though the first shipyard of any significant size wasn't in being until 1791, when William and Hugh Ritchie opened for business. The Lagan Valley gave convenient access to the rest of Ireland for the increase of trade and commerce to encourage development of the port, while the prosperous farms of Down and Antrim fed a rapidly expanding population.

So, at the head of what was becoming known as Belfast Lough, Belfast took off in a big way, a focus for industrial ingenuity and manufacturing inventiveness, and a magnet for entrepreneurs and innovators from all of the north of Ireland, and the world beyond. Its population in 1600 had been less than 500, yet by 1700 it was 2,000, and by 1800 it was 25,000. The city's growth was prodigious, such that by the end of the 19th Century it could claim with justifiable pride to have the largest shipyard in the world, the largest ropeworks, the largest linen mills, the largest tobacco factory, and the largest heavy engineering works, all served by a greater mileage of quays than anywhere comparable, and all contributing to a situation whereby, in 1900, the population had soared through the 300,000 mark.

Expansion had become so rapid in the latter half of the 19th Century that it tended to obliterate the influence of the gentler intellectual and philosophical legacies inspired by the Huguenots and other earlier developers, a case in point being the gloriously flamboyant and baroque Renaissance-style City Hall, which was completed in 1906. It was the perfect expression of that late-Victorian energy and confidence in which Belfast shared with total enthusiasm. But its site had only become available because the City Fathers authorised the demolition of the quietly elegant White Linen Hall, which had been a symbol of Belfast's more thoughtful period of development in the 18th Century.

However, Belfast Corporation was only fulfilling the spirit of the times. And in such a busy city, there was always a strongly human dimension to everyday life. Thus the City Hall may be on the grand scale, but it was nevertheless right at the heart of town. Equally, while the gantries of the shipyard may have loomed overhead as they still do today, they do so near the houses of the workers in a manner which somehow softens their sheer size. Admittedly this theme of giving great projects a human dimension seems to have been forgotten in the later design and location of the Government Building (completed 1932) at Stormont, east of the city. But back in the vibrant heart of Belfast, there is continuing entertainment and accessible interest in buildings as various as the Grand Opera House, St Anne's Cathedral, the Crown Liquor Saloon, Sinclair Seamen's Church, the Linenhall Library, and Smithfield Market, not to mention some of the impressive Victorian banking halls, while McHugh's pub on Queen's Square, and Tedford's Restaurant just round the corner on Donegall Quay, provide thoughtful reminders of the earlier more restrained style.

In modern times, modern technologies and advanced engineering have displaced the old smokestack industries in the forefront of the city's work patterns, with the shipyard today being only a shadow of its former self in terms of employment numbers. However, the energy of former times has been channeled into impressive urban regeneration along the River Lagan. Here, the flagship building is the Waterfront Hall, a large state-of-the-art concert venue which has won international praise. In the southern part of the city, Queen's University (founded 1845) is a beautifully balanced 1849 Lanyon building at the heart of a pleasant university district which includes the city's noted Lyric Theatre as well as the respected Ulster Museum & Art Gallery, while the university itself is particularly noted for its pioneering work in medicine and engineering.

Thus there's a buzz to Belfast which is reflected in its own cultural and warmly sociable life, which includes the innovative energy of its young chefs. Yet in some ways it is still has marked elements of a country town and port strongly rooted in land and sea. The hills of Antrim can be glimpsed from most streets, and the farmland of Down makes its presence felt. They are quickly reached by a somewhat ruthlessly implemented motorway system, relished by those in a hurry who also find the increasingly busy and very accessible Belfast City Airport a convenient boon. So although Belfast may have a clearly defined character, it is also very much part of the country around it, and is all the better for that. And in the final analysis, Belfast is uniquely itself.

Local Attractions and Information

Arts Council of Northern Ireland	028 90 385200
Belfast Castle & Zoo	028 90 776277
Belfast Crystal	028 90 622051
Belfast Festival at Queens (late Oct-early Nov)	028 90 665577
City Airport	028 90 457745
Citybus Tours	028 90 458484
Grand Opera House	028 90 241919
International Airport	028 94 484848
Kings Hall (exhibitions, concerts, trade shows)	028 90 665225
Lagan Valley Regional Park	028 90 491922
Linenhall Library	028 90 321707
Lyric Theatre	028 90 381081
National Trust Regional Office	028 97 510721
Northern Ireland Railways	028 90 899411
Odyssey (entertainment & sports complex)	028 90 451055
Tourism Information	028 90 246609
Ulster Historical Foundation (genealogical res.)	028 90 332288
Ulster Museum & Art Gallery	028 90 383000
Waterfront Hall (concert venue)	028 90 334455
West Belfast Festivals	028 90 313440

Belfast
RESTAURANT ☆

Aldens

229 Upper Newtownards Road Belfast BT4 3JF
Tel: 028 90 650079 Fax: 028 90 650032

A discreet public face belies the warmth and elegance of this contemporary restaurant - and it is greatly to proprietor Jonathan Davis's credit that he had the courage and foresight to introduce this shaft of bright light to an area until then bereft of good eating places. Head chef Cath Gradwell has been here since the restaurant opened in 1998, bringing a raft of cosmopolitan experience (Roux restaurants, Kensington Place, 5th Floor at Harvey Nichols to name but three), showing in lively international menus that change daily and make the most of local and seasonal ingredients. The cooking style is now well established with strong emphasis on flavour combinations, fish and local produce; dishes that combine classic and contemporary influences and employ a wide range of ingredients are well-conceived and executed with flair. Although menus are not overlong, there is plenty of choice: from a selection of around a dozen starters ranging from Thai broth with noodles and coriander to luxurious dishes like sevruga caviar (30g - a starter for two or nibbles for four at £27.50), there are still some affordable classics in there, such as steamed mussels with white wine, parsley & garlic. Main courses offer a similarly wide range and dishes like roast fillet of sea bass with prawn dumplings, fried rice cake, choy sum or grilled pork chop with chilli butter and sweet potatoes are typical of Cath Gradwell's way with fish and humbler everyday foods. Vegetarian dishes are always offered and display the same combination of down to earth qualities and creativity - two or three options on each course are usually vegetarian, typically a starter of rocket, asparagus and artichoke salad with parmesan and a balsamic reduction, and vegetable chilli con carne with a rice pilaff or spanish omelette with tomato, basil & onion salad. Lunch specials and the short dinner menu offer particualrly good value and side dishes are imaginative. Consistently excellent food and and professional service from smartly-uniformed staff make this one of Northern Ireland's finest restaurants. An interesting, well-priced wine list mixing the old and new world, includes an extensive house wine selection and a fair number of half bottles. **Seats 70.** Children welcome. No smoking area; air conditioning. L Mon-Fri,12-2.30; D Mon-Thur 6-10, Fri & Sat 6-11; Set D £14.95, Lunch special (main course & coffee) £7.95; à la carte also available. House wines £10-17; sc discretionary. Closed L Sat, all Sun, 25-26 dec, 2 weeks July. Amex, Diners, MasterCard, Visa, Switch. **Directions:** On the Upper Newtownards Road towards Stormont.

Belfast
B&B

All Seasons Bed & Breakfast

356 Lisburn Road Belfast BT9 6GJ
Tel: 028 90 682814 Email: allseasons@fsmail.net

Well-situated for business or pleasure, this large house near the King's Hall is handy to the city centre and the shops and restaurants of the Lisburn road and university area, yet has the advantages of space (including parking) that are at a premium in the centre. The proprietor, Theodore McLaughlin, speaks fluent French and is very accommodating - airport pickups and any other transport can be arranged, he will organise tours for and guide guests to the golf, fishing and horseriding facilities which are suprisingly close by. Spacious bedrooms have all been recently renovated and have good amenities, including television, tea./coffee-making facilities and trouser press and fax facilities are available on request. Children welcome (under 4s free in parents' room; cots available without charge). No pets. Garden. **Rooms 6** (all en-suite & no smoking). B&B £22.50 pps, ss £2.50. Limited room service. Open all year. MasterCard, Visa. **Directions:** Take Balmoral exit from, M1 motorway.

Belfast
RESTAURANT

La Belle Epoque

61 Dublin Road Belfast BT2 7HE
Tel: 028 90 323244

Since 1984 Alain Rousse's authentic French cooking has been giving Belfast Diners, a flavour of old Paris. Set menus include "Le Petit Lunch" (Mon-Fri), which is terrific value at just £6.25 for a starter and main course from a short à la carte menu (terrine de campagne aux pruneaux, perhaps, and tarte aux légumes, vinaigrette aux tomatoes sechées) and a similarly keenly priced set dinner, which offers a choice of three options within each course and is augmented by an equally fairly priced à la carte. All the timeless French favourites are here - if only there were more places like it. Not suitable for children. **Seats 84.** No smoking area. L Mon-Fri 12-5, Mon-Sat D 5-11. Set L from £6.25; Set D from £15; also à la carte; no sc, Closed L Sat, all Sun, 10-13 Jul & Christmas. Amex, Diners, MasterCard, Visa, Switch. **Directions:** 5 minutes Walk from City Centre

---

Belfast

Benedict's of Belfast

HOTEL

7-21 Bradbury Place Belfast BT7 1RQ **Tel: 02890 591 999**
Fax: 02890 591 990 Web: www.benedictshotel.co.uk

Very conveniently located - a wide range of attractions including the Botanic Gardens, Queen's University, Queen's Film Theatre and Ulster Museum are within a few minutes walk - this new hotel combines comfort and contemporary style with moderate prices. ISDN lines. Parking arrangement with nearby carpark. Not suitable for children after 9pm. No private parking. No pets. **Rooms 32** (12 executive rooms, 2 for disabled) Lift.Wheelchair accessible B&B about £55pps, ss £25. Open all year. Amex, Diners, MasterCard, Visa. **Directions:** City centre hotel situated in Bradbury Place - just off Shaftsbury Place in the heart of Belfast's "Golden Mile."

Belfast

Cargoes Café

CAFÉ

613 Lisburn Road Belfast BT9 7GT **Tel: 02890 665451**

This is a special little place run by partners Radha Patterson and Mary Maw, who take a lot of trouble sourcing fine produce for the delicatessen side of the business and apply the same philosophy to the food served in the café. Modern European, Thai and Indian influences work well together here; simple preparation and good seasonal ingredients dictate menus - where you might find dishes like smokey bacon & potato soup, Moroccan chicken with couscous, vegetarian dishes such as goats cheese & tarragon tart or wild mushroom risotto. There are classic desserts like lemon tart or apple flan, and a range of stylish sandwiches. Children welcome. **Seats 30.** No smoking restaurant. Open Mon-Sat 9 am-5 pm, L 12-3. A la carte; sc discretionary. Toilets wheelchair accessible. Closed Sun, bank hols. MasterCard, Visa.

Belfast

Cayenne Restaurant

RESTAURANT ★

7 Ascot House Shaftesbury Square Belfast BT2 7DB
Tel: 02890 331 532 Fax: 02890 261 575
Email: colm@cayennerestaurant.com Web: www.atdinequick.com

RESTAURANT OF THE YEAR

The Rankin magic is still working in Belfast's Shaftesbury Square and, behind the opaque glass façade of Cayenne, Paul and Jeanne Rankin are offering quality food without frills at accessible prices. It's hard to believe that it is just two short years ago that 'Roscoff' was delighting connoisseurs on this site: but gone is the metal starkness that traditionalists tolerated because the food was so starry good, instead there's something less comfortable but warmer, more modest, friendlier - and the food is still superb. Fine dining this is not: eating is very definitely fun at Cayenne and the anteroom bar is filled with the hungry long before the first sitters have finished their desserts. Given the number of quality restaurants Belfast offers these days, this says much for the quality of Paul Rankin's quick fire cooking - and it is a credit to the legendary teamwork of this kitchen that the food is equally good when he cannot be here himself. Choice is generous, with many dishes having equal appeal, and the menu is constructed to allow flexibility, with soups, salads, rice and noodle dishes offered separately between appetisers and main courses. The flavours are strongly oriental with some Mediterranean touches: Pork Sang Choy Bow with coriander, peanuts and mint served in crunchy lettuce cups; Crab and Lemongrass pot Stickers with Thai dipping sauce; Terrine of Mediterranean Vegetables with pesto and goats cheese fritters, for example. These tantalising tastes and textures from around the world are served with charm and friendliness by a mixed team of locals and 'blow-ins' in a no nonsense environment - bringing accessible excellence to contemporary diners who enjoy an animated environment and don't mind rubbing shoulders with neighbouring Diners, in the café atmosphere of this long narrow, warmly decorated dining room. On a recent visit the Crispy Duck Confit with Thai cucumber and lemongrass salad with chilli oil was outstanding, the duck leg was melt in the mouth tender, and the Vegetable Sushi Rolls with pickled ginger, soy and wasabi really did tickle the taste buds. There are also three soups (£4), four salads and four rice and noodle dishes (as starters or main course £4.50 to £8.50): terrific value. **Seats 90.** No smoking area; air conditioning, L Mon-Fri 12-2.15, D Mon-Sat 6-11.15pm. Set L £10-£13.50; also à la carte. House wine from £12.50. sc discretionary (except 10% on parties of 6+). Closed Sun, Easter Mon, 12-13 July, 25-26 Dec. Amex, Diners, MasterCard, Visa, Switch. **Directions:** 5 mins from Europa Hotel.

Belfast
HOTEL

The Crescent Townhouse

13 Lower Crescent Belfast BT71NR
Tel: 028 90 323 349 Fax: 028 90 320 646
Email: info@crescenttownhouse.co.uk Web: www.crescenttownhouse.co.uk

This is an elegant building on the corner of Botanic Avenue, just a short stroll from the city centre. The ground floor is taken up by the Metro Brasserie and Bar/Twelve, a stylish club-like bar with oak panelling and snugs, particularly lively and popular at night (necessitating 'greeters' for the entrance). The reception lounge is on the first floor. Spacious bedrooms, which have phones with data points, TV and trouser press, are furnished in country house style, with practical furniture, colourful fabrics and good tiled bathrooms. In addition, there are two superior rooms, decorated more elaborately in a period style with canopied beds and luxurious bathrooms with roll-top baths and separate showers. Fax, photocopying and secretarial services are available through reception. Breakfast is taken in the contemporary split-level Metro Brasserie, which is also open for dinner; lunch is available at Bar/Twelve: Mon-Sat 12-3. The wine list includes quite an extensive cocktail menu and a number of wines by the glass. Children welcome (under 12s free in parents' room, cots available without charge). No pets. **Rooms 9** (2 superior, 3 no smoking) 24 hour room service. B&B £50 pps, ss £30. Metro Brasserie **Seats 70.** D Mon-Sat 6-10; Early D £9.50-£12.50, otherwise à la carte sc discretionary. Closed Sun. Amex, MasterCard, Visa, Switch. **Directions:** Opposite Botanic Railway Station on corner of Botanic Avenue, in university area.

Belfast
PUB

Crown Liquor Saloon

46 Great Victoria St. Belfast BT2 7BA
Tel: 02890 279 901 Fax: 02890 279 902

Belfast's most famous pub, The Crown Liquor Saloon, was perhaps the greatest of all the Victorian gin palaces which once flourished in Britain's industrial cities. Remarkably, considering its central location close to the Europa Hotel, it survived The Troubles virtually unscathed. Although now owned by the National Trust (and run by Bass Leisure Retail) the Crown is far from being a museum piece and attracts a wide clientele of locals and visitors. A visit to one of its famous snugs for a pint and half a dozen oysters served on crushed ice, or a bowl of Irish Stew, is a must. The upstairs restaurant section, "Flannigans Eaterie & Bar", is built with original timbers from the SS Britannic, sister ship to the Titanic. Crown: bar food served Mon-Sat 12-3. Flannigans: 11-9. Closed 25-16 Dec. Diners, MasterCard, Visa. **Directions:** City centre, opposite Europa Hotel.

Belfast
RESTAURANT

Deanes Brasserie

36-40 Howard Street Belfast BT1 6PF
Tel: 028 9056 0000 Fax: 028 9056 0001

On the ground floor under Restaurant Michael Deane, this much larger restaurant is all buzz and offers an eclectic contemporary menu, with something for everybody. Risotto of seafood with lemongrass & herb cream and grilled beef sausage with mashed potatoes and brown sauce are both typical, also modish fish & chips - prices are moderate, service slick and efficient and everything on the wine list is under £20. **Seats 100.** Air conditioning. Children welcome. No booking for lunch. L Mon-Sat 12-2.30 (Sat from 12.30), D Mon-Sat 5.30-10.30 (post theatre menus, last orders 11 pm). A la carte; sc charge discretionary (10% on parties of 6+). Closed Sun, Christmas, 1 week Jan, 1 week Jul. **Directions:** City centre, back of City Hall.

Belfast
HOTEL

Dukes Hotel

65-67 University St. Belfast BT7 1HL
Tel: 02890 236 666 Fax: 02890 237 177
Email: info@dukes-hotelbelfast.co.uk Web: dukes-hotel-belfast.co.uk

First opened in 1990, within an imposing Victorian building, the hotel is modern inside with an interesting waterfall descending down one wall, floor by floor, into a rock pool in the foyer. This is flanked on either side by a restaurant/mezzanine bar and the intriguingly-shaped Dukes Bar, a popular rendezvous for locals. Double-glazed bedrooms are spacious with practical furniture and good fabrics, and in addition to the usual facilities there's an ironing board and iron hidden in the wardrobe. Conference/banqueting (120/150) secretarial services. Wheelchair accessible. Street parking (ticketed 8am-6pm). Mini-gym; sauna. Children (Under 12s free in parents' room; cots available). Pets by arrangement. **Rooms 21** (1 executive, 11 no smoking, 1 for disabled) B&B about £55 pps, ss about £40. Amex, Diners, MasterCard, Visa. **Directions:** Behind Queens University on junction of University St. and Botanic Avenue.

Belfast
HOTEL

Express by Holiday Inn

106 University Street Belfast BT7 1HP
Tel: 02890 311 409 Fax: 02890 311 910

Offering budget accommodation in a sought-after area of the city, this hotel has good-size bedrooms with of plenty of workspace, multi-channel satellite TV (including payable in-house movies and radio) and compact bathrooms, most only with shower. This was one of the first hotels to support an environmentally-friendly philosophy, by getting guests to decide if they want their bed linen – duvets here – and towels changed daily, in order to save energy and water resources and reduce detergent pollution. A modest continental breakfast is included in the rate. Conference/banqueting 200/180. Business centre. Video-conferencing & secretarial services by arrangment. Secure parking to the rear. Beer garden. No pets. **Rooms 114** (108 shower only, 30 no-smoking, 6 for disabled) Room rate about £65, max 2 guests. Open all year. Amex, Diners, MasterCard, Visa. **Directions:** From Shaftesbury Square take Botanic avenue, turn left on to University St.

Belfast
HOTEL

Hastings Europa Hotel

Great Victoria St. Belfast Co Antrim BT2 7AP
Tel: 028 9032 7000 Fax: 028 9032 7800
Email: res@eur.hastingshotels.com Web: www.hastingshotels.com

Belfast's tall, central landmark hotel has undergone many changes since it first opened in the'70s. Now owned by Hastings Hotels, it has been renovated and refurbished to a high standard, with a facade that is particularly striking when illuminated at night. Off the entrance foyer, with its tall columns, is the all-day brasserie (6am-midnight) and the lobby bar, featuring Saturday afternoon jazz and other live musical entertainment. Upstairs on the first floor you'll find the Gallery lounge (afternoon teas served here to the accompaniment of a pianist) and a cocktail bar with circular marble-topped counter. Attractive and practical bedrooms offer the usual up-to-date facilities and include 56 recently added executive bedrooms. But perhaps the hotel's greatest assets are the function suites, ranging from the Grand Ballroom to the twelfth floor Edinburgh Suite with its panoramic views of the city. Nearby parking (special rates apply) can be added to your account. Staff are excellent (porters offer valet parking), and standards of housekeeping and maintenance very good. Children welcome (under 14s free in parents' room; cots available without charge). Conference/banqueting (750/600); business centre; secretarial services. Pets by arrangement. **Rooms 240** (5 suites, 56 executive rooms, 2 for disabled). Lifts. B&B £64 pps, ss £52.50; Room rate from £150. Closed 24-25 Dec. Amex, Diners, MasterCard, Visa, Switch. **Directions:** Located in the heart of Belfast.

Belfast
RESTAURANT

Hawthorne Coffee Shop

Fultons Fine Furnishings Store Retail Park Boucher Cres. Belfast BT20 6HU
Tel: 028 90 384705 Fax: 028 90 384701

If you're shopping or have business in the area, this stylish contemporary café in a well known furniture store is great place to know about, as they specialise in real home cooking. There's nothing flashy about the food: expect lovely flavoursome dishes like home-made soup with wheaten bread, quiches - asparagus & salmon, vegetable - seafood pie and streak & mushroom hot-pot. There's always a large selection of salads and home-made desserts like banoffee and lemon meringue pie. **Seats 127.** Mon-Sat: morning cofffee, lunch, afternoon tea. A la carte. MasterCard, Switch. **Directions:** Off M1, take Stockmans Lane exit off roundabout, left into Boucher Road, left again into

Boucher Crescent.

Belfast

HOTEL

Hilton Belfast

4 Lanyon Place Belfast Co Antrim BT1 3LP
Tel: 028 90 277 000 Fax: 028 90 277 277

Occupying a prominent position on a rise beside the Waterfront Hall, the interior of this landmark hotel is impressive: the scale is grand, the style throughout is of contemporary clean-lined elegance - the best of modern materials have been used and the colour palette selected is delicious - and, best of all, it makes the best possible use of its superb waterside site, with the Sonoma Restaurant and several suites commanding exceptional views. Outstanding conference and business facilities include the state-of-the-art Hilton Meeting service tailored to individual requirements and three executive floors with a Clubroom. All rooms have air-conditioning, satellite TV, in-room movies, no-stop check out in addition to the usual facilities. Recreational facilities are also excellent. The absence of private parking could be a problem, as the multi-storey carpark next door is not owned by the hotel. Conference/banqueting (400/260); secretarial services; business centre; video conferencing; ISDN lines. Leisure centre; indoor swimming pool; beauty salon. Children welcome (cots available). Pets by arrangement. **Rooms 195** (6 suites, 7 junior suites, 38 executive rooms, 68 no-smoking, 10 for disabled). Lifts. Room rate (max 2 guests), £165. Open all year. Amex, Diners, MasterCard, Visa, Switch. **Directions:** Belfast city centre, beside Waterfront Hall.

Belfast

HOTEL

Jurys Belfast Inn

Fisherwick Place Great Victoria St. Belfast BT2 7AP
Tel: 02890 533 500 Fax: 02890 533 511
Email: bookings@jurys.com Web: www.jurysdoyle.com

Located in the heart of the city, close to the Grand Opera House and City Hall and just a couple of minutes walk from the major shopping areas of Donegall Place and the Castlecourt Centre, Jurys Belfast Inn set new standards for the city's budget accommodation when it opened in 1997. The high standards and good value of all Jurys Inns applies here too: all rooms are en-suite (with bath and shower) and spacious enough to accommodate two adults and two children (or three adults) at a fixed price. **Rooms (190)** are well-designed and furnished to a high standard, with outstanding amenities for a hotel in the budget class. Room rate about £67, max 3 guests w/o b'fst). Closed 24-26 Dec. Amex, Diners, MasterCard, Visa. **Directions:** City centre, close to Opera House.

Belfast

RESTAURANT

The Manor House Cantonese Cuisine

43/47 Donegall Pass Belfast BT7 1DQ
Tel: 02890 238 755 Fax: 02890 238 755

Easily found just off Shaftesbury Square, this well-established Cantonese restaurant has been in the Wong family since 1982; it has since expanded to meet demand and there have been recent renovations and refurbishment. In common with many other Chinese restaurants, the menu is long, but Joe Wong's menu - which is given in Chinese as well as English - offers more unusual choices in addition to the many well-known popular dishes. There is, for example, a wide range of soups and specialities include Cantonese-style crispy chicken and seafood dishes like steamed whole seafish with ginger and scallions. Children welcome. Parking in nearby carpark. **Seats 70** (private room, 40) L 12.30-2.15 Mon-Fri, D 5.30-11 daily, Set L £5.95, Set D £12.95-17; also à la carte. House wine £8.95. Air conditioning. sc discretionary except for parties of 6+. Closed 25-26 Dec. MasterCard, Visa. **Directions:** Off Shaftesbury Square,within town centre.

Belfast

HOTEL/RESTAURANT

The McCausland Hotel

34–38 Victoria Street Belfast BT1 3GH
Tel: 02890 220200 Fax: 02890 220220 Email: info@mccauslandhotel

Well-located close to the Waterfront Hall, this sister establishment to The Hibernian Hotel in Dublin is in a magnificent landmark building designed by William Hastings in the 1850s in Italianate style -its ornate four storey facade has carvings depicting the five continents and looks particularly impressive when floodlit at night. Classic contemporary design and high quality materials combine to create an exclusive venue for business and leisure guests. Individually appointed bedrooms - decorated in a contemporary country house style, all with some items of antique furniture - include wheelchair-friendly and lady executive rooms (with thoughtful little emergency overnight kits in the bathroom for unplanned visits). Rooms also have fax/modem points and entertainment systems which include TV/CD/radio and VCR. Conference/banqueting (60/64); secretarial services. Children welcome (under 2s free in parents' room; cots available without charge). No pets. **Rooms 60** (9 junior suites, 30 no smoking, 3 for disabled). Lift. Room rate from £120. Parking in nearby carpark (Mon-Sat only). Closed 24-26 Dec. **Marco Polo:** The restaurant of this fine hotel has moved to the mezzanine area over the bar (aka Café Marco Polo, serving bar food 12-9.30 daily). Food is lively and colourful in the contemporary style: a starter of satay chicken on Greek salad with roasted fennel & curried vegetables, perhaps and main course of pan fried salmon wrapped in green lentils and creamed spinach are typical. Food quality, cooking and presentation are all excellent, service is helpful and pleasant - the only problem is noise and smoke coming up from the bar below, which can affect an otherwise enjoyable dining experience. **Seats 60.** L Mon-Fri 12.30-2.30, D daily 7-9.30. D from £27.50; also à la carte. House wine £9.95; sc discretionary. Toilets wheelchair accessible. Closed L Sat & L Sun. & 24-26 Dec. **Seats 60.** Continental-style fare daily, 12 noon-10 pm. Hotel closed 24-27 Dec. Amex, Diners, MasterCard, Visa. **Directions:** On Victoria Street in central Belfast, between Anne Street and Albert Clock.

Belfast
PUB

McHugh's Bar & Restaurant

29 Queen's Square Belfast BT1 3FG
Tel: 02890 247 830 Fax: 02890 249 842
Email: info@botanic-inns.com Web: mchughsbar.com

This remarkable pub is in one of Belfast's few remaining eighteenth century buildings. It has been extensively and carefully renovated allowing the original bar (which has many interesting maps, photographs and other memorabilia of old Belfast) to retain its character while blending in a new café-bar and two restaurants (one in the basement, the other upstairs). Good modern food includes a lunchtime carvery/salad bar, evening meals and light food - soup, sandwiches etc - through the day (11.30 am-1 am). **Seats 100** (private room, 35) Air conditioning. L daily,12-3; D daily 5-10 (Sun to 9); à la carte. House wine from about £9. Toilets wheelchair accessible. Parking in nearby carpark. Closed Christmas and 12 Jul. MasterCard, Visa. **Directions:** Opposite the Albert Clock in central Belfast.

Belfast
PUB

The Morning Star

17-19 Pottinger's Entry Belfast Co Antrim BT1 4DT
Tel: 02890 235 986 Fax: 028 90 329311
Email: morningstar@pottingers-entry.freeserve.co.uk

Situated in a laneway in the middle of the city, The Morning Star is a listed building with many interesting features. It's been trading as a public house since about 1840 (although it was mentioned even earlier in the Belfast Newsletter of 1810 as a terminal for the Belfast to Dublin mail coach). The Morning Star always had a good name for food and, when Corinne and Seamus McAlister took over the business in 1989, they wanted to build on that. With due respect for the special character of the pub, the McAlisters have made changes that now allow an impressive range of menus through the day, beginning with breakfast at 9.30, then Morning Star 'Morning Tea' with a full range of teas and coffees, on to lunch and so on. Between them, an astonishing range of food is served, including traditional specialities like Irish stew, champ and sausage, local Strangford mussels, roast Antrim pork and aged Northern Ireland beef (which is a particular source of pride, cooked and served on cast iron sizzle platters, with grilled tomatoes & sautéed onions), as well as many universal pub dishes. Daily chef's specials, blackboard specials, there seems no end to the choices offered each day. Not surprisingly, this can be a very busy pub and, in the Guide's recent experience, it can be unappealingly untidy at times, especiallly at weekends. There's also a restaurant upstairs where more ambitious meals are served, including themed dinners and special wine evenings. The Morning Star does not knowingly serve any Genetically Modified Foods. Food served Mon-Sat 12-10. Amex, MasterCard, Visa, Switch. **Directions:** 200 yards from Albert Clock. Between Ann Street and High Street.

Belfast
RESTAURANT/PUB

Nick's Warehouse

35-39 Hill St. Belfast BT1 2LB
Tel: 02890 439 690 Fax: 02890 230 514
Email: nicks@warehouse.co.uk Web: www.nickswarehouse.co.uk

Nick's Warehouse is a clever conversion on two floors, with particularly interesting lighting and efficient aluminium duct air-conditioning. It's a lively spot, notable for attentive, friendly service and excellent food, in both the wine bar (where informal light meals and some hot dishes are served) and the restaurant (slightly more formal with structured à la carte menus). A network of trusted suppliers provide the superb ingredients that are the basis for lively contemporary menus offering a wide range of dishes which are consistently interesting and include some unusual items - rare breed pork, for example (with champ and apple & onion gravy perhaps) and game in season. There's always an imaginative selection of vegetarian dishes and menus are considerately marked with symbols indicating dishes containing nuts or oils and also shellfish. The cheese selection is interesting too - you can choose between house cheeses (Brie, Caerphilly & Shropshire Blue) or Irish cheeses (Ardrahan, Cashel Blue & St Brendan). Wide choice of teas of coffees and an informative, well-priced wine list that makes good reading - and includes a special Spanish listing and nine house wines not much over a tenner. Children welcome before 9 pm. Air conditioning. **Seats 45** upstairs, (L Tue-Fri & D Sat only); **Seats 135** downstairs. L 12-3 Mon-Fri, D 6-10 Tue-Sat, all à la carte. House wines from £10.75. Closed Sat L, all Sun, D Mon, 25-26 Dec, 15 Jan, Easter Mon/Tue, 15 May, 12-13 July. Amex, MasterCard, Visa, Diners, Switch. **Directions:** Near St. Anne's Cathedral, off Waring St.

Belfast

The Olive Tree Company

CAFÉ

353 Ormeau Road Belfast Co Antrim BT7 5GL **Tel: 028 90 648898**
Email: oliver@olivetreeco.fsnet.co.uk Web: www.olivetreecompany.com

Olivier Maindroult and Audrey Concannon have run this unique delicatessen/café since 1999. It specialises in freshly marinated olives, handmade cheeses and salamis - and also sells an exclusive range of French specialities, notably from Provence. The café offers authentic French patisserie and food with a Mediterranean flavour, mainly based on the best of local Irish produce. Think sandwiches with tapenade (olive paté with vine-ripened tomatoes & sping onions, or dolmades (vine leaves) salad with organic natrural yogurt and ciabatta bread and you'll get the flavour . Hot dishes include specialities like 'brodetto' a traditional Italian fish stew, or contemporary dishes such as warm duck salad wth chilli & lime dressing. This place is a little gem. **Seats 26.** No smoking restaurant. Open daily: Mon-Sat 9am-6.30pm (Sat 9-5.30, Sun 11-5. L daily, 11-5. (No wine but BYO allowed.) Closed 8-15 July, 24 Dec-2 Jan. **Directions:** From Belfast City Centre take the direction for Newcastle/Downpatrick cross the Ormeau Bridge - spot the Ormeau Bakery landmark and The Olive Tree Company is on the right. No Credit Cards.

Belfast

Posthouse Premier Belfast

HOTEL

22 Ormeau Avenue Belfast Co Antrim BT28HS
Tel: 0870 400 9005 Fax: 028 90 62 6546
Web: www.Posthouse.hotels.com

This new contemporary hotel is conveniently located less than half a mile from most of the main city centre attractions and offers luxurious modern accommodation, with excellent business and health and leisure facilities. The style is classy contemporary and spacious bedrooms are designed particularly with the business guest in mind - the decor is unfussy and warm, with comfort and relaxation to match its use as a workbase; superior rooms all have modem points, fridge, interactive TV with on screen checkout facility and Sky Sports, trouser press, power shower, cotton bathrobe and Neutrogena toiletries, while suites have a hallway as well as a separe sitting/dining room. 'The Academy' offers sate-of-the-art conference and training facilities, and business support. Conference/banqueting (120/100); business centre, secretarial services, video-conferencing. Children welcome (under 6s free in parents' room, cot available without charge). No pets. Swimming pool. **Rooms 170** (2 suites, 168 executive, 60 no smoking, 10 for disabled). Lift. 24 hour room service. B&B £61pps (Room only £109, max 2 adults & 2 children). Special weekend rates available. Open all year. Amex, MasterCard, Visa, Switch. **Directions:** Opposite BBC, 2 minutes walk from City Hall via Bedford Street.

Belfast

Ramada Hotel

HOTEL/RESTAURANT

117 Milltown Road Belfast Co Antrim BT87XP
Tel: 02890 923500 Fax: 02890 923600
Email: mail@ramadabelfast.com Web: www.ramadabelfast.com

This new hotel near Shaws Bridge in Belfast is in the Lagan Valley Regional Park and the setting is beautiful, overlooking the River Lagan The exterior was not quite complete at the time of the Guide's visit, but should mature well. Bedoroms are decorated in a fairly neutral modern style and have all the facilities expected of a new hotel, including in-room safes, TV with satellite and movie channels, telephone with voicemail and either a king-size bed or two singles. There are also executive suites available, intended mainly for business guests. Conference and banqueting facilities include 12 meeting rooms of various sizes, with up-to-date technology, and there is a ballroom (capacity 900) suitable for weddings, conferences and exhibitions. On-site leisure facilities include sauna, steam room spa and fitness suite as well as an indoor swimming pool and there's free parking for 300 cars. Conference/banquetingf 900. **Rooms 120.** Rates from £89; introductory weekend offers (2 B&B, 1D), £99 pps. **Belfast Bar and Grill:** Opened in August 2001 with chef Paul Rankin as consultant (he devised the menu and supervises the chefs cooking for the restaurant), the Belfast Bar & Grill has a small reception area, a large feature bar, and an 'on view' kitchen with an attractive wine cellar beside it, but it doesn't capitalise on the hotel's lovely location, as it is on the first floor at the back of the hotel, and without windows. White linen-clad tables span two levels with booths for four at the top, and an open lower level, which has less atmosphere. Cream walls display prints of Belfast by the noted Irish photographer Christopher Hill - this Belfast theme is carried through to the menu where the food is distinctly Irish traditional with inspiration from land sea and shore: starters begin with Irish broth (£5.75) and Cuan oysters and Cashel Blue soufflé and crubeens and ham hock are all typical, while main courses include aged steaks from the char grill (£11.50), traditional homely favourites like Irish stew (£9.50), pot roast chicken with bacon, mushrooms and herb cream, Finnebrogue venison on a colcannon cake with creamy Guinness sauce (£13.50) and even fish and chips with mushy peas (£8.50). Traditional desserts include many country favourites (apple and blackberry crumble, baked rice pudding with whiskey prunes), and some rather more sophisticated ones, like vanilla cream pots with stewed plums and Irish cheeses. On the Guide's visit (shortly after the hotel opened), the meal was enjoyable (and enhanced by unpretentious presentation) but the cooking a little uneven - and, once the Rankin name is involved, comparisons with Cayenne are inevitable. While the style is totally different, the prices are similar and the Belfast Bar and Grill is not (yet, at any rate) a match for the dining experience of Cayenne.(Function catering has a separate team of chefs and has no connection to the Rankin Belfast Bar and Grill). **Seats 120.** Open for lunch & dinner daily. Amex, Diners, MasterCard, Visa. **Directions:** In Lagan Valley Regional Park near Shaws Bridge.

Belfast
RESTAURANT ★★

Restaurant Michael Deane

34-40 Howard St. Belfast Co Antrim BT1 6PR
Tel: 028 90 331 134 Fax: 02890 560 001

This continues to be Northern Ireland's only serious fine dining restaurant: Michael Deane is uncompromising - a beacon set on a northern rock which is unmoved by the swirling tide of latest trends in a fickle lemongrass-with-everything world. Michael is unshakeable in his resolve to offer meticulously prepared dishes, served with old world efficiency and charm in an elegant ambience. Perhaps the contrast is all the more striking as, to reach the oasis of the restaurant, diners walk through the bustling ground floor brasserie, climb the broad staircase and are admitted to the inner sanctum. Here all is comfort; the fin de siècle sitting room, the elegant dining room, the smart, attentive and knowledgeable staff and that open kitchen with the ever-present Deane meticulously controlling the pace of events and timing food to perfection. So particular and precise is Michael about his cooking that this year he has reduced the number of covers to a maximum of 30 to ensure dishes reach his customers to his satisfaction. To experience the sheer breadth and refinement of Michael Deane's cooking, the eight course Menu Prestige (£55) is the yardstick against which all serious cooking in Ireland should be judged: 'Assiette of Quail'; Velouté of Monkfish; Foie Gras, Potato Bread and Vanilla; Risotto of Squab; Local Lamb, Black Pudding and Parsnip; Selection of Cheese; Dessert du Chef; Coffee & Chocolate. Simply superb. The main menu offers two courses for £29 and dishes tasted on a recent visit which reflect the richness and deftness of the cooking included a starter of Assiette of Quail with Sweetbreads, Foie Gras, Quails Eggs and white Truffle Oil; there were three delicate eggs in this magical dish - one fried, one poached and one boiled - and it is incredible to see such creativity at work, encompassing both the 'architecture' of each dish (its theme and structure, the interaction of elements, its colours, textures and flavours) and seemingly limitless attention to detail. The wide-ranging main courses offered monkfish, turbot, beef, lamb, duck and squab as the starting points for the great chef's genius and there is a thoughtfully crafted Vegetarian Menu (two courses £21). An 'Assiette of Local Lamb, with Black Pudding, Parsnip and Butter Roast Garlic' was perfection and the jus simply lip-smackingly good, while 'Salted Monkfish. Seared Scallops, Ratatouille, Couscous and Curry' was a combination which could very well fail miserably in other hands than maestro Deane's - and these fine dishes are designed to be complete, with no side orders. Desserts a snip for only £7.50, and each one is a jewel - especially a dish in which the versatility of a single ingredient is demonstrated, which is a Michael Deane trademark. A study in chocolate, for example - 'Layered Leaves of Bitter Chocolate, Passionfruit Sorbet and Chocolate Fondant' and 'Orange Muscat Ice Cream and Vanilla' - would set the seal gloriously on a memorable dining experience.

The wine list is grand but not overawing, and the discreet advice given to match wines with the meal is outstanding. This is fine dining in Ireland at its best and extremely good value for what is offered, so head North - and book early. *A private dining room is to be opened before Christmas 2001. **Seats 30.** Air conditioning D Wed-Sat 7-9.30; L Fri only. D £21-£55; sc discretionary (10% added to bills of 6+). Closed Sun-Tue, Christmas & New Year, 1 week Jan, Easter,1 week July. Amex, MasterCard, Visa, Switch. **Directions:** 150 yards on left hand side from back of City Hall.

Belfast

Shu Restaurant

RESTAURANT

253 Lisburn Road Belfast Co Antrim BT9 7EN
Tel: 028 90 381655 Fax: 028 90 681632 Web: www.shu-restaurant.com

Where is the buzz in Belfast this year? Book dinner at Shu on that ever-changing, chameleon strip, Lisburn Road, just out from the centre of Belfast and you'll see where a lot of the greeting and eating is happening. It's in an unassuming terrace, behind a sober facade of traditional Victorian arched windows: inside, contrasting with the stainless steel efficiency of the bar and de rigeur 'on view' kitchen, there's a courteous welcome and guests are led into a large L shaped room which is light and airy, with shiny metal muted by terracotta pillars and discreet covers. Opened in October 2000 by the Boyd family, who have long experience in the restaurant business, this is a smoothly run operation, with many regulars of all age groups. Belfast born head chef, Paul Cotterson (ex Quaglino's and Zinc in London, and La Stampa in Dublin) runs a slick engine room and his 'Classical Brasserie' fare is complemented by restaurant manager Julian Henry's marshalling of a tip top waiting staff. And the food should not disappoint. ?aul provides a menu founded on his classical training but with wider world influences. Smoked haddock, spinach & poached egg and crispy prawn rolls with mango mayonnaise are typical, well-executed starters. Main courses like roast hake, crispy potatoes, chard and salsa verde and confit of duck with organic lettuce, peas, baby onions and potatoes are in the same vein - but there is plenty for the less adventurous dinner too, such as Shu lamb pie, Cumberland sausages and sirloin steak. Lovely classical desserts to finish. Providing the management team maintains the quality of welcome, food and service experienced by the Guide, Shu should buzz reliably on. Not suitable for children under 10 after 7 pm. **Seats 76** (private room 20). L Mon-Sat, 12-2.30, D Mon-Sat 6-10. All à la carte (average main course £14). House wine £11.95;s.c. discretionary (10% on parties of 6+). Closed Sun, 24-26 Dec, 12-14 Jul. Amex, MasterCard, Visa, Laser, Switch. **Directions:** 0.5 mile south of City Centre on Lisburn Road.

Belfast

Sun Kee Restaurant

RESTAURANT

38 Donegall Pass Belfast BT7 1BS **Tel: 02890 312016**

Edmund Lau's little place just off Shaftesbury Square has earned widespread recognition as the city's most authentic Chinese restaurant. What you get here is a combination of the classic Chinese dishes which are already familiar - but created in uncompromising Chinse style, without the usual "blanding down" typical of most oriental restaurants. They also offer more unusual dishes, which offer a genuine challenge to the jaded western palate, be prepared to be adventurous. It is unlicensed (but you may bring your own). The main difficulty is getting a reservation, as its popularity is matched only by its tiny size. Children welcome. **Seats 30.** Air conditioning. D 5-11 daily, all à la carte. Closed mid-Jul – mid-Aug. No Credit Cards. **Directions:** Beside Police Station.

Belfast

Ta Tu

RESTAURANT/PUB

701 Lisburn Road Belfast BT9 7GU
Tel: 028 9038 0818 Fax: 028 9038 0828

Hotelier Bill Wolsey opened Ta Tu in the late spring of 2000 . It immediately became one of 'the' places and both bar and restaurant are packed with the young and young and heart at weekends. Local architect Colin Conn (who also designed Altos) was responsible for the design, which incorporates an ultra-modern high-roofed 'warehouse' with a long bar where the bright young things meet and greet and, at the rear, a more intimate restaurant area reminiscent of photographs depicting pre-war airship lounges, with comfortable high-backed armchairs, sofas and discreet, individual table lighting. Menus from a dynamic kitchen team change monthly and the food is, as one might expect, adventurous and beautifully presented, demonstrating delicous flavour combinations. Millefeuille of crab salad with mango salsa (available as a starter or main course) and roast fillet of hake with aubergine chutney & coriander oil are typical examples. The waiting staff are excellent (and really know the menus); the wine list offers a wide range of carefully chosen wines at reasonable prices (mostly under £20-£25) and there's a long list of wines by the glass - and the price structure throughout offers good value. No children after 7pm. Restaurant: **Seats 90.** Air conditioning. L 12-6, D 6-9.45 (Sun to 8.30). A la carte. House wines from £8.75. Bar food served 12-9.45 daily. Closed 25 Dec. MasterCard, Visa., **Directions:** From the city centre, take Lisburn Road - about 1 mile on the right.

Belfast

TENsq

HOTEL/RESTAURANT

10 Donegal Square South Belfast BT1 5JD

Tel: 028 90 241001

Belfast's most centrally located new hotel, TENsq is just opposite the City Hall and within walking distance of the whole city centre area. It opened in August 2001 so, at the time of going to press, this exclusive hotel, restaurant, bar and private members' club had not yet established itself. There are 23 luxurious rooms, all with excellent facilities including air conditioning, safes, phones with ISDN lines, TV with DVD/video channel, tea/coffee-making facilities and iron/trouser press. **Rooms 23.** (3 junior suites, 20 superior, 15 no smoking, 2 for disabled). Lift. B&B room rate £160-200. **Restaurant Porcelain @ TENsq** In discreetly oriental surroundings on the first floor, with beautifully set (if rather tightly packed) tables, head chef Niall McKenna's food laid on artistically decorated wedge shaped plates is delicious: intimations of the subtle Far East for the western palate with Tempura and Sashimi to the fore but with lots dishes of mixed inspiration on offer. Desserts like warm chocolate and nut samosas with pistachio ice cream and apple & coconut delice are works of art and invention for a fiver - and the chocolate bento box must be seen and tasted to be believed. And for drink - sip from the range of Momokawa Sakes, some chilled and others warmed. **Seats 152.** L Tue-Thu 12-3, Fri 12.30-3; D Tue-Thu 6.30-10.30, Fri & Sat 6.30-11. A la carte. House wine £12.50. s.c. discretionary. [Food to go is available from Deli@TENsq and food is available from 7.30 am-6pm at the Red Bar.] Closed 25 Dec. **Directions:** Corner of Linenhall Street at rear of City Hall.

Belfast

The Water Margin

RESTAURANT

159-161 Donegall Pass Belfast BT7 1DP

Tel: 028 90 326888 Fax: 028 90 327333

A big, brassy 200-seater in a converted church at the bottom of the Ormeau Road is now the biggest Chinese restaurant in Ireland - and this shrine to Oriental cooking quickly attracted hundreds of followers. Inside, East meets West - a comfortable reception lounge with red leather sofas leads into the large open dining space with round tables of vaious sizes, lots of artificial plants and garish stained glass windows, all bright reds and greens and mythical beasts. An open bar runs the length of the inside wall and the dining area is divided between the ground floor and a gallery with purple painted vaulted ceiling and an adjoining opaque glass walled function room. The menu is massive and it pays to either know Chinese food really well or have inside information to find your way about. An extensive Dim Sum menu offers uncompromising authentic Chinese dishes such as steamed ox tripe and steamed fish head (in black bean sauce), a remindinder that there is a large Chinese community in Belfast. Finally you arrive at the safe haven of the set banquets, and the familiar territory of Western favourites: aromatic duck, sesame toast, sweet and sours, sizzlings and fried rice are all here - also desserts like chocolate gateau, mango pudding with cream and the fresh orange segments. At this level the food is pretty average (and by no means cheap), but there is plenty of noisy atmosphere and the Water Margin is somewhere to experience on a busy night for that alone. [There is an older sister restaurant in Coleraine, Co Londonderry.] **Seats 200.** Open 7 daily, 12-11.30. Set menus from £20 per person. House wine £20. Open all year. MasterCard, Visa, Laser.

Belfast

Wellington Park Hotel

HOTEL

2 Malone Road Belfast BT9 6RU

Tel: 02890 381 111 Fax: 02890 38505

Email: wellypark.sales@btinternet.com Web: www.mooneyhotelgroup.com

Situated close to the University, just five minutes from the city centre, this hotel is quite a Belfast institution and has been greatly improved by the recent addition of twenty-five new bedrooms and a dedicated business centre with its own secure parking (the main conference facilities remain on the first floor of the redesigned building). Individual guests need not worry about being overrun by conference delegates, since one of the bars is exclusively for their use. The spacious foyer and public areas are comfortably furnished, as are the refurbished bedrooms, featuring the usual facilities, some with modem points and voice-mail. Guests have free use of Queen's University sports centre, a few minutes from the hotel. The Dunadry Hotel & Country Club, a fifteen minute drive from the city, is in the same ownership and the new Armagh City Hotel is under construction at the time of gong to press. (For further information contact the central reservations office: 021 9038 5050.) Conference (350); secretarial services. Business centre. Own parking. Wheelchair accessible. Children welcome (under 12s free in parents' room; cots available without charge). No pets. **Rooms 75** (3 suites, 12 executive rooms). Lift. 24 hour room service. B&B £65 pps, ss £30 (room-only rate available). Closed 25 Dec. Amex, Diners, MasterCard, Visa. **Directions:** From Queen's University, head South up Malone Road, hotel is on the right hand side.

COUNTY ANTRIM

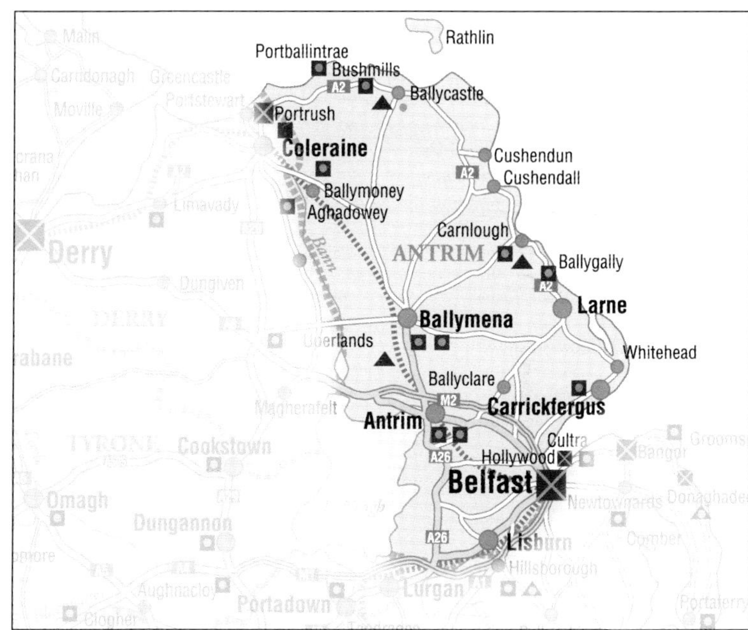

The Antrim Coast may be timeless in its beauty, but 2002 sees its picturesque ports enjoying the fruits of restoration and development at places as various as Ballycastle, Glenarm and Carrickfergus. In particular, the waterfront regeneration of Carrickfergus has been nothing less than a rebirth. In times past, this was the principal port on Belfast Lough. But the rise and rise of Belfast from 1700 onwards saw Carrickfergus becoming - despite its impressive Norman castle - a decidedly workaday sort of place. However, March 2001 saw the official opening of the main centres in the waterfront regeneration around the old harbour and the new marina, and Carrickfergus was born again.

With its boundaries naturally defined by the sea, the River Bann, the extensive lake of Lough Neagh, and the River Lagan, County Antrim has always had a strong sense of its own clearcut geographical identity. This is further emphasised by the extensive uplands of the Antrim Plateau, wonderful for the sense of space with the moorland rising to heights such as Trostan (551m) and the distinctive Slemish (438m), famed for its association with St Patrick.

The plateau eases down to fertile valleys and bustling inland towns such as Ballymena, Antrim and Ballymoney, while the coastal towns ring the changes between the traditional resort of Portrush in the far north, the ferryport of Larne in the east, and Carrickfergus in the south.

In the spectacularly beautiful northeast of the county, the most rugged heights of the Plateau are softened by the nine Glens of Antrim, havens of beauty descending gently from the moorland down through small farms to hospitable villages clustered at the shoreline and connected by the renowned Antrim Coast Road. Between these sheltered bays at the foot of the Glens, the sea cliffs of the headlands soar with remarkable rock formations which, on the North Coast, provide the setting for the Carrick-a-Rede rope bridge and the Giant's Causeway. From the charming town of Ballycastle, Northern Ireland's only inhabited offshore island of Rathlin is within easy reach by ferry, a mecca for ornithologists and perfect for days away from the pressures of mainstream life.

Local Attractions and Information

Antrim town Lough Neagh cruises	028 94 481312
Antrim town Shanes Castle	028 94 428216
Antrim town Tourism Information	028 94 428331
Ballymena Tourism Information	028 25 660300
Ballymoney Leslie Hill Open Farm	028 27 666803
Bushmills Antrim Coast and Glens	028 20 731582
Bushmills Irish Whiskey- World's Oldest Distillery	028 20 731521
Carnlough AlwaysIreland Activity Holidays	028 28 885995
Carrickfergus Castle	028 93 351273
Carrickfergus Waterfront	028 93 366455
Dunluce Castle Visitor Centre	028 20 731938
Giants Causeway	028 20 731855
Giants Causeway & Bushmills Railway	028 20 741157
Glenariff Forest Park	028 21 758232
Larne Carnfunnock Country Park	028 28 270451
Larne Ferryport	028 28 872100
Larne Tourism Information	028 28 260088
Lisburn Irish Linen Centre & Lisburn Museum	028 92 663377
Lisburn Tourism Information	028 92 660038
Portrush Tourism Information	028 70 823333
Rathlin Island Ferries	028 20 769299
Templepatrick Patterson's Spade Mill	028 94 433619

Ballycastle

The House Of McDonnell

PUB 71 Castle Street Ballycastle Co. Antrim BT54 6AS **Tel: 028 2076 2975**
Fax: 028 2076 2586 Email: toms1744@aol.com Web: www.houseofmcdonnell.com

The House of McDonnell has been in the caring hands of Tom and Eileen O'Neill since 1979 and in Tom's mother's family for generations before that – they can even tell you not just the year, but the month the pub first opened (April 1766). Tom and Eileen delight in sharing the history of their long, narrow premises with its tiled floor and mahogany bar: it was once a traditional grocery-bar, and is now a listed building. The only change in the last hundred years or so, says Tom, has been the addition of a toilet block "but outside the premises you understand" and, most recently, some old photographs which have come to light have now been put on display. Music is important too – they have a good traditional music session every Friday and love to see musicians coming along and joining in. They're usually open from 11 am until "late" in summer, but only in the evenings in winter although it's worth checking out at weekends anyway, all year. **Directions:** near the Diamond.

Ballygally

Hastings Ballygally Castle Hotel

HOTEL Coast Road Ballygally Co. Antrim BT40 2Q2 **Tel: 02890 745 251**
Fax: 02890 748 152 Email: info@hastingshotels.com Web: hastingshotels.com

This coastal hotel really has got a (very) old castle at the heart of it - and they've even got a ghost. (You can visit her room at the top of the castle). The whole thing is quite unlike any of the other Hastings hotels, although investment is now going into upgrading accommodation and public areas. At the moment rooms vary quite considerably but all are comfortable, some are quite romantic and the hotel has character. The beach is just a stone's throw away, across the road. Conference/banqueting (200/130) Children welcome; under 14s free in parents' room; cots available). Wheelchair accessible. Parking. Children welcome. Pets by arrangement. **Rooms 44** (2 suites, 8 executive rooms, 6 shower only) B&B about £42 pps, ss about £14.no sc. Toilets wheelchair accessible. Open all year except Christmas. Amex, Diners, MasterCard, Visa. Directions: Situated on the Coast Road between Larne and Glenarm. Amex, Diners, MasterCard, Visa. **Directions:** Situated on the coast road between Larne and Glenarm.

Ballygally

Lynden Heights Restaurant

RESTAURANT 97 Drumnagreagh Rd. Ballygally Co. Antrim BT40 2RR
Tel: 02828 583560 Fax: 02828 583560

On a clear day, this restaurant high up above the coast road has the most amazing views - and the dining room is in a conservatory, to make the most of it. There's a cosy bar, where orders are taken by friendly, neatly uniformed waiting staff. Well-balanced menus offer a wide choice in a fairly classic style given the occasional contemporary twist: medallions of pork fillet coated with honey & ginger sauce is typical. Good ingredients, sound cooking and efficient service all complement this restaurants natural appeal. Children welcome Parking. **Seats 60.** D Wed-Sun; L Sun only. Toilets wheelchair accessible. Closed Mon & Tue. Amex, MasterCard, Visa. **Directions:** Situated between Larne and Glenarm - signed off the coast road.

Ballymena

Adair Arms Hotel

HOTEL

Ballymoney Road Ballymena Co. Antrim BT43 5BS **Tel: 02825 653 674** Fax: 02825 640 436 Email: reservations@adair.com Web: www.adairarms.com

Located in the centre of Ballymena town, this attractive creeper-covered hotel has been owned and managed by the McLarnon family since 1995. Very much the centre of local activities – the bar and lounge make handy meeting places, and there are good conference and banqueting facilities (250/230) – it's also a popular base for visitors touring the Glens of Antrim and the coastal beauty spots. Bedrooms are not especially big, but they are comfortably furnished and well-maintained, with all the usual amenities. Children welcome (under 4s free in parents' room. Pets by arrangement. **Rooms 44** (all en-suite) B&B about £43 pps, ss about £15. Amex, MasterCard, Visa. **Directions:** In the town centre.

Ballymena

Galgorm Manor Hotel

HOTEL

136 Fenaghy Rd. Ballymena Co. Antrim BT42 1EA **Tel: 02825 881 001** Fax: 02825 880 080 Email: mail@galgorm.com Web: www.galgorm.com

Set amidst beautiful scenery, with the River Maine running through the grounds, this converted gentleman's residence was completely refurbished before opening under the present management in 1993,s and it is now one of Ireland's leading country house hotels. Approaching through well-tended parkland, one passes the separate banqueting and conference facilities to arrive at the front door of the original house, (which is a mere 100 yards from the river). An impressive reception area with antiques and a welcoming log fire sets the tone of the hotel, which is quite grand but also friendly and relaxed. Day rooms include an elegant drawing room and a traditional bar, as well as the more informal Ghillies Bar in a characterful converted buildings at the back of the hotel (where light meals are also served). Accommodation includes three suites; two rooms have four-posters. All rooms are very comfortably furnished with good bathrooms, and most have views over the river. The latest phase of development will add 48 new bedrooms, a new conference suite and a leisure centre with swimming pool, jacuzzi and fitness suite. Conference/banqueting (500/500) golf (9/18), fishing, horse-riding,walking & garden.Wheelchair accessible. **Rooms 24** (3 suites, 3 executive rooms,8 for disabled) B&B about £60 pps, ss about £39. Open all year. Restaurant: Galgorm Manor has had a good reputation for its food since opening. Table d'hôte menus with an emphasis on local produce are offered at lunch and dinner. Menus are changed monthly and always include vegetarian dishes. The panelled Board Room has an antique dining table seating 12, for private parties. **Seats 73** (private room, 16). L &D daily. Toilets wheelchair accessible Children welcome. Parking. Amex, Diners, MasterCard, Visa. **Directions:** From the Galgorm roundabout, take the third exit for Cullybackey (Feneghy road). About 2 miles, on the left.

Bushmills

Bushmills Inn

HOTEL/RESTAURANT

9 Dunluce Rd. Bushmills Co. Antrim BT57 8QG **Tel: 028 207 32339** Fax: 028 207 32048 Email: georgi@bushmillsinn.com Web: www.bushmillsinn.com

Only a couple of miles from the Giant's Causeway, Bushmills is home to the world's oldest distillery – a tour of the immaculately maintained distillery is highly recommended. The Bushmills Inn is one of Ireland's best-loved hotels. It has grown since its establishment as a 19th-century coaching inn, but its development under the current ownership – including complete restoration before re-opening in 1987 – has been thoughtful. A recently added wing (with 22 bedrooms, a conference centre, new kitchen and staff facilities, car park and an additional entrance) was so skilfully designed that it is hard to work out where the old ends and the new begins. Inside, it's the same story: all the features which made the old Inn special have been carried through and blended with new amenities. The tone is set by the turf fire and country seating in the hall and public rooms – bars, the famous circular library, the restaurant, even the Pine Room conference room – carry on the same theme. Bedrooms are individually furnished in a comfortable cottage style and even have "antiqued" bathrooms – but it's all very well done and avoids a theme park feel. Conferences are held in an oak-beamed loft. Small conferences (50). Wheelchair accessible. Garden. Fishing. Children welcome. Pets permitted by arrangement. **Rooms 32** (22 in Mill House; 10 shower only in Coaching Inn), 1 for disabled) B&B £49 pps in Coaching Inn, £64 pps in Mill House, ss £10-20. **Restaurant: Seats 120** (private room, 50) D daily 7-9.30 (Sun 6-9), L Sun only, from 12.30; Set D £20-25, house wine £10; sc discretionary. Open all year. Amex, MasterCard, Visa, Switch. **Directions:** On the A2 Antrim coast road, in Bushmills village, as it crosses the river.

Carnlough
HOTEL

Londonderry Arms Hotel

20 Harbour Road Carnlough Co. Antrim BT44 OEU
Tel: 028 28 885 263 Fax: 028 28 885 263
Email: ida@glensofantrim.com Web: www.glensofantrim.com

Carnlough, with its charming little harbour and genuinely old-fashioned atmosphere (they still sell things like candyfloss in the little shops) is one of the most delightful places in Northern Ireland – and, to many people, the Londonderry Arms Hotel is Carnlough. Built by the Marchioness of Londonderry in 1848 as a coaching inn, it was inherited by her great grandson, Sir Winston Churchill, in 1921. Since 1948 it has been in the caring hands of the O'Neill family. The original building and interior remain intact, giving the hotel great character. They do good home-made bar meals or afternoon tea which you can have in the bar or beside the fire in a comfortably old fashioned lounge. Bedrooms, which are all en-suite and include 14 added at the back of the hotel, are comfortable and well-furnished in keeping with the character of the building. Many of the older rooms have sea views. Conferences/banqueting (100/150). Parking. Wheelchair accessible. Children under 4 free in parents' room; cots available. No pets. **Rooms 35** (2 for disabled). Lift. B&B about £55 pps, ss about £25. Closed 25 Dec. **Restaurant:** Local ingredients – wild salmon , crab, lobster and mountain lamb – are used in contemporary international cooking, with an emphasis on seafood. Typical starters, for example, are tempura of prawn, panfried crab cake with avocado guacomole, crème fraîche & sweet potato crisps - but it's not all seafood, as you could equally begin with confit of duck and follow with a main course of char-grilled beef fillet on Chinese greens with beetroot, pesto & saute potatoes. Children welcome. D daily,L Sun only. Barfood served daily. Amex, Diners, MasterCard, Visa. **Directions:** On the A2 Antrim coast road.

Carrickfergus
HOTEL

Quality Hotel Carrickfergus

75 Belfast Road Carrickfergus Co. Antrim BT38 8BX
Tel: 028 93 364556 Fax: 028 93 351620 Email: info@qualityinncarrickco.uk

The opening of the Quality Hotel in 1997 gave a much needed boost to accommodation choices in this area – and at prices which are far from outrageous. Conveniently located to Belfast airport (10 miles) and the scenic attractions of the Antrim coast, the hotel makes a good base for business and leisure visitors. It has good conference facilities (600), meeting rooms (max 60) and in-room amenities (desk, fax/modem line) for business guests. Bedrooms include three suitable for disabled guests, two suites, two junior suites and 20 non-smoking rooms; all are furnished to a high standard with good en-suite bathrooms (all with bath and shower). The Glennan Suite ("simply the best suite on the island") has jacuzzi bath and separate shower, his & hers washbasins, private dining room, leather furniture and a raised American king size bed overlooking Belfast Lough through balcony doors. B&B £45 pps, ss £30. Restaurant open daily 5.30-10; food available in Mac's Pub Mon-Sat 12-3, Mon-Sun 5.30-9.30. Open all year. Amex, Diners, MasterCard, Visa, Switch. **Directions:** Main Coast Road exit Belfast North (8 miles).

Crumlin
HOTEL

Aldergrove Airport Hotel

Belfast International Airport Crumlin Co. Antrim BT29 4ZY
Tel: 02894 422 033 Fax: 02894 423 500

Seventeen miles from Belfast city centre, this pleasant modern hotel opened in 1993 and is just 50 metres from the main terminal entrance at Belfast International Airport. Spacious, attractively furnished bedrooms include three designed for disabled guests and a non-smoking floor; all are double-glazed, sound-proofed and have good bathrooms with bath and shower. Fully air-conditioned throughout, the hotel has spacious public areas and good facilities, including a fitness suite with sauna, conference and banqueting facilities, ample parking, a sun terrace and garden. An extra 60 bedrooms and a public bar are due for construction and, to address the needs of long-stay business guests, also a full leisure centre and games room. High security around the airport is seen as a bonus by the hotel, as it helps guests to feel relaxed. Conference/banqueting (250/200) Children's playground & garden. Children (Under 15s free in parents' room; cots available). Wheelchair accessible. No Pets. **Rooms 108** (all en-suite, 50 no-smoking, 3 for disabled) Lift. B&B £38pps, ss about £20. Open all year. Amex, Diners, MasterCard, Visa. **Directions:** Belfast - follow signs for International Airport.

Dunadry
HOTEL

Dunadry Hotel & Country Club

2 Islandreagh Drive Dunadry Co. Antrim BT41 2HA
Tel: 02894 434 343 Fax: 02894 433 389
Email: info@dunadryhotel.co.uk Web: mooneyhotelgroup.com

The riverside Dunadry Hotel & Country Club was formerly a mill and it succeeds very well in combining the character of the old buildings with the comfort and efficiency of an international hotel. Set in ten acres of grounds, the hotel has excellent business and leisure facilities, plus conferencing/banqueting (350/400). Stylish, spacious bedrooms include three suites and eleven executive rooms – all have good amenities, including satellite TV, and executive rooms have computer points and fax machines. The most desirable rooms have French windows opening on to the gardens or the inner courtyard and a new informal restaurant makes the most of its situation overlooking the river. Leisure facilities within the grounds include a professional croquet lawn, fun bowling, trout fishing and cycling, as well as a leisure centre which rates as one of the best in Britain and Ireland. Sister establishment to the Wellington Park Hotel in Belfast city (see entry) and the new Armagh City Hotel, under construction the the time of going to press. **Rooms 83** (12 executive, 2 for disabled). B&B about £40 pps; room-only rate also available, £67.50 (max 3 guests). Closed 24-26 Dec. Amex, Diners, MasterCard, Visa.

Portballintrae
PUB

Sweeney's Public House & Winebar

Seaport Avenue Portballintrae Co. Antrim BT57 8SB
Tel: 028207 32405 Fax: 028207 31850 Email: seaport@freeuk.com

This attractive stone building is on the sea side of the road as you drive into Portballintrae and is very handy to both the Royal Portrush Golf Club and the Giant's Causeway. It's a pleasant place, with a welcoming open fire in the bar and a choice of places to drink or have a bite to eat. During the day the conservatory is an attractive option, but on chillier days, the fireside in the main bar wins over the conservatory and its view. Unpretentious food in the modern international café/bar style is prepared by Pauline Gallagher (who has been head chef since 1995); seafood, including lobster, wild salmon and locally caught white fish, is a speciality. Although likely to suit all age groups during the day, it can get very busy during the evening, especially on live music nights (folk & country; there is a late licence to 1 am on Friday and Saturday). Children welcome. **Seats 120** (private room, 32) No smoking area; air conditioning. Food available every day (12-9.30pm), à la carte; house wines from £7.50; sc discretionary. Toilets wheelchair accessible. Own parking. No Credit Cards. Open all year. **Directions:** Centre of Village overlooking Bay & Harbour.

Portrush
RESTAURANT/ACCOMMODATION

Academy Restaurant

NI Hotel & Catering College
Ballywillan Road Portrush Co. Antrim BT56 8JL
Tel: 028 708 26201 (Accommodation) 028 708 26200
Fax: 028 708 26207

It is not widely known beyond the immediate area that the renowned Northern Ireland Hotel & Catering College at Portrush is also open to the public as a normal commercially-operated restaurant - and it is one of the best in the province. Lunch in the Academy offers a brasserie style menu with quick, professsional service, while dinner offers fine dining and a more formal style of service including plated dishes, silver service and guéridon preparation and flambé work - their catchphrase "tomorrow's chefs cooking today" is only the beginning of it, as guests have the benefit of tomorrow's best restaurant staff as well. The kitchen and restaurant are staffed by students following higher education programmes in hospitality and the culinary arts under the guidance of professional restaurant manager, Martin Caldwell, and head chef, Martin Devaney. Menus and wine lists are bang up to date, the food is excellent and beautifully presented and service is friendly, attentive - and highly efficient. The quality and value offered are both outstanding, They also do theme evenings, wedding receptions/banqueting and conferences - and even have accommodation. A major refurbishment programme is under way as we go to press. **Seats 80** (private room available on request). No smoking restaurant. L Tue-Sat 12.30-1 (also Sun & Mon in Jun-July); D daily, 7-8. Set L £8.95, Set D £8.95-£14.95; a la carte L&D also available. House wine £8.50. Closed Sun & Mon, except Jun-Jul, Christmas. Accommodation Inexpensive bed & breakfast accommodation is offered in rooms attached to the college. **Rooms 84** (31 en-suite, all no smoking). Lift. B&B £18 pps, no ss. Room-only rate available: £15. Closed Christmas. MasterCard, Visa, Laser, Switch.

Portrush

RESTAURANT/PUB

Harbour Bistro & Harbour Bar

The Harbour Portrush Co. Antrim BT58 8BM
Tel: 028 70 822 430 Fax: 028 70 823 194

The original part of the Harbour Bar is one of the oldest pubs in Northern Ireland and has great character. The McAlpin family, who also own the Ramore Wine Bar, took over the pub a few years ago and have developed it considerably, notably by opening a restaurant at the back with a large lounge bar over it where customers can dance. Menus are more traditional than those at the Wine Bar and include roasts, pies and steaks various ways as well as more contemporary dishes like Mexican chicken kebeb and prawn & chicken laksa (which are the most popular dishes). Here too, what is offfered is good food at very reasonable prices. Children welcome. Restaurant **Seats 95.** No smoking area; air conditioning. Food available Mon-Sat: L 12.30-2.30, D 5.30-10. A la carte. Closed Mon, 25 Dec. No Credit Cards. **Directions:** At the harbour in Portrush.

Portrush

FARMHOUSE

Maddybenny Farmhouse

18 Maddybenny Park Portrush Co. Antrim **Tel: 02870 823 394**
Email: accommodation@maddybennyfreeserve.co.uk
Web: www.maddybenny.freeserve.co.uk

Just two miles from Portrush, Rosemary White's Plantation Period farmhouse was built before 1650. Since extended and now modernised, it makes a very comfortable and exceptionally hospitable place to stay, with a family-run equestrian centre nearby (including stabling for guests' own horses). There is also snooker, a games' room and quiet sitting places, as well as a a garden and an area for outdoor children's games. The accommodation is just as thoughtful. The bedrooms are all en-suite and there are all sorts of useful extras – electric blankets, a comfortable armchair, hospitality tray complete with teacosy, a torch and alarm clock beside the bed, trouser press, hair dryer – and, on the landing, an ironing board, fridge and pay phone for guest use. Across the yard there are also six self-catering cottages, open all year (one wheelchair friendly). No evening meals, but Rosemary guides guests to the local eating places that will suit them best. Maddybenny was the Guide's Farmhouse of the Year in 2000. Golf, fishing, tennis and pitch & putt nearby. Children welcome. No pets. **Rooms 3** (all en-suite) B&B £25pps, ss £5 Parking. Closed Christmas/New Year. MasterCard, Visa. **Directions:** Take the A29 Portrush/Coleraine - signposted to riding centre.

Portrush

RESTAURANT

Ramore Wine Bar

The Harbour Portrush Co. Antrim BT56 8BM
Tel: 02870 824313 Fax: 02870 823194

An upmarket fast food operation is all that remains of the wonderful Ramore Restaurant, which was once the leading light of cosmopolitan fine dining in Northern Ireland. However, the informal style of this large restaurant overlooking the harbour is clearly popular with the holiday market and is a real hit with the young - teenagers, families with young children - who appreciate the fun & friendly atmosphere, the speed and prices which are reasonable for the quality of food. Menus are much the same as the old wine bar - a wide selection of contemporay dishes ranging from tortilla chips with dips, through bang bang chicken with oriental salad, peanut & garlic dips, chilli steak in pitta with salad & garlic mayo or lamb steaks with red pepper & cherry tomato salsa on bruschetta to jumbo prawn salad or vegetarian options like cheese & spinach flan. Prices are very accessible - almost everything is still under £10 - so if you are willing to tolerate noise, discomfort and scanty service for a quick bite of good fast food, this is the place for you. **Seats 170.** L&D daily:L12.15-2.15, D5-10 (Sun,12.15-3 & 5-9). A la carte; house wine £7.50. sc discretionary. Toilets wheelchair accessible. Closed 25 Dec MasterCard, Visa, Switch. **Directions:** At the harbour.

Portrush

HOTEL

Royal Court Hotel

233 Ballybogey Road Portrush Co. Antrim BT56 8NF
Tel: 02870 822 236 Fax: 02870 823 176
Email: royalcourthotel@aol.com Web: royalcourthotel.co.uk

Set in a spectacular clifftop location just outside Portrush, and a 10 minute drive from the Giant's Causeway, the Royal Court offers the most desirable hotel accommodation in the area. Public areas are spacious and comfortable – the dining room has the sea view. Bedrooms are all well-furnished with good bathrooms, but vary considerably in size and outlook – the best are on the sea side and have little private balconies. Very handy to a number of golf links including the Royal Portrush and an excellent base for touring this lovely area. Conference/banqueting (100/140). Wheelchair accessible. Children under 4 free in parents' room; cots available. No pets. **Rooms 18** (4 suites, 3 executive rooms) B&B about £45pps, no ss. Closed 26 Dec. Amex, MasterCard, Visa, Amex, MasterCard, Visa. **Directions:** From Ballymena head north on M2, at Ballymoney roundabout take 3rd exit to Portrush (B62). Hotel at end on right hand side.

Templepatrick
HOTEL

Hilton Templepatrick

Castle Upton Estate Templepatrick Co. Antrim BT39 ODD
Tel: 028 9443 5500 Fax: 028 9443 5511
Web: www.templepatrickhilton.com

This purpose-built hotel and resort is very close to Belfast International Airport, yet it is located in 220 acres of parkland in the Castle Upton Estate, on the banks of Six Mile Water. Business and leisure facilities are very good, especially for golf - in the hotel as well as on the course - and bedrooms have views over the golf course and estate. Hilton hotels have instigated a very interesting 'discovering wine' initiative to encourage guests to be more adventurous with wine and see it as exciting rather than intimidating; instead of an ordinary wine list there's an A4 magazine-style information package, giving background information on wine types and the specific ones offered (with illustrations of the labels) and lots of hints; there's also a wine trolley containing a wide selection of the wines listed, available to sample before ordering. Conference/banqueting (500). Business centre; secretarial services; video conferencing. Leisure centre, swimming pool. Golf (18), pitch & putt, fishing, equestrian, tennis. Garden, walking. Children under 15 free in parents' room; cots available. Pets permitted by arrangement. **Rooms 130** (1 suite, 56 executive rooms, 65 no-smoking, 7 for disabled).Lift. B&B about £75 pps, ss £20; no sc. Open all year. Amex, Diners, MasterCard, Visa, Switch. **Directions:** M2 from Belfast; Templepatrick roundabout, 3rd exit.

Toome
PUB

The Crosskeys Inn

40 Grange Road Ardnaglass Toome Co. Antrim BT41 3QB **Tel: 028 7965 0694**
Email: eamonn@crosskeys.clara.net Web: crosskeys.clara.net

This pretty thatched country pub dates back to 1740 and, despite being devastated by fire in February 2000 the landlord managed to save a lot of the artefacts, and much of the character of the old building has been recreated in the restoration. It is has since changed hands, but the new proprietor, Vincent Hurl, intends to keep things just the way they have always been: it is one of Ireland's most famous pubs for traditional music, with sessions every Saturday night (and other impromptu sessions, with singing and story-telling, that happen at the drop of a hat). There are occasional blues sessions as well as traditional Irish. It's a characterful cottagey place, with a fire in the old kitchen and several small, low-ceilinged rooms that fill up easily on a busy night. Open Mon-Sat, 11.30am-midnight, Sun 11.30-10.30. **Directions:** Between Randalstown and Portglenone.

COUNTY ARMAGH

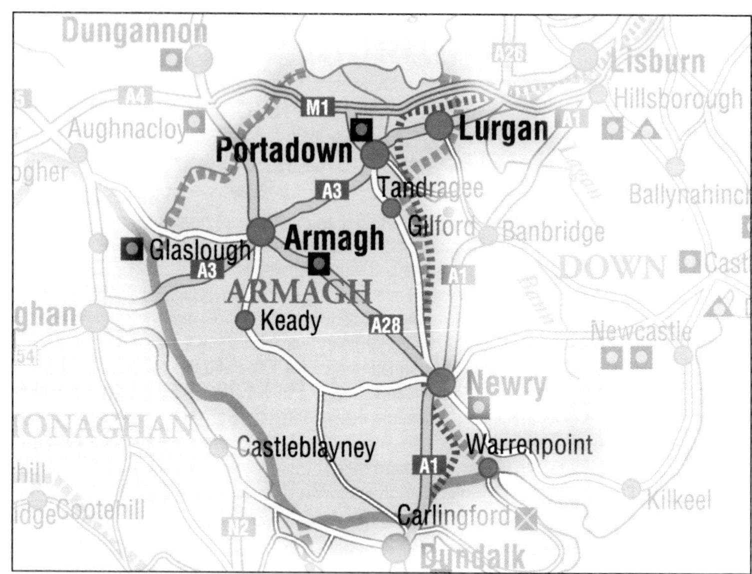

With the miniature cathedral city at its heart determinedly retaining its city status in 2002 despite a population of just 12,000 souls, Armagh county finds itself providing fresh interest for those who like to balance urban days with rural respite. Mention Armagh, and most people will think of apples and archbishops. In the more fertile northern part of the county, orchards are traditionally important in the local economy, and the lore of apple growing and their use is part of County Armagh life.

The pleasant cathedral city of Armagh itself is of course the ecclesiastical capital of all Ireland, and many a mitre is seen about it. But in fact Armagh city's significance long pre-dates Christian times. Emhain Macha - Navan Fort- to the west of the town, was a royal stronghold and centre of civilisation more than 4,000 years ago.

As with anywhere in Ireland, we are never far from water, and even inland Armagh has its own "coastline" of 25 kilometres along the southern shores of Lough Neagh, the largest lake in Britain and Ireland, and the setting for Europe's biggest eel fishery. Today, Lough Neagh provides sand for the construction industry, eels for gourmets, and recreational boating of all sorts. In times past, it was part of the route which brought coal to Dublin from the mines in Coalisland in Tyrone, the main link to the seaport of Newry being the canal from Portadown which, when opened in 1742, was in the forefront of canal technology. That County Armagh was a leader in canal technology is only one of its many surprises - the discerning traveller will find much of interest, whether it be in the undulating farmland and orchards, the pretty villages, or the handsome uplands rising to Carrigatuke above Newtownhamilton, and on towards the fine peak of Slieve Gullion in the south of the county.

Local Information and Attractions

Annaghmore (nr Portadown) Ardress (NT house)	028 38 851236
Armagh County Museum	028 37 523070
Armagh Planetarium	028 37 523689
Armagh Astronomical Observatory	028 37 522928
Armagh Palace Stables Heritage Centre	028 37 529629
Armagh St Patrick's Trian Visitor Centre	028 37 521801
Bessbrook Derrymore House	028 30 830353
Forkhill (Slieve Gullion)Ti chulainn Cultural Centre	028 30 888828
Moy The Argory (NT Mansion)	028 87 784753
Lough Neagh Discovery Centre, Oxford Island	028 38 322205
Portadown Moneypenny's Lock (Newry Canal)	028 37 521800
Slieve Gullion Forest Park	028 30 848226

Armagh

HOTEL

Armagh City Hotel

Friary Road Armagh Co. Armagh BT61 7QJ
Tel: 028 9038 5050

Coming soon - a new sister hotel to the Dunadry Inn, Co Antrim and Wellington Park Hotel, Belfast (see entries) is under construction at the time of gong to press and due to open in 2002, bringing badly needed up-to-date facilties to Ireland's historic ecclesiastical capital. It will have conference facilties for up to 1,200 delegates, with full back up business services and a leisure centre with swimming pool. Telephone for details, including information on any introductory offers and special breaks. **Rooms 85.** Room rate about £80.

Armagh

CAFÉ

Navan Centre

Killylea Road Armagh Co. Armagh BT60
Tel: 02837 525550

In the Navan Centre, the coffee shop in the interpretative centre serves wholesome hot food and light snacks. No smoking restaurant.

Lurgan

RESTAURANT

The Brindle Beam Tea Rooms

House of Brindle 20 Windsor Avenue Lurgan Co. Armagh BT67 9BG
Tel: 028 3832 1721

This in-store self-service restaurant is a real one-off. Nothing is bought in and Alannah Gilpin, who has been head chef for nine years, puts the emphasis firmly on real home cooking. There are two freshly-made soups each day and hot dishes like beef stew, made with well trimmed fat-free chump steak - with no onions. None of the pies or casseroles contain onions as some customers don't like them, but they're still full of flavour. Their salad cart is a special attraction, with anything up to 30 different salads served each day, and several different hot dishes including baked or grilled chicken breasts, salmon and always some vegetarian dishes too. There's also a huge variety of tray bakes and desserts - and only real fresh cream is used. Scrupulously clean, with reasonable prices (not cheap but good value for the quality) and real home cooking, this place is a gem. **Seats 110** (private room 50). No smoking restaurant, Open Mon-Sat, 10-5, L 12-2, Aft Tea 2-4.30 (Sat to 4.45). A la carte self-service except special set menus, eg Christmas. Unlicensed. Closed Sun, 25-26 Dec, Easter, 12-13 Jul. Amex, Diners, MasterCard, Visa, Switch.

Portadown

HOTEL

Seagoe Hotel

Upper Church Lane Portadown Co Armagh BT63 5JE
Tel: 028 3833 3076 Fax: 028 3835 0210

Attractively situated in its own grounds on the edge of Portadown, this fine hotel has been in the same ownership for many years but has recently undergone a complete makeover. The design is innovative and exceptionally easy on the eye and, once inside, the tone of the whole development is set by stylish public areas which are outstanding not only for grace and scale of design, but also the use of extremely high quality materials in construction, furnishing and decor. Easy wheelchair access throughout the building has been thought through in detail (the pay phone in the lobby is wheelchair accessible, for example). Bedrooms have contemporary simplicity teamed with warm, rich fabrics and good work space for business guests; executive rooms also have modem and fax facilities. Business/ conference facilities are equally special - but it's not all work, as there's a separate function entrance (popular for weddings as well as conferences), with its own dramatic lobby/reception area and two superb honeymoon suites. Bar and restaurant areas are designed with equal care, looking on to a delightful courtyard garden in the centre of the building. Own parking. Garden. **Rooms 34** (all en-suite). Wheelchair accessible. Lift. Open all year. Credit cards accepted. **Directions:** Off the A27 (Old Lurgan Road).

COUNTY DOWN

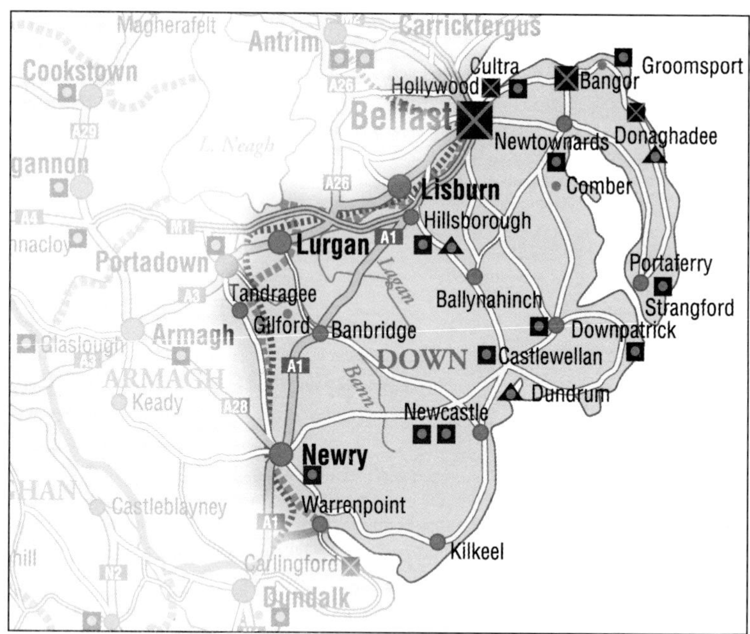

The abiding impression of County Down is of a natural home for the comfortable modern lifestyle, but in fact you can expect to find more scenic variety here than in many other Irish counties. Down County rings the changes in its own quiet way, from its affluent shoreline along Belfast Lough - the "Gold Coast" - through the rolling drumlin country which provides Strangford Lough's many islands, and on then past the uplands around Slieve Croob, with the view southward being increasingly dominated by the purple slopes of the Mountains of Mourne.

But while the Mournes may soar to Northern Ireland's highest peak of Slieve Donard (850m), and provide within them some excellent hill-walking and challenging climbing, nevertheless when seen across Down's patchwork of prosperous farmland they have a gentleness which is in keeping with the county's well-groomed style. In the same vein, Down is home to some of Ireland's finest gardens, notably Mount Stewart on the eastern shore of Strangford Lough, and Rowallane at Saintfield, while the selection of forest and country parks is also exceptional.

Within the contemporary landscape, history is much in evidence. St Patrick's grave is in Downpatrick, while the Ulster Folk and Transport Museum at Cultra near Holywood provides an unrivalled overview of the region's past. The coastline is much-indented, so much so that when measured in detail County Down provides more than half of Northern Ireland's entire shoreline. Within it, the jewel of Strangford Lough is an unmatched attraction for naturalists and boat enthusiasts, while Portaferry has one of Ireland's longest-established saltwater aquariums in Exploris.

Throughout the county, there is greater interaction with the sea than anywhere else in Northern Ireland. Bangor in the north of the county has Ireland's largest marina, an award-winning facility, while all three of Northern Ireland's main fishing ports - Portavogie, Ardglass and Kilkeel - are in County Down, the latter being home to the Nautilus Centre, which provides a living experience of the fishing industry.

Local Attractions and Information

Bangor Events Office	028 91 278051
Bangor Tourism Information	028 91 270069
Bangor North Down Heritage Centre	028 91 271200
Castle Espie Wildfowl and Wetlands Centre	028 91 874146
Cultra Ulster Folk & Transport Museum	028 90 428428
Downpatrick Downpatrick Cathedral	028 44 614922
Dromore Kinallen Craft Centre	028 97 533733
Dundrum Murlough National Nature Reserve	028 43 751467
Greyabbey Mount Stewart House	028 42 788387
Kilkeel Nautilus Centre	028 41 765555
Millisle Ballycopeland Windmill	028 91 861413
Mourne Mountains Guided Wildlife Walks	028 43 751467
Newcastle Tollymore Forest Park	028 43 722428
Newtownards Kingdoms of Down Tourism	028 91 822881
Portaferry Exploris Aquarium	028 42 728062
Rathfriland Bronte Interpretive Centre	028 40 631152
Saintfield Rowallane Gardens	028 97 510131
Strangford Castle Ward	028 44 881204
Strangford Lough Wildlife Centre	028 44 881411

Bangor

Clandeboye Lodge Hotel

HOTEL

10 Estate Road Clandeboye Bangor Co. Down BT19 1UR
Tel: 028 9185 2500 Fax: 028 9185 2772

Set in woodland on the edge of the Clandeboye estate, this comfortable modern hotel fits in well with its rural surroundings. The stylish foyer creates a good impression, with a welcoming fire and plentiful seating areas. Off it is the Lodge Restaurant with gothic-style windows and furnishings (where breakfast is also served). Good-sized bedrooms have neat, well-planned bathrooms (suites have whirlpool baths); standard amenities include phones with voicemail and fax/modem points. A country-style pub, The Poacher's Arms, is in an original Victorian building beside the hotel. Conference/banqueting (300/300) Golf (18/9), walking & garden available. Children under 4 free in parents' room; cots available). Wheelchair accessible. No Pets. Credit card numbers are taken when booking - and the deduction may be made before your arrival. Children welcome. Parking. **Rooms 43** (2 suites, all en-suite,13 no-smoking, 2 for disabled) Lift B&B about £35 pps, ss about £11. Closed 24-26 Dec. Amex, Diners, MasterCard, Visa. **Directions:** 15 minutes from Belfast, on outskirts of Bangor.

Bangor

Marine Court Hotel

HOTEL

Bangor Co Down BT20 5ED **Tel: 028 91 451100** Fax: 028 91 451200

Excellent leisure facilities at the Marine Court's Oceanis Health & Fitness Club are this hotel's greatest strength – these include an 18 metre pool, steam room, whirlpool and sunbeds, plus a well-equipped, professionally-staffed gym. As a result, the club is extremely popular with locals as well as hotel residents. The hotel overlooks the marina (beyond a public carpark) but the first-floor restaurant is the only public room with a real view and only a few bedrooms are on the front – most overlook (tidy) service areas. While the decor is very neutral, furnishings are good quality, with plenty of worktop and tea/coffee tray, hair dryer and trouser press standard in all rooms. Noise from a disco at the back of the hotel may be a problem on some nights. There are three restaurants in the hotel: two informal ones and the first-floor Stevedore Restaurant, overlooking the marina. Conference/banqueting (300/250). Leisure centre; swimming pool. Children welcome (under 6s free in parents' room; cots available). No Pets. **Rooms 52** (2 suites, 15 executive rooms, 1 for disabled). Lift. B&B £45pps, ss £25. Closed 25 Dec. Amex, MasterCard, Visa, Switch. **Directions:** 14 miles from Belfast/10 miles Belfast City Airport.

Bangor

Royal Hotel

HOTEL

26/28 Quay Street Bangor Co. Down BT20 5ED
Tel: 02891 271866 Fax: 02891 467810

This old hotel near the marina came into new ownership a few years ago but has lost none of its friendliness or old-fashioned charm. There's a warm personal welcome, a clear willingness to help guests in any way possible and the building has some endearing idiosyncracies - although, alas, the early 20th century lift with folding grille doors and a mind of its own, which amused the Guide on an earlicr visit, has been replaced by a sleek new early 21st century one. Rooms vary - the best are the new ones on the front, overlooking the marina. Small conferences (40); Children welcome (under 5s free in parents' room; cots available). No Pets. **Rooms 50** (7 executive rooms, 8 shower only, 1 for disabled). Lift. B&B about £48pps, ss £15. Special offers sometimes available. Nearby parking. Closed 25 Dec. Amex, Diners, MasterCard, Visa. **Directions:** A2 from Belfast, at bottom of Main Street turn right (keeping in left lane). Hotel is 300 yards on right facing marina.

Bangor
RESTAURANT ☆

Shanks Restaurant

Blackwood Golf Centre 150 Crawfordsburn Road
Bangor Co Down BT19 1PR **Tel: 028 91 853313** Fax: 028 91 852 493

The setting is unusual for Robbie and Shirley Millar's restaurant, which was designed by Sir Terence Conran's company. On two floors (the first floor is mostly taken up by the bar and reception area, with some tables in use for extra-busy sittings, and a balcony for al fresco eating), the main restaurant is downstairs. The interior has had a makeover recently, with excellent results - the overall effect is warmer, soft mauves and greys upstairs with plush new leather and suede furniture, and warm blue and dove grey walls downstairs with deep red leather banquette seating, lightwood chairs and smart table settings. The windowed kitchen at one end allows you to watch chef-patron Robbie Millar and his team of chefs at work, while Shirley supervises the front-of-house team with quietly attentive efficiency. At its best, Robbie's contemporary cooking brings together the best local ingredients in really creative combinations, often demonstrating Mediterranean influences and some from Asia. The 3-course dinner menu is good value, although some dishes carry a supplement (mostly £2.95); a price structure avoiding this policy might be more customer-friendly. Starters sometimes read like main courses - for example, a first course of hake with crispy artichokes, saffron aïoli, tomato confit experienced on a recent visit could easily have been a main dish; it, like other dishes on the same occasion, was inconsistent as far as the cooking was concerned and not very attractively presented - especially in comparison with other meals here in the past: the hake was cooked to perfection and very tasty and the tomato confit on which it rested was generous in texture and flavour, but the tapenade toast was tough and unattractive in both appearance and taste and the aïoli, drizzled in tram lines across the top, did nothing for the dish. Although good and tasty in a general sense, this was not the cooking this kitchen has previously produced. Main courses followed a similar pattern, desserts included a good but unexceptional crème brulée with apricot & orange compôte, and the cheese - which used to be a high point of a meal here, has become quite good rather than exceptional (and attracts a supplement). This is still one of the best restaurants in the country - food is based on the highest quality ingredients, ambience and service are excellent, the wine list is very well balanced and, for the quality on offer, inexpensive; but the style of cooking has changed and is now more ordinary and not always well-judged. There is a feeling that we are no longer seeing an inspired culinary artist at work - but we hope to be proved wrong on our next visit. Children welcome.; vegetarian menu available. **Seats 60** (private room, 36) L Tue-Fri 12.30-2.30, D Tue -Sat 7-10. Set 3 course L, £19.95. Set D £27-£35. House wine from £13.50; sc discretionary. Closed Sun, Mon; 25-26 dec; Easter Tue.25-26 Dec, 1 Jan & 2 wks in July. Amex, MasterCard, Visa, Switch. **Directions:** 2km off A2 Dual Carriageway from Belfast to Bangor.

Crawfordsburn
HOTEL/RESTAURANT

The Old Inn

Main Street Crawfordsburn Co. Down BT19 1JH
Tel: 048 9185 3255 Fax: 048 9185 2775
Email: info@theoldinn.com Web: www.theoldinn.com

The pretty village setting of this famous 16th century inn – the oldest in continuous use in all Ireland – belies its convenient location close to Belfast and its City Airport. Oak beams, antiques and gas lighting emphasise the natural character of the building, an attractive venue for business people and private guests alike. Individually decorated bedrooms vary in size and style, most have antiques, some have four-posters and a few have private sitting rooms. The conference and banqueting suite has been recently extended: weddings of up to 125 guests can now be accommodated and there's a delightful little garden that is popular for photographs. The Ulster Folk and Transport Museum and the Royal Belfast Golf Club are also nearby. There are several eating areas in the hotel - food is served in the olde worlde bar during afternoon and early evening and Restaurant 1614 is open for dinner and Sunday lunch; the Churn Bistro serves informal evening meals daily (7-9.30). Conference/banqueting (120/125) Ample parking. Garden, walking. Children welcome. Pets allowed by arrangement. Rooms 32 (1 suite, 3 mini-suites, 18 executive) B&B £37.50pps, ss £32.50. Closed Christmas. Amex, Diners, MasterCard, Visa, Switch.

Donaghadee

Grace Neill's

PUB/RESTAURANT

33 High Street Donaghadee Co Down BT21 0AH
Tel: 02891 884595 Fax: 02891 882553

Dating back to 1611, Grace Neill's lays a fair claim to be one of the oldest inns in all Ireland; Grace Neill herself was born when the pub was more than two hundred years old and died in 1916 at the age of 98. Extensions and improvements under the present ownership have been completed with due sensitivity to the age and character of the original front bar, which has been left simple and unspoilt. The back of the building has been imaginatively developed in contemporary style, creating a bright, high-ceilinged restaurant area called **Bistro Bistro**. Delicious easy-going food is along the lines of shredded duck & red onion tortillas with sundried tomato, rack of lamb with chargrilled vegetables and (a great favourite this) homemade pork sausage with mash potato & onion gravy; good desserts follow, all at very reasonable prices. Sunday Brunch is a speciality, with live jazz. Children welcome before 7 pm. Own parking. No smoking area. Toilets wheelchair accessible. **Seats 72.** L Tue-Sat,12-2.30; L Sun 12.30-3.30; D Tue-Sat, 6-9.30; à la carte; sc discretionary. Closed D Sun, all Mon; 25-26 Dec, 1 Jan & 12-13 July. (Please phone to check times.) Amex, MasterCard, Visa. Directions: Through an arch, off the main High Street. Directions:

Donaghadee

Pier 36

PUB RESTAURANT

The Parade Donaghadee Co Down BT2 10HE
Tel: 028 91 884466 Fax: 028 91 884636
Email: info@pier36.co.uk Web: www.pier36.co.uk

Good food, especially seafood, is attracting the crowds to Denis and Margaret Waterworth's harbourside pub. Denis is the front of house part of the team, while Margaret oversees the kitchen - and the food is excellent for pub cooking, with some traditional dishes and also plenty of choice for palates accustomed to flavours from all around the world. Menus change through the day, but fresh home baked breads are a point of pride and simply grilled local lobster is a speciality - but global influences show in dishes like steamed mussels with a Thai fish stock and roast peppered monkfish, which is served with Mediterranean vegetables and and garlic potatoes. The abundance of quality fresh fish on the menu is encouraging but there is plenty else to choose from - wild boar comes from Moyallen foods, there's organic free range chicken and a separate vegetarian menu too, with three starters and six main courses to choose from. Desserts, listed on a blackboard, offer lots of old favourites, from lemon tart and strawberry cheesecake to apple crumble and profiteroles, all served with ice cream, fresh cream or custard - and there's also a nice little coffee menu. Prices are keen, with most evening main courses around £10-12, and you'd better book early at weekends as plenty of people seem to like the idea of a stroll on the pier before supper here. Children welcome. **Seats 130.** No smoking area,L daily 12-2.30, D Mon-Sat 5-9.30 (Sun 12-8.30). A la carte; house wine £8.75. Closed 25 Dec. MasterCard, Visa, Switch. **Directions:** At the Pier, Donaghadee.

Downpatrick

Denvirs

HOTEL/PUB

14 English Street Downpatrick Co. Down BT30 6AB
Tel: 02844 612012

What a gem this ancient place is. It's a wonderful pub with two old bars. There's an interesting informal restaurant, genuinely olde-worlde with an amazing original fireplace and chimney discovered during renovations. There's also delightful accommodation in sympathetically updated rooms. And there's a first floor room, with some remarkable original features, suitable for meetings or private parties. Go and see it - there can't be another place in Ireland quite like it. Conferences (70). Wheelchair accessible.Parking. Children welcome. Pets permitted. **Rooms 6** (all en-suite) B&B about £30pps, ss £5 Bar/Restaurant: Food served from 12-2.30pm daily & 6-8pm Mon-Fri (6-9pm Sat). [Data not confirmed at time of going to press; please phone to check details.] Closed 25 Dec. Amex, Diners, MasterCard, Visa. **Directions:** On same street as Cathedral and Courthouse in Downpatrick.

Downpatrick
HOTEL/RESTAURANT

The Mill At Ballydugan

Drumcullen Road Ballydugan Downpatrick Co Down BT30 8HZ
Tel: 028 44 613654 Fax: 028 44 839754
Web: www.ballyduganmill.com

Hidden away in rolling County Down countryside just outside Downpatrick the site of this 18th century flour mill is very atmospheric: looking out onto ruined stone outbuildings, it is almost like being in a medieval castle courtyard. The Mill would be worth a visit if only to see the magnificent restoration undertaken by the owner, Noel Killen, over more than a decade - but, since opening for business in late summer 2000, there is much more to it than that. The building now houses a bistro/coffee shop on the ground floor, a more formal restaurant on the first floor and, above it, function rooms and accommodation. The bedrooms, which are appropriately furnished in traditional country style, with exposed beams and brass-and-iron beds but also the convenience of phones, TV with video channel, tea/coffee-making facilities and safe. Just a few hundred yards away, Ballydugan Lake is stocked with fish - all round, this is an ideal base for fishing, golfing. Downpatrick races and touring holidays in this lovely area. Conference/banqueting (120/86); secretarial service. Garden. Children welcome, under 5s free in parents' room (cots available free of charge). **Rooms 10** (1 shower only, 6 no smoking, 1 for disabled) **Lecale Restaurant** General Manager Burnett Cooper and head chef David Kenny are working hard to build up the food side of the business, with the emphasis on local produce, especially fish. Quite wide-ranging table d'hôte lunch and à la carte dinner menus are offered daily, typically including starters like an excellent steamed cockles and mussels in a coconut & Thai broth and a seasonal soup such as asparagus & garden pea and main courses of cornfed chicken with spring vgetables, risotto & truffle oil and pan-roasted loin of lamb with basil mash, chunky courgettes & roast pepper jus; interesting vegetarian options are also offered. Prices are not unreasonable (starters from £3.50 and average evening main course about £12) and, bearing in mind that this ambitious project had been operational for less than a year at the time of the Guide's visit, it was promising. Although the cooking is not yet quite consistent and service needs to be sharpened up - while charming and polite, there is a lack of attention to detail - but local reports suggest that it is improving all the time, which is encouraging: Downpatrick needs the Mill. **Seats 50.** No smoking area. L daily, 1-3, D daily 7-9.30. Set L £12.50, D à la carte; house wine £11.50; s.c. discretionary. MasterCard, Visa, Switch. **Directions:** Downpatrick enroute to Newcastle past race course take first right hand turn and follow road to the Mill.

Downpatrick
COUNTRY HOUSE

Pheasants Hill Country House

37 Killyleagh Road Downpatrick Co Down BT30 9BL
Tel: 028 44 617246 Fax: 028 44 617246
Email: info@pheasantshill.com Web: www.pheasantshill.com

In 'St Patrick's country', Pheasants' Hill was a small Ulster farmstead for over 165 years until it was rebuilt in the mid-'90s - and is now an exceptionally comfortable country house on a seven-acre organic small-holding within sight of the Mourne Mountains, 12 miles away. It is in an area of outstanding natural beauty and abundant wildlife bordering the Quoile Pondage (a wetland wildlife reserve and favoured fishing spot) and the property is right on the Ulster Way walking trail. It is an idyllic spot, as guests soon dicover when they are welcomed with tea in front of the fire, or in the orchard on fine summer afternoons. The bedrooms, which are named after flowers and herbs, differ in character and outlook but are all comfortably furnished with generous beds and the advantages of modern facilities, including television, radio alarm clock, tea/coffee making facilties, quality toiletries, hair dryer and books and magazines to read. Breakfast is a major event and worth factoring in as a main meal in your day - the extensive menu even includes a vegetarian cooked breakfast mini-meni within it, although anyone who is not a dedicated vegetarian will find it hard to resist dry-cured bacon and home-made sausages made with their own free range Tamworth pork and many other serious temptations. Perhaps the wisest action is to stay for several nights to allow the opportunity of trying as many variations as possible. Children welcome (babies under 1 free in parents' room; cots available, £5). **Rooms 4** (3 en-suite, 1 with private bathroom). B&B £28.50, ss £10. Closed 19 Dec-2 Jan. Amex, Diners, MasterCard, Visa. **Directions:** On A22, 3 miles north of Downpatrick, 3 miles south of Killyleagh.

Dundrum

RESTAURANT

The Buck's Head Inn

79 Main Street Dundrum Co. Down BT33 0LU
Tel: 028 4375 1868 Fax: 028 44 811323
Email: bucksheadi@aol.com Web: www.thebucksheadinn.co.uk

Michael and Alison Crothers have developed this attractive, welcoming place from a pub with bar food and a restaurant, to its present position as a restaurant with bar. Alison is in charge of the kitchen and sources local produce, especially seafood, including oysters from Dundrum Bay, which might be baked with a garlic & cheddar crust and monkfish, marinated in citrus juices and served with a mussel & cider cream.The dinner menu, which is not over-ambitious but well-balanced, includes many tempting dishes and offers good value for money; desserts are tempting and a short but an imaginative vegetarian menu is also offered. At lunch time there's a shortish à la carte, including some intriguing specialities such as steak & Guinness pie in a giant Yorkshire pudding & champ, plus daily blackboard specials - and they are open for high tea as well as dinner. Regular visits here confirm that the cooking is consistently good (and, indeed, always becoming more interesting) and service under the direction of the proprietor Michael Crothers, is friendly and efficient. The atmosphere is always pleasant but especially so on Saturday nights, when a classical guitarist plays. Interesting wines are supplied by the highly respected wine merchant James Nicholson. Children welcome. **Seats 70** (private room, 28) No smoking area L 12-2.30, D 7-9.30 (Sun 7-8.30). Set Sun L £14.50; otherwise à la carte. House wine from £10; sc discretionary. Closed Mon off-season (Oct- Mar); 25 Dec. Amex, MasterCard, Visa, Switch. **Directions:** On the main Belfast-Newcastle road, approx 3 miles from Newcastle.

Gilford

RESTAURANT

Oriel of Gilford

2 Bridge Street Gilford Co. Down BT63 6HF
Tel: 028 38 831543 Fax: 028 38 831180
Email: orielrestaurant@aol.com Web: www.orielrestaurant.com

Tucked away in a corner of County Down, alongside the River Bann, proprietor-chef Barry Smyth's charming country restaurant is in a series of rooms with a cottage-like atmosphere. A cosy, relaxing bar/reception room has mixed furniture which combines character with comfort - and the restaurant areas alongside are well-lit with a pleasantly contemporary feeling. Round tables are both sociable and pleasing on the eye, set up beautifully with crisp white linen and fine porcelain - and the combination of a warm welcome and caring, professional service gets a visit off to a good start. Barry Smyth previously worked in a number of distinguished kitchens, so his creative contemporary menus and confident cooking should come as no surprise. Menus are characterised by lively, colourful dishes that aren't afraid to be bold with flavours: imaginative starters might include a little lasagne of confit duck and roast pepper with beetroot, tomato passata & basil pesto or an exotic fresh fruit medley, while typical main courses could matured peppered sirloin steak with goat's cheese and basil mash, shredded parsnips, chive bearnaise & Jus of ratatouille. Equally impressive desserts range from traditional hot 'club' puddings to well-made pretty and refreshing offerings such as tangy lemon pudding with Armagh strawberries and fresh cream - and, a nice touch: dessert wines are suggested to partner each dish. The niceties are observed to the end, when little dark and white chocolate petits fours served with cafetière coffee (or any other from a coffee menu) sends guests off with a smile on their faces. A well-priced wine list includes some unusual bottles. **Seats 55** (private room, 16). No smoking area; air conditioning. L Tue-Sun,12-2.30, D Tue-Sun, 6.30-9.30; Set L £16.95; early D £6.95 (5-7); also à la carte. House wine £12.95; sc discretionary. Closed Mon. Amex, Diners, MasterCard, Visa, Switch, Laser. **Directions:** 4 miles from Banbridge, on Tandragee Road.

Groomsport

B&B

Islet Hill

21 Bangor Road Groomsport Co. Down BT19 6JF
Tel: 028 9146 4435 Email: dnmyn@netscapeonline.co.uk

Just outside the town of Bangor, Islet Hill is a lovely old farmhouse set in fields overlooking the North Channel. It is a comfortable place to stay but it is the hospitality offered by Denis and Anne Mayne that make it really special. Children are particularly welcome and can play safely in the lovely garden. Both bedrooms are suitable for family use – one has a double bed and a single, the other a king-size bed and adjoining bunk room; and, in addition to en-suite showers, there's a shared guest bathroom on the landing. Bedrooms have tea/coffee-making facilities and phone, television, video and ironing facilities are available in the house. Short on rules and regulations and long on welcome, there is no set time for breakfast (which is a major event), guests can use the house at any time and there's a fire in the guests' private sitting room in winter. A copy of a 9000 word essay "Fifty-seven Acres and a Rood, A History of Islet Hill Farm" is presented to every guest. Garden, walking. Children under 2 free in parents' room; cots available. Pets permitted by arrangement. **Rooms 2** (both shower only & no-smoking) B&B £25pps, no ss. No Credit Cards. **Directions:** On B511, 1/4 mile west of Groomsport.

Hillsborough
PUB /RESTAURANT

The Plough Inn

3 The Square Main Street Hillsborough Co. Down BT26 6AG
Tel: 02892 682985 Fax: 02892 682472

Established in 1752, this former coaching inn enjoys a fine position at the top of the hill. Since 1984, it has been owned by the Patterson family who have built up a national reputation for hospitality and good food, especially seafood. Somehow they manage to run three separate food operations each day, so pleasing customers looking for a casual daytime meal and more serious evening diners. The evening restaurant is in the old stables at the back of the pub and booking is required; although renowned for seafood,a sprinkling of meat and poultry dishes will always include fine Angus steaks – a fillet with cracked peppercorn crust and Bushmills whiskey cream perhaps – and there's a vegetarian menu available. Unsuitable for children. Parking. **Seats 150** (private room, 40). No smoking area. Air conditioning. L 12-2.30 daily D 5-9.30 daily (Sun 5-8) Closed 25 Dec. *The Pheasant Inn at Annahilt is a sister establishment. Amex, Diners, MasterCard, Visa. **Directions:** Off the main Dublin-Belfast Dual Carriageway.

Hillsborough
HOTEL

White Gables Hotel

14 Dromore Road Hillsborough Co. Down **Tel: 02892 682755**

About ten miles south of Belfast, off the A1 Dublin road, in the historic Georgian village of Hillsborough. The hotel, designed for business travellers, is modern, though already somewhat dated. Uniform and practical bedrooms provide the usual facilities, and there are conference facilities for up to 150. **Rooms 31** (all en-suite). B&B about £65 pps (breakfast extra) Open all year.

Holywood
RESTAURANT

Bay Tree Coffee House

118 High Street Holywood Co. Down BT18 9HW
Tel: 02890 421419

Since 1988 The Bay Tree has been attracting people from miles around to its delightful craft shop and coffee house on the main street. The craft shop, which sells exclusively Irish wares, is a busy, colourful place specialising in pottery, with over two dozen Irish potters represented. There is also a gallery exhibiting the work of Irish artists and – perhaps best of all – Sue Farmer's delicious food. Baking is a strength, especially the cinnamon scones which are a house speciality. There's quite a strong emphasis on vegetarian dishes – soups, pates, main courses such as red bean & aubergine stew with spiced mash – and organic salads, especially in summer, when you can also eat out on a patio in fine weather. No reservations for lunch, but they are required on Friday evenings, when the Bay Tree is open for dinner; it's then that Sue might augment her informal lunch time fare with more serious dishes such as crown of Irish lamb with garlic, redcurrant and rosemary. Children welcome. Parking. Wheelchair accessible. No smoking restaurant. **Seats 34** L 12-2.30 Mon-Sat D 7.30-9.30 Fri only. sc discretionary. Closed Sundays, Christmas & 12,13 July. No Credit Cards **Directions:** Opposite the police station.

Holywood
RESTAURANT

Fontana

61A High Street Holywood Co. Down BT18 9AE
Tel: 02890 809908 Fax: 02890 422475

A first floor restaurant over a classy kitchen shop ("down the alley & up the stairs"), Fontana is fresh and bright, with clear yellow walls which work very well with the polished wood floor and leather seating. Although badly damaged by fire recently, everyone liked it so much the way it was that it was reconstructed using the existing scheme. Proprietor chef Colleen Bennett is one of the new wave of chefs making names for themselves in the area at the moment and she offers lovely zesty, loosely structured menus that suit the atmosphere of the room. Starters and main courses overlap to a great extent, with small and large portions of some dishes offered. A dish like Caesar salad with garlicky croutons, black olives and char-grilled chicken might come in two sizes, for example and appear on both the lunch and dinner menus. Seafood features strongly - in an updated chowder with white wine, coriander & garlic aioli, perhaps, or seared cod on new spinach with baby potatoes and sundried tomato butter. Moderate prices rise quickly when side vegetables and salads are charged separately. Outside eating area. Toilets wheelchair accessible. On street parking. Children welcome **Seats 56** L 12-3 Tues-Sat (Sun 11-3), D 6.30-10 Tues-Sat., all à la carte, house wine from about £9.95; sc discretionary, 10% added on tables of 6+. [Data not confirmed at time of going to press, please phone to check details.] Closed Mon, 25-26 Dec & 1 Jan. MasterCard, Visa. **Directions:** Three doors from the Maypole.

Holywood
HOTEL

Hastings Culloden Hotel

Bangor Road Holywood Co.Down BT18 0EX
Tel: 02890 425 223 Fax: 02890 426 777
Email: res@cull.hastingshotels.com Web: www.hastingshotels.com

Hasting Hotels' flagship property, on the main Belfast to Bangor road, is set in 12 acres of beautifully secluded gardens and woodland overlooking Belfast Lough and the County Antrim coastline. The building was originally the official palace for the Bishops of Down, and is a fine example of 19th-century Scottish Baronial architecture – though we do wonder what the bishops would have made of the glass cabinet containing yellow plastic ducks signed by visiting dignitaries. The elegant and luxurious surroundings include fine paintings, antiques, chandeliers, plasterwork ceilings, stained glass windows and an imposing staircase. The spacious bedrooms include a large proportion of suites (some new ones were recently added) and the Presidential Suite, with the best views; all are lavishly furnished and decorated and offer the usual facilities, plus additional details such as a bowl of fruit and nice touches such as ground coffee and a cafetière on the hospitality tray as well as bathrobes and fine toiletries feature in the splendidly equipped bathrooms. Business and conference faciltities have been further improved recently, making the Culloden an even more attractive venue. The hotel also has a fine health club, the 'Cultra Inn' (an informal bar and restaurant in the grounds), and an association with The Royal Belfast Golf Club, four minutes away by car (book the complimentary hospitality limousine). Conference/banqueting (400/600); business centre, secretarial services, video conferencing. Leisure centre; swimming pool. Hairdresser.Tennis, snooker, walking, pitch & putt, garden. Children welcome (under 14s free in parents' room; cots available). No pets. **Rooms 95** (16 suites, 70 executive rooms, 22 no-smoking) . Lift. B&B £105 pps, ss £60. Open all year. Amex, Diners, MasterCard, Visa, Switch. **Directions:** 6 miles from Belfast city centre on A2 towards Bangor.

Holywood
B&B

Rayanne Country House

60 Demesne Road Holywood Co.Down B18 9EX
Tel: 028 9042 5859 Fax: 028 9042 5859

Situated almost next to the Holywood Golf Club and Redburn Country Park, and with views across Belfast Lough, this is a tranquil spot in which to unwind and a fine alternative to impersonal hotels. Some bedrooms have views of Belfast Lough, all are individually decorated to a high standard with phones and television - and little extras like fresh fuit, spring water, sewing kit, stationery and a hospitality tray with bed-time drinks and home-made shortbread as well as the usual tea & coffee. Numerous other facilities available in the house on request include fax/phocopying, trouser press and minicom telephone for the deaf. It's a relaxing place, family-run and offering an outstanding breakfast, with dishes such as prune soufflé and bacon, Stilton and avocado kedgeree, grilled kippers and baked fresh herring fillets tossed in oatmeal. Garden. Parking. Wheelchair accessible. No Pets. **Rooms 7** (1 for disabled) B&B £45pps, ss £10. Open all year. Visa, MasterCard, Switch. **Directions:** From Belfast City Airport, past Hollywood Barrack turn right,f irst right again. Past Hollywood Golf Club. Rayanne 500 yards on right.

Holywood
RESTAURANT

Sullivans Restaurant

2 Sullivan Place Holywood Co. Down BT18 9JF
Tel: 028 9042 1000 Fax: 028 9042 6664 Web: www.sullivansrestaurant.co.uk

Chef-proprietor Simon Shaw's bright, friendly and informal bar, restaurant & café offers lively lunch and sandwich menus ranging from a choice of home-made soups served with crusty bread to traditional sausages & mash or salmon & sole with mushrooms & sauté potatoes. He seeks out interesting produce from trusted suppliers like Moyallen Foods and North Down Organics and there are some choices for vegetarians on the regular menus as well as a separate vegetarian menu on request. The generous proportions of dishes such marinated pork loin with grilled vegetables or roasted monkfish with aubergine & ratatouille tian are most enjoyable - this is first-class cooking, based on the best local ingredients. Simon has been doing a good job here for nearly ten years now - excellent food, varied menus, a lively atmosphere and fair prices are the secret of his success. **Seats 70.** Air conditioning. L daily 12-2.30, D Tue-Sun 5-9.30. A la carte, except set 2-course D for two £30 incl wine; house wine £11; sc 10% on parties of 6+. Closed D Mon, 1 week Jul. Amex, MasterCard, Visa, Switch. **Directions:** Just off main Belfast-Bangor Dual carriageway.

Newcastle

Burrendale Hotel & Country Club

HOTEL

51 Castlewellan Road Newcastle Co. Down BT33 0JY
Tel: 028 4372 2599 Fax: 028 4372 2328
Email: reservation@burrendale.com Web: www.burrendale.com

Just outside the traditional seaside holiday town of Newcastle, and close to the championship links of the Royal County Down golf course, this area on the edge of the Mourne mountains has a remote atmosphere yet is just an hour's drive from Belfast. Public areas in the hotel are spacious and include the Cottage Bar with an open log fire, welcome on chilly days. Well-appointed accommodation includes family rooms and all rooms are well-equipped with phone, TV with video, tea/coffee making facilities and trouser press; some new superior rooms are furnished to a particularly high standard, and have air conditioning. Golf is a major attraction to the area but a varied programme of other special breaks is also offered throughout the year. The hotel's 'Country Club' health and leisure centre is being refurbished at the time of going to press and is due for completion by the end of 2001. Conference/banqueting (250 /200); business centre, secretarial srvices; video conferencing available. Leisure centre (12 metre pool); beauty salon. Children welcome (under 4s free in parents' room; cots availablewithout charge). **Rooms 68** (18 executive rooms, 20 no smoking, 10 for disabled). Lift. B&B £50 pps, ss £15. Open all year. Diners, MasterCard, Visa, Amex, Switch. **Directions:** On A50 Castlewellan Road.

Newcastle

Hastings Slieve Donard Hotel

HOTEL

Downs Road Newcastle Co. Down BT33 0AH
Tel: 02843 723 681 Fax: 02843 724 830
Email: res@sdh.hastingshotel.com Web: www.hastingshotels.com

This famous hotel stands beneath the Mournes in six acres of public grounds, adjacent to the beach and the Royal County Down Golf Links. The Victorian holiday hotel par excellence, the Slieve Donard first opened in 1897 and has been the leading place to stay in Newcastle ever since. Recent years have seen great improvements in both the public rooms and accommodation. Bedrooms are finished to a high standard and all the bathrooms sport one of the famous yellow Hastings ducks. The nearby Tollymore Forest Park provides excellent walking on clearly marked trails, just one of the many outdoor pursuits that attract guests; should the weather be unsuitable, the Elysium health club has enough facilities to keep the over-energetic occupied for weeks - and is soon to be extended. The hotel also offers a wide range of special breaks. Conference/banqueting (825/440). Business centre; secretarial services. Leisure centre. Tennis, golf (18), fishing, snooker. Own parking. Children under 14 free in parents' room; cots available. No pets. **Rooms 126** (3 suites, 10 junior suites, 114 executive rooms, 10 no-smoking, 1 for disabled). 2 Lifts. B&B about £70 pps, ss about £20. [Data not confirmed at time of going to press.] Open all year. Amex, Diners, MasterCard, Visa. **Directions:** Along sea front from town centre.

Newcastle

Sea Salt Bistro

51 Central Promenade Newcastle Co. Down BT33 0HH
Tel: 028 437 25027 Fax: 028 437 25027

A good meal will add greatly to your enjoyment of a visit to this traditional holiday town on the sea edge of the Mountains of Mourne, so make a point of seeking out Caroline and Andrew Fitzpatrick's restaurant in a seafront terrace, wedged between an ice-cream parlour and a chemist shop. Dressed outside in unmistakeable aquamarine livery, the interior of the daytime deli/café is reminiscent of 60's coffee bars - but all is transformed on Friday and Saturday evenings when it becomes a thriving bistro, with two sittings on each night. Patrick is a chef with varied experience, including working at the late lamented Fitzers at the RDS in Dublin and Caroline has researched food programmes like Gourmet Ireland and Moveable Feast, so it should be no suprise that they have come up with a winning formula here. Anything the decor lacks in refinement is more than made up for with Patrick's excellent value set menus that offer a choice of four or five starters and main courses and half a dozen desserts (not made on the premises unfortunately) or Irish farmhouse and European cheeses (£2 supplement) for a modest £17.50. Typical starters could include oriental crab salad with fresh coriander, chilli and ginger and roasted mediterranean vegetables with melted goat's cheese and summer leaves, while main courseof Japanese style salmon teriyaki with traditional cabbage and bacon and Ardglass Cod with spiced spinach and tomato mash give a fair impression of the tone. With no drinks licence and a modest £1 corkage, everyone brings their own and part of the charm of the evening is to see what diners on adjoining tables have brought in their carrier bags. Booking is essential. **Seats 28.** No smoking restaurant. Open daily in summer 9-6; D Fri & Sat only, 7-9. Amex, MasterCard, Visa, Switch.

Newry

HOTEL

Canal Court Hotel

Merchants Quay Newry Co. Down BT35 8HF
Tel: 028 3025 1234 Fax: 028 3025 1177

This canalside hotel provides Newry with badly needed facilities, including business/conference services as well as a health & leisure complex and spacious, comfortable accommodation. **Rooms 51.** B&B about £55 pps. Open all year.

Newtownards

COUNTRY HOUSE

Edenvale House

130 Portaferry Road Newtownards Co. Down BT22 2AH
Tel: 028 9181 4881 Fax: 028 9182 6192
Email: edenvalehouse@hotmail.com Web: www.edenvalehouse.com

Diane Whyte's charming Georgian house is set peacefully in seven acres of garden and paddock, with views over Strangford Lough to the Mourne mountains and a National Trust wildfowl reserve. The house has been sensitively restored and modernised, providing a high standard of accommodation and hospitality. Guests are warmly welcomed and well fed, with excellent traditional breakfasts and afternoon tea with homemade scones. For evening meals, Diane directs guests to one of the local restaurants. Edenvale is close to the National Trust properties Mount Stewart and Castle Ward. Children welcome (under10s free in parents' room; cots available without charge). Pets permitted. **Rooms 3** (all no-smoking). B&B £27.50pps, ss £7.50. Closed 24 Dec-2 Jan. MasterCard, Visa. **Directions:** 2 miles from Newtownards on A20 going towards Portaferry.

Portaferry

RESTAURANT/ACCOMMODATION

The Narrows

8 Shore Road Portaferry Co. Down BT22 1JY
Tel: 028 4272 8148 Fax: 028 4272 8105
Email: info@narrows.co.uk Web: www.narrows.co.uk

On the Portaferry waterfront, an archway in the middle of a primrose yellow facade attracts attention to the inspired 18th century courtyard development that is central to Will and James Browns' unusual guesthouse and conference facilities. The ground floor includes a cosy sitting room with an open fire and a spacious restaurant; the style throughout is light and bright, with lots of natural materials and local art. Minimalist bedrooms are all different and have a serene, almost oriental atmosphere; all are en-suite but only three have baths. For guests with special needs, all the shower rooms are wheelchair-friendly, eight are specially designed and there is a lift. There are two interconnecting rooms and two family rooms; children's tea is available at 5 pm. A fine room over the archway, opening onto a private balcony, provides banqueting/conference facilities for 50. Own parking. Children under 2 free in parents' room; cots available. Pets by arrangement. **Rooms 13** (all no-smoking, 8 for disabled). Lift. B&B £42.50 pps, ss £15. **Restaurant:** At lunch and dinner every day, head chef Danny Millar presents lively modern menus based on the very best ingredients – notably seafood, including lobster, but also local meats and organic vegetables and herbs from their own garden and other growers nearby, free range eggs and hand-made Irish cheeses. A recent visit indicates that the restaurant is performing extremely well and the transition from the bustle of daytime/family restaurant to the more relaxed bistro dinner venue is achieved with ease. Danny Millar's sensibly limited but thoughtful menus will appeal to all comers; fish is naturally the speciality, but a choice of eight on both first and main courses allows a balanced selection. Excellent home-baked breads with tapenade are offered before starters arrive. Half lobster salad with guacamole & spiced aïoli makes an outstanding first course, while a keenly-priced vegetarian main course of wild mushroom, fennel & truffle crostini is also likely to draw applause. Delicious desserts require some forward planning, as they are substantial, and there's also an Irish cheeseboard. Children welcome. **Seats 80** L daily 12-2.30 (Sun to 3.30); D daily 6-9 (Sun 5.30-8.30). A la carte. House wine from £10.95. sc discretionary. Open all year. Amex, MasterCard, Visa, Switch/ **Directions:** A20 to Portaferry, on shore front.

Portaferry

Portaferry Hotel

HOTE/RESTAURANT

The Strand Portaferry Co. Down BT22 1EP

Tel: 02891 728231 Fax: 02891 728999 Email: info@portaferryhotel.com

This 18th-century waterfront terrace presents a neat, traditional exterior overlooking the Lough to the attractive village of Strangford and the National Trust property, Castleward, home to an opera festival each June. Extensions and refurbishment undertaken by John and Marie Herlihy, who have owned the hotel since 1980, have been sensitively done and the inn is now one of the most popular destinations in Northern Ireland – not least for its food. There's an excellent lunchtime bar menu (including 'Children's Choice') available every day except Sunday. Accommodation is comfortable and most of the individually decorated en-suite bedrooms have views of the water. Small conference/private parties (14/85); Own parking. Children (Under 2s free in parents' room; cots available). No pets. **Rooms 14** (4 no-smoking) B&B about £48 pps, ss £10. Restaurant: A slightly cottagey style provides the perfect background for good unpretentious food. Local produce features prominently in prime Ulster beef, Mourne lamb and game from neighbouring estates – but it is, of course, the seafood from daily landings at the nearby fishing villages of Ardglass and Portavogie that take pride of place. Well-balanced table d'hôte lunch and dinner menus are offered, plus a short carte, providing plenty of choice although majoring on local seafood. Not suitable for children under 12 after 8 pm. **Seats 80.** L&D daily: 12.30-2.30, 5.30-7, 7-9 (Sat to 10). Set menus & à la carte L available; house wine from about £11.50; sc discretionary.Toilets wheelchair accessible. Closed 24-25 Dec. [Data not confirmed at time of going to press, please phone to check details.] Amex, Diners, MasterCard, Visa. **Directions:** On Portaferry seafront.

Rostrevor

Celtic Fjord

RESTAURANT

8 Mary Street Rostrevor Co. Down BT34 3AY

Tel: 028 4173 8005

In an attractive house on the main street, Cathy (front of house) and Michael (the chef) Keenan have been running a pleasing restaurant here since the summer of 2000. Arriving guests are promptly welcomed and offered an aperitif in the reception, then shown into one of the interesting, warmly decorated dining rooms. Michael's menus offer plenty of choice - nine or ten dishes on each course at dinner, and very keenly priced with starters an average £3.75-£4 and most main courses under £10. The style ranges from the traditional - first courses like soup of the day with freshly-baked bread or chicken liver paté with Cumberland sauce and main courses such as crisp fried haddock with tartare sauce - to more contemporary fare typically including chunky fish cakes with pimento & cucumber relish and tangy mayonnaise and garlic pork tossed with crunchy vegetables, soy, spices and pasta. Desserts tend to be classic - French apple flan with crème patissière is typical. Excellent value, good cooking and efficient service make for a very pleasant dining experience. **Seats 75** (private room 25). L Wed-Sat 12-2.45; Sun L 12.30-8.15). D Tue-Sun 6-9.30 (Sun to 8.15). Closed Mon, Tue. MasterCard, Visa, Switch. **Directions:** On Main Street, halfway up the Hill.

Strangford

The Cuan

PUB/GUESTHOUSE/RESTAURANT

Strangford Village Co Down BT30 7ND

Tel: 028 44 88 1222 Fax: 028 44 88 1770

Email: info@thecuan.com Web: www.thecuan.com

On the square, just up from the car ferry that goes over to Portaferry, Peter and Caroline McErleann's village hotel presents a neat, inviting face to the world. Over a century old, it has character with open fires, cosy lounges and a homely bar, where good food is available every day - local seafood is the main speciality, notably dishes like seafood crêpe and scampi - also excellent steaks and hearty traditional food like beef & Guinness casserole and venison sausages with champ. (The hotel restaurant also specialises in seafood but what makes it different is their themed dinners - a different area is selected each month, with matchng wines and the best dishes are selected at the end of the year for New Year's Eve.) Some new bedrooms, including two family rooms, have recently been added, and all are comfortably furnished with good bathrooms (nearly all with bath and shower), television and tea/coffee making facilities. There's also a sitting room for residents, with television and video. Small conferences/banqueting (15/80). Children welcome (under 5s free in parents' room, cots available without charge). **Rooms 9** (2 shower only, all no smoking, 1 for disabled). Limited room service (on request). B&B £34.95, ss £15; Room-only rate also available, £60 (max 2 guests). Bar meals daily 12-9.30. Restaurant L 12.30-2.20 daily, D Mon-Thu 6.30-9, Fri & Sat to 9.30; Sun High Tea 5-9pm. House wine from £10.25. Closed 25 Dec. Amex, MasterCard, Visa, Switch. **Directions:** On the square, near the ferry.

COUNTY FERMANAGH

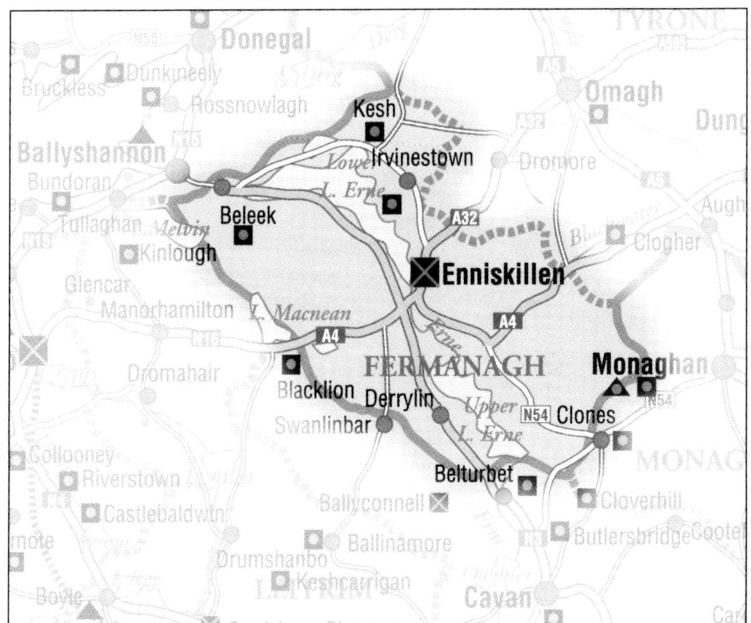

Fermanagh in 2002 is moving into a central role in Ireland's myriad inland waterways system, with the headquarters of Waterways Ireland developing in Enniskillen. Ireland is a watery place of many lakes, rivers and canals. So it's quite an achievement to be the most watery county of all. Yet this is is but one of Fermanagh's many claims to distinction.

It is the only county in Ireland in which you can travel the complete distance between its furthest extremities within the heart of its territory entirely by boat. Elsewhere, rivers often divide one county from another, but Fermanagh is divided - or linked if you prefer - throughout its length by the handsome waters of the River Erne, both river and lake.

Southeast of the county town of Enniskillen, Upper Lough Erne is a maze of small waterways. Northwest of the historic and characterful town, the riverway opens out into the broad spread of Lower Lough Erne, a magnificent inland sea set off against the spectacular heights of the Cliffs of Magho.

Boating has always been central to life in Fermanagh, so much so that in ancient times the leading local family, the Maguires, reputedly had a fleet of pleasure craft on Lough Erne as long ago as the 12th Century. It's a stunningly beautiful county with much else of interest, including the Marble Arch caves, and the great houses of Castle Coole and Florence Court, the latter with its own forest park nestling under the rising heights of Cuilcagh (667m).

And if you think lakes are for fishing rather than floating over, then in western Fermanagh the village of Garrison gives access to Lough Melvin, an angler's heaven. You just can't escape from water in this county. So much so, in fact, that Fermanagh folk will tell you that during the more summery six months of the year, the lakes are in Fermanagh, but in the damper months of winter, Fermanagh is in the lakes..........

Local Attractions and Information

Belleek Porcelain and Explore Erne Exhibition	028 68 659300
Bellanaleck Sheelin Lace Museum	028 66 348052
Enniskillen Ardhowen Lakeside Theatre	028 66 325440
Enniskillen Castle Coole	028 66 322690
Enniskillen Enniskillen Castle	028 66 325000

Enniskillen Florence Court	028 66 348249
Enniskillen Lough Erne Cruises	028 66 322882
Enniskillen Tourism Information	028 66 323110
Enniskillen Waterways Ireland	028 66 323004
Florencecourt Marble Arch Caves	028 66 348855
Garrison Lough Melvin Activity Holiday Centre	028 68 658142
Kesh Ardess Craft Centre	028 68 631267
Kesh Castle Archdale Country Park	028 68 621588
Newtownbutler Crom Castle	028 67 738174

Bellanaleck

The Sheelin

RESTAURANT

Main Street Bellanaleck Co. Fermanagh BT922BA
Tel: 028 6634 8232 Fax: 028 6634 8232
Email: malcolm.cathcart@virgin.net Web: www.irish-lace.com

John and Annett Donnelly's delightful thatched cottage restaurant not only offers good cooking but there's also a fascinating museum of traditional Irish lace (and an antiques shop) to add to the attraction. Most recently, an even more unlikely point of interest has arrived in the form of a "Fairy Landscape" specially created by local sculptor Gordon Johnston. Continental cuisine is the style, as seen in sensibly limited but appealing Table d'Hôte dinner menus that begin with a complimetary amuse-geule compliments of chef Thomas Earl and round off with a choice of desserts that might include a home-baked apple & pecan strudel with vanilla ice cream. In between, you'll be offered a choice of the day's soup or a starter such as zucchini parcels filled with goats cheese, cherry tomatoes with thyme & basil balsamic vinaigrette and main courses that could include roast rack of lamb (in a herb crust, perhaps, served with ratatouille, baby potatoes and fresh herb sauce) or a fish, which might be more exotic than expected - red snapper, for example, is just as likely as a local fish. John Donnelly's particular passion is for wine, so the list is one of many things about this litle place that may surprise you. Children welcome. **Seats 44** (private room 16). No smoking area/ LTue-Sun, 12.30-3, D Tues-Sun 6-10. Set L £8.90; Set D £12.9-£22. House wine from £10. SC discretionary. Closed Mon, except bank hols. MasterCard, Visa, Switch. **Directions:** Main Cavan - Dublin 4km out of Enniskillen.

Belleek

Hotel Carlton

HOTEL

2 Main Street Belleek Co. Fermanagh BT93 3FX **Tel: 028 6665 8282**

Belleek is a smashing little place and one of the friendliest you'll find anywhere.There are several great music pubs, including Moohans/The Fiddlestone and McMorrrows/Franks (both on the main street) and Gilmartins craft shop, which is exceptionally friendly and helpful. Then there's this welcoming waterside hotel, the Carlton which has a welcoming open fire in the bar where meals are served, very helpful staff and comfortable accommodation. **Rooms 19**, all en-suite. B&B about £37.50, no ss. major cards. Open all year. **Directions:** At the bottom of the main street, near the bridge.

Belleek

The Thatch

CAFÉ

Belleek Co. Fermanagh **Tel: 028 686 58181**

This coffee shop is really special: a listed building dating back to the late eighteenth century, it's the only originally thatched building remaining in County Fermanagh. Home-made food has been served here since the early 1900s and the tradition is being well-maintained today, with home-made soups, a range of freshly made sandwiches and toasted sandwiches all made to order, hot specials like stuffed baked potatoes and (best of all) delicious bakes like chocolate squares, carrot cake and muffins. Drinks include a coffee menu and, more unusually, you can also buy fishing tackle, hire a bike - or even a holiday cottage here. **Directions:** On the main street.

Enniskillen

Blakes of the Hollow

PUB

6 Church Street Enniskillen Co. Fermanagh BT746JE
Tel: 028 6632 2143 Fax: 028 6774 8491
Email: blakep@itconnect.com

One of the great classic pubs of Ireland, Blakes has been in the same family since 1887 and, up to now, has always been one of the few places that could be relied upon to be unchanged. Not a food place, a pub. Maybe a sandwich, but mainly somewhere to have a pint and put the world to rights. It will be a great relief to Blakes' many fans all over the world that the building is listed both inside and out because major changes at this historic establishment are under way and, although not complete at the time of going to press, could include three new bars, a café/wine bar and a restaurant. Open all year Diners, MasterCard, Visa, Switch. **Directions:** Main shopping area of Enniskillen.

Enniskillen

RESTAURANT

Francos Pizzeria

Queen Elizabeth Road Enniskillen Co. Fermanagh
Tel: 028 66324424

Striking decor and a dramatic increase in size are the most immediate points noted about Francos on a recent visit; it was one of Enniskillen's first contemporary eating places and remains one of the most popular. Informal food, including pizzas, pastas and barbecues, are the order of the day - and it's all done with great style. Open Mon-Sat, noon-midnight; Sun noon-10.30 pm. All major cards.

Enniskillen

HOTEL

Killyhevlin Hotel

Dublin Road Enniskillen Co. Fermanagh BT74 6RW
Tel: 028 6632 3481 Fax: 028 6632 4726
Email: info@killyhevlin.com Web: www.killyhevlin.com

Just south of Enniskillen, on the A4, this pleasant modern hotel on the banks of the Erne has fishing and river cruising as particular local attractions in addition to other outdoor activities such as golf and horse-riding. The hotel was completely refurbished in 1997 and is spacious, with conference/banqueting facilities (600/400) as well as a warm welcome and comfortable accommodation for private guests. There are also some holiday chalets in the grounds, with private jetties. Fishing, cycling & walking available. Leisure centre. Ample parking. Children under 4 free in parents' room; cots available, about £10. Wheelchair accessible. Pets permitted by arrangement. **Rooms 43** (1 suite, 1 junior suite, 1 for disabled). B&B about £53 pps, ss about £15; sc incl. Closed 24-25 Dec. Amex, Diners, MasterCard, Visa. **Directions:** On the A4 just south of Enniskillen.

Enniskillen

COUNTRY HOUSE

Rossahilly House

Rossahilly Enniskillen Co. Fermanagh BT94 2FP
Tel: 028 6632 2352 Fax: 028 6632 0227
Email: info@rossahilly.com Web: www.rossahilly.com

Just three miles from Enniskillen and very close to the airport, the approach to Monica Poole's beautifully located 1930s guesthouse may take you past an unsightly disused farmyard but, once you get there, it's definitely worth it. It's on an elevated site with panoramic views overlooking Lower Lough Erne: "A little bit of heaven" is what one guest called it and it's easy to see why. The entrance is through a neat conservatory style entrance with comfortable seating overlooking manicured lawns towards the lough - and there's a lovely traditionally tiled hallway too, setting the tone for a house that has been furnished with character. Accommodation in individually decorated bedrooms has been thoughtfully organised for the maximum comfort and security of guests - not only with phone, TV with video, pressing facilities, but also a safe and fax available on request. There is a lot to do in the area - they're specialists in fly-fishing holidays - and there is a tennis court on site.Children welcome (under 4s free in parents' room). **Rooms 3** (1 suite, 1 junior suite, all no smoking). Rooms service all day. Restaurant: This great little restaurant is open to non-residents in summer, offering good home cooking (notably excellent baking) for morning and afternoon "bites" and a proper menu for lunch and dinner. Everything is meticulously sourced and well cooked - presentation is attractive and service, by local waiting staff, both efficient and friendly. Licensed. **Seats 20** (private room 10). Open to non-residents Jul-Sep & Dec, 8.30-6 (L 12.30-2, D 7-8.30. Set Menu £22). MasterCard, Visa. **Directions:** From Enniskillen take A32 then B82, adjacent to Airport.

Kesh

HOTEL

Lough Erne Hotel

Main St. Kesh Co.Fermanagh BT93 1TF
Tel: 028 6863 1275 Fax: 028 6863 1921
Email: loughernehotel@lakelands.net Web: www.lakelands.net/loughernehotel

In a very attractive location on the banks of the Glendurragh River, this friendly town centre hotel has twelve comfortable rooms with en-suite bath/shower rooms, TV and tea/coffee facilities. The hotel is understandably popular for weddings, as the bar and function rooms overlook the river and have access to an attractive paved riverside walkway and garden. Popular for fishing holidays, it would also make a good base for a family break; there is plenty to do in the area, including golf, watersports and horse-riding. Conferences (250). Fishing, cycling, walking. Off-season breaks.

Garden. Limited wheelchair access. Own parking. Children welcome. Pets permitted in some areas. **Rooms 12** (all en-suite) B&B about £35pps, ss about £5; sc discretionary. Closed 25 Dec. Amex, Diners, MasterCard, Visa. **Directions:** On north-eastern corner of Lough Erne, where A42 joins the A35.

Kesh

PUB/ACCOMMODATION

Lusty Beg Island

Boa Island Kesh Co. Fermanagh BT93 8AD
Tel: 028 686 32032 Fax: 028 686 32033

If you arrive by road, a little ferry takes you over to the island (leave your car on the mainland unless you will be staying on the island), or of course, you can call in by boat. It's an unusual place and worth a visit, if only to call into the pleasant waterside pub for a drink, a cup of tea or an informal bite such as smoked salmon and brown bread. However, you could stay much longer as accommodation is available in lodges, chalets and a motel, all spread relatively inconspicuously around the wooded island. Conferences, corporate entertaining and management training is a speciality and all sorts of activity breaks. Leisure centre with swimming pool, tennis court, fitness suite, sauna. Canoes. Mountain bikes for hire. Nature trail. Visiting boats are welcome; phone ahead for details of barbecues and other theme nights; music Saturday nights. Bar food available daily in summer. (No food Mon & Tues off-season). B&B about £32.50 pps. ss about £12.50. Open all year. Amex, Visa.

Killadeas

HOTEL/RESTAURANT

Manor House Country Hotel

Killadeas Co. Fermanagh BT94 1NY
Tel: 028 6862 2211 Fax: 028 6862 1545
Email: manorhousehotel@lakelands.net Web: www.lakelands.net/manorhousehotel

This impressive lakeside period house makes a fine hotel. The scale of the architecture and the style of furnishings and decor lean very much towards the luxurious in both public areas and accommodation. Spacious bedrooms range from interconecting family rooms to deluxe doubles and romantic suites with canopied four-poster beds. Front rooms have stunning views.Leisure centre, indoor swimming pool. Children under 3 free in parents' room. No pets. **Rooms 46** (all en-suite, 6 suites) B&B about £55pps, ss about £30. **The Belleek Restaurant** is also well positioned to make the most of the lovely view, especially at breakfast and lunchtime. Dominic Almond, who has been head chef "for years" is doing a good job and both food and service match the grand surroundings. Bar meals available 12.30-9 pm daily. Restaurant seats 65 (private room 30). Non-smoking restaurant. Air Conditioning. L&D daily. [*Information on the nearby Inishclare restaurant, bar & marina complex is available from the hotel, which is in common ownership.] Open all year. Belleek Restaurant Amex, MasterCard, Visa. **Directions:** 6 miles from Enniskillen on the B82.

Killadeas

Restaurant

The Waterfront Restaurant

Rosigh Bay Killadeas Co. Fermanagh **Tel: 028 6862 1938**

This beautifully located bar and restaurant has an attractive bar, decorated to a fairly nautical theme with antiques and memorabilia, and a sunny waterside seating area for fine weather. The menu - a fairly extensive à la carte - offers a balanced choice of quite upscale dishes, notably seafood but plenty else besides, including vegetarian dishes. Opening times after Easter:Weds-Sat, 6-9 pm & Sun 12.30-3, followed by teas until 5.30, then the evening a la carte menu. Open daily in July & August. Off season, open Fri, Sat & Sun only, 6-9 pm. MasterCard, Visa.

COUNTY LONDONDERRY

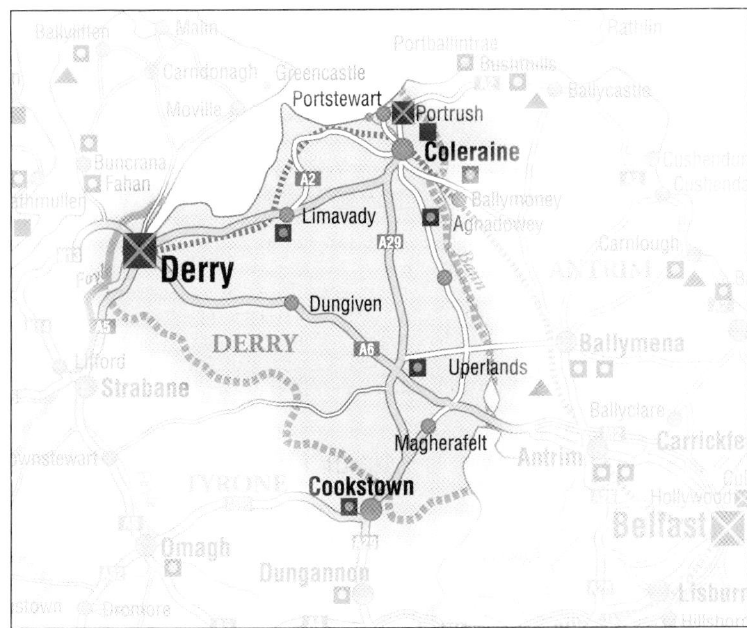

The City of Derry has established itself as a formidable pace-setter as we enter 2002, with the Millennium Complex (opened September 2001) and its impressive Forum Theatre - the largest purpose-built theatre in Ireland - setting the style in architecture, while the renewed interest in the River Foyle has added a fresh dimension to city life.

When the boundaries of its surrounding county were first defined in modern times, this was actually the County of Coleraine, named for the busy little port 30 miles to the northeast, on the River Bann a few miles inland from the Atlantic coast. It was an area long favoured by settlers, for Mountsandel, on the salmon-rich Bann a mile south of Coleraine, is where the 9,000 year old traces of one of the sites of some of the oldest-known houses in Ireland have been found.

Today, Coleraine is the main campus of the University of Ulster, with the vitality of student life spreading to the nearby coastal resorts of Portstewart and Portrush in the area known as the "Golden Triangle", appropriately fringed to the north by the three golden miles of Portstewart Strand. Southwestward from Coleraine, the county - which was re-named after the City of Derry became Londonderry in 1613 - offers a fascinating variety of places and scenery, with large areas of fine farmland being punctuated by ranges of hills, while the rising slopes of the Sperrin Mountains dominate the County's southern boundary.

The road from Belfast to Derry sweeps through the Sperrins by way of the stirringly-named Glenshane Pass, and from its heights you begin to get the first glimpses westward of the mountains of Donegal. This is an appropriate hint of the new atmosphere in the City of Derry itself. This lively place could reasonably claim to be the most senior of all Ireland's modern cities, as it can trace its origins back to a monastery of St Colmcille, otherwise Columba, founded in 546AD. Today, the city - with up-dated port facilities on the River Foyle and a cheerfully restored urban heart - is moving into a vibrant future in which it thrives on the energy drawn from its natural position as the focal point of a larger catchment area which takes in much of Donegal to the west in addition to Londonderry to the east.

The area eastward of Lough Foyle is increasingly popular among discerning visitors, the Roe Valley through Dungiven and Limavady being particularly attractive. The re-establishment of the ferry between Magilligan Point and Greencastle in Donegal across the narrow entrance to Lough Foyle will add a new dimension to the region's infrastructure, as will the up-grading of the increasingly busy City of Derry Airport at Eglinton.

Local Attractions and Information

Bellaghy Bellaghy Bawn (Seamus Heaney centre)	028 79 386812
Castlerock Hezlett House	028 70 848567
City of Derry Airport	028 71 810784
Coleraine Guy L Wilson Daffodil Garden	028 70 344141
Coleraine Tourism Information	028 70 344723
Derry City The Fifth Province - Celtic culture	028 71 373177
Derry City Foyle Arts Centre	028 71 266657
Derry City Foyle Cruises (year round)	028 71 362857
Derry City Foyle Valley Railway Centre	028 71 265234
Derry City The Guildhall	028 71 377335
Derry City Harbour Museum	028 71 377331
Derry City Millennium Forum Theatre	028 71 264426
Derry City Orchard Gallery	028 71 269675
Derry City The Playhouse	028 71 268027
Derry City St Columb's Cathedral	028 71 267313
Derry City Tourism Information	028 71 267284
Derry City Tower Museum	028 71 372411
Downhill Mussenden Temple & Gardens	028 70 848726
Draperstown Plantation of Ulster Visitor Centre	028 79 627800
Garvagh Museum & Heritage Centre	028 29 558216
Limavady Roe Valley & Ness Wood Country Parks	028 77 722074
Limavady Tourism Information	028 77 760307
Magherafelt Tourism Information	028 79 631510
Moneymore Springhill (NT house)	028 86 748210
Sperrin Mountains Sperrins Tourism	028 79 634570

Aghadowey
HOTEL/RESTAURANT

The Brown Trout Golf & Country Inn

209 Agivey Road Aghadowey Co. Londonderry BT51 4AD
Tel: 028 7086 8209 Fax: 028 7086 8878
Email: bill@browntroutinn.com Web: www.browntroutinn.com

Golf is the major attraction at this lively country inn, both on-site and in the locality. Newcomers will soon find friends in the convivial bar, where food is served from noon to 10 pm every day. Spacious en-suite rooms with plenty of space for golfing gear are all on the ground floor, arranged around a garden courtyard. New cottage suites overlooking the golf course (just 100 yards from the main building) are the first of this standard to be completed in Northern Ireland. **Restaurant:** Up a steep staircase (with chair lift for the less able), the restaurant overlooks the garden end of the golf course. Jane O'Hara's good home cooking is based on fresh local ingredients – trout fillet with fresh herbs & lemon butter or sirloin steak with a Bushmills whiskey sauce. High Tea (very popular in this part of the country) is followed by an à la carte dinner menu. Small conference/private parties (40/50); Tennis, horse-riding, golf (9/18), fishing, walking, garden & children's playground available. Children under 4 free in parents' room; cots available). Pets permitted. **Rooms 25** (4 mini-suites, all en-suite) B&B £42.50pps, ss £25. Lift. **Seats 42** (private room, 40). No smoking restaurant. Open all day (7am-10pm) L 12-3 daily, Set Sun L about £10; also à la carte; house wine about £7.95; sc discretionary Toilets wheelchair accessible. Open all year. Amex, Diners, MasterCard, Visa, Switch. **Directions:** Intersection of A54/B66 7 miles south of Coleraine.

Coleraine
RESTAURANT

Charly's Restaurant

34 Newbridge Road Coleraine Co. Londonderry BT52 1TP
Tel: 028 703 52020 Fax: 028 703 55299
Email: chatroom@charlys.com Web: www.charlysrestaurant.com

This big, bright roadside restaurant is inviting, like an American diner, and a great fun place for all age groups, especially the kids. What you get here is good quality fashionable food for all the family - "Charly's Special", a fillet steak with champ, bacon,& garlic mash, is the most expensive dish on the menu at £13.25 - served with speed, efficency and charm. It has heaps of atmosphere and a huge seating capacity but, although tables are turned around quite rapidly, there's no sense that you're being hurried. Most main courses are under £10; it's great quality for the price and service is `terrific - no wonder it's always busy. **Seats 120.** No smoking area; air conditioning. Children welcome. Open daily high season: 11.30-10; (open low season: L&D Tue-Fri, all day Sat & Sun). A la carte except Set Sun L £10.50 (12-2.30, also main menu, 12-9.30). Closed 25-26 Dec & Mon in low season, also Tue-Fri afternoons, 3-5pm. Amex, MasterCard, Visa, Switch. **Directions:** Belfast/Ballymoney line. One mile from New Hospital.

Coleraine

GUESTHOUSE

Greenhill House

24 Greenhill Road Coleraine Co. Londonderry BT51 4EU
Tel: 028 7086 8241 Fax: 028 7086 8365
Email: greenhill.house@btinternet.com Web: www.greenhill.house.btinternet.co.uk

Framed by trees with lovely country views, the Hegarty family's Georgian farmhouse is at the centre of a large working farm. In true Northern tradition, Elizabeth Hegarty is a great baker and greets guests in the drawing room with an afternoon tea which includes a vast array of home-made teabreads, cakes and biscuits. There are two large family rooms and, although not luxurious, the thoughtfulness that has gone into furnishing bedrooms makes them exceptionally comfortable – everything is in just the right place to be convenient. Little touches like fresh flowers, a fruit basket, After Eights, tea & coffee making facilities, hair dryer, bathrobe, good quality clothes hangers and even a torch are way above the standard expected of farmhouse accommodation. There's also a safe, fax machine, iron and trouser press available for guests' use on request. Elizabeth provides a home-cooked residents' dinner based on local ingredients by arrangement, served at 6.30pm – please book by noon. (No wine). Children welcome, cot available. No pets. **Rooms 6** (all en-suite). B&B £25 pps, ss £5. Closed Nov-Feb. MasterCard, Visa. **Directions:** On B66 Greenhill Road off A29 south of Coleraine.

Limavady

RESTAURANT

The Lime Tree

60 Catherine Street Limavady Co. Londonderry BT49 9DB
Tel: 028 7776 4300 Fax: 028 7776 4300
Email: info@limetreerest Web: www.limetreerest.com.

Stanley and Maria Matthews' restaurant is on a main street of this handsome, wide-streeted town in a beautiful and prosperous part of the country. There is a great sense of contentment about The Lime Tree; the room is pleasant but quite modest, Stanley is a fine chef and Maria a welcoming and solicitous hostess. Ingredients are carefully sourced, many of them local; menus are generous, with a classical base that Stanley works on to give popular dishes a new twist, thus sauté lambs kidneys in a puff pastry case with red wine & shallot sauce alongside crab cakes with a chilli oil dressing; perennial favourites include Hunters sirloins steak with a crushed black peppercorn sauce and hake goujons rolled in chopped nuts, with tartare sauce or a lemon mayonnaise dip. Set menus include a keenly-priced busines lunch, and they also offer a good à la carte lunch menu, with a dressier version in the evening. They also do theme nights "to try out different dishes and ideas". Good cooking and good value go hand in hand with warm hospitality at The Lime Tree. Limavady is lucky to have it. Children welcome. **Seats 30.** No smoking area. L 12-2 (Wed-Sun) D 6-9 (Wed-Sat; Sun to 8.30). Set L £7.50; Set Sun L £13.50. Early D £14.50 (6-7 pm only, excl Sat); also à la carte; house wine £9.95; sc discretionary. Toilets wheelchair accessible. Closed Mon,Tue (Sat. lunch booking only), 1 week Feb/Mar, 1 week Jul & Nov. Amex, MasterCard, Visa, Switch. **Directions:** On the outskirts of town, main Derry-Limavady road.

Limavady

B&B

Streeve Hill

25 Dowland Road Limavady Co. Londonderry BT49 9DB
Tel: 02877 766 563 Fax: 02877 768 285

Peter and June Welsh have welcomed guests to their lovely 18th century home since they moved here in 1996. It is a very charming house, with a Palladian facade of rose brick and fine views over parkland towards the Sperrin Mountains – but there is also beauty closer to home, in and around the house itself and in the nearby gardens of their former home, Drenagh. The stylish country house accommodation at Streeve Hill is extremely comfortable and the food and hospitality exceptional. Although the maximum number they can accommodate is six, they are happy for guests to bring friends to dine (provided 24 hours notice is given). They also cater for private dinner parties. Breakfast is another high point and, in the event of fine summer weather, it can be even more enjoyable if served on the terrace outside the drawing room Horse-riding, walking, fishing, garden available. Children welcome (under 3s free in parents' room; cots available). No Pets. Residents D about £30 (inc. their friends). Please give 24hrs notice. **Rooms 3** (all en-suite & no-smoking,1 shower only). B&B £45pps, ss £10; sc discretionary. Closed 21 dec-2 Jan. Amex, MasterCard, Visa. **Directions:** From Limavady take B021 for Castlerock, follow Estate wall on right. 200 yards past lodge turn right at end of wall.

Londonderry
HOTEL
RESTAURANT

Beech Hill Country House Hotel

32 Ardmore Road Londonderry Co. Londonderry BT47 3QP
Tel: 028 71 34 9279 Fax: 028 71 34 5366
Email: info@beech-hill.com Web: www.beech-hill.com

Beech Hill is just a couple of miles south of Londonderry, in a lovely setting of 42 acres of peaceful woodland, waterfalls and gardens. Built in 1729, the house has retained many of its original details and proprietor Patsy O'Kane makes an hospitable and caring hostess. Comfortable bedrooms vary in size and outlook – many overlook the gardens – but all are thoughtfully and attractively furnished with Mrs O'Kane's ever-growing collection of antiques. Public rooms include a good-sized bar, a fine restaurant (in what was originally the snooker room, now extended into a new conservatory overlooking the gardens) and, unusually, a private chapel, now used for meetings, private parties or small weddings. Facilities include picnic areas in the grounds for fine weather and a fitness suite with sauna, steam room, jacuzzi and weight room. The US Marines had their headquarters here in World War II and an informative small museum of the US Marine Friendship Association is housed within the hotel.Conference/banqueting (100); secretarial services. Fitness centre. Tennis, garden, walking. Children welcome (under 1 free in parents' room; cots available). Pets by arrangement. **Rooms 27** (4 suites, 2 junior suites, 8 executive rooms, 1 for disabled).Lift. B&B £60pps, ss £20 sc discretionary. Closed 25 Dec. Amex, MasterCard, Visa, Switch. **Directions:** From main A6 Derry - Belfast road, turn off at Faughan bridge, drive 1 mile to Ardmore chapel - Hotel is opposite.

Londonderry
RESTAURANT

Browns Bar & Brasserie

1-2 Bond Hill Londonderry Co. Londonderry
Tel: 028 71 345180 Fax: 028 71 345180 Email: browns.tinvtee@aol.com

The city's leading contemporary restaurant has a devoted local following and no wonder - the welcome (and service) may be a little on the cool side, but the cooking's cool too and it's the food that keeps them coming back for more. Recent refurbishment has resulted in a relaxed space with subtle blends of natural colours, textures and finishes - and proprietor-chef Ivan Taylor's new menus have also changed, bringing a more pared-down approach to the food, in dishes with a cleaner, fresher taste. His cooking hasn't changed though - as ever, it is terrific. From a wide-ranging menu, dishes that attracted particular praise on a recent visit included a starter of fine beans, Roquefort & walnuts with grilled pancetta & duck 'crackliing' which was an inspired combination and a perfectly cooked main dish: mustard glazed tenderloin of pork with roast apples, mushrooms & sauce charcutière - a good example of how to modernise classics without forgetting the basics. Desserts ring some changes with the classics - or espresso, vin santo & home-made biscotti might make a pleasing alternative. All round, there's imagination, a certain amount of style, dedication and consistency - not bad after 15 years in business.Tue-Sat: L12-2.15; D 5.30-10.30. Closed Sun, Mon. & Closed 1st two weeks Aug. Diners, MasterCard, Visa, Laser, Switch. **Directions:** Opposite the old Waterside railway station.

Londonderry
RESTAURANT

Fitzroy's

3 Carlisle Road/2-4 Bridge Street Londonderry Co. Londonderry
Tel: 028 71 266211 Fax: 028 71264060
Email: fitzroys@lineone.net

This large modern restaurant beside the Foyle Shopping Centre is on two floors and very handy for shoppers, visitors or pre/post-theatre meals. Menus change through the day and offer a wide range of food in the current international fashion - rack of lamb with ratatouille & pesto oil indicates the evening style while a large daytime menu ranges from hot breakfasts and designer sandwiches to a range of substantial 'chef's specialities'. A useful one to know about. Food served all day from 9.30 am (Breakfast to 12.30, lunch to 6, D6-10, à la carte; Sun brasserie menus all day (12-8). Early closing Mon/Tue (7pm). House wine from £7. Closed 26 Dec. Amex, MasterCard, Visa, Laser, Switch. **Directions:** Beside Foyle shopping centre.

Londonderry
HOTEL

Hastings Everglades Hotel

Prehen Road Londonderry Co. Londonderry BT47 2NH
Tel: 02871 346 722 Fax: 02871 349 200
Email: res@egh.hastingshotels.com Web: www.hastingshotels.com

Situated on the banks of the River Foyle, close to City of Derry airport and just a mile from the city centre, this modern hotel is well located for business and pleasure. Like all the Hastings Hotels, Everglades Hotel undergoes an ongoing system of refurbishment and upgrading, a policy which pays off in comfortable well-maintained bedrooms and public areas which never feel dated. Accommodation is all of a high standard, with good amenities including air conditioning and a spacious desk area, although beds are only standard size which is now unusual in a hotel of this class (and unnecessary as rooms are generally spacious). The hotel is well located for golf, with the City of Derry course just a couple of minutes away and six other courses, including Royal Portrush, within driving distance. Conference/banqueting (500/350); secretarial services; video conferencing. Wheelchair accessible. Own parking. Children under 14 free in parents' room; cots available. No pets. **Rooms 64** (2 suites, 4 junior suites, 4 executive, 24 no-smoking, 1 for disabled). Lift. B&B £67pps, ss £30; no sc. Closed 25 Dec. Amex, Diners, MasterCard, Visa, Switch. **Directions:** Situated in norhtwest, take N2 from Belfast then A6 signposted to Londonderry.

Londonerry
HOTEL

The Trinity Hotel

22-24 Strand Road Londonerry Co. Londonerry BT48 7AB
Tel: 02871 271271 Fax: 02871 271277

Entry to this new hotel is a little strange - you by-pass the ground floor bar and head upstairs, as reception is on the first floor. However, once there it's worth the trip, as it's a very pleasant contemporary hotel, conveniently located, moderately priced and a great asset to the city. Bedrooms aren't especially big, but they are cosy and comfortably furnished - a good base for doing Derry on foot. [* A sister hotel, Quality Hotel Da Vinci's, has recently opened, at 15 Culmore Road, Derry city. Tel: 028 71279111. Room rate, about £50].Conference/banqueting (160/80) secretarial services. Children welcome (under 2s free in parents' room; cots available). Wheelchair accessible. No Pets. **Rooms 40** (2 suites, 2 for disabled). Lift. Room rate about £45 pps, ss about £25. Children welcome. Nearby parking. Amex, Diners, MasterCard, Visa. **Directions:** At end of Strand road opposite pedestrianised area.

Upperlands
COUNTRY HOUSE
RESTAURANT

Ardtara Country House

8 Gorteade Road Upperlands
Nr. Maghera Co. Londonderry BT46 5SA
Tel: 028796 44490 Fax: 028796 45080

Former home to the Clark linen milling family, Ardtara is now an attractive, elegantly decorated Victorian country house with a genuinely hospitable atmosphere. Well-proportioned rooms have antique furnishings and fresh flowers. All the large, luxuriously furnished bedrooms enjoy views of the garden and surrounding countryside and have king size beds and original fireplaces, while bathrooms combine practicality with period details, some including freestanding baths and fireplaces. Breakfast is a high point, so allow time to enjoy it. Private parties catered. Tennis, woodland walk, golf practice tee. No dogs. Conferences/Banqueting (40/65). **Rooms 8** (all en-suite) B&B about £75pps, No ss. **Restaurant:** In a dining room converted from its previous use as a snooker room – still with full Victorian skylight and original hunting frieze – the chef continues the philosophy of using seasonal and local ingredients and offers a balanced choice on the menus, with game well represented in season. **Seats 40** (private room, 12) No smoking restaurant. L&D.Ring to check opening times off-season; closed 25-26 Dec. Amex, MasterCard, Visa. **Directions:** A29 to Maghera/Coleraine; follow the sign to Kilrea until reaching Ardtara.

COUNTY TYRONE

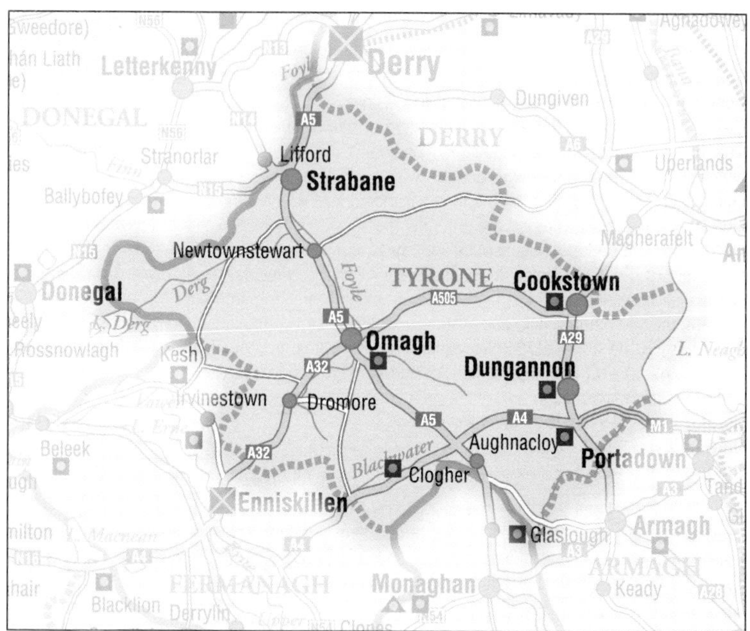

With the USA leading the world into 2002 and the years beyond, it's intriguing to reflect that some of the key people in that great nation's creation had clearcut family roots in Tyrone, and these Transatlantic connections are celebrated at a number of locations.

Tyrone is Northern Ireland's most extensive county, so it is something of a surprise for the traveller to discover that its geography appears to be largely dominated by a range of mountains of modest height, and nearly half of these peaks seem to be in the neighbouring county of Londonderry.

Yet such is the case with Tyrone and the Sperrins. The village of Sperrin itself towards the head of Glenelly may be in Tyrone, but the highest peak of Sawel (678 m), which looms over it, is actually right on the county boundary. But as well, much of the county is upland territory and moorland, giving the impression that the Sperrins are even more extensive than is really the case.

In such a land, the lower country and the fertile valleys gleam like jewels, and there's often a vivid impression of a living - and indeed prosperity - being wrested from a demanding environment. It's a character-forming sort of place, so it's perhaps understandable that it was the ancestral homeland of a remarkable number of early American Presidents, and this connection is commemorated in the Ulster American Folk Park a few miles north of the county town of Omagh.

Forest parks abound, while attractive towns like Castlederg and Dungannon, as well as villages in the uplands and along the charming Clogher Valley, provide entertainment and hospitality for visitors refreshed by the wide open spaces of the moorlands and the mountains. And these communities have a growing sense of local pride - in October 2001, it was confirmed that Dungannon was winner of the Tidiest Town & Village Award.

Local Attractions and Information

Castlederg Visitor Centre (Davy Crockett links)	028 81 670795
Clogher Clogher Valley Rural Centre	028 85 548872
Coagh Kinturk Cultural Centre	028 86 736512
Cookstown Drum Manor Forest Park	028 86 762774
Cookstown Wellbrook Beetling Mill (Corkhill)	028 86 748210
Cranagh (Glenelly) Sperrin Heritage Centre	028 81 648142
Creggan (nr Carrickmore) Visitor Centre	028 80 761112
Dungannon Heritage Centre	028 87 724187
Dungannon Tourism Information	028 87 767259
Dungannon Tyrone Crystal	028 87 725335
Dungannon Ulysses S Grant Ancestral Homestead	028 85 557133
Fivemiletown Clogher Valley Railway Exhibition	028 89 521409
Gortin Ulster History Park	028 81 648188
Newtownstewart Baronscourt Forest Park	028 81 661683
Newtownstewart Gateway Centre & Museum	028 81 662414
Omagh Ulster-American Folk Park	028 82 243292
Omagh Tourism Information	028 82 247831
Strabane Gray's Printing Press (US Independence)	028 71 884094
Strabane Tourism Information	028 71 883735
Strabane President Wilson Ancestral Home	028 71 3844

Cookstown

HOTEL

Tullylagan Country House

40B Tullylagan Road Cookstown Co. Tyrone BT80 8UP

Tel: 028867 65100 Fax: 028867 61715

Halfway between Dungannon and Cookstown, this impressive country house hotel is set in 30 acres of grounds, with the Tullylagan River flowing through the estate. The lovely setting enhances a hotel which is particularly notable for friendly and enthusiastic staff. The public areas include a spacious foyer/reception with a fine staircase leading up to a range of well-appointed bedrooms, which vary according to their position in the house (five are shower only), but are all attractively decorated in country house style. The hotel is within 10 minutes drive of two golf courses, and equestrian activities and fishing are also available nearby; weekend and other special breaks offer good value. Conference/banqueting (150/140); video conferencing. Fishing, Walking. Garden. Children's playground; children under 2 free in parents' room; cots available without charge. Wheelchair accessible. Pets permitted. **Rooms 15** (1 suite, 1 junior suite, 13 no-smoking, 2 for disabled).Lift. B&B £34.95 pps, ss £15.Closed 24-26 Dec. Amex, MasterCard, Visa, Switch. **Directions:** 4 miles from Cookstown.

Dungannon

COUNTRY HOUSE

Grange Lodge

7 Grange Road Dungannon Co. Tyrone BT71 7EJ

Tel: 028 8778 4212 Fax: 028 8778 4313

Email: grangelodge@nireland.com

Norah and Ralph Brown's renowned Georgian retreat offers comfort, true family hospitality and extremely good food. The house is on an elevated site just outside Dungannon, with about 20 acres of grounds; mature woodland and gardens (producing food for the table and flowers for the house) with views over lush countryside. Improvements over the years have been made with great sensitivity and the feeling is of gentle organic growth, culminating in the present warm and welcoming atmosphere. Grange Lodge is furnished unselfconsciously, with antiques and family pieces throughout. Bedrooms (and bathrooms) are exceptionally comfortable and thoughtful in detail. Norah's home cooking is superb and, although they no longer accept bookings from non-residents for dinner, they will cater for groups of 10-30. Grange Lodge is fully licensed and dinner menus change daily (in consultation with guests). Resident dinner (from about £22) must be pre-booked, especially if you want to dine on the day of arrival. Breakfasts are also outstanding, so allow time to indulge: a sumptuous buffet beautifully set out on a polished dining table might typically include a large selection of juices, fruit and cereals and porridge is a speciality, served with a tot of Bushmills whiskey, brown sugar and cream. (Isn't that how everyone takes porridge?) There is, of course, a cooked breakfast menu as well, so go easy on the early temptations, all served with lovely fresh breads and toast and home-made preserves. Just wonderful. (Grange Lodge won the Guide's Denny Breakfast Award for the Ulster Region in 2001.) Banqueting (30) Fishing, walking, garden, snooker. Not suitable for children under 12. Rooms 5 (3 shower only) B&B £39 pps, ss £16. Closed 20 Dec-1 Feb. MasterCard, Visa **Directions:** 1 mile from M1 junction 15. A29 Armagh, left at Grange sign; next right & first white walled entrance on right.

Omagh

GUESTHOUSE/RESTAURANT

Hawthorn House

72 Old Mountfield Road Omagh Co. Tyrone BT79 7EN
Tel: 028 8225 2005 Fax: 028 8225 2005
Email: hawthorn@lineone.net Web: www.hawthornhouse.co.uk

On the edge of the town, in a lovely part of the country at the foot of the Sperrin Mountains, Hawthorn House was only established in the autumn of 1997 and yet is already recognised as one of the leading guesthouses and restaurants in Ulster. Owner-chef Michael Gaine is putting years of experience in the hotel business to work in this fine venture, and is supported by an excellent team. Bedrooms are large and comfortable, with all the amenities expected of quality accommodation; further bedrooms (including one for disabled), a bistro bar and conference facilities were under construction at the time of the Guide's most recent visit and are due for completion for the 2002 season. Public areas are also furnished to a high standard and warm hospitality and helpful staff ensure guests' comfort, in both the accommodation and the restaurant. Conference/banqueting (60/80). Garden. Children welcome (under 10s free in parents' room; cots available without charge). Special breaks offered. No Pets. **Rooms 5** (1 shower only). B&B £30pps, ss £10. Open all year. **Restaurant:** Michael Gaine presents tempting modern menus for both lunch and dinner. Sunday lunch offers a nicely judged combination of traditional and more adventurous dishes. Seats 60 (private room, 20). No smoking area. Children welcome. L 12-2.30 daily, D 7-9.30 daily, Set L £10, Set Sun L & D £15; à la carte also available; house wines from £10. sc discretionary. MasterCard, Visa, Switch. **Directions:** 200 metres from Omagh Leisure Complex.

LOCATION	ESTABLISHMENT	Business Hotel	Conference Centre	Banqueting	Leisure Centre	Golf	Family Friendly	Pet Friendly	No Smoking Restaurant	Sunday Dining	Open Christmas	Off-season Breaks
DUBLIN CITY												
Dublin 1	Chapter One Restaurant			•								
Dublin 1	Clarion Hotel Dublin IFSC	•	•	•	•		•			•		•
Dublin 1	Expresso Bar Café									•		
Dublin 1	Morrison Hotel		•				•			•		•
Dublin 1	Panem									•		
Dublin 2	Alexander Hotel	•	•	•	•							•
Dublin 2	The Bad Ass Café						•			•		
Dublin 2	Bewley's Principal Hotel	•					•					•
Dublin 2	Brooks Hotel		•							•	•	
Dublin 2	Brownes Brasserie and Townhouse		•									
Dublin 2	Buswells Hotel									•		
Dublin 2	Café Mao									•		
Dublin 2	Central Hotel	•	•	•								•
Dublin 2	The Chili Club									•		
Dublin 2	The Clarence Hotel	•	•	•			•			•		
Dublin 2	The Commons Restaurant		•	•								
Dublin 2	Conrad International	•		•								
Dublin 2	Cooke's Café									•		
Dublin 2	Da Pino						•			•		
Dublin 2	The Davenport Hotel	•	•	•	•						•	•
Dublin 2	Dish Restaurant						•			•		
Dublin 2	The Dome Restaurant						•					
Dublin 2	Dunne & Crescenzi									•		
Dublin 2	Elephant & Castle						•			•		
Dublin 2	Fado Restaurant						•					
Dublin 2	The Fitzwilliam Hotel	•	•	•					•		•	•
Dublin 2	The Gotham Cafe									•		
Dublin 2	The Grafton Capital	•	•				•			•		•
Dublin 2	Hilton Dublin Hotel	•	•	•			•			•		•
Dublin 2	Kilkenny Restaurant & Café						•			•		

LOCATION	ESTABLISHMENT	Business Hotel	Conference Centre	Banqueting	Leisure Centre	Golf	Family Friendly	Pet Friendly	No Smoking Restaurant	Sunday Dining	Open Christmas	Off-season Breaks
Dublin 2	La Cave Wine Bar & Restaurant			•						•		
Dublin 2	La Mère Zou						•			•		
Dublin 2	La Stampa Hotel & Restaurant									•		
Dublin 2	Le Meridien Shelbourne	•	•	•			•					
Dublin 2	Les Frères Jacques						•					
Dublin 2	The Mercer Hotel	•	•	•			•					•
Dublin 2	The Merrion Hotel	•		•						•	•	
Dublin 2	The Morgan	•								•		•
Dublin 2	Pasta Fresca						•			•		
Dublin 2	Rajdoot Tandoori						•			•		
Dublin 2	Saagar Indian Restaurant						•		•	•		
Dublin 2	Stephen's Green Hotel	•			•							
Dublin 2	Temple Bar Hotel	•		•								
Dublin 2	Westbury Hotel	•		•						•	•	
Dublin 3	Clontarf Castle Hotel	•	•	•			•			•		•
Dublin 4	Aberdeen Lodge		•								•	•
Dublin 4	Bella Cuba Restaurant									•		
Dublin 4	Berkeley Court Hotel	•	•	•							•	•
Dublin 4	Bewley's Hotel, Ballsbridge	•								•		
Dublin 4	Blakes Townhouse										•	•
Dublin 4	Burlington Hotel	•	•	•						•	•	
Dublin 4	Cedar Lodge											•
Dublin 4	Expresso Bar Cafe									•		
Dublin 4	The Four Seasons Hotel	•	•	•	•					•	•	
Dublin 4	Furama Restaurant			•						•		
Dublin 4	Herbert Park Hotel	•	•				•			•	•	•
Dublin 4	The Hibernian Hotel	•	•	•			•			•		•
Dublin 4	Jurys Ballsbridge The Towers	•	•	•	•							
Dublin 4	Jurys Ballsbridge Hotel		•	•	•		•			•		•
Dublin 4	Jurys Montrose Hotel	•	•				•			•	•	•
Dublin 4	Lansdowne Manor	•	•				•		•			•
Dublin 4	Merrion Hall										•	•
Dublin 4	Merrion Inn									•		

LOCATION	ESTABLISHMENT	Business Hotel	Conference Centre	Banqueting	Leisure Centre	Golf	Family Friendly	Pet Friendly	No Smoking Restaurant	Sunday Dining	Open Christmas	Off-season Breaks
Dublin 4	The Mespil Hotel						•			•		
Dublin 4	O'Connells in Ballsbridge						•			•		
Dublin 4	Pembroke Townhouse	•					•					
Dublin 4	Roly's Bistro						•			•		
Dublin 4	The Schoolhouse Hotel	•	•				•			•		•
Dublin 6	Dunville Place						•			•		
Dublin 6	Nectar Juice Bar						•			•		
Dublin 6	Poppadom Indian Restaurant									•		
Dublin 6	Zen Restaurant									•		
Dublin 7	Chief O'Neill's Hotel	•	•	•			•			•		
Dublin 7	The Hole in the Wall									•		
Dublin 7	Kelly & Ping, Bar & Restaurant			•						•		•
Dublin 7	The Old Jameson Distillery		•	•			•			•		
Dublin 8	Locks Restaurant						•					
Dublin 8	The Old Dublin Restaurant			•								
Dublin 13	Marine Hotel			•	•					•		•
Dublin 14	Indian Brasserie			•			•			•		
Dublin 22	Bewley's Hotel at Newlands Cross	•								•		
Dublin 22	Browns Barn						•			•	•	
Dublin 22	Jurys Green Isle Hotel	•	•	•		•		•		•	•	•
Dublin 22	Kingswood Country House									•		•
Dublin 22	Red Cow Moran's Hotel	•	•	•			•			•		
COUNTY DUBLIN												
Blackrock	Dali's Restaurant									•		
Blackrock	Radisson SAS St Helen's Hotel	•	•								•	
Dalkey	Kish Restaurant									•		
Dalkey	Munkberrys Restaurant									•		
Dalkey	The Queen's Bar & Restaurant									•		
Dalkey	Thai House Restaurant									•		
Dublin Airport	Great Southern Hotel	•	•	•								
Dun Laoghaire	Cumberland Lodge						•					
Dun Laoghaire	Duzy's Cafe									•		

LOCATION	ESTABLISHMENT	Business Hotel	Conference Centre	Banqueting	Leisure Centre	Golf	Family Friendly	Pet Friendly	No Smoking Restaurant	Sunday Dining	Open Christmas	Off-season Breaks
Dun Laoghaire	Gresham Royal Marine Hotel	•	•	•							•	
Dun Laoighaire	Roly @ The Pavilion									•		
Howth	Abbey Tavern		•	•								
Howth	Aqua Restaurant			•						•		
Howth	Casa Pasta						•			•		
Howth	King Sitric Fish Restaurant & Accommodation						•					
Killiney	Fitzpatrick Castle Dublin	•	•	•	•		•			•		
Lucan	Finnstown Country House Hotel	•	•	•	•		•	•		•	•	
Malahide	Beanos									•		
Malahide	Bon Appetit		•						•			
Malahide	Cruzzo Bar & Restaurant						•			•		
Malahide	Le Restaurant 12A									•		
Malahide	Siam Thai Restaurant									•		
Monkstown	The Purty Kitchen									•		
Portmarnock	Portmarnock Hotel & Golf Links	•	•	•		•				•	•	
Saggart	Citywest Hotel Conference Leisure & Golf Resort	•	•	•	•	•				•		
Stillorgan	Stillorgan Park Hotel	•	•	•			•			•	•	
Swords	Lukas Restaurant									•		
Swords	The Old Schoolhouse			•						•		
COUNTY CARLOW												
Bagenalstown	Lorum Old Rectory							•				
Ballon	Sherwood Park House						•		•			
Borris	The Step House							•				
Carlow	The Beams Restaurant						•					
Leighlinbridge	The Lord Bagenal Inn		•	•			•			•		•
COUNTY CAVAN												
Ballinagh	Lacken Mill House & Gardens						•	•				•
Ballyconnell	Slieve Russell Hotel & Country Club	•	•	•	•	•	•			•	•	•
Belturbet	Erne Bistro						•		•	•		
Belturbet	International Fishing Centre						•		•		•	
Blacklion	MacNean House & Bistro						•			•		•

LOCATION	ESTABLISHMENT	Business Hotel	Conference Centre	Banqueting	Leisure Centre	Golf	Family Friendly	Pet Friendly	No Smoking Restaurant	Sunday Dining	Open Christmas	Off-season Breaks
Cavan	Hotel Kilmore	•	•	•			•			•		•
Kingscourt	Cabra Castle Hotel & Golf Club	•	•	•		•	•	•	•			
Mountnugent	Ross House & Castle						•	•				
COUNTY CLARE												
Ballyvaughan	Aillwee Cave									•		
Ballyvaughan	Gregans Castle Hotel									•		•
Ballyvaughan	Hyland's Hotel						•			•		•
Ballyvaughan	Monks Bar & Restaurant						•			•		
Ballyvaughan	Whitethorn Restaurant						•		•	•		
Bunratty	Bunratty Castle Hotel						•					•
Bunratty	Bunratty Manor Hotel	•								•		
Bunratty	Fitzpatrick Bunratty Hotel	•	•	•	•		•			•		•
Clarecastle	Carnelly House		•				•				•	
Corofin	Clifden House						•					
Doolin	Aran View House Hotel						•	•	•	•		•
Doolin	Ballinalacken Castle Country House							•	•	•		
Doolin	Cullinans Restaurant & Guesthouse									•		
Doolin	Doolin Crafts Gallery						•					
Ennis	Newpark House						•	•				
Ennis	Old Ground Hotel	•	•	•			•			•		•
Ennis	Quality Auburn Lodge Hotel	•	•	•			•			•		•
Ennis	Temple Gate Hotel	•	•	•						•		•
Ennis	West County Conference & Leisure Hotel	•	•	•	•		•			•	•	•
Ennis	Woodstock Hotel & Golf Club	•	•	•	•	•	•			•		•
Kilbaha	Anvil Farm Guesthouse						•	•				
Kilkee	Halpins Townhouse Hotel											•
Kilkee	Ocean Cove Golf & Leisure Hotel	•	•	•		•	•			•	•	•
Killaloe	Waterman's Lodge hotel	•	•				•			•		•
Lahinch	Aberdeen Arms Hotel						•			•		•
Lahinch	Barrtra Seafood Restaurant						•					
Lisdoonvarna	Sheedy's Country House Hotel								•	•		
Miltown Malbay	Berry Lodge						•			•	•	

LOCATION	ESTABLISHMENT	Business Hotel	Conference Centre	Banqueting	Leisure Centre	Golf	Family Friendly	Pet Friendly	No Smoking Restaurant	Sunday Dining	Open Christmas	Off-season Breaks
Miltown Malbay	Black Oak										•	
Mountshannon	An Cupán Caifé									•		
Newmarket-on-Fergus	Clare Inn Golf & Leisure Hotel	•	•	•	•	•	•			•	•	•
Newmarket-on-Fergus	Dromoland Castle Hotel		•	•	•	•				•	•	
Shannon	Oakwood Arms Hotel	•	•	•	•					•		•
Shannon	Quality Hotel Shannon						•			•	•	
Shannon	Shannon Great Southern Hotel	•	•	•						•		
Tulla	Flappers Restaurant						•					
CORK CITY												
Cork	Bully's Restaurant						•			•		
Cork	The Crow's Nest Bar & Restaurant									•		
Cork	The Douglas Hide									•		
Cork	Hayfield Manor Hotel	•	•		•				•	•	•	
Cork	Hotel Isaacs	•								•		•
Cork	Imperial Hotel	•	•	•			•			•		•
Cork	Isaacs Restaurant								•			
Cork	The Ivory Tower								•			
Cork	Jurys Cork Hotel	•		•	•		•			•		•
Cork	Jurys Cork Inn						•					
Cork	The Kingsley Hotel	•	•		•					•		•
Cork	Lancaster Lodge						•		•		•	
Cork	Lotamore House							•				•
Cork	Lovetts Restaurant & Brasserie								•			
Cork	Maryborough House Hotel	•	•	•	•					•		•
Cork	Pl Restaurant						•			•	•	
Cork	Proby's Bistro						•					
Cork	Rochestown Park Hotel	•	•	•	•			•		•	•	
Cork	Seven North Mall						•					
COUNTY CORK												
Ahakista	Ahakista Bar						•	•				
Ballinadee	Glebe House						•	•				

LOCATION	ESTABLISHMENT	Business Hotel	Conference Centre	Banqueting	Leisure Centre	Golf	Family Friendly	Pet Friendly	No Smoking Restaurant	Sunday Dining	Open Christmas	Off-season Breaks
Ballycotton	Bayview Hotel			•								
Ballycotton	Spanish Point Restaurant & Accom						•	•		•		
Ballylickey	Larchwood House Restaurant						•					
Baltimore	Baltimore Bay Guest House										•	
Baltimore	Baltimore Harbour Resort Hotel						•					
Baltimore	Bushe's Bar						•			•		
Baltimore	Casey's of Baltimore											•
Baltimore	Customs House Restaurant								•			
Baltimore	The Mews Baltimore									•		
Bantry	O'Connor's Seafood Restaurant									•		
Bantry	Sea View House Hotel						•	•		•		•
Bantry	The Westlodge Hotel	•	•	•	•		•			•		•
Blarney	Blarney Park Hotel	•	•	•	•		•			•	•	•
Butlerstown	Butlerstown House							•				
Butlerstown	Otto's Creative Catering						•	•			•	
Carrigaline	Carrigaline Court Hotel	•	•	•	•					•		
Carrigaline	Glenwood House	•						•				•
Carrigaline	Gregory's Restaurant						•			•		
Castlelyons	Ballyvolane House						•		•	•		
Castletownshend	Bow Hall						•					
Castletownshend	Mary Ann's Bar & Restaurant			•			•			•		
Clonakilty	An Sugan									•		
Clonakilty	Dunmore House Hotel			•			•			•		
Clonakilty	Emmet Hotel									•		•
Clonakilty	Fionnuala's Little Italian Restaurant						•					
Clonakilty	Lodge & Spa at Inchydoney Island			•				•		•		•
Cloyne	Barnabrow Country House		•		•		•		•	•		
Cloyne	The Cross of Cloyne			•								
Cobh	Robin Hill House & Restaurant						•			•		•
Cobh	WatersEdge Hotel	•					•		•	•		•
Cork	Great Southern Hotel Cork Airport	•										
Fermoy	Castlehyde Hotel	•	•							•	•	
Glanmire	The Barn Restaurant									•	•	

LOCATION	ESTABLISHMENT	Business Hotel	Conference Centre	Banqueting	Leisure Centre	Golf	Family Friendly	Pet Friendly	No Smoking Restaurant	Sunday Dining	Open Christmas	Off-season Breaks
Glanworth	Glanworth Mill Country Inn									•		•
Goleen Harbour	The Heron's Cove									•		
Kilbrittain	Casino House		•				•			•		
Kinsale	The Blue Haven Hotel	•					•			•		•
Kinsale	The Bulman						•			•		
Kinsale	Crackpots Restaurant						•			•		
Kinsale	Fishy Fishy & The Gourmet Store								•	•		
Kinsale	Jean Marc's Chow House									•		
Kinsale	Max's Wine Bar									•		
Kinsale	Trident Hotel	•	•	•	•	•				•		•
Kinsale	Vintage Restaurant									•	•	
Macroom	The Castle Hotel & Leisure Centre				•			•		•		•
Mallow	Longueville House		•				•		•	•		•
Midleton	Ballymaloe House						•			•		•
Midleton	Glenview House						•				•	
Midleton	Loughcarrig House						•					
Midleton	Old Midleton Distillery		•	•					•			
Midleton	Rathcoursey House							•		•	•	•
Monkstown	The Bosun	•					•			•		
Oysterhaven	Oz - Haven									•		
Rosscarbery	Celtic Ross Hotel	•	•	•	•		•					•
Rosscarbery	O'Callaghan-Walshe						•					
Schull	Corthna Lodge Country House							•			•	•
Schull	Stanley House						•					
Skibbereen	Kalbo's Bistro						•			•		
Skibbereen	O'Sullivans						•	•				
Skibbereen	Ty Ar Mor Seafood Restaurant									•		
Skibereen	West Cork Hotel						•	•		•		•
Timoleague	Lettercollum House						•					
Union Hall	Dinty's Bar						•	•				
Youghal	Aherne's Seafood Restaurant						•			•		•
Youghal	Ballymakeigh House & Brownes Restaurant						•			•		
Youghal	Old Imperial Hotel with Coachhouse						•			•	•	

LOCATION	ESTABLISHMENT	Business Hotel	Conference Centre	Banqueting	Leisure Centre	Golf	Family Friendly	Pet Friendly	No Smoking Restaurant	Sunday Dining	Open Christmas	Off-season Breaks
COUNTY DONEGAL												
Annagry	Danny Minnie's Restaurant						•		•	•		
Ardara	The Green Gate						•	•			•	
Ardara	Nancy's Bar						•			•		
Ardara	Woodhill House		•				•	•				
Ballybofey	Jackson's Hotel	•	•	•	•		•				•	•
Ballybofey	Kee's Hotel		•	•	•					•	•	•
Bruckless	Bruckless House						•					
Bunbeg	Ostan Gweedore Hotel & Leisure Centre				•		•		•	•		•
Bundoran	Le Chateaubrianne						•		•	•		
Carndonagh	Corncrake Restaurant								•	•		
Donegal	St. Ernan's House Hotel								•			
Dunfanaghy	The Mill Restaurant & Accommodation								•	•		
Dunkineely	Castle Murray House Hotel								•	•		•
Fahan	St. John's Country House						•			•		
Greencastle	Kealys Seafood Bar									•		
Killybegs	Bay View Hotel	•		•	•							•
Laghey	Coxtown Manor						•		•	•	•	
Letterkenny	Castle Grove Country House Hotel								•			•
Letterkenny	Letterkenny Court Quality Hotel						•			•		•
Lough Eske	Ardnamona House		•	•			•	•				
Lough Eske	Harvey's Point Country Hotel			•				•	•		•	•
Lougheske	Rhu - Gorse						•					
Portsalon	Croaghross					•	•		•			
Rathmullan	Fort Royal Hotel							•	•			•
Rathmullan	Rathmullan House						•		•		•	•
Rossnowlagh	Sand House Hotel						•		•	•		•
Rossnowlagh	Smugglers Creek Inn						•		•	•		
COUNTY GALWAY												
Galway City	Ardilaun House Hotel	•	•	•	•			•	•	•		•
Galway City	Brennan's Yard Hotel		•							•		

LOCATION	ESTABLISHMENT	Business Hotel	Conference Centre	Banqueting	Leisure Centre	Golf	Family Friendly	Pet Friendly	No Smoking Restaurant	Sunday Dining	Open Christmas	Off-season Breaks
Galway City	Corrib Great Southern Hotel	•	•	•	•		•			•		•
Galway City	Galway Bay Hotel, Conference & Leisure Centre	•	•	•	•		•			•		•
Galway City	Glenlo Abbey Hotel	•	•	•		•	•		•	•		•
Galway City	Great Southern Hotel		•	•	•					•		
Galway City	Park House Hotel	•								•		•
Galway City	Radisson SAS Hotel	•	•	•	•		•			•	•	•
Galway City	The Malt House									•		
Galway City	Westwood House Hotel	•	•	•						•		•
Aran Islands	Pier House Restaurant & Guest House						•		•			•
Aran Islands	Teach Nan Phaidai									•		
Ballinasloe	Haydens Gateway Business & Leisure Hotel	•	•	•			•				•	•
Barna	O'Grady's on the Pier						•			•		
Cashel	Cashel House Hotel						•	•	•	•	•	•
Cashel	Zetland Country House								•			•
Clarenbridge	Oyster Manor Hotel	•	•	•			•			•		•
Clarenbridge	Paddy Burkes						•			•		
Clifden	Abbeyglen Castle							•			•	
Clifden	Ardagh Hotel & Restaurant						•	•		•		•
Clifden	Dolphin Beach Country House											•
Clifden	Fire and Ice										•	
Clifden	O'Grady's Seafood Restaurant								•			
Clifden	Quay House								•	•		
Clifden	Rock Glen Country House Hotel									•		•
Clifden	Station House Hotel				•		•		•			•
Clonbur	Ballykine House						•					
Craughwell	Raftery's, The Blazers Bar						•			•		
Craughwell	St. Clerans								•		•	•
Furbo	Connemara Coast Hotel		•	•	•		•		•	•		•
Inishbofin	Day's Inishbofin House Hotel						•			•		
Inishbofin	The Dolphin Restaurant						•		•	•		
Kilcolgan	Moran's Oyster Cottage									•		
Kylemore	Kylemore Abbey Restaurant and Tea House						•		•	•		
Leenane	Killary Lodge		•				•		•			

LOCATION	ESTABLISHMENT	Business Hotel	Conference Centre	Banqueting	Leisure Centre	Golf	Family Friendly	Pet Friendly	No Smoking Restaurant	Sunday Dining	Open Christmas	Off-season Breaks
Leenane	Portfinn Lodge									•		
Letterfrack	Rosleague Manor Hotel						•	•	•	•		•
Moycullen	Moycullen Country House & Restaurant		•						•			
Moycullen	White Gables Restaurant						•			•		
Oranmore	Galway Bay Golf & Country Club Hotel	•	•	•		•	•			•	•	•
Oranmore	Quality Hotel & Leisure Centre, Galway	•	•		•		•		•	•		•
Oughterard	Connemara Gateway Hotel						•					•
Oughterard	Corrib Wave Guesthouse						•					
Oughterard	Currarevagh House								•	•		
Portumna	Shannon Oaks Hotel & Country Club	•	•	•	•	•	•			•	•	•
Recess	Ballynahinch Castle Hotel									•		•
Recess	Lough Inagh Lodge						•	•				•
Renvyle	Renvyle House Hotel					•	•	•	•		•	
Tuam	Cré-na-Cille						•					
Tuam	Finns Bar & Restaurant						•			•		
COUNTY KERRY												
Balldavid	Gorman's Clifftop House & Restaurant								•		•	•
Ballybunion	Harty-Costello Townhouse Bar & Restaurant						•					
Ballybunion	Teach de Broc Countryhouse					•						
Ballyferriter	Tigh an Tobair			•			•		•	•		
Beaufort	The Beaufort Bar & Restaurant						•			•		
Beaufort	Hotel Dunloe Castle	•	•	•	•		•	•				
Caherciveen	Brennan's Restaurant						•			•		
Caherciveen	QC's Bar & Restaurant						•			•		
Caherdaniel	Derrynane Hotel						•	•				•
Cahirciveen	The Quarry Restaurant						•			•		
Camp	The Cottage Restaurant						•			•	•	
Camp	James Ashe						•			•		
Camp	Suan Na Mara						•		•			
Caragh Lake	Caragh Lodge								•			
Caragh Lake	Carrig House Country House & Restaurant							•			•	
Caragh Lake	Hotel Ard-na-Sidhe					•			•	•		

LOCATION	ESTABLISHMENT	Business Hotel	Conference Centre	Banqueting	Leisure Centre	Golf	Family Friendly	Pet Friendly	No Smoking Restaurant	Sunday Dining	Open Christmas	Off-season Breaks
Castlegregory	Spillanes						•			•		
Dingle	Beginish Restaurant									•		
Dingle	Benners Hotel											•
Dingle	The Chart House						•					
Dingle	Cleevaun House						•					
Dingle	Dingle Skellig Hotel		•	•	•		•			•		•
Dingle	Greenmount House						•					
Dingle	Heatons House						•					
Dingle	Pax Guest House						•					
Fenit	West End Bar, Restaurant & Accom						•					
Kenmare	Avoca Handweavers									•		
Kenmare	Dromquinna Manor Hotel	•	•	•			•	•				•
Kenmare	The Lodge						•					
Kenmare	Mulcahys Restaurant									•		
Kenmare	The New Delight						•					
Kenmare	Park Hotel Kenmare								•	•	•	•
Kenmare	The Rosegarden											•
Kenmare	Sheen Falls Lodge		•	•	•		•		•	•	•	•
Killarney	Aghadoe Heights Hotel			•	•		•		•	•		
Killarney	Arbutus Hotel						•			•		•
Killarney	Castlerosse Hotel		•	•	•	•						
Killarney	The Cooperage									•	•	
Killarney	Dromhall Hotel		•	•	•		•	•				•
Killarney	Earls Court House						•		•			
Killarney	Fuchsia House						•					
Killarney	Gaby's Seafood Restaurant						•					
Killarney	Great Southern Hotel Killarney		•	•	•		•			•	•	•
Killarney	Hotel Europe	•	•	•	•		•	•		•		•
Killarney	Killarney Lodge						•					
Killarney	Killarney Park Hotel		•	•	•							
Killarney	Killarney Royal						•			•		•
Killarney	Randles Court Clarion Hotel	•			•		•	•				•
Killorglin	Nick's Seafood Restaurant & Piano Bar						•				•	

LOCATION	ESTABLISHMENT	Business Hotel	Conference Centre	Banqueting	Leisure Centre	Golf	Family Friendly	Pet Friendly	No Smoking Restaurant	Sunday Dining	Open Christmas	Off-season Breaks
Listowel	Allo's Restaurant, Bar & Bistro								•			•
Portmagee	The Moorings						•					•
Tahilla	Tahilla Cove Country House						•	•			•	
Tralee	Abbey Gate Hotel		•	•			•		•	•	•	•
Tralee	Ballygarry House Hotel	•	•	•			•			•		•
Tralee	Barrow Guest House		•									•
Tralee	Castlemorris House										•	
Tralee	Quality Hotel Tralee	•					•			•		
Tralee	Restaurant Uno									•		
Ventry	Skipper						•					
Waterville	Butler Arms Hotel			•	•							
Waterville	The Huntsman						•					
Waterville	The Smuggler's Inn						•					•
COUNTY KILDARE												
Athy	Coursetown Country House							•				
Ballymore Eustace	Ballymore Inn						•					
Curragh	Martinstown House								•			
Leixlip	Leixlip House Hotel	•	•	•						•		
Maynooth	Moyglare Manor		•							•		
Naas	Killashee House Hotel	•	•	•	•					•		•
Naas	Les Olives Restaurant									•		
Narraghmore	The Pond House						•	•			•	
Straffan	Barberstown Castle	•	•	•		•				•		
Straffan	The K Club	•	•	•	•	•				•	•	•
COUNTY KILKENNY												
Bennettsbridge	Nicholas Mosse Irish Country Shop						•			•		
Graiguenamanagh	Waterside									•		
Kilkenny	Butler House		•									
Kilkenny	The Hibernian Hotel	•	•							•		
Kilkenny	Hotel Kilkenny	•	•	•	•		•			•		
Kilkenny	Kilkenny Design Centre						•			•		

LOCATION	ESTABLISHMENT	Business Hotel	Conference Centre	Banqueting	Leisure Centre	Golf	Family Friendly	Pet Friendly	No Smoking Restaurant	Sunday Dining	Open Christmas	Off-season Breaks
Kilkenny	Kilkenny Ormonde Hotel	•	•	•	•		•			•		
Kilkenny	Kilkenny River Court Hotel	•	•	•	•				•	•		•
Kilkenny	Lacken House		•				•		•			•
Kilkenny	Rinuccini Restaurant									•		
Kilkenny	Zuni	•								•		•
COUNTY LAOIS												
Abbeyleix	Preston House							•	•	•		
Ballacolla	Foxrock Inn						•					
Mountrath	Roundwood House						•					
COUNTY LEITRIM												
Ballinamore	Glenview House			•			•		•			
Carrick-on-Shannon	The Barge Steakhouse						•		•	•		
Carrick-on-Shannon	Bush Hotel	•	•	•					•	•		
Carrick-on-Shannon	Hollywell Country House								•			•
Carrick-on-Shannon	The Landmark Hotel	•	•	•	•		•			•		•
Keshcarrigan	Canal View House & Restaurant						•	•	•	•	•	•
Kinlough	Courthouse Restaurant									•		
Tullaghan	Tullaghan House						•					
COUNTY LIMERICK												
Limerick	Adare Manor Hotel & Golf Club					•						
Limerick	Castleroy Park Hotel & Conference Ctr	•	•	•	•		•			•		
Limerick	Jurys Inn Limerick		•									
Limerick	Jury's Limerick Hotel	•	•	•	•					•		
Limerick	The Locke Bar & Restaurant									•		
Limerick	South Court Business & Leisure Centre	•	•	•	•		•			•	•	•
Adare	Dunraven Arms Hotel		•	•	•			•	•	•	•	
Adare	Fitzgeralds Woodlands House Hotel	•	•	•	•		•			•		•
Ballingarry	The Mustard Seed at Echo Lodge		•					•				
Castleconnell	Castle Oaks House Hotel		•		•					•		•
Newcastlewest	Arrabrook Bar & Restaurant		•	•		•	•		•		•	

LOCATION	ESTABLISHMENT	Business Hotel	Conference Centre	Banqueting	Leisure Centre	Golf	Family Friendly	Pet Friendly	No Smoking Restaurant	Sunday Dining	Open Christmas	Off-season Breaks
COUNTY LONGFORD												
Granard	Toberphelim House						•			•		
Longford	Aubergine Gallery Cafe									•		
COUNTY LOUTH												
Carlingford	Beaufort House		•								•	•
Carlingford	Georgina's Tearooms									•		
Carlingford	Ghan House		•				•		•			
Carlingford	Kingfisher Bistro						•			•		
Carlingford	The Oystercatcher Lodge & Bistro								•			•
Clogherhead	Little Strand Restaurant						•	•		•		
Collon	Forge Gallery Restaurant						•					
Drogheda	Black Bull Inn									•		
Drogheda	Boyne Valley Hotel & Country Club	•	•	•	•		•	•		•	•	•
Dundalk	Fitzpatrick's Bar & Restaurant						•			•		
COUNTY MAYO												
Achill Island	The Beehive						•					
Achill Island	Gray's Guest House						•	•	•			
Ballina	Gaughans						•	•				
Ballina	Teach Iorrais Hotel		•	•			•			•	•	•
Castlebar	Breaffy House Hotel	•	•	•						•	•	•
Cong	Ashford Castle		•		•	•	•		•		•	•
Crossmolina	Enniscoe House							•				
Foxford	Healy's Hotel	•					•	•		•		•
Lahardane	Leonard's Lahardane						•			•	•	
Mulrany	Rosturk Woods						•	•	•			
Westport	Atlantic Coast Hotel	•	•	•	•		•					•
Westport	Hotel Westport	•	•	•	•		•		•	•	•	•
Westport	Knockranny House Hotel		•									•
Westport	The Lemon Peel									•		

LOCATION	ESTABLISHMENT	Business Hotel	Conference Centre	Banqueting	Leisure Centre	Golf	Family Friendly	Pet Friendly	No Smoking Restaurant	Sunday Dining	Open Christmas	Off-season Breaks
Westport	The Olde Railway Hotel								•	•		•
Westport	Quay Cottage						•			•		
Westport	T.Staunton						•					
COUNTY MEATH												
Bettystown	Bacchus At The Coastgaurd									•	•	
Dunshaughlin	The Old Workhouse						•	•				
Enfield	Johnstown House Hotel & Spa	•	•	•						•		
Kells	Boltown House						•	•				
Kilmessan	The Station House	•	•	•			•	•		•		•
Navan	Hudson's Bistro						•			•		
Navan	Southbank Bistro						•			•		
Slane	Boyle's Licensed Tea Rooms						•		•	•		
Slane	Conyngham Arms Hotel	•	•	•			•	•		•		•
COUNTY MONAGHAN												
Carrickmacross	Nuremore Hotel & Country Club		•	•	•	•				•	•	
Clones	Hilton Park								•			•
Glaslough	Castle Leslie		•	•					•	•	•	•
Monaghan	Andy's Bar and Restaurant						•			•		
Monaghan	Hillgrove Hotel	•	•	•			•			•	•	
COUNTY OFFALY												
Annaharvey	Annaharvey Farm		•				•		•			
Banagher	J.J.Hough's						•	•				
Birr	Dooley's Hotel	•	•	•			•					•
Birr	The Glendine Bistro						•			•	•	
Birr	Spinners Town House & Bistro		•				•			•	•	•
Birr	The Stables Restaurant & Townhouse						•	•	•	•		
Kinnity	Ardmore House						•					
Tullamore	Tullamore Court	•	•	•	•		•			•		•

LOCATION	ESTABLISHMENT	Business Hotel	Conference Centre	Banqueting	Leisure Centre	Golf	Family Friendly	Pet Friendly	No Smoking Restaurant	Sunday Dining	Open Christmas	Off-season Breaks
COUNTY ROSCOMMON												
Castlerea	Clonalis House						•		•			
Knockvicar	The Harbour Lights Café		•				•			•		
Rooskey	Shannon Key West Hotel		•	•					•			•
COUNTY SLIGO												
Ballymote	Temple House						•					
Castlebaldwin	Cromleach Lodge						•		•			•
Collooney	Glebe House Restaurant						•					•
Collooney	Markree Castle						•	•	•	•		
Mullaghmore	Eithna's Seafood Restaurant									•		
Riverstown	Coopershill House						•		•	•	•	
Rosses Point	Austie's						•			•		
Sligo	Bistro Bianconi									•		
Sligo	Coach Lane Restaurant @ Donaghy's Bar					•			•			
Sligo	Garavogue Bar & Restaurant									•		
Sligo	Hargadon Bros.						•					
Sligo	Montmartre									•		
Sligo	Sligo Park Hotel	•	•	•	•		•			•	•	•
Sligo	Tower Hotel Sligo	•	•	•			•		•	•		•
Strandhill	Strand House Bar & Restaurant						•				•	
COUNTY TIPPERARY												
Ardfinnan	Kilmaneen Farmhouse						•			•		
Borrisokane	Dancer Cottage						•				•	
Cahir	Clifford's at The Bell									•		
Cashel	Cashel Palace Hotel	•	•	•			•			•		•
Cashel	Dualla House						•					
Clonmel	Angela's Restaurant						•					
Clonmel	Clonmel Arms Hotel	•		•			•	•				•
Clonmel	Hotel Minella	•	•		•		•			•		
Clonmel	Mr. Bumbles						•			•		
Clonmel	Sean Tierney									•		

LOCATION	ESTABLISHMENT	Business Hotel	Conference Centre	Banqueting	Leisure Centre	Golf	Family Friendly	Pet Friendly	No Smoking Restaurant	Sunday Dining	Open Christmas	Off-season Breaks
Cloughjordan	Charlie Swan Equestrian Centre						•					
Glen of Aherlow	Aherlow House Hotel			•			•			•	•	•
Killaloe	Goosers									•		
Nenagh	Country Choice Delicatessen & Coffee Bar						•					
Nenagh	Kylenoe							•				
Nenagh	Larkins						•	•		•		
Roscrea	Ballycormac House						•	•	•	•	•	
Terryglass	The Derg Inn						•			•		
COUNTY WATERFORD												
Dungarvan	Castle Farm Country House						•	•	•			•
Dungarvan	Gortnadiha House						•	•				
Dungarvan	The Park Hotel	•	•	•	•		•			•		•
Dunmore East	The Ship									•		
Faithlegg	Faithlegg House Hotel		•	•	•	•				•		
Lismore	Ballyrafter Country House Hotel		•	•			•		•	•		•
Waterford	Foxmount Farm & Country House						•	•				
Waterford	Granville Hotel	•	•	•			•			•		
Waterford	O'Grady's			•					•	•		
Waterford	Tower Hotel Waterford			•	•		•					
Waterford	Waterford Castle Hotel & Golf Club		•			•	•		•		•	•
COUNTY WESTMEATH												
Athlone	Hodson Bay Hotel		•	•	•	•	•			•	•	•
Athlone	The Olive Grove						•			•		
Athlone	Restaurant Le Chateau						•			•		
Glasson	Glasson Village Restaurant						•			•		
Glasson	Wineport Lodge		•	•			•			•		
Kinnegad	The Cottage								•			
Mullingar	Crookedwood House						•	•	•	•		
Mullingar	Gallery 29 Cafe						•					
Mullingar	Woodville House						•			•		
Multyfarnham	Mornington House							•				

LOCATION	ESTABLISHMENT	Business Hotel	Conference Centre	Banqueting	Leisure Centre	Golf	Family Friendly	Pet Friendly	No Smoking Restaurant	Sunday Dining	Open Christmas	Off-season Breaks
COUNTY WEXFORD												
Arthurstown	Dunbrody Country House		•	•						•		
Bunclody	Chantry Restaurant						•					
Campile	Kilmokea Country Manor & Gardens		•				•			•		
Enniscorthy	Riverside Park Hotel	•	•	•			•			•		•
Ferrycarrig Bridge	Ferrycarrig Hotel		•	•	•		•			•	•	•
Gorey	Marlfield House						•	•	•	•		•
Kilmore Quay	Quay House Guesthouse								•			•
Rosslare	Kelly's Resort Hotel				•		•			•		
Rosslare Harbour	Great Southern Hotel		•	•	•		•			•	•	•
Tagoat	Churchtown House						•	•				
Wexford	Mange 2 Restaurant						•					
Wexford	Talbot Hotel		•	•	•		•			•	•	•
Wexford	White's Hotel		•	•	•		•			•	•	•
COUNTY WICKLOW												
Arklow	Plattenstown House											•
Arklow	Woodenbridge Hotel	•	•	•			•		•	•		•
Ashford	Ashford House						•			•		
Ashford	Ballyknocken House								•			
Aughrim	Lawless Hotel		•	•			•		•	•		•
Avoca Village	Avoca Handweavers									•		
Bray	The Tree of Idleness Restaurant									•		
Dunlavin	Rathsallagh House Golf & Country Club	•	•	•		•		•				•
Enniskerry	Powerscourt Terrace Cafe									•		
Enniskerry Village	Wingfields Bistro									•		
Glen Of The Downs	Glenview Hotel	•	•	•	•		•					•
Glendalough	Derrymore House								•			
Greystones	The Hungry Monk									•		
Greystones	Vino Pasta									•		
Kilmacnogue	Avoca Handweavers - Kilmacnogue									•		
Kiltegan	Barraderry Country House						•					

LOCATION	ESTABLISHMENT	Business Hotel	Conference Centre	Banqueting	Leisure Centre	Golf	Family Friendly	Pet Friendly	No Smoking Restaurant	Sunday Dining	Open Christmas	Off-season Breaks
Kiltegan	Humewood Castle		•	•				•				
Rathnew	Hunter's Hotel		•				•		•			
Rathnew	Tinakilly Country House & Restaurant		•	•						•	•	
Roundwood	Roundwood Inn						•			•		
Wicklow	The Bakery Restaurant & Cafe									•		
Wicklow	Christy's						•			•		
Wicklow	The Grand Hotel	•	•	•			•			•	•	•
BELFAST												
Belfast	Alden's Restaurant						•					
Belfast	All Season's Bed & Breakfast						•				•	•
Belfast	Benedict's of Belfast		•							•		
Belfast	Cayenne Restaurant						•					
Belfast	The Crescent Townhouse		•				•					•
Belfast	Crown Liquor Saloon						•			•		
Belfast	Dukes Hotel	•	•	•						•		
Belfast	Express by Holiday Inn	•	•	•			•			•	•	
Belfast	Hastings Europa Hotel	•	•	•			•	•	•	•		
Belfast	Hastings Stormont Hotel	•	•							•	•	
Belfast	Hilton Belfast	•	•	•			•			•	•	•
Belfast	Jurys Belfast Inn	•										
Belfast	Manor House Cantonese Cuisine			•			•					
Belfast	McHugh's Bar & Restaurant		•				•			•		
Belfast	The Morning Star						•					
Belfast	Olive Tree Company						•		•	•		
Belfast	Posthouse Premier Belfast		•	•	•						•	•
Belfast	Ramada Hotel	•	•	•								
Belfast	Ta Tu						•			•		
Belfast	Ten sq									•		
Belfast	Wellington Park Hotel	•	•	•			•					

LOCATION	ESTABLISHMENT	Business Hotel	Conference Centre	Banqueting	Leisure Centre	Golf	Family Friendly	Pet Friendly	No Smoking Restaurant	Sunday Dining	Open Christmas	Off-season Breaks
COUNTY ANTRIM												
Ballycastle	The House Of McDonnell						•					
Ballygally	Hastings Ballygally Castle Hotel	•	•	•			•		•	•	•	•
Ballygally	Lynden Heights Restaurant						•			•		
Ballymena	Galgorm Manor Hotel		•	•						•		
Bushmills	Bushmills Inn		•						•	•	•	•
Carnlough	Londonderry Arms Hotel		•				•					•
Carrickfergus	Quality Hotel Carrickfergus	•	•	•			•			•		•
Crumlin	Aldergrove Airport Hotel	•	•	•			•			•	•	
Dunadry	Dunadry Hotel & Country Club	•	•	•	•		•			•		•
Portballintrae	Sweeney's Public House & Winebar						•	•		•		
Portrush	Harbour Bistro & Harbour Bar						•			•		
Portrush	Royal Court Hotel		•	•			•			•	•	•
Portrush/Coleraine	Maddybenny Farmhouse						•					
Templepatrick	Hilton Templepatrick	•	•	•	•	•	•	•		•	•	•
Toome	The Crosskeys Inn										•	
COUNTY DOWN												
Bangor	Marine Court Hotel	•	•	•			•			•		
Belfast	Hastings Slieve Donard Hotel		•		•	•	•			•	•	
Crawfordsburn	The Old Inn Crawfordsburn	•	•	•			•	•	•	•		
Donaghadee	Pier 36						•			•		
Downpatrick	The Mill At Ballydugan	•	•	•			•			•		
Downpatrick	Pheasants Hill Country House							•				
Dundrum	The Buck's Head Inn									•		
Gilford	Oriel of Gilford								•	•		
Groomsport	Islet Hill						•					
Holywood	Hastings Culloden Hotel	•	•	•	•					•		
Holywood	Rayanne Country House						•				•	
Holywood	Sullivans									•		
Newcastle	Burrendale Hotel & Country Club	•	•	•	•	•	•			•	•	
Newtonards	Edenvale House						•					
Newtownards	The Old Schoolhouse Inn	•	•	•			•			•	•	

LOCATION	ESTABLISHMENT	Business Hotel	Conference Centre	Banqueting	Leisure Centre	Golf	Family Friendly	Pet Friendly	No Smoking Restaurant	Sunday Dining	Open Christmas	Off-season Breaks
Portaferry	The Narrows		•				•		•	•		
Rostrevor	Celtic Fjord									•		
COUNTY FERMANAGH												
Bellanaleck	The Sheelin						•			•		
Enniskillen	Killyhevlin Hotel	•	•	•			•	•		•		
Enniskillen	Rossahilly House						•				•	
Kesh	Lough Erne Hotel						•	•				
Killadeas	Manor House Country Hotel	•	•		•		•		•	•	•	
COUNTY LONDONDERRY												
Aghadowey	The Brown Trout Golf & Country Inn		•		•	•	•	•	•	•	•	
Coleraine	Charly's Restaurant	•	•	•	•		•			•		
Limavady	Streeve Hill						•					
Limavady	The Lime Tree						•			•		
Londonderry	Beech Hill Country House Hotel		•	•			•			•		•
Londonderry	Hastings Everglades Hotel	•	•	•			•			•		•
Upperlands	Ardtara Country House		•	•			•		•	•	•	
COUNTY TYRONE												
Dungannon	Grange Lodge			•			•		•			
Omagh	Hawthorn House	•					•			•	•	•

READER'S NOTES

READER'S NOTES

READER'S NOTES

READER'S NOTES

READER'S NOTES